Company Law Compliance and Enforcement

Nessa Cahill BL

publishing

Published by
Tottel Publishing Ltd
Maxwelton House
41–43 Boltro Road
Haywards Heath
West Sussex
RH16 1BJ

Tottel Publishing Ltd
Fitzwilliam Business Centre
26 Upper Pembroke Street
Dublin 2

ISBN 978-1-84592-105-7
© Tottel Publishing Ltd 2008
First published 2008

British Library Cataloguing-in-Publication Data
A catalogue record for this book is available from the British Library

Typeset by Marie Armah-Kwantreng, Dublin, Ireland
Printed and bound in Great Britain by
CPI Antony Rowe Limited, Chippenham, Wiltshire

Foreword

The 1960s was a decade of much needed commercial law reform in this jurisdiction. It saw the enactment of the Income Tax Act 1967, and the Companies Act 1963. As well as providing an appropriate framework for commercial activities, these long overdue reforms constituted the material on which Irish text books could be based and legal education reformulated. In addition they provided a secure foundation for the changes required by the rapid growth in economic activity which was to occur in subsequent years.

The Companies Act 1963 was based on the Companies Commission Report 1958. A particular recommendation of that Commission was that the provisions of the proposed legislation be enforced effectively. There was – and continues to be – a need to persuade those involved in the management of companies that breaches of commercial or administrative law may be as damaging to the community as physical wrongs perpetrated on the individual. Enforcement activity is an important means of raising this awareness and there must be some authority with responsibility for securing compliance by those who may be recalcitrant. In the case of company law, this authority is the Office of the Director of Corporate Enforcement.

Even if violations of the Companies Act were to be prosecuted vigorously, that would not have sufficed. Both domestically and internationally there were calls for higher standards in commercial and financial activities and for a new system of corporate governance. The new regime includes the various legislative enactments that comprise the Companies Acts 1963 to 2006. This system of governance must be known and understood by those to whom it is directed. Compliance is recognised as being in the interest of those engaged in the enterprises and those who benefit from them. "Compliance" has therefore joined "Enforcement" as an essential pillar of corporate governance. It is appropriate that these two words form the title to Ms Cahill's superlative treatise on this subject.

The scheme of Ms Cahill's book is designed with clarity. It is addressed in the first place, to companies, directors, auditors, receivers, liquidators and others who are subject to corporate regulation. It identifies clearly and comprehensively the obligations falling on those parties: the source of those provisions and their impact. In later chapters, the author turns to the means of investigation of breaches of the Companies Acts and the agencies by whom the laws will be enforced and compliance secured. In particular, there is a full analysis of the powers available to the Director of Corporate Enforcement: his rights and duties and the powers which he may exercise.

The treatise considers the sanctions that arise from breaches of the Companies Acts, including detailed treatment of the legislative provisions dealing with the restriction or disqualification of directors, provisions which have been the subject matter of several judicial decisions. The relevant sections underpin the requirement for honesty and responsibility which is now the basis of the required commercial morality. The analyses of these provisions and authorities by the author are impeccable and invaluable.

This book will be welcomed by those who must acquaint themselves with the ever-growing body of obligations and regulations governing commercial activities. It will be indispensable to the lawyers, accountants and compliance officers who must advise on those obligations and regulations as well as the courts and agencies by whom they must be enforced.

Ms Cahill has given us the authoritative guide to enforcement and compliance in Company Law. Her treatise will provide the model for other reference books in allied disciplines. Hopefully Ms Cahill can be persuaded to extend her writing to cover those areas. In the meantime, she is entitled to our best thanks for the present magnificent publication.

Frank Murphy

Dublin

7 January 2008

Preface

It is common for an author of a legal text to describe the area of law he addresses as one that has undergone considerable change and development since previous publications in that area. Without wishing to follow this pattern, it is impossible to ignore the upheaval that has occurred in relation to company law compliance and enforcement in recent years. Since the enactment of the Company Law Enforcement Act 2001, the law and practice of company law enforcement has become virtually unrecognisable from the pre-existing regime. Indeed, in the course of the time spent writing this book, the law in relation to each and every chapter has shifted and morphed between drafts. This is illustrated by a quick reference to the law governing disqualification orders: in 2004, the names of 10 persons appeared on the register of disqualified persons and there were few decisions concerning section 160 of the Companies Act 1990. By the end of 2006, there were 1,781 names on the register of disqualified persons and there are now dozens of significant judgments regarding the interpretation and scope of the relevant provisions.

It is probably inevitable, therefore, that, as this book goes to print, there are developments underway and pending that may further re-draw some of the lines of company law compliance and enforcement. Two of these warrant a special mention. First, the Company Law Review Group's General Scheme of the Draft Companies Consolidation and Reform Bill 2007, if and when enacted into law, promises to consolidate the Companies Acts 1963 to 2006 and to introduce some significant reforms. This Bill is expected to be published in late 2008. Second, an appeal against the High Court decision in *Re Tralee Beef and Lamb Ltd, Kavanagh v Delaney*, was heard by the Supreme Court on the 14th November 2007, and is likely to yield definitive determinations on certain important aspects of company law compliance and enforcement.

In an ideal world (inasmuch as company law features in anyone's idea of utopia), this publication would have awaited these developments. However, in an area of law in which there are such regular developments and amendments, a publication could never anticipate and encapsulate them all. There needs to be a cut-off point. For this book, that cut-off point is the end of October 2007. While I aim and attempt to state the law accurately as of that date, no legal responsibility is accepted for any errors, misstatements, omissions, or misrepresentations which may be contained in this book.

At the culmination of what has been a lengthy writing process, there are certain persons to whom I am indebted. First and foremost, Dr Thomas B. Courtney reviewed earlier drafts of many of the chapters and provided invaluable assistance, insight, and advice regarding individual chapters and the structure and focus of the book more generally. Tricia Sheehy Skeffington reviewed drafts of several of the chapters, providing very useful suggestions and comments in relation to those chapters. I wish to thank them both for their considerable assistance. All errors in, and shortcomings of, the book are, of course, solely attributable to me.

The publishers, Tottel Publishing, deserve my thanks for their patience, professionalism and efficiency, as do Louise Leavy who edited the book, Andrew Turner who indexed it and Marie Armah-Kwantreng who typeset the manuscript. I am particularly grateful to Sandra Mulvey for her encouragement, unwavering support and dedication. I would also like to express my deep gratitude to the Honourable Mr Justice Frank Murphy, for so generously agreeing to write, and so generously writing, the foreword to the book.

The persons to whom I wish to proffer my personal thanks are many. My family in Kilcock has been a source of great support and friendship, and a constant reminder to look at the lighter side (no mean feat where company law is concerned). My friends have, with patience and grace, accepted my occasional hermitic tendencies as I buried myself in the Companies Acts, emerging none the more sociable for it. Above all, my husband, Liam, has held my hand lightly but firmly throughout, always with a smile. I dedicate the book to him.

Nessa Cahill BL

The Law Library

Four Courts

Dublin 7

15 November 2007

Contents

Foreword...v
Preface vii
List of abbreviations xxix
Table of cases xxxi
Table of statutes... xliii
Table of statutory instruments lxxv

Chapter 1: Introduction
  A. Background 1
  B. Scope of Company Law Compliance and Enforcement 3
  C. Future direction of company law compliance and enforcement 5

Part A
Corporate Compliance

Chapter 2: Companies' Obligations: Filing
  A. Introduction 9
  B. Formation of a company 9
    (a) Memorandum of association 9
    (b) Articles of association 10
    (c) Section 3 statement ('Form A1') 11
    (d) Registered office 14
    (e) Activity in State 14
    (f) Effect of registration 16
    (g) Members 16
  C. Annual return 17
    (a) Content of annual return 17
    (b) Annexed documents 22
      (i) Scope of obligation 23
      (ii) Documents to be attached 24
        1. Accounts 24
        2. Reports 25
        3. Translation 25
        4. Date of accounts 25
      (iii) Small companies 26
        1. Criteria 26
        2. Accounts required 26
        3. Requirements of documents delivered to Registrar 27
      (iv) Medium companies 28
    (c) Annual return date 29
      (i) Company formed before 1 March 2002 30
      (ii) Companies formed after 1 March 2002 31
      (iii) Date for delivery of annual return 31
      (iv) Changing the annual return date 33
        1. Earlier annual return date 33

2. Later annual return date 34
(d) Groups of companies 36
   (i) Extension of annual return date 36
   (ii) Accounts 37
     1. Exception for parent companies 37
     2. Exception for subsidiary companies 37
(e) Grounds for rejection of annual returns 38
(f) Consequences of failing to file annual return 40
D. Prospectus 41
(a) Prospectus Regulations 2005 41
(b) Investment Funds, Companies and Miscellaneous
   Provisions Act 2005 41
E. Members 43
(a) Increase in number of members 44
(b) Location of register of members 45
F. Share capital 46
(a) Allotment of shares 46
(b) Alterations in share capital 47
(c) Increase in share capital 49
(d) Reduction of share capital 49
   (i) Notification of Registrar of Companies 50
   (ii) Registration of reduction 50
   (iii) Public limited companies 51
(e) Other share dealings 51
   (i) Variation of rights of shareholders 51
   (ii) Financing acquisition of own shares 52
   (iii) Acquisition of own shares 53
G. Charges 54
(a) Obligation to register 54
(b) Registrable charges 55
   (i) Property outside the State 56
   (ii) Companies incorporated in other jurisdictions 58
   (iii) Series of debentures 59
   (iv) Judgment mortgages 59
(c) Particulars to be registered 60
(d) Commission 61
(e) Time limits for registration 61
(f) Effect of registration 62
(g) Effect of non-registration 66
(h) Register of debenture holders 67
(i) Release from charge 67
H. Resolutions and agreements 68
I. Directors and secretaries 70
(a) Delivery of particulars and consent 70
(b) Share qualifications 70
(c) Notification of changes in directors and secretary 71
(d) Notification of resignation or removal by former officer 72

(e) Irish resident director 74
J. Company name 75
  (a) 'Limited', 'teoranta' or 'plc' 76
    (i) Obligation to use 'limited' or 'plc' 76
    (ii) Improper use of 'limited' or 'plc' 76
    (iii) Exemption from use of 'limited' or 'teoranta' 77
  (b) Prohibited names 81
    (i) Undesirable names 81
    (ii) Similarity to other company names 81
    (iii) Legislative restrictions 82
    (iv) Miscellaneous restrictions 83
  (c) Publication and disclosure 83
  (d) Change of name 84
  (e) Reservation of name 85
  (f) Business name 85
K. Companies incorporated outside the State 86
  (a) Companies that establish a place of business in the State 86
  (b) Companies that establish a branch in the State 87
L. Public limited companies 90
M. Re-registration of companies 92
  (a) Re-registration of private company as public limited company 92
  (b) Re-registration of public limited company as private company 95
N. Form of documents 96
  (a) General requirements 96
  (b) Electronic filing agent 98
  (c) Delivery of defective documents 100

Chapter 3: Companies' Obligations: Maintenance of Registers
A. Introduction 103
B. Form of registers 103
C. Register of members 104
  (a) Contents 104
  (b) Date of registration 106
  (c) Index 106
  (d) Location 107
  (e) Inspection 108
  (f) Refusal to register 110
  (g) Rectification 112
  (h) Closing register of members 115
  (i) Effect of register 115
  (j) Sanctions 117
D. Register of directors and secretaries 118
E. Register of directors' interests in company 120
F. Directors' contracts 122
G. Register of charges 123
H. Register of debenture holders 124

Chapter 4: Books of Account
  A. Introduction 127
  B. Proper books of account 127
     (a) 'Proper books of account' 128
     (b) Form and language 129
     (c) Regularity required 130
     (d) Content of books 130
     (e) Deemed proper books 131
     (f) Currency of books 131
     (g) Location of books 132
     (h) Inspection 132
     (i) Preservation 135
  C. Criminal liability 135
     (a) Company and directors 135
     (b) Officers 137
  D. Personal liability 138
  E. Disqualification 147

Chapter 5: Companies' Obligations: Members' Meetings
  A. Introduction 149
  B. Annual General Meeting 149
     (a) Intervals between AGMs 149
     (b) General business at AGM 150
     (c) Directions to convene AGM 151
     (d) Failure to convene AGM 152
     (e) Notice of AGM 154
         (i) Content of notice 154
         (ii) Addressees of notice 154
         (iii) Timing of notice 155
         (iv) Service of notice 155
         (v) Failure to notify 156
     (f) Location of AGM 156
     (g) Exemption for single member private limited companies 157
  C. Extraordinary General Meeting 158
     (a) Nature of EGMs 158
     (b) Convening EGMs 158
         (i) Requisition of members 159
         (ii) Serious loss of capital 162
     (c) Location of EGM 163
     (d) Notice of EGM 163
  D. Resolutions 164
     (a) Special resolutions 164
     (b) Written resolutions 167
     (c) Extended notice 168
  E. Conduct of business at general meetings 168
     (a) Quorum 168
     (b) Chairman 170

(c) Adjournments 170
(d) Voting 173
(e) Meeting venue 174
F. Direction of Court 175
G. Minutes of meetings 176

Part B
Compliance Obligations of Individuals

Chapter 6: Directors
A. Introduction 181
  (a) General 181
  (b) Qualifications 181
  (c) Irish resident director 184
B. Transactions involving company directors 186
  (a) Introduction 186
  (b) Common law 187
    (i) Common law regulation of directors' interests 187
    (ii) Consequences of conflict of interest at common law 191
  (c) Statutory regulation of transactions with companies 192
    (i) Remuneration 192
    (ii) Loans 193
      1. Scope of prohibition 194
      2. Exceptions 198
      3. Sanctions 205
    (iii) Substantial property transactions 209
      1. Prohibited transactions 209
      2. Exceptions 213
      3. Consequences of violation 216
      4. Defence 217
C. Disclosure obligations 218
  (a) Personal information 219
  (b) Disqualifications in other jurisdictions 220
  (c) Directors' contracts 221
  (d) Interest in contract with company 222
    (i) Scope 222
    (ii) Date for disclosure 223
    (iii) General notice 223
    (iv) Record of disclosure 224
    (v) Penalty 224
    (vi) Interaction with other laws 225
  (e) Interest in shares or debentures 225
  (f) Disclosure of payments to directors 228
  (g) Disclosure of directors' interests in company accounts 229
D. Specific offences 230
  (a) Furnishing false information 231
  (b) Alteration or falsification of books 232
  (c) Criminal fraudulent trading 232

  (i) Introduction 232
  (ii) Respondents 234
  (iii) 'Carrying on of the business of a company' 235
  (iv) Participation required 237
  (v) Requirement of knowledge 239
  (vi) Requisite intention 241
    1. General 241
    2. 'Intent to defraud' 242
    3. Fraudulent purpose 244
  (vii) Sentences 245
 E. Directors' reports 248
  (a) Report accompanying balance sheet 248
  (b) Directors' compliance statement 253
 F. Proceedings against officers of companies in liquidation 256
  (a) Offences by officers of companies in liquidation 256
  (b) Fraud by officers of companies in liquidation 259
 G. Directors of insolvent companies 259
 H. Sanctions 261
 I. Relief 264
 J. Protection against liability 265

Chapter 7: Auditors
 A. Introduction 269
  (a) Background 269
  (b) Appointment of auditors 269
  (c) Removal of auditors 271
  (d) Auditors' rights on removal 272
  (e) Resignation of auditors 274
  (f) Remuneration of auditors 276
 B. Auditor's report 276
  (a) General 276
  (b) Content 277
  (c) Qualifications or adverse opinions 280
  (d) Further considerations 280
  (e) Special Auditor's Report 281
 C. Integrity and independence 282
  (a) Qualifications 282
    (i) Recognition 282
    (ii) Register of Auditors 286
    (iii) Disqualification 292
    (iv) Acting as auditor while not qualified 293
  (b) Independence 300
  (c) Right of access to documents 307
  (d) Right to compel information and explanations 307
  (e) Right to attend meetings 308
 D. Auditors' reporting obligations 308
  (a) Background 308

(b) Proper books of account 311
(c) Duty to report indictable offences 314
    (i) 'in the course and by virtue of' audit work 316
    (ii) Requirement of 'information' 320
    (iii) Opinion to be formed 321
    (iv) 'Reasonable grounds' 322
    (v) Level of certainty required 324
    (vi) Company, officer or agent 325
    (vii) Indictable offence under the Companies Acts 326
    (viii) No discretion 328
    (ix) Exceptions 328
    (x) Timing of notification 329
    (xi) Further information, books and documents 330
(d) Legal professional privilege 331
(e) Protection from liability 334
(f) Report on Directors' Compliance Statements 335
(g) Other reporting obligations 336
E. Audit exemption 339
F. Auditors' liability 342
(a) No exemption 342
(b) Potential liability 343
    (i) In general 343
    (ii) Other companies 345
    (iii) Investors 348
    (iv) Creditors 349
    (v) Standard of care 349
(c) Developments regarding auditors' liability 352

Chapter 8: Receivers
A. Introduction 355
B. Publication of appointment 356
(a) Publication by person appointing receiver 356
(b) General publication requirements 358
(c) Receiver's duty to publicise appointment 358
C. Compliance duties of receivers 360
(a) Qualifications of receivers 360
(b) Statement of affairs 362
(c) Returns 368
(d) Information to the company 370
(e) Sale of assets 372
(f) Distribution of proceeds 379
D. Enforcement under the Companies Acts 383
(a) Examination of receiver's books 383
(b) Directions to comply 384
(c) Report by professional body 385
E. Reporting obligations of receivers 386
F. Remuneration 388

G. Liability 390
H. Resignation/Removal 391

Chapter 9: Liquidators
A. Introduction 395
B. Appointment of liquidators 396
  (a) Means of appointment 396
    (i) Official liquidation 396
    (ii) Obligations of company in voluntary winding up 396
    (ii) Obligations of creditors in voluntary winding up 396
  (b) Qualifications 397
  (c) Creditors' disclosure obligation 399
  (d) Prohibition on inducement for appointment of liquidator 400
  (e) Liquidator's consent and chairman's duty of notification 401
  (f) Removal of liquidator 401
  (g) Notification of appointment 403
    (i) Official liquidator's duty to notify 403
    (ii) Company's duty to publicise appointment of liquidator 403
    (iii) Voluntary liquidator's duty to notify 403
    (iv) General duty to disclose liquidation 404
C. Compliance obligations of liquidators 404
  (a) Duty to convene meetings 404
    (i) Official liquidator 404
    (ii) Members' voluntary liquidation 406
    (iii) Creditors' voluntary liquidation 410
  (b) Duty to make returns 411
  (c) Duty to report to the DCE 412
    (i) Scope of obligation to report 414
      1. Insolvent companies 414
      2. Voluntary liquidations 414
      3. Provisional liquidations 415
      4. Temporal scope 418
    (ii) Information required 418
      1. Liquidator details 420
      2. Company details 421
      3. Company directors 424
      4. Statement of affairs, accounts and report to creditors 427
      5. Proceedings 433
      6. Final report 436
      7. Liquidator's statement 437
    (iii) Additional reports 437
    (iv) Sanctions 438
      1. Prosecution 439
      2. Administrative fine 439
      3. Court order 439
    (v) Approach of the ODCE 440
  (d) Duty to report to the Director of Public Prosecutions 441

(i) Official liquidations 442
    1. Applicants 442
    2. Scope 442
    3. Grounds 443
    4. Liquidator's duties 443
(ii) Voluntary liquidations 444
    1. Voluntary liquidator's report 444
    2. Court directions 445
(iv) Prosecution 446
    1. Obligation to assist 446
    2. Failure to assist 446
    3. Role of the Director of Public Prosecutions 447
    4. Role of the DCE 448
(e) Duty to report to court 448
D. Investigations during winding up 451
  (a) Introduction 451
  (b) Inspection of books 452
    (i) Compulsory liquidations 452
    (ii) Voluntary liquidations 453
  (c) Examination of persons 454
  (d) Power of arrest 455
  (e) Orders for payment, delivery up, search and seizure 457
  (f) Prevention of removal or dissipation of assets 458
  (g) Order for return of company property 460
  (h) Contribution toward debts of related companies 461
  (i) Extension of powers to companies not in liquidation 463
E. Investigation of liquidator 469
  (a) Production of liquidator's books 469
  (b) Investigation by professional body 469

Chapter 10: Examiners' Obligations
A. Introduction 471
B. General provisions regarding examiners 472
  (a) Qualifications 472
  (b) Publication 475
  (c) Termination of office 476
  (d) Title 477
  (e) Contractual liability 477
  (f) Directions 477
  (g) Committee of creditors 478
C. Powers of examiners 478
  (a) Auditors' rights and powers 478
  (b) Meetings 479
  (c) Prevent detriment 479
  (d) Pre-petition contracts 480
  (e) Application for directions 482
  (f) Claims against a company 483

(g) Co-operation of officers and agents 483
  (i) Scope of obligation to co-operate 483
  (ii) Forms of co-operation 485
  (iii) Refusal to co-operate 486
(h) Access to bank details 487
(i) Powers of directors 487
(j) Power to dispose of charged property 489
(k) Related companies 491
(l) Pre-petition debts 492
(m) Costs of examinership 493
  (i) Costs, expenses and remuneration payable 493
  (ii) Application to court 494
  (iii) Court discretion 494
  (iv) Priority of examiner's costs, expenses and remuneration 496
D. Obligations of examiners 497
(a) Formulation of proposals 498
(b) Consideration of proposals 500
(c) Report 504
(d) Dissemination of report 505
(e) Confirmation of report 506
  (i) Time limits 506
  (ii) Hearing 507
  (iii) Court determination 507
  (iv) Consequences of confirmation 509
  (v) Revocation of confirmation 510
(f) Failure of examinership 511
(g) Report regarding irregularities 511

Part C
Enforcement and Investigation

Chapter 11: Agencies of Enforcement

A. Office of the Director of Corporate Enforcement 517
(a) Background 517
  (i) Establishment 517
  (ii) Appointment 518
  (iii) Functions 518
(b) Compliance role 519
  (i) Public presentations 520
  (ii) Publications 520
  (iii) Consultations 520
  (iv) Discussions 521
    1. Submissions on legislation 521
    2. Involvement with IAASA 522
    3. Company Law Review Group 522
    4. Miscellaneous 523
  (v) Interaction with other bodies 523
    1. Joint presentations 523

2. Agreements 523
3. Joint publications 524
(vi) Enforcement 524
(c) Enforcement role 524
(i) Detection 525
1. Reports by other agencies 525
2. Reports by auditors, directors, liquidators 528
3. Reports by professional bodies 528
4. Disclosure of information 529
5. Public complaints 530
(ii) Investigation 531
(iii) Prosecution 531
(iv) Civil sanctions 532
(d) Powers 536
(e) Duties 536
(i) Independence 537
(ii) Accountability 537
1. Annual report 537
2. Information to Minister 539
3. Accounting to Oireachtas Committees 540
(iii) Protection of information 542
1. Information protected 543
2. Exceptions 543
3. Approach of ODCE 544
B. Companies Registration Office 545
(a) Powers of prosecution 545
(b) Striking company off the register 549
(c) Power to seek order of disqualification 550
(d) Power to require compliance 550
(e) Fines/penalties 551
(f) 'Integrated Enforcement Environment' 552
(g) Encouraging compliance 552
C. Director of Public Prosecutions 553
(a) Overview of role of DPP 553
(b) Role of DPP under Companies Acts 554
(i) Before the CLEA 2001 554
1. Criminal functions 554
2. Civil functions 555
(ii) Effect of CLEA 2001 556
1. Criminal role 556
2. Civil functions 557
D. Minister for Enterprise, Trade and Employment 557
(a) Background 557
(b) Transferred functions 558
(i) Functions transferred to DCE 558
(ii) Functions transferred to the CRO 560
(iii) Functions transferred to the IAASA 560

(c) Retained functions 561
    (i) Obligations to show particulars on headed paper 561
    (ii) Investigations 561
    (iii) Postponement of AGM or annual return date 562
E. Irish Auditing and Accounting Supervisory Authority 562

Chapter 12: Powers of Investigation of the Director of Corporate Enforcement
A. Production of books or documents 565
  (a) Introduction 565
  (b) Entities affected 567
    (i) Companies formed and registered under the Companies Acts 567
    (ii) Companies that already exist within the meaning
    of the Companies Acts 567
    (iii) Companies that are covered by CA 1963, s 325 567
    (iv) Companies registered in accordance with Pt IX of CA 1963 568
    (v) Bodies corporate to which provisions of CA 1963
    apply pursuant to CA 1963, s 377 569
    (vi) Bodies corporate incorporated outside Ireland 569
    (vii) Insurance undertakings 569
  (c) Grounds for directing production of books or documents 569
    (i) The necessity of appointing an inspector needs
    to be investigated 570
    (ii) The company's affairs are or were conducted

    with intent to defraud 577
    (iii) The company's affairs are or were conducted
    with a fraudulent purpose 578
    (iv) The company's affairs are or were conducted
    in an unfairly prejudicial manner 578
    (v) Unfairly prejudicial act or omission 579
    (vi) Acts or omissions that have been, are or are likely
    to be unlawful 580
    (vii) Fraudulent purpose 582
    (viii) Unlawful purpose 582
    (ix) Other company 582
  (d) Evidential requirement 583
  (e) Review of decision 585
  (f) Duty to give reasons 588
  (g) Books or documents to be produced 591
  (h) Notice of decision and time periods 594
    (i) Advance notice 594
    (ii) Time limit for compliance 597
  (i) Production of books or documents by third parties 598
    (i) Grounds for directing third parties to produce books
    or documents 598
    1. Possession of s 19(1) books or documents 599
    2. Possession of copies of books or documents 599

    3. Possession of related books or documents 599
    (ii) Documents to be produced by a third party 601
    (iii) Grounds for resisting third party production 603
        1. Privilege 603
        2. Banking documents 603
        3. Lien 603
  (j) Supplemental powers 604
    (i) Copies of books or documents 604
    (ii) Explanations of books or documents 604
    (iii) Location of books or documents 606
    (iv) General assistance 607
  (k) Exceptions 608
    (i) Lien 608
    (ii) Privilege 608
    (iii) Banking documents 609
  (l) Compel compliance 610
  (m) Use of statements in legal proceedings 611
  (n) Offences 614
    (i) Failure to comply 614
    (ii) False or misleading 616
    (iii) Interference 616
  (o) Expenses 617
B. Entry and search of premises 619
  (a) Issue of search warrant 619
  (b) Application for search warrant 620
  (c) Designated officer 621
  (d) Grounds 622
  (e) Material information 625
    (i) Books or documents not produced 625
    (ii) Evidence of offences under the Companies Acts 627
  (f) Execution of search warrant 628
    (i) Duration of validity of search warrant 628
    (ii) Premises 629
    (iii) Use of force 630
    (iv) Material information 631
    (v) Persons at premises 632
    (vi) Retention of information 632
    (vii) Computers 633
  (g) Obstruction and failure to comply 634
C. Disclosure of information 635

Chapter 13: Inspectors and Company Investigations
A. Appointment of inspector to investigate company's affairs 641
  (a) Applicants 641
    (i) Internal applicants 641
    (ii) External 643
  (b) Grounds 645

(c) Evidence 653
    (i) Applications under CA 1990, s 7(2) 653
    (ii) Applications under CA 1990, s 8(1) 653
(d) Companies affected 655
    (i) General definition 655
    (ii) Companies incorporated outside the State 656
    (iii) Winding up 657
    (iv) Related company 657
(e) Request of other authority 661
B. Investigation of membership of company 662
(a) Inspector 662
    (i) Appointment 662
    (ii) Grounds 662
    (iii) Scope of inspection 663
    (iv) Powers 663
    (v) Publication 664
    (vi) Expenses 664
(b) Investigations 665
(c) Share restrictions 666
(d) Investigations of share dealing 666
C. Conduct of investigations 666
(a) Role of inspectors 666
(b) Fair procedure 671
(c) Court directions 672
(d) Information regarding offences 673
(e) Privacy of investigations 674
D. Powers of investigation 675
(a) Production of documents 675
    (i) General 676
    (ii) Officers or agents 677
    (iii) Other persons 678
    (iv) Books or documents to be produced 680
    (v) Time frame 682
    (vi) Lien 683
    (vii) Privilege 683
(b) Attendance, examinations and other assistance 683
    (i) Obligation to attend and assist 683
    (ii) Self-incrimination 684
    (iii) Use of answers 685
(c) Banking documents 688
(d) Failure to comply 691
E. Report 693
(a) Form of report 693
(b) Challenge to report 695
(c) Publication 700
(d) Consequences 704
(e) Use of report 706

F. Expenses 708

Chapter 14: Striking Companies' Names off the Register
A. Grounds for striking off 713
    (a) Failure to file annual returns 713
    (b) Failure to deliver statement to Revenue Commissioners 717
    (c) Ceasing to carry on business 720
    (d) Failure to have an Irish resident director 721
        (i) Irish resident director 721
        (ii) Exceptions 721
        (iii) Consequences 723
    (e) Failure of public limited company to have certificate 725
    (f) Incomplete winding up 727
    (g) Voluntary striking off 728
B. Effect of strike-off 729
    (a) Dissolution 729
    (b) Director and officer liability 730
    (c) Winding up 731
    (d) Company's property 731
    (e) Litigation 733
    (f) Disqualification of directors 734
C. Restoration by court 736
    (a) Section 12B(3) of CA(A) 1982 736
        (i) Scope 737
        (ii) Applicants 737
        (iii) Requirements 739
        (iv) Procedure 739
        (v) Orders 746
    (b) Section 12B(7) of C(A)A 1982 752
        (i) Scope 753
        (ii) Applicants 753
        (iii) Requirements 753
        (iv) Procedure 753
        (v) Orders 754
    (c) Section 311(8) of CA 1963 754
        (i) Scope 755
        (ii) Applicants 755
        (iii) Requirements 756
        (iv) Procedure 756
        (v) Orders 757
D. Restoration by Registrar 758
    (a) Scope of the statutory provisions 758
    (b) Applicants 761
    (c) Requirements 764
    (d) Restoration 766
E. Effect of restoration 766

Chapter 15: Criminal Prosecutions
A. Nature of offences 775
B. Detection of offences 779
C. Potential Defendants 779
    (a) Company 780
    (b) Officer in default 782
D. Pre-trial 786
    (a) Commencement of prosecution 786
        (i) Laying a complaint or information 786
        (ii) Administrative procedure 788
        (iii) Arrest without warrant 788
    (b) Limitation periods 789
    (c) Collecting evidence 791
    (d) Arrest 791
E. Trial 793
    (a) Venue 793
    (b) Jury 796
    (c) Documentary evidence 797
    (d) Double jeopardy 799
F. Sanctions 800
G. Illustration of criminal prosecution under the Companies Acts 802
H. Proposed reforms 803

Part D
Declarations of Restriction

Chapter 16: Nature and scope of restriction proceedings
A. Introduction 807
B. Nature of restriction proceedings 808
    (a) Introduction 808
    (b) Public interest 809
    (c) Non-adversarial 809
    (d) Role of applicant 813
    (e) Burden of proof 813
    (f) Lack of discretion 816
    (g) Extra-territorial jurisdiction 817
C. Persons affected 817
    (a) Onus of proving fact of directorship 818
    (b) Directors at date of winding up 819
        (i) Executive and non-executive directors 820
    (c) Former directors 824
        (i) Justifications for restricting former directors 824
        (ii) Resignation 825
        (iii) Temporal scope of restriction 826
        (iv) Obligation to restrict former directors 828
    (d) Shadow Directors 828
        (i) Definition 828
        (ii) Restriction of shadow directors 829

(iii) Companies as shadow directors 831
(e) De facto directors 833
(f) Nominee directors 839

Chapter 17: Defences to restriction proceedings
A. Introduction 841
B. Honesty and responsibility 842
   (a) Scope of directors' 'honesty and responsibility' 843
      (i) Relevant period of time 843
      (ii) Conduct in relation to other companies 845
   (b) General interpretation of 'honestly and responsibly' 846
      (i) Failure of company 846
      (ii) Compliance with Companies Acts 847
      (iii) 'La Moselle' test 848
      (iv) The extension of 'La Moselle' 851
   (c) Relevant factors 854
      (i) Proper books and records 855
      (ii) Financial affairs 859
      (iii) Non-financial information 862
      (iv) Board meetings 863
      (v) Relationship with other companies 863
      (vi) Dealings with Revenue Commissioners 868
      (vii) Dealings between director and company 872
      (viii) Miscellaneous factors 873
C. 'Just and equitable' 875
D. Delay 877
E. Relief 881

Chapter 18: Procedure of restriction proceedings
A. Applicants under s 150 887
B. Parties to restriction proceedings 888
C. Rules of procedure 891
D. Practice direction 892
E. Service of restriction proceedings 893
   (a) General rule 893
   (b) Service out of the jurisdiction 894
F. Discovery in restriction proceedings 897
G. Restriction undertakings 898

Chapter 19: Consequences of declarations of restriction
A. Period of restriction 903
B. Effect of declaration of restriction 904
C. Notification and reporting requirements 905
   (a) Restricted person's notification duty 905
   (b) Liquidator's reporting duty 905
D. Consequences for restricted companies 906
   (a) Capital requirements 906
   (b) Limitations on a restricted company 909

(i) Funding purchase of company's shares 909
(ii) Loans to directors 910
(iii) Consideration for transfer of non-cash assets by members 913
(c) Relief for a restricted company 913
E. Register of restricted persons 914
F. Breach of declaration of restriction 915
G. Costs 916
(a) Costs recoverable under s 150(4B) 918
(b) Costs of unsuccessful applications 922
(c) Order of costs in favour of respondent 924
(d) Applicant's liability for costs 927
(e) Recovery of costs in a winding up 929
(f) Notice party costs order 930

Part E
Disqualification Orders

Chapter 20: Deemed disqualifications
A. Introduction 933
B. Conviction on indictment 935
(a) Offences which trigger disqualification 936
(b) Period of disqualification 936
(c) Role of the court 938
(d) Implementation of deemed disqualification 938
(e) Notification by director 940
(f) Persons affected 942
(g) Discretion to substitute restriction order 942
(h) Comparative legislation 943
C. Failure to disclose disqualification in other jurisdiction 944
(a) Duty to notify of disqualification in other jurisdiction 944
(b) Automatic disqualification for failure to notify 948
D. Acting in breach of order of restriction or under instructions
of disqualified or restricted person 950
(a) Breach of declaration of restriction 951
(b) Acting under the directions of a disqualified or restricted person 952
E. Undischarged bankruptcy 952

Chapter 21: Applications for Disqualification Orders
A. Introduction 955
B. Purpose of a disqualification order 957
C. Discretion of the Court 960
D. Onus of proof 961
E. Procedure 962
(a) Initiation of disqualification applications 963
(b) Delay 963
(c) Hearing of disqualification applications 964
(d) Undertakings 967
F. Test of fitness 969

G. Considerations 977
  (a) Seniority 977
  (b) Experience and qualifications 980
  (c) Attempts to rectify or stop the misconduct 982
  (d) Impact of disqualification order 983
  (e) Lapse of time 984
  (f) Attitude in the proceedings 985

Chapter 22: Grounds of discretionary disqualification
A. Fraud in relation to company, creditors or members 987
  (a) Respondents under s 160(2)(a) 987
  (b) Applicants under s 160(2)(a) 988
  (c) Meaning of 'guilty' 988
  (d) Applications under s 160(2)(a) 989
B. Breach of duty 989
  (a) Respondents under s 160(2)(b) 989
  (b) Applicants 991
  (c) Scope of s 160(2)(b) 991
  (d) Applications under s 160(2)(b) 991
  (e) Requirement of 'guilty' 995
  (f) Relationship between s 160(2)(b) and other grounds 996
C. Civil liability for fraudulent and reckless trading 997
  (a) Respondents under s 160(2)(c) 998
  (b) Applicants under s 160(2)(c) 998
  (c) Applications under s 160(2)(c) 999
  (d) Comparative 999
D. Unfit to be concerned with the management of a company 1000
  (a) Respondent under s 160(2)(d) 1001
  (b) Applicant under s 160(2)(d) 1001
  (c) Conduct in other companies 1001
  (d) Overlap between ss 150 and 160 1002
  (e) Factors 1004
E. Finding of unfitness in inspector's report 1008
  (a) Respondents under s 160(2)(e) 1008
  (b) Applicants under s 160(2)(e) 1008
  (c) Scope of s 160(2)(e) 1009
  (d) Applications under s 160(2)(e) 1009
F. Persistent default 1010
  (a) Respondents under s 160(2)(f)) 1010
  (b) Applicants under s 160(2)(f) 1010
  (c) Means of proof under s 160(2)(f) 1010
  (d) Applications under s 160(2)(f) 1012
G. Failing to keep proper books of account 1013
  (a) Respondents under s 160(2)(g) 1013
  (b) Applicants under s 160(2)(g) 1014
  (c) Offence of failing to keep proper books of account 1014
  (d) Applications under s 160(2)(g) 1016

H. Company struck off the register 1016
    (a) Respondents under s 160(2)(h) 1017
    (b) Applicants under s 160(2)(h) 1017
    (c) Criteria of s 160(2)(h) 1017
    (d) Defence to disqualification application under s 160(2)(h) 1019
    (e) Applications under s 160(2)(h) 1020
I. Disqualification in another state 1025
    (a) Applicants under s 160(2)(i) 1026
    (b) Overview 1026
    (c) Interaction with automatic disqualification 1026
    (d) Period of disqualification 1027
J. Undischarged bankruptcy 1028
    (a) Information gathering 1028
    (b) Interaction with Pt VII of CA 1990 1028
K. Restricted persons 1029

Chapter 23: Consequences of Disqualification Orders
A. General 1031
B. Conditional disqualification 1032
C. Period of disqualification 1036
D. Substitution of restriction order 1044
E. Costs 1046
F. Relief 1047
G. Register of disqualified persons 1049
H. Acting while disqualified 1050
    (a) Offence of acting while disqualified 1050
    (b) Extension of period of disqualification 1051
    (c) No relief 1051
    (d) Repayment of consideration 1052
    (e) Liability for company's debts 1053
    (f) Acting under directions of a disqualified person 1054

Index... 1057

List of Abbreviations

Primary Legislation

CA 1963–2006	Companies Acts 1963 to 2006
CA 1963	Companies Act 1963
CA 1990	Companies Act 1990
C(AA)A 2003	Companies (Auditing and Accounting) Act 2003
C(A)(No 1)A 1999	Companies (Amendment) (No 1) Act 1999
C(A)(No 2)A 1999	Companies (Amendment) (No 2) Act 1999
C(A)A 1977	Companies (Amendment) Act 1977
C(A)A 1982	Companies (Amendment) Act 1982
C(A)A 1983	Companies (Amendment) Act 1983
C(A)A 1986	Companies (Amendment) Act 1986
C(A)A 1990	Companies (Amendment) Act 1990
CLEA 2001	Company Law Enforcement Act 2001
EC(BD)R 1993	European Communities (Branch Disclosure) Regulation s 1993
EC(C)R 2004	European Communities (Companies) Regulations 2004
EC(FVA)R 2004	European Communities (Fair Value Accounting) Regulations 2004
EC(IFRSMA)R 2005	European Communities (International Financial Reporting Standards and Miscellaneous Amendments) Regulations 2005
FA	Finance Act
IA 2005	Interpretation Act 2005
IFCMPA 2005	Investment Funds, Companies and Miscellaneous Provisions Act 2005
IFCMPA 2006	Investment Funds, Companies and Miscellaneous Provisions Act 2006
TCA 1997	Taxes Consolidation Act 1997

Other

AG	Attorney General
AGM	annual general meeting
ARD	annual return date
ASB	Accounting Standards Board
CLRG	Company Law Review Group
CRO	Companies Registration Office

Other

DCE	Director of Corporate Enforcement
DETE	Department of Enterprise, Trade and Employment
DPP	Director of Public Prosecutions
EGM	extraordinary general meeting
IAASA	Irish Auditing and Accounting Supervisory Authority
ICAI	Institute of Chartered Accountants in Ireland
ICLSA	Irish Current Law Statutes Annotated
IEX	Irish Enterprise Exchange
IFRS	International Financial Reporting Standards
ISA	International Standard on Auditing
ODCE	Office of the Director of Corporate Enforcement
plc	public limited company
RSC	Rules of the Superior Courts 1986

Table of Cases

360Atlantic (Ireland) Ltd, O'Ferral v Coughlan, Re
[2004] IEHC 410, [2004] 4 IR 266 .... 4.036, 16.015, 16.019, 16.020,
17.010, 17.039, 17.044, 17.048, 17.050,
17.052, 17.053, 17.055, 17.056, 17.057, 17.065
360Networks (Ireland) Ltd, O'Ferral v Coughlan, Re
[2004] IEHC 412 .... 17.010, 17.044, 17.050, 17.055, 17.057

A

Adam Eyton Ltd, Re (1887) 36 Ch D 299 ....9.016
Aerospares Ltd v Thompson [1999] IEHC 76 ....6.016, 6.017, 6.018, 6.019
AG (McDonnell) v Higgins [1964] IR 374 ....15.020
Airscape Ltd v Powertech Logistics Ltd [2007] IEHC 43..................................9.126, 9.127
Al Saudi Banque & Ors v Clark Pixley (a firm) [1990] Ch 313, [1990] 2 WLR 344,
[1989] All ER 361, [1990] BCLC 46 ....7.143
Allied Mechanical Holdings Ltd, Director of Corporate Enforcement v Mongey, Re
(5 July 2005, ex tempore), HC 22.087
Amantiss Enterprises Ltd, Framus Ltd v CRH plc, Re
[2000] 2 ILRM 177 .... 14.034, 14.046, 14.099, 14.100, 14.101
Anderson v Hogg [2002] SLT 634; [2002] BCC 923 ....13.013
Andrew & Ors v Kounnis Freeman (a firm) [1999] 2 BCLC 641 ....7.138
Anois Couriers Ltd v Hannigan (28 July 2000, unreported), HC 6.020
Ansbacher (Cayman) Ltd, Director of Corporate Enforcement v Collery, Re
[2006] IEHC 67 .... 13.124, 21.007, 21.008, 21.010,
21.012, 21.023, 21.038, 22.051, 23.018
Ansbacher (Cayman) Ltd, Director of Corporate Enforcement v Stakelum, Re
(31 July 2007, unreported), HC 1.001, 21.005, 21.007, 21.008,
21.027, 21.034, 21.041, 21.044
Ansbacher (Cayman) Ltd, Re [2002] IEHC 27, [2002] 2 IR 517 ....13.113, 13.114
Anthony & Ors v Wright & Ors [1995] 1 BLCL 236, [1995] BCC 768 ....7.142
Ardmore Studios (Ireland) Ltd v Lynch [1965] IR 1 ....8.075
Arulchelvan & Wright v Wright (7 February 1996, unreported), HC 3.030, 5.011, 5.036
Ashclad Ltd, Ashclad Ltd v Harrington, Re [2000] IEHC 174 ....4.030, 4.035, 6.022, 6.162
Atlantic Magnetics Ltd (in Receivership), Re [1993] 2 IR 561 ....10.047
Augustus Barnett & Son Ltd, Re [1986] BCLC 170 ....6.129

B

Balaghat Gold Mining Company Ltd, Re [1901] 2 KB 665 ....3.016
Bamfords Ireland Ltd, Stewart v Campbell, Re (13 June 1986, unreported), HC 8.065
Banco Ambrosiano SPA v Ansbacher & Co Ltd [1987] ILRM 669 ....4.028
Bank of Credit and Commerce International SA (in liq), Re [2004] 2 BCLC 236 ....6.131
Bank of Credit and Commerce International SA, Morris v Bank of India, Re
[2004] EWHC 528 (Ch), [2005] EWCA (Civ) 693, (2005) Times (19 July) 6.131, 6.132
Barings PLC (No 5), Secretary of State For Trade and Industry v Baker, Re
[1991] BCLC 433 ....16.065
Barnroe Ltd, Director of Corporate Enforcement v Rogers, Re
[2005] IEHC 433 .... 12.111, 21.027, 21.036, 22.006, 22.008,
22.021, 23.021, 23.022
Barrowland Ltd, Re [2003] IEHC 54 ....14.056, 14.081, 14.102, 14.104
Bath Glass Ltd, Re [1988] BCLC 329 ....22.030
Battle v Irish Art Promotion Centre Ltd [1968] 1 IR 254 ....15.009
Berg Sons & Co Ltd v Mervyn Hampton Adams & Ors [1993] BCLC 1045 ....7.025, 7.140

Bevan v Webb [1901] 2 Ch 59, 74 LJ Ch 300 ....4.016, 7.099

Bloomberg Developments Ltd, Bloomberg Developments Ltd v Philips Electrical
  (Ireland) Ltd, Re [2002] IESC 56, [2002] 2 IR 613 .... 14.069, 14.070

Bray v Ford [1896] AC 44 ....6.015

Brosnan v Sommerville [2006] IEHC 329 ....4.017, 11.038

Bula Ltd v Crowley (No 3) [2003] IESC 10, [2003] 1 IR 396 ....8.001

Bula Ltd v Crowley (No 4) [2003] IESC 28, [2003] 2 IR 430 ....8.050

Burke Clancy & Co Ltd, Re (23 May 1974, unreported), HC 6.023

Business Communications Ltd v Baxter
  (21 July 1995, unreported), HC 4.036, 17.012, 17.013, 17.030, 17.032, 17.033,
                                    17.077, 19.002, 19.003, 19.015, 19.022, 22.037, 22.042

Byng v London Life Assurance Ltd [1990] Ch 170,
  [1989] 2 WLR 738 ....5.042, 5.043, 5.044, 5.048

Byrne v Grey [1988] IR 31 ....12.100, 12.107

C

C (N) (A Bankrupt), Re [1999] IEHC 203 (26 November 1999) 22.046

Camoate Construction Ltd, Coyle v Callanan, Re [2005] IEHC 346 ....17.064

Canadian Aeroservices v O'Malley [1974] SCR 592 ....6.018

Candler v Crane, Christmas & Co Ltd [1951] 1 All ER 426,
  [1951] 2 KB 164 .... 7.025, 7.136, 7.138

Caparo Industries plc v Dickman [1990] 2 AC 605,
  [1990] All ER 568, [1990] BCLC 273 ....7.025, 7.137, 7.138, 7.140, 7.142, 7.143

Capital Auto Group Ltd, Foster v Swords, Re [2005] IEHC 434 ....17.037

Carecraft Construction Co Ltd, Re [1994] 1 WLR 172, [1994] 4 All ER 499 ....21.020

CB Readymix Concrete Ltd, Cahill v Grimes, Re
  [2002] IESC 12, [2002] 1 IR 372 ....6.162, 21.005, 21.011, 21.024, 21.025,
                            21.026, 21.027, 21.028, 21.030, 21.033, 21.034,
                            22.008, 22.016, 22.035, 22.036, 22.042, 22.043,
                            22.047, 23.002, 23.003, 23.004, 23.007, 23.008,
                            23.009, 23.010, 23.027, 23.029

Champion Telecom Ltd, Director of Corporate Enforcement v Allen, Re
  (19 February 2007, ex tempore), HC 22.087, 22.088

Chapman (JA) & Co Ltd, Secretary of State for Trade and Industry v Amiss, Re
  [2003] EWHC 532 (Ch), [2003] All ER (D) 317 Mar, [2003] 2 BCLC 206 ....23.017

Charnley Davies Ltd (No 2), Re [1990] BCLC 760 ....13.013

Chaulk v R [1990] 3 SCR 1303 ....12.121

Cherby Ltd, Kavanagh v Cooke, Re [2005] IEHC 219 ....6.014, 17.058

Chestvale Properties Ltd v Glackin [1993] 3 IR 35 .... 13.039, 13.043, 13.054, 13.055,
                                    13.070, 13.075, 13.078

Chestvale Properties Ltd v Glackin (No 2) (10 March, 1992, unreported), HC 13.040, 13.073

City Car Sales Ltd, Re [1995] 1 ILRM 221 ....8.072, 8.073

City Equitable Fire Insurance Co Ltd Re (No 1) (1925) Ch 407 ....22.019

Clare Textiles Ltd, Re [1993] 2 IR 213 ....10.030, 10.042, 10.048, 10.052, 10.054

Clarkes of Ranelagh Ltd, Re [2004] IEHC 320, [2004] 3 IR 264 ....14.033

Clawhammer Ltd, Re Director of Corporate Enforcement v McDonnell;
  Re Shinrone Food Market Ltd, Director of Corporate Enforcement v Hoctor;
  Re Cautious Trading Ltd, Director of Corporate Enforcement v Forristal
  [2005] IEHC 85, [2005] 1 IR 503 ....14.037, 19.024,
                                        19.028, 20.009, 20.033, 22.077, 22.080, 22.082,
                                        22.085, 22.086, 23.006, 23.007, 23.012, 23.013,
                                        23.014, 23.017, 23.019, 23.021, 23.025,
                                        23.026, 23.027, 23.028, 23.029
Club Tivoli Ltd Foster v Davies, Re [2005] IEHC 468 .... 17.058, 17.065
Clune v DPP [1981] ILRM 17 ....15.004
CMC (Ireland) Ltd, Carolan v Fennell, Re [2005] IEHC 340 .... 17.078, 17.079, 17.080
CMC (Ireland) Ltd, Fennell v Carolan, Re [2005] IEHC 59 .... 17.006, 17.007, 17.008,
                                        17.009, 17.065, 17.068
Comhlucht Páipéar Ríomhaireachta Teo v Údarás na Gaeltachta [1990] 1 IR 320 ....19.045
Comet Food Machinery Company Ltd, Re [1999] 1 IR 485.............................. 9.126, 9.127
Company, Re A [1980] Ch 138, [1980] 2 WLR 241, [1980] 1 All ER 284 ....22.011
Company, Re A [1983] Ch 178, [1983] 2 WLR 381, [1983] 2 All ER 36 ....13.013
Company, Re A [1986] BCLC 376 ....13.013
Cook v Deeks [1916] 1 AC 554 ....6.015
Cooke's Events Co Ltd, Kavanagh v Cooke, Re [2005] IEHC 225 ....6.014, 17.040,
                                        17.065, 22.038
Coulthard v Neville Russell [1997] All ER (D) 92, [1998] 1 BCLC 143 ....7.135
Countyglen plc v Carway [1998] 2 IR 540 ....13.101, 13.115, 13.122, 13.123
Countyglen plc, Re [1995] 1 IR 220 .... 13.039, 13.065
Cunard Steamship Co v Hopwood [1908] 2 Ch 564 ....2.102
Currie v Cowdenbeath Football Club Ltd [1992] BCLC 1029 ....5.018
Cyona Distributors Ltd, Re [1967] 1 All ER 281, [1967] Ch 889 ....6.142

D

DCS Ltd, Fitzpatrick v Henley, Re [2006] IEHC 179 .... 16.031, 17.065
Deauville Communications Worldwide Ltd, Re, Orlaford Ltd v Wetherhill
  [2002] 2 IR 32 ....14.044, 14.045, 14.046, 14.047, 14.057, 14.058, 14.075
Demite Ltd v Protec Health Ltd [1998] BCC 638 ....8.041
Desmond v Glackin [1993] 2 IR 106 ....10.027
Desmond v Glackin (No 1) [1993] 3 IR 1 ....13.098
Desmond v Glackin (No 2) [1993] 3 IR 67 ....13.040, 13.045, 13.082, 13.083, 13.098, 13.099
Diamond Telecom Ltd, Director of Corporate Enforcement v Banks, Re
  (16 February 2007, ex tempore), HC 22.087, 22.088
Director of Corporate Enforcement v Anderson (19 January 2006, unreported),
  Dublin District Court 6.118
Director of Corporate Enforcement v Cloudbury Developments Ltd
  (unreported, 22 June 2007), Newport District Court 15.010
Director of Corporate Enforcement v Curran [2007] IEHC 181 ....21.022
Director of Corporate Enforcement v Gannon [2002] 4 IR 439 .... 7.044, 7.045, 7.046, 7.047,
                                        7.048, 7.054, 15.049
Director of Corporate Enforcement v Gannon (18 March 2004, unreported),
  Naas District Court 6.147
Director of Corporate Enforcement v Jeffrey Norman Burton
  (6 May 2003, unreported), Dublin District Court 20.040
Director of Corporate Enforcement v McCormack (1 November 2002, unreported),
  Edenderry District Court 3.034, 3.041

Director of Corporate Enforcement v Mediasatellite Ireland Ltd
(20 June 2007, unreported), Cork District Court 15.010
Director of Corporate Enforcement v Muhammad Sabir Hafeez
(21 June 2006, unreported), Dublin District Court 7.051
Director of Corporate Enforcement v O'Brien (2 March 2006, unreported),
Midleton District Court 6.096, 20.033
Director of Corporate Enforcement v O'Donohue (6 December 2005, unreported),
Swords District Court 19.023
Director of Corporate Enforcement v Rogers [2005] IEHC 443 ....4.036
Director of Corporate Enforcement v Scanlon (20 December 2005, unreported),
Dunshaughlin District Court 19.023
Director of Corporate Enforcement v This N' That Athenry Ltd
(14 November 2006, unreported), Athenry District Court 15.010
Document Imagining Systems Ltd, Re [2005] IEHC 250,
[2005] 3 IR 103 ....18.005, 18.006, 18.007
Doherty Advertising Ltd, Stafford v Beggs, Re [2006] IEHC 258 .... 19.042, 19.043, 19.044
Don Bluth Entertainment Ltd, Re [1994] 3 IR 141 ....10.040, 10.043, 10.044, 14.069
DPP v Byrne [1995] 1 ILRM 279 ....6.145
DPP v Clarkin (10 February 2003, unreported), Court of Criminal Appeal 6.137
DPP v Gaffney [1987] IR 173 ....12.110
Dublin Sports Cafe Ltd, Farrell v Long, Re [2005] IEHC 458 ....16.036, 17.013,
17.032, 17.065
Duignan v Carway [2001] 4 IR 550 ....17.074
Dunleckney Ltd, Re [1999] IEHC 109 .... 16.009, 17.064, 17.068
Dunnes Stores (ILAC) v Houlihan [2003] IEHC 619 .... 12.002, 12.038
Dunnes Stores Ireland Co Ltd v Maloney [1999] 3 IR 542 .... 12.040, 12.043, 12.044, 12.046,
12.048, 12.050, 12.053, 12.059, 12.060,
12.061, 13.029, 13.076, 13.080
Dunnes Stores Ireland Co Ltd v Ryan [1999] IEHC 184, [2000] 2 IR 60,
[2002] 2 IR 60, [2000] IEHC 141, [2000] IESC 46..........................12.002, 12.015, 12.017,
12.018, 12.019, 12.021, 12.024, 12.025,
12.027, 12.030, 12.031, 12.034, 12.041,
12.042, 12.045, 12.046, 12.054, 12.056,
12.079, 12.089, 12.099, 12.132, 13.001,
13.019, 13.020, 13.021, 13.022, 13.023,
13.029, 13.031, 13.045, 13.077

E

East Donegal Co-Operative Livestock Mart Ltd v Attorney General
[1970] IR 317 .... 12.044, 13.090, 18.014
Edenfell Holdings Ltd, Re [1999] 1 IR 443 ....8.045, 8.050
E-Host Europe Ltd, Coyle v O'Brien, Re [2003] 2 IR 627 ....17.070
Eisc Teoranta, Re [1991] ILRM 760 ....8.057, 8.059
El Sombrero Ltd, Re [1958] Ch 900, [1958] 3 WLR 349 ....5.050
Enron Corporation Securities, Re 258 F Supp 2d 576; 2003 US Dist LEXIS 3786;
Fed Sec L Rep (CCH) P92,296 (SD Tex March 12, 2003) 1.001, 7.001
Eurofood IFSC Ltd, Re [2004] 4 IR 370 .... 9.043, 9.044, 9.046
Eurofood IFSC Ltd, Re C-341/04, [2006] ECR I-03813, [2006] 3 WLR 309 ....9.046

Euroking Miracle (Ireland) Ltd (In Voluntary Liquidation),
  Fennell v Frost , Re [2003] IEHC 15, [2003] 3 IR 80 ....16.020, 17.059, 17.065, 18.002,
  18.003, 18.008, 18.011, 18.012,
  18.015, 18.016, 18.017

F

Fayed v UK (Case 28/1993/423/502) (A/294-B) (1994) 18 EHRR 393 ....12.092, 13.053
Ferngara, Robinson v Forrest, Re [1999] IEHC 103 [1999] 1 IR 429,
  [1999] 2 ILRM 169 ....17.077
Ferreira v Levin [1996] ISA 484 ....13.088
Finchley Construction Ltd, Roache v Culloo, Re [2005] IEHC 448 ....17.058
First Class Toy Traders Ltd, Re (in liq), Gray v McLoughlin
  [2004] IEHC 289 ....16.056, 16.063, 16.064, 16.065, 17.065
Fomento (Sterling Area) Ltd v Selsdon Fountain Pen Co Ltd and Others
  [1958] 1 WLR 45, [1958] 1 All ER 11, [1958] RPC 8 ....7.099, 7.147
Foss v Harbottle (1843) 2 Hare 461 ....5.023, 13.013
Friends of the Curragh Environment Ltd, Re [2006] IEHC 243 ....15.009
Fruit and Vegetable Growers' Association Ltd v Kekewich [1912] 2 Ch 52,
  81 LJ Ch 499 ....5.020
Funke v France Series A, No 256-A, [1993] 1 CMLR 897, 16 EHRR 297 ....12.091
Fyffes plc v DCC plc [2005] IESC 3, [2005] 1 IR 59....................................1.008, 7.121

G

Gallagher v National Maternity Hospital [1998] 2 IR 267 ....7.119
Galoo Ltd (In Liq) v Bright Grahame Murray (a firm) [1994] 1 WLR 1360,
  [1995] 1 All ER 16, [1994] 2 BCLC 492 ....7.072, 7.142
Gasco Ltd, Re [2001] IEHC 20, [2001] 5 ICLMD 21 ....16.042, 16.043, 16.045,
  16.046, 16.052, 16.053, 17.004,
  17.035, 17.036, 17.065
Gerald Cooper Chemicals Ltd, Re [1978] Ch 262 ....6.123, 6.126
Glackin v Trustee Savings Bank [1993] 3 IR 55 ....12.087, 13.073, 13.075
GMT Engineering Services Ltd (in voluntary liquidation) Luby v McMahon, Re
  [2003] 4 IR 133 ....19.028, 19.029,
  19.035, 19.036, 19.037
Gomba Holdings Ltd v Minories Finance Ltd [1988] 1 WLR 1231,
  [1989] 1 All ER 261 ....8.001
Greenmount Holdings Ltd, Stafford v O'Connor, Re
  [2007] IEHC 246 .... 17.013, 17.064, 17.065
Greycaine Ltd, Re [1946] Ch 269, [1946] 2 All ER 30 ....8.073
Guinness plc v Saunders [1988] 2 All ER 940 ....6.106

H

Haltone (Cork) Ltd, Re [1996] 1 IR 32 .... 14.062, 14.063, 14.064
Hanafin v The Minister for the Environment [1996] 2 IR 321, [1996] 2 ILRM 161 ....4.028
Hanahoe v Hussey [1998] 3 IR 69 ....12.109, 12.110
Harrison (JJ) (Properties) Ltd v Harrison [2002] 1 BCLC 162 ....6.022
Harrison (Saul D) & Sons plc, Re [1995] 1 BCLC 14 ....13.013
Hartley Baird Ltd, Re [1955] Ch 143, [1954] 3 WLR 946 ....5.036
Haughey v Moriarty [1999] 3 IR 1 ....12.059, 12.060
Haughey, Re [1971] IR 217 ....13.054, 13.059, 13.098, 13.099
Hayes Homes Ltd, Re [2004] IEHC 124, [2004] 10 ICLMD 45 ....9.005

Healy v Healy Homes Ltd [1973] IR 309 ....4.014, 4.015, 4.016, 4.017
Heaney v Ireland [1994] 3 IR 593 ....12.121, 13.086
Heaney v Ireland [1996] 1 IR 580 ....13.086
Hedley Byrne & Co Ltd v Heller & Partners Ltd [1964] AC 465,
    [1963] 2 All ER 575 ....7.137, 7.138
Hely-Hutchinson v Brayhead Ltd [1967] 3 All ER 98 ....6.106
Hennessy v National Agricultural and Industrial Development Association Ltd
    [1947] IR 159 ....5.037
Holidair Ltd, Re [1994] 1 IR 434 ....10.020
Honiball v McGrath [2000] IEHC 33, [2000] 6 ICLMD 59 ....13.119
Horgan (John) Livestock Ltd, O'Mahony v Horgan, Re [1995] IESC 6,
    [1995] 2 IR 411, [1996] 1 ILRM 161 ....9.117, 9.118
Hunting Lodges Ltd, Re [1984] IEHC 3,
    [1985] ILRM 75 ....6.122, 6.124, 6.125, 6.126, 6.128, 6.129, 6.136
Hydrodam (Corby) Ltd, Re [1994] 2 BCLC 180, [1994] BCC 166 ....6.035, 16.051

                                                        I

Iarnrod Éireann v Ireland [1996] IESC 221, [1996] 3 IR 321 ....7.133
Inner House Conti v UeberseeBank AG, (2000) Times Law Reports, 15 March 14.091
INS Realisations Ltd; Secretary of State for Trade and Industry v Jonkler, Re
    [2006] EWHC 135 (Ch), [2006] 1 WLR 3433, [2006] 2 All ER 902 ....21.020
International Fishing Vessels Ltd v Minister for Marine [1989] IR 149 ....12.048, 12.049
International Retail Ltd, Re (19 September 1974, unreported), HC 2.087
Inverdeck Ltd, Re [1998] 2 BCLC 242 ....3.018
Irish Oil & Cake Mills Ltd v Donnelly [1983] HC 798
    (27 March 1983, unreported), HC 8.001, 8.023, 8.033, 8.037
Isle of Wight Ry Co v Tahourdin [1883] 25 Ch D 320 ....5.021, 5.023

                                                        J

Jacob (Walter L) & Co Ltd, Re [1989] BCLC 345, 5 BCC 244 ....13.120
JEB Fasteners Ltd v Marks Bloom & Co [1981] 3 All ER 289 ....7.141
Jesner v Jerrad Properties Ltd [1993] BCLC 1032, [1992] BCC 807 ....13.013
JN 2 Ltd, Re [1978] 1 WLR 183, [1977] All ER 1104 ....3.031
Jones v Gunn [1997] IEHC 27, [1997] 3 IR 1 ....9.122

                                                        K

Kaytech International plc, Secretary of State for Industry v Kaczer, Re
    [1998] All ER (D) 655, [1999] 2 BCLC 351, [1999] BCC 390 ....16.064, 16.065
Kelly Technical Services (Ireland) Ltd, Kavanagh v Kelly, Re
    [2005] IEHC 421 ....16.056, 17.058
Kelly v Haughey Boland [1985] IEHC 209, [1989] ILRM 373,
    (30 July 1985, unreported), HC 7.025, 7.141
Kelly's Carpetdrome Ltd, Re (1 July 1983, unreported), HC 22.029
Kennedy v Law Society [2000] 2 IR 204 (HC), [2002] 2 IR 458 (SC) 7.073, 7.145
Kent Coalfields Syndicate Ltd, Re [1898] 1 QB 754 ....3.015
Kentford Securities Ltd, Director of Corporate Enforcement v McCann, Re
    [2006] IEHC 57; [2007] IEHC 1 ....7.052, 21.005, 21.010, 21.01621.035, 21.042,
                                    21.043, 21.046, 21.047, 21.048, 21.049, 21.051,
                                                            22.010, 22.020, 23.027
Kingston Cotton Mills Co (No 2), Re [1896] 2 Ch 279 ....7.071, 7.073, 7.145, 7.146

Kinsella Hire Ltd, Director of Corporate Enforcement v Kinsella, Re
(16 April 2007, ex tempore), HC 22.087
Kinsella v Somers [1999] IEHC 44, [2000] ICLMD 3 ....8.039
Knocklofty House Hotel Ltd, Re [2005] IEHC 105, [2005] 7 ICLMD 25 ....17.075

L

La Moselle Clothing Co Ltd v Soualhi [1998] IEHC 66,
[1998] 2 ILRM 345 ....6.025, 6.167, 6.168, 16.046, 16.058,
17.001, 17.002, 17.005, 17.006, 17.012,
17.013, 17.016, 17.018, 17.019, 17.022, 17.025,
17.028, 17.030, 17.032, 17.034, 17.059, 17.063,
17.064, 17.065, 17.067, 21.025, 22.037, 22.038

Lambert Jones Estates Ltd v Donnelly [1982] IEHC 47
(5 November 1982, unreported), HC 8.042, 8.043
Lavender v Lavender (1875) 9 Ir Eq 593 ....8.077
Leeds Estate Building and Investment Co v Shepherd [1887] 36 Ch D 787 ....7.073
Leitch (William C) Bros Ltd, Re [1932] 2 Ch 71 ....6.139, 6.140
Lo-Line Electric Motors Ltd, Re [1988] Ch 477, [1998] 3 WLR 26,
[1998] 2 All ER 692, [1988] BCLC 698 .... 16.057, 17.019, 21.005, 21.025,
21.026, 21.027, 21.028, 21.030, 21.032,
21.033, 21.034, 21.036, 22.017, 22.036,
22.037, 22.038, 22.039
Lombard & Ulster Banking (Irl) Ltd v Amurec Ltd [1976–1977] ILRM 222 ....2.105
London and General Bank (No 2), Re [1895] 2 Ch 673 .... 7.073, 7.145, 7.146
London School of Electronics, Re [1986] Ch 211, [1985] 3 WLR 474,
[1985] BCLC 273 ....13.013
Lonrho plc, Re [1990] 2 AC 154, [1989] 3 WLR 535, [1989] 2 All ER 1100 ....13.117
Lynch v Cooney [1982] IR 337 .... 12.040, 12.044, 13.029
Lynrowan Enterprises Ltd, Re [2002] IEHC 90,
[2002] 10 ICLMD 16 .... 6.006, 6.025, 6.035,6.167, 16.033, 16.035,
16.051, 16.057, 16.058, 16.061, 16.062, 16.063,
16.064, 17.044, 17.045, 17.064, 17.065, 17.069
Lyons v Curran [1993] ILRM 375 ....13.103

M

Maidstone Building Provisions Ltd, Re [1971] 1 WLR 1085,
[1971] 3 All ER 363 ....6.129, 6.130
Man Nutzfahrzeuge Aktiengesellschaft and others v Freightliner Ltd
[2003] EWHC 2245 (Comm), [2003] All ER (D) 105 ....7.148
Manifest Shipping Co Ltd v Uni-Polaris Shipping Co Ltd [2001] UKHL 1,
[2003] 1 AC 469 ....6.131
Manning Furniture Ltd, Re [1996] 1 ILRM 13 ....8.058, 8.059
Mantruck Services Ltd, Mehigan v Duignan, Re [1996] IEHC 18,
[1997] 1 IR 340, [1997] 1 ILRM 171 .... 4.027, 4.028, 4.029, 4.030, 4.035, 17.033
Maxwell v Department of Trade and Industry [1974] QB 523,
[1974] 2 WLR 338, [1974] 2 All ER 122 .... 13.058, 13.108, 13.109
MC Plant Sales Ltd, Director of Corporate Enforcement v Christy, Re
(27 November 2006, ex tempore), HC 22.087
McCarter (WP) & Co Ltd v Roughan [1986] ILRM 447 ....8.044

McCormack v The Garda Síochána Complaints Board [1997] 2 IR 489,
    [1997] 2 ILRM 321 ....12.048
McKenna v E H [2001] IEHC 139 ....18.014
McNaughton (James) Papers Group Ltd v Hicks Anderson & Co (a firm)
    [1991] 2 QB 113, [1991] 2 WLR 641, [1991] 1 All ER 134, [1991] BCLC 163 ....7.139
Merit Marketing Ltd and Royal Associates Ltd,
    Director of Corporate Enforcement v Browne, Re (30 July 2007, ex tempore), HC 22.087
Miley v Flood [2001] 2 IR 50, [2001] 1 ILRM 489 ....7.119
Minister for Industry and Commerce v Hales [1967] IR 50 ....19.040
Minister for Justice v Siucre Éireann cpt [1992] 2 IR 215 ....13.033, 13.127, 13.128, 13.129
Mitek Holdings Ltd, Grace v Kachkar, Re [2005] IEHC 160, [2005] 4 IR 522 ....19.030
Mitek Holdings Ltd, Grace v Kachkar, Re [2005] IEHC 63 ....6.167, 16.015, 16.020,
    17.010, 17.056, 17.057, 17.065
Money Markets International Stock Brokers Ltd, Re [2006] IEHC 350 ....17.012
Motor Racing Circuits Ltd, Re [1997] IESC 59................................. 8.002, 8.003, 8.079
Moypool Ltd, Gannon v O'Hora, Re [2006] IEHC 149 .... 19.031, 19.032, 19.033
Muckross Park Hotel Ltd, Re (21 February 2001, unreported), Killarney District Court 5.007
Murph's Restaurants Ltd, Re [1979] ILRM 141 ....6.172
Musselwhite v Musselwhite & Son Ltd [1962] Ch 964, [1962] 2 WLR 374 ....5.014

N

National Irish Bank (Under Investigation) v Companies Acts [2006] IEHC 35,
    2 ILRM 263 ....13.001, 13.109
National Irish Bank Ltd (No 1), Re [1999] 3 IR 145,
    [1999] ILRM 321 .... 13.056, 13.058, 13.059, 13.085, 13.087, 13.088,
    13.089, 13.090, 13.105
National Irish Bank Ltd (No 2), Re [1999] 3 IR 190,
    [1999] 2 ILRM 443 ....13.057, 13.058, 13.059, 13.060, 13.061,
    13.062, 13.105, 13.106
National Irish Bank Ltd (No 3), Re [2004] IEHC 287, [2004] 4 IR 186 ....13.116, 13.120
National Irish Bank Ltd, Director of Corporate Enforcement v Curran, Re
    [2007] IEHC 181 .... 21.019, 21.022, 21.027, 21.033, 21.039,
    21.040, 21.044, 21.045, 22.021, 22.022
National Irish Bank Ltd, Director of Corporate Enforcement v Seymour, Re
    [2006] IEHC 369, [2007] IEHC 102 .... 21.005, 21.006, 21.027, 21.032,
    21.033, 21.034, 21.038, 21.043, 21.044,
    21.047, 21.050, 22.019, 22.021,
    22.022, , 23.020
National Irish Bank Ltd, Director of Corporate Enforcement, Re v D'Arcy
    [2006] 2 IR 163; [2005] IEHC 333 .... 13.124, 21.004, 21.005, 21.007,
    21.010, 21.012, 21.021, 21.023,
    21.027, 21.029, 21.030, 21.031,
    21.038, 21.039, 22.011, 22.012,
    22.021, 22.022, 23.019
National Irish Bank Ltd, Re [2006] IEHC 35, 2 ILRM 263 ....13.109
National Provincial & Union Bank of England v Charnley [1924] 1 KB 431 ....2.102
Nelson Car Hire Ltd, Re (1971) 107 ILTR 97 ....14.046
New Ad Advertising Company Ltd, Re [2006] IEHC 19 .... 14.034, 14.064, 14.065,
    14.067, 14.068
New Millennium Experience Co Ltd, Re [2003] EWHC 1823
    (Ch, 23 July 2003) [2004] 1 AER 687 ....3.027

New Timbiqui Gold Mines Ltd, Re [1961] 1 Ch 319, [1961] All ER 865 .... 14.043, 14.092

Newcastle Timber (in liq), Re [2001] IEHC 146, [2001] 4 IR 586 ....6.167, 6.168,
16.015, 17.038, 17.062, 17.065,
20.004, 21.011, 21.025, 21.026, 21.030,
22.016, 22.017, 22.018, 22.022, 22.024,
22.039, 22.044, 22.045, 22.047, 23.022

Niemietz v Germany (1993) 16 EHRR 97 ....12.100

Norse Security Ltd, Re (15 November 2004, unreported), HC 22.081, 23.014

Norwest Holst Ltd v Secretary of State for Trade [1978] 1 Ch 201,
[1978] 3 WLR 73, [1978] 3 All ER 280 .... 12.042, 12.046, 12.051, 12.062, 13.031

Nye (CL) Ltd, Re [1971] Ch 442, [1970] 3 WLR 158, [1970] 3 All ER 1061 .... 2.102, 2.105

O

O'Keeffe v Ferris [1993] 3 IR 165 ....6.121, 6.122, 22.027

O'Neill (Colm) Engineering Services Ltd, Re [2004] IEHC 83 .... 6.166, 16.005, 17.020,
17.042, 17.045, 17.069

O'Neill v Beaumont Hospital Board [1990] ILRM 419 ....13.054

O'Neill v Phillips [1999] 1 WLR 1092, [1999] 2 All ER 961, [1999] 2 BCLC 1 ....13.013

Official Receiver v Stern [2001] EWHC Civ 1787, [2001] All ER (D) 278 (Nov),
[2002] 1 BCLC 119 ....23.017

Olhausen v Powderley [1943] IR 426 ....3.019, 3.020

Opera Photographic Ltd, Re [1989] 1 WLR 634, [1989] BCLC 763 ....5.051

P

Pamstock Ltd, Re [1994] 1 BCLC 716 ....21.007

Patrick & Lyon Ltd, Re [1933] 1 Ch 786 .... 6.135, 6.139, 6.140

Pearce Duff & Co Ltd, Re [1960] 3 All ER 222, [1960] 1 WLR 1014 ....5.032

Pelling v Families Need Fathers Ltd [2001] EWCA Civ 1280, [2002] 2 All ER 440 ....3.017

People (Attorney General) v Cummins [1972] IR 312 ....13.089

People (DPP) v Kenny [1990] 2 IR 110 ....12.110

People (DPP) v Clarkin (10 February 2003, unreported),
Court of Criminal Appeal 6.145, 6.146, 6.147

People (DPP) v McCormack [2000] 4 IR 356 ....6.145

People (DPP) v WC [1994] 1 ILRM 321 ....6.145

Performing Right Society Ltd, Re [1978] 1 WLR 1197, [1978] 3 All ER 972 ....3.006

Pergamon Press Ltd, Re [1971] Ch 388, [1970] 3 All ER 535 .... 13.054, 13.107, 13.109

Philippou (1989) 89 Cr App R 290 ....6.123

Phoenix Shannon v Purkey (No 5) [1997] IEHC 214, [1998] 4 IR 597,
[1997] 2 ILRM 381 .... 5.008, 5.009

Pierce (James) & Sons Ltd, Director of Corporate Enforcement v Pierce, Re
(18 December 2006, ex tempore), HC 22.087

Pineroad Distribution Ltd, Stafford v Fleming, Re [2007] IEHC 55 ....17.058, 17.065

PNC Telecom plc v Thomas [2002] EWHC 2848 (Ch), [2002] All ER 315(D),
[2004] 1 BCLC 88 ....5.020

Potters Oils Ltd (No 2), Re [1986] 1 WLR 201, [1986] 1 All ER 890 ....8.073

Primor plc v Stokes Kennedy Crowley [1996] 2 IR 459 .... 17.072, 17.073, 17.075

Probets v Glackin [1993] 3 IR 134 ....13.045

Q

Quickson (South and West) Ltd v Katz & Anor CA 1963, [2004] EWHC 2443 (Ch)
(25 August 2004), [2004] All ER (D) 138 (Aug), [2006] 1 BCLC 9 ....9.016

R

R (Clegg) v Secretary of State [2002] EWCA Civ 519, [2002] All ER (D) 114 (Apr) 13.107
R v Cox [1983] BCLC 169 ....6.135
R v Grantham [1984] QB 675 ....6.140
R v IRC Ex p Rossminster [1980] AC 952, [1980] 2 WLR 1, [1980] 1 All ER 80 ....12.110
R v Kemp [1988] QB 645, [1988] 2 WLR 975 ....6.142
R v Landy [1981] 1 All ER 1172 ....6.135
R v Registrar of Companies, ex p Central Bank of India [1986] QB 1114,
    [1986] 1 All ER 105 ....2.104
R v Registrar of Companies, ex p Esal Commodities Ltd [1986] QB 1114,
    [1985] 2 WLR 447 ....2.103
R v Secretary of State, ex p Lonrho [1989] 1 WLR 525, [1989] 2 All ER 609 ....13.117
R v Secretary of State, ex p Perestrello [1981] QB 19 [1980] 3 WLR 1 ... 12.046, 12.055, 12.056
R v Smith [1996] 2 BCLC 109 .... 6.141, 6.144, 6.146
R v Ward (27 November 2000, unreported) 6.144
Rayhill Property Company Ltd, Conroy v Corneill, Re
    [2003] 3 IR 588 ....4.031, 4.032, 4.033, 4.034, 4.035
Red Sail Frozen Foods Ltd, Re [2006] IEHC 328 ....8.054, 8.072
Regal (Hastings) v Gulliver [1967] 2 AC 134 ....6.015
Regal (Hastings) v Gulliver, Re [1942] 1 All ER 378 ....6.021
Registrar of Companies v Anderson [2004] IESC 103, [2005] 1 IR 21 ....2.058, 11.068, 15.045
Rex Williams Leisure, Re [1994] Ch 1, [1993] 2 All ER 741, [1993] 3 WLR 685,
    [1993] BCLC 568 ....12.090
Richborough Furniture Ltd, Re (1996) 1 BCLC 507 ....16.057, 16.061, 16.063, 16.064
Richmond Building Products Ltd v Soundgables Ltd [2004] IEHC 382,
    [2005] 3 IR 321, [2005] 1 ILRM 497 ....14.106, 14.107, 14.109
Ridsdel, Ridsdel v Rawlinson, Re [1947] 2 All ER 312 ....7.099
RMF (Ireland) Ltd, Kavanagh v Riedler, Re [2004] IEHC 334,
    [2004] 3 IR 498 ....16.028, 16.030, 16.031, 16.032, 17.062
Rogers v Maloney [2005] IEHC 433 ....7.099, 12.002, 12.054, 12.063, 12.105,
                                                                                     12.111, 12.117, 12.123, 12.125
Rose v McGivern [1998] 2 BCLC 593 ....5.021
Ruby Property Company Ltd v Kilty
    [1999] IEHC 50... 6.001, 6.031, 6.054, 8.046, 8.047, 8.048

S

Sasea Finance Ltd (In Liq) v KPMG [2000] 1 All ER 676, [2000] 1 BCLC 236 ....7.072
Saunders (TH) & Co Ltd, Re [1908] 1 Ch 415 ....3.008
Saunders v United Kingdom (Case 43/1994/490/572) (1996) 23 EHRR 313,
    [1998] 1 BCLC 362 ....12.092, 13.053, 13.086, 13.088
Scottish Co-Operative Society Ltd v Meyer [1959] AC 324, [1958] 3 WLR 404,
    [1958] 3 All ER 66 ....13.013
SEC v Solucorp, 2002 WL 741660 (SDNY 26 April 2002) 7.104
SEC v WorldCom Inc 273 F Supp 2d 431&& 2003 US Dist LEXIS 11394;
    Fed Sec L Rep (CCH) P92,456 (SDNY 7 July 2003) 1.001, 7.001
Secretary of State for Trade and Industry v Ashcroft [1998] Ch 71,
    [1997] 3 WLR 319, [1997] 3 All ER 86 ....12.002, 12.090
Secretary of State for Trade and Industry v Rogers [1996] 1 WLR 1569,
    [1996] 4 All ER 854 ....21.020
Secretary of State for Trade and Industry v Swan [2005] EWHC 603 (Ch),
    [2005] All ER (D) 102 (Apr) 23.017

Secretary of State for Trade and Industry v Tjolle [1998] 1 BCLC 333,
[1998] BCC 282 .... 16.064, 16.065
Sevenoaks Stationers (Retail) Ltd, Re [1991] Ch 164, [1990] 3 WLR 1165,
[1991] All ER 578, [1991] BCLC 325 .... 23.015, 23.016, 23.017, 23.019
Silken Construction Ltd, Kavanagh v O'Donoghue, Re [2003] 4 IR 443 .... 18.018
Smith Ltd v Middleton [1979] 3 All ER 842 .... 8.037
Somers v Kennedy [1998] 1 IR 1 .... 8.018, 8.019, 8.020
South London Greyhound Racecourses Ltd v Wake [1931] 1 Ch 496 .... 3.028
Specified Aluminium Ltd, Director of Corporate Enforcement v Donoghue, Re
(16 February 2007, ex tempore), HC 22.087, 22.088
SPH Ltd, Fennell v Shanahan, Re [2005] IEHC 152 .... 16.013, 16.046, 17.004, 17.013,
17.016, 17.022, 17.032, 17.040,
17.041, 17.061, 17.065
Springline Ltd (In liq), Re [1999] 1 IR 467, [1999] 1 ILRM 15 .... 10.046
Squash (Ireland) Ltd, Re [2001] IESC 200, [2001] 3 IR 35 .... 16.015, 16.046, 17.004, 17.016,
21.025, 22.037, 22.038
St George's Estate, Re (1887) 19 LR Ir 556 .... 8.077
State (Lynch) v Cooney [1982] IR 337, [1982] ILRM 190 .... 12.044, 12.109, 12.110, 13.045
State (O) v O'Brien [1973] IR 50 .... 13.065
State of Wyoming Syndicate Ltd, Re [1901] 2 Ch 431 .... 5.022
Steamline Ltd (In Voluntary Liquidation), Re [2001] 1 IR 103 .... 18.006
Supreme Oil Co Ltd, Hughes v Duffy, Re [2005] IEHC 145,
[2005] 1 IR 571 .... 17.073, 17.074
Sussex Brick Co Ltd, Re [1904] 1 Ch 598 .... 3.027
Swaledale Cleaners Ltd, Re [1968] 1 WLR 1710, [1968] 3 All ER 619 .... 3.018
Swanpool Ltd, McLaughlin v Lannen, Re [2005] IEHC 341, [2006] 2 ILRM 217 .... 17.065

T

Tangney v Clarence Hotels Co Ltd [1933] IR 51 .... 3.022
TDI Metro Ltd v Delap (No 1) [2000] 4 IR 337, TDI Metro Ltd v Delap
(No 2) [2000] 4 IR 520 .... 15.004, 18.005
Tenants First (Ireland) Ltd, Director of Corporate Enforcement v McGovern, Re
(12 October 2004, unreported), Dundalk District Court 20.040, 22.070
Thomas Gerrard, Re [1968] Ch 455, [1967] 2 All ER 525 .... 7.025
Times Newspapers Ltd v United Kingdom (1979) 2 EHRR 245 .... 12.121
Tipperary Fresh Foods Ltd, O'Riordan v O'Connor, Re [2005] IEHC 96,
[2005] 1 IR 551 .... 19.025, 19.026, 19.029, 19.030
Todd (L), Re [1990] BCLC 454 .... 6.140
Tournier v National Provincial and Union Bank of England [1924] 1 KB 461 .... 12.087
Tralee Beef and Lamb Ltd, Kavanagh v Delaney, Re
[2004] IEHC 139, [2005] 1 ILRM 34 .... 16.008, 16.015, 16.028, 16.030,
16.031, 16.034, 16.035, 16.046, 16.066,
17.004, 17.010, 17.013, 17.022, 17.024,
17.025, 17.029, 17.030, 17.032, 17.040,
17.043, 17.045, 17.046, 17.047, 17.065
Tuama v Allied Metropole Hotel Ltd (19 December 1988, unreported), HC 3.032
Tuskar Resources plc, Re [2001] IEHC 27 [2001] 1 IR 668 .... 10.003

U

Ultramares Corp v Touche 174 NE 444, (1931) 255 NY 170 .... 7.135, 7.142

Union Music Ltd v Watson [2003] EWCA Civ 180, [2003] All ER (D) 328 (Jan),
[2003] 1 BCLC 453 ....5.051
USIT Ireland Ltd, Re [2003] IEHC 44, [2003] 2 IR 635, [2004] 1 ILRM 296 ....16.048
USIT World plc, Re [2005] IEHC 285 ....15.016, 16.014, 16.016, 16.018, 16.019,
17.002, 17.012, 17.014, 17.015,
17.017, 17.021, 17.065, 18.010

V

Verit Hotel and Leisure (Ireland) Ltd, Duignan v Carway, Re
[2001] IESC 74; [2002] IEHC 1, [2001] 4 IR 550 .... 16.005, 16.007, 16.011,
16.012, 17.060, 17.065, 17.071,
17.072, 17.073, 17.075, 18.001,
18.009, 18.010
Via Net Works Ireland Ltd [2002] IESC 24, [2002] 2 IR 47 ....3.033
Visual Impact and Displays Ltd, Murphy v Murphy, Re
[2003] IEHC 91, [2003] 4 IR 451 .... 16.023, 16.024, 19.028, 19.036,
19.038, 19.039, 19.040, 19.041, 19.042,
19.044, 19.045, 19.046, 19.047, 19.048

W

Welham v DPP [1961] AC 103 ....6.138
West Canadian Collieries, Re [1962] Ch 370, [1961] 3 WLR 1416,
[1962] 1 All ER 26 ....5.014
Westmid Packing Ltd, Re [1998] 2 All ER 124 .... 21.007, 23.018, 23.019
White v Bristol Aeroplane Co Ltd [1953] Ch 65, [1953] 2 WLR 144 ....5.030
Wise Finance Company v O'Regan [1998] IEHC 105 .... 8.004, 8.009
Wogans (Drogheda) Ltd (No 3), Re (9 February 1993, unreported), HC 10.003
Wood Products (Longford) Ltd, Director of Corporate Enforcement, Re v McGowan
[2005] IEHC 41 ....11.037, 20.005, 21.028, 21.030, 22.056, 22.059, 22.061, 23.023
Worldport (Ireland) Ltd, Re [2005] IEHC 467 ....16.054

X

XNet Information Systems Ltd, Higgins v Stafford, Re [2006] IEHC 289 ....17.081

Y

Yolland, Husson and Birkett, Re [1908] 1 Ch 152 ....2.102

Z

Z Ltd v A-Z and AA-LL [1982] 1 QB 558, [1982] 2 WLR 288, [1982] 1 All ER 556,
[1982] 1 Lloyd's Rep 240 ....9.117

Table of Statutes

ACC Bank Act 2001
  s 12 .... 2.023

Bills of Sale (Ireland) Act 1879
  s 4 .... 2.089

Broadcasting Act 1990
  s 14 .... 12.100

Building Societies Act 1989 .... 7.127

Central Bank Act 1971 .... 2.023
  s 7 (4) 10.029, 13.091, 13.096
   9 .... 7.129, 13.091, 13.111

Central Bank Act 1989
  s 47 (1) 7.126

Central Bank Acts 1942 to 1998 .... 12.135

Central Bank and Financial Services
  Authority of Ireland Act 2003 ..... 6.149
  s 35 (1) 6.149
  Sch 1 Pt 4 .... 6.149

Central Bank and Financial Services
  Authority of Ireland Acts 2003 .... 1.008

Central Bank and Financial Services
  Authority of Ireland Acts 2004 .... 1.008

Charities Act 1960 .... 3.031

Civil Liability Act 1961 .... 7.133

Criminal Justice (Theft and Fraud Offences)
  Act 2001
  s 59 .... 7.071, 7.126

Committees of the Houses of the
  Oireachtas (Compellability,
  Privileges and Immunities
  of Witnesses) Act 1997 .... 12.136

Companies (Amendment)
  (No 2) Act 1999 .... 10.001, 10.039,
              10.047, 10.050, 10.054,
              10.055, 10.059, 10.060,
              10.062, 10.064, 10.068,
              10.072, 14.015, 14.020,
              14.060, 14.062, 14.063
  s 7 .... 10.039, 10.064, 10.072
   9 .... 10.040
   12 .... 10.037, 10.038

14 .... 10.002, 10.004
15 .... 10.039
16 .... 10.002, 10.004
  (a) 8.080
18 .... 10.020, 10.022
  (4) 10.002
19 .... 10.027
20 .... 10.008
21 .... 10.072
22 .... 10.002, 10.050, 10.051,
          10.055, 10.059, 10.061,
          10.062, 10.063, 10.071
23 .... 10.058
24 .... 10.066, 10.067, 10.071
26 .... 10.053, 10.068
27 .... 10.070
28 .... 10.046, 10.049
29 .... 10.069, 10.072
30 (2) 10.069
32 .... 7.129, 7.132
  (1) (a) 7.130
  (3) 7.129
32A–32B 7.129
33 .... 7.129, 7.132
  (1)–(2), (7) 7.131
41 .... 15.024, 15.025
42 (1) 2.013
  (2) 2.013, 2.014
  (3) 2.013
  (4) 2.014
  (7) 2.013
43 .... 2.057, 2.117, 2.119,
         6.006, 11.061, 11.062,
        14.017, 14.019, 14.020,
              14.078, 14.080
  (1) 14.014
   (c) 6.153
  (3) 2.021, 2.121, 6.009,
              14.015, 14.016
  (4) 14.015
  (5)–(6) 14.016
  (8) 14.017
   (a)–(b) 2.121, 6.009
  (9) 2.117, 2.120,
             6.008, 14.017
  (10) 2.120, 6.008
  (11) 2.120, 6.008, 14.017
  (13)–(14) 14.019

Companies (Amendment) (No 2) Act 1999
(contd)
  s 43 (cond)
       (15) 14.019, 14.027,
                 14.084, 14.086
         (b) 14.078, 14.080
       (16) 6.006
    44 .... 2.021, 2.122, 14.020
       (1)–(3) 2.122, 6.010, 14.018
       (4) 2.122, 14.018
       (5)–(7) 2.122, 14.018
       (8) (a) 14.014
         (i)–(iii) 6.007
       (9) 6.007
       (10) 6.007, 14.014
    45 .... 6.004, 11.061
    46 .... 2.058, 11.062, 14.004,
               14.005, 14.006, 14.012,
               14.024, 14.025, 14.027,
               14.028, 14.029, 14.040,
               14.041, 14.043, 14.049,
               14.057, 14.059, 14.061,
               14.063, 14.066, 14.069,
               14.071, 14.073, 14.075,
               14.076, 14.083, 14.084,
               14.089, 14.094, 14.097,
               14.098, 14.099, 14.107,
               14.108
    47 .... 2.116, 2.117
    48 .... 14.013, 14.084
    49 .... 11.062, 14.089
       (a) 14.040, 14.077, 14.078,
               14.080, 14.082, 14.098
    50 .... 11.062, 14.083, 14.089,
               14.095, 14.097
    53 .... 12.131, 12.133, 13.111
       (2) 12.130, 12.135,
               12.136, 12.137
    Pt III 4.001
    Sch 2 .... 7.129

Companies (Amendment) Act 1977
  s 4 .... 5.052
       (1) 3.003

Companies (Amendment)
  Act 1982 .... 6.009, 8.009, 11.061
  s 2 .... 2.006, 2.007
    3 .... 2.004, 2.010, 2.012, 2.014,
          2.112, 2.121, 6.094, 14.017,
          20.020, 20.021, 20.025

       (3) 2.011, 2.112, 6.002
       (4) 2.011
       (5) 2.011, 6.094
       (5A) 20.022
  3A 2.011, 6.094
       (1) 2.011, 20.021, 20.024,
          20.026, 20.027, 20.028,
          20.029, 20.030, 22.091
  4 ....2.012, 2.124, 11.061
  5 ....2.083, 2.109
  6 ....7.028
  7 ....2.057
  8 ....6.092, 20.020
  10 ....8.053
  11 ....11.062, 14.013, 14.025
  12 ....2.058, 11.062, 14.004,
          14.007, 14.008, 14.009,
          14.024, 14.025, 14.035,
          14.044, 14.086, 22.071,
          22.072, 22.074, 22.077
       (1) 14.006, 14.009,
          21.001, 22.074
       (2) 14.005, 14.006, 22.076
       (3) 14.005, 14.006, 14.027,
          14.029, 14.041, 14.061,
          14.071, 14.084, 14.087,
          14.107, 22.076
       (6) 14.046, 14.060, 14.063,
          14.081, 14.099, 14.100,
          14.101
       (7) 14.098
  12A 14.044, 14.094
       (1)–(2) 14.012
       (3) 14.012, 14.027, 14.029,
          14.041, 14.071,
          14.084, 14.094
  12B 14.009, 14.057, 14.063,
          14.089, 14.107
       (1) 14.004, 14.027, 14.028
       (2) 14.004, 14.027, 14.029
       (3) 14.040, 14.041, 14.043,
          14.045, 14.047, 14.048,
          14.049, 14.050, 14.051,
          14.053, 14.054, 14.059,
          14.061, 14.064, 14.068,
          14.069, 14.070, 14.073,
          14.081, 14.098, 14.099

Companies (Amendment) Act 1982 (contd)
  s 12B (cond)
      (4) 14.069, 14.098
      (5) 14.066, 14.067
        (a)–(b) 14.061
      (6) 14.053, 14.065,
                    14.066,14.067
        (a) 14.061, 14.063
        (b) 14.061
      (7) 14.040, 14.050, 14.071,
                14.072, 14.073, 14.074,
                14.075, 14.076, 14.089,
                14.098, 14.099
      (9) 14.057, 14.075
      (10) 14.059
      (11) 14.075
    12C 14.083, 14.084, 14.085,
                14.089, 14.091, 14.092,
                14.093, 14.094, 14.096,
                14.097, 14.098, 14.107
      (1) 14.083, 14.089,
                14.094, 14.097, 14.107
      (2) 14.094,14.097,
                14.098, 14.109
      (3) 14.108, 14.109
    12D 14.094
    15 .... 2.009, 2.067, 2.070,
                2.071, 2.073, 2.075, 2.083,
                2.085, 2.089, 2.106, 2.107,
                2.109, 2.111, 2.142, 2.143,
                2.149, 3.010, 3.014, 3.034,
                3.044, 3.045, 3.047, 5.007,
        8.002, 8.083, 10.056, 10.058,
                          15.047
    16 .... 8.021, 9.017, 9.027,
                9.032, 11.061
    19 .... 2.071
    20 .... 3.004, 3.005
  Sch 1 .... 2.111, 8.005, 9.029

Companies (Amendment)
  Act 1983 .... 2.065, 2.157, 2.162,
                          20.020
  s 2 .... 19.011, 19.013
    3 .... 2.084, 2.109, 2.123,
                2.124, 2.161
    4 .... 2.123
    5 (1) 2.004
      (2) 2.005, 2.015
      (4) 2.015
      (5) 2.004

    6 .... 14.024
      (1) 14.021
      (2) 2.156, 14.022
      (3) 14.021
      (4)–(5) 14.022
      (6)–(8) 14.023
    8 .... 11.062, 14.024, 14.027
      (1) 14.024, 14.084
    9 .... 5.030
      (1) (a)–(b) 2.158
         (c) 2.159
      (2) 2.158
      (3)–(4) 2.159
      (5) 2.158, 2.159
      (6) –(9) 2.160
    10 (1) 2.159
        (a)–(d) 2.158
    11 .... 2.157
    12... 2.157
      (3) (a) 2.109
    12B(1) 14.028
    13 .... 2.157
    14 .... 5.030
      (1) (d) 2.162
      (2)–(5) 2.162
    15 .... 2.162
    16 .... 2.157
    17... 2.079
      (4) 2.080
    20 .... 2.156
      (6) 2.109
    24 .... 5.030
    26 (4) 19.013
    31 (2) 2.156
    32 .... 19.019
    33 (2) 2.156, 19.019
    34 .... 19.012
    36 .... 19.019
    38 .... 5.030
    39 .... 2.156
    40 .... 5.018, 5.026
      (1) 5.026, 7.019
      (2)–(3) 5.026
    41 .... 6.153
    42 .... 6.183
    43 (3) 2.109
    44 (2) 6.153
    47 .... 11.061
    52 .... 2.157
    53 .... 2.157, 5.030

Companies (Amendment) Act 1983 (contd)
s 55 .... 2.156, 11.061
   (1) (a) 2.156, 14.021
  56 .... 2.126
  57 .... 15.005
  58 .... 2.156
   (1)–(2) 2.134
 Sch 1 .... 2.109
    para 16 .... 6.183

Companies (Amendment)
  Act 1986 .... 2.023, 6.148, 6.151,
        6.152, 6.154, 7.129
 s 2 .... 2.023
   (1) 6.148
    (a)–(c) ... 2.023, 7.026, 7.129
   (2)–(3) 2.023, 2.024
  3 .... 2.024, 4.001
   (1) (e) 6.148
  4 .... 2.024, 10.037, 10.038
   (5) 10.037
    (a)–(f) 10.025
  5 .... 2.024
   (1) 10.002, 10.004,
        10.059, 10.063
   (2)–(4) 10.002
   (5B) 10.027
  5A 10.039
  6 .... 10.002
   (1) 8.080, 10.004
  7 .... 2.022, 2.023, 2.030,
       2.032, 2.055, 2.056
   (1) 2.057, 10.016
    (a) 2.023, 2.025
     (i)–(iii) 2.024
    (b) 2.026
   (1A) 2.023, 2.055, 2.057
   (1B) 2.055
   (1C) 2.028
    (a)–(b) 2.027
   (2) 10.017
   (3) 2.022
   (4) 10.017
   (5) 10.018, 10.019
   (5A) 10.020, 10.022
   (5B)–(5C) 10.020
   (6) 10.014, 10.023
   (7) 10.024
  8 .... 10.025, 10.027, 10.037
   (1) 10.026
    (b) 2.032
   (2) 2.029, 10.025, 10.026

   (3) 2.032, 10.029
   (4) 10.026
   (5) 10.027, 10.028
   (5A)(a)–(b) 10.027
   (6) 10.025
  9 .... 10.022, 10.029, 10.031
   (1)–(2) 10.030
   (3)–(4) 10.031
  10 .... 2.031, 2.057, 6.148, 6.155
   (1) 2.030, 6.148
  11 .... 2.031, 2.057, 6.148, 6.155
   (1) 2.032
  12 .... 2.031, 2.057
  13 .... 6.155
   (1) 6.155
    (a) 6.151, 6.154
    (b)–(f) 6.152
   (2) 6.151, 6.152
  14 .... 6.153, 6.155
  15 .... 7.023
  16 .... 2.057, 6.155
  17 .... 2.056
   (3)–(4) 2.080
  18 .... 6.155
   (1)–(2) 2.031
   (3)–(5) 2.031, 7.027
  22 .... 4.001, 6.155
   (3) 21.042
 Schedule 2.024

Companies (Amendment)
  Act 1990 .... 10.001, 10.002, 10.005,
       10.008, 10.022, 10.025,
       10.026, 10.037, 10.054,
       10.060, 22.027
 s 1 .... 10.072
  2 .... 10.037
   (b)–(c) 10.064, 10.072
  3 (3B)(k) 10.039
   (6) 8.080
  3A 10.002, 10.040
  10 .... 10.040
  11 .... 10.032
   (1)–(2) 10.033
   (3) 10.034
   (4) 10.035, 10.036
   (5) 10.035
   (6) 10.033, 11.061
   (7)–(8) 10.033
  12 .... 10.008, 11.061
   (1)–(2) 10.008
   (3) 10.004, 10.008

Companies (Amendment) Act 1990 (contd)
s 12 (cond)
    (4) 10.008
    (5) 10.008, 11.061
  13 (1) 10.010, 10.011
    (2)–(3) 10.011
    (4) 10.012
    (5) 10.007
    (6) 10.013
    (7) 10.014
  13A 10.072
  15 .... 10.054
  18 .... 10.015, 10.060, 10.062
    (1) (a) 10.051
      (b) 10.050
    (2) 10.051, 10.055,
                 10.059, 10.063
    (3) 10.002, 10.059, 10.063
    (4) 10.060, 10.063
    (5) 10.062
      (a) 10.059, 10.062
    (7)–(8) 10.062
    (9) 10.071
  19 .... 10.061
  20 .... 10.021, 10.022
  21 .... 10.015
  22 .... 10.051
    (5) 10.051, 10.067
  23 .... 10.056, 10.058
    (2) 10.057
    (4)–(6) 10.058
    (7) 10.056, 10.058
    (8) 10.056
  24 .... 10.014, 10.052
    (1) 10.063
    (2) 10.064
    (3) 10.065, 10.071
    (4) 10.066
    (4A) 10.067
    (5)–(7) 10.069
    (8) 10.065
    (9) 10.009, 10.053, 10.069
    (10) 10.069
    (11) 10.071
    (12) 10.066
  25 .... 10.064
  25B 10.053, 10.068
  25B 10.053, 10.068
  26 .... 10.009
  27 .... 10.070
  28 (1) 10.004, 10.005

    (2) 10.006
  29 .... 10.041, 10.048
    (1)–(2) 10.040
    (3) 10.046, 10.047
    (3A)–(3B) 10.046
    (4)–(5) 10.041, 10.045
  30 .... 11.061
    (1) 10.069, 10.072
    (2) 10.072
    (3) 11.061
  36A 11.061
  172 .... 8.045, 8.050

Companies (Amendment) Act 1996 ....6.155

Companies (Amendment)
  (No 2) Act 1999
  Pt III 7.132

Companies (Auditing and Accounting)
  Act 2003 ....1.005, 4.001, 6.006,
            6.156, 6.157, 6.183, 6.186,
            6.187, 7.001, 7.030, 7.032,
            7.034, 7.037, 7.040, 7.050,
            7.083, 7.113, 7.124, 11.004,
            11.084
s 5 ....11.089
  8 (1) 11.089
  9 ....11.089
  23 ....11.089
  32 ....7.028
    (1) 7.028, 7.031, 7.034,
            7.037, 7.040
    (2) 7.032
  35 ....7.030, 7.035, 7.040, 11.035
    (b) 7.039
    (c) 7.030, 7.033
  37 ....7.079, 7.101
    (a)–(b) 7.079
    (c) 7.077, 7.080
    (d) 1.007, 7.071, 7.083,
            7.096, 7.101, 7.113
    (e) 7.116, 7.119
  38 ....7.034, 7.035, 7.036, 7.037
    (1) 7.037
  39 ....7.032, 7.033, 7.034
    (a)–(c) 7.032
    (d) 7.033
    (e) 7.032
  40 ....7.032, 7.033, 7.034
    (a) 7.032
    (b) 7.034
    (c) 7.032

Companies (Auditing and Accounting)
  Act 2003 (contd)
  s 42 .... 6.151, 7.058
     43 .... 7.124
     44 .... 7.055, 7.056, 7.057,
                            7.058, 7.063
     45 .... 6.156, 6.157, 7.124, 7.125
     46 .... 2.037, 2.046, 11.061
       (a) 2.035, 2.037
       (b) 2.039
       (c) 2.046
     47 .... 2.025, 7.026
     48 (1) (j) 7.055
     51 .... 11.004
     52 .... 15.042, 15.043, 15.044
     53 .... 7.132
       (b)–(c) 7.129
       (e) 7.129
     54 .... 7.129
     56 .... 6.182, 6.186, 6.187, 7.133
     57 .... 2.009, 2.012, 2.067, 2.070,
              2.071, 2.073, 2.075, 2.083,
              2.097, 2.106, 2.107, 2.109,
              2.111, 2.142, 2.143, 3.043,
              3.045, 3.047, 5.007, 8.002,
              8.005, 8.009, 8.083, 9.007,
              9.010, 9.012, 9.013, 9.019,
              9.020, 9.021, 9.026, 9.031,
              9.033, 10.033, 11.061
       (2) 2.089
     57 .... 2.143
     59 .... 7.032, 7.033, 7.034, 7.040
    Sch 1 .... 7.028, 7.031, 7.032,
                 7.034, 7.037, 7.040
    Pt 1 .... 11.084
     2 .... 2.074, 2.113, 3.002,
              3.036, 3.044, 5.007, 6.005,
              8.002, 8.005, 8.009, 8.083,
              9.012, 9.019, 9.020, 9.021,
              9.026, 9.031, 9.033, 10.033,
              10.056, 10.058, 11.061,
              11.089
       para 1 .... 9.007, 9.010, 9.013

Companies (Consolidation)
  Act 1908 .... 12.005, 12.006,
                  12.007, 13.032

Companies Act 1862 .... 3.008, 12.005,
                 12.006, 12.007, 13.032
  s 30 .... 3.008
     32 .... 3.015

Companies Act 1948
  s 135 .... 5.050
     165 .... 12.042
     322 .... 6.129
     332 .... 6.120, 6.140
     455 .... 22.011

Companies Act 1960
  s 160(6A) 20.028

Companies Act 1962
  s 234 .... 18.008

Companies Act 1963 ..... 2.018, 2.124, 2.136,
              3.031, 4.015, 5.003,
              5.010, 5.012, 5.014,
              5.018, 5.029, 5.036,
              5.038, 5.039, 5.047,
              6.183, 7.028, 9.106,
          11.083, 12.006, 12.137,
              13.032, 13.078
  s 1 (b) 2.045
     2 .... 12.004, 12.006
       (1) 4.013, 6.006, 6.151,
             7.107, 12.005, 12.006,
            13.032, 14.057, 14.075,
            16.026, 16.051, 16.056,
                  20.038
       (b) 2.034, 2.036,
                 2.042, 2.046
     3 (1) 13.069
     6 .... 14.023
       (1) 2.123, 2.124
       (3) 14.021, 14.022
     10 .... 5.030
       (8) 11.083
     11 .... 2.006, 2.007
     12 (1)–(2) 2.008, 2.067
       (3) 2.009, 2.067
     15 .... 5.030
       (1) 2.067
     17 .... 2.002
     18 .... 2.015
     20 (5) 6.182
     21 .... 2.123, 2.136, 11.083
     22 (1) 2.146
     23 .... 2.123, 2.131, 5.030,
           11.035, 11.061, 11.083
       (1) 2.144
       (2) 2.138
       (3)–(4), (6) 2.144
       (7) 2.138

Companies Act 1963 (contd)
s 24 .... 2.127, 2.128, 2.129, 2.131,
          2.132, 2.133, 2.134, 2.156,
          11.061, 11.083, 15.004
      (1) 2.128, 2.130
        (a) 2.127, 2.130, 2.131
        (b) 2.130
          (i) –(iii) 2.127
        (c) 2.130
      (2) 2.124
        (a) 2.128
      (3) 2.130
      (4) 2.130
      (5)–(6) 2.131
      (7) 2.133
      (8) 2.133
    27 .... 2.041
    28 .... 5.030
    31 .... 3.030, 3.032, 5.011
      (1) 2.016, 2.066
      (2) 2.016, 2.066, 3.030, 5.011
    33 (1) (b) 2.021
    35 .... 2.161
    47 (1) 2.059
    56 .... 9.039, 9.040, 9.085
    57 .... 9.128
    58 .... 2.066, 9.129
      (1) 2.071, 2.156
      (2)–(4) 2.071
    60 .... 2.084, 2.085, 3.041, 5.030,
              17.064, 19.017, 19.020
      (2) 2.084, 19.017, 19.020
        (a) 2.084
        (b) 2.085
      (3) 19.017
      (4) 2.084, 19.017
      (13) 19.017
      (15) 2.085
    65 .... 5.030
    67 .... 5.030
    68 .... 2.074
      (1)–(2) 2.072
    69 .... 2.073, 2.074
      (1) 2.073, 2.156
    70 .... 2.057, 2.074, 2.075
    72 .... 5.030
      (1) 2.076
      (2) 2.076, 2.156
    75 (1) 2.077, 2.078
      (2) 2.078
      (4)–(5) 2.078

    78 .... 2.082
      (5) 2.083
    90 .... 15.008
    91 (1)–(2) 3.045
      (3)–(4) 2.107, 3.045
      (5) 2.107, 3.045, 3.047
    92 (1) 3.046
      (2)–(5) 3.047
      (6) 3.046
    95 .... 2.102
      (1) 2.104
    98 .... 8.054, 8.056, 8.057,
                    8.058, 8.059
      (1) 8.052
      (2) 2.103, 2.104
      (3) 8.055
      (5) 8.056
    99 .... 2.089, 2.090, 2.096, 2.097,
                  2.106, 11.061
      (1) 2.088, 2.089, 2.097,
                    2.100, 2.106
      (2)–(2B) 2.089
      (3) 2.100
      (5) 2.094
      (8) 2.096, 2.098
      (9) 2.099
      (10)(a) 2.088
        (b) 2.089
    100 .... 11.061
      (1)–(2) 2.088
      (3)–(4) 2.106
    101 .... 2.089
      (1) 2.100
    102 .... 2.089, 2.097, , 3.044
    103 .... 2.088
      (1)–(2) 2.098
    104 .... 2.101, 2.104, 2.105
    105 .... 2.108
    106 .... 2.100
    107 .... 8.003, 8.008, 8.012
      (1) 8.002, 8.008
      (2) 8.083
      (3) 8.002, 8.083
    109 .... 3.044
    110 .... 3.044
    111 .... 2.095
    113 .... 2.010, 11.061
      (1)–(3), (5)–(6) 2.012
    114 .... 2.123
      (1)–(2) 2.142
      (3)–(4) 2.143

Companies Act 1963 (contd)

s 115 ....2.065
    (1) 2.064
    (2)–(3) 2.065
    (6) 2.065
  116 ....2.066, 3.006
    (1) 3.004
      (a) 3.004, 3.005
      (b)–(c) 3.004, 3.009
    (2)–(3) 3.009
    (4) 3.005
    (5) 2.068, 3.011
      (b) 2.068, 2.070, 3.011
    (6)–(8) 2.069, 3.011
    (9) 2.070, 3.011, 3.034
  117(1)–(2) 3.010
    (3) 3.010, 3.011, 3.012
    (4) 3.010, 3.034
  118 ....3.005
  119 ....3.012, 3.015, 3.034,
                  3.041, 11.035
    (1) 3.013
    (2) 3.013, 4.017
    (3) 3.013, 3.014, 3.034
    (4) 3.014, 3.017, 3.034
  120 ....2.070, 3.012, 3.014, 3.034
  121 ....3.013, 3.029
  122 ....3.023, 3.025, 3.026
    (5) 3.024
  123 ....3.007, 3.008
  124 ....3.030
  125 ....2.018, 2.020, 2.021, 2.057,
             11.035, 11.061, 14.004,
             15.045, 15.049, 22.056,
                    22.060, 22.074
    (1) 2.018, 2.020, 2.057, 7.113
    (2) 2.058, 7.113, 15.007
    (3) 2.058
  126 ....2.018, 2.020, 11.061,
                 14.004, 22.074
  127 ....2.020, 2.034, 2.038, 2.039,
             7.129, 11.061, 15.007
    (1) ...2.035, 2.036, 2.037, 2.042,
                 2.045, 2.046
    (2) (b) 2.041
    (3)–(4) 2.043
    (5) 2.039
    (6) 2.040
    (7) 2.022
    (8) 2.045, 2.046

    (9) 2.044, 2.048, 2.049,
                    2.051, 2.052
      (a) 2.047, 2.050
      (b) 2.047
    (10) 2.044, 2.051, 2.052
    (11)......................................2.052
    (12) 7.113, 15.007
  128 ....2.022, 2.025, 2.057, 11.061
    (1) 2.057
    (4) (a) 7.026
      (c) 2.023, 2.025,
                 7.026, 7.129
    (5) 2.023, 2.025, 7.026, 7.129
    (6A) 2.025
      (a)–(c) 7.026
    (6B) 2.025, 7.026
    (6C) 7.026
  131 ....5.002, 5.008, 5.009, 5.016
    (1) 5.002, 5.007, 5.010
    (2) 5.002
    (3) 5.004, 5.006,
                 5.009, 11.082
    (4) 5.005, 5.006,
                 5.009, 11.082
    (5) 5.005
    (6) 5.007, 11.082
  132 ....5.018, 5.019, 5.020
    (1) 5.019, 5.021
    (2) 5.020
    (3) 5.021, 5.023
    (4) 5.024
    (5) 5.024, 5.025
    (6) 5.021
  133(1) 5.012, 5.028
      (a) 5.012
      (b) 5.028
    (2) 5.028
      (a) 5.012
      (b) 5.028
    (3) 5.012
  133A 14.108
  134 ....5.036, 5.045
    (a) 5.011, 5.013
    (c) 5.014, 5.038
    (d) 5.029, 5.040
    (e) 5.045
  135 ....5.050
    (1)–(2) 5.049
  137 ....5.046
  140 ....5.015, 5.027

Companies Act 1963 (contd)

s 141 .... 5.021, 5.030, 5.033
    (1) 5.010, 5.031
    (2) 5.028, 5.032
    (3) 5.032
    (4) 5.030
    (8) 5.033
142 .... 7.002, 7.003
    (1)–(2) 5.035
143 .... 2.109, 2.110, 2.156
    (1)–(3) 2.110
    (4) 2.083
    (a)–(j) 2.109
    (5)–(7) 2.111
144 .... 10.058
145 .... 5.054
    (1) 5.052
    (2) 5.052, 6.104
    (3) 5.052
146(1)–(2) 5.053
    (3)–(4) 5.055
147 .... 4.010, 4.014
148 .... 6.148
150 .... 15.016
153 .... 2.053
    (1) 2.053, 11.088
    (2) 2.054, 11.088
155(5) 10.025
156(1) (a) 2.031
158 .... 6.148, 6.150, 6.155, 6.156,
            6.158, 7.023, 7.058
    (2)–(6B) 6.149
    (7) 6.150, 6.155
159 .... 7.011, 7.014
160 .... 5.033
    (1) 7.002, 7.129, 19.017
    (2) 7.002
    (c) 7.011
    (3) 7.002, 7.003
    (4) 7.002
    (5) 7.003
    (5A) 7.002
    (a) (ii) 7.004
    (b) 7.002, 7.004
    (6) 7.002, 7.008
    (a) 7.003
    (b) 7.002
    (7) 7.002
    (8) 7.017
    (9) 7.002, 7.045

161 .... 5.034, 7.007
    (1) 5.034
    (a)–(b) 7.003
    (c) 7.002
    (2) 7.003
    (c) 7.002
    (2A) 7.006
    (3) 7.009
    (4) 7.010
    (5) 7.008
162 .... 7.028
165–173 .... 13.001
172 .... 13.122
176 .... 6.004, 8.079
179 .... 2.113
180 .... 6.005
182 .... 5.033, 5.034, 20.039
    (1) 16.039
    (2) 5.034
182A(4) 22.099
183 ...6.004, 11.035, 20.039, 20.040,
             20.041, 22.070
    (1) 10.007, 20.038, 20.039,
             20.040
    (2) 10.007, 20.005, 20.038,
      20.039, ... 20.040
183A 22.099, 22.100
    (3) 22.098
184 .... 20.039, 22.029, 23.001
    (7) 15.010
185 .... 6.025
186 .... 6.025
187 .... 6.025
    (9) 15.003
188 .... 6.025
190(8) 4.017
191 .... 6.112, 7.023
    (8) 7.023
193 .... 2.031, 18.017
194 .... 6.099, 6.100, 6.103,
             6.105, 6.106
    (1) 6.099
    (2) 6.102
    (3) 6.103
    (4) 6.103, 6.104
    (5) (a) 6.105
    (b) 6.106
    (6) 6.106
    (7) 6.107

Companies Act 1963 (contd)
s 195 .... 2.010, 2.114, 18.015,
20.020
(1) ...., 6.092
(2) ...., 6.092, 20.020, 20.025
(3) 6.092
(4) 2.010
(6) 2.114, 6.092, 16.038,
20.020, 20.021,
20.023, 20.025
(6A) 2.115
(7) 2.114, 6.002, 20.021
(8) 2.114, 6.095, 20.021,
20.022, 20.024, 20.025,
20.026, 20.027, 20.028,
20.029, 20.030, 22.091
(9) 2.114
(10) 3.035
(10A) 3.035, 3.036, 4.017
(11) .... 2.114, , 6.093
(11A) 2.116, 2.118
(11B) 2.116, 2.117
(11C) 2.117
(11D) 2.116
(11E 2.117
(12) 2.148, 3.036
(13) 3.036
(14) 3.036, 6.093
196 .... 11.086
198 .... 5.030
199 .... 5.030
200 .... 6.182, 6.184, 6.185,
6.186, 7.149
(1) 6.182, 7.133
(a)–(b) 6.183
(2) 6.186, 7.133
(3)–(4) 6.187
201 .... 10.058
202 .... 10.058
(2)–(3) 10.056
(6) 4.012, 10.056
205 .... 3.032, 3.033, 10.002,
14.064, 14.065
208 .... 9.023
213(a) 5.030
214 .... 9.039
215 .... 9.088
216(1) 9.043
218 .... 8.079, 9.067
220(2) 9.043
222 .... 8.079

224 .... 8.018
225 .... 9.002
226(1) 9.002
(2) 9.002, 9.044
227 .... 9.020, 11.061
(1)–(2) 9.018
228 .... 9.014
231(1) 9.023
(a) 19.045
(3)–(4) 9.023
232 .... 9.023
234 .... 11.061
236 .... 6.160, 6.179
240(7) 9.027
243 .... 9.106, 9.107, 9.108, 9.122
(1) 6.118, 9.107, 15.027
(1A) 9.107, 9.108, 15.027
245 .... 9.106, 9.110, 9.112, 9.113,
9.114, 9.122, 9.126, 9.127
(1) 9.109, 9.126
245A 9.113, 9.122
(1) 9.113, 9.114
(2) 9.113, 9.115
(3)–(6) 9.113
247 .... 9.106, 9.111, 9.112,
9.122, 9.127
249 .... 11.061
(1) 9.047
251(1) (b) 2.109, 5.030
(c) 2.109
252 .... 11.061
(1)–(2) 9.019
254A 9.125
256 .... 9.025
(8) 8.031
258(1) 9.003
260 .... 5.030
261 .... 9.025, 9.030, 9.040
(3) 9.026
(7) 9.026
262 .... 9.027, 11.061
263 .... 9.028, 9.029, 11.061
264(1) 9.030
(2) 9.030, 9.040
266 .... 9.004, 9.031, 9.101
267(1) 9.004, 9.006
(2) 9.006, 9.010
(3) 9.005
272 .... 9.030, 9.032, 11.061
(2) 9.010, 9.032

Companies Act 1963 (contd)

s 273 .... 11.061
    (1) 9.033, 9.047
  276 .... 5.030
    (1) (b) 19.045
  276A 9.013
  277(2) 9.012, 9.014
  278 .... 11.061
    (1)–(2) 9.020
  280 .... 11.061
  281 .... 19.048
  282A 9.108
  282B 9.109, 9.112,
             9.114, 15.027
  282B(1) 9.109
    (2)–(7) 9.110
    (8) 9.110, 9.112
  282C 9.113
    (1) 9.113, 9.114, 9.115
    (3)–(4) 9.115
    (5)–(6) 9.113
  282D 9.111, 9.112
  285 .... 8.053, 8.054, 8.055, 10.043
    (7) 8.056
    (14) 8.053
  286 .... 6.168, 9.067, 9.119
  293 .... 6.162
    (1) 6.161
  294 .... 6.118, 6.161
  295 .... 6.163, 9.122, 9.123, 9.127
  297 .... 6.119, 6.120, 6.121, 6.122,
             6.129, 6.130, 6.137, 6.138,
             6.139, 6.146, 9.122, 9.127,
             11.035, 15.049
    (2) 6.119, 6.144, 6.146
  297A 6.119, 6.121, 6.136, 8.031,
             9.122, 9.125, 9.127, 20.015,
             21.001, 22.026, 22.031
    (1) 6.171, 9.122
  298 .... 6.174, 9.122, 9.125,
             9.127, 9.122
    (1) 6.174
    (2) 6.175
  299 .... 8.068, 9.073, 9.074, 9.086,
             9.088, 9.089, 9.092, 9.095,
             9.096, 9.099, 9.100, 15.049
    (1) ... 9.073, 9.086, 9.087, 9.088,
             9.089, 9.090, 9.091,
             9.096, 11.027
    (1A) 9.086, 9.087, 9.091,
             9.096, 9.100, 11.027

    (2) 8.068, 8.069, 9.074, 9.086,
             9.091, 9.092, 9.093,
             9.094, 9.095,
             9.096, 11.027
    (2A) 8.068, 9.074, 9.086,
             9.091, 9.092, 9.093,
             9.094, 9.096, 9.100
    (3) 8.069, 9.086, 9.092,
             9.094, 9.095, 11.027
    (4) 8.068, 9.097, 9.098
    (5) 8.068, 9.095, 9.098
  300 ....9.007
    (a)–(b) 9.007, 10.004
  300A 9.007, 9.008, 9.009, 9.011,
             10.004, 10.005, 10.006
    (3) 9.008, 9.011,
             10.005, 10.010
    (4) 9.009, 10.010, 15.007
  301 ....9.012
  301A 9.010, 9.011
  302...9.036
  303 ....9.017, 9.021
  305(1) (b) 5.030
  306 ....9.024, 11.061
    (2) 9.024, 15.007
  310 ....14.046
  311 ....11.062, 14.004, 14.013,
             14.019, 14.026, 14.027,
             14.028, 14.078, 14.082,
             14.084, 14.086, 14.087,
             14.088
    (1)–(2) ...14.013, 14.019, 14.084
    (3) 14.025
    (5) 14.013, 14.019, 14.024,
             14.025, 14.027, 14.084
    (7) 14.029
    (8) 14.019, 14.040, 14.050,
             14.077, 14.078, 14.079,
             14.080, 14.081, 14.082,
             14.084, 14.089
             14.098, 14.099
    (8A) 14.082, 14.098
    (9) 14.013, 14.025
  311A 14.083, 14.084, 14.085,
             14.086, 14.087, 14.088,
             14.089, 14.092, 14.093,
             14.095, 14.096, 14.097,
             14.098, 14.107
    (1) 14.084, 14.089,
             14.095, 14.097

Companies Act 1963 (contd)
s 311A (contd)
(2) 14.095, 14.097, 14.098
(3) 14.108
314 .... 8.009
315(1) 8.009, 8.010
(2)–(3) 8.012
(5) 8.013, 15.007
316 .... 8.045, 8.050
(2) 8.074, 8.075
(3) 8.076
316A 8.041, 8.042, 8.045, 8.046,
8.048, 8.050, 8.051
(1)–(2)............................... 8.040
317 .... 8.005
318 .... 8.070, 8.072, 8.073
(2) 8.071
(3) 2.125, 8.071
319 .... 8.003, 8.006, 8.008, 8.018,
8.023, 8.026, 8.027, 8.065,
11.061
(1) 8.007, 8.008, 8.014,
8.026, 8.032
(b) 8.006, 8.014, 8.022
(c) 8.006, 8.008, 8.024
(2) ... 8.008, 8.012, 8.025, 8.026,
8.027, 8.028, 8.029,
8.030, 8.066
(2A) 8.028, 8.084
(4) 8.007
(6) 8.029
(7) 8.008
(8) 8.006, 8.024, 8.030,
8.066, 15.007
320 .... 8.014, 8.015, 8.022, 8.023,
8.065, 11.061
(1) 8.015
(2)–(4) 8.017
(5) 8.021, 8.022, 11.061
320A 8.022
321 .... 8.012, 8.029, 11.061
(1) 8.025, 8.026, 8.027,
8.028, 8.030
(2) 8.030, 15.007
322 .... 8.065, 8.066
(1) (a) 8.064
322A(1) 8.077
(2) 8.078
322B(1)–(4) 8.079
322C 8.081
(2) –(3)............................... 8.082

323(1) 8.001
323A(1) 8.060
(2) 8.061
(3) 8.060
(4) 8.061
325 .... 12.006
328 .... 6.081
(1)–(4) 12.007
330(a) 2.066
332 .... 2.066
334 .... 2.136, 11.083
351 .... 2.147
352–353 .... 2.148
355 .... 2.149
357 .... 2.148
358 .... 2.149
360 .... 2.147
369 .... 2.164
(2) 8.075
371 .... 3.014, 5.054, 6.178, 9.082,
11.037, 11.038, 11.066,
12.088, 22.054, 22.056,
22.057, 22.061
(1) 2.058, 6.178, 9.082,
11.037, 11.066, 22.057
(2)–(3) 6.178, 11.037
(4) 11.037
371A 12.067, 12.088
377 .... 12.008
378(1) 3.002, 5.052
(2) 3.002
381 .... 2.126, 11.067
(1) 2.125
(2) 2.125, 11.067
(3) 2.125
382 .... 15.010
383 ..... 3.034, 6.115, 15.011, 15.012,
15.013, 15.014,
15.015, 15.016
(1) 4.024, 15.015
(2) .... , 4.024, 4.029,
15.015, 15.016
(3) 15.016
384 .... 15.027
(1) 11.082, 15.027
(2)–(4) 15.027
386 .... 15.047
389 .... 2.015
391 .... 6.180, 6.183
(2) 6.181
437 .... 12.090

Companies Act 1963 (contd)
s 447 .... 12.002, 12.090
448 .... 12.090
Sch 1 .... 6.025
5 .... 2.019, 2.021
6 .... 7.019
9 .... 12.008
Pt IX 6.081, 12.007
VI 8.054
VII 8.041

Companies Act 1963–2001 .... 9.061

Companies Act 1963–2006 ..... 1.007, 1.008,
2.060, 2.061, 2.066,
3.014, 6.001,
6.115, 14.081

Companies Act 1990 .... 2.114, 2.163,
3.041, 4.001, 4.013, 6.044,
6.119, 7.007, 7.019, 7.029,
7.031, 7.033, 7.034, 7.040,
7.044, 7.082, 9.057, 9.106,
11.076, 12.043, 12.100,
12.116, 13.005, 13.052,
13.063, 13.078, 13.090,
13.091, 13.097, 13.118,
13.122, 14.086, 14.088,
16.001, 18.001, 18.002,
18.014, 22.029, 23.013
s 2 (3) 16.055
3 (1) 13.025, 13.032,
13.036, 13.037
6 .... 4.010, 20.039
7 .... 12.022, 13.007, 13.008, 13.015,
13.032, 13.035, 13.034,
13.036, 13.047, 13.048,
13.052, 13.063,
13.083, 13.087, 13.101,
13.111, 13.121, 13.128
(1) 12.022, 13.003, 13.004,
13.005, 13.009, 13.017,
13.025, 13.026, 13.101
(2) 13.009, 13.025, 13.026
(3) 13.004
(4) 13.007, 13.060, 13.061,
13.062, 13.064, 13.065

8 .....11.081, 12.013, 12.020, 12.022,
13.006, 13.007, 13.008,
13.013, 13.014, 13.015,
13.016, 13.017, 13.018,
13.021, 13.022, 13.023,
13.028, 13.030, 13.033,
13.034, 13.036, 13.047,
13.048, 13.052, 13.063,
13.065, 13.069, 13.083,
13.087, 13.101, 13.111,
13.121, 13.127, 13.128
(1) 11.082, 12.019, 13.007,
13.009, 13.011, 13.012,
13.019, 13.024, 13.027,
13.030, 13.031, 13.085,
13.101, 13.105, 13.113
(a) 12.013, 12.014,
13.012, 13.020,
13.023, 13.024
(b) ...12.013, 13.012, 13.024
(c) 12.013, 13.012, 13.024
(2) 13.027
(a) 13.022, 13.035
(b) 13.024
9 ....9.068, 13.007, 13.036,
13.037, 13.038, 13.039,
13.041, 13.047, 13.052,
13.060, 13.065,
13.066, 13.069, 13.083,
13.102, 13.127
10 ....10.043, 10.044, 13.033,
13.040, 13.052, 13.073,
13.075, 13.076, 13.077,
13.079, 13.082, 13.083,
13.086, 13.090
(1) 13.066, 13.067, 13.068,
13.069, 13.074, 13.079,
13.081, 13.083, 13.087,
13.096
(2) 10.040, 13.066, 13.067,
13.069, 13.072, 13.073,
13.074, 13.079, 13.081,
13.083, 13.087, 13.096,
13.098
(3) 13.047, 13.091, 13.093,
13.095, 13.096
(4) 13.066, 13.087
(5) 10.027, 13.047, 13.060,
13.066, 13.071, 13.079,
13.084, 13.097, 13.098,
13.099, 13.100

Companies Act 1990 (contd)
  s 10 (contd)
       (6) 13.047, 13.066, 13.097,
                         13.099, 13.100
       (7) 13.069
     11 .... 13.033, 13.047, 13.117,
                         13.119, 13.120
       (1) 10.033, 13.101
       (2) 10.033, 13.063
       (3) 11.082, 13.111, 13.117
         (b) 13.112
           (ii)-(iv) 13.116
           (v) 13.116, 13.117
           (vi) 13.116
         (ba) 13.116
         (c) 13.112
       (4) 13.112, 13.115, 13.116,
                 13.117, 13.122, 13.123
     12 .... 13.109, 13.119
       (1) (a) 13.120, 13.121
       (2) 11.082
     13 .... 13.033, 13.110,
                         13.127, 13.128
       (1) 13.126, 13.129
       (2)–(3) 13.126
     14 .... 12.012, 12.014, 12.020,
                 12.022, 12.102, 12.112,
                 12.137, 13.040, 13.045,
                 13.046, 13.047, 13.048,
                 13.049, 13.050, 13.051,
                 13.052, 13.054, 13.066,
                 13.070, 13.087, 13.103
       (1) 11.082, 13.044, 13.098,
                         13.101, 13.103
       (2) 11.082, 12.012, 13.045
       (5) 9.121, 11.082, 13.047,
                         13.070, 13.083
       (6) 13.129
     15 ...... 7.055, 9.070, 12.102, 12.112,
                 12.137, 13.050, 13.051
       (1) 11.082, 13.050
     16 .... 11.082, 13.051, 13.052
       (2) (h) 14.038
     17 .... 13.033, 13.034, 13.052
     18 .... 13.033, 13.052, 13.090
     19 ...... 4.013, 8.062, 11.082, 12.001,
                 12.002, 12.003, 12.005,
                 12.006, 12.007, 12.008,
                 12.013, 12.014, 12.015,
                 12.016, 12.017, 12.022,

                 12.027, 12.032, 12.038,
                 12.039, 12.040, 12.041,
                 12.042, 12.043, 12.044,
                 12.045, 12.046, 12.047,
                 12.048, 12.050, 12.051
                 12.052, 12.053, 12.054,
                 12.055, 12.056, 12.057,
                 12.058, 12.059, 12.060,
                 12.061, 12.063, 12.072,
                 12.075, 12.079, 12.081,
                 12.082, 12.083, 12.084,
                 12.086, 12.088, 12.089,
                 12.091, 12.092, 12.093,
                 12.094, 12.097, 12.098,
                 12.099, 12.102, 12.111,
                 12.112, 12.113, 12.115,
                 12.125, 12.130, 12.133,
                 12.137, 12.138, 13.014,
                 13.015, 13.016, 13.017,
                 13.018, 13.019, 13.020,
                 13.021, 13.029, 13.032,
                 13.045, 13.076, 13.080,
                         15.017, 15.018
       (1) 12.008, 12.010, 12.011,
                 12.064, 12.065, 12.066,
                 12.068, 12.069, 12.070,
                         12.099, 12.114
         (a) 12.003, 12.021
         (b) 12.004
         (f) 12.009
       (2) 12.011, 12.014, 12.034,
                 12.038, 12.039, 12.040,
                 12.041, 12.047, 12.064,
                 12.065, 12.068, 12.093,
                         12.099, 12.113,
                         13.028, 13.031
         (a) 12.011, 12.012,
                         12.014, 12.015,
                         12.016, 12.019,
                         12.020, 12.023,
                         12.024, 12.025,
                         12.113, 12.138
         (b) 12.025, 12.026,
                         12.027, 12.038,
                                 12.132
           (ii) 13.020
           (iii) 13.015
         (b)–(i) 12.014
         (c) 12.027, 12.028,
                                 12.038

Companies Act 1990 (contd)
  s 19 (contd)
    (2) (contd)
      (d) 12.028, 12.029,
                12.030, 12.031,
                12.038, 13.021
      (da) 12.011, 12.029,
                12.030, 12.031
      (e) 12.031, 12.032,
                12.035, 12.038,
                12.113
      (f) 12.021, 12.032,
                12.033, 12.034,
                12.035, 12.038,
                13.016, 13.022
      (g) 12.035, 12.036,
                12.038
      (h) 12.036, 12.037
      (i) 12.011, 12.025,
                12.037, 12.038,
                12.082
    (3) 12.064, 12.065, 12.068,
            12.069, 12.070, 12.073,
            12.075, 12.076, 12.082,
            12.088, 12.093, 12.099
      (a) .. 12.060, 12.066, 12.067,
                12.069, 12.071
      (b) 12.040, 12.047,
                12.067, 12.069,
                12.088
    (4) 12.040, 12.057, 12.067,
            12.070, 12.071
      (a) 12.047, 12.067
      (b) 12.047, 12.057,
                12.058, 12.067
    (5) 12.075, 12.076, 12.081,
            12.096, 12.099
      (a) 12.077, 12.081
        (ii) 12.076, 12.077,
                12.078, 12.081,
                12.086, 12.093,
                12.095, 12.096
      (b) 12.077, 12.080,
                12.081, 12.093,
                12.095, 12.096
    (6) 12.061, 12.063, 12.089,
            12.093, 12.094, 12.095,
            12.096, 12.111, 15.018
    (7) 12.089

(8) 12.097
(8)–(9) 15.018
(9) 12.098
(10) 12.052, 12.099
(11) 12.099
(12) 12.099
19A 12.052, 12.098
20 ...11.082, 12.001, 12.063, 12.100,
        12.102, 12.104, 12.105,
        12.106, 12.108, 12.110,
        12.111, 12.113, 12.114,
        12.116, 12.118, 12.120,
        12.121, 12.122, 12.123,
        12.124, 12.125, 12.126,
        12.129, 12.130, 12.133,
        12.137, 15.017, 15.049
  (1) 12.100, 12.101, 12.104,
           12.106, 12.117,
           12.122, 12.124
  (2) 12.100, 12.104, 12.119,
           12.126
    (a) 12.105, 12.122, 12.124
  (3) 12.127
  (4) 12.125
    (a) 12.128
    (b) 12.129
  (6)................................12.129
  (7) 12.104, 12.106, 12.112,
           12.115, 12.116, 12.117,
           12.125, 12.128
21 ....11.082, 12.094, 12.132,
        12.138, 13.111,
        15.017, 15.018
  (1) 12.130, 12.131,
           12.133, 12.138
    (a) 11.058, 12.135
    (a)–(fb) 13.111, 13.117
    (a)–(j) 12.130
    (b)–(d) 11.058, 12.136
    (e)–(fb) 12.136
    (g)–(j) 12.137
  (2) 12.138
  (3) 11.049, 12.131
    (a)–(j) 13.111, 13.117
    (i) 12.131, 13.111,
           13.117
22 ....13.033, 13.052, 13.110,
        13.115, 13.122, 13.123
    (b) 21.019

Companies Act 1990 (contd)
s 23 .... 12.084, 12.086
    (1) 10.025, 10.027, 12.084,
                13.052, 13.082
    (2) 12.072, 12.085,
                12.086, 12.087
    (3) 12.130, 13.052
    (4) 12.085
        (a)–(b) 13.081
  23A 13.042
  24 (1) 15.017
  25 (1) 6.030
    (2) 6.028
    (3) 6.029
    (4) 6.038
        (c) 6.076
    (5) 6.039
  26 .... 6.034, 6.067, 6.068, 7.055,
           10.029, 13.091, 13.096
    (1) 8.041, 13.096
        (a)–(c) 6.034, 6.068
        (2)–(4) 6.034, 6.068
  27 ...... 6.035, 6.069, 16.049, 16.051,
           16.053, 16.054
    (1) 6.035, 6.069, 6.100, 9.057
    (3) 6.100
  28 .... 6.025
  29 .... 6.066, 6.070, 6.071, 6.072,
         6.073, 6.074, 6.075, 6.076,
         6.078, 6.079, 6.084, 6.085,
         6.086, 6.087, 6.088, 6.089,
         6.090, 8.041, 9.067, 10.043
    (1) ... 6.066, 6.071, 6.072, 6.078,
         6.083, 6.086, 6.089, 9.067
    (2) 6.040, 6.076, 6.089,
           8.041, 19.018
    (3) 6.071, 6.085, 6.088
        (c) 6.085, 6.086
    (4) 6.087
        (b) 6.085
    (5) 6.088, 6.089, 6.090
    (6) 6.081
    (7) (a) 6.082
        (b) 6.083
    (8) 6.084
    (9) (a) 6.075, 8.041
        (b) 6.072, 6.073
        (c) 6.076
  30 .... 13.052
    (8) 19.019

31 ....5.030, 6.014, 6.049, 6.052,
        6.054, 6.055, 6.056, 6.063,
        6.064, 6.070, 6.101, 6.113,
        13.092, 13.094, 19.018
    (1) 6.034
      (a)–(b) 6.027, 13.092
      (c) 6.027, 6.030,
         6.031, 13.092
    (2) 6.032, 13.092
    (3) 6.032, 6.033, 13.092
      (a) 6.034
  32 ....6.001, 6.037, 6.038, 6.057,
        6.060, 6.061, 6.062, 6.076,
        11.082, 19.018
    (1) 6.037, 19.018
    (2) 6.062, 19.018
  33 ....6.042, 6.043
    (1) 6.041, 6.061
    (2) 6.041
    (3) 6.043, 6.061
  33AK 6.149
  34 ....5.030, 6.044, 6.080, 19.018
    (1) 6.080
      (b) 6.047
    (2) 6.045
    (3) 6.045, 6.080
    (4) 6.080
      (a) 6.046
      (b) 6.046
    (5) (a) 6.048, 6.171
      (b) 6.048
    (7) 6.047, 6.048, 6.080
    (8) 6.047
    (9) 6.047, 6.080
    (10) 6.047
    (11) 6.047, 6.080
  35 ....6.049, 19.018
  36 (1)–(3) 6.050, 19.018
  37 ....6.051, 19.018
  38 (1) 6.043, 6.053, 6.054,
        19.018
    (2) 6.056, 19.018
    (3) 19.018
  39 ....6.059, 6.062, 8.031, 19.018
    (1) 6.001, 6.057, 19.018
    (2) 6.058
    (3) 6.056, 6.058, 6.062
  40 ....6.064, 19.018
    (1)–(2) 6.063, 19.018

Companies Act 1990 (contd)

s 41 .... 4.001, 6.114, 7.024, 13.091,
13.092, 13.093,
13.094, 13.095
   (1) 6.113
     (a) 6.113, 13.093
     (b) 6.113
     (c) 6.113, 13.093
   (2) 6.113
   (3) 6.114, 13.093
   (5) (b) 6.113, 13.093
   (6) 6.113, 13.094
   (7) 6.114, 13.094
   (8) 6.113
42 ..... 6.114, 13.092, 13.093, 13.095
43 ..... 7.024, 13.092, 13.094, 13.095
44 ... 13.091, 13.092, 13.094, 13.095
45 .... 6.114, 13.092
46 .... 4.001, 7.024
47 .... 6.103
   (1)–(2) 6.101
50 .... 3.043
   (1) 3.043
     (a)–(d) 3.042, 6.097
   (2)–(4) 3.043, 6.097
   (5) 3.042, 6.097
   (6) 3.043, 6.097
   (7)–(8) 3.043, 6.098
   (9) 3.043, 6.097
51 .... 2.114, 2.116, 2.117, , 3.035,
3.036, , 6.092, 6.093, 6.095,
20.020, 20.021
53 .... 3.037, 6.108, 6.111
   (2) 6.110
   (7) 6.111
   (9) 6.108
54 .... 3.037, 6.109, 6.111
   (9) (c) 9.125
55 .... 3.037, 6.109, 6.111
56 .... 3.037, 6.110, 6.111
57 .... 3.037, 6.108, 6.111
58 .... 3.037, 6.111, 6.150
   (1) 6.108
59 .... 3.040, 3.041
   (1) 3.037, 6.111
   (2) 3.037, 6.111
   (3) 3.037, 6.111
   (4) 3.037
60 .... 9.071, 11.035, 12.137
   (1) 3.040

   (2) 3.037, 3.040, 6.111
   (5) 3.038
   (6) 3.038, 3.040
   (7) 3.038, 3.040
   (8) 3.038
   (9) 3.038, 3.040
   (10) 3.040
   (11) 3.040
61
   (1) 3.039
   (2) 3.039
   (3) 3.040
62
   (1) 3.039
   (2) 3.039
63 .... 3.039
64 ....3.039, 6.108
   (3) 13.052
   (5) 13.052
   (6) 6.111
66 .... 13.052
   (1) 11.082
   (4) 11.082
   (5) 11.082
79 ....12.094, 15.017, 15.018
85 (6) 11.082
90 .... 11.024
91 .... 11.024
92 ....11.024, 11.026
   (2) 11.024, 11.025
94 (2) 11.082
99 .... 3.044
103 .... 3.044
107 ....11.025, 11.031
115 ....6.119, 7.121, 11.025,
11.026, 11.031, 11.082
   (1)–(2), (4) 11.025
   (5) 11.082
116 .... 6.119
   (3) 11.082
117 ....11.023, 11.031
   (1) 11.082
118(1) 11.031
   (2) 11.031, 11.082
   (2A) 11.031
119(3) 3.034
122 .... 2.089,
125 .... 9.119
   (1) 7.083
   (2) 7.083, 7.113

Companies Act 1990 (contd)

s 126 .... 9.109, 9.110, 9.112,
9.122, 9.126

127 .... 9.113, 9.115, 9.122

(12) 7.083, 7.113

128 .... 9.025

129 .... 9.025, 9.026, 9.040

130 .... 9.031, 9.101

131 .... 9.101

(2) 9.031

133 .... 9.013

134 .... 8.053

135 .... 6.168, 9.067

137 .... 6.119, 6.121, 6.129, 6.144,
6.146, 9.122, 11.035

138 .... 6.119, 6.121, 6.171, 7.003,
9.122, 9.125, 21.001,
22.026, 22.027

139 .... 8.027, 9.119, 9.122, 9.125,
9.127, 10.039,
10.072, 18.008

(1) 9.067, 9.119

(2)–(3) 9.119

140 .... 9.120, 9.122, 9.125, 9.127,
13.036, 13.038

(5) 9.120, 13.037

(6) 9.120

(7) 10.033

141 .... 9.121

142 .... 6.174, 6.175, 9.122

143 .... 8.068, 9.073, 9.086, 9.091,
9.092, 9.093, 9.094, 9.095,
9.096, 9.097, 9.098,
9.100, 11.027

144 .... 9.034

(1) 8.031, 9.034

(2) 8.031, 9.034, 15.007

145 .... 8.003, 8.030, 9.024, 9.027,
9.029, 9.032

(1) 9.035

146 .... 9.007, 9.008, 9.009, 9.011,
10.004, 10.005, 10.010

147 .... 4.017, 9.010

148 .... 6.175, 9.122, 9.127

149 .... 9.122, 16.001, 16.013,
16.014, 16.019, 16.026,
16.038, 16.043, 18.014

(1) 9.102, 16.003

(2) 16.003, 16.020,
16.026, 16.037

(5) 16.003, 16.049

149A 9.122

150 .... 4.029, 4.030, 6.014, 6.035,
6.162, 9.037, 9.070, 9.102,
16.001, 16.002, 16.003,
16.005, 16.007, 16.011,
16.012, 16.014, 16.015,
16.016, 16.019, 16.020,
16.021, 16.024, 16.027,
16.029, 16.030, 16.032,
16.036, 16.037, 16.039,
16.040, 16.043, 16.044,
16.045, 16.052, 16.054,
16.055, 16.064, 16.065,
17.003, 17.004, 17.006,
17.008, 17.009, 17.013,
17.017, 17.020, 17.021,
17.033, 17.040, 17.043,
17.044, 17.047, 17.048,
17.053, 17.060, 17.068,
17.069, 17.070, 17.073,
17.074, 17.076, 17.077,
17.080, 18.002, 18.006,
18.007, 18.008, 18.009,
18.010, 18.011, 18.014,
18.018, 19.002, 19.004,
19.007, 19.023, 19.025,
19.029, 19.031, 19.032,
19.033, 19.036, 19.038,
19.039, 19.042, 19.043,
19.044, 20.002, 20.004,
20.017, 21.011, 21.047,
22.017, 22.036, 22.037,
22.039, 22.040, 22.041,
22.042, 22.084, 22.101,
22.102, 23.013, 23.014,
23.022, 23.034, 23.037

(1) 16.003, 17.012, 17.067,
18.002, 18.006, 19.001,
19.005, 19.035, 22.101

(2) 16.014, 16.015, 16.032,
16.034, 17.001,
18.014, 19.001

(a) 17.001, 17.002,
17.010, 17.011,
17.016, 17.019,
17.022, 17.031,
17.050, 17.051,
17.054, 17.059,
17.065, 17.066,
17.067, 22.040,
22.041

Companies Act 1990 (contd)
  (2) (contd)
      (b) ... 16.013, 16.067, 18.010
      (c) 16.067, 19.011
  (3) 17.033, 17.068, 19.001,
                19.013, 19.014,
                19.020, 22.0102
      (a) 19.004, 19.010
      (b) 19.010, 19.011
      (c) 19.010, 19.012
  (4) 16.015
  (4A) 16.025, 16.013, 18.003,
          18.006, 18.007, 18.010,
             18.014, 19.045
  (4B) 19.024, 19.025, 19.026,
          19.027, 19.028, 19.029,
          19.030, 19.031, 19.032,
          19.034, 19.035, 19.036,
          19.037, 19.038, 19.040,
          19.041, 19.042, 19.045,
             19.047, 23.026
  (5) 19.007
151 .... 9.102, 9.104, 9.105, 19.004
  (1) 9.103, 19.008
  (3) 9.103, 15.007, 19.008
152 .... 17.076, 17.077, 17.078,
         17.079, 17.080, 18.015,
         19.021, 23.006, 23.028
  (1) 17.080, 19.004
  (2) 17.076
  (3) 17.076, 17.080
  (4) 17.078, 17.080
  (5) 17.076
153 .... 19.021
154 .... 9.104
155 .... 19.011, 19.012, 19.016,
                     19.020
  (3) 19.012, 19.019
  (4) 19.018
  (5) 19.007, 19.020
156(1) 19.011
  (2) 19.012
  (3)–(4) 19.013
  (5) 19.011
  (6) 19.013
157 .... 19.020
158 .... 19.014
159 .... 3.034, 11.037, 11.064,
         20.001, 20.006, 20.039,
         22.011, 22.012, 22.057,

         22.098, 23.001, 23.003,
         23.004, 23.006, 23.034
  (a) 10.007
160 ....6.004, 6.146, 7.041, 7.052,
       9.009, 9.083, 11.037, 11.072,
       11.076, 11.077, 11.080,
       13.124, 14.035, 16.011,
       16.015, 18.001, 18.009,
       19.003, 21.005, 21.006,
       21.010, 21.011, 21.013,
       21.024, 21.025, 21.026,
       21.028, 21.030, 21.032,
       21.033, 22.016, 22.046,
       22.096, 23.004, 23.005,
       23.007, 23.013, 23.022,
           23.027, 23.029
  (1) 19.006, 20.005, 20.006,
       20.007, 20.008, 20.009,
       20.010, 20.011, 20.012,
       20.013, 20.014, 20.015,
       20.016, 20.017, 20.018,
       20.019, 20.029, 21.010,
       22.006, 22.007, 23.013
  (1A) 2.011, 6.096, 20.005,
       20.026, 20.029, 20.033,
       22.093, 22.094, 22.097
  (1B) 20.030, 20.032, 20.033,
           22.093, 22.094
  (2) 11.082, 14.035, 18.006,
       18.008, 20.004, 20.015,
       21.001, 21.010, , 21.010,
       21.011, 21.012, 21.013,
       21.024, 21.050, 22.001,
       22.012, 22.017, 22.023,
       22.024, 22.025, 22.066,
       22.092, 23.005, 23.011,
          23.014, 23.022
  (a) 21.036, 22.002,
           22.003, 22.004,
           22.005, 22.006,
           22.007, 22.008,
           22.021, 22.023
  (b) ...., 21.026, 21.036,
           21.039, 22.008,
           22.009, 22.010,
           22.013, 22.014,
           22.015, 22.016,
           22.018, 22.019,
           22.021, 22.022

Companies Act 1990 (contd)
 s 160(2)(contd)
  (c) 22.026, 22.028,
                    22.030, 22.031
  (d) 11.076, 17.019,
                    21.006, 21.024,
                    21.026, 21.032,
                    21.036, 21.039,
                    22.006, 22.008,
                    22.012, 22.015,
                    22.016, 22.019,
                    22.021, 22.023,
                    22.030, 22.031,
                    22.032, 22.033,
                    22.034, 22.036,
                    22.039, 22.040,
                    22.041, 22.042,
                    22.046, 22.059
  (e) .... 11.076, , 21.006,
                    21.008, 21.024,
                    21.030, 21.031,
                    21.032, 21.034,
                    21.039, 22.012,
                    22.015, 22.019,
                    22.023, 22.048,
                    22.049, 22.050,
                    22.051, 23.018
  (f) 2.058, 11.064,
                    22.023, 22.053,
                    22.054, 22.055,
                    22.056, 22.058,
                    22.059, 22.060,
                    22.061, 22.068
  (g) 4.036, 22.023,
                    22.062, 22.063,
                    22.064, 22.065,
                    22.066, 22.068,
                    22.069, 22.070
  (h) 14.035, 14.036,
                    14.037, 22.071,
                    22.072, 22.073,
                    22.075, 22.076,
                    22.077, 22.078,
                    22.079, 22.081,
                    22.082, 22.083,
                    22.084, 22.085,
                    22.086, 22.087,
                    22.088, 22.089,
                    22.093, 23.012,
                    23.014

  (i) 20.027, 22.090,
                    22.093, 22.094,
                    22.095, 22.096,
                    22.097
  (3) 22.056, 22.060, 22.061
  (a) 22.068
  (3A) 14.035, 14.037, 22.071,
                    22.078, 22.079, 22.082
  (3B) 22.090
  (4) 18.001, 18.003, 18.006,
                    22.013, 22.026,
                    22.028, 22.034
  (a) 22.050, 22.055
  (b) 18.006
  (4)–(6) 11.076
  (5) 22.050, 22.066
  (6) 11.064, 22.055
  (6A) 11.080, 22.005, 22.013,
                    22.028, 22.034, 22.050,
                    22.055, 22.066,
                    22.073, 22.091
  (7) 21.014, 22.079,
                    22.100, 23.005
  (8) 18.008, 20.017, 20.034,
                    20.041, 22.084, 22.100,
                    23.004, 23.005, 23.006
                    23.014, 23.019, 23.022,
                    23.027, 23.028, 23.029,
                    23.031, 23.036
  (9A) 20.017, 21.047, 22.083,
                    22.100, 23.013, 23.014,
                    23.022, 23.023
  (9B) 19.028, 23.024,
                    23.025, 23.026
  (b) 22.021
  161 ....9.105, 11.035, 20.005,
                    20.032, 20.036, 23.013
  (1) 6.096, 7.007, 9.105,
                    19.023, 20.033, 20.035,
                    20.036, 22.0102,
                    23.031, 23.034
  (1A) 6.096, 20.033
  (2) 19.023, 20.035, 22.0102
  (3) 7.007, 20.033, 23.035,
                    23.036, 23.038
  (4) 20.034, 23.036
  (5) 9.105, 19.023,
                    22.101, 22.0102
  (6) 9.105, 22.0102
  162 ....20.036, 20.039

Companies Act 1990 (contd)

s 163 .... 20.032, 23.037
    (2) 19.023, 23.037, 23.038
    (3) 8.031, 19.020, 19.023,
                        23.038, 23.039
    (5) 23.038, 23.039, 23.043
  164 .... 20.005, 20.037, 23.031,
                        23.040, 23.041
    (1) 20.037, 23.040, 23.042
  165 .... 8.031, 23.040
    (1) 23.041
    (2) 23.041, 23.043
  166 .... 20.015
    (1) 20.014
  167 .... 20.012, 20.013,
                        23.031, 23.032
  168 .... 23.031
  169 .... 6.004, 10.007, 20.005,
                     20.038, 20.039, 20.040
  170 .... 8.009, 8.012, 8.013
  172 .... 8.040, 8.041
  173 .... 8.021, 11.061
  175 .... 8.022, 8.077, 8.078
  176 .... 8.079
  177 .... 8.081, 8.082
  178 .... 8.027, 9.119
  179 .... 8.068
  180 .... 8.080, 10.002, 10.025,
                 10.027, 10.029, 10.040,
                                10.058
    (2) 9.119, 10.039, 10.072
  181 .... 10.025, 10.035, 11.061
  182(2) 7.055
  183 .... 7.002, 7.004
  184 .... 5.034, 7.002, 7.003, 7.006
    (2) 7.008
  185 .... 7.011, 7.013
    (2)(b) 7.011, 7.013, 7.014
    (4) 7.011, 7.012
  186 .... 5.018, 7.013
    (1) 7.013, 7.014
    (3) 7.014
    (4) 7.015
    (5) 7.016
    (6) 7.013, 7.014, 7.016
  187 .... 7.028, 7.030, 7.039, 7.042,
                    7.048, 7.052, 7.149,
                   11.035, 11.089, 15.040
    (1) 7.034, 7.035, 7.041
      (a) 7.040, 11.084

      (iv) 7.028, 7.029,
                            7.034
      (v) 7.028
      (vi) 7.028, 7.031,
                            7.034
    (b) 7.032
  (1A) 7.040, 7.055
  (1B) 7.035, 7.040
  (2) 6.004, 7.039, 7.046, 7.054
    (a) 2.165
    (g) 7.040, 7.133
  (6) 7.042, 7.045
  (7) 7.042
  (9) 7.050, 15.003, 15.007
    (a) 7.043
  (12) 7.049
    (a) 7.049, 15.007
  (13) 7.050
  (14)–(15) 7.030, 7.033
  189 .... 7.028, 7.031, 7.034
    (1)–(2), (4) 11.084
  190 .... 7.028
    (1) 11.084
    (2) 11.084, 21.013
  191 .... 7.028, 7.032, 11.084
    (1)–(2) 6.112
    (3) 6.112, 7.032
    (4)–(5), (8) 6.112
  192(1)–(4) 11.084
    (6) 11.029
    (7) 11.029
  193 .... 2.031, 5.026, 7.019, 7.023,
               7.025, 7.026, 7.027, 7.056
    (1) 7.018
    (2) 7.018, 7.068
    (3) 4.013, 5.054, 7.067, 7.068
    (4)–(4A) 7.019
    (4B)(a) 7.020, 7.069
      (b)–(c) 7.019
      (d) 7.020
      (e) 7.019
    (4C)(i) 7.019
        (I)–(III) 7.020
      (ii) 7.019
    (4D)(a) 7.019
      (b)–(c) 7.021
    (4E) 7.021
    (5) 5.011, 7.070
    (6) 7.025, 7.144

Companies Act 1990 (contd)

s 194 .... 4.024, 7.078, 7.079, 7.081,
7.101, 7.108, 7.119, 7.122,
7.123, 7.126, 11.022
  (1) 7.077, 7.078, 7.112, 7.114
    (a) 7.077
    (b) 7.077, 11.022
  (2) 7.078, 7.112
  (3) 7.078, 7.112
  (3A) 7.079, 7.080
  (3B) 7.081, 7.118
  (4) 4.024, 7.077, 7.080,
7.093, 15.007
  (5) ... 1.007, 7.071, 7.083, 7.084,
7.085, 7.086, 7.087, 7.088,
7.089, 7.090, 7.092, 7.093,
7.094, 7.096, 7.097, 7.098,
7.100, 7.101, 7.102, 7.103,
7.105, 7.106, 7.109, 7.110,
7.111, 7.113, 7.114, 7.115,
7.118, 15.003
  (5A) 7.101, 7.116
  (5B) 7.119
  (6) 7.123
195(1) 7.052
  (2) 7.053
  (5A) 7.103
  (6A) 6.093
197 .... 4.024, 7.067
  (1)–(4) 7.068
  (5) 4.013, 7.068
198 .... 7.035, 7.037
  (3) 7.034, 7.035
  (5) 7.036
199 .... 7.032, 7.033, 7.037, 7.041
  (3) 7.033, 7.034

200 .... 7.032, 7.034, 7.037, 7.041
  (1) 7.032, 7.037
  (2) 7.032
  (2A) 7.032
  (3) 7.033, 7.034
  (3A) 7.034
  (4) 7.032
202 .... 4.001, 4.002, 4.005, 4.007,
4.009, 4.010, 4.011, 4.014,
4.017, 4.019, 4.020, 4.021,
4.023, 4.024, 4.027, 4.028,
4.029, 4.030, 4.031, 4.032,
4.034, 4.035, 6.149, 7.077,
7.078, 7.079, 11.035,

11.038, 15.049, 17.032,
17.033, 17.065, 20.040,
22.064, 22.067, 22.069
  (1) 7.077
    (a) 4.003, 22.069
    (b) 4.003, 4.007
  (2) 4.007, 7.077
  (5) 4.012
  (6) 4.005, 4.012, 17.039
  (7) 4.005, 4.006, 4.013
  (8) 4.013
  (9) 4.018
  (10) 4.019, 4.036, 11.038,
21.001, 22.062, 22.063,
22.064, 22.065, 22.067,
22.069, 22.070
203 .... 4.021, 4.022, 4.024, 7.064,
9.122, 9.127, 17.032
  (1) 4.021
    (b) 4.021
      (i) 4.023
  (2) (a) 4.021
    (b) 4.022
204 .... 4.024, 4.025, 4.027, 4.028,
4.029, 4.030, 4.031, 4.034,
4.035, 6.162, 6.171, 8.031,
9.122, 9.125, 9.127, 22.065
  (1) 4.024, 4.025,
22.065, 22.069
  (2) 4.024
  (3) 4.026
  (4) 4.025
    (a) 22.069
    (b) 4.031
  (5) 4.025
205 .... 6.156
205A 7.055
205B 6.151, 7.055
  (2) (m) 7.058
205C 7.055
205D 7.055, 7.057, 7.063
  (1) 7.055, 7.056
  (2) 7.055
    (c)–(d) 7.056
  (3) 7.056
  (4) 7.055
  (5) 7.057, 7.063
  (6)–(7) 7.058
  (8)–(9) 7.055
  (11) 7.058
  (12) 7.055

Companies Act 1990 (contd)

s 205E 6.157, 6.158, 7.055, 7.124
   (3) 6.156, 7.124
   (5)–(6) 6.156
205F 6.157, 7.124, 7.125
207 .... 2.073, 2.086
209(6) (d) 5.030
210-211 .... 2.086
212(3) 11.058
213 .... 5.030, 5.046
214 .... 5.030
215(2) 2.109
221 .... 2.073
226 .... 2.086, 11.061
230 .... 11.026, 11.082
231 .... 2.076
233 .... 6.153
235 .... 14.057, 14.075
236 .... 11.088
237(2) 8.011
240 .... 2.106, 6.063, 11.034,
       15.046, 15.047, 23.034
   (1) 4.019, 9.080, 15.028,
        15.032, 15.046
   (3) 15.005
   (4) 11.034, 11.081,
        11.082, 15.004
   (5) 15.024, 15.026
     (c) 15.025
   (5A) 15.025
   (6) 15.046
   (7) ... 2.009, 2.012, 2.067, 2.070,
       2.071, 2.073, 2.075, 2.083,
       2.085, 2.089, 2.107, 2.109,
       2.111, 2.113, 2.126, 2.138,
       2.142, 2.143, 2.149, 2.156,
       2.161, 3.002, 3.010, 3.014,
       3.034, 3.036, 3.040, 3.044,
       3.047, 4.023, 5.007, 5.055,
       6.119, 6.144, 6.150, 6.161,
       7.002, 7.004, 8.002, 8.005,
       8.009, 8.013, 8.021, 8.030,
       8.082, 8.083, 9.010, 9.012,
       9.013, 9.018, 9.105, 10.006,
       10.008, 10.056, 10.058,
       10.069, 10.072, 14.023,
       15.003, 15.008, 15.047,
       19.008, 19.019, 22.0102
   (8) 2.085, 2.161, 15.028,
        15.032, 15.047
240A 15.034, 15.036, 15.037

241 .... 12.094, 12.138, 15.017,
       15.018
   (1) 12.063, 15.017
   (2) 15.017
242 .... 2.118, 4.024, 6.116, 11.035,
       12.094, 15.017, 15.018,
       21.042
   (1) ...4.024, 6.116, 6.117, 15.018
   (1A) 2.166, 6.116, 6.117
   (2) 6.117, 15.018
243 .... 6.118, 7.018
245 .... 11.062, 22.074
   (1) 9.122
246 .... 14.083, 14.089, 14.095,
       14.097, 14.098, 14.108
248 .... 2.163, 2.167
   (1) 2.163, 2.164
249(2) (a) 2.167
249A 2.167, 2.170
250(1) (a) 12.008
   (7) 7.043
251 .... 6.119, 6.163, 6.169, 6.175,
       8.031, 9.067, 9.122, 9.123,
       9.124, 9.125, 9.126, 9.127
   (1) 6.163, 9.122, 9.124
     (a) 9.122, 9.123
   (2) (a) 9.122
     (b) 6.175, 9.122, 9.123
   (2A) 6.175, 9.124
   (4) (a) 9.125, 9.127
     (b) 9.124
   (5)................................. 9.123
280(8) 6.161
297 .... 22.027
297A 22.027, 22.029, 22.031
   (1) 22.027
     (b) 6.121
   (10) 22.027
300A 9.008
352(1) (c) 2.164
Pt II 11.082, 12.084, 12.137, 13.001,
       13.036, 13.038, 13.042,
       13.054, 13.060, 13.078,
       13.085
V 7.121, 11.023
VII 18.006, 20.037, 20.039,
       20.041, 22.082, 22.100,
       23.013
   Ch 1 .... 9.122, 16.003
XI 2.086, 11.026

Companies Act 2001
  s 30 .... 12.127

Companies Act 2005 .... 2.059, 2.062

Companies Act 2006
  s 993 .... 6.120, 6.123, 6.129

Companies Acts
  1963–1990 .... 7.073, 11.081,
                       17.016, 17.028

Companies Acts
  1963 to 2001 .... 7.109, 11.004

Companies Acts 1963 to 2005 .... 2.012,
              5.027, 7.109, 14.051

Companies Acts
  1963–2006 .... 2.001, 2.068, 2.104,
          2.123, 3.001, 3.018, 3.047,
          4.001, 4.010, 5.001, 5.002,
          5.015, 5.030, 5.049, 7.002,
          7.003, 7.005, 7.041, 7.062,
          7.066, 8.009, 8.067, 9.022,
          9.089, 10.001, 10.023,
          11.005, 11.019, 11.021,
          11.023, 11.027, 11.037,
          12.134, 14.027, 14.089,
          15.001, 15.003, 15.005,
          15.006, 15.007, 15.008,
          15.010, 15.011, 15.014,
          15.020, 15.021, 15.022,
          15.024, 15.027, 15.029,
          15.032, 15.034, 15.035,
          15.039, 15.040, 15.046,
              15.048, 15.049,
              17.013, 20.007

Companies and Miscellaneous
  Provisions Act 2005 .... 2.165

Company Directors Disqualification
  Act 1986 .... 13.122, 21.020, 23.011
  s 1 (2) 23.011
    1A 21.020
    2 .... 20.019
      (1) 20.011, 20.019
      (3) 20.019, 23.011
    3 (5) 23.011
    4 (3) 23.011
    5 (5) 23.011
    6 .... 21.023, 22.030
      (4) 23.011
    10 .... 22.030

Company Law Enforcement
  Act 2001 .....1.005, 2.020, 2.038, 2.045,
        2.123, 2.127, 2.128, 3.034,
        6.043, 6.044, 6.049, 7.049,
        7.050, 7.052, 7.080, 7.082,
        7.083, 9.001, 9.005, 9.009,
        9.020, 9.037, 9.047, 9.074,
        9.100, 9.106, 9.107, 9.108,
        9.110, 9.113, 9.116, 11.002,
          11.027, 11.030, 11.039,
          11.041, 11.072, 11.076,
          11.078, 11.079, 11.081,
          11.082, 11.083, 12.018,
          12.034, 12.043, 12.047,
          12.048, 12.061, 12.076,
          12.077, 12.089, 12.116,
          12.119, 12.122, 12.124,
          12.125, 13.006, 13.081,
          13.097, 15.028, 15.037,
          15.041, 15.047, 16.001,
          16.007, 16.010, 16.011,
          18.001, 18.002, 18.003,
          18.004, 19.014, 19.015,
          19.024, 20.021, 20.029,
          22.062, 22.071, 22.073,
             22.090, 23.022
  s 3 (1) 13.032
    7... 11.003
    8 ....11.003
    9 (2) 13.041
    12 ....11.017, 11.034, 11.079
      (1) 9.048, 11.004, 11.020
        (a) 9.100, 11.001, 11.034,
               11.079, 15.004
        (f)–(g) 11.004
      (2) 11.041
      (5) 11.043, 11.052
        (d) 11.017, 11.034
    13 ....12.002
    14 ....5.004, 5.005, 5.009, 12.012,
          12.020, 13.045, 13.050,
          13.051, 13.070, 13.119,
            15.027, 21.001
    16 ....11.048, 11.050, 11.053
      (1) 11.045, 11.052
      (2) 11.043, 11.045, 11.047,
            11.050, 11.053
      (3) 11.043, 11.051, 11.053
      (4) 11.043, 11.052,
            11.053, 11.054

Company Law Enforcement
  Act 2001 (contd)
  s 17 .... 11.047, 11.048, 11.049,
            11.050, 11.055, 11.056,
                      11.057
      (1) 11.047, 11.055,
                  11.056, 11.058
      (2) 11.048, 11.049
        (b)–(c) 11.058
      (3) 11.058
      (4) 11.047, 11.055, 11.056
  18 .... 11.030, 13.087
  19 .... 5.054
  20 .... 12.022, 13.004, 13.036
  21 .... 11.082, 12.013, 12.020,
             13.006, 13.012, 13.036
  22 .... 13.038, 13.066
  23 .... 13.066, 13.067, 13.069
      (b) 13.072
      (c) 13.071, 13.084,
                13.097, 13.100
      (d) 13.069
  24 (1) 13.111
      (2) 13.112
  25 .... 13.126
  26 ... 12.012, 12.020, 13.049, 13.129
  27 .... 13.051
  28 .... 13.087
  29 .... 4.013, 11.082, 12.001, 12.002,
            12.003, 12.004, 12.005,
            12.006, 12.007, 12.008,
            12.009, 12.011, 12.015,
            12.025, 12.027, 12.028,
            12.031, 12.032, 12.033,
            12.034, 12.035, 12.036,
            12.037, 12.038, 12.039,
            12.047, 12.050, 12.052,
            12.057, 12.058, 12.060,
            12.061, 12.063, 12.064,
            12.065, 12.067, 12.070,
            12.073, 12.075, 12.076,
            12.077, 12.080, 12.081,
            12.082, 12.088, 12.089,
            12.093, 12.096, 12.097,
            12.098, 12.099, 12.113,
            12.138, 13.015, 13.016,
                  13.032, 13.045,
                  13.076, 15.018

  30 ...11.082, 12.001, 12.100, 12.104,
               12.105, 12.106, 12.116,
               12.122, 12.124, 12.125,
               12.127, 12.128, 12.129
  31 ....11.082, 12.133, 12.135,
               12.136, 12.137, 13.111
      (a) 11.058, 12.137
  32 ....11.082, 12.084, 12.085
      (a) 12.072, 12.085
  33 ....13.042
  34 ....11.087
  36 ....11.024
      (b) 11.024
  37 ....11.025, 11.082
      (1) 11.082
        (b) 11.025
  38 ....11.031
  39 ....11.026, 11.082
  40 ....22.098, 22.099
  41 .....9.102, 18.003, 18.006, 19.025,
               19.026, 19.029
      (1) 19.004, 19.010, 19.014,
            19.024, 19.028, 19.030,
            19.034, 19.038, 19.040,
            19.041, 19.045, 22.0102
        (c) 16.013, 16.025
  42 .....6.004, 11.080, 14.035, 21.001,
            21.024, 22.071, 22.075
      (a) 2.011, 6.096, 20.005,
            20.029, 20.030, 22.093
      (b) (ii) 14.035, 20.027,
            22.062, 22.071, 22.072,
               22.076, 22.090
      (c) 14.035, 22.071, 22.078
      (e) 11.080, 20.028, 22.005,
            22.013, 22.028, 22.034,
            22.050, 22.055, 22.066,
              22.073, 22.091
      (f) 20.017, 22.083, 22.100,
            23.013, 23.022, 23.024
  43 ....9.107, 15.027
  44 ....9.109, 9.110, 9.112
  45 ....9.113, 9.115
  46 ....9.111, 9.122
  47 ....9.005
  48 ....9.020
  49 ....9.108, 9.109, 9.110, 9.111,
         9.112, 9.113, 9.115, 15.027

Company Law Enforcement
  Act 2001 (contd)
  s 51 .... 8.068, 9.073, 9.074, 9.086,
          9.087, 9.091, 9.092, 9.093,
          9.094, 9.095, 9.096, 9.097,
          9.098, 9.100, 11.027
     52 .... 8.024, 8.028, 8.030,
          8.066, 8.084
        (b) 8.006, 8.008
     53 .... 8.060, 8.061
     54 .... 6.169, 9.122
        (6) 6.175
        (b) 9.124
        (c) 9.124, 9.125
     55 .... 9.116, 9.117, 9.118
     56 .... 9.037, 9.038, 9.039, 9.042,
          9.043, 9.044, 9.045, 9.047,
          9.048, 9.049, 9.051, 9.052,
          9.053, 9.057, 9.062, 9.064,
          9.067, 9.075, 9.076, 9.079,
          9.080, 9.082, 9.083, 9.084,
          15.049, 16.008, 16.013,
          16.015, 16.024, 16.025,
          16.040, 16.048, 18.004,
          18.010, 18.015, 18.018,
          19.030, 19.039, 19.041,
          19.045, 19.046, 19.050
        (1) 9.037, 9.041, 9.077
        (2) 9.037, 16.006, 16.048,
          17.070, 18.004
        (3) 9.037, 17.070
     57 .... 9.108, 9.128
     58 .... 8.067, 9.129, 11.029
     59 .... 2.018, 2.020, 2.058, 11.035,
          11.061
     60 .... 2.022, 2.037, 2.039, 2.041,
          2.042, 2.043, 2.044, 2.045,
          2.046, 2.047, 2.050, 2.051,
          2.052, 11.061
     61 .... 2.054, 11.088
     63 (2) 2.021
     64 .... 2.027, 2.028, 2.057
     65 .... 2.056
     66 ..... 2.058, 11.039, 11.065, 11.068
     72 .... 7.040, 11.035
        (a) 7.028
        (b) 7.049, 7.050
     73 .... 11.029
        (2) (d) 7.083

        (3) 7.083
     74 .... 7.077, 7.079, 11.022
        (a) 7.077
        (b) 7.077, 11.022
        (c) 7.079, 7.081, 7.118
        (d) 7.077, 7.080, 7.093
        (e) 1.007, 7.071, 7.083, 7.096,
          7.101, 7.113, 7.114, 7.123
     76 .... 6.034, 6.067, 6.068
        (a) 8.041
     77 .... 6.043, 6.061
     78 .... 5.030, 6.044, 6.045, 6.046,
          6.047, 6.048, 6.080, 6.171
     79 .... 6.049
     80 .... 2.002, 2.003
     83 .... 2.002
     84 (a) 2.034, 2.042, 2.046
        (b) 20.038
     85 .... 11.083
     86 .... 2.123, 2.136, 11.083
     87 .... 2.138, 2.144, 11.035,
          11.061, 11.083
     88 .... 2.127, 2.129, 2.134,
          11.061, 11.083
        (1) 2.124, 2.127, 2.130,
          2.131, 2.133
     89 .... 2.084, 19.017
     90 .... 6.149
     91 .... 3.035, 3.036, 20.020, 20.021,
          20.027, 20.028
        (a) 2.114, 6.095, 20.021
     96 .... 2.058, 6.178, 9.082, 11.037,
          11.066, 12.088
     97 .... 12.067, 12.088
     98 .... 2.125, 11.067
     100 .... 4.029, 6.115, 15.013,
          15.015, 15.016
     101 .....2.011, 6.094, 20.020, 20.021,
          20.027, 20.028
     102 .... 13.052
     104 ....4.019, 6.119, 6.144, 6.161,
          8.002, 8.005, 8.009, 8.013,
          8.082, 8.083, 9.080, 9.105,
          10.006, 10.008, 10.033,
          10.056, 10.069, 15.005,
          15.028, 15.032, 15.046,
          15.047, 22.0102
        (1) 19.019

Company Law Enforcement
Act 2001 (contd)
s 104 (1) (contd)
(c) ... 2.009, 2.012, 2.067, 2.070,
2.071, 2.073, 2.075, 2.083,
2.085, 2.089, 2.106, 2.107,
2.109, 2.111, 2.113, 2.126,
2.138, 2.142, 2.143, 2.149,
2.156, 2.161, 3.002, 3.010,
3.014, 3.034, 3.036, 3.040,
3.044, 3.047, 4.023, 5.007,
5.055, 6.150, 7.002, 7.004,
7.043, 8.021, 8.030, 9.010,
9.012, 9.013, 9.018, 9.027,
10.058, 10.072, 14.023,
15.003, 15.008, 15.032,
15.047, 19.008
105 .... 15.034, 15.037
106 ..... 6.116, 6.117, 11.035, 15.018
107 .... 2.167, 2.168
109 .... 4.024, 6.176, 9.081, 11.039
110 .... 15.041
110A 15.042, 15.043, 15.044
Sch 11.082, 13.044
Pt 2 .... 11.034
Pt VII 1.009

Competition Act 1991 .... 20.007, 20.013

Competition Act 2002 .... 1.008, 9.089

Constitution of Ireland
Art 8 .... 4.005
30.3 .... 11.034, 15.004
34 .... 11.034
34.1 .... 13.113, 13.114, 13.122
38 .... 13.087
38.1 .... 13.086
40 .... 12.079
40.3 .... 13.086, 13.087
40.3.2 .... 13.113
40.5 .... 12.100
40.6 .... 13.086
40.6.1 .... 13.086
43.2.1 .... 13.070
49 .... 14.030

Consumer Credit Act 1995
s 4 (3) 11.045
(4) 11.051
106 .... 12.120
149(12) 12.085

Conveyancing Act 1881 .... 8.073
s 19-24 .... 8.072

Copyright Act 1963
s 27 .... 12.100

Corporation Act 2001
s 206B 20.018

Courts (No 3) Act 1986 .... 15.021
s 1 .... 15.021

Courts Act 1971
s 15 .... 15.033, 15.034

Credit Union Act 1997 .... 2.140

Criminal Acts 1963–1990 .... 7.109

Criminal Assets Bureau Act 1996 ..... 12.119
s 14 .... 12.100, 12.105, 12.114
(1) 12.108, 12.122

Criminal Damage Act 1991
s 13 .... 12.120

Criminal Justice (Administration) Act 1924
s 9 (1) 11.034, 15.004

Criminal Justice (Scotland) Act 1987
s 52 .... 12.090

Criminal Justice (Terrorist Offences) Act
2005 .... 7.127

Criminal Justice (Theft and Fraud
Offences) Act 2001 .... 7.126, 12.119
s 48 .... 12.100, 12.105, 12.114
(2) 12.108, 12.122
(3) (a) 12.119
(c) 12.125
(8) 12.128
59 .... 7.128

Criminal Justice Act 1851
s 7 .... 15.026

Criminal Justice Act 1951 .... 15.023

Criminal Justice Act 1984 .... 15.032
s 4 .... 15.031

Criminal Justice Act 1987
s 2 .... 12.090

Criminal Justice Act 1993
s 2 (1) 6.145
57 .... 7.126

Criminal Justice Act 1994
  s 57 .... 7.128
    64 .... 12.100, 12.105, 12.114

Criminal Justice Act 2006 .... 15.023

Criminal Law Act 1997 .... 15.028, 15.032
  s 2 (1) 15.028
    4 .... 15.003
     (2) 15.029
     (3) 15.030
     (4) 15.029

Dáil Éireann (Privilege and Procedure)
  Act 1970
  s 3 (4) 13.098

Designated Investment Funds Act 1985
  s 5 .... 11.088

Electoral Act 1997
  s 22 (2) (a) 2.021
    26 .... 2.021

Electronic Commerce Act 2000
  s 12 .... 2.165
    13 (2) (a) 2.165
    27 .... 12.105

European Communities Act 1972 .... 12.010,
  12.131, ... 12.135

European Convention of Human Rights Act
  2003 .... 12.091, 12.100

Exchange Control Acts 1954 to 1986 ....
  11.058, ... 12.135

F

Finance (No 2) Act 1959 .... 8.053

Finance Act 1999
  s 82 .... 14.010
    83 .... 14.010, 14.011

Finance Act 2000
  s 78 .... 14.010, 14.011

Finance Act 2003
  s 48 .... 7.055

Financial Services Act 1986
  s 94 .... 12.090

  105 .... 12.090
  177 .... 12.090

Financial Services Authority of Ireland
  Act 2004
  s 33 .... 2.098

Fisheries (Consolidation) Act 1959 ...12.049

Friendly Societies Acts 1896 to 1977
  .... 23.001

Gaming and Lotteries Act 1956
  s 39 .... 12.100

Human Rights Commission Act 1975
  s 15 (2) 11.054

Human Rights Commission Act 2000
  s 4 (2) 11.053
    15 .... 11.046, 11.053
    23 .... 11.045

ICC Bank Act 2000
  s 7 .... 2.023

Industrial and Provident Societies
  Acts 1893 to 1978 .... 23.001

Insolvency Act 1986 .... 9.015
  s 108(2) 9.015, 9.016
    213 .... 6.131
    214 .... 22.030

Insolvency Act 2000 .... 21.020, 21.023
  Sch 4 Pt I 20.011

Insurance Act 1989 .... 7.127

Insurance Acts 1909
  to 1990 .... 11.058, 12.135

Insurance Acts 1909 to 2000 .... 12.010

Interpretation Act 1937
  s 11 (d) 16.054

Interpretation Act 2005 .... 15.008, 15.018
  s 6 .... 2.021
    18 (c) 15.018
     (j) 15.008, 15.018
  Sch Pt I 5.002

Investment Funds, Companies and
Miscellaneous Provisions
Act 2005 ..... 1.005, 7.083, 7.109, 7.113,
12.032, 12.033, 12.034,
12.088, 12.127, 20.015
s 11 (2) 23.024
31 .... 11.023
38 .... 2.062
49 .... 2.062
56 .... 5.030
57 .... 2.165
58 .... 2.166
59 .... 2.123
(2)–(6) 2.145
60 .... 2.123
(1)–(2) 2.145
61 .... 2.025, 7.026, 11.061
62 .... 2.115, 6.093
63 .... 9.036
64 .... 6.178, 12.088
65 .... 14.009
67 .. 12.002, 12.011, 12.030, 12.031,
12.032, 12.033,
12.034, 12.039
(a) 12.029
(c) 13.016
68 .... 12.001, 12.127
69 .... 12.131
70 .... 20.015
(a) 20.014
71 .... 4.024, 6.116, 6.117, 11.035
(b) 2.166
72 .... 2.156, 8.002, 9.018,
9.019, 9.025, 10.008,
10.069, 10.072, 11.061,
11.062, 14.004, 14.005,
14.006, 14.012, 14.013,
14.019, 14.021, 14.024,
14.025, 14.027, 14.040,
14.041, 14.043, 14.049,
14.061, 14.069, 14.077,
14.078, 14.080, 14.082,
14.083, 14.084, 14.089,
14.098
73 .... 22.0102
(1) 2.065
(2) (a) 11.035
(d) 1.007, 7.071, 7.083,
7.096, 7.101, 7.113
(3) 1.007, 7.083, 7.096,
7.101, 7.113

74 ......2.058, 11.037, 11.066, 15.042
Pt 5 ....2.059

Investment Funds, Companies and
Miscellaneous Provisions
Act 2006 ....1.005, 2.021, 7.129,
11.011, 15.040, 19.024,
19.026, 19.029, 19.030,
21.022
s 7 ....2.021
9 ....7.129, 7.131, 7.132
11 ....19.024, 19.026, 19.030, 19.049

Investment Intermediaries Act 1995 ....7.127
s 75 ....12.120

Investment Limited Partnerships Act 1994
s 44 ....11.088

Joint Stock Banking Companies
Act 1857 ....12.006

Joint Stock Companies Act 1844 ....11.060

Joint Stock Companies Act 1956 ....12.006

Joint Stock Companies Acts 1856 .....12.006

Joint Stock Companies
Acts 1856–1857 ....12.006

Law Reform Commission Act 1975
s 6 ....11.045

Local Government (Planning and
Development) Act 1963
s 80 (1) 15.004

Local Government (Planning and
Development) Act 1982
s 9 ....15.005
13 ....15.004

Minimum Notice and Terms
of Employment Act 1973
s 13 (1) 8.054

Minimum Notice and Terms
of Employment Act 1993 ....8.054

Misuse of Drugs Act 1977 ....12.107
s 27 (2) 12.120

Oireachtas (Compellability, Privileges and
    Immunities of Witnesses) Act 1997
  s 3 .... 11.054

Partnership Act 1890 .... 4.016

Pensions (Amendment) Act 1996
  s 83 .... 7.128
     (1) 7.126

Petty Sessions (Ireland) Act 1851
  s 10 .... 15.020
     (4) 15.023, 15.024

Police Property Act 1897
  s 9 .... 15.049

Probation of Offenders
  Act 1907 .... 6.064, 15.048

Property Act 1954
  s 29 .... 14.033

Prosecution of Offences Act 1974 .... 11.071
  s 2 (5) 11.043

Prospectus Regulations 2005 .... 2.062

Provident Societies Acts 1893
  to 1978 .... 20.006

Public Company Accounting Reform and
  Investor Protection
  Act 2002 .... 7.060, 7.064

Redundancy Payments
  Acts 1967–1979 .... 8.054

Registration of Business Names Act 1963
  s 4 .... 2.146
    14 .... 2.146

Regulation of Information (Services
  Outside the State for Termination
  of Pregnancies) Act 1995
  s 9 .... 12.120

Safety, Health and Welfare at Work
  Act 2005 .... 1.008

Social Welfare Act 1991
  s 37 .... 8.053

Stamp Duty Consolidation Act 1999
  s 162 .... 2.071

State Property Act 1954
  s 27 .... 14.030
    28 .... 14.030, 14.033, 14.034
    29 (3) 14.030
    30 .... 14.031
    31 .... 14.032, 14.033, 14.034

Stock Exchange Act 1995 .... 7.129
  s 66 .... 12.120

Taxes Consolidation Act 1997 .... 2.121,
            6.009, 12.135, 21.034
  s 110 .... 7.055
    207 .... 2.129
    23A 14.010
    819 .... 6.007
     (3) 14.014
     (a) 6.007
    882 .... 14.010, 14.011, 14.012,
            14.015, 14.042, 14.048,
            14.054, 14.055, 14.060,
            14.061, 14.072, 14.084,
                        14.094
     (3) 14.011, 14.094
    883 .... 14.061
    1071 .... 14.015
    1073 .... 14.015
    1078 .... 14.015
     (1) 12.135
    1079 .... 7.126

Trade Union Acts, 1871 to 1990 .... 7.129

Trustee Savings Act 1989 .... 7.127

Trustee Savings Banks
  Acts 1863 to 1965 .... 2.023

Unfair Dismissals Act 1977 .... 8.054
  s 12 (1) 8.054

Video Recordings Act 1989
  s 25 .... 12.100

Workmen's Compensation
  Acts 1934 to 1955 .... 8.053

Australia

Corporation Act 2001
  s 206B(1).........................(b)(ii) 20.018

United Kingdom

Companies Act 1862 .... 3.015, 3.026
  s 32 .... 3.016
     35 .... 3.026

Companies Act 1929 (Eng) 6.139

Companies Act 1948 .... 22.012
  s 110 .... 3.006
     165 .... 12.051, 13.031
        (b) (ii) 12.042
     353 .... 14.092
     369(2) 8.075

Companies Act 1967
  s 109 .... 12.046, 12.055, 12.056

Companies Act 1985 .... 5.048, 12.090,
                               12.092, 13.007,
                               13.008, 13.013,
                               13.117, 13.086
  s 293 .... 6.002
     300 .... 17.019
     389A(1) 7.067
        (2) 7.068
     390 (1) 7.070
     431 .... 13.005, 13.007, 13.041,
                           13.064, 13.117
        (3) 13.009, 13.010, 13.025
        (4) 13.004
     432 .... 13.007, 13.041, 13.064,
                       13.117, 13.118, 13.035
        (1) 13.007, 13.008, 13.117
        (2) 12.042, 13.007, 13.012,
                       13.031, 13.053, 13.117

     (2A) 13.118
     (4) 13.024
  433 .... 13.007, 13.041
  437 .... 13.007, 13.064, 13.117
     (1) 13.101
     (3) 13.118
  441 .... 13.122
  442 .... 13.117
  447 .... 12.002, 12.083, 12.090
  458 ....6.120, 6.123, 6.129, 6.141
  459 .... 13.012, 13.013
  460 .... 13.012

Companies Act 1989
  s 55 .... 13.118
     63 .... 12.083
     83 .... 12.090

Company Directors Disqualification Act
  1986
  s 6 ....22.030, 22.040, 23.011
  8   (1) 12.090

New Zealand

Companies Act 1955
  s 245(1) (a) 9.120

Companies Act 1993
  s 271(1) 9.120

South Africa

Companies Act 1973
  s 417 .... 13.088

USA

Securities Exchange Act 1934 .... 7.060
  s 10A 7.064
     (b)...................................... 7.114
     (1) (f) 7.104
  13 (2) (b) 7.068

Table of Statutory Instruments

CLEA 2001 (Section 58) Regulations 2002
(SI 544/2002) 11.029

Companies (Amendment) (No 2) A 1999
Bonding Order 2000
(SI 64/2000) 14.015

Companies (Auditing and Accounting)
Act 2003 (Commencement)
Order 2004 (SI 132/2004) 2.037

Companies (Auditing and Accounting)
Act 2003 (Commencement) (No 2)
Order 2005 .... 7.055

Companies (Auditing and Accounting)
Act 2003 (Commencement)
Order 2006
(SI 56/2006) 7.028, 7.032, 11.089

Companies (Auditing and Accounting)
Act 2003 (Commencement) Order 2007
(SI 61/2007) 7.079, 7.080,
7.116, 7.119

Companies (Fees Order) 2001
(SI 477/2001) 2.164

Companies (Fees) (No 3) Order 2005
(SI 179/2005) 2.088

Companies (Fees) Order 1997
(SI 358/1997)
reg 4 .... 14.095

Companies (Fees) Order 2000
(SI 63/2000)
reg 4 .... 14.094

Companies (Fees) Order 2001 (SI 477/2001)
reg 6 .... 14.095
7 .... 14.094

Companies (Forms) (No 2) Order 2004
(SI 829/2004) 2.010, 2.012, 2.075
Sch 5 .... 2.075

Companies (Forms) Order (No 2) 2002
(SI 54/2002) 2.057

Companies (Forms) Order 2000
(SI 62/2000) 14.018

Companies (Forms) Order 2004
(SI 133/2004) 2.021

Companies (Forms) Regulations 1991
(SI 162/1991)
Sch 2.086

Companies Act 1990 (Auditors)
Regulations 1992
(SI 259/1992) 7.033, 7.034, 7.038,
7.040
reg 3 ....7.028
4 ....7.040
7 (1) (a) 7.032
(b) 7.033, 7.034

Companies Act 1990 (Form and Content of
Documents Delivered to Registrar)
Regulations 2002 (SI 39/2002)
reg 1 ....2.057
4 ....2.164
5 ....2.164
6...2.164
7 ....2.164
8 ....2.164
9 ....2.164
10 ....2.164
11 ....2.164
12 ....2.057, 2.164
13...2.164
14 (1) 2.164
(2) 2.057, 2.164
(4) 2.164
15 ....2.164
(1) 2.164
(2) 2.057, 2.164
(3) 2.057
(a) 2.057, 2.164
(b) 2.164
18 ....2.004
21 ....2.057, 2.164
23 (1) 2.164

Companies Act 1990 (Parts IV and VII)
Regulations 1991
(SI 209/1991) 20.012, 20.013
reg 3 (1) 19.021
Sch 19.021

Companies Act 1990 (Section 34)
Regulations 2001 (SI 524/2001)... 6.046

Company Law Enforcement Act 2001
(Commencement) (No 2)
Order 2001
(SI 438/2001) 2.003, 2.039

Company Law Enforcement Act 2001
(Commencement)
(No 5) Order 2002
(SI 53/2002) 20.021, 22.071

Company Law Enforcement Act 2001
(Section 56) Regulations 2002
(SI 324/2002) 9.048, 9.051, 9.052,
9.053, 9.054, 9.055,
9.056, 9.057, 9.058,
9.059, 9.062, 9.063,
9.066, 9.067, 9.069,
9.070, 9.071, 9.072,
9.073, 9.075

Company Law Enforcement Act 2001
(Section 58) Regulations 2002
(SI 544/2002) 8.067, 9.129

Company Law Enforcement Act 2001
(Winding-up and
Insolvency Provisions)
(Commencement) Order 2003
(SI 217/2003) 9.047

Criminal Justice Act (Section 32)
Regulations 2003 (SI 242/2003) .. 7.126

District Court (Company Law
Enforcement) Rules 2002
(SI 207/2002) 12.101, 12.102
reg 3 .... 12.101

District Court (Summonses) Rules 2005
(SI 167/2005)
reg 3 .... 15.020

District Court Rules 1997
(SI 93/1997) 15.001
ord 13 r 1 .... 15.033, 15.037
2 .... 15.033
15 .... 15.020
16 .... 15.020
17 .... 15.022
34 .... 12.101

European Communities (Accounts)
Regulations 1993 (SI 396/1993) ..4.001

European Communities
(Branch Disclosure) Regulations
1993 (SI 395/1993) 7.106
reg 3 .... 2.151
4 .... 2.152
5 .... 2.154
6 .... 2.151
7 .... 2.152
8 .... 2.154
10 .... 2.154
11 .... 2.154
12 .... 2.154
19 .... 2.155

European Communities (Companies)
Regulations 2004 (SI 839/2004)
reg 5 .... 2.154

European Communities (Companies
Group Accounts) Regulations 1992
(SI 201/1992) 2.057, 4.001, 7.129
reg 37 .... 6.151
45 .... 2.056
Sch 6.112

European Communities (Credit Institutions
Accounts) Regulations 1992
(SI 294/1992)
reg 7 .... 6.112

European Communities (Fair Value
Accounting) Regulations 2004
(SI 765/2004)
reg 3 .... 6.154
5 .... 6.152

European Communities (Insurance
Undertakings: Accounts) Regulations
1996 (SI 23/1996) 7.129
reg 10 .... 6.112
20 .... 2.023

European Communities (International
Financial Reporting Standards
and Miscellaneous
Amendments)
Regulations 2005
(SI 116/2005) 2.024, 2.032, 4.001,
7.019, 11.035
reg 4 .... 6.148

European Communities (International Finan-
cial Reporting Standards
and Miscellaneous
Amendments)
Regulations 2005
(SI 116/2005) (contd)

reg 5 .... 2.023, 2.024, 2.025,
2.027, 2.028, 2.030,
2.031, 2.032, 2.055,
2.056, 7.021, 7.023,
7.027
(f) 6.148
(g) (i) 6.151, 6.154
(ii) 6.151, 6.152
8 .... 7.019, 7.020, 7.021, 7.069
9............... 2.031, 4.003, 4.005,
4.012, 6.076
Sch 1.............. 2.031, 4.003, 4.005,
4.012, 6.076, 11.089

European Communities (Public Limited
Companies Subsidiaries) Regulations
1997 (SI 67/1997)
reg 6 .... 6.153

European Communities (Single-Member
Private Limited Companies)
Regulations 1994
(SI 275/1994) 2.057, 5.016
reg 5 .... 2.057
6 .... 2.057
8–9 .... 5.016
10 .... 5.016, 5.038

Investment Funds, Companies and
Miscellaneous Provisions Act 2005
(Commencement) Order 2005
(SI 323/2005) 7.113

Investment Funds, Companies and
Miscellaneous Provisions Act 2006
(Commencement) Order 2007
(SI 23/2007) 19.026

Prospective (Directive 2003/17/EC)
Regulations 2005 (SI 324/2005) .. 2.059
reg 8 (1) (h) 2.062

38 (1) 2.060

Rules of the District Court
ord 34 .... 12.102, 12.103
r 7................................. 12.101

Rules of the Superior Courts (No 4) 1991
(SI 278/1991) 9.119, 9.124,
13.002, 13.036,
13.051, 13.060,
13.101, 13.121,
13.126, 18.008, 21.014
ord 40 .... 21.014
r 1 .... 21.018, 21.019
75B 3 .... 18.008, 21.014
7 .... 21.014, 21.019
9 .... 21.015

Rules of the Superior Courts
(SI 15/1986) 9.005, 18.005
ord 9 .... 18.011, 18.012
r 2, 16 .... 18.011

11............................... r 1 18.012
12 .... 18.013
18 (1)–(2) 10.055
(3) 10.055, 10.057
(4)–(5) 10.055
(6)–(9), (13)–(15) 10.057
(17)................................... 10.061
19 .... 10.021
22 .... 10.041
74 r 49 .... 6.175
75 r 4 .... 14.060
(n) 14.081
75A r 10 .... 10.028
12 .... 10.032
13 (1) 10.010
(2)–(3) 10.011
17 .... 10.060
(3) 10.061
18 .... 10.055

Rules of the Superior Courts
   (SI 15/1986) (contd)
    ord 75B r 3 (a)—(b) 13.002
             (c) 13.036
             (d) 13.126
             (dd) 9.124
             (e) 13.051

         4 .... 13.121
         5 (a) 13.060
         7 .... 13.060
           (c)—(d) 13.101
     99 .... 19.024, 23.025
      r 1 ... 19.024, 19.037, 19.038,
                  19.040, 19.047

Chapter 1

INTRODUCTION

A. Background

[1.001] The Irish Companies Acts are replete with mandatory requirements and attendant sanctions. Until recent years, however, these requirements were infrequently enforced and the sanctions rarely imposed. This situation was highlighted by the reports of *ad hoc* bodies, such as the Working Group on Company Law Compliance and Enforcement[1] and the Review Group on Auditing.[2] There were further high profile events, particularly the investigations into the affairs of companies such as *National Irish Bank Ltd*[3] and *Ansbacher (Cayman) Ltd*,[4] which also illustrated the need to utilise the Companies Acts more effectively in the prevention and redress of corporate wrong doing. Internationally, the awareness of the need for strong external regulation and oversight of companies was also acute after the collapse of *Enron Corporation*[5] and *Worldcom Inc*[6] and other corporations.

[1.002] The establishment of the Working Group on Company Law Compliance and Enforcement by the Minister for Enterprise Trade and Employment in August 1998 had a particularly significant impact on compliance with, and enforcement of, company law in Ireland. The Report of the Working Group emphasised the importance of compliance with, and effective enforcement of, company law:

> 'Compliance and enforcement are the means by which all legal duties, rights and protections are lifted from the dusty page and have life breathed into them, and without which such duties, rights and protection all return to dust.'[7]

The Working Group set out a number of 'particular reasons' why it is important for company law to be complied with and enforced.[8] First, a higher standard of compliance and enforcement enhances the protection of the public; of employees; of traders and suppliers; of the State's revenue; of investors; of legitimate business; and of Ireland's

---

[1]   The establishment of the Working Group on Company Law Compliance and Enforcement was announced by the Minister for Enterprise, Trade and Employment on the 7 August 1998. The Report of the Working Group was published on the 30 November 1998.

[2]   *Report of the Review Group on Auditing* (July 2000).

[3]   See further Pt E, Disqualification Orders.

[4]   See further Pt E, Disqualification Orders.

[5]   See *Re Enron Corporation Securities* 258 F Supp 2d 576; 2003 US Dist LEXIS 3786; Fed Sec L Rep (CCH) P92,296 (SD Tex March 12, 2003) for background.

[6]   See *SEC v WorldCom Inc* 273 F Supp 2d 431; 2003 US Dist LEXIS 11394; Fed Sec L Rep (CCH) P92,456 (SDNY 7 July 2003).

[7]   *Report of the Working Group on Company Law Compliance and Enforcement* at p 5.

[8]   *Report of the Working Group on Company Law Compliance and Enforcement* at para 1.19.

business and trading reputation.[9] Second, 'a compliant corporate sector should yield substantial returns in business efficiency, solvency, revenue yield, social solidarity and in terms of public and private time saved in dealing with the consequences of non-compliance'.[10]

Third, compliance with company law is beneficial to the company itself, as it ensures the company records its transactions, keeps accurate and up-to-date accounts and complies with the requirements of transparency imposed by the Companies Acts. The Group records that, 'any enterprise which takes compliance seriously is also likely to identify and avoid problems in good time which otherwise might threaten its viability'.[11]

[1.003] There are other advantages and benefits of a high level of compliance with, and enforcement of, company law, including the prevention, detection and punishment of abuses of limited liability. Whether the potential benefits of enhancing compliance with, and enforcement of, company law, have been achieved by the measures which have been introduced into the Companies Acts for that purpose, remains to be seen in some areas of compliance and enforcement. It is undeniable, however, that the level of compliance with, and enforcement of, company law in Ireland has risen significantly since the publication of the *Report of the Working Group on Company Law Compliance and Enforcement* in November 1998.

[1.004] In its Report, the Working Group made some stark findings regarding the attitude in Ireland towards compliance with, and enforcement of, the Companies Acts at that time. The Working Group found that, 'Irish company law has been characterised by a culture of non-compliance and a failure by companies and their officers to meet their obligations in respect of the filing of annual returns on time'[12] and that, 'most statutory offences have never been the subject of prosecutions, and those which have been prosecuted have resulted in only a handful of convictions'.[13] The Group further found that:

> 'Those who are tempted to make serious breaches of company law have little reason to fear detection or prosecution. As far as enforcement is concerned, the sound of the enforcer's footsteps on the beat is simply never heard.'[14]

In light of these findings, the Group regarded 'action to counter a culture of under-enforcement, non-enforcement and non-compliance as an urgent economic, social and legislative priority'.[15]

[1.005] Since the publication of the Report of the Working Group, there have been several developments that have strengthened compliance with, and enforcement of, the

---

9   *Report of the Working Group on Company Law Compliance and Enforcement* at para 1.19.
10   *Report of the Working Group on Company Law Compliance and Enforcement* at para 1.20.
11   *Report of the Working Group on Company Law Compliance and Enforcement* at para 1.22.
12   *Report of the Working Group on Company Law Compliance and Enforcement* at para 2.4.
13   *Report of the Working Group on Company Law Compliance and Enforcement* at para 2.5.
14   *Report of the Working Group on Company Law Compliance and Enforcement* at para 2.5.
15   *Report of the Working Group on Company Law Compliance and Enforcement* at para 2.27. The Group made specific recommendations for such 'action', many of which are reflected in subsequent legislation. Wherever relevant, these recommendations are considered in subsequent chapters.

Companies Acts. First, there have been many amendments to the Companies Acts which have enhanced the enforcement of the Acts, by creating new enforcement mechanisms and procedures and new sanctions for non-compliance. The Companies Acts have been amended by, among other legislative enactments, the Company Law Enforcement Act 2001 ('CLEA 2001'), the Companies (Auditing and Accounting) Act 2003 ('C(AA)A 2003'), the Investment Funds, Companies and Miscellaneous Provisions Act 2005 ('IFCMPA 2005'), and the Investment Funds, Companies and Miscellaneous Provisions Act 2006 ('IFCMPA 2006').

Second, there have been important regulatory changes, particularly the establishment of the Office of the Director of Corporate Enforcement ('ODCE'), with responsibility for enforcing the Companies Acts. Third, there has been a significant increase in the instances of enforcement of the Acts. Finally, there has been a marked enhancement of awareness of the need to comply with the provisions of the Acts, and the risks of non-compliance.

[1.006] While there may be some debate and divergence regarding the efficiency and proportionality of some of the means of enforcement and the sanctions that now exist under the Companies Acts,[16] it is incontrovertible that those who commit serious breaches of company law may no longer assume that they will not hear 'the sound of the enforcer's footsteps on the beat'.[17]

B. Scope of *Company Law Compliance and Enforcement*

[1.007] The primary objective of this book is to examine the means and mechanisms of enforcement of the provisions of the Companies Acts 1963–2006 ('CA 1963–2006'). 'Enforcement', as that term is used for the purpose of this book, refers to enforcement of the provisions of the CA 1963–2006 by external agencies, such as the Director of Corporate Enforcement ('DCE'), the Director of Public Prosecution ('DPP') or the Companies Registration Office ('CRO'); or by persons vested with responsibility for such enforcement, such as liquidators. While the requirements of the CA 1963–2006 may be considered and relied upon in a variety of proceedings, including private civil litigation, this book does not address such private litigation, but focuses solely on enforcement proceedings by external regulatory agencies or by persons vested by the CA 1963–2006 with responsibility for such enforcement.

In examining enforcement, the book also considers the related topic of compliance with the CA 1963–2006. The compliance obligations that are addressed here have two dimensions. First, the book considers those obligations imposed by the CA 1963–2006 to enhance or strengthen compliance with the requirements of the Acts.[18] Second, the book considers certain categories of statutory obligation, which have been significant in

---

[16] See, for example, Irish Times 15 April 2005 'Taking Corporate Laws Too Far' and Sunday Times, 1 June 2003 'Enforcer's Legal Move to Feather Lawyers Nests'.

[17] *Report of the Working Group on Company Law Compliance and Enforcement* at para 2.5.

[18] This aspect of 'compliance' includes the duties to report suspected breaches of the CA 1963–2006, or suspected offences, to regulatory agencies. See eg, the duty of an auditor to report suspected indictable offences to the DCE under CA 1990, s 194(5), as inserted by CLEA 2001, s 74(e), as amended by C(AA)A 2003, s 37(d), IFCMPA 2005, s 73(3), and by IFCMPA 2005, s 73(2)(d). See Ch 7.

the context of the enforcement of company law, such as companies' filing obligations. The term 'compliance' as it is used here, does not, however, intend to encapsulate every requirement of the CA 1963–2006 and the book does not purport to contain an exhaustive treatment of every obligation under the CA 1963–2006 with which there must be compliance.[19]

[1.008] There are certain matters and areas of law that are beyond the scope of this book. First, the enforcement and compliance that is addressed in this book relates solely and exclusively to the CA 1963–2006. While there is a body of company law that is derived from, and governed by, common law, this is beyond the scope of this book.[20] Second, there are numerous legislative enactments, other than the CA 1963–2006, which may impact on companies, but which do not fall within the category of 'company law'. The requirements and restrictions of legislation such as the Competition Act 2002, the Safety, Health and Welfare at Work Act 2005, and the Central Bank and Financial Services Authority of Ireland Acts 2003 and 2004, among others, are accordingly not considered here. Third, topics of general company law, which are not relevant to compliance with, or enforcement of, the CA 1963–2006, are addressed elsewhere.[21] Fourth, there is no detailed treatment of accountancy standards and regulations.[22] The obligation to keep proper books of account is however considered separately in Ch **4**, as this is a topic which has given rise to, and been considered in, numerous enforcement proceedings.[23] Fifth, the provisions of the CA 1963–2006 applicable to share transfers and share dealings, including the law governing insider dealing and market abuse,[24] are not considered here. This is a significant body of law, but it is an area in which there has not yet been significant enforcement activity.[25] Sixth, topics that are uniquely relevant to

---

[19] For a broader treatment of the requirements of the CA 1963–2006, see, eg, Courtney, *The Law of Private Companies* (2nd edn, Tottel Publishing, 2002) and Keane, *Company Law* (4th edn, Tottel Publishing, 2007).

[20] For the common law rules applicable to companies, see, eg, Courtney, The Law of Private Companies (2nd edn, Tottel Publishing, 2002) and Keane, Company Law (4th edn, Tottel Publishing, 2007); Forde, *Company Law* (3rd edn, Round Hall Sweet and Maxwell, 1999).

[21] See, eg, Courtney, *The Law of Private Companies* (2nd edn, Tottel Publishing, 2002) and Keane, *Company Law* (4th edn, Tottel Publishing, 2007); Forde, *Company Law* (3rd edn, Round Hall Sweet and Maxwell, 1999).

[22] See Courtney, *The Law of Private Companies* (2nd edn, Tottel Publishing, 2002) at Ch **13**.

[23] See, eg, Ch **17**.

[24] See Market Abuse (Directive 2003/6/EC) Regulations, 2005 (Market Abuse Regulations).

[25] There has only been one attempted criminal prosecution for the offence insider dealing, a prosecution which was unsuccessful. See DETE, *Companies Report 2001* at p 66. See also the decision of the Supreme Court in *Fyffes v DCC* [2007] IESC 36 (27 July 2007, unreported), SC in which the provisions applicable to insider dealing were considered in the context of private civil litigation. The DCE is examining the decision of the Supreme Court. The relevance of the provisions on insider dealing in the sphere of company law enforcement may change in the wake of the Supreme Court's decision and the DCE's examination of it, but for the present, the area of share transfers and share dealings comprises a large body of law, which has not played a central role in company law enforcement.

public limited companies, such as the prospectus regulations[26] and listing rules,[27] relate to a small minority of such companies that are formed in Ireland and are beyond the scope of this book.[28] Finally, internal corporate governance is not addressed in this book, other than insofar as it falls within one of the chapters in Corporate Compliance Obligations, Pt A, or Compliance Obligations of Individuals, Pt B.[29]

C. Future Direction of Company Law Compliance and Enforcement

[1.009] Among the recommendations of the Working Group on Company Law Compliance and Enforcement was the establishment of a Company Law Review Group ('CLRG').[30] On 8 December 1999, the Minister for Enterprise, Trade and Employment announced the establishment of the CLRG on an administrative basis. The CLRG was formally established upon the commencement of Pt VII of the CLEA 2001 on 1 October 2001.

The CLRG has produced a General Scheme of the Companies Consolidation and Reform Bill 2007 together with a Report on this General Scheme.[31] The General Scheme sets out in Pillar A, Pt 13, the provisions applicable to Compliance, Investigation and Enforcement. Many of the provisions of this chapter replicate existing provisions of the Companies Acts.[32] There are, however, certain innovations in the General Scheme, such as Head 57 of Pillar A, Pt 13, which recommends the categorisation of most offences under the Companies Acts into category one, two, three

---

26 Prospectus (Directive 2003/71/EC) Regulations, 2005 (Prospectus Regulations).

27 Irish Stock Exchange, Revised Listing Rules (1 November 2007). Available at www.ise.ie.

28 According to the CLRG, Report on the General Scheme of the Companies Consolidation and Reform Bill 2007, at p 15, only 0.62% of the companies formed in Ireland are public limited companies. Available at www.clrg.org.

29 See guidance such as the Combined Code of Corporate Governance (2003); the UK Financial Reporting Council, Revised Turnball Guidance (October 2005); and the OECD, Principles of Corporate Governance.

30 *Report of the Working Group on Company Law Compliance and Enforcement* (30 November 1998) at para 5.29.

31 Both are available at www.clrg.org. Note that, according to the Government Legislation Programme for Autumn Session 2007 (25 September 2007), Pt B, the Company Law Consolidation and Reform Bill is expected to be published in late 2008. Available at www.taoiseach.gov.ie.

32 The CLRG, *Report on General Scheme of Companies Consolidation and Reform Bill* (March 2007) states, for example, that Heads 2 to 20 of Ch 2 of Pillar A, Pt 13, 'substantially re-enact the existing provisions which regulate investigations under the Companies Acts' and that, in Ch 5 of Pillar A, Pt 13, which deals with restriction and disqualification of company directors and officers, 'the existing provisions have been substantially re-enacted with some changes'. See CLRG, *Report on General Scheme of Companies Consolidation and Reform Bill* (March 2007) at Ch 6.13.

or four offences.[33] Insofar as the General Scheme does propose changes to the Companies Acts that are significant from the perspective of compliance with, or the enforcement of, the Acts, these proposals will be examined in the context of the existing legislative provisions.[34]

---

[33] See CLRG, *Report on General Scheme of Companies Consolidation and Reform Bill* (March 2007) at Ch 6.13. The exceptions to this categorisation relate to the most serious offences, such as market abuse and fraudulent trading.

[34] Unless otherwise specified, the amendments that are proposed in the General Scheme and referred to, relate to private companies limited by shares, as that is the form of company which is addressed in Pillar A of the General Scheme. See CLRG, Report on the General Scheme of the Companies Consolidation and Reform Bill 2007, at p 27. Available at www.clrg.org.

PART A
CORPORATE COMPLIANCE

Chapter 2: Companies' Obligations: Filing
A. Introduction 9
B. Formation of a company 9
C. Annual return 17
D. Prospectus 41
E. Members 43
F. Share capital 46
G. Charges 54
H. Resolutions and agreements 68
I. Directors and secretaries 70
J. Company name 75
K. Companies incorporated outside the State 86
L. Public limited companies 90
M. Re-registration of companies 92
N. Form of documents 96

Chapter 3: Companies' Obligations: Maintenance of Registers
A. Introduction 103
B. Form of registers 103
C. Register of members 104
D. Register of directors and secretaries 118
E. Register of directors' interests in company 120
F. Directors' contracts 122
G. Register of charges 123
H. Register of debenture holders 124

Chapter 4: Books of Account
A. Introduction 127
B. Proper books of account 127
C. Criminal liability 135
D. Personal liability 138
E. Disqualification 147

Chapter 5: Companies' Obligations: Members' Meetings
A. Introduction 149
B. Annual General Meeting 149
C. Extraordinary General Meeting 158
D. Resolutions 164
E. Conduct of business at general meetings 168
F. Direction of Court 175
G. Minutes of meetings 176

PART A

Chapter 2

COMPANIES' OBLIGATIONS: FILING

A. Introduction

[2.001] This chapter considers some of the obligations that the Companies Acts 1963 to 2006 ('CA 1963–2006') impose on companies to make returns, make filings, send notifications, and deliver documents to the Registrar of Companies.[1] These regulatory obligations ensure that a company's structure and affairs are transparent and publicly accessible. While the filing requirements imposed by the Companies Acts are burdensome, they must be complied with in exchange for the benefits of incorporation.

The obligations considered in this chapter are generically referred to as 'filing obligations' and are treated under distinct sub-headings, ranging from the obligation to file an annual return to filing obligations in relation to the company name. Other topics such as the form in which documents should be presented to the Companies Registration Office ('CRO') are also considered.

B. Formation of a company

(a) Memorandum of association

[2.002] Every company must send a copy of its proposed memorandum of association to the Registrar of Companies. CA 1963, s 17 provides that:

> The memorandum and the articles, if any, shall be delivered to the registrar of companies in an entire format or in a form pursuant to s 80 of the Company Law Enforcement Act, 2001, and he shall retain and register them.[2]

[2.003] The Company Law Enforcement Act 2001, s 80 ('CLEA 2001') provides that the Registrar 'may accept for registration a document containing standard form text from the objects clause of a memorandum of association or from articles of association',[3] which need not relate to a particular company or contain the company's

---

[1] This chapter does not purport to examine every filing obligation which the Companies Acts impose on companies, but focuses on what are considered to be the principal filing obligations of which companies should be aware. It should also be noted that certain topics, such as filing obligations in the context of liquidations, receiverships and in relation to restriction and disqualification orders, are considered under the heading of the chapters which are dedicated to those topics.

[2] CA 1963, s 17, as amended by CLEA 2001, s 83.

[3] CLEA 2001, s 80(1), as commenced by the CLEA 2001 (Commencement) (No 2) Order 2001 (SI 438/2001) on 1 October 2001.

registered number (this is known as a 'standard form memorandum and articles of association').[4]

A company's memorandum and articles of association may incorporate the text of the standard form memorandum and articles of association as previously registered with the Registrar, including the reference number of those documents.[5] These documents may then be read as one entire document.[6] This procedure renders it unnecessary to register a complete memorandum and articles of association in respect of every company which is registered.

[2.004] Where a memorandum is delivered to the Registrar, it will not be registered unless it complies with all of the requirements of the Companies Acts regarding registration and related matters.[7] A statutory declaration by a solicitor engaged in the formation of the company, or a person named as a director or secretary in the statement delivered to the Registrar under s 3 of the C(A)A 1982,[8] that the relevant requirements have been complied with, should be delivered to the Registrar.[9] The Registrar may, but is not required to, accept such a declaration as sufficient evidence of compliance with the Companies Acts.[10]

[2.005] In the case of public limited companies it is essential that the amount of share capital with which the company proposed to be registered, as stipulated in its memorandum of association, must not be less than the authorised minimum share capital.[11]

(b) Articles of association

[2.006] Not every company is obliged to register its articles of association with the Registrar of Companies. According to CA 1963, s 11 companies limited by shares and companies limited by guarantee and not having a share capital, may, but are not required to, register the company's articles of association, with the memorandum of association.[12]

---

4   CLEA 2001, s 80(2).

5   CLEA 2001, s 80(3).

6   CLEA 2001, s 80(4).

7   C(A)A 1983, s 5(1).

8   The statement required by C(A)A 1982, s 3, is considered further below at paras **[2.010]** to **[2.011]**.

9   C(A)A 1983, s 5(5). Companies Act 1990 (Form and Content of Documents Delivered to Registrar) Regulations 2002 (SI 39/2002), reg 18 provides that a statutory declaration under s 5(5) shall be made on or after the date of the form prescribed for the purposes of the Companies Acts in relation to the registration of a company, or the date of the memorandum and articles of association of the company concerned, whichever is the later.

10   C(A)A 1983, s 5(5).

11   C(A)A 1983, s 5(2).

12   CA 1963, s 11, as substituted by C(A)A 1982, s 2.

Companies limited by guarantee and having share capital or unlimited companies, are both required to register articles of association with their memoranda of association.[13]

[2.007] A company which registers its articles of association with the Registrar of Companies, whether voluntarily or compulsorily, must ensure that it is signed by the subscribers to the company's memorandum of association.[14]

[2.008] There are certain additional requirements for the articles of association of unlimited companies and companies limited by guarantee having a share capital. In the case of an unlimited company, the articles must state the number of members with which the company will be registered and the amount of its share capital, if applicable.[15]

CA 1963, s 12(2) provides that the articles of a company limited by guarantee 'must state the number of members with which the company proposes to be registered.'[16] It is curious to note that the scope of s 12(2) is not restricted to companies limited by guarantee having a share capital, but refers simply to companies limited by guarantee. This suggests that while companies limited by guarantee and not having a share capital are not obliged to register their articles of association, if they do so, the articles must state the number of members of the company.

[2.009] If a company which is obliged to state the number of its members in its articles of association (unlimited companies or companies limited by guarantee) increases the number of its members beyond that registered number, it must notify the Registrar of Companies of that increase.[17] The form to be used for this purpose is Form No 11.[18] This notice must be given to the Registrar within 15 days of the increase or the resolution to introduce the increase in the number of members and must be signed by the secretary or a director of the company.[19] It is an offence for a company and every officer in default to fail to comply with this notification requirement.[20]

(c) Section 3 Statement ('Form A1')

[2.010] Whenever a memorandum of association is delivered to the Registrar of Companies for registration, it must be accompanied by a statement setting out certain particulars regarding the company. This information must be presented on what is

---

[13] CA 1963, s 11, as substituted by C(A)A 1982, s 2.

[14] CA 1963, s 11, as substituted by C(A)A 1982, s 2.

[15] CA 1963, s 12(1).

[16] CA 1963, s 12(2).

[17] CA 1963, s 12(3) as amended by C(AA)A 2003, s 57.

[18] Referred to as Form B9/11. This form may be downloaded from the Companies Registration Office website, www.cro.ie.

[19] CA 1963, s 12(3) as amended by C(AA)A 2003, s 57.

[20] CA 1963, s 12(3), as amended by C(A)A 1982, s 15 and CA 1990, s 240(7) as inserted by CLEA 2001, s 104(c). CA 1963, s 12(3) provides that a person who is convicted of the offence of failing to notify the Registrar of an increase in the number of members, is liable to a fine not exceeding €1904.61.

known as 'Form A1'.[21] This form must be completed correctly, in full and in accordance with the notes provided for this purpose by the CRO.[22]

The Companies (Amendment) Act 1982 ('C(A)A 1982'), s 3 requires this statement to contain the following information:

- the names of the first directors of the company;[23]

- all particulars of the directors required to be kept by CA 1963, s 195;[24]

- the name of the first secretary of the company;[25]

- all particulars of the secretary which are required by CA 1963, s 195(4);[26]

- the particulars of the registered office which are required to be given to the Registrar under CA 1963, s 113.[27]

---

[21] Companies (Forms) No 2 Order 2004 (SI 829/2004). This form may be downloaded at www.cro.ie.

[22] See Notes to Form A1, 'This form must be completed correctly, in full and in accordance with the following notes. Every section of the form must be completed.' The Notes also give the following general guidance: 'Where "not applicable", "nil" or "none" is appropriate, please state. Where €/_ appears, please insert/delete as appropriate. Where /_ applies, give the relevant currency, if not euro. Where the space provided on Form A1 is considered inadequate, the information should be presented on a continuation sheet in the same format as the relevant section in the form. The use of a continuation sheet must be so indicated in the relevant section.' See www.cro.ie.

[23] C(A)A 1982, s 3(1). This must be the full name and it should be noted that initials will not suffice. It should also be noted that 'Where the secretary is a firm, the name of the firm and registered address ought to be stated. Where a person is signing on behalf of a company which is the secretary, he/she should state that he/she is signing for and on behalf of the company which is acting as secretary. His/her name should be printed in bold capitals or typescript below the signature' (Note Three to Form A1 at www.cro.ie). In addition, any former forename or surname must be stated, unless the change in name occurred before the person attained the age of 18, or has been disused for 20 years. A married woman is not obliged to state the name or surname by which she was known prior to her marriage. See Note Four to Form A1 at www.cro.ie.

[24] C(A)A 1982, s 3(2)(a).

[25] C(A)A 1982, s 3(1). This must be the full name and it should be noted that initials will not suffice. It should also be noted that 'Where the secretary is a firm, the name of the firm and registered address ought to be stated. Where a person is signing on behalf of a company which is the secretary, he/she should state that he/she is signing for and on behalf of the company which is acting as secretary. His/her name should be printed in bold capitals or typescript below the signature' (Note Three to Form A1 at www.cro.ie). In addition, any former forename or surname must be stated, unless the change in name occurred before the person attained the age of 18, or has been disused for 20 years. A married woman is not obliged to state the name or surname by which she was known prior to her marriage. See Note Four to Form A1 at www.cro.ie.

[26] C(A)A 1982, s 3(2)(b).

[27] C(A)A 1982, s 3(2)(c). This must be a full postal address and a PO Box, eg, will not suffice. See Note Three to Form A1 at www.cro.ie.

[2.011] The Form A1 must also state the name of the company as it appears on the memorandum and articles of association.[28] This statement must be signed by or on behalf of the subscribers[29] and accompanied by a consent signed by each of the persons named in it as a director, secretary or joint secretary to act in that capacity.[30] If the memorandum of association is delivered to the Registrar by a person acting as agent for the subscriber(s), the name of this person should also be specified in the s 3 statement ('Form A1').[31]

The persons who are named in the statement delivered to the Registrar as the directors and secretary of the company are deemed, from the incorporation of the company, to have been so appointed.[32] Any indication in the articles of association, which are delivered with the memorandum, that any other persons hold such positions, will be void.[33]

If any of the persons whose names are notified to the Registrar in Form A1 as directors of the company are disqualified from being so appointed or so acting in another state, this fact must be disclosed in a separate statement to the Registrar.[34] It is the duty of the disqualified person to ensure that this statement is made. The statement must specify the jurisdiction in which he is disqualified and the date and period of such disqualification.[35] It must also be signed by the disqualified person.[36] The form prescribed for this statement is Form B74.[37] While s 3A specifies no sanction for a failure to deliver Form B74, the director in question will be deemed to be disqualified in Ireland and may face prosecution for acting as a director while disqualified.[38]

---

[28] See Note One to Form A1: 'The proposed company name must be given in full and must correspond exactly with the company name given on the accompanying memorandum and articles of association.'

[29] It should be noted in this regard that, 'The subscribers in this section must correspond with the subscribers to the accompanying memorandum and articles of association except where an agent signs this section on behalf of the subscriber(s).' (Note Eleven to Form A1 at www.cro.ie).

[30] C(A)A 1982, s 3(3).

[31] C(A)A 1982, s 3(4).

[32] C(A)A 1982, s 3(5).

[33] C(A)A 1982, s 3(5).

[34] C(A)A 1982, s 3A, as inserted by CLEA 2001, s 101. See Note Six to Form A1: 'Where a person who has consented to be a director of this company is currently disqualified under the law of another state from being appointed or acting as a director or secretary of a body corporate or undertaking, he/she must complete Form B74 which must be submitted to CRO with Form A1. Otherwise he/she will be deemed to be disqualified from acting as a director of an Irish-registered company for the balance remaining of his/her foreign disqualification'. See further Ch **20**.

[35] C(A)A 1982, s 3A(1), as inserted by CLEA 2001, s 101.

[36] C(A)A 1982, s 3A(1), as inserted by CLEA 2001, s 101.

[37] This form may be downloaded from the Companies Registration Office website, www.cro.ie.

[38] CA 1990, s 160(1A), as inserted by CLEA 2001, s 42(a). See Ch **20**.

(d) Registered office

[2.012] A company which is incorporated under the Companies Acts 1963 to 2005, must have a registered office in the State to which communications and notices may be sent.[39] The location of this office must be disclosed in the statement which is delivered to the Registrar in accordance with C(A)A 1982, s 3.[40] Any change in the location of the company's registered office must be notified to the Registrar within 14 days.[41] This notification must be made on Form B2.[42] It is not sufficient to include this information in the company's annual return.[43] If there any default in complying with this requirement, the company and every defaulting officer is guilty of an offence, which may be brought and prosecuted by the Registrar, and liable to a fine of up to €1904.61.[44]

(e) Activity in State

[2.013] A company may not be formed and registered under the Companies Acts unless it appears to the Registrar of Companies that the company, when it is registered, will carry on an activity[45] in the State.[46] This activity must be within the scope of the company's memorandum of association.[47] A statutory declaration may be filed for this purpose on Form A1. The declaration should state the following:

– the declaration must be included in Form A1;[48]

– the declaration must state that the purpose, or one of the purposes, of the company, is the carrying on of an activity in the State;[49]

– if it appears to the person making the declaration that the activity is one which belongs to a division, group or class appearing in the 'relevant classification

---

[39] CA 1963, s 113(1), as substituted by C(A)A 1982, s 4.

[40] CA 1963, s 113(2), as substituted by C(A)A 1982, s 4. See further para **[2.010]**.

[41] CA 1963, s 113(3), as substituted by C(A)A 1982, s 4.

[42] Companies (Forms) No 2 Order 2004 (SI 829/2004). This form may be downloaded from the Companies Registration Office website, www.cro.ie and may be filed online.

[43] CA 1963, s 113(3), as substituted by C(A)A 1982, s 4.

[44] CA 1963, s 113(5) and (6), as substituted by C(A)A 1982, s 4, and as amended by C(AA) 2003, s 57, and by CA 1990, s 240(7) as inserted by CLEA 2001, s 104(c).

[45] C(A)(No 2)A 1999, s 42(7) defines an 'activity' as 'any activity that a company may be lawfully formed to carry on and includes the holding, acquisition or disposal of property of whatsoever kind …'

[46] C(A)(No 2)A 1999, s 42(1).

[47] C(A)(No 2)A 1999, s 42(1).

[48] C(A)(No 2)A 1999, s 42(2).

[49] C(A)(No 2)A 1999, s 42(2).

system',[50] the declaration should state the general nature of the activity and the division, group or class to which it belongs;[51]

- if the person making the declaration does not consider that the activity falls within a division, group or class, the declaration should state a precise description of the activity;[52]

- the declaration must state the place or places in the State in which the company proposes to carry on the activity;[53] and

- the declaration must state where the central administration of the company will normally be carried on, whether in the State or not.[54]

[2.014] The function and importance of this statutory declaration has been described as follows by the CRO:

> The statutory declaration is a declaration of compliance with all the legal requirements relating to the incorporation of a company. It must be signed by either a solicitor who is forming the company or the director or secretary in the presence of either a commissioner of oaths, notary public, solicitor or peace commissioner. As the declaration confirms that all other registration requirements have been completed, it must be signed after the form has been completed in full, and so the date of declaration must not predate the dates of other signatures which appear on the form and accompanying memorandum and articles of association.[55]

Such a statutory declaration may be accepted by the Registrar as sufficient evidence that a company will carry on an activity in the State.[56] The Registrar is not obliged to accept, as sufficient evidence, a statutory declaration under s 42. This statutory declaration

---

50 C(A)(No 2)A 1999, s 42(7) defines the 'relevant classification system' as 'NACE Rev 1, that is to say, the common basis for statistical classifications of economic activities within the European Community set out in the Annex to Council Regulation (EEC) No 3037/90 of 9 October 1990 on the statistical classification of economic activities in the European Community, as amended for the time being.' The CRO describes this classification as follows: 'The NACE code is the common basis for statistical classifications of economic activities within the EU' and clarifies that, 'the four digit NACE code and general nature of the activity must correspond with the proposed company's principal objective in the accompanying memorandum of association. Where there are two or more activities, give details of the principal activity in the State.' See Note Sixteen to Form A1 at www.cro.ie.

51 C(A)(No 2)A 1999, s 42(2)(a). If the company's purpose, or one of its purposes, is the carrying on of two or more activities in the State, this information should refer to whichever of those activities the person making the declaration considers to be the 'principal activity for which the company is being formed to carry on in the State' (C(A)(No 2)A 1999, s 42(3)).

52 C(A)(No 2)A 1999, s 42(2)(b). C(A)(No 2)A 1999, s 42(3) also applies to this aspect of the statutory declaration and requires this information to relate to the 'principal activity' in the State, if there are more than one such activities.

53 C(A)(No 2)A 1999, s 42(2)(c). C(A)(No 2)A 1999, s 42(3) also applies to this aspect of the statutory declaration and requires this information to relate to the 'principal activity' in the State, if there are more than one such activities.

54 C(A)(No 2)A 1999, s 42(2)(d).

55 Note Fourteen to Form A1 at ww.cro.ie.

56 C(A)(No 2)A 1999, s 42(2).

should be made by any person named as a director or secretary of the company in the s 3 statement or by a solicitor engaged in the formation of the company.[57]

(f) Effect of registration

[2.015] The effect of registration of a company's memorandum of association with the Registrar is the following:

> On the registration of the memorandum of a company the registrar shall certify under his hand that the company is incorporated and, in the case of a limited company, that the company is limited.[58]

From the date of incorporation specified in the certificate of incorporation issued by the Registrar, the subscribers shall be a body corporate with all of the ensuing consequences of such incorporation.[59]

A certificate of incorporation is, according to C(A)A 1983, s 5(4), conclusive evidence that the requirements of the Companies Acts in connection with the registration have been complied with and that the company is duly registered under the Companies Acts.[60] If the certificate states that the company is a public limited company it shall also be conclusive evidence of that fact.[61]

(g) Members

[2.016] The persons who are named in the memorandum of association that is delivered to the Registrar of Companies, are deemed to have agreed to become members of the company and their names are entered on the register as members of the company.[62] According to CA 1963, s 31(2), 'Every other person who agrees to become a member of a company, and whose name is entered in its register of members, shall be a member of the company.'

---

[57]   C(A)(No 2)A 1999, s 42(4).

[58]   CA 1963, s 18(1). Note that pursuant to CA 1963, s 389, 'A certificate signed by any person purporting to hold the office of registrar of companies or assistant registrar of companies or any office similar thereto in any country prescribed by the Minister for the purposes of this section, certifying that a company named in such certificate has been incorporated in that country, shall be *prima facie* evidence of such incorporation without proof of the signature of the person signing such certificate and without proof that the person signing such certificate holds that office.'

[59]   CA 1963, s 18(2).

[60]   C(A)A 1983, s 5(4)(a).

[61]   C(A)A 1983, s 5(4)(b). If the company is a public limited company, the amount of the share capital stated in the memorandum must not be less than the authorised minimum and the certificate of incorporation shall include a statement that the company is a public limited company (C(A)A 1983, s 5(2)).

[62]   CA 1963, s 31(1).

C. Annual return

[2.017] Every company, whether trading or not, is obliged to file an annual return with the Registrar of Companies at least once in every calendar year.[63] The form to be used for this purpose is Form B1.[64] This is designed to give a snapshot of the company and its affairs on an annual basis, to enable the Registrar and the public to be aware of a range of information regarding the company.

(a) Content of annual return

[2.018] The CA 1963 contained a Schedule (the Fifth Schedule), which set out the matters that needed to be included in a company's annual return. CA 1963, s 125 as originally enacted, provided that:

> Every company having a share capital shall, once at least in every year, make a return to the registrar of companies containing in relation to the registered office of the company, registers of members and debenture holders, shares and debentures, indebtedness, past and present members and directors and secretary, the matters specified in Part I of the Fifth Schedule.[65]

The matters which needed to be addressed in the annual return were therefore the following:

- the registered office of the company;
- the register of members;
- the register of debenture holders;
- shares;
- debentures;
- indebtedness;
- past and present members;
- directors; and
- secretary.[66]

[2.019] CA 1963, Sch 5 provided that an annual return must contain the following:

(a) the address of the registered office;

(b) the address at which the register of members is kept (if not (a) above);

---

[63] For a practical overview of the obligation to file an annual return, see CRO, 'Filing an Annual Return in the CRO' (Information Leaflet No 22, December 2005).

[64] Available at www.cro.ie. Note that annual returns may be filed electronically. See further paras **[2.165]** to **[2.166]**.

[65] CA 1963, s 125(1). CA 1963, s 126 imposed a similar obligation on companies without a share capital. This distinction is no longer of any relevance in the context of the obligation to file an annual return. See CLEA 2001, s 59.

[66] CA 1963, s 125(1).

(c)   the address at which the register of debenture holders is kept (if not (a) above);

(d)   a summary, distinguishing between shares issued for cash or otherwise, stating the amount of share capital; the number of shares; the number of shares taken; the amount called up on each share; the total amount of calls received; the total amount of calls unpaid, the amount of commission paid in respect of any shares or debentures; any discounts allowed on the issue of any shares; the total amount of any discounts in respect of debentures; and the total number of shares forfeited;

(e)   particulars of the total amount of the company's indebtedness in respect of all mortgages and charges which are required to be registered with the CRO;

(f)   a list of the names, addresses and occupations of all persons who are existing members of the company and the shares held by each, specifying shares transferred since the last return by such members and the dates of registration of such transfers (if this list is not alphabetical, it should be accompanied by an index enabling the name to be easily found);

(g)   a list of the names, addresses and occupations of all persons who have ceased to be members since the date of the last return and specifying the shares transferred since that date and the dates of registration of such transfers (if this list is not alphabetical, it should be accompanied by an index enabling the name to be easily found);

(h)   all particulars relating to the directors and secretaries of the company at the date of the return, as are required to be included in the register of the directors and secretaries of a company.[67]

[2.020] CA 1963, ss 125 and 126 have been repealed and replaced by CLEA 2001, and s 125(1) now imposes the same obligation on both companies which have a share capital and those which do not, to file an annual return, as follows: 'Every company shall, once at least in every year, subject to s 127, make a return to the Registrar of companies, being its annual return, in the prescribed form.'[68]

[2.021] CA 1963, Sch 5 was repealed by CLEA 2001, s 63(2). The Companies (Forms) Order 2004 (SI 133/2004) now provides for the content and form of annual returns which are prescribed for the purposes of CA 1963, s 125. This form is known as 'Form B1'[69] and the matters which must be included therein are the following:

(a)   the name of the company;

(b)   the date to which the return is made;

---

[67] See CA 1963, Sch 5, Pt I.

[68] CA 1963, s 125(1), as inserted by CLEA 2001, s 59.

[69] This form may be downloaded from the Companies Registration Office website, www.cro.ie and filed online.

    (c)   if the return is made up to a date earlier than the Annual Return Date ('ARD'), the company must state whether it wishes to retain the original ARD;[70]

    (d)   the financial year to which the return relates;

    (e)   the registered office of the company at the date of the return;

    (f)   if other than (d) above, the address at which the register of members; of debenture holders; register of directors' and secretaries' interests in shares or debentures; and copies of directors' service contracts, are kept;

    (g)   the full name and usual residential address of the company's secretary, including any former names and addresses[71] (if the secretary is a company, the registered name and office must be included and if the secretary is a firm and all partners are joint secretaries, the name and principal office of the firm must be included);

    (h)   details of the recipient and value of any donations[72] made by the company for political purposes to a political party, a member of Dáil Éireann, Seanad Éireann, or an MEP, a candidate for the Dáil, Seanad or European Parliament, where the total value of all such donations in the period to which the annual return relates exceeds €5,079.00;[73]

---

[70] See further paras **[2.033]** to **[2.052]** below regarding the 'ARD'.

[71] The former names of the secretary that must be included do not include: (a) if the person is usually known by a title other than his surname, the name by which he was known before this title (b) if the former name or surname was changed or disused before the person attained the age of 18 or more than 20 years prior to making the return or (c) in the case of a married woman, the name by which she was known prior to the marriage, if different. See Note Seven to Sch 1 to SI 133/2004 'Companies (Forms) Order 2004.

[72] 'Donation' is widely defined in the Electoral Act 1997, s 22(2)(a) as follows: '"donation" means any contribution given for political purposes by any person, whether or not a member of a political party, to a political party, a member of either House of the Oireachtas, a representative in the European Parliament or a candidate at a Dáil, Seanad or European election and includes all or any of the following, namely—

    (i)   a donation of money,
    (ii)   a donation of property or goods,
    (iii) conferring the right to use, without payment or other consideration, indefinitely or for a specified period of time, any property or goods,
    (iv) the supply of services without payment or other consideration therefor,
    (v)   the difference between the commercial price and the price charged for the purchase, acquisition or use of property or goods or the supply of any service where the price, fee or other consideration is less than the commercial price, or
    (vi) in the case of a contribution made by a person in connection with an event organised for the purpose of raising funds for a political party, a member of either House of the Oireachtas, a representative in the European Parliament or a candidate at a Dáil, Seanad or European election, the proportion attributable to that contribution of the net profit, if any, deriving from the event …'

[73] The Electoral Act 1997, s 26 requires disclosure in the annual return of contributions for political purposes which exceed in aggregate €5,079.00, to any political party, member of the Dáil or Seanad, MEP or candidate for the Dáil, Seanad or European Parliament. The disclosure must be sufficiently detailed to identify the value and recipient of each individual donation.

(i)   the details of the presenter, including name, address, telephone number, email address, fax number;

(j)   the authorised share capital of the company, stating the class of shares, the number in each class and the nominal value of each share;[74]

(k)   the total issued share capital, broken down into the following (which figures must equal the total issued share capital):

  – The amount paid up on shares issued for cash,

  – The amount considered to be paid on other shares,

  – The total calls on shares not yet paid,

  – The total number of shares not yet called;

(l)   the shares which have been issued for cash consideration, listing, in respect of each, the following:

  – the class of shares,

  – the number of shares,

  – the total nominal value,

  – the total premium paid,

  – the total amount paid;

(m)   the shares which have been issued other than for cash consideration, listing, in respect of each, the following:

  – the class of shares,

  – the total number of shares held,

  – the total nominal value of the shares,

  – the total premium considered to have been paid,

  – the total amount considered to have been paid for the shares;

(n)   the total number of shares issued for both cash and non-cash consideration, which must equal the total number of shares held by existing members of the company;

(o)   the total amount of consideration (cash and non-cash) which has been paid, considered paid, called but unpaid and not yet called;

(p)   other details of shares and debentures, which should include the class, number and amounts of any shares or debentures that were forfeited, issued at a discount, or on which commission was paid;[75]

(q)   a full list of all past and present members of the company, including, in respect of each,[76] the following:

  – name,

---

[74]   If a company has transferred its shares to stock, the references to shares should be taken to refer to stock. See Sch 1, Note Nine, to SI 133/2004, Companies (Forms) Order 2004.

[75]   See Note Eleven to Sch I to SI 133/2004, Companies (Forms) Order 2004.

[76]   In the case of joint shareholders, the names of each of the shareholders can be included, or the names can be listed as the first named shareholder 'and another'. See Sch 1, Note Twelve, to the Companies (Forms) Order 2004 (SI 133/2004).

– address,

– class of shares held,

– total number of shares held;

(r) in the case of private companies only, the return must include the following particulars regarding the transfer of any shares by existing or past members of the company:

– particulars of shares transferred,

– date of registration of each transfer,

– number of shares transferred on each date since the last annual return (or since incorporation, if it is the company's first return);[77]

(s) in the case of each director, including shadow or alternate directors,[78] the following particulars must be furnished:

– full names,[79]

– former names,[80]

– date of birth,

– whether Irish resident,[81]

– whether alternate director,[82]

– residential address,

---

[77] See Sch 1, Note Fifteen, Companies (Forms) Order 2004 (SI 133/2004).

[78] See definitions in Ch **6** below. See also Courtney, *The Law of Private Companies* (2nd edn, Tottel Publishing, 2002) Ch 8.

[79] If the director is a body corporate, the name and registered office of the company must be included; if the director is a firm, and all the partners are directors of the company making the return, the name and principal office of the firm should be included. See Sch 1, Note Six, Companies (Forms) Order 2004 (SI 133/2004).

[80] The former names of the directors that must be included do not include: (a) if the person is usually known by a title other than his surname, the name by which he was known before this title; (b) if the former name or surname was changed or disused before the person attained the age of 18 or more than 20 years prior to making the return; or (c) in the case of a married woman, the name by which she was known prior to the marriage, if different. See Sch 1, Note Seven, Companies (Forms) Order 2004 (SI 133/2004).

[81] This is included in the annual return to verify compliance with C(A)(No 2)A 1999, ss 43(3) and 44. See Sch 1, Note Sixteen, Companies (Forms) Order 2004 (SI 133/2004).

[82] The requirement to state whether the director is an alternate director is explained as follows in Sch 1, Note 17, Companies (Forms) Order 2004 (SI 133/2004): 'The appointment of any person to act as director is notifiable by a company to the CRO, regardless of how the appointment is described. The company is statutorily obliged to notify the CRO of the addition to and removal of each person from its register. In the event that a full-time director who has appointed an alternate director ceases to act as director, the company is required to notify the CRO of the termination of appointment of the full-time director and of his/her alternate.'

     – business occupation,

     – nationality;

     – particulars of any other directorships held (company number, name and, if other than Ireland, place of incorporation);[83]

(t) the directors of the company must furnish a certificate to the effect that the form was duly completed in accordance with the attached 'Notes on Completion of Form B1'; that it contains the relevant particulars as of the date of making up the annual return; and confirming if any of the following applies to the company:

     – the company is not a private company,

     – the company is private and has not issued any invitation to the public to subscribe for shares or debentures in the company in the period to which the annual return relates,

     – the company is a private company with in excess of 50 (or, under the amended ss 33(1)(b), 99) members, which excess consists wholly of persons who are not counted within the threshold of 50 (or under the amended ss 33(1)(b), 99) members in accordance with CA 1963, s 33(1)(b).[84]

(b) Annexed documents

[2.022] There are certain documents which must be annexed to a company's annual return. The first annual return of a company is however exempt from this requirement. CA 1963, s 127(7) provides that:

> Notwithstanding anything to the contrary in the Companies Acts, companies incorporated on or after the commencement date shall not be required to annex accounts to the first annual return delivered to the registrar after the commencement date in compliance with the Companies Acts.[85]

---

[83] This obligation does not apply to bodies corporate (a) of which the person has not been a director for ten years; (b) of which the company is a wholly owned subsidiary; or (c) which are or were wholly owned subsidiaries of the company. See Sch 1, Note Eighteen, Companies (Forms) Order 2004 (SI 133/2004).

[84] CA 1963, s 33(1)(b), as substituted by IFCMPA 2006, s 7 provides that the limit of 99 members for a private company does not include 'persons who are in the employment of the company and persons who, having been formerly in the employment of the company, were, while in that employment, and have continued after the determination of that employment to be, members of the company ...'. Prior to the enactment of IFCMPA 2006, the limit for private companies was 50 members. To date, the raising of this limit has not been reflected in Form B1 or SI 133/2004. The Interpretation Act 2005, s 6, allows for the construction of statutory instruments in light of a change in the law, as long as the text, purpose and content of the statutory instrument permit. It is possible therefore to read this section of Form B1 and SI 133/2004 as if the stated limit in them has been raised to 99. However it is to be hoped that the relevant amendments to Form B1 and its governing statutory instrument are made expeditiously to avoid any unnecessary confusion.

[85] CA 1963, s 127(7), as substituted by CLEA 2001, s 60.

The precise scope of the documents which must be attached to a company's annual return vary depending on the nature and size of the company. By way of example, a small company is not obliged to attach a profit and loss account or a directors' report, but is obliged to attach to its annual return an abridged balance sheet.[86]

C(A)A 1986, s 7 is generally the governing provision with regard to the documents that must be attached to a company's annual return. CA 1963, s 128 does also contain some provisions regarding the necessary attachments to an annual return. However, the scope of s 7 is broad and applies to all companies with some limited exceptions.[87] In light of the fact that s 7(3) provides that 's 128 of the Principal Act shall not apply to a company to which this section applies', the scope of the latter must necessarily be limited and is not therefore considered here in any detail.[88]

(i) Scope of obligation

[2.023] C(A)A 1986, s 7 governs the documents which must be attached to the annual returns of particular companies. The companies to which s 7 relates are defined as follows:[89]

First, C(A)A 1986 contains particular provisions for the documents that must be attached to the annual returns of companies that hold licences under the Central Bank Act 1971; companies that are certified under the Trustee Savings Banks Acts, 1863 to 1965; companies engaged solely in the making of hire-purchase agreements and credit-sale agreements; companies engaged in the business of accepting deposits or other repayable funds or granting credit for its own account or Fóir Teoranta ('s 2(2) companies').[90]

Secondly, s 7 contains provisions regarding the documents, which must be attached to the annual return of undertakings to which the European Communities (Insurance Undertakings: Accounts) Regulations 1996 apply ('s 2(3) companies').[91]

Finally, s 7 governs the documents which must be attached to the annual returns of companies other than s 2(2) companies or s 2(3) companies.

C(A)A 1986 expressly excludes from the scope of s 7 the following companies:

  — a company not trading for the acquisition of gain by the members;[92]

---

[86] See paras **[2.029]** to **[2.031]**.

[87] See further below paras **[2.029]** to **[2.032]**.

[88] See C(A)A 1986, s 7(3). See further Courtney, *The Law of Private Companies* (2nd edn, Tottel Publishing, 2002), Ch 13; Keane, *Company Law* (4th edn, Tottel Publishing, 2007), Ch 30.

[89] See C(A)A 1986, s 7(1)(a).

[90] C(A)A 1986, s 2(2), as amended by ACC Bank Act 2001, s 12 and ICC Bank Act 2000, s 7.

[91] C(A)A 1986, s 2(3), as substituted the European Communities (Insurance Undertakings: Accounts) Regulations 1996 (SI 23/1996), reg 20.

[92] C(A)A 1986, s 2(1)(a).

–   a company to which CA 1963, s 128(4)(c) applies;[93]

–   a company in respect of which there is in force an order under CA 1963, s 128(5);[94] and

–   parent companies which prepare group accounts under the Companies Acts.[95]

(ii) Documents to be attached

1. ACCOUNTS

[2.024] The documents which must be attached to the annual return of companies which fall within the scope of s 2(2) and whose financial years commence after 1 January 2005 include 'a copy of the company's individual accounts which shall be either IFRS[96] individual accounts or Companies Act individual accounts prepared in accordance with the Credit Institutions Regulations.'[97] A company within the scope of s 2(3) and whose financial year commences after 1 January 2005, must attach 'a copy of the undertaking's individual accounts which shall be either IFRS individual accounts or Companies Act individual accounts prepared in accordance with the Insurance Undertakings Regulations.'[98]

All companies, other than those within the scope of C(A)A 1986, s 2(2) or (3) must attach 'a copy of the company's individual accounts which shall be either IFRS individual accounts or Companies Act individual accounts prepared in accordance with ss 3, 4 and 5 of, and the Schedule to, this Act'.[99]

---

[93]   C(A)A 1986, s 2(1)(b). CA 1963, s 128(4)(c) refers to 'a company, not having a share capital, which is formed for an object that is charitable and is under the control of a religion recognised by the State under Article 44 of the Constitution, and which exercises its functions in accordance with the laws, canons and ordinances of the religion concerned.'

[94]   C(A)A 1986, s 2(1)(c). CA 1963, s 128(5) refers to the following order: 'The Commissioners of Charitable Donations and Bequests for Ireland may, if they think fit, by order exempt, either altogether or for a limited period, from the application of this section a specified company, formed for charitable purposes, not having a share capital.'

[95]   See C(A)A 1986, s 7(1A), as substituted by the European Communities (International Financial Reporting Standards and Miscellaneous Amendments) Regulations 2005 (SI 116/2005), reg 5.

[96]   'International financial reporting standards'.

[97]   C(A)A 1986, s 7(1)(a)(ii) as substituted by the European Communities (International Financial Reporting Standards and Miscellaneous Amendments) Regulations 2005 (SI 116/2005), reg 5.

[98]   C(A)A 1986, s 7(1)(a)(iii) as substituted by the European Communities (International Financial Reporting Standards and Miscellaneous Amendments) Regulations 2005 (SI 116/2005), reg 5.

[99]   C(A)A 1986, s 7(1)(a)(i) as substituted by the European Communities (International Financial Reporting Standards and Miscellaneous Amendments) Regulations 2005 (SI 116/2005), reg 5.

2. REPORTS

[2.025] In the case of each of these companies, the accounts must be accompanied by a copy of the auditor's and directors' report on the accounts and the copies submitted must be certified by a director and the company's secretary, as true copies of the accounts and reports laid before the company's annual general meetings.[100]

Certain charitable companies as defined by CA 1963, s 128(4)(c) and (5) fall under the reporting obligations of s 128 of that Act, which are defined in sub-ss (6A), (6B) and (6C).[101] Auditor's reports will now be required to be submitted by the company and annexed to the annual return of companies who are not required to file accounts with their return pursuant to CA 1963 or C(A)A 1986.

3. TRANSLATION

[2.026] If the accounts and reports attached to the annual return are in a language other than English or Irish they must be accompanied by a translation, certified as a proper translation of the document in question.[102]

4. DATE OF ACCOUNTS

[2.027] Every document, whether a balance sheet, profit and loss account, report or statement, which is annexed to an annual return, must cover the period since the end of the period to which the same documents submitted with the preceding annual return, related.[103] This ensures that there is no gap in the reporting periods of the documents which are submitted to the Registrar of Companies. In the case of a company's first annual return, the company's annual return date will be six months from the date of its incorporation. However, the company is not obliged to submit accounts with its first annual return. The result is that the first accounts a company has to submit after incorporation, is 18 months from the date of incorporation. For this reason, s 7(1C)(a) provides that when a company submits its first annual report with accounts attached, these accounts must date since the incorporation of the company.[104] Unless the company extends the annual return date, this will therefore require a company's first accounts as

---

[100] C(A)A 1986, s 7(1)(a), as substituted by the European Communities (International Financial Reporting Standards and Miscellaneous Amendments) Regulations 2005 (SI 116/2005), reg 5. See further Chs **6** and **7**.

[101] CA 1963, s 128(6A) and (6B) as inserted by C(AA)A 2003, s 47 (substituting the original s 128(6)) and as amended by IFCMPA 2005, s 61.

[102] C(A)A 1986, s 7(1)(b).

[103] C(A)A 1986, s 7(1C)(b) was inserted as s 7(1A) by CLEA 2001, s 64, and renumbered as s 7(1C) by the European Communities (International Financial Reporting Standards and Miscellaneous Amendments) Regulations 2005 (SI 116/2005), reg 5.

[104] C(A)A 1986, s 7(1C)(a) was inserted as s 7(1A) by CLEA 2001, s 64, and renumbered as s 7(1C) by the European Communities (International Financial Reporting Standards and Miscellaneous Amendments) Regulations 2005 (SI 116/2005), reg 5.

delivered to the Registrar, to cover the first 18 months of the company's existence and to be delivered to the Registrar within 28 days of that date.

[2.028] A further point to note about the period of time to which the accounts attached to a company's annual return must relate, is that the accounts must be made up to a date which is not more than nine months earlier than the date to which the annual return is made up.[105] The CRO has cautioned that this rule may require a company to bring forward or extend its annual return date.[106] By way of example, assuming a company's financial year end is 31 December, if its annual return date is 4 November, it will be necessary to change the latter date to ensure that the accounts are not more than nine months old.

(iii) Small companies

1. CRITERIA

[2.029] A company may qualify as a 'small company' in respect of a financial year if it satisfies two of the following criteria in that year and the preceding financial year:

– its balance sheet total for that year did not exceed €1,904,607.10;

– its turnover for that year did not exceed €3,809,214.20; and

– the average number of persons employed by the company in that year did not exceed 50.[107]

2. ACCOUNTS REQUIRED

[2.030] In the context of a company's annual return, the significance of this designation is that a 'small company' can, instead of complying with the requirements of s 7:

> … annex to the annual return … a copy of the abridged balance sheet of the company drawn up in accordance with sub-s (2) of this section in respect of the period to which the return refers and, notwithstanding s 7 of this Act, the company shall not be required to annex to the return a copy of the profit and loss account of the company or the report of the directors accompanying the balance sheet of the company.[108]

---

[105] C(A)A 1986, s 7(1C) was inserted as s 7(1A) by CLEA 2001, s 64, and renumbered as s 7(1C) by the European Communities (International Financial Reporting Standards and Miscellaneous Amendments) Regulations 2005 (SI 116/2005), reg 5.

[106] CRO, 'Filing an Annual Return with the CRO' (Information Leaflet No 22, December 2005).

[107] C(A)A 1986, s 8(2).

[108] C(A)A 1986, s 10(1) as substituted by the European Communities (International Financial Reporting Standards and Miscellaneous Amendments) Regulations 2005 (SI 116/2005), reg 5, which apply to the preparation of annual accounts by a company whose financial year commences on or after 1 January 2005.

A small company is also relieved of the obligation to attach a copy of the company's profit and loss account to the annual return and is moreover not obliged to attach a report of the directors to accompany the company's balance sheet.[109]

3. REQUIREMENTS OF DOCUMENTS DELIVERED TO REGISTRAR

[2.031] If a company does submit abridged accounts, such as the abridged balance sheet which a small company is entitled to attach to its annual return, there are certain specific requirements which these accounts must satisfy.

First, any abridged accounts that are attached to a company's annual return must be signed on behalf of the directors by two of the directors of the company.[110] Secondly, any abridged balance sheet attached to an annual return must include a statement by the directors that they have availed of a particular exemption under C(A)A 1986 ss 10 to 12, on the ground that the company is a small or medium company, as appropriate.[111] Thirdly, this directors' statement should appear immediately above the signature of the directors.[112] Fourth, the company must submit a copy of the report of the auditors in relation to the abridged accounts.[113] This report is not obliged to comply with the requirements of a full report of the auditors.[114] There must be a special auditors report which must contain a copy of the report of the auditors on the company's individual

---

[109] C(A)A 1986, s 10(1) as substituted by the European Communities (International Financial Reporting Standards and Miscellaneous Amendments) Regulations 2005 (SI 116/2005), reg 5, which apply to the preparation of annual accounts by a company whose financial year commences on or after 1 January 2005.

[110] C(A)A 1986, s 18(1), as substituted by the European Communities (International Financial Reporting Standards and Miscellaneous Amendments) Regulations 2005 (SI 116/2005), reg 5, applying CA 1963, s 156(1)(a) as substituted by the European Communities (International Financial Reporting Standards and Miscellaneous Amendments) Regulations 2005 (SI 116/2005), reg 9 and Sch.

[111] C(A)A 1986, s 18(2), as amended by the European Communities (International Financial Reporting Standards and Miscellaneous Amendments) Regulations 2005 (SI 116/2005), reg 5,

[112] C(A)A 1986, s 18(1), as substituted by the European Communities (International Financial Reporting Standards and Miscellaneous Amendments) Regulations 2005 (SI 116/2005), reg 5, applying CA 1963, s 156(1)(a) as substituted by the European Communities (International Financial Reporting Standards and Miscellaneous Amendments) Regulations 2005 (SI 116/2005), reg 9 and Sch.

[113] C(A)A 1986, s 18(1), as substituted by the European Communities (International Financial Reporting Standards and Miscellaneous Amendments) Regulations 2005 (SI 116/2005), reg 5.

[114] According to C(A)A 1986, s 18(3), as substituted by the European Communities (International Financial Reporting Standards and Miscellaneous Amendments) Regulations 2005 (SI 116/2005), reg 5, 'Abridged accounts delivered to the registrar of companies need not be accompanied by the report of the auditors under s 193 of the Companies Act 1990 on the company's individual accounts'.

accounts, prepared in accordance with CA 1963, s 193,[115] as well as a report in the following terms:

> Where the directors of a company propose to annex to the annual return abridged accounts for any accounting period prepared pursuant to any of the provisions of ss 10 to 12 of this Act and the auditors of the company are satisfied that the directors of the company are entitled, for that purpose, to rely on exemptions specified in ss 10 to 12 of this Act and that the abridged accounts have been properly prepared pursuant to those provisions, it shall be the duty of the auditors of the company to provide the directors of the company with a report in writing stating that, in the opinion of the auditors of the company, the directors of the company are entitled to annex those abridged accounts to the annual return and that the abridged accounts so annexed are properly prepared as aforesaid.[116]

Finally, the 'special report' of the auditors referred to above must be accompanied by a certification by a director and the secretary of the company that the copy furnished is a true copy.[117]

These requirements apply equally in the case of abridged accounts submitted on behalf of medium companies.

(iv) Medium companies

[2.032] A company may be designated as a 'medium' company in respect of a given financial year if, in respect of that year and the preceding year, its satisfies two of the following criteria:[118]

- its balance sheet total for that year shall not exceed €7,618,428.40;
- the amount of its turnover for that year shall not exceed €15,236,856.00; and
- the average number of persons employed by the company in that year shall not exceed 250.[119]

A medium company is not obliged to comply with all of the requirements of s 7 regarding the accounts and reports to be attached to the annual return. On the contrary, a medium company is entitled to attach an abridged balance sheet and abridged profit and loss or income statement to its annual return.[120]

---

[115] C(A)A 1986, s 18(3)(b), as substituted by the European Communities (International Financial Reporting Standards and Miscellaneous Amendments) Regulations 2005 (SI 116/2005), reg 5.

[116] C(A)A 1986, s 18(4), as amended by the European Communities (International Financial Reporting Standards and Miscellaneous Amendments) Regulations 2005 (SI 116/2005), reg 5.

[117] C(A)A 1986, s 18(5).

[118] C(A)A 1986, s 8(1)(b).

[119] C(A)A 1986, s 8(3).

[120] C(A)A 1986, s 11(1) as substituted by the European Communities (International Financial Reporting Standards and Miscellaneous Amendments) Regulations 2005 (SI 116/2005), reg 5, which Regulations apply to the preparation of annual accounts in the case of a company or undertaking the financial year of which commences on or after 1 January 2005. See further Courtney, *The Law of Private Companies* (2nd edn, Tottel Publishing, 2002) Ch 13; Keane, *Company Law* (4th edn, Tottel Publishing, 2007), Ch 30.

(c) Annual return date

[2.033] The date up to which a company is obliged to prepare its annual return is an important one, particularly in light of the late filing penalties and other sanctions that may be imposed on a company which fails to deliver its annual return by the prescribed date.[121] The date of a company's annual return has become known as a company's 'ARD' or 'annual return date'.

[2.034] The 'annual return date' is defined as '... the date in each year not later than that to which the annual return shall be made up, the calculation of which is provided for in s 127.'[122] This definition suggests that the annual return date is the same, or earlier, than the date to which the annual return shall be made up. In light of the function and content of an annual return, it is difficult to see how it could be feasible for the annual return date to predate the date to which it is made up. The definition contained in the Companies Acts therefore suggests that the annual return date and the date to which the annual return is made up should be the same date. This interpretation has logical appeal, in that it ensures that the information included in an annual return is valid on the date on which the legislative obligations largely hinge, namely the annual return date.[123]

[2.035] However, the definition of the 'annual return date' is not without complications. Section 127(1) provides that every company must ensure that the annual return of the company is made up to a date not later than the annual return date.[124] This permits the possibility that the annual return may be made up to a date which pre-dates the annual return date. There is no limit to how far in advance of the annual return date the annual return may be made up. This suggests that a company may make its annual return up to a date that precedes the annual return date by a period of days, weeks or months.

[2.036] The combination of the definition of the 'annual return date' in CA 1963, s 2(1)(b) and CA 1963, s 127(1), is that the annual return date must be not later than the date to which the annual return is made up, and the annual return must be made up to a date which is not later than the annual return date. Another way of expressing this is that the annual return date must be the same, or earlier, than the date to which the annual return is made up, and the annual return must be made up to the same, or an earlier, date than the annual return date. The only way of reconciling these provisions is that the annual return date and the date to which the annual return is made up, must be the same date. While this does appear to be logical, it is not entirely consistent with some of the formulations of the law governing the annual return date and it also begs the question of why there are two different formulations of the relationship between the annual return date and the date to which the annual return is made up.

---

[121] See below pars **[2.058]**.

[122] CA 1963, s 2(1)(b), as inserted by CLEA 2001, s 84(a).

[123] It may be noted that the definition of an 'annual return date' in the General Scheme of the Companies Consolidation and Reform Bill 2007 is more straightforward. Pt A4, Head 53(2) provides: '... an annual return date shall fall in each year in respect of every company on the anniversary of the company's previous annual return date'. Available at www.clrg.org.

[124] CA 1963, s 127(1), as substituted by C(AA)A 2003 s 46(a).

[2.037] One qualification to the power of a company to make its annual return up to a date prior to the annual return date is that the first annual return of a company incorporated after 17 May 2004,[125] must be made up to the same date as the company's first annual return date.[126] There is no such requirement in respect of subsequent annual returns.

[2.038] The annual return date of a company was originally determined in accordance with CA 1963, s 127. Section 127(1) provided that:

> The annual return must be completed within 60 days after the annual general meeting for the year, whether or not that meeting is the first or only ordinary general meeting, or the first or only general meeting, of the company in the year, and the company must forthwith forward to the registrar of companies a copy signed both by a director and by the secretary of the company.

The annual return date was therefore 60 days after the company's AGM. The CLEA 2001 changed this means of computing the ARD. Section 127 now provides for two different means of computing the annual return date and the date for delivery of the annual return, depending on the date of formation of the company.

It is interesting to note that the General Scheme of the Companies Consolidation and Reform Bill 2007 recommends the simplification of the law governing the ARD and includes a provision that 'every company shall deliver to the Registrar for registration an annual return ... not later than 28 days after each annual return date of the company, unless it is made up to an earlier date in which case it shall be delivered to the Registrar not later than 28 days after that earlier date'.[127]

(i) Company formed before 1 March 2002

[2.039] For a company incorporated before 1 March 2002,[128] the annual return date is the anniversary of the date to which the previous annual return was made up. Section 127(5) provides in this regard:

> For companies incorporated before the commencement date, the annual return date is, subject to sub-s (8), each anniversary of the date to which the then most recent annual return delivered to the registrar by the company was made up.[129]

If a company incorporated before 1 March 2002, has not delivered any annual return to the Registrar of Companies, the first annual return date is '... subject to sub-s (8), the first day after the commencement date that is six months after the date on which the

---

125 The date of commencement of C(AA)A 2003, s 46 was May 17, 2004, pursuant to SI 132/ 2004, as referred to in CA 1963, s 127(1), as substituted by C(AA)A 2003, s 46(a).

126 See CA 1963, s 127(1), as substituted by CLEA 2001, s 60 and C(AA)A 2003, s 46(a).

127 General Scheme of the Companies Consolidation and Reform Bill 2007, Pt A4, Head 52. Available at www.clrg.org.

128 CA 1963, s 127 was substituted by CLEA 2001, s 60, which came into effect on 1 March 2002, by means of SI 438/2001.

129 CA 1963, s 127(5) as substituted by CLEA 2001, s 60 and amended by C(AA)A 2003 s 46(b). Sub-s (8) is discussed below at paras **[2.045]** to **[2.046]**.

anniversary of incorporation of the company falls …'.[130] Therefore, the annual return date becomes the date which is 18 months from the date of the company's incorporation.

Each company incorporated before 1 March 2002 received a notification from the CRO specifying the relevant annual return date. In some instances it was necessary for these companies to amend the assigned dates. The reason for this was that the accounts attached to the annual return must be dated no more than nine months prior to the annual return date.[131]

For companies incorporated before 1 March 2002, the subsequent annual return dates fall on the anniversary of the first annual return date.[132]

(ii) Companies formed after 1 March 2002

[2.040] For companies incorporated on or after 1 March 2002, the first annual return date is six months from the date of the incorporation of the company.[133] Each ensuing annual return date will then fall on the anniversary of the first annual return date.[134] This is subject to the qualification that a company may elect to change the annual return date to a date earlier than its assigned date.[135]

(iii) Date for delivery of annual return

[2.041] The rules governing the delivery of annual returns to the Registrar of Companies depend upon the date of formation of the company. A company that is formed before 1 March 2002 must deliver the first annual return that is prepared after that date, to the Registrar of Companies within 28 days after the annual return date or three months from 1 March 2002, whichever was the later.[136] If, however, the annual return is made up to an earlier date, it must be delivered to the Registrar of Companies within 28 days of that date.[137]

With regard to companies which are formed after 1 March 2002, the general rule is that the annual return must be delivered to the Registrar of Companies not later than 28 days after the annual return date.[138] This is subject to the caveat that, if the return is made up

---

[130] CA 1963, s 127(5), as substituted by CLEA 2001, s 60 and amended by C(AA)A 2003 s 46(b).

[131] See further para **[2.028]** above. With regard to the means of amending the assigned annual return date, see below paras **[2.047]** to **[2.052]**.

[132] CA 1963, s 127(5).

[133] CA 1963, s 127(6).

[134] CA 1963, s 127(6).

[135] See further below paras **[2.045]** to **[2.046]**.

[136] CA 1963, s 27(2)(a), as substituted by CLEA 2001, s 60.

[137] CA 1963, s 27(2), as substituted by CLEA 2001, s 60.

[138] CA 1963, s 127(2)(b), as substituted by CLEA 2001, s 60.

to a date earlier than the annual return date, it must be delivered to the Registrar of Companies within 28 days of that date.[139]

[2.042] The CRO has issued guidance to the effect that, 'in all cases, an annual return delivered to the CRO has to be filed within 28 days of the "return made-up-to" date.'[140] This confirms that the material date for delivery of the annual return is in fact the date to which the annual return was made up. This does not sit easily with the fact that the annual return date and the date to which the return is made up, are not necessarily the same date, a fact which is apparent from the Companies Acts (albeit with some inconsistency and ambiguity regarding the precise relationship between the two dates).[141] Moreover, the significance of the date to which the return is made up, as a means of calculating the obligation to deliver the annual return, is in conflict with the definition of the 'annual return date' which is 'the date in each year not later than that to which the annual return shall be made up, the calculation of which is provided for in s 127'.[142]

[2.043] The court may extend the date for delivery of the annual return if the company makes an application for such an extension and the court is satisfied that it is just to extend time for delivery of the annual report.[143] As soon as practicable after an order is made extending time for delivery of the annual return, the company must deliver a copy of the order to the Registrar of Companies.[144] Failure to comply with this obligation will render the company and every defaulting officer guilty of an offence.[145]

[2.044] It should be noted that while the time for delivery of the annual return may be extended, there is no corresponding provision for an extension by the court of the annual return date itself. There is a particular provision of the Companies Acts which enables companies to extend their annual return date.[146] This provision may be invoked no more than once in every five years.[147] No such limitation exists in respect of the right to apply to court for an extension of the date for delivery of the annual return. Moreover, the right of a company to extend its annual return date requires the company to file the current annual return by the prescribed date, namely 28 days from the annual return date, with a

---

[139] CA 1963, s 27(2), as substituted by CLEA 2001, s 60.

[140] See CRO, 'Filing and Annual Return in the CRO' (Information Leaflet No 22, December 2005).

[141] See, eg, CA 1963, ss 2(1)(b) and 127(1), as substituted by CLEA 2001, ss 84(a) and 60. See further above paras **[2.033]** to **[2.037]**.

[142] CA 1963, s 2(1)(b), as substituted by CLEA 2001, s 84(a).

[143] CA 1963, s 127(3) as substituted by CLEA 2001, s 60.

[144] CA 1963, s 127(4), as substituted by CLEA 2001, s 60.

[145] CA 1963, s 127(4), as substituted by CLEA 2001, s 60.

[146] CA 1963, s 127(9), as substituted by CLEA 2001, s 60. See further below paras **[2.047]** to **[2.052]**.

[147] CA 1963, s 127(10), as substituted by CLEA 2001, s 60. See further below paras **[2.047]** to **[2.052]**.

form nominating a new annual return date for the subsequent annual return. There is little flexibility in this mechanism and no accommodation of considerations of what is 'just'.

It may be noted that the delivery of the annual return is a matter of public record and is capable of objective confirmation. By contrast, the annual return date is not amenable to such objective assessment. It may be seen as unproductive to facilitate the extension of the date for delivery of the annual return, but not such flexible extension of the annual return date itself. For a court to extend the former, insisting on adherence to the latter, appears neither logical nor enforceable.

(iv) Changing the annual return date

1. EARLIER ANNUAL RETURN DATE

[2.045] Since the enactment of the CLEA 2001, a company has had the power to amend its annual return date. As introduced in 2001, s 127(8) provided that:

> Where the annual return of a company is made up to a date earlier than 14 days before its annual return date, the annual return date shall thereafter be each anniversary of the date to which that annual return is made up.[148]

If a company had made its annual return up to a date prior to 1 March 2002, it was not affected by this change in legislation and the next annual return date was the anniversary of the date to which the previous return was made up.[149]

Section 127(8) appears to equate the annual return date and the date to which the return must be made up. As noted above, CA 1963, ss 1(b) and 127(1), expressly and somewhat inconsistently distinguish between these two dates. Section 127(1) moreover envisages the possibility that the annual return may be made up to any date prior to the annual return date, without expressing any limitation in this regard.

The CRO issued guidance on this issue in 2002. According to the CRO, if a company wished to bring its annual return date forward, it could do so by making the return up to a date which predated the existing annual return date by more than 14 days.[150] This return must then be delivered within 28 days of being made up, or by 1 June 2002, whichever was later.

[2.046] Section 127(8) was further amended in 2004. C(AA)A 2003, s 46 substitutes the following provision for s 127(8):

> Where the annual return of a company is made up to a date earlier than its annual return date, the annual return date shall thereafter be each anniversary of the date to which that annual return is made up, unless the company elects in the annual return to retain its existing annual return date or establishes a new annual return date pursuant to sub-s (9).[151]

---

[148] CA 1963, s 127(8), as substituted by CLEA 2001, s 60. This provision is substantially reproduced in the General Scheme of the Companies Consolidation and Reform Bill 2007, Pt A4, Head 54. Available at www.clrg.org.

[149] See CRO, 'Filing an Annual Return' (June 2002).

[150] CRO, 'Filing an Annual Return' (June 2002).

[151] CA 1963, s 127(8), as substituted by CLEA 2001, s 60 and C(AA)A 2003, s 46(c).

This provision has two notable effects. First, it equates the annual return date and the date to which the annual return is made up. According to the definition of the 'annual return date' and the effects of the annual return date, as set out elsewhere in the Companies Acts, it is by no means clear that the annual return date and the date to which the annual return should be made up are the same date.[152] Secondly, this provision indicates that a company can decide to prepare an annual return on a date prior to its annual return date. In this event, the company can choose whether to adopt that earlier date as its annual return date from that date onwards, or alternatively the company may revert to its original return date.

A final point to note about the power of companies to bring forward the annual return date is that companies incorporated on or after 1 March 2002, are not, according to the CRO, entitled to bring forward the date of their first annual return.[153] It is not clear what the legislative basis for this position is, but it is a position of which companies should be aware.

2. LATER ANNUAL RETURN DATE

[2.047] A company is entitled to extend its annual return date. This requires two steps. First, the company must deliver an annual return to the Registrar of Companies not later than 28 days after the annual return date.[154] Secondly, the company must nominate to the Registrar a new annual return date, which must be no more than six months after the existing date.[155] The second step requires the company to fill out what is known as a 'Form B73'.[156] This form requires the company to state its name; company number; the new nominated annual return date (not being six months after the existing date) and the date to which the attached annual return is made up.

[2.048] It is curious to note that, whereas s 127(9) does not specify that the annual return which is delivered 28 days after the annual return date, together with a Form B73, must be made up to the annual return date, Form B73 does make this assumption. The consequence of this is that a company that wishes to extend its annual return date is essentially obliged to prepare and deliver its annual return in accordance with the existing annual return date. It is not obliged to file accounts with this return and it is the filing of the Form B73 that actually effects the change of date.

[2.049] A further ambiguity in the formulation of the procedure for the extension of the annual return date relates to the date on which the next annual return must be prepared and delivered. Section 127(9) states that the annual return date shall be extended to a

---

[152] See CA 1963, ss 2(1)(b), as substituted by CLEA 2001, s 84(a) and 127(1), as substituted by C(AA)A 2003, s 46. See further above paras **[2.033]** to **[2.037]**.

[153] See CRO, 'Filing and Annual Return in the CRO' (Information Leaflet No 22, December 2005).

[154] CA 1963, s 127(9)(a) as substituted by CLEA 2001, s 60.

[155] CA 1963, s 127(9)(b) as substituted by CLEA 2001, s 60.

[156] This form may be downloaded from the Companies Registration Office website, www.cro.ie. The form may be filed online, but the CRO states on its website that it may only be filed online on the same day and after the associated annual return has been filed.

date not more than six months later than the existing annual return date. It does not specify when the next annual return must be filed. It could be inferred from the language of the provision that the company has up to 18 months (depending upon the extended annual return date which is nominated) to deliver its next annual return. Otherwise, a company which nominated an extended annual return date a matter of weeks later than the existing date, would be faced with the obligation of filing two annual returns (one with accounts, one without) within weeks of each other.

[2.050] On the other hand, the CRO advise companies that, 'The effect of extending the first ARD, however, is to accelerate the date by which accounts have to be filed with CRO from 18 months and 28 days post-incorporation to an earlier date. Companies should not extend the first ARD without taking account of this.'[157] This advice suggests that the extended annual return must be filed when it first falls due after the extension of the previous annual return date. By way of example, a company with an annual return date of 1 March 2004, which wished to extend its annual return date to July 1 would be obliged to deliver its annual return (without any accounts) within 28 days of 1 March 2004, with the completed Form B73 indicating this extended date. The CRO advice quoted above suggests that this company would be obliged to file its next annual return, with accounts annexed, by 1 July 2004.

It is important to be aware that if a company wishes to take this step it is not required to annex accounts to the return.[158] However, it must also bear in mind that the accounts to be attached to the ensuing annual return must be made up to a date not more than nine months before the next annual return date.

[2.051] A company which has extended its annual return date under s 127(9) cannot do so again until at least five years have passed 'since the establishment of the first mentioned new annual return date'.[159] This language suggests that the five year period runs from the new annual return date itself, although it is sufficiently ambiguous to allow an argument be made that time should begin to run from the date on which the Form B73 was filed.

[2.052] A company which was incorporated before 1 March 2002 may also extend its annual return date by delivering to the Registrar of Companies, its first annual return, within 28 days after its first annual return date, together with a Form B73 nominating a new annual return date, which shall be no more than six months from the assigned annual return date.[160] A company is not obliged to annex accounts to such an annual return.[161] If a company avails of this mechanism, it cannot use the s 127(9) procedure for extending the annual return date 'before such time as it has delivered to the Registrar an

---

[157] See CRO, 'Filing and Annual Return in the CRO' (Information Leaflet No 22, December 2005).

[158] CA 1963, s 127(9)(a) as substituted by CLEA 2001, s 60.

[159] CA 1963, s 127(10), as substituted by CLEA 2001, s 60.

[160] CA 1963, s 127(11)(a), as substituted by CLEA 2001, s 60.

[161] CA 1963, s 127(11)(a)(i), as substituted by CLEA 2001, s 60.

annual return made up to the new annual return date nominated' by the company in the Form B73.[162] A company incorporated before 1 March 2002, which does so extend its annual return date, is not therefore subject to the limitation that it cannot extend its annual return date until the expiry of five years. The position can be contrasted with companies incorporated after 1 March 2002, which may only extend the annual return date once in every five year period.[163]

(d) Groups of companies

(i) Extension of annual return date

[2.053] There are certain specific provisions in the Companies Acts for addressing the situation of groups of companies and their obligation to prepare and deliver annual returns. Section 153 provides that a holding company should take steps to ensure that the financial years of each of its subsidiaries coincide with the company's own financial year.[164]

[2.054] For the purpose of facilitating the financial year of the holding company and its subsidiaries coinciding, there is a particular procedure which may be used. This procedure enables the holding company or its subsidiary to extend its financial year and postpone the annual return date among other matters. Section 153(2) provides as follows:

> Where it appears to the Minister desirable for a holding company or a holding company's subsidiary to extend its financial year so that the subsidiary's financial year may end with that of the holding company, and for that purpose to postpone the submission of the relevant accounts to an annual general meeting from one calendar year to the next, or for a holding company or a holding company's subsidiary to extend its annual return date so that the subsidiary's annual return date may correspond with that of the holding company, the Minister may—
>
> (a) on the application or with the consent of the directors of the company whose financial year is to be extended, direct that in the case of that company, the submission of accounts to an annual general meeting or the holding of an annual general meeting shall not be required in the earlier of the calendar years, or
>
> (b) on the application or with the consent of the directors of the company whose annual return date is to be extended, direct that an extension is to be permitted in the case of that company.[165]

A decision to amend the financial year and the annual return date of a company can therefore only be taken by the Minister for Enterprise, Trade and Employment. The application for such an extension must be made by or with the consent of the directors of the company whose annual return date is to be so extended.

---

162 CA 1963, s 127(11)(b), as substituted by CLEA 2001, s 60.

163 CA 1963, s 127(10), as substituted by CLEA 2001, s 60.

164 CA 1963, s 153(1).

165 CA 1963, s 153(2), as substituted by CLEA 2001, s 61.

(ii) Accounts

1. EXCEPTION FOR PARENT COMPANIES

[2.055] C(A)A 1986, s 7 also contains a provision for the accommodation of company groups. Section 7(1A) provides that the obligation to attach accounts prepared in accordance with the Companies Acts to a company's annual return does not apply to parent companies which prepare group accounts. Section 7(1A) provides that the obligations described in s 7(1), do not apply to the profit and loss account or income statement of a company where:

    (a) the company is a parent undertaking,

    (b) the company prepares group accounts in accordance with s 150 of the Principal Act, and

    (c) the notes to the company's individual balance sheet show the company's profit or loss for the financial year determined in accordance with this Act or s 149A of the Principal Act, as appropriate.[166]

A further condition to the right to avail of this carve-out is that the company must disclose in the notes to the company's own individual accounts and the notes to the group accounts the fact that the company is availing of the opportunity not to deliver to the Registrar of company its individual profit and loss account and income statement.[167]

2. EXCEPTION FOR SUBSIDIARY COMPANIES

[2.056] A private company which is a subsidiary of a parent undertaking may be exempt from the requirement to attach the accounts required by C(A)A 1986, s 7, if certain conditions are met.[168]

First, every shareholder at the next AGM or annual return date after the end of that financial year, whichever is earlier, must declare his consent to the exemption.[169] Secondly, there must be in place for the entire financial year, an irrevocable guarantee by the parent undertaking of the company's liabilities.[170] Thirdly, the company's annual

---

   [166] C(A)A 1986, s 7(1A) as substituted by the European Communities (International Financial Reporting Standards and Miscellaneous Amendments) Regulations 2005 (SI 116/2005), reg 5.

   [167] C(A)A 1986, s 7(1B) as substituted by the European Communities (International Financial Reporting Standards and Miscellaneous Amendments) Regulations 2005 (SI 116/2005), reg 5.

   [168] C(A)A 1986, s 17(1), as substituted by the European Communities (Companies: Group Accounts) Regulations 1992 (SI 201/1992), reg 45, with effect from 16 July 1992 and amended by CLEA 2001, s 65 and the European Communities (International Financial Reporting Standards and Miscellaneous Amendments) Regulations 2005 (SI 116/2005), reg 5.

   [169] C(A)A 1986, s 17(1)(a), as substituted by the European Communities (Companies: Group Accounts) Regulations 1992 (SI 201/1992), reg 45, with effect from 16 July 1992 and amended by CLEA 2001, s 65.

   [170] C(A)A 1986, s 17(1)(b), as substituted by the European Communities (Companies: Group Accounts) Regulations 1992 (SI 201/1992), reg 45 and substituted by the European Communities (International Financial Reporting Standards and Miscellaneous Amendments) Regulations 2005 (SI 116/2005), reg 5.

accounts for that financial year must be consolidated in the group accounts prepared by the parent company and the subsidiaries' exemption must be disclosed in a note to the group accounts.[171] Fourthly, there must be annexed to the annual return which is delivered to the Registrar of Companies, a notice to the effect that the company has availed of the s 17 exemption, a copy of the parent company's guarantee and a declaration by the company that the shareholders have duly consented to the exemption.[172]

Finally, the group accounts of the parent company must be drawn up and audited in accordance with the Seventh Council Directive 83/349/EEC of 13 June 1983 or in accordance with international financial reporting standards, and these group accounts must be annexed to the annual return of the subsidiary.[173]

(e) Grounds for rejection of annual returns

[2.057] The CRO has issued guidance stipulating a number of grounds on which annual returns may be rejected.[174] These include the following:

- the address of the company's registered office is incorrect;[175]
- the names of the directors or secretary do not accord with the names previously delivered to the CRO;[176]
- previous annual returns are outstanding;[177]
- there is a period for which accounts have not been filed;[178]
- accounts have not been filed with the annual return;[179]
- audited accounts have not been filed with the annual return (the exemption from audit not having been claimed or not having been claimed successfully);[180]

---

[171] C(A)A 1986, s 17(1)(c), as substituted by the European Communities (Companies: Group Accounts) Regulations 1992 (SI 201/1992), reg 45.

[172] C(A)A 1986, s 17(1)(d), as substituted by the European Communities (Companies: Group Accounts) Regulations 1992 (SI 201/1992), reg 45.

[173] C(A)A 1986, s 17(1)(e) and (f), as substituted by the European Communities (Companies: Group Accounts) Regulations 1992 (SI 201/1992), reg 45 and the European Communities (International Financial Reporting Standards and Miscellaneous Amendments) Regulations 2005 (SI 116/2005), reg 5 (in the case of s 17(1)(e)).

[174] CRO, 'Grounds for Returning Documents to Presenters' (Information Leaflet No 21, September 2004). The general requirements of documents delivered to the Registrar are considered at para **[2.164]**.

[175] Companies Act 1990 (Form and Content of Documents Delivered to Registrar) Regulations 2002 (SI 39/2002), reg 14(2).

[176] SI 39/2002, reg 21.

[177] CA 1963, s 125.

[178] C(A)A 1982, s 7(1A) (inserted by CLEA 2001, s 64).

[179] C(A)A 1982, s 7, CA 1963, s 128 (as applicable).

[180] C(A)A 1982, s 7, CA 1963, s 128 (as applicable).

- the authorised capital is incorrect;[181]

- the return does not state the date up to which it is made or the commencement and end of the financial year;[182]

- the commencement and end of financial year are not consistent with the accounts attached to the return;[183]

- the accounts predate the annual return date by more than nine months;[184]

- the details of the issued capital are entered in the wrong section of the return;[185]

- the issued capital and number of shares held by shareholders do not tally;[186]

- the details of shares transferred are not entered on the return;[187]

- the details of the directors are omitted;[188]

- the Irish resident director box is not ticked, there is no Irish resident director and no bond is attached;[189]

- no list of directorships is attached;[190]

- the business rather than residential address of a director is given;[191]

- the form is not signed or dated;[192]

- the form is signed by a person who is not currently registered with CRO as an officer of the company;[193]

- the company has become or ceased to be a single member company or vice versa and the requisite form has not been filed (Form M1/M2, as applicable);[194]

---

[181] CA 1963, s 70.

[182] Companies Act 1990 (Form and Content of Documents Delivered to Registrar) Regulations 2002 (SI 39/2002), reg 12.

[183] CA 1963, s 125; Companies (Forms) Order (No 2) 2002 (SI 54/2002).

[184] C(A)A 1986, s 7(1A) (inserted by CLEA 2001, s 64).

[185] CA 1963, s 125; Companies (Forms) Order (No 2) 2002 (SI 54/2002).

[186] CA 1963, s 125; Companies (Forms) Order (No 2) 2002 (SI 54/2002).

[187] Companies Act 1990 (Form and Content of Documents Delivered to Registrar) Regulations 2002 (SI 39/2002), reg 12.

[188] Companies Act 1990 (Form and Content of Documents Delivered to Registrar) Regulations 2002 (SI 39/2002), reg 12.

[189] C(A)(No 2)A 1999, s 43.

[190] CA 1963, s 125(1); Companies (Forms)(No2) Order 2002 (SI 54/2002).

[191] Companies Act 1990 (Form and Content of Documents Delivered to Registrar) Regulations 2002 (SI 39/2002), reg 15(2).

[192] Companies Act 1990 (Form and Content of Documents Delivered to Registrar) Regulations 2002 (SI 39/2002), reg 15(3).

[193] Companies Act 1990 (Form and Content of Documents Delivered to Registrar) Regulations 2002 (SI 39/2002), reg 21.

[194] EC (Single-Member Private Limited Company) Regulations 1994, regs 5 or 6.

- the accounts are not certified as true copies or full accounts are not filed[195] without an exemption from the obligation to file full accounts being claimed;[196]

- group accounts are not filed;[197] or

- there are no original signatures certifying the accounts.[198]

(f) Consequences of failing to file annual return

[2.058] If a company fails to file its annual return 'once at least in every year',[199] the company, every officer who is in default and 'any person in accordance with whose directions or instructions the directors of the company are accustomed to act and to whose directions or omissions the default is attributable',[200] shall be guilty of an offence.[201] Proceedings in respect of this offence may be brought and prosecuted by the Registrar of Companies.[202] In addition to criminal prosecutions, the company will face a late filing penalty if its annual return is filed late.[203] The CRO generates sizeable receipts from late filing penalties, amounting to €20.7m in 2006.[204] The CRO may also bring proceedings to compel compliance with the requirements of the CA 1963–2006[205] and may impose fines in respect of defaults in delivering, filing or making returns under the Acts.[206]

Further sanctions that may arise from a failure to file a company's annual return, are that the company's officers or directors may face disqualification proceedings,[207] and the company's name may be struck off the register of companies.[208]

---

[195] C(A)A 1986, s 7(1).

[196] C(A)A 1986, ss 10 to 12.

[197] C(A)A 1986, s 16; EC (Companies: Group Accounts) Regulations 1992.

[198] Companies Act 1990 (Form and Content of Documents Delivered to Registrar) Regulations 2002, reg 15(3)(a); Companies Act 1963, s 128(1), C(A)A 1986, s 7(1) as applicable.

[199] CA 1963, s 125(1), as substituted by CLEA 2001, s 59.

[200] CA 1963, s 125(2)(b), as substituted by CLEA 2001, s 59.

[201] CA 1963, s 125(2), as substituted by CLEA 2001, s 59.

[202] CA 1963, s 125(3), as substituted by CLEA 2001, s 59.

[203] According to the CRO, the late filing penalty of €140 (for paper filing) or €120 (for electronic filing) becomes due on the day after the expiry of the filing deadline, together with a daily penalty of €3, up to a maximum of €1,200 per return. See CRO, Filing an Annual Return in the CRO, Information Leaflet No. 22/December 2005 at p 2. Available at www.cro.ie. Note that it is now established that the levying of late filing penalties does not preclude the institution of criminal proceedings under CA 1963, s 125(3). See *Registrar of Companies v Anderson* [2004] IESC 103. See also Ch **15**.

[204] CRO, Annual Report 2006, at p 1. Available at www.cro.ie.

[205] CA 1963, s 371(1), as amended by CLEA 2001, s 96 and IFCMPA 2005, s 74. See Ch **11**.

[206] CLEA 2001, s 66. See Ch **11**.

[207] CA 1990, s 160(2)(f). See further Ch **22**.

[208] C(A)A 1982, s 12, as substituted by C(A)(No 2)A 1999, s 46. Ch **14**.

D. Prospectus

[2.059] The Registrar of Companies formerly had an important role in relation to the registration of prospectuses for the offer of shares to the public.[209] However, the enactment of the so-called 'Prospectus Regulations'[210] and Pt 5 of the Investment Funds, Companies and Miscellaneous Provisions Act 2005, have altered this position significantly.

(a) Prospectus Regulations 2005

[2.060] The only role retained by the Registrar under the Prospectus Regulations 2005 is that if the company issuing shares is a company registered under the CA 1963–2006 and the prospectus has been approved by the competent authority and filed and published in accordance with the Regulations, the company must file a copy of the prospectus with the Registrar of Companies within 14 days of its publication.[211]

(b) Investment Funds, Companies and Miscellaneous Provisions Act 2005

[2.061] There are a number of exemptions from the requirement to file a prospectus in connection with the offer of shares to the public. Of relevance in the present context is the fact that a company may issue shares in what is referred to as a 'local offer' without complying with the requirements of the Prospectus Regulations and the CA 1963–2006. When a company avails of this possibility, the offering document must be delivered to the Registrar of Companies.

[2.062] Section 38(1), Investment Funds, Companies and Miscellaneous Provisions Act 2005 ('IFCMPA 2005'), defines a 'local offer' as an offer of securities to the public in which 'the offer expressly limits the amount of the total consideration for the offer to less than €2,500,000'.[212] An offering document in respect of a 'local offer' is not bound to comply with the requirements of IFCMPA 2005 and the Prospectus Regulations 2005.

---

[209] See, eg, CA 1963, s 47(1), which provided, before the enactment of the CA 2005, that 'No prospectus shall be issued by or on behalf of a company or in relation to an intended company unless, on or before the date of its publication, there has been delivered to the registrar for registration a copy thereof signed by every person who is named therein as a director or proposed director of the company, or by his agent authorised in writing …'.

[210] Prospective (Directive 2003/17/EC) Regulations 2005 (SI 324/2005) ('Prospectus Regulations'), introduced to give effect to Directive 2003/17/EC ('the Prospectus Directive').

[211] Prospectus Regulations 2005, reg 38(1). The CRO has introduced a new form B18 for this purpose, which may be downloaded from the CRO website, www.cro.ie.

[212] See also the Prospectus Regulations 2005, reg 8(1)(h). This is subject to the qualification that securities referred to in art 1(2)(a) to (g) or art 1(2)(i) to (j) (which are transposed by the Prospectus Regulations 2005, reg 8) are not covered and the offer must not be of a type described by art 3(2) of the Prospectus Directive (which is transposed by reg 9 of the Prospectus Regulations). See IFCMP 2005, s 38(1)(c).

Section 49 provides that such an offering document must comply with certain specific requirements, including the following:

- the offering document must state, on the front cover or other prominent position, that it was not prepared in accordance with the Prospectus Directive or legislation in implementation of that Directive;[213]

- the offering document must state, on the front cover or other prominent position, that the offering document has not been reviewed, prior to its being issued, by any regulatory authority in Ireland or any other member state of the European Union;[214]

- the offering document must state, on the front cover or other prominent position, that it may not contain all of the information required of a document which has been prepared in accordance with the Prospectus Directive, or implementing laws;[215]

- the offering document must state, wherever there is information regarding past performance, that 'past performance may not be a reliable guide to future performance'[216] among numerous other such requirements.

It is an offence for an offeror to fail to include all of the requisite statements in the offering document.[217] Summary proceedings for offences under s 49 may be brought and prosecuted by the Financial Regulator[218] or by the Registrar of Companies.[219]

[2.063] In terms of filing requirements, the rule is that no offering document can be issued in respect of a local offer unless, on or before the date of publication, a copy of this offering document has been delivered to the Registrar of Companies for registration.[220] It should be noted that the requirement that the offering document be delivered to the Registrar of Companies does not import any review or supervisory role for the Registrar of Companies. This interpretation is supported by the fact that s 49(1)(a) requires an offering document in a local offer to state expressly that it has not been reviewed by any regulatory authority.

[2.064] A company which has issued a prospectus inviting public subscriptions for its shares should not commence business or exercise borrowing powers unless certain

---

213 IFCMPA 2005, s 49(1)(a).

214 IFCMPA 2005, s 49(1)(a).

215 IFCMPA 2005, s 49(1)(a).

216 IFCMPA 2005, s 49(1)(b)(i).

217 IFCMPA 2005, s 49(3).

218 IFCMPA 2005, s 49(5) refers to 'the competent authority designated under Irish prospectus law', which is the Irish Financial Services Regulatory Authority ('the Financial Regulator').

219 IFCMPA 2005, s 49(5).

220 IFCMPA 2005, s 49(4). The CRO has introduced a new Form B18A for the presentation of offering documents in local offers. This form essentially verifies that certain information is included in the offering document and is available to download from the CRO website, www.cro.ie.

conditions have been met[221] and a statutory declaration by a director or secretary has been delivered to the Registrar of Companies for registration, confirming that those conditions have been complied with. This declaration must be made on Form A2/ 44.[222]

[2.065] If a public unlimited company[223] has not issued a prospectus, it shall not commence business or exercise any borrowing power unless a statement in lieu of a prospectus has been delivered to the Registrar of Companies; every director who has taken shares in the company has paid the proportion of cash payable on the allotment of such shares; and a statutory declaration by a director or secretary of the company confirming compliance with the latter conditions has been delivered to the Registrar for registration.[224] This declaration must be made on Form A3/44A.

On receipt of such a statutory declaration and statement in lieu of prospectus, if applicable, the Registrar shall certify that the company is entitled to commence business and the certificate is conclusive evidence of such entitlement.[225] If a company commences business or exercises borrowing powers before the issue of such a certificate, every person responsible for such a contravention is guilty of an offence and liable to a fine of a maximum fine of €1,904.61.[226]

E. Members

[2.066] Every memorandum of association which is registered by a company will include a list of the 'subscribers'. These persons are deemed to be members of the company.[227] In addition to these persons, any person who agrees to become a member, is, according to s 31(2), a member of the company. However, there is no specific

---

[221] CA 1963, s 115(1) requires that '(a) shares held subject to the payment of the whole amount thereof in cash have been allotted to an amount not less in the whole than the minimum subscription; and (b) every director of the company has paid to the company on each of the shares taken or contracted to be taken by him and for which he is liable to pay in cash, a proportion equal to the proportion payable on application and allotment on the shares offered for public subscription; and (c) no money is or may become liable to be repaid to applicants for any shares or debentures which have been offered for public subscription by reason of any failure to apply for or to obtain permission for the shares or debentures to be dealt in on any stock exchange.'

[222] This form may be downloaded from the Companies Registration Office website, www.cro.ie.

[223] Note that the requirements described in this paragraph derive from CA 1963, s 115, which, according to s 115(7) does not apply to private companies or to public limited companies, registered as such under the C(A)A 1983. Section 115 therefore only applies to public limited companies.

[224] CA 1963, s 115(2).

[225] CA 1963, s 115(3).

[226] CA 1963, s 115(6), as substituted by IFCMPA 2005, s 73(1).

[227] See CA 1963, s 31(1) ('The subscribers of the memorandum of a company shall be deemed to have agreed to become members of the company, and, on its registration, shall be entered as members in its register of members.')

obligation on companies to register with the Registrar of Companies details of each such member of the company.[228] The only members whose names must be notified to the Registrar are therefore the subscribers to the company's memorandum of association.[229] However, every company limited by shares or by guarantee is under a separate obligation to notify details of share transfers to the Registrar of Companies and the names and addresses of all members are therefore furnished to the Registrar.[230]

There are a limited number of matters regarding its members, of which a private company, whether limited by shares, by guarantee, or unlimited, must notify the Registrar of Companies.

(a) Increase in number of members

[2.067] Certain companies must notify the Registrar of certain changes in the number of members stated in the company's memorandum of association. In the case of an unlimited company or a company limited by guarantee, the articles of association must state the number of members with which the company proposes to the registered.[231] If this number is exceeded, the company must notify the Registrar of this increase. The form to be used for this purpose is Form No 11.[232] CA 1963, s 12(3) accordingly provides:

> Where an unlimited company or a company limited by guarantee has increased the number of its members beyond the registered number, it shall, within 15 days after the increase was resolved on or took place, give to the registrar notice of the increase, and he shall record the increase.

The company therefore has 15 days from either the passing of, or the giving effect to, the resolution to increase the number of members, to notify the Registrar of this fact. It is difficult to understand the inclusion of these alternative means of computing the time limit for notification. As a special resolution is necessary to alter a company's articles of association[233] it would be expected that any amendment to increase the number of members would require a resolution. Furthermore, any such resolution should precede the implementation of the increase. It therefore appears inevitable that the time period from the 'taking place' of the increase will be longer than the time from the resolution

---

[228] This is subject to the caveat that 'joint stock' companies wishing to register under the CA 1963–2006, must deliver to the Registrar 'a list showing the names, addresses and occupations of all persons who, on a day named in the list, not being more than six clear days before the day of registration, were members of the company, with the addition of the shares or stock held by them respectively, distinguishing, in cases where the shares are numbered, each share by its number' (CA 1963, s 330(a)). This list must be verified by a statutory declaration of two directors or principal officers of the company (CA 1963, s 332).

[229] The distinct obligation on companies to keep a register of members pursuant to CA 1963, s 116 *et seq*, is addressed further in Ch **3**.

[230] See CA 1963, s 58.

[231] CA 1963, s 12(1) and (2).

[232] Referred to as Form B9/11. Available at www.cro.ie.

[233] See CA 1963, s 15(1).

authorising such increase, and the latter, shorter, time limit, will therefore rarely if ever be applicable.

If there is a default in notifying the Registrar of an increase in the number of members of an unlimited company, or a company limited by guarantee, the company and every defaulting officer is guilty of an offence and liable to a fine of a maximum of €1904.61.[234]

(b) Location of register of members

[2.068] Every company is obliged to keep a register of its members and the form and content of this register are prescribed by the CA 1963–2006.[235] While the content of the register of members does not have to be notified to the Registrar of Companies, the location of the register does. In this regard, s 116(5) provides that the general rule is that the register of members should be kept at the company's registered office. This is subject to the exception that, if the register is made up at an office other than the registered office, whether an office of the company, or an office of a person who makes up the register on behalf of the company, the register may be kept at that office, provided it is not outside the jurisdiction.[236]

[2.069] Section 116(7) provides that, 'every company shall send notice to the Registrar of Companies of the place where its register of members is kept and of any change in that place.' This obligation does not arise if the register is, and has at all times since its creation been, located at the company's registered office.[237] Therefore, if a company hires another person to compile, maintain and house its register of members, it must notify the Registrar of this fact and of the location of the register. Conversely, if a company moves its register of members to the company's registered office, the Registrar must be notified. If it is necessary to notify the Registrar of the location of the register of members, this should be done on Form B3.[238]

[2.070] It is an offence for a company and every officer in default to fail to comply with this notification requirement and they may be liable to a fine of up to €1904.61.[239] According to this provision, it is an offence to fail to notify the Registrar of the location of the register of members for 14 days. While it is not clear when the period of 14 days begins to run, it appears likely that it refers to 14 days from the date of the change of the location of the register of members. A company must therefore notify the Registrar within 14 days of any change in the location of the register of members.

---

[234] CA 1963, s 12(3), as amended by C(A)A 1982, s 15, C(AA)A 2003, s 57 and CA 1990, s 240(7) as inserted by CLEA 2001, s 104(c).

[235] See CA 1963, ss 116 to 124. See further Ch **3**.

[236] CA 1963, s 116(5)(a), (b) and (6).

[237] CA 1963, s 116(8).

[238] This form may be downloaded from the CRO website, www.cro.ie.

[239] CA 1963, s 116(9), as amended by C(A)A 1982, s 15, C(AA)A 2003, s 57 and CA 1990, s 240(7) as inserted by CLEA 2001 s104(c).

A default in complying with this notification requirement may constitute an offence by persons other than the company and the officers in default. According to s 120, there are three pre-conditions to liability for this offence being imposed on a third party. First, the company's register of members must be made up, and kept at, the office of a person other than the company ('an agent'). Secondly, there must be a default in notifying this location to the Registrar. Thirdly, this failure must be by reason of the default on the part of the agent. If these circumstances arise, that agent is exposed to the same potential liability as an officer of the company.[240]

F. Share capital

(a) Allotment of shares

[2.071] Allotments of shares by companies limited by shares or companies limited by guarantee having a share capital, must be notified to the Registrar of Companies within one month of the allotment.[241] The return must state the following:

- the number and nominal amount of shares allotted;[242]

- the name and address of the persons to whom the shares were allotted;[243] and

- the amount, if any, paid or due on each share.[244]

If the allotted shares are paid up (fully or partly) other than by means of cash, the company must deliver to the Registrar the following:

- a contract in writing demonstrating the title of the person to whom the shares were allotted;[245]

- any duly stamped contract of sale, for services, or other consideration, in respect of which the allotment was made;[246]

- a return stating the number and nominal amount of shares allotted, the extent to which they are treated as being paid up, and the consideration paid.[247]

---

[240] CA 1963, s 120, referring to CA 1963, s 116(5)(b).

[241] CA 1963, s 58(1). This is subject to the caveat that, 'where shares are allotted to the members of a company on a capitalisation or provisionally allotted on a rights issue, it shall not be necessary to make a return of the particular allottees, notwithstanding that in either case there may be a right of renunciation.' CA 1963, s 58(1).

[242] CA 1963, s 58(1)(a) as amended by C(A)A 1982, s 19.

[243] CA 1963, s 58(1)(a) as amended by C(A)A 1982, s 19.

[244] CA 1963, s 58(1)(a) as amended by C(A)A 1982, s 19.

[245] CA 1963, s 58(1)(b). If there is no contract in writing, the company must deliver to the Registrar the particulars of the contract, stamped as if the contract had been duly reduced to writing. CA 1963, s 58(2) as amended by Stamp Duty Consolidation Act 1999, s 162.

[246] CA 1963, s 58(1)(b).

[247] CA 1963, s 58(1)(b).

This return should be made on Form B5.[248] If a company fails to comply with the obligations to make a return and deliver specified documents to the Registrar regarding the allotment of shares, every officer of the company who is in default is guilty of an offence and liable to a fine of up to €1904.61.[249] There is no reference to such a default constituting an offence on the part of the company. However, s 58(4) does provide that where there is a default in delivering any of the documents required by s 58, the company, or any officer in default, may apply to the court for relief.[250] On such an application, if the court is satisfied that the omission was accidental, due to inadvertence or that it is otherwise just and equitable, the court may extend the time for delivery of the requisite documents to the Registrar.[251]

It seems incongruous that, where there has been failure to deliver the requisite documents regarding the allotment of shares to the Registrar of Companies, this does not constitute an offence on the part of the company, but the company may nonetheless apply to the court for relief.

(b) Alterations in share capital

[2.072] A company which is limited by shares or which is limited by guarantee and has a share capital, is entitled to alter its share capital in certain circumstances.[252] First, the company must be authorised by its articles of association to make the alteration in question. Secondly, the company must pass a resolution in general meeting altering the condition of its memorandum of association.[253] If those conditions are met, the company may make the following alterations:

- increase its share capital by such amount as it considers expedient;[254]

- consolidate and divide any of its share capital into shares of larger amounts;[255]

- convert any of its paid up shares into stock and re-convert stock into paid up shares;[256]

- subdivide any shares into shares of smaller amounts than fixed by the memorandum;[257] or

---

[248] This form may be downloaded from the CRO website, www.cro.ie.

[249] CA 1963, s 58(3), as amended by C(A)A 1982, s 15, C(AA)A 2003, s 57 and CA 1990, s 240(7) as inserted by CLEA 2001, s 104(c).

[250] CA 1963, s 58(4).

[251] CA 1963, s 58(4).

[252] CA 1963, s 68(1).

[253] CA 1963, s 68(1).

[254] CA 1963, s 68(1)(a).

[255] CA 1963, s 68(1)(b).

[256] CA 1963, s 68(1)(c).

[257] CA 1963, s 68(1)(d) (this is subject to the caveat that, 'in the subdivision the proportion between the amount paid and the amount, if any, unpaid on each reduced share shall be the same as it was in the case of the share from which the reduced share is derived').

- cancel shares which, at the date of the resolution, had not been taken or agreed to be taken by any person, and reduce the amount of share capital by the amount of cancelled shares.[258]

[2.073] A company which alters its share capital must notify the Registrar of Companies of this fact, stating the shares altered, and the nature of the alteration.[259] The alterations and notifications which are addressed by s 69 are the following:

- consolidation or division of the company's share capital into shares of larger amounts;[260]

- conversion of shares into stock;[261]

- reconversion of stock into shares;[262]

- subdivision of any shares;[263]

- redemption of any redeemable preference shares or other preference shares;[264] or

- Cancellation of any shares, other than by means of reduction of share capital.[265]

When a company makes any of the alterations referred to in s 69, it must notify the Registrar on Form B7/28[266] within one month of such alteration, of the shares which have been consolidated, divided, converted, subdivided, redeemed or cancelled, or the stock which has been reconverted.[267]

If there is default in notifying the Registrar of such alterations of its share capital, the company and its officers in default are guilty of an offence and liable to a fine not exceeding €1904.61.[268]

---

[258] CA 1963, s 68(1)(e). Any such cancellation of shares 'shall not be deemed to be a reduction of share capital within the meaning of this Act', CA 1963, s 68(2).

[259] CA 1963, s 69.

[260] CA 1963, s 69(1)(a).

[261] CA 1963, s 69(1)(b).

[262] CA 1963, s 69(1)(c).

[263] CA 1963, s 69(1)(d).

[264] CA 1963, s 69(1)(e) and (f). CA 1990, s 221 provides that a reference to redeemable preference shares in this section shall be construed as a reference to redeemable shares. CA 1990, s 207 provides that companies may issue redeemable shares, subject to the restrictions set out in that section.

[265] CA 1963, s 69(1)(g).

[266] This form may be downloaded from the CRO website, www.cro.ie.

[267] CA 1963, s 69(1).

[268] CA 1963, s 69(2), as amended by C(A)A 1982, s 15, C(AA)A 2003, s 57 and CA 1990, s 240(7) as inserted by CLEA 2001, s 104(c).

(c) Increase in share capital

[2.074] The power of a company to increase its share capital, as contained in s 68, is the only power to alter the share capital contained in that section, which does not trigger the notification obligation of s 69. This is because any increase in a company's share capital must be notified to the Registrar of Companies separately in accordance with s 70.[269] The form for this notification is Form B4.[270]

[2.075] Section 70 provides that if a company passes a resolution to increase its share capital above the registered capital it must deliver a notice to the Registrar of Companies within 15 days of that resolution.[271] According to the Companies (Forms) (No 2) Order 2004,[272] the particulars which must be disclosed include the following:

- the company name;
- company number;
- the date of the resolution to increase the nominal share capital;
- the existing authorised share capital of the company;
- value by which the authorised share capital is to be increased;
- a description of the division of the additional share capital, according to the class of the shares (such as voting rights, rights in winding up, dividend rights);
- whether any of the new shares are preference and, if so, whether they are redeemable;
- the number of shares;
- the nominal amount of each share; and
- the conditions subject to which the new shares are to be, or have been, issued.[273]

A current director or secretary of the company must then sign, date and verify the accuracy of, the return.

If the Registrar of Companies does not receive a notice of an increase in a company's share capital within 15 days of such increase, the company and every officer in default are guilty of an offence and liable to a fine of up to €1904.61.[274]

(d) Reduction of share capital

[2.076] It is generally unlawful for a company limited by shares or a company limited by guarantee having a share capital to reduce its share capital.[275] This restrictive

---

[269] CA 1963, s 70, as amended by C(AA)A 2003, Sch 2, Item 1.

[270] This form may be downloaded from the CRO website (www.cro.ie) and filed online.

[271] CA 1963, s 70(1).

[272] Companies (Forms) (No 2) Order 2004 (SI 829/2004).

[273] Companies (Forms) (No 2) Order 2004 (SI 829/2004), Sch 5.

[274] CA 1963, s 70(3), as amended by C(A)A 1982, s 15, C(AA)A 2003, s 57 and CA 1990, s 240(7) as inserted by CLEA 2001 s104(c).

[275] CA 1963, s 72(1), as amended by CA 1990, s 231.

approach is guided by the need to protect the interests of the company's creditors. However, if certain steps are taken a company make reduce its share capital. The requisite steps may be summarised as follows: the company must have the authority to reduce its share capital pursuant to its articles of association, it must pass a special resolution approving this reduction, and the court must confirm this reduction.[276]

(i) Notification of Registrar of Companies

[2.077] If the court has confirmed the duly authorised reduction of a company's share capital, this reduction must be notified to the Registrar of Companies. The documents which must be delivered to the Registrar are a copy of the court order itself and a minute, approved by the court, demonstrating with regard to the altered share capital, the following:

- the amount of the share capital;
- the number of shares into which it is to be divided;
- the amount of each share; and
- the amount, if any, deemed to be paid up on each share.[277]

(ii) Registration of reduction

[2.078] Upon receipt of these documents, the Registrar shall register the court order and the minute regarding the altered share capital.[278] The Registrar must also certify this registration and the certificate shall be conclusive evidence that all of the requirements of the Companies Acts have been complied with and that the company's share capital is as it is stated in the minute.[279] Upon registration, the minute containing the details of the reduced share capital, shall be deemed to be substituted for the relevant part of the company's memorandum of association.[280]

While there is no time limit for notifying the Registrar of the reduction of share capital, and no penalty for failing to so notify the Registrar, this may be explained by the fact that it is not until this registration occurs that the special resolution which the company passed to authorise the reduction of its share capital, as confirmed by court order, may take effect.[281] It is therefore in the interests of a company which wishes to reduce its share capital to act expeditiously and deliver the requisite documents to the Registrar promptly upon receipt of the court order.

---

[276] CA 1963, s 72(2).

[277] CA 1963, s 75(1).

[278] CA 1963, s 75(1).

[279] CA 1963, s 75(4).

[280] CA 1963, s 75(5).

[281] CA 1963, s 75(2).

(iii) Public limited companies

[2.079] A public limited company is not permitted to reduce its allotted share capital below the authorised minimum.[282] If a court confirms a reduction of a public limited company's share capital which has the effect of bringing the nominal value of the allotted share capital below the authorised minimum, C(A)A 1983, s 17 provides that the Registrar of Companies should not register this reduction. The only situations in which the Registrar may register such a reduction are if the court makes an order to that effect,[283] or if the company is first re-registered as a form of company, other than a public limited company.[284]

[2.080] With regard to the court order, it is interesting to note that s 17(4) provides that a court making 'any such order' may do two things. First, the court order may authorise the re-registration of the company as a company other than a public limited company, without the passing of a special resolution. Secondly, if the court order does permit such re-registration, it 'shall' specify the alterations to the company's memorandum and articles of association which must be made for the purpose of such re-registration.[285] While s 17(4) is framed in permissive language and purports to suggest what the court order may direct, its formulation and the fact that it is the only explanation of the vague reference to an order of court in s 17(3), combined with the fact that it can hardly be expected that a court can simply override the legal prohibition on a public limited company reducing its allotted share capital below the authorised minimum, indicate that the only court order which can properly be made under s 17(3), directing the Registrar of Companies to register an otherwise illegal reduction of share capital, is the court order described in s 17(4).

(e) Other share dealings

[2.081] There are certain other dealings in a company's shares which must be notified to the Registrar of Companies. The following are merely examples of the dealings which must be so notified.

(i) Variation of rights of shareholders

[2.082] A company which has shares of different classes may, subject to certain conditions, vary the rights of the holders of a particular class of shares. The conditions can be briefly described as follows: the variation must be provided for in the articles or memorandum of association; a specified proportion of the shareholders in question must consent to the variation, or the affected shareholders must pass a resolution to that effect; and disgruntled shareholders, holding at least 10 per cent of the shares in

---

[282] C(A)A 1983, s 17(1) provides that, 'a public limited company may not reduce its allotted share capital below the authorised minimum and s 72 (1) of the Principal Act shall be construed accordingly.'

[283] C(A)A 1983, s 17(3).

[284] C(A)A 1983, s 17(3).

[285] C(A)A 1983, s 17(4).

question, have the right to apply to court,[286] upon which application the court may confirm or disallow the variation in question.[287]

[2.083] If such an application is made to court, the company must, within 21 days of the court order, forward a copy to the Registrar of Companies.[288] A failure to deliver a copy of the court order constitutes an offence on the part of the company and every officer in default, and is punishable by a fine of up to €1904.61.[289]

The obligation to deliver a copy of the court order to the Registrar applies whether the court disallows or confirms the variation. It is not entirely clear why the Registrar needs to be notified of a court decision to disallow a variation of share rights. It is also less than clear why the obligation to notify the Registrar is only triggered by a court order, and does not arise if the variation is effected by consent or the resolution of the shareholders affected by the variation. This seems particularly strange in light of the fact that, while a resolution varying shareholders' rights must be notified to the Registrar,[290] there appears to be no provision by which the Registrar will become aware of the variation of the rights of a class of shareholders by consent of a defined proportion of such shareholders.

(ii) Financing acquisition of own shares

[2.084] There is a general prohibition on companies funding the acquisition of their own shares. CA 1963, s 60, accordingly provides that:

> ... it shall not be lawful for a company to give, whether directly or indirectly, and whether by means of a loan, guarantee, the provision of security or otherwise, any financial assistance for the purpose of or in connection with a purchase or subscription made or to be made by any person of or for any shares in the company, or, where the company is a subsidiary company, in its holding company.

There is a notable exception to this rule, which bears some relevance to the present context. A company may furnish assistance for the purchase of its own shares, if, within 12 months previously, it passes a special resolution authorising such assistance.[291] There are a number of pre-conditions to passing such a resolution. In particular, a statutory declaration must be made at a meeting of the directors held not more than 24 days before the meeting at which the resolution is passed.[292] This resolution must state the

---

[286] Such an application must be made within 28 days of the consent or resolution in question. See CA 1963, s 78(2).

[287] CA 1963, s 78(1). The decision of the court is final, but an appeal may lie to the Supreme Court on a point of law (CA 1963, s 78(4)).

[288] CA 1963, 78(5), as amended by C(A)A 1982, s 15, C(AA)A 2003, s 57 and CA 1990, s 240(7) as inserted by CLEA 2001 s104(c).

[289] CA 1963, s 78(5), as amended by C(A)A 1982, s 15, C(AA)A 2003, s 57 and CA 1990, s 240(7) as inserted by CLEA 2001, s 104(c).

[290] CA 1963, s 143(4), as amended by C(A)A 1982, s 5.

[291] CA 1963, s 60(2)(a). This exception does not apply to public limited companies. See CA 1963, s 60(15A), as inserted by C(A)A 1983, s 3.

[292] CA 1963, s 60(3).

form, recipient and purpose of the assistance in question.[293] The declaration must also state that the directors have made a full inquiry into the affairs of the company and have formed the opinion that the company will be able to pay its debts as they fall due, after the assistance in question has been provided.[294]

A copy of this statutory declaration must be sent to the members of the company, together with the notice of the meeting at which the resolution is to be proposed. In the event that the special resolution authorising the assistance is passed and the financial assistance is furnished, the company must deliver a copy of the directors' statutory declaration to the Registrar of Companies, within 21 days of providing the assistance.[295]

[2.085] According to s 60(15), if a company acts in contravention of s 60, every officer of the company who is in default is liable to imprisonment for up to five years or a fine of up to €3,174.35, if convicted on indictment, or imprisonment for up to six months or a fine of up to €1904.61, on summary conviction.[296] There are a few points that may be noted about this provision. First, it refers to contraventions of s 60 in broad terms. The requirement to deliver a copy of the statutory declaration to the Registrar of Companies is not among the most onerous or notable aspects of the procedure governed by s 60 and, taking this aspect of the provision in isolation, the sanctions stipulated in s 60(15) seem severe. However, as there is no alternative sanction for failing to deliver the statutory declaration to the Registrar within the requisite timeframe, the sanctions of s 60(15) must be taken to apply to such a failure.

Secondly, the sanctions set out in s 60(15), as applied to a failure to deliver a copy of the statutory declaration to the Registrar, appear disproportionate, particularly when a comparison is drawn with the sanctions and fines generally applicable to failures to deliver documents to the Registrar within stipulated timeframes. Thirdly, only officers in default may be prosecuted for the offence of contravening s 60. Section 60(2)(b) requires the company to deliver a copy of the statutory declaration to the Registrar, but, according to s 60(15), it is not an offence for the company to fail to do so.

(iii) Acquisition of own shares

[2.086] Part XI of the CA 1990 contains provisions regarding the acquisition by a company of its own shares.[297] The relevance of these provisions in the present context is that, whenever these provisions are availed of, the company must deliver a return to the Registrar of Companies.[298] Section 226 accordingly requires that every company which has acquired shares under Pt XI must, within 28 days after delivery to the company of

---

[293] CA 1963, s 60(4)(a), (b), (c).

[294] CA 1963, s 60(4)(d).

[295] CA 1963, s 60(2)(b), as substituted by CLEA 2001, s 89.

[296] CA 1963, s 60(15), as amended by C(A)A 1982, s 15, CA 1990, s 240(7) and (8) as inserted by CLEA 2001, s 104(c).

[297] See, eg, CA 1990, ss 207 (power to issue redeemable shares), 210 (power to convert shares into redeemable shares) and 211 (power of company to purchase own shares).

[298] CA 1990, s 226.

the shares, deliver to the Registrar of Companies a return setting out the following information:

- the number of shares of each class;

- the nominal value of shares of each class; and

- the date on which the shares were delivered to the company.[299]

In the case of a public limited company, the return must also state the aggregate amount paid by the company for the shares and the maximum and minimum prices paid for each class of share purchased.[300]

The form of the return required under s 226 is set out in the Companies (Forms) Regulations 1991.[301] Particulars of shares delivered to the company making the return, on different dates and under different contracts, may be included in a single return.[302] It is an offence for the company and every officer in default to fail to comply with the requirements of s 226.[303]

G. Charges

[2.087] There are a number of important provisions regarding the obligation of a company to deliver to the Registrar of Companies particulars of charges which the company has created, and to keep a register of such charges.[304] These provisions are designed to ensure that creditors and other persons dealing with a company have information regarding the company's financial condition.[305]

(a) Obligation to register

[2.088] Every company must send to the Registrar of Companies for registration the particulars of every charge[306] created by the company within 21 days after the date of its creation.[307] This notification should be presented on Form C1. Such registration may also be effected on the application of the person with an interest in the charge.[308] The

---

[299] CA 1990, s 226(1).

[300] CA 1990, s 226(2).

[301] Companies (Forms) Regulations 1991 (SI 162/1991), Sch.

[302] CA 1990, s 226(3).

[303] CA 1990, s 226(4).

[304] See Courtney, *The Law of Private Companies* (2nd edn, Tottel Publishing, 2002) Ch 20 and Johnston, *Banking and Security Law in Ireland* (Butterworths, 1998).

[305] Kenny J stated in *Re International Retail Ltd* (19 September 1974, unreported), HC that the purpose of s 99 is to ensure that creditors dealing with the company should know that the company had given security for its indebtedness.

[306] 'Charge' includes mortgage. See CA 1963, s 99(10)(a).

[307] CA 1963, s 100(1). The time limit of 21 days is contained in CA 1963, s 99(1).

[308] CA 1963, s 100(1). Where such other person effects the registration, they are entitled to recover from the company any fees paid in relation to such registration. See CA 1963, s 100(2).

Registrar keeps a register of charges in respect of every company.[309] The fee for registering a charge is €40.[310]

(b) Registrable charges

[2.089] There are various categories of charges which must be registered under the Companies Acts. The general rule is that every charge that is created by the company[311] must be registered.[312] The following charges are covered by this obligation:[313]

- charges for the purpose of securing any issue of debentures;[314]
- charges on uncalled share capital of the company;[315]
- charges created or evidenced by instruments which would require registration as bills of sale, if executed by an individual;[316]
- charges on, or interests in, land (other than charges for rent or other such periodic sums);[317]
- charges on the company's book debts;[318]
- floating charges on the company's property or undertaking;[319]

---

[309] CA 1963, s 103.

[310] Companies (Fees) (No 3) Order 2005.

[311] CA 1963, s 99(1) refers to 'charges created after the fixed date' and the 'fixed date' is defined in s 99(10)(b) as 1 July 1908, or the operative date of the provisions in question, neither of which are likely to be of continued relevance.

[312] CA 1963, s 99(1).

[313] The charges which are within the scope of s 99, and the description of those charges, may be amended by regulation according to CA 1963, s 99(2A) and (2B), as inserted by CA 1990, s 122.

[314] CA 1963, s 99(2)(a).

[315] CA 1963, s 99(2)(b).

[316] CA 1963, s 99(2)(c). Note that, according to the Bills of Sale (Ireland) Act 1879, s 4 a 'bill of sale' shall not include transfers or assignments of any 'ship or vessel'.

[317] CA 1963, s 99(2)(d). According to CA 1963, s 99(7), 'The holding of debentures entitling the holder to a charge on land shall not, for the purposes of this section, be deemed to be an interest in land.'

[318] CA 1963, s 99(2)(e). CA 1963, s 99(6) clarifies that, 'Where a negotiable instrument has been given to secure the payment of any book debts of a company, the deposit of the instrument for the purpose of securing an advance to the company shall not, for the purposes of this section, be treated as a charge on those book debts.' A 'negotiable instrument' includes such instruments as cheques. This provision therefore means that the deposit of such instruments to secure the payment to the company of debts owed to it, is not treated as a charge on those debts. See further regarding charges on book debts: Breslin, 'Company charges over book debts after Holidair and New Bullas Trading' (1995) 2(2) CLP 32; Byrne, 'Charges on the book debts of a company' (1986) ILT 49; Breslin, 'Brumark Investments Ltd: Charges Over Book Debts, Divisibility of Assets, and the Role of Conduct in Interpretation of Contracts' (2001) 8(9) CLP 207.

[319] CA 1963, s 99(2)(f).

- charges on calls made but not paid;[320]

- charges on ships or aircrafts or any shares in a ship or aircraft;[321]

- charges on intellectual property, such as goodwill, patents, trademarks, copyright, or licences under patents or copyright;[322]

- charges existing on property when it is acquired by the company;[323]

- judgment mortgages.[324]

(i) Property outside the State

[2.090] There are certain inconsistencies and ambiguities regarding the application of s 99 to charges created over property located in other jurisdictions.

In the first instance, s 99(1)(d) specifies that the duty to register applies to charges on land 'wherever situate'. No such specificity appears with regard to the other categories of charges, such as floating charges over the property and undertaking of a company.[325] On the basis of the principle of interpretation that '*expressio unius est exclusio alterius*',[326] it appears from the terms of s 99(1) that only land that is situated outside the jurisdiction is captured by the registration requirement. This would appear to excuse property other than land, located outside Ireland, from the registration requirement.

[2.091] Secondly, s 99(3) provides that:

> In the case of a charge created out of the State comprising property situate outside the State, 21 days after the date on which the prescribed particulars could, in due course of post, and if despatched with due diligence, have been received in the State shall be substituted for 21 days after the date of the creation of the charge as the time within which the particulars are to be delivered to the registrar.

This suggests that charges over property situated in other jurisdictions must be registered, which is not entirely consistent with the terms of s 99(1) itself, as noted above. However, the explicit terms of s 99(3) are more persuasive than an interpretation of s 99(1), based on the inclusion of the phrase 'wherever situate' in s 99(1)(d) and it is suggested that the soundest interpretation of the scope of s 99 is that it does require

---

[320] CA 1963, s 99(2)(g).

[321] CA 1963, s 99(2)(h), as substituted by CA 1990, s 122.

[322] CA 1963, s 99(2)(i). See F Hackett, 'Taking Security Over Intellectual Property Rights in Ireland' (1994) CLP 50.

[323] This applies to charges which, if created by the company, would have been within the scope of the registration requirement of s 99. CA 1963, s 101. If a company fails to comply with this registration requirement, the company and every officer in default is guilty of an offence and liable to a maximum fine of €1904.61. CA 1963, s 101(2) as amended by C(A)A 1982, s 15, C(AA)A 2003, s 57(2) and CA 1990, s 240(7) as inserted by CLEA 2001 s104(c). Form C3/47B, which can be downloaded from www.cro.ie, should be used for this purpose.

[324] CA 1963, s 102.

[325] CA 1963, s 99(1)(f).

[326] Roughly translates as the 'expression of one thing is the exclusion of another'.

registration of charges created by companies to which s 99 applies, over property which is located outside Ireland.

[2.092] Thirdly, s 99(4) provides that:

> Where a charge is created in the State but comprises property outside the State, the prescribed particulars may be sent for registration under this section, notwithstanding that further proceedings may be necessary to make the charge valid or effectual according to the law of the country in which the property is situate.

At first glance, this provision could be interpreted as permitting, but not requiring, the registration of a charge related to property situated in another jurisdiction. However, in light of the terms of s 99(3), the more compelling interpretation is that s 99(4) permits the particulars of such a charge to be sent for registration even though further steps may be required to validate the charge in the jurisdiction in which the property is situated. This is probably necessary to ensure that it is possible to comply with the time limit specified in s 99(1), as extended by s 99(3), namely that the particulars must be registered within 21 days of the date on which the particulars could with diligence, have been received in Ireland. The policy which appears to underlie s 99(4) is compelling, in light of the fact that there could be no guarantee that the proceedings which may be required to validate a charge in the jurisdiction in which the property is situated, could be completed within 21 days of the creation of the charge. The terms of s 99(4) are therefore necessary to ensure that the registration requirements applicable in this jurisdiction can be satisfied, irrespective of the requirements of the jurisdiction in which the property is located.

[2.093] The fourth provision to note is s 99(5) which provides that:

> Where a charge comprises property situate outside the State and registration in the country where the property is situate is necessary to make the charge valid or effectual according to the law of that country, a certificate in the prescribed form stating that the charge was presented for registration in the country where the property is situate on the date on which it was so presented shall be delivered to the registrar of companies for registration.

This provision essentially provides that, if it is necessary to register a charge to make it valid or effective under the law of the jurisdiction in which the property is situate, a certificate must be delivered to the Registrar of Companies stating that the charge was presented for registration in that country and the date of such presentation.[327] This certificate should be presented in Form C2/47C.[328]

[2.094] Section 99(5) is a curious provision, for a number of reasons. This registration obligation is triggered if there is an obligation to register a charge in the jurisdiction in which it is created. As pointed out by Nolan, this is anomalous insofar as there is no equivalent requirement to register the instrument of charge itself in Ireland.[329] In addition, this provision assumes that other jurisdictions have a similar registration

---

[327] CA 1963, s 99(5).

[328] Available to download at www.cro.ie.

[329] S Nolan, 'Registration of Company Charges over Foreign Property: Who needs s 99(5) of the Companies Act 1963?' (1995) ILT 9.

procedure to that applicable in Ireland, which may not be an accurate assumption.[330] Further, if registration according to the laws of other jurisdictions requires a sequence of steps, rather than a single act of registration, it is difficult to see how the terms of s 99(5) could be complied with and it may require repeated registration of each such step.[331] A final issue in this regard is that there is no specified time limit for the registration of a charge over property located in another jurisdiction. Nolan cautions that, if the delivery of the certificate under s 99(5) falls within the 'particulars' required to be registered under s 99(1), it may be impossible to comply with the usual 21 day time limit, if, for example, the foreign registration could not be completed within 21 days of the creation of the charge in question.[332] On the other hand, it seems more likely that s 99(5) is not intended to come within the scope of s 99(1) and that the 21 day time limit does not therefore apply to the obligation to file a certificate demonstrating registration in the jurisdiction in which the charged property is situated. While Nolan relies on two distinct justifications for this conclusion, it appears that the most persuasive factors are the acknowledgement in s 99(3) that it may not be possible to register charges on property located in other jurisdictions within the 21 day time limit and the recognition in s 99(4) that it may not be possible to make a charge valid or effective according to the law of the country in which it is situated within the 21 day time limit.[333]

(ii) Companies incorporated in other jurisdictions

[2.095] A company incorporated in a jurisdiction other than Ireland, but having an established place of business in Ireland, must notify the Registrar of Companies of any of the following:

- the creation of a charge over property located in Ireland;[334]

- the registration of a judgment mortgage in respect of property located in Ireland;

---

[330] See S Nolan, 'Registration of Company Charges over Foreign Property: Who needs s 99(5) of the Companies Act 1963?' (1995) ILT 9.

[331] As noted by Nolan, 'The requirement to make a filing in the Companies Registration Office is triggered by each act whereby the charge is presented for registration not by the act whereby the charge is first presented for registration. The exclusion of the word 'first' would seem to be a material omission in the legislation.' ('Registration of Company Charges over Foreign Property: Who needs s 99(5) of the Companies Act 1963?' (1995) ILT 9.)

[332] See S Nolan, 'Registration of Company Charges over Foreign Property: Who needs s 99(5) of the Companies Act 1963?' (1995) ILT 9.

[333] Nolan also relies on the requirement in s 99(1) that the particulars must be verified in the prescribed manner and the fact that the Companies (Forms) Order 1964 does not require verification of the particulars under s 99(5) and notes that the CRO does not as a matter of practice require the registration of a s 99(5) certificate, where applicable, within the 21 day time limit.

[334] The appropriate form for this purpose is Form F8/8E, available to download at www.cro.ie.

– the acquisition of property in Ireland which is subject to a charge; or

– the appointment of a receiver in respect of property in Ireland.[335]

Section 111 curiously states that, 'for the purpose of these provisions, the principal place of business of such a company in the State shall be deemed to be its registered office.' The criterion for the application of s 111 is that the company must have 'an established place of business in the State'.

(iii) Series of debentures

[2.096] If a company creates a series of debentures containing charges to which the holders are entitled *pari passu*, these debentures can be registered cumulatively.[336] The appropriate form for this purpose is Form C4/47A.[337] Where there is more than one issue of debentures in the same series, the amount and date of each such issue must be notified separately to the Registrar of Companies, although a failure to comply with this requirement will not render such debentures invalid.[338] Where such a series of debentures is registered with the Registrar of Companies, the following particulars must be supplied:

– the total amount secured by the entire series of debentures;[339]

– the dates of the resolutions authorising the issue of the series of debentures;[340]

– the date of the covering deed, if any, creating or defining the security;[341]

– a general description of the property which is charged;[342] and

– the names of the trustees for the debenture holders, if applicable.[343]

(iv) Judgment mortgages

[2.097] If a creditor converts a judgment obtained against a company, into a judgment mortgage over any property of the company, the company must notify the Registrar of

---

[335] CA 1963, s 111.

[336] CA 1963, s 99(8) provides as follows: 'Where a series of debentures containing, or giving by reference to any other instrument, any charge to the benefit of which the debenture holders of that series are entitled *pari passu* is created by a company, it shall, for the purposes of this section, be sufficient if there are delivered to or received by the registrar, within 21 days after the execution of the deed containing the charge, or, if there is no such deed, after the execution of any debentures of the series ...' the particulars prescribed by that section.

[337] This may be downloaded from www.cro.ie.

[338] CA 1963, s 99(8).

[339] CA 1963, s 99(8)(a).

[340] CA 1963, s 99(8)(b).

[341] CA 1963, s 99(8)(b).

[342] CA 1963, s 99(8)(c).

[343] CA 1963, s 99(8)(d).

Companies of this fact.[344] The procedure is that the creditor must send to the company two copies of the affidavit that was filed in support of the application for the judgment mortgage, which must be certified as correct copies by the Land Registry or the Registry of Deeds, as appropriate. The company must then send one of these copies to the Registrar of Companies. The time limits applicable to the registration of judgment mortgages are that the creditor must send copies of the affidavit to the company within 21 days of its registration and the company then has three days within which to deliver this affidavit to the Registrar of Companies.[345]

It is an offence for a creditor to fail to deliver the affidavit to the company within 21 days of its registration or for the company and every officer in default to fail to deliver the affidavit to the Registrar within three days of receipt. These offences attract a maximum fine of €1,904.61.[346] No further consequences are attached to a failure to comply with s 102. This can be contrasted with s 99, pursuant to which a failure to register a charge will render it void.[347]

The Law Reform Commission Consultation Paper on Judgment Mortgages[348] provisionally recommends the repeal of s 102:

> The Commission provisionally recommends that a judgment mortgage should be subject to the same registration requirements as applied to the other forms of security set out in section 99 of the Companies Act 1963. Accordingly failure by the judgment creditor to register particulars of the charge within 21 days of its creation should render the judgment mortgage void as against a liquidator and other creditors of the company.

(c) Particulars to be registered

[2.098] The register of charges that is maintained by the Registrar of Companies in respect of every company is open to inspection by the public[349] and contains the following particulars:[350]

- the date of creation of the charge;[351]
- if the charge was on property acquired by the company, the date of such acquisition;[352]

---

[344] CA 1963, s 102(1).

[345] CA 1963, s 102(1).

[346] CA 1963, s 102(2), as substituted by C(AA)A 2003, s 57.

[347] CA 1963, s 99(1). See further para **[2.106]**.

[348] Law Reform Commission, Consultation Paper on Judgment Mortgages (LRC CP 30–2004) at para 2.73.

[349] CA 1963, s 103(2).

[350] CA 1963, s 103(1). Note that the particulars that must be registered in respect of a series of debentures within the meaning of s 99(8) are stipulated in that subsection. CA 1963, s 103(1)(a).

[351] CA 1963, s 103(1)(b)(i). This only applies if the charge was created by the company and does not apply if the charge existed before the property was acquired by the company, for example.

[352] CA 1963, s 103(1)(b)(ii).

- if the charge was a judgment mortgage, the date of creation;[353]

- the amount of the charge;[354]

- particulars of the property charged;[355]

- the persons entitled to the charge.[356]

In addition to these particulars, if the company grants a floating charge to the Central Bank and Financial Services Authority as collateral, particulars of any provision of the charge that prohibit or restrict the company from issuing further securities ranking equally with that charge or modifying the ranking of that charge in relation to previously issued securities, must be entered on the register.[357]

(d) Commission

[2.099] If a company grants any commission, allowance or discount[358] to any person in consideration of his subscribing or agreeing to subscribe, procuring or agreeing to procure subscriptions, for debentures in the company within the meaning of s 99, the rate and amount of any such payment or discount must be included in the notice which is sent to the Registrar of Companies.[359] An omission to comply with this requirement does not affect the validity of the debentures subscribed for.[360]

(e) Time limits for registration

[2.100] Section 99(1) provides that all charges must be registered within 21 days of their creation. There are certain exceptions to this general rule. First, where property is acquired which is already subject to a charge, the company has 21 days from the acquisition of the property to register the charge.[361] Secondly, if a company acquires property located in another jurisdiction which is subject to a charge, the deadline for registration is '21 days after the date on which the prescribed particulars could, in due course of post and if despatched with due diligence, have been received in the State'.[362] Thirdly, if a company creates a charge over property which is located in another

---

[353] CA 1963, s 103(1)(b)(iii).

[354] CA 1963, s 103(1)(b)(iv).

[355] CA 1963, s 103(1)(b)(v). This provision refers to 'short particulars of the property charged', but does clarify what is envisaged by 'short particulars'.

[356] CA 1963, s 103(1)(b)(vi).

[357] CA 1963, s 103(1)(b)(iiia) as inserted by the Central Bank and Financial Services Authority of Ireland Act 2004, s 33.

[358] Note that, according to CA 1963, s 99(9), 'the deposit of any debentures as security for any debt of the company shall not, for the purposes of this subsection, be treated as the issue of the debentures at a discount.'

[359] CA 1963, s 99(9).

[360] CA 1963, s 99(9).

[361] CA 1963, s 101(1).

[362] CA 1963, s 101(1).

jurisdiction, particulars of this charge must similarly be registered within 21 days of the date on which the particulars could, in due course and with due diligence, have been received in Ireland.[363]

The final exception to the time limit of 21 days from the creation of the charge for its registration, is contained in s 106.[364] According to this provision, a company or an interested person may apply to court for an extension of time for registration of a charge.[365] If the court is satisfied that the failure to register the charge, or any of the requisite particulars, within the 21 day time limit, was for one of the following reasons, the court may extend the time for registration of the charge:

- the omission was accidental or inadvertent or for some other 'sufficient cause',

- the omission is not of a nature to prejudice the position of the company's shareholders or creditors; or

- on other grounds, it is just and equitable to grant relief.[366]

If satisfied of any of these grounds, the court may extend time or rectify the omission on such terms and conditions as the court deems just and expedient.[367] However, it is of interest to note that such a court order does not relieve the company or its officer in default of liability for failing to comply with the obligation to register charges.[368]

(f) Effect of registration

[2.101] Upon registration of a charge, the Registrar of Companies will issue a certificate stating the amount secured by the charge. Such a certificate is conclusive evidence that the requirements of the Companies Acts in relation to the registration of charges have been complied with.[369]

[2.102] The effect of a certificate of registration was considered by the Court of Appeal in England in *Re CL Nye Ltd*.[370] In that case a charge created in favour of a bank was not registered within 21 days of its creation due to inadvertence on the part of the bank's solicitors. The solicitors did register the charge some months after its creation, inserting a false date to create the impression that the charge was registered within the requisite timeframe. The Registrar issued a certificate of registration in respect of the charge. When the company subsequently went into liquidation, the liquidator claimed that the charge was void, as it was not registered within 21 days of its actual creation. The two

---

[363] CA 1963, s 99(3).

[364] CA 1963, s 106(1).

[365] CA 1963, s 106(1).

[366] CA 1963, s 106(1).

[367] CA 1963, s 106(1).

[368] CA 1963, s 106(1), (2) provides in this regard, 'The grant of relief by the court under this section shall, if the court so directs, not have the effect of relieving the company or its officers of any liability already incurred under s 100.'

[369] CA 1963, s 104.

[370] *Re CL Nye Ltd* [1970] 3 WLR 158.

issues were the proper date of creation of the charge and the effect of the certificate of registration, particularly whether it remedied any defect in the registration of the charge.

The Court of Appeal held that the date of creation of the charge was the date on which the company first drew down the borrowed funds and that, the fact that the charge was not registered within 21 days of that date notwithstanding, the certificate of registration was conclusive as to all of the particulars contained in the register, including the date of creation.

The Court considered cases such as *National Provincial & Union Bank of England v Charnley*[371] in which the particulars sent for registration were incomplete. In that case, Scrutton LJ referred to the possibility of errors being made in the registration of a charge by the company or the Registrar and the injustice that would ensue if the beneficiary of the charge was not protected against the consequences of such errors. Scrutton LJ concluded that:

> 'The result of the legislation as it appears to me is that if the document sent in for registration does contain a charge on particular property, even if the company sending it in has misstated that charge, or the registrar considering it judicially has misunderstood it, when once the certificate has been given the grantees are safe. Though one can see that this may cause great hardship to a person who gives credit to the company in reliance on a defective register, one can also see that equal hardship would be caused to secured creditors if their security was to be upset for reasons connected with the action of persons over whom they had no control. For these reasons I take the view which was taken in *In re Yolland, Husson and Birkett* [1908] 1 Ch 152 and *Cunard Steamship Co v Hopwood* [1908] 2 Ch 564 that the giving of the certificate by the registrar is conclusive that the document creating the charge was properly registered, even if in fact it was not properly registered.'[372]

Harman LJ analysed the effect of a certificate of registration of a charge as follows:

> 'The whole point of creating the register under s 95 is to give security to persons relying on the certificate. If it were possible to go behind the certificate and show that the date of the creation of the charge made it out of time, no lender on the faith of the charge could be secure and sure that it would not thereafter be attacked by somebody who could successfully prove that there was in fact an interval of more than 21 days between the charge's creation and its registration. This would be disastrous in my opinion and is not a view to be taken unless the language positively compels it. I find no such compulsion and see no reason why the word "conclusive" should not mean what it says. The legislature in 1900 imposed on limited liability companies the obligation to disclose the charges they created. This was to the great advantage of the unsecured creditors but a limit was put to that advantage by giving a responsible official the right to judge whether all the prescribed particulars were in order, once he has done this, in order they are, even though the company has mis-stated them or the registrar has taken a wrong view.'[373]

These cases demonstrate the importance of the principle that a certificate of registration of a charge is conclusive and the strength of the protection such certificates offer secured creditors.

---

[371] *National Provincial & Union Bank of England v Charnley* [1924] 1 KB 431.

[372] *National Provincial & Union Bank of England v Charnley* [1924] 1 KB 431 at 447–448.

[373] *Re CL Nye Ltd* [1970] 3 WLR 158 at 168.

[2.103] As a result of a subsequent decision in England, this line of authority was thrown into some doubt.[374] In *R v Registrar of Companies, ex p Esal Commodities Ltd*[375] a bank filed an application for registration of a charge which failed to specify the date and description of the instrument which created the charge. An official within the office of the Registrar of Companies indicated these deficiencies to the bank, which subsequently delivered an amended application. The certificate of registration issued by the Registrar recorded the date of registration as the date of receipt of the first application.

The company was wound up and judicial review proceedings were instituted, seeking an order of certiorari quashing the decision of the Registrar to issue a certificate of registration, on the grounds that the requirements of the Companies Acts were not complied with.

Mervyn Davies J considered the arguments that the certificate of registration was issued without jurisdiction; that it was defective; and that it violated the requirements of natural justice, as the company was not notified or given the opportunity to make representations, among other arguments. The Court determined that it did have jurisdiction to issue an order of certiorari in respect of a decision of the Registrar, as the Registrar was a person with authority to make decisions which affected the rights of other persons, such as the secured creditors as against those of unsecured creditors in relation to the registration of charges.[376] The Court proceeded to question whether the conclusiveness of a certificate of registration could be queried in judicial review proceedings. In this regard, the Court considered the reasons for the 'conclusiveness' of a certificate of registration and noted that:

> 'These reasons of policy which seem to have influenced the legislature in making a s 98(2) certificate unassailable in private litigation have some weight when one is asked, in judicial review proceedings, whether or not the actions of the registrar leading to the issue of a s 98(2) certificate are reviewable. The mischief sought to be avoided by s 98(2), commercial uncertainty, will be brought alive if judicial review is allowed. That is a consequence it is desirable to avoid.'[377]

This policy notwithstanding, the Court determined that the interests of commercial certainty must give way to public policy in judicial review proceedings. The Court concluded that there was an error of law, as the Registrar registered a charge without receipt of the requisite particulars and did not have jurisdiction to extend time for receipt of those particulars. The Court noted that extensions of time were matters for the court, and that the Registrar did not have the power to extend time, as charges were automatically void if not registered within the prescribed 21 day time limit.[378] The Court therefore granted an order quashing the Registrar's decision to issue a certificate of registration.

---

[374] See *R v Registrar of Companies, ex p Esal Commodities Ltd* [1985] 2 WLR 447. See also an article regarding this case: S Pye, 'The s 104 certificate of registration: An impenetrable shield no more?' (1985) ILT 213.

[375] *R v Registrar of Companies, ex p Esal Commodities Ltd* [1985] 2 WLR 447.

[376] *R v Registrar of Companies, ex p Esal Commodities Ltd* [1985] 2 WLR 447 at 459–460.

[377] *R v Registrar of Companies, ex p Esal Commodities Ltd* [1985] 2 WLR 447 at 462.

[378] *R v Registrar of Companies, ex p Esal Commodities Ltd* [1985] 2 WLR 447 at 465–466.

[2.104] On an appeal by the Registrar of Companies, the Court of Appeal considered whether it was possible to go behind the Registrar's certificate on an application for judicial review of his decision to register a charge. Lawton LJ stated:

'In my judgment, the registrar did act without jurisdiction when he decided to register the debenture without having had delivered to him within 21 days of 9 February 1984 the original of the instrument by which the debenture was created or evidenced.'[379]

The Court concluded that the conclusiveness of the certificate of registration had the effect that no evidence should have been admitted regarding what occurred after the date of registration. The courts have no jurisdiction to enquire whether the requirements of the Companies Acts were complied with, once a certificate of registration is issued. As noted by Slade LJ:

'the legislature, in enacting s 98(2) [the equivalent of s 104], has, in my opinion, evinced a clear intention that no one ... should be entitled to adduce evidence for the purpose of attacking the correctness of the Registrar's answer, once it has been incorporated in a s 98 certificate.'[380]

The Court noted that it may be possible to challenge a certificate of registration in cases of fraud, but that errors of law by the Registrar were within the scope of his jurisdiction and did not prevent the certificate being conclusive.[381] The trial judge (Mervyn Davies J) was therefore in error in admitting evidence regarding the application for registration. The Registrar's appeal was allowed and the certificate of registration was restored.

Slade LJ considered the consequences of this position and noted that there were two factors which prevented the conclusiveness of the Registrar operating in an unduly harsh or unjust fashion.

First, the conclusive effect of the certificate registration is of a limited nature and does not confer validity on a charge which is invalid for reasons other than lack of registration. The effect of the certificate is that, once a charge is registered, whether incorrectly or not, persons intending to advance money or credit to the company will have notice of its existence. Slade LJ noted that:

'Even if a charge has been incorrectly registered (eg, because the prescribed particulars were delivered out of time) I think there are likely to be very few, if any, creditors who could, on the subsequent liquidation of the company, show that they had suffered any substantial injustice as a result of this erroneous registration.'[382]

---

[379] *R v Registrar of Companies, ex p Central Bank of India* [1986] QB 1114 at 1165.

[380] *R v Registrar of Companies, ex p Central Bank of India* [1986] QB 1114 at 1176.

[381] *R v Registrar of Companies, ex p Central Bank of India* [1986] QB 1114 at 1178: 'Section 98(2), in my opinion, by itself shows the intention of the legislature that the registrar is to have jurisdiction finally and conclusively to determine the question whether or not the requirements of s 95(1) have been complied with in any given case, and that he cannot be said to be acting beyond his powers even if he made an honest error of fact or of law or mixed fact and law in the course of determining this question' (*per* Slade LJ).

[382] *R v Registrar of Companies, ex p Central Bank of India* [1986] QB 1114 at 1177.

The second reason for believing the conclusiveness of the certificate of registration would not operate unfairly or harshly was that it had been indicated on behalf of the Registrar of Companies in that case that the conclusiveness of the certificate did not bind the Crown, and the Attorney General could therefore intervene by way of judicial review, if there was evidence available to show that the Registrar had erred in the discharge of his functions. It has not been established whether this possibility would be open under the Irish CA 1963–2006.

[2.105] The conclusiveness of a certificate of registration appears to remain intact and immune from challenge. In Ireland, the case of *Re CL Nye Ltd*[383] was applied in *Lombard & Ulster Banking (Irl) Ltd v Amurec Ltd*[384] In that case, an attempt to challenge the validity of a certificate of registration on the ground that the charge was not registered within 21 days of its creation was rejected by Hamilton J. The Court confirmed that s 104 was conclusive evidence that the requirements of the Companies Acts were complied with.

(g) Effect of non-registration

[2.106] If a company fails to deliver the requisite particulars of every charge over the company's property to the Registrar of Companies, there are two important consequences. First, the charge will be rendered void. Section 99 provides in this regard that every charge which there is an obligation to register, shall 'be void against the liquidator and any creditor of the company, unless the prescribed particulars of the charge … are delivered to or received by the Registrar of Companies.'[385]

This only applies insofar as the charge creates security on the company's property or undertaking.[386] It should also be noted that the avoidance of a charge under s 99 does not affect any contract or obligation to repay the monies secured.[387] Moreover, as soon as a charge becomes void, the monies secured by that charge become immediately payable.[388]

Secondly, if a company fails to comply with the obligation to deliver particulars of charges to the Registrar of Companies, and no such registration is effected by any other person, the company and officer in default is guilty of an offence and liable to a fine of up to €1904.61.[389] Proceedings in this regard may be brought and prosecuted by the Registrar of Companies.[390]

---

[383] *Re CL Nye Ltd* [1970] 3 WLR 158.

[384] *Lombard & Ulster Banking (Irl) Ltd v Amurec Ltd* [1976]–1977 ILRM 222.

[385] CA 1963, s 99(1). Note that this consequence does not ensue in respect of a failure to register a judgment mortgage. See CA 1963, s 102. See Law Reform Commission, Consultation Paper on Judgment Mortgages (LRC CP 30–2004).

[386] CA 1963, s 99(1).

[387] CA 1963, s 99(1).

[388] CA 1963, s 99(1).

[389] CA 1963, s 100(3), as amended by C(A)A 1982, s 15, C(AA)A 2003, s 57 and CA 1990, s 240 as inserted by CLEA 2001, s 104(c).

[390] CA 1963, s 100(4).

(h) Register of debenture holders

[2.107] In addition to the obligation to register particulars of charges secured on the company's property, every company is also obliged to keep a register of debenture holders and must notify the Registrar of Companies of the place where the register is kept and any change in that location.[391] This obligation does not arise if the register has at all times been kept at the company's registered office.[392] If it is necessary to notify the Registrar of the location of the register, this should be done on Form B3. If the company does not notify the Registrar of the location of the register of debenture holders within 14 days of a change in that location, the company and every officer in default is guilty of an offence and liable to a maximum fine of €1904.61.[393]

(i) Release from charge

[2.108] There is a mechanism whereby the register of charges may be adapted to reflect satisfaction or release of charges. If the Registrar of Companies is satisfied that either the debt secured by the charge has been repaid or satisfied in whole or in part, or that the property which was subject to the charge has been released from the charge or is no longer owned by the company,[394] the Registrar may record this fact on the register of charges.[395] This can only be done if the Registrar has first given notice to the holder of the charge or the judgment creditor of his intention to record the charge as satisfied.[396] The matters that may be recorded by the Registrar are the following:

- a memorandum of satisfaction in whole or in part;[397]

- a memorandum that part of the company's property or undertaking has been released from the charge; or

- a memorandum that the property or undertaking subject to the charge has ceased to form part of the company's property or undertaking.[398]

---

[391] CA 1963, s 91(3). See further Ch **3**.

[392] CA 1963, s 91(4).

[393] CA 1963, s 91(5), as amended by C(A)A 1982, s 15, C(AA)A 2003, s 57 and CA 1990, s 240(7) as inserted by CLEA 2001 s104(c).

[394] Statutory declarations of satisfaction of the charges may be made by a secretary and director of the company and delivered to the CRO for this purpose. The appropriate form of the statutory declaration is Form C6, if the charge has been wholly satisfied and Form C7 should be delivered if there has been partial satisfaction of the charge. Both these forms may be downloaded from www.cro.ie.

[395] CA 1963, s 105.

[396] CA 1963, s 105.

[397] CA 1963, s 105. If a memorandum of satisfaction in whole is entered, the Registrar must, if required, send a copy of this to the company.

[398] CA 1963, s 105.

H. Resolutions and agreements

[2.109] Every company is obliged to send copies of certain resolutions and agreements to the Registrar of Companies.[399] The following are the resolutions and agreements which must be so registered:

- special resolutions;[400]

- resolutions which have been agreed by all members, and which would otherwise have been required to be special resolutions;[401]

- resolutions and agreements which have been agreed by all members of a class of shareholders, and which would otherwise have been required to be passed by some particular majority or in some particular manner;[402]

- resolutions and agreements which bind all of the members of a particular class of shareholders, although not agreed by all such members;[403]

- resolutions increasing the company's share capital;[404]

- resolutions to wind up the company voluntarily;[405]

- resolutions attaching or varying the rights of restrictions attached to any share;[406]

- resolutions classifying any unclassified share;[407]

- resolutions converting shares of one class into another class;[408]

- resolutions of the directors re-registering an old public liability company as a public limited company;[409]

- resolutions of the directors of a public limited company cancelling shares and reducing the share capital and, if necessary, re-registering the company in another form;[410]

---

[399] CA 1963, s 143, as amended by C(A)A 1982, ss 5, 15, C(A)A 1983, s 3, C(AA)A 2003, s 57 and CA 1990, s 240(7) as inserted by CLEA 2001 s104(c).

[400] CA 1963, s 143(4)(a).

[401] CA 1963, s 143(4)(b).

[402] CA 1963, s 143(4)(c).

[403] CA 1963, s 143(4)(c).

[404] CA 1963, s 143(4)(d).

[405] CA 1963, s 143(4)(e), referring to CA 1963, s 251(1)(b) and (c).

[406] CA 1963, s 143(4)(f) and (g), as inserted by C(A)A 1982, s 5.

[407] CA 1963, s 143(4)(h), as inserted by C(A)A 1982, s 5.

[408] CA 1963, s 143(4)(i), as inserted by C(A)A 1982, s 5.

[409] CA 1963, s 143(4)(j), as inserted by C(A)A 1983, Sch 1, para 15, referring to C(A)A 1983 s12(3)(a).

[410] CA 1963, s 143(4)(j), as inserted by C(A)A 1983, s 3, referring to Sch 1, para 15 applying C(A)A 1983, s 43(3).

- an ordinary resolution of a company to give, vary, revoke or renew the authority of directors to allot shares not originally subscribed for or rights to subscribe for, or convert other security into, shares;[411] and

- a resolution of a company authorising a market purchase by the company of its own shares.[412]

[2.110] Within 15 days of the passing of any such resolution or the formation of any such agreement, the company must send a printed copy of the resolution or agreement to the Registrar of Companies.[413] There are two other devices in s 143 to ensure that there is transparency regarding any of the resolutions or agreements listed above. First, if the company's articles of association have been registered with the Registrar of Companies, every copy of the articles issued after the formation of an agreement or passing of a resolution within the scope of s 143, must embody or attach a copy of such agreement or resolution.[414] This only applies if the articles are registered and does not pertain to company's whose articles are not registered with the Registrar of Companies.[415] Secondly, a copy of every such resolution and agreement must be forwarded to any member of the company, if requested, on payment of a fee of one shilling (€0.06) or 'such less sum as the company may direct'.[416] It is difficult to imagine a company directing payment of a fee of less than €0.06.

The forms for notification of resolutions to the Registrar of Companies are Form G1, in respect of special resolutions, and Form G2, in respect of ordinary resolutions.[417]

[2.111] If a company fails to deliver a copy of a resolution or agreement within the scope of s 143 to the Registrar, the company and every defaulting officer is guilty of an offence and liable to a fine of up to €1904.61[418] If a company, whose articles are registered, fails to attach to, or include in, those articles, any resolution or agreement within the scope of s 143, the company and every defaulting officer is guilty of an offence and liable to a fine of up to €1904.61 for each defaulting copy.[419] The same penalties apply if the company fails to comply with a request to forward a copy of such

---

[411] C(A)A 1983, s 20(6).

[412] CA 1990, s 215(2).

[413] CA 1963, s 143(1).

[414] CA 1963, s 143(2).

[415] For the distinction between companies that are and are not obliged to register the articles of association, see further paras **[2.006]** to **[2.009]**.

[416] CA 1963, s 143(3).

[417] Both forms are available to download from www.cro.ie and may be filled in and filed online.

[418] CA 1963, s 143(5), as amended by C(A)A 1982, s 15, C(AA)A 2003, s 57 and CA 1990, s 240(7) as inserted by CLEA 2001, s 104(c).

[419] CA 1963, s 143(6), as amended by C(A)A 1982, s 15 and C(AA)A 2003, s 57 and CA 1990, s 240(7) as inserted by CLEA 2001, s 104(c). In this section, the blanket increase in maximum fines provided for by CA 1990, s 240(7), as inserted by CLEA 2001, s 104(c), operates to increase the previous maximum fine from €6.35 (as provided for by C(A)A 1982, Sch 1) to €1904.61.

resolution or agreement to a member of the company.[420] If a company is in liquidation at the time of any default under s 143, the liquidator is deemed to be an officer of the company and may be guilty of the offences specified in s 143(5) and (6).[421]

I. Directors and secretaries

(a) Delivery of particulars and consent

[2.112] Every company must furnish particulars of its directors and secretary on Form A1, which is forwarded to the Registrar of Companies together with the company's memorandum of association, when it is first incorporated.[422] The consent of the directors and secretary to act as such must also be forwarded to the Registrar.[423]

(b) Share qualifications

[2.113] Directors of public limited companies[424] must take certain steps before they can be appointed or named as directors or proposed directors in the company's prospectus or statement in lieu of the prospectus.[425] They must deliver to the Registrar for registration a signed consent in writing to act as director[426] and they must further demonstrate compliance with the share qualification requirements in one of the following ways:

- sign the memorandum for the requisite number of shares;[427]

- take and pay, or agree to pay, for the qualification shares;[428]

- sign and deliver to the Registrar an undertaking in writing to take and pay for the qualification shares;[429] or

- make and deliver to the Registrar a statutory declaration that the requisite number of shares are registered in his name.[430]

---

[420] CA 1963, s 143(6), as amended by C(A)A 1982, s 15 and C(AA)A 2003, s 57 and CA 1990, s 240(7) as inserted by CLEA 2001, s 104(c).

[421] CA 1963, s 143(7).

[422] See C(A)A 1982, s 3. See further paras **[2.010]** to **[2.011]**.

[423] C(A)A 1982, s 3(3). See further para **[2.011]**.

[424] This provision applies to companies other than companies without share capital, private companies, companies which were private companies before becoming public companies and prospectuses issued more than one year after the company was entitled to commence business. See CA 1963, s 179(5).

[425] CA 1963, s 179(1).

[426] CA 1963, s 179(1)(a).

[427] CA 1963, s 179(1)(b)(i).

[428] CA 1963, s 179(1)(b)(ii).

[429] CA 1963, s 179(1)(b)(iii).

[430] CA 1963, s 179(1)(b)(iv).

On an application to register the company's memorandum and articles of a company, a list of the persons who have consented to act as directors must be delivered to the Registrar of Companies.[431]

(c) Notification of changes in directors and secretary

[2.114] Every company must keep a register of its directors and secretary.[432] If there is any change in the directors or secretary of the company, or any particulars of such directors or secretary, the company must notify the Registrar of this occurrence.[433] The notification must be sent within 14 days of the change in question and must set out the change that occurred and the date on which it occurred.[434] The form to be used for this purpose is Form B10.[435]

To facilitate company's compliance with the obligation to notify the Registrar of changes in directors' or secretaries' particulars, s 195(11) provides that every director and secretary is under a duty 'to give information in writing to the company as soon as may be of such matters as may be necessary to enable the company to comply with this section.'[436]

Where the change to be notified to the Registrar involves the appointment of a new director or secretary, the notification must be accompanied by a signed consent of that person to so act.[437] Further, if the person whose appointment as a director is notified to the Registrar, is disqualified under the law of another state from being appointed, or acting, as a director, it is the duty of that disqualified person to ensure that the notification of their appointment is accompanied by a separate statement.[438] This statement must be signed by the disqualified person and must state the jurisdiction in which they are disqualified and the date and period of such disqualification.

---

[431] CA 1963, s 179(4) as amended by C(AA)A 2003, Sch 2, Item 1 and CA 1990, s 240(7) as inserted by CLEA 2001, s 104(c). It is an offence to include the name of any person as director, who has not consented to so act.

[432] CA 1963, s 195, as substituted by CA 1990, s 51. See further Ch **3**.

[433] CA 1963, s 195(6), as substituted by CA 1990, s 51. CA 1963, s 195(9), as substituted by CA 1990, s 51, sets out the following rule regarding transition from the registration requirements as they existed before the introduction of CA 1990, to the rules applicable thereafter: 'Sub-s (6) shall not apply to any change in the particulars contained in a company's register of directors and secretaries made solely by reason of the coming into force of s 51 of the Companies Act, 1990 but if after any such change has occurred and before the company makes its next annual return, any other change in those particulars occurs, the company shall send to the registrar of companies a notification in the prescribed form of any such earlier changes and the date on which they occurred at the same time as it notifies the registrar of the later changes in accordance with this section.'

[434] CA 1963, s 195(6), as substituted by CA 1990, s 51.

[435] This form, which is available at www.cro.ie, may be filled in and filed online.

[436] CA 1963, s 195(11), as substituted by CA 1990, s 51.

[437] CA 1963, s 195(7), as substituted by CA 1990, s 51.

[438] CA 1963, s 195(8), as substituted by CA 1990, s 51, and as substituted by CLEA 2001, s 91(a).

[2.115] When the relevant section is commenced, a person who is a director of more than one company will be able to avail of a particular procedure which allows that person to notify the Registrar of Companies of changes in their name or address, relieving the companies of the obligation to notify this change individually. Section 195(6A) provides that a director of several companies may send a notification to the Registrar of a change in their residential address or their name, the date on which the change occurred and a list of the companies of which the person is director.[439] If the Registrar receives such a notification, he may record the change or changes notified in relation to each of the companies listed in the notification.[440] These companies will then be relieved of the obligation to notify that change to the Registrar, but only in respect of the change or changes specifically notified.[441] To date, s 195(6A) has not been commenced.

(d) Notification of resignation or removal by former officer

[2.116] While it is the company's primary responsibility to notify the Registrar of any changes in the company's board of directors or secretary, there is a mechanism which enables a former director to ensure that his removal or resignation is notified to the Registrar, where the company fails to do so.[442] According to s 195(11A), if a company fails to file a Form B10 notifying the Registrar of the fact that a person has ceased to be a director or secretary, that former director or secretary may serve a notice on the company. This notice should state the following three matters:

1.   it should require the company to comply with this requirement forthwith;[443]

2.   it should state that, if the company fails to comply with this requirement within 21 days of the notice, the former director or secretary will forward to the Registrar documentary proof of his ceasing to be a director or secretary of the company, such as a copy of the notice of resignation, together with such other information as may be prescribed;[444] and

3.   it should state that, if the company fails to file the Form B10 within 21 days, the former director or secretary will forward to every person who is, to his knowledge, an officer of the company, documentary proof of his ceasing to be a

---

[439]   CA 1963, s 195(6A)(a), as inserted by IFCMPA 2005, s 62.

[440]   CA 1963, s 195(6A)(b)(ii), as inserted by IFCMPA 2005, s 62.

[441]   CA 1963, s 195(6A)(b)(i), as inserted by IFCMPA 2005, s 62.

[442]   Note that the death of a director or secretary should be notified to the CRO on Form B70.

[443]   CA 1963, s 195(11A)(a), as substituted by CA 1990, s 51, as inserted by C(A)(No 2)A 1999, s 47.

[444]   CA 1963, s 195(11A)(b) and (b)(i), as substituted by CA 1990, s 51, as inserted by C(A)(No 2)A 1999, s 47. Note that information which is furnished to the Registrar under this provision is not capable of being defamatory. CA 1963, s 195(11D), as substituted by CA 1990, s 51, as inserted by C(A)(No 2)A 1999, s 47 provides as follows: 'No additional information referred to in sub-s (11A)(b)(i) that is included in a notice of resignation or other documentary proof referred to in this section which is forwarded, under and in accordance with the foregoing provisions, to the registrar of companies shall, of itself, be regarded as constituting defamatory matter.'

director or secretary, together with a written request to that officer to take steps to ensure that the company's failure to comply with the notice is rectified.[445]

If the company does fail to file the Form B10 within 21 days of the service of a notice by the former director or secretary under s 195(11A), that person may proceed to deliver the above-mentioned documents to the Registrar of Companies and to the persons who are, to the knowledge of the former director or secretary, officers of the company.[446]

[2.117] It is essential that the additional documents referred to above, must accompany the documentary evidence of ceasing to be a director or secretary of the company.[447] A former director or secretary cannot therefore simply serve a copy of his letter of resignation to the Registrar or the company's officers. It should also be noted that this is the only means by which a former director or secretary[448] can deliver documentary proof of ceasing to be a director or secretary to the Registrar of Companies. In only one other circumstance will the Registrar consider such evidence.[449] By contrast with the general limitations on the notification by former directors or secretaries of their ceasing to act as such, any person can notify the Registrar when a director or secretary of a company dies.[450]

[2.118] The notification to be sent to the Registrar must be on Form B 69,[451] which constitutes a statutory declaration by the former director or secretary that the company has failed, despite the service of a request under s 195(11A), to file a Form B 10. In this declaration, the former director or secretary must declare that they ceased to act as a director or secretary of the company, and the date of such cessation. The declaration must also include a list of the names and addresses of the officers of the company, to the best of the knowledge of the person making the declaration. There are two documents which must be attached to this declaration: documentary evidence of the cessation, such as a letter of resignation, and a copy of the notice which was sent to the company under s 195(11A). The declaration must be signed and witnessed.

---

[445] CA 1963, s 195(11A)(b)(ii), as substituted by CA 1990, s 51, as inserted by C(A)(No 2)A 1999, s 47.

[446] CA 1963, s 195(11B), as substituted by CA 1990, s 51, as inserted by C(A)(No 2)A 1999, s 47.

[447] CA 1963, s 195(11B), as substituted by CA 1990, s 51, as inserted by C(A)(No 2)A 1999, s 47.

[448] The only qualification to this is that the sole Irish resident director of a company may notify the Registrar of his resignation or removal. See C(A)(No 2)A 1999, s 43.

[449] CA 1963, s 195(11C), as substituted by CA 1990, s 51, as inserted by C(A)(No 2)A 1999, s 47: 'No notice of resignation or other documentary proof of a person's having ceased to be a director or secretary of a company which is forwarded to the registrar of companies by that person (other than such a notice or other proof which is forwarded by him under and in accordance with sub-ss (11A) and (11B), or s 43(9) of the Companies (Amendment) (No 2) Act, 1999) shall be considered by the registrar.'

[450] This notice must be accompanied by such proof as may be prescribed. (CA 1963, s 195(11E), as substituted by CA 1990, s 51, as inserted by C(A)(No 2)A 1999, s 47. Form B70 is the appropriate form for the notification of the death of a director or secretary.

[451] This form is available to download on www.cro.ie.

The CRO has drawn attention to a practice of certain directors filing Forms B69, without having resigned as director of the company. This is done to avoid enforcement measures by the CRO. The CRO has advised that such a use of the Form B69 procedure is an abuse of that procedure and is a breach of CA 1990, s 242, and constitutes a false statutory declaration.[452]

(e) Irish resident director

[2.119] Subject to certain exceptions, every company is generally required to have at least one director who is resident in Ireland.[453]

[2.120] If the company's sole Irish resident director is removed or resigns, he must notify the Registrar of this fact, within 14 days of its occurrence.[454] It is important for Irish resident directors to be aware of this requirement, as s 43(11) provides that:

> If a person fails to comply with sub-s (9), he or she shall be jointly and severally liable with the company of which he or she has ceased to be a director for any fine or penalty referred to in sub-s (3) imposed on the company or which it is held liable to pay after that cessation, and any such fine or penalty for which that person is so liable may be recovered by the registrar of companies or the Revenue Commissioners, as appropriate, from him or her as a simple contract debt in any court of competent jurisdiction.[455]

[2.121] If the company does not have at least one Irish resident director, it must hold a bond in the amount of €25,394.74, which would cover any fine imposed on the company for offences under the Companies Acts prosecutable by the Registrar of Companies or fines for specified offences under the Taxes Consolidation Act 1997.[456] A copy of the bond must be attached to any of the following, if applicable:

- if there are no Irish resident directors on the incorporation of the company, the statement which a company is obliged to register under C(A)A 1982, s 3;[457]

- if the company's sole Irish resident director notifies the Registrar of his resignation or removal, that notification;[458] and

- if there is no Irish resident director during the period to which an annual return relates, to that annual return.[459]

[2.122] There is a procedure whereby a company may obtain an exemption from the requirement to have an Irish resident director or hold a bond in the sum of

---

[452] See Sunday Business Post, 29 May 2005, 'File on Time or Face Huge Penalties'.

[453] C(A)(No 2)A 1999, s 43. See further Ch **6**.

[454] C(A)(No 2)A 1999, s 43(9). This notification cannot of itself be regarded as constituting defamatory material. (C(A)(No 2)A 1999, s 43(10)).

[455] C(A)(No 2)A 1999, s 43(11).

[456] C(A)(No 2)A 1999, s 43(3).

[457] C(A)(No 2)A 1999, s 43(8)(a).

[458] C(A)(No 2)A 1999, s 43(8)(b).

[459] C(A)(No 2)A 1999, s 43(8)(c).

€25,394.75.[460] This exemption is obtained if the Registrar of Companies grants a certificate stating that the company has a 'real and continuous link with one or more economic activities that are being carried on in the State'.[461] The company must tender evidence to satisfy the Registrar of the existence of such a link and must attach the requisite evidence to a completed 'Form B 67'.[462] That form envisages the provision of the following statement, which is deemed to be proof of the requisite link:[463]

> a statement in writing that has been given to the company concerned by the Revenue Commissioners within the period of two months ending on the date on which an application is made under sub-s (2) by the company and which states that the Revenue Commissioners have reasonable grounds to believe that the company has a real and continuous link with one or more economic activities being carried on in the State.[464]

If the Registrar forms the opinion, on foot of information which has come into his possession, that a company in possession of a certificate of exemption under s 44 has ceased to have the requisite link with the State, the certificate can be revoked.[465] One possible source of such information is the Revenue Commissioners and s 44(7) provides specifically in this regard that if the Revenue form the opinion that the company has ceased to have the requisite link with the State, they may notify the Registrar of this fact, any secrecy or disclosure restrictions notwithstanding.[466]

J. Company name

[2.123] Every company is required to have a name, which must be stated in the company's memorandum of association, as forwarded to the Registrar of Companies at the time of incorporation.[467] There are certain rules that apply to the name of companies incorporated under the CA 1963–2006. First, the company name must generally include an indication of its incorporation, and the type of company it is, such as 'limited', 'teoranta' or 'plc'.[468] Secondly, there are certain restrictions on the company name which may be selected. For example, the name may not be misleading, undesirable, or excessively similar to the name of another company, among other restrictions.[469] Thirdly, the name of a company must be published and disclosed in accordance with particular requirements of the Companies Acts.[470] Fourthly, if a company wishes to change its

---

[460] C(A)(No 2)A 1999, s 44(1).

[461] C(A)(No 2)A 1999, s 44(2).

[462] C(A)(No 2)A 1999, s 44(3).

[463] C(A)(No 2)A 1999, s 44(4).

[464] C(A)(No 2)A 1999, s 44(5).

[465] C(A)(No 2)A 1999, s 44(6).

[466] C(A)(No 2)A 1999, s 44(7).

[467] CA 1963, s 6(1) as substituted by C(A)A 1983, s 3.

[468] CA 1963, ss 6(1)(a) and (b), as substituted by C(A)A 1983, s 3 and C(A)A 1983, s 4.

[469] See CA 1963, s 21.

[470] CA 1963, s 114.

name, particular steps must be taken and notified to the Registrar.[471] Fifth, it may be possible to reserve a company name.[472]

The Registrar of Companies bears general responsibility for issues concerning company names, many of these functions having been transferred from the Minister for Enterprise, Trade and Employment to the Registrar, by the CLEA 2001.[473]

(a) 'Limited', 'teoranta' or 'plc'

(i) Obligation to use 'limited' or 'plc'

[2.124] The general rule is that every company which is incorporated under the CA 1963–2006, must include 'limited', 'teoranta', 'public limited company' or 'cuideachta phoibli theoranta', or abbreviations of these words, after its name. CA 1963, s 24(2) provides in this regard that, 'The registrar shall refuse to register as a limited company any association about to be formed as a limited company by a name which does not include the word "limited" or "teoranta"'.[474] CA 1963, s 6(1), similarly provides that the name of a company which is limited by guarantee or shares must have 'limited' or 'teoranta' as the last word of the name and public limited companies must have 'public limited company' or 'cuideachta phoibli theoranta' as the last words of the name.[475]

(ii) Improper use of 'limited' or 'plc'

[2.125] It is an offence for any person, not being a duly incorporated company with limited liability, to trade or carry on business under a name of which the words 'limited' or 'teoranta' or abbreviations, versions or imitations of those words, appear at the end.[476] If such a person receives a notice to desist from carrying on business or trading under such a name and fails to comply with that notice within 14 days, the Registrar or the DCE may apply to court for an order directing compliance with that notice within a specified period of time.[477] If such an order is made, the court may direct that all costs incurred in connection with the application should be borne by the person against whom the order is made.[478] The court has a discretion whether to make the order sought and whether to director the payment of costs by the person guilty of the offence.[479]

---

[471] See CA 1963, s 23.

[472] See IFCMPA 2005, ss 59 and 60.

[473] See, eg, CLEA 2001, s 86. See Ch **11**.

[474] CA 1963, s 24(2), as substituted by CLEA 2001, s 88(1). This obligation is expressly subject to the qualification that it does not apply if 'a declaration as provided for under sub-s (1)(c) has been delivered to the Registrar' (CA 1963, s 24(2), as substituted by CLEA 2001, s 88(1)). See further below.

[475] CA 1963, ss 6(1)(a) and (b), as substituted by C(A)A 1983, s 3 and C(A)A 1982, s 4.

[476] CA 1963, s 381(1), as substituted by CLEA 2001, s 98.

[477] CA 1963, s 381(2), as substituted by CLEA 2001, s 98.

[478] CA 1963, s 318(3), as substituted by CLEA 2001, 98.

[479] CA 1963, s 381(2) and (3), as substituted by CLEA 2001, s 98, provide that the court 'may' make the order in question and that the order 'may' provide for costs to be borne by the person against whom the order is made.

[2.126] It is also an offence for a person who is not a public limited company[480] to carry on any trade, profession or business under a name which includes, as its last words, the words 'public limited company' or 'cuideachta phoibli theoranta' or abbreviations of those words.[481] The scope of this offence is narrower than that applicable to use of the words 'limited' or 'teoranta' as the use of any abbreviation, version or imitation of those words is prohibited by s 381, whereas only abbreviations of 'public limited company' or 'cuideachta phoibli theoranta' are captured by s 56.

Conversely, it is an offence for a public limited company to use a name 'which may reasonably be expected to give the impression that it is a company other than a public limited company', in circumstances where the fact that it is a public limited company is likely to be material to any person.[482] This offence is punishable on summary conviction by a fine of €1904.61, and a daily fine for continuing contraventions of €63.49, up to a total of €1,904.61.[483] If the person guilty of the offence is a company, every defaulting officer is also liable to conviction.[484]

(iii) Exemption from use of 'limited' or 'teoranta'

[2.127] Certain companies may be exempt from the requirement to use the words 'limited' or 'teoranta' at the end of their name. CA 1963, s 24 originally provided that the Minister for Enterprise, Trade and Employment had the power to grant exemptions from the use of 'Ltd,' 'limited', 'teoranta,' or other such designations, as part of a company's name upon applications made on behalf of the company. CLEA 2001, s 88 substituted this provision with a new s 24, which now provides that companies which fall within its scope are automatically exempt from the obligation to use 'limited' or 'teoranta' as part of their names. Section 88(2) expressly continues in force any licences that were granted by the Minister prior to the enactment of the CLEA 2001.[485]

The company to which s 24 applies is one that meets the following criteria:

- – its objects are the promotion of commerce, art, science, education, religion, charity or any other prescribed object;[486]

- – its memorandum and articles of association require all profits and income to be applied in the promotion of its objects;[487]

---

[480] This offence also applies if the person in question is an old public limited company. See C(A)A 1983, s 56(1).

[481] C(A)A 1983, s 56(1).

[482] C(A)A 1983, s 56(2).

[483] C(A)A 1983, s 56(5), as amended by CA 1990, s 240(7) as inserted by CLEA 2001, s 104(c).

[484] C(A)A 1983, s 56(5) as amended by CA 1990, s 240(7) as inserted by CLEA 2001, s 104(c).

[485] CLEA 2001, s 88(2) accordingly provides, 'Notwithstanding the repeal effected by sub-s (1), a licence granted by the Minister pursuant to s 24(1) or (2) of the Act of 1963 as in force immediately before the commencement of this section shall continue to have effect …'.

[486] CA 1963, s 24(1)(a), as substituted by CLEA 2001, s 88(1).

[487] CA 1963, s 24(1)(b)(i), as substituted by CLEA 2001, s 88(1).

  – its memorandum and articles of association prohibit the payment of dividends
     to its members;[488] and

  – its memorandum and articles of association require that, on its winding up, the
     assets which would otherwise be available to the members, be transferred to
     another company which meets the above criteria.[489]

[2.128] The objects to which the company is restricted are narrow and appear to be
strictly limited to those listed in s 24(1)(a). The previous version of s 24, as it existed
before the enactment of CLEA 2001, required the company to have the objects of the
promotion of 'commerce, art, science, religion, charity or any other useful object.'[490] In
addition, s 24(2) formerly provided that the Minister could licence a company to change
its name by removing 'limited' or 'teoranta' where a company fulfilled certain criteria,
such as having objects of the promotion of 'commerce, art, science, religion, charity or
any other useful object' or other objects which were 'conducive or incidental thereto'.[491]
Section 24 therefore allowed a company with 'any other useful object' or objects
'conducive or incidental' to the objects specified in that section, to apply for a licence
not to use the words 'limited' or 'teoranta' in its name. This is significantly broader than
the category of objects to which a company is now restricted, before it can avail of an
exemption from the use of the words 'limited' or 'teoranta' under s 24.

[2.129] The fact that the Minister had a licensing role under s 24 before the
commencement of s 88, ensured there was some level of discretion in the application of
that provision, and this may have justified a more broad formulation of the relevant
criteria. However, the present formulation of the objects which a company can have in
its memorandum of association, in order to avail of s 24, appears to be excessively
limited. In particular, it seems very restrictive not to permit a company to have objects
which are incidental and conducive to the other objects required by s 24. It may be of
interest to note that the model articles and memorandum of association which the
Revenue Commissioners supply to bodies which are seeking to register as companies
and apply for charitable status, include the possibility of listing of objects supplemental
and ancillary to the company's charitable objects.[492]

[2.130] If a company meets these criteria and wishes to avail of the exemption from the
use of 'limited' or 'teoranta' as part of its name, a director or secretary of the company
must deliver to the Registrar of Companies a statutory declaration to the effect that the

---

488 CA 1963, s 24(1)(b)(ii), as substituted by CLEA 2001, s 88(1).

489 CA 1963, s 24(1)(b)(iii), as substituted by CLEA 2001, s 88(1).

490 CA 1963, s 24(1) (as it existed before the enactment of CLEA 2001).

491 CA 1963, s 24(2)(a) (as it existed before the enactment of CLEA 2001).

492 See Revenue Commissioners, 'Standardised Memorandum and Articles of Association for a
     Company Limited by Guarantee and Seeking Tax Exemption as a Charity under the
     Provisions of s 207, Taxes Consolidation Act 1997' at www.revenue.ie.

company does comply, or will comply, with the criteria of s 24(1).[493] This declaration must be made on Form G5.[494]

A company which meets the requirements of s 24(1)(a) and (b), and which avails of the exemption from the requirement to use the words 'limited' or 'teoranta' as part of its name, is prohibited from subsequently altering its memorandum or articles of association so as to cease to comply with the requirements of s 24(1)(a) and (b).[495] This has the entirely sound consequence that a company which formulates its memorandum and articles of association so as to come within the letter of CA 1963, s 24(1), and avails of the benefit of that provision, is not entitled subsequently to remove those restrictions from its constitution, without also losing the benefit of not having 'limited' or 'teoranta' as part of its company name.

[2.131] There are certain additional safeguards to ensure that a company which has availed of s 24 does not abuse that procedure. Section 24(5) provides that the Registrar of Companies may direct a company which has availed of the exemption from the use of 'limited' or 'teoranta' as part of its name, to change its name to include 'limited' or 'teoranta', if it appears to the Registrar that the company has done one of the following:[496]

- carried on any business other than in promotion of commerce, art, science, education, religion, charity or any other prescribed object;[497]

- applied any of the company's profits or income other than in promotion of commerce, art, science, education, religion, charity or any other prescribed object;[498] or

- paid a dividend to any of its members.[499]

A direction by the Registrar to change the company's name to include 'limited' or 'teoranta' will be in writing and will specify the timeframe within which the change of name must be effected. The change of name must be made in accordance with CA 1963, s 23.[500] Where a company has been the subject of such a direction, it cannot be registered by a name which does not include 'limited' or 'teoranta' without the Registrar's approval.[501]

---

[493] CA 1963, s 24(1)(c), as substituted by CLEA 2001, s 88(1). If a company wishes to change its name to omit the use of 'limited' or 'teoranta' this statutory declaration must also be furnished. CA 1963, s 24(3), as substituted by CLEA 2001, s 88(1).

[494] This form may be downloaded at www.cro.ie.

[495] CA 1963, s 24(4), as substituted by CLEA 2001, s 88(1).

[496] CA 1963, s 24(5), as substituted by CLEA 2001, s 88(1).

[497] CA 1963, s 24(5)(a), as substituted by CLEA 2001, s 88(1), referring to the objects cited in CA 1963, s 24(1)(a), as substituted by CLEA 2001, s 88(1).

[498] CA 1963, s 24(5)(b), as substituted by CLEA 2001, s 88(1).

[499] CA 1963, s 24(5)(c), as substituted by CLEA 2001, s 88(1).

[500] CA 1963, s 24(5), as substituted by CLEA 2001, s 88(1).

[501] CA 1963, s 24(6), as substituted by CLEA 2001, s 88(1).

[2.132] It should be noted that the sanction envisaged by s 24(5) must involve the company acting in breach of its own articles and memorandum of association. This can be inferred from the fact that a company which satisfied the criteria of s 24(1) is prohibited by s 24(4) from altering its memorandum and articles of association and must therefore still have in its memorandum and articles of association the objects set out in s 24(1) and the restrictions on the application of its profits and income and the payment of dividends which are the pre-conditions to the right not to use 'limited' or 'teoranta' as part of the company name. Any actions by the company in breach of these restrictions and in contravention of the objects of the company are therefore not only subject to the possible sanction of a direction from the Registrar of Companies to change the company's name, but are also *ultra vires* the company itself.

[2.133] A further potential consequence of infringing the provisions of s 24 is that the person responsible may be guilty of an offence. The following violations of s 24 are offences which are amenable to summary prosecution by the Registrar of Companies:[502]

- the provision of incorrect, false or misleading information in a statutory declaration submitted to avail of the exemption from the use of 'limited' or 'teoranta' as part of the company name;[503]

- alteration of the memorandum or articles of association so as to cease to comply with the requirements of s 24(1);[504] or

- failure to comply with direction by Registrar to change company name to include 'limited' or 'teoranta'.[505]

[2.134] It is not possible for a public limited company to avail of the exemptions under s 24 and no such exemptions may be effective in respect of such a company.[506] If a licence has been issued to a company, or an exemption availed of, and the company subsequently re-registers as a public limited company, the licence or exemption will cease to have effect.[507]

Furthermore, the European Communities (Companies) Regulations 1973 which implemented the first EU Directive on Company Law, provide that a company that has an exemption from the obligation to use the word 'limited' or 'teoranta' in its name, must nonetheless show on its letters and order forms that it is a limited company.[508]

---

[502] CA 1963, ss 24(7) and (8), as substituted by CLEA 2001, s 88(1).

[503] CA 1963, s 24(7)(a), as substituted by CLEA 2001, s 88(1).

[504] CA 1963, s 24(7)(b), as substituted by CLEA 2001, s 88(1).

[505] CA 1963, s 24(7)(c), as substituted by CLEA 2001, s 88(1).

[506] C(A)A 1983, s 58(1). Note, while this section relates to the licences which the Minister could grant under CA 1963, s 24, since its substitution by CLEA 2001, s 88 the only logical way to read s 58 is as if it referred to the dispensations or exemptions now provided for in s 24, rather than the licences previously provided for.

[507] C(A)A 1983, s 58(2).

[508] See CRO, Information Leaflet Number 24, 'Exemption from use of 'limited' or 'teoranta' as part of company name' (June 2006).

(b) Prohibited names

[2.135] There are four general grounds on which the Registrar may refuse to register a company's name. First, the Registrar will not register a company by a name which the Registrar considers to be undesirable. Secondly, the Registrar will also refuse to register a name which is identical or excessively similar to a name of another existing company. Thirdly, the Registrar will not register a company name which suggests state sponsorship. Finally, there are certain words which are generally inadmissible in company names, pursuant to particular pieces of legislation.

(i) Undesirable names

[2.136] If the Registrar considers a name to be undesirable, no company may be registered under that name.[509] An appeal lies to court against a refusal by the Registrar to refuse to register a company name.[510]

(ii) Similarity to other company names

[2.137] The Registrar has advanced detailed guidance for the assistance of companies in the selection of names which are not excessively similar to the names of existing companies.[511] This guidance includes the following general rules:

- it is not sufficient to distinguish between company names by the use of accents or punctuation marks;

- certain words and their abbreviations are not sufficient to distinguish between company names (the examples given are 'the,' 'company', 'co', 'corporation', 'and', '&', 'service', 'services', 'limited');

- place names are not sufficient to distinguish between company names (the examples of Dublin, Ireland, West are given);

- the use of similar descriptions is not sufficient to distinguish between company names (the examples of press/printing, staff/employment agency are given);

- the use of weak or general qualifications are not sufficient to distinguish between company names (the examples given are the words 'holding', 'group', 'system', 'services', 'international');

- particular care should be taken with names which are distinctive, such as made-up words or words which do not appear in the dictionary;

---

[509] CA 1963, s 21, as amended by CLEA 2001, s 86. Note that companies which were registered by names that the Registrar considered to be undesirable, before the enactment of the CA 1963, are permitted to change their name with the approval of the Registrar and the members, which change will be effective from the date of registration of the company. See CA 1963, s 334, as amended by CLEA 2001, s 95.

[510] CA 1963, s 21, as amended by CLEA 2001, s 86.

[511] CRO, Information Leaflet No 1, 'Company Incorporation' (May 2006). Available at www.cro.ie.

    –   names which are phonetically or visually similar to the names of existing companies will be refused (this includes slight variation in spellings);

    –   a number is not of itself a sufficient means of distinguishing between company names, unless the companies are members of the same group;

    –   the use of a year in numbers (such as 2006) as a means of differentiating between companies of the same name, is prohibited.

This list does not claim to be exhaustive. It is interesting to note that the only carve-out for companies in the same group relates to the use of numbers. Therefore, according to this guidance, a company cannot establish a subsidiary with the same name as its own, save for the insertion of a word such as 'company' or a place name, but it may incorporate a subsidiary by its name, with the addition of a number. It is difficult to explain this distinction.

[2.138] If the Registrar, through inadvertence or otherwise, registers a name which it considers to be too similar to the name of an existing company, that existing company may object on the ground of such similarity within six months of the registration of that name. The Registrar may then direct the company in respect of which the name was most recently registered, to change its name. If such a direction is issued, the company must change its name within six weeks or such longer period as the Registrar may permit.[512] If a company defaults in complying with such a direction, it is liable to a fine of up to €1904.61.[513] Summary proceedings for this offence may be prosecuted by the Registrar of Companies.[514]

(iii) Legislative restrictions

[2.139] The word 'bank' or any variation thereof may not be used in a company name, unless approved by the Central Bank of Ireland. The CRO lists the following words as related examples of words which are prohibited: 'banc', 'banking', 'banker,' 'hollybank', 'sweetbank', 'canal bank', 'bancorp', and the surname 'Banks'.[515] This list seems excessive, particularly as these words are prohibited whether or not the company intends to carry on banking business. It is difficult to imagine a person being misled and assuming that a company by the name of 'Hollybank Nursery Ltd' was engaged in the business of banking.

[2.140] A further restriction is that words such as 'insurance', 're-insurance' and 'assurance' cannot be used in a company name unless the Irish Financial Services Regulatory Authority has granted permission for the use of such words. Thirdly, the words 'society', 'co-op' or 'co-operative' cannot be used unless permission has been granted by the Registrar of Friendly Societies. Fourthly, the words 'University' and

---

[512] CA 1963, s 23(2), as amended by CLEA 2001, s 87.

[513] CA 1963, s 23(2), as amended by CLEA 2001, s 87 and CA 1990, s 240(7) as inserted by CLEA 2001 s 104(c).

[514] CA 1963, s 23(7), as amended by CLEA 2001, s 87.

[515] See CRO, Information Leaflet No 1, 'Company Incorporation' (May 2006). Available at www.cro.ie.

'Institute of Technology' or 'Regional Technical College' cannot be used unless permission has been sought from and granted by the Department of Education. Fifthly, the use of the term 'credit union' is prohibited by the Credit Union Act 1997.

(iv) Miscellaneous restrictions

[2.141] If a company wishes to register under a name which includes the word 'holding', 'group' or other such words which suggest specific functions, the Registrar may require additional information to support that application.[516] The Registrar also prohibits the use of the word 'standard' in any company name.[517]

(c) Publication and disclosure

[2.142] Every company is obliged to display its company name in a number of particular locations and means. First, the company name as registered must be painted or affixed at all times on the outside of every office or place in which the company's business is carried on.[518] The name must be in easily legible letters and located in a conspicuous position.[519] If a company fails to paint or affix its name, the company and every defaulting officer is guilty of an offence and liable to a fine of up to €1904.61. If a company fails to keep its name painted or affixed, the company and every defaulting officer is guilty of an offence and liable to a fine of not more than €1904.61.[520]

Secondly, every registered company must have its name engraved in legible letters on its seal.[521] Thirdly, every company must place its name legibly on all of the following:

- its business letters, notices and official publications;

- bills of exchange, promissory notes, endorsements, cheques, money orders, orders for goods, which are signed by or on behalf of the company; and

- invoices, receipts and letters of credit of the company.[522]

[2.143] If a company fails to have its name engraved on a seal or to place its name on the requisite documents, the company is guilty of an offence and liable to a fine of up to €1904.61.[523] There are specific provisions governing the liability of the company's

---

[516] See CRO, Information Leaflet No 1, 'Company Incorporation' (May 2006).

[517] See CRO, Information Leaflet No 1, 'Company Incorporation' (May 2006).

[518] CA 1963, s 114(1)(a).

[519] CA 1963, s 114(1)(a).

[520] CA 1963, s 114(2), as amended by C(A)A 1982, s 15, and C(AA)A 2003, s 57 and CA 1990, s 240(7) as inserted by CLEA 2001 s104(c). Note, the blanket increase inserted by CLEA s104(c) in this instance increased the fines from €31.74 for the first offence and €158.72 for the continuing offence to €1,904.61.

[521] CA 1963, s 114(1)(b).

[522] CA 1963, s 114(1)(c).

[523] CA 1963, s 114(3), as amended by C(A)A 1982, s 15, and C(AA)A 2003, s 57 and CA 1990, s 240(7) as inserted by CLEA 2001, s 104(c). Note, the blanket increase inserted by CLEA 2001, s 104(c) in this instance increased the fine from €317.43 to €1,904.61.

officers, or other persons acting on their behalf, for such defaults. If is an offence for an officer of the company, or other person acting on his behalf, to do any of the following:

- use or authorise the use of a seal of the company which does not have the company name engraved thereon;[524]

- issue or authorise the issue of any business letter, notice, official publication, without the company's name legibly thereon;[525]

- sign or authorise to be signed on behalf of the company any bill of exchange, promissory note, endorsement, cheque, order for money or goods, which does not state the company's name in clearly legible form;[526] or

- issue or authorise the issue of any invoice, receipt or letter of credit of the company which does not state the company's name legibly.[527]

A person who is found guilty of any of these offences is liable to a fine of up to €1904.61.[528] He is moreover personally liable to the holder of any bill of exchange, promissory note, cheque, order for money or for goods, which does not state the name of the company legibly, for the amount of such document, unless the company discharges that liability.[529]

(d) Change of name

[2.144] A company may change its name but there are particular steps which must be taken before such a change can take effect.[530] First, the members of the company must authorise the change of the company's name by means of a special resolution, as this will constitute an amendment of the company's memorandum of association.[531] This should be communicated to the Registrar on Form G1Q.[532] Secondly, the name change must be approved in writing by the Registrar of Companies.[533] When these steps have been taken, the Registrar will enter the new name on the register and issue a certificate

---

[524] CA 1963, s 114(4)(a), as amended by C(A)A 1982, s 15 and C(AA)A 2003, s 57.

[525] CA 1963, s 114(4)(b), as amended by C(A)A 1982, s 15 and C(AA)A 2003, s 57.

[526] CA 1963, s 114(4)(b), as amended by C(A)A 1982, s 15 and C(AA)A 2003, s 57.

[527] CA 1963, s 114(4)(c), as amended by C(A)A 1982, s 15 and C(AA)A 2003, s 57.

[528] CA 1963, s 114(4)(c), as amended by C(A)A 1982, s 15 and C(AA)A 2003, s 57 and CA 1990, s 240(7) as inserted by CLEA 2001, s 104(c). Note, the blanket increase inserted by CLEA s104(c) in this instance increased the fine from €317.43.

[529] CA 1963, s 114(4)(c), as amended by C(A)A 1982, s 15 and C(AA)A 2003, s 57.

[530] Note that, according to CA 1963, s 23(4), 'A change of name by a company under this section shall not affect any rights or obligations of the company, or render defective any legal proceedings by or against the company, and any legal proceedings which might have been continued or commenced against it by its former name may be continued or commenced against it by its new name.'

[531] CA 1963, s 23(1), as amended by CLEA 2001, s 87.

[532] This form, which is available at www.cro.ie, may be filled in and filed online.

[533] CA 1963, s 23(1), as amended by CLEA 2001, s 87.

of incorporation amended to reflect the change of name.[534] If the company is wound up within 12 months of the change of name, the notices and advertisements of the winding up shall include both names.[535]

(e) Reservation of name

[2.145] Once the relevant sections are commenced, a person will be able to apply to the Registrar of Companies to reserve a particular company name for a company which he proposes to incorporate under that name.[536] On such an application, the Registrar may decide that the name in question should be reserved for that purpose[537] and will notify the applicant specifying the period for which the name will be reserved.[538] This period will not exceed 28 days, but the person seeking the reservation may apply for an extension for a specified period, before the expiry of the preceding period of reservation.[539] The Registrar may grant the extension, if he considers it appropriate to do so, and the extended period shall not exceed 28 days.[540] During the reservation period, no company may be incorporated by the reserved name, except on the application of the person who reserved the name.[541]

(f) Business name

[2.146] Companies are entitled to conduct business under a name other than their registered company name. If a company wishes to avail of this possibility, it must register that name on the register of business names.[542] Form RBN1B is the appropriate form for the registration by a body corporate of a business name under the Registration of Business Names Act 1963, s 4.[543]

---

[534] CA 1963, s 23(3). According to the CRO, Information Leaflet No 8 'Change of Company Name' (September 2005), what the Registrar will issue is a 'certificate of change of name'. This is not wholly consistent with the terms of s 23(3) which states that the Registrar shall 'issue a certificate of incorporation altered to meet the circumstances of the case.'

[535] CA 1963, s 23(6).

[536] IFCMPA 2005, s 59(3).

[537] IFCPMA 2005, s 59(4). The qualification to the power of the Registrar to reserve a name is that no names which he considers to be undesirable may be registered (IFCMPA 2005, s 59(6)).

[538] IFCPMA 2005, s 59(5).

[539] IFCMPA 2005, s 60(1).

[540] IFCMPA 2005, s 60(2).

[541] IFCMPA 2005, s 59(2).

[542] CA 1963, s 22(1).

[543] Note that, according to the Registration of Business Names Act 1963, s 14, the Minister for Enterprise Trade and Employment may refuse to register a business name which is undesirable.

K. Companies incorporated outside the State

(a) Companies that establish a place of business in the State

[2.147] In certain circumstances, companies which are incorporated outside Ireland may be under an obligation to make particular returns and filings with that Registrar of Companies. The company must establish a place of business in the State for these obligations to arise.[544] A 'place of business' is defined by s 360 as follows: "'place of business" includes a share transfer or share registration office'.[545] The carrying on of business in the State is therefore not sufficient to trigger the filing obligations considered below.

[2.148] Within one month of establishing a place of business in the State, a company must deliver to the Registrar for registration, on Form F1, the following documents:[546]

–   a certified copy of the constitution of the company, whether in the form of a charter, statute or articles and memorandum and a certified translation thereof, if not in English or Irish;[547]

–   a list of the company's directors, stipulating their full names, past and present; their address; their nationality (if not Irish); occupation; any directorships of companies incorporated in the State; if a body corporate, the company name and registered or principal office;[548]

–   particulars of the company secretary, stating the full name, past and present; usual residential address and if a body corporate, the company name and registered or principal office;[549]

---

[544] CA 1963, s 351.

[545] CA 1963, s 360.

[546] CA 1963, s 352(1).

[547] CA 1963, s 352(1)(a).

[548] CA 1963, s 352(1)(b) and (2)(a). CA 1963, s 352(2) states that CA 1963, s 195(12) applies for the purpose of the construction of references to present and former names and surnames. Section 195(12) does not address the interpretation of names. However, it must be presumed that the reference to s 195(12) was intended to refer to s 195(15) which provides as follows:

'For the purposes of this section – (a) in the case of a person usually known by a title different from his surname, the expression 'surname' means that title; (b) references to a 'former forename' or 'surname' do not include— (i) in the case of a person usually known by a title different from his surname, the name by which he was known previous to the adoption of or succession to the title; or (ii) in the case of any person, a former forename or surname where that name or surname was changed or disused before the person bearing the name attained the age of 18 years or has been changed or disused for a period of not less than 20 years; or (iii) in the case of a married woman, the name or surname by which she was known previous to the marriage.'

[549] CA 1963, s 352(1)(b) and (2)(b). If all the partners in a firm are joint secretaries of the company, the name and principal office of the firm may be stated instead of these particulars (CA 1963, s 352(3)).

- the names and address of one or more persons resident in the State who are authorised to accept service on behalf of the company;[550]

- the address of the company's principal place of business in the State.[551]

If there is any alteration in any of these documents or particulars, the company must make a return to the Registrar of Companies containing particulars of the alteration and the date of the change.[552] If the alteration relates to the company's memorandum or articles of association (or equivalent document), it must be notified on Form F2; if it relates to a change in the directors or secretaries of the company, it must be notified on Form F3; and if it relates to changes such as changes in the names or addresses of the persons resident in the State who may accept service on behalf of the State or in the address of the place of business in the State, the return must be made on Form F4.[553]

If a company which fell within the scope of these filing obligations, ceases to have a place of business in Ireland, it must forthwith notify the Registrar of Companies of this fact, and all such filing obligations cease from the date of that notice.[554]

[2.149] Any company incorporated in another jurisdiction which establishes a place of business in the State must ensure that its name, the country in which it is incorporated and the fact that the liability of its members is limited (if applicable)[555] are displayed on each of the following:

- any prospectus inviting subscriptions in the State;[556]

- every place in which the company carries on business in the State;[557] and

- all bills, letters, notices and other official publications of the company.[558]

If a company which has a place of business in Ireland fails to comply with these filing obligations, the company and every officer who 'knowingly and wilfully authorises or permits the default' shall be guilty of an offence and liable to a fine of not more than €1904.61.[559]

(b) Companies that establish a branch in the State

[2.150] A company which is incorporated outside Ireland but which establishes a branch in Ireland, is subject to certain filing obligations. These are governed by the

---

[550] CA 1963, s 352(1)(c).

[551] CA 1963, s 352(1)(c).

[552] CA 1963, s 353.

[553] These forms are available to download from www.cro.ie.

[554] CA 1963, s 357.

[555] CA 1963, s 355(d).

[556] CA 1963, s 355(a).

[557] CA 1963, s 355(b).

[558] CA 1963, s 355(c).

[559] CA 1963, s 358, as amended by C(A)A 1982, s 15 and CA 1990, s 240(7) as inserted by CLEA 2001, s 104(c).

European Communities (Branch Disclosure) Regulations 1993.[560] A 'branch' is not defined in the Regulations, but the term has been interpreted as involving a more active operation than that which is required to establish a 'place of business'.[561] The common view is that, 'although every "branch" will be regarded as an "established place of business", not every 'established place of business' will be a branch.'[562]

[2.151] There are two different categories of company to which these filing obligations apply. First, a limited company which is incorporated in another Member State and which establishes a branch in Ireland is bound by Pt II of the EC(BD)R 1993.[563] Second, a limited company which is incorporated outside the EU and which establishes a branch in Ireland, is bound by Pt III of the Regulations.[564]

[2.152] A limited liability company which is incorporated in another Member State must, within one month of the date on which it establishes a branch in Ireland, deliver to the Registrar, 'a certified copy of the memorandum and articles of association or the charter, statutes or other instrument constituting or defining the constitution of the company.'[565] At the same time, the company must notify the Registrar on Form F12 of the following:

- the company's name and legal form;

- the name of the company's branch, if different to the company's name;

- the company's certificate of incorporation;

- the address of the branch;

- the activities of the branch;

- the company's place and number of registration;

- a list and details of the persons who are authorised to represent the company, including their full name (and former names); date of birth; usual residential address; nationality; business occupation, if any; particulars of any other directorships; that person's powers in relation to the branch;

- the name and addresses of one or more persons who are resident in the State and authorised to accept service on behalf of the company;

- the name and address of every person who is resident in the State and authorised by the company to ensure compliance with the provisions of these Regulations, together with a consent signed by each such person to act in this capacity;

---

[560] These Regulations give effect to Council Directive 89/666/EC.

[561] See MacCann and Courtney, *Companies Acts 1963 to 2006* (Tottel Publishing, 2007) at p 1963.

[562] MacCann and Courtney, *Companies Acts 1963 to 2006* (Tottel Publishing, 2007) at p 1963.

[563] EC(BD)R 1993, reg 3.

[564] EC(BD)R 1993, reg 6.

[565] EC(BD)R 1993, reg 4(1).

– copies of the company's latest accounting documents prepared in relation to a financial year of the company to have been publicly disclosed in accordance with the law of the State in which it is incorporated.[566]

A limited liability company which establishes a branch in Ireland, and which is incorporated in another Member State, must also send certain notices and documents to the Registrar within 14 days of certain events occurring, such as an alteration of the company's articles or memorandum of association; an alteration of a change of the branch's address; the closure of the branch or the winding up of the company.[567]

A limited liability company which is incorporated outside the EU and which establishes a branch in the State, is bound by similar filing obligations.[568] The form prescribed for this purpose is Form F13.[569]

[2.153] The CRO requires the copy of the company's memorandum and articles of association (or, if no memorandum and articles exist, the instrument constituting or defining the constitution of the company) to be certified as a true copy in the country in which the company is incorporated by either the Registrar, a notary public, or by an officer of the company, on oath, before a person having authority to administer an oath. The CRO further requires that:

'For countries other than Great Britain or Northern Ireland, the memorandum and articles of association must be authenticated. For other countries which are not party to the E.U. Convention, Council of Europe Convention or the Hague Convention, when certified by the Registrar of Companies, his/her seal or signature must be authenticated by a government official and then stamped as seen at the Irish Embassy. When certified by a notary public an Irish Embassy official should authenticate the signature or seal. When certified by an officer of the company on oath, an Irish Embassy official should authenticate the status of the person administering the oath.'[570]

If the memorandum and articles of association (or equivalent documents) are in a language other than Irish or English, these documents must also be translated and, if the translation is conducted outside Ireland, the CRO requires that 'it should be certified to be a correct translation by an Irish diplomatic or consular officer or by any person whom the officer can certify is competent to translate it.' If the translation is conducted in Ireland, it should be certified by a solicitor or notary public.[571]

---

[566] EC(BD)R 1993, reg 4(2).

[567] EC(BD)R 1993, reg 4(3).

[568] See EC(BD)R 1993, reg 7(1) and (2). An example of a distinction between the obligations on companies that are incorporated outside the EU is that, rather than being obliged to notify the Registrar of the company's place of registration and registration number, reg 7(2)(f) requires the notification of '... the State in which the company is incorporated and, where the law of that State so provides, the place of registration of the company and the number with which it is registered ...'.

[569] Available at www.cro.ie.

[570] See www.cro.ie.

[571] See www.cro.ie.

[2.154] A company that establishes a branch in Ireland and delivers either Form F12 or Form F13 to the Registrar, together with the requisite documents, must publish a notice in the Companies Registration Office Gazette, within 21 days of such delivery.[572] Such companies are also bound to deliver certain accounting and related documents to the Registrar on an annual basis.[573] Finally, companies which establish a branch in Ireland and which are bound by the EC(BD)R 1993, should be mindful of the obligation to disclose certain information on the letters and forms that are used by the branch, such as the place of registration, and registration number, of the branch.[574]

[2.155] It is an offence for a person to contravene the provisions of EC(BD)R 1993, which is punishable by a maximum fine of €1,904l.61 on summary conviction, or, at the discretion of the court in the case of an individual, by a term of imprisonment not exceeding 12 months, or both.[575] A term of imprisonment shall not be imposed unless the court is of the opinion that the offence was committed willfully.[576] If an offence, which has been committed by or on behalf of a body, is proved to have been committed 'with the consent or connivance of or to be attributable to, or to have been facilitated by, any neglect' by an officer or employee of that body, that person shall also be guilty of an offence.[577]

L. Public limited companies

[2.156] Public limited companies generally bear the same duty to deliver documents to the Registrar of Companies that are imposed on private companies. However, there are important additional obligations on public limited companies. By way of example, C(A)A 1983, s 55[578] provides that public limited companies must publish in the Companies Registration Office Gazette notice of the delivery to the Registrar of Companies of the following:

  - a statutory declaration under s 6(2);[579]

---

[572] EC(BD)R 1993, reg 10, as amended by EC(C)R 2004, reg 5.
[573] See EC(BD)R 1993, regs 11, 12.
[574] EC(BD)R 1993, regs 5 and 8. Note that the obligations imposed on companies incorporated in the EU are slightly more onerous in this regard and require information regarding the company itself.
[575] EC(BD)R 1993, reg 19.
[576] EC(BD)R 1993, reg 19(3).
[577] EC(BD)R 1993, reg 19(4).
[578] C(A)A 1983 s 55 as amended by IRCMPA 2005, s 72.
[579] C(A)A 1983, s 55(1)(a). C(A)A 1983, s 6(2) provides that:

> 'The registrar shall issue a public limited company with a certificate under this section if, on an application made to him in the prescribed form by the company, he is satisfied that the nominal value of the company's allotted share capital is not less than the authorised minimum, and there is delivered to him a statutory declaration complying with sub-s (3).'

This statutory declaration is therefore one which confirms that the company's allotted share capital is at least at the level of the authorised minimum.

- a copy of a resolution which gives, varies, revokes or renews an authority to allot particular securities for the purposes of s 20;[580]

- a copy of a special resolution under s 24(1), (2) or (3);[581]

- any expert's valuation report on a non-cash consideration under s 31(2);[582]

- any expert's valuation report on a non-cash asset acquired from a subscriber under s 33(2);[583]

- any statement or notice under s 39(1), (3) or (4);[584]

- any return of allotments under CA 1963, s 58(1);[585]

- any notification of the redemption of preference shares under CA 1963, s 69(1);[586]

- a copy of a special resolution to reduce its share capital under CA 1963, s 72(2);[587]

- a copy of any resolution or agreement to which CA 1963, s 143, applies and which states or varies rights attached to any shares in the company or assigns a name or designation, or new name or designation to any class of shares in the company.[588]

These notices must be published within six weeks of their delivery to the Registrar.[589] If a company fails to comply with this obligation, the company and every defaulting

---

[580] C(A)A 1983, s 55(1)(b).

[581] C(A)A 1983, s 55(1)(c). This provision concerns resolutions for the allotment of shares by the directors.

[582] C(A)A 1983, s 55(1)(d). This valuation concerns consideration for shares of public limited companies, other than in the form of cash.

[583] C(A)A 1983, s 55(1)(e).

[584] C(A)A 1983, s 55(1)(f). C(A)A 1983, s 39(1) provides that:

> 'Where a company allots shares with rights which are not stated in its memorandum or articles or in any resolution or agreement to which s 143 of the Principal Act applies, the company shall, unless the shares are in all respects uniform with shares previously allotted, deliver to the registrar of companies within one month from allotting the shares a statement in the prescribed form containing particulars of those rights.'

A notification under C(A)A 1983, s 39(1) should be made on Form B11/80. C(A)A 1983, s 39(3) and (4) deal with the obligation to notify the Registrar of the variation of rights attached to shares and the assignment of designations to classes of shares. Notifications of changes of the names of classes of shares under C(A)A 1983, s 39(4) should be notified to the CRO on Form B13/82.

[585] C(A)A 1983, s 55(1)(g). C(A)A 1983 s 58 provides that no licence under s 24, to dispense with the use of the word 'limited', can have effect in respect of a public limited company.

[586] C(A)A 1983, s 55(1)(h). Such a redemption should be notified to the Registrar on Form B 7/28.

[587] C(A)A 1983, s 55(1)(i).

[588] C(A)A 1983, s 55(1)(j).

[589] C(A)A 1983, s 55(2).

officer is guilty of an offence and liable to a fine of up to €1904.61.[590] The Registrar of Companies may bring and prosecute such proceedings.[591]

M. Re-registration of companies

[2.157] There are mechanisms in the Companies Acts for the conversion of a company from one form to another, such as for the conversion of a private company to a public limited company.[592] There are detailed rules in the C(A)A 1983 regarding such conversions. These rules include obligations to notify the Registrar of Companies, or file with the Registrar, certain documents and returns. These filing obligations are addressed in this section.

(a) Re-registration of private company as public limited company

[2.158] A private company may re-register as a public limited company. The company must pass a special resolution authorising such re-registration[593] and must file Form D1/71 with the Registrar of Companies.[594] Certain conditions must also be satisfied. These conditions may be summarised as follows:

– where shares are allotted by the company between the balance sheet date and the passing of the special resolution, as fully or partly paid up, other than in cash, the consideration must have been valued and a report of its value must have been made to the company;[595]

– the nominal value of the company's allotted share capital must be not less than the authorised minimum;[596]

– each of the company's allotted shares must be paid up at least as to one-quarter of the nominal value and the premium on it;[597]

---

[590] C(A)A 1983, s 55(3), as amended by CA 1990, s 240(7) as inserted by CLEA 2001 s104(c).

[591] C(A)A 1983, s 55(4).

[592] There are certain forms of company conversions which are considered to be beyond the scope of this publication. By way of example, C(A)A 1983, ss 12, 13 and 16, which deal with the re-registration of 'old public companies' and C(A)A 1983, ss 11, 52 and 53, which deal with the conversion of limited companies to unlimited companies are not considered here.

[593] C(A)A 1983, s 9(1)(a). According to C(A)A 1983, s 9(2), the special resolution must alter the memorandum of association to state that the company is a public limited company and to ensure that the memorandum complies with the requirements of a public limited company and it must alter the articles of association as appropriate.

[594] C(A)A 1983, s 9(1)(b). This form is available to download at www.cro.ie.

[595] C(A)A 1983, s 9(5).

[596] C(A)A 1983, s 10(1)(a).

[597] C(A)A 1983, s 10(1)(b).

– where any share in the company or premium payable on it has been fully or partly paid up by an undertaking to do work or perform services for the company or another, the undertaking must have been performed or otherwise discharged;[598]

– where shares have been allotted as fully or partly paid up to their nominal value or any premium payable other than by way of cash and the consideration includes an undertaking, that undertaking must have been performed or discharged or there must be a contract with the company for the performance of that undertaking within five years.[599]

[2.159] In addition, Form D1/71 must be accompanied by the following documents:

– a copy of the amended articles and memorandum of association;[600]

– a written statement by the auditors that the balance sheet shows that the company's net assets are not less than the aggregate of its called-up share capital and undistributable reserves;[601]

– a copy of the relevant balance sheet, with a copy of an unqualified auditor's report;[602]

– if the company has allotted shares between the previous balance sheet date and the passing of the resolution, which are paid up other than for cash, a copy of the report regarding the value of that consideration that was made to the company;[603]

– a statutory declaration by a director or secretary of the company that the requisite special resolution has been passed; that the conditions specified in s 9(1)(c) have been satisfied;[604] and that there has been no change in the financial position of the company since the last balance sheet date, that has resulted in the amount of the company's net assets becoming less than the aggregate of its called-up share capital and undistributable reserves.[605] This declaration should be made on CRO Form D1/72.

---

[598] C(A)A 1983, s 10(1)(c).

[599] C(A)A 1983, s 10(1)(d).

[600] C(A)A 1983, s 9(3)(a).

[601] C(A)A 1983, s 9(3)(b).

[602] C(A)A 1983, s 9(3)(c).

[603] C(A)A 1983, s 9(3)(d) and (5)(b).

[604] C(A)A 1983, s 9(1)(c) refers to the conditions specified in s 9(5)(a) and (b) and s 10(1)(a) to (d).

[605] C(A)A 1983, s 9(3)(e).

The statutory declaration may, but not must, be accepted by the Registrar as sufficient evidence that the requisite conditions have been satisfied and special resolution passed.[606]

[2.160] If the Registrar of Companies is satisfied that the company may be re-registered as a public limited company he must retain the application and other documents and issue the company with a certificate of incorporation stating that the company is a public limited company.[607] Upon the issue of such a certificate, the company becomes a public limited company and the alterations of the memorandum and articles of association take effect accordingly.[608] The certificate of incorporation is conclusive evidence that the requirements of the C(A)A 1983 regarding re-registration have been complied with and that the company is a public limited company.[609]

[2.161] A company which ceases to a private company must also deliver a statement in lieu of prospectus to the Registrar of Companies.[610] This statement must be made on Form B32/55.[611] If there is a default in this regard, the company and every defaulting officer is guilty of an offence and liable on summary conviction to a maximum fine of €1904.61.[612] If there is any untrue statement in the statement in lieu of prospectus,[613] any person who authorised the delivery of the statement is guilty of an offence and liable on conviction on indictment, to imprisonment for up to five years or a maximum fine of €3,174.35, or both; and on summary conviction, is liable to six months' imprisonment and a maximum fine of €1904.61, or both.[614] If the person who authorised the statement can prove that the untrue statement was immaterial or that he had reasonable grounds to

---

[606] C(A)A 1983, s 9(4).

[607] C(A)A 1983, s 9(6). Note that, according to C(A)A 1983, s 9(7):

> 'The registrar shall not issue a certificate of incorporation under sub-s (6) if it appears to him that the court has made an order confirming a reduction of the company's capital which has the effect of bringing the nominal value of the company's allotted share capital below the authorised minimum.'

[608] C(A)A 1983, s 9(8).

[609] C(A)A 1983, s 9(9).

[610] CA 1963, s 35(3), as substituted by C(A)A 1983, s 3.

[611] This form may be downloaded from www.cro.ie.

[612] CA 1963, s 35(6), as substituted by C(A)A 1983, s 3 and amended by CA 1990, s 240(7) as inserted by CLEA 2001, s 104(c).

[613] CA 1963, s 35(8), as substituted by C(A)A 1983, s 3, provides that:

> '(a) a statement included in a statement in lieu of prospectus shall be deemed to be untrue if it is misleading in the form and context in which it is included, and (b) a statement shall be deemed to be included in a statement in lieu of prospectus if it is contained therein or in any report or memorandum appearing on the face thereof, or by reference incorporated therein.'

[614] CA 1963, s 35(7), as substituted by C(A)A 1983, s 3 and amended by CA 1990, s 240(7) and (8) as inserted by CLEA 2001 s104(c).

believe, and did believe, that the untrue statement was true, he will not be guilty of this offence.[615]

(b) Re-registration of public limited company as private company

[2.162] A public limited company may be re-registered as a private company if the following conditions are met:

– a special resolution is passed altering the memorandum and articles of association as necessary;[616]

– Form D4/76, signed by a director or secretary, is delivered to the Registrar of Companies, together with a copy of the articles and memorandum of association;[617]

– a period of 28 days, within which an application could be made for the cancellation of the special resolution, has expired without any such application being made;[618]

– if an application for the cancellation of the special resolution has been made, this application has been withdrawn or rejected and a copy of the order has been delivered to the Registrar of Companies.[619]

If the Registrar of Companies is satisfied that the public limited company may be re-registered, he shall retain the application and accompanying documents[620] and issue the company with a certificate of incorporation appropriate to a private company.[621] Upon the issue of such a certificate, the company becomes a private company and the alterations of the memorandum and articles of association take effect accordingly.[622] The certificate of incorporation is conclusive evidence that the requirements of the C(A)A 1983 regarding re-registration have been complied with and that the company is a private company.[623]

---

[615] CA 1963, s 35(7), as substituted by C(A)A 1983, s 3.

[616] C(A)A 1983, s 14(1)(a) and (2). An application may be made by the holders of not less than five per cent in nominal value of the company's issued share capital; or if the company is not limited by shares, by five per cent of the company's members; or 50 of the company's members, to cancel such a resolution within 28 days. The company must notify the Registrar of any such application and deliver a copy of any order made to the Registrar, within 15 days of such order. The company and every defaulting officer is guilty of an offence if there is a default in this regard (C(A)A 1983, s 15). The appropriate form for notification of such an application is Form D13/65.

[617] C(A)A 1983, s 14(1)(b). This form may be downloaded from www.cro.ie.

[618] C(A)A 1983, s 14(1)(c).

[619] C(A)A 1983, 14(1)(d).

[620] C(A)A 1983, s 14(3)(a).

[621] C(A)A 1983, s 14(3)(b).

[622] C(A)A 1983, s 14(4).

[623] C(A)A 1983, s 14(5).

N. Form of documents

[2.163] Documents which are presented to the Registrar of Companies must fulfil certain requirements, in terms of their form and layout. CA 1990, s 248 sets out certain specific requirements including the requirement that the documents delivered to the Registrar must be legible[624] and that they must state the registered number of the company in a prominent position.[625] Section 248 also requires that any requirements prescribed regarding the form and content of documents to be delivered to the Registrar must be complied with[626] and s 248(6) specifies that regulations may be introduced to provide for the form and content of different types of documents. In this regard, the Companies Act 1990 (Form and Content of Documents Delivered to Registrar) Regulations 2002 stipulate detailed requirements that must be met by documents delivered to the Registrar.

(a) General requirements

[2.164] The following is a non-exhaustive list of the general requirements applicable to documents which are delivered to the Registrar:[627]

- the documents must be legible and suitable for scanning and electronic copying;[628]
- the documents must be in A4 size[629] and on white paper of matt finish weighing not less than 80 grams/mm2;[630]
- the print must be black,[631] not less than 1.8 mm in height,[632] and suitable for electronic scanning;[633]
- the margin around the printed matter must be not less than 1cm;[634]
- the document must contain no colour other than black print on white paper;[635]

---

[624] CA 1990, s 248(1).

[625] CA 1990, s 248(2)(a).

[626] CA 1990, s 248(2)(b).

[627] The requirements that documents delivered to the Registrar must satisfy are considered in detail in an information leaflet issued by the CRO in September 2002 entitled, 'Grounds for Returning Documents to Presenters' (Information Leaflet No 21). For a complete list of the rules applicable to documents presented to the CRO, this document is a useful point of reference.

[628] CA 1990, s 248(1); Companies Act 1990 (Form and Content of Documents Delivered to Registrar) Regulations 2002 (SI 39/2002), reg 4.

[629] SI 39/2002, reg 5(a).

[630] SI 39/2002, reg 5(b).

[631] SI 39/2002, reg 6(a).

[632] SI 39/2002, reg 6(b).

[633] SI 39/2002, reg 6(c).

[634] SI 39/2002, reg 7.

[635] SI 39/2002, reg 8.

- if the original document contains coloured print or its pages consist of glossy paper, a copy of the document or a printer's proof which complies with the Regulations must be delivered;[636]

- pages must be kept together by means of a clip or a staple at top left hand corner and must not be stitched together or bear adhesive tape;[637]

- documents must not consist of or contain carbon copies or photocopies or printed matter from dot matrix computer printers;[638]

- there must be no blank spaces in the documents where information should have been inserted and the words 'not applicable', 'nil' or 'none' must be inserted if appropriate;[639]

- any amendments to documents must be initialled and dated by at least one of the signatories to the document (or if there are no signatories by at least one person who authorised its production);[640]

- if the CRO returns a document for amendment, amendments must be initialled and dated or a new document prepared, as requested by the CRO;[641]

- the company name and its registered office address must be displayed in a prominent position on the first page of the document;[642]

- any individual named in a document delivered must be named by his full first name and surname and, if an address is required, the residential address must be stated;[643]

- if a document must be signed, an original handwritten signature is necessary[644] and this signature must be dated;[645]

- a document shall not refer to a person who is an officer, liquidator, receiver, or examiner, of a company or a person referred to in s 352(1)(c) unless the

---

[636] SI 39/2002, reg 9.

[637] SI 39/2002, reg 10.

[638] SI 39/2002, reg 11.

[639] SI 39/2002, reg 12.

[640] SI 39/2002, reg 13(1).

[641] SI 39/2002, reg 13(2). Note that if the document which requires amendment is a statutory declaration, the person who made the declaration must make a fresh statutory declaration (SI 39/2002, reg 13(3)).

[642] SI 39/2002, reg 14(1). The name and address must correspond to information previously furnished to the CRO (SI 39/2002, reg 14(2)) and the registered address may not be a post office box number (SI 39/2002, reg 14(4)).

[643] SI 39/2002, reg 15(1) and (2).

[644] SI 39/2002, reg 15(3)(a).

[645] SI 39/2002, reg 15(3)(b).

Registrar has been notified, as required under the Acts, of the name and appointment of the person;[646]

– a resolution that is delivered shall be signed either by a director or secretary of the company, whose appointment has been notified to the Registrar;[647] and

– the document must be accompanied by the requisite fee.[648]

(b) Electronic filing agent

[2.165] The CRO has put in place systems for the electronic filing of certain documents, such as the annual return.[649] By virtue of the Companies (Forms) Order 2002, a company's director or secretary can complete a Form J2 to obtain a personal identification number and identity code for the purpose of electronic signing of CRO documents.[650] This enables that person to affix an electronic signature to documents to be delivered to the CRO pursuant to CA 1963–2006 and the Electronic Commerce Act 2000, s 12.

The Investment Funds, Companies and Miscellaneous Provisions Act 2005 further enables a company to appoint a so-called 'electronic filing agent'.[651] Section 57 provides that a company may appoint such an agent to sign electronically documents that are required or authorised to be delivered to the Registrar of Companies[652] and deliver such documents to the Registrar by electronic means.[653] Such an act shall be valid as if done by the company, subject to the following conditions:[654]

– the company's authorisation of the agent must be notified to the Registrar before the first instance of electronic filing by the agent;[655] and

---

[646] SI 39/2002, reg 21.

[647] SI 39/2002, reg 23(1).

[648] CA 1963, s 369 and Companies (Fees Order) 2001 (SI 477/2001).

[649] See CRO, Annual Report 2006, at p 6 for details of the rate of e-filing.

[650] This form is available to download on www.cro.ie.

[651] It should be noted that the appointment of a electronic filing agent does not render that person a servant or officer of the company for the purpose of CA 1990, s 187(2)(a), which disqualifies servants or officers from appointment as auditors. Section 57(6) accordingly provides, 'An electronic filing agent shall not, by virtue of his or her authorisation under this section to act as such, be regarded as an officer or servant of the company concerned for the purposes of s 187(2)(a) of the Act of 1990.' A company's auditor can therefore also act as its electronic filing agent.

[652] IFCMPA 2005, s 57(2)(a).

[653] IFCMPA 2005, s 57(2)(b).

[654] IFCMPA 2005, s 57(3) and (4).

[655] This is done on CRO Form B77.

– the act must comply with any requirements imposed by the Registrar of Companies similar to those stipulated by of the Electronic Commerce Act 2000, ss 12(2)(b)[656] and 13(2)(a)[657].

[2.166] If a person wishes to become an electronic filing agent, he must file a Form J1A with the CRO, which is an application for a digital certificate and which must name one or two persons within the agent's organisation who will verify the agent's signature using CRO identification numbers and PINs.[658] The company must then file a Form B77 notifying the CRO of the authorisation of the electronic filing agent.[659]

It should be noted that a company can only have one electronic filing agent at a given time, and must revoke the authority of an existing agent before a new one may be appointed.[660] A company is entitled to revoke the authorisation of an electronic filing agent,[661] but such a revocation only becomes valid when it is notified to the CRO.[662]

---

[656] Electronic Commerce Act 2000, s 12(2)(a) provides: 'where the information is required or permitted to be given to a public body or to a person acting on behalf of a public body and the public body consents to the giving of the information in electronic form, whether as an electronic communication or otherwise, but requires—(i) the information to be given in accordance with particular information technology and procedural requirements, or (ii) that a particular action be taken by way of verifying the receipt of the information, if the public body's requirements have been met and those requirements have been made public and are objective, transparent, proportionate and non-discriminatory.'

[657] Electronic Commerce Act 2000, s 13(2)(a) provides that an electronic signature may be used only if, '… the signature is required or permitted to be given to a public body or to a person acting on behalf of a public body and the public body consents to the use of an electronic signature but requires that it be in accordance with particular information technology and procedural requirements (including that it be an advanced electronic signature, that it be based on a qualified certificate, that it be issued by an accredited certification service provider or that it be created by a secure signature creation device)— if the public body's requirements have been met and those requirements have been made public and are objective, transparent, proportionate and non-discriminatory …'.

[658] See CRO, 'Electronic Filing Agents' (Information Leaflet No 15, December 2005). Available at www.cro.ie.

[659] See also Form J3 which permits directors or secretaries of a company who have CRO identification numbers and PINs, to appoint electronic filing agents, including the appointment of firms as such agents. These forms are available to download on www.cro.ie. B77 may be filed online.

[660] See CRO, 'Electronic Filing Agents' (Information Leaflet No 15, December 2005). Available at www.cro.ie.

[661] IFCMPA 2005, s 58(1). Note that, according to IFCMPA 2005, s 58(4), 'If a revocation … of an authorisation under s 57 constitutes a breach of contract or otherwise gives rise to a liability being incurred— (a) the fact that it constitutes such a breach or otherwise gives rise to a liability being incurred does not affect the validity of the revocation for the purposes of s 57, and (b) the fact of the revocation being so valid does not remove or otherwise affect any cause of action in respect of that breach or the incurring of that liability.' The power to revoke an authorisation is therefore distinct and separate from any liability which may arise as a result of such revocation.

[662] IFCMPA 2005, s 58(2) and (3).

Unless and until the revocation is notified to the CRO on Form B77, the authorisation is deemed to be in force.[663]

It should also be noted that the control of any documents filed by an electronic filing agent remains the joint responsibility of the agent and the company.[664] Finally, it should be noted that the provision of false information to an electronic filing agent is an offence. CA 1990, s 242(1A) provides that:

> A person who knowingly or recklessly furnishes false information to an electronic filing agent that is subsequently transmitted in a return made, on the person's behalf, to the registrar of companies shall be guilty of an offence.[665]

(c) Delivery of defective documents

[2.167] If a document which is delivered to the Registrar does not satisfy the requirements applicable to such document, whether imposed by CA 1990, s 248 or s 249; by any other provision of the Companies Acts; or by any other enactment related to the completion and delivery of documents to the Registrar,[666] the person who delivered the document ('the presenter') may be given an opportunity to rectify this defect.[667]

CA 1990, s 249A provides that, where such a defect is detected by the Registrar, he may serve on the presenter (or one of them, if there are several), a notice stipulating the defect in the document.[668] Within 14 days of service of such a notice, the presenter should deliver a replacement document, which rectifies the defect identified by the Registrar.[669] Unless the Registrar receives such a replacement document which is not rejected for failure to comply with any of the applicable requirements, the document which was originally received 'shall be deemed not to have been delivered to him.'[670]

[2.168] Many of the requirements in relation to the filing of documents with the Registrar of Companies are accompanied by penalties for non-compliance. In some instances, the failure to deliver, or late delivery of documents, gives rise to penalties for continued contraventions or higher registration fee for late delivery of documents. Where such penalties apply, the period between the delivery of the original (defective) document and the expiry of the period of 14 days after the service of the defect notice,

---

[663] IFCMPA 2005, s 58(3). This form (which is available at www.cro.ie,) may be filed online.

[664] IFCMPA 2005, s 57(5).

[665] CA 1990, s 242(1a), as inserted by IFCMPA 2005, s 71(b).

[666] CA 1990, s 249A(1), as inserted by CLEA 2001, s 107.

[667] Note that, according to CA 1990, s 249A(4), as inserted by CLEA 2001, s 107: 'Nothing in this section shall have the effect of making valid any matter which a provision of the Companies Acts or of any other enactment provides is to be void or of no effect in circumstances where a document in relation to it is not delivered to the registrar within the period specified for the document's delivery to him.'

[668] CA 1990, s 249A(1), as inserted by CLEA 2001, s 107.

[669] CA 1990, s 249(2)(a), as inserted by CLEA 2001, s 107.

[670] CA 1990, s 249A(2), as inserted by CLEA 2001, s 107.

shall not be reckoned.[671] This exemption only applies if a replacement document is delivered within 14 days of the defect notice.[672] The effect of this exemption is that, if a document is filed within the stipulated deadline, but is subsequently the subject of a defect notice, the penalties of daily fines, or increased registration fees, if otherwise applicable, shall not apply, until the expiry of 14 days from the service of the notice, provided a replacement document is filed within that period.

[2.169] While there is an exemption from penalties for continuing contraventions and increased registration fees, there is no general exemption from penalties applicable to non-compliance with filing requirements. Therefore, the fact that a notice of defect has been served does not appear to afford any protection against the imposition of general penalties for late filing, or non filing, of requisite documents. However, as against this, it is not until the expiry of the 14 day period that the original document is deemed not to have been delivered. It therefore appears that the original document will be deemed to have been duly delivered, for the purpose of the imposition of penalties for non-delivery or late delivery, until the expiry of 14 days from the service of a defect notice.

[2.170] One point to note about the notification and rectification of defective documents, is that the Registrar is not obliged to notify the presenter of such defects. Section 249A states that the Registrar 'may' serve such a notice. This leaves open the possibility that the Registrar may simply reject a document for non-compliance with requirements of the Companies Acts, for example, without furnishing the presenter with notice of the defect or an opportunity to present a replacement document.

---

[671] CA 1990, s 249A(3), as inserted by CLEA 2001, s 107.

[672] CA 1990, s 249A(3), as inserted by CLEA 2001, s 107.

Chapter 3

COMPANIES' OBLIGATIONS: MAINTENANCE OF REGISTERS

A. Introduction

[3.001] Every company must keep certain registers, such as a register of members, of directors and secretaries, of interests held by directors and secretaries and of debenture holders. These registers must contain certain specific information and must be open to inspection as required by the Companies Acts 1963–2006. Similar obligations for the purpose of transparency apply to directors' service contracts. This chapter considers the scope and content of these statutory obligations.

B. Form of registers

[3.002] The Companies Acts contain a general requirement that 'any register, index, minute book or book of account required by this Act to be kept by a company or by the registrar of companies may be kept either by making entries in bound books or by recording the matters in question in any other manner'.[1] If any such documents are kept other than in a bound book, the Companies Acts require that 'adequate precautions shall be taken for guarding against falsification and facilitating its discovery'.[2] If there is a default in relation to this requirement, such as if a register is kept in a loose-leaf form, with no secure means of protecting it against interference, the company and every officer in default is guilty of an offence and liable to fine.[3]

[3.003] According to C(A)A 1977, s 4(1), the power of a company to keep a register other than in bound books, includes the power to keep such a register, 'by recording the matters in question otherwise than in a legible form so long as the recording is capable of being reproduced in a legible form.'[4] This permits companies to keep the company registers electronically.

---

[1]   CA 1963, s 378(1).

[2]   CA 1963, s 378(2).

[3]   CA 1963, s 378(2) as amended by C(AA)A 2003, Sch 2 and CA 1990, s240(7) as inserted by CLEA 2001, s 104(c).

[4]   C(A)A 1977, s 4(1).

C. Register of members

(a) Contents

[3.004] Every company is required to keep a register of its members.[5] This register must include the name and address of each member.[6] The register of members should also state the date on which each person was entered on the register as a member[7] and the date on which any person ceased to be a member of the company, if applicable.[8]

[3.005] In the case of companies limited by shares, the register must contain a statement of the shares held, stating the amount paid or agreed to be considered as paid, on each member's shares.[9] If a company issues share warrants, the names of the members registered as holding the shares included in such warrants should be removed from the register of members.[10] The register should instead contain notice of the fact of the issue of the warrant, the shares included in the warrant and the date of its issue.[11] The bearer of the share warrant may be deemed to be a member of the company, if, and to the extent that the articles of the company so provide.[12] Upon surrendering the share warrant for cancellation, the bearer shall be entitled to have his name restored to the register of members.[13] The date of surrender of the share warrant should be entered on the register.[14]

[3.006] The information that must be included on the register of members of a company not having a share capital was considered in *Re Performing Rights Society Ltd*.[15] The issue in that case was whether the register of members of a company limited by guarantee not having a share capital should disclose the different classes of membership. The relevant legislative provision was s 110 of the English Companies Act 1948, which

---

5   CA 1963, s 116(1). The terms of s 116 are substantially reproduced in the General Scheme of the Companies Consolidation and Reform Bill 2007, Pt A4, Head 36. Available at www.clrg.org.

6   CA 1963, s 116(1)(a), as amended by C(A)A 1982, s 20.

7   CA 1963, s 116(1)(b).

8   CA 1963, s 116(1)(c).

9   CA 1963, s 116(1)(a), as amended by C(A)A 1982, s 20. Note that, if the company has converted its shares into stock and notified to Registrar of Companies of this conversion, the register should show the amount of stock held by each members and the other particulars required by CA 1963, s 116(1)(a) (CA 1963, s 116(4)).

10   CA 1963, s 118(1)(a), (b) and (c).

11   CA 1963, s 118(1).

12   CA 1963, s 118(5).

13   CA 1963, s 118(2). This entitlement is subject to the articles of the company and the company is 'responsible for any loss incurred by any person by reason of the company entering in the register the name of a bearer of a share warrant in respect of the shares therein specified without the warrant being surrendered and cancelled' (CA 1963, s 118(3)).

14   CA 1963, s 118(4).

15   *Re Performing Rights Society Ltd* [1978] 2 All 712; [1978] 1 WLR 1197.

is substantially the same as CA 1963, s 116. Buckley LJ analysed this provision as follows:

> 'In my judgment, it turns entirely upon the terms of s 110, from which it is clear that a company having a share capital is required to do things in relation to its register of members which are not required in the case of a company which has not a share capital. Upon the terms of the section, a company which has no share capital is only required to enter in its register particulars of the names and addresses of the members, the date at which each person was entered in the register as a member and the date at which any person ceased to be a member.'[16]

Applying a literal interpretation of the terms of s 110, the Court noted:

> 'It may, I think, be very inconvenient in the case of a company which has no share capital but has its membership divided into different classes that that fact should not appear in the register and that the composition of the various classes should not be ascertainable from the register. I cannot find in this subsection, in the way in which it is framed at the present time, any requirement on a company which has not a share capital to disclose more than the matters to which I have already referred, the names and addresses of the members, the date when they became members and the date when any person ceased to be a member.'[17]

If this case was followed in Ireland, companies without share capital would only have to disclose the matters which fall strictly within the scope of s 116, namely the name and address of members, the date of entry on the register and the date of cessation of membership.

[3.007] One matter that should be neither recorded on the register of members, nor notified to the Registrar of Companies, is the existence of any trust regarding the ownership of shares.[18] Section 123 provides: 'No notice of any trust, express, implied or constructive, shall be entered on the register or be receivable by the registrar.'[19]

[3.008] The manner in which interests in shares should be recorded on the register of members has been considered in a number of cases. In *Re TH Saunders & Co Ltd*,[20] for example, the executors of the estate of a deceased shareholder sought to have the register rectified by the insertion of their names as members of the company. The directors of the company refused to register the interests of the executors in anything other than a representative capacity. The governing legislation in that case, the Companies Act 1862, contained in s 30 a provision almost identical to CA 1963, s 123.[21] Warrington J noted that:

> 'Of course the company is entitled to preserve in its books a record of the mode in which the shares come to be transmitted. The question is, Is it entitled to put it on the register, that is to say – is it entitled to qualify in the register the insertion of

---

16 *Re Performing Rights Society Ltd* [1978] 1 WLR 1197 at 1203.

17 *Re Performing Rights Society Ltd* [1978] 1 WLR 1197 at 1204.

18 CA 1963, s 123.

19 CA 1963, s 123.

20 *Re TH Saunders & Co Ltd* [1908] 1 Ch 415.

21 Companies Act 1862, s 30 provided, 'No notice of any trust, expressed, implied, or constructive, shall be entered on the register, or be receivable by the registrar, in the case of companies under this Act and registered in England or Ireland.'

the name of the executors as members, and qualify it in such a way that the qualification will also appear on the certificate of the shares? In my opinion it is not.'[22]

The Court considered the terms of s 30 and concluded that:

'Section 30 of that Act in terms prevents the placing on the register of members any statement which would qualify the entry of their names so as to shew that they do not hold as absolute owners. They are entitled to have their names put on the register, in my opinion, without qualification if they so insist.'[23]

This decision confirms that the register of members should only record the names of members, or persons entitled to be recorded as members, without qualification.

(b) Date of registration

[3.009] The name and address of a new member, and the shares held by such member, should be entered on the register of members within 28 days after 'the conclusion of the agreement with the company to become a member'.[24] If the member is a subscriber to the memorandum of association of the company, their details should be recorded in the register of members within 28 days of the registration of the company.[25]

The combined effect of s 116(1)(b) and (2) is that the date of the entry of the member's name on the register, must be recorded on the register within 28 days of the member attaining that status. There is no requirement that the date on which a person became a member must be recorded. This can be contrasted with s 116(1)(c) and (3). The register of members must, according to s 116(3), record the 'date at which any person ceased to be a member'. Section 116(3) requires that this entry must be made within 28 days of the date on which the person ceased to be a member of the company, or within 28 days of the production to the company of satisfactory evidence of the 'occurrence of an event whereby he ceased to be a member'.[26]

The effect of these provisions is that the date on which a person actually ceased to be a member of the company, rather than the date on which the name was removed from the register, should be recorded. To ensure strict compliance with the obligation to keep a register of members, companies should record the date of entry of a member's name on the register, rather than the date on which the person became a member of the company, and should record the actual date of cessation of membership, rather than the date of entering such cessation on the register.

(c) Index

[3.010] Every company with 50 or more members must also keep an index of the names of the members,[27] which shall enable the account of each member to be readily found in

---

[22] *Re TH Saunders & Co Ltd* [1908] 1 Ch 415 at 422.

[23] *Re TH Saunders & Co Ltd* [1908] 1 Ch 415 at 423.

[24] CA 1963, s 116(2).

[25] CA 1963, s 116(2).

[26] CA 1963, s 116(3).

[27] CA 1963, s 117(1).

the register of members.[28] This is not necessary if the register of members is in such a form as to constitute an index of itself.[29] Within 14 days of any alteration to the register of members, the company must amend the index accordingly.[30] The index of members must be kept at the same place as the register of members.[31] If there is a default in complying with these obligations, the company and every officer in default is guilty of an offence and liable to a maximum fine of €1904.61.[32]

(d) Location

[3.011] The register must be kept at the registered office of the company[33] or at the office at which it is compiled, whether an office of the company or the office of another person who is retained to make up the register on behalf of the company.[34] A company is generally obliged to send notice to the Registrar of Companies of the place at which the register of members is kept and of any change in that location, within 14 days of such change occurring.[35] However, no such notice is necessary if the register has at all times since the registration of the company, been kept at the registered office of the company.[36] The register of members must be kept in Ireland[37] and the index must be kept in the same place as the register.[38]

[3.012] If the register of members is kept at the office of a person (an 'agent') whom the company has retained to make up the register, and, due to the default of that agent, the Registrar is not notified of this fact, the agent is liable to the same penalties as an officer in default would be and orders may accordingly be made against that agent.[39] CA 1963–2006 do not relieve the company and other officers who may be in default of liability in these circumstances.

---

[28] CA 1963, s 117(2).

[29] CA 1963, s 117(1).

[30] CA 1963, s 117(1).

[31] CA 1963, s 117(3).

[32] CA 11963, s 117(4) as amended by C(A)A 1982, s 15 and CA 1990, s 240(7) as inserted by CLEA 2001, s 104(c).

[33] CA 1963, s 116(5).

[34] CA 1963, s 116(5)(a) and (b). If the register is kept at the office of a person who makes up the register for the company, it must be kept at the office at which it is made up. If the person making up the register has a number of offices, the register must be kept at the office at which it is made up (CA 1963, s 116(5)(b)).

[35] CA 1963, s 116(7) and (9). This notification must be on CRO Form B3, which is available to download from www.cro.ie.

[36] CA 1963, s 116(8).

[37] CA 1963, s 116(6).

[38] CA 1963, s 117(3).

[39] CA 1963, s 120. This provision also permits liability to be imposed on the agent for failure to comply with ss 117(3) and 119 and any requirements as to the production of the register. Section 120 further provides for orders to be made against the agent and his officers and servants under s 119(4). See further below paras [3.010] to [3.014].

(e) Inspection

[3.013] The register and index of members must be open to free inspection by members and by others on payment of a fee,[40] for at least two hours daily, during business hours.[41] This right of inspection is subject to the right of companies to close the register for a maximum of 30 days in each year in accordance with CA 1963, s 121. [42]

Any person is entitled to a copy of the register, or part thereof, on payment of a nominal charge.[43] According to CA 1963, s 119(2), 'The company shall cause any copy so required by any person to be sent to that person within a period of ten days commencing on the day next after the day on which the requirement is received by the company.'

These provisions require a company to send to any person, within ten days of receipt of a request from that person, a copy of the register of members, or part thereof. The costs chargeable for such copies are so low that it appears unlikely that a company would recover the costs of sending copies of the register.

[3.014] If a request for inspection of the register or index or for a copy of the register is refused, or not acceded to within the requisite period, the company and every officer in default is liable, in respect of each offence, to a maximum fine of €1904.61.[44] The court may further compel an immediate inspection of the register and index or direct that copies be sent to persons requesting them.[45]

Applications to court for the right to inspect the register or obtain copies of such register must be made by means of special summons in accordance with Order 75, rule 5 of the Rules of the Superior Courts.

The right to inspect the register of members is reproduced in substantially the same terms as s 119 in the General Scheme of the Companies Consolidation and Reform Bill 2007. The right to make a court application to compel such inspection does not, however, appear in the General Scheme, on the basis that the court has a general power under CA 1963, s 371 to compel compliance with the requirements of CA 1963–2006.[46]

---

[40] CA 1963, s 119(1) prescribes a fee of one shilling (€0.06) or such 'less sum as the company may prescribe for each inspection' (CA 1963, s 119(1)).

[41] CA 1963, s 119(3). This right of inspection may be subject to such reasonable restrictions as the company in general meeting may impose but not less than two hours a day must be allowed for inspection (CA 1963, s 119(1)).

[42] CA 1963, s 121. See further para **[3.029]**.

[43] The charge referred to in CA 1963, s 119(2) is 'sixpence (€0.08), or such less sum as the company may prescribe, for every 100 words or fractional part thereof required to be copied.'

[44] CA 1963, s 119(3) as amended by C(A)A 1982, s 15 and CA 1990, s 240(7) as inserted by CLEA 2001, s 104(c).

[45] CA 1963, s 119(4). Note that such an order may be made against an agent who is making up the register on behalf of the company (CA 1963, s 120).

[46] See General Scheme of the Companies Consolidation and Reform Bill 2007, Pt A4, Head 38. Available at www.clrg.org.

[3.015] The English Companies Act 1862 contained a provision almost identical to s 119.[47] This provision was considered in *Re Kent Coalfields Syndicate Ltd*,[48] in which a person who was neither a member nor a creditor of the company sought the right to inspect the register of a company which was in liquidation. The issue before the Court was whether the right of inspection ceased upon the commencement of liquidation. The Court of Appeal determined that it was not reasonable to apply the right of inspection to a company in liquidation as the company was no longer a going concern and the liquidator, rather than the directors, had control of the register. The Court concluded that the directors and the company should not be held liable for a default for which they were not responsible and that the right of inspection therefore ceased to have effect upon the commencement of the liquidation.

[3.016] In *Re Balaghat Gold Mining Company Ltd*,[49] a different aspect of s 32 of the English Companies Act 1862 was considered. The issue in that case was whether a person, not being a member of the company, was entitled to take copies of the register of members. The Court of Appeal determined that:

> 'The whole right that the Act gives as to copies is the express right to be furnished with a copy on payment. It seems to me that, under these circumstances, the right to take copies himself without paying for them is excluded.'[50]

This case suggests that the right to request the company to send out copies of the register, is in lieu of the right to take copies during an inspection of the register of members.

[3.017] In a more recent case the Court of Appeal considered the English equivalent of s 119(4) and noted that the court has a discretion whether to order a company to furnish copies of the register. In *Pelling v Families Need Fathers Ltd*[51] the Court of Appeal noted that the court will generally make an order to give effect to the right to receive copies of

---

[47] Companies Act 1862, s 32: 'The register of members ... except when closed as hereinafter mentioned, it shall during business hours, but subject to such reasonable restrictions as the company in general meeting may impose, so that not less than two hours in each day be appointed for inspection, be open to the inspection of any member gratis, and to the inspection of any other person on the payment of one shilling, or such less sum as the company may prescribe, for each inspection; and every such member or other person may require a copy of such register, or of any part thereof, or of such list or summary of members as is hereinbefore mentioned, on payment of sixpence for every hundred words required to be copied.'

[48] *Re Kent Coalfields Syndicate Ltd* [1898] 1 QB 754.

[49] *Re Balaghat Gold Mining Company Ltd* [1901] 2 KB 665.

[50] *Re Balaghat Gold Mining Company Ltd* [1901] 2 KB 665 at 668 *per* Vaughan Williams J. See also the following dicta of AL Smith MR at p 667: 'It seems to me that the statute fenced the right of the person inspecting, with regard to copies, by saying that he may require a copy of any portion of the register. That is not language to describe taking a copy, and, further, there is another restriction that he is to pay 6d. *per* hundred words for such portions of the register as he requires to be copied. In my opinion, it is not the true construction of the statute, on which alone the right to copies of the register depends, to say that the person inspecting is entitled to take a copy and to take it without paying anything.'

[51] *Pelling v Families Need Fathers Ltd* [2001] EWCA Civ 1280, [2002] 2 All ER 440.

the register, but that this right is not unqualified. The Court went on to note that the scope of the judicial discretion to refuse such an order is narrow. Examples of situations in which the court could refuse to order copies of the register of members to be supplied included where the request had already been complied with; where it was not possible to accede to the request, due to the destruction or loss of the register; or where an undertaking had been provided to the court that the copies would be furnished.[52]

(f) Refusal to register

[3.018] While CA 1963–2006 do not expressly provide for the refusal of the directors to register a transfer of shares, this is a matter which may be addressed by the articles of association of a company. Model Reg 3 of Pt II of Table A provides in this regard that: 'The directors may, in their absolute discretion, and without assigning any reason therefor, decline to register any transfer of any share, whether or not it is a fully paid share.'

It should be noted that, if the company directors intend to refuse to register a transfer of shares, they should do so promptly. *Re Inverdeck Ltd*[53] suggests that a delay in registering the name of the new shareholder, or responding to the request for registration, may entitle the transferee of the shares to have their name entered on the register.[54]

The difficulty of challenging the exercise of directors' discretion to refuse to register a share transfer was described as follows by MacCann:

> 'The discretion conferred on the directors is extremely wide and is only assailable if the proposed transferee can prove that they exercised their discretion against him either for an improper purpose or in bad faith. It may be extremely difficult to prove the existence of either of these factors on the part of the directors.'[55]

[3.019] In *Olhausen v Powerly,*[56] the Supreme Court considered the refusal of a company to register a transfer to a beneficiary under the will of a deceased member.[57] This refusal was challenged on the ground that it was not a *bona fide* exercise of the powers of the directors, a ground which is frequently invoked to challenge the exercise

---

[52]   See also Courtney, 'Company Law Update' (2002) 9(6) CLP 138.

[53]   *Re Inverdeck Ltd* [1998] 2 BCLC 242.

[54]   In that case a delay of two months was held to be excessive and to give rise to the right to be included on the register of members. See *Re Swaledale Cleaners Ltd* [1968] 1 WLR 1710 in which a delay of four months was held to be excessive ('… since there is an obligation on directors, who refuse to register a transfer, to inform the persons who are aggrieved within two months of such a refusal, the Act of 1948 clearly indicates that a reasonable time, other things being equal, within which directors must make up their minds either to accept the transfer or to refuse it must be the two months within which they must make an answer' *per* Harman LJ at p 1715). See also Courtney, (Company Law Update) (1999) 6(1) CLP 30.

[55]   MacCann, '*Locus Standi* and Section 205 of the Companies Act 1963' (1989) 7 ILT 195.

[56]   *Olhausen v Powderley* [1943] IR 426.

[57]   Article 6 of the company's articles of association provided that: 'The directors may, in their absolute and uncontrolled discretion and without assigning any reason, refuse to register any transfer of shares, and clause 20 of Table A shall be modified accordingly.'

of directors' discretion not to register transfers of shares. Among the relief sought, was an order that the plaintiff's name be entered on the register of members.

The Supreme Court noted that:

> 'In seeking to establish that the action of the directors was not *bona fide* in exercise of the fiduciary power conferred upon them by Art 6, the plaintiff was faced with the difficulty that under that Article the directors need not assign any reason for their refusal to register the transfer, and that the mere omission of the directors to state their reasons would not entitle the Court to infer that their reasons were not proper and legitimate.'[58]

This demonstrates the extent to which any challenge to the refusal of directors to register share transfers, depends on the precise terms of the company's articles of association and that it may be difficult to demonstrate that the exercise of this discretion was not *bona fide*.

On the evidence presented in that case, the Court did conclude that there was sufficient material from which to infer that the refusal to register the transfer was not the result of the *bona fide* exercise of the directors' discretion. The refusal was therefore not a valid exercise of the directors' powers under the articles of association.

[3.020] A further issue which required resolution was whether the directors could invoke the right of pre-emption contained in the articles.[59] The Supreme Court concluded that, if the directors wished to exercise their right to acquire the shares, they should have done so, rather than exercising their discretion not to register the transfer. By refusing to register the transfer, the directors were deemed to have waived their right to acquire the shares in accordance with the articles of association. O'Sullivan CJ accordingly held:

> 'In the present case the directors could, in our opinion, waive their right to require that the shares should be first offered to them. They would, admittedly, do so if they registered the transfer to the plaintiff, and we think that they also do so if, instead of calling upon the plaintiff to offer the shares to them, they proceed to deal with and dispose of the application for registration under Art 6 by refusing to register the transfer. We are of opinion that the directors should consider and decide whether they will exercise their option to purchase the shares under Art 7 before they proceed to consider the exercise of their discretionary power under Art 6.'[60]

The Court concluded:

> 'Accordingly it seems to us that the fact that the directors have considered and disposed of an application to register a transfer under Art 6, whether such application is granted or refused, indicates clearly that the directors have waived

---

[58] *Olhausen v Powderley* [1943] IR 426 at 471 (*per* O'Sullivan CJ).

[59] Article 7 of the articles of association provided that: 'No member may transfer or dispose of his shares or any of them without first offering them to the directors of the company, who shall have the first option of purchasing same at a fair market price to be fixed, in the event of dispute, by the auditors of the company at the expense of the vendor. On payment of the price so fixed, the registered owner shall forthwith transfer the shares in manner directed by the directors.'

[60] *Olhausen v Powderley* [1943] IR 426 at 476 (*per* O'Sullivan CJ).

their rights under Art 7, as those rights should have been exercised before the application was finally disposed of.'[61]

[3.021] If a company wishes to resist an application to register a share transfer, it should therefore ensure that any rights of pre-emption which may overcome the need to register such a transfer be exercised, before relying on any discretionary power to refuse such registration. The exercise of the latter power may be viewed as a waiver of any right of pre-emption that is vested in the directors. It is not clear whether this consequence would flow from a right of pre-emption vested in the individuals in their capacity as members, rather than directors, of the company. In such circumstances, the exercise of the right of pre-emption would be a right of the members and may be distinguished from the right of the directors to refuse to register a transfer. This question depends primarily on the wording and the construction of a company's articles of association.

[3.022] The considerations are different when the share transfer which the company refuses to register is a transfer to an existing member. In *Tangney v Clarence Hotels Co Ltd*[62] the directors refused to register a transfer of shares on the basis that the transferee, who was an existing member of the company, was an undesirable person. The company's articles of association did contain rights of pre-emption and permitted the directors to refuse to admit a person who they considered to be 'undesirable' as a member of the company. The Court noted that, while the articles did give the directors the right to refuse to register share transfers, this envisaged the registration of new members, not existing members. Johnston J stated:

> 'That device has been adopted by company draftsmen in many different forms – that is, to place no restrictions upon the circulation of the shares amongst the members of the company, but to enable the heavy hand of the Directors to come down when a stranger seeks to enter into the charmed circle.'[63]

The Court concluded that the directors had no power to refuse to register the transfer of the shares to the transferee, as he was an existing member of the company. This case demonstrates that the power of a company to refuse to register share transfers is not unrestricted and that a refusal to register a transfer to an existing member may be subject to particularly close scrutiny.

(g) Rectification

[3.023] Rectification of the register of members may be sought in any of the three following circumstances:

- if the name of a person is entered on the register 'without sufficient cause';[64]

- if the name of a person is omitted from the register 'without sufficient cause';[65] or

---

[61] *Olhausen v Powderley* [1943] IR 426 at 477 (*per* O'Sullivan CJ).

[62] *Tangney v Clarence Hotels Co Ltd* [1933] IR 51.

[63] *Tangney v Clarence Hotels Co Ltd* [1933] IR 51 at 63.

[64] CA 1963, s 122(1)(a).

[65] CA 1963, s 122(1)(a).

    — if the fact that a person has ceased to be a member is not entered on the register within 28 days of such cessation.[66]

According to s 122, an application may be made to court for the rectification of the register in these circumstances and the persons who may make such an application are the person aggrieved by the error, any member of the company, or the company itself.[67] There is no procedure envisaged by s 122 for such persons to request the company to rectify the register, although it may be expected that, in practice, such a request would be made before the issue of a court application.

[3.024] In this regard, s 122(5) provides that:

> A company may, without application to the court, at any time rectify any error or omission ... in the register but such a rectification shall not adversely affect any person unless he agrees to the rectification made.

Where the company does rectify the register without a court application, it must notify the Registrar of Companies of this change within 21 days, if the error or omission rectified was reflected in any document forwarded to the Registrar.[68]

[3.025] When an application is made to court for the rectification of the register, the court may refuse the application or it may order rectification of the register.[69] In determining such an application:

> '... the court may decide any question relating to the title of any person who is a party to the application to have his name entered in or omitted from the register, whether the question arises between members or alleged members, or between members or alleged members on the one hand and the company on the other hand, and generally may decide any question necessary or expedient to be decided for rectification of the register.'[70]

This provision confers a wide discretion on the court to assess the title to shares in any company, irrespective of the nature of, and parties to, the dispute.[71]

In considering an application for rectification of the register, the court may also direct the company to pay compensation for any loss sustained by the party aggrieved by the error or omission.[72]

Applications to court for the rectification of the register of members under s 122 must be made by means of special summons in accordance with Order 75, rule 5 of the Rules of the Superior Courts.

---

[66] CA 1963, s 122(1)(b).

[67] CA 1963, s 122(1).

[68] CA 1963, s 122(5).

[69] CA 1963, s 122(2).

[70] CA 1963, s 122(3).

[71] According to CA 1963, s 122(4), if the company is required to send a list of its member to the Registrar of Companies, 'the court when making an order for rectification of the register shall by its order direct notice of the rectification to be given to the registrar.'

[72] CA 1963, s 122(2).

[3.026] The provision of the English Companies Act 1862 which provided for the rectification of the register of members was similar in terms to CA 1963, s 122. Section 35 of that Act provided that an aggrieved person, any member of a company, or the company itself, may make an application to court for rectification of the register:

> 'If the name of any person is, without sufficient cause, entered in or omitted from the register of members of any company under this Act, or if default is made or unnecessary delay takes place in entering on the register the fact of any person having ceased to be a member of the company.'

[3.027] There is authority in English law that the register may be rectified with retrospective effect and that rectification may be ordered in respect of a company in liquidation.[73] In *Re Sussex Brick Co Ltd*[74] a transfer of shares was not entered on the register of members, due to an apparent oversight and error, including the intervening replacement of the company secretary. Before the transfer was registered, the company passed a resolution for its voluntary winding up. In the mistaken belief that the transfer had been registered, the transferees of the shares sought to dissent from this resolution and, upon learning that the transfer was not registered, made an application to court for the rectification of the register of the company, which was then in liquidation.

The Court of Appeal considered whether the names of the transferees could only be entered on the list of contributories of the company in liquidation or whether the register of members should be rectified. The Court concluded that the names of the transferees should have appeared on the register of members before the passing of the resolution to wind up the company and that there was nothing in the governing legislation which prevented the exercise of the court's power to rectify the register of members after the commencement of the liquidation of a company.

Vaughan Williams LJ considered the effect of such an order as follows:

> 'If I thought here that such an order would work injustice to other persons, especially to persons who are not in any way bound by the mistake of the company, I should feel considerable hesitation in making the order; but in the present case there is no evidence before us that any injustice will be caused at all.'[75]

The court considered the operative date of the rectification of the register as follows: 'in a proper case the court has power to fix a date as from which the change in the register is to be made operative.'[76] The court concluded that courts have full discretion in determining whether, and from when, the register of members should be rectified.

---

[73] See *Re New Millennium Experience Co Ltd* [2003] EWHC 1823 (Ch, 23 July 2003); [2004] 1 ER 687, in which the register was rectified retrospectively to include the name of a member who had passed a resolution for the liquidation of the company, unaware of the fact that his name was erroneously omitted from the register. An application to set arise this rectification order was dismissed on the basis that the applicant did not have standing to challenge the rectification of the register.

[74] *Re Sussex Brick Co Ltd* [1904] 1 Ch 598.

[75] *Re Sussex Brick Co Ltd* [1904] 1 Ch 598 at 607.

[76] *Re Sussex Brick Co Ltd* [1904] 1 Ch 598 at 608 *per* Stirling LJ.

As a general matter, it is important to note that the court in *Re Sussex Brick Co Ltd*[77] held that the list of contributories and the register of members are distinct matters and that the suggestion that the register of members ceased to exist on the commencement of the liquidation of a company was not tenable.[78]

[3.028] In *South London Greyhound Racecourses Ltd v Wake*[79] a director and secretary of a company registered a transfer of shares to a person to whom they were both indebted, without procuring the requisite authorisation of the board of directors of the company. There was also no entry on the register recording the transfer of the shares or the cessation of membership of the alleged transferor. The company applied to court for the rectification of the register. The court held that the certificate certifying the share transfer was not duly sealed on behalf of the company and was a forgery. The court therefore made an order rectifying the register by the deletion of the name of the alleged transferee of the shares.

(h) Closing register of members

[3.029] A company is entitled to close the register of members for any time or times during a year, for not more than 30 days in each year.[80] Before closing the register in this manner, the company must publish an advertisement in a newspaper circulating in the district in which the company's registered office is located.[81]

(i) Effect of register

[3.030] According to CA 1963, s 124, the register of members is *prima facie* (as opposed to conclusive) evidence of any matters which the Companies Acts require or authorise to be included in the register.[82]

The importance of the register of members is also apparent from the terms of CA 1963, s 31, which defines a 'member' as follows: 'Every other person who agrees to become a member of a company, and whose name is entered in its register of members, shall be a member of the company.'[83]

---

[77] *Re Sussex Brick Co Ltd* [1904] 1 Ch 598.

[78] Cozens-Hardy LJ noted in this regard: 'It seems to me that Mr Gore-Browne's argument is really based on this hypothesis, that the register of members is a thing which ceases to have any real operation or existence after the winding-up order; that the only right which can be dealt with after a winding-up order is one with regard to making some change in the position of persons on the list of contributories. Now on looking at the scheme and method of the Act, it is clear that the list or register of members is one thing, and the list of contributories is an entirely different thing.' *Re Sussex Brick Co Ltd* [1904] 1 Ch 598 at 609.

[79] *South London Greyhound Racecourses Ltd v Wake* [1931] 1 Ch 496.

[80] CA 1963, s 121.

[81] CA 1963, s 121.

[82] CA 1963, s 124. This provision is reproduced in the General Scheme of the Companies Consolidation and Reform Bill 2007, Pt A4, Head 41. Available at www.clrg.org.

[83] CA 1963, s 31(2). See *Arulchelvan & Wright v Wright et al* (7 February 1996, unreported), HC, (Carroll J).

[3.031] The effect of the register of members, and the status of persons who claim to be entitled to appear on the register, but do not, was considered in *Re JN 2 Ltd*.[84] In that case, a person who claimed to be a member of the company wished to present a petition for the winding up of the company, on the ground that there was oppression and it was just and equitable that the company be wound up. The person's name did not appear on the register of members and it had to be determined as a preliminary question whether that person had status to bring the petition. The Chancery Division considered the governing provisions of the English equivalent of the Companies Act 1963 as follows:

> 'The register is only *prima facie* evidence of the matters directed or authorised to be inserted therein: see s 118. It is liable to be rectified under s 116. It is not even conclusive evidence until rectified (in contradistinction to the register maintained under, for example, the Charities Act 1960). Every person who holds shares will, save in exceptional circumstances, know that they have been allotted or transferred to him. But not one shareholder in a thousand is likely to peruse the register of members, or to know for certain that his name is entered therein. I do not feel inclined to go out of my way to decide that a petitioning contributory must be *de facto* on the register, except in the one case where the statute makes this obligatory.'[85]

The Court therefore concluded that it would be excessively legalistic to deny the allottee the status of member because of an omission from the register of members and further concluded that, 'a winding up petition may be presented by an allottee, although his membership of the company is not recorded in the register of members.'[86]

[3.032] In *Tuama v Allied Metropole Hotel Ltd*[87] an application was made to strike out a petition under CA 1963, s 205, on the ground that the petitioner was not registered as a member of the company. Gannon J held that it was necessary to come within the scope of CA 1963, s 31, in order to qualify as a member of a company and that a person whose name did not appear on the register of members could not pursue a petition under s 205.

[3.033] A related question arose for consideration in the more recent case of *Via Net Works Ireland Ltd*[88] The specific issue in that case was whether persons whose names continued to appear on the register of members, despite having voluntarily disposed of their entire shareholding, had standing to bring proceedings for oppression under s 205.

---

[84] *Re JN 2 Ltd* [1978] 1 WLR 183.

[85] *Re JN 2 Ltd* [1978] 1 WLR 183 at 187, *per* Brightman J.

[86] *Re JN 2 Ltd* [1978] 1 WLR 183 at 187, *per* Brightman J. On the facts of that case, the allotment itself was in dispute and the Court determined that, 'It therefore seems to me to be all the more important that he should not be permitted to present a petition and thereby interfere with dispositions by the company of its assets and risk damaging the financial standing of the company, so long as his right to be a shareholder of the company is in dispute' (*Re JN 2 Ltd* [1978] 1 WLR 183 at 188). The status of the alleged allottee therefore had to be resolved before the petition could be presented and the petition was accordingly dismissed.

[87] *Tuama v Allied Metropole Hotel Ltd* (19 December 1988, unreported), HC, Gannon J. See MacCann, 'Locus Standi and Section 205 of the Companies Act 1963' (1989) 7 ILT 195.

[88] *Via Net Works Ireland Ltd* [2002] IESC 24; [2002] 2 IR 47 at 55–56.

The Supreme Court made the following determination:

> 'Section 205 is a valuable protection against the misuse by shareholders, usually constituting the majority, of their powers in a manner which is oppressive to the other shareholders or fails to have regard to their interests. Persons, such as the respondents, who have voluntarily disposed of their entire shareholding in a company could not conceivably have been contemplated by the legislature as persons who would be entitled to relief under the section. Nor is it any answer to say that, because the respondents have not transferred their shares, as they are contractually bound to do, they remain registered as members of the company. It is undoubtedly the case that a person who has become entitled to be registered as a shareholder may be unable to exercise any of his rights as a shareholder until his name has been entered on the register. But it does not follow that a person who, conversely, has voluntarily divested himself of all his shares in the company, but remains on the register must be treated as a member of the company for all purposes. I have no doubt that, when the legislature enacted s 205(1), it was not envisaged that persons without any interest in the company but who, for whatever reason, remained on the register as members would be entitled to present a petition grounded on alleged oppression of them as members.'[89]

This case is therefore authority for the proposition that, while a person whose name incorrectly does not appear on the register may not be entitled to exercise the rights of membership, there is no principle or rule to the effect that every person whose name appears on the register of members is automatically entitled to the benefits of membership.

(j) Sanctions

[3.034] Where a company is in default of any of the requirements relating to the register or index of members, the company and every officer who is in default is guilty of an offence and liable to a fine.[90] In addition, if there is a default or refusal in relation to the inspection, or taking of copies, of the register or index of members, the court may make

---

[89]   *Via Net Works Ireland Ltd* [2002] IESC 24; [2002] 2 IR 47 at 55–56, *per* Keane CJ.

[90]   CA 1963, s 116(9) (as amended by C(A)A 1982, s 15 and CA 1990, s 240(7) as inserted by CLEA 2001, s 104(c)), 117(4) (as amended by C(A)A 1982, s 15 and CA 1990, s 240(7) as inserted by CLEA 2001, s 104(c)) and 119(3) (as amended by C(A)A 1982, s 15). A company or officer who is in default of the requirements to maintain an index of the register of members is liable to a maximum fine of €1904.61 (CA 1963, s 117(4), as amended by C(A)A 1982, s 15 and CA 1990, s 240(7) as inserted by CLEA 2001, s 104(c)); a company or officer in default in relation to the maintenance of the register of members and disclosure of the location of the register is liable to a maximum fine of €1904.61 (CA 1963, s 116(9) as amended by C(A)A 1982, s 15 and CA 1990, s 240(7) as inserted by CLEA 2001, s 104(c)); and a company and defaulting officer in default in relation to the rights of inspection and to get copies of the register is liable to a maximum fine of €1904.61 (CA 1963, s 119(3), C(A)A 1982, s 15 and CA 1990, s 240(7) as inserted by CLEA 2001, s 104(c)).

an order compelling an immediate inspection of the register and index or directing that the copies requested be sent to the person making the request.[91]

Directors have been the subject of prosecutions under s 119 for failing to allow inspections of the register of members.[92] Directors should be aware that the shifting of the burden of proving a director was in default of the requirements of the Companies Acts by s 383, is likely to lead to considerably more prosecutions of any offences of which officers in default may be prosecuted.[93]

D. Register of directors and secretaries

[3.035] Every company is obliged to keep at its registered office a register of its directors and secretaries.[94] In relation to each director, this register must contain his full name (and any former names), date of birth, residential address, nationality and business occupation (if any), and the particulars of any other directorships of companies, which he holds or has held within the previous ten years.[95]

In relation to individuals who hold the office of secretary, the register should state their full name and former names and their usual residential address.[96] If there are joint secretaries, this information should be disclosed in relation to each of them.[97] If the

---

[91] CA 1963, s 119(4). Note that this extends to making orders against an agent in default, his officers or servants. See CA 1963, s 120.

[92] Eg, two directors were prosecuted for violations of CA 1990, s 159, and violations of CA 1963, s 119, on 22 January 2002. Each director was fined €100 and one of the directors was also ordered to pay expenses of €254 to the DCE and prosecution costs of €952. A further two directors were prosecuted under CA 1963, s 119 on 1 November 2002, one of whom was fined €100 for that offence (*Director of Corporate Enforcement v McCormack* (1 November 2002, unreported), Edenderry District Court.)

[93] See CA 1963, s 383(2), as substituted by CLEA 2001, s 100. '... an officer shall be presumed to have permitted a default by the company unless the officer can establish that he took all reasonable steps to prevent it or that, by reason of circumstances beyond his control, was unable to do so.' See Ch **6**.

[94] CA 1963, s 195(1), as substituted by CA 1990, s 51. Note that the obligation to keep a register of directors and secretaries is substantially reproduced in the General Scheme of the Companies Consolidation and Reform Bill 2007, Head 19. Available at www.clrg.org. See further Ch **2**.

[95] CA 1963, s 195(2) and (3)(a), as substituted by CA 1990, s 51. According to CA 1963, s 195(3)(b), the register does not have to contain information regarding directorships 'which is held or was held by a director in bodies corporate of which the company is or was the wholly owned subsidiary or which are or were the wholly owned subsidiaries either of the company or of another body corporate of which the company is or was the wholly owned subsidiary.'

[96] CA 1963, s 195(4)(a), as substituted by CA 1990, s 51.

[97] CA 1963, s 195(4), as substituted by CA 1990, s 51. Note however that, according to CA 1963, s 195(5), as substituted by CA 1990, s 51, 'Where all the partners in a firm are joint secretaries of a company, the name and principal office of the firm may be stated instead of the said particulars.'

secretary is a body corporate, the register should state the registered name and office of the company.[98]

Every director and secretary is under a duty to furnish to the company, as promptly as possible, such information as may be necessary to enable the company to comply with the requirement to keep this register of directors and secretaries.[99]

The register of directors and secretaries must be open to inspection by members of the company for at least two hours during business hours without payment of a fee, and to other persons, on payment of a fee.[100] In addition, any person is entitled to require the company to furnish them with a copy of the register, or part of the register, on payment of a charge, and the company is obliged to send such copies within ten days of the request.[101]

[3.036] There are a number of sanctions associated with the register of directors and secretaries. First, if there is default in relation to any of the requirements relating to the register of directors and secretaries, the company and every officer in default is guilty of an offence and liable to a once-off fine and to a daily default fine for continued contraventions.[102] Secondly, if inspection of the register of directors and secretaries is refused, the company and every officer in default is similarly liable to a once-off and a daily default fine.[103] Thirdly, if there is a refusal to allow inspection of the register, the court may compel an immediate inspection of the register.[104] Fourthly, it is an offence for the company to fail to comply with the requirement to furnish copies of the register, when requested to do so.[105] Finally, it is an offence for a director or secretary to fail to furnish to the company, as promptly as possible, such information as may be necessary to enable the company to comply with the requirement to keep the register of directors and secretaries.[106]

---

[98] CA 1963, s 195(4)(b), as substituted by CA 1990, s 51.

[99] CA 1963, s 195(11), as substituted by CA 1990, s 51.

[100] CA 1963, s 195(10), as substituted by CA 1990, s 51, which provides that the inspection may be 'subject to such reasonable restrictions as the company may by its articles or in general meeting impose, so that not less than two hours in each day be allowed for inspection'.

[101] CA 1963, s 195(10A), as substituted by CLEA 2001, s 91.

[102] CA 1963, s 195(12), as substituted by CA 1990, s 51, and amended by C(AA)A 2003, Sch 2 and CA 1990, s 240(7) as inserted by CLEA 2001, s 104(c).

[103] CA 1963, s 195(12), as substituted by CA 1990, s 51 and amended by C(AA)A 2003, Sch 2 and CA 1990, s 240(7) as inserted by CLEA 2001, s 104(c).

[104] CA 1963, s 195(13), as substituted by CA 1990, s 51.

[105] CA 1963, s 195(10A), as substituted by CLEA 2001, s 91. Note that s 195(10A) does not provide that it is an offence for an officer in default to fail to provide the copy of the register requested under that provision. This can be contrasted with failing to provide copies of the register of members and of debenture holders, for which both the company and officers in default may be fined.

[106] CA 1963, s 195(14), as substituted by CA 1990, s 51.

E. Register of directors' interests in company

[3.037] Every company is required to keep a register of all of the shares and debentures which are owned by its directors.[107] There are certain particular matters which the company must enter on this register. First, whenever a company director fulfils his duty to furnish information to the company regarding his interest in the company's shares or debentures, the company must, within three days of that notification, enter on the register, beside that person's name, the information furnished and the date on which it was entered on the register.[108]

Secondly, if a company grants a director or secretary the right to subscribe for the company's shares or debentures, the company must enter on the register, the date on which that right was conferred, the period for which it is exercisable, the consideration paid, and a description of the shares or debentures at issue.[109] Thirdly, if the director or secretary subsequently exercises that subscription right, the company is required to enter on the register the fact that the right was exercised, the number or amount of shares or debentures subscribed for, and the names in which they are registered.[110]

[3.038] The register of directors' interests must be readily open to inspection and easily located. There are a number of means by which CA 1963–2006 seek to ensure this transparency. First, the register must be kept at the company's registered office, or at the same place as the register of members, if that register is not kept at the registered office.[111] Secondly, the Registrar of Companies must be notified of its location.[112] Thirdly, the register must be open to inspection for at least two hours during business hours, such inspection to be free of charge for members and subject to a fee for other persons.[113] Fourthly, the register must further be open and accessible to any person attending the company's annual general meeting for at least fifteen minutes before the commencement of such meeting and for the duration of the meeting.[114] Fifthly, any person is also entitled to a copy of the register, or parts thereof, on payment of a fee, and the company must send such copies within ten days of receipt of the request.[115] Finally,

---

[107] CA 1990, s 59(1). CA 1990, ss 53 to 58 concern the obligation of directors to notify companies of their interests in the company's shares or debentures and are addressed in more detail in Ch **6**.

[108] CA 1990, s 59(2). This must be done within three days of the day following such notification (CA 1990, s 60(2)).

[109] CA 1990, s 59(3)(a) to (d). This must be done within three days commencing on the day following the day on which that right is conferred (CA 1990, s 60(2)).

[110] CA 1990, s 59(4). This must be done within three days commencing on the day following the date on which that right was exercised (CA 1990, s 60(2)).

[111] CA 1990, s 60(5).

[112] CA 1990, s 60(6). There is no obligation to notify the Registrar of Companies of the register's location, if it has at all times been kept at the company's registered office (CA 1990, s 60(6)).

[113] CA 1990, s 60(5).

[114] CA 1990, s 60(9).

[115] CA 1990, s 60(8).

to ensure ease of reference, the company must compile an index of the names entered on the register, which must be kept with the register and which must be updated within 14 days of any changes to the register.[116]

[3.039] The circumstances in which entries may be deleted from the register of directors' interests are exhaustively set out in ss 63 and 64. A company can remove an entry if more than six years have lapsed since the entry was made and either the entry stated that the director ceased to have an interest in the company[117] or it was superseded by a later entry made in respect of the same person.[118] These are the only two circumstances in which an entry can be removed.[119] If an entry is removed from the register, other than in these two circumstances, the company is required to restore that entry 'as soon as is reasonable and practicable.'[120] If a name is removed from the company's register the company must, within 14 days, amend the index accordingly.[121]

[3.040] There are various penalties and sanctions for failing to comply with the requirements regarding the register of directors' interests. If the register is not available before and during the company's AGM, the company and every officer in default are guilty of an offence and liable to a fine.[122] If there is a default in notifying the Registrar of Companies of the location of the register, which default continues for 14 days, the company and every officer in default is liable to a fine.[123] If there is a default with regard to the keeping of the register, with regard to the index, or if an inspection or copy of the register is refused, the company and every officer in default is liable to a fine.[124] Furthermore, if there is a refusal to allow an inspection of the register, or to send a copy thereof, the court may make an order compelling compliance with those requirements.[125] Finally, if there is a default in relation to the amendment of the index or the removal of an entry from the register of interests in shares, the company and every officer who is in default is guilty of an offence and liable to a fine.[126]

---

[116] CA 1990, s 60(7).

[117] CA 1990, s 61(1). In this circumstance, the name of the person can also be removed from the register.

[118] CA 1990, s 61(1).

[119] According to CA 1990, s 62(1), 'entries in a company's register of interests in shares and debentures … shall not be deleted except in accordance with s 61.'

[120] CA 1990, s 62(2).

[121] CA 1990, s 61(2).

[122] CA 1990, s 60(10) as amended by CA 1990, s 240(7) as inserted by CLEA 2001, s 104(c), referring to CA 1990, s 60(9).

[123] CA 1990, s 60(10), CA 1990, s 240(7) as inserted by CLEA 2001, s 104(c), referring to CA 1990, s 60(6).

[124] CA 1990, s 60(10), CA 1990, s240(7) as inserted by CLEA 2001, s 104(c), referring to CA 1990, ss 59, 60(1), 60(2), 60(7).

[125] CA 1990, s 60(11).

[126] CA 1990, s 61(3) and (3).

[3.041] Directors of companies have faced prosecution in relation to the register of directors' interests. On 22 January 2002, two directors[127] were each convicted of an offence under s 59 (register of directors' interests) of the Companies Act 1990. There were also separate offences in relation to the keeping of the register of members, as required by CA 1963, s 119. Each director was fined €100 and one of them was also ordered to pay expenses of €254 to the DCE and prosecution costs of €952. A further two directors were prosecuted and convicted of offences under CA 1963, s 60 on 1 November 2002, one of those convicted being fined €100 in respect of that contravention.[128]

F. Directors' contracts

[3.042] A company is obliged to keep any contracts of service with its directors available for inspection. While there is no obligation to keep a register of such contracts, the duty to have contracts available for inspection, is of the same nature as the obligation to keep registers, and it is therefore included in this chapter.

The documents which must be kept available for inspection are the following:

- if a director's contract of service is in writing, a copy of that contract;[129]
- if a director's contract is not in writing, a written memorandum setting out its terms;[130]
- if the contract is with a subsidiary of the company, a copy or written memorandum of that contract;[131] and
- if there is any variation of the contract of service, a copy or written memorandum of such variation.[132]

This is subject to the qualification that, if the contract required the work to be carried out wholly or mainly outside the State, such documents do not have to be kept, but the company must instead keep a memorandum setting out the following:[133]

- if the contract is with the company, the director's name and the duration of the contract;[134] and
- if the contract is with a subsidiary, the director's name, the name and place of incorporation of the subsidiary, and the duration of the contract.[135]

---

[127] Vincent and Sheila Mayock, being directors of 2001 Domain Trading Ltd, as reported on www.odce.ie.

[128] *Director of Corporate Enforcement v McCormack*, (1 November 2002, unreported), Edenderry District Court.

[129] CA 1990, s 50(1)(a). These provisions apply equally if the contract is partly in writing (CA 1990, s 50(2)).

[130] CA 1990, s 50(1)(b).

[131] CA 1990, s 50(1)(c).

[132] CA 1990, s 50(1)(d).

[133] CA 1990, s 50(5).

[134] CA 1990, s 50(5)(a).

[135] CA 1990, s 50(5)(b).

[3.043] There is a further qualification that a company is not required to keep any such documents regarding a contract of service which has less than three years left unexpired, or which can be terminated by the company without payment of compensation in the ensuing three years.[136] This may be interpreted as exempting from the requirements of s 50, any contracts of service of less than three years' duration.

All such documents must be kept at the same place,[137] which may be the company's registered office, principal place of business or the place where the register of members is kept (if other than the registered office).[138] Unless these documents have always been kept at the registered office, the company must notify the Registrar of Companies of their location and any change in such location within 14 days of such change occurring.[139]

Every document required to be kept under CA 1990, s 50, must be open to inspection by any member of the company during business hours, for at least two hours daily, free of charge.[140] This entitlement only applies to members and does not extend to the right to require copies of any such contracts.

If there is a default in complying with any of the obligations regarding directors' service contracts, the company and every defaulting officer is guilty of an offence and liable, on summary conviction, to a maximum fine of €1,904.61, and a daily default fine of up to €63.49 for continued contraventions.[141] In addition, if the company refuses to allow a member to inspect these documents, the court may make an order compelling immediate inspection.[142]

G. Register of charges

[3.044] The particulars of charges created by a company must be delivered to the Registrar of Companies and the latter then maintains a register of all such charges.[143] The company is also required to keep, at its registered office, a copy of every instrument creating a charge which is so registered.[144] If there is a series of uniform debentures, a copy of the one of the debentures from the series is adequate to comply with this obligation.[145]

---

[136] CA 1990, s 50(9).

[137] CA 1990, s 50(1).

[138] CA 1990, s 50(3).

[139] CA 1990, s 50(4) and (7).

[140] CA 1990, s 50(6). The company in general meeting may resolve to impose reasonable restrictions on such inspections, but inspection must be permitted for not less than two hours daily.

[141] CA 1990, s 50(7), as substituted by C(AA)A 2003, s 57.

[142] CA 1990, s 50(8).

[143] CA 1963, ss 99 and 103. See Ch 2.

[144] CA 1963, s 109. Such documents must be accompanied by any affidavits that were delivered under CA 1963, s 102.

[145] CA 1963, s 109.

These instruments must be open to inspection by the company's creditors and members during business hours for a minimum of two hours daily.[146] No fee may be charged for such inspection.[147] It should be noted that, by contrast with the register of members, inspection of the instruments creating charges is only open to a company's members or creditors.

If such inspection is refused, every officer of the company who is in default is guilty of an offence and liable to a fine.[148] It should be noted that there is no specific offence of failing to keep copies of the instruments creating the charges at the company's registered office. It is only a refusal to allow inspection that constitutes an offence. It should moreover be noted that there is no provision to the effect that the company itself is liable for such defaults.[149] Where such a refusal occurs, the court may make an order compelling an immediate inspection.[150]

H. Register of debenture holders

[3.045] Every company is required by the Companies Acts to keep a register of holders of debentures, containing their names, addresses and the amount of the debentures held by each debenture holder.[151] This register may be kept at the company's registered office[152] or at the office at which it is compiled, whether an office of the company or the office of a person who compiles the register on behalf of the company.[153] If the register is not being kept at the company's registered office,[154] the company is required to notify the Registrar of Companies of where it is kept and any change in that location, within 14 days of such change occurring.[155] The location of the register, and any change in its location, should be notified on CRO Form B3.[156]

---

[146] CA 1963, s 110(1) provides as follows: 'The copies of instruments referred to in s 109 may be inspected during business hours (but subject to such reasonable restrictions as the company in general meeting may impose, so that not less than two hours in each day shall be allowed for inspection) by any creditor or member of the company without fee.'

[147] CA 1963, s 110(1).

[148] CA 1963, s 110(2), as amended by C(A)A 1982, s 15, and C(AA)A 2003, Sch 2 and CA 1990, s 240(7) as inserted by CLEA 2001, s 104(c).

[149] CA 1963, s 110(2), as amended by C(A)A 1982, s 15 and C(AA)A 2003, Sch 2 and CA 1990, s 240(7) as inserted by CLEA 2001, s 104(c).

[150] CA 1963, s 110(3).

[151] CA 1963, s 91(1). According to s 91(1), 'For the purposes of this subsection, debentures do not include any debenture which does not form part of a series ranking *pari passu* nor any debenture which is transferable by delivery.'

[152] CA 1963, s 91(2).

[153] CA 1963, s 91(3) and (4).

[154] CA 1963, s 91(4) provides in this regard, 'A company shall not be bound to send notice under sub-s (3) where the register has, at all times since it came into existence, or, in the case of a company which came into existence after the operative date, at all times since then, been kept at the registered office of the company.'

[155] CA 1963, s 91(3) and (5), as amended by C(A)A 1982, s 15 and C(AA)A 2003, s 57.

[156] This form is available to download from www.cro.ie.

[3.046] The register of debenture holders must be open to inspection by the debenture holders and the company's members, free of charge, and by any other person, on payment of a fee.[157] This is subject to the qualification that the register may be closed, and

> 'shall be deemed to be duly closed if closed in accordance with provisions contained in the articles or in the debentures or, in the case of debenture stock, in the stock certificates, or in the trust deed or other document securing the debentures or debenture stock, during such period or periods, not exceeding in the whole 30 days in any year, as may be therein specified.'[158]

[3.047] A company's members, debenture holders or any other person, may also, on payment of a nominal fee,[159] require the company to furnish copies of the register of debenture holders, or parts thereof.[160] There is no time specified in the Companies Acts 1963–2006, within which such copies must be supplied.

Companies must forward a copy of any trust deed for securing any issue of debentures to any holder of such debentures at his request.[161] This is subject to the payment of €0.32 'or such less sum as may be prescribed by the company' for a printed trust deed' or payment of €0.08 for every 100 words copies, if the trust deed has not been printed.[162]

If the company fails to maintain a register of debenture holders in the requisite location, or fails to notify the Registrar of Companies of the location of that register, if applicable, the company and every officer in default is guilty of an offence and liable to a maximum fine of €1904.61.[163]

If the company refuses to allow inspection of the register of debenture holders, or fails or refuses to send a copy,[164] the company and every defaulting officer is guilty of an offence and liable to a maximum fine of €1904.61.[165] In such circumstances, the court

---

[157] CA 1963, s 92(1). The register may be closed but only subject to reasonable restrictions, in particular, the register must be open for inspection for at least two hours daily (CA 1963, s 92(1)). The fee prescribed by CA 1963, s 92(1) is one shilling, which equates with €0.06, 'or such less sum as may be prescribed by the company', CA 1963, s 92(1).

[158] CA 1963, s 92(6).

[159] CA 1963, s 92(2) provides that the fee chargeable for receipt of copies of the register of debenture holders is six pence (€0.08) for every 100 words copied. There is no discretion on the part of the company to vary this charge.

[160] CA 1963, s 92(2).

[161] CA 1963, s 92(3).

[162] CA 1963, s 92(3).

[163] CA 1963, s 91(5), as amended by C(A)A 1982, s 15, and C(AA)A 2003, s 57 and CA 1990, s 240(7) as inserted by CLEA 2001, s 104(c).

[164] The language used in CA 1963, s 92(4) is general and refers to 'a copy' which could, it appears, encompass both copies of the register requested under s 92(2) and copies of trust deeds required under s 92(3).

[165] CA 1963, s 92(4), as amended by C(A)A 1982, s 15 and C(AA)A 2003, s 57 and CA 1990, s 240(7) as inserted by CLEA 2001, s 104(c).

may make an order compelling an immediate inspection of the register or directing the copies required to be sent to the person requiring them.[166]

---

[166] CA 1963, s 92(5).

Chapter 4

BOOKS OF ACCOUNT

A. Introduction

[4.001] Every company is required to keep certain documents and books which reflect the company's financial situation and dealings. The failure of many companies to keep basic financial records in the past was cited as a factor in corporate collapses and the Companies Acts 1963–2006 ('CA 1963–2006') now contain detailed and stringent requirements in this regard.[1] Every company must keep books of account, which are the primary documents reflecting the company's income and expenditure. A company must also keep annual accounts which comprise balance sheets and profit and loss accounts.[2]

It is beyond the scope of this work to examine companies' accounting obligations in detail. One aspect of this topic which has been prominent in the enforcement of the CA 1963–2006, however, is the obligation to keep proper books of account and the focus of this chapter will therefore be on that requirement.

B. Proper books of account

[4.002] Books of account are essentially the primary books or internal books which a company is obliged to keep. The obligation of a company to keep proper books of account is a highly significant one in the context of the enforcement of company law, which is illustrated by the fact there have been many criminal prosecutions of companies and their directors for failure to keep proper books of account. As the ODCE recorded in its Annual Report 2006, failure to keep proper books of account accounted for ten per cent of the total number of suspected defaults that were reported to the ODCE in 2006. In light of this finding, the ODCE described the obligation to keep proper books of account as follows:

> 'This obligation is fundamental to the maintenance of a sound company from a financial and operational perspective. Because failures in this area can distort business markets by creating unfair and unwarranted advantages on some companies and their stakeholders to the detriment of others, the question of enforcement action is seriously considered in each such case'.[3]

---

[1] See *Companies Act 1990*, annotated by McCormack, 1990 ICLSA.

[2] The most relevant legislative provisions are CA 1963, ss 148 to 159 (as amended); C(A)A 1986, ss 3 to 22 and Schedule (as amended); CA 1990, ss 41 to 46 (as amended); EC (Companies: Group Accounts) R 1992; EC (Accounts) R 1993; C(A)(No2)A 1999, Pt III (as amended); EC(IFRSMA)R 2005. See also the C(AA)A 2003. See generally, Courtney, *The Law of Private Companies* (2nd edn, Tottel Publishing, 2002), Ch 13.

[3] ODCE Annual Report 2006 at p 14.

CA 1990, s 202 is the provision which governs the obligation of companies to keep books of account. The various aspects of this obligation will now be considered in turn.

(a) 'Proper books of account'

[4.003] Every company, whether public, private, limited or unlimited, is required to keep proper 'books of account'. These documents must achieve the following:

–   correctly record and explain the company's transactions;[4]

–   enable the company's financial position to be determined with reasonable accuracy at any given time;[5]

–   enable the directors to ensure that the company's annual accounts comply with the requirements of the Companies Acts and the IAS Regulations, if applicable;[6]

–   enable the company's annual accounts to be readily and properly audited.[7]

[4.004] The ODCE set out, in an appendix to its Decision Notice on Companies, the following list of matters which should, at a minimum, be included in a company's primary financial statements.

First, a payments book should reflect all payments made by the company and should include the date, cheque number, payee and amount paid. The amount should then be broken down into the VAT and net amount, and then categorised into a predefined expenditure heading, such as heat and light or telephone, for example.

Second, a receipts book should set out all monies received by the company, including the date; name of payor; amount; the amount exclusive of VAT; a description of the category into which the receipt falls (whether trading receipt or bank interest for example); and a statement of the amount lodged to the bank, with an explanation where there are joint lodgments.[8]

Third, all bank documents evidencing the company's payments and receipts should be retained by the company, including statements, cheque stubs, lodgment slips and correspondence.

---

⁴   CA 1990, s 202(1)(a).

⁵   CA 1990, s 202(1)(b).

⁶   CA 1990, s 202(1)(c), as amended by European Communities (International Financial Reporting Standards and Miscellaneous Amendments) Regulations 2005, reg 9 and Sch. Note these Regulations apply to companies whose financial years commence on or after 1 January 2005.

⁷   CA 1990, s 202(1)(d), as amended by European Communities (International Financial Reporting Standards and Miscellaneous Amendments) Regulations 2005, reg 9 and Sch.

⁸   ODCE, Decision Notice on Companies, D/2002/1, Information Book 1.

Furthermore, it will, according to the ODCE, be necessary to perform a stocktake at the end of each year to assess the amount of physical stock at hand. The ODCE cautioned however that:

> '... the system as set out above is very basic and, generally, will not provide the requisite level of management information for all but the smallest of companies. Where the above system is not adequate to enable the company and its directors to determine at any time and with reasonable accuracy the financial position of the company, a more sophisticated accounting system will be required in order to fulfil the company's legal obligations to maintain proper accounting records.'[9]

The information that the ODCE specifically requires a company to keep may therefore be regarded as the bare minimum and any company which fails to keep a payments and receipts book and copies of bank documents, may be found to be in default of its obligations.

(b) Form and language

[4.005] It is not necessary that the books of account which a company keeps must be in a physical form. On the contrary, s 202(1) refers to the obligation of companies to keep proper books of account 'whether in the form of documents or otherwise'. A company may therefore comply with the requirements of s 202 by having a computer file which includes the information required by that provision.

If the books of account are kept in written form, they must be in one of the official languages of the State, Irish or English.[10] If the books of account are kept outside the State, the accounts and returns which must be sent to, and kept in, the State must also be in one of the State's official languages.[11] It appears that books of account which are kept outside the State do not themselves have to be in an official language of the State.

[4.006] If a company's books of account (or accounts or returns, in the case of books of account which are kept outside the State) are not in written form, they must be kept in a form which enables them 'to be readily accessible and readily convertible into written form in an official language of the State.'[12] While this could be interpreted as permitting the books to be kept in a different language so long as they are readily convertible into

---

[9] ODCE, Decision Notice on Companies, D/2002/1. Information Book 1. It should also be noted that the ODCE includes the following qualification to the guidance contained in that Decision Notice: 'The guidance set out in this appendix is general in nature and does not purport to be an all-encompassing guide. Companies and their directors are strongly advised to seek professional accountancy advice when setting up their accounting and internal control systems in order to ensure that the systems implemented enable the company and its directors to comply with their legal requirements in this regard'.

[10] CA 1990, s 202(7). See Art 8 of the Constitution: '(1) The Irish language as the national language is the first official language. (2) The English language is recognised as a second official language.'

[11] CA 1990, s 202(6), as amended by as amended by the European Communities (International Financial Reporting Standards and Miscellaneous Amendments) Regulations 2005, reg 9 and Sch. See para [4.012].

[12] CA 1990, s 202(7).

Irish or English, this interpretation appears strained, as, if a document which needed to be fully translated into Irish or English could be described as 'readily convertible,' this would render the requirement to keep books in Irish or English meaningless.

It appears that the provision requires that while books, accounts or returns may be kept other than in written form, they must nonetheless be in an official language of the State, and must be readily accessible and convertible into written form. An electronic file which stores the books, accounts or returns would therefore be sufficient, so long as the language used is English or Irish and the file can be easily accessed, read and printed into paper form.

(c) Regularity required

[4.007] It is evident from the terms of s 202 that books of account must be kept updated. In particular, the requirement that the books of account must 'at any time enable the financial position of the company to be determined with reasonable accuracy'[13] illustrates that books of account are not matters which should be tended to purely for the purpose of preparation of annual accounts, or on any other such sporadic basis. Section 202(2) clarifies this requirement further. It provides:

> 'The books of account of a company shall be kept on a continuous and consistent basis, that is to say, the entries therein shall be made in a timely manner and be consistent from one year to the next.'[14]

The requirement that the books be kept on a 'continuous' basis and that the entries be made 'in a timely manner' demonstrates that a company should enter transactions into its books of account and maintain any necessary records promptly after the transaction in question.

[4.008] The requirement of consistency in the keeping of books of account was explained by the ODCE as follows:

> 'The requirement that accounts be prepared in a consistent manner from one year to the next is to allow accounts covering different periods to be compared. Where they are not directly comparable due to, for example, a change in the manner in which they have been prepared (eg due to a change in accounting policy), this must be stated in the accounts.'[15]

Therefore, if a company does introduce a change to the manner in which it keeps its books of account, it must state this change in its accounts, to ensure that a proper means of comparing different periods may be arrived at.

(d) Content of books

[4.009] Section 202(3) sets out some specific matters which a company's books of account must contain. This is without prejudice to the generality of the requirements of s 202(1) and (2) and should not therefore be assumed to be a finite list of matters to be

---

[13]   CA 1990, s 202(1)(b).

[14]   CA 1990, s 202(2).

[15]   ODCE, Decision Notice on Companies D/2002/1, Information Book 1.

included in a company's books. The matters which must be included in a company's books, according to s 202(3) are the following:

(a) entries from day-to-day of all sums of money received and expended by the company and the matters in respect of which the receipt and expenditure takes place,

(b) a record of the assets and liabilities of the company,

(c) if the company's business involves dealing in goods—

    (i) a record of all goods purchased, and of all goods sold (except those sold for cash by way of ordinary retail trade), showing the goods and the sellers and buyers in sufficient detail to enable the goods and the sellers and buyers to be identified and a record of all the invoices relating to such purchases and sales,

    (ii) statements of stock held by the company at the end of each financial year and all records of stocktakings from which any such statement of stock has been, or is to be, prepared, and

(d) if the company's business involves the provision of services, a record of the services provided and of all the invoices relating thereto.

(e) Deemed proper books

[4.010] –A company's books of account will be deemed to be proper if three conditions are met.[16] First, the books must give comply with the requirements of s 202(1), (2) and (3). Second, the books must give a 'true and fair view of the state of the affairs of the company'. Thirdly, the books must explain the company's transactions.[17] The requirement that a company's books of account give a 'true and fair view of the state of affairs of the company' is an overriding one and is often the definitive criterion applied in assessing a company's books. While there is no definition in the CA 1963–2006, of a 'true and fair view', compliance with the applicable accounting standards will be a strong indication that the books do give such a view.[18] Compliance with such standards may not, however, be sufficient to render a company's books a 'true and fair' reflection of the company's state of affairs.

(f) Currency of books

[4.011] The CRO has adopted the position that a company's books of account (referred to by the CRO as the 'internal books of account') should be maintained 'in a currency which will enable the financial position of the company to be determined with reasonable accuracy, and an audit to be carried out without difficulty' in order to comply

---

[16] CA 1990, s 202(4).

[17] It is interesting to note that the predecessor to CA 1990, s 202, CA 1963, s 147 had a provision which was essentially the reverse of s 202(4). Section 147(2) provided that, 'For the purposes of sub-s (1), proper books of account shall not be deemed to be kept in relation to the matters aforesaid if there are not kept such books as are necessary to give a true and fair view of the state of the company's affairs and to explain its transactions.' Section 147 was repealed by CA 1990, s 6.

[18] See Courtney, *The Law of Private Companies* (2nd edn, Tottel Publishing, 2002) at para 13.022.

with s 202.[19] By contrast, a company's 'formal books of account,' which includes annual and group accounts, must be prepared in 'a currency which has legal effect as at the date on which the financial year ends are accepted for filing by the CRO'.[20]

(g) Location of books

[4.012] The general rule is that a company's books of account must be kept at the company's registered office. However, the books may be kept at 'such other place as the directors think fit.'[21] This is subject to the qualification that if the books of account are kept outside of Ireland, certain additional steps must be taken.[22] In particular, accounts and returns relating to the company must be sent to a place in the State and kept there open for inspection at all reasonable times by the directors. These accounts and returns must meet the following criteria:

– relate to the business of the company which is dealt with in the books of account which are kept outside the State;

– disclosure 'with reasonable accuracy' the financial position of that business;

– reflect the financial position at intervals not exceeding six months;

– enable the company's accounts and any annexes to be prepared in accordance with the Companies Acts or the IAS Regulation; and

– give information required, and permitted to be given, by the Companies Acts.[23]

(h) Inspection

[4.013] An interesting point to note about a company's books of accounts is that there is a limited category of persons who are entitled to inspect these books. Section 202(8) provides in this regard:

> A company shall make its books of account, and any accounts and returns referred to in sub-s (6), available in written form in an official language of the State at all reasonable times for inspection without charge by the officers of the company and by other persons entitled pursuant to the Companies Acts to inspect the books of account of the company.

There are a number of points to note about this provision. First, it requires a company to make its books, accounts, or returns (if applicable), available in written form in Irish or English. This seems somewhat inconsistent with the terms of s 202(7) which states that a company may keep its books, accounts or returns, in a form other than written form, so long as they are 'readily accessible and readily convertible into written form in an

---

[19]   CRO, Company's Accounts, at www.cro.ie.

[20]   CRO, Company's Accounts, at www.cro.ie.

[21]   CA 1990, s 202(5).

[22]   CA 190, s 202(6), as amended by the European Communities (International Financial Reporting Standards and Miscellaneous Amendments) Regulations 2005, reg 9 and Sch.

[23]   CA 1990, s 202(6), as amended by the European Communities (International Financial Reporting Standards and Miscellaneous Amendments) Regulations 2005, reg 9 and Sch.

official language of the State.'[24] The only reasonable interpretation of s 202(8) is that, while a company is not obliged to keep its books of account (or accounts or returns in the case of books kept outside the State) in a written form, it must make the books available in written form if an officer, or other person entitled to do so, wishes to inspect the books. This leads to a second point that may be noted about s 202(8), which is that it appears that notice must be given of an intention to inspect the books. There is nothing in the provision which stipulates such a notice requirement, but if a company is to have the time to make the books, accounts or returns available in written form, it must be entitled to some time to convert the documents into that form.

A third point to note in relation to s 202(8) is that inspection can only occur at 'reasonable times' and that a company cannot therefore be taken by surprise by an out-of-hours demand to inspect its books of account. Fourth, no charge can be levied for the right to inspect a company's books of account, irrespective of the cost which may be incurred by the company in converting the books into a written form, as required by s 202(8). Fifth, there is no reference in s 202(8) to a right to take copies of a company's books of account.

Finally, the persons who are entitled to inspect a company's books of account (or accounts or returns where the books are kept outside the State) are primarily the officers of the company.[25] Other persons who are entitled, pursuant to the Companies Acts, to inspect the books include inspectors,[26] the DCE[27] and the company's auditors.[28]

[4.014] In *Healy v Healy Homes Ltd*[29] the right of a director to inspect a company's books of account, under the predecessor to s 202, CA 1963, s 147 (now repealed) was considered. In relation to the right of inspection, s 147(3) provided, 'the books of account shall be kept at the registered office of the company or at such other place as the directors think fit, and shall at all reasonable times be open to inspection by the directors.' This provision was more limited in the right of inspection it conferred than s 202(8), being confined as it was to 'directors', but the point which arose in *Healy v Healy Homes Ltd* is equally applicable to s 202(8).

In *Healy v Healy Homes Ltd*[30] the company sought to prevent a director from inspecting the books of account, on the ground that he was accompanied by his accountant and a

---

[24] CA 1990, s 202(7).

[25] Note that CA 1963, s 2(1) describes an officer as including a director or secretary.

[26] Note that CA 1990, imposes no limit on the scope of the documents or books of which an inspector may require production. Section 10(1) simply refers to '... all books or documents of or relating to the company ...'. See Ch **13**.

[27] See CA 1990, s 19, as substituted by CLEA 2001, s 29. See Ch **12**.

[28] CA 1990, s 193(3) ('every auditor shall have a right of access at all reasonable times to the books, accounts and vouchers of the company and shall be entitled to require from the officers (within the meaning of s 197(5)) of the company such information and explanations that are within their knowledge or can be procured by them as he thinks necessary for the performance of the duties of the auditors.'). See Ch **7**.

[29] *Healy v Healy Homes Ltd* [1973] IR 309.

[30] *Healy v Healy Homes Ltd* [1973] IR 309.

director's right of inspection of the books was a personal right. Kenny J considered the nature of the requirement that a company keep proper books of account and to make those books open to inspection as follows:

> 'The purpose of the section is to compel companies to keep proper books of account: one of the ways in which this important object is achieved is by imposing an obligation on each director to make sure that this is being done. But a director who has not had a training in accountancy cannot decide whether proper books of account are being kept unless an accountant is allowed to inspect them; the phrase "proper books of account" means books which give a true and fair view of the state of the company's affairs and which explain its transactions. It follows that a director's right to inspect the books of account necessarily involves that an accountant nominated by him may do this.'

This demonstrates that one of the reasons for requiring that books of account be open to inspection is to police and enforce the duty of companies to keep proper books of account, and that a right of inspection may only be effective if it is carried out by someone with the suitable qualifications.

[4.015] Another reason cited by Kenny J for allowing directors to inspect a company's books of account relates to the potential liability of such directors for failures to keep such proper books. In this regard, Kenny J held:

> 'The right of a director to inspect the books of a company, when he has an obligation imposed on him the breach of which may involve him in criminal liability, necessarily implies that he has the right to employ a qualified agent to advise him. The question whether proper books are being kept is one on which an accountant is the only person qualified to advise as most directors would not be able to form a correct judgment on the matter.'

In light of the significant increase in the severity of the sanctions which directors may face for 1990 failure to keep proper books of account since CA 1990, and the possibility that the possibility that directors may now face orders of personal liability for the company's debts, as well as criminal prosecution, for failures to keep proper books of account, the rationale for allowing a director to be accompanied by someone to help him to understand the content of the books, is all the more compelling.

The Court in *Healy v Healy Homes Ltd* therefore strongly endorsed the importance of a director's right to carry out an effective and meaningful inspection of the company's books of account and established that a director has the right to be accompanied by someone who can advise him and assist him in ascertaining whether proper books of account are being kept.

[4.016] There are two further points to note about the decision of Kenny J in *Healy v Healy Homes Ltd*. While the director in that case sought only to be accompanied by an accountant in his inspection of the books of account, the Court went a step further and stated, in what must be an *obiter dictum*, that a director may authorise an accountant to inspect the books on his behalf. If a director did choose to given written authority to an accountant to inspect the books on his behalf, Kenny J stated that the accountant may 'be required to give a written undertaking that the knowledge which he gets will not be used for any purpose except that of giving confidential advice to his employer in relation to the matter in connection with which he has been retained.' The Court further noted that the case of *Bevan v Webb*,[31] which concerned inspection under the Partnership Act 1890, 'decided that the accountant is entitled to make the inspection though he is not accompanied by his employer if he has the necessary authority from him.'

[4.017] A further aspect of the decision of Kenny J which is noteworthy is the statement that 'The director and his accountant are also entitled to make copies of the books of account or any part of them.' There is no express provision in s 202 which confers a right on officers to take or require copies of a company's books of account. Section 147 similarly conferred no right on directors to take or require copies of the books. While the headnote to the judgment of Kenny J in *Healy v Healy Homes Ltd*[32] indicates that the director did seek to take copies of the books of account, there is no reference in the judgment to this aspect of the case and it is not clear whether the right to take copies was raised as an issue before the High Court. It is possible that the statement that a director is entitled to take copies of the books of account is *obiter*. Moreover, the fact that s 202 does not confer any express right to copies of the books of account can be contrasted with the provisions applicable to the right to inspect the company's registers, such as the register of members,[33] directors[34] and directors' shareholdings.[35] This reservation notwithstanding, the decision of *Healy v Healy* was cited in *Brosnan v Summerville*[36] as authority for the proposition that, 'a director is entitled to be accompanied by his/her accountant for the purpose of inspecting the books of account, and to make copies thereof.

(i) Preservation

[4.018] A company must preserve any books of account, or accounts or returns, in the case of companies which keep their books of account outside the State, for at least six years. This date is calculated from the latest date to which the books, accounts or returns relate.[37]

C. Criminal liability

(a) Company and directors

[4.019] If there is a contravention of CA 1990, s 202, both the company and its directors may face criminal prosecution.[38] There are two categories of offences of which

---

[31] *Bevan v Webb* [1901] 2 Ch 59.

[32] *Healy v Healy Homes Ltd* [1973] IR 309.

[33] CA 1963, s 119(2). See further Ch **3**.

[34] CA 1963, s 195(10A), as substituted by CA 1990, s 51 and as inserted by CLEA 2001, s 91.

[35] CA 1963, s 190(8). See further Ch **3**.

[36] *Brosnan v Summerville* [2006] IEHC 329.

[37] CA 1990, s 202(9).

[38] It may be noted that s 202(10) refers to 'company that contravenes this section' which leaves open the possibility that directors may be prosecuted for a failure of a company to comply with requirements such as making the books open to reasonable inspection by officers of the company.

directors may be convicted under s 202. First, if a director fails to take 'all reasonable steps' to secure the company's compliance with s 202, he may be convicted of an offence.[39] This is subject to the qualification that it will be a defence to prove that he had 'reasonable grounds for believing and did believe that a competent and reliable person was charged with the duty of ensuring that those requirements were complied with and was in a position to discharge that duty.'[40] If a company has an accountant, for example, who bears responsibility for ensuring that the company keeps proper books of account, its directors can raise this as a defence to a prosecution for failing to take reasonable steps to secure compliance with s 202. Furthermore, according to s 202(10)(b), a director 'shall not be sentenced to imprisonment for such an offence unless, in the opinion of the court, the offence was committed willfully.' The effect of this provision is essentially that a director who is prosecuted for failing to take 'reasonable steps' to secure compliance with s 202 will not be sentenced to imprisonment.

The second ground on which a director may face prosecution under s 202 is if he is the cause of the company's default by 'his own willful act'.[41] On such a prosecution, it is no defence for the director to believe that a reliable and competent person was responsible for ensuring proper books of account were kept. When a director is convicted of causing a default under s 202 by 'his own willful act' he may moreover face imprisonment.[42]

An offence under s 202 is punishable by a maximum fine of €1,904.61, or a maximum sentence of imprisonment for 12 months, or both, on summary conviction.[43] On conviction on indictment, a maximum fine of €12,697.38 or a maximum sentence of imprisonment of five years, or both, may be imposed.[44]

[4.020] There have been a large number of convictions of directors and companies arising from non-compliance with s 202. In most of these cases the charges were prosecuted by the ODCE and were tried summarily, resulting in the imposition of fines and orders for the payment of legal costs. The ODCE reports in its Annual Report 2006 the 'importance for the conduct of commercial relations that the transactions of companies are properly recorded and described, so that relevant company stakeholders (such as banks, creditors and other stakeholders) with access to the company's prepared financial statements can rely on the associated information.' The ODCE further states in its Annual Report that, 'Due to the importance of the obligation, the ODCE gives priority in its investigations to detected breaches of these requirements.' Thirteen cases for failures to keep proper books of account in accordance with s 202 were concluded in 2006, of which only one was unsuccessful. The ODCE records that, of the 42 charges prosecuted in 2006, there were convictions of nine directors on 25 charges in respect of nine companies. A further eight charges were deemed by the District Court to have been

---

[39] CA 1990, s 202(10).

[40] CA 1990, s 202(10)(a).

[41] CA 1990, s 202(10).

[42] CA 1990, s 202(10)(b) only exempts from imprisonment directors who are not guilty of wilfulness.

[43] CA 1990, s 240(1), as amended by CLEA 2001, s 104.

[44] CA 1990, s 240(1), as amended by CLEA 2001, s 104.

proven, and five charges were taken into account by the court. Fines totalling over €10,000 were imposed in respect of these offences.[45]

(b) Officers

[4.021] An officer of a company may face prosecution for a company's failure to keep proper books of account in certain circumstances.[46] First, the company must be in the process of being wound up.[47] Second, the company must be unable to pay all of its debts.[48] Third, the company must have contravened s 202. Finally, the court must consider that the contravention of s 202 had one of the following consequences:

- it contributed to the company's inability to pay all of its debts;

- it caused substantially uncertainty as to the company's assets or liabilities; or

- it substantially impeded the orderly winding up of the company.[49]

If these conditions are met, every officer of the company who is in default shall be guilty of an offence. However, there are certain defences open to such officers. First, if an officer shows that he took all reasonable steps to secure compliance with s 202, this will relieve him of liability under s 203.[50] This defence renders the scope of the liability of directors under s 202(10) similar to that of officers under s 203. While the focus is different, in both cases, there must be a failure to take 'reasonable steps' to ensure compliance with s 202 before a conviction will be secured.

[4.022] The second defence which an officer may invoke under s 203 is that:

> ... he had reasonable grounds for believing and did believe that a competent and reliable person, acting under the supervision or control of a director of the company who has been formally allocated such responsibility, was charged with the duty of ensuring that that section was complied with and was in a position to discharge that duty.[51]

This defence is similar to the defence which directors, not being charged with wilfulness, may invoke under s 202. However, there are two points of distinction to note. First, any officer charged under s 203 may invoke this defence, whether or not wilfulness is found to exist on the part of the officer. This can be contrasted with the position pertaining to directors of companies which are not being wound up, who are charged with causing the company's default by means of 'willful act'. Such directors cannot invoke the defence of believing that a competent and reliable person was responsible for ensuring s 202 was complied with.

---

[45] ODCE Annual Report 2006 at pp 20 to 21.

[46] CA 1990, s 203.

[47] CA 1990, s 203(1)(a).

[48] CA 1990, s 203(1)(a).

[49] CA 1990, s 203(1)(b).

[50] CA 1990, s 203(2)(a).

[51] CA 1990, s 203(2)(b).

A second point of distinction is that an officer who wishes to invoke this defence under s 203, must not only show that he believed, on reasonable grounds, that a competent and reliable person was responsible for ensuring compliance with s 202, and in a position to do so, but also that this person was acting under the supervision or control of a director who was formally allocated responsibility for such supervision or control. As an illustration, it is not sufficient for an officer to show that he believed that the company retained an accountant with responsibility for keeping proper books of account. The officer must also believe on reasonable grounds that a director of the company was responsible for supervising or controlling that accountant and did in fact do so.

[4.023] If an officer is convicted summarily under s 203, he may face a maximum fine of €1,904.61 or maximum sentence of six months, or both.[52] On conviction on indictment, he may face a maximum fine of €12,697.38, or a maximum sentence of imprisonment of five years, or both.[53] In contrast to the conviction of directors of companies which are not being wound up, under s 202, there is no pre-requisite that wilfulness be found for an officer to face a sentence of imprisonment on conviction under s 203.

D. Personal liability

[4.024] The possibility of personal liability arises where the criteria for the criminal prosecution of an officer under s 203 are met, namely that a company which is in insolvent liquidation, was in violation of s 202, and that this violation contributed to the inability to pay debts; impeded the orderly winding up of the company; or resulted in substantial uncertainty as to the company's assets and liabilities.[54] If these criteria are met, a liquidator, creditor or contributory of the company may make an application to the court to have officers of the company who are in default declared personal liable for the company's debts.[55] Such an application may relate to one or more present or former officers of the company.

An officer is in default under this provision if he 'authorises or … in breach of his duty as such officer, permits, the default mentioned in the provision.'[56] An officer is 'presumed to have permitted a default by the company unless the officer can establish that he took all reasonable steps to prevent it or that, by reason of circumstances beyond his control, was unable to do so.'[57]

The category of 'officers' in respect of whom declarations of personal liability may be sought under s 204 is wider than the 'officers' who may be subject to criminal

---

[52]   CA 1990, s 203(1)(b)(i), as amended by CA 1990, s 240(7), as inserted by CLEA 2001, s 104(c).

[53]   CA 1990, s 203(1)(b)(ii).

[54]   CA 1990, s 204(1).

[55]   Note that, pursuant to s 204(2), 'On the hearing of an application under this subsection, the person bringing the application may himself give evidence or call witnesses.'

[56]   CA 1963, s 383(1), as substituted by CLEA 2001, s 109. See Ch **6**.

[57]   CA 1963, s 383(2), as substituted by CLEA 2001, s 109.

prosecution under s 203. Section 204(6) provides that 'officer', for the purpose of that section, 'includes a person who has been convicted of an offence under s 194, 197 or 242 in relation to a statement concerning the keeping of proper books of account by the company.' Section 194 deals with the duty of auditors to report a failure by a company to comply with s 202. If an auditor fails to discharge his duties under that provision, he shall be guilty of an offence.[58] If this occurs, an auditor convicted under s 194, may also face a declaration of personal liability for the company's debts under s 204.

Section 197(5) provides that an officer includes an employee of a company. If and insofar as an employee has been prosecuted under s 197 for making a misleading, false or deceptive statement to an auditor in a material particular, that person may also face the risk of a declaration of personal liability under s 204.

Section 242 creates the offence of furnishing false information and provides for the prosecution of any person 'who answers a question, provides an explanation, makes a statement or completes, signs produces, lodges or delivers any return, report, certificate, balance sheet or other document false in a material particular, knowing it to be false, or recklessly answers a question, provides an explanation, makes a statement or completes, signs produces, lodges or delivers any such document false in a material particular shall be guilty of an offence.'[59]

Insofar as any person is convicted under s 242 in connection with a statement concerning the keeping of proper books of account by a company, that person may also be the subject of a declaration of personal liability under s 204.

[4.025] If the court thinks it proper to do so, it may declare such officer or officers (as broadly defined in s 204) to be personally liable, without any limitation, for all of the company's debts or liabilities, or such part of those debts or liabilities as the court may specify.[60] A court shall not make such a declaration however, if it considers that one of the defences mentioned in s 203, and repeated in s 204, are applicable. Therefore, if the officer took 'all reasonable steps' to secure compliance with s 202, or believed on reasonable grounds, that a competent and reliable person, under the supervision or control of a director, was responsible for ensuring compliance with s 202, and was in a position to discharge that duty, a declaration of personal liability should not be made.[61] However, if such defences are not applicable, the fact that an officer may be criminally liable for the default in question, will not prevent a declaration of personal liability being made under s 204.[62]

---

[58] CA 1990, s 194(4). See further Ch 7.

[59] CA 1990, s 242(1), as amended by IFCMPA 2005, s 71.

[60] CA 1990, s 204(1).

[61] CA 1990, s 204(4).

[62] CA 1990, s 204(5) ('this section shall have effect notwithstanding that the person concerned may be criminally liable in respect of the matters on the ground of which the declaration is to be made.')

[4.026] The court may further give directions to give effect to the declaration of personal liability, including the following:

> ... make provision for making the liability of any such person under the declaration a charge on any debt or obligation due from the company to him, or on any mortgage or charge or any interest in any mortgage or charge on any assets of the company held by or vested in him or any company or other person on his behalf, or any person claiming as assignee[63] from or through the person liable under the declaration or any company or person acting on his behalf, and may from time to time make such further order as may be necessary for the purpose of enforcing any charge imposed under this subsection.[64]

[4.027] The courts have shown their willingness to make declarations of personal liability under s 204 in a number of decisions. In *Re Mantruck Services Ltd*[65] a liquidator sought an order under s 204 against a director and shareholder of a company, alleging significant and extensive omissions in the company's books and stating that it took eighty per cent of his time as liquidator to attempt to assess the company's assets and liabilities as a result of these omissions. In the application to court he averred that the failure to keep proper books of account substantially impeded the orderly winding up of the company and caused substantial uncertainty as to the company's assets and liabilities. In particular, the liquidator stated that the deficiencies in the books and records did not enable him to determine the financial position of the company with reasonable accuracy; did not enable the company to be readily and properly audited; the books and records did not properly record the assets and liabilities of the company; the books and records did not properly record all goods purchased and sold by the company in sufficient detail to enable the goods' sellers and buyers to be identified and did not properly record all the invoices relating to such purchases and sales; and the books and records did not properly record all sums of money received and expended by the company.[66]

Shanley J considered the scope of s 204, stating that the company must first be found to have contravened s 202:

> 'In other words, the court must be satisfied that a criminal offence has been committed by the company. Section 202, sub-s 10 makes it an offence for a company to contravene the section. Section 202 details the nature and extent of the accounting records which a company is obliged to keep. It is clear from the words of the section that the obligation of a company to "keep" proper books of account is not an obligation to act as a mere passive custodian of books and papers but rather the positive obligation to create books and records in a particular form with

---

[63]   Note that, according to CA 1990, s 204(3)(b), '"assignee" includes any person to whom or in whose favour, by the directions of the person liable, the debt, obligation, mortgage or charge was created, issued or transferred or the interest created, but does not include an assignee for valuable consideration (not including consideration by way of marriage) given in good faith and without notice of any of the matters on the ground of which the declaration is made.'

[64]   CA 1990, s 204(3)(a).

[65]   *Re Mantruck Services Ltd, Mehigan v Duignan* [1997] 1 IR 340.

[66]   *Re Mantruck Services Ltd, Mehigan v Duignan* [1997] 1 IR 340 at 345–346.

specified contents. It is also clear from the wording of the section that the obligation to keep proper books of account is necessarily a continuing obligation.'[67]

[4.028] The Court went on to consider the matters that must be established before a declaration could be made under s 204 and noted that:

'The section, on its face, does not require that there be any causal relationship between the s 202 contravention and the liability declared under s 204. Nor does the section, on its face, make any allowance for different degrees of blameworthiness which might attend contraventions of s 202. As to the absence of a causal connection between a contravention of s 202 and the liability imposed under s 204, there may well be a significant number of situations where the contravention bears little or no relationship to the amount of the debts of the insolvent company. For example, where the insolvency is the direct result of unwise foreign exchange transactions and it is discovered that the auditors and directors have knowingly and consistently *undervalued* the assets of the company (thereby resulting in a contravention of s 202) such that, while insolvent, the company's indebtedness is less than it would have been had the assets been properly valued. Where such an undervaluation results in substantial uncertainty as to the assets of the company or substantially impedes the orderly winding up of the company liability under s 204 is established, yet it would be clearly unjustifiable in principle to impose liability for all the debts of the company (caused by injudicious foreign exchange dealings) on the auditors and directors responsible for the company's contravention of s 202. On the other hand, where a particular contravention of s 202 can be seen to have a particular financial consequence resulting in a particular debt of the insolvent company, it is difficult to see how it could be argued that imposing liability for such a debt works any injustice.'[68]

Shanley J further expressed the concern that:

'... on its face, s 204 appears to allow that a court, in the exercise of its discretion, can impose unlimited liability on an officer of a company in respect of all the debts of a company where the s 202 contravention has not in itself resulted in any loss to the company, but has substantially impeded the orderly winding up of the company, or resulted in substantial uncertainty as to its assets and liabilities. There may be circumstances where, if the court's discretion is exercised in this way, the result achieved would be so harsh, unfair and disproportionate, having regard to the wrong committed, as to constitute an unjust attack on the personal rights of the affected officers.'[69]

The Court considered the presumption of constitutionality, noting that the court's discretion under s 204 must be exercised in a manner which respects the provisions of the Constitution. Applying this requirement, Shanley J stated that, in applying s 204, 'the Court in the exercise of this discretion must have regard to (but not necessarily exclusively) the extent to which the contravention of s 202 resulted in financial loss and, if it did, whether or not such losses were reasonably foreseeable by the officer as a

---

[67] *Re Mantruck Services Ltd, Mehigan v Duignan* [1997] 1 IR 340 at 356.

[68] *Re Mantruck Services Ltd, Mehigan v Duignan* [1997] 1 IR 340 at 358.

[69] *Re Mantruck Services Ltd, Mehigan v Duignan* [1997] 1 IR 340 at 358–359.

consequence of the contravention.'[70] Shanley J further concluded that, 'save in exceptional circumstances, liability should not be imposed for contraventions not resulting in loss, or for losses not reasonably foreseeable as a consequence of the contravention.'[71]

With regard to the standard of proof applicable to an application under s 204, the Court observed that no argument was raised that it was a criminal sanction or was other than a civil wrong, and the standard applicable to a civil wrong was therefore applied. In light of decisions such as *Banco Ambrosiano SPA v Ansbacher & Co Ltd*[72] and *Hanafin v The Minister for the Environment,*[73] 'no higher degree of probability of a contravention of s 202 is required than in any other civil matter.'[74]

[4.029] Having assessed the scope of s 204 and the exercise of the court's discretion under that provision, Shanley J distilled the issues to be determined on an application under s 204 into the following helpful list:

'(1) Whether the company contravened any of the provisions of s 202 of the Companies Act, 1990, in relation to the keeping of proper books of account?

(2) If it did contravene s 202, was the company at the time of its winding up unable to pay all its debts?

(3) If it did contravene s 202, did such contravention result in substantial uncertainty as to the assets and liabilities of the company or, alternatively, did such contravention substantially impede the orderly winding up of the company?

(4) Whether, if there was a contravention by the company of s 202 of the Act of 1990 resulting in either of the matters at (3) above, the respondent is an officer of the company who knowingly and wilfully authorised or permitted the contravention?[75]

(5) Whether the respondent can avail of any defence under s 204 of the Act of 1990?

---

[70] *Re Mantruck Services Ltd, Mehigan v Duignan* [1997] 1 IR 340 at 359.

[71] *Re Mantruck Services Ltd, Mehigan v Duignan* [1997] 1 IR 340 at 360.

[72] *Banco Ambrosiano SPA v Ansbacher & Co Ltd* [1987] ILRM 669 at 701 ('I am unable therefore to discern, in principle or in practice, any rational or cogent reason why fraud in civil cases should require a higher degree of proof than is required for the proof of other issues in civil claims,' *per* Henchy J)

[73] *Hanafin v The Minister for the Environment* [1996] 2 IR 321.

[74] *Re Mantruck Services Ltd, Mehigan v Duignan* [1997] 1 IR 340 at 361.

[75] It is significant to note that the definition of 'officer in default' at the time of the decision in *Re Mantruck Services Ltd, Mehigan v Duignan* [1997] 1 IR 340, was 'any officer of the company who knowingly and wilfully authorises or permits the default, refusal or contravention mentioned in the provision.' This was amended by the CLEA 2001, s 100 and now provides for the lower threshold that an officer is 'in default' if he 'authorises or … in breach of his duty as such officer, permits, the default mentioned in the provision.' According to CA 1963, s 383(2), as it now exists, an officer is 'presumed to have permitted a default by the company unless the officer can establish that he took all reasonable steps to prevent it or that, by reason of circumstances beyond his control, was unable to do so.'

(6) If not, and the matters at paras (1) to (4) are established, what order, if any, should the court in its discretion make against the respondent?'[76]

Applying these questions, the Court concluded that the books provided to the liquidator were deficient in a number of important respects and, in particular, noted that certain creditors' ledgers, debtors' ledgers, credit notes, records of stock and records to enable the company's liabilities to be assessed, were missing.

Shanley J concluded that:

> 'These deficiencies were such that the financial position of the company could not at any time be determined with reasonable, or indeed any, accuracy or enable the company to be readily and properly audited. I am satisfied further that the deficiencies were such that the assets and liabilities of the company could not be recorded and that there was not a sufficient recording or proper record of goods purchased and sold or of the purchasers and sellers of those goods or of invoices relating to all purchases and sales ... Finally, I am satisfied that the books of account were not kept in a continuous and consistent basis and are deficient in failing to enter daily all sums of money received and expended by the company and the matters in respect of which such took place. Because I am satisfied as to the foregoing, I conclude that there have been contraventions by the company of s 202, sub-s (1)(a), (b) and (d), s 202, sub-ss (2), (3)(a), (b) and (c) of the Companies Act, 1990.'[77]

The Court further concluded that the company was unable to pay its debts and that the contraventions of s 202 'were such as to result in substantial uncertainty as to the assets and liabilities of the company and also substantially impeded the orderly winding up of the company.' With regard to the respondent's role, the Court held that he 'knowingly and wilfully authorised and permitted the s 202 contraventions' and could not invoke any defence under s 204.

Applying the rationale that personal liability should not be imposed unless the default under s 202 contributed to the loss suffered, and the latter was reasonably foreseeable, Shanley J commented that it was not possible to separate out the liabilities of the company which resulted from those violations. However, it was established that the liquidator expended eighty per cent of his time in attempting to overcome the deficiencies in the company's books and records. The Court assessed that the losses resulting from this expenditure of time amounted to £91,239.80 and were reasonably foreseeable by the officer, as a consequence of the contraventions of s 202. Shanley J therefore made an order that the respondent be personally liable to the company in the amount of £91,239.80, and further made a declaration under s 150 that the respondent be restricted from acting as a company director.[78]

---

[76] *Re Mantruck Services Ltd, Mehigan v Duignan* [1997] 1 IR 340 at 361.

[77] *Re Mantruck Services Ltd, Mehigan v Duignan* [1997] 1 IR 340 at 363.

[78] Note that in this regard, Shanley J considered that he had no discretion but to impose the five year restriction, 'having regard to the mandatory words of s 150 of the Act of 1990' and the fact that the respondent did not bring himself within any of the exceptions thereto. *Re Mantruck Services Ltd, Mehigan v Duignan* [1997] 1 IR 340 at 364.

[4.030] In *Re Ashclad Ltd*[79] the liquidator made an application to the court under s 204 for orders of personal liability to be made against officers of the company. The liquidator pointed to gaps in the books and records which were provided to him, including the lack of proper records in relation to sales and purchases. He indicated that the books of account failed to show daily records of the monies received and expended by the company and that there were no statements of stock in the records, among other deficiencies. He further stated that, as a result of the gaps and deficiencies in the books of account, he could not accurately determine the company's financial position; identify the suppliers of goods or services; identify the quantities of goods or services supplied to the company; identify how the monies were used; identify the recipients of cash payments; ascertain the extent of the company's assets or liabilities; or form a judgment as to the sums received or expended by the company.

Geoghegan J concluded that the orderly winding up of the company was being substantially impeded, noting that eighty per cent of the liquidator's time was spent attempting to assess the company's books and records and overcoming the deficiencies therein. The Court further concluded that, as a result of these deficiencies, there was 'quite obviously substantial uncertainty as to the assets and liabilities of the Company.'[80]

In relation to the financial situation of the company in liquidation, Geoghegan J found that sums of at least £100,000.00 were wrongly withdrawn from the company and appropriated for other purposes. Geoghegan J referred to the judgment of Shanley J in *Re Mantruck Services Ltd*,[81] stating 'I broadly accept the approach which he adopted and the principles which he said had to be applied particularly having regard to the Constitution.' Geoghegan J was of the view that 'To some extent he [Shanley J] lays down quite a strict onus of proof in relation to causality.' However, giving the respondents the benefit of the doubt, Geoghegan J was satisfied as a matter of probability that the cash withdrawals in the range of £100,000.00, which were not for the company's benefit, very substantially affected the company's liabilities. The Court added to this figure a further £12,000.00 in respect of the liquidator's expenses in trying to ascertain the assets and liabilities of a company, as a consequence of the failures to comply with s 202 of the 1990 Act. The Court therefore concluded that the liquidator had discharged the onus of proof to obtain a declaration under s 204 and made a declaration that:

> '... the respondents should be made personally liable to the extent of £112,000 for the debts of the Company on the grounds that the Company failed to keep proper books of account as required by s 202 of the Companies Act, 1990 and that such contravention of s 202 has resulted in substantial uncertainty as to the Company's assets and liabilities and/or has impeded the orderly winding up of the Company and/or has contributed to the Company's inability to pay all of its debts.'

The Court further, with 'no hesitation', made an order for the restriction of the respondents under CA 1990, s 150.

---

[79] *Re Ashclad Ltd, Ashclad Ltd v Harrington* [2000] IEHC 174.

[80] *Re Ashclad Ltd, Ashclad Ltd v Harrington* [2000] IEHC 174.

[81] *Re Mantruck Services Ltd, Mehigan v Duignan* [1997] 1 IR 340.

[4.031] In *Re Rayhill Property Company Ltd*[82] the High Court considered an application by a liquidator for an order of restriction and an order of personal liability against a director under s 204 ('the second respondent'). This application followed an investigation by the Department of Enterprise, Trade and Employment into the affairs of three companies, including Rayhill Property Company Ltd ('Rayhill'), which were involved in a retirement home. Following the investigation, a liquidator was appointed to all three companies. The second respondent failed to deliver the company's books and records, despite requests, and failed to deliver a statement of affairs to the liquidator, despite a court order to do so. There were conflicting statements regarding the location of the books and records, but the Court found as a fact that they were removed to the United Kingdom after the date of the liquidator's demand for their production. The Court further rejected the director's representations that he had only a limited role in Rayhill's affairs and found that he was a director of the company at all material times.

In relation to the application under s 204, the second respondent argued that there was no infringement of s 202; that he took all reasonable steps to secure compliance with that provision; and that he believed, on reasonable grounds, that a competent and reliable person bore responsibility for ensuring compliance with that provision, under the supervision or control of a director, and was in a position to do so, within the meaning of s 204(4)(b).

[4.032] Smyth J determined that the person who the second respondent claimed fulfilled the latter role was a management consultant not a bookkeeper or accountant and the Court rejected the contention that he bore responsibility for ensuring that the company was keeping proper books of account. The Court also determined in this regard that it was neither reasonable for the respondent to believe that he was so responsible, nor did the second respondent in fact hold such a belief. The Court further found that the company failed to keep proper books of account under s 202, as the 'keeping' of such books was 'spasmodic and so infrequent and muddled with the affairs of other companies or enterprises' and failed 'to meet the objectives intended to be achieved by the observance of the statutory requirements.' The Court went on to consider the issue of causation:

> 'Equally, I am satisfied that there is a causative connection between the failure to keep the proper books and records which could and should have permitted the company to make informed decisions as the occasion arose (because of the muddled state of affairs there were no records extant to which reference could be made) and the inability of the company to pay debts – as was immediately clear when the applicant was appointed. No meaningful proper records were available as such. The "bits and scraps" of information, as he was able to work up into a set of records, clearly indicated that the company could not pay its debts because not only was it carrying on business while insolvent, but this was either being done knowingly and with deliberation or because it had no records on a receipts and payment basis or income and expenditure basis, or any other basis, such as could enable it to know or to pay its debts.'[83]

---

[82] *Re Rayhill Property Company Ltd, Conroy v Corneill* [2003] 3 IR 588.

[83] *Re Rayhill Property Company Ltd, Conroy v Corneill* [2003] 3 IR 588 at 596–597.

[4.033] The Court stated:

'Likewise, I am satisfied that the absence of keeping proper accounts and records must have created substantial uncertainties as to its assets and liabilities and was a substantial impediment to the winding up of the company. I am unable to accept the second respondent's evidence that he did nothing wrong – the level of laxity in the keeping of records amounts, in my judgment, to almost total disregard and was wholly unreasonable and irresponsible conduct on his part. He came to the company when it was in real difficulty and instead of being assiduous in his care of its affairs, he caused or permitted matters to go further adrift.'[84]

[4.034] The second respondent raised the argument that the appointment of the liquidator impeded his ability to help the company, an argument which the Court rejected outright, finding:

'There was no evidence to show that the company could have, in either the short or long term, traded out of its difficulties. The evidence is of business being conducted in a haphazard manner – no clear distinctions being kept between the companies, of a hand-to-mouth existence and corporate and personal affairs being confused.'[85]

The Court concluded that the evidence did not support the claim that any records were written or kept up, such as would or could give a 'true and fair view of the state of affairs of the company and/or explain its transactions.' The Court further concluded that:

'it was reasonably foreseeable by the second respondent that losses would result from his involvement in the s 202 contravention; and such losses did so arise. I am also satisfied that the second respondent knowingly and wilfully authorised or permitted the contraventions of s 202 of the Act of 1990. I have, nonetheless, also considered his defence under s 204 of the Act of 1990 and am satisfied that it is unsustainable.'[86]

[4.035] Having reached the findings, Smyth J made an order in the following terms:

'I am satisfied that the evidence establishes failure under s 202(1)(a), (b), (c) and (d), and under sub-ss (2) and (3)(a) and (b). I am satisfied beyond any doubt that the liabilities of the company were substantially and most adversely affected by the manner in which the business of the company was conducted by the second respondent and his wholly irresponsible attitude to the keeping of records by it and that he is wholly responsible for the sum proven in evidence. While the amount pleaded is such that there may be some element of doubt, I have taken the view that even on the most charitable and lenient view that can be taken, his liability is no less than €203,334, made up as to €72,551 plus €137,083, as referred to in evidence, and for the avoidance of doubt I declare the second respondent to be personally liable to the company in the sum of €203,334.'[87]

---

84   *Re Rayhill Property Company Ltd, Conroy v Corneill* [2003] 3 IR 588 at 597–598.

85   *Re Rayhill Property Company Ltd, Conroy v Corneill* [2003] 3 IR 588 at 598.

86   *Re Rayhill Property Company Ltd, Conroy v Corneill* [2003] 3 IR 588 at 598.

87   *Re Rayhill Property Company Ltd, Conroy v Corneill* [2003] 3 IR 588 at 599.

In this judgment, the decisions of Shanley J in *re Mantruck Services Ltd*[88] and that of Geoghegan J in *Re Ashclad Ltd*[89] were cited with approval. The rules applicable to an application under s 204 are now relatively well defined and it appears that an element of causation must be found to exist between the breach of s 202 and the loss claimed. It further appears that it must be reasonably forseeable that such loss would flow from that contravention before personal liability will be imposed under s 204.

E. Disqualification

[4.036] A further consequence which may flow from a failure to keep proper books of account is an order of disqualification. CA 1990, s 160(2)(g) stipulates that a court may make an order of disqualification in respect of a person, for such period as it sees fit, if it is satisfied that the person 'has been guilty of 2 or more offences under s 202(10)'.[90]

There have been numerous cases in which a failure to keep proper books of account has been invoked as a ground for making an order of disqualification. In *Director of Corporate Enforcement v Rogers*,[91] for example, the finding that there was a failure to keep proper books of account was one of the grounds on which the Court made an order of disqualification of five years' duration.

A finding that there has been a failure to keep proper books of account contrary to s 202 can also be a ground for imposing an order of restriction, as occurred in *Re 360 Atlantic (Ireland) Ltd.*[92]

---

[88]   *Re Mantruck Services Ltd, Mehigan v Duignan* [1997] 1 IR 340.

[89]   *Re Ashclad Ltd, Ashclad Ltd v Harrington* [2000] IEHC 174.

[90]   See Ch **22**.

[91]   *Director of Corporate Enforcement v Rogers* [2005] IEHC 443. See Ch **22**.

[92]   *Re 360 Atlantic (Ireland) Ltd: O'Ferral v Coughlan* [2004] 4 IR 266. See *Business Communications Ltd v Baxter & Anor* (21 July 1995, unreported), HC. See Ch **17**.

Chapter 5

COMPANIES' OBLIGATIONS: MEMBERS' MEETINGS

A. Introduction

[5.001] Every company (with the exception of a single member private limited company) is obliged to hold meetings of its members at least once a year. This requirement acts as an important control and monitor on the conduct of the company's affairs; it also allows members to play a role in ensuring their company is in compliance with the Companies Acts 1963–2006 ('CA 1963–2006'). The requirements that effective notice be given and quorums formed for such meetings, also ensures a level of transparency in the running of a company. Moreover, there are certain members' powers, such as the power to requisition the convening of an EGM, which may assist in the effective detection and enforcement of the Companies Acts.[1]

B. Annual General Meeting

(a) Intervals between AGMs

[5.002] Every company, other than a single member private limited company, is obliged to hold an annual general meeting ('AGM') every year and not more than 15 months may elapse between AGMs.[2] Section 131(1) provides in this regard:

> Subject to sub-s (2), every company shall in each year hold a general meeting as its annual general meeting in addition to any other meetings in that year and shall specify the meeting as such in the notices calling it and not more than 15 months shall elapse between the date of one annual general meeting of a company and that of the next.[3]

According to s 131(2), the following exception applies to this general requirement:

> So long as a company holds its first annual general meeting within 18 months of its incorporation, it need not hold it in the year of its incorporation or in the following year.[4]

While there is no definition of 'year' in the CA 1963–2006, the Interpretation Act 2005 defines a 'year', when used without qualification, as 'a period of 12 months beginning

---

[1]   See generally, Courtney, *The Law of Private Companies* (2nd edn, Tottel Publishing, 2002), Ch 9; Keane, *Company Law* (4th edn, Tottel Publishing, 2007), Ch 25; Forde, *Company Law* (3rd edn, Round Hall Sweet and Maxwell, 1999), Ch 4.

[2]   CA 1963, s 131(1). This requirement is replicated in the General Scheme of the Companies Consolidation and Reform Bill 2007, Pt A4, Head 46. Available at www.clrg.org.

[3]   CA 1963, s 131(1). See also reg 48, Table A, CA 1963.

[4]   CA 1963, s 131(2).

on 1 January in any year.'[5] Adopting this interpretation, every company must hold an AGM between 1 January and 31 December every year and no more than 15 months may expire between such AGMs.[6] This is subject to the exception that a company may avoid the obligation to hold an AGM in its first two calendar years (the calendar year within which it was incorporated and the ensuing year) so long as an AGM is held within 18 months of the company's incorporation.[7] By way of illustration, if a company is incorporated in early October of year one, it may be exempt from the requirement to hold an AGM in that calendar year and the following year, provided the AGM is held by the end of March of the third year. In practice, therefore, the exemption from holding an AGM in the calendar year following the year of a company's incorporation, will only apply to companies incorporated after the end of June in the first year, as otherwise the expiry of 18 months will occur within the ensuing calendar year.

(b) General business at AGM

[5.003]   There are certain types of business that must be transacted at every AGM of a company. These matters may be referred to as 'general business'.[8] All other business is deemed to be 'special business'. The following are examples of the general business that may be transacted at an AGM:

– declaration of a dividend;

– consideration of accounts and balance sheets;

– consideration of the directors' reports;

– consideration of the auditor's report;

– election of directors to replace retiring directors;

– re-appointment of retiring auditors; and

– fixing remuneration of auditors.

---

[5]   Interpretation Act 2005, Sch, Pt I.

[6]   CA 1963, s 131(1).

[7]   CA 1963, s 131(2).

[8]   Reg 53, Table A, CA 1963 provides: 'All business shall be deemed special that is transacted at an extraordinary general meeting, and also all that is transacted at an annual general meeting, with the exception of declaring a dividend, the consideration of the accounts, balance sheets and the reports of the directors and auditors, the election of directors in the place of those retiring, the re-appointment of the retiring auditors and the fixing of the remuneration of the auditors'. Note that the General Scheme of the Companies Consolidation and Reform Bill 2007 removes references to 'general business' or 'special business' and sets out, in Pt A4, Head 57, the business that must be conducted at an AGM. Available at www.clrg.org.

(c) Directions to convene AGM

[5.004] If a company fails to hold an AGM within a calendar year, or within 15 months of the preceding AGM, the ODCE may, on the application of a member of the company, call or direct the calling of an AGM.[9] Section 131(3) of CA 1963 provides:

> If default is made in holding a meeting of the company in accordance with sub-s (1), the Director may, on the application of any member of the company, call or direct the calling of a general meeting of the company and give such ancillary or consequential directions as the Director thinks expedient, including directions modifying or supplementing in relation to the calling, holding and conducting of the meeting, the operation of the company's articles, and ... the directions which may be given under this subsection include a direction that one member of the company present in person or by proxy shall be deemed to constitute a meeting.[10]

The ODCE has exercised this power on a number of instances. The ODCE reports that in October 2005, for example, a member of a management company contacted the ODCE indicating that no AGM of the company had been held. On further investigation the ODCE discovered that financial statements appended to the company's annual return suggested that they had been laid before the AGM, but that members of the company were not present at any such meeting. The ODCE therefore concluded that no AGM had been held. The ODCE directed the company to hold an AGM and further directed that (a) members be informed that the AGM was convened at the direction of the ODCE; (b) members be permitted to be accompanied by financial advisers; (c) auditors be notified in advance of the meeting to secure their attendance; (d) the statutory registers be available for inspection 30 minutes before and after the meeting; and (e) the directors be obliged to have the company's bank statements and block insurance policy available for inspection.[11]

[5.005] A meeting held at the direction of the ODCE shall, subject to any directions of the ODCE, be deemed to be an AGM.[12] However, if the meeting is not held in the year in which the default occurred, it will only be treated as an AGM for the year in which it is held if the company passes a resolution at that meeting to that effect.[13] Section 131(4) accordingly provides:

> A general meeting held in pursuance of sub-s (3) shall, subject to any directions of the Director, be deemed to be an annual general meeting of the company but, where a meeting so held is not held in the year in which the default in holding the company's annual general meeting occurred, the meeting so held shall not be

---

[9] See CA 1963, s 131(3), as amended by CLEA 2001, s 14.

[10] CA 1963, s 131(3), as amended by CLEA 2001, s 14.

[11] See ODCE, *Annual Report 2006* at p 15. See also ODCE, *Annual Report 2005* at p 25; ODCE, *Annual Report 2004* at p 14 for further examples of directions by the ODCE to convene AGMs.

[12] CA 1963, s 131(4) as amended by CLEA 2001, s 14.

[13] CA 1963, s 131(4) as amended by CLEA 2001, s 14. Note that, if a company passes such a resolution '... a copy of the resolution shall, within 15 days after the passing thereof, be forwarded to the registrar of companies and recorded by him' (CA 1963, s 131(5)).

treated as the annual general meeting for the year in which it is held unless at that meeting the company resolves that it shall be so treated.

The wording of this provision suggests that the meeting will be deemed to have been held in the year in which the default occurred, even if it was not in fact held until later. No resolution appears to be necessary for this effect to occur. However, if the company wants the meeting to constitute an AGM for the year in which it is actually held, in addition to being an AGM for a previous year, a resolution is required. If such a resolution is passed, a copy of it must be delivered to the Registrar of Companies within 15 days.[14]

[5.006] There are two issues which are not clear from the wording of s 131(4). First, there is ambiguity as to whether an AGM can be deemed to be an AGM for several years. By way of example, if a company is in default of s 131(1) by not having held an AGM for a period of five years, and the ODCE issues a direction that an AGM be held under s 131(4), whether the meeting consequently held may be deemed to be an AGM for each of those five years of default as well as the year in which it is held, if the company passes a resolution to that effect, is not addressed.

Secondly, it is only meetings which are convened at the direction of the ODCE under s 131(3) that may be deemed to be AGMs of the company, according to the language of s 131(4). The situation of companies which are in default of their obligations to hold AGMs, but in respect of which no directions of the ODCE are made, is not considered. If a company wishes to voluntarily remedy its own failure to hold an AGM as required by s 131(1), the language of s 131(4) does not seem to be of any assistance and there is accordingly no mechanism for such a company to convene a meeting that may be deemed to be an AGM of the company for the years of default.

(d) Failure to convene AGM

[5.007] If there is a failure to hold an AGM as required by s 131(1), the company and every defaulting officer is guilty of an offence and liable to a maximum fine of €1904.61.[15] If the ODCE gives a direction requiring an AGM to be held under s 131(3), which is not complied with, the company and every defaulting officer is guilty of a further offence and liable to a maximum fine of €1904.61.[16] In addition, if a resolution is passed to treat a meeting as an AGM for the year in which it is held, pursuant to s 131(4), and a copy of this resolution is not sent to the Registrar of Companies, the

---

[14]   CA 1963, s 131(5).

[15]   CA 1963, s 131(6), as amended by CA)A 1982, s 15, C(AA)A 2003, s 57 and Sch 2 and CA 1990, s 240(7) as inserted by CLEA 2001 s104(c).

[16]   See CA 1963, s 131(6), as amended by C(A)A 1982, s 15, C(AA)A 2003, s 57 and Sch 2 and CA 1990, s 240(7) as inserted by CLEA 2001, s 104(c). See also Courtney, *The Law of Private Companies* (2nd edn, Tottel Publishing, 2002) at para 9.010: 'Although the instances of criminal prosecutions under the Companies Acts have been rare, prosecutions are not unknown ...'. At fn 18 to para 19.010, Courtney notes the case of *Re Muckross Park Hotel Ltd* (21 February 2001, unreported), Killarney District Court, in which a company and its directors were prosecuted successfully and fined for failing to hold an AGM in 1999.

company and every defaulting officer is guilty of an offence and liable to a maximum fine of €1904.61.[17]

[5.008] The consequences of failing to convene an AGM within 15 months of the preceding AGM were considered by the High Court in *Phoenix Shannon plc v Purkey (No 5)*[18]. The circumstances of this case were that the company was in financial difficulties and its financiers co-opted a number individuals on to the board of directors (the defendants). At the time, there were three other remaining directors on the board (the plaintiffs), one of whom subsequently resigned. The company's articles of association provided that any co-opted director had to vacate office automatically at the date for holding an AGM. Similarly, one of the plaintiffs was due, as a matter of rotation, to resign at the AGM. No AGM was held by the company within 15 months of the previous AGM, as required by s 131. For this reason, the one remaining director purported to co-opt one of the other plaintiffs as a director, as mandated by the articles of association where the number of directors fell below the quorum. The two directors then purported to appoint the third plaintiff to the board of directors. Together, the three directors then co-opted another three persons to the company's board of directors.

[5.009] The plaintiff issued proceedings seeking a number of reliefs, including an injunction to prevent the defendants from acting as the company's directors. Costello P stated that it was:

> 'clear that the company is required to hold an annual general meeting every year and that not more than 15 months may elapse between the date of one annual general meeting and that of the next annual general meeting.'[19]

However, the Court noted that the company's articles of association were silent as to the consequences of failing to convene a meeting. The Court regarded the plaintiffs' submissions as an attempt to require the Court to imply a provision that the failure to convene a general meeting caused the co-opted directors to automatically vacate their office. The Court refused to do this for two reasons. First, the Court stated that CA 1963, s 131(3), 'makes express provision as to what is to happen should the directors default in convening an annual general meeting.'[20] These consequences, as noted above, are that the ODCE (formerly the Minister)[21] may call or direct the calling of a meeting, on the application of a member of the company, which shall then be deemed to be an AGM of the company.[22]

---

[17] CA 1963, s 131(6), as amended by C(A)A 1982, s 15, C(AA)A 2003, s 57 and Sch 2 and CA 1990, s 240(7) as inserted by CLEA 2001, s 104(c).

[18] *Phoenix Shannon v Purkey (No 5)* [1997] IEHC 214, [1998] 4 IR 597, [1997] 2 ILRM 381.

[19] *Phoenix Shannon v Purkey (No 5)* [1997] IEHC 214, [1998] 4 IR 597 at 603, [1997] 2 ILRM 381.

[20] *Phoenix Shannon v Purkey (No 5)* [1997] IEHC 214, [1998] 4 IR 597 at 603, [1997] 2 ILRM 381.

[21] Note that the functions of the Minister under CA 1963, s 131 were transferred to the ODCE, by CLEA 2001 s 14.

[22] CA 1963, s 131(3) and (4).

Costello P noted that '[t]hese provisions not only provide a practical remedy should the directors fail to convene an annual general meeting but also a means by which the default can be legally rectified.'[23] On the facts of the case, the Court observed that any member of the company could request the holding of a meeting after the lapse of the 15 month period, which would then be treated as the company's AGM. The Court concluded: 'In the light of this express statutory provision should default occur I do not think the court should imply into the article the suggested provision of automatic resignations.'[24] The directors who were co-opted onto the board of directors could not therefore be deemed to have vacated office and the defendants continued, together with the two plaintiffs who had not resigned from office, to comprise the company's board of directors.

(e) Notice of AGM

(i) Content of notice

[5.010] A notice calling an AGM must specify that it is an AGM.[25] Companies which have adopted Table A (or the relevant regulations of it)[26] as their articles of association must also state the place, the day and the hour of the meeting.[27] The notice must further describe the nature of any special business to be conducted at the meeting.[28] If it is proposed to move a special resolution at an AGM, this intention must also be stated in the notice calling the AGM.[29]

(ii) Addressees of notice

[5.011] The notice must be sent in writing to every person who is entitled to receive such notices.[30] In the case of Table A companies, reg 136 provides further that:

> ... notice of every general meeting shall be given in any manner hereinbefore authorised to
>
> (a) every member; and

---

23 *Phoenix Shannon v Purkey (No 5)* [1997] IEHC 214, [1998] 4 IR 597 at 604, [1997] 2 ILRM 381.

24 *Phoenix Shannon v Purkey (No 5)* [1997] IEHC 214, [1998] 4 IR 597 at 604, [1997] 2 ILRM 381.

25 CA 1963, s 131(1).

26 Whereas public companies rarely adopt Table A, Pt I articles of association without amending them substantially,' many private companies adopt them wholesale by virtue of their express adoption of Table A, Pt II which, in regulation 1, applies the vast majority of the Table A, Pt I regulations. See MacCann and Courtney, *Companies Acts 1963–2006* (Tottel Publishing, 2007) p 653.

27 Model reg 51, Table A, CA 1963.

28 Reg 51, Table A, CA 1963. See further para **[5.017]** regarding distinction between special and general business.

29 CA 1963, s 141(1). See paras **[5.031]** to **[5.032]**.

30 CA 1963, s 134(a), referring to reg 51 of Table A.

(b) every person upon the ownership of a share devolves by reason of his being a personal representative of the Official Assignee in bankruptcy of a member, where the member but for his death or bankruptcy would be entitled to receive notice of the meeting; and

(c) the auditor for the time being of the company.[31]

No other person shall be entitled to receive notices of general meetings.

'Members' are broadly defined in s 31 as persons whose names appear on the register of members.[32]

(iii) Timing of notice

[5.012] At least 21 days' notice in writing must be given before the date of the meeting, although the company's articles of association may provide for a longer period of notice.[33] Any provision of a company's articles of association which envisages a shorter notice period is void.[34] The notice must be calculated on the basis that the period is exclusive of the day on which it is served and the date for which the notice is given.[35]

There is a notable exception to the requirement that a company must furnish 21 days' notice of an AGM. If all of the members who are entitled to attend an AGM and vote at such a meeting, and the auditors of the company, agree that notice of less than 21 days may be provided, such shorter notice will be permissible.[36]

(iv) Service of notice

[5.013] According to CA 1963, s 134(a), unless the articles of the company provide otherwise, 'notice of the meeting of a company shall be served on every member of the company in the manner in which notices are required to be served by Table A.' Table A requires that notice of a meeting may either be given personally to a member or it may

---

[31] Note the provisions of CA 1990, s 193(5) which require auditors to receive notice of a company's AGM. See further Ch **7**. Note that under the General Scheme of the Companies Consolidation and Reform Bill 2007, Pt A4, Head 41, the persons entitled to notice of general meetings also include its directors and secretary. Available at www.clrg.org.

[32] CA 1963, s 31(2) provides in this regard: 'Every other person [other than subscribers to the memorandum] who agrees to become a member of a company, and whose name is entered in its register of members, shall be a member of the company'. On the authority of *Arulchelvan v Wright* (7 February 1995, unreported), HC, this definition of 'member' is strictly construed and persons, such as personal representatives, who are entitled to have their names entered on the register of members, but whose names have not been so registered, may not attend meetings, form part of the quorum for general meetings or exercise other rights attendant on membership.

[33] CA 1963, s 133(1)(a) and (2)(a).

[34] CA 1963, s 133(1).

[35] Model reg 51, Table A, CA 1963.

[36] CA 1963, s 133(3).

be delivered by post to the member's registered address. Regulation 133 of Table A provides in this regard:

> ... a notice may be given by the company to any member either personally or by sending it by post to him to his registered address. Where a notice is sent by post, service of the notice shall be deemed to be effected by properly addressing, prepaying and posting a letter containing the notice ...

(v) Failure to notify

[5.014] If a member is accidentally not notified of a meeting, or does not receive notice of a meeting, the meeting is not rendered invalid. Regulation 52 of Table A states that, 'the accidental omission to give notice of a meeting to, or the non-receipt of notice of a meeting by, any person entitled to receive notice shall not invalidate the proceedings at the meeting.' Where such an omission occurs, the meeting will be deemed to have been duly convened.[37] This is subject to the caveat that there must be a quorum of members who are validly notified of, and present at, the meeting. Otherwise, the proceedings at the meeting would be automatically invalid.[38]

It is established that a deliberate omission to notify members of a meeting, or an omission which is based on a misapprehension of fact or of law, will render the meeting invalid and will not be overcome by provisions in a company's articles of association in the terms of reg 52.[39]

(f) Location of AGM

[5.015] A company which is registered and formed under the CA 1963–2006 must hold its AGM in the State. CA 1963, s 140 provides that 'any business transacted at a meeting held in breach of this requirement shall be void.'[40]

There are four exceptions to this rule. First, if all of the members entitled to attend and vote at the AGM consent to its being held outside the State, this may be valid. The

---

[37] *Re West Canadian Collieries* [1961] 3 WLR 1416 at 1420 ('It must, I think, be implicit in art 75 that a meeting, the proceedings of which are to be taken to be valid notwithstanding the omission to give notice to members, is to be deemed to have been duly convened for the purposes of the articles, including in those purposes the manner of convening the meeting. It seems to me that, in the absence of such an implication, there would be no meeting the proceedings of which could be validated by the articles.')

[38] See reg 54, Table A, CA 1963: 'No business shall be transacted at any general meeting unless a quorum of members is present at the time when the meeting proceeds to business; save as herein otherwise provided, three members present in person shall be a quorum.' Note that reg 5 of Table A, Pt II, provides that, in the case of private companies, two persons present in person or by proxy shall be a quorum, whereas CA 1963, s 134(c) provides that 'in the case of a private company two members, and in the case of any other company three members, personally present shall be a quorum.'

[39] See *Musselwhite v Musselwhite & Son Ltd* [1962] 2 WLR 374, [1962] Ch 964.

[40] CA 1963, s 140(1).

consent of the members for this purpose must be in writing.[41] Secondly, if a resolution is passed at the preceding AGM that the meeting be held outside the State, this may be valid.[42] Third, if the company's articles of association do not require the AGM to be held in the State, an AGM outside the State will be valid.[43] It should be noted in this regard that reg 47 of Table A provides that, 'All general meetings of the company shall be held in the State'. The General Scheme of the Companies Consolidation and Reform Bill 2007 contains a modification at s 140(1). Under Pt A4, Head 47, a general meeting can only be held outside the State if all members entitled to attend and vote consent. The company must make the requisite arrangements to enable members to participate by 'technological means' without leaving the State, arrangements which must be made at the expense of the company.[44]

Finally, the requirement that every AGM be held in the State does not apply to the first AGM of a company held after the coming into effect of CA 1963.[45]

(g) Exemption for single member private limited companies

[5.016] The European Communities (Single-Member Private Limited Companies) Regulations 1994[46], permit the sole member of a single member company to dispense with the requirement to hold AGMs.[47] Regulation 9(1) provides that:

> 'all the powers exercisable by a company in general meeting under the Companies Acts or otherwise shall be exercisable, in the case of a single-member company, by the sole member without the need to hold a general meeting for that purpose.'[48]

Any decision which may otherwise be taken or resolved by a company in general meeting may be taken by the single member and a copy of this written decision must be communicated to the company.[49] Within 15 days of exercising any such right under the

---

[41] CA 1963, s 140(1)(a).

[42] CA 1963, s 140(1)(a).

[43] CA 1963, s 140(1)(b).

[44] The General Scheme of the Companies Consolidation and Reform Bill 2007, Pt A4, Head 47(1). Available at www.clrg.org.

[45] CA 1963, s 140(2) provides: 'Sub-s (1) shall not apply to the first annual general meeting of a company held on or after the operative date.'

[46] SI 275/1994.

[47] A decision to dispense with the requirement to hold an AGM shall be valid for the year it is made and subsequent years but does not have retrospective effect: European Communities (Single Member Private Limited Company Regulations) 1994, reg 8(2).

[48] When this occurs, the single member is exempt from the provisions of CA 1963, s 131: European Communities (Single Member Private Limited Company Regulations) 1994, reg 8(1).This is subject to the exception that the sole member cannot remove an auditor from office without holding the requisite general meeting: European Communities (Single Member Private Limited Company Regulations) 1994, reg 9(2).

[49] European Communities (Single Member Private Limited Company Regulations) 1994, reg 9(3) and (4). Note that the company is obliged to record and retain the notification of any such decisions, in a book or by other suitable means. reg 9(5).

Regulations, the company must notify the Registrar of Companies in writing of this fact.[50] Any failure by a single member or a single member company to comply with these requirements is an offence.[51] When there are meetings in a single member company, one person present in person or by proxy is a quorum, irrespective of any provision to the contrary in the articles of association.[52] The General Scheme of the Companies Consolidation and Reform Bill 2007 introduces a new power for all private companies limited by shares to pass resolutions signed by all members entitled to attend and vote, dispensing with the need to hold an AGM in a given year.[53]

C. Extraordinary General Meeting

(a) Nature of EGMs

[5.017] Every meeting of a company that is not an AGM, is an extraordinary general meeting ('EGM'). Regulation 49 of Table A provides in this regard that 'All general meetings other than annual general meetings shall be called extraordinary general meetings.' All business transacted at an EGM is deemed to be special business.[54]

(b) Convening EGMs

[5.018] There is no general obligation on a company to convene EGMs. Directors have a discretion to convene such meetings whenever they consider it appropriate to do so; it is generally at the initiative of directors that EGMs are convened, to obtain the members' vote regarding a proposed course of action.[55]

There are three circumstances in which it is compulsory for directors to convene an EGM. First, an EGM must be convened on the requisition of the company's members.[56] Secondly, the directors must convene an EGM if the company suffers a serious loss of

---

[50] European Communities (Single Member Private Limited Company Regulations) 1994, reg 9(6).

[51] European Communities (Single Member Private Limited Company Regulations) 1994, reg 9(7).

[52] European Communities (Single Member Private Limited Company Regulations) 1994, reg 10.

[53] See the General Scheme of the Companies Consolidation and Reform Bill 2007, Pt A4, Head 46(3). Available at www.clrg.org.

[54] Reg 53 of Table A provides 'All business shall be deemed special that is transacted at an extraordinary general meeting.'

[55] Reg 50 of Table A, CA 1963. See *Currie v Cowdenbeath Football Club Ltd* [1992] BCLC 1029 for an example of a case in which the directors convened an EGM on the basis they considered it appropriate to do so.

[56] CA 1963, s 132. See further below paras **[5.019]** to **[5.025]**.

capital.[57] Thirdly, the directors must convene an EGM if the resigning auditors of the company requisition such a meeting.[58] According to reg 50 of Table A:

> If at any time there are not within the State sufficient directors capable of acting to form a quorum, any director or any two members of the company may convene an extraordinary general meeting in the same manner as nearly as possible as that in which meetings may be convened by the directors.

This ensures that if the directors are obliged, or consider it necessary, to convene an EGM but cannot form a quorum to do so, any director or any two members of the company can convene such a meeting.

The General Scheme of the Companies Consolidation and Reform Bill 2007 includes a new provision whereby a court can direct a company to hold a general meeting, on the application of a member, director, personal representative of a deceased member, or Official Assignee in Bankruptcy of a bankrupt member of the company, or on its own initiative.[59]

(i) Requisition of members

[5.019] The members of a company who hold a sufficient interest in the company may compel the directors to convene an EGM.[60] This right to requisition an EGM is independent of, and cannot be curtailed by, the company's articles of association.[61] The level of interest that the requisitioning members must hold is strictly defined and depends on whether the company has a share capital or not. If the company has a share capital, the members making the requisition must hold at least one tenth of the paid up capital of the company which, at the date of deposit of the requisition, carries the right to vote at general meetings of the company.[62] If the company does not have share capital, the requisitioning members must represent not less than one tenth of the total voting rights of the members who, at the date of the deposit of the requisition, have a right to vote at the company's general meetings.[63] The members must hold this level of interest in the company at the date of the deposit of the requisition.

---

[57] C(A)A 1983, s 40. See below para **[5.026]**. Note that the General Scheme of the Companies Consolidation and Reform Bill 2007 contains this requirement to convene an EGM when there is a serious loss of capital only in the case of public limited companies. There is no such provision in the General Scheme in respect of private companies. See General Scheme of the Companies Consolidation and Reform Bill 2007, Pt 32, Head 67. Available at www.clrg.org.

[58] CA 1990, s 186. See further Ch **7**.

[59] See General Scheme of the Companies Consolidation and Reform Bill 2007, Pt A4, Head 50. Available at www.clrg.org.

[60] CA 1963, s 132.

[61] This is apparent from the wording of CA 1963, s 132(1), which states that, 'the directors of a company, notwithstanding anything in its articles, shall …' convene an EGM on the requisition of the members.

[62] CA 1963, s 132(1).

[63] CA 1963, s 132(1).

[5.020] The requisition must meet certain requirements, which are set out in s 132(2) as follows:

> 'The requisition must state the objects of the meeting and must be signed by the requisitionists and deposited at the registered office of the company and may consist of several documents in like form each signed by one or more requisitionists.'

With regard to the statement of the objects of the meeting, it appears that a general description of the matters to be raised at the meeting is sufficient. In *Fruit and Vegetable Growers Association Ltd v Kekewich*[64] the following description of the objects of a requisition was held to be sufficient and the validity of the requisition was upheld: 'for the purpose of considering the reconstitution of the board and resolutions concerning the directorate and officers of the company'.

It appears from *PNC Telecom plc v Thomas*[65] that a faxed copy of a requisition may be sufficient to constituted 'delivery' for the purposes of s 132, on the basis that, 'there is nothing inherent in a fax transmission to make it more or less reliable than the post.'[66]

[5.021] If the conditions for a valid requisition are met, the directors must convene the EGM. This is subject to the qualification that if the objects for which the meeting is sought are unlawful and could not be carried out in a lawful manner the directors are not bound to convene the meeting.[67]

Upon receipt of a valid requisition, the directors of the company must 'forthwith proceed to duly convene an extraordinary general meeting of the company'.[68] There are three components of the obligation imposed on directors by this provision. First, the term 'forthwith' may be interpreted as allowing the directors a maximum of 21 days to convene the meeting, as it is only after the expiry of 21 days that the consequences of failing to act 'forthwith' take effect.[69]

Secondly, the meeting should be held within two months of the date of the deposit of the requisition.[70] Thirdly, if a special resolution is to be proposed at the EGM, the directors

---

[64] *Fruit and Vegetable Growers Association Ltd v Kekewich* [1912] 2 Ch 52 at 53.

[65] *PNC Telecom plc v Thomas* [2004] 1 BCLC 88.

[66] *PNC Telecom plc v Thomas* [2004] 1 BCLC 88 at 94 *per* Sir Andrew Morritt VC ('The ultimate result is exactly the same as if it had been transmitted in person or by post').

[67] See *Isle of Wight Railway Co v Tahourdin* (1884) LR 25 Ch D 320 ('If the object of a requisition to call a meeting were such that in no manner and by no machinery could it be legally carried into effect, the directors would be justified in refusing to act on it', *per* Fry LJ). See also *Rose v McGivern* [1998] 2 BCLC 593.

[68] CA 1963, s 132(1).

[69] CA 1963, s 132(3) provides that 'If the directors do not within 21 days from the date of the deposit of the requisition proceed duly to convene a meeting to be held within two months from the said date, the requisitionists, or any of them representing more than one half of the total voting rights of all of them, may themselves convene a meeting, but any meeting so convened shall not be held after the expiration of three months from the said date.' It is therefore apparent that a delay of up to 21 days in convening the EGM is not of consequence.

[70] CA 1963, s 132(3) refers to the convening of an EGM within two months. This envisages the directors convening a meeting within 21 days to be held up to two months later.

must give notice in accordance with CA 1963, s 141. If the directors fail to furnish such notice, the meeting will be deemed not to have been duly convened.[71]

[5.022] During the 21 day period after the delivery of the requisition, only the directors may convene an EGM. The case of *Re State of Wyoming Syndicate Ltd*[72] illustrates this principle. In that case, the company's secretary purported to convene a meeting within 21 days of receipt of a requisition from members of the company. Wright J held that, until the expiry of that 21 day period, only the directors could convene a meeting and the secretary could not summon a meeting without their authority. The fact that the directors did not convene the meeting was more than a 'mere question of informality' and rendered the meeting and the resolution passed invalid.[73]

[5.023] Section 132(3) sets out the consequences of failing to duly convene an EGM:

> If the directors do not within 21 days from the date of the deposit of the requisition proceed duly to convene a meeting to be held within two months from the said date, the requisitionists, or any of them representing more than one half of the total voting rights of all of them, may themselves convene a meeting, but any meeting so convened shall not be held after the expiration of three months from the said date.

This permits the requisitioning members to convene an EGM directly if the directors either fail to duly convene an EGM within 21 days or fail to convene a meeting to be held within two months of the date of the requisition. Such an EGM must be held within three months of the date of deposit of the requisition.

The courts have traditionally been reluctant to interfere with the rights of shareholders to convene meetings in these circumstances. In *Isle of Wight Ry Co v Tahourdin*,[74] Lindley LJ considered this issue in the following terms:

> 'We must bear in mind the decisions in *Foss v Harbottle* and the line of cases following it, in which this Court has constantly and consistently refused to interfere on behalf of shareholders, until they have done the best they can to set right the matters of which they complain, by calling general meetings. Bearing in mind that line of decisions, what would be the position of the shareholders if there were to be another line of decisions prohibiting meetings of the shareholders to consider their own affairs? It appears to me that it must be a very strong case indeed which would justify this Court in restraining a meeting of shareholders.'[75]

[5.024] If the requisitioning members wish to convene the EGM directly, they must do so 'in the same manner as nearly as possible as that in which meetings are to be convened by directors.'[76]

---

[71] CA 1963, s 132(6). See further paras **[5.030]** to **[5.033]** regarding CA 1963, s 141.

[72] *Re State of Wyoming Syndicate Ltd* [1901] 2 Ch 431.

[73] Note that Wright J did consider that 'a mere question of informality with reference to the constitution of the board which summoned the meeting' may not render a resolution invalid. *Re State of Wyoming Syndicate Ltd* [1901] 2 Ch 431 at 437.

[74] *Isle of Wight R. Co v Tahourdin* [1883] 25 Ch D 320.

[75] *Isle of Wight Ry Co v Tahourdin* [1883] 25 Ch D 320 at 333.

[76] CA 1963, s 132(4). See further paras **[5.028]** to **[5.029]** regarding requirements for convening EGMs.

Any reasonable expenses that the requisitioning members incur as a result of the failure of the directors to convene an EGM shall be paid by the company.[77] This right to recover expenses is not premised on, or related to, the members convening an EGM, although it is difficult to see how expenses may be incurred as a result of the directors' failure, unless the members do convene the EGM.

[5.025] While there is no direct penalty imposed on directors for failing to convene an EGM, and there is nothing in CA 1963–2006 designating such a failure as an offence or breach of duty, there is an indirect penalty contained in s 132(5). According to this provision, where the company pays the reasonable expenses of the requisitioning members, the company may have the right to recover these monies from the directors who were in default. Section 132(5) accordingly provides that any sums paid to the requisitioning members, '… shall be retained by the company out of any sums due or to become due from the company by way of fees or other remuneration in respect of their services to such of the directors as were in default.' This penalty is limited, as it can only be imposed if and to the extent that the company owes monies to the directors.

(ii) Serious loss of capital

[5.026] If a company suffers a loss of capital of a particular magnitude, the directors of the company must convene an EGM. This obligation is triggered if the company's net assets are half or less of the company's called up share capital.[78] Where this occurs, the directors must convene an EGM. In particular, the directors must ensure the following requirements are complied with:

- the meeting must be convened within 28 days of the earliest date on which a director of the company is aware of this fact;

- the meeting must be held within 56 days of the earliest date on which a director of the company is aware of this situation; and

- the meeting must be for the purpose of considering whether and what measures should be taken to address the situation.[79]

Only one director must be aware of the fact that the net assets are less than half of the company's share capital for the obligation to be triggered, and for time to begin to run. It is not necessary for the board of directors as a whole to have formed the view that the net assets were less than half of the company's called up share capital. It is moreover not necessary for the individual director in question to have communicated this view to other directors or to the board of directors.

---

[77] CA 1963, s 132(5).

[78] C(A)A 1983, s 40(1).

[79] C(A)A 1983, s 40(1). Note that the meeting may not consider any matters which it would not otherwise be permitted to consider. C(A)A 1983, s 40(3) provides in this regard, 'Nothing in this section shall be taken as authorising the consideration, at a meeting convened in pursuance of sub-s (1), of any matter which could not have been considered at that meeting apart from this section.'

If the directors fail to convene an EGM in accordance with s 40(1), each of the directors who 'knowingly and wilfully authorises or permits that failure'[80] or who 'knowingly and wilfully authorises or permits that failure to continue' after the expiry of the period of 28 days within which the meeting should have been convened,[81] is guilty of an offence.

One of the means by which a failure by the directors in this regard may be detected and prosecuted, is the auditors' report. The auditors' report which is made to the members and laid before the company's general meeting,[82] is required to state, among other things, whether, in the opinion of the auditors, there existed a financial situation which required the convening of an EGM within the meaning of C(A)A 1983, s 40.[83]

(c) Location of EGM

[5.027] There is no provision of CA 1963–2006, which stipulates where an EGM of a company registered and formed in Ireland must be held.[84] However, reg 47 of Table A does provide that, 'All general meetings of the company shall be held in the State'. The provisions of the General Scheme of the Companies Consolidation and Reform Bill 2007 applicable to holding an AGM outside the State apply equally to EGMs.[85]

(d) Notice of EGM

[5.028] In the case of a private company or an unlimited company, at least seven days' notice in writing must be given in advance of an EGM.[86] If the company is neither private nor unlimited, at least 14 days' notice is required.[87] Any provision of a company's articles of association which provides for a shorter period of notice is void, although the articles may require a longer period of notice.[88] If a special resolution is to be passed at an EGM of the company, 21 days' notice must be furnished.[89] By way of exception to the general rule, shorter periods of notice may be furnished if the auditors of the company and every member who is entitled to attend meetings and vote, agree to such shorter notice.[90]

---

[80] C(A)A 1983, s 40(2)(a).

[81] C(A)A 1983, s 40(2)(b).

[82] See CA 1990, s 193. See further Ch **7**.

[83] CA 1990, s 193(2)(g).

[84] This can be contrasted with the position governing AGMs, which, according to CA 1963, s 140, must generally be held in the State. See para **[5.015]**.

[85] See the General Scheme of the Companies Consolidation and Reform Bill 2007, Pt A4, Head 47(1). See para **[5.015]**.

[86] CA 1963, s 133(1)(b) and (2)(b).

[87] CA 1963, s 133(1)(b) and (2)(b).

[88] CA 1963, s 133(1) and (2). This rule does not apply to adjourned meetings, for which shorter notice may be given.

[89] CA 1963, s 141(2); reg 51 of Table A, CA 1963. See paras **[5.030]** to **[5.032]**.

[90] CA 1963, s 133(2).

[5.029] In the case of Table A companies, the notice of an EGM must be exclusive of the day on which the notice is served and the day on which the meeting is to be held.[91] The notice must state the place, date and hour of the meeting and the general nature of the business to be conducted at the meeting.[92]

An accidental failure to give notice of a meeting to a member, or the non-receipt of notice by a member, will not invalidate the proceedings at the meeting.[93]

D. Resolutions

(a) Special resolutions

[5.030] CA 1963, s 141 stipulates that particular rules apply to special resolutions.[94] The CA 1963–2006 require special resolutions to be passed for certain purposes, including, but not limited to, the following:

- alteration of a company's memorandum of association;[95]

- alteration of a company's articles of association;[96]

- change of a company's name;[97]

- provision of financial assistance by a company for the purchase of its own shares;[98]

- redemption of preference shares issued before 5 May 1959;[99]

- rendering the uncalled share capital of a limited company incapable of being called up;[100]

---

91   Reg 51 of Table A, CA 1963.

92   Reg 51 of Table A, CA 1963. The persons to whom such notice must be sent are the same persons to whom notice of an AGM must be sent. See further para **[5.011]**. The means of service are also the same. Note that, according to CA 1963, s 134(d), 'notice of the meeting of a company shall be served on every member of the company in the manner in which notices are required to be served by Table A and for the purpose of this paragraph 'Table A' means that Table as for the time being in force.' See para **[5.013]**.

93   Reg 52 of Table A, CA 1963. See further above para **[5.014]**. These provisions are largely reproduced in the General Scheme of the Companies Consolidation and Reform Bill 2007, Pt A4, Head 52. Available at www.clrg.org.

94   Note that, according to CA 1963, s 141(4), 'For the purposes of this section, notice of a meeting shall be deemed to be duly given and the meeting to be duly held when the notice is given and the meeting held in manner provided by this Act or the articles.'

95   CA 1963, ss 10 and 28.

96   CA 1963, s 15.

97   CA 1963, s 23.

98   CA 1963, s 60, as amended by IFCMPA 2005, s 56.

99   CA 1963, s 65.

100   CA 1963, s 67.

- reduction of a company's share capital;[101]

- rendering the liability of a company's directors unlimited;[102]

- assignment of the office of director to another person;[103]

- resolution that the company be wound up by the court;[104]

- resolution that the company be wound up voluntarily;[105]

- authority for voluntary liquidator to accept shares as consideration for sale of company's property;[106]

- sanction for the exercise of the powers of a voluntary liquidator;[107]

- resolution directing the means of disposal of the company's books and papers in a voluntary liquidation;[108]

- authorisation of a credit arrangement with a director, by way of exception to the prohibition of CA 1990, s 31;[109]

- variation or renewal of determinations regarding the re-issue of treasury shares;[110]

- authorisation of off-market purchase of the company's own shares;[111]

- authorisation of purchase of company's own shares in contingent purchase contracts;[112]

- re-registration of private company as public limited company;[113]

- re-registration of public limited company as private company;[114]

- re-registration of unlimited company as limited company;[115]

---

[101] CA 1963, s 72.

[102] CA 1963, s 198.

[103] CA 1963, s 199.

[104] CA 1963, s 213(a).

[105] CA 1963, s 251(1)(b).

[106] CA 1963, s 260.

[107] CA 1963, s 276.

[108] CA 1963, s 305(1)(b).

[109] CA 1990, s 34 as substituted by CLEA 2001, s 78.

[110] CA 1990, s 209(6)(d).

[111] CA 1990, s 213.

[112] CA 1990, s 214.

[113] C(A)A 1983, s 9.

[114] C(A)A 1983, s 14.

[115] C(A)A 1983, s 53.

- variation of rights attached to class of shares;[116] and

- decisions modifying or overriding rights of pre-emption on allotments of shares.[117]

[5.031] There are three particular requirements that apply to special resolutions. First, such resolutions must be passed by three fourths of the votes cast by such members as, being entitled to vote, vote in person or by proxy at a general meeting.[118] Secondly, at least 21 days notice of the meeting at which a special resolution is to be proposed must have been given.[119] Thirdly, the notice of such a meeting must specify the intention to propose the special resolution.[120]

[5.032] The requirement of 21 days' notice of a meeting at which a special resolution is to be proposed may be avoided by the agreement of the requisite majority of the members of the company.[121] In the case of a company with share capital, this majority must comprise the majority in number of the members of the company who are entitled to attend and vote at such a meeting, and who hold ninety per cent in nominal value of the shares that carry the right to attend and vote.[122] If the company has no share capital, the majority that must agree to less than 21 days' notice, must represent the majority in number of the members of the company who are entitled to attend at vote at such meetings and this majority must represent at least ninety per cent of the total voting rights of all members at that meeting.[123]

---

[116] C(A)A 1983, s 38. Note that only the holders of the class of shares affected by the variation should vote on the resolution: C(A)A 1983, s 38. The question of whether shareholders' rights were affected by a resolution was posed and answered by Evershed LJ in *White v Bristol Aeroplane Co Ltd* [1953] Ch 65, [1953] 2 WLR 144 at 150–151 as follows: "The question then is – and, indeed, I have already posed it – are the rights which I have already summarised 'affected' by what is proposed? It is said in answer – and I think rightly said – No, they are not; they remain exactly as they were before; each one of the manifestations of the preference stockholders' privileges may be repeated without any change whatever after, as before, the proposed distribution. It is no doubt true that the enjoyment of, and the capacity to make effective, those rights is in a measure affected; for as I have already indicated, the existing preference stockholders will be in a less advantageous position on such occasions as entitle them to register their votes, whether at general meetings of the company or at separate meetings of their own class. But there is to my mind a distinction, and a sensible distinction, between an affecting of the rights and an affecting of the enjoyment of the rights, or of the stockholders' capacity to turn them to account."

[117] C(A)A 1983, s 24.

[118] CA 1963, s 141(1).

[119] CA 1963, s 141(1).

[120] CA 1963, s 141(1).

[121] CA 1963, s 141(2).

[122] CA 1963, s 141(2).

[123] CA 1963, s 141(2).

There is authority to the effect that the consent of the members to less than 21 days' notice must be knowingly given and that consent to short notice will not be valid unless the members know the effect of their consent.[124]

Unless a poll is demanded, a declaration by the chairman of the meeting that the special resolution has been carried will be conclusive evidence of that fact and it is not necessary to prove the number or proportion of votes in favour of, or against, the resolution.[125]

(b) Written resolutions

[5.033] A company's articles of association may permit its members to pass a resolution, whether special or ordinary, by means of a written procedure.[126] This requires the written resolution to be signed by every member who is for the time being entitled to attend and vote on the resolution at a general meeting.[127] Such a resolution has the same effect as if it were passed at a duly convened and held meeting of the members and is deemed to have been passed on the date on which the last member signed the resolution.[128]

The only specific exceptions to s 141 are that it is not possible to pass resolutions under s 160[129] or s 182[130] by means of written resolution.[131]

---

[124] *Re Pearce Duff & Co Ltd* [1960] 1 WLR 1014: 'In my judgment, that proviso requires the persons who agree to a resolution being passed on short notice to appreciate that the resolution is being passed on short notice and to agree to its being so passed with that consideration in their minds. I think that it is clear that in the present case the shareholders who signed the consent did not have it in their mind at all that the initial notice was defective in point of time. So, in my judgment, this consent does not cure the matter in that way' (*per* Buckley LJ at 1016) On the facts of that case, the special resolution was subsequently confirmed by the consent of 100% of the members of the company and the court gave effect to the resolution in that exceptional situation.

[125] CA 1963, s 141(3).

[126] CA 1963, s 141(8). See, eg, reg 6, Pt II of Table A, CA 1963 ('a resolution in writing signed by all the members for the time being entitled to attend and vote on such resolution at a general meeting ... shall be as valid and effective for all purposes as if the resolution had been passed at a general meeting of the company duly convened and held ...'.)

[127] CA 1963, s 141(8)(a).

[128] CA 1963, s 141(8). Note that 'where the resolution states a date as being the date of his signature thereof by any member the statement shall be *prima facie* evidence that it was signed by him on that date': CA 1963, s 141(8)(b).

[129] CA 1963, s 160 concerns the appointment, removal and remuneration of a company's auditors.

[130] CA 1963, s 182 concerns the removal of directors from office.

[131] CA 1963, s 141(8)(c). The General Scheme of the Companies Consolidation and Reform Bill 2007 introduces a new power to pass a majority resolution by means of a written procedure, Pt A4, Head 65. Available at www.clrg.org.

(c) Extended notice

[5.034] Before certain resolutions may be passed, extended notice must be furnished. The matters for which extended notice are required principally concern the appointment of auditors and the removal of directors. CA 1963, s 161 requires extended notice to be given of a resolution at an AGM to appoint a new auditor, remove an auditor or filling a casual vacancy in the office of auditor.[132] Section 182 requires extended notice to be furnished of a resolution to remove a director from office or to appoint a director in place of the removed director.[133]

[5.035] Where such notice is required, the resolution will not be effective unless notice of the intention to move that resolution has been given to the company at least 28 days before the meeting at which that resolution is to be proposed.[134] The company must send notice of this resolution to the members of the company, together with, and in the same manner as, the notice of the meeting.[135] If this is not practicable, the company must give the members 21 days' notice of the resolution either by advertisement in a daily newspaper in the district in which the company's registered office is located, or by such other manner as is permitted by the company's articles of association.[136]

There are two forms of exception to the requirement of 28 days' notice of resolutions for which extended notice is required. First, the directors may resolve to submit such a resolution without the extended notice of 28 days' being given to the company.[137] Second, if after extended notice of the intention to move a resolution is given to the company, a meeting of the company is called sooner than the expiry of the requisite 28 days, the notice shall be deemed to have been properly given, even though it was not given 28 days before the meeting.[138]

E. Conduct of business at general meetings

(a) Quorum

[5.036] There must be a quorum of members present at a general meeting and no business may be transacted unless such quorum is present at the time when the meeting

---

[132] CA 1963, s 161(1), as substituted by CA 1990, s 184.

[133] CA 1963, s 182(2).

[134] CA 1963, s 142(1).

[135] CA 1963, s 142(1) ('the company shall give its members notice of any such resolution at the same time and in the same manner as it gives notice of the meeting').

[136] CA 1963, s 142(1).

[137] CA 1963, s 142(1) ('the resolution shall not be effective unless (except when the directors of the company have resolved to submit it) notice of the intention to move it has been given to the company not less than 28 days before the meeting at which it is moved').

[138] CA 1963, s 142(2).

proceeds to business.[139] In *Re Hartley Baird Ltd*[140] the company's articles of association contained this requirement. While a quorum was present when the meeting proceeded to business, a member departed before a particular resolution was passed, reducing the number present beneath the quorum. The validity of the resolution was challenged on that basis. The Court held that the meeting and the resolution were valid, 'because at the beginning of the meeting, that is, when the meeting proceeded to business, there was present a quorum as provided by article 46 of the articles of association.'[141] On this interpretation, it would not undermine the validity of a meeting or the business conducted thereat, if a quorum was not present for the voting on resolutions, so long as the quorum was present when the meeting proceeded to business.

[5.037] *Hennessy v National Agricultural and Industrial Development Association Ltd*[142] demonstrates a different interpretation of the requirement that a quorum be present at a meeting. In that case, there was a quorum present at the commencement of the meeting and three members left before the resolution at issue was voted upon. The articles of association specified the quorum that must be present, but did not specify when the quorum must be present. Overend J stated that 'in my opinion the common law requires the quorum to be present at the one time and place when the corporate act is done', and determined that the resolutions which were passed were 'null and void for want of a quorum'.[143]

[5.038] Unless the articles of the company provide otherwise, the quorum for private companies limited by shares is generally two members present in person.[144] In the case of a public company limited by shares the quorum is three members present in person.[145] In a single member private limited company, one person present in person or by proxy shall be a quorum, any provision to the contrary in the company's articles of association notwithstanding.[146]

---

139 CA 1963, s 134. This is subject to any provision to the contrary in a company's articles of association. See reg 5, Pt II of Table A, CA 1963; reg 54, Pt I of Table A, CA 1963. *Arulchelvan v Wright* (7 February 1996, unreported), HC demonstrates that there is no exception to the requirement of a quorum in relation to personal representatives whose names have not been entered on the register of members: such persons are entitled to notice of general meetings under reg 136(b), Table A, but do not contribute towards the formation of a quorum.

140 *Re Hartley Baird Ltd* [1955] Ch 143, [1954] 3 WLR 946.

141 *Re Hartley Baird Ltd* [1955] Ch 143 at 147, [1954] 3 WLR 946 at 967.

142 *Hennessy v National Agricultural and Industrial Development Association Ltd* [1947] IR 159.

143 *Hennessy v National Agricultural and Industrial Development Association Ltd* [1947] IR 159 at 198 to 199.

144 CA 1963, s 134(c). Note that reg 5, Pt II of Table A, CA 1963, envisages the possibility that the members comprising the quorum may be present in person or by proxy.

145 CA 1963, s 134(c). reg 54, Table A, CA 1963.

146 EC(SMPLC)C 1994, reg 10.

[5.039] If a quorum is not present within half an hour of the time at which the meeting was scheduled to commence, one of two consequences may ensue in the case of companies which have adopted Table A as their articles of association. First, if the meeting was convened on the requisition of the members, it will be dissolved.[147] Secondly, in all other cases, it will be adjourned to the same day, time and place in the following week, or to such other day, time and place as the directors may determine. If a quorum is not present within half an hour of the time scheduled for commencement of the adjourned meeting, the members who are present will be a quorum.[148] In the case of a private company limited by shares, this therefore envisages a single member comprising a quorum for the purpose of a general meeting of the company.

(b) Chairman

[5.040] CA 1963, s 134(d) states that 'any member elected by the members present at a meeting may be chairman thereof.' This provision is subject to any provision of a company's articles of association to the contrary. According to reg 56 of Table A, the chairman of the board of directors shall preside as chairman of every general meeting of the company. There are three exceptions to this general rule. First, there may be no chairman of the board of directors. Secondly, if the chairman is not present within 15 minutes of the time of commencement of the meeting, he shall not be chairman of the general meeting. Thirdly, if the chairman of the board of the directors does not wish to act as the chairman of the general meeting, he is not obliged to do so.[149] If any of these exceptions applies, there are two possible outcomes. First, the directors may elect one of them to act as chairman.[150] However, if there are no directors present within 15 minutes of the time of commencement of the meeting, or none who are willing to act as chairman, the members may choose one of the members to be chairman of the meeting.[151]

(c) Adjournments

[5.041] The adjournment of general meetings is a matter which may be addressed by a company's articles of association. According to Table A, there are two circumstances in which a general meeting which is quorate and which has been duly convened and commenced, may be adjourned.[152] First, the chairman may adjourn the meeting with the consent of the meeting. Secondly, the meeting may direct the chairman to adjourn the meeting, a direction with which the chairman is obliged to comply. In such circumstances, the meeting may be adjourned to a different time and to a different place. However, the only business that may be discussed at an adjourned meeting is business that was left unfinished at the previous meeting.

---

[147] Reg 55, Table A, CA 1963.

[148] Reg 55, Table A, CA 1963.

[149] Reg 56, Table A, CA 1963.

[150] Reg 56, Table A, CA 1963.

[151] Reg 57, Table A, CA 1963.

[152] Reg 58, Table A, CA 1963.

While it is not generally necessary to give notice to the members of the adjourned meeting or the business to be transacted at the adjourned meeting, if the meeting is adjourned for more than 30 days, it is necessary to give notice of this meeting in the same manner as the meeting from which it was adjourned.[153]

[5.042] In *Byng v London Life Assurance Ltd*[154] the venue for a general meeting was inadequate, as the members of the company who attended could not be accommodated in the room in which the meeting was to be conducted. Arrangements were in place for members to be accommodated in overflow rooms but the audiovisual connections between these rooms and the meeting did not function. In these circumstances, the chairman of the meeting decided to adjourn the meeting to a later time on the same day at a venue sufficiently sizeable to accommodate the members. This was objected to, as several of the members who attended at the place and time of the scheduled meeting could not attend the adjourned meeting and could not arrange for proxies to attend on such short notice. The meeting resumed at the adjourned time and the members challenged the validity of that meeting and the resolutions passed. The company's articles of association (art 18) permitted the chairman to adjourn a meeting with the consent of the meeting.

The Court of Appeal considered the nature of the original meeting and determined that, while members were excluded and the meeting could not proceed to business, it was nonetheless a meeting.[155] The Court used the analogy of meetings lacking a quorum, which may not proceed to business but which nonetheless constitute meetings.[156] The Court then considered whether the chairman had the power to adjourn the meeting without the consent of the meeting. In this regard, Sir Nicolas Browne-Wilkinson VC referred to the chairman's overriding duty to regulate the proceedings in general meetings and concluded as follows:

> 'In my judgment art 18 regulates the chairman's powers of adjournment to the extent that its machinery is effective to cover the contingencies which occur. Therefore if the circumstances are such that it is possible to discover whether or not the meeting agrees to an adjournment, art 18 lays down a comprehensive code.

---

[153] Reg 58, Table A, CA 1963.

[154] *Byng v London Life Assurance Ltd* [1990] Ch 170, [1989] 2 WLR 738. See further paras **[5.043]** to **[5.044]** and **[5.048]**.

[155] Mustill LJ dissented from this view and stated that the events that transpired did not amount to a meeting. *Byng v London Life Assurance Ltd* [1990] Ch 170 at 193, [1989] 2 WLR 738 at 754 ('I think it equally plain that on no view could these fragments be regarded as a meeting of any kind, even one with the very limited capacity previously described').

[156] *Byng v London Life Assurance Ltd* [1990] Ch 170, [1989] 2 WLR 738 ('The fact that a meeting cannot pass a valid resolution in certain circumstances does not necessarily mean that there has been no meeting at all. Thus in many cases (including the present) the articles of a company provide that, in the event of there being no quorum present at a meeting, the meeting shall be adjourned for a fixed period. In such a case it is clear that the inquorate meeting was a meeting notwithstanding the fact that it could conduct no business. In my judgment there is no absolute rule of law that a meeting from which members are wrongly excluded is a nullity. The meeting, as such, can conduct no business, but it is nevertheless a meeting.' Sir Nicolas Browne-Wilkinson VC at 184, 746).

> But if the circumstances are such that the wishes of the meeting cannot be validly
> ascertained, why should art 18 be read as impairing the fundamental common law
> duty of the chairman to regulate proceedings so as to enable those entitled to be
> present and to vote to be heard and to vote? … the contrary result would produce
> manifest absurdities. Say that there was a disturbance in a meeting which
> precluded the taking of any vote on a motion to adjourn. Would this mean that the
> meeting had to be abandoned even though a short adjournment would have
> enabled peace to be restored and the meeting resumed?'[157]

The Court concluded that the existence of a provision in a company's articles of
association which regulates adjournments, when the views of the meeting can be
ascertained, does not preclude the chairman having an implied power to adjourn the
meeting when the consent of the meeting cannot be obtained.

[5.043] The exercise of a chairman's residual discretion to adjourn general meetings is
not without limitation however. In *Byng v London Life Assurance Ltd*[158] this power was
described as follows: 'a residual power exercisable only when the machinery provided
by the articles had broken down. This residual common law power is itself tightly
circumscribed by reference to the objects for which it exists.'[159] These objects include
giving all persons entitled to vote, a reasonable opportunity to do so; ensuring no
damage or injury is caused; and ensuring all members have a right to hear and be heard
in the debate. The Court moreover noted that:

> '… the impact of the proposed adjournment on those seeking to attend the original
> meeting and the other members must be a central factor in considering the validity
> of the chairman's decision to adjourn.'[160]

[5.044] In relation to challenging the exercise of the chairman's powers, the Court of
Appeal determined that the appropriate standard is that applicable in judicial review and
that:

> 'The chairman's decision will not be declared invalid unless on the facts which he
> knew or ought to have known he failed to take into account all the relevant factors,
> took into account irrelevant factors or reached a conclusion which no reasonable
> chairman, properly directing himself as to his duties, could have reached.'[161]

Applying this standard, the Court of Appeal determined that the chairman's decision to
adjourn the meeting to a time later on the same day, without taking into account the fact
of central importance that numerous members would be unable to attend, was
unreasonable and was not a valid exercise of the chairman's discretion to adjourn
general meetings.

---

[157] *Byng v London Life Assurance Ltd* [1990] Ch 170 at 187 to 188, [1989] 2 WLR 738 at 750.

[158] *Byng v London Life Assurance Ltd* [1990] Ch 170, [1989] 2 WLR 738.

[159] *Byng v London Life Assurance Ltd* [1990] Ch 170 at 188, [1989] 2 WLR 738, at 750–751.

[160] *Byng v London Life Assurance Ltd* [1990] Ch 170 at 189, [1989] 2 WLR 738 at 751.

[161] *Byng v London Life Assurance Ltd* [1990] Ch 170 at 189, [1989] 2 WLR 738 at 751 *per* Sir
Nicolas Browne-Wilkinson VC.

(d) Voting

[5.045] CA 1963, s 134, which applies except insofar as it conflicts with any provisions of a company's articles of association, provides that every member of a company with share capital shall have one vote for each share held or each stock to the value of €12.69 held by him. If the company does not have share capital or stock, every member has one vote.[162]

[5.046] A company must respect the right to demand a poll on any question other than the election of the chairman or the adjournment of the meeting.[163] CA 1963, s 137 renders void any provision of a company's articles of association which would:

- exclude the right to demand a poll at a general meeting;[164]

- render ineffective a demand for a poll by five or more members who have the right to vote at the meeting;[165]

- render ineffective a demand for a poll by members who represent at least one tenth of the total voting rights of all members having a right to vote at the meeting;[166]

- render ineffective a demand for a poll by members who hold shares with a right to vote on which a sum has been paid up which amounts to at least one tenth of the total sum paid up on all such shares.[167]

[5.047] Regulation 59 of Table A provides that, as a general rule, votes at general meetings should be decided by a show of hands unless a poll is demanded by one of the following:

- the chairman of the meeting;

- at least three members present in person or by proxy;

---

[162] CA 1963, s 134(e).

[163] Note that, according to CA 1963, s 137(2), 'The instrument appointing a proxy to vote at a meeting of a company shall be deemed also to confer authority to demand or join in demanding a poll.' A proxy therefore has the same right to demand a poll as a member of the company present in person.

[164] CA 1963, s 137(1)(a). Note that reg 62 provides that a poll may be demanded on the appointment of a chairman or the adjournment of meeting ('A poll demanded on the election of a chairman or on a question of adjournment shall be taken forthwith. A poll demanded on any other question shall be taken at such time as the chairman of the meeting directs, and any business other than that on which a poll is demanded may be proceeded with pending the taking of the poll.')

[165] CA 1963, s 137(1)(b)(i).

[166] CA 1963, s 137(1)(b)(ii).

[167] CA 1963, s 137(1)(b)(iii). Note that CA 1990, s 213, which concerns special resolutions authorising companies to purchase their own shares in off-market transactions, provides that nothing in s 137 shall prevent a member demanding a poll under s 213.

   –   any members present in person or by proxy representing at least one tenth of the
       total voting rights of all members with a right to vote at the meeting; or

   –   members holding shares with a right to vote on which a sum has been paid that
       amounts to at least one tenth of the total sum paid up on all such shares.[168]

The general rule is that, where a poll is so demanded, it should be taken at such time as
the chairman directs and other business may proceed pending the taking of the poll.[169]

In Table A companies, unless a poll is demanded, a declaration by the chairman that the
resolution has been carried on a show of hands, or lost, and the margin by which it was
won or lost, accompanied by an entry to that effect in the minute book, shall be
conclusive evidence of that fact.[170]

If there are equal votes, whether on a show of hands or a poll, the chairman is entitled to
a casting vote.[171]

(e) Meeting venue

[5.048] It has been established that a general meeting may be held in different rooms,
without all members meeting face to face, provided there is some form of audio visual
communication between the rooms, enabling all members to see and hear the
proceedings at the meeting. The question of whether a meeting may be held without any
members being in the same room, such as by video link, remains open. In *Byng v
London Life Assurance Ltd*[172] a meeting was held in a number of rooms with
arrangements made for audiovisual links between the rooms. While there were
difficulties with the arrangements for audiovisual communications in that case, and the
meeting did not proceed as planned, Mustill LJ considered the acceptability of such
meetings as follows:

> '... it is possible to have a meeting, not all of whose members are present in the
> same room. It is unnecessary to consider the extreme case where none of the
> participants are face to face, but are linked by simultaneous audio-visual
> transmissions. This would require consideration of whether it is possible to
> convene a meeting which does not take place in any single location, and which
> consists only of the exchange of electronic impulses. No such problem arises here.
> If the arrangements had gone according to plan, and if the participants had first
> occupied Cinema 1 until it was full, and had then all found a place in the adjacent
> rooms by the time the business had commenced, and if they all had been able to

---

[168] Reg 59, Table A, CA 1963.

[169] Reg 62, Table A, CA 1963. This is subject to the following logical exceptions: 'A poll
demanded on the election of a chairman or on a question of adjournment shall be taken
forthwith.' Reg 62, Table A, CA 1963.

[170] Reg 59, Table A, CA 1963.

[171] Reg 61, Table A, CA 1963.

[172] *Byng v London Life Assurance Ltd* [1990] Ch 170, [1989] 2 WLR 738. See further
paras **[5.042]** to **[5.044]**.

see, hear and communicate with the other participants I would have seen no intellectual and practical objection to regarding this as a "meeting".'[173]

Browne Wilkinson VC similarly held:

'The rationale behind the requirement for meetings in the Companies Act 1985 is that the members shall be able to attend in person so as to debate and vote on matters affecting the company. Until recently this could only be achieved by everyone being physically present in the same room face to face. Given modern technological advances, the same result can now be achieved without all the members coming face to face: without being physically in the same room they can be electronically in each other's presence so as to hear and be heard and to see and be seen. The fact that such a meeting could not have been foreseen at the time the first statutory requirements for meetings were laid down, does not require us to hold that such a meeting is not within the meaning of the word "meeting" in the Act of 1985 …

I have no doubt therefore that, in cases where the original venue proves inadequate to accommodate all those wishing to attend, valid general meetings of a company can be properly held using overflow rooms provided, first, that all due steps are taken to direct to the overflow rooms those unable to get into the main meeting and, second, that there are adequate audio-visual links to enable those in all the rooms to see and hear what is going on in the other rooms.'[174]

The General Scheme of the Companies Consolidation and Reform Bill 2007 includes a provision that a meeting may be held in two or more venues 'using any technology that provides members as a whole with a reasonable opportunity to participate'.[175]

F. Direction of Court

[5.049] If it is 'impracticable' for any reason for a company to call or conduct a meeting in the manner required by the CA 1963–2006, or the company's articles of association, the court may intervene.[176] This may occur of the court's own motion, or on the application of a director of the company or a member who is entitled to vote at such meeting.[177] In these circumstances, the court may order a meeting to be called, held and conducted in such manner as the court considers fit.[178] The court may also 'give such ancillary or consequential directions as it thinks expedient,' including the direction that one member of the company may constitute meeting.[179]

---

[173] *Byng v London Life Assurance Ltd* [1990] Ch 170 at 192, [1989] 2 WLR 738 at 754.

[174] *Byng v London Life Assurance Ltd* [1990] Ch 170 at 183, [1989] 2 WLR 738 at 745.

[175] The General Scheme of the Companies Consolidation and Reform Bill 2007, Pt A4, Head 47(c). Available at www.clrg.org.

[176] CA 1963, s 135(1).

[177] CA 1963, s 135(1).

[178] CA 1963, s 135(1). Note that, according to CA 1963, s 135(2), any such meeting shall be treated as if it were a duly called and convened meeting of the company. ('Any meeting called, held and conducted in accordance with an order under sub-s (1) shall for all purposes be deemed to be a meeting of the company duly called, held and conducted'.) See also General Scheme of the Companies Consolidation and Reform Bill 2007, Pt A4, Head 50. Available at www.clrg.org.

[179] CA 1963, s 135(1).

[5.050] In *Re El Sombrero Ltd*[180] a majority shareholder of a company sought a direction of the court for an AGM to be convened in circumstances where the two directors (also members) had never held a members' meeting and never filed an annual return. The Court considered the meaning of the term 'impracticable' as it appeared in the English equivalent of s 135 (Companies Act 1948, s 135). Wynn Parry J noted that the word 'impracticable' was not synonymous with the word 'impossible' and that the appropriate approach was to 'examine the circumstances of the particular case and answer the question whether, as a practical matter, the desired meeting of the company can be conducted, there being no doubt, of course, that it can be convened and held.'[181] The Court also noted that there was no reason for the court not to exercise its jurisdiction under s 135 despite the opposition of other shareholders. The Court referred to the member's statutory right to remove the directors, and the directors' breach of their statutory duties, and directed an AGM to be held.

[5.051] In *Re Opera Photographic Ltd*[182] an application was made to court to direct the holding of a general meeting. This application was made on the basis that there was deadlock between the two members of the company. The Court determined that no one member should have a veto in respect of the management of the company and that it was necessary to convene a meeting to break the deadlock. The Court therefore made the order sought.[183]

G. Minutes of meetings

[5.052] Every company is obliged to keep the minutes of every meeting of the company and of its board of directors in books kept for that purpose.[184] These minutes should be entered into the books as soon as possible after the meetings.[185] There are no other requirements stipulated in the CA 1963–2006 regarding the manner or form in which minutes should be recorded and kept.[186] In particular, there is no requirement that the

---

[180] *Re El Sombrero Ltd* [1958] Ch 900, [1958] 3 WLR 349.

[181] *Re El Sombrero Ltd* [1958] Ch 900 at 904, [1958] 3 WLR 349 at 351.

[182] *Re Opera Photographic Ltd* [1989] BCLC 763, [1989] 1 WLR 634.

[183] See also *Union Music Ltd v Watson* [2003] 1 BCLC 453.

[184] CA 1963, s 145(1). This includes the obligation to keep minutes of any meeting of a committee of the directors. See also General Scheme of the Companies Consolidation and Reform Bill 2007, Pt A4, Head 69. Available at www.clrg.org. Head 69 also requires all resolutions to be entered in the minute books.

[185] CA 1963, s 145(1).

[186] It should be noted however, that the power to keep documents other than in legible form, as conferred by C(A)A 1977, s 4, does not apply to the minutes of members' meetings. Section 4(1) provides, 'It is hereby declared that the power conferred on a company by s 378 (1) of the Act of 1963 to keep a register or other record by recording the matters in question otherwise than by making entries in bound books includes power to keep the register or other *record other than minute books kept pursuant to s 145 of the Act of 1963* by recording the matters in question otherwise than in a legible form so long as the recording is capable of being reproduced in a legible form' (emphasis added).

minutes must be signed. The effect of the minutes is greatly strengthened, however, if the minutes are signed by the chairman of the meeting to which they relate, or the chairman of the subsequent meeting: they shall then be evidence of what transpired at that meeting.[187] Once the minutes are signed, they are also a sufficient note or memorandum for the purposes of the Statute of Frauds.[188]

The minute books are important from the perspective of the company and its directors. First, if the minutes are signed by the chairman of the meeting at which they were taken, or the chairman of the following meeting, they shall be evidence of the proceedings at that meeting.[189] If disputes arose regarding what had transpired at a meeting, properly kept minutes could play an important role in resolving these disputes. Secondly, where proper minute books are kept, the meeting and the proceedings at the meeting, are deemed to have been duly held, unless the contrary is proved.[190]

[5.053] The minute books are also important from the perspective of the company's members. The books containing the minutes of the company's general meeting must be kept at the company's registered office and must be available for inspection by the members, free of charge, for at least two hours a day during business hours.[191] A member is also entitled, upon payment of a charge, to a copy of the minutes and this copy must be furnished to the member within seven days of the request.[192] It should be noted that members have no corresponding entitlement to inspect and request copies of, the minutes of directors' meetings.

[5.054] The DCE has the right to require a company to produce its minute books for inspection and must be given facilities for inspecting and taking copies of the content of those books.[193] A company's auditor has the right to inspect its books and, therefore, its minute books.[194] The potential importance of the right of inspection of a company's minutes can be seen in aspects of the ODCE's enforcement activity. The ODCE reports, for example, that an inspection of one company's minutes under s 145, demonstrated that the company had failed to convene an AGM and led to the ODCE issuing a direction that such a meeting be convened, in exercise of the ODCE's powers under s 131. When it became clear that the company would not comply with that direction, the

---

[187] According to CA 1963, s 145(2), minutes which are so signed are evidence of the proceedings at the meeting.

[188] See MacCann and Courtney, *Companies Acts 1963–2006* (Tottel Publishing, 2007) at p 299.

[189] CA 1963, s 145(2). Note, however, that they are not conclusive evidence of the proceedings at the meeting and may be rebutted. See MacCann and Courtney, *Companies Acts 1963–2006* (Tottel Publishing, 2007) at p 299.

[190] CA 1963, s 145(3).

[191] CA 1963, s 146(1).

[192] CA 1963, s 146(2).

[193] CA 1963, s 145(3A), as inserted by CLEA 2001, s 19(a). For an example of a case in which this power was exercised, see *ODCE Annual Report 2005* at p 25. It is an offence for the company and every officer in default to fail to comply with a requirement of the DCE under s 145(3A). See CA 1963, s 145(4), as amended by CLEA 2001, s 19(b).

[194] CA 1990, s 193(3).

ODCE issued proceedings against the company and one director under CA 1963, s 371, to compel compliance with its direction, and an AGM was duly convened.[195]

[5.055] A company and its officers can face a number of sanctions in connection with the obligation to keep and display the minute books. First, if the company fails to comply with the requirement to keep minutes of each meeting of the company and its directors, the company and every officer in default is guilty of an offence and liable to a fine. Secondly, if the company refuses to allow an inspection or fails to furnish a copy of the minutes within seven days, the company and every officer in default is liable to a fine.[196] Thirdly, the court may make an order compelling an immediate inspection of the minute books or the delivery of copies of those books, where there has been a failure or refusal to do so.[197]

---

[195] ODCE *Annual Report 2005* at p 25 ('Grangewood Estate Services (Rosslare) Limited – Need for High Court proceedings to secure the calling of its AGM')

[196] CA 1963, s 146(3) as amended by CA 1990 s 240(7) as inserted by CLEA 2001 s104(c).

[197] CA 1963, s 146(4).

PART B
COMPLIANCE OBLIGATIONS OF INDIVIDUALS

Chapter 6: Directors
A. Introduction 181
B. Transactions involving company directors 186
C. Disclosure obligations 218
D. Specific offences 230
E. Directors' reports 248
F. Proceedings against officers of companies in liquidation 256
G. Directors of insolvent companies 259
H. Sanctions 261
I. Relief 264
J. Protection against liability 265

Chapter 7: Auditors
A. Introduction 269
B. Auditor's report 276
C. Integrity and independence 282
D. Auditors' reporting obligations 308
E. Audit exemption 339
F. Auditors' liability 342

Chapter 8: Receivers
A. Introduction 355
B. Publication of appointment 356
C. Compliance duties of receivers 360
D. Enforcement under the Companies Acts 383
E. Reporting obligations of receivers 386
F. Remuneration 388
G. Liability 390
H. Resignation/Removal 391

Chapter 9: Liquidators
A. Introduction 395
B. Appointment of liquidators 396
C. Compliance obligations of liquidators 404
D. Investigations during winding up 451
E. Investigation of liquidator 469

Chapter 10: Examiners' Obligations
A. Introduction 471
B. General provisions regarding examiners 472
C. Powers of examiners 478
D. Obligations of examiners 497

Chapter 6

DIRECTORS

A. Introduction

(a) General

[6.001] There is a vast body of law regarding the role of a company director and the duties of directors in general.[1] This chapter does not address these general topics: the focus here is upon the enforcement of directors' duties and director's duties in enhancing company law compliance. With regard to the enforcement of directors' duties under the CA 1963–2006, there is a wide range of means and mechanisms by which these duties may fall to be considered. There is also considerable diversity in the persons who may invoke the Companies Acts and allege breaches of duty by company directors.[2]

The focus of this chapter is upon the duties of directors that are significant from the perspective of company law enforcement, and which fall to be enforced by the ODCE or other enforcement agencies.

(b) Qualifications

[6.002] There are no particular qualifications which a person must possess to be appointed as a director. There is no legislative provision in this regard. The only obvious constraint is that a director must sign a consent to so act and must therefore have legal capacity to do so.[3] This ensures that the person accepting nomination to a board of directors will have legal capacity and be of sound mind. In this regard, it is of interest to note that the Draft Companies Consolidation and Reform Bill 2007 contains an explicit

---

[1]   It is beyond the scope of this text to analyse every obligation which the Companies Acts and the common law impose on directors. For directors' duties generally, see Courtney, *The Law of Private Companies* (2nd edn, Tottel Publishing, 2002), Chs 9, 10, 11; Keane, *Company Law* (3rd edn, Tottel Publishing, 2000), Ch 27; Ussher, *Company Law in Ireland* (1986, Sweet and Maxwell), Ch 7. See also CLRG, Draft Companies Consolidation and Reform Bill 2007, Pt A5, Head 9 which codifies directors' fiduciary duties. Available at www.clrg.org.

[2]   Allegations that a company director has acted in breach of CA 1963–2006 may be made in a variety of proceedings and contexts and are often taken into account, for example, in restriction and disqualification proceedings. See Pts **D** and **E**.

[3]   See C(A)A 1982, s 3(3) and CA 1963, s 195(7).

provision requiring that a director must be over 18 years of age.[4] However, there is nothing preventing wholly unsuitable and ill-equipped persons from serving as directors of companies.[5] The standards of care, skill and diligence which directors are expected to meet takes account of the fact that a director may possess no relevant qualifications or experience. As noted by MacCann:

> 'it is clear that the courts have insisted on framing the director's duty to exercise care and skill by reference to his own personal abilities and qualifications. Whether liability can be imposed for failure to take reasonable care depends on a personal assessment of the individual director. In essence the level of skill which may legitimately be expected is as high or as low as the actually possessed by the director in question.'[6]

[6.003] The lack of qualifications notwithstanding, there is a heavy onus on directors to understand their duties and to discharge them with the requisite skill, care and diligence, particularly in the present environment of strong enforcement of company law. There are publications by the ODCE and CRO which emphasise the onus on directors to be aware of their duties and to ensure their companies' compliance with the Companies Acts.[7] The ODCE has prepared numerous information and decision notices, including a Consultation Paper[8] and Decision Notice[9] regarding directors' duties. The latter was distributed to every registered company.[10] The ODCE also issues statements and releases regarding prosecutions and proceedings for breaches of company law. The duties of company directors to ensure compliance with company law have therefore been widely publicised.

---

4   CLRG, General Scheme of Draft Companies Consolidation and Reform Bill 2007, Pt A4, Head 5(1). Available at www.clrg.org.

5   See Davies, *Gower and Davies' Principles of Modern Company Law* (7th edn, 2003) at p 308: 'the Cohen Committee tried to ensure that directors should normally retire when they attained the age of 70, but as finally enacted the provision [CA 1985, s 293] is so riddled with exceptions that it has proved of little value. Nor, it seems is any minimum age required required ...'. Among the exceptions to the age of retirement of directors in England and Wales, is that it does not apply to private companies unless they are subsidiaries of public limited companies (CA 1985, s 293(1)).

6   MacCann, 'Directors' duties of care, skill and diligence' (1991) ILT 56 at p 60.

7   See ODCE, '*Corporate Health Check: Ten Steps that every Company Director should take to help secure their Compliance with Company Law*'; See CRO, '*Six things that every director should know about company registration*' (Information Leaflet No 2, September 2005).

8   ODCE, *The Principal Duties and Powers of Companies, Directors, Company Secretaries, Members/Shareholders, Auditors, Creditors, Liquidators, Receivers and Examiners under the Companies Acts 1963–200*', Consultation Paper C/2002/1.

9   ODCE, *The Principal Duties and Powers of Company Directors under the Companies Acts 1963–200*' (Decision Notice D/2002/1, Information Book 2).

10   See ODCE, *The Principal Duties and Powers of Company Directors under the Companies Acts 1963–2001* (Decision Notice D/2002/1, Information Book 2). See also Ch **2**.

[6.004] There are certain persons who are not permitted to act as directors of companies. Persons who are bankrupt,[11] bodies corporate,[12] a company's auditor,[13] and anyone who is subject to an order of disqualification[14] are prohibited from being appointed to a company's board of directors. In addition, as seen in Ch **19**, if a person is subject to a declaration of restriction, they can only act as a director of a company which is capitalised to the requisite extent.[15] It should also be noted that there is a limit on the number of directorships of Irish-registered private limited companies that one person may hold, which includes positions as shadow director. Subject to certain exceptions, the most such directorships that a person may hold at a given time is 25.[16] It is an offence for a person to exceed this limit, an offence that may be prosecuted summarily by the Registrar of Companies.[17]

[6.005] A final point to note is that a director may be required to own a certain amount of shares in the company. Whether this qualification requirement is imposed on directors depends on each company's articles of association. If the articles do require directors to own a certain level of shareholding, CA 1963, s 180 provides that the directors must acquire these shares within two months of appointment to the office, or such shorter time as the articles may prescribe.[18] The office of director 'shall be vacated' if the director does not meet this requirement[19] and if an unqualified person continues to act as director beyond the designated period, he is guilty of an offence and liable to a fine.[20]

---

[11] CA 1963, s 183, as substituted by CA 1990, s 169. A person who acted as a director of three companies while an undischarged bankrupt was prosecuted in Dublin District Court on 6 May 2003. Jeffrey Norman Burton was fined a total of €1,200 and disqualified for five years. The prohibition on bankrupts acting as directors is proposed to be continued in force by the Draft Companies Consolidation and Reform Bill 2007. See Pt A4, Head 6. Available at www.clrg.org. Note, however, that the Draft Companies Bill envisages the possibility of a person who has been declared bankrupt obtaining the leave of the court to act as a director (Pt IV, s 6(1)).

[12] CA 1963, s 176. Note that the Draft Companies Consolidation and Reform Bill 2007, proposed by the CLRG retains this prohibition on bodies corporate acting as directors. See Pt A4, Head 4. Available at www.clrg.org.

[13] CA 1990, s 187(2): 'None of the following shall be qualified for appointment as auditor of a company– (a) an officer or servant of a company, (b) a person who has been an officer or servant of the company within a period in respect of which accounts would fall to be audited by him if he were appointed auditor of the company …'.

[14] CA 1990, s 160, as amended by CLEA 2001, s 42. See Ch **23**.

[15] Other restrictions also apply to companies of which a restricted person is a director. See further Ch **19**.

[16] C(A)(No 2)A 1999, s 45.

[17] C(A)(No 2)A 1999, s 45(8) and (13).

[18] CA 1963, s 180(1).

[19] CA 1963, s 180(3).

[20] CA 1963, s 180(5), as amended by C(AA)A 2003, Sch 2.

(c) Irish resident director

[6.006] Subject to certain exceptions, every company is required to have at least one director who is resident in Ireland.[21] While 'director' is usually defined to include, '*any person occupying the position of director by whatever name called*',[22] since the enactment of the C(AA)A 2003, this resident director must not be an 'alternate director.'[23] This leaves open the possibility that a nominee or a *de facto* director who is resident in Ireland may fulfil the requirement that the company have a director resident in Ireland. The characterisation of a '*de facto*' director is not always a straightforward matter.[24] This may leave scope for some ambiguity in the application of the requirement to have an Irish resident director.

[6.007] A person is considered to be 'resident' in Ireland at a given time, in any of the following three circumstances:

- he is present in Ireland for 183 days or more during the preceding 12 month period;[25]

- he is present in Ireland in the preceding 12 month period and 12 month period previous to that, for an aggregate period of 280 days or more;[26] or

- in that year of tax assessment, he has made an election to be treated as resident in the State.[27]

---

[21]   C(A)(No 2)A 1999, s 43.

[22]   CA 1963, s 2(1).

[23]   C(AA)A 2003, s 54 inserts the following new s 43(16) into C(A)(No 2)A 1999: 'In this section "director" does not include an alternate director.' An alternate director is someone who takes the place of an appointed director who is unable to act. See Model Reg 9 of Pt II of Table A.

[24]   See *Re Lynrowan Enterprises Ltd* [2002] IEHC 90, ('A *de facto* director, I repeat, is one who claims to act and purports to act as a director although not validly appointed as such' *per* O'Neill J). See Ch **16**. See Courtney, *The Law of Private Companies* (2nd edn, Tottel Publishing, 2002) at paras 8.054 to 8.058.

[25]   C(A)(No 2)A 1999, s 44(8)(a)(i). Note that this mirrors one of the criteria for residence for taxation purposes. See TCA 1997, s 819(1)(a).

[26]   C(A)(No 2)A 1999, s 44(8)(a)(ii). This mirrors one of the criteria for residence for taxation purposes. See TCA 1997, s 819(1)(b).

[27]   C(A)(No 2)A 1999, s 44(8)(a)(iii). This provision refers to elections made pursuant to TCA 1997, s 819. Note that TCA 1997, s 819(3)(a) provides that, '... an individual (i) who is not resident in the State for a year of assessment, and (ii) to whom paragraph (b) applies, may at any time elect to be treated as resident in the State for that year and, where an individual so elects, the individual shall for the purposes of the Acts be deemed to be resident in the State for that year. (b) This paragraph shall apply to an individual who satisfies an authorised officer that the individual is in the State— (i) with the intention, and (ii) in such circumstances, that the individual will be resident in the State for the following year of assessment.'

If a person is resident in Ireland for less than 30 days in the year preceding a given date, he shall not qualify as a resident at that time, and that period cannot be counted for the purpose of the 280-day aggregate referred to above.[28] A person is considered to be 'present' in Ireland on a given day, if he is personally present in the country at the end of the day.[29]

[6.008] If the company's sole Irish resident director is removed or resigns, he must notify the Registrar of this fact within 14 days of its occurrence.[30] It is important for Irish resident directors to be aware of this requirement, as s 43(11) provides that:

> If a person fails to comply with sub-s (9), he or she shall be jointly and severally liable with the company of which he or she has ceased to be a director for any fine or penalty referred to in sub-s (3) imposed on the company or which it is held liable to pay after that cessation, and any such fine or penalty for which that person is so liable may be recovered by the registrar of companies or the Revenue Commissioners, as appropriate, from him or her as a simple contract debt in any court of competent jurisdiction.[31]

This has the effect that a former director may be personally liable for fines imposed on a company which are unrelated to the director's conduct and which may postdate the director's removal or resignation from the company, on the sole basis that the director, being the only Irish resident director, failed to notify the Registrar of his resignation or removal. From the formulation of the governing provisions, it appears that the only defence which may be open to such a former director is that he was not aware that there were no other Irish resident directors.[32] It is interesting to note that a sole Irish resident director is under no equivalent notification obligation if he ceases to reside in Ireland, although the consequences of such a change are the same, from the perspective of the company, the Registrar and the Revenue Commissioner.

[6.009] If a company does not have at least one Irish resident director, it must hold a bond in the amount of €25,394.74, which would cover any fine imposed on the company for offences under the Companies Acts prosecutable by the Registrar of Companies or fines for specified offences under TCA 1997.[33]

A copy of the bond must be attached to any of the following, if applicable:

- if there are no Irish resident directors on the incorporation of the company, the statement which a company is obliged to register under C(A)A 1982, s 3;[34]

---

[28] C(A)(No 2)A 1999, s 44(9). This mirrors the terms of TCA 1997, s 819(2).

[29] C(A)(No 2)A 1999, s 44(10).

[30] C(A)(No 2)A 1999, s 43(9). This notification cannot of itself be regarded as constituting defamatory material. (C(A)(No 2)A 1999, s 43(10)).

[31] C(A)(No 2)A 1999, s 43(11).

[32] C(A)(No 2)A 1999, s 43(9) refers to the requirement that there must be no other Irish resident director and that this must be within the knowledge of the person ceasing to act as a director of the company.

[33] C(A)(No 2)A 1999, s 43(3).

[34] C(A)(No 2)A 1999, s 43(8)(a).

  – if the company's sole Irish resident director notifies the Registrar of his resignation or removal, that notification; [35] and

  – if there is no Irish resident director during the period to which an annual return relates, to that annual return.[36]

[6.010] There is a procedure whereby a company may obtain an exemption from the requirement to have an Irish resident director or to hold a bond in the sum of €25,394.75.[37] This exemption is obtained if the Registrar of Companies grants a certificate stating that the company has a 'real and continuous link with one or more economic activities that are being carried on in the State'.[38] The company must tender evidence to satisfy the Registrar of the existence of such a link and must attach the requisite evidence to a completed 'Form B67'.[39]

B. Transactions involving company directors

(a) Introduction

[6.011] Both the common law and the Companies Acts devote considerable attention to the ways in which a director can profit from a company, or be personally involved in a company's transactions. Publications by the ODCE confirm that the treatment by directors of a company's property and, in particular, the taking of loans from the company, is one of the areas in which breaches of company law are particularly prevalent.[40] This topic is therefore a very important one for company directors in the context of the enforcement of company law.

[6.012] There are various ways of analysing the law's treatment of dealings between a company and its directors. Before analysing the content of the substantive law in this regard, however, it is important to understand the logic behind regulating so closely a director's involvement with his company. The fiduciary position which a director occupies in a company has a number of consequences for any dealings between the

---

[35] C(A)(No 2)A 1999, s 43(8)(b).

[36] C(A)(No 2)A 1999, s 43(8)(c).

[37] C(A)(No 2)A 1999, s 44(1).

[38] C(A)(No 2)A 1999, s 44(2).

[39] C(A)(No 2)A 1999, s 44(3). See further Ch **2**.

[40] See ODCE, *Annual Report 2006* at p 14: 'some 268 reported defaults (or about 80 per cent of the total reported in mandatory reports) involved excessive directors' transactions. The associated sums amounted to over €70 million.' See also ODCE, *A Guide to Transactions involving Directors*, at p 5: 'During 2002, the Office of the Director of Corporate Enforcement (ODCE) received 27 reports from auditors in which the opinion was expressed that there were grounds for believing that indictable offences1 had been committed in relation to companies' transactions with their directors. An analysis of those reports indicated that a significant proportion of the instances reported related to the issue of unlawful loans to directors. This trend accelerated in 2003 with the reporting of approximately 200 cases to the ODCE.'

director and the company. This can be summarised as involving three broad principles. First, a director should not allow his own personal interests to conflict with those of the company. Secondly, a director should not gain a secret profit from his position. Thirdly, a director should remain independent in the discharge of his functions.[41] As will be seen, these principles have a number of very concrete implications for company directors.

(b) Common law

(i) Common law regulation of directors' interests

[6.013] The common law imposes strict controls on the conduct of directors and their dealings with companies. The primary rule is that a director must not allow a situation to arise in which the interests of the company and his own personal interests are in conflict.[42] There is both an internal and an external dimension to this rule. First, a director cannot derive profits from the company which are not disclosed to and, if necessary, authorised by, the company. Secondly, a director cannot derive profits from a company's dealings with third parties, such as by usurping an opportunity which rightfully belonged to the company.

[6.014] *Re Cooke's Events Company Ltd*[43] is an example of a case in which an allegation was made that the director acted in breach of his fiduciary duty by allowing a conflict to arise between his interests and those of the company. The liquidator alleged that the director was in breach of his common law and statutory duties because of the treatment of a particular debt, which a company of which he was the managing director, owed to the company in liquidation.[44] The High Court (McMenamin J) stated that the position regarding this debt, while unclear, was 'indicative of a clear conflict of interest and a failure on the part of [the director] to realise his duties towards this, specific company.'[45]

McMenamin J further noted that it was for the director to realise this issue, among others, and 'to act in the interest of the company and for the protection of its creditors'.[46]

---

[41] See Courtney, *The Law of Private Companies* (2nd edn, Tottel Publishing, 2002) at Chs 9, 10 and 11.

[42] See Ussher, *Company Law in Ireland* (1986, Sweet and Maxwell) at pp 207–218; See also Forde, *Company Law* (3rd edn, Round Hall Sweet & Maxwell, 1999) at pp 184–194.

[43] *Re Cooke's Events Company Ltd, Kavanagh v Cooke* [2005] IEHC 225.

[44] It may be queried why the apparent breach of CA 1990, s 31, which this loans seems to represent, was not referred to in the judgment. If the director had sufficient control over the company in debt, for that to represent a conflict of interest, it is likely he had sufficient control to warrant a finding that the company was a 'person connected with a director' for the purposes of CA 1990, s 31. See further paras **[6.062]** to **[6.064]**. See also *Re Cherby Ltd, Kavanagh v Cooke* [2005] IEHC 225, a related case, in this regard.

[45] *Re Cooke's Events Company Ltd, Kavanagh v Cooke* [2005] IEHC 225.

[46] *Re Cooke's Events Company Ltd, Kavanagh v Cooke* [2005] IEHC 225.

The Court concluded that the director demonstrated a want of proper standards in the conduct of the company and further concluded:

> 'it is clear that in at least one instance [the debt owed to the company of which he was managing director] the director did not comply with the fiduciary duties imposed on him *qua* director of the company.'[47]

The relief sought in the case was a declaration of restriction in CA 1990, s 150, which the Court duly granted.

[6.015] A director cannot take for himself an opportunity that would have advanced the interests of the company.[48] This rule is strict and has been applied even in circumstances where the company had considered and rejected the business opportunity in question or where the company lacked the resources to avail of the opportunity.[49] In *Bray v Ford*, Herschell LJ described this rule as follows:

> 'It is an inflexible rule of a Court of Equity that a person in a fiduciary position, such as the respondent's, is not, unless otherwise expressly provided, entitled to make a profit; he is not allowed to put himself in a position where his interest and duty conflict.'[50]

The general principle, which has been adhered to in subsequent cases, was stated as follows by Lord Cranworth LC in *Aberdeen Rly Co v Blaikie Bros:*[51]

> 'A corporate body can only act by agents, and it is of course the duty of those agents so to act as best to promote the interests of the corporation whose affairs they are conducting. Such agents have duties to discharge of a fiduciary nature towards their principal. And it is a rule of universal application, that no one, having such duties to discharge, shall be allowed to enter into engagements in which he has, or can have, a personal interest conflicting, or which possibly may conflict, with the interests of those whom he is bound to protect. So strictly is this principle adhered to, that no question is allowed to be raised as to the fairness or unfairness of a contract so entered into ... so inflexible is the rule that no inquiry on that subject is permitted.'

[6.016] *Aerospares Ltd v Thompson*[52] was a case in which the plaintiff was a company which was engaged in the business of purchasing and supplying aircraft parts and components for airlines around the world. The defendants were three directors of the plaintiff (who had since resigned those positions); a company formed, and run by, those directors, which was engaged in the same business as the plaintiff ('the defendant company'); and a company formed in the Seychelles under the same name as the

---

[47]   *Re Cooke's Events Company Ltd, Kavanagh v Cooke* [2005] IEHC 225.

[48]   *Cook v Deeks* [1916] 1 AC 554.

[49]   *Regal (Hastings) v Gulliver* [1967] 2 AC 134 ('the rule of equity which insists on those, who by use of a fiduciary position make a profit, being liable to account for that profit, in no way depends on fraud, or absence of *bona fides* ...')

[50]   *Bray v Ford* [1896] AC 44 at 51–52, [1895–9] All ER Rep 1009 at 1011.

[51]   *Aberdeen Rly Co v Blaikie Bros* (1854) 1 Macq 461 at 471–472, [1843–60] All ER Rep 249 at 252–253.

[52]   *Aerospares Ltd v Thompson* [1999] IEHC 76, Kearns J.

plaintiff ('the Seychelles company'). The plaintiff essentially alleged that the defendant directors perpetrated a fraud on it, by diverting monies which were properly due to the plaintiff from its customers, to accounts in the name of the Seychelles company. The plaintiff also claimed damages for business poached by the defendant directors, while they were still directors of the plaintiff and thereafter.

[6.017] In the first instance, the High Court (Laffoy J) granted an injunction preventing the defendants from dealing with the monies which were alleged to have been wrongfully diverted from the plaintiff and precluding the dissipation of the defendants' assets. The plaintiff subsequently sought a continuance of this injunction and applied for it to be made a worldwide injunction.

Kearns J considered the submission by the defendants that the payments related to contracts they had entered independently of the plaintiff. The Court noted in this regard, that:

> 'it strikes me as extraordinary that such a contract could have been placed in position by any of the first three named Defendants at this point in time, when two of the three Defendants were still working for the Plaintiff Company and the first named Defendant had resigned a mere few weeks previously.'

While the Court did not determine finally whether the goods to which the payments related, were manufactured by the plaintiff, Kearns J held:

> 'this seems to me somewhat immaterial. [The customers] were, at a critical point in time, clearly given to understand that they were still dealing with the servants or agents of the Plaintiff Company and there is nothing in the contemporaneous documentation to indicate that [the customers] believed that there had been a parting of the ways between the Plaintiff and its employees. On the contrary, all of the contemporaneous documentation, including, in particular, the documentation supplied from Barclays Bank in London, supports the Plaintiff's interpretation of events at this time.'[53]

Kearns J concluded:

> 'I am satisfied therefore that the Plaintiff has made out a good arguable case both for a proprietary claim and for the proposition that the first three named Defendants acted dishonestly in breach of contract and in breach of fiduciary duty in relation to this particular payment, and that they diverted monies wrongfully from the Plaintiff.'[54]

[6.018] With regard to the appropriate remedy, the scale of potential damages at issue and the continuance of the mareva injunction, the Court made a number of observations.

First, Kearns J considered the possible scale of damages which could be awarded to the company. In this regard, the company argued that it was entitled, not just to an account, but to a return of any monies and profits which were diverted from the company and any profits of which the company was deprived. The company relied upon the decision of

---

[53] *Aerospares Ltd v Thompson* [1999] IEHC 76 (13 January 1999).

[54] *Aerospares Ltd v Thompson* [1999] IEHC 76 (13 January 1999) at para 26.

the Canadian Supreme Court in *Canadian Aeroservices v O'Malley*[55] in which two officers resigned and then entered a contract with a former customer of the company. Those officers were made liable to the company for the profits they made as a result of usurping the company's business.[56]

Kearns J distinguished that case from the facts which pertained in *Aerospares Ltd v Thompson*,[57] on the basis that the former involved a very specific and complex contract of which the officers had acquired detailed and confidential knowledge while working at the company. This was distinguished from the latter case in which two of the directors were on routine service contracts, in a non-exclusive area of trade, in which the directors could not have been restrained from entering into competition with the company.[58] The Court therefore concluded that the damages to which the company would be entitled must be confined to so-called specific 'poached' business, rather than profits made during an ongoing indefinite period of time, as contended for by the company. There were accordingly definite limits to the damages recoverable by the company. [59]

[6.019] Secondly, the Court considered submissions by the defendants to the effect that damages would be an adequate remedy and that the injunction should be discharged. Kearns J weighed these arguments against:

> '... my belief, on the evidence at this stage only, that the first three named Defendants behaved dishonestly, both in re-routing certain payments destined for the Plaintiff and in holding themselves out as working for the Plaintiff while in fact operating on their own account.'

While the Court was inclined on this basis to continue the injunction, there were a number of undertakings which were furnished by the defendants,[60] which the Court regarded as sufficient to assuage the concerns of the plaintiff. The injunction was therefore discontinued.

---

[55] *Canadian Aeroservices v O'Malley* [1974] SCR 592.

[56] In *Aerospares Ltd v Thompson* [1999] IEHC 76, Kearns J at para 34, Kearns J described the decision in *Canadian Aeroservices v O'Malley* [1974] SCR 592 as follows: 'it was stated by the Court that a director or a senior officer of a company is disqualified from usurping for himself or diverting to another person or company with which he is associated a maturing business opportunity which his company is actively pursuing; he is also precluded from so acting even after his resignation where the resignation may fairly be said to have been prompted or influenced by a wish to acquire for himself the opportunity sought by the company or where it was his position with the company rather than a fresh initiative that led him to the opportunity which he later acquired.'

[57] *Aerospares Ltd v Thompson* [1999] IEHC 76 (13 January 1999), Kearns J.

[58] *Aerospares Ltd v Thompson* [1999] IEHC 76 (13 January 1999), Kearns J at paras 35 and 36.

[59] *Aerospares Ltd v Thompson* [1999] IEHC 76 (13 January 1999), Kearns J.

[61] In particular, the defendants gave an undertaking to lodged into Court the sum of £100,000.00 to meet any possible award against them in the case; an undertaking not to try to dispose of their shares in the plaintiff's parent company; and an undertaking not to move any of their assets in this jurisdiction abroad or to dissipate any assets they own in this jurisdiction or any other jurisdiction for the purpose of defeating execution of any judgment obtained in the case. (contd \...)

[6.020] Another case which demonstrates the duty of directors not to usurp the company's business opportunities is *Anois Couriers Ltd v Hannigan*.[61] In that case, a director formed a business in competition with that of the company. Morris P granted an injunction to restrain the director from soliciting courier business from the company's customers and from making use of any of the company's customer list and confidential information, on the basis that the director owed a duty of confidentiality and fiduciary duty to company.

[6.021] The rule prohibiting conflicts of interests between a director and the company also prohibits directors from deriving profits from their position, which are not disclosed to the company, its directors and its members.[62]

(ii) Consequences of conflict of interest at common law

[6.022] The general rule is that where a director breaches his common law duty to avoid a conflict of interest between his personal interests and those of the company, the company can set aside any contracts thus formed and the director can be liable to account for any profit made.[63]

The application of this rule can be seen in *Re Ashclad Ltd*.[64] One of the reliefs sought by the liquidator in that case was the return of certain property to the company in liquidation by its former directors. The property in question, a crane and a 'bending machine,' were originally the subject of a lease executed in October 1989, between two companies, the lessee ('Harrington Roofing Ltd') bearing the director's surname and another company. The lessee assigned the lease to the company in liquidation in September 1992. The Court noted that, between October 1992, and November 1996, the company in liquidation made rental payments amounting to £65,448. At that stage, the lessor then sold the crane and the bending machine to the director for the sum of £121. The director argued that that property was his property, as he personally paid the sum of £121. Geoghegan J considered this submission and concluded as follows:

> 'I do not think that this is correct in law and I think that the Official Liquidator's view that Mr Harrington was under a fiduciary duty to the Company at the time that he paid the £121 is correct. In my view, he is a trustee of the machines for the Company. I will … specifically order that the said machines vest in the liquidator by his official name.'

---

[60] (contd) See *Aerospares Ltd v Thompson* [1999] IEHC 76 (13 January 1999), Kearns J at paras 45 and 46. The Court concluded at para 46, 'These undertakings, if clarified in a satisfactory way, go far enough in my view to meet the requirements of this case.'

[61] *Anois Couriers Limited v Hannigan* (28 July 2000, unreported), HC, Morris P.

[62] *Re Regal Hastings v Gulliver* [1942] 1 All ER 378.

[63] *JJ Harrison (Properties) Ltd v Harrison* [2002] 1 BCLC 162 ('He is trustee of the property because it has become vested in him; but his obligations to deal with the property as a trustee arise out of his pre-existing duties as a director; not out of the circumstances in which the property was conveyed.')

[64] *Re Ashclad Ltd, Aschclad v Harrington* [2000] IEHC 174.

[6.023] While these common law duties to avoid a conflict of interest and the duty not to profit from the office of director, as well as the consequences of breaching these duties, are strict, they arise by virtue of a director's position as a fiduciary of the company. As such, the company is free to reach a decision to release a director from these duties and to exonerate him from the consequences of any infringements.[65]

(c) Statutory regulation of transactions with companies

[6.024] In parallel with the common law principles which disfavour any conflict of interest between a director and the company and which regard profits made by directors from their position as such with caution, the Companies Acts also contain very precise and detailed provisions regulating how and to what extent a director may derive benefits from his position as such, and the interests which he may have in the company's transactions. First, the Companies Acts regulate the remuneration and other payments which a director may receive. Secondly, the Acts control the circumstances in which, and the extent to which, a director may obtain a loan from the company. Thirdly, the Acts contain certain provisions regarding transactions to which the company is party, and in which the director has an interest. Fourthly, there are certain disclosure requirements imposed on directors with a view to ensuring that any means by which the director may profit from, or be interested in, the company itself, or its transactions, are made known to potentially interested parties. It should finally be noted that the Companies Acts contain certain restrictions regarding directors' interests in, and transfers of, shares. In the context of company law enforcement, each of these topics is an important one for company directors and is examined in turn.

(i) Remuneration

[6.025] A director can be paid for the services he renders to a company, if, and to the extent that, this is permitted by the company's articles of association.[66] Any amendment in this regard can only be implemented by means of a special resolution.[67] While the Companies Acts do not provide for the payment of remuneration to directors, the Acts do contain certain restrictions on the remuneration which a director may receive. First, a director is not entitled to receive remuneration free from liability to taxation.[68] Secondly,

---

[65]   See *Re Burke Clancy & Co Ltd* (23 May 1974. unreported), HC, Kenny J.

[66]   It is important to note in this regard that the Draft Companies Consolidation and Reform Bill 2007, Pt A4, Head 24, provides that, '(1) Unless the constitution otherwise provides the remuneration of the directors shall from time to time be determined by the company in general meeting and such remuneration shall be deemed to accrue from day to day. (2) The directors may also be paid all travelling, hotel and other expenses properly incurred by them in attending and returning from meeting of the directors or any committee of the directors or general meetings of the company or in connection with the business of the company.' As stated in the explanatory memorandum to this provision it imports Reg 76 of Pt I of Table A of the First Schedule to the CA 1963.

[67]   See MacCann, 'Directors' Remuneration and Loans' (1991) ILT.

[68]   CA 1963, s 185. Note that this prohibition is also contained in the Draft Companies Consolidation and Reform Bill 2007, Pt A4, Head 25. Available www.clrg.org.

a director cannot be engaged on a contract which exceeds five years' duration, without the approval of the company in general meeting.[69] Thirdly, there are also prohibitions on payments which a director can receive upon vacating the office.[70] The Companies Acts provide in this regard that it is unlawful for a company to make any payment to a director by way of compensation for loss of office, or in connection with retirement from the office of director.[71] This prohibition applies equally to any attempt to compensate a director for loss of office in connection with the transfer of the company's undertaking or property.[72] The only way of overcoming these prohibitions is for the details of the proposed payment, including the amount, to be disclosed to, and approved by, the company's members in general meeting.[73]

If compensation is paid illegally to a director in connection with the loss of office, the monies received are deemed by the Companies Acts to have been received by the director in trust for the company.[74] Another consequence of a violation of the law applicable to remuneration of directors, is that it may be a factor in restriction or disqualification proceedings.[75]

(ii) Loans

[6.026] The Companies Acts contain very precise restrictions on the credit which a company may advance to a director. This has been identified by the ODCE as one of the primary areas in which directors of companies in Ireland breach the requirements of the Companies Acts. While the rules and formulae are complex and tortuously formulated in some instances, it is crucial for directors to have an understanding of the law governing loans to directors.

---

[69] CA 1990, s 28(2) refers to 'any term by which a director's employment with the company of which he is the director or, where he is the director of a holding company, his employment within the group is to continue, or may be continued, otherwise than at the instance of the company (whether under the original agreement or under a new agreement entered into in pursuance of the original agreement), for a period exceeding five years during which the employment (a) cannot be terminated by the company by notice; or (b) can be so terminated only in specified circumstances.' CA 1990, s 28(1) requires that any such term must first be approved by the company in general meeting and a written memorandum setting out this agreement must be available for inspection by members of the company (CA 1990, s 28(4)).

[70] CA 1963, s 186.

[71] CA 1963, s 186.

[72] CA 1963, s 187(1). It was noted by MacCann that, 'the purpose of the restrictions imposed by ss 187 and 188 is to prevent an abuse by directors of their position in a takeover either of the company itself or of the company's business'. See MacCann, 'Directors' remuneration and loans (Pt I)' (1991) ILT.

[73] CA 1963, s 186.

[74] CA 1963, s 187(2).

[75] See, eg, *Re La Moselle Clothing Ltd, La Moselle Clothing Ltd v Soualhi* [1998] IEHC 66; *Re Lynrowan Enterprises Ltd* [2002] IEHC 90 (31 July 2002). See further Pt **D** and Pt **E**.

1. SCOPE OF PROHIBITION

[6.027] The CA 1963–2006 prohibit the giving of any form of credit by any means to a company director. This is a broadly formulated rule, which prohibits various forms of credit, not limited to direct loans, and which affects a wider range of people than a company's formally appointed directors.[76] The legislation reflects an anxiety to ensure that the prohibition could not be circumvented or evaded by the use of devices or strategies.

The basic rule is that the following transactions between a company and a director are not permitted:

– A loan from the company to the director;[77]

– A quasi-loan from the company to the director;[78]

– A credit transaction, in which the company is creditor for the director;[79]

– The provision of a guarantee or security by the company for the director, in connection with a loan, quasi-loan or credit transaction by another person.[80]

With the exception of the first category, namely direct loans, each of these transactions require further explanation. The terminology used by the Companies Acts in this regard is technical and the definitions are, in some instances, convoluted. Furthermore, the circumstances in which the prohibitions apply are extended by the Companies Acts to cover any possible means by which the ban on loans to directors may be circumvented or evaded. The scope of this ban will now be considered.

[6.028] The first definition to be considered is that of the term 'quasi-loan,' which is as follows:

(a) a quasi-loan is a transaction under which one party ('the creditor') agrees to pay, or pays otherwise than in pursuance of an agreement, a sum for another ('the borrower') or agrees to reimburse, or reimburses otherwise than in pursuance of an agreement, expenditure incurred by another party for another ('the borrower')—

    (i) on terms that the borrower (or a person on his behalf) will reimburse the creditor; or

    (ii) in circumstances giving rise to a liability on the borrower to reimburse the creditor;

(b) any reference to the person to whom a quasi-loan is made is a reference to the borrower; and

(c) the liabilities of a borrower under a quasi-loan include the liabilities of any person who has agreed to reimburse the creditor on behalf of the borrower.[81]

---

[76] The term 'director' is used in this section, but the category of persons affected by s 31 is much broader. See paras **[6.034]** to **[6.035]**.

[77] CA 1990, s 31(1)(a).

[78] CA 1990, s 31(1)(a).

[79] CA 1990, s 31(1)(b).

[80] CA 1990, s 31(1)(c).

[81] CA 1990, s 25(2).

This can be summarised as the payment of money or expenses, for a person, who is then obliged to reimburse those monies, whether or not there is an agreement to this effect. It essentially refers to a loan, without the formal use of that title.

[6.029] The term 'credit transaction' is defined as follows in CA 1990, s 25(3):

> ... a credit transaction is a transaction under which one party ('the creditor')—
>
> (a) supplies any goods or sells any land under a hire-purchase agreement or conditional sale agreement;
>
> (b) leases or licenses the use of land or hires goods in return for periodical payments;
>
> (c) otherwise disposes of land or supplies goods or services on the understanding that payment (whether in a lump-sum or instalments or by way of periodical payments or otherwise) is to be deferred.

This essentially refers to the conveyance of any interest in goods or land, for which payment is deferred.

[6.030] The final category of credit which is prohibited is the provision of guarantees or security in connection with a loan, quasi-loan or credit transaction. The first point to note is that a 'guarantee' includes an indemnity.[82] The second point is that there is no definition of what it means for a company to 'enter into a guarantee or provide any security in connection with a loan, quasi-loan or credit transaction made by any other person'.[83] These terms must therefore be given their ordinary and natural meaning. A company is therefore prohibited from guaranteeing the indebtedness of a director to another, or from furnishing security in connection with any such indebtedness.

[6.031] Section 31(1)(c) was invoked in the case of *Ruby Property Company Ltd v Kilty*.[84] The circumstances of that case, which are of relevance in the present context, were that the two sole shareholders and directors of a company used the company's real property to secure their own liability to a bank. When the director/shareholders failed to discharge this liability, the bank appointed a receiver over the company's property (the first defendant), who subsequently sold that property to the second defendant. The director/shareholders and the company issued proceedings challenging, among other matters, the legality of the security which had been furnished by the company.

McCracken J held that, while 'there is no doubt in the present case that the company did enter into a guarantee and provide security in connection with loans by the Bank to the Second and Third Plaintiffs, who were it's directors, however, this section only came into force on the 1st day of February 1991, while the guarantee and security were granted on the 3rd day of August 1990.'[85]

---

82 CA 1990, s 25(1).

83 CA 1990, s 31(1)(c).

84 *Ruby Property Company Ltd v Kilty* [1999] IEHC 50.

85 *Ruby Property Company Ltd v Kilty* [1999] IEHC 50.

The plaintiffs argued that the amount and terms of the loan were revised after 1 February 1991, which constituted the giving of a new security. The Court accepted that it was possible, although unlikely, that this argument could succeed, but proceeded to conclude that:

> 'any issue of this nature would be an issue between the First Plaintiff and the Bank, and not between the Plaintiffs and the Defendants in these proceedings. Unless and until the transaction has been avoided as against the Bank, the debenture and the appointment of the Receiver remain valid.'

This is an interesting insight into the effect of a violation of s 31(1)(c):[86] a transaction remains valid unless and until it is avoided under s 31.

[6.032] The scope of the prohibition on loans to directors is extended further by s 31(2) and (3). Section 31(2) provides that:

> 'A company shall not arrange for the assignment to it or the assumption by it of any rights, obligations or liabilities under a transaction which, if it had been entered into by the company, would have contravened subsection (1); but for the purposes of this Part the transaction shall be treated as having been entered into on the date of the arrangement.'[87]

The result of this provision is that if a director gets credit, security or a guarantee from a third party, the company cannot subsequently replace the third party as creditor, security-provider or guarantor. The premise of this rule is clearly that if it would have been illegal for the company to enter the transaction at the date it was entered, it is just as illegal for the company to enter it subsequently.

[6.033] Another means by which the ban on credit to directors is extended is that a company cannot participate in an arrangement whereby:

(a) another person enters into a transaction which, if it had been entered into by the company, would have contravened subsection (1) or (2); and

(b) that other person, in pursuance of the arrangement, has obtained or is to obtain any benefit from the company or its holding company or a subsidiary of the company or its holding company.[88]

According to this provision, a company is not permitted to give some benefit to someone else in return for them furnishing credit, security or a guarantee to a director. This is to ensure that companies do not circumvent the prohibition on loans to directors by paying someone else to enter the prohibited transactions. It should be noted that any benefit emanating from the company, its holding company, or a subsidiary of either of them, will cause the transaction to fall within the scope of the prohibition.

[6.034] The prohibition on credit to directors can be summarised as a prohibition on a company entering, guaranteeing, securing, assuming, receiving assignment of, or paying for, any transaction under which a director of the company receives credit.

---

86 *Ruby Property Company Ltd v Kilty* [1999] IEHC 50. See further paras **[6.054]** to **[6.055]** regarding the Court's analysis of the bank's position.

87 CA 1990, s 31(2).

88 CA 1990, s 31(3).

The prohibition on credit to directors does not merely affect persons who are formally appointed to the company's board of directors. On the contrary, the scope of the legislation is far broader, which is another reflection of the legislature's concern to ensure that the prohibition cannot be circumvented or evaded.

Section 31 refers to loans to 'a director of the company or of its holding company or to a person connected with such a director.'[89] The first point is that a director of the company's holding company cannot receive any form of credit from the company. The second point to note is the breadth of the term 'person connected with such a director', which is defined extensively in s 26.[90] The persons who are deemed by the Companies Acts to be 'connected with a director' (unless they are directors of the company themselves) are the following:

- a member of the director's family (spouse, parent, sibling, child);[91]

- a trustee (acting in that capacity) of a trust of which the director, his wife or child, or company which he controls, is the principal beneficiary;[92]

- a partner of the director; [93] and

- a company controlled by the director.[94]

Any of these persons, if connected to a director of a company or of its holding company, cannot receive any form of credit in any guise from the company.

[6.035] The third point to note regarding the persons who are affected by the prohibition on loans, is that the Companies Acts expressly extend this prohibition to include so-called 'shadow directors'. This term is defined in s 27 as:

> '... a person in accordance with whose directions or instructions the directors of a company are accustomed to act ... unless the directors are accustomed so to act by reason only that they do so on advice given by him in a professional capacity.'[95]

---

[89] CA 1990, s 31(3)(a). The same category of persons is referred to in each of the three limbs of the prohibition on credit. See CA 1990, s 31(1)(b) and (c).

[90] CA 1990, s 26, as amended by CLEA 2001, s 76.

[91] CA 1990, s 26(1)(a), as substituted by CLEA 2001, s 76.

[92] CA 1990, s 26(1)(b), as substituted by CLEA 2001, s 76.

[93] CA 1990, s 26(1)(c), as substituted by CLEA 2001, s 76.

[94] CA 1990, s 26(2). According to CA 1990, s 26(3), as substituted by CLEA 2001, s 76, 'For the purposes of this section, a director of a company shall be deemed to control a body corporate if, but only if, he is, alone or together with any other director or directors of the company, or any person connected with the director or such other director or directors, interested in one-half or more of the equity share capital of that body or entitled to exercise or control the exercise of one-half or more of the voting power at any general meeting of that body.' This definition is further expended by CA 1990, s 26(4)(b), which provides that, 'references to voting power exercised by a director shall include references to voting power exercised by another body corporate which that director controls.'

[95] CA 1990, s 27(1).

This encompasses persons who are not formally appointed to the company's board of director but who do in fact exercise some measure of control over the company's affairs.[96]

The definition of 'shadow director' was considered by the High Court in the context of restriction proceedings under CA 1990, s 150. In *Re Lynrowan Enterprises Ltd*,[97] O'Neill J quoted the following dicta of Millett LJ in *Re Hydrodan (Corby) Ltd*:[98]

'A *de facto* director, I repeat, is one who claims to act and purports to act as a director although not validly appointed as such. A shadow director by contrast does not claim or purport to act as a director. On the contrary claims not to be a director. He lurks in the shadows, sheltering behind others who he claims, are the only directors of the company to the exclusion of himself.'[99]

2. EXCEPTIONS

[6.036] There are a number of circumstances in which companies are permitted to give credit to directors, by way of exceptions to the general prohibition on such transactions.

1. Value of transaction

[6.037] The first exception to the prohibition on loans to directors is that a company is permitted to give loans and quasi-loans to, and enter credit transactions with, its directors if the value of that transaction is within prescribed limits. It should be noted at the outset that there is no such value-based exception for the provision of guarantees or security in favour of directors.

Section 32 of CA 1990 provides that loans, quasi-loans and credit transactions are permitted if their value, together with the total amount outstanding under any other such arrangement with any of the company's directors, is less than ten per cent of the company's 'relevant assets'.[100] The effect of this exception is that a certain number of loans and other forms of credit can be freely extended to a company's directors, but the first such loan to push the total amount outstanding under all such transactions over the ten per cent limit, will be prohibited. The previous transactions will remain intact.

[6.038] The calculation of the value of a transaction and of the company's 'relevant assets' are governed by particular provisions of the Companies Acts. Section 25(4) of CA 1990 defines the value of a transaction, for the purpose of determining whether it comes within the scope of s 32 as follows:

(a) in the case of a loan, the principal of the loan;

---

[96] See further Ch **16**.

[97] *Re Lynrowan Enterprises Ltd* [2002] IEHC 90 (31 July 2002, unreported), HC. See further Ch **16**.

[98] *Re Hydrodan (Corby) Ltd* (1994) 2 BCLC 180, cited in *Re Lynrowan Enterprises Lt*d [2002] IEHC 90 (31 July 2002, unreported), HC at para 20.

[99] In that case, the Court concluded that the person in question was a '*de facto*' director, rather than a shadow director. See Ch **16**.

[100] CA 1990, s 32(1).

(b) in the case of a quasi-loan, the amount, or maximum amount, which the person to whom the quasi-loan is made is liable to reimburse the creditor;

(c) in the case of a transaction or arrangement, other than a loan or quasi-loan ..., the price which it is reasonable to expect could be obtained for the goods, land or services to which the transaction or arrangement relates if they had been supplied at the time the transaction or arrangement is entered into in the ordinary course of business and on the same terms (apart from price) as they have been supplied or are to be supplied under the transaction or arrangement in question ...[101]

In the case of a loan or quasi-loan, its value should be easily ascertained. In the case of a credit transaction, the value will be the price which it would be reasonable to expect to be paid for the goods or land to which the credit relates at the date of that transaction.

[6.039] This is supplemented by s 25(5), which provides that:

'... the value of a transaction or arrangement which is not capable of being expressed as a specific sum of money (because the amount of any liability arising under the transaction is unascertainable, or for any other reason) shall, whether or not any liability under the transaction has been reduced, be deemed to exceed €63,486.90.'

This provision has the effect that, where the value of a loan cannot be ascertained for whatever reason, it is presumed, on an apparently wholly random basis, to be worth more than €63,486.90.

[6.040] Section 29(2) defines a company's relevant assets as follows:

(a) except in a case falling within paragraph (b), the value of its net assets determined by reference to the accounts prepared and laid in accordance with the requirements of section 148 of the Principal Act in respect of the last preceding financial year in respect of which such accounts were so laid;

(b) where no accounts have been prepared and laid under that section before that time, the amount of its called-up share capital.

Most Irish companies have a low level of called-up share capital, so the benefit of the value-based exception would be very limited if such companies rely on the second limb of the definition of a company's relevant assets. It is more likely that companies will invoke the value of the company's net assets as set out in the company's accounts.

[6.041] There is a particular provision of the Companies Acts which takes account of the possibility of a decrease in the value of the company's net assets, and the effect this has on the application of the value-based exception to the prohibition on directors' loans. Section 33 provides that, if the total outstanding value of the loans, quasi-loans and credit transactions, comes to exceed ten per cent of the value of the company's assets, corrective measures must be taken.[102] The obligation is triggered if the directors become aware, or ought reasonably to have become aware, of such a situation. This has the consequence that the directors must remain mindful of any outstanding loans and their value relative to the company's assets and must ensure that any fluctuations are

---

[101] CA 1990, s 25(4).

[102] CA 1990, s 33(1).

monitored, particularly if the value of the outstanding loans is close to the ten per cent limit.[103] It should be noted that, while s 33 does make reference to a fall in the value of the company's assets being a possible cause of the value of the loans exceeding the ten per cent threshold, it is not limited to that situation.[104]

The steps which must be taken are clear and unequivocal. Within two months of the date on which the directors become aware (or should reasonably have become aware) of a relevant fall in value of the company's assets, the credit arrangements must be amended to bring their value within the ten per cent threshold. Section 33(2) provides in this regard:

> ... it shall be the duty of the company, its directors and any persons for whom the arrangements referred to in that subsection were made, to amend, within two months, the terms of the arrangements concerned so that the total amount outstanding under the arrangements again falls within the percentage limit referred to in that subsection.[105]

[6.042] The duty to amend the credit arrangements is widely imposed. The company, its directors and any persons in whose favour the arrangements were made, must take the steps required by s 33. When one considers that the obligation is triggered by the state of knowledge, actual or constructive, of the company's directors, this may be harsh. As an illustration, a sister of a director of a holding company may receive a loan from the company which is worth a very small percentage of the company's net assets. If, in conjunction with numerous other loans to directors, and due to a slight fall in the value of the company's assets, the total level of credit comes to exceed ten per cent of the company's net assets, in a manner which should come to the notice of the directors, the sister is under a direct obligation to amend the credit arrangements, within a period of two months.

There are a number of issues to be considered in this regard. First, the means of knowledge of the company's affairs that is possessed by a person, such as the sister of the director of the holding company, may be very limited. Secondly, the loan received by a particular individual, such as the sister in the example cited, may play an extremely minor, inconsequential role in the state of affairs whereby the loans exceed the prescribed threshold. However, there is nothing in the provision which confines its scope to those recipients of loans which are material to the increase in the overall level of credit. Thirdly, the obligation is to amend the 'the terms of the arrangements concerned'. This is vague and may be difficult to implement. Every loan, quasi-loan and credit arrangement into which the company had entered is relevant to the attainment of the ten

---

[103] CA 1990, s 33(1).

[104] CA 1990, s 33(1) provides, 'This section applies to a company in respect of which the total amount outstanding under any arrangements ... comes to exceed 10 per cent of the company's relevant assets *for any reason, but in particular because the value of those assets has fallen*' (emphasis added).

[105] CA 1990, s 33(2).

per cent threshold. There is no clarification in s 33 as to how it should be determined which transactions to amend, and in what manner.

[6.043] The CLEA inserted a new provision into s 33 and s 33(3) now provides that:

> 'Where the terms of the arrangements referred to in subsection (2) are not amended within the period specified in that subsection, the arrangements shall be voidable at the instance of the company unless s 38(1)(a) or (b) applies.'[106]

This has the curious consequence that, where the total value of the directors' loans comes to exceed ten per cent of the value of the company's relevant assets, and no remedial action is taken within two months of the date on which this should have come to the notice of the company's directors, every loan, quasi-loan or credit transaction, of which any amount remains outstanding, irrespective of how little, is voidable. It is conceivable that a loan given to a person connected to a director of the company's holding company, some considerable time previously, of which little remained outstanding, could be entirely avoided by the company. This could present an incentive for unscrupulous companies to allow loans to exceed the ten per cent threshold, without notifying the recipient of loans which are largely discharged, and who would not be aware of this fact (such as a former director or director of a holding company) and thereby allowing the company to avoid the transaction in its entirety.

2. Special resolution

[6.044] As enacted, the CA 1990 contained no means for a company to authorise the provision of a guarantee or security in connection with a loan, quasi-loan or credit transaction in favour of a company director. While loans, quasi-loans and credit transactions worth less than ten per cent of the company's net assets were permitted,[107] this exception did not encapsulate guarantees and security and there was no corresponding exception for the provision of a guarantee or security.

The CLEA 2001 introduced a significant change to this area of the law. According to s 34, as inserted by CLEA 2001, s 78, a company is permitted to provide security or a guarantee in connection with a loan, quasi-loan or credit transaction where the provision of the security or the guarantee is given under the authority of a special resolution of the company which has been passed within the preceding 12 months, and the company has provided each member with a copy of a statutory declaration satisfying all of the following criteria.[108]

---

[106] CA 1990, s 33(3), as inserted by CLEA 2001, s 77. See further below paras [6.053] to [6.061].

[107] See above paras [6.037] to [6.043].

[108] This declaration must be sent to the members with the notification of the meeting at which the special resolution is to be considered or, if the resolution is passed without a meeting of the members, the statutory declaration must be appended to the resolution. See CA 1990, s 34, as substituted by CLEA 2001, s 78.

[6.045] The declaration must be made by the directors (or a majority of the directors) at a meeting of the directors held within 24 days of the meeting at which the special resolution is to be considered by the members.[109] The declaration must state:[110]

(a)   the circumstances in which the guarantee or security is to be provided;

(b)   the nature of the security or guarantee;

(c)   the person(s) to or for whom the loan, quasi-loan or credit transaction (in connection with which the guarantee or security is to be provided) is to be made;

(d)   the purpose for which the company is providing the security or guarantee;

(e)   the benefit that will accrue to the company directly or indirectly from providing the security or guarantee; and

(f)   that the directors making the declaration have made a full inquiry into the affairs of the company and, having done so, have formed the opinion that the company, having provided the security or guarantee, will be able to pay its debts in full as they fall due.[111]

[6.046] The directors' statutory declaration has no effect unless it is accompanied by a report drawn up by an independent person who is qualified at the time of the report to act as the company's auditor.[112] The independent report must state whether, in the opinion of the independent person, the statutory declaration is reasonable.[113] The report of the independent person must be in the form prescribed by CA 1990 (Section 34) Regulations 2001.[114]

[6.047] The passing of a special resolution is not necessarily the last step in the process of securing or guaranteeing a director's indebtedness. First, while the passing of a special resolution requires a majority of 75 per cent of those members voting, unless all of the members entitled to vote at general meetings vote in favour of the special

---

109   CA 1990, s 34(2), as inserted by CLEA 2001, s 78. Note that, if the resolution is passed without a meeting of the members, the meeting of the directors at which the statutory declaration was made, must have been held not more than 24 days before the date on which the resolution is signed by the members (CA 1990, s 34(2), as substituted by CLEA 2001, s 78).

110   CA 1990, s 34(3), as substituted by CLEA 2001, s 78.

111   CA 1990, s 34(3), as substituted by CLEA 2001, s 78.

112   CA 1990, s 34(4)(a), as substituted by CLEA 2001, s 78.

113   CA 1990, s 34(4)(b), as substituted by CLEA 2001, s 78.

114   The CA 1990 (Section 34) Regulations 2001 (SI 439/2001). It should be noted that the accountancy bodies comprising the Consultative Committee of Accountancy Bodies – Ireland (CCAB-I) (ie the Institute of Chartered Accountants in Ireland (ICAI), the Association of Chartered Certified Accountants (ACCA) and the Institute of Certified Public Accountants in Ireland (ICPAI)), have advised their members not to sign these reports on the basis that the required reports are too open-ended and pose an unacceptable risk to their practices. Consequently, directors seeking to avail of this exemption are advised to discuss the matter with their auditors in advance.

resolution to authorise the provision of the security or guarantee, the company must allow a period of 30 days to lapse before it can provide the security.[115] For 28 days from the passing of the resolution, the holders of not less than ten per cent of the nominal value of the company's issued share capital, or a class thereof,[116] may apply to court for the cancellation of the special resolution.[117] The resolution will then only have effect to the extent to which it is confirmed by the court.[118]

A second step which must be taken is that the company must deliver a copy of the statutory declaration to the Registrar of Companies within 21 days of the provision of such guarantee or security.[119]

[6.048] Directors must think carefully about the making of a statutory declaration in support of the provision of a guarantee or security for the benefit of one of the directors. If the declaration is not reasonable, the jurisdiction of the court may be invoked under s 34(8). Furthermore, if a director makes a statutory declaration without having reasonable grounds for forming the opinion that the company, having provided the security or guarantee, will be able to pay its debts as they fall due, a court may declare that the director be held personally liable, without limitation of liability, for the debts and other liabilities of the company.[120] In this regard, it is very important for directors to be aware that if the company is wound up within 12 months of the making of the statutory declaration, and the company's debts have not been fully paid or provided for within 12 months of the commencement of the winding up, it is presumed, unless the contrary is shown, that the director did not have reasonable grounds for his opinion.[121]

3. Group loans

[6.049] A company is not prohibited by the Companies Acts from entering any of the arrangements otherwise prohibited by s 31, if the beneficiary is the company's holding company, its subsidiary or a subsidiary of its holding company.[122] As originally enacted, this exception only applied to a holding company. The CLEA 2001 extended the scope

---

[115] CA 1990, s 34(7), as substituted by CLEA 2001, s 78.

[116] CA 1990, s 34(9), as substituted by CLEA 2001, s 78. Note that an application for cancellation of the special resolution cannot be made by a person who has consented to, signed, or voted in favour of, that resolution (CA 1990, s 34(10), as substituted by CLEA 2001, s 78).

[117] CA 1990, s 34(11), as substituted by CLEA 2001, s 78.

[118] CA 1990, s 34(8), as substituted by CLEA 2001, s 78.

[119] CA 1990, s 34(1)(b), as inserted by CLEA 2001, s 78.

[120] CA 1990, s 34(5)(a), as substituted by CLEA 2001, s 78(a). An application for such an order may be made by a liquidator, member, creditor or contributory of the company.

[121] CA 1990, s 34(5)(b), as substituted by CLEA 2001, s 78.

[122] CA 1990, s 35, as amended by CLEA 2001, s 79.

of the exception to include a company's subsidiary and any subsidiary of its holding company.[123] Section 35 provides:

> Section 31 shall not prohibit a company from—
>
> (a) making a loan or quasi-loan to its holding company or entering into a guarantee or providing any security in connection with a loan or quasi-loan made by any person to any company which is its holding company, subsidiary or a subsidiary or its holding company;
>
> (b) entering into a credit transaction as creditor for its holding company or entering into a guarantee or providing any security in connection with any credit transaction made by any other person for any company which is its holding company, subsidiary or a subsidiary or its holding company.[124]

4. Expenses

[6.050] A company is permitted to provide its directors with funds to pay for expenses, subject to certain conditions. These expenses must be vouched and they must be, or be about to be, properly incurred, either for the purposes of the company or to enable him properly to perform his duties as an officer.[125] Alternatively, a company can provide its directors with funds to enable them to avoid incurring such expenses.[126] When the company does provide such funding for expenses, any liability to repay the money must be discharged within six months of the date it was incurred.[127] It is an offence for a person to fail to repay the monies within that timeframe.[128]

5. Ordinary course of business

[6.051] A company is permitted to provide a loan or quasi-loan or to enter a credit transaction if it does so in the ordinary course of business. Section 37 provides that a company can enter into such transactions on the fulfilment of the following conditions:

- it must do so in the ordinary course of business;

- the value of the transaction must be no greater than those which the company ordinarily offers or which it would be reasonable for the company to offer to a person of the same financial status, who was unconnected with the company; and

- the terms of the transaction must be no more favourable than those which the company ordinarily offers or which it would be reasonable for the company to offer to a person of the same financial status, who was unconnected with the company.[129]

---

[123] CA 1990, s 35, as amended by CLEA 2001, s 79.

[124] CA 1990, s 35, as amended by CLEA 2001, s 79.

[125] CA 1990, s 36(1).

[126] CA 1990, s 36(1).

[127] CA 1990, s 36(2).

[128] CA 1990, s 36(3).

[129] CA 1990, s 37(2).

3. SANCTIONS

[6.052] The Companies Acts and those responsible for the enforcement of company law in Ireland treat breaches of s 31 severely.[130] There are a number of different means by which such violations are sanctioned.

1. Avoidance of transaction

[6.053] Where a company enters in a transaction or arrangement that is in breach of the prohibition, the transaction or arrangement is voidable at the instance of the company.[131] A transaction cannot however be avoided, if restitution is no longer possible; if the company has been indemnified for the loss or damage suffered by it; or if a third person has legitimately, for value and without notice, acquired rights which would be affected by avoiding the transaction or arrangement.[132]

[6.054] *Ruby Property Co Ltd v Kilty*[133] is an example of the application of the latter rule. In that case, the directors who had obtained security from the company to secure their debts to a bank, on foot of which the bank appointed a receiver and the company's property was sold, attempted to challenge the power of the bank to do so. The Court doubted the strength of their claim on a number of grounds, particularly the fact that the security was originally granted before s 31 came into effect,[134] and went on to make the following observations:

> 'Finally, in the context of the possibility of the security being in breach of section 31 of the Companies Act, 1990, I am quite satisfied that even if that were the case, the Plaintiffs would not have any remedy against either of the Defendants in the present case.'[135]

McCracken J quoted the text of CA 1990, s 38(1) in full and concluded:

> 'Firstly, the transaction which could be said to contravene section 31 is the transaction between the company and the Bank. As I have said, the Bank is not a party to these proceedings, and they do not seek to avoid that transaction as against the Bank. Secondly, I have no doubt whatever that the Second Defendant acquired the property *bona fide* and for value without actual notice of any contravention of section 31, if there has been such a contravention. Therefore, any challenge to the sale on the basis of a possible contravention of section 31 must fail.'[136]

---

[130] These sanctions are in addition to other sanctions for breaches of the Companies Acts that can be imposed upon directors. In particular, if a company goes into insolvent liquidation, the directors may be restricted as directors and, in serious circumstances, disqualified from so acting. See further Pts **D** and **E**.

[131] CA 1990, s 38(1).

[132] CA 1990, s 38(1)(a) and (b).

[133] *Ruby Property Company Ltd v Kilty* [1999] IEHC 50. See further above para **[6.031]**.

[134] See further above para **[6.031]** regarding this aspect of the decision of McCracken J.

[135] *Ruby Property Company Ltd v Kilty* [1999] IEHC 50 at para 11.

[136] *Ruby Property Company Ltd v Kilty* [1999] IEHC 50 at para 12.

[6.055] This decision will provide comfort to banks and other parties which have accepted securities or guarantees offered by companies in respect of the indebtedness of the company's directors. However, the increased vigilance of the ODCE and the enhanced publicity of the requirements of the Companies Acts, generally, and the prohibitions on credit to directors, in particular, may undermine the claim of any financial institution or other entity that it lacked notice of the fact that security furnished by a company to its directors was a breach of CA 1990, s 31.

2. Liability to account and indemnify

[6.056] If an arrangement is made in contravention of s 31, the director[137] for whose benefit the arrangement was made, and any director who authorised the arrangement, is liable to account to the company for any gain made directly or indirectly as a result of the transaction or arrangement and is further obliged to indemnify the company for any loss or damage suffered.[138] There are some mechanisms in the legislation by which a director may avoid this liability. First, if the arrangement is with a person connected with a director, and the director can show that he took all reasonable steps to secure the company's compliance with s 31, he shall not be liable to account for gains made or to indemnify for the losses suffered.[139] Secondly, if a connected person or any other director of the company (not being the director to whom the persons are connected) can show that, at the time the transaction or arrangement was entered into, they did not know the relevant circumstances constituting the contravention, they shall not be liable for gains made and losses suffered.[140]

3. Personal liability for debts of company

[6.057] An individual who benefits from a loan, quasi-loan or credit transaction from a company may be held personally liable, without any limitation of liability, for some or all of the company's debts and liabilities.[141] There are a number of criteria which must be met before this liability may be triggered. First, the arrangement in question must be a loan, quasi-loan, or credit transaction, which was entered into on the basis that its value, combined with the total outstanding value of all such arrangements, was worth less than ten per cent of the company's net assets.[142] Secondly, the company must be in the course of being wound up.[143] Thirdly, the company must be unable to pay its debts.[144] Fourthly,

---

137 Note that the word 'director' as used in this context includes shadow directors, directors of the holding company and persons connected with such directors. See further above paras **[6.034]** to **[6.035]**.

138 CA 1990, s 38(2).

139 CA 1990, s 39(3).

140 CA 1990, s 39(3).

141 CA 1990, s 39(1).

142 CA 1990, s 39(1), referring to CA 1990, s 32, which contains the value-based exception to the prohibition on loans to directors. See further above paras **[6.037]** to **[6.043]**.

143 CA 1990, s 39(1).

144 CA 1990, s 39(1).

a liquidator, creditor or contributory must apply to court for a declaration of personal liability.[145] Fifthly, the court must be satisfied either that the arrangement has contributed materially to the company's inability to pay its debts or that the arrangement has substantially impeded the orderly winding up of the company.[146]

[6.058] In determining whether to make a declaration of personal liability, the court is required to have particular regard to the following matters:

– whether and to what extent, the outstanding liabilities in question were discharged before the commencement of the winding up;[147]

– the extent to which the arrangements in question contributed materially to the company's inability to pay its debts; [148] and

– The extent to which the arrangements substantially impeded the orderly winding up of the company.[149]

[6.059] A number of points should be noted about the imposition of personal liability for the debts of a company under s 39.

First, it is only possible to bring an application for such a declaration, when a loan, quasi-loan or credit transactions is at issue. There is no provision for such liability to be imposed when a guarantee or security was furnished by a company in insolvent liquidation. In light of the fact that the invocation of a guarantee could have severe consequences for a company and could conceivably cause a company's insolvency, and in light of the fact that responsibility for such an occurrence would rest directly and squarely on the shoulders of the director in question, it is inexplicable why the provision of guarantees and securities cannot give rise to personal liability.

[6.060] Secondly, a declaration of personal liability can only be made where the loan, quasi-loan or credit transaction was of a category which is expressly permitted by the Companies Acts, as an exception to the prohibition against loans to directors.[150] A loan, quasi-loan or credit transaction which openly violates the prohibition against loans to directors, without purporting or attempting to come within the exceptions to that prohibition set out in s 32, cannot give rise to a declaration of personal liability. This is entirely anomalous and unjust.

[6.061] Thirdly, the formulation of the sanction does not expressly require that the loan, quasi-loan or credit transaction at issue must have come outside the scope of the s 32 exception, by exceeding the ten per cent threshold for a defined period during the life of the company, or at all. Section 33 envisages such a situation and addresses the

---

[145] CA 1990, s 39(1).
[146] CA 1990, s 39(1).
[147] CA 1990, s 39(2).
[148] CA 1990, s 39(3).
[149] CA 1990, s 39(3).
[150] CA 1990, s 32 is addressed further above paras **[6.037]** to **[6.043]**.

consequences of the value of the relevant outstanding loans, quasi-loans and credit arrangements, exceeding the permitted threshold.[151] Where that does occur and no remedial steps are taken, it is appropriate that sanctions should be imposed. This is achieved by the terms of s 33(3), which renders such transactions voidable after the expiry of two months.[152] This can be seen as conferring a two-month period of grace within which the company, the directors and the beneficiaries of the loan, have time to make the necessary amendments. By contrast, the sanction of imposing personal liability under s 39 is not predicated on the loans exceeding the ten per cent threshold during the life of the company. In particular, the imposition of personal liability is not precluded by the fact that two months may not yet have lapsed since the date on which the arrangements came to exceed the permitted threshold. The logic behind imposing the very severe penalty of unlimited personal liability on a person who may not have been party to any infringement of the Companies Acts is questionable.

[6.062] A fourth point to note about the law governing the imposition of personal liability is that the factors to which the court should have regard in relation to an application for a declaration of personal liability, do not include any reference to the culpability or responsibility of the person against whom the declaration is sought. As envisaged by s 32(2), it is entirely conceivable that a fall in the value of the company's assets, or other external factors, may cause the value of the relevant outstanding loans, quasi-loans and credit transactions, to exceed ten per cent of the value of the company's assets.[153] In the context of s 39, it is similarly possible that a recipient of a lawful loan may become, due to factors and circumstances beyond his control, the subject of a declaration of personal liability for the company's debts.

As an illustration, if a director did obtain a valid, lawful, loan from a company, which was permitted under s 32, and shortly thereafter, the company's business dramatically collapsed due to factors entirely beyond the control of the director in question, it seems unfair and extremely harsh that the director, not being in a position to repay the loan earlier than the agreed repayment schedule, and not being responsible of the company's ill fate, should be personal liable without limitation for all of the company's debts. While the court will have regard to the extent to which the arrangement contributed to the inability of the company to repay its debts,[154] it is recommended that a court should also, in an appropriate case, have regard to the extent to which the director in question is responsible for that state of affairs.

4. Criminal sanctions

[6.063] An officer of a company who authorises or permits the company to enter into a transaction or arrangement knowing, or having reasonable cause to believe, that the

---

[151] CA 1990, s 33(1). See further above paras **[6.037]** to **[6.043]**.

[152] CA 1990, s 33(3), as inserted by CLEA 2001, s 77. See further above paras **[6.037]** to **[6.043]**.

[153] CA 1990, s 32(2). See further above paras **[6.037]** to **[6.043]**.

[154] See CA 1990, s 39(3).

company was contravening s 31, is guilty of an offence.[155] Similarly, a person who procures a company to enter into a transaction or arrangement knowing, or having reasonable cause to believe, that the company was, as a result, breaching the prohibition is also guilty of an offence.[156]

The maximum penalty on summary conviction is €1,904 and/or 12 months imprisonment. On conviction on indictment, the maximum penalty is €12,697 and/or five years imprisonment.[157]

[6.064] Directors of companies have faced prosecution under s 40 on a number of occasions. For example, on 21 October 2005, District Judge John Neilan, sitting at Granard District Court in Co Longford heard a case in which a director of a company was charged by the ODCE with six counts of having, as an officer of a company, authorised or permitted the company to lend sums of money to herself, knowing or having reasonable cause to believe that the company was thereby contravening CA 1990, s 31. The defendant pleaded guilty and, under the Probation of Offenders Act 1907, the charges were dismissed, the court noting the defendant's contribution to a charitable organisation. Similarly, on 8 July 2003, District Judge Brian Kelly heard a case involving 16 separate charges against a director of having authorised or permitted the company to lend money to himself, knowing or having reasonable cause to believe that the company was thereby contravening CA 1990, s 31. The defendant pleaded guilty and the court dismissed the charges under the Probation of Offenders Act 1907, noting the defendant's contribution of €3,000 to charity.[158]

(iii) Substantial property transactions

[6.065] The Companies Acts prohibit certain transactions of a specific value between a company and its directors. While there are exceptions to the prohibition and mechanisms whereby it can be overcome, directors should be aware that the legislation does prohibit a director from entering into specific transactions with a company.

1. PROHIBITED TRANSACTIONS

[6.066] CA 1990, s 29 is the provision which governs the prohibition on directors' transactions with the company. Section 29(1) provides that:

a company shall not enter into an arrangement—

(a) whereby a director of the company or its holding company or a person connected with such a director acquires or is to acquire one or more non-cash assets of the requisite value from the company; or

(b) whereby the company acquires or is to acquire one or more non-cash assets of the requisite value from such a director or a person so connected ...[159]

---

[155] CA 1990, s 40(1).

[156] CA 1990, s 40(2).

[157] CA 1990, s 240.

[158] See www.odce.ie for details of all prosecutions by the ODCE.

[159] CA 1990, s 29(1).

[6.067] The effect of this provision is that any arrangement for the acquisition by, or from, a company of 'non-cash assets of the requisite value' is prohibited if the other party to the arrangement is one of the following:

-   a director of the company;

-   a person connected with a director of the company;

-   a director of the company's holding company;

-   a person connected with a director of the company's holding company.[160]

[6.068] The expression 'person connected with such a director' is defined in s 26.[161] The persons who are deemed by the Companies Acts to be 'connected with a director' (unless they are directors of the company themselves) are the following:

-   a member of the director's family (spouse, parent, sibling, child);[162]

-   a trustee (acting in that capacity) of a trust of which the director, his wife or child, or company which he controls, is the principal beneficiary;[163]

-   a partner of the director;[164] and

-   a company controlled by the director.[165]

[6.069] The prohibition on substantial property transactions also extends to include so-called 'shadow directors'. This term is defined in s 27 as:

> … a person in accordance with whose directions or instructions the directors of a company are accustomed to act … unless the directors are accustomed so to act by reason only that they do so on advice given by him in a professional capacity.[166]

---

160 See paras **[6.034]** to **[6.035]** regarding the definition of persons 'connected with a director' (CA 1990, s 26, as amended by CLEA 2001, s 76). For the purposes of this section, the term 'director' should be read as encapsulating directors, directors of holding companies and persons connected with such directors.

161 CA 1990, s 26, as amended by CLEA 2001, s 76. See further paras **[6.034]** to **[6.035]**.

162 CA 1990, s 26(1)(a), as substituted by CLEA 2001, s 76.

163 CA 1990, s 26(1)(b), as substituted by CLEA 2001, s 76.

164 CA 1990, s 26(1)(c), as substituted by CLEA 2001, s 76.

165 CA 1990, s 26(2). According to CA 1990, s 26(3), as substituted by CLEA 2001, s 76, 'For the purposes of this section, a director of a company shall be deemed to control a body corporate if, but only if, he is, alone or together with any other director or directors of the company, or any person connected with the director or such other director or directors, interested in one-half or more of the equity share capital of that body or entitled to exercise or control the exercise of one-half or more of the voting power at any general meeting of that body.' This definition is further expended by CA 1990, s 26(4)(b), which provides that, 'references to voting power exercised by a director shall include references to voting power exercised by another body corporate which that director controls.'

166 CA 1990, s 27(1).

This encompasses persons who are not formally appointed to the company's board of director but who do in fact exercise some measure of control over the company's affairs.[167]

1. Acquisition by companies

[6.070] There are a number of points to note about s 29. The first issue to highlight is that it prohibits the acquisition by, or from, a company of the relevant assets. In addition to a director being prohibited from acquiring assets from the company, the company is also prohibited from acquiring such assets from its directors. This can be contrasted with the prohibition on loans, which only affects loans from the company to the director and not loans from the director to the company.[168]

2. Arrangements

[6.071] Section 29 prohibits a broad range of dealings between a company and its directors. This is immediately apparent from the fact that the provision prohibits 'arrangements' for the acquisition of the relevant assets. This is a term of which there is no definition in the Companies Acts. It must therefore be given its ordinary and natural meaning. In this regard, the fact that 'arrangements' rather than 'transactions' is the term used suggests that there does not need to be a formal contract or agreement. The word 'arrangement' would capture more informal dealings, or planned dealings, between a company and its director. This is apparent from the references in s 29 to 'an arrangement entered into by a company... and any transaction entered into in pursuance of the arrangement ...'.[169] and to arrangements whereby the company or the director 'acquires or is to acquire' the relevant assets.[170] The arrangements that are captured by s 29 therefore clearly include collaborations or plans which are formed before any transaction is entered.

The language used throughout s 29 confirms that the prohibition on arrangements between a company and director for the acquisition of non-cash assets of the requisite value, includes informal arrangements which do not immediately effect the transfer of the assets. Indeed, it appears that such arrangements are prohibited whether or not they are ever put into effect in the form of an executed transaction.

3. Acquisition

[6.072] The word 'acquisition' would ordinarily connote gaining or obtaining something. In the context of s 29, it is provided that:

> any reference to the acquisition of a non-cash asset includes a reference to the creation or extinction of an estate or interest in, or a right over, any property and

---

[167] See further Ch **16**.

[168] CA 1990, s 31. See further above paras **[6.026]** to **[6.064]**.

[169] CA 1990, s 29(3).

[170] CA 1990, s 29(1).

also a reference to the discharge of any person's liability other than a liability for a liquidated sum ....[171]

Applying this definition of 'acquisition', s 29(1) therefore prohibits an arrangement whereby a director or a company creates or extinguishes any estate or interest in, or any right over, any property and whereby a director or a company discharges any person's liability other than a liability for a liquidated sum.

[6.073] This is not an interpretation that one would commonly attach to the word 'acquisition' and a number of ambiguities arise from it. For example, s 29(9)(b) does not specify to whom the property in which the interest, estate or right is created or extinguished, must belong and to whom the interest, estate or right, which is created or extinguished, must belong. In addition, the act of creating or extinguishing an estate, interest or right, does not necessarily confer anything on the person doing that act. The reference to the discharge of another's liability is also very vague. This is inconsistent with the purpose of s 29, which is premised on the existence of an arrangement between two persons, one being the company and the other its director, for the acquisition of an asset.

4. Prohibition on company

[6.074] A fourth matter that may be noted in relation to s 29 is that it is formulated as a prohibition on the company entering in the arrangements described in that section. Section 29(1) begins with the phrase, 'a company shall not enter into an arrangement ...'. It is curious that the prohibition is expressed as being imposed on the company, particularly in light of the fact that sanctions for a violation of s 29 focus entirely on the director.[172] The prohibition would more appropriately be formulated as a prohibition on a director entering into the arrangements in question. This is, however, more a point of semantics than substance.

5. 'Non-cash assets

[6.075] A 'non-cash asset' is defined in s 29(9)(a) as 'any property or interest in property other than cash, and for this purpose "cash" includes foreign currency ...'.

This definition is broad and ensures that only transactions founded on cash are not captured by s 29. It leaves open the possibility that negotiable instruments, savings certificates and other means by which money may be represented or exchanged, may be within the scope of s 29.

6. Requisite value

[6.076] CA 1990, s 25(4)(c) clarifies that the 'value of a transaction or arrangement' for transactions or arrangements within the scope of s 29 is:

> the price which it is reasonable to expect could be obtained for the goods, lands or services to which the transaction or arrangement relates if they had been supplied

---

[171] CA 1990, s 29(9)(b).

[172] See further below paras **[6.085]** to **[6.087]**.

at the time the transaction or arrangement is entered into in the ordinary course of business and on the same terms (apart from price) as they have been supplied or are to be supplied under the transaction or arrangement in question.

The value which an asset must hold to come within the scope of s 29 is defined as follows in s 29(2):

non-cash asset is of the requisite value if at the time the arrangement in question is entered into its value is not less than €1.269.74 but, subject to that, exceeds €63.486.90 or ten per cent of the amount of the company's relevant assets.[173]

There are two maximum value thresholds and one overriding minimum threshold. If the value of the assets exceeds either one of the two maximum thresholds, namely €63,486.90 or the value of ten per cent of the company's relevant assets, it will come within the scope of s 29. However, if the value of the assets is less than €1,269.74 (by virtue of ten per cent of the company's net assets being worth less than that amount) its acquisition by a company or its director will not violate s 29.[174]

2. EXCEPTIONS

[6.077] The prohibition on acquisition of non-cash assets by a company from a director and vice versa, is by no means absolute. There are a number of exceptions to the rule that such acquisitions are prohibited. Moreover, any arrangements for the acquisition of non-cash assets by or from the company can be approved by the company in general meeting.

1. Company approval

[6.078] A company can pass a resolution to approve the acquisition, between a company and director, of a non-cash asset, irrespective of its value. When such a resolution is passed, an arrangement which would otherwise violate s 29, is removed

---

[173] CA 1990, s 29(2). The value of the relevant assets are: '(a) except in a case falling within para (b), the value of its net assets determined by reference to the accounts prepared and laid in accordance with the requirements of s 148 of the Principal Act in respect of the last preceding financial year in respect of which such accounts were so laid; (b) where no accounts have been prepared and laid under that section before that time, the amount of its called-up share capital' (CA 1990, s 29(2)). 'Net assets' are defined in CA 1990, s 29(9)(c), as substituted by EC(IFRSMA)R 2005, reg 9, Sch 1, Pt 4, as 'the aggregate of the company's assets less the aggregate of its liabilities'.

[174] MacCann illustrates the operation of this rule as follows: '... if the company had net assets of £25,000, approval would be required for transactions in respect of non-cash assets worth more than £2,500 (ie, worth more than 10% of the net assets). On the other hand, if the company had net assets of £9,000, transactions in respect of non-cash assets worth £901would not require approval although exceeding 10 per cent of the net assets, since they would come below the £1,000 minimum threshold. Conversely if the company had non-cash assets of £1,000,000, transactions in respect of non-cash assets worth £75,000, although representing less than 10% of the net assets would still require approval since they would exceed the £50,000 threshold'. MacCann, *Companies Acts 1963–1990* (1993, Tottel Publishing) at p 907.

from the scope of that provision. Section 29(1) provides in this regard, that the acquisition of non-cash assets of the requisite value is prohibited:

> unless the arrangement is first approved by a resolution of the company in general meeting and, if the director or connected person is a director of its holding company or a person connected with such a director, by a resolution in general meeting of the holding company.[175]

The resolution must be passed by the company in general meeting. It must also be passed before the arrangement in question is made or entered into. If the director (or person connected with him) who is entering into the arrangement with the company, is in fact a director of a holding company, the latter must also pass a resolution approving the arrangement.

[6.079] This provision is not very exacting or specific and it does not contain any safeguards or stipulations regarding the circumstances surrounding the passing of the resolution. There are a number of matters which one may expect to be addressed in a provision permitting a director to enter into an arrangement of a sizeable value with the company that are not included in s 29(1). For example, there is nothing in this provision which requires any particular notice of the resolution to be circulated with the notice of the meeting. A simple majority resolution is sufficient to approve a transaction under s 29; there is no requirement that a special resolution be passed. There is no requirement that the directors must state the impact the transaction will have on the company. There is no requirement of, or opportunity for, an independent valuation of the asset in question. Finally, there is nothing in s 29 which permits dissatisfied shareholders to challenge the resolution and the arrangement which it approves.

[6.080] The terms of s 29(1) contrast sharply with CA 1990, s 34, as inserted by CLEA 2001, s 78. That provision allows a company to pass a special resolution permitting a company to furnish a guarantee or security in favour of a director, and is subject to a number of conditions and restrictions. Section 34 requires, among other stipulations, that the resolution must be a special resolution, which must have been passed in the 12 months preceding the transaction.[176] In addition, the directors must make a detailed statutory declaration regarding the proposed transaction and its effect on the company, which must be accompanied by an auditors' report confirming its reasonableness.[177] This declaration must be sent to the members with the notice of the meeting and must be registered with the Registrar of Companies.[178] A final protection that is contained in s 34 is that members who do not vote in favour of the resolution have the right to apply to court for the cancellation of the resolution.[179]

---

[175] CA 1990, s 29(1).

[176] CA 1990, s 34(1), as inserted by CLEA 2001, s 78. See further paras **[6.044]** to **[6.048]**.

[177] CA 1990, s 34(3) and (4), as inserted by CLEA 2001, s 78. See further paras **[6.044]** to **[6.048]**.

[178] CA 1990, s 34(1), as inserted by CLEA 2001, s 78. See further paras **[6.044]** to **[6.048]**.

[179] CA 1990, s 34(7) to (11), as inserted by CLEA 2001, s 78. Note that such an application may only be made by the 'holders of not less in the aggregate than 10 per cent in nominal value of the company's issued share capital or any class thereof' (CA 1990, s 34(9), as inserted by CLEA 2001, s 78). See further paras **[6.044]** to **[6.048]**.

If a company proposes to sell to, or acquire from, a director, a non-cash asset of a certain value, a shareholder may not be aware of this proposal until the day of the general meeting. The shareholders will not necessarily receive any detailed or verified information regarding the proposed arrangement. Furthermore, there is no recourse for a dissatisfied shareholder if the resolution is passed successfully. While it would clearly constitute a breach of the duties of a director, and may violate other provisions of the Companies Acts, for a director to arrange for a resolution to be passed approving the sale of an asset to the company at a gross over-value, there is nothing in s 29 itself which protects against such a risk.

2. Bodies corporate

[6.081] The scope of the prohibition on arrangements for the acquisition of assets of a particular value between a company and a director only applies to companies incorporated under the Companies Acts. Section 29(6) provides in this regard:

> No approval is required to be given under this section by any body corporate unless it is a company within the meaning of The Principal Act or registered under Part IX of that Act[180] or, if it is, for the purposes of section 150 of that Act, a wholly owned subsidiary of any body corporate, wherever incorporated.[181]

3. Group arrangements

[6.082] It is not prohibited for companies in the same group, in which the subsidiaries are wholly owned, to enter into an arrangement for the acquisition of a non-cash asset. Section 29(7)(a) provides that the prohibition shall not apply:

> if the non-cash asset in question is or is to be acquired by a holding company from any of its wholly owned subsidiaries or from a holding company by any of its wholly owned subsidiaries or by one wholly owned subsidiary of a holding company from another wholly owned subsidiary of that same holding company.[182]

3. Company in liquidation

[6.083] It is not prohibited for a company which is being wound up to enter into an arrangement which would otherwise be prohibited by s 29(1). This is subject to the caveat that such a transaction continues to be prohibited if the company is being wound up in a members' voluntary winding up.[183]

4. Capacity as member

[6.084] The final exception to s 29 is that it does not prevent a person from acquiring an asset from a company if he does so in his capacity as a member of the company.[184] There

---

[180] CA 1963, Pt IX deals with companies which are capable of registration under that Act, such as companies formed under the Joint Stock Companies Acts. See CA 1963, s 328.

[181] CA 1990, s 29(6).

[182] CA 1990, s 29(7)(a).

[183] CA 1990, s 29(7)(b).

[184] CA 1990, s 29(8).

is no corresponding exception permitting a person to sell an asset to the company in his capacity as a member of the company. Section 29(8) provides in this regard:

> Subsection (1)(a) shall not apply in relation to any arrangement whereby a person acquires or is to acquire an asset from a company of which he is a member if the arrangement is made with that person in his character as such member.[185]

There is nothing in this provision regulating how and when it should be invoked. In most Irish companies the same persons own the company and sit on its board of directors. The roles are often treated interchangeably. The fact that s 29(8) permits one role, that of member, to be exempt from the terms of s 29, may be anomalous and may encourage shareholder/directors to purport to acquire assets from the company in their capacity as a member, rather than as a director, to circumvent the terms of s 29.

3. CONSEQUENCES OF VIOLATION

1. Voidable arrangement and transaction

[6.085] If an arrangement is entered in violation of s 29, that arrangement and any transaction that may ensue, are voidable at the instance of the company.[186] There are four exceptions to this general rule. The arrangement and transaction are not voidable if one of the following situations exists:

- restitution of any money or other asset which is the subject matter of the arrangement or transaction, is not possible;[187]

- the company has been indemnified for any loss or damage suffered;[188]

- its avoidance would affect the rights of a person, not being a party to the arrangement or transaction, which were acquired *bona fide* for value and without notice of the contravention; [189] or

- within a reasonable period after the arrangement, it is affirmed by the company in general meeting.[190]

[6.086] The last of these exceptions, the possibility of a company affirming the arrangement after it is made, is worthy of some comment. First, it only purports to allow the affirmation of the arrangement. It does not exempt any transaction which may have ensued from the arrangement from the possibility of being avoided by the company. This has the curious consequence that an arrangement to enter into a transaction could

---

[185] CA 1990, s 29(8).

[186] CA 1990, s 29(3).

[187] CA 1990, s 29(3)(a).

[188] CA 1990, s 29(3)(a). Note that the company must have been indemnified pursuant to CA 1990, s 29(4)(b).

[189] CA 1990, s 29(3)(b).

[190] CA 1990, s 29(3)(c). Note that, if the transfer involves a the director of a holding company (or a person connected with such a director), the holding company must also pass a resolution in general meeting.

be affirmed, but the transaction itself could not. Secondly, the resolution must be passed within a 'reasonable period after the arrangement'. This expression is vague and may be difficult to apply in practice. However, this may be the explanation for the failure to permit ratification of a transaction. It is possible that the intention behind s 29(3)(c) is that the arrangement can be affirmed within a reasonable time, but if the arrangement has gone so far as to have been implemented, and a transaction has been formed, a 'reasonable time' must have lapsed and the arrangement and the transaction would then be incapable of affirmation by the company. A final point to recall is that a company can pass a resolution to approve the arrangement in advance.[191] The fact that s 29(3)(c) creates a power to affirm an arrangement after it has been made in breach of s 29, seems to give a company and its director a second chance to use the same mechanism.

2. Liability to account and indemnify

[6.087] If an arrangement is made in contravention of s 29, the person who entered into the arrangement with the company (whether a director of the company, of a holding company, or a person connected with such directors) and 'any other director of the company who authorised the arrangement or any transaction entered into in pursuance of such an arrangement' are liable to account to the company for any gain made, directly or indirectly, by the arrangement or transaction and they are also liable to indemnify the company for any loss or damage which has resulted from the arrangement or transaction.[192]

4. DEFENCE

[6.088] Where an arrangement is made in violation of s 29, between a person connected with a director of a company or of its holding company, the director shall not be liable to indemnify the company for loss suffered and account for gains made, 'if he shows that he took all reasonable steps to secure the company's compliance with this section'.[193] Furthermore, a person connected to a director and any other director who authorised the arrangement or transaction, 'shall not be so liable if he shows that, at the time the arrangement was entered into, he did not know the relevant circumstances constituting the contravention.'[194] While these defences protect persons against liability to account for gains made, and to indemnify for losses suffered, they do not prevent the arrangement or resulting transaction, being avoided by the company pursuant to s 29(3).[195] There are therefore two different types of defence, depending upon the person seeking to escape liability for an arrangement which was made in contravention of s 29.

[6.089] The first type of defence which may be relied upon is that all reasonable steps were taken to secure compliance with the requirements of s 29.[196] This defence can only be invoked when the arrangement in question was made between a person connected

---

[191] CA 1990, s 29(1). See further above paras **[6.078]** to **[6.080]**.
[192] CA 1990, s 29(4).
[193] CA 1990, s 29(5).
[194] CA 1990, s 29(5).
[195] CA 1990, s 29(3). See above paras **[6.085]** to **[6.086]**.
[196] CA 1990, s 29(5).

with a director (whether a director of the company or its holding company) and the company. It does not apply when the arrangements are made between a company and its own director or a director of its holding company. Moreover, this defence can only be invoked by the director to whom the person who made the relevant arrangement, is connected. What constitutes 'reasonable steps' is not clarified. It must be assumed that an unsuccessful attempt to have a resolution passed by the company approving the arrangement, within the meaning of s 29(1), would not constitute 'reasonable steps to secure the company's compliance.' Otherwise, a director could make an arrangement for the acquisition of an asset, which the company had refused to approve in general meeting, acting in complete disregard of the company's vote on the matter, and subsequently escape liability on the basis of having placed the resolution before the general meeting. The only other steps which could be taken to ensure compliance with s 29 would be to discourage and seek to prevent the arrangement being made, such as by voting against it, and bringing it to the company's attention. Alternatively, a director could take steps to attempt to ensure that the value of the arrangement was lower than the threshold stipulated in s 29(2).[197]

[6.090] The second defence is based on a lack of knowledge of the relevant circumstances constituting the contravention at the time the arrangement was made.[198] This defence can be invoked in any circumstances in which there is a breach of s 29.[199] A person connected with a director (whether a director of the company with which the arrangement is made or its holding company) can avoid liability on this basis. By way of example, it may be conceivable that a person could sell an asset to a company without being aware that his sister was a director of its holding company. A director who authorised the arrangement or transaction may also rely on this defence. An example of a situation in which this may arise is where a director is not aware that an individual who is buying an asset from the company is in a partnership with a director of the company's holding company. It should be emphasised that the basis of this defence is a lack of knowledge of the relevant circumstances, not a lack of knowledge of the law. If the person was aware of their connection to the company, they cannot invoke the defence that they did not know it was a violation of the Companies Acts to make an arrangement with that company for the acquisition of an asset of a certain value.

C. Disclosure obligations

[6.091] Directors are obliged to make disclosure of certain matters to the company which the company may then be required to keep on a register or notify to the Registrar of Companies.[200] The information that must be disclosed regarding directors may be divided into the following categories:

   (a)   Personal information;

---

[197] CA 1990, s 29(2). See further above para **[6.076]**.

[198] CA 1990, s 29(5).

[199] CA 1990, s 29(5). This is indicated by the words 'in any case' in relation to this defence.

[200] It should be noted that a director may also be required to furnish information to certain persons, such as the company's auditors, liquidators, the Registrar of Companies and the ODCE. Each of these obligations are very important to the enforcement of company law and are addressed in detail in Chs **2**, **7** and **9**, respectively.

(b) Disqualifications in other jurisdictions;

(c) Directors' contracts;

(d) Interests in contracts with company;

(e) Interests in shares or debentures;

(f) Payments to directors; and

(g) Disclosure in company accounts.

(a) Personal information

[6.092] Every company is obliged to keep at its registered office a register of its directors and secretaries.[201] In relation to each director, this register must contain his full name (and any former names); date of birth; residential address; nationality; business occupation (if any); and the particulars of any other directorships of companies, which he holds or has held within the previous ten years.[202] Within 14 days of any change in these particulars, the company is obliged to notify the Registrar of Companies of this change and the date on which it occurred.[203] The form to be used for this purpose is Form B10.[204]

[6.093] Every director and secretary is under a duty to furnish to the company, 'as soon as may be' and 'in writing', such information as may be necessary to enable the company to comply with these requirements.[205] A director must therefore notify the company to which it is appointed of all of the particulars listed above.[206] A director must furthermore notify a company promptly of any change in these particulars. Such notification must be given to the company quickly enough to enable the company to notify the Registrar of the change within 14 days of its occurrence. It is an offence for a director or secretary to fail to comply with these requirements.[207]

---

[201] CA 1963, s 195(1), as substituted by CA 1990, s 51. Note that the obligation to keep a register of directors and secretaries is contained in the Draft Companies Bill, available at www.clrg.ie. See further Ch **2**.

[202] CA 1963, s 195(2) and (3)(a), as substituted by CA 1990, s 51. According to CA 1963, s 195(3)(b), the register does not have to contain information regarding directorships 'which is held or was held by a director in bodies corporate of which the company is or was the wholly owned subsidiary or which are or were the wholly owned subsidiaries either of the company or of another body corporate of which the company is or was the wholly owned subsidiary.'

[203] CA 1963, s 195(6), as substituted by C(A)A 1982, s 8.

[204] This form, which is available at www.cro.ie, may be filled in and filed online.

[205] CA 1963, s 195(11), as substituted by CA 1990, s 51.

[206] Note that, when CA 1990, s 195(6A), as inserted by IFCMPA 2005, s 62, is commenced, a person who is a director of several companies can notify the Registrar of Companies directly of changes in their names or addresses, relieving those companies of the obligation to notify such changes separately. See Ch **2**.

[207] CA 1963, s 195(14), as substituted by CA 1990, s 51.

(b) Disqualifications in other jurisdictions

[6.094] The persons who are named as directors on the Form A1, which a company delivers to the Registrar, are deemed to have been appointed as the company's directors.[208] If any of these persons are disqualified in another state from being so appointed or so acting, this fact must be disclosed in a separate statement to the Registrar.[209] It is the duty of the disqualified person to ensure that this statement is made. The statement must specify the jurisdiction in which he is disqualified, the date and period of such disqualification.[210] It must also be signed by the disqualified person.[211] The form prescribed for this statement is Form B74.[212]

[6.095] If a person is appointed as a director of a existing company, and is disqualified under the law of another state from being appointed, or acting, as a director, it is the duty of that disqualified person to ensure that the notification of their appointment which the company must send to the Registrar, is accompanied by a separate statement.[213] This statement must be signed by the disqualified person and must state the jurisdiction in which they are disqualified and the date and period of such disqualification. The form that must be used for this purpose is Form B74.[214]

[6.096] A person who is a director of a company being registered in Ireland, or who is appointed as a director of a company already registered in Ireland, and who fails to ensure that a separate statement is sent to the Registrar of Companies specifying that he is subject to a disqualification order in another jurisdiction, shall be deemed to be disqualified in Ireland. According to CA 1990, s 160(1A),[215] if such a person fails to ensure the notification requirements are complied with, or permits the requisite statement or notification to be accompanied by a statement signed by him which is 'false or misleading in a material respect,' he shall be deemed to be disqualified.[216] To

---

[208] C(A)A 1982, s 3(5). The Form A1 is the form which a company is required by C(A)A 1982, s 3, to deliver to the Registrar, together with the company's memorandum of association, for the purpose of first registering the company. Ch **2**.

[209] C(A)A 1982, s 3A, as inserted by CLEA 2001, s 101. See Note Six to Form A1: 'Where a person who has consented to be a director of this company is currently disqualified under the law of another state from being appointed or acting as a director or secretary of a body corporate or undertaking, he/she must complete Form B74 which must be submitted to CRO with Form A1. Otherwise he/she will be deemed to be disqualified from acting as a director of an Irish-registered company for the balance remaining of his/her foreign disqualification'. See Ch **20**.

[210] C(A)A 1982, s 3A(1), as inserted by CLEA 2001, s 101.

[211] C(A)A 1982, s 3A(1), as inserted by CLEA 2001, s 101.

[212] This form may be downloaded from www.cro.ie.

[213] CA 1963, s 195(8), as substituted by CA 1990, s 51, and as substituted by CLEA 2001, s 91(a).

[214] Available at www.cro.ie.

[215] CA 1990, s 160(1A), as inserted by CLEA 2001, s 42(a).

[216] CA 1990, s 160(1A), as inserted by CLEA 2001, s 42(a). See Ch **20**.

date, one person has been prosecuted for acting as a director without notifying the Registrar that he was disqualified in England and Wales.[217]

(c) Directors' contracts

[6.097] Every company is required by the Companies Act to keep copies of its directors' contracts of service,[218] together with any variations of those contracts,[219] at the company's registered office; its principal place of business; or at the place where the register of members is kept.[220] If these contracts are kept somewhere other than the company's registered office, the Registrar of Companies must be notified of their location and any change in their location.[221] It should be noted that there is no obligation to keep such copies or memoranda if the contract of service will expire within three years or if the contract may be terminated, without payment of compensation, within three years.[222]

The obligation to keep copies or memoranda of the directors' contracts of service applies to the company's own directors and to directors who are employed under contracts of service with subsidiaries of the company.[223] If the contract of service requires a director to work wholly or mainly outside Ireland, the company is not required to keep a copy or memorandum of that contract, but must keep a memorandum setting out certain details about the director's contract of service.[224] These memoranda must be

---

[217] In the case of *Director of Corporate Enforcement v O'Brien*, the defendant was charged at Midleton District Court with contravening CA 1990, s 161(1) by acting as a director of two Irish companies while deemed to be disqualified under s 161(1A), due to his failure to ensure that the Registrar of Companies was notified of his disqualification in England and Wales. On conviction, he was fined €1,900 on each charge and ordered to pay prosecution costs of €1,000. His disqualification from acting as a director in the State was extended to 1 January 2008. This matter is currently under appeal by way of case stated to the High Court. The conviction and disqualification have been suspended pending the outcome of this appeal. See further Chs **20** and **23**.

[218] If the contract is written, a copy of the contract must be kept (CA 1990, s 50(1)(a)). If there is no written contract of service, a written memorandum setting out the terms of the oral contract must be kept (CA 1990, s 50(1)(b)). If the contract is partially in writing, these requirements apply to such a contract (CA 1990, s 50(2)).

[219] CA 1990, s 50(1)(d) requires a copy or written memorandum of such variations to be kept.

[220] CA 1990, s 50(3). For further information regarding the places where the register of members may be kept, see Ch **3**.

[221] CA 1990, s 50(4).

[222] CA 1990, s 50(9).

[223] CA 1990, s 50(1)(c).

[224] CA 1990, s 50(5). The memorandum must state, '(a) in the case of a contract of service with the company, setting out the name of the director and the provisions of the contract relating to its duration; (b) in the case of a contract of service with a subsidiary of the company setting out the name of the director, the name and place of incorporation of the subsidiary and the provisions of the contract relating to its duration.'

kept in the same place as the copies or memoranda of the other directors' contracts of service.[225]

Every copy and memorandum of a director's service contract which the company is required to keep, must be open to inspection, free of charge, by the company's members for at least two hours daily during business hours.[226]

[6.098] If the company fails to keep the requisite copies or memoranda of the directors' contracts of service, or refuses to allow inspection of these copies of memoranda, the company and every officer in default is liable on summary conviction to a once-off fine and to a daily default fine for continued contraventions.[227] If the company fails to notify the Registrar of Companies of the location, or change in location, of these documents, within 14 days, the company and every officer in default is liable to a fine and a daily default fine for continuing contraventions.[228] Furthermore, in the event of a refusal to allow inspection of the copies or memoranda of the service contracts, the court may make an order compelling immediate inspection of those documents.[229]

(d) Interest in contract with company

[6.099] It is the duty of every director to declare to the directors of the company any interest he has in any contract or proposed contract with the company. Section 194 provides in this regard:

> It shall be the duty of a director of a company who is in any way, whether directly or indirectly, interested in a contract or proposed contract with the company to declare the nature of his interest at a meeting of the directors of the company.[230]

It should be noted at the outset that this provision only requires a director to disclose his interest in a contract to the directors of the company. There is nothing in s 194 which requires the directors to vote in favour of, sanction, or approve the interest held by the director. Moreover, there is no explicit requirement that the director must disclose the interest to the members of the company.

(i) Scope

[6.100] There are two matters to consider with regard to the scope of s 194. First, the category of directors who are obliged to make disclosure of their interests in contracts with the company includes shadow directors.[231] In this regard, the Companies Acts

---

[225] CA 1990, s 50(5).

[226] CA 1990, s 50(6).

[227] CA 1990, s 50(7).

[228] CA 1990, s 50(7).

[229] CA 1990, s 50(8).

[230] CA 1963, s 194(1).

[231] CA 1990, s 27(3). A shadow director is defined as '...a person in accordance with whose directions or instructions the directors of a company are accustomed to act' (CA 1990, s 27(1)). See Ch **16**.

acknowledge that shadow directors are not formally appointed directors and do not have the right to attend meetings of a company's board of directors. Shadow directors are therefore obliged to make disclosure of their interests by notice in writing to the directors, rather than at a meeting of the directors.[232]

[6.101] Secondly, the requirement to disclose an interest in a contract includes a duty to disclose any interest in any transaction or arrangement, whether or not it amounts to a contract.[233] In addition, a director must disclose if there are any loans, quasi-loans, credit transactions, guarantees or securities within the meaning of CA 1990, s 31, between the company and him or a person connected with him.[234] This obligation of disclosure arises whether or not the transaction in question was prohibited by s 31.[235]

(ii) Date for disclosure

[6.102] There are three different means to determine the timing of the meeting at which a director must disclose his interest in a contract. The first rule is that the interest in a proposed contract must be disclosed at the meeting at which the question of entering into that contract is first considered.[236] The second rule is that, if the director was not interested in the contract at the date of that first meeting at which it was considered, but subsequently acquires such an interest, he must disclose this interest at the next meeting thereafter.[237] The third rule is that a director who becomes interested in a contract after it is made, must declare that interest at the first meeting of the directors held after he obtained that interest.[238]

(iii) General notice

[6.103] Section 194 does permit directors to make general declarations of disclosure in two circumstances. First, a director can give the directors of the company a general notice of the fact that he is a member of a particular company or firm or that he is to be regarded as interested in any contract formed with a particular company or firm.[239] Secondly, a director can furnish general notice of the fact that he is to be regarded as

---

[232] CA 1990, s 27(3). Note that this notice must be either, '(a) a specific notice given before the date of the meeting at which, if he had been a director, the declaration would be required by subsection (2) of that section to be made; or (b) a notice which under sub-s (3) of that section falls to be treated as a sufficient declaration of that interest or would fall to be so treated apart from the proviso' (CA 1990, s 27(3)).

[233] CA 1990, s 47(1).

[234] CA 1990, s 47(2).

[235] CA 1990, s 47(2).

[236] CA 1963, s 194(2).

[237] CA 1963, s 194(2).

[238] CA 1963, s 194(2).

[239] CA 1963, s 194(3)(a), as substituted by CA 1990, s 47.

interested in any contract formed with a particular person, with whom he is connected.[240]

Any such general notice must be given at a meeting of the directors.[241] Alternatively, the director must take reasonable steps to ensure that the notice is brought up and read at the next meeting after it is given. The notice is of no effect unless one of these steps has been taken.[242]

[6.104] Finally, a notice declaring a general interest in all contracts with a particular firm, company, or person, should be reflected in the minutes of the meeting at which the notice is given or read. The minutes of such meetings if duly signed are deemed to be evidence of what transpired at the meeting.[243] In the case of a general notice of interest in a contract, it may be very significant for a director to be able to present the signed minutes demonstrating that notice being brought to the attention of the directors. This is particularly true in light of the fact that the notice is not of effect unless it has been presented at a meeting of the directors.[244]

(iv) Record of disclosure

[6.105] Every time a director discloses an interest in a contract with the company, that disclosure must be entered in a book kept for this purpose.[245] This must be done within three days of the making or giving of the notice.[246] This book must be readily accessible. Section 194 contains three specific requirements in this regard. First, the book must be open to inspection by any director, secretary, auditor or member of the company, free of charge, at the company's registered office.[247] Secondly, the book of directors' interests must be produced at every general meeting of the company. Thirdly, if any director makes a request in sufficient time, the book must be produced at a meeting of the directors.[248]

(v) Penalty

[6.106] A director who fails to make a declaration of interest or to ensure that it is disclosed at the meeting of the company's directors, is liable to a fine.[249]

---

[240] CA 1963, s 194(3)(b), as substituted by CA 1990, s 47.

[241] CA 1963, s 194(4).

[242] CA 1963, s 194(4).

[243] CA 1963, s 145(2). See Ch **5**.

[244] CA 1963, s 194(4).

[245] CA 1963, s 194(5)(a).

[246] CA 1963, s 194(5)(a).

[247] CA 1963, s 194(5)(a).

[248] CA 1963, s 194(5)(a).

[249] CA 1963, s 194(6).

If a company fails to keep a book containing all such declarations of interest, or fails to make this book available for inspection at the company's registered office, at the company's general meetings, or, if requested, at meetings of the company's directors, the company and every officer in default is liable to a fine and the court may make an order compelling the immediate inspection or production of the book.[250]

In addition to the possibility of a fine for any infringement of s 194, a failure to comply with this provision may cause the contract to become voidable and the director may be liable to account for profits made.[251]

(vi) Interaction with other laws

[6.107] Even if a director complies with the requirement to make disclosure of his interest in a contract with the company, this does not necessarily absolve him of legal responsibility for his interest in a contract with the company. In particular, s 194(7) provides that:

> Nothing in this section shall be taken to prejudice the operation of any rule of law restricting directors of a company from having any interest in contracts with the company.[252]

(e) Interest in shares or debentures

[6.108] Every company director is obliged to notify the company of any interests he holds in its shares or debentures.[253] A director is also obliged to notify the company if he ceases to hold an interest in any shares or debentures, or is contracting to sell, assign or have assigned to him, any such shares or debentures.[254]

The provisions applicable to directors' duties to disclose interests in a company's shares or debentures are detailed and complex and are not addressed in detail here.[255] There are, however, certain points that may be noted regarding the scope of this obligation. First, if a director owns shares in, or debentures of, the company, its subsidiary, holding company or a subsidiary of its holding company, these are regarded as shares and

---

[250] CA 1963, s 194(5)(b).

[251] *Guinness plc v Saunders* [1988] 2 All ER 940; *Hely-Hutchinson v Brayhead Ltd* [1967] 3 All ER 98.

[252] CA 1963, s 194(7).

[253] CA 1990, s 53(1). The Company Law Review Group identified a number of anomalies in relation to this obligation of disclosure and noted the low level of compliance with this notification requirement. The CLRG made a number of recommendations for the law to be changed in this regard, 'the effect of which will be to disapply the existing law from the vast majority of private companies limited by shares.' See CLRG, *First Report*, at paras 11.10.1 to 11.10.8.

[254] CA 1990, s 53(2). CA 1990, s 57 contains detailed provisions regarding how these occurrences need to be notified, and these requirements must be strictly complied with. CA 1990, s 58(1) also contains provisions regarding the consequences of acquiring, or disposing of, shares through an agent.

[255] See Courtney, *The Law of Private Companies* (2nd edn, Tottel Publishing, 2002) at paras 8.090 to 8.093.

debentures in the company.[256] Secondly, the requirement to notify the company of interests in shares and debentures applies to shadow directors as well as directors.[257] Thirdly, if the spouse or a minor child of a director or secretary acquires an interest or right of subscription for, or contracts or subscribes for, or takes assignment or grant of, shares or debentures of the company, the director or secretary is obliged to notify the company of this fact within five days of the date on which that occurrence came to his knowledge.[258]

[6.109] Fourthly, a director is considered to have an interest in shares and debentures in each of the following circumstances:[259]

- irrespective of any restriction or restraint to which the interest may be subject;[260]
- where he is the beneficiary of a trust which includes an interest in shares or debentures;[261]
- when he enters into a contract to purchase shares;[262]
- if he is entitled to exercise or control any right conferred by the holding of shares, without being the registered holder;[263]
- if a company which acts in accordance with his instructions or directions, holds shares or debentures;[264]
- if a company of which he controls or exercises at least one third of the voting power, holds such shares or debentures;[265]

---

[256] CA 1990, s 53(1).

[257] CA 1990, s 53(9) provides, 'This section applies to shadow directors as to directors, but the making of a notification by a person under this section shall not, in itself, be proof that the person making the notification is a shadow director'. See Ch **16**.

[258] CA 1990, s 64(1) to (5). Note that the director or secretary must furnish the same information as is required by CA 1990, s 53.

[259] There are a number of specific exclusions from the scope of situations in which a director is considered to have an interest in shares. CA 1990, s 55 lists the interests which are exempt from the notification requirement. These include interests in reversion or remainder or of a bare trustee; any discretionary interests where the shares or debentures are held on trust (CA 1990, s 55(1)(a)); an interest for life under a settlement (CA 1990, s 55(1)(c)); an interest held as security for a transaction by a stockbroker, in the ordinary course of business (CA 1990, s 55(1)(d)), among others.

[260] CA 1990, s 54(2).

[261] CA 1990, s 54(3).

[262] CA 1990, s 54(4)(a).

[263] CA 1990, s 54(4)(b). According to CA 1990, s 54(8), 'For the purposes of sub-s (4)(b) a person shall be taken to be entitled to exercise or control the exercise of any right conferred by the holding of shares or debentures if he has a right (whether subject to conditions or not) the exercise of which would make him so entitled or is under an obligation (whether so subject or not) the fulfilment of which would make him so entitled.' Note that this does include situations in which a person is appointed as a proxy to vote or appointed to act as a representative of a company at a meeting (CA 1990, s 54(9)).

[264] CA 1990, s 54(5)(a).

[265] CA 1990, s 54(5)(b).

- if a company of which he controls or exercises at least one third of the voting power, is entitled to exercise or control the exercise of any voting power in the company of which he is director;[266]
- if he has a right to call for delivery of the shares or debentures;[267] and
- if he has a right or obligation to acquire an interest in shares or debentures.[268]

[6.110] Fifthly, a director must notify a company of the fact that he holds an interest in its shares or debentures within very tightly defined timeframes.[269] Every director must notify a company of any interest he holds in its shares and debentures within a period of five days.[270] This period of time commences the day after the date the legislation came into force, or the date of his appointment, whichever is the later, if he is aware of the interest on that date. Otherwise, the period of five days runs from the day following the day on which he does become aware of that interest.

[6.111] A number of consequences flow from a director failing to notify the company of his interest in shares or debentures within the requisite period of time. First, it is an offence for a director to fail to comply with these notification requirements.[271] Secondly, no right or interest of any kind in respect of the shares or debentures shall be enforceable by the director, directly or indirectly, in any action or proceeding.[272]

Every company is required to keep a register of all of the shares and debentures which are owned by its directors.[273] Whenever a company director fulfils his duty to furnish

---

[266] CA 1990, s 54(6).

[267] CA 1990, s 54(7)(a). Note that, according to CA 1990, s 54(10), '… rights or obligations to subscribe for any shares or debentures shall not be taken for the purposes of sub-s (7) to be rights to acquire, or obligations to take, any interest in shares or debentures.'

[268] CA 1990, s 54(7)(b).

[269] CA 1990, s 56(1). The same timeframes apply to the obligation to notify the company of an event by which the director is assigning, or acquiring shares or debentures in the company. CA 1990, s 56(2) provides, 'An obligation imposed on a person by s 53(2) to notify the occurrence of an event must, if at the time at which the event occurs he knows of its occurrence, be fulfilled before the expiration of the period of five days beginning with the day next following that on which it occurs; otherwise, it must be fulfilled before the expiration of the period of five days beginning with the day next following that on which the occurrence of the event comes to his knowledge.'

[270] CA 1990, s 56(1).

[271] CA 1990, s 53(7). It is also an offence to fail to notify the company of the interests of a spouse or minor child of the director (CA 1990, s 64(6)).

[272] CA 1990, s 58(3). Where this occurs, the defaulting director or other affected person, may apply to court for relief and '… the court on being satisfied that the default was accidental, or due to inadvertence, or some other sufficient cause, or that on other grounds it is just and equitable to grant relief, may grant such relief either generally, or as respects any particular right or interest on such terms and conditions as it sees fit' (CA 1990, s 58(4)). Note that the court will not grant relief if the applicant for relief is the director and the failure to notify was the result of a deliberate act or omission (CA 1990, s 58(5)).

[273] CA 1990, s 59(1). CA 1990, ss 53 to 58 concern the obligation of directors to notify companies of their interests in the company's shares or debentures and are addressed in more detail in Ch 3.

information to the company regarding his interest in the company's shares or debentures, the company must, within three days of that notification, enter on the register, beside that person's name, the information furnished and the date on which it was entered on the register.[274]

(f) Disclosure of payments to directors

[6.112] The accounts of every company, as laid before the company's general meeting, must include certain information in relation to the payments and salaries which have been received by the company's directors.[275]

CA 1963, s 191(1) requires the following matters to be so disclosed:

    (a)   the aggregate amount of the directors' emoluments;[276]

    (b)   the aggregate amount of directors' or past-directors' pensions;[277] and

---

[274] CA 1990, s 59(2). This must be done within 3 days of the day following such notification (CA 1990, s 60(2)). If a company grants a director or secretary the right to subscribe for the company's shares or debentures, the company must also enter on the register, the date on which that right was conferred, the period for which it is exercisable, the consideration paid, and a description of the shares or debentures at issue. CA 1990, s 59(3)(a) to (d). This must be done within 3 days commencing on the day following the day on which that right is conferred (CA 1990, s 60(2)). See further Ch **3**.

[275] CA 1963, s 191(1). This obligation only relates to such information as appears in the company's books and records or which the company has a right to obtain from the directors (CA 1990, s 191(1)). Section 191 does not apply to group accounts prepared in accordance with EC(CGA)R 1992, Sch, Pt 2, para 16(a) or companies to which EC(CI:A)R 1992, reg 7 or EC(IUA)R 1996, reg 10 applies.

[276] According to CA 1990, s 191(2) this '(a) shall include any emoluments paid to or receivable by any person in respect of his services as director of the company or in respect of his services, while director of the company, as director of any subsidiary thereof or otherwise in connection with the management of the affairs of the company or any subsidiary thereof; and (b) shall distinguish between emoluments in respect of services as director, whether of the company or of its subsidiary, and other emoluments; and, for the purposes of this section, "emoluments" in relation to a director, includes fees and percentages, any sums paid by way of expenses allowance in so far as those sums are charged to income tax, any contribution paid in respect of him under any pension scheme, and the estimated money value of any other benefits received by him otherwise than in cash in so far as the same are charged to income tax.'

[277] According to CA 1990, s 191(3), 'The amount to be shown under para (b) of sub-s (1)— (a) shall not include any pension paid or receivable under a pension scheme if the scheme is such that the contributions thereunder are substantially adequate for the maintenance of the scheme, but save as aforesaid, shall include any pension paid or receivable in respect of any such services of a director or past-director of the company as are mentioned in subsection (2), whether to or by him or, on his nomination or by virtue of dependence on or other connection with him, to or by any other person; and (b) shall distinguish between pensions in respect of services as director, whether of the company or its subsidiary, and other pensions; and, for the purposes of this section, "pension" includes any superannuation allowance, superannuation gratuity or similar payment ...'

(c) the aggregate amount of any compensation to directors or past-directors in respect of loss of office.[278]

These amounts include any sums paid by the company, its subsidiary, or any other person. In the case of payments in respect of loss of office, the amounts shown must distinguish between sums paid by or receivable from the company, its subsidiary, and other persons.[279] The amounts shown must reflect the sums which are receivable during the financial year to which the accounts relate.

If the requirements to disclosure these payments in the company's accounts are not complied with, the company's auditors are obliged to include in their report, insofar as it is possible for them to do so, a statement of the required particulars.[280]

(g) Disclosure of directors' interests in company accounts

[6.113] A company's accounts[281] must disclose any transaction or arrangement within the scope of s 31 (whether or not prohibited by s 31)[282] entered into by a company or its subsidiary or holding company for the benefit of a director,[283] and any agreement to enter into such a transaction or arrangement, during the relevant accounting period.[284] The accounts must also disclose any other transaction or arrangement entered into by the company or its subsidiary or holding company in which a director has a direct or indirect material interest.[285] Section 41(5)(b) clarifies that:

an interest in such a transaction or arrangement is not material if in the opinion of the majority of the directors (other than that director) of the company which is

---

[278] CA 1990, s 191(4) provides, 'The amount to be shown under para (c) of sub-s (1)—(a) shall include any sums paid to or receivable by a director or past-director by way of compensation for loss of office as director of the company or for the loss, while director of the company, or on or in connection with his ceasing to be a director of the company, of any other office in connection with the management of the company's affairs or of any office as director or otherwise in connection with the management of the affairs of any subsidiary thereof; and (b) shall distinguish between compensation in respect of the office of director, whether of the company or of its subsidiary, and compensation in respect of other offices; and, for the purposes of this section, references to compensation for loss of office shall include sums paid as consideration for or in connection with a person's retirement from office.'

[279] CA 1990, s 191(5)(a) and (b).

[280] CA 1990, s 191(8). See Ch 7.

[281] CA 1990, s 41(1) requires a holding company to include these matters in the group accounts. CA 1990, s 41(2) also requires these matters to be disclosed in the accounts prepared by a company other than a holding company.

[282] CA 1990, s 41(8)(a).

[283] Each of these obligations applies whether or not the person was a director, or the subsidiary was a subsidiary, at the date of the transaction or arrangement in question (CA 1990, s 41(8)(b) and (c)).

[284] CA 1990, s 41(1)(a) and (b); CA 1990, s 41(2)(a) and (b). These disclosure requirements do not apply to holding companies of licensed banks (CA 1990, s 41(6)).

[287] CA 1990, s 41(1)(C); CA 1990, s 41(2)(c). See ODCE, *A Guide to Transactions Involving Directors*, at p 28: 'In deciding whether an unlawful transaction or arrangement is material in the context of the financial statements, directors should have regard to the Accounting Standards Board's *"Statement of Principles"*, (contd \...)

preparing the accounts in question it is not material (but without prejudice to the question whether or not such an interest is material in any case where those directors have not considered the matter).[286]

[6.114] The particulars which companies are obliged to disclose must be contained in the accounts by way of notes to the accounts[287] and must include the principal terms of the transaction, arrangement or agreement.[288] There are a number of specific exceptions,[289] definitions and qualifications in relation to the scope of the obligation to disclose these matters in a company's accounts.[290]

D. Specific offences

[6.115] The prosecution of offences under the Companies Acts is the most direct form of enforcement of directors' duties. There are two preliminary points to note regarding the prosecution of directors of companies. First, there are many offences under the CA 1963–2006 with which companies and 'officers in default' may be charged. A definition of an 'officer in default' in CA 1963, s 383 was substituted by CLEA 2001, s 100.[291] The definition of an 'officer of default' in s 383 as amended makes it significantly easier for a prosecutor to proceed against an officer of a company. Rather than the prosecutor bearing the burden of proving that the officer knowingly and wilfully authorised or permitted the offence in question to be committed, the burden now lies on a company's officer to show that he took reasonable steps to prevent the commission of the offence, or was unable to prevent it.[292]

---

[285] (contd) which states: "An item of information is material to the financial statements if its misstatement or omission might reasonably be expected to influence the economic decisions of users of those financial statements, including their assessment of management's stewardship. Whether information is material will depend on the size and nature of the item in question judged in the particular circumstances of the case'.' Available at www.odce.ie.

[286] CA 1990, s 41(5)(b).

[287] CA 1990, s 41(3).

[288] CA 1990, s 42. CA 1990, s 42(1) to (h) contain more detailed specifications in this regard, which are expressly without prejudice to the general obligation to disclose the principal terms of the transaction, arrangement or agreement in question.

[289] See, eg, CA 1990, s 41(7) 'Sub-s (1) and (2) do not apply in relation to the following transactions, arrangements and agreements— (a) a transaction, arrangement or agreement between one company and another in which a director of the first company or of its subsidiary or holding company is interested only by virtue of his being a director of the other; (b) a contract of service between a company and one of its directors or a director of its holding company or between a director of a company and any of that company's subsidiaries; (c) a transaction, arrangement or agreement which was not entered into during the relevant period for the accounts in question and which did not subsist at any time during that period; and (d) a transaction, arrangement or agreement which was made before the commencement of this section and which does not subsist thereafter.'

[290] See CA 1990, ss 41 to 45.

[291] See Ch **15**.

[292] CA 1963, s 383, as substituted by CLEA 2001, s 100. See further Ch **15**.

In addition to the vulnerability of directors to prosecution for offences for which they are in default, as officers of the company, there are several further offences of which officers of the company may be convicted. The following are a sample of such offences, which are selected as they are among the offences with which directors have been prosecuted by the ODCE. This is by no means a complete list of the offences with which a company's directors may be charged.

(a) Furnishing false information

[6.116] Any person who does any of the following is guilty of an offence:

> in purported compliance with any provision of the Companies Acts, answers a question, provides an explanation, makes a statement or completes, signs, produces, lodges or delivers any return, report, certificate, balance sheet or other document false in a material particular, knowing it to be false, or recklessly answers a question, provides an explanation, makes a statement or completes, signs produces, lodges or delivers any such document false in a material particular.[293]

This encompasses a broad range of acts or omissions and essentially renders it an offence for any person to knowingly or recklessly make a representation in a document or statement, which is false in a material particular. It is also an offence to knowingly or recklessly furnish false information to an electronic filing agent, which is then transmitted on that person's behalf to the Registrar of Companies.[294]

Two persons were prosecuted by the ODCE in 2006 for offences under s 242, both of which involved directors submitting annual returns to the CRO which were falsely represented as having been audited.[295] The ODCE has stated that it:

> 'will continue to give priority to the investigation and prosecution of cases involving the provision of materially false information in purported compliance with a provision in the Companies Acts due to the potential impact which these practices have for increasing market risk for all company stakeholders.'[296]

[6.117] If a person is convicted on indictment under either s 242(1) or (1A), and the act, omission or conduct in question had, in the opinion of the court, one of the following effects, he shall be liable to imprisonment for a maximum term of seven years imprisonment or a maximum fine of €12,697.38, or both:[297]

- it substantially contributed to the company being unable to pay its debts;
- it prevented or seriously impeded the company's orderly winding up; or
- it substantially facilitated the defrauding of the company's creditors or the creditors of any other person.[298]

---

[293] CA 1990, s 242(1), as amended by CLEA 2001, s 106 and IFCMPA 2005, s 71.

[294] CA 1990, s 242(1A), as inserted by IFCMPA 2005, s 71.

[295] See ODCE, *Annual Report 2006* at p 21.

[296] See ODCE, *Annual Report 2006* at p 21.

[297] CA 1990, s 242(2), as amended by CLEA 2001, s 106 and IFCMPA 2005, s 71.

[298] CA 1990, s 242(2), as amended by CLEA 2001, s 106 and IFCMPA 2005, s 71.

(b) Alteration or falsification of books

[6.118] A further category of offences with which directors of a company may be charged, concerns the alteration or falsification of a company's books or documents. CA 1963, s 294 formerly applied this offence only to officers and contributories of companies which were being wound up. This was replaced by CA 1990, s 243 which renders it an offence for an officer to do, or be privy to the doing of, any of the following, whether or not the company in question is being wound up:

- destroy, mutilate or falsify any book or document regarding the company's affairs or property;[299]
- make a false entry in any such book or document;[300]
- fraudulently part with, alter or make an omission in any such book or document.[301]

This offence was prosecuted by the ODCE for the first time in 2006 in the case of a company director who used a set of financial statements, in support of an application to renew an overdraft facility, which were falsely represented to the company's bank as having been audited by a firm of auditors, no such audit having been conducted.[302]

(c) Criminal fraudulent trading

(i) Introduction

[6.119] A person who is 'knowingly a party to the carrying on of the business of a company' with fraudulent intent, may be convicted either on indictment or summarily of the offence of fraudulent trading. CA 1963, s 297(1) provides:

> If any person is knowingly a party to the carrying on of the business of a company
> with intent to defraud creditors of the company or creditors of any other person or
> for any fraudulent purpose, that person shall be guilty of an offence.[303]

---

[299] CA 1963, s 243(1). It is a defence for the officer to prove that he had no intention to defeat the law (CA 1963, s 243(1)).

[300] CA 1963, s 243(1). It is a defence for the officer to prove that he had no intention to defeat the law (CA 1963, s 243(1)).

[301] CA 1990, s 243(2).

[302] *DCE v Anderson* (19 January 2006, unreported), Dublin District Court. See ODCE, *Annual Report 2006* at p 18. Available at www.odce.ie.

[305] CA 1963, s 297(1), as substituted by CA 1990, s 137. Prior to the commencement of CA 1990, criminal and civil liability for fraudulent trading were combined in the same provision. As the then Minister for Industry and Commerce (Desmond O'Malley) recorded in the Dáil: 'Section 297 has been criticised in the past because both the criminal and civil offences of fraudulent trading were contained in the same section. Civil plaintiffs, therefore, tended to be reluctant to embark on proceedings because the same strict standards of proof might be required by the court in respect of civil proceedings as for criminal proceedings. In an effort to overcome this alleged difficulty, to facilitate court proceedings and to encourage liquidators and creditors to be more confident about civil proceedings, ss 115 and 116 provide for the separation of the civil and criminal elements of s 297 of the Principal Act. (contd \...)

There is no requirement that the company must be insolvent or in liquidation for this provision to apply.[304] A director is clearly one of the persons who may come within the scope of this offence. The criteria are the following:

- the person must be a party to the carrying on of the company's business with the fraudulent intent;

- he must 'knowingly' occupy that role; and

- the business of the company must be carried on with intent to defraud the company's creditors, the creditors of any other person, or for any fraudulent purpose.[305]

Upon summary conviction, the defendant may be sentenced to a maximum term of imprisonment of 12 months or a maximum fine of €1,904.61, or both. Upon conviction on indictment, he may face a maximum term of imprisonment of seven years or a maximum fine of €64,486.90, or both.[306]

[6.120] There have been few prosecutions under s 297. A similar situation in England has been attributed to a number of factors.[307] These include, first, the interest of victims of fraudulent trading in recouping monies from the persons who participated in the fraud, combined with the absence of any such direct interest in criminal prosecutions of such persons.[308] The second factor cited was the absence of an appetite on the part of the police for prosecuting commercial fraud, a reluctance compounded by uncertainty as to

---

[303] (contd) Thus, the criminal offence of fraudulent trading is contained in s 115, The essential element of the offence is, as heretofore, the existence of an intent to defraud'. (*Dáil Debates*, Stage 3).

[304] Note that a company must be in examinership or liquidation for the civil consequences of fraudulent or reckless trading to apply. CA 1963, s 297A, as inserted by CA 1990, s 138. Note, however, that CA 1990, s 251 permits proceedings for fraudulent trading under s 297A to be commenced in respect of a company which not being wound up, but which meets the criteria of that provision.

[305] CA 1963, s 297, as substituted by CA 1990, s 137.

[306] CA 1963, s 297(2), as substituted by CA 1990, s 137, and as amended by CA 1990, s 240(7), as inserted by CLEA 2001, s 104.

[307] The same position existed under the English equivalent of s 297, CA 1948, s 332 (replaced by CA 1985, s 458, and CA 2006, s 993). As R Leng noted, 'The offence of fraudulent trading in s 332(3) of the Companies Act 1948 occupies the twilight zone of criminal law: more often threatened than prosecuted; less feared than the associated civil remedy in s 332(1) by which company directors and managers may be made personally liable for the company's bad debts. As was pointed out by the Cork Committee in paragraph 1898, this state of affairs does not reflect either the seriousness or the prevalence of the offence.' R Leng, 'The Element of Fraud in Fraudulent Trading' (1985) ILT 140.

[308] Leng commented in this regard, '… it may be thought that resort to the criminal law might prejudice rather than assist any attempt to recover losses by means of the civil procedure.' R Leng, 'The Element of Fraud in Fraudulent Trading' (1985) ILT 140.

the scope of the offence. A third factor was the unsuitability of a criminal trial forum for resolving questions involving complex commercial dealings.[309]

[6.121] The criteria for civil fraudulent trading under s 297A(1)(b)[310] and criminal fraudulent trading under s 297 are similar, although the standard of proof obviously varies depending upon whether the proceedings are civil or criminal.[311] In particular, both provisions refer to a person being 'knowingly a party to the carrying on' of a company's business with 'intent to defraud creditors of the company, or creditors of any other person or for any fraudulent purpose.'[312] Cases decided under s 297A may therefore be of assistance in interpreting the criteria of s 297.

(ii) Respondents

[6.122] The category of persons who may be convicted of the offence of fraudulent trading is not defined or limited by s 297. In *O'Keeffe v Ferris*,[313] Murphy J described the persons who may come within the scope of the provisions on fraudulent trading, as follows:

> 'The burden imposed by the sub-section is not confined to or indeed directly related to the shareholders in or proprietors of the company. The liability, where it arises, is imposed upon persons 'who are knowingly parties to the carrying on of the business' of the company with intent to defraud creditors thereof. That is to say the executives or management of the company whether or not they were shareholders therein. Effectively what the section does is to withdraw, in certain circumstances and to a certain extent, the right of an executive to plead that he was acting merely as an agent of a corporate body and to make him personally liable in certain circumstances for the activities for which he was directly responsible.'[314]

The Law Commission for England and Wales has stated:

> 'The only people who may be guilty of fraudulent trading are those who exercise some control or managerial function within the company: employees who exercise no such functions, such as junior managers or branch managers, are not regarded as being party to the carrying on of the company's business.'[315]

---

[309] R Leng, 'The Element of Fraud in Fraudulent Trading' (1985) ILT 140.

[310] CA 1963, s 297A(1)(b), as inserted by CA 1990, s 138. See more generally Courtney, *The Law of Private Companies* (2nd edn, Tottel Publishing, 2002) at pp 565–572; MacCann and Courtney (general eds), *Companies Acts 1963 to 2006* (2007, Tottel Publishing) at pp 545–551.

[311] For an analysis of the nature of the civil wrong of fraudulent trading, see the judgment of Murphy J in *O'Keeffe v Ferris* [1993] 3 IR 165.

[312] See CA 1963, s 297(1), as substituted by CA 1990, ss 137, and 297A(1)(b), as inserted by CA 1990, s 138.

[313] *O'Keeffe v Ferris* [1993] 3 IR 165.

[314] *O'Keeffe v Ferris* [1993] 3 IR 165 at 174.

[315] Law Commission for England and Wales, 'Legislating the Criminal Code: Fraud and Deception' (LLCP 155, 27 April 2004) at para 2.34, citing Miles [1992] CrimLR 657.

The persons within a company who will typically come within the scope of s 297 are therefore the directors and officers of the company, rather than its employees or shareholders. It is not only a company's directors or officers who may be guilty of fraudulent trading: persons who engage in transactions or dealings with the company may also be so guilty.[316]

(iii) 'Carrying on of the business of a company'

[6.123] The requirement that the fraudulent trading must relate to the 'carrying on of the business of the company' has been broadly construed. In particular, it is firmly established that a single transaction can suffice. The Law Commission for England and Wales has commented, in relation to the equivalent provision in that jurisdiction, of CA 1985, s 458:[317]

> Although the wording of the section might suggest that it applies only where the whole business is fraudulently conducted, the approach of the courts has been that a single transaction will suffice, and the offence is committed where only one part of the business of the company is fraudulently conducted.[318]

[6.124] The most important Irish case on the interpretation of the components of 'fraudulent trading' is *Re Hunting Lodges Ltd*.[319] That case concerned a company of which a husband and wife (Mr and Mrs Porrit) were the sole directors and which was heavily indebted to the Revenue Commissioners, having suffered losses as a result of a fire on one of the company's premises. The company's auditor held discussions with the Revenue Commissioners, during which it was made clear that the company should not dispose of any properties, without paying the debts owed to the Revenue. Shortly after these discussions, negotiations were initiated, through an auctioneer, for the sale of a licensed premises which the company owned (known as 'Durty Nelly's). Mr Porrit sought to have a sizeable amount of the proceeds paid on the side and the purchaser

---

[316] See, eg, *Re Hunting Lodges Ltd* [1984] IEHC 3, [1985] ILRM 75, in which a person who purchased an asset from the company was held to have participated in fraudulent trading. See further below.

[317] CA 1985, s 458 provides: 'If any business of a company is carried on with intent to defraud creditors of the company or creditors of any other person, or for any fraudulent purpose, every person who was knowingly a party to the carrying on of the business in that manner is liable to imprisonment or a fine, or both.' This has now been replaced by CA 2006, s 993 (England and Wales).

[318] Law Commission for England and Wales, 'Legislating the Criminal Code: Fraud and Deception' (LCCP 155, 27 April 2004) at para 2.32, citing the dicta of Templeman J in *Re Gerald Cooper Chemicals Ltd* [1978] Ch 262 at 268: a single transaction could suffice as 'it does not matter ... that only one creditor was defrauded, and by one transaction, provided that the transaction can properly be described as a fraud on a creditor perpetrated in the course of carrying on business.' The Law Commission cited the example of *Philippou* (1989) 89 Cr App R 290, in which, according to the Law Commission, 'it was held that the fraudulent obtaining of an air travel organiser's licence from the Civil Aviation Authority involved the carrying on of business for a fraudulent purpose, as the licence was essential to that business.'

[319] *Re Hunting Lodges Ltd* [1984] IEHC 3, [1985] ILRM 75.

agreed. Before this transaction was completed, the Revenue issued a letter threatening to liquidate the company if the Revenue debt was not paid.

The sale of the licensed premises proceeded, with Mr and Mrs Porrit duly countersigning the affixing of the company's seal. Mr Porrit subsequently opened 13 different bank accounts under the false names of Mr and Mrs Atkinson, for which he and his wife signed the mandates. The monies that were paid on the side for the licensed premises were paid into these accounts. A few days later, the Revenue Commissioners began to make enquiries about the sale of Durty Nelly's and, information not being forthcoming, the Revenue made a successful application to the High Court for the appointment of a provisional liquidator to the company. The company was subsequently wound up.

[6.125] The liquidator made an application for declarations of personal liability against Mr and Mrs Porrit, the purchaser of Durty Nelly's and the company, which was the vehicle through which the purchaser acquired the premises. While the proceedings concerned civil, rather than criminal, liability for fraudulent trading, the criteria are the same and the analysis in *Re Hunting Lodges Ltd* is instructive in interpreting s 297.

[6.126] Among the issues which the High Court was called upon to consider in *Re Hunting Lodges Ltd*,[320] was whether each of the respondents was knowingly a party to the carrying on of the company's business with fraudulent intent.[321] The Court made a number of significant determinations regarding the meaning of the expressing 'carrying on the business of the company.' First, it is not 'synonymous with trading'.[322] Second, it is not necessary that all of a company's business must be carried on with fraudulent intent. Third, there does not have to be a course of dealing or a series of transactions for fraudulent trading to occur. Fourth, 'one single transaction can properly be described as "business of the company"'.[323] Fifth, the constituent parts of a transaction can also be the 'business of the company.'[324] Sixth, 'one single act' may amount of fraudulent trading. Finally, if the business conducted is the sale of the entirety of the company's assets, this does not prevent the application of s 297.[325]

Carroll J broke down the 'business of the company' for the purposes of *Re Hunting Lodges Ltd*, into a number of constituent parts as follows: 'There are the negotiations culminating in the signing of the contract, the closing of the sale and the disposition of the purchase money.' [326] The Court concluded that, '[e]ach of these elements can be designated together or separately as "business of the company".'[327] The Court further

---

[320] *Re Hunting Lodges Ltd* [1984] IEHC 3, [1985] ILRM 75. Other important issues, which were considered in this case are analysed further below. See paras **[6.128]** to **[6.130]**.

[321] [1985] ILRM 75 at para 40.

[322] [1984] IEHC 3, [1985] ILRM 75 at para 39.

[323] [1984] IEHC 3, [1985] ILRM 75 at para 39.

[324] [1984] IEHC 3, [1985] ILRM 75 at para 39.

[325] [1984] IEHC 3, [1985] ILRM 75 at para 39, citing *In re Gerald Cooper Chemicals Ltd* [1978] Ch 262.

[326] [1984] IEHC 3, [1985] ILRM 75 at para 43.

[327] [1984] IEHC 3, [1985] ILRM 75 at para 43.

stated that, '[h]aving decided that any business of the company includes a single transaction or part thereof I intend to refer to the "business" in this case as the sale or a constituent part thereof. This is the common denominator between Mr and Mrs Porrit and Mr O'Connor and Plage Services Ltd.'[328]

This decision indicates clearly the breadth of the expression 'carrying on the business of the company.'

(iv) Participation required

[6.127] The person who faces a prosecution for fraudulent trading under s 297, must have been a 'party' to the fraud in question. What it means to be a 'party' to the carrying on a company's business in a fraudulent manner, is not defined in the Companies Acts or elsewhere. It has, however, been considered in a number of judicial determinations.

[6.128] In *Re Hunting Lodges Ltd*,[329] Carroll J considered whether each of the respondents was knowingly a party to the carrying on of business with fraudulent intent.[330] Having determined that the transactions at issue constituted the carrying on of the 'business of the company', Carroll J was satisfied that, 'all four parties were "parties" to the sale within the meaning of the section.'[331] She also stated that there was no difficulty in proving positive steps on the part of the respondents, as each of them participated in the sale of Durty Nelly's.[332]

Considering the position of each of the respondents individually, the High Court held that Mr Porrit participated from start to finish in the relevant 'business', having participated in the negotiations; required payment on the side; countersigned the affixing of the company's seal to the conveyance; taken the money which was paid on the side; and opened accounts under false names.[333]

With regard to Mrs Porrit, the Court held that she attended the closing of the sale of Durty Nelly's, countersigned the affixing of the company's seal and signed a false name for the purpose of the bank accounts. On this basis, the Court held that she took an active part in the closing of the sale and the disposition of the purchase money.[334]

Both the purchaser and the company through which he acquired the property from the company in liquidation, were held to have participated in the sale. The purchaser was also held to have negotiated, and agreed, the payment of monies on the side, and to have executed that agreement.[335]

---

[328] [1984] IEHC 3, [1985] ILRM 75 at para 44.

[329] [1984] IEHC 3, [1985] ILRM 75.

[330] [1984] IEHC 3, [1985] ILRM 75 at para 40.

[331] [1984] IEHC 3, [1985] ILRM 75 at para 45.

[332] [1984] IEHC 3, [1985] ILRM 75 at para 46.

[333] [1984] IEHC 3, [1985] ILRM 75 at para 46.

[334] [1984] IEHC 3, [1985] ILRM 75 at para 47.

[335] [1984] IEHC 3, [1985] ILRM 75 at para 48.

[6.129] *Re Hunting Lodges Ltd* demonstrates the breadth of the category of persons who may be held to have been 'party' to a company's fraudulent activities. While it may be expected that only a company's executive directors, with a direct role in the affairs in question, should be held liable for a company's fraudulent business, the decision in *Re Hunting Lodges* is clear authority for the proposition that anybody, whether involved in the company or not, may be held liable for fraudulent trading.[336]

The High Court in *Re Hunting Lodges Ltd* relied on one English authority in relation to the interpretation of 'party' to a company's fraudulent trading. The decision of *Re Maidstone Building Provisions Ltd*,[337] decided under the English equivalent of CA 1963, s 297[338] was cited as authority for the proposition that the requirement that a person be 'a party' to the business in question indicates 'no more than "participates in", "takes part in" or "concurs in"' and that it involved 'some positive steps of some nature'.[339]

[6.130] In decisions concerning the English equivalent of s 297, the courts have emphasised that active or positive participation in the carrying on of the company's business is required. The failure of a company's secretary or financial advisor to draw the company's insolvency to the attention of its directors, for example, is not a form of participation that would give rise to a finding of fraudulent trading.[340] It also appears from English authorities that advancing money to enable a company's business to be carried on, will not be sufficient participation to invite the application of the provisions on fraudulent trading, unless the person advancing the finance has a role in the company's decision making.

---

[336] See also *Re Augustus Barnett & Son Ltd* [1986] BCLC 170, which illustrates that a person may be liable for fraudulent trading if he is knowingly party to a fraudulent act by the company despite not being involved in carrying on the company's business.

[337] *Re Maidstone Building Provisions Ltd* [1971] 1 WLR 1085.

[338] CA 1963, s 297, as substituted by CA 1990, s 137. The English equivalent at the time *Re Maidstone Building Provisions Ltd* [1971] 1 WLR 3 was decided was the CA 1948, s 322, which was replaced, although on similar terms, by the CA 1985, s 458, which provides, 'If any business of a company is carried on with intent to defraud creditors of the company or creditors of any other person, or for any fraudulent purpose, every person who was knowingly a party to the carrying on of the business in that manner is liable to imprisonment or a fine, or both. This applies whether or not the company has been, or is in the course of being, wound up.' This provision has now been replaced by CA 2006, s 993 (England and Wales).

[339] *Re Hunting Lodges Ltd* [1984] IEHC 3, [1985] ILRM 75 at para 45 (Re Carroll J stated in this regard, 'The phrase in the corresponding section to the English Act (s 322 of the Companies Act, 1948) has been defined in *In Re Maidstone Buildings Provisions Ltd* [1971] 1 WLR 1085, at p 1092 as indicating no more than "participates in", "takes part in" or "concurs in". Pennycuick VC added that it seemed to him that involved some positive steps of some nature.')

[340] See *Tolley's Company Law Service*, Insolvency, Pt IV, 'Malpractice', citing *Re Maidstone Building Provisions Ltd* [1971] 3 All ER 363.

(v) Requirement of knowledge

[6.131] For a person to be found guilty of fraudulent trading, he must be have been 'knowingly' a party to the fraudulent conduct or transactions in question. Buckley has described this criterion as follows:

> 'A person can be liable under s 458 if "knowingly a party" to the fraudulent purpose. To be liable, a party must be "knowingly" a party and mere negligence that fraud was being perpetrated will not suffice.[341] Knowledge includes deliberately shutting one's eyes to the obvious but in order to show "blind-eye" knowledge it is essential that the "suspicion [of fraud] must be firmly grounded and targeted on specific facts".[342] For one company (the outsider company) to be knowingly a party to the carrying on of fraud by another company, it is not necessary for the outsider company to have acted through its board of directors; the acts of a senior manager who had responsibility for entering into the transaction could be attributed to the outsider company.'[343,344]

[6.132] In *Re Bank of Credit and Commerce International SA, Morris v Bank of India*,[345] Patten J described the level of knowledge that a bank must have before being responsible for fraudulent trading, as follows:

> 'The liquidators have to show that BOI (through its relevant officers and employees) knew that the six transactions (or one or more of them) were being entered into either to defraud the creditors of BCCI or for a fraudulent purpose. They did not have to know every detail of the fraud or the precise mechanics of

---

[341] Citing *Re Bank of Credit and Commerce International SA (in liq)* [2004] 2 BCLC 236 at 11, upheld on appeal, *sub nom Morris v Bank of India* [2005] EWCA (Civ) 693. This case dealt with the Insolvency Act 1986, s 213.

[342] Citing *Manifest Shipping Co Ltd v Uni-Polaris Shipping Co Ltd* [2001] UKHL 1, [2003] 1 AC 469 at 116. In that case, 'blind eye knowledge' was defined by Lord Scott of Foscote as follows: 'In summary, blind-eye knowledge requires, in my opinion, a suspicion that the relevant facts do exist and a deliberate decision to avoid confirming that they exist. But a warning should be sounded. Suspicion is a word that can be used to describe a state of mind that may, at one extreme, be no more than a vague feeling of unease and, at the other extreme, reflect a firm belief in the existence of the relevant facts. In my opinion, in order for there to be blind-eye knowledge, the suspicion must be firmly grounded and targeted on specific facts.'

[343] Citing *Morris v Bank of India* [2005] EWCA (Civ) 693. Acts will not be so attributed to the company where the company agent is defrauding the company: *Morris v Bank of India* [2005] EWCA (Civ) 693 at 114.

[344] *Buckley on the Companies Acts*, Pt XVI, 'Fraudulent trading'. Available at www.lexisnexis.com.

[345] *Re Bank of Credit and Commerce International SA, Morris v Bank of India* [2004] EWHC 528 (Ch), [2005] 1 All ER (Comm) 209. This case essentially concerned six separate transactions by which large sums of money were deposited into accounts held in the name of BCCI, at the Bank of India, for fixed periods of time. These sums were then loaned by BOI to borrowers, for which no security, other than a guarantee, was furnished. In a serious of civil proceedings, BCCI was found to have been responsible for fraudulent trading and was made liable for the company's debts. In proceedings taken against the BOI, the Bank denied that it was knowingly a party to this trading.

how it would be carried out, but clearly they did have to know, either from their own observation of what was being done or from what they were told, that BCCI was intent on a fraud. Knowledge, for this purpose, means what it says. There must have been an actual realisation on the part of BOI that BCCI would, or was likely to, engage in false accounting. A failure to recognise the truth of what was going on is not enough, however obvious that may now seem to have been.'[346]

The Court went on to find that:

'But both sides accept that knowledge, for these purposes, includes so-called blind-eye knowledge, which exists when the party in question shuts its eyes to the obvious because of a conscious fear that to inquire further will confirm a suspicion of wrongdoing which already exists.'[347]

Dismissing the appeal against the judgment of Patten J, Mummery LJ of the Court of Appeal confirmed that, 'there is no dispute about the relevant alleged knowledge in question being "blind-eye" knowledge'.[348] In an earlier decision arising from the same transactions, Patten J similarly stated:

'Knowledge includes deliberately shutting ones eyes to the obvious, provided that the fraudulent nature of the transactions did in fact appear obvious to those who dealt with these matters at SBI at the relevant time. It is well established that it is no defence to say that one declined to ask questions, when the only reason for not doing so was an actual appreciation that the answers to those questions would be likely to disclose the existence of a fraud'[349]

It is also worth noting the comment of Patten J in *Re Bank of Credit and Commerce International SA, Morris v Bank of India*[350] that, 'subsequent knowledge based on hindsight is not enough, nor is negligence the test of liability.'

[6.133] There are a number of general points that may be noted about the requirement that a person must be 'knowingly' a participant in the carrying on of a company's business with a fraudulent intent or purpose. First, negligence that fraud was being committed is not sufficient. Second, 'turning a blind eye' will be sufficient to constitute knowledge, if there are specific facts which indicated the fraud in question, from which it can be said that the person in question must have actually realised the existence of the intent to defraud or deliberately shut his eyes to that fact.

---

[346] *Re Bank of Credit and Commerce International SA, Morris v Bank of India* [2004] EWHC 528 (Ch), [2005] 1 All ER (Comm) 209 at 276, *per* Patten J. The appeal against this judgment was dismissed by the Court of Appeal. *Bank of India v Morris* [2005] EWCA Civ 693.

[347] *Re Bank of Credit and Commerce International SA, Morris v Bank of India* [2004] EWHC 528 (Ch), [2005] 1 All ER (Comm) 209 at 276, *per* Patten J.

[348] *Bank of India v Morris* [2005] EWCA Civ 693 at para 14.

[349] *Re Bank of Credit and Commerce International SA, Morris v State Bank of India* [2004] 2 BCLC 236.

[350] *Re Bank of Credit and Commerce International SA, Morris v Bank of India* [2004] EWHC 528 (Ch), [2005] 1 All ER (Comm) 209.

(vi) Requisite intention

1. GENERAL

[6.134] There are three distinct forms of fraudulent intention which may lead a person to be convicted of fraudulent trading: an intent to defraud the company's creditors; an intent to defraud the creditors of any other person; or any other fraudulent purpose. There are certain common features of these three forms of intention.

First, it is not necessary that there be a definite intention to cause financial loss to another person. It is sufficient if another person's property or interests are placed at risk. As the Law Commission for England and Wales stated:

> 'The offence does not require an intent to cause financial loss to another person: deliberately and dishonestly putting another's property and financial interests in jeopardy will suffice. Deception is not required.'[351]

[6.135] Second, it is established law in England that there must be dishonesty before a conviction for fraudulent trading may be obtained. The dicta of Maugham J in *Re Patrick & Lyon Ltd*,[352] is notable in this regard:

> 'I will express the opinion that the words "defraud" and "fraudulent purpose", where they appear in the section in question, are words which connote actual dishonesty involving, according to current notions of fair trading among commercial men, real moral blame.'

In *R v Cox*[353] the Court of Appeal confirmed that:

> 'The reported cases make it clear that in both the civil and the criminal jurisdictions the allegation of an intent to defraud contains the ingredient of dishonesty, without which finding no jury would be entitled to convict a defendant of the offence charged, and no judge in the civil jurisdiction would be entitled to find for a person who fails to prove dishonesty on the part of him by whom he alleges he has been defrauded.'[354]

---

[351] Law Commission for England and Wales, 'Legislating the Criminal Code: Fraud and Deception' (LCCP 155, 27 April 2004) at para 2.32.

[352] *Re Patrick & Lyon Ltd* [1933] 1 Ch 786 at 790.

[353] *R v Cox* [1983] BCLC 169.

[354] *R v Cox* [1983] BCLC 169 at 175, *per* Watkins LJ The Law Commission for England and Wales has also confirmed that, in the context of the offence of fraudulent trading, 'there must be dishonesty.' Law Commission for England and Wales, 'Legislating the Criminal Code: Fraud and Deception' (LCCP 155, 27 April 2004) at para 2.32. See also the decision delivered by Lawton LJ in *R v Landy* [1981] 1 All ER 1172 at 1181: 'What the Crown had to prove was a conspiracy to defraud which is an agreement dishonestly to do something which will or may cause loss or prejudice to another. The offence is one of dishonesty. This is the all important ingredient which must be stressed by the judge in his directions to the jury and must not be minimised in any way. There is always a danger that a jury may think that proof of an irregularity followed by loss is proof of dishonesty. The dishonesty to be proved must be in the minds and intentions of the defendants.'

[6.136] Third, it is not necessary that all persons charged with the offence of fraudulent trading must have a common agreed fraudulent intent. As Carroll J stated in *Re Hunting Lodges Ltd*:[355]

> '... in order for the section to apply, it is not necessary that there should be a common agreed fraudulent intent. If each of the participants acts for a fraudulent purpose then each may be liable ... every person is deemed to intend the natural and probable consequences of his acts.'

Each individual who is charged with fraudulent trading, or who faces civil proceedings for fraudulent trading under s 297A, must have a specific fraudulent intent.

[6.137] Fourth, it is corporate fraud that is at issue in proceedings under s 297: there is no requirement that the defendant must have benefited personally from the fraud in question. As the Court of Criminal Appeal noted in *DPP v Clarkin*:[356]

> 'The charge under s 297 relates only to the actions of the respondent in the course of carrying on the business of a company, and therefore relates to corporate fraud as opposed to individual fraud. This distinction is clearly exemplified in the present case, as there is no suggestion by the prosecution that the respondent personally benefited in any way from the fraud.'[357]

2. 'INTENT TO DEFRAUD'

[6.138] For a person to be convicted of fraudulent trading under s 297, one of the conditions is that he must have been a party to the carrying on of the company's business with 'intent to defraud creditors of the company or creditors of any other person.'[358] In a number of cases, the courts have considered whether the incurring of debts at a time when there is no prospect of payment, amounts to an 'intent to defraud.'

[6.139] In *Re Leitch (William C) Bros Ltd*,[359] Maugham J referred to the then English equivalent of s 297, under the Companies Act 1929:

> 'In my opinion I must hold with regard to the meaning of the phrase carrying on business "with intent to defraud creditors" that, if a company continues to carry on business and to incur debts at a time when there is to the knowledge of the

---

[355] *Re Hunting Lodges Ltd* [1984] IEHC 3, [1985] ILRM 75.

[356] *DPP v Clarkin* (10 February 2003, unreported), Court of Criminal Appeal.

[357] *DPP v Clarkin* (10 February 2003, unreported), Court of Criminal Appeal.

[358] An 'intent to defraud' may be defined as an intention to prejudice or take the risk of prejudicing the rights of another, knowing that you have no right to do so. See, eg, *Welham v DPP* [1961] AC 103 at 123 ('Now I think that there are one or two things that can be said with confidence about the meaning of this word "defraud". It requires a person as its object; that is, defrauding involves doing something to someone. Although in the nature of things it is almost invariably associated with the obtaining of an advantage for the person who commits the fraud, it is the effect on the person who is the object of the fraud that ultimately determines its meaning,' *per* Lord Radcliffe). It may also include inducing a person to act to his own economic detriment. See Leng, 'The Element of Fraud in Fraudulent Trading' (1985) ILT 140.

[359] *Re Leitch (William C) Bros Ltd* [1932] 2 Ch 71.

directors no reasonable prospect of the creditors ever receiving payment of those debts, it is, in general, a proper inference that the company is carrying on business with intent to defraud ...'

In his decision in *Re Patrick & Lyon Ltd*,[360] Maugham J stated:

'... I will express the opinion that the words "defraud" and "fraudulent purpose", where they appear in the section in question, are words which connote actual dishonesty involving, according to current notions of fair trading among commercial men, real moral blame. No judge, I think, has ever been willing to define "fraud", and I am attempting no definition. I am merely stating what, in my opinion, must be one of the elements of the word as used in this section.'

[6.140] *R v Grantham*[361] is an example of the application of these tests. In that case, a company took delivery of supplies of potatoes at a time when the person running the company knew that the supplier would not be paid. The appellant was a consultant and responsible for the administration of the company. In an appeal against his conviction under CA 1948, s 332, the Court of Appeal concluded that the following direction was appropriate:

'Members of the jury, if a man honestly believes when he obtains credit that although funds are not immediately available he will be able to pay them when the debt becomes due or within a short time thereafter, no doubt you would say that is not dishonest and there is no intent to defraud but if he obtains or helps to obtain credit or further credit when he knows there is no good reason for thinking funds will become available to pay the debt when it becomes due or shortly thereafter then, though it is entirely a matter for you this question of dishonesty, you might well think that is dishonest and there is an intent to defraud.'[362]

On these authorities, incurring debts at a time when there is no reasonable prospect of their repayment will typically be evidence of 'actual dishonesty' and of an 'intent to defraud' and could form the basis for a conviction of fraudulent trading.

[6.141] The creditors who it is intended to defraud are broadly defined. In addition to creditors of the company, the persons defrauded may be creditors of 'any other person.' The former has been interpreted to include any person to whom a debt is owed, whether or not that debt can presently be sued for. In *R v Smith*,[363] the defendant was a managing director of a company which was wound up leaving debts of approximately £92 million.

---

[360] *Re Patrick & Lyon Ltd* [1933] 1 Ch 786 at 790.

[361] *R v Grantham* [1984] 1 QB 675.

[362] *R v Grantham* [1984] 1 QB 675. Another example of the application of the decisions of Maugham J in *Re Patrick & Lyon Ltd* [1933] 1 Ch 786 and *Re Leitch (William C) Bros Ltd* [1932] 2 Ch 71, is the decision of Harman J in *Re L Todd* [1990] BCLC 454, in which he stated at p 458: 'In my judgment, to deliberately set out to cheat HM Commissioners of Customs and Excise of large sums for VAT must be regarded by all commercial men (even those who wish they could get away with such an act) as requiring real moral blame. In addition to failing to make any provision for PAYE on wages is liable to mean that the wage earner is deprived of rights and that must be a matter of real moral blame. I therefore have no difficulty in holding that this case falls within the requirements set by Maugham J'.

[363] *R v Smith* [1996] 2 BCLC 109.

The company had been involved in bogus transactions with another company controlled by the defendant, the result of which was to artificially inflate the company's profits and size. The prosecution case was essentially that the company was insolvent and could only pay its creditors by 'robbing Peter to pay Paul.'

Rose LJ considered the terms of s 458 of the Companies Act 1985 (UK), noting that, 'In a charge under s 458 the offence is a continuing one and if trading is carried on fraudulently, future as well as present creditors may be prejudiced.' The Court of Appeal expanded upon the scope of the word 'creditor' in the context of the offence of fraudulent trading:

> 'In our judgment the word creditor in s 458, in its ordinary meaning, denotes one to whom money is owed: whether that debt can presently be sued for is immaterial. This is sufficient to decide the present case. But we see no reason in principle why other kinds of creditors should not be within the scope of s 458 because such may come into existence after the fraudulent trading has first begun. Such a construction is consonant with the purpose of the first part of the section which is aimed at preventing insolvent trading to the prejudice of those who are induced to do business.'[364]

The reference to a company's creditors in the context of the offence of fraudulent trading may therefore include potential as well as actual creditors.

3. FRAUDULENT PURPOSE

[6.142] Where persons other than creditors of a company or of any other person are defrauded, it is possible to obtain a conviction for fraudulent trading, on the ground that there was a 'fraudulent purpose.'[365] An example of such a case is *R v Kemp*.[366] In that case, the defendant had engaged in the practice of delivering goods to persons on the pretext that they had ordered them. These persons did not pursue civil remedies against the defendant.

Appealing against a conviction for fraudulent trading, the defendant argued that these persons were customers not creditors, as they had obtained no judgment against him, and that the conduct complained of did not fall within the scope of the offence of fraudulent trading. The defendant's argument in this regard was that:

> 'While all affected customers doubtless had unliquidated claims for recoverable damage caused by the excess stock they had to acquire, until they had obtained judgment in respect of their unliquidated damages they were not creditors. A defrauded customer is initially merely a potential creditor.'[367]

---

[364] *R v Smith* [1996] 2 BCLC 109 at 122.

[365] See Law Commission for England and Wales, 'Legislating the Criminal Code: Fraud and Deception' (LCCP 155, 27 April 2004) at para 2.33, citing *R v Kemp* [1988] QB 645: 'The courts have construed this offence very widely. The Court of Appeal has held that the mischief aimed at is fraudulent trading generally. The offence can consist in the defrauding of customers as well as creditors.'

[366] *R v Kemp* [1988] 2 WLR 975.

[367] *R v Kemp* [1988] 2 WLR 975 at 977.

The Court of Appeal rejected this narrow interpretation of the offence of fraudulent trading. The Court referred to the breadth of the wording 'or for any fraudulent purpose'[368] and noted: 'It seems to us that the mischief aimed at is fraudulent trading and not fraudulent trading just in so far as it affects creditors ...'[369]

The Court then addressed the defendant's argument that the words 'or any fraudulent purpose' should be construed *ejusdem generis* with the words 'where the business of the company has been carried on with intent to defraud creditors of the company or creditors of any other person.' The Court refused to allow this interpretation on the following grounds:

> 'The difficulty with that submission is this, that the *genus* there is creditors. The category of creditors listed exhaust the *genus* and leaves no room for any others. Even if the category of creditors listed did not exhaust the genus, the argument could not prevail, first, because if it did not exhaust the *genus*, that *genus* would certainly include potential creditors, for the reasons set out in *Reg v Seillon,* and secondly, on any construction one could only exclude potential creditors by simply ignoring the additional words to be found in the statute which is impermissible. If words add anything to the section, they must apply to potential creditors as being the nearest thing to creditors and therefore they must apply to customers.'[370]

[6.143] The words 'any fraudulent purpose' are therefore a stand-alone ground for seeking a conviction for fraudulent trading and do not have to relate to the defrauding of a company's creditors.

(vii) Sentences

[6.144] A person convicted of the offence of fraudulent trading may, upon summary conviction, be sentenced to a maximum term of imprisonment of twelve months or a maximum fine of €1,904.61, or both. Upon conviction on indictment, he may face a maximum term of imprisonment of seven years or a maximum fine of €64,486.90, or both.[371]

---

[368] The Court noted that, 'the wording 'or for any fraudulent purpose' in a section could not be wider.' *R v Kemp* [1988] 2 WLR 975 at 978. The Court also referred to the decision of Lord Denning MR in *Re Cyona Distributors Ltd* [1967] 1 All ER 281 at 284, [1967] Ch 889 at 902, in which 'he said of the section that it was deliberately in wide terms to enable the court to bring fraudulent persons to book, and added that the words of the section were to be given their full width.'

[369] *R v Kemp* [1988] 2 WLR 975 at 982.

[370] *R v Kemp* [1988] 2 WLR 975 at 983.

[371] CA 1963, s 297(2), as substituted by CA 1990, s 137 and as amended by CA 1990, s 240(7), as inserted by CLEA 2001, s 104. See decisions of the English courts regarding the appropriate level of sentence for the offence of fraudulent trading, such as the decision of the Court of Appeal in *R v Smith* [1996] 2 BCLC 109, in which six years' imprisonment was deemed not to be excessive, and *R v Ward* (27 November 2000, unreported) in which the Court of Appeal determined that a sentence of imprisonment of four years for two counts of fraudulent trading, resulting in losses to creditors of hundreds of thousands of pounds, should be reduced to three years.

[6.145] The appropriate level of sentence was considered by the Court of Criminal Appeal in *People (DPP) v Clarkin*.[372] The respondent, who pleaded guilty to a charge on indictment of fraudulent trading, was sentenced to one year imprisonment, which was suspended for two years. The DPP applied to the Court of Criminal Appeal for a review of that sentence on the basis that it was unduly lenient.[373] The DPP argued that the failure to impose a custodial sentence was an error of principle.

Delivering the judgment of the Court, McCracken J noted at the outset that there was no precedent to assist the Court in determining the appropriate sentence.

The fraud to which the respondent pleaded guilty, was 'a large scale and sophisticated fraud' involving bogus invoices, which resulted in a loss to Ulster Bank Commercial Services Ltd of over £1,000,000. The Court considered the rules applicable to applications by the DPP for review of sentences and, in particular, the deference that must be paid to the decisions of the trial judge regarding sentencing.[374] The Court also emphasised the absence of any 'scheme of rigid sentencing rules' and that each case must turn on its own facts.[375]

[6.146] Applying these principles to the facts of *People (DPP) v Clarkin*,[376] the Court noted that the trial judge heard a considerable amount of evidence and reserved his decision on sentencing to consider that evidence. The matters taken into account by the judge included that the respondent himself approached Ulster Bank Commercial Services Ltd and supplied them with full details of what had been going on; that he sold his family home; that he entered into an arrangement with his creditors, including consenting to an order of disqualification under CA 1990, s 160; that the respondent

---

[372] *People (DPP) v Clarkin* (10 February 2003, unreported), Court of Criminal Appeal.

[373] This application was made under the Criminal Justice Act 1993, s 2(1), which provides: 'If it appears to the Director of Public Prosecutions that a sentence imposed by a court (in this Act referred to as the "sentencing court") on conviction of a person on indictment was unduly lenient, he may apply to the Court of Criminal Appeal to review the sentence.'

[374] In this regard, the Court referred to the decision of O'Flaherty J in *DPP v Byrne* [1995] 1 ILRM 279 at 287, including the dicta that: 'the court should always afford great weight to the trial judge's reasons for imposing the sentence that is called in question. He is the one who receives the evidence at first hand ... He may detect nuances in the evidence that may not be as readily discernible to an appellate court. In particular, if the trial judge has kept a balance between the particular sentences of the commission of the offence and the relevant personal circumstances of the person sentenced what Flood J has termed the "constitutional principle of proportionality" (see *People (DPP) v WC* [1994] 1 ILRM 321), his decision should not be disturbed.'

[375] In this regard, the Court referred to the *People (DPP) v McCormack* [2000] 4 IR 356 ('Each case must depend upon its special circumstances. The appropriate sentence depends not only upon its own facts but also upon the personal circumstances of the accused. The sentence to be imposed is not the appropriate sentence for the crime, but the appropriate sentence for the crime because it has been committed by that accused. The range of possible penalties is dependant upon those two factors. It is only when the penalty is below the range as determined on this basis that the question of undue leniency may be considered.')

[376] *People (DPP) v Clarkin* (10 February 2003, unreported), Court of Criminal Appeal.

obtained no personal benefit from the fraud; that his motive was to try to save a company which employed over 50 people; and that the respondent was highly unlikely to reoffend.

The trial judge was, according to McCracken J, entitled to take all of these matters into account. The Court also noted that, unless imposed by statute, there is no minimum sentence in Ireland. In the context of fraudulent trading, the Court moreover noted that the reference in s 297 to imprisonment and/or a fine indicates that a fine may be a sufficient sentence.[377] In *People (DPP) v Clarkin*,[378] the trial judge clearly believed that a sentence of imprisonment was appropriate, but suspended that sentence on the basis of the factors listed above.

[6.147] McCracken J noted that, 'Possibly the best argument put forward on behalf of the Director of Public Prosecutions is that there should be a serious deterrent element in the sentence in cases of this nature.' In relation to this point the Court concluded:

> 'Certainly this Court would not like this sentence to be interpreted in a way as to imply that a person can conduct the affairs of a company in a fraudulent manner and not have any serious penalty imposed. There may be many cases in which a custodial sentence is appropriate, but the real question is whether in the circumstances of this particular case and this particular accused that is so.'

While the sentence imposed by the trial judge may well be said to be lenient and the members of the Court of Criminal Appeal may well have imposed a custodial sentence, McCracken J pointed out that that is not the test to be applied. The Court concluded:

> 'A trial judge is entitled to be lenient if he considers that it is just to do so in all the circumstances of any particular case, and in the present case the learned trial Judge spelt out the reasons for his leniency and we can see no error in principle in

---

[377] The Court noted in this regard that, 'Clearly in the present case there would have been little point in imposing a fine on the respondent, as he had in effect contributed all his assets towards restitution.' *People (DPP) v Clarkin* (10 February 2003, unreported), Court of Criminal Appeal. This position can be contrasted sharply with the approach which has been adopted in England. In particular, see the decision of the Court of Appeal in *R v Smith* [1996] 2 BCLC 109 at 130 ('By raising from two to seven years the maximum sentence for fraudulent trading – a maximum, it is to be noted, which is higher than that for simple theft – Parliament has clearly signalled to the courts the seriousness with which this offence should be viewed. This was a very grave example of fraudulent trading: the period was long; there was dishonesty throughout the 12-month period; the fraudulent machinery was skilful and complex; and the sums of money involved were huge; there was no plea of guilty. The offences of obtaining by deception likewise involved very large sums of money, which were obtained by telling lies. In our judgment, it is impossible successfully to contend that the sentence of six years' imprisonment passed concurrently on each count was in any way excessive,' *per* Rose LJ). Note that, in Ireland, the maximum sentence for fraudulent trading has also been raised from two years to seven years, an increase which may be taken to indicate the seriousness with which the offence should be viewed. CA 1963, s 297(2), as substituted by CA 1990, s 137.

[378] *People (DPP) v Clarkin* (10 February 2003, unreported), Court of Criminal Appeal.

applying those reasons to the present case and in suspending the sentence on the respondent.'[379]

It may be noted that a suspended sentence was also imposed in the only case to date in which the ODCE has secured a conviction for fraudulent trading.[380]

E. Directors' reports

(a) Report accompanying balance sheet

[6.148] The directors of a company must generally ensure that a balance sheet is prepared and laid before the company in annual general meeting.[381] This balance sheet must be accompanied by a directors' report.[382] Section 158(1) provides:

> 'There shall be attached to every balance sheet laid before the annual general meeting of a company a report by the directors on the state of the company's affairs and, if the company is a holding company, on the state of affairs of the company and its subsidiaries as a group, the amount, if any, which they recommend should be paid by way of dividend and the amount, if any, which they propose to carry to reserves within the meaning of the Sixth Schedule.'[383]

---

[379] *People (DPP) v Clarkin* (10 February 2003, unreported), Court of Criminal Appeal.

[380] *ODCE v Gannon* (18 March 2004, unreported), Naas District Court. See press statement dated 18 March 2004, available at www.odce.ie.

[381] CA 1963, s 148, as replaced by EC(IFRSMA)R 2005, reg 4. Note, however, that 'small companies' or 'medium-sized companies' within the meaning of the C(A)A 1986, may instead prepare an abridged balance sheet. See C(A)A 1986, ss 10 and 11, respectively, as substituted by EC(IFRSMA)R 2005, reg 5(f). See further Ch **2**.

[382] CA 1963, s 158. This requirement applies whether the accounts are prepared in accordance with the Companies Acts or the IFRS. See CA 1963, s 148(2), as replaced by EC(IFRSMA)R 2005, reg 4. Not that, while the directors' report does not have to be annexed to the annual return of 'small companies', such companies are not exempt from the requirement to attach a directors' report to the abridged balance sheet, as laid before the company's annual general meeting. See C(A)A 1986, s 10(1). 'Medium-sized companies' must annex a directors' report to the annual return, as well as laying that report before the annual general meeting. There are certain particular provisions applicable to directors' reports on group accounts and public limited companies, which are addressed below. See paras **[6.151]** to **[6.155]**.

[383] The Sixth Schedule appears to apply to only the limited categories of companies which are excluded from the scope of C(A)A 1986, namely: '(a) a company not trading for the acquisition of gain by the members, (b) a company to which sub-s (4)(c) of s 128 of the Principal Act applies, (c) a company in respect of which there is in force an order under sub-s (5) of that section' (C(A)A 1986, s 2(1)). See MacCann and Courtney (Gen Eds), *Companies Acts 1963 to 2006* (2007, Tottel Publishing) at 733. For companies to which C(A)A 1986 applies, the reference to the Sixth Schedule in s 158(1), is replaced by a reference to the corresponding provisions of C(A)A 1986. See C(A)A 1986, s 3(1)(e).

[6.149] The directors' report must be signed by two directors on behalf of all of the directors.[384] It must include a number of specific matters. First, the directors' report must address a change in any of the following:

 – the business of the company during the relevant financial year;

 – the business of the company's subsidiaries during the financial year; or

 – the classes of business in which the company has an interest, as a member of another company or otherwise.

This only applies insofar as that change is 'material for the appreciation of the state of the company's affairs.'[385]

Secondly, the directors' report must include (a) a list of any bodies corporate which are subsidiaries of the company at the end of the financial year; and (b) a list of bodies corporate in which the company is beneficially entitled to at least 20 per cent in nominal value of the shares carrying voting rights.[386] The report must distinguish between bodies corporate listed under category (a) or (b) and must specify, in relation to each body listed, its name; place of incorporation; and the nature of its business.[387]

Third, the directors' report must contain a statement of the measures that the directors have taken to secure the company's compliance with CA 1990, s 202.[388]

Finally, the directors' report under s 158 must contain, 'a copy of any Disclosure Issue Notice issued under s 33AK (inserted by the Central Bank and Financial Services Authority of Ireland Act 2003) during the financial year ending with the relevant balance sheet date.'[389]

[6.150] A director who fails to take 'all reasonable steps to comply with the requirements of' s 58, shall be liable on summary conviction, in respect of each such offence, to imprisonment for a maximum term of 6 months or to a maximum fine of €1,904.61, or both.[390] A director can only receive a sentence of imprisonment, if the court is of the opinion that the offence was committed 'wilfully'.[391]

---

[384] CA 1963, s 158(2).

[385] CA 1963, s 158(3).

[386] CA 1963, s 158(4).

[387] CA 1963, s 158(5). CA 1963, s 158(4) and (5), do not apply to any company that is, 'principally engaged in the acquisition and underwriting of shares or other securities of companies carrying on a trade or industry in the State and which holds a certificate of exemption issued by the Minister from the requirements of those subsections' (CA 1963, s 158(6)).

[388] CA 1963, s 158(6A), as inserted by CLEA 2001, s 90. See further Ch **4**.

[389] CA 1963, s 158(6B), as inserted by Central Bank and Financial Services Authority of Ireland Act 2003, s 35(1) and Sch 1, Pt 4.

[390] CA 1963, s 158(7), as amended by CA 1990, s 240(7), as inserted by CLEA 2001, s 104(c).

[391] CA 1963, s 158(7)(b).

When a company fails to prepare a directors' report, or prepares a report which is false or misleading, its directors are not automatically liable for that default. It is only if it is proven that an individual director failed to take 'all reasonable steps' to comply with the requirements of s 158, that he may be convicted of an offence. Two points may be noted in relation to the formulation of s 158(7). First, the onus is on the prosecutor to demonstrate that there was a default under s 158 and that the director charged, failed to take 'all reasonable steps' to comply with that provision. Second, the reference to 'all reasonable steps' is curious: it suggests that the prosecutor must prove that the director in question failed to take all steps that he could reasonably have taken to secure compliance with s 158, not just that he failed to take any such reasonable steps.

Furthermore, if summary proceedings are initiated against a director under s 158(7), he may avail of the defence that:

> 'he had reasonable ground to believe and did believe that a competent and reliable person was charged with the duty of seeing that the provisions of this *section* were complied with and was in a position to discharge that duty.'[392]

[6.151] Additional matters must be included in the directors' reports of particular companies. In the case of public limited companies, for example, there must be information regarding the company's audit committee.[393] For companies to which C(A)A 1986 applies,[394] there are numerous additional matters that must be included in the directors' report. First, s 13(1)(a) requires that the report must contain, in relation to the company and its subsidiaries, a 'fair review' of their development; the performance of their business; and their position.[395] This 'fair review' must relate to the financial year ending on the relevant balance sheet date and it must fulfil the dual requirements of being 'a balanced and comprehensive analysis' of these matters, and of being 'consistent with the size and complexity of the business.'[396] The review must also include an analysis of financial and, where appropriate, non financial, key performance indicators relevant to that business, to the extent that such analysis is necessary to understand the

---

[392] CA 1963, s 158(7)(a).

[393] See CA 1990, s 205B, as inserted by C(AA)A 2003, s 42 Note that this provision has not yet been commenced. Large private companies and 'relevant undertakings' as defined in CA 1990, s 205B(1), must also state whether they have audit committees; if not, the reason; and the responsibility of such a committee. CA 1990, s 205B(4), as inserted by C(AA)A 2003, s 42 (yet to be commenced).

[394] C(A)A 1986 applies to all private and public limited companies, other than those specifically excluded by s 2(1), namely: '(a) a company not trading for the acquisition of gain by the members, (b) a company to which sub-s (4)(c) of s 128 of the Principal Act applies, (c) a company in respect of which there is in force an order under sub-s (5) of that section.' Similar requirements apply to directors' reports accompanying group accounts. See EC(CGA)R 1992, reg 37.

[395] C(A)A 1986, s 13(1)(a), as substituted by EC(IFRSMA)R 2005, reg 5(g)(i).

[396] C(A)A 1986, s 13(1)(a)(i), as substituted by EC(IFRSMA)R 2005, reg 5(g)(i).

company's development, performance or position, or that of its subsidiaries.[397] The directors of a company which is treated as a small or medium-sized company are not, however, obliged to provide this analysis of key performance indicators in their report.[398]

[6.152] Second, s 13(1)(f) requires that, if the company or its subsidiaries use financial instruments and it is material for the assessment of the company's or the group's assets, liabilities, financial position, and profit or loss, the directors' report must state 'the financial risk management objectives and policies of the company and the group' and 'the exposure of the company and the group to price risk, credit risk, liquidity risk and cash flow risk.'[399] The directors of a company which is treated as a small or medium-sized company under the C(A)A 1986, are not required to include this category of information in their report.[400]

[6.153] Third, if a company acquires its own shares,[401] the directors' report for that financial year must state:

- the number and nominal value of those shares;[402]

- the maximum number and nominal value of such shares, whether acquired during that year or preceding years, which are held at any time by the company during the relevant year;[403]

- the number and nominal value of such shares which are disposed of or cancelled during that year, whether acquired during that year or preceding years;[404]

- if shares of a particular description are acquired or disposed of, the percentage of the called up share capital of the company which shares of that description represent;[405]

---

[397] C(A)A 1986, s 13(1)(a)(ii), as substituted by EC(IFRSMA)R 2005, reg 5(g)(i). The indicators that should be analysed include information relevant to environmental, or employee matters.

[398] C(A)A 1986, s 13(2), as inserted by EC(IFRSMA)R 2005, reg 5(g)(ii).

[399] C(A)A 1986, s 13(1)(f), as inserted by EC(FVA)R 2004, reg 5.

[400] C(A)A 1986, s 13(2), as inserted by EC(IFRSMA)R 2005, reg 5(g)(ii).

[401] This applies to situations where a company acquires its own shares by forfeiture or surrender in lieu of forfeiture; pursuant to C(A)A 1983, s 41; in the circumstances referred to in s 43(1)(c) (nominee of a public limited company acquiring shares from a third party) or C(A)A 1983, s 41(1)(d) (acquisition of shares by a person with financial assistance by a public limited company, the company having a beneficial interest in those shares); or where the shares in the company are subject to a lien or charge taken by the company, as permitted by C(A)A 1983, s 44(2)(a), (c) or (d). C(A)A 1986, s 14. If the company is a public limited company and its subsidiary acquires shares in it, this must also be disclosed. EC(PLCS)R 1997, reg 6.

[402] C(A)A 1986, s 14(i).

[403] C(A)A 1986, s 14(ii).

[404] C(A)A 1986, s 14(iii).

[405] C(A)A 1986, s 14(iv).

- if the acquisition is in the form of a charge, the amount of the charge in each case;[406]

- if the shares are acquired or disposed of for money or money's worth, the amount or value of such consideration for each transaction;[407] and

- the reasons for the acquisition, lien or charge.[408]

[6.154] Finally, there are other assorted matters that must be included in the directors' report of a company to which C(A)A 1986 applies:

- a description of the principal risks and uncertainties that the company and its subsidiaries face;[409]

- where appropriate, the report must include additional explanations of amounts contained in the annual accounts;[410]

- particulars of any important events affecting the company or any of its subsidiaries, which have occurred since the end of that year;[411]

- an indication of likely future developments in the business of the company and any of its subsidiaries;[412]

- an indication of any activities of the company or its subsidiaries, in research and development; [413] and

- an indication of any branches of the company outside the State and the country in which they are located.[414]

[6.155] There is no sanction for non-compliance with ss 13 or 14 specified in the C(A)A 1986.[415] These requirements are supplemental to the requirements of s 158.[416] The sanction for non-compliance with s 158, however, is expressly stated to apply to

---

[406] C(A)A 1986, s 14(v).

[407] C(A)A 1986, s 14(vi), as amended by CA 1990, s 233.

[408] C(A)A 1986, s 14(vii), as inserted by CA 1990, s 233.

[409] C(A)A 1986, s 13(1)(a), as substituted by EC(IFRSMA)R 2005, reg 5(g)(i).

[410] C(A)A 1986, s 13(1)(a), as substituted by EC(IFRSMA)R 2005, reg 5(g)(i).

[411] C(A)A 1986, s 13(1)(b).

[412] C(A)A 1986, s 13(1)(c), as inserted by EC(FVA)R 2004, reg 3.

[413] C(A)A 1986, s 13(1)(d), as inserted by EC(FVA)R 2004, reg 3.

[414] C(A)A 1986, s 13(1)(e), as inserted by EC(FVA)R 2004, reg 3. This provision refers to branches 'within the meaning of Council Directive 89/666/EEC)(OJ No L395, 30.12.1989, p 36.'

[415] C(A)A 1986, s 22, stipulates that it is an offence, by a company and officers in default, when there is a failure to comply with particular sections of that Act, including ss 10, 11, 16 and 18, but the list of provisions does not include ss 13 or 14.

[416] C(A)A 1986, s 13(1), clearly states: 'the report of the directors of a company under s 158 of the Principal Act shall contain, in addition to the information specified in that section, the following information ...'.

failures to comply with the requirements of that section: the sanctions set out in s 158(7) apply only 'if any person, being a director of a company, fails to take all reasonable steps to comply with *the requirements of this section* …'. (emphasis added). Sections 13 and 14 do not invite the interpretation that s 158 should be extended to include their requirements. If ss 13 and 14 stated that 'section 158 shall be interpreted as including the following requirements …', s 158(7) may be applicable to failures to comply with those provisions. As C(A)A 1986, ss 13 and 14 and CA 1963, s 158(7) are formulated, however, there is no apparent sanction where a directors' report fails to include the matters required by ss 13 and 14.

(b) Directors' compliance statement

[6.156] The Review Group on Auditing included in its Report the recommendation that directors of companies should be required to prepare an annual statement confirming 'the company's compliance with its obligations under company law, taxation law or other relevant statutory or regulatory requirements'.[417]

The C(AA)A 2003 accordingly inserted a new s 205E into the CA 1990, introducing the concept of a directors' compliance statement ('DCS') into Irish company law. In broad terms, s 205E requires the directors of all companies to which it applies, to prepare a statement at least once every three years, setting out the company's policies and internal procedures regarding its 'relevant obligations' and its arrangements for implementation of such policies and procedures.[418] Section 205E also requires the directors to include in the directors' report under s 158, a statement acknowledging their responsibility for ensuring the company's compliance with its 'relevant obligations'; confirming, among other matters, that the directors have reviewed the effectiveness of the company's procedures for securing compliance with these obligations; and specifying whether the directors used all reasonable endeavours to secure such compliance.[419]

[6.157] Section 205E provoked considerable debate and was faced with sizeable opposition. Among the contentious aspects of this provision were the number of companies to which it applied[420] and the broad definition of 'relevant obligations', which includes 'the company's obligations under (a) the Companies Acts, (b) tax law,

---

[417] *Report of the Review Group on Auditing* (July 2000) at recommendation 14.1.

[418] CA 1990, s 205E(3), as inserted by C(AA)A 2003, s 45.

[419] CA 1990, s 205E(5) and (6), as inserted by C(AA)A 2003, s 45.

[420] According to CA 1990, s 205E(9), as inserted by C(AA)A 2003, s 45, only private limited companies with balance sheet totals of less than €7,618,428 and turnover of less than €15,236,856, are exempt from the requirements of s 205E. These thresholds were originally much lower, but, during the passage of the C(AA)A 2003 through the Dáil and Seanad, they were revised upwards to quell concerns as to cost. The ICLSA records that, 'To address concerns as to cost, the thresholds for private companies were increased dramatically. They were initially pitched at the audit exemption threshold figures… but were dramatically increased at Dáil Committee Stage by the Minister of State.' ICLSA, C(AA)A 2003, s 45.

and (c) any other enactments that provide a legal framework within which the company operates and that may materially affect the company's financial statements.'[421]

The debate surrounding s 205E prompted the Minister for Trade and Commerce, on 21 April 2005, to refer the provision to the Company Law Review Group ('CLRG') for consideration. The CLRG prepared a report, which analysed the DCS, the risks associated with it, and its regulatory impact, among other matters.[422] In the *Report on Directors' Compliance Statement*, the CLRG concluded that 'the risks associated with not repealing or modifying 45/2003 [s 45, C(AA)A 2003] greatly outweighed in terms of seriousness the risks associated with not commencing 45/2003 [s 45, C(AA)A 2003].'[423]

The CLRG accordingly recommended that C(AA)A 2003, s 45 should be repealed. In its Report on the topic, the CLRG also advances an alternative model for a DCS. [424] This model differs from s 205E in the following respects, among others: First, the new model amends the definition of 'relevant obligations' to refer only to the tax acts, or to obligations under the Companies Acts, failure to comply with which are indictable offences. Second, the thresholds that must be met before a private company will come within the scope of the DCS requirements have been increased to a balance sheet total of €12,500 and a turnover of €25,000,000, and are now cumulative requirements.[425] Third, whereas CA 1990, s 205F as inserted by C(AA)A 2003, s 45, included a requirement

---

[421] CA 1990, s 205E(1), as inserted by C(AA)A 2003, s 45. These concerns were also raised in the debates in the Dáil and Seanad preceding the enactment of the C(AA)A 2003. The annotations to C(AA)A 2003, s 45, state that, 'Many opposition deputies and senators felt that the burden of the compliance statement on directors would prove so unattractive that companies would have severe difficulty in attracting non-executive directors.' See ICLSA, C(AA)A 2003, s 45.

[422] CLRG, *Report on Directors' Compliance Statement* (2005). Available at www.clrg.ie. The CLRG concluded, among other matters, that, 'there is a clear and imminent risk that the commencement of 45/2003 will result in a substantial cost to those Irish companies within the scope of the DCS'; that 'there is a clear and imminent risk that investment in the Irish economy through Irish registered companies will be curtailed'; and that, 'there is no evidence to suggest that a stance by Ireland on corporate compliance that is so far-reaching and above the recognised standards applying at EU and international level will be accepted by the international community and it is likely that such would operate to encourage foreign companies to incorporate in an alternative jurisdiction.' CLRG, *Report on Directors' Compliance Statement* (2005) at pp 10 and 127.

[423] CLRG, *Report on Directors' Compliance Statement* (2005) at pp 10 and 127.

[424] It should be noted that a majority of the CLRG recommended that C(AA)A 2003, s 45 should be repealed and not replaced 'pending any EU initiative on compliance verification by directors of companies.' The Group did, however, advance an alternative form of DCS, if the Minister did not accept that primary recommendation (referred to in the Report as 'section X'). CLRG, *Report on Directors' Compliance Statement* (2005) at p 128.

[425] See CLRG, *Report on Directors' Compliance Statement* (2005) at pp 12 and 134 and Ch 10 generally. This revised form of DCS is now largely reflected in the Draft Companies Consolidation and Reform Bill 2007, Pt A5, Head 7. Available at www.clrg.org.

that a company's auditor must review the DCS, the CLRG does not recommend the retention of any such requirement.[426]

[6.158] Another change proposed by the CLRG is that company directors will not be required to prepare a statement of policies and procedures at least every three years, as envisaged by s 205E. This aspect of s 205E is not reflected in the model proposed by the CLRG. By contrast, the 'compliance statement' proposed by the CLRG will only be included in the directors' report under s 158 and will include a statement by the directors:

–   acknowledging that they are responsible for securing the company's compliance with its relevant obligations;

–   confirming that the company has in place a compliance policy statement that is, in the opinion of the directors, appropriate for the company and, if this is not the case, specifying the reasons;

–   confirming that the company has in place appropriate arrangements or structures that are, in the opinion of the directors, designed to secure material compliance with its relevant obligations,[427] which arrangements or structures may (at the discretion of the directors) include the company's reliance upon internal and/or external advisors who appear to the directors to have the requisite knowledge and experience to advise the company on compliance with its relevant obligations and if this is not the case, specifying the reasons; and

–   confirming that the company's arrangements or structures referred to above have been reviewed during the financial year to which the report relates, and if this is not the case, specifying the reasons.[428]

[6.159] On 1 December 2005, the Minister for Trade and Commerce announced that the Government has agreed to take forward in legislation the proposal for a new model of DCS, in accordance with the recommendations of the CLRG.[429] Announcing this

---

[426] The CLRG recommends, 'the removal of the requirement that a company's auditors must specifically opine on the reasonableness or otherwise of the proposed revised Annual Statement on Compliance in Directors' Reports'. See CLRG, *Report on Directors' Compliance Statement* (2005) at p 130. Available at www.clrg.org.

[427] The CLRG model, referred to as 'section X', also provides in subsection (4) that, 'For the purposes of this section, a company's arrangements or structures are considered to be designed to secure material compliance with its relevant obligations if they provide a reasonable assurance of compliance in all material respects with those obligations.' See also CLRG, Draft Companies Consolidation and Reform Bill 2007, Pt A5, Head 7(3). Available at www.clrg.org.

[428] See CLRG, *Report on Directors' Compliance Statement* (2005) at p 134. See also CLRG, Draft Companies Consolidation and Reform Bill 2007, Pt A5, Head 7(2). Both available at www.clrg.org.

[429] Press Release, 'Minister Michael Ahern Announces Reform of Directors' Compliance Statement', 1 December 2005. The release describes the revised model DCS as follows: 'It differs from existing 45/2003 in restricting and clarifying the obligations on which directors must report, in being less prescriptive about the methods a company uses to review its compliance procedures, and in not requiring review of the compliance statement by an external auditor.' Available at www.entemp.ie.

decision, the new model for the DCS was described as 'an integral feature of the systemic reform and simplification of the company law code'. The revised form of DCS proposed by the CLRG is now reflected in the General Scheme of the Draft Companies and Reform Bill 2007.[430]

F. Proceedings against officers of companies in liquidation

[6.160] Officers of companies which are in liquidation are under very stringent obligations to co-operate with the liquidation and not to do, or have done, anything which undermines the liquidation process or damages the interests of the company's creditors. Failure to comply with these obligations is an offence and may be taken into account in other proceedings, such as restriction and disqualification proceedings.[431] There are also several offences with which directors of companies in liquidation may be charged. The following are merely an example of such offences.

(a) Offences by officers of companies in liquidation

[6.161] CA 1963, s 293(1) provides that it is an offence for a past or present officer of a company[432] which is at the time of the relevant conduct, or subsequently, the subject of winding up proceedings, to do any of the following:

- fail, when requested to do by the liquidator, to make full and true disclosure, to the best of his knowledge and belief, of all the real and personal property of the company and of all information regarding the disposal of such property, except insofar as the disposal was done in the ordinary course of business;[433]

- fail to comply with a direction of the liquidator, to deliver up real or personal property of the company in his custody or under his control, when required by the law to do so;[434]

---

[430] CLRG, Draft Companies Consolidation and Reform Bill 2007, Pt A5, Head 7. Available at www.clrg.org.

[431] Note that the court may also make an order directing an officer to 'pay, deliver, convey, surrender or transfer forthwith, or within such time as the court directs, to the liquidator any money, property or books or papers in his hands to which the liquidator is *prima facie* entitled' (CA 1963, s 236). See further Pts **D** and **E**.

[432] 'Officer' is defined for the purposes of this section to include any person in accordance with whose instructions or directions the directors have been accustomed to act (CA 1963, s 294(4)).

[433] CA 1963, s 293(1)(a). It is a defence to a charge under this heading, for the director to prove that he had no intent to defraud (CA 1963, s 294(2)).

[434] CA 1963, s 293(1)(b). It is a defence to a charge under this heading, for the director to prove that he had no intent to defraud (CA 1963, s 294(2)).

    – fail to comply with a direction of the liquidator to deliver up all books and papers in his custody or control which belong to the company and which he is legally required to deliver;[435]

    – within 12 months preceding the commencement of the winding up, or thereafter, conceal any part of the company's property (above a particular value), or any debts due to or from the company;[436]

    – within 12 months preceding the commencement of the winding up, or thereafter, fraudulently remove any part of the company's property worth above a prescribed amount;[437]

    – make any material omission in any statement regarding the company's affairs;[438]

    – fail, for a month, to inform the liquidator of his knowledge or belief that a false debt was proved by any person during the winding up;[439]

    – prevent the production of any book or paper relating to the company's property or affairs, after the commencement of the winding up;[440]

    – within the 12 months preceding the commencement of the winding up, or thereafter, conceal, destroy, mutilate or falsify any book or paper regarding the company's affairs or property, or is privy to any such conduct;[441]

    – within 12 months preceding the commencement of the winding up, or thereafter, make or be privy to the making of, any false entry in any book or paper regarding the company's affairs or property;[442]

    – within 12 months preceding the commencement of the winding up, or thereafter, fraudulent part with, alter or make any omission in, any document regarding the company's affairs or property, or be privy to any such conduct;[443]

---

[435] CA 1963, s 293(1)(c). It is a defence to a charge under this heading, for the director to prove that he had no intent to defraud (CA 1963, s 294(2)).

[436] CA 1963, s 293(1)(d). The value stipulated in s 294(1)(c) is £10. It is a defence to a charge under this heading, for the director to prove that he had no intent to defraud (CA 1963, s 294(2)).

[437] CA 1963, s 293(1)(e).

[438] CA 1963, s 293(1)(f). It is a defence to a charge under this heading, for the director to prove that he had no intent to defraud (CA 1963, s 294(2)).

[439] CA 1963, s 293(1)(g).

[440] CA 1963, s 293(1)(h). It is a defence for a director to prove that he had no intent to conceal the true state of affairs of the company or to defeat the law (CA 1963, s 294(2)).

[441] CA 1963, s 293(1)(i). It is a defence for a director to prove that he had no intent to conceal the true state of affairs of the company or to defeat the law (CA 1963, s 294(2)).

[442] CA 1963, s 293(1)(j). It is a defence for a director to prove that he had no intent to conceal the true state of affairs of the company or to defeat the law (CA 1963, s 294(2)).

[443] CA 1963, s 293(1)(k).

– at a meeting of creditors within 12 months preceding the commencement of the winding up, or after the commencement of the winding up, attempt to account for any part of the company's property by fictitious losses or expenses;[444]

– within 12 months preceding the commencement of the winding up or thereafter, obtain, for or on behalf of the company, property on credit which the company does not subsequently pay for, on the false pretence that the company is carrying on business;[445]

– within 12 months preceding the commencement of the winding up or thereafter, pawn, pledge or dispose of any property which was obtained by the company on credit and which was not paid for, other than in the ordinary course of business;[446] or

– be guilty of any false representation or fraud for the purpose of obtaining from the creditors or any of them consent to an agreement regarding the affairs of the company or the winding up.[447]

Each of these offences may be prosecuted summarily or on indictment.[448] The maximum penalties vary depending on the particular offence.[449]

[6.162] In addition to the possibility of prosecution for specific offences of thwarting the course of the liquidation, the extent to which a director co-operates with a duly appointed liquidator and facilitates the liquidation process, may be considered more generally by the court in the context of proceedings taken against such a director. Allegations of non-cooperation or any of the other conduct criminalised by s 293 would be damaging in applications for declarations of restriction,[450] orders of disqualification[451] and in the context of fraudulent and reckless trading proceedings.

---

[444] CA 1963, s 293(1)(l).

[445] CA 1963, s 293(1)(n). It is a defence to a charge under this heading, for the director to prove that he had no intent to defraud (CA 1963, s 294(2)).

[446] CA 1963, s 293(1)(o). It is a defence to a charge under this heading, for the director to prove that he had no intent to defraud (CA 1963, s 294(2)). Every person who receives the property, knowing the circumstances described in s 294(1)(o), is guilty of an offence and liable to the same sanction as if he committed the offence directly (CA 1963, s 294(3)).

[447] CA 1963, s 293(1)(p).

[448] CA 1963, s 293(1).

[449] See CA 1963, s 293(1), as amended by CA 1990, ss 240(7) and 280(8), as inserted by CLEA 2001, s 104.

[450] See *Ashclad v Harrington* [2000] IEHC 174, in which the court accepted the liquidator's allegation that the directors provided no assistance in connection with the liquidation. Declarations of restriction under CA 1990, s 150 and personal liability under CA 1990, s 204 were made in that case. See Pt **D**.

[451] See, eg, *Re CB Readymix Ltd, Cahill v Grimes* [2002] 1 IR 372. See further Pt **E**.

(b) Fraud by officers of companies in liquidation

[6.163] It is an offence for an officer of a company which subsequently goes into liquidation (whether voluntary or compulsory) to do any of the following:[452]

- to induce a person to give credit to the company, by means of fraud or false pretences;[453]

- to make a gift of, transfer, create a charge, or cause or connive the levying of execution against, the company's property, with intent to defraud the creditors;[454] or

- to conceal or remove any part of the company's property within two months of any unsatisfied judgment or order for payment against the company, with intent to defraud creditors.[455]

These provisions may also apply to companies which are not being wound up, if the criteria of CA 1990, s 251 are met. These criteria are that:

- a judgment, decree or order is made in favour of a creditor of a company and execution or other process on such a judgment, decree or order is returned unsatisfied, in whole or in part,

- or the court is satisfied that the company is unable to pay its debts, taking into account the company's contingent and prospective liabilities

- and that it appears to the court that the sole or principal reason for the company not being wound up is the insufficiency of its assets.[456]

G. Directors of insolvent companies

[6.164] When a company ceases to be able to pay its debts as they fall due, this has particular consequences for the directors and gives rise to a distinct set of duties. As this is a particularly important area in the context of company law enforcement, certain aspects of directors' duties on insolvency are examined separately in Pt **D**. In particular, this Part addresses the restriction of directors and it is in that context that Irish company law has set out most comprehensively the duties and standards which are expected of directors of insolvent companies. The following list illustrates some of the duties and standards which company law imposes on directors when the company becomes incapable of paying its debts as they fall due.

[6.165] First, when a company has become insolvent, the courts will examine closely the extent to which the directors held regular meetings and discussed the financial situation of the company, particularly during the period in which the company's predicament has become apparent. While there is no statutory obligation on directors to

---

[452] CA 1963, s 295.

[453] CA 1963, s 295(a).

[454] CA 1963, s 295(b).

[455] CA 1963, s 295(c).

[456] CA 1990, s 251(1).

hold meetings at prescribed intervals of time, the failure of a company's board to hold meetings and discuss a company's worsening financial situation, when a company is insolvent, has been taken into account by courts as a gauge of the directors' conduct and has been a factor in relation to the imposition of such penalties as declarations of restriction.[457]

[6.166] Second, it is highly advisable for a company's directors to enlist the assistance of professional advisors, if the company is insolvent, or at risk of insolvency. This is particularly advisable where the directors do not possess the requisite education, training or experience to deal with the company's situation. While this cannot be stated as an affirmative duty of directors of insolvent companies, the fact that the directors of a company solicited and acted upon professional advice, may be an important point in the directors' defence against applications for declarations of restriction or orders of disqualification, or in the context of proceedings for reckless trading.[458]

[6.167] Third, there are a number of consequences of a company continuing to trade while insolvent.[459] Directors which allow a company to continue to trade in those circumstances should be particularly aware of the possibility of restriction proceedings, disqualification proceedings and proceedings for fraudulent and reckless trading.[460]

[6.168] Fourth, the law frowns upon preferential treatment of any creditors, particularly when the company becomes insolvent.[461] In this regard, there have been particular cases in which the directors paid the debts owing to trade creditors in preference to discharging liabilities owed to the Revenue Commissioners. The courts have criticised such conduct and have taken it into account in imposing sanctions on directors, such as declarations of restriction.[462]

[6.169] Fifth, if a company is unable to pay its debts, but is not being wound up, and it appears that the principal reason for its not being wound up is the insufficiency of the

---

[457] See Pt **D**.

[458] *Re Colm O'Neill Engineering Services* (in liq) [2004] IEHC 83 (13 February 2004, unreported), HC is an example of a case in which the directors, having retained an external financial controller, were found not to have acted irresponsibly in proceedings for a declaration of restriction. See Pt **D**.

[459] See, as examples of the attitude towards directors permitting companies to continue to trade while insolvent: *Re Mitek Ltd, Grace v Kachkar* [2005] IEHC 63; *Re La Moselle Clothing Ltd, La Moselle Clothing Ltd v Soualhi* [1998] IEHC 66; *Re Lynrowan Enterprises Ltd* [2002] IEHC 90 (31 July 2002, unreported), HC; *Re Newcastle Timber Ltd* [2001] IEHC 146.

[460] See Pts **D** and **E**.

[461] See, eg, CA 1963, s 286, as substituted by CA 1990, s 135.

[462] See, eg, *Re Newcastle Timber Ltd* [2001] IEHC 146; *Re La Moselle Clothing Ltd, La Moselle Clothing Ltd v Soualhi* [1998] IEHC 66. See Pt **D**.

company's assets, certain provisions that may otherwise only be invoked in liquidations, may also be invoked in respect of those companies.[463]

H. Sanctions

[6.170] There are a variety of sanctions which may be imposed on a director who is found to be guilty of an infringement of the Companies Acts or in breach of his duties at common law.

First, a director who has infringed the Companies Acts or otherwise failed to act honestly and responsibly, may face proceedings for a declaration of restriction or, in appropriate circumstances, an order of disqualification.[464]

[6.171] Second, there are certain provisions of the Companies Acts which allow unlimited personal liability for the debts of the company to be imposed on a defaulting director. For example, such liability may be imposed for a failure to keep proper books of account and where a director made a false statutory statement in connection with the provision of a guarantee or security in favour of a director.[465] Another example of an area in which personal liability for the debts of a company may be imposed, is if a director is found to have been guilty of fraudulent or reckless trading.[466]

[6.172] Third, if a director has committed infringements of the Companies Acts or of his duties at common law, this may have direct consequences for the company's status. In particular, a company may be wound up,[467] or struck off the register of companies,[468] as a result of certain actions or inaction of the company's directors.

[6.173] Fourth, a director who has acted in breach of his duties as a director, or has otherwise infringed the requirements of the Companies Acts or the common law, may be liable in damages for that misconduct. For example, a director may be made liable to account to the company for gains which he made as a result of his breach of company law, and may be made liable for losses suffered by the company as a result of such

---

[463] See CA 1990, s 251, as amended by CLEA 2001, s 54. Note that, 'A lot of emphasis was laid on this provision during the course of the Parliamentary Debates. The section basically applies certain provisions of this legislation and of the Companies Act 1963 to companies who go out of business without formally going into liquidation. The Minister had adverted to the situation where insolvent companies deliberately run down their affairs and then simply close their doors without any formal winding up so as to leave creditors high and dry (383 *Dáil Debates* Col 1702). This section is designed to deal with that problem.' ICLSA, Companies Act 1990 (Thomson Roundhall).

[464] These topics are addressed in detail in Pts **D** and **E**.

[465] CA 1990, s 204; CA 1990, s 34(5)(a), as inserted by CLEA 2001, s 78. See further Ch **4** and paras **[6.044]** to **[6.048]**.

[466] CA 1963, s 297A(1), as inserted by CA 1990, s 138.

[467] See, eg, *Re Murph's Restaurants Ltd* [1979] ILRM 141.

[468] See Ch **4**.

misconduct.[469] A director may also face punitive damages for particularly egregious breaches of duty.

[6.174] When a company is being wound up, directors may be ordered to pay damages pursuant to CA 1963, s 298, when they are found to have been guilty of a breach of trust, of duty, misfeasance, or of having misapplied or retained the company's money or property.[470] The criteria for making an order under s 298 are set out as follows in s 298(1):

> ... in the course of winding up a company it appears that any person who has taken part in the formation or promotion of the company, or any past or present officer, liquidator, receiver or examiner of the company, has misapplied or retained or become liable or accountable for any money or property of the company, or has been guilty of any misfeasance or other breach of duty or trust in relation to the company.

It is necessary therefore that persons who have taken part in the formation or promotion of the company or any past or present officer, liquidator, examiner or receiver of the company[471] must have done one of the following:

– misapplied or retained any money or property of the company;

– become accountable or liable for any money or property of the company;

– been guilty of misfeasance in relation to the company;

– committed a breach of duty in relation to the company; or

– committed a breach of trust in relation to the company.[472]

[6.175] When these criteria are met, the company's liquidator or a creditor or contributory of the company may make an application to court for one of two types of orders.[473] Section 298(2) provides:

> The court may, on the application of the liquidator, or any creditor or contributory, examine the conduct of the promoter, officer, liquidator, receiver or examiner, and compel him—
>
> (a) to repay or restore the money or property or any part thereof respectively with interest at such rate as the court thinks just, or
>
> (b) to contribute such sum to the assets of the company by way of compensation in respect of the misapplication, retainer, misfeasance or other breach of duty or trust as the court thinks just.[474]

---

[469] See eg para **[6.087]**. See also CLRG, General Scheme of Draft Companies Consolidation and Reform Bill 2007, Pt A5, Head 13, which introduces a general liability to account for gains made by directors as a result of breaches of duty.

[470] CA 1963, s 298, as inserted by CA 1990, s 142.

[471] CA 1963, s 298(1), as substituted by CA 1990, s 142.

[472] CA 1963, s 298(1), as substituted by CA 1990, s 142.

[473] CA 1963, s 298(2), as substituted by CA 1990, s 142. An application under s 298 should be by way of notice of motion, together with such reports and affidavits as the motion is grounded upon. Rules of the Superior Courts (SI 15/1986), ord 74, r 49.

[474] CA 1963, s 298(2), as substituted by CA 1990, s 142.

The same power to award damages against a director arises, if a subsidiary is being wound up and it appears to the court that a director of the holding company was guilty of misfeasance, breach of duty, breach of trust, or misapplication or retention of property or money, or liability or accountability or liability for such property or money which belonged to the subsidiary.[475]

Section 298 also applies to companies that are not being wound up, if the criteria of s 251 are met.[476] An application for an order under s 298, in the circumstances addressed by CA 1990, s 251 may be made by the DCE.[477]

[6.176] A fifth form of sanction that may be imposed on a company director is the service of a compliance notice by the DCE requiring him to remedy the default and make a prescribed payment.[478] Such a notice may only be served if the DCE believes, on reasonable grounds, that the person in question has committed an offence which 'is subject to summary prosecution.'[479] Following the delivery of a notice from the DCE under s 109, the person to whom it is directed may pay the prescribed sum and remedy the default complained of. If this is done, to the satisfaction of the DCE, within the time specified in s 109, namely 21 days, no criminal proceedings will be taken in respect of that default.[480]

This provision has not yet been commenced, and the DCE has no power at present to serve compliance notices requiring the rectification of defaults and the payment of administrative fines. The DCE does, however, already employ certain comparable tools.[481] First, the DCE accepts remedial measures or voluntary rectification of minor or inadvertent defaults. Second, the DCE issues 'caution warnings' informing the person in default that repeated defaults will be treated seriously. Third, the DCE may send a 'warning letter' urging rectification of defaults, failing which High Court proceedings will be instituted to compel compliance with the relevant requirements. These are all measures which may be employed in respect of a company director who is in default of his obligations under the Companies Acts.

---

[475] CA 1990, s 148. Note that CA 1990, s 251, extends the application of s 148 to companies which are not being wound up, if the criteria of s 251 are met. See para **[6.163]**.

[476] See CA 1990, s 251(2)(b). See further para **[6.163]**.

[477] CA 1990, s 251(2A), as inserted by CLEA 2001, s 54(6).

[478] CLEA 2001, s 109. In 2002, the Minister for Enterprise, Trade and Employment stated that, 'Section 109 will be commenced following further discussions with the Director of Corporate Enforcement' (Dáil Éireann. *Written Answers*. Vol. 549. 27 February 2002). The Minister commented in September 2005 that the provision 'will be commenced when the Office of the Director of Corporate Enforcement, ODCE, confirms that it is in a position to implement this provision.' (Dáil Éireann, *Written Answers*, Vol 606 No 1, 28 September 2005). As of October 2007, this provision has not been commenced.

[479] CLEA 2001, s 109.

[480] CLEA 2001, s 109(2)(c).

[481] See ODCE, *Annual Report 2006* at p 20.

[6.177] Sixth, a director may face imprisonment and fines for many violations of the Companies Acts for which he may be liable. These sanctions are addressed in Ch **15**.

[6.178] Seventh, if a director[482] is in default in relation to a requirement of the Companies Acts, he may be served with a notice requiring him to comply with that requirement. If he does not comply with the requirement in question, within 14 days of service of the notice or such greater period as is specified in the notice, the court may, on an application by any member or creditor of the company, or the DCE or the Registrar of Companies, make an order directing compliance with the requirement, within such time as the court may specify.[483] This power to order compliance with the Companies Acts is specifically without prejudice to any other penalties which may be imposed on the responsible director, such as the restriction or disqualification of the director.[484] The court may order that the costs of the application should be borne by the director in default.[485]

[6.179] There are other forms of injunctions and orders which a court may grant in respect of a director in specific circumstances. For example, when a company is being wound up, the court may make an order directing an officer to 'pay, deliver, convey, surrender or transfer forthwith, or within such time as the court directs, to the liquidator any money, property or books or papers in his hands to which the liquidator is *prima facie* entitled.'[486]

I. Relief

[6.180] An officer[487] who is facing proceedings for negligence, default, breach of duty or breach of trust may be excused from liability on the ground that he acted honestly and reasonably and that it would be fair to so excuse him.[488] This provision does not have any application in respect of the criminal liability of directors.

Section 391 of CA 1963 provides:

> If in any proceeding for negligence, default, breach of duty or breach of trust against an officer of a company or a person employed by a company as auditor, it

---

[482] This power to order compliance also applies to the company and the term 'officer' as it used in s 371 is defined to include a 'director, a shadow director, an officer, a promoter, a receiver, a liquidator or an auditor of a company' (CA 1963, s 371(4), as inserted by CLEA 2001, s 96). CA 1963, s 371, as amended by CLEA 2001, s 96.

[483] CA 1963, s 371(1), as amended by CLEA 2001, s 96, and IFCMPA 2005, s 64.

[484] CA 1963, s 371(3), as amended by CLEA 2001, s 96.

[485] CA 1963, s 371(2), as amended by CLEA 2001, s 96.

[486] CA 1963, s 236.

[487] This provision also applies to persons employed as the company's auditor (CA 1963, s 391).

[488] CA 1963, s 391. If the case is being tried by a judge and a jury and the judge is satisfied that relief should be granted in whole or in part, the judge may 'withdraw the case in whole or in part from the jury, and direct judgment to be entered for the defendant on such terms as to costs or otherwise as the judge may think proper.'

appears to the court hearing the case that that officer or person is or may be liable in respect of the negligence, default, breach of duty or breach of trust, but that he has acted honestly and reasonably, and that, having regard to all the circumstances of the case, including those connected with his appointment, he ought fairly to be excused for the negligence, default, breach of duty or breach of trust, that court may relieve him, either wholly or partly from his liability on such terms as the court may think fit.[489]

[6.181] The premise of this relief from liability is that, while the director is or may be liable, he acted honestly and reasonably and that, in all of the circumstances, he should be excused, in whole or in part, from liability for his conduct. If an officer 'has reason to apprehend that any claim will or might be made against him in respect of any negligence, default, breach of duty or breach of trust', he may make an anticipatory application to court for relief. The court has the same power to grant relief on the same grounds, as it would have, if the proceedings were in being before the court.[490]

J. Protection against liability

[6.182] The Companies Acts prohibit any attempt to exempt or indemnify an officer of a company in respect of liability for any negligence, default, breach of duty or breach of trust of which he is guilty.[491] CA 1963, s 200 provides in this regard:

> any provision whether contained in the articles of a company or in any contract with a company or otherwise for exempting any officer of the company or any person employed by the company as auditor from, or indemnifying him against, any liability which by virtue of any rule of law would otherwise attach to him in respect of any negligence, default, breach of duty or breach of trust of which he may be guilty in relation to the company shall be void ….[492]

[6.183] Before the enactment of the C(AA)A 2003, there were only two situations in which this prohibition did not apply. First, it does not apply where the action or inaction in question occurred while a provision of the articles of association or of a contract, which exempted or indemnified the officer, was still in force.[493]

Secondly, a company may include a provision in its articles of association, or in a contract, to indemnify an officer against any liability incurred in relation to legal proceedings taken against that officer in a number of distinct situations. The first situation is that an officer may be indemnified in respect of the liability incurred in the course of civil legal proceedings, if judgment is entered in his favour in such

---

[489] CA 1963, s 391(1).

[490] CA 1963, s 391(2).

[491] CA 1963, s 200, as amended by C(AA)A 2003, s 56. Note that the term 'officer' as it used in s 200 includes former officers of the company (the references to auditors in the section also includes former auditors) (CA 1963, s 20(5), as inserted by C(AA)A 2003, s 56).

[492] CA 1963, s 200(1).

[493] CA 1963, s 200(1)(a). This is unlikely to be of much relevance any longer, as the provision could only have been validly in force before the enactment of the CA 1963.

proceedings. The second situation in which indemnification of the costs of proceedings is permitted, is where an officer is acquitted in criminal proceedings. The third possibility is that an officer who makes a successful application for relief in respect of any actual or anticipated proceedings for negligence, default, breach of duty or breach of trust, on the basis that he acted honestly and reasonably, is entitled to be indemnified.[494] Finally, a company may indemnify a director who successfully applies for relief from the obligation to pay for shares which were issued to him as a nominee, on the basis that he acted honestly and reasonably.[495]

[6.184] One of the important issues which arose from the original terms of s 200 was the effect it had on the power of a director, and a company, to execute a policy of insurance to protect the director against liability. While s 200 on its face would certainly cause any such contracts to be void, it was acknowledged by the CLRG that there was, 'an active market in the provision of directors' and officers' insurance, as well as a frequent practice of directors of Irish subsidiaries of overseas companies receiving indemnities from those overseas companies.'[496]

[6.185] The CLRG further noted that there was a general practice that insurers underwriting the insurance of directors and officers would include in the contract of insurance a statement to the effect that the insurer would not invoke CA 1963, s 200, as a means of invalidating the contract of insurance.[497] As noted by the CLRG:

> 'The flaw in this practice is that it is not for an insurer, or any person for that matter, to decide whether or not a contract is void under the section – the section states "void", not "voidable" – if a contract such as a contract of insurance falls under the section, then it will be void, and there is nothing an insurer or the intended insured can do.'[498]

To overcome this frailty, it appears that the market practice which developed was that the policy would be written under the laws of another jurisdiction, such as England and Wales. The CLRG observed that:

> 'This would appear to offer a better possibility of the insurance overcoming s 200 in order to be enforceable against the insurer, but does not address the breach of duty by the directors in contravening the section: the underlying philosophy of the section being that the company ought not spend its money in bailing out negligent directors and other officers.'[499]

---

[494] CA 1963, s 200(1)(b), referring to CA 1963, s 391. See further paras **[6.180]** to **[6.181]**.

[495] CA 1963, s 200(1)(b), as amended by C(A)A 1983, Sch 1, para 16, referring to C(A)A 1983, s 42.

[496] CLRG, *First Report*, at para 11.6.1. Available at www.clrg.org.

[497] CLRG, *First Report*, at para 11.6.2.

[498] CLRG, *First Report*, at para 11.6.2.

[499] CLRG, *First Report*, at para 11.6.3.

[6.186] In line with the recommendations of the CLRG, the C(AA)A 2003 introduced an important change in this regard. Section 200(2) now provides that:

> Notwithstanding subsection (1), a company may purchase and maintain for any of its officers or auditors insurance in respect of any liability referred to in that subsection.[500]

[6.187] Section 200(3) provides that a director may vote, and may not be precluded from voting, on any resolution to purchase or maintain insurance which may be to his benefit.[501] Furthermore, s 200(4) ensures that any contracts of insurance which were formed before the C(AA)A 2003 came into effect, are valid. It provides:

> Any directors' and officers' insurance purchased or maintained by a company before the date on which the amendments made to this section by the Companies (Auditing and Accounting) Act 2003 came into operation is as valid and effective as it would have been if those amendments had been in operation when that insurance was purchased or maintained.[502]

---

[500] CA 1963, s 200(2), as inserted by C(AA)A 2003, s 56.

[501] CA 1963, s 200(3), as inserted by C(AA)A 2003, s 56. This provision states expressly that a director is entitled to so vote 'notwithstanding any provision contained in an enactment, the articles of a company or otherwise.'

[502] CA 1963, s 200(4), as inserted by C(AA)A 2003, s 56.

Chapter 7

AUDITORS

A. Introduction

(a) Background

[7.001] In recent years, the role of the auditor of a company has attracted considerable scrutiny. Events such as the spectacular collapse of Enron[1] and WorldCom[2] in the US, among other high profile events, have led to a significant heightening of the emphasis placed upon the functions and responsibilities of a company's auditor.

In Ireland, attention was initially drawn to the role of auditors as a result of the discovery and investigation of bogus non-resident accounts that were established for the purpose of evading Deposit Income Retention Tax ('DIRT'). These investigations culminated in the establishment of the Review Group of Auditing. This body embarked on a study of the role of external auditors in 2000 and published its Report in July of that year. The Report noted:

> 'In examining the auditor/client relationship, the Review Group was aware that many international bodies and jurisdictions, such as the EU and USA are considering similar issues at present. The Review Group's view is that Ireland should be at the forefront of international best practice in establishing and implementing rules governing auditor independence while at the same time maintaining Ireland's competitive position as a small extremely open economy.'[3]

The law governing auditors has accordingly seen considerable changes in recent years, both at an Irish and a European level. The C(AA)A 2003, and the establishment of the IAASA in December 2005 are among the important developments that have taken place,[4] and there are indications that there will be further changes in relation to issues such as auditors' liability in the future. The role of an auditor in the enforcement of company law has taken on particular significance, as obligations are increasingly imposed on auditors to report suspected offences to the appropriate regulatory authorities.

(b) Appointment of auditors

[7.002] The general rule is that every company must appoint an auditor at an AGM of the company, to hold office until the next such meeting.[5] CA 1963, s 160(1) provides,

---

[1] See *Re Enron Corporation Securities* 258 F Supp 2d 576; 2003 US Dist LEXIS 3786; Fed Sec L Rep (CCH) P92,296 (SD Tex March 12, 2003) for background.

[2] See *SEC v WorldCom Inc* 273 F Supp 2d 431; 2003 US Dist LEXIS 11394; Fed Sec L Rep (CCH) P92,456 (SDNY 7 July 2003).

[3] *Report of the Review Group of Auditing* (July 2000), p 16.

[4] The incorporation of the IAASA on 20 December 2005 heralded an important development in the regulation of the auditing profession.

[5] This is subject to the qualification that certain companies may avail of an exemption from the obligation to appoint auditors. See paras **[7.129]** to **[7.132]**.

'every company shall at each annual general meeting appoint an auditor or auditors to hold office from the conclusion of that until the conclusion of the next annual general meeting.'[6]

There should be no vacancy in the office of auditor of a company. There are a number of provisions of the CA 1963–2006 designed to ensure this does not occur. First, after a company's formation and before its first AGM, its directors may appoint the company's first auditors, to hold office until the end of that first meeting.[7] If the directors fail to do so, the company in general meeting may appoint the first auditors.[8] Secondly, the general rule is that a retiring auditor will be re-appointed automatically at any AGM, without a resolution to that effect,[9] unless he is not qualified to be re-appointed; a resolution has been passed providing that he shall not be re-appointed or appointing someone else to that role;[10] or he has written to the company indicating his unwillingness to be re-appointed.

Thirdly, if a casual vacancy arises in the office of auditor (such as by reason of the death or resignation of the company's auditor) the directors or the company in general meeting may fill any such vacancy and while the vacancy continues, the surviving or continuing auditor or auditors, if such exist, may act.[11] A resolution of a general meeting to fill a casual vacancy in the office of auditor, must be notified to the company at least 28 days before the meeting and the company must give the members at least 21 days' notice of the resolution.[12] Upon receipt of such notice, the company must forthwith send a copy to the person (if any) whose cessation as auditor caused the vacancy to arise.[13]

Fourthly, if no auditor is appointed or re-appointed at a company's AGM, the company must, within one week, give the Minister notice of that fact[14] and the Minister has the power to appoint an auditor.[15] If a company fails to provide the Minister with this notice,

---

6   Note that 'The appointment of a firm by its firm name to be the auditors of a company shall be deemed to be an appointment of those persons who shall from time to time during the currency of the appointment be the partners in that firm as from time to time constituted and who are qualified to be auditors of that company' CA 1963, s 160(9).

7   CA 1963, s 160(6).

8   CA 1963, s 160(6)(b).

9   CA 1963, s 160(2).

10   Note that if the proposed replacement auditor cannot be appointed, the retiring auditor shall be automatically re-appointed. CA 1963, s 160(3) provides, 'Where notice is given of an intended resolution to appoint some other person or persons in place of a retiring auditor, and by reason of the death, incapacity or disqualification of that person or of all those persons, as the case may be, the resolution cannot be proceeded with, the retiring auditor shall not be automatically re-appointed by virtue of sub-s (2).'

11   CA 1963, s 160(7), as substituted by CA 1990, s 183.

12   CA 1963, s 161(1)(c), as substituted by CA 1990, s 184, applying CA 1963, s 142.

13   CA 1963, s 161(2)(c), as substituted by CA 1990, s 184.

14   CA 1963, s 160(5A(a)(i), as inserted by CA 1990, s 183.

15   CA 1963, s 160(4).

the company and every officer in default is guilty of an offence and liable on summary conviction to a maximum fine of €1,904.61.[16]

(c) Removal of auditors

[7.003] While the general rule is that a retiring auditor is automatically re-appointed at each AGM, there are three means by which a company may resolve otherwise. First, in the case of the first auditors of a company, being auditors appointed by the directors before the first annual general meeting of the company, the company in general meeting may remove the auditors appointed by the directors and appoint persons nominated by any member of the company, provided 14 days' notice of that nomination has been given to the members.[17]

Second, a company may pass a resolution at its AGM providing that the auditor appointed at the previous AGM shall not be re-appointed or appointing someone else to that role.[18] If it is intended to move a resolution at an AGM, to appoint a person other than the retiring auditor, or to provide that the retiring auditor shall not be re-appointed, the company must be given 28 days' notice of this resolution and the company must give the members notice of the resolution at least 21 days before the meeting.[19] Upon receipt of such notice, the company must forthwith send a copy of the notice to the retiring auditor.[20]

Third, a company may remove an auditor from office before the expiry of his term, by passing an ordinary resolution at a general meeting of the company, appointing in his place any other person who has been nominated by a member of the company. Notice of this nomination must be given to the members and the nominee must be qualified for such appointment under the CA 1963–2006.[21] In addition, the company must receive notice of this resolution at least 28 days before the general meeting; the company must forthwith send a copy of this notice to the auditor proposed to be removed;[22] and the company must provide to members at last 21 days' notice of the resolution.[23]

[7.004] If a resolution is passed removing an auditor, the company must give notice of this fact to the Registrar of Companies within 14 days of the meeting at which the

---

[16] CA 1963, s 160(5A)(b), as inserted by CA 1990, s 183 and as amended by CA 1990, s 240(7), as inserted by CLEA 2001, s 104(c).

[17] CA 1963, s 160(6)(a).

[18] Note that, if the proposed replacement auditor cannot be appointed, the retiring auditor shall be automatically re-appointed. CA 1963, s 160(3) provides, 'Where notice is given of an intended resolution to appoint some other person or persons in place of a retiring auditor, and by reason of the death, incapacity or disqualification of that person or of all those persons, as the case may be, the resolution cannot be proceeded with, the retiring auditor shall not be automatically re-appointed by virtue of sub-s (2).'

[19] CA 1963, s 161(1)(a), as substituted by CA 1990, s 184, applying CA 1963, s 142.

[20] CA 1963, s 161(2), as substituted by CA 1990, s 184.

[21] CA 1963, s 160(5), as substituted by CA 1990, s 138.

[22] CA 1963, s 161(2)(b), as substituted by CA 1990, s 184.

[23] CA 1963, s 161(1)(b), as substituted by CA 1990, s 184.

resolution was passed.[24] The form prescribed for this purpose is Form H3, which must be signed by a director or secretary of the company and must state the date on which the resolution was passed.[25] If a company fails to provide the Registrar with this notice, the company and every officer in default is guilty of an offence and liable on summary conviction to a maximum fine of €1,904.61.[26]

[7.005] There is nothing in the CA 1963–2006 which limits the grounds on which a company may remove its auditor and Form H3 does not require an explanation of the grounds on which an auditor is being removed. While an auditor who faces removal has certain rights, such as the right to attend and be heard at meetings of the company, and the right to make written representations, there is no obligation on him to do so and he has no right to require reasons to be furnished.[27] European Council Directive 2006/43/EC, which must be transposed into Irish law by 29 June 2008, contains more specific provisions in this regard.

Article 38 requires that:

> 1. Member States shall ensure that statutory auditors or audit firms may be dismissed only where there are proper grounds. Divergence of opinions on accounting treatments or audit procedures shall not be proper grounds for dismissal.
>
> 2. Member States shall ensure that the audited entity and the statutory auditor or audit firm inform the authority or authorities responsible for public oversight concerning the dismissal or resignation of the statutory auditor or audit firm during the term of appointment and give an adequate explanation of the reasons therefor.

These requirements, particularly the requirement of 'proper grounds' and 'an adequate explanation of the reasons' in respect of an auditor's removal, do not appear to be reflected in Irish law at present and it is foreseeable that more stringent measures governing the removal of auditors will be required.

(d) Auditors' rights on removal

[7.006] If an auditor is removed during his term in office, he has certain rights in respect of both the next annual general meeting of the company (the meeting at which his term would otherwise have expired) and the general meeting at which it is proposed to fill the vacancy arising from his removal.[28] First, he is entitled to receive all communications and notices regarding these meetings, which a member would be entitled to receive.[29] Second, he is entitled to attend both such meetings.[30] Third, he is

---

[24]   CA 1963, s 160(5A)(a)(ii) as inserted by CA 1990, s 183.

[25]   Form H3. Available at www.cro.ie.

[26]   CA 1963, s 160(5A)(b), as inserted by CA 1990, s 183 and as amended by CA 1990, s 240(7), as inserted by CLEA 2001, s 104(c).

[27]   See paras **[7.006]** to **[7.010]**.

[28]   CA 1963, s 161(2A), as inserted by CA 1990, s 184.

[29]   CA 1963, s 161(2A), as inserted by CA 1990, s 184.

[30]   CA 1963, s 161(2A), as inserted by CA 1990, s 184.

entitled 'to be heard at any general meeting that such a member attends on any part of the business of the meeting which concerns him as former auditor of the company.'[31]

[7.007] Section 161(3) further provides that a 'retiring auditor' may make written representations in relation to 'intended resolutions'. CA 1963, s 161(1) and (2), indicate that an 'intended resolution' encompasses:

(a) a resolution at an AGM to appoint an auditor other than 'a retiring auditor', or not to re-appoint a 'retiring auditor';

(b) a resolution at a general meeting removing an auditor before the expiry of his term; and

(c) a resolution at a general meeting filling a casual vacancy in the office of auditor.

It is only in relation to (a) that an auditor is described as a 'retiring auditor'. Section 161(1), as it existed before the enactment of CA 1990, referred only to '... a resolution at a company's annual general meeting appointing as auditor a person other than a retiring auditor or providing expressly that a retiring auditor shall not be re-appointed.' Despite the amendments to s 161(1) in 1990 to introduce categories (b) and (c) above, s 161(3) has not been amended and, from its wording, continues to apply only to retiring auditors who face resolutions not to be re-appointed, or to be replaced at a company's AGM.

[7.008] This narrow interpretation has been overcome by both CA 1963, s 161(5), and CA 1990, s 184(2). Section 161(5) provides that, 'sub-ss (3) and (4) shall apply to a resolution to remove the first auditors by virtue of sub-s (6) of s 160 as they apply in relation to a resolution that a retiring auditor shall not be re-appointed.' Section 184(2) provides, 'The reference in sub-s (5) of the said s 161 to a resolution to remove the first auditors by virtue of sub-s (6) of s 160 of the Principal Act shall be construed as including a reference to a resolution to remove an auditor other than the first auditors before the expiration of his term of office.' The provisions applicable to written representations therefore apply to first auditors and subsequently appointed auditors, who face resolutions of the company in general meeting, to remove them as auditors, as well as to retiring auditors who face resolutions not to be re-appointed or to be replaced.

[7.009] The right to make written representations in relation to the intended resolution, consists of the right to make representations which do not exceed 'a reasonable length', requesting they be notified to the members. Provided these representations are not received too late to do so, the company shall include with the notice to members of the intended resolution, a statement that the auditor has made written representations, and shall further send a copy of the representations to every member entitled to notice of the meeting.[32]

If copies of the representations are not sent to the members, either because they are received too late, or due to default on the company's part, the auditor may further require that the representations be read out at the meeting.[33]

---

[31] CA 1963, s 161(2A), as inserted by CA 1990, s 184.

[32] CA 1963, s 161(3).

[33] CA 1963, s 161(3).

[7.010] The company or any person who claims to be aggrieved by the representations, may apply to court for an order that the written representations do not need to be distributed or read out at the company's meeting.[34] Before granting such an order the court must be satisfied that the auditor's rights to make written representations are 'being abused to secure needless publicity for defamatory matter.'[35] In addition to ordering that the representations not be disseminated or read out at the meeting, the court may also order the auditor to pay the company's costs on the application in whole or in part, in spite of the fact that the auditor is not a party to the application.[36] It is interesting to note that the court has no power to order the auditor to pay the costs of any other aggrieved party who may bring a successful application to court to prevent the oral or written publication of the written representations.

(e) Resignation of auditors

[7.011] An auditor of a company can resign as such by serving a notice in writing on the company.[37] The notice of resignation will take effect upon the date of service or such later date as it specifies.[38] He may also resign by serving a notice on the company of his unwillingness to be re-appointed at the company's AGM.[39]

The resigning auditor must send a copy of the notice to the Registrar of Companies within 14 days after sending it to the company.[40] The notice must either state that there are no circumstances connected with the resignation that the auditor considers should be brought to the attention of the company's members and creditors; or it must contain a statement of any such circumstances.[41] The latter will be referred to as a 's 185(2)(b) notice'. It is an offence for an auditor to fail to comply with the requirements regarding the content of the notice and its delivery to the Registrar.[42]

If the notice is a s 185(2)(b) notice, the company must, within 14 days of the service of that notice on the company, send a copy of it to every person who is entitled to receive notice of the company's general meetings and every member and holder of debenture of the company (whether or not entitled to notice of general meetings).[43] It is an offence for the company and every officer in default if there is a failure to distribute this notice.[44]

---

[34] CA 1963, s 161(4).

[35] CA 1963, s 161(4).

[36] CA 1963, s 161(4).

[37] CA 1990, s 185(1).

[38] CA 1990, s 185(1).

[39] CA 1963, s 160(2)(c). The provisions of CA 1990, s 185 are applied to s 160(2)(c) by means of CA 1990, s 185(5).

[40] CA 1990, s 185(3)(a).

[41] CA 1990, s 185(2).

[42] CA 1990, s 185(6).

[43] CA 1990, s 185(3)(b), applying CA 1963, s 159. This is subject to CA 1990, s 185(4).

[44] CA 1990, s 185(7).

[7.012] If a company or other person who claims to be aggrieved, does not wish the notice to be sent to the members, debenture holders and other persons entitled to notice of the general meetings, they may make an application to court to excuse the company from the duty to make such distribution.[45] If the court is satisfied that the notice 'contains material which has been included to secure needless publicity for defamatory matter,' it may order that the notice does not need to be sent to such persons. The court may also order the auditor to pay the company's costs on the application in whole or in part, the fact that the auditor is not a party to the application notwithstanding.[46] The court has no power to order the auditor to pay the costs of an aggrieved party other than the company who may bring a successful application under s 185.

[7.013] An important power of a resigning auditor is the power to requisition a general meeting.[47] If an auditor sends a s 185(2)(b) notice, the auditor may also requisition the convening of a meeting by the directors of the company 'for the purpose of receiving and considering such account and explanation of the circumstances connected with his resignation from the office of auditor to the company as he may wish to give to the meeting.'[48] If an auditor makes such a requisition, the directors are obliged to convene a meeting within 14 days of the service of the notice on the company under s 185, with the meeting to be held within a period of 28 days of such service.[49] If there is a default in this regard, the company and every director who is in default, is guilty of an offence.[50]

[7.014] If an auditor serves a s 185(2)(b) notice, he may prepare a further statement in writing connected with his resignation, that he considers should be brought to the attention of the company's members.[51] He may then request the company to circulate this statement to its members before:[52]

- the next general meeting at which the auditor's term would otherwise expire;

- any general meeting at which it is proposed to fill the vacancy created by his resignation; or

- a general meeting convened in accordance with a requisition from the auditor under s 186(1).

The company must then, in the notice of the meeting that is sent to its members, state the fact that the statement was made and must further send a copy of this statement to every person entitled to receive notice of the company's general meetings, every member and debenture holder (whether or not entitled to notice of the general meetings) and to the

---

[45] CA 1990, s 185(4).

[46] CA 1990, s 185(4).

[47] CA 1990, s 186.

[48] CA 1990, s 186(1).

[49] CA 1990, s 186(2).

[50] CA 1990, s 186(6).

[51] CA 1990, s 186(3).

[52] CA 1990, s 186(3)(b).

Registrar of Companies.[53] No time limit is specified for this distribution. However, if there is a default in this regard, the company and every officer in default is guilty of an offence.[54]

[7.015] The company does, however, have some recourse against the duty to notify its members of, or to circulate, a resigning auditor's statement. If the company or another aggrieved party makes an application to court and establishes to the satisfaction of the court that the auditor's right to make a statement was 'being abused to secure needless publicity for defamatory matter,' the court will relieve the company of the duty to circulate the statement.[55] The court may, moreover, order that the auditor pay the company's costs of the application (but not those of the other aggrieved party), in whole or in part.

[7.016] With regard to the meetings of the company, the resigning auditor has a right to attend the AGM at which his term of office would have expired but for his resignation; the meeting at which the appointment of a replacement auditor is discussed; and the meeting which was requisitioned by the resigning auditor. He is also entitled to receive such notices and communications regarding these meetings, as any member would be entitled to receive.[56] Finally, a resigning auditor is entitled to be heard on any part of the business of such meetings which concern him as the company's former auditor.[57] If a resigning auditor is not accorded any of these rights to attend, be heard at, and receive notices and communications regarding, company meetings, the company and every officer in default is guilty of an offence.[58]

(f) Remuneration of auditors

[7.017] An auditor's remuneration may be fixed by the directors (or by the Minister, if the auditor is appointed by the Minister) and, subject to this, shall be fixed by the company at its AGM, or 'in such manner as the company at the annual general meeting may determine.'[59] Any sums which are paid to an auditor by way of expenses are deemed to be included in the term 'remuneration'.

B. Auditor's report

(a) General

[7.018] The main function of an auditor is to examine and prepare a report on a company's accounts. This is an important assurance to the members of a company that

---

53   CA 1990, s 186(3)(b), applying CA 1963, s 159.

54   CA 1990, s 186(6).

55   CA 1990, s 186(4).

56   CA 1990, s 186(5).

57   CA 1990, s 186(5).

58   CA 1990, s 186(6).

59   CA 1963, s 160(8).

the company's accounts have been prepared properly and accurately reflect the company's financial situation.

The importance of a company's accounts being examined by a duly appointed auditor has been highlighted in enforcement cases taken by the ODCE. By way of example, an individual who falsely represented a company's financial statements to a bank as having been audited was prosecuted in the District Court under CA 1990, s 243, fined and ordered to pay costs. The ODCE commented:

> 'We were particularly anxious in this case to uphold the integrity of audited financial statements. An auditor's opinion provides valuable independent assurance for the public at large of the state of affairs of a company. We cannot tolerate a director representing a set of financial statements as having been audited by a recognised firm of auditors when this was not the case.'[60]

The ODCE has also prosecuted a number of individuals who filed annual returns with the CRO, and falsely represented the financial statements attached thereto as having been audited, or attached false auditors' reports to the returns.[61] The ODCE emphasised the importance of auditor's reports as follows:

> 'The ODCE will continue to give priority to the investigation and prosecution of cases involving the provision of materially false information in purported compliance with a provision of the Companies Acts due to the potential impact which these practices have for increasing market risk for all company stakeholders.'[62]

An auditor's report must be prepared in relation to the company's individual accounts which are examined by the auditors, and every balance sheet, profit and loss account, income statement, and group account, which are laid before the company in general meeting during the auditors' tenure in office.[63] The auditors' report must be read at the company's annual general meeting and must be open to inspection by every member of the company.[64]

(b) Content

[7.019] The auditors' report must begin with an introduction identifying the individual accounts and, where appropriate, the group accounts that are the subject of the audit; the financial reporting framework applied;[65] and it must describe the scope of the audit and the auditing standards applied.[66] The report must then contain certain statements and

---

[60] ODCE, 'First ODCE Conviction Secured for Falsely Representing Company Financial Statements as having been audited,' 19 January 2006. Available at www.odce.ie.

[61] There were two prosecutions in 2005, and two in 2006, arising from the filing of financial statements with the CRO which were falsely represented as having been audited, contrary to s 242, CA 1990. See ODCE, *Annual Report 2006* at p 21. Available at www.odce.ie.

[62] *ODCE Annual Report 2006* at p 21. Available at www.odce.ie.

[63] CA 1990, s 193(1).

[64] CA 1990, s 193(2).

[65] CA 1990, s 193(4)(a), as substituted by EC(IFRSMA)R 2005, reg 8.

[66] CA 1990, s 193(4)(b), as substituted by EC(IFRSMA)R 2005, reg 8.

opinions and must be signed and dated by the auditors.[67] It is notable that certain matters on which the auditors were previously required to provide their opinion, must now be the subject of statements, without any qualification as to the 'opinion' of the auditors.[68]

The auditors must state their opinion as to the following:

- whether the annual accounts have been properly prepared in accordance with the Companies Acts and, if applicable, the IAS Regulation;[69]

- in the case of a company which does come under Pt III of the Sixth Schedule to the CA 1963, whether the annual accounts (or group accounts, if applicable) have been properly prepared in accordance with the Companies Acts and, if applicable, art 4 of the IAS Regulations,[70] and give a true and fair view of the state of the company's affairs and its profit and loss for the yea;[71]

---

[67] CA 1990, s 193(4D)(a), as inserted by EC(IFRSMA)R 2005, reg 8.

[68] See, in particular, CA 1990, s 193(4C)(i), as substituted by EC(IFRSMA)R 2005, reg 8, which requires particular statements as to whether the annual accounts give a true and fair view of the company's affairs, profits and losses. As previously formulated, s 193(4)(e) required the auditors to state '... whether, in their opinion, the company's balance sheet and profit and loss account and (if it is a holding company submitting group accounts) the group accounts have been properly prepared in accordance with the provisions of the Companies Acts and give a true and fair view ...' of the company's affairs and profits and losses (emphasis added). The reference to 'opinion' does not appear in s 193(4C)(i).

[69] CA 1990, s 193(4A)(a), as inserted by EC (IFRSMA)R 2005, reg 8 (this subsection does not apply to companies which have availed of Pt III of the Sixth Schedule of the CA 1963, such as banking or discount companies and assurance companies). The 'IAS' Regulations refers to Regulation (EC) 1606/2002, on the application of international accounting standards, which is implemented in Ireland by EC(IFRSMA)R 2005.

[70] Regulation (EC) 1606/2002 provides that, 'For each financial year starting on or after 1 January 2005, companies governed by the law of a Member State shall prepare their consolidated accounts in conformity with the international accounting standards adopted in accordance with the procedure laid down in art 6(2) if, at their balance sheet date, their securities are admitted to trading on a regulated market of any Member State within the meaning of art 1(13) of Council Directive 93/22/EEC of 10 May 1993 on investment services in the securities field.'

[71] CA 1990, s 193(4A)(b), as inserted by EC(IFRSMA)R 2005, reg 8. Note that this provision refers to the requirement that the auditors' report in the case of companies within the scope of CA 1963, Sch 6, Pt III, must state whether the annual and group accounts, 'give a true and fair view of the matters referred to in sub-s (4B)(e)(i) and (ii) and, where appropriate, sub-s (4B)(e)(iii) subject to the non-disclosure of any matters (to be indicated in the report) which by virtue of the said Part III are not required to be disclosed.' There is no s 193(4B)(e) in the CA 1990. No sub-s (4B)(e) appears in the IAS Regulations, in the EC(IFRSMA)R 2005, or in CA 1963, Sch 6, Pt III. The only sub-s (4)(e) that could be referred to is s 193(4)(e), as it existed before the introduction of EC(IFRSMA)R 2005. CA 1990, s 193(4)(e) formerly required an auditors' report to state, 'except in the case of a company that has taken advantage of any of the provisions of Part III of the Sixth Schedule to The Principal Act, whether, in their opinion, the company's balance sheet and profit and loss account and (if it is a holding company submitting group accounts) the group accounts have been properly prepared in accordance with the provisions of the Companies Acts and give a true and fair view— (cont .../

–   whether proper books of account have been kept by the company;[72]

–   whether proper returns adequate for their audit were received from any branches of the company that the auditor did not visit;[73] and

–   whether there existed at the balance sheet date a financial situation which under C(A)A 1983, s 40(1) would require an extraordinary general meeting to be convened (ie that the net assets of the company are half or less than half of the company's called-up share capital at the balance sheet date).[74]

[7.020] The auditors' report must also state:

–   whether, to the best of their knowledge and belief, the auditor obtained all of the information and explanations that are necessary for the audit;[75]

–   whether the company's balance sheet and profit and loss account are in agreement with the books of accounts and returns;[76]

–   whether the individual balance sheet gives a true and fair view in accordance with the relevant financial reporting network, of the state of the affairs of the company at the end of the financial year;[77]

–   whether the individual profit and loss account gives a true and fair view in accordance with the relevant financial reporting framework, of the profit or loss of the company for the financial year;[78]

–   whether, in the case of group accounts having been submitted, such accounts give a true and fair view in accordance with the relevant financial reporting network, of the state of affairs at the end of the financial year, and of profit and loss for the financial year of the undertakings included in the consolidation as a whole, so far as it concerns members of the company.[79]

---

[71]   (cont) (i) in the case of the balance sheet, of the state of the company's affairs as at the end of its financial year, (ii) in the case of the profit and loss account (if it is not framed as a consolidated profit and loss account), of the company's profit and loss for its financial year, (iii) in the case of group accounts submitted by a holding company, of the state of affairs and profit or loss of the company and its subsidiaries dealt with thereby, so far as concerns members of the company.' If EC(IFRSMA)R 2005, intends to include a reference in the new s 193(4A)(b) to aspects of s 193 as it existed before the amendment, this would be anomalous and render the interpretation of the provision difficult. The only alternative, and most likely, interpretation, is that the reference to sub-s (4B)(e) in s 193(4A)(b) is wholly erroneous, and s 193(4A)(b) should refer to sub-s (4C)(i)(I), (II), and (III).

[72]   CA 1990, s 193(4B)(b), as inserted by EC(IFRSMA)R 2005, reg 8.

[73]   CA 1990, s 193(4B)(c), as inserted by EC(IFRSMA)R 2005, reg 8.

[74]   CA 1990, s 193(4C)(ii), as inserted by EC(IFRSMA)R 2005, reg 8.

[75]   CA 1990, s 193(4B)(a), as inserted by EC(IFRSMA)R 2005, reg 8.

[76]   CA 1990, s 193(4B)(d), as inserted by EC(IFRSMA)R 2005, reg 8.

[77]   CA 1990, s 193(4C)(i)(I), as inserted by EC(IFRSMA)R 2005, reg 8.

[78]   CA 1990, s 193(4C)(i)(II), as inserted by EC(IFRSMA)R 2005, reg 8.

[79]   CA 1990, s 193(4C)(i)(III), as inserted by EC(IFRSMA)R 2005, reg 8.

(c) Qualifications or adverse opinions

[7.021] In relation to each matter that must be addressed in the report, the statement or opinion furnished must be either qualified or unqualified.[80] A statement or opinion may be qualified 'where there is a disagreement or limitation in scope of work.'[81] Where an opinion or statement is qualified, this can go so far as to consist of an adverse opinion or a disclaimer of the opinion set out in the report. If, on the other hand, there are matters to which the auditors wish attention to be drawn, without qualifying the report, they must include a reference to any such matters by way of emphasis.[82]

[7.022] The Auditing Practices Board ('APB'), a body which prepares standards and guidance for auditors in Ireland and the United Kingdom, issued a Bulletin in 2006 to assist auditors in drafting reports in light of the changes to the Companies Acts. According to the APB, matters to be emphasised, without affecting the report, include matters such as litigation, the effect of which could not be quantified financially. Items which could warrant a qualified opinion include disagreement regarding the accounting treatment of debtors; a qualification in a prior period which remains unresolved and requires a modification of the report; or a qualification arising from a limitation as to scope, such as the auditor not being appointed during a relevant stock take. A disclaimer in the report would arise if an auditor was unable to physically observe the stock or to confirm the trade debtors; or if there are multiple material or significant uncertainties. According to the APB, an adverse opinion would be warranted if, for example, no provision is made for losses expected to arise on certain long term contracts; or if there is a significant level of concern about the company's ability to continue as a going concern that is not disclosed in the financial statements, and the financial statements have been prepared on a 'going concern' basis.[83]

(d) Further considerations

[7.023] There are certain other matters that must be considered in an auditor's report under CA 1990, s 193. By way of example, an auditor is obliged to consider whether the information given in the directors' report, under CA 1963, s 158, in relation to the company's financial year, is consistent with the company's accounts for that year. The auditor must state their opinion as to whether the information given in the directors' report is consistent with the reports.[84]

An auditor must also consider whether the accounts display particulars of the directors' salaries and payments made to directors in compliance with CA 1963, s 191. If these requirements are not complied with, it is the duty of the company's auditor to include in their report on the company's balance sheet a statement giving the required particulars, insofar as they are reasonably able to do so.[85]

---

[80] CA 1990, s 193(4D)(b), as inserted by EC(IFRSMA)R 2005, reg 8.

[81] CA 1990, s 193(4E), as inserted by EC(IFRSMA)R 2005, reg 8.

[82] CA 1990, s 193(4D)(c), as inserted by EC(IFRSMA)R 2005, reg 8.

[83] Auditing Practices Board, 'Auditors' Reports on Financial Statements in the Republic of Ireland', *Bulletin* 2006/1, 1 January 2006. App 2 at p 56 and App 3 at p 73.

[84] C(A)A 1986, s 15, as amended by EC(IFRSMA)R 2005, reg 5.

[85] CA 1963, s 191(8).

[7.024] A further matter which an auditor must address in his report under s 193 is the requirement in CA 1990, s 46, that an auditor must consider whether group accounts which he is auditing comply with the requirement to disclose information regarding substantial contracts, loans, credit agreements, guarantees, and other such transactions, with directors or persons connected with directors. If these requirements, as specified in CA 1990, ss 41 and 43, are not met, the auditor examining those group or other accounts, must include in their report on the balance sheet of the company, insofar as they are reasonably able to, a statement containing the requisite particulars.[86]

[7.025] A final example of a matter which an auditor must address is set out in reg 38 of the EC(Companies: Group Accounts) Regs 1992 as follows:

> it shall be the duty of auditors of a parent undertaking, in preparing the report on group accounts required by s 193 of the Companies Act 1990, to consider whether the information given in the report of the directors on the state of affairs of the parent undertaking and its subsidiary undertakings, as a group, relating to the financial year concerned is consistent with the group accounts for that year and they shall state in the report whether, in their opinion, such information is consistent with those accounts.

In furnishing a report, an auditor should be mindful of the fact that he owes a general duty of care regarding the conduct of the audit and this extends wholly to the preparation of the report.[87] As provided in s 193(6): 'A person who is appointed as auditor of a company or as a public auditor shall be under a general duty to carry out such audit with professional integrity.' It has been held in this regard that, '[a]n auditor must not form an opinion on unverified representations.'[88] It is also established law that, 'auditors cannot be justified in making a report containing a statement the truth of which they have not had the opportunity of ascertaining.' They 'must either refuse to make a report at all or make an appropriately qualified report.'[89]

(e) Special Auditor's Report

[7.026] Certain companies are not obliged to append annual accounts to their annual return and must instead attach a special auditor's report to the annual return. These companies are the following:

(i) a private company which is not trading for the acquisition of gain by its members;[90]

---

86   CA 1990, s 46.

87   See *Caparo Industries plc v Dickman* [1990] BCLC 273, 282, [1990] 2 AC 605; *Kelly v Haughey Boland* (30 July 1985, unreported), HC, Lardner J; *Candler v Crane Christmas* [1951] 1 All ER 426.

88   *Berg Sons & Co Ltd v Mervyn Hampton Adams & Ors* [1993] BCLC 1045, 1073.

89   *Re Thomas Gerrard* [1967] 2 All ER 525, [1968] Ch 455 (*per* Pennycuick J). See also *Candler v Crane Christmas* [1951] 1 All ER 426.

90   CA 1963, s 128(4)(a) and (6A)(a), as inserted by C(AA)A 2003, s 47, and C(A)A 1986, s 2(1)(a).

(ii)   a charitable company without share capital, under the control of a recognised
       religion;[91] and

(iii) a charitable company without share capital, to which the Commissioners of
       Charitable Donations and Bequests for Ireland has granted an exempted from
       the requirement to annex to its annual return, the company's accounts and an
       auditor's report.[92]

In respect of these companies the auditor must prepare a separate report to the directors
confirming that they audited the accounts for the relevant year and this report must
include the report made to the members under s 193 (the so-called 'special auditor's
report').[93] This report must then be certified by the directors and the secretary of the
company to be a true copy and must be attached to any annual return which is delivered
to the CRO by such companies.[94]

[7.027] In the case of medium or small companies which avail of the right to append
abridged accounts to the annual return, but which do not have an audit exemption, a
special auditor's report must also be prepared, certified by the directors and secretary
and delivered to the Registrar with the abridged accounts.[95] This report must state that,
in the opinion of the auditor, the directors are entitled to annex abridged accounts to the
annual return and that the abridged accounts have been properly prepared.[96] It must be
accompanied by a copy of the auditor's report to the members under CA 1990, s 193.[97]

C. Integrity and independence

(a) Qualifications

(i) Recognition

[7.028] CA 1990, s 187 sets out the specific qualifications that a person must possess in
order to be appointed to act as auditor. The actions of the ODCE to date indicate a
determination to enforce the qualification requirements that company law imposes on

---

91   CA 1963, s 128(4)(c), and (6A)(b), as inserted by C(AA)A 2003, s 47, and C(A)A 1986,
     s 2(1)(b), applying CA 1963, s 128(4)(c). (Such a company must also 'exercise its functions
     in accordance with the laws, canons, and ordinances of the religion concerned.')

92   CA 1963, s 128(5)(a) and (6A)(c), as inserted by C(AA)A 2003, s 47, and C(A)A 1986,
     s 2(1)(c), applying CA 1963, s 128(5).

93   CA 1963, s 128(6B), as inserted by C(AA)A 2003, s 47 and as amended by IFCMPA 2005,
     s 61.

94   CA 1963, s 128(6C), as inserted by C(AA)A 2003, s 47.

95   C(A)A 1986, s 18(3) and (5), as substituted by EC(IFRSMA)R 2005, reg 5.

96   C(A)A 1986, s 18(4), as substituted by EC(IFRSMA)R 2005, reg 5.

97   C(A)A 1986, s 18(3), as substituted by EC(IFRSMA)R 2005, reg 5.

auditors practising in Ireland, so it is important to be mindful of these requirements. The qualifications that an individual must possess to act as an auditor are as follows:

- he must be a member of a body of accountants recognised by the IAASA and hold a valid practising certificate from such body;[98]
- he must hold an accountancy qualification which is, in the opinion of the IAASA, of a standard not less than that required by a recognised body of accountants, which would entitle him to a practising certificate by that body, if he were a member, and he is authorised for the time being by the IAASA;[99] or
- he was, on 31 December 1990, a member of body of accountants recognised under CA 1963, and holds a valid practising certificate from such body;[100]
- he was authorised by the Minister to so act before 3 February 1983, and is for the time being authorised by the IAASA;[101]
- he holds a qualification from another state which the IAASA has declared to qualify him for appointment in Ireland and is for the time being authorised by the IAASA to act;[102] or
- he was undergoing training on 1 January 1990, within the meaning of Council Directive 84/253/EC.[103]

---

[98] CA 1990, s 187(1)(a)(i), as amended by C(AA)A 2003, s 32(1) and Sch 1. Section 32 and Sch 1 were commenced by Companies (Auditing and Accounting) Act 2003 (Commencement) Order 2006, SI 56/2006. The bodies recognised by the IAASA for the purposes of CA 1990, s 191, are the Institute of Chartered Accountants in Ireland; Institute of Chartered Accountants in England and Wales; the Institute of Chartered Accountants of Scotland; the Institute of Certified Public Accountants in Ireland; the Association of Chartered Certified Accountants; and the Institute of Incorporated Public Accountants.

[99] CA 1990, s 187(1)(a)(ii), as amended by C(AA)A 2003, s 32(1) and Sch 1.

[100] CA 1990, s 187(1)(a)(iii), as amended by CLEA 2001, s 72(a) and C(AA)A 2003, s 32(1) and Sch 1. Note that pursuant to CA 1990 (Auditors) Regulations 1992, reg 3, 'Sub-para (iii) of s 187(1)(a) of the Act shall not be regarded as having been complied with by a person appointed to be the auditor of a company or a public auditor unless, both on the 31st day of December, 1990, and on the date of such appointment, he was a member of a body referred to in that subparagraph and on the later date he held a valid practising certificate from that body.'

[101] CA 1990, s 187(1)(a)(iv), as substituted by C(AA)A 2003, s 32(1) and Sch 1. Note that these so-called 'grandfather rights' originate from the fact that the then Minister for Industry and Commerce was permitted under CA 1963, s 162, to authorise individual persons to be company auditors subject to certain conditions. This power was withdrawn by C(A)A 1982, s 6, which became effective on 3 February 1983.

[102] CA 1990, s 187(1)(a)(vi), applying CA 1990, s 189, as amended by C(AA)A 2003, s 32(1) and Sch 1.

[103] The relevant provision of the so called 'Eight Company Law Directive' (since repealed and replaced by Council Directive 2006/46/EC) was art 18, which provided in material part: 'For six years after the application of the provisions referred to in art 30(2), Member States may apply transitional measures in respect of persons already undergoing professional or practical training when those provisions are applied who, on completion of their training, would not fulfil the conditions imposed by this Directive and would therefore be unable to carry out statutory audits of the documents referred to in art 1(1) for which they had been trained.' (contd .../)

[7.029] Persons who were granted individual authorisations by the Minister to act as auditors before 3 February 1983, within the meaning of s 187(1)(a)(iv) are referred to as 'individually recognised' auditors for the purpose of the register of auditors that is maintained by the Registrar of Companies. The Review Group on Auditing commented on the problem of 'individually authorised' auditors, as the Group referred to them, who were granted such authorisation before the enactment of CA 1990, and who are not members of a recognised body of accountants (so-called 'grandfather rights'). The Group noted:

> '... that it was unsatisfactory that the individual auditors who are not members of a recognised accountancy body but who were authorised prior to 3 February, 1983 by the then Minister are not subject to any regular monitoring. Even if the numbers involved are only about 50 at this time, the Review Group is of the opinion that the absence of ongoing regulation in this area should be resolved in the public interest.'[104]

The Group noted the experience in England, where there were several thousand individually authorised auditors. Part of the solution adopted was that these persons were compelled to join a recognised accountancy body, which led to the formation and recognition of the Association of Authorised Public Accountants (AAPA), which subsequently became a subsidiary of the Association of Chartered Certified Accountants (ACCA).[105] In relation to the situation in Ireland, where the number of individually authorised auditors is significantly fewer, the Review Group made the following recommendation:

> 'The Review Group does not consider the UK approach to be a practical option having regard to the small numbers involved and the likelihood that some of them at least may not be very active auditors at this stage. Having made enquiries, the Review Group is nevertheless satisfied that a number of the present recognised accountancy bodies would be prepared to consider applications for membership or regulation from individually authorised auditors. Having taken legal advice, the Group is satisfied that:
>
> • it would be a reasonable use of statutory power to compel individually authorised auditors either to become members of recognised accountancy bodies or at a minimum to be regulated by them;
>
> • an individual authorisation could be suspended or revoked for failure to comply or to meet the body's competency and other standards for the conduct of audit work; and
>
> • such a move was unlikely to be regarded as constitutionally objectionable by the Courts.
>
> The Review Group appreciates that there may be situations where an individually authorised auditor may not immediately attain the present standards required by the body for the issue or continuance of an audit practising certificate. Clearly,

---

[103] (contd) To come within this category, the person must also have been admitted to membership of a body of accountants which is recognised by the IAASA before 1 January 1996, and have subsequently been awarded a practising certificate which remains valid. CA 1990, s 187(1)(a)(v), applying CA 1990, s 190.

[104] *Report of the Review Group on Auditing* at p 159.

[105] *Report of the Review Group on Auditing* at p 159.

some period of grace (say three years) should be permitted to the individual to reach the acceptable auditing standards, before any final decision is made to suspend or withdraw his/her individual authorisation.'[106]

[7.030] The C(AA)A 2003 enacts this recommendation in the form of a new s 187(14) and (15), which provide:

(14) An authorisation granted to a person under sub-s (1)(a)(iv) ceases to have effect on the expiry of three years after the commencement of this subsection unless, within that three year period, the person becomes a member of, or becomes subject to the regulations of, a body of accountants recognised for the purposes of s 187.

(15) On an authorisation ceasing to have effect under sub-s (14), the person to whom it was granted ceases to be qualified for appointment as auditor of a company or as a public auditor.[107]

It should be noted that this three year grace period will only run from the commencement of these new subsections. As of October 2007, C(AA)A 2003, s 35 has not been commenced.

[7.031] There is another category of individual authorisations provided for by CA 1990. Section 187(1)(a)(vi) refers to persons to whom s 189 applies and who are 'for the time being authorised by the Supervisory Authority to so act.'[108] Section 189 applies to persons who are hold qualifications which entitle them to act as auditors, or qualifications which are recognised as such, in another country and provides that the IAASA (formerly the Minister) may declare such persons to be qualified in Ireland, subject to the conditions stipulated in that provision. This provision implements Council Directive 89/48/EEC, which provides for the mutual recognition of higher education qualifications among Member States. The Review Group on Auditing describes this category of qualification as follows:

'Despite the withdrawal of the right of individual authorisation by the Minister in the 1982 Act, this power had to be re-introduced on foot of Directive 89/48/EEC of 21 December, 1988 which provides for the mutual recognition by EU Member States of certain higher education qualifications. Thus, an auditor recognised in one Member State had to be capable of being recognised to provide services as an auditor in another Member State. However, the Directive permits the Member State in which a person wishes to achieve authorisation to impose tests to ensure that he/she is fully conversant with local taxation and company law. This power was transposed into Irish law under s 187(1)(a)(vi) of the Companies Act, 1990, and requests for authorisation under the Companies Acts are addressed to the Minister for Enterprise, Trade and Employment.'[109]

---

[106] *Report of the Review Group on Auditing* at p 160.

[107] CA 1990, s 187(14) and (15), as inserted by C(AA)A 2003, s 35(c).

[108] CA 1990, s 187(1)(a)(vi), as amended by C(AA)A 2003, s 32(1) and Sch 1.

[109] *Report of the Review Group on Auditing* at p 160. It is interesting to note the Report's finding that, 'no such persons have been authorised to date under this provision. The Review Group understands that any persons who have enquired about the matter have been encouraged by the Department to become a member of a recognised accountancy body.'

(ii) Register of Auditors

[7.032] In respect of each of the means by which a person may be qualified for appointment as an auditor, it is also necessary that particulars about that person have been delivered to the Registrar of Companies.[110] Unless this has been done, he will not be qualified for appointment as an auditor. The particulars that must be delivered to the Registrar are the following:

- a body of accountants which attains the recognition of the IAASA[111] must deliver to the Registrar, within one month of such recognition, the names and addresses of each of its members who are qualified for appointment as auditors;[112]

- a body of accountants based outside the State, the recognition of which is continued by the C(AA)A 2003,[113] or granted under CA 1990, s 191, must notify the Registrar of the names of its members who wish to practice in the State;[114]

---

[110] CA 1990, s 187(1)(b).

[111] Note that recognition by the IAASA is governed by CA 1990, s 191, as substituted by C(AA)A 2003, Sch 1, which provides, 'The Supervisory Authority may grant recognition to a body of accountants but only if satisfied— (a) that the standards relating to training, qualifications and repute required by that body for the awarding of a practising certificate to a person are not less than those specified in arts 3 to 6, 8 and 19 of the Council Directive, and (b) as to the standards that body applies to its members in the areas of ethics, codes of conduct and practice, independence, professional integrity, auditing and accounting standards and investigation and disciplinary procedures.' Note that the Council Directive referred to, Council Directive 84/253/EEC has been repealed and replaced by Council Directive 2006/46/EC, which must be transposed into Irish law by 29 June 2008.

[112] CA 1990, s 199(1), as substituted by C(AA)A 2003, s 39(a). Note that, as of August 2007, C(AA)A 2003, s 39 has not been commenced. However, the current formulation of CA 1990, s 199(1) is similar in effect. ('(1) Subject to sub-s (2), a body of accountants whose recognition has been renewed by the Minister under section 191(1) or which has been recognised under section 191(3) shall, within one month after such renewal or recognition, deliver to the registrar of companies the name and address of each of its members who is qualified for appointment under the Companies Acts as auditor of a company or as a public auditor.')

[113] C(AA)A 2003, s 32(2), provides in this regard, 'Subject to sub-ss (3) to (5), each body that was a recognised body of accountants immediately before the commencement of this section is a recognised accountancy body immediately after the commencement of this section.' This provision was commenced by Companies (Auditing and Accounting) Act 2003 (Commencement) Order 2006, SI 56/2006.

[114] CA 1990, s 199(2), as amended by C(AA)A 2003, s 39(b). Note that as of August 2007, C(AA)A 2003, s 39 has not been commenced, but the amendment is inconsequential, as it merely incorporates a reference to s 32(2) (it substitutes 'whose recognition is continued under section 32(2) of the Act of 2003' for 'whose recognition is renewed'). CA 1990, s 200(2) similarly provides, 'Without prejudice to the generality of sub-s (1), a recognised body of accountant based outside the State shall notify details of those of its members who wish to practise in the State.'

– if a person becomes qualified for appointment as an auditor, by virtue of his membership of a recognised body of accountants, that body must, within one month of his qualification, deliver his name and address to the Registrar;[115]

– as soon as possible and, at the latest, within six months, a recognised body of accountants must notify the Registrar of any change in the particulars previously delivered to him.[116]

In addition to preventing the individual being qualified to act as an auditor, it is also an offence for the body of accountants to fail to comply with the applicable notification requirements.[117]

[7.033] If a person was given an individual authorisation by the Minister to act as an auditor before the date of commencement of CA 1990, otherwise than through membership of a recognised body of accountants, his name must appear on a register kept by the Registrar of Companies.[118] The following notification requirements apply to such individuals:

– he must have delivered to the Registrar within one month of the commencement of the Act, his name and address;[119]

---

[115] CA 1990, s 200(1).

[116] CA 1990, s 199(2A), as inserted by C(AA)A 2003, s 39(c). CA 1990, s 200(2A) as inserted by C(AA)A 2003, s 40(a) similarly provides, 'A body of accountants referred to in sub-s (1) or a recognised body of accountants referred to in sub-s (2) shall, as soon as possible but not later than six months after the event, notify the registrar of companies of any change in the particulars previously provided to him under the applicable sub-s.' Note that, as of August 2007, neither C(AA)A 2003, s 39 nor s 40 were commenced. However, the CA 1990 (Auditors) Regulations 1992, reg 7(1)(a) provides in similar terms that ss 199 and 200 shall be construed as 'requiring a body of accountants referred to therein, to notify the registrar of companies of any change in the particulars previously furnished to him pursuant to those sections, as soon as may be, but not later than six months after its occurrence.' While the CA 1990 (Auditors) Regulations 1992 are repealed by C(AA)A 2003, s 59, that provision has not, as of August 2007, been commenced. It may be expected that C(AA)A 2003, ss 39, 40, and 59, would be commenced contemporaneously and effectively enshrine the provisions of the 1992 Regulations as primary legislation. This, however, is subject to the qualification that Council Directive 84/253/EEC, which the 1992 Regulations implemented, has now been repealed and replaced by Council Directive 2006/46/EC, which must be transposed into Irish law by 29 June 2008.

[117] CA 1990, s 199(4), as substituted by C(AA)A 2003, s 39(e), provides, 'If default is made in complying with sub-s (1) or (2A), the body of accountants concerned shall be guilty of an offence.' Note that, while s 39 was not commenced as of October 2007, its predecessor provided in materially similar terms, 'If default is made in complying with sub-s (1), the body of accountants concerned shall be guilty of an offence.' CA 1990, s 200(4) (which was identical in terms to s 199(4)), has also been substituted by C(AA)A 2003, s 40(c), which provides 'If default is made in complying with sub-s (1) or (2A), the body of accountants concerned, or the recognised body of accountants concerned, shall be guilty of an offence.' C(AA)A 2003, s 40(c) has not, as of October 2007, been commenced.

[118] The Department of Enterprise, Trade and Employment records that there are 46 such individually authorised auditors. See www.entemp.ie.

[119] CA 1990, s 199(3).

    – he must at least once a year notify the Registrar of the fact that he holds that authorisation;

    – he must as soon as possible and, at the latest, within one month, notify the Registrar of any change in these particulars; and

    – he must as soon as possible and, at the latest, within one month, notify the Registrar of ceasing to hold that authorisation.[120]

[7.034] According to CA 1990, s 200, the same notification requirements apply to an individual who is granted authorisation by the Minister to act as an auditor after the commencement of that provision. The only category of persons to whom individual authorisations could be granted after the commencement of CA 1990, are persons who are qualified as auditors in other countries within the meaning of s 189, to whom authorisations to so act in Ireland are granted under s 187(1)(a)(iv). While it seems that s 200(3) must be intended to refer to such persons, there is a difficulty in interpretation, as s 200(3) refers to authorisations granted by the 'Minister', a reference which has not been amended by the C(AA)A 2003, whereas s 187(1)(a)(vi) and s 189 refer to authorisations by the 'Supervisory Authority'.[121] This appears to be an oversight, as evidenced by the reference in CA 1990, s 198(3), as inserted by C(AA)A 2003, s 38, to the fact that a person's name is 'deemed to be entered in the register of auditors: (a) if the person becomes qualified for appointment as an auditor or is granted an authorisation *by the Supervisory Authority* under s 187(1) *and if the time allowed under s 200(1), (2) or (3)* for forwarding that person's particulars to the registrar of companies has not yet expired ...' (emphasis added). Under the current formulation of s 200(3), it is a person authorised by the Minister, whose particulars must be forwarded to the

---

[120] CA 1990, s 199(3A), as inserted by C(AA)A 2003, s 39(d). Note that, as of August 2007, this provision was not commenced. However, CA 1990 (Auditors) Regulations 1992, reg 7(1)(b) provides that persons who are granted individual authorisations to act as auditors, whether under s 199(3) (before the commencement of CA 1990) or under s 200(3) (after the commencement of CA 1990), must notify the Registrar of Companies, '(i) at least once in each year, if it be the case, that he holds an authorisation referred to in those sub-ss, and (ii) as soon as may be, but not later than one month after its occurrence, of his ceasing to hold such an authorisation or of any change in the particulars delivered by him to the registrar of companies under either of those sections.' While the CA 1990 (Auditors) Regulations 1992 are repealed by C(AA)A 2003, s 59, that provision has not, as of October 2007, been commenced. It may be expected that C(AA)A 2003, ss 39, 40, and 59, would be commenced contemporaneously and effectively enshrine the provisions of the 1992 Regulations, regarding notification to the Registrar by individually authorised auditors, as primary legislation. This, however, is subject to the qualification that Council Directive 84/253/EEC, which the 1992 Regulations implemented, has now been repealed and replaced by Council Directive 2006/46/EC, which must be transposed into Irish law by 29 June 2008. See *IAASA Annual Report* 2006 at p 105 and Table F.1 which sets out details of so-called 'individually authorised auditors.' It should also be noted that, pursuant to CA 1990, s 187(14) and (15), as inserted by C(AA)A 2003, s 35(c), such individually authorised auditors must become a member of a recognised body of accountants within three years of the commencement of that provision. See further para **[7.030]**.

[121] CA 1990, s 200(3); CA 1990, ss 187(1)(a)(iv) and 189, as amended by C(AA)A 2003, s 32(1) and Sch 1 (substituting 'Supervisory Authority' for 'Minister').

Registrar under s 200(3). Assuming that s 200(3) is intended to refer to individuals who are authorised by the IAASA to act as auditors, within the meaning of s 187(1)(a)(vi), such individuals are bound by the following notification requirements:

- he must deliver to the Registrar, within one month of being granted authorisation, his name and address;[122]

- he must at least once a year notify the Registrar of the fact that he holds that authorisation;

- he must as soon as possible and, at the latest, within one month, notify the Registrar of any change in these particulars; and

- he must as soon as possible and, at the latest, within one month, notify the Registrar of ceasing to hold that authorisation.[123]

[7.035] CA 1990, s 198, as replaced by C(AA)A 2003, s 38, governs the register of auditors that must be maintained by the Registrar of Companies.[124] This requires the Registrar to keep a register with all the names of persons or firms which have been notified to him as qualified for appointment as auditor.[125] A person must not act or describe himself as an auditor or so hold himself out 'as to indicate, or be reasonably understood to indicate, that he is, or is registered as, an auditor ...' unless his name is entered on the register of auditors, or deemed to be so entered, and he holds the requisite practising certificate.[126] A person may also act or represent himself as an auditor if he is

---

[122] CA 1990, s 200(3).

[123] CA 1990, s 200(3A), as inserted by C(AA)A 2003, s 40(b). Note that, as of August 2007, this provision was not commenced. However, CA 1990 (Auditors) Regulations 1992, reg 7(1)(b) provides that persons who are granted individual authorisations to act as auditors, whether under s 199(3) (before the commencement of CA 1990) or under s 200(3) (after the commencement of CA 1990), must notify the Registrar of Companies, '(i) at least once in each year, if it be the case, that he holds an authorisation referred to in those sub-ss, and (ii) as soon as may be, but not later than one month after its occurrence, of his ceasing to hold such an authorisation or of any change in the particulars delivered by him to the registrar of companies under either of those sections.' While the CA 1990 (Auditors) Regulations 1992 are repealed by C(AA)A 2003, s 59, that provision has not, as of August 2007, been commenced. It may be expected that C(AA)A 2003, ss 39, 40, and 59, would be commenced contemporaneously and effectively enshrine the provisions of the 1992 Regulations, regarding notification to the Registrar by individually authorised auditors, as primary legislation. This, however, is subject to the qualification that Council Directive 84/253/EEC, which the 1992 Regulations implemented, has now been repealed and replaced by Council Directive 2006/46/EC, which must be transposed into Irish law by 29 June 2008. See *IAASA Annual Report 2006* at p 105 and Table F.1 which sets out details of so-called 'individually authorised auditors.'

[124] Note that, as of October 2007, C(AA)A 2003, s 38 has not been commenced.

[125] CA 1990, s 198(1), as substituted by C(AA)A 2003, s 38.

[126] CA 1990, s 198(2), as substituted by C(AA)A 2003, s 38.

a member of a firm that holds a practising certificate within the meaning of s 187(1B) and he is deemed to hold such a certificate.[127]

A person's name is deemed to be entered on the register if the person becomes qualified for appointment as an auditor and is granted authorisation by the IAASA under CA 1990, s 187(1), and the time for forwarding his particulars to the Registrar has not expired; or if he is entitled to have his name entered on the register and his particulars have been forwarded to the Registrar for that purpose, but his name has not yet been entered.[128]

[7.036] While the obligation to forward particulars about qualified auditors rests on the recognised body of accountants of which he is a member (or on the individually authorised auditor himself if applicable), it is an offence for the person himself to act as an auditor, or so describe or hold himself out, unless his name is registered on the register of auditors. If found guilty of this offence, he may be liable, on summary conviction, to a maximum fine of €2,000 and a daily default fine of up to €60 for continued contravention.[129] On conviction on indictment, he may be liable to a maximum fine of €12,500 and a daily default fine of €300 for continued contraventions.[130]

[7.037] Section 198, as it existed before the enactment of C(AA)A 2003, required the Registrar to maintain a register containing the names and addresses of persons who were notified to him as qualified for appointment as auditors.[131] Consistently with this requirement, ss 199 and 200 require the name and address of qualified auditors to be delivered to the Registrar.[132] By contrast, the amendment introduced by C(AA)A 2003 only requires the names of auditors to be included on the register of auditors.[133] This is

---

[127] CA 1990, s 198(2)(ii), as substituted by C(AA)A 2003, s 38. CA 1990, s 187(1B), as inserted by C(AA)A 2003, s 35, provides, 'A body referred to in sub-s (1A) may grant a practising certificate to a firm that satisfies the conditions in that subsection, and, if a practising certificate is granted— (a) each member of the firm who from time to time during the currency of the certificate is qualified for appointment as auditor of a company or as a public auditor is deemed to hold the certificate, and (b) the name of such a member is deemed to be entered in the register of auditors.' Note that, as of October 2007, s 35 has not been commenced.

[128] CA 1990, s 198(3), as substituted by C(AA)A 2003, s 38. As of October 2007, s 38 was not yet commenced.

[129] CA 1990, s 198(5)(a), as substituted by C(AA)A 2003, s 38. As of October 2007, s 38 was not yet commenced.

[130] CA 1990, s 198(5)(b), as substituted by C(AA)A 2003, s 38. As of October 2007, s 38 was not yet commenced.

[131] CA 1990, s 198(1).

[132] See CA 1990, s 199(1), as amended by C(AA)A 2003, s 32(1) and Sch 1; CA 1990, s 200(1).

[133] C(AA)A 2003, s 38(1) does not refer to addresses. As of October 2007, s 38 was not yet commenced.

particularly curious in light of the fact that s 198(6) contains a definition of 'address' and states:

> In this section and ss 199 and 200, 'address' in relation to a person means—
>
> (a) the person's usual business address, and
>
> (b) if the person is a partner or employee of a firm, the name of the firm and the address of its head office.[134]

This clearly envisages the use of the word 'address' in s 198, but, from the date on which s 38 is commenced, the word 'address' will not appear in s 198 and there will be no requirement that the register of auditors include an auditor's address.

[7.038] Many of the obligations to update information furnished to the Registrar are contained in CA 1990 (Auditors) Regulations 1992, and are derived from Council Directive 84/253/EEC. That Directive has now been repealed and replaced by Council Directive 2006/46/EC, which must transposed into Irish law by 29 June 2008. The following are among the requirements that will then apply to the registration of information regarding auditors in Ireland:

- every auditor and audit firm must be entered onto a public register and identified by an individual number;[135]

- the registration information must be stored electronically and be electronically accessible to the public;[136]

- the auditors' register must include, at a minimum, their names, addresses, registration number; if applicable, the name, address, website address, registration number of the audit firm by which they are employed, or with which they are associated; all registrations in other Member States and third countries, including registration numbers;[137]

- the register of audit firms must include, at a minimum, the name, address, registration number; legal form; contact information; website address (if applicable); address of each office in the Member State; name and registration number of all statutory auditors employed by or associated with the firm; name and business address of all owners, shareholders, members of management and administration; any memberships of networks, names and addresses of affiliates or member firms, or indications of where such information is publicly accessible; and all registrations of the firm in other Member States or third countries, including registration numbers;[138]

- any change in information must be notified to the competent authority in charge of the register (at present, the Registrar of Companies) without undue delay and the register must be updated without undue delay after such notification;[139]

---

[134] CA 1990, s 198(6), as substituted by C(AA)A 2003, s 38.

[135] Council Directive 2006/46/EC, arts 15(1) and 15(2).

[136] Council Directive 2006/46/EC, art 15(2).

[137] Council Directive 2006/46/EC, art 16(1).

[138] Council Directive 2006/46/EC, art 17(1).

[139] Council Directive 2006/46/EC, art 18.

    — the information furnished must be signed by the auditor or audit firm (which can be done by electronic signature, if permitted by the relevant authority).[140]

The matters which are required by s 198 to be included on the register of auditors will clearly need to be expanded to give effect to Council Directive 2006/46/EC.

(iii) Disqualification

[7.039] In addition to the qualifications that a person must attain to be appointed as an auditor, and the requirement that certain information must be notified to the Registrar, before he can so act, there are further limitations in CA 1990, s 187(2). This provides that none of the following persons may act as a company's auditor:

    (a) an officer or servant of the company,

    (b) a person who has been an officer or servant of the company within a period in respect of which accounts would fall to be audited by him if he were appointed auditor of the company,

    (c) a parent, spouse, brother, sister or child of an officer of the company,

    (d) a person who is a partner of or in the employment of an officer of the company,

    (e) a person who is disqualified under this subsection for appointment as auditor of any other body corporate that is a subsidiary or holding company of the company or a subsidiary of the company's holding company, or would be so disqualified if the body corporate were a company,

    (f) a person who is disqualified under sub-s (3) for appointment as a public auditor of a society that is a subsidiary or holding company of the company or a subsidiary of the company's holding company,

    (g) a body corporate,

    (h) a person in whose name a share in the company is registered, whether or not that person is the beneficial owner of the share.[141]

[7.040] A body corporate is disqualified under CA 1990 from acting as a company's auditor.[142] Auditors cannot therefore avail of the protection of limited liability in Ireland. This disqualification was abrogated by the Companies Act 1990 (Auditors) Regulations 1992 which permits the appointment of a firm of auditors, provided at least one member of that firm has a certificate to practise with a recognised body of accountants.[143] While

---

[140] Council Directive 2006/46/EC, art 19.

[141] CA 1990, s 187(2). Note that C(AA)A 2003, s 35(b), which inserts s 187(2)(h) was not commenced as of October 2007. The prohibition on shareholders acting as auditors is therefore not applicable until such time as that provision is commenced.

[142] CA 1990, s 187(2)(g).

[143] Companies Act 1990 (Auditors) Regulations 1992 (SI 259/1992), reg 4.

those Regulations were repealed by the C(AA)A 2003,[144] s 187(1A) and (1B) now provide in similar terms:

> (1A) A firm shall be qualified for appointment as auditor of a company or as a public auditor if—
>
> (a) at least one member of the firm is entitled to hold a practising certificate from a body referred to in sub-para (i), (ii) or (iii) of sub-s (1)(a)[145] and is otherwise qualified under the applicable subparagraph for appointment as auditor of a company or as a public auditor, and
>
> (b) the particulars required by ss 199 and 200 in respect of such a member have been forwarded to the registrar of companies.
>
> (1B) A body referred to in sub-s (1A) may grant a practising certificate to a firm that satisfies the conditions in that subsection, and, if a practising certificate is granted—
>
> (a) each member of the firm who from time to time during the currency of the certificate is qualified for appointment as auditor of a company or as a public auditor is deemed to hold the certificate, and
>
> (b) the name of such a member is deemed to be entered in the register of auditors.[146]

(iv) Acting as auditor while not qualified

[7.041] From the foregoing, it is clear that a person who wishes to be appointed as an auditor of a company must meet a number of criteria. First, he must be a member of a recognised body of accountants and hold a valid practising certificate from such body, or meet one of the other conditions of s 187(1).[147] Second, particulars must have been

---

[144] C(AA)A 2003, s 59, which repeals the CA 1990 (Auditors) Regulations 1992, was not commenced as of October 2007. Note that the Council Directive 84/253/EEC, which the 1992 Regulations implemented, has now been repealed and replaced by Council Directive 2006/46/EC, which must be transposed into Irish law by 29 June 2008.

[145] As noted above, CA 1990, s 187(1)(a)(i), (ii) and (iii), as amended by CLEA 2001, s 72, and C(AA)A 2003, s 32(1) and Sch 1, provide that a person is not qualified for appointment as an auditor unless, '(i) he is a member of a body of accountants for the time being recognised by the Supervisory Authority for the purposes of this section and holds a valid practising certificate from such a body, or (ii) he holds an accountancy qualification that is, in the opinion of the Supervisory Authority, of a standard which is not less than that required for such membership as aforesaid and which would entitle him to be granted a practising certificate by that body if he were a member of it, and is for the time being authorised by the Supervisory Authority to be so appointed, or (iii) he was, on the 31st day of December, 1990, a member of a body of accountants for the time being recognised under section 162(1)(a) of The Principal Act and holds a valid practising certificate from such a body.'

[146] CA 1990, s 187(1A) and (1B), as inserted by C(AA)A 2003, s 35(a). Note that, as of October 2007, s 35 was not commenced. However, while CA 1990 (Auditors) Regulations 1992 contain similar provisions, Council Directive 84/253/EEC, on which the 1992 Regulations implemented, has now been repealed and replaced by Council Directive 2006/46/EC, which must be transposed into Irish law by 29 June 2008.

[147] See paras **[7.028]** to **[7.031]**.

delivered to the Registrar of Companies in accordance with CA 1990, ss 199, 200, including his name, address, and any changes in particulars previously notified to the Registrar.[148] Third, he must not have a prohibited connection with the company in question, such as a familial connection with an officer of the company or hold an office or employment with the company.[149] Finally, any person who is disqualified under CA 1990, s 160, must not act as an auditor of a company.[150]

[7.042] A person who is disqualified, on any of the grounds listed in s 187, from being appointed as an auditor of a company must not act as an auditor while so disqualified.[151] Section 187(6) provides in this regard, '... a person shall not act as auditor of a company or as a public auditor at a time when he is disqualified under this section for appointment to that office.'

The disqualification of an auditor extends to situations in which a person may become disqualified during the currency of their appointment as auditor of a company.[152] In such circumstances, the person must vacate the office of auditor upon becoming so disqualified, notifying the company in writing that they are resigning for that reason. Section 187(7) provides:

> If, during his term of office as auditor of a company or public auditor, a person becomes disqualified under the Companies Acts for appointment to that office, he shall thereupon vacate his office and give notice in writing to the company, society or friendly society that he has vacated his office by reason of such disqualification.

[7.043] It is an offence for a person to act as an auditor while disqualified from so acting or to continue acting as an auditor after becoming disqualified. Upon summary conviction, a person may be liable to a maximum fine of €1,904.61 and a daily default fine of up to €63.49 for continued contraventions.[153] If convicted on indictment, he may be liable to a maximum fine of €6,348.69 and a daily default fine of up to €126.97 for continued contraventions.[154]

[7.044] The decision of the High Court in *Director of Corporate Enforcement v Gannon*[155] establishes some important principles regarding the offence of acting as an

---

[148] See paras **[7.032]** to **[7.038]**.

[149] See paras **[7.039]** to **[7.040]**.

[150] See Pt **E**. Note that the reference to auditors' being disqualified from acting, is used in the specific sense of auditors not meeting the qualification criteria of the Companies Acts 1963–2006, and is not generally intended to refer to persons who are subject to disqualification orders, although such persons are also disqualified from acting as auditors. The consequences of breaching orders of disqualification are considered in more detail in Ch **23** and are not addressed here.

[151] CA 1990, s 187(6).

[152] CA 1990, s 187(7).

[153] CA 1990, s 187(9)(a), as amended by CA 1990, s 250(7), as inserted by CLEA 2001, s 104(c). See also para **[7.050]**.

[154] CA 1990, s 187(9)(b).

[155] *Director of Corporate Enforcement v Gannon* [2002] 4 IR 439.

auditor while disqualified. In that case, a firm of auditors (the second defendant), and each of the partners in the firm, were charged in the District Court with charges of acting as auditors while disqualified, as one of the seven partners in the firm (the first defendant) was a director of two companies of which the firm was alleged to have acted as auditor. The second defendant was appointed as auditor of companies of which the first defendant was a director prior to the commencement of the CA 1990. It was submitted that, after that date, none of the defendants were appointed as auditors of those companies. However, the financial statements filed by the companies in 1997 were accompanied by auditors' reports on the headed paper and bearing the name of the second defendant, in which the second defendant was described as the companies' auditors. The District Court dismissed the prosecutions on the ground that there was no case to answer and stated the case for the opinion of the High Court as to whether the Court was correct in law in reaching this determination.

[7.045] Among the issues that fell to be considered in that case were whether the firm of auditors were 'acting as auditors' within the meaning of s 187(6), which provides, 'Subject to sub-s (5), a person shall not act as auditor of a company or as a public auditor at a time when he is disqualified under this section for appointment to that office'. The defendants argued that there was a distinction between being an auditor and acting as an auditor and that 'not everything that an auditor does necessarily involves acting as auditor of a company'. [156] The defendants further argued that: 'if a person who holds the office of auditor takes no steps in that capacity and discharges none of his duties, then it cannot be said the auditor has "acted" as auditor.'[157] The defendants submitted, conversely, that 'if a person does not hold the office of auditor and has not been appointed to the office of auditor of a company, then any carrying out of some or all of the tasks which are the duties of an auditor is merely a person carrying out those tasks and is not "acting as auditor"'.[158]

O'Caoimh J considered the facts in light of the submissions made and reached the following conclusions:

> While it is clear that the District Court Judge was correct in stating that there was no evidence as to which of the partners of the defendant firm had acted as auditor it is clear from the evidence before the District Court that at the relevant dates the defendant firm had acted as auditors to both Brodericks Ltd and Sligo County Enterprise Fund. The evidence before this court and before the District Court shows that at the relevant dates the defendant firm was auditor to the two companies. It is clear that in the circumstances the evidence also shows that the first defendant was, at the relevant dates, an officer of the two companies. Accordingly, I am satisfied that he was not qualified for appointment as auditor of either company and accordingly, I am satisfied that at the relevant dates the defendant firm was not qualified for appointment as auditors of either company having regard to the provisions of s 160(9) of the Act of 1963. Accordingly, the firm should have ceased to act as auditors upon the coming into force of the Act of

---

[156] [2002] 4 IR 439 at 456.

[157] [2002] 4 IR 439 at 457.

[158] [2002] 4 IR 439 at 457.

1990 and it (and each of the partners of the firm) were required to vacate their office as auditors.[159]

[7.046] The Court interpreted the prohibition on 'acting' as auditor to extend beyond the persons who were formally appointed as auditors and further held:

> 'I do not believe that it would in any circumstances be difficult for a person asked to act as auditor to establish whether he or she, or any partner of the firm of which they may be a member, is disqualified to act as auditor having regard to the limited category of disqualified persons referred to in s 187(2) of the Act of 1990.'[160]

With regard to the position of the first defendant's partners, O'Caoimh J held that: 'As each of the partners of the defendant constituted "a person who is a partner of ... an officer of each company" none of them were qualified for appointment as auditor of either company at the relevant time, having regard to the provisions of s 187(2)(d) of the Act of 1990'. [161]

[7.047] Another significant issue the Court was called upon to consider in *Director of Corporate Enforcement v Gannon*[162] was whether the offence of acting as an auditor while not qualified was one of strict liability. The prosecution contended that the offence was one of strict liability and that, in any case, the knowledge of the auditor who drew up an auditors' report or acted as an auditor must be imputed to his partners who share in his profits. The defendants argued the offence was not specified as one of strict liability and that, as many large firms of accountants had hundreds of partners operating in different countries, it could not be claimed that an irregularity of the type alleged in this case could lead to criminal prosecutions of all of the partners in the various jurisdictions.

O'Caoimh J noted that 'In light of the relatively limited penalties capable of being imposed in this case I am satisfied ... that the statutory offences at issue in these proceedings cannot be classified as being 'truly criminal' in character.'[163] The Court concluded that:

> 'I am satisfied that the provisions of the Companies Acts at issue in these proceedings, as reinforced by the terms of the Eighth Council Directive, are addressed to an issue of social concern and I am satisfied that the creation of strict liability will be effective to promote the objects of the statute by encouraging greater vigilance to prevent the commission of the prohibited acts, the subject matter of the charges herein.'[164]

[7.048] *Director of Corporate Enforcement v Gannon*[165] illustrates the potential severity of s 187. Before accepting appointment as, or carrying out the duties of, a company's

---

[159] [2002] 4 IR 439 at 460 to 461.

[160] [2002] 4 IR 439 at 461.

[161] [2002] 4 IR 439 at 461.

[162] [2002] 4 IR 439.

[163] [2002] 4 IR 439 at 462.

[164] [2002] 4 IR 439 at 462.

[165] [2002] 4 IR 439.

auditor, a person must verify carefully that they do not fall within any of the categories specified in s 187(2). Furthermore, any violation of this restriction by one individual will be visited upon each person with whom they are in partnership, irrespective of the state of knowledge or intention of those partners.

[7.049] It may be noted that the CLEA 2001 introduced certain evidential presumptions and rules regarding proof of qualification, which are designed to facilitate the prosecution of persons acting as auditors without the requisite qualifications and render it more difficult to refute allegations of having so acted.

The DCE can now demand a person who is acting, or purporting to be qualified to so act, as auditor to produce proof of their qualification to so act.[166] Section 187(12) provides in this regard:

(a) The Director may demand of a person acting as an auditor of a company or as a public auditor, or purporting to be qualified to so act, the production of evidence of his qualifications under sub-s (1) in respect of any time or period during which he so acted or purported to be qualified to so act, and if the person refuses or fails to produce the evidence within 30 days of the demand, or such longer period as the Director may allow, he shall be guilty of an offence.

(b) In a prosecution for an offence under this subsection, it shall be presumed, until the contrary is shown by the defendant, that the defendant did not, within 30 days, or any longer period allowed, after the day on which the production was demanded, produce evidence in accordance with para (a).[167]

This provision may operate severely, in that a refusal or failure to comply with the demand within 30 days, or such longer period as the Director may permit, constitutes an offence.[168] Moreover, in the prosecution of such an offence, it shall be presumed that no proof of qualification was produced during the requisite timeframe, unless the defendant proves to the contrary.[169] This clearly shifts the burden of proof onto the defendant with regard to the essential ingredient of the offence.

[7.050] The CLEA 2001 also inserts s 187(13), which deals with prosecutions of persons who have acted as auditor while disqualified from so acting:[170]

(a) Where a person is the subject of a prosecution under sub-s (9) for a contravention of sub-s (6) or (7), it shall be sufficient evidence, until the contrary is shown by the person, of non-membership of a body of accountants for the time being recognised by the Minister[171] for the purposes of this section for any or all such bodies to certify in writing to the court such non-membership, provided that the first-mentioned person is provided by the

---

[166] CA 1990, s 187(12)(a), as inserted by CLEA 2001, s 72(b).

[167] CA 1990, s 187(12), as inserted by CLEA 2001, s 72(b).

[168] CA 1990, s 187(12)(a), as inserted by CLEA 2001, s 72(b).

[169] CA 1990, s 187(12)(b), as inserted by CLEA 2001, s 72(b).

[170] CA 1990, s 187(9); See above para **[7.043]**.

[171] There does not appear to be a provision of the C(AA)A 2003 which substitutes 'Supervisory Authority' for 'Minister' in CA 1990, s 187(13)(a), although that would appear to be the more accurate reference.

> prosecutor with a copy of the certificate or certificates, served by registered post, not later than 21 days before any such certificate is presented in evidence to the court.
>
> (b) Where a person the subject of a prosecution proposes to contest the certification of non-membership contained in a certificate provided for by para (a), he shall give written notice thereof, served by registered post, to the prosecutor within 21 days, or such longer period as the court may allow, of receipt of the certificate from the prosecutor.[172]

Under this provision, the burden of proving that someone is not qualified to act as auditor is considerably lightened. If 'any or all' of the bodies of accountants then recognised by the Minister[173] certifies in writing that the individual under suspicion is not a member of their organisation, that shall be sufficient evidence that the person is not a member of a recognised body of accountants. This appears to suggest that if one recognised body of accountants certifies that a person acting as an auditor is not a member of their organisation, this will be sufficient proof that he is not a member of any such recognised body. While it is unlikely that this is the intended effect of s 187(13), it is an interpretation to which the provision is open, as the provision is currently formulated. The more plausible interpretation of s 187(13), is that 'any or all' of the recognised bodies of accountants can certify that an individual is not a member of any such body.

There are certain protections available to the person facing prosecution. First, they must receive copies of each of the certifications at least 21 days before they are presented in court. Secondly, the evidence is not conclusive and the person in question can seek to disprove it. However, where a person seeks to contest the certification of non-membership, advance written notice of this fact must be furnished to the prosecutor.[174] Thirdly, the evidential rule introduced in s 187(13) only addresses membership of a body of accountants and does not affect prosecutions of individuals who are alleged not to be qualified, or to be disqualified, as auditors on the various other grounds contained in s 187. For instance, a person who is alleged to be disqualified from acting as auditor of a company on the grounds that they are connected with that company, does not appear to be affected by s 187(13).

[7.051] There have been a number of prosecutions of persons who acted as auditors while disqualified from so acting, including 14 such convictions in 2006.[175] The ODCE reports that:

> 'A feature of this type of enforcement case is that many of the persons involved are offering accounting services of some character and could reasonably be expected to be aware of the reserved nature of the auditing function.'[176]

---

[172] CA 1990, s 187(13), as inserted by CLEA 2001, s 72(b).

[173] As noted above, there does not appear to be a provision of the C(AA)A 2003 which substitutes 'Supervisory Authority' for 'Minister' in CA 1990, s 187(13)(a), although it would appear more appropriate that the Supervisory Authority be referred to in this context

[174] CA 1990, s 187(13)(b), as inserted by CLEA 2001, s 72(b).

[175] *ODCE Annual Report 2006* at p 23.

[176] *ODCE Annual Report 2006* at p 23.

An example of such a prosecution was the conviction of one individual in 2006 on fourteen charges (five further counts having been taken into account by the Court), related to eight different companies, of acting as an auditor while disqualified. Fines totalling €4,000 were imposed, and costs of €1,000 were also awarded against him.[177]

In relation to the prohibition on persons who are connected with a company acting as auditor of that company, the ODCE prosecuted five persons on fifteen charges in one set of proceedings. The ODCE reports that one of the individuals was convicted on three of the charges in the District Court of acting as an auditor while a director of the company, while the Probation Act was applied to four partners of the same auditing firm, on similar charges, by a District Court judge sitting in a different District. The person convicted on the charges appealed to the Circuit Court, where the conviction was quashed and the Probation Act applied. The five persons in question were ordered to pay a total of €5,000 in charitable donations.

Commenting on the outcome of the case, the ODCE reports that, it:

'has recommended a change in the law which would further enable similar cases arising from common facts or circumstances to be disposed of in one District Court hearing rather than (as sometimes still happens) their having to be heard in two or more District Court areas. As well as removing the scope for what might be perceived a inconsistent outcomes at District Court level, this change would save Court time and legal costs. It is hoped that the Department of Enterprise Trade and Employment will approve this proposal in 2007 following its consideration by the Company Law Review Group.'[178]

[7.052] In addition to the prosecutions that persons who act as auditors while not qualified or disqualified, in the sense of s 187, may face, they may also be the subject of orders of disqualification[179] and furthermore, there is a strict prohibition on persons who are subject to disqualification orders acting as auditors. CA 1990, s 195(1), provides in this regard:

If a person who is subject or deemed to be subject to a disqualification order—

(a) becomes, or remains after 28 days from the date of the making of the order, a partner in a firm of auditors,

---

[177] *Director of Corporate Enforcement v Muhammad Sabir Hafeez* (21 June 2006, unreported), Dublin District Court. See *ODCE Annual Report 2006* at p 23.

[178] *ODCE Annual Report 2006* at p 23. See further Ch **15**.

[179] See *Re Kentford Securities Ltd* [2006] IEHC 57, in which a person who acted as a company's auditor while also a director of the company, faced disqualification proceedings on numerous grounds, including that, contrary to the statement in the auditor's report, the accounts did not provide a true and fair view of the company's affairs; that the auditor was guilty of forgery; that he failed to comply with proper auditing standards; and that the audits were generally deficient (that case concerned an unsuccessful motion to dismiss the prosecution on the ground of delay). Note that the Company Law Enforcement Bill, as it was originally formulated, gave the DCE a right to apply for the removal of a person from the register of auditors. However, this was not enacted in the CLEA 2001, and the DCE instead retains the power to apply for the disqualification of an auditor under CA 1990, s 160. See Company Law Enforcement Act 2001 Annotated, ICLSA. See Pt **E**, 'Disqualification Orders'.

(b) gives directions or instructions in relation to the conduct of any part of the audit of the accounts of a company, or

(c) works in any capacity in the conduct of an audit of the accounts of a company,

he shall be guilty of an offence.[180]

This prohibition is wide in its ambit and precludes a person who is subject to a disqualification order from being involved in any capacity in relation to auditing a company's accounts. It also requires the immediate resignation from a firm of auditors of a partner in respect of whom an order of disqualification is made.

[7.053] If a person is convicted of an offence within the meaning of s 195, he faces an extension of the period of disqualification by a further ten years from the date of conviction, or such further period as the court may order, in addition to such criminal penalties as may be imposed.[181] The formulation of this provision is interesting as it states that, upon conviction, 'the period for which he was disqualified shall be extended for a further period of ten years from such date, or such other further period as the court, on the application of the prosecutor and having regard to all the circumstances of the case, may order.' It is only the prosecutor who may therefore apply for the disqualification to be extended for any period other than ten years. In light of the severity of the consequences for a professional auditor, this provision could operate particularly harshly, depending on the view taken by the prosecutor.

(b) Independence

[7.054] An issue with regard to the appointment of auditors that has caused considerable debate in recent years is the extent to which a person appointed as a company's auditor must be independent of the company.[182] There are two aspects to this debate. First, there is an argument that a firm or individual that act as auditors for a company should not conduct non-audit work for that company. Secondly, there is an argument that the same person or firm should not conduct audit work for the same company for more than a defined period of time. A third aspect of the protection of auditors' independence which may be recalled is the disqualification of persons who have a prescribed connection with the company, from being appointed as the company's auditor.[183]

With regard to the first issue, there was a concern that auditors who provided a variety of non-audit services, as well as conducting audit work for a client, may become financially dependent on the client and may be too heavily involved in the client's affairs. The concern was at its highest in relation to firms of auditors acting as auditors, consultants and actuaries for the same client. In the US there was evidence that some of

---

[180] CA 1990, s 195(1). See further Pt **E**, 'Disqualification Orders'.

[181] CA 1990, s 195(2).

[182] See Eighth Council Directive 84/253/EEC of 10 April 1984, OJ 1984 L 126, p 20, art 24: 'Member States shall prescribe that such persons shall not carry out statutory audits which they have required if such persons are not independent in accordance with the law of the Member State which requires the audit.'

[183] CA 1990, s 187(2). See further paras **[7.039]** to **[7.040]**. See also *Director of Corporate Enforcement v Gannon* [2002] 4 IR 439.

the large accounting firms earned more revenue for the non-audit work they conducted for clients than the audit work.[184] This presented the danger that the auditors would be reluctant to antagonise a client and risk losing the non-audit revenue. Many jurisdictions have required the disclosure of all audit and non-audit revenue earned in an attempt to overcome these concerns.

[7.055] In Ireland, the Review Group on Auditing considered this matter and concluded that:

> 'it is not feasible or practicable for a small open economy such as Ireland to adopt rules completely out of line with current international practices or the forthcoming EU Recommendation by requiring a complete separation of the audit function from all other consultancy activities.'[185]

The solution that has been adopted in Ireland is set out in CA 1990, s 205D.[186] This provision imposes an obligation on a company to disclose, in the notes to its annual accounts,[187] all remuneration paid to its auditors, directly or indirectly, in connection with audit and non-audit work conducted for the company in the financial year to which the accounts relate and the preceding year.[188]

The information that must be disclosed is the remuneration for all work that was carried out for the company itself or a subsidiary, associated company or joint venture partner[189] of the company, during that financial year or the preceding financial year, by the

---

[184] Eg, it has been reported that in 2001 KPMG billed electronics manufacturer Motorola Inc. $3.9 million for audit services and $62.3 million for other services. E&Y was reported to have billed Sprint Corp $2.5 million for audit work and $63.8 million for non-audit work. PWC reportedly billed AT&T $7.9 million for audit work and $48.4 for other services.

[185] *Report of the Review Group on Auditing* at p 178. The Group also noted, 'Due to the increasing complexity of the business environment and regulatory requirements most companies require external assistance in order to remain competitive and to meet their various obligations. A prohibition on auditors providing such services to audit clients could limit the source of advice available to companies and increase costs.'

[186] This provision was inserted by C(AA)A 2003, s 44, which has not, as of October 2007, been commenced.

[187] CA 1990, s 205D(2) as inserted by C(AA)A 2003, s 44. Note that, as of October 2007, s 44 has not been commenced.

[188] This obligation applies to all companies, other than those which are specifically exempted by Regulation under C(AA)A 2003, s 48(1)(j), which provides that the Minister may make regulations, 'exempting from all or any of ss 15 and 26 of this Act and ss 205A, 205B, 205C, 205D and 205E of the Act of 1990— (i) qualifying companies within the meaning of s 110 of the Taxes Consolidation Act 1997 (as inserted by s 48 of the Finance Act 2003), and (ii) classes of other companies and other undertakings, if the extent to which or the manner in which they are or may be regulated under any enactment makes it, in the Minister's opinion, unnecessary or inappropriate to apply those provisions to them.' Section 48 was commenced by C(AA)A 2003 (Commencement) (No 2) Order 2005, SI 791/2005.

[189] CA 1990, s 205D(1), as inserted by C(AA)A 2003, s 44, defines 'connected undertaking' as 'an undertaking that under the 1992 Regulations, or under those Regulations as applied by Regulation 9 of the 1993 Regulations, is— (a) a subsidiary undertaking of the relevant undertaking, (b) a joint venture of the relevant undertaking proportionally consolidated in accordance with Regulation 32 of the 1992 Regulations, or (c) an associated undertaking of the relevant undertaking.'

company's auditor, or any firm or individual to which the auditor was affiliated[190] during the relevant year.[191] It should be noted that if the auditor of the company is a firm, any work which is carried out by a partner of the firm, is considered to have been carried out by the auditor.[192] With regard to identifying an auditor's affiliates, s 205D(9) requires that the auditor must provide the company's directors with the requisite information to make such an identification. It is an offence for an auditor to fail to do so.[193] It should also be noted that, if the company retains more than one firm or individual as its auditor in a single financial year, the remuneration paid to each of them and their affiliates must be disclosed separately in the notes to the company's annual accounts.[194]

[7.056] The 'work' to which this disclosure obligation applies is threefold.[195] First, it encompasses 'audit work', which means the work which an auditor is obliged to do to discharge his duties under CA 1990, s 193.[196] Secondly, it encompasses 'audit-related work', which is broader and covers any work, other than audit work, that a person is required to do, as a result of his position as a company's auditor.[197] The final category of work to which this disclosure obligation applies is 'non-audit' work, which refers to any work other than audit or audit-related work.[198] If the disclosure relates to non-audit work, the nature of the work that was conducted by the auditor, his firm or affiliates must also be disclosed.[199]

The remuneration which must be disclosed is not just monetary remuneration, but includes benefits in kind and payments in cash.[200] If the remuneration which must be disclosed was wholly or partly in the form of a benefit in kind, the nature and estimated monetary value of the benefit must also be disclosed in the notes to the company's financial statements.[201]

---

[190] CA 1990, s 205D(1), as inserted by C(AA)A 2003, s 44, defines 'affiliate' as 'a firm, body corporate or partnership considered under section 182(2) to be an affiliate of the auditor,' and defines 'firm' as 'a firm that qualifies for appointment as auditor of a company or as a public auditor under section 187(1A).' See para **[7.040]**.

[191] CA 1990, s 205D(2), as inserted by C(AA)A 2003, s 44. Note that, as of August 2007, s 44 has not been commenced.

[192] CA 1990, s 205D(4), as inserted by C(AA)A 2003, s 44.

[193] CA 1990, s 205D(12), as inserted by C(AA)A 2003, s 44.

[194] CA 1990, s 205D(8), as inserted by C(AA)A 2003, s 44.

[195] See CA 1990, s 205D(3), as inserted by C(AA)A 2003, s 44.

[196] CA 1990, s 205D(1), as inserted by C(AA)A 2003, s 44.

[197] CA 1990, s 205D(1), as inserted by C(AA)A 2003, s 44, defines 'audit-related work' as, 'work required by any relevant undertaking, body or person to be done by an auditor of the relevant undertaking by virtue of his or her position as auditor of that undertaking, but does not include audit work.'

[198] CA 1990, s 205D(1), as inserted by C(AA)A 2003, s 44.

[199] CA 1990, s 205D(2)(c), as inserted by C(AA)A 2003, s 44.

[200] CA 1990, s 205D(1), as inserted by C(AA)A 2003, s 44.

[201] CA 1990, s 205D(2)(d), as inserted by C(AA)A 2003, s 44.

[7.057] If a company fails to make the disclosure required by s 205D, 'each company or other entity that forms all or part of that undertaking is guilty of an offence.'[202] However, there are thresholds which must be reached before this disclosure obligation arises. This disclosure obligation is only triggered if the aggregate remuneration for all work conducted of the relevant category (ie audit, non-audit or audit-related) in each of the financial year in question, and in the preceding year, exceeds €1,000.[203] Section 205D(5) provides in this regard:

> The disclosure requirements of this section apply in relation to a financial year of the relevant undertaking only if—
>
> (a) the aggregate of the remuneration for all work in each specified category that was carried out as described in sub-s (2)(a) in that financial year exceeds €1,000, and
>
> (b) the aggregate of the remuneration for all work in each specified category that was carried out as described in sub-s (2)(b) in the preceding financial year exceeds €1,000.

This limitation is formulated in a cumulative rather than an alternative fashion and suggests that unless the €1,000 threshold is passed in both the financial year to which the accounts relate, and the preceding one, in respect of a particular category of work, there is no obligation of disclosure. If this interpretation was adopted, it would easily facilitate the circumvention of the disclosure obligation, as a company could remunerate its auditors amply for each of the categories of audit, non-audit and audit-related work, in one financial year, and stay within the €1,000 threshold on alternate years. As s 205D(5) is drafted, so long as the remuneration for each category of work does not exceed €1,000 in successive years, the disclosure obligation will not apply.

[7.058] There is a separate, but related, obligation that arises if the remuneration which a company is obliged to disclose for non-audit work paid to its auditor exceeds the aggregate remuneration which it is obliged to disclose in respect of audit and audit-related work, in a financial year. Section 205D(6) provides that, in such circumstances, the audit committee must state in a report under s 205B(2)(m):[204]

> (a) whether it has satisfied itself that the carrying out of the non-audit work by the auditor or an affiliate of the auditor has not affected the auditor's independence from the relevant undertaking, and
>
> (b) if it has satisfied itself to that effect, the reasons for the decision to have the non-audit work carried out by the auditor or an affiliate of the auditor.[205]

In the case of a company that does not have an audit committee, the statement which directors are required to attach to every balance sheet laid before the company's AGM, must include the same statements as to whether the directors are satisfied that the

---

[202] CA 1990, s 205D(10), as inserted by C(AA)A 2003, s 44.

[203] CA 1990, s 205D(5), as inserted by C(AA)A 2003, s 44.

[204] CA 1990, s 205B(2)(m), as inserted by C(AA)A 2003, s 42 refers to the requirement that the audit committee satisfy itself that, '... the arrangements made and the resources available for internal audits are in the committee's opinion suitable.' Note that, as of October 2007, s 42 has not been commenced.

[205] CA 1990, s 205D(6), as inserted by C(AA)A 2003, s 44.

auditor's non-audit work has not affected his independence and the reasons for employing the auditor or an affiliate to carry out the non-audit work.[206]

If a company's auditors are paid more for non-audit than for audit, or audit-related work, but no statements are included in the audit committee report or directors' report, as applicable, confirming the auditor's independence and explaining this fact, each member of the audit committee, or member of the board of directors, to whom the failure is attributable, is guilty of an offence.[207]

[7.059] The Irish approach is to require disclosure of all remuneration paid to auditors for audit and non-audit work, subject to minimum thresholds. Where the remuneration for non-audit work exceeds that payable for audit and audit-related work in a given year, it must be confirmed by the directors (or an audit committee, if one exists) whether they are satisfied of the auditor's independence and they must explain why the auditor or an affiliate of the auditor is retained for the non-audit work.

[7.060] In the US, the Sarbanes-Oxley Act[208] goes further and prohibits auditors from offering certain specified non-audit services to audit clients, including human resources consultancy; actuarial services; accounting and bookkeeping services; work related to financial information systems; and internal audit services.[209] There are certain other non-audit services, including tax services, that an auditor may be permitted to provide if they are approved by the audit committee.

[7.061] In the EU, Council Directive 2006/43/EC addresses this issue of auditor independence, noting that, 'Examples of threats to the independence of a statutory auditor or audit firm are a direct or indirect financial interest in the audited entity and the provision of additional non-audit services' and that 'Statutory auditors and audit firms should refuse to undertake any additional non-audit service that compromises their independence.'[210] Article 22 of the Directive moreover provides that:

> 1. Member States shall ensure that when carrying out a statutory audit, the statutory auditor and/or the audit firm is independent of the audited entity and is not involved in the decision-taking of the audited entity.
>
> 2. Member States shall ensure that a statutory auditor or an audit firm shall not carry out a statutory audit if there is any direct or indirect financial, business, employment or other relationship – including the provision of additional non-audit services – between the statutory auditor, audit firm or network and the audited entity from which an objective, reasonable and informed third party would conclude that the statutory auditor's or audit firm's independence is compromised. If the statutory auditor's or audit firm's independence is affected by threats, such

---

[206] CA 1990, s 205D(7), as inserted by C(AA)A 2003, s 44, referring to the directors' statement under CA 1963, s 158.

[207] CA 1990, s 205D(11), as inserted by C(AA)A 2003, s 44.

[208] Public Company Accounting Reform and Investor Protection Act of 2002, Pub L No 107–204 § 804(b), 116 Stat. 745 (July 30, 2002).

[209] Section 201, amending Securities Exchange Act 1934 (15 USC 78 j–1), s 10A.

[210] Council Directive 2006/43/EC, recital 10. Note that this Directive must be transposed into Irish law by 29 June 2008.

as self-review, self-interest, advocacy, familiarity or trust or intimidation, the statutory auditor or audit firm must apply safeguards in order to mitigate those threats. If the significance of the threats compared to the safeguards applied is such that his, her or its independence is compromised, the statutory auditor or audit firm shall not carry out the statutory audit.

[7.062] The test to determine whether an auditor may conduct non-audit work for a company should therefore be whether 'an objective, reasonable and informed third party' would conclude that the auditor's independence would be compromised thereby. Disclosure alone is not sufficient, nor is it sufficient that a company's audit committee or board of directors may subjectively be satisfied that the auditor's independence is not compromised. CA 1963–2006 will have to be amended to reflect this standard by 29 June 2008.

[7.063] Council Directive 2006/43/EC further amends Directive 78/660/EEC, which concerns companies' annual accounts, by requiring that the notes to companies' annual accounts must include 'the total fees for the financial year charged by the statutory auditor or audit firm for the statutory audit of annual accounts, the total fees charged for other assurance services, the total fees charged for tax advisory services and the total fees charged for other non-audit services.'[211] There does not appear to be a *de minimus* exception to this obligation, and, among other necessary changes, CA 1990, s 205D, will therefore have to be adapted by the deletion of s 205D(5).[212]

[7.064] With regard to the second perceived threat to the independence of an auditor, namely the risk that an auditor who audits a client's accounts for longer than a defined period of time may lose objectivity, the Sarbanes-Oxley Act[213] requires that the partner in a firm who is responsible for a particular audit must rotate every five years.[214]

[7.065] At the European level, there is also recognition of the need to safeguard the independence of auditors. On 16 May 2002, the EC Commission issued a recommendation on the issue of auditor independence.[215] One of the primary recommendations is that an auditor should not conduct an audit of a company if they have a relationship, such a business, employment, economic link, with the company that could compromise their independence as auditor. The recommendation requires an auditor, prior to accepting an engagement, to list any potential risks or threats to their independence and the means of mitigating such risks or threats. The recommendation

---

[211] Council Directive 2006/43/EC, art 49(1), inserting Directive 78/660/EEC, art 34(15). The same requirement is introduced with regard to consolidated accounts by Directive 2006/43/EC, art 49(2), inserting Directive 83/349/EEC.

[212] CA 1990, s 205D(5), as inserted by C(AA)A 2003, s 44. See para [7.057].

[213] Public Company Accounting Reform and Investor Protection Act 2002, Pub L No 107–204 § 804(b), 116 Stat 745 (30 July 2002).

[214] Section 203, amending Securities Exchange Act 1934 (15 USC 78 j–1), s 10A. See also APB, Ethical Standard 3, 'Long Association with the Audit Engagement', which requires a five year rotation cycle for audit engagement partners in the case of listed companies.

[215] Commission Recommendation (2002/590/EC) of 16 May 2002 on 'Statutory Auditors' Independence in the EU: A Set of Fundamental Principles' 2002 OJ L 191/22.

also lists certain risks to the independence of an auditor that are considered to be unacceptable, such as a family connection, a financial interest, or the fact that they receive an unduly high proportion of their income from one client. Key audit partners must also rotate at least every seven years, according to the recommendation.

Internal Market Commissioner, Frits Bolkestein, speaking on the introduction of the Recommendation, stated that:

> 'Trust in the independence and objectivity of auditors is vital for the efficient functioning of the EU's capital market. It is essential for business integrity, shareholder confidence and consumer and employee protection. Audits must be seen as adding credibility to financial statements.'

[7.066] Council Directive 2006/43/EC now reflects this concern. Article 42(2) of the Directive provides as follows:

> Member States shall ensure that the key audit partner(s) responsible for carrying out a statutory audit rotate(s) from the audit engagement within a maximum period of seven years from the date of appointment and is/are allowed to participate in the audit of the audited entity again after a period of at least two years.

This requires that the key persons responsible for a company's audit must rotate every seven years and there must be a break of at least two years between such rotations. The definition of 'key audit partner(s)' includes an individual auditor who signed the audit report,[216] so while a partner in an audit firm has the option of rotating the responsibility for auditing a particular company to a partner in the same firm, it appears that an individual auditor will be obliged to resign this office every seven years for a period of at least two years.

Article 42(3) of Council Directive 2006/43/EC further provides:

> The statutory auditor or the key audit partner who carries out a statutory audit on behalf of an audit firm shall not be allowed to take up a key management position in the audited entity before a period of at least two years has elapsed since he or she resigned as a statutory auditor or key audit partner from the audit engagement.

The effect of this provision is that when an auditor, or a partner in an auditing firm, resign from acting as the auditor of a particular company, they must not take up a 'key management position' until the expiry of two years from that resignation. This is a further safeguard designed to avoid situations in which an auditor's self-interest may come into conflict with his duties as an auditor.

In Ireland, there is no provision of the CA 1963–2006 at present that restricts the length of time for which a person may serve as a company's auditor or the right of a person to take up a senior office with a company of which he was auditor. The implementation of Council Directive 2006/43/EC will necessitate changes on both these fronts.

---

[216] Council Directive 2006/43/EC, art 1(16), provides that 'key audit partner(s)' means '(a) the statutory auditor(s) designated by an audit firm for a particular audit engagement as being primarily responsible for carrying out the statutory audit on behalf of the audit firm; or (b) in the case of a group audit, at least the statutory auditor(s) designated by an audit firm as being primarily responsible for carrying out the statutory audit at the level of the group and the statutory auditor(s) designated as being primarily responsible at the level of material subsidiaries; or (c) the statutory auditor(s) who sign(s) the audit report'.

(c) Right of access to documents

[7.067] Another means by which an auditor's ability to discharge his functions is strengthened is the requirement that '[e]very auditor of a company shall have a right of access at all reasonable times to the books, accounts and vouchers of the company...'.[217] However, there is no specific provision of the Companies Acts that addresses the enforcement of this obligation or creates a penalty for non-compliance. This can be contrasted with the penalties that the law imposes on an officer of a company who either furnishes materially misleading, false or deceptive information or explanations in response to a request by an auditor, or who fails to furnish any information or explanations in response to such a request.[218]

(d) Right to compel information and explanations

[7.068] An auditor is entitled to require the officers and employees[219] of the company to furnish such information and explanations as are within their knowledge or procurement and which the auditor considers to be necessary for the performance of their duties.[220] Section 193(2) provides that every auditor:

> ... shall be entitled to require from the officers (within the meaning of s 197(5)) of the company such information and explanations that are within their knowledge or can be procured by them as he thinks necessary for the performance of the duties of the auditors.

This power is supported by strong penalties for non-compliant officers. Section 197(1) of CA 1990 provides that '[a]n officer of a company who knowingly or recklessly makes a statement to which this section applies[221] that is misleading, false or deceptive in a material particular shall be guilty of an offence.'[222] This can operate particularly harshly in practice, as an officer who fails to provide an auditor with the requested information or explanation that is within their knowledge or procurement, within a mere two days is

---

[217] CA 1990, s 193(3). This provision is similar to the English Companies Act 1985, s 389A(1) of which grants the auditors a right of access at all times to the company's books, accounts and vouchers and entitles them to require, from the officers of the company, the information and explanations that they consider necessary in order to perform their duties as auditors.

[218] CA 1990, s 197. See below para **[7.068]**.

[219] Note that CA 1990, s 197(5) provides that, 'In this section 'officer', in relation to a company, includes any employee of the company'.

[220] CA 1990, s 193(3).

[221] CA 1990, s 197(2) clarifies that the section applies to '...any statement made to the auditors of a company (whether orally or in writing) which conveys, or purports to convey, any information of explanation which they require under the Companies Acts, or are entitled to so require, as auditors of the company.'

[222] In England, CA 1985, s 389A(2) similarly provides that it is an offence for a company officer knowingly or recklessly to make a statement to the auditors, either orally or in writing, which conveys (or purports to convey) information or explanations which the auditors are entitled to require and which is misleading, false or deceptive. An officer who commits such an offence is liable to imprisonment or a fine or both. In the US, the Exchange Act, s 13(b)(2) and rule 13b2–2 similarly prohibit making materially false or misleading statements to auditors.

guilty of an offence.[223] This is mitigated somewhat by the fact that an officer who has not complied with the auditor's request within two days shall have a defence against prosecution, if it is shown not to have been reasonably possible for the officer to comply with the request within that timeframe.[224] To avail of this defence, the officer must also show that they complied with the request as soon as possible after the expiry of the two-day period.

[7.069] In addition to the penalisation of officers who do not comply with the request of an auditor to provide information or explanations, the auditor's powers in this regard are further strengthened by the fact that the auditor's report must state whether the auditor obtained all information and explanations which, to the best of their knowledge and belief, are necessary for the purpose of the audit.[225] Any dissatisfaction that the auditor may experience regarding the level of disclosure will therefore be made known directly to the members of the company. There is no such provision regarding access to company documents.

(e) Right to attend meetings

[7.070] CA 1990, s 193(5) provides that a company's auditor is entitled to attend any general meeting of the company and to receive the notices and communications related to such meetings as the members of the company are entitled to receive. An auditor is also entitled to address any meeting he attends on any part of the company's business which concerns him as auditor. The same right is conferred on auditors in the UK by CA 1985, s 390(1). An auditor also enjoys the rights to address meetings at which his resignation or removal are under consideration.[226]

D. Auditors' reporting obligations

(a) Background

[7.071] The detection of fraud has always formed part of the responsibilities of an auditor.[227] The focus on this aspect of an auditor's responsibilities has heightened in the wake of recent legislative amendments.[228] Some auditors prefer not to bear the responsibility for detecting and reporting fraud and,[229] to borrow the language used in *Re*

---

[223] CA 1990, s 197(3).

[224] CA 1990, s 197(4).

[225] CA 1990, s 193(4B)(a), as inserted by EC(IFRSMA)R 2005, reg 8.

[226] See paras **[7.006]** to **[7.010]** and **[7.013]** to **[7.016]**.

[227] 'From the time of the Pharaohs until the turn of the 20th century, auditors were responsible for fraud prevention and detection', J Wells, 'The Fraud Beat', *Journal of Accountancy* (October 2000).

[228] CA 1990, s 194(5), as amended by CLEA 2001, s 74(e), C(AA)A 2003, s 37(d) and IFCMPA 2005, s 73(2)(d); and CJ (TFO)A 2001, s 59.

[229] Statement by CEO of Ernst & Young (Philip Lawkawy) to the Washington Post in mid-1990s ('We don't want to be in the business of being fraud detectors').

Kingston Cotton Mill (No 2),[230] prefer the role of watch-dogs rather than bloodhounds.[231] However, a proper regime for the enforcement of company law depends on effective mechanisms for the detection of potential contraventions of those laws. The auditor plays a unique role in the context of a company, being a person who gains access to company documentation and information, while remaining independent and accountable for the representation of the company affairs to the outside world.

As such, an auditor is an ideal position to assist in the detection and reporting of infringements of company law which may not otherwise come to the attention of the authorities responsible for enforcing those laws.

[7.072] The role of an auditor in detecting and reporting matters of relevance to a company's affairs has been acknowledged by the English courts. The obligation was described in *Galoo Ltd (in liq) v Bright Grahame Murray (a firm)*[232] as follows:

> 'If auditors in the course of an audit come across matters which satisfy them that, unless they are disclosed, for example, to directors or even to regulators, the company is suffering and will continue to suffer losses, I do not think it would be right to say they have no duty to take any action until the audit is completed. An obvious example would be material which established, at least *prima facie*, that the managing director was stealing the company's property. To take no action so that the defalcations were able to and did continue should, it seems to me result in liability.'

This matter was further considered by the Court of Appeal in the decision of *Sasea Finance Ltd (in liq) v KPMG.*[233] Kennedy LJ examined the duties of an auditor, with particular reference to the obligations of an auditor to take action when fraud is detected in the course of the audit:

> 'When a firm of accountants accepts instructions to audit the accounts of a company for a fiscal year its primary obligation is within a reasonable time to exercise an appropriate level of skill and care in reporting to the company's members on the accounts of the company, stating, in their opinion, whether the accounts of the company give a true and fair view of the company's financial affairs. As mentioned, solely for the purposes of this application KPMG accepts that in certain circumstances a different type of obligation can arise. If, for example, the auditors discover that a senior employee of a company has been defrauding that company on a grand scale, and is in a position to go on doing so, then it will normally be the duty of the auditors to report what has been discovered to the management of the company at once, not simply, when rendering the auditors' report, to record what has been discovered weeks or months later.'[234]

---

[230] [1896] 2 Ch 279.

[231] Lopes LJ in *Re Kingston Cotton Mills Co* (No 2) [1896] 2 Ch 279, 288–289, described the auditor's role as follows: 'An auditor is not bound to be a detective, or, as was said, to approach his work with suspicion or with a foregone conclusion that there is something wrong. He is a watchdog, but not a bloodhound.'

[232] *Galoo Ltd (in liq) v Bright Grahame Murray (a firm)* [1994] 2 BCLC 492, [1995] 1 All ER 16, [1994] 1 WLR 1360.

[233] *Sasea Finance Ltd (in liq) v KPMG* [2000] 1 BCLC 236.

[234] *Sasea Finance Ltd (in liq) v KPMG* [2000] 1 BCLC 236, 240.

In the course of that decision, the Court of Appeal also noted that an auditor may be required to report a discovery of fraud directly to a third party without the consent or knowledge of management. This would arise if the management appeared to have a role in the fraud or irregularities, for instance, and would depend on the extent to which the fraud could result in material gain or loss, among other considerations.[235]

[7.073] In Ireland, the fact that an auditor must be mindful of the possibility of encountering fraud or error was acknowledged in the High Court decision of Kearns J in *Kennedy v Law Society*.[236] Having considered various authorities regarding the duty of auditors, such as *Re London and General Bank (No 2)*,[237] *Re Kingston Cotton Mill (No 2)*,[238] and *Leeds Estate Building and Investment Co v Shepherd*,[239] Kearns J noted that:

> 'All these cases go to show that the limits of an auditor's function are not to be narrowly interpreted. The auditor must go further and at times must go into areas which would not appear to be within his expertise and ascertain whether actual payments are lawful or permissible. If he needs to get advice on that, he is entitled to do so as the guidelines demonstrate. By implication, if he has the necessary expertise himself it may not be necessary to retain an expert for that purpose.'

While *Kennedy v Law Society*[240] concerned the role of an investigating accountant, appointed pursuant to the Solicitors' Accounts Regulations, and not the role of an auditor, the Supreme Court also endorsed the decision of Lopes LJ in *Re Kingston Cotton Mills (No 2)*, describing as a 'principle of utmost importance' the principle that:

> '... where an accountant is appointed as auditor of a company pursuant to the provisions of the Companies Acts 1963–1990, or engaged by a taxpayer to ascertain his profits for tax purposes, that he will be bound in certain circumstances to investigate dubious transactions. Lawyers and accountants alike have accepted the conclusion expressed by Lopes LJ in *In Re Kingston Cotton Mill (No 2)* [1896] 2 Ch 279, at pp 288 and 289 of the report, in the colourful and oft quoted simile that while an auditor is "a watchdog but not a blood hound ... if there is anything calculated to excite suspicion, he should probe it to the bottom".'[241]

[7.074] The Review Group on Auditing considered the role of an auditor in detecting breaches of laws and regulations and expressed the reservation that:

> '... given that the primary purpose of an audit is to express an opinion on the financial statements, its focus in relation to compliance would generally be on non-compliance with law and regulations where the financial impact is material to the company's financial statements. To expect that an audit could uncover all instances of non compliance would require a significant extension of the scope of the audit and consequently involve considerable extra cost. Therefore the Review

---

235 *Sasea Finance Ltd (in liq) v KPMG* [2000] 1 BCLC 236, 241.

236 *Kennedy v Law Society* [2000] 2 IR 204 (HC); [2002] 2 IR 458 (SC).

237 *Re London and General Bank (No 2)* [1895] 2 Ch 673.

238 *Re Kingston Cotton Mill (No 2)* [1896] 2 Ch 279.

239 *Leeds Estate Building and Investment Co v Shepherd* [1887] 36 Ch D 787.

240 *Kennedy v Law Society* [2000] 2 IR 204 (HC); [2002] 2 IR 458 (SC).

241 *Kennedy v Law Society* [2000] 2 IR 204 (HC); [2002] 2 IR 458 (SC) at 471 (*per* Murphy J).

Group accepts that without a fundamental shift in the scope and nature of the audit, it cannot, in itself, ensure full compliance with all statutory provisions.'[242]

The Group further stated:

'While the Review Group was anxious to strengthen the role of auditors in relation to compliance with statutory obligations, it felt that this should be achieved in a balanced manner that would not impose significant additional costs on companies.'[243]

[7.075] There are various Statements of Auditing Standards (SAS) and International Standards on Auditing (ISAs) that relate to the detection, identification and reporting of issues such as compliance with laws and regulations that may arise during an audit. These indicate the procedures and steps that should be followed by an auditor in this regard and indicate the scope of the relevant professional duties.[244]

[7.076] The importance of an auditor's role in detecting and reporting breaches of company law is acknowledged in the Strategy Statement of the ODCE for 2003–2005, which lists the second goal of the Office as the uncovering of suspected breaches of company law and which moreover recognises the important role that persons such as auditors play in the reporting of such breaches.[245] It is in this area of company law compliance and enforcement that an auditor plays the most significant role.

(b) Proper books of account

[7.077] Section 194(1) imposes an obligation on an auditor to notify the company and the Registrar of Companies if he forms the opinion that there is or has been a contravention of the duty to keep proper books of account, as required by CA 1990, s 202. [246] It is an offence for an auditor to fail to comply with this requirement.[247] Section 194(1) provides:

If, at any time, the auditors of a company form the opinion that the company is contravening, or has contravened, s 202 by failing to cause to be kept proper books of account (within the meaning of that section) in relation to the matters specified in sub-s (1) and (2) of that section, the auditors shall—

(a) as soon as may be, by recorded delivery, serve a notice in writing on the company stating their opinion, and

(b) not later than seven days after the service of such notice on the company, notify the registrar of companies in the prescribed form of the notice and the registrar shall forthwith forward a copy of the notice to the Director.[248]

---

[242] *Report of the Review Group on Auditing* at p 217.

[243] *Report of the Review Group on Auditing* at p 217.

[244] See, eg, SAS 110, 120, 620; ISA 220, 250.

[245] Office of the Director of Corporate Enforcement, *Strategy Statement 2003–2005*, at p 11. Available at www.odce.ie.

[246] This obligation is contained in CA 1990, s 202.

[247] CA 1990, s 194(4), as amended by CLEA 2001, s 74(d) and C(AA)A 2003, s 37(c).

[248] CA 1990, s 194(1), as amended by CLEA 2001, s 74.

The obligation to notify arises if the auditor forms the opinion, at any time, that a company is contravening, or has contravened, s 202, by failing to keep proper books of account in relation to matters specified in s 202(1) and (2).[249] This obligation is not confined to opinions formed in the course of conducting an audit, as is apparent from the phrase 'at any time', nor is it confined to suspicions of recent or on-going violations of the duty to keep proper books of account.

Upon formation of such opinion, the auditor must, 'as soon as may be' serve a notice in writing on the company, by means of recorded delivery, such as registered post, stating this opinion.[250] Within seven days after the service of this notice, the auditor must notify the Registrar of Companies of the fact that the notice was served.[251]

The form prescribed for this purpose is Form H4 which requires the auditor to state his opinion that either the company is contravening s 202 or has contravened s 202 by failing to keep proper books of account in relation to the matters specified in s 202(1) or (2). This form must be dated, signed, and provide the address and telephone number of the person presenting it.[252] When a Form H4 is delivered to the Registrar, he must forthwith forward a copy of this form to the DCE.[253]

[7.078] There are two circumstances in which an auditor is not obliged to serve a notice referred to in s 194(1), despite having formed the opinion that there is or was a contravention of s 202.

First, an auditor will be excused from the obligation to notify the Registrar of a contravention of s 202, if the auditor forms the opinion that, after such contravention, the directors of the company took the necessary steps to ensure that proper books of account are kept as required by s 202.[254] The exemption from the requirement to serve a Form H4 on the Registrar only applies if an auditor forms the opinion that a company is contravening, or has contravened, s 202; serves a notice to that effect on the company under s 194(1)(a); and, either before sending the notice to the company, or within the ensuing seven days, forms the opinion that the directors of the company have taken the necessary steps to ensure that proper books of account are kept. If an auditor forms the opinion from the outset that a company has contravened s 202 in the past, but necessary steps have since been taken to ensure that proper books of account are kept, s 194(2) suggests that he must nonetheless serve a notice on the company under s 194(1)(a), but will be exempt from the requirement to notify the Registrar.

Secondly, an auditor is not obliged to serve a notice on the company or on the Registrar under s 194(1), if the auditor is of the opinion that the contraventions are 'minor and otherwise immaterial in nature.'[255]

---

[249] See further Ch **4**.

[250] CA 1990, s 194(1)(a), as substituted by CLEA 2001, s 74(a).

[251] CA 1990, s 194(1)(b), as amended by CLEA 2001, s 74(b).

[252] Form H4 available at www.cro.ie-downloads-forms.

[253] CA 1990, s 194(1)(b), as amended by CLEA 2001, s 74(b).

[254] CA 1990, s 194(2).

[255] CA 1990, s 194(3).

[7.079] Upon receipt of a Form H4 from the Registrar of Companies, there are particular procedures that the DCE can avail of to assist in the investigation and prosecution of suspected infringements of the duty to keep proper books of account. Section 194(3A) provides:

> Where the auditors of a company file a notice pursuant to sub-s (1)(b), they shall, if requested by the Director—
>
> (a) furnish to the Director such information, including an explanation of the reasons for their opinion that the company had contravened s 202, and
>
> (b) give to the Director such access to books and documents, including facilities for inspecting and taking copies,
>
> being information, books or documents in their possession or control and relating to the matter the subject of the notice, as the Director may require.[256]

According to this provision, upon receipt of a s 194(1) notice, the DCE may request the auditor to provide information relating to the subject matter of the notice and the auditor must comply with this request.[257] The information that an auditor can be required to furnish includes an explanation of the grounds for the formation of the opinion that there is or was a contravention of s 202.[258]

Secondly, the DCE can require an auditor to provide access to books and documents relating to the subject matter of the notice.[259] In addition to access to books and documents, the DCE can also request the provision of facilities for inspection and copying of such books and documents.[260] The information, books and documents which the DCE can request under the amended s 194, are confined to such information, books and documents as are in the possession and control of the auditor.[261]

[7.080] While s 194(3A), as inserted by CLEA 2001, refers to the provision of such information, books and documents as 'requested' by the DCE, it also states that an auditor 'shall' furnish such information, books and documents 'as the Director may require'. It is clear from the wording of s 194(3A) that it is mandatory for an auditor to comply with any request made by the DCE under that subsection. This further evidenced by the fact that an auditor who fails to comply with such a request is guilty of an offence.[262]

---

[256] CA 1990, s 194(3A), as inserted by CLEA 2001, s 74, as amended by C(AA)A 2003, s 37.

[257] CA 1990, s 194(3A), as inserted by CLEA 2001, s 74(c) and as amended by C(AA)A 2003, s 37(b), which by C(AA)A 2003 (Commencement) Order 2007, SI 61/2007, came into effect on 1 March 2007.

[258] CA 1990, s 194(3A)(a), as inserted by CLEA 2001, s 74(c).

[259] CA 1990, s 194(3A)(b) as inserted by CLEA 2001, s 74(c), and as amended by C(AA)A 2003, s 37(a).

[260] CA 1990, s 194(3A)(b), as inserted by CLEA 2001, s 74(c) and as amended by C(AA)A 2003, s 37(a).

[261] CA 1990, s 194(3A), as inserted by CLEA 2001, s 74(c) and as amended by C(AA)A 2003, s 37(b).

[262] CA 1990, s 194(4), as amended by CLEA 2001, s 74(d), and as amended by C(AA)A 2003, s 37(c), which by C(AA)A 2003 (Commencement) Order 2007, SI 61/2007, came into effect on 1 March 2007.

[7.081] Any written information that an auditor provides to the DCE pursuant to s 194(3A) is deemed to be admissible in all legal proceedings as evidence of any facts contained in such information.[263] Section 194(3B) provides:

> Any written information given in response to a request of the Director under sub-s (3A) shall in all legal proceedings be admissible without further proof, until the contrary is shown, as evidence of the facts stated therein.[264]

This provision permits the admissibility into evidence of 'written information.' 'Information' is referred to in s 194(3A)(1)(a), whereas 'books and documents' are referred to in s 194(3A)(1)(b). It must be assumed that the use of the term 'information' in s 194(3B) is not accidental and that it only encompasses information, other than books and documents, insofar as the auditor has reduced such information to writing. An example of 'written information' that may be supplied to the DCE would be a written explanation by an auditor for the formation of the opinion that a company was not keeping proper books of account. The admissibility of such evidence could expose a company to a prosecution founded largely on the opinion of the auditor and his explanations for such an opinion. While such evidence is only admissible to the extent that it is not disproved,[265] s 194(3A) clearly envisages an auditor having possession and control of relevant documents and this possession and control may render it difficult for a company to disprove an auditor's opinion that the company contravened s 202.

[7.082] Prior to the enactment of CLEA 2001, the only obligation that the Companies Acts imposed on an auditor to report a company's affairs to an outside body was the obligation to report suspected failures to keep proper books of account to the Registrar of Companies. It is of note that very few such reports appear to have been filed in the years between the enactment of the CA 1990 and the enactment of the CLEA 2001. The Minister for Enterprise, Trade and Employment remarked that fewer than ten such reports were filed in most years and that auditors could do more to report any improper behaviour of which a company or its directors may be guilty.[266]

(c) Duty to report indictable offences

[7.083] An auditor is under an obligation to make a report to the DCE if he forms the opinion that an indictable offence under the Companies Acts has been committed. This reporting obligation was first introduced by the CLEA 2001. It has since been amended

---

[263] CA 1990, s 194(3B), as inserted by CLEA 2001, s 74(c).

[264] CA 1990, s 194(3B), as inserted by CLEA 2001, s 74(c).

[265] CA 1990, s 194(3B), as inserted by CLEA 2001, s 74(c) provides that the written information referred to is admissible 'until the contrary is shown'.

[266] Remarks by the DCE, Mr Paul Appleby, to the Leinster Society of Chartered Accountants Luncheon (14 May 2002), p 5. The Director commented, at p 7 that, '... [t]he number of reports by auditors of improper books of account has since increased from less than ten to more than fifty *per* year.'

by the C(AA)A 2003, an amendment which was repealed by the IFCMPA 2005, before it was commenced.[267] Section 194(5) now provides as follows:

> Where, in the course of, and by virtue of, their carrying out an audit of the accounts of the company, information comes into the possession of the auditors of a company that leads them to form the opinion that there are reasonable grounds for believing that the company or an officer or agent of it has committed an indictable offence under the Companies Acts (other than or indictable offence under s 125(2) or 127(12) of the Principal Act), the auditors shall, forthwith after having formed it, notify that opinion to the Director and provide the Director with details of the grounds on which they have formed that opinion.[268]

[7.084] This is a significant requirement from the perspective of company law enforcement and it has been the subject of considerable debate and analysis. In interpreting s 194(5), it is important to have regard to the decision notice on this topic which the ODCE prepared together with the APB and the Consultative Committee of Accountancy Bodies – Ireland ('CCAB-I').[269] It is also important to have regard to the International Auditing Standards (IAS), particularly as these standards are regarded by the law as an indication of and guide to the standards that the law expects of auditors.[270]

The following aspects of this provision will now be considered:

(i) 'in the course of and by virtue of' audit work;

(ii) requirement of 'information';

(iii) 'opinion' to be formed;

(iv) 'reasonable grounds';

(v) level of certainty;

(vi) company, officer or agent;

(vii) indictable offence under the Companies Acts;

---

[267] CA 1990, s 194(5), as inserted by CLEA 2001, s 74(e), was amended by C(AA)A 2003, s 37(d) (to insert '(other than an indictable offence under section 125(1) or 127(12) of the Principal Act)' (never commenced); it was further amended by IFCMPA 2005, s 73(3), which repealed C(AA)A 2003, s 37(d); and by IFCMPA 2005, s 73(2)(d) (to insert '(other than an indictable offence under section 125(2) or 127(12) of the Principal Act)'). By the IFCMPA 2005 (Commencement) Order 2005, ss 73(2)(d) and (3) came into effect on 1 September 2005. All of these amendments were necessitated by the fact that C(AA)A 2003, s 37(d) contained an erroneous reference to CA 1963, s 125(1), rather than to s 125(2).

[268] CA 1990, s 194(5), as inserted by CLEA 2001, s 74(e), as amended by C(AA)A 2003, s 37(d), IFCMPA 2005, s 73(3), and by IFCMPA 2005, s 73(2)(d).

[269] ODCE 'Revised Guidance on the Duty of Auditors to Report Suspected Indictable Offences to the Director of Corporate Enforcement' Decision Notice D/2006/2, which is largely identical to APB, 'The Duty of Auditors in the Republic of Ireland to Report to the Director of Corporate Enforcement' Bulletin 2007/2 (March 2007).

[270] See, eg, the heavy reliance placed by the ODCE on the relevant IASs in its 'Revised Guidance on the Duty of Auditors to Report Suspected Indictable Offences to the Director of Corporate Enforcement' Decision Notice D/2006/2.

(viii)   no discretion;

 (ix)   timing of notification;

  (x)   further information, books and documents; and

 (xi)   legal professional privilege.

(i) 'in the course and by virtue of' audit work

[7.085] Section 194(5) is only triggered if an auditor comes into possession of the relevant information '… in the course of, and by virtue of, their carrying out an audit of the accounts of the company …'. Two conclusions may be drawn from this. First, information which comes into the possession of an auditor during the conduct of non-audit work for the company will not trigger s 194(5). Secondly, the reporting obligation will not arise if information comes into the auditor's possession during the conduct of an audit, but which did not result from the audit work itself.

[7.086] With regard to the inference that information obtained in the course of non-audit work does not trigger s 194(5), there are three different scenarios to consider. First, the position of a person who conducts solely non-audit work for a company needs to be considered. Second, the same person may conduct non-audit and audit work for a company, whether contemporaneously or otherwise. Third, a member of a firm may come into possession of relevant information in the course of conducting non-audit work for a company of which one of his colleagues is acting as auditor.

[7.087] The language of s 194(5) clearly limits its application to information which is obtained during, and as a result of, the conduct of an audit of a company. With regard to a person who conducts exclusively non-audit work, there is no apparent basis for applying s 194(5). The ODCE has indicated that, 'In general … the reporting obligation does not apply to a person providing non-audit services to a company'.[271] A person who provides non-auditing services to a company, and who never provides auditing services, is not therefore affected by s 194(5).

The formulation of s 194(5) similarly appears to exclude from its scope information which comes into the possession of a person in the course of conducting non-audit work for a company, for which he also conducts audit work.

The applicable auditing standard is ISA 250B, which explains that:

> '… the statutory duty to report to a regulator applies to information which comes
> to the attention of the auditor in the auditor's capacity as auditor. In determining
> whether information is obtained in that capacity, two criteria in particular need to
> be considered: first, whether the person who obtained the information also
> undertook the audit work; and if so, whether it was obtained in the course of or as
> a result of undertaking the audit work.'[272]

---

[271] See, eg, ODCE, 'Revised Guidance on the Duty of Auditors to Report Suspected Indictable Offences to the Director of Corporate Enforcement' Decision Notice D/2006/2 at p 7.

[272] ISA (UK and Ireland), ISA 250B at para 4.

This ISA further advises that, if information comes into an individual's possession other than in the course of conducting an audit, which suggests that there would be a duty to make a report to a regulatory authority, if the information was obtained in his capacity as auditor:

> '... it will be prudent for them to make enquiries in the course of their audit work in order to establish whether this is the case from information obtained in that capacity.'[273]

The effect of this guidance is that, unless the information comes into an individual's possession in the course of conducting audit work, there is no obligation to report the information to the appropriate regulatory authority. However, if, in the course of non-audit work, a person becomes aware of information which may give rise to an auditor's duty to report, and that person subsequently conducts an audit of the company, it would be 'prudent' for him to enquire, from information obtained in his capacity as auditor, whether such a duty to report does exist. It is notable that this report would not therefore be based on information obtained in the course of non-audit work.

[7.088] The ODCE's interpretation of this aspect of the scope of s 194(5) is that:

> '... where a person performs, or has performed, non-audit work for a company for whom s/he also acts, or subsequently accepts appointment, as auditor, that auditor, acting as such, has certain responsibilities in relation to any information suggesting the commission of an indictable offence which came to attention during the course of the non-audit work.'[274]

This guidance adopts a different emphasis to that which appears in ISA 250B in one important respect. ISA 250B limits the reporting obligation to information which is obtained in the course of the conduct of the audit, even if the enquiry is prompted by information otherwise obtained. By contrast, the ODCE suggests that an auditor has a particular responsibility in relation to information 'which came to attention during the course of the non-audit work'. There is no qualification or statement to the effect that this information must also come into the auditor's possession in his capacity as such before the reporting obligation will be triggered.

[7.089] However, in relation to the timing of the reporting obligation, the ODCE makes is clear that if issues are first identified in the course of non-audit work, it is only when the information comes into the person's possession in his capacity as auditor that the reporting obligation arises:

> 'With regard to the point in time at which auditors' reporting obligations arise in respect of matters first identified in the course of providing non-audit services:
>
> - where a person providing non-audit services to a company becomes aware of an indictable offence and s/he also acts as the auditor of that company, the obligation to report the suspected indictable offence will arise when the auditor comes into possession of the information in question as part of the undertaking of the audit, and

---

[273] ISA (UK and Ireland), ISA 250B, App 2 at para 8.

[274] ODCE, 'Revised Guidance on the Duty of Auditors to Report Suspected Indictable Offences to the Director of Corporate Enforcement' Decision Notice D/2006/2 at para 4.2.

- where a person providing non-audit services to a company becomes aware of
  an indictable offence and s/he is subsequently appointed to act as the auditor
  of that company, the obligation to report the suspected indictable offence will
  arise when the auditor comes into possession of the information in question
  as part of the undertaking of the audit.'[275]

It is therefore only when the information comes into an auditor's possession in his
capacity as such, that the obligation to report under s 194(5) arises. While the ODCE
guidance appears to be premised on the assumption that this information will come into
his hands as auditor, this may not necessarily be the case. As previously acknowledged
by the ODCE, '…it is possible that the information suggesting an indictable offence may
not come to attention as part of the normal audit process.'[276] If an auditor does not come
into possession of the requisite information in the course of the audit, there will be no
duty to make a report to the DCE, irrespective of his prior or present suspicion of the
commission of an indictable offence from information otherwise obtained.

[7.090] The third and final situation in which the application of s 194(5) to non-audit
work falls to be considered relates to members of the same firm carrying out audit and
non-audit work for the same company. The issue here is the extent, if any, to which an
individual conducting non-audit work, who comes into possession of information which
would give rise to a reporting duty if detected in the course of audit work, should convey
that information to members of the same firm who are conducting such audit work. The
Review Group on Auditing addressed this issue as follows:

> 'Where non-audit partners of an audit firm have information in relation to a client
> company which may be relevant to their audit of that company, the audit
> engagement partner's responsibility to take account of such information for the
> purposes of the audit is not clear, particularly where that information is withheld
> from the audit partner. The Review Group recommends that this should be
> rectified in the appropriate audit standards.'[277]

The Review Group's recommendation was as follows:

> 'The audit engagement partner and staff of a firm should be presumed to know
> everything relevant to the audit of a client company that other partners in the firm
> or an associated firm are aware of in relation to the company. A firm appointed as
> auditor of a company needs to have in place appropriate procedures to ensure that
> the partner responsible for the audit function is made aware of any other
> relationship which exists between any department of the audit firm and the
> company when that relationship could affect the audit firm's responsibilities as
> auditors.'[278]

[7.091] ISA 250 issued the following guidance in this regard:

> 'The right and duty to report to a regulator applies to information of which the
> auditor becomes aware in the auditor's capacity as such. They do not extend

---

[275] ODCE, 'Revised Guidance on the Duty of Auditors to Report Suspected Indictable
Offences to the Director of Corporate Enforcement' Decision Notice D/2006/2 at para 4.12.

[276] ODCE Consultation Paper C/2002/2, p 5.

[277] *Report of the Review Group on Auditing* at p 185.

[278] *Report of the Review Group on Auditing* at p 186 (recommendation 12.6).

automatically to any information obtained by an accounting firm regardless of its source. Consequently partners and staff undertaking work in another capacity are not required to have detailed knowledge of the regulator's requirements (unless necessary for that other work) nor to bring information to the attention of the partner responsible for the audit on a routine basis.'[279]

This suggests that there is no requirement that partners in the same firm who are conducting non-audit and audit work in respect of the same company must exchange information. This guidance is qualified by the following:

'However ... firms need to establish lines of communication, commensurate with their size and complexity, sufficient to ensure that non-audit work undertaken for a regulated entity which is likely to have an effect on the audit is brought to the attention of the partner responsible for the audit, who will need to determine whether the results of non-audit work undertaken for a regulated entity ought to be assessed as part of the audit process.'[280]

[7.092] The ODCE notes that s 194(5), 'does not impose a legal obligation on persons undertaking non-audit services to inform the auditors within the firm of the information which has come into their possession.'[281] However, the ODCE also quotes the ISA guidance to the effect that a firm which is appointed as auditor must treat information in a responsible manner; the partner responsible for the audit should conduct all necessary enquiries, including enquiries regarding those aspects of the non-audit work which may be relevant to the audit; and should consider whether information obtained in other capacities should be assessed as part of the audit process, particularly because of the legal position that the knowledge obtained by one partner may be imputed to the entire partnership.[282]

While neither ISA 250B nor the ODCE's Decision Notice contain an express requirement that partners in a firm must exchange information obtained during non-audit work for a company with partners responsible for auditing the company all information which may be relevant to an audit should be exchanged and taken into account, and there is an obligation to handle such information appropriately and in a responsible manner.

[7.093] A final point to note about this aspect of s 194(5) is that it refers to information obtained 'by virtue of' the carrying out of a company's audit. This suggests that information that an auditor obtains incidentally while carrying out an audit, rather than in the discharge of his functions as auditor, is excluded from s 194(5). The line between information that arises 'by virtue' of audit work and information incidental to such work may be a narrow one and a difficult one by which to determine whether an obligation to report a suspected offence will arise. Moreover, in light of the fact that a failure by an

---

[279] ISA (UK and Ireland), ISA 250B, at para 37.

[280] ISA (UK and Ireland), ISA 250B, at para 38.

[281] ODCE, 'Revised Guidance on the Duty of Auditors to Report Suspected Indictable Offences to the Director of Corporate Enforcement' Decision Notice D/2006/2 at para 4.1.

[282] ODCE, 'Revised Guidance on the Duty of Auditors to Report Suspected Indictable Offences to the Director of Corporate Enforcement' Decision Notice D/2006/2 at paras 4.5 and 4.7.

auditor to comply with the reporting obligations of s 194, as amended, is an offence,[283] it is unlikely that an auditor will rely on the niceties of whether the information arose by virtue of the audit work itself, or some other aspect of the work conducted, in order to justify not making a report under s 194(5).

(ii) Requirement of 'information'

[7.094] The obligation to make a report under s 194(5) only arises:

> [w]here, in the course of, and by virtue of, their carrying out an audit of the accounts of the company, information comes into the possession of the auditors of a company that leads them to form the opinion that there are reasonable grounds for believing that the company or an officer or agent of it has committed an indictable offence.

There are four points to note about the requirement in s 194(5) that an auditor must come into possession of 'information'. First, this requirement indicates an important aspect of an auditor's obligation to detect the commission of possible indictable offences. Information must come into the auditor's possession during and as a result of the audit work he is undertaking. It is only if and when that occurs that an auditor must enquire further and conduct investigations. No action on the part of the auditor is necessary. He is not obliged to find such information, seek it out, or conduct investigations to determine whether any such information may exist. This interpretation is confirmed by the ODCE – 'the Director does not regard the obligation as requiring auditors to seek out possible indictable offences as part of the audit process.'[284]

[7.095] Secondly, the 'information' must come into the auditor's possession during the audit. A suspicion that pre-dates the auditor's appointment or arises from information received outside the scope of the audit is excluded from s 194(5), as the formulation of that provision indicates that the suspicion must arise from 'information' received during the audit.[285]

[7.096] Thirdly, the terms 'information' and 'grounds' in s 194(5) seem at first sight, to be repetitive and duplicative. However, on closer analysis, they do achieve different purposes. The requirement of 'information' relates to the initial discovery that an indictable offence may have been committed. The fact that this information must 'lead to the formation of an opinion that there are reasonable grounds' suggests that, upon receipt of the initial information, the auditor must investigate matters further and determine that there are 'reasonable grounds' before the obligation to report the opinion arises. While the 'information' itself may be sufficiently probative to constitute 'reasonable grounds', this will not always occur and the formulation of s 194(5) ensures that an auditor should go beyond the initial 'information' and determine whether

---

[283] CA 1990, s 194(4), as amended by CLEA 2001, s 74(d).

[284] ODCE, 'Revised Guidance on the Duty of Auditors to Report Suspected Indictable Offences to the Director of Corporate Enforcement' Decision Notice D/2006/2 at para 5.1.

[285] See, however, ODCE, 'Revised Guidance on the Duty of Auditors to Report Suspected Indictable Offences to the Director of Corporate Enforcement' Decision Notice D/2006/2, regarding duty to investigate information that came into an auditor's possession during non-audit work. See further para **[7.088]**.

'reasonable grounds' exist, before making a report to the DCE. The ODCE supports this interpretation:

> '... auditors react to information coming into their possession which suggests that a possible indictable offence has occurred and to make the necessary enquiries to enable them to form a considered opinion on the question.'[286]

This interpretation is further supported by the final phrase of s 194(5), which states that a reporting auditor must 'provide the Director with details of the grounds on which they have formed that opinion'.[287] It is not the initial information that prompted the auditor's suspicion, with which the DCE is concerned, but the actual grounds on which the auditor considered it necessary to make a report under s 194(5).

[7.097] A final point is that the 'information' which prompts an auditor's enquiries under s 194(5), must not take any particular form, as it does not need to be communicated to the DCE as such. The 'information' obtained could be in written or oral form, and may be inconclusive and equivocal in nature. The only requirement is that it must prompt the auditor to assess whether there are 'reasonable grounds' to form an opinion that an indictable offence has been committed.

(iii) Opinion to be formed

[7.098] An auditor must obtain information that leads him to 'to form the opinion that there are reasonable grounds for believing that the company or an officer or agent of it has committed an indictable offence' before the reporting obligation of s 194(5) will arise. The language used to describe the opinion that must be formed appears circular, as opinions and beliefs are similar in effect.[288] Section 194(5) essentially requires an auditor to believe that there are reasonable grounds to believe a state of affairs exists. The effect of this, however, is that the auditor himself does not have to state his opinion or belief that an offence has been committed. He merely has to have the opinion that one could believe, on reasonable grounds, that an indictable offence was committed. The conclusion does not need to be a subjective one.

[7.099] An auditor is entitled to obtain assistance in forming his opinion as to whether there are reasonable grounds to believe an offence has been committed. While the opinion must be his own and he must exercise his own professional judgment, he can seek legal and other professional advice in forming it. There is no obligation or duty on an auditor to seek such outside advice. However, in light of the fact that an auditor is bound by a duty of confidentiality and is not permitted to disclose information to third parties, other than when statutorily obliged to do so, he would be well advised to ensure

---

[286] ODCE, 'Revised Guidance on the Duty of Auditors to Report Suspected Indictable Offences to the Director of Corporate Enforcement' Decision Notice D/2006/2 at para 5.1.

[287] CA 1990, s 194(5), as inserted by CLEA 2001, s 74(e), as amended by C(AA)A 2003, s 37(d), IFCMPA 2005, s 73(3), and by IFCMPA 2005, s 73(2)(d).

[288] An 'opinion' may be defined as a 'belief stronger than impression and less strong than positive knowledge' and to 'believe' something may be defined as 'to hold an opinion.' Merriam Webster Online Dictionary.

any uncertainty or ambiguity is carefully resolved, before making a report to the ODCE under s 194(5).

The dicta of Lord Denning in *Fomento (Sterling Area) Ltd v Selsdon Fountain Pen Co Ltd*[289] would be of assistance to an auditor in this regard:

> Take, for instance, a point of law arising in the course of auditing a company's accounts. He may come on a payment which, it appears to him, may be unlawful, in that it may not be within the powers of the corporation, or improper in that it may have no warrant or justification. He is, then, not only entitled but bound to inquire into it and, if need be, to disallow it; see *Roberts v Hopwood* (at p 605), *Re Ridsdel, Ridsdel v Rawlinson* ([1947] 2 All ER 312 at p 316). It may be, of course, that he has sufficient legal knowledge to deal with it himself, as many accountants have, but, if it is beyond him, he is entitled to take legal advice on the principle stated in *Bevan v Webb* ([1901] 2 Ch 59 at p 75), that 'permission to a man to do an act, which he cannot do effectually without the help of an agent, carries with it the right to employ an agent'.

[7.100] The ODCE notes:

> While there is no obligation on auditors to obtain legal or other professional advice before forming that opinion, the Director recognises that auditors may wish to seek such independent advice as part of the process of forming their opinion. Where legal or other professional advice is obtained by the company in relation to the matter(s) about which the auditor has concerns, the auditor is similarly required to exercise professional judgement in determining if the information is reportable to the Director of Corporate Enforcement. While in many cases auditors could expect to be satisfied with legal advice emanating from a reputable source, auditors would not be entitled to rely on such advice if, having taken it into account, they formed the opinion that the advice was in error, incomplete or otherwise inadequate by reference to the information in their possession.[290]

This guidance makes it clear that the ODCE will not consider it to be a good defence to a charge of failing to make a report under s 194(5), that the auditor received legal advice to the effect that such a report was not necessary, if the auditor himself formed a contrary opinion. An auditor would be well advised to document carefully the information they receive and their own opinion as to its impact, and to assess any advice received in the exercise of their own professional duties. An auditor cannot delegate to a third party responsibility for determining whether there are 'reasonable grounds for believing' that an indictable offence has been committed.

(iv) 'Reasonable grounds'

[7.101] Having come into possession of information which leads an auditor to suspect the possible commission of an indictable offence, he must assess whether there are 'reasonable grounds' to support this suspicion before an obligation to report under

---

[289] *Fomento (Sterling Area) Ltd v Selsdon Fountain Pen Co Ltd and Others* [1958] 1 All ER 11, at 22.

[290] ODCE, 'Revised Guidance on the Duty of Auditors to Report Suspected Indictable Offences to the Director of Corporate Enforcement' Decision Notice D/2006/2 at paras 6.1 and 6.2.

s 194(5) will arise. There is no definition or illustration of what 'grounds' would suffice. However, the grounds must be objectively verifiable and must be sufficiently detailed to support an opinion under s 194(5). This is apparent from the requirement that the auditor must 'provide the Director with details of the grounds on which they have formed that opinion.'[291]

The DCE originally interpreted the phrase 'details of the grounds' to include an obligation to provide relevant documents in support of the opinion formed by the auditor.[292] The DCE also regarded the provision as permitting an auditor to provide 'clarification or amplification of the information submitted by the auditor' and as permitting the DCE to require such additional information, including any or all of the auditor's working papers.[293] While there was no such provision in s 194(5), s 194(5A) now provides, in similar terms as s 194(3A), for the provision of additional information, books and documents, by an auditor.[294]

[7.102] The ODCE states that 'Auditors should provide sufficient information in support of their opinion to enable the Director to evaluate properly the circumstances suggesting the commission of an indictable offence.'[295] The ODCE further refers to the requirement that an auditor provide 'details of the grounds' for the opinion, as follows: 'Auditors should ensure that this description is of sufficient detail to facilitate appropriate action by the Director.'[296]

The ODCE form to be used by an auditor in making a report under s 194(5), similarly requires the following information to be submitted:

> 'Details of the grounds on which you have formed the opinion that an indictable offence has been committed (you should ensure that the details provided are of sufficient detail to facilitate appropriate action by the Director).'[297]

This requirement that an auditor 'should ensure that the details provided are of sufficient detail to facilitate appropriate action by the Director' goes further than the terms of s 194(5) itself. While s 194(5) requires 'reasonable grounds' to exist and requires that 'details of the grounds' on which the auditor formed his opinion must be furnished, it does not specify that the details of the grounds must be sufficient to facilitate action by the DCE. However, the ODCE purports to require that level of detail. The meaning of 'appropriate action by the Director' and what would comprise 'sufficient detail to facilitate' such action, are not clear. If this suggests that an auditor must provide sufficient information for the DCE to prosecute the offence, this would require

---

[291] CA 1990, s 194(5), as inserted by CLEA 2001, s 74(e), as amended by C(AA)A 2003, s 37(d), IFCMPA 2005, s 73(3), and by IFCMPA 2005, s 73(2)(d).

[292] ODCE, Consultation Paper C/2002/2, p 11.

[293] ODCE, Consultation Paper C/2002/2, p 11.

[294] CA 1990, s 194(5A), as inserted by C(AA)A 2003, s 37.

[295] ODCE, 'Revised Guidance on the Duty of Auditors to Report Suspected Indictable Offences to the Director of Corporate Enforcement' Decision Notice D/2006/2 at para 11.1.

[296] ODCE, 'Revised Guidance on the Duty of Auditors to Report Suspected Indictable Offences to the Director of Corporate Enforcement' Decision Notice D/2006/2 at para 11.2.

[297] ODCE, Indictable Offences Report Form, Decision Notice D/2002/2, App 3, Item 5.

considerable detail and would appear to exceed what is required by s 194(5). The 'reasonable grounds' that may be required to form an opinion that one could believe an offence has been committed, are not of the same level of depth and detail as the grounds that would be required to facilitate the prosecution of such an offence.

[7.103] The interpretation that the 'details' which an auditor is required to furnish under s 194(5) are not as extensive as the ODCE suggests, is bolstered by the fact that s 195(5A) now permits the DCE to specifically request additional information, books and documents.[298] The ODCE describes this provision as follows:

> 'The purpose of this additional provision is to enable the Director to acquire on an efficient and effective basis the quality of information and evidence which initially led the auditor to report the suspected offence and thereby to facilitate the Director in reaching an informed decision as to what enforcement action (if any) is warranted by him as a result of the indicated circumstances.'

If the purpose of s 195(5A) is to facilitate the DCE in deciding what, if any, enforcement action is warranted, it seems unnecessary and excessive to interpret s 194(5) as imposing an obligation on auditors 'to ensure that this description [under s 194(5)] is of sufficient detail to facilitate appropriate action by the Director.'[299]

It seems more appropriate and accurate to interpret the obligation imposed by s 194(5) in a narrow manner, as requiring a description of the 'reasonable grounds' on which the auditor formed an opinion. Insofar as the DCE may require further information, books and documents, to decide what, if any, course of action to take, he can make an appropriate request under s 194(5A).

(v) Level of certainty required

[7.104] An auditor must form the opinion that an offence 'has been committed'. An auditor's opinion that an offence may have been committed will not give rise to the obligation to report the offence to the DCE. This is confirmed by the ODCE in its 'Revised Guidance on the Duty of Auditors to Report Suspected Indictable Offences to the Director of Corporate Enforcement,' wherein the ODCE notes that the terminology used on s 194(5) requires a higher degree of certainty than 'may' or 'might' have committed.[300] The level of certainty required is however diluted by the fact that an auditor must form the opinion that there are reasonable grounds to believe that an indictable offence 'has been committed.' The auditor is not required to form or state his own opinion that such an offence 'has been committed.'

---

[298] See further paras **[7.116]** to **[7.118]**.

[299] ODCE, 'Revised Guidance on the Duty of Auditors to Report Suspected Indictable Offences to the Director of Corporate Enforcement' Decision Notice D/2006/2 at para 11.2.

[300] ODCE, 'Revised Guidance on the Duty of Auditors to Report Suspected Indictable Offences to the Director of Corporate Enforcement' Decision Notice D/2006/2 at para 8.1.

This requirement can be contrasted with the applicable reporting provision in the US, which refers to '… an illegal act which has or may have occurred'.[301] While the reference to 'has been committed' is more limited, it may be criticised for obliging the auditor to make a definitive assessment of fact, rather than allowing the levels of certainty to be assessed in the investigation and prosecution process.

(vi) Company, officer or agent

[7.105] An opinion under s 194(5) must be to the effect that 'the company or an officer or agent of it has committed an indictable offence under the Companies Acts'. 'The company' referred to in s 194(5) can only be the company under audit. Information which comes into the possession of an auditor during an audit, which relates to a company other than the company under audit, will not therefore trigger the obligation to investigate and report under s 194(5). The ODCE confirms in this regard:

> 'In the subsection, "the company" is the company which is being audited by the auditor ("Company A"). Subject to what follows, the reporting obligation does not therefore extend to another company ("Company B"), which the auditor of Company A may believe has committed a reportable offence.'[302]

[7.106] The ODCE also confirms that a 'company' must be a company formed and registered under the Companies Acts to come within the scope of s 194(5) and that:

> 'The reporting obligation on auditors imposed by the subsection does not extend to companies formed outside the State, even where they may be registered as having an established place of business within the State under the Companies Acts or where they operate through a branch (under the European Communities (Branch Disclosure) Regulations 1993).'[303]

The only 'company' which can be reported under s 194(5), is therefore a company formed and registered under the Companies Acts, which is the subject of the audit in question. The only qualification to this is that an audit of the consolidated financial statements of a group of companies, may give rise to a duty to report any of them individually under s 194(5).[304]

---

[301] 'Actual knowledge of an illegal act is not a required element for imposition of liability under Section 10A,' *SEC v Solucorp*, 2002 WL 741660 (SDNY 26 April 2002). 'Illegal act' means '…an act or omission that violates any law, or any rule or regulation having the force of law', Securities Exchange Act 1934, s 10A(f).

[302] ODCE, 'Revised Guidance on the Duty of Auditors to Report Suspected Indictable Offences to the Director of Corporate Enforcement' Decision Notice D/2006/2 at para 7.1.

[303] ODCE, 'Revised Guidance on the Duty of Auditors to Report Suspected Indictable Offences to the Director of Corporate Enforcement' Decision Notice D/2006/2 at para 7.4.

[304] ODCE, 'Revised Guidance on the Duty of Auditors to Report Suspected Indictable Offences to the Director of Corporate Enforcement' Decision Notice D/2006/2 at para 7.7.

[7.107] The term 'officer' as it appears in s 194(5), covers directors and secretaries.[305] It may also, depending on the offence at issue, extend to shadow directors.[306] An agent of a company includes any person authorised to bind the company and would encompass its solicitor in certain circumstances, but will not include counsel.[307]

[7.108] If an auditor detects during an audit of a company that an offence may have been committed by another company, this is not within the scope of s 194(5). However, if, during the audit of a company, the auditor forms an opinion that an officer or agent committed an indictable offence in relation to a different company, this is within the scope of s 194(5). This arises from the wording of s 194(5) which addresses offences committed by 'the company or an officer or agent of it', without any requirement that the offence must have been committed in connection with the company under audit. The ODCE describes this interpretation as follows: 'In other words, a suspected indictable offence by an officer [or agent] of Company A relating to his or her involvement in Company B is eligible to be reported by the auditor of Company A.'[308]

(vii) Indictable offence under the Companies Acts

[7.109] The reporting obligation of s 194(5) applies to any indictable offence under the Companies Acts. An auditor may find this criterion difficult to apply in practice, as it pre-supposes a knowledge and understanding on the part of an auditor of a company of each and every indictable offence under the Companies Acts, the distinction between those that are indictable and those that are not, and the indicia of each.[309] An auditor is now also supposed to be aware of the dates at which offences were created or amended by legislation, and, the fact that certain offences may have been repealed notwithstanding, is expected to report matters which were criminalised at the date of commission. The ODCE refers to the fact that certain offences have been repealed by

---

[305] CA 1963, s 2(1).

[306] See ODCE, 'Revised Guidance on the Duty of Auditors to Report Suspected Indictable Offences to the Director of Corporate Enforcement' Decision Notice D/2006/2 at para 7.6.

[307] See CA 1963, s 2(1) ('"Agent" does not include a person's counsel acting as such') See ODCE, 'Revised Guidance on the Duty of Auditors to Report Suspected Indictable Offences to the Director of Corporate Enforcement' Decision Notice D/2006/2 at para 7.9.

[308] ODCE, 'Revised Guidance on the Duty of Auditors to Report Suspected Indictable Offences to the Director of Corporate Enforcement' Decision Notice D/2006/2 at paras 7.8 and 7.10. Note that this interpretation has been the subject of criticism. See Irish Times, 'Company law move generates wide concern' 12 June 2006, quoting report prepared by PriceWaterhouseCoopers: 'We do not believe that company auditors would be empowered by the Companies' Acts to obtain information relating to other companies or actions by directors or agents outside their capacity as directors or agents of the company being audited.'

[309] As noted in the Report of the Working Group on Company Law Enforcement and Compliance (30 November 1998), there are 280 separate criminal offences under the Criminal Acts 1963–1990. The ODCE 'The Duty of Directors to Report to the Director of Corporate Enforcement' (Decision Notice D/2002/2) at pp 23–38 lists the indictable offences that exist under the Companies Acts 1963–2001, as of 2002. There are 128 such offences listed.

the IFCMPA 2005, noting that, 'such offences continue to be offences which auditors are obliged to report to the ODCE pursuant to s 194(5) of the Companies Act, 1990 (as amended) where such offences were committed prior to the date of commencement of the Investment Funds Companies and Miscellaneous Provisions Act, 2005.'[310] This requires a detailed knowledge of the CA 1963–2006, including the commencement dates of particular provisions, not an easy knowledge to acquire. However, the list of indictable offences under the Companies Acts that has been prepared by the ODCE should be of assistance to auditors.[311]

[7.110] The recommendation of the Review Group on Auditing would be a notable aid in ensuring that auditors are aware of the offences which may trigger the reporting obligation of s 194(5):

> 'As part of the continuing professional development programme for their auditing members, each of the recognised accountancy bodies should include refresher courses on auditors' statutory obligations under the Companies Acts ... and similar legislation and on their duties under the body's code of ethics.'[312]

[7.111] The ODCE attempts to limit the scope of the matters which an auditor must consider under s 194(5), stating it is not necessary for an auditor to evaluate the seriousness or otherwise of the offence and that the following matters are not relevant to the formation of an opinion under s 194(5):[313]

– 'whether the suspected offence has any impact on the company's financial statements or on the auditor's opinion as to whether or not the financial statements give a true and fair view of the state of affairs of the company';

– 'what the policy of the Director of Corporate Enforcement or the Director of Public Prosecutions is with respect to the prosecution of indictable offences of a particular type. In other words even if it is their policy to prosecute certain offences summarily, this is not a matter which should affect the formation of the auditor's opinion in respect of the reporting of any suspected indictable offence';

– 'the extent to which the suspected indictable offence might involve a financial or other loss to any person';

– 'whether the suspected offence may or may not have already been brought to the attention of the Director of Corporate Enforcement by the company, one of its officers or agents or another party';

– 'whether or not circumstances giving rise to the offence have been rectified or otherwise settled.'[314]

---

[310] ODCE, 'List of Indictable Offences pursuant to the Companies Acts 1963–2005.'

[311] Available at www.odce.ie.

[312] *Report of the Review Group on Auditing* at p 220. Recommendation 14.4.

[313] ODCE, 'Revised Guidance on the Duty of Auditors to Report Suspected Indictable Offences to the Director of Corporate Enforcement' Decision Notice D/2006/2 at para 9.4.

[314] ODCE, 'Revised Guidance on the Duty of Auditors to Report Suspected Indictable Offences to the Director of Corporate Enforcement' Decision Notice D/2006/2 at para 9.4.

Offences that may be prosecuted summarily or on indictment, are fully within the scope of the s 194(5) reporting obligation: an auditor does not have to assess or determine whether the offence is likely to be prosecuted on indictment.[315]

(viii) No discretion

[7.112] There is no scope for an auditor to exercise discretion before reporting an opinion that there are reasonable grounds for believing that an indictable offence was committed. Under CA 1990, s 194(1), an auditor is not obliged to notify a suspected violation of the duty to keep proper books of account[316] in two defined circumstances, namely where the auditor is satisfied that the directors have taken necessary steps to ensure compliance[317] and where the contraventions are minor or immaterial in nature.[318] By contrast, where an auditor forms the belief that there are reasonable grounds for believing a company has committed an indictable offence, this must be notified to the DCE forthwith. Even if an auditor could liaise with the company prior to reporting any suspicions to the DCE, there are no grounds on which that reporting obligation is considered by law to be inapplicable. It is significant that there is no provision for the auditor to consider the impact of the offence and its level of materiality before the obligation to report an opinion under s 194(5) arises.

(ix) Exceptions

[7.113] There are two specific exceptions to the duty to report under s 194(5). These were introduced by the C(AA)A 2003, repealed by IFCMPA 2005, before being commenced, and replaced by the latter.[319] The two offences which are excluded from the scope of the reporting obligation are indictable offences under CA 1963, ss 125(2) and 127(12).[320] Sections 125(2) and 127(12) render it an offence for a company, every

---

[315] See further Ch **15**.

[316] CA 1990, s 194(1).

[317] CA 1990, s 194(2).

[318] CA 1990, s 194(3).

[319] CA 1990, s 194(5), as inserted by CLEA 2001, s 74(e), was amended by C(AA)A 2003, s 37(d) (to insert '(other than an indictable offence under section 125(1) or 127(12) of the Principal Act)' (never commenced); it was further amended by IFCMPA 2005, s 73(3), which repealed C(AA)A 2003, s 37(d); and by IFCMPA 2005, s 73(2)(d) (to insert '(other than an indictable offence under section 125(2) or 127(12) of the Principal Act)'). By the IFCMPA 2005 (Commencement) Order 2005, ss 73(2)(d) and 73(3) came into effect on 1 September 2005. All of these amendments were necessitated by the fact that C(AA)A 2003, s 37(d) contained an erroneous reference to CA 1963, s 125(1), rather than to s 125(2).

[320] It should be noted that the transitional approach to these new exceptions was that, any opinions formed before 31 August 2005, must nonetheless be notified to the DCE. ODCE, 'Exemption for Auditors Reporting Annual Return Defaults to the ODCE,' Information Notice I/2005/3 ('Cases may possibly arise where an auditor will have formed the relevant opinion on or before 31 August 2005 but will not have notified it to the ODCE by 1 September 2005. In those instances, notwithstanding the amendment in Section 73(2)(d) of the 2005 Act, the auditor's obligation to 'forthwith notify that opinion' must be discharged even though this calls for action on the auditor's part on or after 1 September 2005.')

defaulting officer, and any person in accordance with whose instructions or directions the directors of the company are accustomed to act, and to whose directions or omissions the default is attributable, to fail to file an annual return in every year made up to the company's annual return date, in the prescribed form.[321]

There were a significant number of notifications under s 194(5) that related to ss 125(2) and 127(12) and the ODCE reports that they accounted for 60% of all reports and complaints made to the ODCE. The ODCE further reports that 'as these defaults were proper to the work of the Companies Registration Office (CRO), the exemption naturally lead to a welcome substantial reduction in overall numbers for 2006' and that the figures, excluding annual return defaults, 'give a more representative picture of the volume of cases which are potentially appropriate for ODCE examination'.[322]

(x) Timing of notification

[7.114] The procedure for reporting a suspected indictable offence neither refers to nor envisages the company itself being notified of the formation of such an opinion. Whereas an auditor who suspects a failure to keep proper books of account is required to send a notice regarding the formation of that opinion to the company itself before sending a notice to the Registrar of Companies,[323] a company whose auditor suspects the commission of an indictable offence will not be aware of such suspicions and will have no opportunity to make representations to the auditor or the enforcement authorities at the notification stage.[324] The exclusion of any interaction between an auditor and a company in connection with the formation of any opinion regarding the commission of an indictable offence, is reinforced by the fact that an auditor is obliged to notify the DCE immediately upon the formation of such an opinion.[325]

The DCE acknowledged that:

> 'While there will be circumstances where is readily apparent that an indictable offence has been committed and that a report is required, there will be other circumstances where the immediate formation of an opinion may not be possible by virtue of auditors having to obtain and assess additional information from the company, its officers and employees.'[326]

[7.115] Despite this apparent flexibility, there is still no scope for an auditor to disclose the suspicions to the company first and ascertain whether a legitimate explanation exists, before referring the matter to the DCE.

---

[321] See Ch **2**.

[322] *ODCE Annual Report 2006* at p12. Available at www.odce.ie.

[323] CA 1990, s 194(1). See paras **[7.077]** to **[7.082]**.

[324] This can be contrasted with the law of the United States, where a procedure is prescribed which envisages the auditor interacting with the company's management and audit committee, and only reporting the matter to the SEC if no action is taken by them. See Securities Exchange Act 1934, s 10A(b)(1)(B).

[325] CA 1990, s 194(5), as inserted by CLEA 2001, s 74(e).

[326] Office of the Director of Corporate Enforcement, 'The Duty of Directors to Report to the Director of Corporate Enforcement' (Decision Notice D/2002/2) at p 14.

However, the form that the ODCE has prepared for the purpose of an auditor's report under s 194(5) includes the following question:

> 'Has the matter been discussed with the directors, officer(s) or agent(s)? If yes, please indicate whether those persons have exercised the option to furnish a separate statement to the Director, and if so, whether that statement accompanies your report or is expected to follow under separate cover.'[327]

The 'statement' referred to has no basis or origin in s 194(5). The ODCE's Decision Notice, however, states that:

> 'Auditors may afford the company's officer(s) or agent(s), as appropriate, the opportunity to compile a statement for submission to the Director of Corporate Enforcement together with the auditor's report. Issues that the officer(s) or agent(s) may wish to address if they choose to prepare such a statement might include, for example, their views on the report's subject matter and details of any corrective or remedial action taken or proposed.'[328]

While it may appear that this step would delay the auditor's submission of his opinion to the DCE, and prevent the opinion being reported 'forthwith', the DCE clarifies that this should not occur and that auditors should only allow a period of two days for the submission of such a statement by the company's officers or agents, before submitting the report under s 194(5).[329]

(xi) Further information, books and documents

[7.116] Section 194(5A) permits the DCE to request further information, books and documents, from an auditor who makes a report under that provision.

> Where the auditors of a company notify the Director of any matter pursuant to sub-s (5), they shall, in addition to performing their obligations under that subsection, if requested by the Director—
>
> (a) furnish the Director with such further information in their possession or control relating to the matter as the Director may require, including further information relating to the details of the grounds on which they formed the opinion referred to in that subsection,
>
> (b) give the Director such access to books and documents in their possession or control relating to the matter as the Director may require, and
>
> (c) give the Director such access to facilities for the taking of copies of or extracts from those books and documents as the Director may require.[330]

[7.117] This obligation only extends to such information, books and documents as are in the auditor's possession or control and should not require the auditor to undertake

---

[327] ODCE, Indictable Offences Report Form, Decision Notice D/2002/2, App 3, Item 3.

[328] ODCE, 'Revised Guidance on the Duty of Auditors to Report Suspected Indictable Offences to the Director of Corporate Enforcement' Decision Notice D/2006/2 at para 11.4.

[329] ODCE, 'Revised Guidance on the Duty of Auditors to Report Suspected Indictable Offences to the Director of Corporate Enforcement' Decision Notice D/2006/2 at para 11.5.

[330] CA 1990, s 194(5A), as inserted by C(AA)A 2003, s 37(e), which by C(AA)A 2003 (Commencement) Order 2007, SI 61/2007, came into effect on 1 March 2007.

further investigations. It may extend to information which is stored electronically as well as physical books, documents and information.[331] The purpose of this provision was described as follows by the ODCE:

> 'The purpose of this additional provision is to enable the Director to acquire on an efficient and effective basis the quality of information and evidence which initially led the auditor to report the suspected offence and thereby to facilitate the Director in reaching an informed decision as to what enforcement action (if any) is warranted by him as a result of the indicated circumstances.'[332]

The ODCE advances the following illustrations of the types of books and documents which the DCE may request the auditor to furnish:

> 'Books and documents may include records of meetings or discussions considering the issue directly, documentation on how the opinion that there are reasonable grounds for believing that an indictable offence has been committed was reached, working papers that highlight the matter as part of the audit fieldwork, as well as any other documents in the possession or control of the auditors that relate to the matter. Other documents may include client records and files or other documents relating to non audit services provided to the company and that relate to the matter reported and are in the possession or control of the auditor.'[333]

[7.118] It should be noted that there is nothing in the Companies Acts that addresses the admissibility in legal proceedings of evidence arising from an auditor's report of a suspected indictable offence. Written information that an auditor furnishes to the DCE regarding a suspected failure to keep proper books of account is admissible in evidence as truth of the facts contained therein, subject to proof to the contrary.[334] There is no provision that affords such treatment to information obtained in connection with the report of a suspected indictable offence. Under the Companies Acts, there is no provision that permits information and grounds that cause an auditor to form the opinion that such an offence has been committed to be admitted in evidence in subsequent legal proceedings. It must therefore be assumed that information, books or documents that have been obtained as a result of a report under s 194(5), are not admissible as evidence of the facts set out therein.

(d) Legal professional privilege

[7.119] It may be noted that nothing in s 194 can overcome the protection of legal professional privilege. Section 194(5B) provides in this regard:

> Nothing in this section compels the disclosure by any person of any information that the person would be entitled to refuse to produce on the grounds of legal

---

[331] See ODCE, 'Revised Guidance on the Duty of Auditors to Report Suspected Indictable Offences to the Director of Corporate Enforcement' Decision Notice D/2006/2 at para 12.4.

[332] ODCE, 'Revised Guidance on the Duty of Auditors to Report Suspected Indictable Offences to the Director of Corporate Enforcement' Decision Notice D/2006/2 at para 12.2.

[333] ODCE, 'Revised Guidance on the Duty of Auditors to Report Suspected Indictable Offences to the Director of Corporate Enforcement' Decision Notice D/2006/2 at para 12.7.

[334] CA 1990, s 194(3B), as inserted by CLEA 2001, s 74(c). See para **[7.081]**.

professional privilege or authorises the inspection or copying of any document containing such information that is in the person's possession.[335]

An auditor cannot therefore be required to disclose, or allow the inspection or copying of, information, which is protected by legal professional privilege. The Supreme Court has defined this legal professional privilege as follows: 'The privilege attaches to confidential communications passing between lawyer and client for the purpose of obtaining legal advice or assistance and also where litigation is contemplated or pending.'[336] The importance of this privilege has been explained by the High Court: 'Legal Professional Privilege is more than a mere rule of evidence. It is a fundamental condition on which the administration of justice as a whole rests.'[337]

The ODCE examined this matter in some detail and recommends that this is a matter which an auditor should consider carefully and, if an auditor wishes to assert legal professional privilege, he should consider taking legal advice in advance. The ODCE comments that:

> 'it is unlikely that the audit work carried out and documented by the auditor which resulted in the identification of a reportable matter will be privileged. This is because such audit work would not have been in contemplation of litigation; identification of a reportable matter is incidental to the audit.'[338]

With regard to the categories of legal privilege, the ODCE guidance is that legal advice privilege 'prevents the disclosure of communications between a lawyer and a client where such communications are made for the purpose of obtaining legal advice' and that, 'the circumstances in which this form of legal professional privilege will apply to an auditor are likely to be rare.'[339]

The ODCE further states that litigation privilege only arises when documents are created when litigation is pending, contemplated or reasonably apprehended, and the dominant purpose of the document in question was for that litigation. The ODCE notes that:

> 'Where the auditor or his/her firm has sought legal advice (including from the audit firm's professionally qualified in-house lawyers), such advice clearly attracts legal professional privilege, and it is for the auditor to decide whether or not to assert the privilege. The same situation applies where the auditor or his/her firm is a party to pending or contemplated litigation and documents have been created for the dominant purpose of that litigation.'[340]

---

[335] CA 1990, s 194(5B), as inserted by C(AA)A 2003, s 37(e), which by C(AA)A 2003 (Commencement) Order 2007, SI 61/2007, came into effect on 1 March 2007.

[336] *Gallagher v National Maternity Hospital* [1997] IESC 65 (*per* O'Flaherty J).

[337] *Miley v Flood* [2001] 2 IR 50, [2001] 1 ILRM 489 (*per* Kelly J).

[338] ODCE, 'Revised Guidance on the Duty of Auditors to Report Suspected Indictable Offences to the Director of Corporate Enforcement' Decision Notice D/2006/2 at App 2.

[339] ODCE, 'Revised Guidance on the Duty of Auditors to Report Suspected Indictable Offences to the Director of Corporate Enforcement' Decision Notice D/2006/2 at App 2.

[340] ODCE, 'Revised Guidance on the Duty of Auditors to Report Suspected Indictable Offences to the Director of Corporate Enforcement' Decision Notice D/2006/2 at App 2.

[7.120] A distinct issue that arises in the context of auditors is the extent to which documents in the auditor's possession, over which the audit client wishes to assert privilege, are protected by that privilege. The ODCE observes that, '... if a client has opted to substantially publicise those communications the privilege may be lost or may be taken to have been waived.' Therefore, if the audit client has made otherwise privileged documents, widely available, they may have relinquished their claim of privilege. However, the ODCE notes:

> 'it is thought that confidential disclosure by a company to its statutory auditors of material over which it (the company) enjoys legal professional privilege will not ordinarily give rise to a loss or waiver of the company's privilege'.[341]

[7.121] The Supreme Court considered the issue of waiver of legal professional privilege in the context of insider dealing in *Fyffes plc v DCC plc*.[342] The defendants sought to prevent the disclosure of information, by way of discovery, of documentation which they had supplied to the Stock Exchange and over which they claimed legal professional privilege. The Supreme Court considered the claim that the defendants had waived the privilege by forwarding the documents in question to the Stock Exchange, which they did with the intention of influencing the DPP not to institute proceedings.[343]

Fennelly J determined that there was no principle of law to the effect that any communication to a third party causes legal privilege to be lost and commented, '... no legal basis has been advanced for its loss in the circumstances of the present case, when disclosure was made for a particular purpose and subject to express conditions as to confidentiality.'[344] The Court further observed, '... express stipulations of confidentiality, such as in the present case, will necessarily be a material factor. They will obviously negative any claim of express waiver and most cases of implied waiver.'[345]

McCracken J observed that, 'There may be many situations in which it is desirable, or even mandatory, that privileged documents be disclosed to a third party for a limited purpose.'[346] In considering a submission that 'fairness' should determine whether or not there was waiver in a particular case, McCracken J held:

> 'While one cannot lay down absolute rules in matters such as this, it is essential that there should be as great a degree of certainty as possible, so that parties can reasonably foresee the result of actions of disclosure taken by them. Were that not so, it is possible that serious injustices could occur because a party might fail to

---

[341] ODCE, 'Revised Guidance on the Duty of Auditors to Report Suspected Indictable Offences to the Director of Corporate Enforcement' Decision Notice D/2006/2 at App 2.

[342] *Fyffes plc v DCC plc* [2005] IESC 3, [2005] 1 IR 59.

[343] It may be noted that the analogy between the situation of the Stock Exchange and the duty of an auditor under consideration is a close one, as the Stock Exchange was obliged under CA 1990, s 115, to report to the DPP if it appears that a person has committed an offence under CA 1990, Pt V (insider dealing). The Stock Exchange's responsibility regarding the information at issue was therefore similar to that of an auditor under s 194.

[344] *Fyffes plc v DCC plc* [2005] IESC 3, [2005] 1 IR 59 at 69.

[345] [2005] IESC 3, [2005] 1 IR 59 at 72 (para 40).

[346] [2005] IESC 3, [2005] 1 IR 59 at 84 (para 65).

make a disclosure due to the fear that it might lose the benefit of a legal privilege to which it was entitled.'[347]

[7.122] The same rationale could be applied to information which is made available to an auditor for the purpose of conducting an audit of a company. The disclosure of such information is clearly subject to restrictions as to confidentiality, and it is provided for a limited purpose. These considerations should negate any claim that a company waived its privilege by disclosing otherwise privileged information to its auditor for the purpose of conducting the audit, or, indeed, if such information was supplied to the auditor in an attempt to influence his decision whether to make a report under s 194.

(e) Protection from liability

[7.123] If an auditor makes a report to the DCE of a failure to keep proper books of account or of an opinion regarding the commission of an indictable offence, or furnishes further information, books or documents to the DCE in connection with such reports, this will not give rise to liability or a breach of any duty on his part. Section 194(6) provides:

> No professional or legal duty to which an auditor is subject by virtue of his appointment as an auditor of a company shall be regarded as contravened by, and no liability to the company, its shareholders, creditors or other interested parties shall attach to, an auditor, by reason of his compliance with an obligation imposed on him by or under this section.[348]

This is consistent with the following observation of the Review Group on Auditing:

> Confidentiality is an implied term of auditors' contracts with their clients. However, in the circumstances where there is a legal duty to report, auditors are entitled to communicate to regulators in good faith information or opinions relating to the business or affairs of the regulated entity or any associated enterprise without contravening the duty of confidence owed to the regulated entity.[349]

This is also reflected in ISA 250B as follows:

> 'Confidentiality is an implied term of the auditor's contracts with client entities. However, in the circumstances leading to a right or duty to report, the auditor is entitled to communicate with regulators in good faith information or opinions relating to the business or affairs of the entity or any associated body without contravening the duty of confidence owed to the entity.'[350]

The protection of s 194(6) will only apply if the auditor is bound by an obligation to make a report or furnish information, books or documents, to the DCE, under s 194. If an auditor misconceives the scope of this provision and makes a report which is not obligatory, s 194(6) will not protect him from liability or claims of breach of duty. It is

---

[347] *Fyffes plc v DCC plc* [2005] IESC 3, [2005] 1 IR 59 at 85 (para 65).

[348] CA 1990, s 194(6), as inserted by CLEA 2001, s 74(e).

[349] *Report of the Review Group on Auditing* at p 228.

[350] ISA (UK and Ireland) 250(B), App 1 para 9.

therefore important for auditors to have a thorough understanding of the scope of their reporting obligations under s 194.

(f) Report on Directors' Compliance Statements

[7.124] C(AA)A 2003, s 45[351] inserts ss 205E and 205F into CA 1990. These provisions concern the obligation of a company's directors to prepare a 'directors' compliance statement' and the obligation of its auditor to review this statement and prepare a report confirming whether it is 'fair and reasonable'.[352]

Section 205E provides for the imposition of an obligation on directors to prepare a compliance statement, which would contain particular information regarding a company's policies and procedures. In particular, the statement should describe the company's policies and procedures for ensuring compliance with 'its relevant obligations' and any arrangements the company has in place to implement and review the effectiveness of these policies and procedures.[353] The relevant obligations are defined as 'the Companies Acts, tax law and any other enactments that provide a legal framework within which the company operates and that may materially affect the company's financial statements.'[354]

Section 205F then requires the auditor to conduct an annual review of the directors' compliance statement, and to prepare a report confirming whether, in the opinion of the auditor and in light of the information available to the auditor from audit, audit related, or non audit work, these statements are fair and reasonable.[355] The auditors are also required to include in their report a review of, and their conclusions regarding, the review they conducted of the directors' compliance statement.[356] If any statement contained in the compliance statement is not, in the opinion of the auditors, fair and reasonable, the auditors must report that fact to the directors and include it in their auditors' report appended to the annual accounts.[357] According to s 205F(3), where an auditor forms the opinion that directors have failed to prepare a compliance statement or to include it in the directors' report, the auditor will be obliged to report that opinion and the reasons for it, to the DCE.[358]

[7.125] These provisions prompted considerable controversy and the Government referred the matter to the Company Law Review Group ('CLRG'), which produced a Report on the topic, recommending a revised form of the directors' compliance statement.[359] The Government has indicated that it will not commence C(AA)A 2003,

---

[351] Inserting a proposed new CA 1990, s 205E.

[352] See further Ch **6**.

[353] C(AA)A 2003, inserting CA 1990, s 205E(3).

[354] C(AA)A 2003, inserting CA 1990, s 205E(1). See Ch **6**.

[355] C(AA)A 2003, s 43, inserting CA 1990, s 205F(1).

[356] C(AA)A 2003, s 43, inserting CA 1990, s 205F(2)(a).

[357] C(AA)A 2003, s 43, inserting CA 1990, s 205F(2)(b).

[358] C(AA)A 2003, s 43, inserting CA 1990, s 205F(3).

[359] CLRG Report on Directors' Compliance Statement, 2005. www.entemp.ie.

s 45 and that the recommendations of the CLRG will be reflected in the new consolidated Companies Act.[360] With regard to the auditor's report, the CLRG made the following observations:

> 'To require the company's auditors to review this is unnecessary and, because of the cost involved, undesirable, particularly when it is now the case that a company's auditors are required to report suspected indictable offences that they encounter in the course of their audit work to the ODCE, which would include the failure by the directors of a company in scope to include a DCS in their Directors' Report. The Review Group further noted that auditors would continue to have responsibility to consider the directors' Annual Statement on Compliance under both company law and auditing standards.'[361]

The CLRG recommends in this regard:

> 'The removal of the requirement that a company's auditors must specifically opine on the reasonableness or otherwise of the proposed revised Annual Statement on Compliance in Directors' Reports.'[362]

It may therefore be expected that the requirement for an auditor's report on the Directors' Compliance Statement will not appear in the Consolidated Companies Bill when published and that there will no equivalent of CA 1990, s 205F.[363]

(g) Other reporting obligations

[7.126] In addition to the obligation imposed by CA 1990, s 194, there are other pieces of legislation that also impose reporting obligations on auditors. While the focus here is on the Companies Acts, these other reporting obligations are mentioned to illustrate the extent to which auditors are required to assist in the detection and reporting of offences.

– Criminal Justice (Theft and Fraud Offences) Act 2001, s 59, requires an auditor to make a report to An Garda Síochána, if there is an 'indication' that certain offences under that Act, involving theft, fraud or other related offences, may have been committed;

– Taxes Consolidation Act 1997, s 1079, requires an auditor to draw the company's attention to any material tax offences of which he becomes aware during the conduct of the audit. If the company does not remedy the situation within six months, the auditor must report the offences to the Revenue Commissioners. In such a situation, the auditor must also resign as auditor of that company for a period of three years, or until such time as the tax issues are rectified. The company must be notified of the reasons for the resignation and the Revenue Commissioners must receive a copy of this notification;

---

[360] See press release, 'Minister Michael Ahern Announces Reform of Directors' Compliance Statement' (1 December 2005) available at www.entemp.ie.

[361] CLRG Report on Directors' Compliance Statement, 2005. www.entemp.ie at p 132.

[362] CLRG Report on Directors' Compliance Statement, 2005. www.entemp.ie at p 132.

[363] See CLRG, General Scheme of Draft Companies Consolidation and Reform Bill 2007, Pt A5, Head 7.

- Criminal Justice Act 1993, s 57, as amended by the Criminal Justice Act (Section 32) Regulations 2003, requires an auditor to report to An Garda Síochána if they suspect that a money laundering offence under s 31 or s 32 of the Act has been or is being committed;

- Central Bank Act 1989, s 47(1) requires the auditor of a bank to send a written report to the Central Bank of any circumstances of which the auditor becomes aware during the course of the audit that affect the ability of the bank to fulfil its obligations to depositors. A bank's auditor must also report any material defects in the financial systems or controls of the bank and any material inaccuracies or omissions in the financial returns to the Central Bank. Finally, an auditor of a bank must notify the Central Bank if they propose to resign from acting as such. The reports required by s 47(1) must be sent without delay. There is no procedure for notifying the company as a preliminary step;

- Pensions (Amendment) Act, 1996, s 83(1), requires an auditor of a pension scheme to make a written report to the Pensions Board where he has 'reasonable cause to believe that a material misappropriation or a fraudulent conversion of the resources of the scheme ... has occurred, is occurring or is to be attempted ...'.

[7.127] There are certain other pieces of legislation that impose obligations on auditors to report circumstances related to the company to an outside regulator. These include the Insurance Act 1989; the Trustee Savings Act 1989; the Building Societies Act 1989; the Criminal Justice (Terrorist Offences) Act 2005; and the Investment Intermediaries Act 1995. However, the Report of the Review Group of Auditing regards, '... the degree of reporting by external auditors under the above specific pieces of legislation as extremely low' and considers that, '[i]t is likely that some auditors are failing to respect their statutory obligations.'[364]

[7.128] The Institute of Chartered Accountants in Ireland ('ICAI') is critical of the range of reporting duties to which an auditor is subject and notes that:

> '... it detracts from the basic role of the auditor if they have to manage a myriad of conflicting reporting requirements to a variety of reporting bodies, with differing thresholds and uncertain parameters. Auditors are willing and prepared to support important public interest initiatives, as they carry out audits on behalf of shareholders, and report to regulators and others on critical issues that arise during the audit process. But to enhance the effectiveness of that reporting duty, we now need to stand back and see if we can develop a more coherent reporting framework.'[365]

---

[364] *Report of the Review Group of Auditing* (July 2000), p 216.

[365] ICAI Publication, 'The 'whistleblowing' obligations of certain professionals in the Republic of Ireland' (May 2005) available at www.icai.ie.

The ICAI identifies particular difficulties for auditors arising from the fact that there are different thresholds of proof or certainty to trigger the various reporting obligations;[366] different reporting procedures and frameworks;[367] and a multiplicity of regulatory bodies to which the reports must be made.[368]

The ICAI made the observation that:

'The imposition on certain professionals of these reporting obligations has developed haphazardly. Whatever about the merits of, or necessity for, these obligations, legislation drafted by different sponsoring government departments has resulted in a number of real practical difficulties for those affected.'

In light of these practical concerns, the ICAI recommends the harmonisation of auditors' reporting obligations.

'The harmonisation of these reporting obligations is not just in the interest of our members. We believe it is in the public interest as well as in the interest of regulators and other statutory authorities. Clarity and simplicity will ensure more effective adherence to these requirements.'[369]

---

[366] The ICAI cites the further examples: 'Under section 194 of the Companies Act, 1990 as amended by section 74 of the Company Law Enforcement Act, 2001, the statutory duty to report to the Director of Corporate Enforcement arises when "…information comes into the possession of the auditors of a company that leads them to form the opinion that there are reasonable grounds for believing that…" an indictable offence under companies legislation has been committed. Under section 59 of the Criminal Justice (Theft and Fraud Offences) Act, 2001, the obligation on "relevant persons," as defined in the legislation, to make a report, in this case to the Garda Síochána, arises when there is an 'indication' in any document or information used for the preparation or the auditing of the accounts of an entity that an offence under that Act has been committed. Section 57 of the Criminal Justice Act, 1994, requires the reporting of a suspicion that a money laundering offence has been or is being committed.' ICAI Publication, 'The 'whistleblowing' obligations of certain professionals in the Republic of Ireland' (May 2005) available at www.icai.ie.

[367] The ICAI notes that, 'No standard framework for making reports exists between the various Acts. Section 83 of the Pensions (Amendment) Act, 1996 stipulates that reports must be made in writing. On the other hand, the Company Law Enforcement Act, the Criminal Justice (Theft and Fraud Offences) Act, and the anti-money laundering reporting obligation are silent on how reports should be made – in theory they could be oral or in writing.' ICAI Publication, 'The 'whistleblowing' obligations of certain professionals in the Republic of Ireland' (May 2005) available at www.icai.ie.

[368] 'Under the anti-money laundering regulations auditors and other designated bodies are obliged to report the same offence to two different regulators or statutory bodies – the Revenue Commissioners and An Garda Síochána. Companies Act offences are reportable to the ODCE and, in some instances, to the Registrar of Companies.' ICAI Publication, 'The 'whistleblowing' obligations of certain professionals in the Republic of Ireland' (May 2005) available at www.icai.ie.

[369] ICAI Publication, 'The "whistleblowing" obligations of certain professionals in the Republic of Ireland' (May 2005) available at www.icai.ie.

E. Audit exemption

[7.129] While the general rule is that a company must have its annual accounts audited,[370] this requirement does not apply to every company. If a company meets a number of specific conditions, it will be entitled to a so-called 'audit exemption'.[371] These conditions must be met both in respect of the current financial year and the preceding financial year, unless the exemption is claimed in respect of the company's first financial year.[372]

- The company must be a company to which C(A)A 1986 applies.[373] This excludes:

    (i)   a company which is not trading for the acquisition of gain by its members;[374]

    (ii) a charitable company without share capital, under the control of a recognised religion;[375]

    (iii) a charitable company without share capital, to which the Commissioners of Charitable Donations and Bequests for Ireland has granted an exempted from the requirement to annex to its annual return, the company's accounts and an auditor's report;[376]

- The company must have a turnover of less than €7.3 million during its financial year[377] (for financial years ending before 24 February 2007, the turnover must have been less than €1.5 million);

- The balance sheet total of the company must be less than €3.65 million at the end of its financial year[378] (for financial years ending before 24 February 2007, the balance sheet total must have been less than €1,904,607.10);

- The company must have an average of less than 50 employees *per* year;[379]

---

[370] See CA 1963, s 160(1): '... every company shall at each annual general meeting appoint an auditor or auditors to hold office from the conclusion of that until the conclusion of the next annual general meeting'.

[371] C(A)(No2)A 1999, s 32, as amended by C(AA)A 2003, s 54 and IFCMPA 2006, s 9. Note that s 9 was commenced on the passing of the IFCMPA 2006, on 24 December 2006.

[372] C(A)(No2)A 1999, s 32(1)(b).

[373] C(A)(No2)A 1999, s 32(3)(a)(i).

[374] C(A)A 1986, s 2(1)(a).

[375] C(A)A 1986, s 2(1)(b), applying CA 1963, s 128(4)(c). Such a company must also 'exercise its functions in accordance with the laws, canons, and ordinances of the religion concerned'.

[376] C(A)A 1986, s 2(1)(c), applying CA 1963, s 128(5).

[377] C(A)(No2)A 1999, s 32(3)(a)(ii), as amended by C(AA)A 2003, s 53(b) and IFCMPA 2006, s 9.

[378] C(A)(No2)A 1999, s 32(3)(a)(iii), as amended by C(AA)A 2003, s 53(b) and IFCMPA 2006, s 9.

[379] C(A)(No2)A 1999, s 32(3)(a)(iv).

- The company's annual return (and the annual return for the preceding financial year, if applicable) must be made up to the correct annual return date and delivered to the Registrar before the requisite date;[380]

- There must have been no notice by members holding shares that carry at least one tenth of the total voting rights, stating that they do not wish the company to avail of the audit exemption;[381]

- The company must not be:

  (i)   A parent or subsidiary undertaking, within the meaning of the EC(CGA)R 1992,[382]

  (ii) A holder of a licence under Central Bank Act 1971, s 9, or of an exemption from holding such licence,[383]

  (iii) An insurance company to which EC(IUA)R 1996 applies,[384]

  (iv) A company referred to in C(A)(No2)A 1999, Second Schedule.[385]

[7.130] If a company wishes to avail of the audit exemption, the directors of the company must form the opinion that the company will satisfy these conditions in respect of the current financial year or a future financial year. Such a decision cannot be taken

---

[380] C(A)(No2)A 1999, s 32A, applying CA 1963, s 127, as inserted by C(AA)A 2003, s 53(e).

[381] C(A)(No2)A 1999, s 32B, applying C(A)(No2)A 1999, s 33, as inserted by IFCMPA 2006, s 9. See Ch **2**.

[382] C(A)(No2)A 1999, s 32(3)(a)(v)(I).

[383] C(A)(No2)A 1999, s 32(3)(a)(v)(II).

[384] C(A)(No2)A 1999, s 32(3)(a)(v)(III).

[385] C(A)(No2)A 1999, s 32(3)(a)(v)(IV), as amended by C(AA)A 2003, s 53(c). The Second Schedule refers to: A company that is a member firm within the meaning of the Stock Exchange Act 1995; A company that is a stock exchange; A company that is an associated undertaking or a related undertaking of a member firm or stock exchange; A company that is an investment business firm; A company that is an associated undertaking or a related undertaking of an investment business firm; A company to which the Central Bank Act 1989, Pt II, Ch VII, VIII or IX, applies; A company that is engaged in the business of accepting deposits or other repayable funds or granting credit for its own account; A company that is an associated body of a building society; A company that is an associated enterprise of a credit institution; An investment company; A company that is a management company or trustee; A company that is an undertaking for collective investment in transferable securities; A company that is a management company or trustee of an undertaking for collective investment in transferable securities; A company that is a management company or trustee of a unit trust scheme; A company that is a general partner or custodian of an investment limited partnership; A company that is an undertaking with close links with a financial undertaking; Any other company the carrying on of business by which is required, by virtue of any enactment or instrument thereunder, to be authorised by the Central Bank; A company that is an insurance intermediary; A company that is an excepted body within the meaning of the Trade Union Acts, 1871 to 1990.

in respect of past financial years. The decision to avail of the exemption must be recorded in the minutes of the meeting at which that decision is taken.[386]

[7.131] Members of the company holding shares carrying at least one tenth of the total voting rights[387] may serve a notice on the company stating that they do not wish the company to avail of the audit exemption in the financial year specified in the notice.[388] Such a notice may be served on the company either during the financial year preceding, or not later than one month before the end of, the year for which the members do not wish an audit exemption to be availed of.[389]

[7.132] If a company does avail of the audit exemption in a given financial year, the directors must include particular statements in the company's balance sheet for that year.[390] These statements must appear immediately above the directors' signatures.[391] It is an offence by the company and every officer in default, if these statements do not appear in the company's balance sheet:[392]

- that the company is availing itself of 'the exemption provided for by Pt III of the Companies (Amendment)(No 2) Act 1999' (in that precise language);[393]

- that the company is availing of the exemption on the ground that it satisfies the conditions specified in C(A)(No2)A 1999, s 32 (as amended by C(AA)A 2003, s 53 and IFCMPA 2006, s 9);[394]

- that the holders of shares carrying one tenth of the total voting rights have not served a notice on the company under C(A)(No2)A 1999, s 33(1) in accordance with s 33(2);[395] and

- the directors must also acknowledge that the company's obligations under the Companies Acts to keep proper books of account and prepare accounts which give a true and fair view of the state of affairs of the company at the end of its financial year and of its profit or loss for such a year and to otherwise comply

---

[386] C(A)(No2)A 1999, s 32(1)(a).

[387] A 'voting right' in this context shall 'be construed as a reference to a right exercisable for the time being to cast, or to control the casting of, a vote at general meetings of members of the company, not being such a right that is exercisable only in special circumstances.' C(A)(No2)A 1999, s 33(7).

[388] C(A)(No2)A 1999, s 33(1), as substituted by IFCMPA 2006, s 9, which came into effect on 24 December 2006.

[389] C(A)(No2)A 1999, s 33(2), as substituted by IFCMPA 2006, s 9, which came into effect on 24 December 2006.

[390] C(A)(No2)A 1999, s 33(4).

[391] C(A)(No2)A 1999, s 33(5).

[392] C(A)(No2)A 1999, s 33(6).

[393] C(A)(No2)A 1999, s 33(4)(a).

[394] C(A)(No2)A 1999, s 33(4)(b).

[395] C(A)(No2)A 1999, s 33(4)(c), as substituted by IFCMPA 2006, s 9.

with the provisions of those Acts relating to accounts so far as they are applicable to the company.[396]

F. Auditors' liability

(a) No exemption

[7.133] An auditor currently has no protection from liability in Ireland. CA 1963, s 200(1) enshrines this position:

> ... any provision whether contained in the articles of a company or in any contract with a company or otherwise for exempting any officer of the company or any person employed by the company as auditor from, or indemnifying him against, any liability which by virtue of any rule of law would otherwise attach to him in respect of any negligence, default, breach of duty or breach of trust of which he may be guilty in relation to the company shall be void ...

It should also be recalled that a body corporate cannot be qualified for appointment as an auditor as the law stands at present in Ireland, so auditors cannot avail of the protection of limited liability.[397]

A third consideration that widens the scope of auditors' exposure to liability in Ireland, is the system of joint and several liability, whereby a plaintiff may sue concurrent wrongdoers jointly in the same action and recover judgment obtained against all of them, in full against any one of them.[398] As noted by the European Commission:

> 'Liability of the auditor and the audited company towards others (shareholders, creditors) is joint and several in the legislation of nearly all Member States. These joint and several liability regimes are designed in such a way that the statutory auditors and the audit firms may also bear a portion of charges resulting from the misconduct of the audited company, in particular if that company goes bankrupt.

---

[396] C(A)(No2)A 1999, s 33(4)(d).

[397] CA 1990, s 187(2)(g). See para **[7.040]**. Note that Accountancy Ireland reports, 'All EU Member States except Ireland allow auditors to adopt the structure of the limited liability company. This protects individual auditors from liability beyond their capital contribution to the company and allows partners (directors) with no involvement in a particular audit to protect themselves from civil liability.' Lambe 'Auditor Liability – the time for reform,' *Accountancy Ireland*, Vol 37, No 5.

[398] In *Iarnrod Éireann v Ireland* [1996] IESC 221, [1996] 3 IR 321, the Supreme Court upheld the constitutionality of the principle of joint and several liability, as it appears in the Civil Liability Act 1961 as follows: 'The legislation provides that once a wrong is established, the wrongdoer or wrongdoers must take the consequences. The wrong done to the plaintiff is regarded as indivisible. As between defendants, it is provided that there can be an apportionment of blame but if a deficiency has to be made up, in the payment of damages, it is better that it should be made up by someone in default than that a totally innocent party should suffer anew. For the Oireachtas so to provide is within its competence in what is truly an area of policy.'

> In consequence, plaintiffs can claim damages from the auditor, regardless of the degree of involvement of the auditor.'[399]

The Department of Enterprise, Trade and Employment in a press release announcing the referral of the issue of auditor liability to the CLRG, described the combined effect of these provisions and principles as follows:

> 'The situation in Ireland for statutory auditors is that they are prohibited from exempting or limiting liability in respect of audits carried out, or from obtaining an indemnity from the companies being audited. This, in addition to a ban on corporate bodies acting as auditors and the legal principle of joint and several liability leaves Irish auditors potentially accountable on a personal basis for losses not just arising from their own actions or omissions but also for those of persons – for example company directors – who may be significantly responsible for such losses, but who do not have the resources to meet claims against them. In summary, the position at the moment is that, arising from these circumstances, the auditing profession in Ireland is the only profession that cannot limit its liability under domestic law.'[400]

The only form of protection against liability which is available to auditors in Ireland is that a company may purchase auditors' insurance for liability its auditor may incur 'by virtue of any rule of law would otherwise attach to him in respect of any negligence, default, breach of duty or breach of trust of which he may be guilty in relation to the company'.[401]

(b) Potential liability

[7.134] The potential scope of an auditor's liability is broad and persons ranging from investors, creditors, and persons acquiring companies under audit, have attempted to fix auditors with liability arising from companies' accounts.

(i) In general

[7.135] It is a general rule of law that an auditor owes a duty of care to the company the subject of the audit. An auditor only owes a duty to other persons, if certain additional circumstances exist. The underlying rationale behind this limitation is that, without it, an auditor could incur '… liability in an indeterminate amount for an indeterminate time to an indeterminate class.'[402] This rationale has been undermined by the events surrounding

---

[399] DG for Internal Market and Services, 'Consultation on Auditors' Liability and its Impact on the European Capital Markets' Commission Staff Working Paper, January 2007 at para 2.1.

[400] DETE Press release, 'Minister Michael Ahern refers current auditor liability regime to the Company Law Review Group (CLRG)' 3 January 2007. Available at www.entemp.ie.

[401] CA 1963, s 200(2), as inserted by C(AA)A 2003, s 56. See further Ch **6**.

It may be noted that the study commissioned by the Commission into Auditor Liability systems in Member States records that insurance is mandatory in Ireland, by means of professional association, and that depending on the professional association, it must be 2.5 times gross practice income to a maximum of €1.3m or to €1.5m (max €15,000 or €38,000).

[402] *Ultramares Corp v Touche* 174 NE 444, (1931) 255 NY 170, 179 (*per* Cardozo CJ).

the collapse of Enron and the subsequent class action law suits that were filed against Arthur Anderson, among others.

The current state of flux of the law applicable to auditors was acknowledged by Chadwick LJ in *Coulthard v Neville Russell*[403] as follows:

> '... the liability of professional advisers, including auditors, for failure to provide accurate information or correct advice can, truly, be said to be in a state of transition or development. As the House of Lords has pointed out, repeatedly, this is an area in which the law is developing pragmatically and incrementally. It is pre-eminently an area in which the legal result is sensitive to the facts ...'[404]

[7.136] The most influential statement of the scope of liability for negligent misstatement by a professional was made by Denning LJ in a dissenting judgment in *Candler v Crane Christmas & Co Ltd*.[405] Having considered the duties of accountants, Denning LJ stated:

> 'They owe the duty, of course, to their employer or client, and also, I think, to any third person to whom they themselves show the accounts, or to whom they know their employer is going to show the accounts so as to induce him to invest money or take some other action on them. I do not think, however, the duty can be extended still further so as to include strangers of whom they have heard nothing and to whom their employer without their knowledge may choose to show their accounts. Once the accountants have handed their accounts to their employer, they are not, as a rule, responsible for what he does with them without their knowledge or consent.'

The caveat to this was that:

> '... there are some cases – of which the present is one – where the accountants know all the time, even before they present their accounts, that their employer requires the accounts to show to a third person so as to induce him to act on them, and then they themselves, or their employers, present the accounts to him for the purpose. In such cases I am of opinion that the accountants owe a duty of care to the third person.'

[7.137] This statement of the law was endorsed strongly by the House of Lords in *Caparo Industries plc v Dickman*[406] and in *Hedley Byrne & Co Ltd v Heller & Partners Ltd*.[407] In the former decision, Lord Bridge held that that common feature of decisions that acknowledged a duty of care to exist between the auditor and a third party was that the defendant/auditor in such cases was:

> '... fully aware of the nature of the transaction which the plaintiff had in contemplation, knew that the advice or information would be communicated to him directly or indirectly and knew that it was very likely that the plaintiff would

---

[403] *Coulthard v Neville Russell* [1998] 1 BCLC 143.

[404] *Coulthard v Neville Russell* [1998] 1 BCLC 143, at 155.

[405] *Candler v Crane Christmas & Co Ltd* [1951] 1 All ER 426, [1951] 2 KB 164.

[406] *Caparo Industries plc v Dickman* [1990] BCLC 273, [1990] 2 AC 605.

[407] *Hedley Byrne & Co Ltd v Heller & Partners Ltd* [1963] 2 All ER 575, [1964] AC 465.

rely on that advice or information in deciding whether or not to engage in the transaction in contemplation.'[408]

In such circumstances, the court considered that the defendant/auditor could be expected to anticipate that the plaintiff would place reliance on such information or advice for the purpose for which it was provided. The plaintiff would also be entitled to assume that they could rely on that information or advice for that purpose. This is subject to any disclaimer made by the defendant/auditor.

(ii) Other companies

[7.138] There have been many cases in which different categories of person claimed to have an actionable claim against an auditor. In *Andrew & Ors v Kounnis Freeman (a firm)*[409] entities that were involved in licensing and supporting travel companies (the Civil Aviation Authority and trustees of the Air Travel Trust) brought an action against the auditors of a travel company (Flight Co (UK) plc), on the basis that the auditors provided certain assurances and furnished accounts on behalf of the company, knowing the reliance that the plaintiffs would place upon those assurances and accounts. The central issue that arose in that case was whether the provision of information directly to a third party implied that the auditor assumed a duty of care towards that third party. The Court of Appeal considered various authorities, including *Candler v Crane Christmas & Co Ltd*,[410] *Hedley Byrne & Co Ltd v Heller & Partners Ltd*[411] and *Caparo Industries plc v Dickman*,[412] and concluded that:

> '[i]t is at least a reasonable inference that in certifying Flight's accounts, the defendants were doing so not merely to the company and its shareholders but also to the authority with the intention that the authority should act upon them in deciding whether or not to renew the licence.'[413]

The Court refused to dismiss the plaintiffs' claim.

[7.139] Similarly, in *James McNaughton Papers Group Ltd v Hicks Anderson & Co (a firm)*[414] the plaintiff company sought to bring an action against the auditor of a group of companies with which the plaintiff was in take-over negotiations. The plaintiff claimed the answers the auditors gave to questions asked of them were misleading. This claim was rejected, on the basis that the answers were general and the transactions in question were between experienced businessmen who could have been reasonably expected to obtain accountancy advice from independence sources.

---

[408] *Caparo Industries plc v Dickman* [1990] BCLC 273, 282, [1990] 2 AC 605, at 620.

[409] *Andrew & Ors v Kounnis Freeman (a firm)* [1999] 2 BCLC 641.

[410] *Candler v Crane Christmas & Co Ltd* [1951] 1 All ER 426, [1951] 2 KB 164.

[411] *Hedley Byrne & Co Ltd v Heller & Partners Ltd* [1963] 2 All ER 575, [1964] AC 465.

[412] *Caparo Industries plc v Dickman* [1990] BCLC 273, [1990] 2 AC 605.

[413] *Andrew & Ors v Kounnis Freeman (a firm)* [1999] 2 BCLC 641, 653 (*per* Beldam LJ).

[414] *James McNaughton Papers Group Ltd v Hicks Anderson & Co (a firm)* [1991] 2 QB 113, [1991] 2 WLR 641, [1991] 1 All ER 134, [1991] BCLC 163.

[7.140] In *Berg Sons & Co Ltd v Mervyn Hampton Adams & Ors*[415] banks and discount houses, among others, sought to sustain an action against the auditors of a company on the basis that the auditors negligently and in breach of duty gave an unqualified certificate and categorised as bills receivable certain sums which were unrecoverable. The court observed that audited accounts are '... only one of the sources of information which a prudent banker takes into account'.[416] The court quoted extensively from *Caparo Industries plc v Dickman*,[417] and concluded:

> '... the purpose of the statutory audit is to provide a mechanism to enable those having a proprietary interest in the company or being concerned with its management or control to have access to accurate financial information about the company. Provided that those persons have that information, the statutory purpose is exhausted.'[418]

The court considered the circumstances in which a bank could invoke the duties of an auditor and, applying authorities such as *Caparo Industries plc v Dickman*,[419] stated:

> '... it will only be in very clear and immediate circumstances that it will be possible to say that a statutory auditor owes a duty of care to a banker who may at some later date choose to lend money to a company. The present case is not such a case.'[420]

No duty was owed to the banks and the claim against the auditors could not therefore be sustained.

[7.141] In Ireland, *Kelly v Boland*[421] sets the parameters of an auditor's duties to third parties. In that case, the plaintiffs were directors of a company (Company A) which entered into an agreement in 1977 to purchase another company (Company B). Before concluding the agreement in November 1977, they received the accounts of Company B, which has been audited by a member of the defendant firm of accountants, Company B's auditors. The plaintiffs held a number of meetings with the defendants before acquiring Company B, during which the stock figures were explained. However, after taking over the company, the plaintiffs became aware that the stock figures for 1973 and 1974 were understated, and were carried forward to 1976, producing an exaggerated view of the company's trading position at the date of purchase. The plaintiffs issued proceedings against the defendants, claiming damages for breach of the defendants' duty of care to them.

---

[415] *Berg Sons & Co Ltd v Mervyn Hampton Adams & Ors* [1993] BCLC 1045.

[416] *Berg Sons & Co Ltd v Mervyn Hampton Adams & Ors* [1993] BCLC 1045, at 1054 (*per* Hobhouse J).

[417] *Caparo Industries plc v Dickman* [1990] BCLC 273, [1990] 2 AC 605.

[418] *Berg Sons & Co Ltd v Mervyn Hampton Adams & Ors* [1993] BCLC 1045, at 1063 (*per* Hobhouse J).

[419] *Caparo Industries plc v Dickman* [1990] BCLC 273, [1990] 2 AC 605.

[420] *Berg Sons & Co Ltd v Mervyn Hampton Adams & Ors* [1993] BCLC 1045, at 1068 (*per* Hobhouse J).

[421] *Kelly v Boland* [1985] IEHC 209.

Lardner J considered the liability of the defendants to the plaintiffs and adopted the following statement of law from the judgment of Woolfe J in *JEB Fasteners Ltd v Marks Bloom & Co*[422] as the 'appropriate test of liability':

> '... the appropriate test for establishing whether a duty of care exists appears in this case to be whether the Defendants knew or reasonably should have foreseen at the time the accounts were audited that a person might rely on those accounts for the purpose of deciding whether or not to take over the company and therefore could suffer loss if the accounts were inaccurate. Such an approach does place a limitation on those entitled to contend that there has been a breach of duty owed to them. First of all, they must have relied on the accounts and, second, they must have done so in circumstances where the auditors either knew that they would or ought to have known that they might. If the situation is one where it would not be reasonable for the accounts to be relied on, then, in the absence of express knowledge, the auditor would be under no duty. This places a limit on the circumstances in which the audited accounts can be relied on and the period for which they can be relied on. The longer the period which elapses prior to the accounts being relied on, from the date on which the auditor gave his certificate, the more difficult it will be to establish that the auditor ought to have foreseen that his certificate would, in those circumstances, be relied on.'

Applying this test to the facts of *Kelly v Haughey Boland & Co*,[423] the defendants did not dispute that they owed a duty of care to the plaintiffs in respect of the financial year 1976, as the audit was conducted in April and May 1977, and the defendants were made aware prior to certifying the accounts, that there were potential purchasers and that the plaintiff were considering acquiring the company. However, the defendants refuted any claim of liability to the plaintiffs in respect of preceding years. Lardner J noted that the defendants did put forward the accounts from 1975 in the context of the bids to acquire Company B, and that 'the auditors in auditing the 1975 accounts should reasonably have foreseen and considered that there might be a sale of the business and the persons interested in purchasing it might rely on the 1975 accounts.' However, with regard to the financial years ending 31 December 1973 and 31 December 1974, the company itself forwarded accounts for 1974 and 1973 to the potential purchasers, but the defendants did not put forward those accounts for the purpose of the purchase negotiations. With regard to these accounts, the Court concluded:

> 'At the times they were prepared, I am not satisfied from any evidence which I have heard, that any sale of the business was in contemplation by the O'Sullivan family [Company B] or might reasonably have been foreseen by the Defendants as auditors. And in the circumstances of this case I do not think it has been established that any duty of care lay upon the Defendants in the preparation of the accounts for these years, in regard to the Plaintiffs as intending purchasers or in regard to intending purchasers in general.'

The liability of auditors' to third parties in Ireland is therefore limited to situations in which the auditors could reasonably have foreseen that the third party in question would rely on those accounts. *Kelly v Haughey Boland & Co* may also be interpreted somewhat more broadly in the sense that, if an auditor furnishes accounts which he audited to

---

[422] *JEB Fasteners Ltd v Marks Bloom & Co* [1981] 3 All ER 289, at 296–297.

[423] *Kelly v Haughey Boland & Co* [1985] IEHC 209.

potential purchasers, in the context of takeover negotiations, he may be liable in respect of those accounts, even though the purchase was not necessarily in contemplation when those accounts were audited.

(iii) Investors

[7.142] There have been cases in which investors in listed companies have sought to invoke breaches of duty by auditors as a basis for their right of action. As described above, the general rule is that auditors owe duties to the company alone, unless they have has assumed a particular obligation towards third parties.[424]

An important case that clarified the position of investors is *Caparo Industries plc v Dickman*,[425] referred to above.[426] In that case, the House of Lords considered the proximity that must exist before an action can be sustained against the auditor of a company. Lord Bridge observed that, to render the maker of a statement liable to the world at large in respect of the accuracy of that statement, is to subject him to 'liability in an indeterminate amount for an indeterminate time to an indeterminate class' as warned against in *Ultramares Corp v Touche*.[427] Lord Bridge noted that imposing such liability would also confer on the world at large the unwarranted right to appropriate the benefit of the statement, and the knowledge and expertise underlying it, to their own ends.[428] Lord Oliver stated emphatically, 'I can see nothing in the statutory duties of a company's auditor to suggest that they were intended by Parliament to protect the interests of investors in the market ...'.[429] The court concluded that '... auditors of a public company's accounts owe no duty of care to members of the public at large who rely on the accounts in deciding to buy shares in the company.'[430] The court also concluded that the duties an auditor owes to the shareholders of company are owed to the shareholders as a body and not in their capacity as individual shareholders.

In *Anthony & Ors v Wright & Ors*[431] persons who invested in a company, without reliance on the audits conducted in respect of that company, claimed that the auditors owed a duty of care to them, as well as to the company. Rejecting this claim, Lightman J stated:

'[a] special relationship is required and in particular intention (actual or inferred) on the part of the auditors that the third party shall rely, and reliance by the third party, on the audit, before a claim in negligence against the auditor can be maintained.'[432]

---

[424] See para **[7.135]**.

[425] *Caparo Industries plc v Dickman* [1990] BCLC 273, [1990] 2 AC 605.

[426] See para **[7.137]**.

[427] *Ultramares Corp v Touche* (1931) 255 NY 170, 179 (*per* Cardozo CJ).

[428] *Caparo Industries plc v Dickman* [1990] BCLC 273, 282, [1990] 2 AC 605, 629.

[429] *Caparo Industries plc v Dickman* [1990] BCLC 273, 309, [1990] 2 AC 605.

[430] *Caparo Industries plc v Dickman* [1990] BCLC 273, 284, [1990] 2 AC 605.

[431] *Anthony & Ors v Wright & Ors* [1995] 1 BLCL 236.

[432] *Anthony & Ors v Wright & Ors* [1995] 1 BLCL 236, 236, citing *Galoo Ltd (in liq) v Bright Grahame Murray (a firm)* [1994] 2 BCLC 492, [1995] 1 All ER 16, [1994] 1 WLR 1360.

In that case the existence of a trust of which the investors were beneficiaries and the company was trustee, was submitted as a basis for the claim. The court held that the most appropriate action in those circumstances was an action against the directors of the company, not the auditors. The action was accordingly struck out.

(iv) Creditors

[7.143] The general rule applicable to the rights of third parties to invoke an alleged breach of duty by an auditor applies equally to creditors of a company. In *Al Saudi Banque & Ors v Clark Pixley (a firm)*[433] the preliminary issue that came before the court was whether an auditor of a company, in carrying out its duties as such, owes a duty of care to lending banks which they knew or ought to know would rely on their accounts and reports when considering the provision of facilities to the company.

The Court considered the law that governs the duty of care of an auditor, placing particular reliance on *Caparo Industries plc v Dickman*.[434] The Court gave a number of reasons for considering that authority to be binding, among them that there must be a sufficient nexus between the parties to establish a duty of care; that forseeability is a necessary but not sufficient condition for imposing liability; and that a sufficient nexus may exist if the auditor impliedly represented the accuracy of the accounts to the third party. *Caparo Industries plc v Dickman*[435] was viewed as the furthest limit of the law regarding the duty of care for negligent misstatement.

Applying that authority to the creditors' claim before it, the Court held that, while it may have been foreseeable that a bank would request and receive copies of the audited accounts, there was no proximity between the auditors and the banks in question. Knowledge of the existence of a third party was not sufficient to establish proximity between an auditor and that third party. As no proximity was established, no duty of care was owed to the company's creditors.

On the authority of *Al Saudi Banque & Ors v Clark Pixley (a firm)*[436] and more general authorities regarding the duty of care owed by an auditor to third parties, it will be difficult if not impossible for a creditor to establish sufficient proximity to make out a claim against a company's auditor.

(v) Standard of care

[7.144] The general rule with regard to the duty of auditors is set out in the CA 1990, s 193(6), which provides:

> 'A person who is appointed as auditor of a company or as a public auditor shall be under a general duty to carry out such audit with professional integrity.'

There is no statutory definition of 'professional integrity' or of the standard of care that is expected of an auditor. However, the Statements of Accounting Standards and other

---

[433] *Al Saudi Banque & Ors v Clark Pixley (a firm)* [1990] BCLC 46.

[434] *Caparo Industries plc v Dickman* [1990] BCLC 273, [1990] 2 AC 605.

[435] *Caparo Industries plc v Dickman* [1990] BCLC 273, [1990] 2 AC 605.

[436] *Al Saudi Banque & Ors v Clark Pixley (a firm)* [1990] BCLC 46.

guidance issued by the Auditing Practices Board can be called in aid in defining the scope and extent of skill and care that should be expected of an auditor. This approach has been endorsed by the ODCE.[437]

[7.145] From the common law perspective, there have been some authoritative descriptions of the duties of an auditor.[438] One classic statement of the law is the following statement by Lopes LJ in *Re Kingston Cotton Mills Co (No 2)*:[439]

> 'It is the duty of an auditor to bear on the work he has to perform that skill, care and caution which a reasonably competent, careful and cautious auditor would use. What is reasonable skill, care and caution must depend on the particular circumstances of the case. An auditor is not bound to be a detective, or, as was said, to approach his work with suspicion or with a foregone conclusion that there is something wrong. He is a watchdog, but not a bloodhound. He is justified in believing tried servants of the company in whom confidence is placed by the company. He is entitled to assume that they are honest, and to reply upon their representations, provided he takes reasonable care. If there is anything calculated to excite suspicion he should probe it to the bottom; but in the absence of anything of that kind he is only bound to be reasonably cautious and careful.'[440]

The other leading statement of the law applicable the duties of an auditor was set forth by Lindley LJ in *Re London and General Bank (No 2)*[441] in the following terms:

> 'An auditor, however, is not bound to do more than exercise reasonable care and skill in making inquiries and investigations. He is not an insurer; he does not guarantee that the books do correctly show the true position of the company's affairs; he does not even guarantee that his balance sheet is accurate according to the books of the company. If he did, he would be responsible for error on his part, even if he were himself deceived without any want of reasonable care on his part, say, by the fraudulent concealment of a book from him. His obligation is not so onerous as this. Such I take to be the duty of the auditor: he must be honest – ie he must not certify what he does not believe to be true, and he must take reasonable care and skill before he believes that what he certifies is true. What is reasonable care in any particular case must depend on the circumstances of that case. Where there is nothing to excite suspicion very little inquiry will be reasonably sufficient, and in practice I believe businessmen select a few cases at haphazard, see that they are right, and assume that others like them are correct also. Where suspicion is

---

[437] See ODCE, 'The Duty of Auditors to Report to the Director of Corporate Enforcement' (Decision Notice D/2002/2), in which considerable reliance is placed on the Statements of Accounting Standards, and ODCE, Revised Guidance on the Duty of Auditors to Report Suspected Indictable Offences to the Director of Corporate Enforcement' Decision Notice D/2006/2, where the IAS are heavily relied upon.

[438] These statements of the duty owed by an auditor of a company were cited by Kearns J in *Kennedy v Law Society* [2000] 2 IR 104.

[439] *Re Kingston Cotton Mills Co (No 2)* [1896] 2 Ch 279.

[440] *Re Kingston Cotton Mills Co (No 2)* [1896] 2 Ch 279, at 288–289.

[441] *Re London and General Bank (No 2)* [1895] 2 Ch 673.

aroused more care is obviously necessary; but, still, an auditor is not bound to exercise more than reasonable care and skill, even in a case of suspicion, and he is perfectly justified in acting on the opinion of an expert where special knowledge is required.'

[7.146] The general rule emerging from these decisions is that an auditor owes the usual standard of care owed by a professional, namely the duty to use such skill, care and caution which a reasonably competent, careful auditor would use. What reasonable care and skill are, will depend on the circumstances of audit. With regard to information provided to the auditor, he is entitled to rely on the honesty of officers of the company, where such reliance is reasonable. However, where there is anything in the information or documents that arouse a suspicion, an auditor is under a duty to investigate such suspicions. There is a divergence between the decisions cited above with regard to the level of care that an auditor must exercise when pursuing a suspicion. In *Re Kingston Cotton Mills Co (No 2)*,[442] Lopes LJ stated that such suspicions must be probed to the bottom, whereas Lindley LJ in *Re London and General Bank (No 2)*[443] held that more care was necessary if suspicious circumstances arose, but not more than a duty of reasonable care and skill.

[7.147] In *Fomento (Sterling Area) Ltd v Selsdon Fountain Pen Co Ltd*[444] Lord Denning explained the duty of an auditor in the following terms:

'An auditor is not to be confined for the mechanics of checking vouchers and making arithmetic computations. He is not to be written off as a professional "adder upper and subtractor". His vital task is to take care to see that errors are not made, be they errors of computation, or errors of omission or commission, or downright untruths.'

This suggests that the responsibility for detecting any errors or wrongdoing applies to an auditor in the usual discharge of his functions and is not confined to situations where something arouses the suspicions of the auditor.

[7.148] A final point that should be noted regarding the duties owed by auditors is that the law is in a considerable state of flux in this area. As stated in *Man Nutzfahrzeuge Aktiengesellschaft & Ors v Freightliner Ltd*:[445]

'The law in the field of auditors' negligence and auditors' duties is in a state of development and transition and there are therefore real difficulties in deciding cases on a summary basis without a full investigation of the detailed facts, unless they fall fairly and squarely within the decided authorities.'

---

[442] *Re Kingston Cotton Mills Co (No 2)* [1896] 2 Ch 279, at 288–289.

[443] *Re London and General Bank (No 2)* [1895] 2 Ch 673.

[444] *Fomento (Sterling Area) Ltd v Selsdon Fountain Pen Co Ltd* [1958] 1 DPP 45.

[445] *Man Nutzfahrzeuge Aktiengesellschaft and others v Freightliner Ltd* [2003] EWHC 2245 (Comm), [2003] All ER (D) 105 (QBD, October 7, 2003)(*per* Cooke J).

(c) Developments regarding auditors' liability

[7.149] An increasing amount of attention is being paid to the issue of auditors' liability.[446] The EU commissioned research on the topic, as reflected in art 31 of Council Directive 2006/43/EC:

> Before 1 January 2007 the Commission shall present a report on the impact of the current national liability rules for the carrying out of statutory audits on European capital markets and on the insurance conditions for statutory auditors and audit firms, including an objective analysis of the limitations of financial liability. The Commission shall, where appropriate, carry out a public consultation. In the light of that report, the Commission shall, if it considers it appropriate, submit recommendations to the Member States.

The Commission accordingly published a study on the economic impact of regimes governing auditors' liability in September 2006.[447] Following the publication of this study, on 3 January 2007, the Minister for Enterprise, Trade and Employment referred the issue of auditor liability to the CLRG, noting that, 'the publication of this EU Report opens the debate on the situation on auditor liability generally and with reference to individual Member States.' The scope of the referral is as follows:

> '... broadly speaking, I have requested CLRG to develop an understanding of the issues associated with the current regime of auditor liability in Ireland, and to consider whether this is in need of reform, having regard to the policy issues and other considerations that are relevant, including those concerning the continuity of supply of audit services to the Irish economy.'[448]

The ICAI presented a discussion paper on the topic of auditor liability in February 2007, opposing the current legal provisions applicable to auditor liability in Ireland and describing the joint effect of CA 1963, s 200, CA 1990, s 187 and the principle of joint and several liability as follows:

> 'So, for example, in an action arising as a result of a corporate collapse where the directors and other senior management of a company have been found to be principally at fault, and where the auditors' culpability has been relatively minor, the auditors may well still have to bear 100% of the loss arising due to the insignificant resources of the other defendants to the claim. Furthermore, the prohibition on bodies corporate from acting as auditors means that the personal assets (including, for example, private residences) of all partners in audit firms are exposed in the event of a 'catastrophic loss', notwithstanding that most partners will have no involvement or culpability in the matter giving rise to that loss. The current liability regime encourages plaintiffs to go after those defendants (in this case the auditors) with the 'deepest pockets', even though the auditors may be

---

[446] See Lambe 'Auditor Liability – the time for reform,' *Accountancy Ireland*, Vol 37, No5 ('Auditor liability has been an increasing concern for the auditing profession for a considerable number of years. It is now being recognised that excessively onerous liability regimes are unfair and unjust to auditors. Consequently, a number of jurisdictions in recent years have introduced measures aimed at reforming their auditor liability regimes.')

[447] London Economics, 'Study on the Economic Impact of Auditors' Liability Regimes' Final report to EC-DG Internal Market and Services (September 2006).

[448] DETE Press release, 'Minister Michael Ahern refers current auditor liability regime to the Company Law Review Group (CLRG)' 3 January 2007. Available at www.entemp.ie.

held to have been responsible for the loss to a much lesser extent than any other defendant.'[449]

In January 2007, the Commission initiated a consultation on auditors' liability and invited submissions on four possible means of reforming auditors' liability:

(1)   a single monetary cap fixed at EU level;

(2)   a cap based on the size of the audited company;

(3)   a cap based on a multiple of the audit fees charged by the auditor;

(4)   the introduction of the principle of proportionate liability, whereby each party (auditor and audited company) is liable only for the portion of loss that corresponds to the party's degree of responsibility.[450]

In Ireland the ICAI presented its position paper on this topic to the Commission:

'ICAI supports the introduction of statutory liability caps for auditors, as set out in the Directorate's paper as a measure required to ensure the viability of, and promote competition within, the audit market. We support ultimately a single auditor liability regime across all EU Member States to promote a fair and equitable audit market within the EU. Such a regime should encompass not only liability caps but also proportionate liability – auditors being liable only for the proportion of the loss for which they are responsible.'[451]

The ODCE also responded to the Commission consultation paper, acknowledging the problem of auditor liability in Ireland:

'Ireland currently does not have any limitation to auditor liability. In addition audit firms are prohibited from establishing limited liability partnerships, and the issue is compounded by the existence of joint and several liability. The ODCE accepts the arguments that have been made as to the potential risks this exposes auditors to.'[452]

In addition, the ODCE cautioned that reform of the principle of joint and several liability may not be straightforward:

'However, in Ireland the principle of joint and several liability for persons who are concurrently responsible for losses arising from negligence is one which is deeply embedded in our legal system and has survived constitutional challenge. In the circumstances any proposal to take audit firms outside its scope might give rise to implications in other areas, and demands by other groups or sectors that they too should not be subject to the regime of joint and several liability. Because the

---

[449] ICAI, 'Auditor Liability – the Reform Imperative' (February 2007). Available at www.icai.ie.

[450] DG for Internal Market and Services, 'Consultation on Auditors' Liability and its Impact on the European Capital Markets' Commission Staff Working Paper, January 2007.

[451] ICAI, 'Consultation on Auditors' Liability and its Impact on the European Capital Markets' (March 2007). Available at www.icai.ie.

[452] ODCE, 'ODCE Response to Commission Staff Working Paper: Consultation on Auditors' Liability and its Impact on European Capital Markets'. Available at www.odce.ie.

ODCE has competence only in the field of company law we are not in a position to assess the full implications of the proposal from this wider perspective.'[453]

The debate on auditors' liability is still open and the direction of Irish law on this topic remains undetermined.

---

[453] ODCE, 'ODCE Response to Commission Staff Working Paper: Consultation on Auditors' Liability and its Impact on European Capital Markets'. Available at www.odce.ie.

Chapter 8

RECEIVERS

A. Introduction

[8.001] This chapter considers the compliance obligations that arise when a receiver is appointed over a company's assets. While it is beyond the scope of this chapter to provide a broader insight into the role and duties of receivers,[1] there are some general points that should be noted. First, a receiver acts as an agent, but not in the ordinary sense of that term. On the contrary, while a receiver has the power to deal with third parties on behalf of the company, and to bind the company by such dealings, the receiver's duties are owed to the debenture holder who appointed him. The role of a receiver was described as follows in a passage from the judgment of Fox LJ in *Gomba Holdings Ltd v Minories Finance Ltd*,[2] which has been adopted by the Irish Supreme Court:[3]

> 'The agency of a receiver is not an ordinary agency. It is primarily a device to protect the mortgagee or debenture holder. Thus, the receiver acts as agent for the mortgagor in that he has power to affect the mortgagor's position by acts which, though done for the benefit of the debenture holder, are treated as if they were the acts of the mortgagor. The relationship set up by the debenture, and the appointment of the receiver, however, is not simply between the mortgagor and the receiver. It is tripartite and involves the mortgagor, the receiver and the debenture holder. The receiver is appointed by the debenture holder, upon the happening of specified events, and becomes the mortgagor's agent whether the mortgagor likes it or not. And, as a matter of contract between the mortgagor and the debenture holder, the mortgagor will have to pay the receiver's fees. Further, the mortgagor cannot dismiss the receiver, since that power is reserved to the debenture holder as another of the contractual terms of the loan. It is to be noted also that the mortgagor cannot instruct the receiver how to act in the conduct of the receivership.'

The proposition that a receiver owes a duty to the debenture holder responsible for his appointment is subject to the qualification that if a receiver is appointed by the court, he is an officer of the court and owes a duty of care to each of the creditors of the company.

A second preliminary point to note about receivers is that there is a distinction between receivers who are appointed in respect of part only of the company's property, by holders of debentures secured by fixed charges over those assets, and receivers who are appointed over the whole or substantially the whole of the company's assets, by holders of debentures which are secured by floating charges. The former are receivers, whereas

---

[1] For a more general analysis of the law applicable to receivers, see Courtney, *The Law of Private Companies* (2nd edn Tottel Publishing, 2002), Ch 22. See also ODCE, 'Information Book 7 – Liquidators, Receivers & Examiners', Decision Notice D/2002/1.

[2] *Gomba Holdings Ltd v Minories Finance Ltd* [1988] 1 WLR 1231 at 1233–1234.

[3] *Bula Ltd v Crowley (No 3)* [2003] 1 IR 396 at 423–424 (*per* Denham J).

the latter are referred to as 'receiver-managers'.[4] For the purposes of the Companies Acts, CA 1963, s 323(1) provides that:

> ... unless the contrary intention appears ... any reference in this Act to a receiver of the property of a company includes a reference to a receiver and manager of the property of a company and to a manager of the property of a company and includes a reference to a receiver or to a receiver and manager and to a manager, of part only of that property, and to a receiver only of the income arising from that property or from part thereof.

B. Publication of appointment

(a) Publication by person appointing receiver

[8.002] Upon the appointment of a receiver, the person who obtained the court order, or exercised a power contained in an instrument for such appointment, must publish a notice in the *Companies Registration Office Gazette*[5] and in at least one newspaper circulating in the district in which the company's registered office is located.[6]

He must also deliver a notice to the Registrar of Companies. Form 53, the appropriate form for this purpose, requires that the following information be furnished to the Registrar:

- the name of the company;

- whether the company is incorporated in Ireland or outside the State;

- the name of the person presenting the notice;

- a signed statement that the receiver has been appointed;

- the means by which the receiver was appointed, whether by court order or pursuant to a power in an instrument;

- the name of the receiver;

- whether the appointment is for receiver, manager or receiver-manager;

- the date of appointment;

- whether the receivership applies to the whole or substantially the whole of the company's property; part of the company's property; or the income from the company's property or part thereof;

---

[4] See *Irish Oil and Cake Mills Ltd v Donnelly* [1983] IEHC 199 (27 March 1983, Costello J,) for an example of a case in which the holders of debentures secured by a floating charge appointed a receiver-manager over the whole of the company's assets. See further Lightman & Moss, *The Law of Receivers and Administrators of Companies* (Sweet & Maxwell, 2000) at para 1-004.

[5] This was substituted for *Iris Oifigiúil* by IFCMPA 2005, s 72.

[6] CA 1963, s 107(1).

– a full description of the instrument which gives rise to the receivership, including a statement that it is a debenture secured by a floating charge, if applicable; and

– the date of the notice.[7]

These notices must be published and delivered within seven days of the court order or the appointment of the receiver pursuant to a debenture.[8] It is an offence to fail to publish or deliver the requisite notices regarding the appointment of a receiver, an offence punishable by a maximum fine of €1,904.61.[9] However, a failure to deliver or publish the requisite notices will not invalidate the appointment of the receiver. In *Re Motor Racing Circuits Ltd*,[10] one of the arguments made in challenging the appointment of a receiver was that there was a failure to notify the company of his appointment. Delivering the judgment of the Supreme Court, Blayney J stated that:

'It is clear from the section of the company under which notice has to be given that a failure to give notice has a sanction simply attached to it, a fine of £100. It is clear under the particular section that notice has to be given but there is no provision that if notice is not given that the appointment of the receiver is in any way affected. So even if the situation was that notice was not given then the appointment of the receiver would not be affected.'

[8.003] It is not wholly clear from the decision of the Supreme Court which provision of the Companies Acts is referred to. The reference to a failure to notify the company suggests that it was CA 1963, s 319. However, while s 319 originally referred to a fine of £100, this was increased to £1,000 by CA 1990, s 145. The fine under s 107, which requires notification to the Registrar of the appointment of a receiver, was also originally £100, but increased to £500 by 1997. This ambiguity does not undermine the fact that, on the authority of *Re Motor Racing Circuits Ltd*,[11] a failure to deliver a notice of the appointment of a receiver will not affect the validity of the appointment of a receiver.

[8.004] It is also established that the delivery of a notice of appointment of a receiver will not cure any invalidity in such appointment. In *Wise Finance Company v O'Regan*,[12] the person who was purportedly appointed as a receiver of a company was also its secretary and was therefore ineligible for appointment. This invalidity in the

---

[7] Form No 53, 'Notice of Appointment of a Receiver (pursuant to s 107(1))'. This form may be downloaded from the Companies Registration Office website 'downloads' section: see www.cro.ie.

[8] CA 1963, s 107(1).

[9] CA 1963, s 107(3), as amended by C(A)A 1982, s 15; CA 1990, s 240(7) as inserted by CLEA 2001, s 104; C(AA)A 2003, s 57 and Sch 2.

[10] *Re Motor Racing Circuits Ltd* [1997] IESC 59 (31 January 1997, unreported), SC.

[11] *Re Motor Racing Circuits Ltd* [1997] IESC 59 (31 January 1997, unreported), SC.

[12] *Wise Finance Company v O'Regan* [1998] IEHC 105, Laffoy J.

appointment of the receiver was not cured by the delivery of the notice of the appointment. As stated by Laffoy J, the notice of appointment:

> 'could not, on its own and without satisfactory evidence of the power and authority of the person purporting to make the appointment, be regarded as sufficient proof of the valid appointment of an eligible individual as receiver and manager of the Company.'

(b) General publication requirements

[8.005] When a receiver has been appointed to a company, this fact must be displayed on documents issued by the company. In particular, every invoice, order for goods, or business letter issued by or on behalf of the company itself, its receiver or liquidator, and on which the company's name appears, must contain a statement that a receiver has been appointed.[13]

If there is a failure to comply with this requirement, the company and any officer, receiver or liquidator who 'knowingly and wilfully authorises or permits the default', shall be guilty of an offence and liable to a maximum fine of €1,904.61.[14]

(c) Receiver's duty to publicise appointment

[8.006] CA 1963, s 319 sets out certain obligations that arise from the appointment of receivers over the whole or substantially the whole of the property of a company pursuant to debentures secured by a floating charge.[15] Where a receiver is so appointed, the receiver must forthwith send a notice to the company of his appointment.[16] Within 14 days of the notice of the appointment being received by the company, or such longer period as the court (if the receiver is court-appointed)[17] or the receiver may permit, the company must make out and submit to the receiver a statement of the affairs of the company.[18] Within two months after the receipt of that statement of affairs, the receiver must send a copy of the statement, with any comments he considers fit in relation to it, to the Registrar of Companies; the company; the court (if the receiver is court-appointed); if he knows their addresses, the debenture holders on whose behalf he was appointed; and to the debenture holders' trustees.[19] It is an offence for the receiver to fail to comply with this requirement.[20]

---

13   CA 1963, s 317(1).

14   CA 1963, s 317(2), as amended by C(A)A 1982, Sch 1; CA 1990, s 240(7), as inserted by CLEA 2001, s 104; and C(AA)A 2003, s 57 and Sch 2.

15   Note that these obligations apply, with the necessary modifications, if the company is being wound up and the receiver is also appointed as liquidator, CA 1963, s 319(5).

16   CA 1963, s 319(1)(a).

17   CA 1963, s 319(3) clarifies that, 'Where a receiver is appointed under the powers contained in any instrument, this section shall have effect with the omission of the references to the court in sub-s (1), and in any other case, references to the court shall be taken as referring to the court by which the receiver was appointed.'

18   CA 1963, s 319(1)(b).

19   CA 1963, s 319(1)(c).

20   CA 1963, s 319(8), as inserted by CLEA 2001, s 52(b).

[8.007] If a receiver is appointed to act together with an existing receiver, or in place of a receiver who has died or ceased to act, there is no requirement to send the above mentioned notice to the company, or for the company to deliver a statement of its affairs to the receiver.[21] This is subject to the qualification that, if a receiver dies or ceases to act before a statement of affairs is received from the company and sent, with comments, to the requisite recipients, the newly appointed receiver shall be substituted for his predecessor.[22]

[8.008] CA 1963, s 319(7) as substituted by CLEA 2001, s 52(b), contains the curious requirement that 'Where the registrar of companies becomes aware of the appointment of a receiver under this section, he shall forthwith inform the Director of the appointment.' It would be more appropriate and logical for this requirement to be included in s 107, rather than s 319, for three reasons.

First, the notices and documents which must be sent to the Registrar of Companies under s 319 relate to the company's affairs and the conduct of the receivership, rather than the details of the appointment of the receiver.[23] Section 319(1)(a) only requires the receiver to notify the company of his appointment. There is no requirement that the Registrar of Companies be notified of the appointment of a receiver under s 319. This can be contrasted with s 107, which requires the person responsible for the appointment of a receiver, to deliver to the Registrar, a particular form (Form 53), containing specific information about the appointment of the receiver.

Secondly, the earliest date at which s 319 envisages the Registrar of Companies being notified of the appointment of a receiver is when the receiver delivers to the Registrar a copy of the company's statement of affairs. The receiver has at least ten weeks from the date of his appointment to fulfil this requirement.[24] If the company receives an extension of the 14 day limit for delivery of the statement of affairs, this period will be longer. It is difficult to reconcile the late stage at which the Registrar may receive any communication under s 319, with the obligation that the Registrar notify the Director 'forthwith' upon becoming aware of the appointment of a receiver under that provision. This is particularly anomalous in light of the fact that s 107(1) requires the notice regarding the appointment of the receiver, to be delivered by the person responsible for the appointment to the Registrar of Companies within seven days of such appointment.

Thirdly, the language used in s 319(7) demonstrates its incompatibility with the terms of s 319. Section 319(7) refers to the Registrar becoming 'aware of the appointment of a receiver under this section'. As noted above, the first communication to the Registrar under s 319 is the delivery of a copy of the company's statement of affairs, some ten

---

[21] CA 1963, s 319(4).

[22] CA 1963, s 319(4) provides that, 'where that subsection [s 319(1)] applies to a receiver who dies or ceases to act before it has been fully complied with, the references in paras (b) and (c) thereof to the receiver shall (subject to sub-s (5)) include references to his successor and to any continuing receiver.'

[23] See CA 1963, s 319(1)(c), which requires the statement of the company's affairs, with comments, to be delivered to the Registrar, and s 319(2), which requires abstracts regarding the company's assets to be sent to the Registrar.

[24] See CA 1963, s 319(1).

weeks after the date of the appointment. By contrast, the Registrar of Companies should be aware of the appointment of a receiver within seven days of such appointment, pursuant to s 107(1). The Registrar will not, therefore, become 'aware' of a receiver by virtue of any of the information or notices required by s 319.

If the objective of s 319(7) is to ensure that the DCE is notified promptly of the appointment of a receiver this objective would be better achieved if the Registrar was required to notify the DCE of receipt of a notice under s 107(1). However, s 319(7) as it is formulated does not require that the DCE be notified of the appointment of a receiver until at least ten weeks after such appointment. In practice, therefore, the Registrar may notify the DCE of the appointment of a receiver, upon receipt of Form 53 under s 107, rather than waiting for receipt of a company's statement of affairs under s 319(1)(c).

C. Compliance duties of receivers

(a) Qualifications of receivers

[8.009] There is nothing in the Companies Acts 1963–2006 regarding the qualifications which a person must possess to act as receiver. However, there are certain persons who are disqualified from acting as receivers:[25]

(1) A body corporate may not act as a receiver and it is an offence for a body corporate to so act,[26] an offence which is punishable by a maximum fine of €1,904.61;[27]

(2) An undischarged bankrupt may not act as a receiver;[28]

(3) A person who is or who was within 12 months before the commencement of the receivership, an officer or servant of the company, may not be a receiver of that company;[29]

(4) A parent, spouse, brother, sister or child of an officer of the company cannot act as a receiver[30] (family members of a servant of a company are not disqualified from acting as its receiver);

---

[25] Note that according to CA 1963, s 315(4), as substituted by CA 1990, s 170, persons who were appointed to the position of receiver before the commencement of CA 1990, s 170, are not required to vacate that position.

[26] CA 1963, s 314, as amended by C(AA)A 2003, s 57 and Sch 2.

[27] CA 1963, s 314, as amended by C(A)A 1982, and CA 1990, s 240(7), as inserted by CLEA 2001, s 104.

[28] CA 1963, s 315(1)(a), as substituted by CA 1990, s 170.

[29] CA 1963, s 315(1)(b), as substituted by CA 1990, s 170. See *Wise Finance Company v O'Regan* [1998] IEHC 105, Laffoy J, for an example of a case in which the appointment of an officer of a company as receiver was found to be invalid under CA 1963, s 315(1), as substituted by CA 1990, s 170.

[30] CA 1963, s 315(1)(c), as substituted by CA 1990, s 170.

(5) An employee, servant, or business partner, of an officer or servant of the company is disqualified from acting as a receiver;[31]

(6) If a person is disqualified from acting as a receiver of a company, he is also disqualified from so acting in respect of that company's parent company, subsidiary or a company which is a subsidiary of the same holding company;[32] and

(7) The disqualifications applicable to officers or servants of a company also apply to auditors. Section 315(1) provides in this regard, 'references in this subsection to an officer or servant of the company include references to an auditor'. Section 315(1)(b) and (d) include the specific phrase 'an officer or servant of the company' and must clearly include auditors. A person who is or was within the preceding 12 months, an auditor of a company cannot therefore act as its receiver. Similarly, a partner or employee of an auditor of a company cannot be appointed as receiver.

[8.010] The prohibition on parents, spouses, brothers, sisters or children acting as receivers refers to 'officers' alone and does not refer to 'an officer or servant of the company.' There are two possible interpretations of this aspect of s 315(1). First, the statement that 'references in this subsection to an officer or servant of the company include references to an auditor' could be interpreted as being limited to references to 'an officer or servant' as a composite expression. Under this interpretation, family members of auditors would not be disqualified from acting as receivers of companies. The second possible interpretation of s 315(1) is that any reference to an officer or to a servant of the company in that subsection shall include references to an auditor. This would disqualify family members of auditors from acting as receivers, as s 315(1)(c) refers to 'a parent, spouse, brother, sister or child of an officer of the company.'

While this aspect of the provision is ambiguous, it appears on balance that the former interpretation is to be preferred. This interpretation is favoured by the fact that the composite expression 'an officer or servant of the company 'is used in relation to two of the categories of persons disqualified in s 315(1) and it is unlikely that the use of the same phrase in relation to auditors is not referable to its precise use elsewhere in the subsection. In addition, there is no isolated reference in s 315(1) to 'a servant of the company.' The inclusion of this reference in relation to auditors would therefore be meaningless unless it was employed as part of the composite expression 'an officer or a servant of the company'.

On this interpretation, a parent, spouse, brother, sister or child of an auditor of a company is not disqualified from acting as the company's receiver.

[8.011] A final category of persons who are disqualified from acting as receivers, are those who are subject to disqualification orders, a topic which is addressed in detail in Pt E, Disqualification Orders. The list of persons who are disqualified from acting as receivers may be expanded by means of regulations introduced by the Minister for Enterprise, Trade and Employment, if he considers it 'necessary or expedient to do so in

---

[31] CA 1963, s 315(1)(d), as substituted by CA 1990, s 170.

[32] CA 1963, s 315(1)(e), as substituted by CA 1990, s 170.

the interests of the orderly and proper regulation of receiverships generally.'[33] No such regulations have been introduced to date.

[8.012] If a person, having been duly appointed as receiver of the property of a company, subsequently becomes disqualified from so acting under s 315, he must vacate his office and give written notice within 14 days to the company; the Registrar of Companies, and either the debenture holder who appointed him, or the court, if he was court-appointed, that he has vacated the office of receiver due to such disqualification.[34] Therefore, if a receiver becomes bankrupt; is appointed to the board of directors of the company; takes a position of employment with the company; enters into partnership or employment with an officer or servant of the company; if a parent, spouse, sibling or child of the receiver becomes an officer of the company; or if the receiver becomes an auditor, or enters into employment or partnership with an auditor of the company, he must vacate the position of receiver.

This obligation to notify the company, the Registrar and the court or debenture holder, of ceasing to act as receiver does not displace the obligations that are imposed on the receiver by virtue of CA 1963, ss 107, 319(2) and 321 and is expressly without prejudice to those obligations.[35]

[8.013] It is an offence for a person to act, or to continue to act, as a receiver when disqualified from so doing, or to fail to furnish the requisite notifications that he has ceased to act due to becoming so disqualified.[36] On summary conviction, this offence is punishable by a maximum fine of €1,904.61 and a maximum daily fine of €63.49 for continuing defaults. On conviction on indictment, the offence is punishable by a maximum fine of €5,348.60 and a maximum daily fine of €317.43 for continuing defaults.[37]

(b) Statement of affairs

[8.014] When a receiver who has been appointed in respect of the whole or substantially the whole of the property of the company on behalf of holders of debentures which are secured by a floating charge, notifies a company of his appointment, in accordance with CA 1963, s 319(1), the company has 14 days within which to deliver a statement of its affairs to the receiver.[38] This requirement does not apply when a receiver is appointed in respect of a part only of the company's assets, on behalf of holders of debentures which are secured by fixed charges.

---

[33] CA 1990, s 237(2).

[34] CA 1963, s 315(2), as substituted by CA 1990, s 170.

[35] CA 1963, s 315(3), as substituted by CA 1990, s 170. See paras **[8.002]**, **[8.025]** to **[8.028]** in relation to the obligations imposed by these provisions.

[36] CA 1963, s 315(5), as substituted by CA 1990, s 170.

[37] CA 1963, s 315(5), as substituted by CA 1990, s 170; amended by CA 1990, s 240(7), as inserted by CLEA 2001, s 104.

[38] CA 1963, s 319(1)(b). This time may be extended by the court or by the receiver. Every reference to 'receiver' in s 320 includes a receiver's successor.

[8.015] Section 320 stipulates that the following information, as it exists on the date of the receiver's appointment, must be contained in the statement of affairs:

- particulars of the company's assets, debts and liabilities;

- the names and addresses of the company's creditors;

- the securities held by each of the creditors respectively;

- the dates on which each of the securities were given to each of the creditors;

- such further or other information as may be prescribed.[39]

[8.016] Form 17 is the form that must be used for the preparation of a company's statement of affairs and sets out in detail the information which is required, including the particulars of the company's assets which are not specifically pledged; assets that are specifically pledged and the creditors whose claims are secured by such assets; estimated total assets available for preferential creditors, floating charge holders and unsecured creditors; the estimated realisable values of each of the company's assets; the preferential creditors, debenture holders secured by floating charges, and unsecured creditors; the estimated surplus or deficiency as regards creditors; the company's issued and called up share capital; and the estimated surplus or deficiency as regards members, among other information.[40]

[8.017] The statement must be submitted by one or more persons who are directors of the company at the date of the receiver's appointment and by the secretary of the company at that date.[41] Alternatively, the receiver may require the following persons to submit the statement of affairs:

- past or present officers of the company;[42]

- persons who were involved in the formation of the company within one year prior to the receiver's appointment; [43]

- employees of the company who, in the opinion of the receiver, are capable of providing the requisite information;[44]

- persons who were employed by the company within one year prior to the receiver's appointment and who, in the opinion of the receiver, are capable of providing the requisite information;[45] or

---

[39] CA 1963, s 320(1). No such additional information has been prescribed to date.

[40] Form 17, 'Statement of Affairs to be Annexed to Affidavit or Statutory Declaration (pursuant to ss 319(1)(b) and 320)'. See www.cro.ie.

[41] CA 1963, s 320(2).

[42] CA 19763, s 320(2)(a).

[43] CA 1963, s 320(2)(b).

[44] CA 1963, s 320(2)(c).

[45] CA 1963, s 320(2)(c).

– persons who are or were within one year prior to the receiver's appointment, officers or employees of a company which is itself, or was within one year prior to the receiver's appointment, an officer of the company in question.[46]

The formulation of the provision suggests that every person who is involved in submitting the statement of affairs must furnish a verifying affidavit. There may therefore be several verifying affidavits. Such affidavits must confirm the position of the person making the affidavit; their means of knowledge of the information contained in the statement of affairs; and the veracity and accuracy of the information contained in the statement. If the receiver is appointed pursuant to a power in a debenture rather than by court appointment, a statutory declaration must be prepared verifying the statement of affairs instead of an affidavit to the same effect.[47]

Any person who submits the statement and furnishes a verifying affidavit will be allowed such costs and expenses as the receiver may consider reasonable, to be paid by the receiver out of his receipts.[48] The receiver's determination as to what are the reasonable costs and expenses of preparing and making a statement of affairs and verifying affidavit, is subject to an appeal to the court.[49]

[8.018] In *Somers v Kennedy*[50] the receiver initiated plenary proceedings seeking a mandatory injunction to compel the directors of the company to prepare and deliver a statement of affairs. The High Court ordered that the directors submit and verify the statement of affairs forthwith. The directors complied with this order and submitted a bill of costs in the amount of £31,318.75, for the costs and expenses of preparing and verifying the statement of affairs. This included valuation fees, accountancy fees, and a fee paid to a specialist contractor. The receiver did not consider that sum to be reasonable and allowed a total of £10,000 for the costs and expenses claimed.

The directors appealed this decision to the High Court, where the decision of the receiver was confirmed. Costello J approached the question of the appropriate level of costs and expenses as follows:

> '... I would approach this case on the basis that I can myself examine whether or not in my view the fees charged are reasonable or not but in reaching that decision I have to take into account the fact that an experienced accountant and a person experienced in insolvency matters has expressed a view that they are not reasonable. This does not bind me in any way, but I take it into account in reaching my conclusion on the issue.'[51]

The High Court considered that the fees paid to valuers and specialist contractors should not be allowed as the purpose of the statement of affairs was for the directors to relate to the receiver their view of the value of the company and its liabilities. While the directors

---

[46] CA 1963, s 320(2)(d).

[47] CA 1963, s 320(4).

[48] CA 1963, s 320(3).

[49] CA 1963, s 320(3).

[50] *Somers v Kennedy* [1998] 1 IR 1.

[51] *Somers v Kennedy* [1998] 1 IR 1, as recorded by Murphy J at p 5 of his Supreme Court decision.

were obliged to act prudently, they were not required to obtain expert opinions as to valuations.

This decision was appealed by the director to the Supreme Court. Delivering the judgment of the Court, Murphy J referred to the significance of a company's statement of affairs as follows:

'... the nature of the duties imposed on directors and other officers of companies in relation to the preparation of a statement of affairs under s 319 of the Act of 1963, where a receiver is appointed, or under s 224, where a winding up order has been made or a provisional liquidator appointed, is a matter of considerable importance to business men generally and their legal and professional advisers.'[52]

The Court noted that the purpose of s 319 is to provide information about the company to the receiver and went on to state:

'The relevant sections must be construed and applied in the context that the persons to whom the information must be submitted will be experts and have access to any necessary additional expertise. Furthermore, they will be in control of the company concerned and will or should have possession of all of the documents of the company material to the performance of their official functions. The information provided by the directors may be of considerable value in the realisation and distribution of the assets of the company but it could never be suggested that a liquidator or receiver would rely exclusively upon it. In the nature of the duties, statutory and fiduciary, performed by receivers and liquidators they would be required to satisfy themselves as to the extent of the assets of the company and its liabilities in so far as they may be material. With regard to the realisation of assets it is difficult to believe that this would be undertaken without the liquidator or receiver satisfying himself by independent professional advice as to the value thereof and the appropriate means of realising the same. The only duty on those making the statement of affairs is to provide the information within their own knowledge as officers or servants of the company and to provide their estimate as to the realisable value thereof. As the learned trial judge pointed out, the trading of the company and its own financial records would provide the directors with a substantial body of information as to the potential value of its assets so that the directors should be in a position to express a commercial view, if not a professional one, as to the value of those assets.'[53]

This decision sets out clearly that the purpose of the statement of affairs is to give the receiver the directors' views and estimates regarding the company's assets and liabilities and the value of such assets. The receiver will be in possession of all relevant documentation, information, expertise, and can obtain his own valuations and external expert opinions regarding the company and its assets. On the basis of this decision, it would not be advisable for a receiver to rely on the content of the statement of affairs, without obtaining independent valuations and advice.

[8.019] In *Somers v Kennedy*,[54] the directors did not argue that expert valuations would ordinarily be required in the preparation of a statement of affairs, but that it was prudent to obtain such independent verification due to the factual circumstances of the case.

---

[52] *Somers v Kennedy* [1998] 1 IR 1 at 5.

[53] *Somers v Kennedy* [1998] 1 IR 1 at 5 to 6.

[54] *Somers v Kennedy* [1998] 1 IR 1.

Murphy J considered this submission and concluded that, while there were differences regarding a system of management and financial control in operation in the company, 'these circumstances did not justify or explain the necessity or even the desirability of obtaining valuations for any part of the assets of the companies.'[55] The Court further stated that, even if the receiver was unlikely to agree with the directors' valuations of the company's assets, 'provided that they have expressed a fair and honest opinion, the attitude of the receiver would be irrelevant' and 'if the defendants wished to protect themselves against any misunderstanding as to the basis on which they arrived at their valuation they could have given, as indeed they did, any appropriate explanation by annotation to the statement delivered by them'.[56] The Court concluded on this basis that the retention of experts to advise on the value of the company's assets was 'unnecessary and unwarranted' and that 'the costs and expenses incurred thereby could not be considered reasonable.'[57]

[8.020] The other category of expense that was considered by the Supreme Court were the expenses claimed by the directors themselves for the preparation of the statement of affairs. The Court noted that 'a statement of affairs may appear as a formidable document' and that, 'it does require the extraction from the books and records of a company of a considerable body of information'.[58] However, the Court also noted that much of this work is 'essentially clerical or administrative work'. The Court also referred to the fact that a fee of £10,000, considerably more than was usual in such cases, was allowed in respect of the accountancy fee. The Court inferred from correspondence between the accountants and the receiver that the accountants undertook the bulk of the work in connection with the preparation of the statement. The fee allowed to the accountants, according to Murphy J, 'may reflect in part the very substantial assets and liabilities of the companies or the troublesome background to the appointment of the receiver. It may reflect too the extent to which the accountants concerned relieved the defendants of the burden imposed upon them by the statute.' Taking these considerations into account, the Court concluded that the level of the fee paid to the accountants left 'no room' for an additional fee to be allowed to the directors themselves. The appeal was therefore dismissed and the fee of £10,000 was allowed.

[8.021] If a person who is required to prepare and submit the statement of affairs and verifying affidavit or statutory declaration defaults in so doing, he is liable to either summary conviction or conviction on indictment. The sanction on summary conviction is a maximum term of six months and/or a maximum fine of €1,904.61 and, for conviction on indictment, a maximum term of three years and/or a maximum fine of €6,348.69.[59] It is a defence to a prosecution under s 320, for a person to prove to the satisfaction of the court that it was not possible for him to comply with the requirement to prepare and make the statement of affairs and verifying affidavit or statutory

---

[55] *Somers v Kennedy* [1998] 1 IR 1 at 6.

[56] *Somers v Kennedy* [1998] 1 IR 1 at 6.

[57] *Somers v Kennedy* [1998] 1 IR 1 at 6.

[58] *Somers v Kennedy* [1998] 1 IR 1 at 7.

[59] CA 1963, s 320(5), as substituted by CA 1990, s 173 and as amended by CA 1990, s 240(7), as inserted by CLEA 2001, s 104(c).

declaration.[60] Such an offence is among those which may be prosecuted by the Registrar of Companies.[61]

[8.022] Where there is a failure to submit the statement of affairs in the prescribed form to the receiver, as well as the individuals responsible being liable to conviction under s 320(5), the court may also make whatever other order it thinks fit.[62] The receiver or a creditor of the company may make an application to the court in this regard. Among the orders which the court may make, is an order compelling compliance with the requirements of ss 319(1)(b) and 320.[63]

[8.023] In *Irish Oil & Cake Mills Ltd v Donnelly*[64] two companies sought a mandatory injunction to compel a receiver-manager to furnish certain information regarding the receivership to the companies. In denying the relief sought, the Court referred to the statutory duty imposed on directors of companies by ss 319 and 320 to furnish a statement of the company's affairs to the receiver. The directors of the plaintiffs had failed to discharge this duty. According to Costello J, the duty to prepare and deliver a statement of affairs 'cannot be regarded in this case as a mere formality whose breach the Court should readily excuse.' The Court referred to a number of factual reasons for which the statement of affairs was 'specially required here'. The Court moreover noted that the information sought by the directors related almost exclusively to the receivership and non-receipt of that information could not be invoked as an excuse for the failure to prepare and deliver a statement of the companies' affairs.

The Court concluded, 'as the relief claimed now is a discretionary one the failure of the Companies through their Directors to comply with this important statutory requirement would in my judgment in any event have disentitled them to relief.'

The decision in *Irish Oil & Cake Mills Ltd v Donnelly*[65] demonstrates the importance of the delivery of a company's statement of affairs to a receiver. It moreover demonstrates that, when a person fails to comply with the obligation to prepare and deliver a statement of affairs, they may not only be the subject of court orders compelling compliance and criminal prosecutions, they may also be refused equitable relief on that ground.

[8.024] From the date on which the receiver receives a company's statement of affairs, he has two months to consider the statement and make any comments in relation to it as he sees fit. Within two months after receipt of the statement of affairs, he must forward it, together with any such comments, to the company; to the Registrar of Companies; to the court (if he was court-appointed); to the trustees for the debenture holders on whose

---

[60] CA 1963, s 320(5), as substituted by CA 1990, s 173.

[61] C(A)A 1982, s 16.

[62] CA 1963, s 320A, as inserted by CA 1990, s 175.

[63] CA 1963, s 320A, as inserted by CA 1990, s 175.

[64] *Irish Oil & Cake Mills Ltd v Donnelly* [1983] HC 798 (27 March 1983, unreported), HC.

[65] *Irish Oil & Cake Mills Ltd v Donnelly* [1983] HC 798 (27 March 1983, unreported), HC.

behalf he was appointed; and, insofar as he has their addresses, to such debenture holders.[66] It is an offence for the receiver to fail to comply with this requirement.[67]

(c) Returns

[8.025] A receiver who is appointed over the whole or substantially the whole of a company's property must deliver periodic returns to the Registrar of Companies pursuant to CA 1963, s 319(2). A receiver who is appointed over a part only of the company's property is obliged by s 321(1) to deliver an abstract containing the same information. The form to be used for both purposes is Form 57.[68] The statutorily required information which must be included in the abstract to be delivered by a receiver is as follows:

– the assets of the company of which he has taken possession;

– the estimated value of such assets;

– the proceeds of sale of any such assets since the receiver's appointment;

– the receiver's receipts and payments during the relevant period;

– the aggregate amounts of all receipts and payments during all periods since his appointment.[69]

[8.026] However, Form 57 contains more specific directions as to the information which the receiver is required to furnish. In particular, Form 57 requires that, if it is a receivership in respect of the whole or substantially the whole of the company's assets under s 319, the information to be included in the abstract must be set out so that it can be identified with the equivalent information in the statement of affairs that was delivered on behalf of the company pursuant to s 319(1).[70]

[8.027] In relation to the requirement to show the assets of which he has taken possession, Form 57 requires an itemised description of these assets, the date on which possession was taken, and an estimated value of such assets. This estimate must be as stated in the statement of affairs if it is a receivership of the whole or substantially the whole of the company's property within s 319. Otherwise, the estimated value of the assets at the date of taking possession should be stated.[71] In relation to assets which the receiver has sold, the abstract must state the date of such realisation, the proceeds, and

---

[66] CA 1963, s 319(1)(c).

[67] CA 1963, s 319(8), as inserted by CLEA 2001, s 52.

[68] Form 57, 'Receivers Abstract (pursuant to s 319(2) or 321(1))'. See www.cro.ie.

[69] CA 1963, s 319(2) and CA 1963, s 321(1).

[70] Note 1 to Form 57, 'Receivers Abstract (pursuant to s 319(2) or 321(1))' states, 'In a case to which s 319(2) of the Act applies, each entry must be set out so that it can be identified with the appropriate entry in the lists and schedules in Form No 17.'

[71] Note 2 to Form 57, 'Receivers Abstract (pursuant to s 319(2) or 321(1))'. See www.cro.ie. It should be noted that, in the course of a receivership, a court may direct a person to return property to the receiver, if the court is satisfied that the disposal of that property perpetrated a fraud on the company, its creditors or members. CA 1990, s 139, as applied by CA 1990, s 178. See Ch 9.

the name of the purchaser. The abstract must also set out the payments and receipts during the period covered by the abstract and all preceding periods.[72]

[8.028] The first of these abstracts must be delivered to the Registrar of Companies, within one month after the expiration of the first six-month period since the receiver's appointment.[73] An abstract must then be delivered within one month of every subsequent six-month period. In effect, therefore, a receiver must deliver an abstract within seven months of the date of his appointment, which will relate to the first six-month period; within 13 months, which will relate to the second six-month period; and so on.

When the receiver ceases to act as receiver, he must deliver a final abstract to the Registrar of Companies within one month of that date.[74] This final abstract must set out the receipts and payments during the period to which the last abstract related, up until the date on which he ceased to act as receiver. In the case of a receivership to which s 319(2) relates, the final abstract must also be accompanied by a statement from the receiver of his opinion as to whether or not the company is solvent.[75] While there is no requirement that the Registrar of Companies forward copies of receivers' abstracts to the DCE, a statement by a receiver as to whether or not a company formerly in receivership is solvent must be forwarded to the DCE.[76] There is no obligation on a receiver who was appointed in respect of only part of the company's assets, to make a statement as to the company's solvency.

[8.029] The obligation of a receiver of the whole or substantially the whole of a company's assets, to deliver abstracts to the Registrar of Companies in accordance with s 319(2), is expressly without prejudice to his obligation to render accounts of his receipts and payments to persons to whom he is otherwise required to deliver such accounts. Section 319(6) provides in this regard that, 'Nothing in sub-s (2) shall be taken to prejudice the duty of the receiver to render proper accounts of his receipts and payments to the persons to whom, and at the times at which, he may be required to do so apart from that subsection.'[77] There is no such stipulation in s 321 in relation to receivers appointed in respect of part of a company's property.

[8.030] It is an offence for a receiver to fail to deliver an abstract as prescribed, under s 319(2) or 321(1).[78] A default in this regard is punishable by a maximum fine of €1,904.61 and a daily default fine of €63.49 for continued contraventions, on summary

---

[72] According to Note 3 to Form 57, 'Receivers Abstract (pursuant to s 319(2) or 321(1)),' 'where s 319(2) of the Act applies, each entry under the heading of 'payments' must be so set out that it can be identified with the appropriate entry in the lists in Form No 17.'

[73] CA 1963, ss 319(2) and 321(1).

[74] CA 1963, ss 319(2) and 321(1).

[75] CA 1963, s 319(2A), as inserted by CLEA 2001, s 52.

[76] CA 1963, s 319(2A), as inserted by CLEA 2001, s 52.

[77] CA 1963, s 319(6).

[78] CA 1963, s 319(8), as inserted by CLEA 2001, s 52 and CA 1963, s 321(2).

conviction, and, on conviction on indictment, by a maximum fine of €12,697.42 and a daily default fine of €317.49 for continued contraventions.[79]

[8.031] When a receiver is obliged to file a return, abstract, statement or account, he must specifically state whether any past or present officer, director or member of the company, has been made subject to an order of personal liability under the Companies Acts[80] or has been made subject to an order of disqualification. CA 1990, s 144(1) provides in this regard:

> Where a receiver or liquidator of a company is obliged by the Companies Acts to make a periodic account, abstract, statement or return in relation to his activities as receiver or liquidator he shall incorporate in such account, abstract, statement or return a report as to whether, at the date of such account, abstract, statement or return any past or present director or other officer, or any member, of the company is a person—
>
> (a) in respect of whom a declaration has been made under any provision of the Companies Acts that he should be personally liable for all or any part of the debts of a company,
>
> (b) who is, or is deemed to be, subject to a disqualification order.

It is an offence for a receiver to fail to include in a return, abstract, statement or return, a report as to whether any past or present director, officer or member of the company is subject to such an order of personal liability or disqualification, for which the receiver will be liable to a fine.[81]

(d) Information to the company

[8.032] There is no general statutory duty on a receiver to furnish information to the company regarding the conduct of the receivership. The only information which the receiver is expressly required to provide to the company under the Companies Acts is a notice of his appointment, and this only arises if the receiver is appointed in respect of the whole or substantially the whole of the company's property, on behalf of holders of debentures which are secured by floating charges.[82]

[8.033] *Irish Oil & Cake Mills Ltd v Donnelly*[83] was a case in which two companies sought a mandatory injunction to compel a receiver-manager to furnish certain information regarding the receivership to the companies. The plaintiffs advanced three principal arguments in support of their claim, all three of which were rejected by the Court.

---

[79] CA 1990, s 145, as amended by CA 1990, s 240(7), as inserted by CLEA 2001, s 104(c).

[80] The provisions of the Companies Acts which provide for the imposition of personal liability include CA 1963, ss 256(8) and 297A and CA 1990, ss 39, 163(3), 165, 204 and 251.

[81] CA 1990, s 144(2).

[82] CA 1963, s 319(1).

[83] *Irish Oil & Cake Mills Ltd v Donnelly* [1983] HC 798 (27 March 1983, unreported), HC.

First, the plaintiffs claimed that the receiver-manager was under a contractual duty to furnish the information sought, as he was agent for the plaintiffs under the terms of the floating charges pursuant to which he was appointed ('the contract argument'). Costello J referred to the fact that it was agreed that the receiver was the agent of the plaintiffs. However, the Court found no basis for implying into the contract between the plaintiffs and the receiver-manager a term which required the latter to furnish the information sought. The 'contract argument' was rejected.

[8.034] Second, the plaintiffs contended that the receiver-manager owed a duty of care to the plaintiffs which required him to furnish the information sought (the 'duty of care argument'). This argument was based on the duty of a receiver to obtain the best price reasonably obtainable in the sale of a company's assets and encompassed three separate submissions, which are referred to here as the three sub-sets of the plaintiffs' 'duty of care' argument. The first sub-set of the 'duty of care argument,' was that the information sought could facilitate a reconstruction of the company which could enhance its value. The Court observed that there was a lack of evidence in support of this contention, noting that, in the time before and since the appointment of the receiver, the directors of the company had not succeeded in implementing a rescue package for the company and there was nothing to indicate the information sought could alter this situation. The Court stated that it was not:

> 'sufficient on a motion of this sort for a Company merely to assert the possibility
> that such a scheme would be forthcoming with the assistance of the information
> sought and that a Receiver is under a duty to await the formulation of such a
> scheme before selling the assets.'

[8.035] The second sub-set of the plaintiffs' 'duty of care argument' was that the information sought would facilitate two directors of the company in submitting a competing and higher bid for the companies' assets. The Court noted that there was no evidence in support of such a contention; that the receiver was willing to furnish the same information to any prospective purchasers; and that in the time that the assets had been advertised for sale, no such offer had been submitted. Costello J observed that the receiver was 'entitled to make a commercial judgment in the matter and decide that it would not conducive to procuring an enhanced price to give these Directors any more information' and that there was no breach of duty on the receiver's part.

[8.036] The third sub-set of the plaintiffs' 'duty of care argument' was that the general duty of receiver-managers to take reasonable steps to secure the best possible price for a company's assets includes a duty 'to keep the Company appraised of how the business of the Company is going'. The Court rejected this contention outright, stating, 'This is a very far-reaching proposition, unsupported by any authority and I must reject it.' However, the following observation qualifies this finding to some extent:

> 'There may well be special circumstances in which, to ensure that the best price
> possible is obtained for the assets, trading information since the appointment of a
> Receiver should be given to the Company's Directors. But in the absence of
> special circumstances which might favourably affect the price, a Receiver/
> Manager is not under any duty of care which involves him in reporting as
> suggested to the Directors on his management of the business.'

This suggests that, if events occurred in the course of the management of a company by a receiver-manager, which enhanced the value of the company's assets, the receiver-manager may be under a duty to furnish this information to the company's directors. However, there is no general duty on a receiver-manager to report to directors of the company regarding the management of the company's business.

[8.037] The third argument advanced by the plaintiffs in *Irish Oil & Cake Mills Ltd v Donnelly*[84] was that the receiver-manager was bound by an equitable duty to account, on the authority of *Smith Ltd v Middleton*[85] (the 'duty to account argument'). In this regard, Costello J considered that, 'it cannot be said that a Receiver/Manager is under no duty to account to the Company whose affairs he is managing' and that, 'the extent and nature of the duty and the extent and nature of the accounts he must furnish will depend on the facts of each individual case.' The Court refrained from laying down any general principles in this regard, holding that the claim for information made by the plaintiffs was 'wholly exceptional' and that there was a lack of evidence to support it.

[8.038] In the absence of special circumstances, a company is not entitled to receive information about the conduct of the receivership from the receiver and, while the receiver may in certain circumstances be under a duty to account to the company, there is no such general obligation.

[8.039] In *Kinsella v Somers*[86] the High Court also confirmed that, in the absence of special circumstances, such as allegations of bad faith on the part of the receiver, a company's shareholders and directors have no right to receive documents and accounts from the receiver.

(e) Sale of assets

[8.040] There are certain statutory requirements and restrictions that exist in relation to the sale of a company's assets by the receiver. First, a receiver is under an obligation to get the best price reasonably obtainable in the sale of the company's property. Section 316A(1) provides that, 'a receiver, in selling property of a company, shall exercise all reasonable care to obtain the best price reasonably obtainable for the property as at the time of sale.'[87] It is not a defence to proceedings arising from a failure to obtain the best price reasonably obtainable, that the receiver was acting as an agent of, or under a power of attorney from, the company.[88] In addition, a receiver is not entitled to be compensated or indemnified by the company for any liability incurred as a result of such a failure.[89]

---

84   *Irish Oil & Cake Mills Ltd v Donnelly* [1983] HC 798, (27 March 1983, unreported), HC.

85   *Smith Ltd v Middleton* [1979] 3 All ER 842.

86   *Kinsella v Somers* [1999] IEHC 44, (23 November 1999, unreported), HC.

87   CA 1963, s 316A(1), as inserted by CA 1990, s 172.

88   CA 1963, s 316A(2)(a), as inserted by CA 1990, s 172.

89   CA 1963, s 316A(2)(b), as inserted by CA 1990, s 172.

[8.041] Second, a receiver is not permitted to enter into a private contract to sell a 'non-cash asset of the requisite value'[90] to a person who is or who was in the three years before the appointment of the receiver, an officer[91] of the company.[92] Such a sale is only permitted if the receiver gives at least 14 days' notice of his intention to do so, to all creditors of the company of whose existence he is aware. It is not specified that such notice must be in writing. The interaction between this provision and CA 1990, s 29 was described as follows by Courtney:

'... it is thought that s 316A(3) implicitly *displaces* the operation of s 29 to sales by receivers. Whereas Pt III of the 1990 Act (where s 29 is located) regulates 'Transactions Involving Directors', Pt VII of the 1963 Act regulates 'Receivers' and when a receiver proposes to dispose of company property his powers of sale are only regulated by s 316A of the 1963 Act.'[93]

[8.042] The obligation on receivers to obtain the best price reasonably obtainable in the sale of a company's assets, has received some judicial consideration. *Lambert Jones Estates Ltd v Donnelly*[94] was a case in which a company's directors took the unusual step of requesting the company's bank to appoint a receiver over the assets of the company that were subject to charges or mortgages in favour of the bank, including a valuable property. Having obtained the advice of relevant professionals, the receiver decided to sell the property in a single lot by way of public tender. A number of parties, including

---

90 According to CA 1963, s 316A(3)(b)(i), "non-cash asset" and "requisite value" have the meanings assigned to them by s 29 of the Companies Act 1990.' CA 1990, s 29(2) provides: '(2) For the purposes of this section a non-cash asset is of the requisite value if at the time the arrangement in question is entered into its value is not less than €1,269.74 but, subject to that, exceeds €63,486.90 or ten per cent of the amount of the company's relevant assets, and for those purposes the amount of a company's relevant assets is— (a) except in a case falling within para (b), the value of its net assets determined by reference to the accounts prepared and laid in accordance with the requirements of s 148 of the Principal Act in respect of the last preceding financial year in respect of which such accounts were so laid; (b) where no accounts have been prepared and laid under that section before that time, the amount of its called-up share capital.' According to CA 1990, s 29(9)(a), '"non-cash asset" means any property or interest in property other than cash, and for this purpose "cash" includes foreign currency.'

91 CA 1963, s 316A(3)(b)(ii) states that, '"officer" includes a person connected, within the meaning of s 26 of the Companies Act 1990, with a director, and a shadow director.' According to CA 1990, s 26(1), as substituted by CLEA 2001, s 76(a), '... a person is connected with a director of a company if, but only if, the person (not being himself a director of the company) is— (a) that director's spouse, parent, brother, sister or child; (b) a person acting in his capacity as the trustee of any trust, the principal beneficiaries of which are the director, his spouse or any of his children or any body corporate which he controls; or **(c)** in partnership, within the meaning of s 1(1) of the Partnership Act, 1890, with that director.'

92 CA 1963, s 316A(3)(a), as inserted by CA 1990, s 172.

93 Courtney, 'Receiverships in Ireland in the Wake of *Demite Ltd v Protec Health Ltd*' (1998) 5(10) CLP 255.

94 *Lambert Jones Estates Ltd v Donnelly* [1982] IEHC 47, (5 November 1982, unreported), HC.

---

the company; its directors; certain unsecured creditors; and a minority shareholder, sought to restrain this sale on the basis that it would be more profitable to divide the property into separate lots, apply for planning permission for these lots, and sell them individually. While this case pre-dates the commencement of s 316A, it is nonetheless illustrative of the principles to be applied in determining whether a receiver has discharged his duty to exercise reasonable care to obtain the best price reasonably obtainable for a company's assets.

[8.043] The Court determined that the plaintiffs had no real prospect of success and rejected the interlocutory relief sought on that basis. This decision was based on the following analysis of the case:

> 'I can see very clearly on the affidavits that the Plaintiffs have radically different ideas from the Defendant as to the best way of realising the assets of the Company, and that they have the support of a prominent firm of Chartered Valuation Surveyors for the opinion they have formed. It is equally clear, however, that the Defendant has also taken expert advice and has acted upon it in deciding how he should proceed with the sale of the property. He is anxious to sell, if at all possible, at an early date, to minimise the enormous burden of interest on the bank debt which is accumulating against the Company with each day and month that pass. He does not want to take a course which will involve him in new and costly and protracted planning applications for multiple units of property. He says he has no funds available to finance such transactions and the Plaintiffs have not suggested that any source of finance is available to him. Finally, he has stated through his Counsel in the course of the hearing, that if and when he is allowed to proceed with sale by tender it is his intention to seek the approval of the Court before accepting the highest or any tender.'[95]

[8.044] In *WP McCarter & Co Ltd v Roughan*,[96] a company's receiver entered into an agreement to sell the company's factory to the plaintiff. This sale was never completed, but the plaintiff did enter into possession of the factory pending completion of the sale, and paid a weekly rent for a period of over eight years. The company issued proceedings seeking to have the contract set aside and preventing the sale of the company's assets, proceedings which were not pursued. When the plaintiff subsequently brought proceedings for specific performance of the contract, the company challenged the contract on a number of grounds, including the ground that no expert valuation was conducted; that the assets were not advertised before the sale; and that it was a sale at a gross undervalue.

The Court considered that there were infirmities in the manner in which the receiver sold the company's assets, as there was no proper valuation and no advertising conducted. The Court concluded that the receiver did not obtain the best price reasonably obtainable. However, the company had control of the situation, by means of the proceedings they originally instituted to have the contract declared null and void, and should have had those proceedings re-entered. The Court also took notice of the long delay of seven or eight years in prosecuting those proceedings and the fact that the plaintiff, to the knowledge of the company, was in occupation of the factory and

---

[95]   *Lambert Jones Estates Ltd v Donnelly* [1982] IEHC 47, (5 November 1982, unreported), HC.

[96]   *WP McCarter & Co Ltd v Roughan* [1986] ILRM 447.

expending money on it. The Court therefore concluded that it 'would be inequitable to set aside this contract at this stage'. The Court directed the specific performance of the contract of sale and stated that the company could pursue its claim for such damages or other relief to which it may be entitled as against the receiver in the other proceedings. This demonstrates the importance of receivers obtaining independent valuations of a company's property and advertising the property before entering into a contract for its sale.

[8.045] In *Re Edenfell Holdings Ltd*[97] a company issued proceedings seeking specific performance of a contract it claimed to have entered for the purchase of a property from a company which had since gone into liquidation and receivership. While the appeal to the Supreme Court was pending in those proceedings, the receiver entered into a contract to sell the property at issue to a third party, one of the terms being that this party would pay £100,000 to procure the discontinuance of the proceedings for specific performance.

The receiver brought a motion under s 316 seeking directions that the contract of sale be completed, while a shareholder and director of the company in receivership brought a motion seeking to prevent the completion of the contract. The High Court (Laffoy J) determined that the receiver did fail to clear all encumbrances to the sale of the property and failed to obtain the best price reasonably obtainable for the sale of the property. The High Court therefore directed that the contract should not be completed.

Keane J, delivering the judgment of the Supreme Court observed:

> 'It is clear that, at common law, a receiver owed a duty of care in relation to the sale of the property, comprised in the charge by virtue of which he was appointed, to any persons interested in the property. That common law duty was given statutory force by s 316A of the Act of 1963, which was inserted by the Companies (Amendment) Act 1990, s 172.'[98]

In reaching the decision that the receiver should complete the proposed sale, the Supreme Court described the approach to be adopted in such applications as follows:

> 'It is not the function of the court in a case such as this to decide, with the benefit of hindsight, whether it might have been better for the creditors and anyone else interested in the property had the receiver rejected the Astra offer and continued to deal with Anglo Éire or anyone else who might be interested. The court was dealing with the matter with the advantage of hindsight: the receiver had to deal with the matter then and there and in the light of the expert advice available to him from a valuer. Having tested the market again, without any response in the form of an unconditional offer, he was entitled, in all the circumstances, to take the view he did, that accepting the Astra proposal was the more prudent course.'[99]

[8.046] In *Ruby Property Company Ltd v Kilty*,[100] the sale of the company's property by the receiver was challenged on a number of grounds, including that the sale should have been publicly advertised; that the property should have been sold by public tender; that

---

[97] *Re Edenfell Holdings Ltd* [1999] 1 IR 443.

[98] *Re Edenfell Holdings Ltd* [1999] 1 IR 443 at 464.

[99] *Re Edenfell Holdings Ltd* [1999] 1 IR 443 at 466.

[100] *Ruby Property Company Ltd v Kilty* [2003] IEHC 433, (31 January 2003, unreported), HC.

the bids were secured privately and not openly; that a billboard should have been placed on the property; that there was no bargaining with third parties; and that the market was not tested. The plaintiffs alleged that, on one or more of these grounds, the sale was not at the best price reasonably obtainable, and was at a considerable discount.

The High Court (McKechnie J) considered these submissions in light of s 316A and set out a number of general principles which should guide a court in determining whether a receiver complied with the duty to obtain the best price reasonably obtainable. McKechnie J stated that, as a starting point, 'the duty of a receiver is to exercise reasonable care to obtain, at the time of the sale, the best price reasonably obtainable for the property in question.'

In applying this standard, receivers should, according to the decision of McKechnie J, be allowed a considerable margin of discretion. For example, there is no obligation on a receiver to follow a 'specified approach'. The Court stated in this regard: 'In assessing the exercise of this duty a receiver is not bound in any preset way to adopt a specified approach in how he particularises the property or asset in sale.' The Court also made the observation that:

> '... there are no predetermined, fixed or rigid rules by which such disposal of property must take place. Public auction, exposure by media or billboard, market strategy, expenditure of money, generous time limits, and the hiring of experts are all matters for consideration, as are many others, but not for mandatory engagement. In each situation, an individual assessment must be made, but provided the duty resting upon the receiver or mortgagee is discharged, the actual method of disposal is not determinative.'

[8.047] Among the other principles cited by the Court in *Ruby Property Company Ltd v Kilty*,[101] was that, 'In deciding what offer to accept, a receiver is obliged to give due weight to and consider, not only the monetary aspect of such offer but also any qualifications, demands or conditions attached thereto or other benefits linked therewith: this so that the full, true and total value of such offer can be evaluated.'

The Court also stated that the duty of a receiver should be appraised at the date of the sale of the assets in question, and the receiver is not obliged to postpone, defer or cancel a sale in the hope of the market improving. Conversely, a receiver is not obliged to sell immediately to avoid a risk of depreciation in the value of the asset. With regard to the timing of the sale, the Court also pointed out, that 'the court of trial must judge the conduct in question at the time of and in the light of the facts and circumstances as these previously existed. Hindsight should not be used.'

On the basis of the principles cited by McKechnie J, a receiver has a wide margin of discretion regarding the manner and timing of the sale of the company's property and regarding the factors to be taken into account in relation to such a sale.

[8.048] The decision in *Ruby Property Company Ltd v Kilty*,[102] also confirms that the burden of proof in a case concerning s 316A rests on the party alleging that the receiver did not exercise reasonable care to obtain the best price reasonably obtainable for the

---

[101] *Ruby Property Company Ltd v Kilty* [2003] IEHC 433, (31 January 2003, unreported), HC.

[102] *Ruby Property Company Ltd v Kilty* [2003] IEHC 433, (31 January 2003, unreported), HC.

company's property. The plaintiffs in that case alleged that the company was at a serious disadvantage in mounting proceedings to challenge the sale, and that the receiver should have the responsibility of satisfying the court that he was not in breach of s 316A. The Court rejected this submission, stating: 'I cannot see how the demands of justice would sustain the argument of imposing the burden on the receiver.'

[8.049] In that case, the kernel of the plaintiffs' case was that the receiver failed to advertise the property in a full public manner and, in particular, failed to advertise the company's property for sale in the public media and failed to place a billboard on the site. The Court recalled that:

> 'the relevant case law permits a receiver or a mortgagor considerable latitude in disposing of an owner's property provided there is no breach of the duty in so doing

and that:

> 'it is of course permissible for the court to consider alternative methods of disposal and alternative valuations, but the exercise involved is not one to resolve differences between such approaches or such valuations, but rather, in light of the totality of the evidence, to decide whether or not the alleged breach has been established or made out.'

The Court referred to the fact that the receiver put in place a team of professionals, covering all the relevant areas of expertise, to advise and assist him in the sale of the property, and took into account the advice of such professionals. The Court also referred to the fact that the decisions of the receiver were kept under constant review and were reconsidered as the situation regarding the property evolved. The Court concluded that:

> '... it was reasonable on his part, in consultation with Messrs Jones Lang and Wootton, to identify the existence of special purchasers or persons with a special interest in the property and to have this group as the primary focus of their initial attention. This decision was made having considered and reviewed other options. This method was pursed in a context that if success did not result other alternatives would be utilised. At no stage prior to the generation of a market or prior to receiving substantial bids form that market, was a decision taken not to advertise this site or to dispose of it by way of public tender. I believe that this was reasonable, and whilst the receiver could not have been faulted for expending a sum on public marketing nonetheless, given the professional advices available to him, likewise in my view he could not be faulted for declining to so do. Accordingly whilst other individuals have expressed different view on the marketing strategy for this property, nevertheless I am firmly of the opinion that the approach adopted by the receiver, was in the circumstances both reasonable and justified.'

This case illustrates both the importance of receivers obtaining independent professional advice in the sale of a company's property and the wide margin of discretion which is allowed to receivers in relation to the manner in which they discharge their functions.

[8.050] In *Bula v Crowley (No 4)*,[103] the issue was whether the sale of a company's assets was in compliance with the receiver's duty to obtain the best price reasonably obtainable. On an application by the receiver under s 316, seeking confirmation of the

---

[103] *Bula v Crowley (No 4)* [2003] 2 IR 430.

sale of the company's assets, the High Court approved the sale and determined that there was no breach of the receiver's duties under s 316A. This decision was appealed to the Supreme Court. The appellants argued that the price was not the best price obtainable, as the receiver put the property on the market at the wrong time; did not obtain specialist valuations; used a gross undervaluation of the assets; and failed to exploit the position of the purchaser. The appellants also invoked a right to fair procedures and argued that the refusal of the High Court to permit cross-examinations on the affidavits was a violation of this right.

Denham J, delivering a judgment with which the other members of the Supreme Court concurred, noted that s 316A 'gives statutory force to common law'[104] and quoted the following dicta of Keane J in *Re Edenfell Holdings Ltd*:[105]

> 'It is clear that, at common law, a receiver owed a duty of care in relation to the sale of the property, comprised in the charge by virtue of which he was appointed, to any persons interested in the property. That common law duty was given statutory force by s 316A of the Act of 1963, which was inserted by s 172 of the Companies (Amendment) Act, 1990 ...'

The Court also quoted the decision of Keane J in *Re Edenfell Holdings plc* to the effect that a court should not assess the receiver's decisions regarding the sale of a company's property 'with the benefit of hindsight.' Denham J described the function of a court as follows:

> 'Under s 316, the function of the court is to consider whether the receiver has taken all reasonable care to obtain the best price reasonably obtainable for the property at the time of sale. Applying *Edenfell*, the receiver had to deal with the matter then and there and in the light of the expert advice available to him. The appropriate date is the date of sale. The receiver does not have a general obligation to wait for the market to rise.'[106]

With regard to the timing of the sale of a company's assets, Denham J held that, '... the receiver has a duty to take all reasonable care to obtain the best price reasonably possible at the time of sale. However, he is not obliged to postpone a sale to obtain a better price.'[107] The Court also made the observation that: 'The receiver is entitled to choose the time at which he will sell the asset. He is not obliged to postpone a sale until the markets may rise or other possible events. However, the receiver is obliged to fairly expose the asset to the market'[108] and that, '... in proceeding to sale, the receiver may put the secured creditors' interests first. The receiver was not under a duty to wait for the market to rise.'[109]

---

[104] *Bula v Crowley (No 4)* [2003] 2 IR 430 at 448.

[105] *Re Edenfell Holdings Ltd* [1999] 1 IR 443 at p 464.

[106] *Bula v Crowley (No 4)* [2003] 2 IR 430 at 449.

[107] *Bula v Crowley (No 4)* [2003] 2 IR 430 at 449.

[108] *Bula v Crowley (No 4)* [2003] 2 IR 430 at 449 at 451.

[109] *Bula v Crowley (No 4)* [2003] 2 IR 430 at 449 at 451.

The receiver therefore is not obliged to postpone a sale to obtain a better price or to wait for the market to rise. Applying this approach, the Court determined that:

> 'The receiver took a rational decision in all the circumstances to proceed to sell the asset. Indeed, also, on the evidence, it is clear that he took reasonable care in the timing of the sale. Therefore, the submissions on behalf of the appellants that the receiver went to the market at the wrong time must fail.'[110]

The Court rejected the other arguments raised by the appellants and determined that the receiver discharged his duties and obtained the best price reasonably obtainable in the sale of the company's assets.

[8.051] The decisions which have been delivered by the Irish courts under s 316A, indicate that a receiver has a wide margin of discretion in determining when and how to sell a company's assets. However, it is advisable for receivers to act upon the advice of suitably qualified experts, particularly if the receiver proposes to act in a manner which is at variance with the wishes of the company, its directors, creditors or members.

(f) Distribution of proceeds

[8.052] Where a receiver is appointed by the holders of a debenture which is secured by a floating charge over the property of a company which is not being wound-up, he must discharge certain debts prior to the debenture holders' claims, from the assets of which he has taken possession. This requirement does not apply to receivers appointed by the holders of debentures which are secured by fixed charges.

CA 1963, s 98(1) provides:

> Where either a receiver is appointed on behalf of the holders of any debentures of a company secured by a floating charge, or possession is taken by or on behalf of those debenture holders of any property comprised in or subject to the charge, then, if the company is not at the time in course of being wound up, the debts which in every winding up are, under the provisions of Pt VI relating to preferential payments to be paid in priority to all other debts, shall be paid out of any assets coming to the hands of the receiver or other person taking possession as aforesaid in priority to any claim for principal or interest in respect of the debentures.

[8.053] CA1963, s 285 sets out the preferential payments that must be made in priority to all other debts in the winding up of a company.[111] In particular, according to s 285(2), the following must be paid in priority to all other debts:

– rates and taxes, including all local rates due from the company at the date of the order or resolution to wind up the company, or appoint the provisional liquidator, and within the preceding 12 months; all assessed taxes, assessed on the company up to the 5th day of April preceding the date of the order or resolution to wind up the company, or appoint a provisional liquidator, not

---

[110] *Bula v Crowley (No 4)* [2003] 2 IR 430 at 449 at 453.

[111] In a winding up, the priority conferred on certain debts by s 285(2), only applies to those debts which the liquidator becomes, or is made, aware of, within six months after advertising for claims in at least two daily newspapers circulating in the district in which the company's registered office is situated. CA 1963, s 285(14), as inserted by CA 1990, s 134.

exceeding one year's assessment; any sums due from an employer under the Finance (No 2) Act 1959;[112]

– all wages and salaries of any clerk or servant in respect of services rendered to the company during the four months preceding the order or resolution to wind up the company, or the appointment of the provisional liquidator;[113]

– all wages of any workman or labourer in respect of services rendered to the company during the four months preceding the order or resolution to wind up the company, or the appointment of the provisional liquidator;[114]

– all accrued holiday pay becoming payable to any clerk, servant, workman or labourer on the termination of his employment before or as a result of the winding up order or resolution;[115]

– social welfare contributions payable during the 12 months preceding the order or resolution to wind up the company, or the appointment of a provisional liquidator;[116]

– any payments which have accrued under the Workmen's Compensation Acts 1934 to 1955, before the order or resolution to wind up the company, or the appointment of the provisional liquidator, to the extent that such payments are not covered by insurance;[117]

---

[112] CA 1963, s 285(2)(a).

[113] CA 1963, s 285(2)(b). According to s 285(3), '... the sum to which priority is to be given under [s 285(2)(b)] respectively shall not, in the case of any one claimant, exceed [£2,500 [€3,174.35]].'

[114] CA 1963, s 285(2)(c). According to s 285(3), '... the sum to which priority is to be given under [s 285(2)(b)] respectively shall not, in the case of any one claimant, exceed [£2,500 [€3,174.35]]'. Note that this is subject to s 285(4), which provides, 'Where a claimant under para (c) of sub-s (2) is a farm labourer who has entered into a contract for payment of a portion of his wages in a lump sum at the end of the year of hiring, he shall have priority in respect of the whole of such sum, or such part thereof as the court may decide to be due under the contract, proportionate to the time of service up to the relevant date.'

[115] CA 1963, s 285(2)(d). Note that in the case of the appointment of a receiver, rather than a liquidator, s 98(2) provides: 'In the application of the said provisions s 285 of this Act shall be construed as if the provision for payment of accrued holiday remuneration becoming payable on the termination of employment before or by the effect of the winding up order or resolution, were a provision for payment of such remuneration becoming payable on the termination of employment before or by the effect of the appointment of the receiver or possession being taken as aforesaid.' Holiday remuneration which becomes payable on the termination of employment before or by the effect of the appointment of a receiver, is therefore a payment which must be made in preference to claims of debenture holders.

[116] CA 1963, s 285(2)(e), as substituted by Social Welfare Act 1991, s 37. This does not apply if the company is being wound up voluntarily merely for the purpose of reconstruction or amalgamation with another company.

[117] CA 1963, s 285(2)(f). This does not apply if the company is being wound up voluntarily merely for the purpose of reconstruction or amalgamation with another company. Note that, according to s 285(5), 'Where any compensation under the Workmen's Compensation Acts, 1934 to 1955 is a weekly payment, the amount due in respect thereof shall, for the purposes of para (f) of sub-s (2) be taken to be the amount of the lump sum for which the weekly payment could be redeemed if the employer made an application for that purpose under the said Acts. '

– all amounts due or liability in respect of damages and costs payable to an employee in connection with an accident which occurred in the course of such employment, before the order or resolution to wind up the company, or the appointment of a provisional liquidator, to the extent that such damages or costs are not covered by insurance;[118]

– all sums due to an employee under any scheme or arrangement for payments during absences from employment owing to ill health; [119] and

– any payments due under any scheme or arrangement for the provision of superannuation benefits for employees.[120]

[8.054] There are other preferential payments that must be made by a liquidator in a winding up, such as payments under certain employment statutes, and these are to be included among the payments referred to in s 285.[121] Therefore, while s 98 only refers to the payments specified in Pt VI of CA 1963, that Act has been extended by those employment statutes and must be interpreted accordingly. A receiver must also discharge payments due under the Minimum Notice and Terms of Employment Act 1993, the Unfair Dismissals Act 1977 and the Redundancy Payments Acts 1967–1979, in priority to the claims of the debenture holders, where the debentures are secured by floating charges.[122]

[8.055] The terms of s 285 are adjusted in the case of receivers, so that periods of time are calculated in relation to the date of the appointment of the receiver, rather than the date of the order or resolution to wind up the company or the date of appointment of a provisional liquidator.[123] For example, the obligation to pay all wages and salaries in respect of services rendered to the company, will relate to the four month period preceding the date of the appointment of the receiver, rather than the date of the order or resolution to wind up the company, or the appointment of the provisional liquidator.[124]

---

[118] CA 1963, s 285(2)(g). This does not apply if the company is being wound up voluntarily merely for the purpose of reconstruction or amalgamation with another company.

[119] CA 1963, s 285(2)(h), as inserted by C(A)A 1982, s 10.

[120] CA 1963, s 285(2)(i), as inserted by C(A)A 1982, s 10.

[121] See, eg, Unfair Dismissals Act 1977, s 12(1). ('There shall be included among the debts which, under s 285 of the Companies Act, 1963, are, in the distribution of the assets of a company being wound up, to be paid in priority to all other debts, all compensation payable under this Act by the company to an employee, and that Act shall have effect accordingly, and formal proof of the debts to which priority is given under this subsection shall not be required except in cases where it may otherwise be provided by rules made under that Act') and Minimum Notice and Terms of Employment Act 1973, s 13(1) ('There shall be included among the debts which, under s 285 of the Companies Act, 1963, are, in the distribution of the assets of a company being wound up, to be paid in priority to all other debts, all compensation payable under s 12 of this Act by the Company to an employee, and that Act shall have effect accordingly, and formal proof of the debts to which priority is given under this subsection shall not be required except in cases where it may otherwise be provided by rules made under that Act.')

[122] See *Re Red Sail Frozen Foods Ltd* [2006] IEHC 328.

[123] CA 1963, s 98(3).

[124] See CA 1963, s 285(2)(b).

[8.056] The preferential payments that must be made by a receiver under s 98 must be recouped 'so far as may be out of the assets of the company available for payment of general creditors.'[125] Section 285(7) provides that, the debts listed in that section 'rank equally among themselves' and, if the assets are insufficient to meet them, 'abate in equal proportions.'[126] Section 285(7) further provides that, 'so far as the assets of the company available for payment of general creditors are insufficient to meet them, [the foregoing debts] have priority over the claims of holders of debentures under any floating charge created by the company, and be paid accordingly out of any property comprised in or subject to that charge.'[127] When a company is being wound-up, therefore, the general rule is that the preferential debts must be paid from the assets of the company available for general creditors. However, if and to the extent that those assets are insufficient to discharge the preferential debts, and the company has assets which are subject to floating charges, the preferential debts have priority over the holders of the debentures which are secured by those charges. This is consistent with the requirement in s 98(5) that the preferential debts should be discharged so far as is possible from the assets available for the payment of general creditors.

[8.057] If a liquidator is appointed after the appointment of a receiver, the requirements of s 98 still apply and the receiver must discharge preferential debts in priority to the claims of the debenture holders whose debentures are secured by floating charges.[128] This requirement applies whether or not the claims of the debenture holders have already been fully satisfied.[129] In *Re Eisc Teoranta*,[130] Lardner J considered the position of a receiver who had discharged the monies owing under a floating and a fixed charge, from the proceeds of sale of the assets subject to the fixed charge, and who sought directions as to whether the proceeds of the assets subject to the floating charge should be paid to preferential creditors, or should be paid to a liquidator who was appointed after the date of appointment of the receiver. The Court concluded that the terms of s 98 were clear and imposed a duty on the receiver to discharge the preferential debts from assets which were subject to a floating charge.

---

[125] CA 1963, s 98(5).

[126] CA 1963, s 285(7)(a).

[127] CA 1963, s 285(7)(b).

[128] See *Re Eisc Teoranta* [1991] ILRM 760. ('This duty having once been imposed in unqualified terms by the section, was not terminated or affected by the circumstance either that a winding up order was made three months after the appointment of the receiver or that the receiver did not in fact require to make any payment out of the assets the subject of the floating charge. The section refers not to the payment out of the assets but to claims for principle or interest. I think such a claim clearly exists at the time of the receiver's appointment and that the duty was then imposed upon the receiver by the section,' *per* Lardner J.)

[129] See *Re Eisc Teoranta* [1991] ILRM 760. ('It is noteworthy that the duty is to make these payments in priority to any claim for principal or interest in respect of the debentures. In my view such a claim is the basis of the appointment of the receiver. It is a claim which exists at the time of his appointment,' *per* Lardner J.)

[130] *Re Eisc Teoranta* [1991] ILRM 760.

[8.058] In *Re Manning Furniture Ltd*[131] a similar issue arose. In that case, the receiver discharged the monies due to the debenture holder, under both a floating and a fixed charge, from the proceeds of sale of the assets which were subject to the fixed charge. The receiver intended to apply the proceeds of sale of the assets which were subject to the floating charge, towards the discharge of the preferential debts. A mortgagee who held a fixed charge over certain of the company's assets sought to claim an entitlement to the proceeds of sale of the assets subject to the floating charge, in priority to the rights of preferential creditors under s 98. The fixed charge in question was not registered until after the date of appointment of the receiver.

[8.059] The Court considered the application of s 98 to the distribution of the proceeds of sale of the company's assets and noted that, 'the present case is similar to the *Eisc Teoranta* case in that the receiver in fact discharged the debenture holder's debt out of the fixed assets, but he did take possession of the assets which were subject to the floating charge'.[132] While there was an attempt to distinguish *Re Eisc Teoranta*[133] on the ground that it concerned a liquidator rather than a mortgagee, the Court rejected this argument. The Court also rejected the argument that, as the assets which were subject to the floating charge were not used to discharge the monies due to the debenture holders, s 98 did not apply. McCracken J followed the decision of Lardner J in *Re Eisc Teoranta* that, 'once a claim has been made under the debenture, the obligation arises under s 98'.[134] The decision in *Re Manning Furniture* demonstrates clearly that the obligation on a receiver to discharge the debts due to preferential creditors arises upon the appointment of the receiver and such creditors are given priority under s 98 as of that date.

D. Enforcement under the Companies Acts

(a) Examination of receiver's books

[8.060] The DCE may request a receiver to produce his books for examination. CA 1963, s 323A(1) accordingly provides:

> The Director may, where he considers it necessary or appropriate, request (specifying the reason why the request is being made) the production of a receiver's books for examination, either in regard to a particular receivership or to all receiverships undertaken by the receiver.[135]

Such a request must therefore be supported by a statement of the reason for requiring a receiver to produce his documents. It seems clear that this provision is directed towards the conduct of the receiver, rather than the affairs of the company. This is apparent from the fact that the DCE may require a receiver to produce books in relation to all receiverships which he has undertaken, other than those which concluded more than six

---

[131] *Re Manning Furniture Ltd* [1996] 1 ILRM 13.

[132] *Re Manning Furniture Ltd* [1996] 1 ILRM 13.

[133] *Re Eisc Teoranta* [1991] ILRM 760.

[134] *Re Manning Furniture Ltd* [1996] 1 ILRM 13.

[135] CA 1963, s 323A(1), as inserted by CLEA 2001, s 53.

years prior to the date of the request.[136] A request from the DCE may cover a receivership which commenced more than six years previously.

[8.061] If the DCE makes a request for the production of a receiver's books, there are four distinct obligations which may flow from this request. First, the receiver must furnish the books to the DCE. Secondly, he must answer any questions which he is reasonably able to answer, in relation to the content of the books. Thirdly, he must answer any questions which he is reasonably able to answer in relation to the conduct of a particular receivership or receiverships. Fourthly, the receiver must give to the DCE all assistance as he is reasonably able to give.[137]

It is an offence for a receiver to fail to comply with any of these requirements.[138]

[8.062] There are a number of ambiguities in the formulation of the obligation of a receiver to comply with requests of the DCE. First, there is no definition or clarification of the 'books' which a receiver may be required to produce. Secondly, there is no reference to confidentiality or privilege or any other such grounds which may be invoked by a receiver to resist the production of books. Thirdly, there is no reference to any grounds on which a receiver may refuse to answer questions posed by the DCE. Finally, there is no explanation of the purpose of the provision and, in particular, the type of reasons which may ground such a request. This can be contrasted with the terms of CA 1990, s 19, which sets out the situations in which the DCE may require a company to produce documents.[139]

(b) Directions to comply

[8.063] If a receiver of a company, whether appointed over the whole or part only of a company's assets and whether appointed pursuant to a floating or a fixed charge, defaults in the performance of his duties, an order may be made to compel compliance with such duties. There are two particular categories of default which trigger this enforcement provision.

[8.064] First, if a receiver makes a default in filing, delivering or making any return, account or other document or in giving any notice which he is required by law to file, deliver, make or give, a notice may be served on him requiring him to make good this default. If the receiver fails to comply with the obligation in question within 14 days of receipt of such notice, the court may make an order directing the receiver to make good the default.[140]

[8.065] Secondly, if a liquidator of a company at any time requires a receiver who was appointed pursuant to an express power in a debenture, to render proper accounts of his

---

[136] CA 1963, s 323A(3), as inserted by CLEA 2001, s 53, provides in this regard, 'A request under sub-s (1) may not be made in respect of books relating to a receivership that has concluded more than six years prior to the request.'

[137] CA 1963, s 323A(2), as inserted by CLEA 2001, s 53.

[138] CA 1963, s 323A(4), as inserted by CLEA 2001, s 53.

[139] See further Ch **12**.

[140] CA 1963. s 322(1)(a).

receipts and payments; to vouch such receipts and payments; and to pay over to the liquidator the amount properly payable to him; and fails to do so, the court may make an order directing the receiver to comply with the liquidator's requirements.[141] Such an application was made by a liquidator in *Re Bamfords Ireland Ltd*,[142] who was seeking to compel a receiver to render receipts and payments in respect of his own term as receiver, and that of his predecessor. The Court was therefore called upon to determine whether the receiver was responsible for rendering receipts and payment in respect of his predecessor. Carroll J noted that there was no reference in s 322 to successors or continuing receiverships, by contrast with the terms of ss 319 and 320. The Court concluded that the reference to 'receiver' in s 322 does not include receivers' predecessors and a receiver is therefore only responsible for rendering receipts and payments in respect of his own tenure. As Carroll J stated:

> 'The statutory duty to render proper accounts is referable to receipts and payments received or made by him personally and does not include a duty to render proper accounts of receipts and payments made by his predecessor.'

The liquidator's application was refused and no order was made as to costs.

[8.066] The persons who may make an application in respect of the first category of default under s 322(1), are members or creditors of the company or the Registrar of Companies.[143] The appropriate applicant in relation to the second category is the company's liquidator.[144] On such an application, the order of the court may require that the receiver make good the default; it may specify the time within which this must be done; and it may provide that the receiver must bear all costs of and incidental to the application.[145] Such an enforcement order is without prejudice to any provision which imposes penalties on receivers for defaults.[146] A receiver who has failed to deliver an abstract required by s 319(2), for example, may face criminal proceedings for that failure, under s 319(8),[147] and may also face enforcement proceedings under s 322.

(c) Report by professional body

[8.067] Another important provision of the CA 1963–2006 regarding enforcement against receivers, is CLEA 2001, s 58. As has been seen, a receiver is not obliged to possess any particular qualifications or to be a member of a professional body. However, if a receiver is a member of one of the prescribed professional bodies, certain reporting obligations are imposed on that body.

---

[141] CA 1963, s 322(1)(b).

[142] *Re Bamfords Ireland Ltd (in receivership and in liquidation), Stewart v Campbell* [1986] 4 1506 (13 June 1986, unreported), HC.

[143] CA 1963, s 322(2).

[144] CA 1963, s 322(2).

[145] CA 1963, s 322(2).

[146] CA 1963, s 322(3).

[147] CA 1963, s 319(8), as inserted by CLEA 2001, s 52.

CLEA 2001, s 58 provides:

> Where a disciplinary committee or tribunal (however called) of a prescribed professional body finds that a member conducting a liquidation or receivership has not maintained appropriate records, or it has reasonable grounds for believing that a member has committed an indictable offence under the Companies Acts during the course of a liquidation or receivership, the body shall report the matter, giving details of the finding or, as the case may be, of the alleged offence, to the Director forthwith and if the body fails to comply with this section it, and every officer of the body to whom the failure is attributable, is guilty of an offence.

The DCE recommended that the following bodies be prescribed for the purposes of s 58:[148]

- the Institute of Chartered Accountants in Ireland;
- the Institute of Certified Public Accountants in Ireland;
- the Association of Chartered Certified Accountants;
- the Institute of Incorporated Public Accountants Ltd;
- the Law Society of Ireland;
- the Bar Council;
- the Institute of Taxation in Ireland; and
- the Chartered Institute of Management Accountants.

The CLEA (Section 58) Regulations 2002 prescribe the above mentioned bodies for the purpose of s 58, with the exception of the Bar Council, which is not therefore a prescribed body for the purposes of s 58.[149]

The effect of this provision is that if a receiver is a member of one of the bodies mentioned above, and a disciplinary committee or tribunal of that body 'finds' that he has not maintained 'appropriate records' or that the committee or tribunal has 'reasonable grounds' to believe he committed an indictable offence under the Companies Acts during the receivership, the body must report this matter to the Director. This report must be made forthwith, and it must include details of the finding that there was a failure to keep appropriate records, or of the alleged indictable offence. It is an offence for the professional body and every responsible officer, to fail to make such a report.

E. Reporting obligations of receivers

[8.068] CA 1963, s 299 imposes an obligation on a liquidator to make a report to the Director of Public Prosecutions ('DPP') if it appears to him that an officer or member of the company is guilty of an offence in relation to the company.[150] CA 1990, s 179

---

[148] Consultation Paper C/2002/3, 'The Liquidation-Related Functions of the Director of Corporate Enforcement' at p 23.

[149] CLEA 2001 (Section 58) Regulations 2002, SI 544/2002.

[150] See Ch **9** for detailed analysis of CA 1963, s 299.

provides that s 299(2), (4) and (5) apply, 'with the necessary modifications' to receivers. While s 299(2A) now extends the obligation of a liquidator to include an obligation to report a suspected offence to the DCE, no such extension is provided for in the case of receivers: receivers are therefore only obliged to report suspected offences to the DPP.[151]

Section 299(2), as modified, provides:

> If it appears to the receiver [liquidator] in the course of a receivership [voluntary winding up] that any past or present officer, or any member, of the company has been guilty of any offence in relation to the company for which he is criminally liable, he shall forthwith report the matter to the Director of Public Prosecutions and shall furnish to the Director of Public Prosecutions such information and give to him such access to and facilities for inspecting and taking copies of any documents, being information or documents in the possession or under the control of the receiver [liquidator] and relating to the matter in question, as the Director of Public Prosecutions may require.[152]

Section 299(4), as modified, provides:

> If, where any matter is reported or referred to the Director of Public Prosecutions [and the Director under this section, either] and the Director of Public Prosecutions [or the Director] considers that the case is one in which a prosecution ought to be instituted and institutes proceedings accordingly, it shall be the duty of the receiver [liquidator] and of every officer and agent of the company past and present (other than the defendant in the proceedings) to give all assistance in connection with the prosecution which he is reasonably able to give.[153]

Finally, s 299(5), as modified, provides:

> If any person fails or neglects to give assistance in the manner required by sub-s (4), the court may, on the application of the Director of Public Prosecutions [or of the Director], direct that person to comply with the requirements of that subsection, and where any such application is made in relation to a receiver [liquidator] the court may, unless it appears that the failure or neglect to comply was due to the receiver [liquidator] not having in his hands sufficient assets of the company to enable him to do so, direct the costs of the application shall be borne by the liquidator personally.[154]

[8.069] The effect of these provisions is that a receiver must make a report to the DPP if it appears to him that a past or present officer, or a member, of the company is guilty of an offence in relation to the company, for which he is criminally liable. The receiver must also furnish to the DPP such information and access to such documents, relating to the matter, as are in his possession as receiver. Furthermore, if the DPP does issue proceedings against the officer or member, the receiver must provide all assistance

---

[151] See CA 1963, s 299(2A), as inserted by CLEA 2001, s 51. See further Ch **9**.

[152] CA 1963, s 299(2), as substituted by CA 1990, s 143 and amended by CLEA 2001, s 51. The words in square brackets are appropriate to liquidators and should be omitted in the context of receivers.

[153] CA 1963, s 299(4), as substituted by CA 1990, s 143, and as amended by CLEA 2001, s 51. The words in brackets relate to liquidators and should be omitted in the context of receivers.

[154] CA 1963, s 299(5), as substituted by CA 1990, s 143 and as amended by CLEA 2001, s 51. The words in brackets relate to liquidators and should be omitted in the context of receivers.

which he is reasonably able to provide, in connection with that prosecution. If the receiver fails to comply with the obligation to assist the DPP in the prosecution of the offence, an application may be made to court to direct such assistance be provided.

It is interesting to note that, whereas a liquidator may be compelled to make a report to the DPP under s 299(3), this power does not exist in respect of a receiver. It is only if a receiver makes a report under s 299(2) and then fails or refuses to assist in the prosecution of the offence, that the DPP has any recourse against the receiver.

F. Remuneration

[8.070] The instrument pursuant to which a receiver is appointed may specify the remuneration of the receiver. However, there is a procedure whereby the court may intervene in respect of such remuneration. Section 318 permits a company's liquidator, creditor or member to make an application to court to fix the remuneration of a receiver who was appointed over the company's property under the terms of a debenture. Section 318(1) accordingly provides:

> The Court may, on an application made to it by the liquidator of a company or by any creditor or member of the company, by order fix the amount to be paid by way of remuneration to any person who, under the powers contained in any instrument, has been appointed as receiver of the property of the company notwithstanding that the remuneration of such receiver has been fixed by or under that instrument.[155]

[8.071] If no previous order has been made fixing the receiver's remuneration, the court may fix the remuneration of the receiver for any period prior to the application or order, even if the receiver has died or ceased to act before the date of the application or the order.[156] If, before the date of the court order, the receiver has been paid, or has retained from monies received, remuneration that exceeds the amount fixed by that order, the court may direct the receiver to account for the excess amount or such part of it as the court may specify.[157] If the receiver has died, this order may be directed to his personal representative. The power to direct a receiver or his personal representative to account for remuneration already received, shall not extend to remuneration for any period before the making of the application to have the remuneration fixed.[158]

The general power to direct a receiver to account for remuneration received, therefore, only relates to monies received in respect of the period between the date of the application and the date of the court order. This is subject to the qualification that, if there are special circumstances which make it proper to direct the receiver or his personal representative to account for remuneration received in respect of periods that pre-date the application, the court may make an order to that effect.[159] There are no

---

[155] CA 1963, s 318(1).

[156] CA 1963, s 318(2)(a) and (b).

[157] CA 1963, s 318(2)(c).

[158] CA 1963, s 318(3).

[159] CA 1963, s 318(3).

reported Irish decisions considering the nature of the 'special circumstances' which would justify such a finding. However, it may be expected that if a receiver receives or retains remuneration which is considered to be grossly excessive, this would justify a court order to account for such remuneration.

At any time after the making of a court order to fix a receiver's remuneration, a liquidator, creditor or member of the company may apply to have that order varied or amended.[160]

[8.072] The purpose of s 318 was considered by Geoghegan J in *Re City Car Sales Ltd*.[161] The liquidator in that case brought an application regarding the appropriate level of the receiver's remuneration. The debenture under which the receiver was appointed stipulated that the remuneration should be calculated in accordance with ss 19 to 24 of the Conveyancing Act 1881. While these provisions apply to receivers appointed over a company's income, and the receiver in that case was appointed over the company's property and assets, the Court held that those provisions nonetheless applied to the receiver's remuneration, in accordance with the terms of the debenture. Geoghegan J stated:

> 'Notwithstanding that the receivership in this case was a receivership of the property and assets of the company and not merely of the income, it was clearly intended by the debenture that those statutory provisions cited above would apply to it and that there was deemed to be a variation and extension of the provisions of ss 19 to 24 inclusive of the 1881 Act so as to achieve this.'[162]

Section 24 of the Act of 1881 specified that a receiver should receive a maximum remuneration of 5 per cent of the value of the proceeds of the receivership. The Court decided to exercise its jurisdiction under s 24(6) of the Act of 1881 to increase this threshold and allowed the receiver a rate of remuneration higher than 5 per cent. In *Re Red Sail Frozen Foods Ltd*,[163] the same issue arose for consideration and the Court again determined that the terms of ss 19 to 24 of the Conveyancing Act 1881 were applicable to the receiver's remuneration, but that the Court should exercise its discretion to allow a rate of remuneration in excess of 5 per cent of the proceeds of the receivership.

[8.073] In *Re City Car Sales Ltd*[164] further arguments were addressed to the Court regarding CA 1963, s 318. While the case was determined under the Conveyancing Act 1881, the Court went on to consider whether the remuneration of the receiver could be

---

[160] CA 1963, s 318(4).

[161] *Re City Car Sales Ltd* [1995] 1 ILRM 221.

[162] *Re City Car Sales Ltd* [1995] 1 ILRM 221.

[163] *Re Red Sail Frozen Foods Ltd* [2006] IEHC 328 ('I am satisfied that the Receiver conducted the receivership in a proper and *bona fide* manner and that the basis on which the remuneration is claimed conforms with the normal practice in the accountancy profession. Accordingly, on that basis, ... I am prepared to adopt the course adopted by Geoghegan J and make an order under s 24(6) of the Act of 1881, as applied and extended by the debentures, allowing the Receiver such rate higher than 5% which results in his being lawfully entitled to remuneration ...' in the amounts set out in the judgment. *per* Laffoy J).

[164] *Re City Car Sales Ltd* [1995] 1 ILRM 221.

increased by means of a court order under s 318. Geoghegan J made the following observations in this regard:

> 'The section is quite clearly designed to curb excessive remuneration being retained by a receiver rather than for the purposes of increasing his remuneration. I would adopt the passage of Hoffmann J in *In Re Potters Oils Ltd (No 2)* [1986] 1 All ER 890 at p 895. That passage dealing with the equivalent provision in England reads as follows:
>
>> "In exercising these discretions I bear in mind the following considerations. First, the exercise of the power involves interference with contractual rights in the interest of the unsecured creditors. As Andrew Clark KC said in argument in *In Re Greycaine Ltd* [1946] Ch 269 at p. 274, the mischief at which the section is aimed is that:
>>
>>> unsecured creditors may find themselves bound by an improvident bargain entered into by the directors and see the assets frittered away on the agent of the secured creditors."
>>
>> I respectfully adopt this description, which suggests to me that interference should be confined to cases in which the remuneration can clearly be seen as excessive rather than take the form of a routine taxation by the court of receivers' remuneration.'[165]

On the basis of this authority, a court order on an application under s 318 cannot increase the receiver's remuneration.

G. Liability

[8.074] The general rule applicable to a receiver's liability on contracts is that he is personally liable on any contract he enters into in the performance of his functions.[166] This applies whether the receiver enters into the contract in his own name, in the name of the company or otherwise. A receiver shall not however be personally liable if the contract contains a provision to that effect. Where a receiver is personally liable on a contract, he is entitled to be indemnified out of the assets.[167] These provisions regarding the contractual liability of a receiver, do not limit any other right to indemnity which the receiver would otherwise have.[168] Furthermore, if a receiver enters into a contract without authority, the terms of s 316(2) neither limit the liability of a receiver in relation to such a contract, nor confer any right to be indemnified in respect of such liability.[169]

[8.075] The effect of s 316(2) was considered in *Ardmore Studios (Ireland) Ltd v Lynch*[170] as follows:

> 'This subsection is similar to sub-s (2) of s 369 of the English Companies Act, 1948, as to the effect of which I have been referred to *Palmer's Company Precedents* (16th edn, 1952, Pt 3), at p 19:— "It is usual to provide that the

---

[165] *Re City Car Sales Ltd* [1995] 1 ILRM 221.

[166] CA 1963, s 316(2).

[167] CA 1963, s 316(2).

[168] CA 1963, s 316(2).

[169] CA 1963, s 316(2).

[170] *Ardmore Studios (Ireland) Ltd v Lynch* [1965] IR 1.

receiver shall be the agent of the company so as to prevent him being held to be the agent of the debenture holders or being personally liable on contracts entered into by him". Section 369(2), however, now provides that he is to be personally liable to the same extent as if he had been appointed by the Court, on any contract entered into by him in the performance of his functions, "except in so far as the contract otherwise provides".[171]

[8.076] If it transpires, after the appointment of a receiver, that the charge pursuant to which he was appointed was not effective as a charge on the property, or part of the property, the receiver may make an application for a court order that he be relieved from personal liability in respect of anything done or omitted to be done in relation to the property.[172] Section 316(3) provides as follows:

> Where a receiver of the property of a company has been appointed or purported to be appointed and it is subsequently discovered that the charge or purported charge in respect of which he was so appointed or purported to be appointed was not effective as a charge on such property or on some part of such property, the court may, if it thinks fit, on the application of such receiver, order that he be relieved wholly or to such extent as the court shall think fit from personal liability in respect of anything done or omitted by him in relation to any property purporting to be comprised in the charge by virtue of which he was appointed or purported to be appointed which if such property had been effectively included in such charge or purported charge would have been properly done or omitted by him and he shall be relieved from personal liability accordingly, but in that event the person by whom such receiver was appointed or purported to be appointed shall be personally liable for everything for which, but for such order, such receiver would have been liable.[173]

The effect of this provision is that, if it is discovered that the charge in respect of which a receiver was appointed was not effective, some or all of the liability arising from things done in relation to the property covered by the charge, during the purported receivership, may be imposed by court order on the person who was responsible for the receiver's appointment, rather than the receiver himself.

H. Resignation/Removal

[8.077] The court can remove and replace a receiver if cause is shown.[174] This applies whether the receiver is appointed by debenture holders or by the court.[175] While the Companies Acts do not specify the grounds on which receivers may be removed, it may be expected that a receiver could be removed on the ground that he was not validly appointed[176] or that he was guilty of misconduct.[177]

---

[171] *Ardmore Studios (Ireland) Ltd v Lynch* [1965] IR 1 at 38.

[172] CA 1963, s 316(3).

[173] CA 1963, s 316(3).

[174] CA 1963, s 322A(1), as inserted by CA 1990, s 175.

[175] See *Annotated Companies Act 1990*, ICLSA.

[176] See *Lavender v Lavender* (1875) 9 Ir Eq 593.

[177] See *Re St. George's Estate* (1887) 19 LR Ir 556.

[8.078] Where proceedings are taken for the removal of a receiver, notice of these proceedings must be served on the receiver and on the person who appointed him, at least seven days before the hearing of the proceedings, and they may appear and be heard at such proceedings.[178]

The background to this provision has been explained as follows:

'During the Dáil Special Committee debates it was explained that the power of removal involves a significant intrusion into the normal practices of commerce (Col 896, April 3, 1990). Consequently, the right of removal was tempered by the *locus standi* accorded both receiver and debenture holder. The relevant provision was further amended at Dáil Report Stage so that notice of the proceedings must be served on the receiver and on the person who appointed him not less than seven days before the hearing of such proceedings (403 Dáil Debates Cols 1122–1123).'[179]

[8.079] A liquidator of a company can also apply for an order that a receiver should cease to so act; that no further receiver should be appointed; or that a receiver should act only in relation to certain specified assets.[180] Such an order shall not however affect the security or charges over the company's undertaking or property.[181] It is notable that this power of a liquidator to seek to terminate or limit a receivership, arises whether the receiver was appointed before or after the commencement of the winding up.[182] It does not however arise if a liquidator is appointed in a members' voluntary winding up. The court order may specify the terms and conditions which apply and the order may moreover be rescinded or amended on the application of the liquidator or the receiver.[183]

---

[178] CA 1963, s 322A(2), as inserted by CA 1990, s 175.

[179] *Annotated Companies Act 1990*, ICLSA.

[180] CA 1963, s 322B(1), as inserted by CA 190, s 176.

[181] CA 1963, s 322B(4), as inserted by CA 1990, s 176.

[182] Note that the appointment of a liquidator does not affect or prevent the appointment of a receiver. This matter was considered by the Supreme Court in *Re Motor Racing Circuit Ltd* [1997] IESC 59 (31 January 1997, unreported), SC where the issue was whether the presentation of the petition for the winding up of the company precluded the appointment of a receiver to a company, as a result of the terms of CA 1963, ss 218 and 222. The Court concluded, 'The position here is that there was no alteration in any way in the property of the company effected by the appointment of the receiver. The alteration in regard to the assets of the company was effected when the debenture was executed. As a result of the debenture being executed the bank had a charge on the particular property which was the subject of the debenture. So the bank from the date of the execution of the debenture was the mortgagee of the property in question. The property in question had been vested in the bank as security for the monies owing to the bank. The appointment of a receiver simply amounted to the normal way for a bank to recover what is due to it on foot of its charge. But there was no change whatsoever in regard to the ownership of the asset that had already been vested in the company under the debenture when the debenture was executed. The position is that the appointment of a receiver does not in any way come within s 218. It does not in any way represent any disposition of the property of the company; this disposition had taken place when the debenture was executed.'

[183] CA 1963, s 322B(2), as inserted by CA 1990, s 176.

If a liquidator makes an application to terminate or limit a receivership, he must serve a copy of this application on the receiver and the person who appointed him, at least seven days before the hearing, and those persons may appear and be heard at that hearing.[184]

[8.080] If a petition is presented for the appointment of an examiner to a company which is in receivership, whether over the whole or any part of the company's property or undertaking, C(A)A 1990, s 6(1), provides that the court may make such orders as it thinks fit, including an order that the receiver cease to so act; that the receiver act only in respect of specified assets; directing the receiver to deliver to the examiner, within a specified period, all books, papers and other records relating to the property or undertaking of the company, that are in the receiver's possession or control; or directing the receiver to give full particulars of all his dealings with the property or undertaking of the company to the examiner.[185] This provision demonstrates clearly that, while receivers and liquidators may operate in respect of the same company, there is less scope for examiners and receivers to co-exist. This is also apparent from the terms of C(A)A 1990, s 3(6), which provides:

> 'The court shall not give a hearing to a petition under s 2 if a receiver stands appointed to the company the subject of the petition and such receiver has stood so appointed for a continuous period of at least three days prior to the presentation of the petition.'[186]

[8.081] A receiver who is appointed pursuant to the terms of a debenture, as opposed to by the court, may resign from that office, provided he furnishes one month's notice of such resignation to the holders of any fixed or floating charges over the part or the whole of the company's property and the company or its liquidator.[187] Prior to the enactment of s 322C, it appears that receivers appointed by debenture holders could only resign if the debenture or the terms of appointment contained a provision to that effect.[188]

[8.082] A receiver who is appointed by the court can only resign with the authority of the court, and on such terms and conditions as may be stipulated by the court.[189] This is consistent with the fact that a receiver who is appointed by the court is an officer of the court, and the terms of the receivership are determined by the court. If a receiver is

---

[184] CA 1963, s 322B(3), as inserted by CA 1990, s 176.

[185] C(A)A 1990, s 6(1), as amended by C(A)(No 2) A 1999, s 16(a).

[186] C(A)A 1990, s 3(6), as amended by CA 1990, s 180.

[187] CA 1963, s 322C(1), as inserted by CA 1990, s 177. Note that the requirement that the receiver furnish notice of the resignation to the holders of charges over the company's property originated with a recommendation of the Cork Committee to the effect that a debenture holder should be able to appoint a replacement receiver immediately (Cmnd 8558 at para 401). See Annotated Companies Act 1990, ICLSA.

[188] See Picarda, *The Law Relating to Receivers, Administrators and Managers* (2nd edn, Tottel Publishing, 1990) at pp 250–251.

[189] CA 1963, s 322C(2), as inserted by CA 1990, s 177.

guilty of a default in relation to the manner in which he resigns from that position, he is liable to a maximum fine of €1,904.61.[190]

[8.083] If a receiver ceases to so act, whether as a result of removal or resignation, he must deliver to the Registrar of Companies a notice specifying this fact.[191] Form 57A is the form prescribed for this purpose. This form simply requires a signed statement by the receiver that he has ceased to act as such, and the date of such cessation.[192] It is an offence to fail to publish or deliver the requisite notices regarding the cessation of a receivership, an offence punishable by a maximum fine of €1,904.61.[193]

[8.084] A further return that must be made by a receiver who has ceased to so act, is that the abstract which he is required to deliver to the Registrar of Companies within one month of ceasing to act as receiver, must be accompanied by a statement by the receiver of his opinion as to whether the company is solvent.[194] The Registrar, upon receipt of this statement of the company's solvency, must forward a copy of the statement to the DCE.[195]

---

[190] CA 1963, s 322C(3), as inserted by CA 1990, s 177, as amended by CA 1990, s 240(7), as inserted by CLEA 2001, s 104.

[191] CA 1963, s 107(2).

[192] See Form E11/57A, 'Notice of Cessation by Receiver', at www.cro.ie.

[193] CA 1963, s 107(3), as amended by C(A)A 1982, s 15; CA 1990, s 240(7) as inserted by CLEA 2001, s 104; C(AA)A 2003, s 57 and Sch 2.

[194] CA 1963, s 319(2A), as inserted by CLEA 2001, s 52. See further para **[8.028]**.

[195] CA 1963, s 319(2A), as inserted by CLEA 2001, s 52.

Chapter 9

LIQUIDATORS

A. Introduction

[9.001] There are certain aspects of the functions of liquidators and the liquidation process under the Companies Acts that are of potentially great significance in the detection of breaches of company law, the prosecution of such breaches and the enforcement of company law generally. In this chapter, these aspects of a liquidation and the duties of a liquidator are addressed under a number of headings.

In section [B], the rules applicable to the appointment of liquidators and the importance of the publication and notification of such appointments are addressed. The publication and notification requirements clearly assist in the transparency that is necessary for the consistent and thorough enforcement of company law.

In section [C], some of the compliance obligations of liquidators in the conduct of a liquidation, which are of relevance to the enforcement of company law, are examined. These duties include the duty to make certain returns and to convene meetings at defined intervals in a winding up. These meetings are an important means of ensuring relevant information is communicated to the liquidators and to the members or the creditors of the company, and that there is openness and disclosure in the liquidation process.

Section [C] also addresses the significant duties of a liquidator to report certain matters that may come to light in the course of a liquidation. The duties of liquidators to make reports to the Director of Corporate Enforcement ('DCE') and to the Director of Public Prosecutions, among others, are of great importance to the effective enforcement of company law by those entities. This aspect of a liquidator's function has become more onerous and the emphasis placed upon it has been heightened significantly since the enactment of CLEA 2001. There are many other duties that are assumed by a company's liquidator, such as the central task of distributing the company's assets. These duties are treated extensively elsewhere[1] and will only be addressed in this chapter to the extent that they are relevant to the enforcement of company law.

Section [D] deals with investigations that may take place when a company is being wound up, whether compulsorily or voluntarily. This encompasses wide ranging powers which may be used against the officers of the company, among others, including the power of arrest; the power to prevent the removal or dissipation of assets; and the power to summon persons to appear before the court.

Finally, section [E] considers the investigation of liquidators and the means by which a liquidator's failure to comply with his obligations, or the commission of certain offences by liquidators, may be brought to light.

---

[1]   See, eg, Courtney, *The Law of Private Companies* (2nd edn, Tottel Publishing, 2002), Ch 26.

With regard to the sanctions that may be imposed on liquidators, it should be noted that they are may face many of the same sanctions and penalties as other company officers, such as declarations of restriction and disqualification orders. These topics are considered separately.[2]

B. Appointment of liquidators

(a) Means of appointment

(i) Official liquidation

[9.002] In a court-ordered winding up, the court has the power to appoint a liquidator or liquidators to conduct the winding up of a company and carry out any duties that the court may impose in respect of the winding up.[3]

Before exercising the power to appoint a liquidator or liquidators to carry out the winding up of a company, the court can appoint a provisional liquidator.[4] This can be done at any time between the presentation of the winding up petition and the appointment of a liquidator or liquidators.[5] The powers of a provisional liquidator can be limited and restricted by the court order appointing such liquidator.[6]

(ii) Obligations of company in voluntary winding up

[9.003] Where a company is being wound up by virtue of a resolution of the company's members, the company is obliged to appoint one or more liquidators to wind up the company's affairs and distribute the company's assets.[7] This appointment must be done by the company in general meeting.[8] It is not expressly required that the liquidator or liquidators be appointed at the same meeting at which the company resolves to wind up the company.

(ii) Obligations of creditors in voluntary winding up

[9.004] In the case of a creditor's voluntary winding up of a company, the creditor and the company at their respective meetings[9] can nominate a person to act as liquidator and

---

2   See Pt **D** 'Declarations of Restriction, and Pt **E**, Disqualification Orders'.

3   CA 1963, s 225.

4   CA 1963, s 226(1).

5   CA 1963, s 226(1).

6   CA 1963, s 226(2).

7   CA 1963, s 258(1).

8   CA 1963, s 258(1).

9   The meetings in question are the meetings referred to in CA 1963, s 266.

to wind-up the company's affairs and distribute the company's assets.[10] If the creditors do not nominate a liquidator, the company's nominee shall be appointed as liquidator.[11]

[9.005] Before the introduction of the CLEA 2001, the creditors could only replace the liquidator nominated by the company in general meeting if a majority in number and in value of the creditors voted in favour of such a proposal. This requirement rendered it very difficult in practice for the creditors to replace the company's nominee. This situation was amended by CLEA 2001, s 47, which inserted a new provision to the effect that, when the first creditor's meeting is held in a voluntary winding up and:

> a resolution as to the creditors' nominee as liquidator is proposed, it shall be deemed to be passed when a majority, in value only, of the creditors present personally or by proxy and voting on the resolution have voted in favour of the resolution.[12]

[9.006] If the company and the creditors nominate different persons to act as liquidator, the general rule is that the person nominated by the creditors shall be liquidator.[13] Where this occurs, a director, creditor or member of the company can apply to the court for an order that the liquidator nominated by the company act in the place of, or in conjunction with, the liquidator nominated by the creditors, or an order directing that a person, other than the persons nominated by the company or the creditors, be appointed to act as liquidator.[14] This application must be made within 14 days of the nomination by the creditors.[15]

(b) Qualifications

[9.007] There is no provision of the Companies Acts that stipulates the qualifications that a liquidator must possess,[16] however there are certain persons who cannot act as liquidators of a company. The first restriction is the exclusion of bodies corporate, which are never qualified to act in that capacity, whether the company is wound-up by

---

10 CA 1963, s 267(1).

11 CA 1963, s 267(1).

12 CLEA 2001, s 47, inserting a new CA 1963, s 267(3). This provision, and its interaction with O 74 of the Rules of the Superior Courts (SI 15/1986) were considered by the High Court in *Re Hayes Homes Ltd* (8 July 2004, unreported), HC, O'Neill J.

13 CA 1963, s 267(1).

14 CA 1963, s 267(2).

15 CA 1963, s 267(2).

16 This can be contrasted with the position in England and Wales, where, as noted by the Company Law Review Group, 'an individual must be a member of a recognised professional body in order to practise as an insolvency practitioner he must also hold a qualification in insolvency, achieved on foot of examination', *First Report of the Company Law Review Group* (February 2002) at para 13.9.7. The Report recommended in this regard that, '... the appropriate route to take with regard to regulating liquidators, examiners and receivers is to provide for regulation through the medium of recognised professional bodies (RPBs)', at para 13.9.8. See also CLRG, General Scheme of the Draft Companies Consolidation and Reform Bill 2007, Pt A11, Head 68, which sets out the criteria for qualification as a liquidator. Available at www.clrg.org.

court order or voluntarily.[17] Any attempt to appoint a body corporate to act as liquidator is void and a body corporate purporting to so act is liable to a fine.[18]

The category of persons who are disqualified from acting as liquidators was extended considerably by CA 1990, s 146, which created a new s 300A. The following categories of person are now precluded from acting as liquidator:

1. A person who is or was within 12 months before the winding up commenced, an officer[19] or servant of the company;

2. A parent, spouse, brother, sister or child of an officer of the company;[20]

3. A partner or employee of an officer or servant of the company;[21] and

4. A person who is not qualified by virtue of their above-listed relationships for appointment as liquidator of another body corporate which is the company in liquidation's subsidiary, holding company or a subsidiary of that company's holding company, or would be so disqualified if the body corporate were a company.[22]

It is of interest to note that the only exception to this list is the proviso that a parent, spouse, brother, sister or child of an officer of the company can act as liquidator of that company, with the leave of the court.[23] Such an application must be supported by such evidence as the court may require.[24]

[9.008] Where a liquidator becomes disqualified under this provision he is obliged to resign as liquidator.[25] There is no time period specified within which the liquidator must vacate his office and it appears that it must occur immediately upon his becoming disqualified within the meaning of CA 1990, s 300A. The liquidator must also, within 14 days of vacating his office, furnish written notice of the disqualification and ensuing resignation to the court (in an official liquidation), to the company (in the member's voluntary liquidation) or the company and the creditors (in the creditor's voluntary liquidation).[26] There are few situations in which this obligation will arise. First, a liquidator may become disqualified as a result of marrying an officer or servant of the company. Secondly, a liquidator may become disqualified as a result of becoming a partner or employee of an officer or servant of the company or its holding company or

---

[17] CA 1963, s 300.

[18] CA 1963, s 300(a) and (b) as amended by C(AA) A 2003, s 57 and Sch 2, para 1.

[19] CA 1963 s 300A (1)(a) as inserted by CA 1990, s 146. The section states expressly that, 'References in this subsection to an officer or servant of the company include references to an auditor.'

[20] CA 1963 s 300A (1)(b) as inserted by CA 1990, s 146.

[21] CA 1963 s 300A (1)(c) as inserted by CA 1990, s 146.

[22] CA 1963 s 300A (1)(d) as inserted by CA 1990, s 146.

[23] CA 1963, s 300A(1)(b), as inserted by CA 1990, s 146.

[24] CA 1963, s 300A(2), as inserted by CA 1990, s 146.

[25] CA 1963, s 300A(3), as inserted by CA 1990, s 146.

[26] CA 1963, s 300A(3), as inserted by CA 1990, s 146.

subsidiary. It is difficult to envisage other situations in which this provision will be relevant. For instance, a liquidator is unlikely to become an officer or servant of a company which is in the process of being wound up and certainly cannot become the parent, sister, brother or child of an officer or servant.

There are clearly compelling grounds for stipulating means by which a liquidator can become disqualified from acting in the course of a winding up and requiring a liquidator to resign for such reasons. However, the extension of the existing grounds of disqualification under s 300A is largely redundant and does not address the other grounds of disqualification that would be more likely to arise in the course of a liquidation than at its inception. For instance, a liquidator may discover a connection with a creditor that was not apparent upon appointment and such a discovery may be a ground for requiring a liquidator to vacate his position.[27] Finally, the disqualification of bodies corporate does not appear to extend beyond the initiation of the liquidation. The requirement that a liquidator resign upon becoming disqualified is confined to the terms of CA 1963, s 300A. It is a conceivable that a liquidator may become incorporated as a body corporate in the course of a liquidation and the legislation does not address this possibility directly. In light of the fact that a body corporate which acts as liquidator is liable to a fine, there is a deterrent and punishment in place to prevent this risk. However, no obligation to resign exists at present.

[9.009] A person who acts as a liquidator when disqualified from so acting for one of the reasons set out in CA 1963, s 300A, or who fails to resign having become disqualified within the meaning of that section, is guilty of an offence and is liable to a fine, including a daily fine for continuing offences.[28]

A person who is subject to a disqualification order under CA 1990, s 160, or is deemed to be disqualified under that provision, is also precluded from acting as a liquidator and will face sanction if he acts as liquidator despite such disqualification.[29]

(c) Creditors' disclosure obligation

[9.010] CA 1963, s 301A[30] imposes a particular obligation on creditors in relation to the appointment of a liquidator in a creditors' voluntary winding up. Where a resolution for the appointment of a liquidator is proposed at a meeting of creditors, any creditor[31] who has 'a connection' with the nominated liquidator is obliged to declare this to the chairman of the meeting before the resolution is put to the meeting. The chairman is then required to disclose the details of the connection to the meeting. For the purposes of this requirement, a 'connection' with a proposed liquidator exists if the person is a

---

[27] With regard to connections between liquidators and creditors, see below paras **[9.010]** to **[9.011]**.

[28] CA 1963, s 300A(4), as inserted by CA 1990, s 146 and as amended by CLEA 2001.

[29] See Pt E.

[30] Inserted by CA 1990, s 147.

[31] According to CA 1963, s 301A(2) and (3), creditors include any representatives of creditors attending the meeting, and the chairman of the meeting is also bound by the duty to disclose any connection with the proposed liquidator.

parent, spouse, brother, sister or child, employee or partner of, the proposed liquidator.[32] A creditor who fails to make the disclosure required by s 301A is guilty of an offence and liable to a fine of €1,904.61.[33] In addition, any failure to comply with this requirement may be taken into account by a court in relation to the removal or appointment of a liquidator.[34]

[9.011] There are a few points to note about this provision. First, a connection between a creditor and a liquidator does not disqualify the latter from acting as such. This can be contrasted with connections between liquidators and officers of a company, which disqualifies the liquidator from acting as such.[35] Secondly, there is no corresponding obligation on members of a company to disclose any connection with a proposed liquidator before the company appoints that liquidator in general meeting. There is a justification for this distinction in the context of an insolvent liquidation, as only creditors have a vested interest in the outcome of such a liquidation. However, in a member's voluntary winding up, the members are likely to gain in the liquidation, and it may be queried whether there should be a requirement to disclose connections with the proposed liquidator in those circumstances.

A final point to note about the disclosure requirement of s 301A is that there is no provision whereby any connection that may arise between the liquidator and a creditor subsequent to the appointment of the liquidator, needs to be notified to the company and/or the other creditors. This can be contrasted with the requirement that, where any ground for disqualification of a liquidator arises during the winding up of a company, that liquidator is thereby obliged to resign.[36] The lack of any ongoing disclosure requirement in s 301A, could lead to a situation where a creditor and a liquidator get married or enter into partnership, for instance, while the winding up is in a progress. The development of such a connection is something that other creditors should arguably be aware of, but, on the current state of the law, there is no obligation to disclose any connections that arise after the appointment of the liquidator.

(d) Prohibition on inducement for appointment of liquidator

[9.012] The Companies Acts prohibit the payment of any inducements to secure the appointment of particular liquidators. CA 1963, s 301, provides:

> Any person who gives or agrees or offers to give to any member or creditor of a company any valuable consideration with a view to securing his own appointment or nomination or to securing or preventing the appointment or nomination of some

---

[32] CA 1963, s 301A(4), as inserted by CA 1990, s 147.

[33] CA 1963, s 301A(5), as inserted by CA 1990, s 147 and amended by CA1990 s 240(7) (as inserted by CLEA 2001, s104(c)) and C(AA) A 2003, s 57 and Sch 2 para 1.

[34] According to CA 1963, s 301A(6), as inserted by CA 1990, s 147, '(6) In exercising its jurisdiction under s 267(2) or 272(2) (which relate to the appointment or removal of a liquidator) the court may have regard to any failure to comply with this section.'

[35] See CA 1963, s 300A. See above para **[9.007]**.

[36] CA 1963, s 300A(3), as inserted by CA 1990, s 146. See further above para **[9.008]**.

person other than himself as the company's liquidator shall be guilty of an offence and liable to a fine not exceeding €1904.61.[37]

The penalty for paying of consideration in connection with the appointment of a liquidator is a fine. It does not appear to be a ground for disqualification of the liquidator. This could result in a liquidator who was appointed by means of corruption retaining that office. Given the increasingly costly and lucrative nature of liquidations, a fine may not be an adequate deterrent against the use of inducements. This is, of course, subject to the overriding jurisdiction of the court to remove a voluntary liquidator where cause is shown.[38]

(e) Liquidator's consent and chairman's duty of notification

[9.013] There are not many formalities surrounding the appointment of a liquidator. One requirement that should be noted, however, is that a liquidator must consent in writing before appointment to that post.[39] Failing such consent, the appointment will be of no effect.[40] A further requirement is that the chairman of the meeting at which a liquidator is appointed must, within seven days of that meeting, notify the liquidator in writing of this appointment.[41] A person who fails to comply with this notification requirement shall be guilty of an offence and liable to a fine not exceeding €1904.61.[42] It appears that the only person who can be held liable for failing to notify the liquidator of his appointment, is the person on whom that obligation is imposed, namely the chairman of the meeting.

However, it should be noted that this, and other possible infirmities in the appointment or qualifications of a liquidator, do not affect the validity of any acts carried out by the liquidator before the discovery of that defect. Any such acts are deemed by the Companies Acts to be valid.[43]

(f) Removal of liquidator

[9.014] The court has the power to remove a liquidator, whether the liquidator was appointed by the court, in a members' voluntary winding up or in a creditors voluntary winding up. In relation to compulsory liquidations, CA 1963, s 228 provides that a court may remove a liquidator 'on cause shown'.[44] In the context of a voluntary winding up,

---

[37] As amended by CA1990 s 240(7) (as inserted by CLEA 2001, s 104(c)) and C(AA) A 2003, s 57 and Sch 2 para 1. See also CLRG, General Scheme of Draft Companies Consolidation and Reform Bill 2007, Pt A11, Head 76.

[38] CA 1963, s 277(2) provides, 'The court may, on cause shown, remove a liquidator and appoint another liquidator.'

[39] CA 1963, s 276A(1), inserted by CA 1990, s 133.

[40] CA 1963, s 276A(1), inserted by CA 1990, s 133.

[41] CA 1963, s 276A(2), inserted by CA 1990, s 133.

[42] CA 1963, s 276A(3), inserted by CA 1990, s 133 and amended by CA 1990 s 240(7) (as inserted by CLEA 2001, s 104(c)) and C(AA) A 2003, s 57 and Sch 2 para 1.

[43] CA 1963, s 228(g).

[44] CA 1963, s 228(c).

the court may also 'on cause shown' remove the liquidator and appoint another.[45] There is no definition or illustration of what causes may warrant the removal of a liquidator and the court therefore has an appropriately broad discretion in this regard.

[9.015] While the power to remove a liquidator has not been invoked by the Irish courts, there are a number of useful decisions in the courts of England and Wales which consider the equivalent provision of the Insolvency Act 1986, s 108(2) which provides, 'The court may, on cause shown, remove a liquidator and appoint another.'

[9.016] As noted by the High Court of England and Wales in *Quickson (South and West) Ltd v Katz & Anor*,[46] the language of s 108(2) has 'appeared in substantially the same form in company legislation for over 140 years'.[47] In that case, the High Court noted that:

> 'The burden is on the applicant to show a good cause for removal of a liquidator, but it is well established that the statutory provision confers a wide discretion on the court which is not dependent on the proof of particular breaches of duty by the liquidator.'[48]

The Court further noted that, 'it is inappropriate to lay down what facts will and what facts will not constitute sufficient grounds for removal under s 108(2)'[49] and that, 'the creditors' lack of confidence in the liquidator must be reasonable, and the court will pay due regard to the impact of removal on the liquidator's professional standing and reputation.'[50]

The High Court concluded that, 'it is quite clear from the entire line of authority stretching back to 1867 that, in appropriate circumstances, there may be good cause to remove a liquidator, notwithstanding the failure of the applicant to prove misfeasance as such, and even though no reasonable criticism can be made of his conduct'[51] and that 'the touchstone for an appraisal of whether good cause has been shown for the removal of a liquidator is the principle stated by Bowen LJ in *Re Adam Eyton*:[52]

> 'The due cause is to be measured by reference to the real, substantial, honest interests of the liquidation, and to the purpose for which the liquidator is appointed.'[53]

---

45. CA 1963, s 277(2).

46. *Quickson (South and West) Ltd v Katz & Anor* CA 1963 [2004] EWHC 2443 (Ch) (25 August 2004) (Etherton J); [2004] All ER (D) 138 (Aug); [2006] 1 BCLC 9.

47. CA 1963 [2004] EWHC 2443 (Ch); [2004] All ER (D) 138 (Aug); [2006] 1 BCLC 9 at para 155.

48. CA 1963 [2004] EWHC 2443 (Ch); [2004] All ER (D) 138 (Aug); [2006] 1 BCLC 9 at para 156.

49. CA 1963 [2004] EWHC 2443 (Ch); [2004] All ER (D) 138 (Aug); [2006] 1 BCLC 9 at para 166.

50. CA 1963 [2004] EWHC 2443 (Ch); [2004] All ER (D) 138 (Aug); [2006] 1 BCLC 9 at para 166.

51. CA 1963 [2004] EWHC 2443 (Ch); [2004] All ER (D) 138 (Aug); [2006] 1 BCLC 9 at para 167.

52. *Re Adam Eyton Ltd* (1887) 36 Ch D 299 at 306.

53. *Quickson (South and West) Ltd v Katz & Anor* CA 1963 [2004] EWHC 2443 (Ch); [2004] All ER (D) 138 (Aug); [2006] 1 BCLC 9 at para 168.

(g) Notification of appointment

[9.017] One important aspect of the appointment of a liquidator from the perspective of the enforcement of company law is the obligation on the company and the liquidator to notify particular persons and bodies of the appointment, and otherwise to publicise the fact that the company is being wound up.[54] Proceedings in relation to default of each of these notification requirements may be prosecuted by the Registrar of Companies.[55]

(i) Official liquidator's duty to notify

[9.018] Certain notification requirements depend on the nature of the winding up. A court-appointed liquidator must publish a notice of his appointment in the *Companies Registration Office Gazette*.[56] He must also deliver a copy of the court order by which he was appointed to the Registrar of Companies.[57] Both of these steps must be taken within 21 days after the liquidator's appointment. In the event that a liquidator fails to comply with these requirements, he shall be guilty of an offence and liable to a fine of €1,904.61.[58]

(ii) Company's duty to publicise appointment of liquidator

[9.019] When the company passes a resolution to wind up the company in a voluntary winding up, it must advertise this resolution in the *Companies Registration Office Gazette* within 14 days of passing the resolution.[59] If this requirement is not complied with, the company and every officer of the company who is in default, including the liquidator, shall be guilty of an offence and liable to a fine.[60]

(iii) Voluntary liquidator's duty to notify

[9.020] A voluntary liquidator is also under an obligation to deliver to the Registrar of Companies a notice of his appointment.[61] This notice must be served within 14 days of appointment and, upon receipt, will be registered by the Registrar.[62] It is an offence for a liquidator to fail to comply with this notification requirement, and a fine may be

---

[54] These obligations are also contained, in amended form, in the CLRG, General Scheme of the Draft Companies Consolidation and Reform Bill 2007, Pt A11, Head 77.

[55] C(A)A 1982, s16. This does not extend to the obligation to display the fact that a company is in liquidation on the company's stationary, as required by CA 1963, s 303. See para **[9.021]**.

[56] CA 1963, s 227(1), as amended by IFCMPA 2005 s 72, which substituted the reference to *Iris Oifigiúil* for the reference to the *Companies Registration Office Gazette*.

[57] CA 1963, s 227(2).

[58] CA 1963, s 227(2), as amended by CA 1990, s 240(7), as inserted by CLEA 2001 s 104(c).

[59] CA 1963, s 252(1), as amended by IFCMPA 2005 s 72, which substituted the reference to *Iris Oifigiúil* for the reference to the *Companies Registration Office Gazette*.

[60] CA 1963, s 252(2), as amended by C(AA)A 2003, s 57 and Sch 2.

[61] CA 1963, s 278(1).

[62] CA 1963, s 278(1).

imposed.[63] Since the enactment of the CLEA 2001, the Registrar will forward a copy of this notice to the DCE.[64]

(iv) General duty to disclose liquidation

[9.021] There are other such requirements that are common to both compulsory and voluntary liquidations. According to CA 1963, s 303, where a company is being wound up either by the court or voluntarily:

> ... every invoice, order for goods or business letter issued by or on behalf of the company or a liquidator of the company, or a receiver of the property of the company, being a document on or in which the name of the company appears, shall contain a statement that the company is being wound up.[65]

If this requirement is not complied with, the company and any officer, liquidator or receiver of the company who has knowingly and wilfully authorised or permitted the default, shall be guilty of an offence and liable to a fine.[66]

C. Compliance obligations of liquidators

[9.022] This section addresses some of the requirements of the CA 1963–2006 with which liquidators must comply. The essential functions of a liquidator, ie to gather in the company's assets and distribute those assets in accordance with law, are addressed elsewhere.[67] This section does not purport to provide an exhaustive account of all such steps which a liquidator must take, but aims to highlight some of the compliance obligations that are most relevant to the enforcement of the Companies Acts. Particular focus is placed on the obligation of liquidators to report certain matters to the DPP or the ODCE. As a result of these expanded obligations, a liquidator may now find himself cast in the role of watchdog and investigator, as well as the administrator of a company's winding up.

(a) Duty to convene meetings

(i) Official liquidator

[9.023] When the liquidator is appointed by court order, there is little scope for direct supervision or oversight by the company or its creditors. The general rule is that decisions and directions that would be within the competence of the company or its creditors in a voluntary liquidation are taken by the court or a court-appointed

---

[63]   CA 1963, s 278(2), as amended by C(AA)A 2003, s 57 and Sch 2.

[64]   CA 1963, s 278(1), as amended by CLEA 2001, s 48. It should be noted that no amendment was introduced to CA 1963, s 227. There is therefore no legislative requirement that the Registrar forward to the DCE copies of notices received in respect of compulsory liquidations.

[65]   CA 1963, s 303(1).

[66]   CA 1963, s 303(2) as amended by C(AA)A 2003, s 57 and Sch 2.

[67]   See Courtney, *The Law of Private Companies* (2nd edn, Tottel Publishing, 2002), Ch 26.

committee of inspection, in a compulsory liquidation. For instance, as will be seen below, a liquidator must convene certain meetings at particular stages of a voluntary liquidation. By contrast, these stages are generally marked by court involvement in an official liquidation.

The general rule is that an official liquidator is subject to the control of the court or a committee of inspection, if one exists, in the exercise of the powers conferred by the Companies Acts.[68] The court can direct the liquidator to summon a meeting of the creditors or contributories to determine whether a committee of inspection should be formed to act with the liquidator and, if so, how it should be constituted.[69] If it is decided to form a committee of inspection, there must be an application to court to make the necessary order and appointment.[70] Where such a committee of inspection is appointed, the powers of the liquidator can be exercised subject to the sanction of that committee, rather than the court.[71] Where no committee is appointed, the court can make an order to the effect that certain of the liquidator's powers, which are generally subject to the sanction of the court, can be exercised without such sanction or approval.[72] The powers of which the requirement of court sanction can be waived by court order in this manner, are the power to bring or defend legal proceedings on behalf of the company and the power to carry on the company's business so far as is necessary for the winding up.[73]

It should be noted that, while the exercise of an official liquidator's powers is generally subject to the sanction of the court or a committee of inspection, and not the company's members or creditors directly, a creditor or contributory[74] of the company can apply to the court in relation to the exercise or proposed exercise of these powers.[75]

[9.024] Finally, in an official liquidation, while meetings of the company and the creditors do not play the same role as in voluntary liquidations, liquidators are still under a duty to account for the progress of the liquidation. For instance, an official liquidator is under a similar duty to that of voluntary liquidators to send an account of the winding up to the Registrar of Companies. If a liquidation continues for more than two years, CA 1963, s 306 requires the liquidator, whether official or voluntary, to send statements to the Registrar of Companies at prescribed intervals. The statements must be in the form

---

[68] CA 1963, s 231(1).

[69] CA 1963, s 232(1).

[70] CA 1963, s 232(2).

[71] CA 1963, s 231(1).

[72] CA 1963, s 231(4).

[73] CA 1963, s 231(1)(a) and (b).

[74] 'Contributory' is defined in CA 1963, s 208 as follows: 'The term "contributory" means every person liable to contribute to the assets of a company in the event of its being wound up, and for the purposes of all proceedings for determining, and all proceedings prior to the final determination of, the persons who are to be deemed contributories, includes any person alleged to be a contributory.'

[75] CA 1963, s 231(3).

required by the Registrar and must contain such information and particulars about the liquidation and its progress as may be prescribed.[76]

A liquidator who fails to comply with the requirement to provide statements to the Registrar of Companies, is guilty of an offence.[77] This offence can be prosecuted by the Registrar of Companies.[78]

(ii) Members' voluntary liquidation

[9.025] A liquidator who is appointed pursuant to a members' resolution to wind up the company, is under a particular obligation to creditors. This obligation arises where the liquidator forms the view that, contrary to the company's declaration of solvency as required under CA 1963, s 256,[79] the company will not be able to pay all of its debts. Where this occurs, the liquidator is obliged to call a meeting of the creditors. CA 1963, s 261[80] contains detailed provisions regarding the duty of a liquidator in this regard and this is an important aspect of the duties of a liquidator in a members' voluntary winding up to be vigilant in the application of the requirements of company law and to make it known if those requirements are not met.

Where the liquidator forms the opinion that the company will not be able to pay its debts in full within the time frame designated in the statutory declaration, he must do the following:

- call a meeting of the creditors to be held within 14 days of the formation of the opinion;[81]

- at least seven days before the meeting, send notices of the meeting to the creditors by post;[82]

- cause a notice of the meeting to be published in the *Companies Registration Office Gazette* at least ten days before the meeting;[83]

---

[76] CA 1963, s 306(1).

[77] CA 1963, s 306(2), as amended by CA 1990, s 145.

[78] CA 1963, s 306(3).

[79] CA 1963, s 256(1), as substituted by CA 1990, s 128. 'Where it is proposed to wind up a company voluntarily, the directors of the company or, in the case of a company having more than two directors, the majority of the directors may, at a meeting of the directors, make a statutory declaration to the effect that they have made a full inquiry into the affairs of the company, and that having done so, they have formed the opinion that the company will be able to pay its debts in full within such period not exceeding 12 months from the commencement of the winding up as may be specified in the declaration.' See further Courtney, *The Law of Private Companies* (2nd edn, Tottel Publishing, 2003), p 1416.

[80] As substituted by CA 1990, s 129.

[81] CA 1963, s 261(1)(a), as substituted by CA 1990, s 129.

[82] CA 1963, s 261(1)(b), as substituted by CA 1990, s 129.

[83] CA 1963, s 261(1)(c), as substituted by CA 1990, s 129 and amended by IFCMPA 2005, s 72.

- cause a notice of the meeting to be published at least once in two daily newspapers that circulate in the area where the company's principal place of business in Ireland was located, at least ten days before the meeting;[84]

- in advance of the meeting, provide the creditors with any information regarding the company's affairs which they may reasonably require;[85]

- make a statement of the company's affairs, including a statement of the company's assets and liabilities, a list of creditors and their estimated claims;[86]

- lay that statement of the company's affairs before the creditors' meeting;[87] and

- attend and preside at the creditors' meeting.[88]

[9.026] When this meeting has taken place, the liquidation will be converted from a members' voluntary winding up to a creditors' voluntary winding up and will proceed as if the statutory declaration of solvency had never been made by the company.[89]

A liquidator in a members' voluntary winding up, who, having formed the opinion that the company will not be able to pay its debts, fails to fulfil his duty to call a creditors' meeting and to disseminate the requisite notices in advance of such meeting, is guilty of an offence and liable to a fine.[90]

[9.027] Where a members' voluntary winding up continues for more than a year, the liquidator is under a duty to convene a general meeting of the company within three months of the end of the first year and each successive year.[91] The liquidator must lay before this meeting an account of his acts and dealings and the conduct of the winding up.[92] Within seven days after the meeting, the liquidator must send a copy of this account to the Registrar.[93] This duty may be a useful and effective means of ensuring that a liquidator is subject to supervision and checks in the discharge of his functions and that the company has an opportunity to become aware of, and address, any breaches of company law by the liquidator. The obligation to send an account of the winding up to the Registrar of Companies ensures that the conduct of the liquidation can also be subject to external oversight. This is underlined by the fact that the Registrar of

---

[84] CA 1963, s 261(1)(c), as substituted by CA 1990, s 129.

[85] CA 1963, s 261(1)(d), as substituted by CA 1990, s 129. This information must be furnished free of charge. The notice of the meeting must state that the liquidator is under an obligation to furnish such information. CA 1963, s 261(1).

[86] CA 1963, s 261(2)(a), as substituted by CA 1990, s 129.

[87] CA 1963, s 261(2)(b), as substituted by CA 1990, s 129.

[88] CA 1963, s 261(2)(c), as substituted by CA 1990, s 129.

[89] CA 1963, s 261(3), as substituted by CA 1990, s 129.

[90] CA 1963, s 261(7), as substituted by CA 1990, s 129 and amended by C(AA)A 2003, s 57 and Sch 2.

[91] CA 1963, s 262(1).

[92] CA 1963, s 262(1).

[93] CA 1963, s 262(1).

Companies is empowered to bring and prosecute proceedings for offences under CA 1963, s 262.[94] The offence that can be prosecuted under that section is set out in s 262(2), which provides that a liquidator who fails to call a general meeting of the company at the end of each year of the liquidation, or to lay an account of the winding up before that meeting, or to send a copy of the account to the Registrar of Companies, is guilty of an offence.[95]

[9.028] A liquidator in a members' voluntary winding up must call a general meeting of the company at the end of the liquidation which is governed by the terms of CA 1963, s 263. This requires the liquidator to do the following:

–   prepare an account of the winding up showing how it was conducted and how the company's property was disposed of;[96]

–   call a general meeting of the company;[97]

–   lay before the meeting the account of the winding up and provide explanations;[98]

–   at least 28 days before the meeting, publish a notice of the meeting in two daily newspapers circulating in the district in which the company's registered office is situated, specifying the time, place and object of the meeting;[99]

–   within one week after the meeting, send to the Registrar of Companies a copy of the account;[100]

–   within one week after the meeting, make a return to the Registrar of Companies of the holding of the meeting and its date;[101] and

–   in the event that there was not a quorum present at the meeting, make a return to the Registrar of Companies that the meeting was called and no quorum was present.[102]

[9.029] Upon receipt of this return and account, the Registrar of Companies registers them and, within three months from such registration, the company shall be deemed to

---

[94]   C(A)A 1982, s 16.

[95]   A liquidator in default under this section is liable, on summary conviction to a fine not exceeding €1904.61 and, for continued contravention, to a daily default fine not exceeding €63.49 and, on conviction on indictment, to a fine not exceeding €12,697.38 and, for continued contravention, to a daily default fine not exceeding €317.44. CA 1963, s 262(2), as amended by CA 1990, s 145 and CA 190, s 240(7) as inserted by CLEA 2001 s 104(c).

[96]   CA 1963, s 263(1).

[97]   CA 1963, s 263(1).

[98]   CA 1963, s 263(1).

[99]   CA 1963, s 263(2).

[100] CA 1963, s 263(3).

[101] CA 1963, s 263(3).

[102] CA 1963, s 263(3).

be dissolved.[103] The date of dissolution can be deferred by court order.[104] It is an offence for the liquidator to fail to call a general meeting or to fail to send a copy of the account or the return to the Registrar as required by s 263.[105]

[9.030] Where the liquidator has formed the view that the company is unable to pay its debts and has followed the procedures required by s 261,[106] the rules for convening meetings differ. One of the effects of summoning a creditors' meeting under s 261 is to convert a members' voluntary winding up into a creditors' voluntary winding up.[107] Where this occurs, the liquidator is obliged to apply the rules applicable to convening meetings in creditors' voluntary winding up, rather than the rules applicable to a members' voluntary winding up.[108] In the case of meetings which must be convened where a liquidation continues for longer than a year, as well as final meetings upon completion of the winding up, the provisions that apply to creditors' and members' voluntary liquidations are very similar. The most apparent difference is that a liquidator must summon meetings of the company and the creditors in a creditors' voluntary winding up, whereas only meetings of the company are necessary in a members' voluntary winding up. There is one deviation allowed in respect of a members' voluntary winding up that has been converted to a creditors' winding up. CA 1963, s 264(2) provides that:

> The liquidator shall not be required to summon a meeting of creditors under s 272 at the end of the first year from the commencement of the winding up, unless the meeting held under s 261 is held more than three months before the end of that year.

This essentially acknowledges the practical reality that, where a liquidation only becomes a creditors' winding up within three months or less before the end of the first year of the liquidation or indeed, after the expiry of the first year, it is not realistic, or not necessary, to require a meeting of the creditors to be summoned at the end of that year, as otherwise required by s 272. This provision does not provide a similar carve-out in respect of the obligation in s 272(1) to summon a meeting of creditors at the end of each successive year of the liquidation and this could be problematic in the event that a liquidator does not form the view that the company is not going to be able to pay its debts, within the meaning of s 261, until more than two years after the commencement of the liquidation, for example. In light of the fact that it is an offence for a liquidator to fail to comply with s 272, this could be invidious in practice.

---

[103] CA 1963, s 263(4).

[104] CA 1963, s 263(5): 'The court may, on the application of the liquidator or of any other person who appears to the court to be interested, make an order deferring the date at which the dissolution of the company is to take effect for such time as the court thinks fit.' Where this occurs, the applicant must within 24 days of the order, deliver a copy of the order to the Registrar for registration. Failure to comply with this requirement is an offence. CA 1963, s 263(6), as amended by C(A)A 1982, Sch 1.

[105] CA 1963, s 263(3) and (7), as amended by C(A)A 1982, Sch 1. An default under CA 1963, s 263 may also constitute and offence under CA 1990, s 145.

[106] See above para **[9.025]**.

[107] See above para **[9.026]**.

[108] CA 1963, s 264(1).

(iii) Creditors' voluntary liquidation

[9.031] The first meeting that must be held in respect of a creditors' voluntary liquidation, after the resolution has been passed by the company in general meeting, is the meeting of the creditors.[109] While this is not within the scope of the liquidator's duties, it is an important avenue for ensuring that there is transparency and vigilance in the initiation of the liquidation process. It also has a direct implication for a liquidator who was appointed by the company in general meeting. CA 1990, s 131(2), provides that the powers conferred on such a liquidator shall not be exercised before the holding of the creditors' meeting, except with sanction of the court.

The obligation to call a meeting of the creditors is imposed on the company and requires the company to call a meeting of the creditors for the day, or the day after, the meeting at which the resolution for voluntary winding up is to be proposed.[110] At least ten days before the meeting, the company is under specific duties to send notices by post to the creditors[111] and to cause notices of the meeting to be published once or more in two daily newspapers circulating in the district in which the registered office or principal place of business of the company is located.[112] The directors of the company must cause to be laid before the meeting a full statement of the position of the company's affairs, with a list of the creditors and their estimated claims[113] and must appoint a director who is under a duty to attend and preside over the creditors' meeting.[114]

It is an offence for the company or the directors, or any of them, to default in their duties with regard to the creditors' meeting under CA 1963, s 266.[115]

[9.032] A liquidator appointed in a creditors' voluntary winding up is under a duty to summon meetings of the company and of the creditors, in the event that the winding up process continues for more than a year. This obligation is framed in almost identical terms to the duty of a liquidator to summon general meetings of the company in a members' voluntary winding up that continues for more than a year.[116] In summary, a liquidator appointed by the creditors must convene a general meeting of the company and a meeting of the creditors within three months of the end of the first year and each successive year.[117] The liquidator must lay before these meetings an account of his acts and dealings and the conduct of the winding up.[118] Within seven days after the later of the two meetings, the liquidator must send a copy of this account to the Registrar.[119] As

---

109 CA 1963, s 266.

110 CA 1963, s 266(1).

111 CA 1963, s 266(1).

112 CA 1963, s 266(2), as amended by CA 1990, s 130.

113 CA 1963, s 266(3)(a).

114 CA 1963, s 266(3)(b) and (4).

115 CA 1963, s 266(6), as amended by C(AA)A 2003, s 57 and Sch 2.

116 See above para **[9.027]**.

117 CA 1963, s 272(1).

118 CA 1963, s 272(1).

119 CA 1963, s 272(1).

noted above, this duty may be an important means of ensuring that a liquidator is subject to supervision in the discharge of his functions and that the company and the creditors have an opportunity to detect and address any breaches of company law or of duty that may have been committed by the liquidator. The offence that can be prosecuted under that section is set out in s 272(2), which provides that a liquidator who fails to call a general meeting of the company or of the creditors at the end of each year of the liquidation, or to lay an account of the winding up before those meetings, or to send a copy of the account to the Registrar of Companies, is guilty of an offence.[120] The Registrar of Companies is empowered to bring and prosecute proceedings for offences under CA 1963, s 272.[121]

[9.033] When the winding up is complete, the liquidator must call a meeting of the company and of the creditors and he must lay before these meetings an account of the winding up, showing how it was conducted and how the company's property was disposed of, and provide explanations of this account.[122] The provisions governing the convening of these meetings and their consequences are almost identical to those that govern the final meeting in a members' voluntary winding up.[123] In summary, at least 28 days before these meetings, the liquidator must cause notices to be advertised in two daily newspapers circulated in the district in which the registered office of the company is located, stating the time, place and object of the meetings.[124] The liquidator must send a copy of the account, and make a return regarding the meetings, to the Registrar of Companies within one week of the later of the two meetings.[125] It is an offence for the liquidator to fail to call a meeting of the company or of the creditors, or to fail to send the account and make the return to the Registrar of Companies.[126]

(b) Duty to make returns

[9.034] The Companies Acts impose certain obligations on liquidators to make returns, statements, abstracts or accounts. Some aspects of these obligations have a direct bearing on the enforcement of company law. CA 1990, s 144 provides that where such a return, account, statement or abstract is required to be made, the liquidator making that return, account, statement or abstract must report as to whether, at that date, any past or present director, officer or member of the company has been disqualified or has been

---

[120] A liquidator in default under this section is liable, on summary conviction to a fine not exceeding €1,904.61 and, for continued contravention, to a daily default fine not exceeding €63.49 and, on conviction on indictment, to a fine not exceeding €12,697.38 and, for continued contravention, to a daily default fine not exceeding €317.44. CA 1963, s 272(2), as amended by CA 1990, s 145.

[121] CA(A) 1982, s 16.

[122] CA 1963, s 273(1).

[123] See above para **[9.028]**.

[124] CA 1963, s 273(2).

[125] CA 1963, s 273(3).

[126] CA 1963, s 273(3) and (7), as amended by C(AA)A 2003, s 57 and Sch 2.

declared personally liable for all or part of the debts of the company.[127] A failure to comply with this requirement is an offence.[128]

[9.035] Where an obligation to make a return, statement, abstract or account is imposed on a liquidator, and the liquidator fails to comply with that obligation, this constitutes an offence and the liquidator is liable to summary conviction or conviction on indictment.[129] In addition to providing for the imposition of fines, the Companies Acts provide for daily default fines in respect of continuing contraventions.

[9.036] Where there is such a default by a liquidator, a notice may also be served on the liquidator requiring him to comply with the obligation in question. In the event that the liquidator does not rectify the default within 14 days of receipt of the notice, or any greater period allowed for by the notice, the court may order the liquidator to remedy the default.[130] A member or creditor of the company may apply to court for such an order to be made and the order will specify the time within which the default must be made good.[131] As an additional penalty, the liquidator may be ordered to pay the costs of the application to court.[132]

(c) Duty to report to the DCE

[9.037] A liquidator was obliged to report certain matters to the court or the Registrar of Companies before the enactment of the CLEA 2001. However, in practical terms, the most important reporting obligation imposed on liquidators was created by CLEA 2001. CLEA 2001, s 56(1) imposes the following duty on liquidators:

> A liquidator of an insolvent company shall, within six months after his or her appointment or the commencement of this section, whichever is the later, and at intervals as required by the Director thereafter, provide to the Director a report in the prescribed form.[133]

This provision imposes very specific and onerous duties on a liquidator to report to the DCE in the course of the liquidation. In the first instance, a liquidator is obliged to

---

[127] CA 1990, s 144(1). This obligation is retained in the CLRG, General Scheme of Draft Companies Consolidation and Reform Bill 2007, Pt A11, Head 81.

[128] CA 1990, s 144(2).

[129] CA 1990, s 145(1).

[130] CA 1963, s 302(1), as amended by IFCMPA 2005 s 63. This is without prejudice to any offences that may be committed by the default in question. Section 302(3) provides, 'Nothing in this section shall be taken to prejudice the operation of any enactment imposing penalties on a liquidator in respect of any such default as aforesaid.'

[131] CA 1963, s 302(1).

[132] CA 1963, s 302(2).

[133] This provision is substantially reproduced in the CLRG, General Scheme of the Draft Companies Consolidation and Reform Bill 2007, Pt A11, Head 113, subject to the amendment that it applies to all creditors' voluntary windings up and official liquidations, with no stipulation that the company must be insolvent. This removes the requirement for the liquidator to assess the company's solvency at the outset. See www.clrg.org.

report to the DCE within six months of his appointment.[134] This report must adopt a particular format and must contain very particular information.[135] A liquidator can also be required to report to the DCE at such intervals as the DCE may require.[136] A liquidator who fails to comply with these reporting requirements is guilty of an offence.[137] Section 56 also imposes obligations on liquidators to apply to court for the restriction of directors of the company in liquidation, unless relieved of such obligation by the DCE.[138] Failure to comply with this obligation also constitutes an offence.[139]

[9.038] There are a number of points to note regarding the reporting obligation created by CLEA 2001, s 56. Some of the issues that are raised by this provision will now be considered under the following headings:

   (i)   Scope of obligation to report:

        1.   Insolvent companies;

        2.   Voluntary liquidations;

        3.   Provisional liquidations;

        4.   Temporal scope.

   (ii)   Information required:

        1.   Liquidator details;

        2.   Company details;

        3.   Company directors;

        4.   Statement of affairs, accounts and report to creditors;

        5.   Proceedings;

        6.   Final report;

        7.   Liquidator's statement.

   (iii)   Additional reports.

   (iv)   Sanctions:

        1.   Prosecution;

---

[134] There was particular provision made for the commencement of this section to ensure existing liquidations were brought within its ambit. This is addressed below. See para **[9.047]**.

[135] See further below paras **[9.048]** to **[9.076]**.

[136] CLEA 2001, s 56(1).

[137] CLEA 2001, s 56(3).

[138] 'A liquidator of an insolvent company shall, not earlier than three months nor later than five months (or such later time as the court may allow and advises the DCE) after the date on which he or she has provided to the DCE a report under sub-s (1), apply to the court for the restriction under s 150 of the Act of 1990 of each of the directors of the company, unless the DCE has relieved the liquidator of the obligation to make such an application.' CLEA 2001, s 56(2).

[139] CLEA 2001, s 56(3).

> 2.   Administrative fine;
>
> 3.   Court order.
>
> (v)   Approach of ODCE.

(i) Scope of obligation to report

1. INSOLVENT COMPANIES

[9.039] Section 56 only applies to insolvent companies in liquidation. This would therefore include creditors' liquidations and official liquidations, where the company was unable to pay its debts as they fell due at the date of the liquidation.[140] The definition of a company being unable to pay its debts is set out in CA 1963, s 214.

2. VOLUNTARY LIQUIDATIONS

[9.040] With regard to voluntary liquidations, there may be some difficulty in determining the applicability of s 56. As noted above, a liquidator in a members' voluntary winding up may form the view that the company is in fact unable to pay its debts and may summon a creditors' meeting to address this issue.[141] There is no guarantee that such a realisation will occur within six months, or any other defined time frame, of the appointment of the liquidators. This is acknowledged by the terms of CA 1963, s 264(2), which provides that:

> The liquidator shall not be required to summon a meeting of creditors under s 272
> at the end of the first year from the commencement of the winding up, unless the
> meeting held under s 261 is held more than three months before the end of that
> year.

As noted above, this provision envisages situations in which a liquidation may only be converted to a creditors' winding up within the final three months of the first year of the liquidation.[142] Section 56, on the other hand, defines a single time frame within which the report must be issued to the DCE and does not accommodate situations in which a members' voluntary liquidation may convert into a creditors' voluntary liquidation. The insolvent status of a company is not necessarily known at the date of the appointment of the liquidator and imposing the obligation to report on a liquidator within six months of his appointment may be unworkable in some situations.

The fact that s 56 envisages each liquidator making an initial report and then such other reports as the DCE may require confirms the interpretation that the obligation to make the initial report is not discretionary or capable of being substituted by later reports. If the obligation to make the initial report and the subsequent reports were framed in the

---

[140] The interpretation of s 56 as applying to both voluntary and compulsory liquidations was recommended by the McDowell Report: 'It is recommended that the law should provide that the liquidators of all insolvent companies (whether compulsory or creditors' voluntary) should be required to bring an application under s 150(1) of the 1990 Act ...'. *Report of the Working Group on Company Law Compliance and Enforcement* (1998) at para 6.41.

[141] CA 1963, s 261, as substituted by CA 1990, s 129. See above paras **[9.025]**–**[9.026]**.

[142] See above para **[9.030]**.

alternative, it would permit liquidators of companies, the winding up of which is converted from a members' voluntary winding up to a creditors' winding up during the liquidation, to file reports as may be required by the DCE, after the date of such conversion, without regard being had to the six month time limit for the initial report. Section 56 does not allow of this interpretation.

[9.041] The ODCE has considered this issue in the context of the date from which the obligation to report runs and concluded that:

> If a liquidator in a member's voluntary liquidation discovers following his or her appointment as liquidator that the company is insolvent, the obligation to file a report exists from the date of his or her appointment as liquidator and not from the date of determination of the insolvency of the company.[143]

As noted above, this could be impractical and unworkable where the discovery of the company's insolvency occurs at some date later than the expiry of six months after the liquidator's appointment. Moreover, the imposition of such a strict time limit exposes a liquidator to potential liability for the commission of the offence of non-compliance with the obligation to report under s 56(1), when he was not and could not have been aware of the existence of that obligation.

3. PROVISIONAL LIQUIDATIONS

[9.042] Where a provisional liquidator is appointed to an insolvent company, it may be questioned whether and when the duty to file a s 56 report arises. The DCE has expressed the following view on this topic:

> 'In the case of an official liquidator whose appointment was preceded by appointment as provisional liquidator, the official liquidator will be required to file the report within the period specified following the date of his or her appointment as provisional liquidator.'[144]

The ODCE has further observed that, in circumstances where a provisional liquidator of an insolvent company continues to act as such six months after appointment, the provisional liquidator must comply with the obligation to file the report within the six month time limit.[145]

[9.043] This treatment of the effect of the appointment of a provisional liquidator is consistent with the view of the role of provisional liquidators in Irish company law in

---

[143] Decision Notice D/2002/3: 'The Liquidation-Related Functions of the Director of Corporate Enforcement' at para 3.5. See also Consultation Paper C/2002/3 'The Liquidation-Related Functions of the Director of Corporate Enforcement'.

[144] Decision Notice D/2002/3: 'The Liquidation-Related Functions of the Director of Corporate Enforcement' at para 3.5. See also Consultation Paper C/2002/3 'The Liquidation-Related Functions of the Director of Corporate Enforcement'.

[145] 'Where a provisional liquidator is appointed and an appointment as official liquidator has not been made within six months of his or her appointment as provisional liquidator, then the provisional liquidator will be required under s 56 to file the prescribed report.' Consultation Paper C/2002/3 'The Liquidation-Related Functions of the Director of Corporate Enforcement'.

some respects, but not in others. First, the Companies Acts regard an official winding up of a company to have commenced 'at the time of the presentation of the petition for the winding up'.[146] This has the consequence that the liquidation can be viewed as commencing at the time of the appointment of a provisional liquidator and before the appointment of the official liquidator. It is consistent with this approach that the time for filing a report under CLEA 2001, s 56, should run from the date of the appointment of the provisional liquidator, whether or not an official liquidator has been appointed.

However, the effect of the appointment of a provisional liquidator is not always so clear. It cannot be taken for granted that the appointment of a provisional liquidator will result in the winding up of the company or the appointment of an official liquidator. This is evident from the terms of CA 1963, s 216(1), which confirms that:

> On hearing a winding-up petition, the court may dismiss it, or adjourn the hearing
> conditionally or unconditionally, or make any interim order, or any other order that
> it thinks fit, but the court shall not refuse to make a winding-up order on the
> ground only that the assets of the company have been mortgaged to an amount
> equal to or in excess of those assets, or that the company has no assets.

[9.044] If there is a chance that the appointment of a provisional liquidator will not be followed by an order winding up the company, the justification for requiring a provisional liquidator to file a report under CLEA 2001, s 56, or for allowing time to run from the date of the appointment of the provisional liquidator, is not entirely clear. This is reinforced by the fact that the rationale for the appointment of a provisional liquidator is usually to prevent the imminent dissipation of the company's assets.[147] The role of a provisional liquidator can also be distinguished from that of an official liquidator. CA 1963, s 226(2) provides that, 'Where a liquidator is provisionally appointed by the court, the court may limit and restrict his powers by the order appointing him.' The obligation to file a report under s 56 and to accumulate the information necessary to file such a report, could not override the power of the court to limit the scope of the powers of the provisional liquidator. In addition, if the powers of a provisional are capable of being limited by court order, it may not be realistic to expect provisional liquidators to file reports as required by CLEA 2001, s 56. This also renders it potentially unjust to cause the time for filing a report under s 56 to run from the date of the appointment of a provisional liquidator, where that liquidator may have had limited powers and where the official liquidator may only be appointed close to the expiry of the six month time limit for submitting the report under s 56.

[9.045] A final concern that can be voiced regarding the rule that the time for filing a report under s 56 runs from the date of the appointment of the provisional liquidator, even against a subsequently-appointed official liquidator, is that there can be no grounds for assuming that an official liquidator appointed to a company will be the same individual as the provisional liquidator formerly appointed to the same company. To back-date the obligation to file a report under CLEA 2001, s 56, to the appointment of the provisional liquidator may operate unfairly and unworkably against a newly appointed official liquidator, who will have to bear responsibility for work done before

---

[146] CA 1963, s 220(2). See further *Re Eurofoods IFSC Ltd* [2004] 4 IR 370.

[147] See *Re Eurofoods IFSC Ltd* [2004] 4 IR 370, 406. See further below para **[9.046]**.

his involvement with the company commenced. Moreover, an official liquidator may be appointed to replace a provisional liquidator close to the expiry of the six month time limit for filing a s 56 report. A liquidator who has acted as such for no more than a matter of weeks, could be faced with a choice between filing a report with inadequate time to satisfy himself of the necessary information and inadequate time to form the views required, or risking prosecution for the offence of non-compliance with CLEA 2001, s 56.

[9.046] Considerable judicial attention has recently been paid to the legal effect of the appointment of a provisional liquidator under Irish company law and EU insolvency law.[148] In *Re Eurofoods IFSC Ltd* the High Court and the Supreme Court were called upon to consider, among other matters, whether the appointment of a provisional liquidator represented the opening of insolvency proceedings, within the meaning of EU insolvency law.[149] In that case, two sets of insolvency proceedings were commenced in respect of the same company, one set of proceedings in Italy and another in Ireland. The EU insolvency regulation addresses the issue of where insolvency proceedings are deemed to have first commenced and which state should have jurisdiction with regard to those proceedings. In the High Court, Kelly J relied upon the fact that the EU insolvency regulation categorised provisional liquidators as 'liquidators' for the purposes of that regulation and the fact that the appointment of a provisional liquidator clearly involved a judgment opening insolvency proceedings, within the meaning of the regulation. He concluded:

> '... it is in my view beyond argument that for the purposes of the Regulation a decision of the Irish High Court appointing a provisional liquidator is a judgment in relation to the opening of insolvency proceedings within the meaning of Art 3.1.'[150]

In the Supreme Court, having heard submissions on when insolvency proceedings should be deemed to have opened for the purposes of the EU insolvency regulation, the Court considered the role of a provisional liquidator under Irish company law. Fennelly J, delivering the judgment of the Court, stated, 'The grounds for appointment of a Provisional Liquidator are usually that the assets of the Company are in danger and that it is necessary to take action to prevent them from being dissipated.'[151] The Court further noted that, 'The legal effect of the appointment of a Provisional Liquidator is that the directors of the company no longer have any power to deal with assets of the Company covered by the order of the court.'[152] However, an important aspect of the effect of the appointment of a provisional liquidator, which was noted in the Supreme Court in *Re Eurofoods IFSC Ltd*, is that the appointment of a provisional liquidator does not necessarily mean that a winding up order will in fact be made.[153] The Supreme Court concluded that, whether the appointment of a provisional liquidator can be regarded as

---

[148] See *Re Eurofoods IFSC Ltd* [2004] 4 IR 370.

[149] Council Regulation (EC) No 1346/2000.

[150] See *Re Eurofoods IFSC Ltd* [2004] 4 IR 370 at 387.

[151] *Re Eurofoods IFSC Ltd* [2004] 4 IR 370 at 406.

[152] *Re Eurofoods IFSC Ltd* [2004] 4 IR 370 at 406.

[153] *Re Eurofoods IFSC Ltd* [2004] 4 IR 370 at 406.

opening insolvency proceedings requires interpretation of provisions of the EU insolvency regulation, and a preliminary ruling of the European Court of Justice was therefore sought on that question, among others. The ECJ interpreted the opening of insolvency proceedings as involving the divestment of a debtor of his power of management over his assets, and as such could be dated back to the appointment of a provisional liquidator.[154]

4. TEMPORAL SCOPE

[9.047] Section 56 was brought into force in three phases. First, the Company Law Enforcement Act 2001 (Winding-up and Insolvency Provisions) (Commencement) Order 2002, provided that s 56 came into force on 1 June 2002 in respect of all liquidators who were appointed on or after 1 June 2002.[155] Secondly, the Order provided that s 56 came into force on 1 June 2002, in respect of liquidators who were appointed between 1 June 2001, and 1 June 2002, where the liquidations were still ongoing on 1 June 2002.[156]

The third phase of the introduction of CLEA 2001, s 56 was effected by the Company Law Enforcement Act 2001 (Winding-up and Insolvency Provisions) (Commencement) Order 2003.[157] This Order provides that s 56 came into force on 1 June 2003, in respect of all liquidators of insolvent companies who were appointed between 1 January 2000, and 1 June 2001, where those liquidations were still ongoing on 1 June 2003.[158]

For the purposes of both commencement orders, a liquidation is deemed not to be ongoing on a particular date, and therefore not to be subject to s 56, if an order has been made under CA 1963, s 249(1) or if the meetings required by CA 1963, s 273(1) have been held, before the relevant commencement date. It is not necessary for the final statutory return to have been made to the Companies Registration Office or, in the case of voluntary liquidations, for the three months after the registration of the return, that is necessary for the dissolution of the company, to have lapsed.[159]

Where s 56 applies to a liquidation that is ongoing at the date of its commencement, the liquidator must file the report within six months of the applicable commencement date.

(ii) Information required

[9.048] The information that must be contained in a liquidator's report is not defined in s 56. That provision merely requires the reports to be in the 'prescribed form'. This is

---

[154] C–341/04 *Re Eurofoods Ltd* [2006] ECR I-03813, paras 54–55.

[155] SI 263/2002.

[156] Company Law Enforcement Act 2001 (Winding-up and Insolvency Provisions) (Commencement) Order 2002 (SI 263/2002).

[157] SI 217/2003.

[158] Company Law Enforcement Act 2001 (Winding-up and Insolvency Provisions) (Commencement) Order 2003 (SI 217/2003).

[159] See Decision Notice D/2002/3: 'The Liquidation-Related Functions of the Director of Corporate Enforcement' at para 3.7.

highly ambiguous and could be seen as unfairly broad and mutable. However, the DCE has produced a form, with guidance notes, which set out the information required and means of presentation of a s 56 report. This form has been 'prescribed', within the meaning of s 56, by means of statutory instrument.[160]

The type of information which is required ranges from the basic, such as the name of the company and its directors, to the more probing, such as information concerning the grounds on which the liquidator may propose to apply for the restriction or disqualification of directors of the company. The DCE describes the information that must be included in the report form as an attempt:

> '... to strike a reasonable balance between: providing information on directors to a sufficiently high level of detail to enable the ODCE to discharge its functions effectively and efficiently and minimising the demands on the liquidator.'[161]

It is entirely logical that the information to be contained in the liquidator's report should facilitate the discharge of the functions of the ODCE regarding the investigation, detection and prosecution of breaches of company law.[162] The description of this information as relating to directors exclusively may be too limited, as information that comes to light in the course of the liquidation may disclose breaches of company law other than breaches by directors. In addition, the requirement that the level of detail be sufficiently precise to enable the ODCE to discharge its functions may be too onerous. Finally, the stated objective of minimising the demands on the liquidator does not sit easily with the introduction and formulation of CLEA 2001, s 56. The obligation this provision imposes on a liquidator to file a report with the DCE within six months of appointment and thereafter as may be required, is undeniably an increased burden on a liquidator and adds considerably to the tasks that a liquidator must undertake. The proposal that the scope of the information that a liquidator must include in a report could minimise the demands on the liquidator does not seem entirely feasible, particularly not if such information is intended to be sufficiently detailed to facilitate the discharge of its functions by the ODCE.

[9.049] With regard to the objectives of a s 56 report, the DCE has described the function of the report form as follows:

> 'The essential purpose of the Report Form is to distinguish the circumstances of honest and responsible business failure (which do not merit any form of sanction of the company directors) from those where directors have known or ought to have known that the company was insolvent or that they were otherwise conducting the company's business affairs in a manner which was contrary to the interests of creditors, other parties or the general public interest.'[163]

---

[160] Company Law Enforcement Act 2001 (Section 56) Regulations 2002 (SI 2002/324).

[161] Decision Notice D/2002/3: 'The Liquidation-Related Functions of the Director of Corporate Enforcement' at para 4.1. See also Consultation Paper C/2002/3 'The Liquidation-Related Functions of the Director of Corporate Enforcement'.

[162] See CLEA 2001, s 12(1). See further Ch **12**.

[163] Decision Notice D/2002/3: 'The Liquidation-Related Functions of the Director of Corporate Enforcement' at para 4.5. See also Consultation Paper C/2002/3 'The Liquidation-Related Functions of the Director of Corporate Enforcement'.

This description of the function of the report suggests that it is less an overall review and analysis of the liquidation than an attempt to ascertain the level of blameworthiness, if any, of the directors of the company, for its insolvency and consequent liquidation.

[9.050] The report is divided into seven sections. The headings are:

1. Liquidator details;

2. Company details;

3. Company directors;

4. Statement of affairs, accounts and report to creditors;

5. Proceedings;

6. Final report; and

7. Liquidator's statement.

These are now examined in detail below.

1. LIQUIDATOR DETAILS

[9.051] Particular information about the liquidator must be furnished in the first section of a report under CLEA 2001, s 56. This information must be contained in the initial report filed under s 56 and in any subsequent reports, if changes in these details have occurred.[164] The information required is straightforward. The liquidator must state his name, address, telephone number and other contact details, such as fax number and email address.[165] The liquidator must also state the name of the firm and professional body to which he belongs, if applicable.[166] With regard to the liquidation, the liquidator must state the date of his appointment as liquidator and whether the liquidation is an official or a creditor's voluntary winding up.[167] In a creditor's winding up, the liquidator must state specifically whether he was nominated by the members or the creditors.[168] If the liquidator has vested a member of staff with responsibility for the liquidation, he must furnish the name of this individual and may furnish this employee's contact details in substitution for the liquidator's own contact details.[169]

---

[164] Company Law Enforcement Act 2001 (Section 56) Regulations 2002 (SI 2002/324).

[165] Company Law Enforcement Act 2001 (Section 56) Regulations 2002 (SI 2002/324), items 1, 3, 9.

[166] Company Law Enforcement Act 2001 (Section 56) Regulations 2002 (SI 2002/324), items 2 and 4.

[167] Company Law Enforcement Act 2001 (Section 56) Regulations 2002 (SI 2002/324), items 5 and 7.

[168] Company Law Enforcement Act 2001 (Section 56) Regulations 2002 (SI 2002/324), item 6. See above paras **[9.004]** to **[9.006]**.

[169] Company Law Enforcement Act 2001 (Section 56) Regulations 2002 (SI 2002/324), items 8 and 9.

2. COMPANY DETAILS

[9.052] The second section of a report under CLEA 2001, s 56, must contain certain information about the company. This information must be included in the initial report and, if changes in the details have occurred, it must also be included in any subsequent report. The information required varies from basic information to more probing material. The basic information that must be provided includes the company's business or trading name, the address of the registered office[170] and the principal trading address of the company, and any other names or addresses which the company used in the 12 months prior to the liquidation.[171] The report must also state the number of employees;[172] the company's turnover for the three financial years preceding the commencement of the liquidation;[173] the date on which the company started trading; and the date on which the company ceased trading, if applicable.[174] The statement of turnover for the three financial years must be based on the accounts that are required to be attached to the report form by virtue of section four of the report form.[175]

[9.053] The liquidator must also state the nature of the company's business and he must describe the company's activities.[176] The company's business must be defined, according to the report form, by reference to coding system that is employed by the Companies Registration Office. The report form formulates the question as follows: 'please state the most relevant NACE Classification at the date of commencement of the liquidation'.[177] In the draft report form prepared by the DCE the question was

---

[170] The registered address must be as it is registered with the Companies Registration Office. See ODCE, 'Guidance Notes for the Completion of Liquidator's Reports under section 56 of the Company Law Enforcement Act 2001.'

[171] Company Law Enforcement Act 2001 (Section 56) Regulations 2002 (SI 2002/324), items 10, 11, 12, 13.

[172] Company Law Enforcement Act 2001 (Section 56) Regulations 2002 (SI 2002/324), item 15. According to the Draft Notice, what was required was the average number of employees over the three years before the winding up commenced. The Report Form, as introduced, refers to the number of employees at the date of the commencement of the liquidation. However, the Guidance Notes states that, 'if this figure is significantly different from employment numbers in the company over the past three years, you should indicate this fact and explain the variance.' ODCE, 'Guidance Notes for the Completion of Liquidator's Reports under section 56 of the Company Law Enforcement Act 2001.'

[173] Company Law Enforcement Act 2001 (Section 56) Regulations 2002 (SI 2002/324), item 16.

[174] Company Law Enforcement Act 2001 (Section 56) Regulations 2002 (SI 2002/324), item 17.

[175] This is stated expressly in the ODCE, 'Guidance Notes for the Completion of Liquidator's Reports under section 56 of the Company Law Enforcement Act 2001.' See further below paras **[9.062]** to **[9.064]**.

[176] Company Law Enforcement Act 2001 (Section 56) Regulations 2002 (SI 2002/324), item 14.

[177] Company Law Enforcement Act 2001 (Section 56) Regulations 2002 (SI 2002/324), item 14(a).

formulated differently. It required the nature of the company's business to be described using the most relevant classification, as outlined in the Guidance Notes.[178] The merit of allowing flexibility in the system of designation used is obvious and it is not clear why that change was introduced to the Report Form prescribed for reports under CLEA 2001, s 56. In any case, the NACE classification system is annexed to the Guidance Notes, which describes this system as 'the business classification system used by the Central Statistics Office'.[179] In addition to stating the nature of the company's business, the liquidator must also provide 'a precise description of the Company's activities that the Company was engaged in at the date of commencement of the liquidation.'[180] According to the Guidance Notes, what is required here is a narrative summary of the company's business, describing the company's day-to-day activities at the time of the commencement of the liquidation.[181] In a large company with diverse operations, this summary could be very lengthy, particularly if precision is required, as the report form suggests.

[9.054] A further category of information about the company which the liquidator must provide relates to certain types of intervention that may have occurred in respect of the company prior to the liquidation. If there has been any examinership, receivership, scheme of arrangement or liquidation of the company in the 36 months before the submission of the report, this fact must be stated in the second section of the report.[182] The report must also contain particular information regarding such proceedings, including the type of proceedings; the name and address of the office holder so appointed; the dates of appointment; and termination of appointment.[183] Copies of notices of the appointment of such office holders and reports compiled by them during the 36 month period before the commencement of the winding up must also be furnished.[184]

[9.055] On a more elaborate level, the liquidator must state his opinion as to the reasons for the liquidation of the company and he must cite the evidence in support of this opinion on a separate sheet.[185] The report form, as prescribed by statutory instrument,

---

[178] See draft Report Form, attached to ODCE, Consultation Paper C/2002/3 'The Liquidation-Related Functions of the Director of Corporate Enforcement'.

[179] ODCE, 'Guidance Notes for the Completion of Liquidator's Reports under section 56 of the Company Law Enforcement Act 2001.'

[180] Company Law Enforcement Act 2001 (Section 56) Regulations 2002 (SI 2002/324), item 14(b).

[181] ODCE, 'Guidance Notes for the Completion of Liquidator's Reports under section 56 of the Company Law Enforcement Act 2001.'

[182] Company Law Enforcement Act 2001 (Section 56) Regulations 2002 (SI 2002/324), item 19.

[183] Company Law Enforcement Act 2001 (Section 56) Regulations 2002 (SI 2002/324), item 19.

[184] Company Law Enforcement Act 2001 (Section 56) Regulations 2002 (SI 2002/324), item 19.

[185] Company Law Enforcement Act 2001 (Section 56) Regulations 2002 (SI 2002/324), item 18.

varies from the wording proposed by the DCE in this regard. The draft report form required the liquidator to 'specify in detail (on a separate sheet) the reasons for the liquidation of the company'.[186] Rather than being obliged to state definitively the reasons for a liquidation, the report form, as prescribed, requires a liquidator to offer his opinion, supported by evidence, as to the reasons for the liquidation. The approach that was adopted, it is submitted, is entirely more sensible, as there could be many alternative or cumulative reasons for a liquidation, and a variety of valid views as to why it occurred.

The Guidance Notes provide more detailed analysis of the type of information that is required to support a liquidator's opinion as to the reasons for a liquidation. The Notes state, 'This information should specify the particular circumstances, including the actions of the company, its officers and senior executives, which led to the company's liquidation.'[187] This suggests that while the evidence is required as support for the opinion of the liquidator, rather than as evidence of affirmatively established facts, the information itself must specify 'particular circumstances ... which led to the company's liquidation'. This seems to require a particularly high level of direct evidence, rather than such evidence as may be sufficient to support the conclusion reached by the liquidator. While it is clear that the liquidator should not form unsubstantiated views as to the reason for a company's liquidation, it is by no means clear that an opinion properly formed will be based on evidence of particular circumstances which definitively lead to the liquidation. The caveat that a liquidator can state his opinion as to reasons for the liquidation, rather than stating the reasons for the liquidation definitively, acknowledges that such unequivocal conclusions may not be feasible. If a liquidation can be explained by reference to several factors and varying views are possible as to its ultimate cause, the liquidator may form a valid opinion as to the cause of the liquidation, which may not be capable of proof by reference to specific circumstances which uncontrovertibly led to the liquidation.

This concern over the level of evidence that must be presented by a liquidator in support of his opinion for the reasons for the liquidation, is heightened when one considers the following direction that is contained in the Guidance Notes: 'It is not sufficient to make general references to "poor market conditions" or "loss of customer base", etc.'[188]

The liquidator clearly bears a heavy burden to establish why the liquidation occurred, to form an opinion as to the reasons for the liquidation, and to produce firm and specific data in support of this conclusion. This is an onerous task, particularly if the liquidation is one which is expected to last considerably longer than six months. In such instances, to oblige the liquidator to spend time and effort assessing the cause of the liquidation and accumulating evidence in support of his opinion in this regard, may be seen as too backward-looking and as absorbing the liquidator's time, which could better be spent administering the liquidation of the company. This concern is heightened by the fact that

---

[186] Consultation Paper C/2002/3 'The Liquidation-Related Functions of the Director of Corporate Enforcement'.

[187] ODCE, 'Guidance Notes for the Completion of Liquidator's Reports under section 56 of the Company Law Enforcement Act 2001.'

[188] ODCE, 'Guidance Notes for the Completion of Liquidator's Reports under section 56 of the Company Law Enforcement Act 2001.'

the liquidator is under separate and well-established duties to report the commission of any offences of which he becomes aware in the course of the liquidation.[189] The benefit of assessing where responsibility lies for a company's liquidation is not obvious, particularly as any wrongdoing associated with the cause of the company's liquidation should be detected by other means.

[9.056] In section two of the report, the liquidator must also furnish certain information which involves the liquidator directly in the detection and reporting of suspected breaches of the law of taxation. In particular, the liquidator must state whether there is any deficiency in the company's tax affairs or the payment of taxes by the company.[190] If such deficiencies do exist, the liquidator must state the periods for which the returns are overdue and the amounts that are due.

[9.057] There is a final category of information that a liquidator must furnish in section two of a report under CLEA 2001, s 56. This category relates to the issue of so-called 'shadow directors'. As has been seen, a 'shadow director' is defined in CA 1990 as '… a person in accordance with whose directions or instructions the directors of a company are accustomed to act'.[191] A liquidator must state whether there is any information which would lead to the belief that the company had a shadow director.[192] If such a belief does exist, the liquidator must furnish the name and address of the shadow director and must state what that person's role in the company was. In this section, the liquidator must finally state whether the shadow director has demonstrated that he has acted honestly and responsibly in relation to the conduct of the company's affairs.[193] All information relevant to this issue, including details of the factors that support the conclusion reached, must be provided. It seems curious that this category of information was included under the heading of 'company details' rather than 'director details', as was proposed in the Consultation Paper of the ODCE,[194] but the difference is not one of substance.

3. COMPANY DIRECTORS

[9.058] In the third section of the report, the liquidator must furnish certain information about any persons who appear to the liquidator to be, or to have been, directors of the company during the 12 months before the commencement of the winding up.[195] The

---

[189] See below paras **[9.086]** to **[9.100]**.

[190] Company Law Enforcement Act 2001 (Section 56) Regulations 2002 (SI 2002/324), item 20.

[191] CA 1990, s 27(1). This can include individuals or bodies corporate. Such persons are treated as directors of the company within the meaning of CA 1990. CA 1990, s 27(1). See Ch **16**.

[192] Company Law Enforcement Act 2001 (Section 56) Regulations 2002 (SI 2002/324), item 21.

[193] Company Law Enforcement Act 2001 (Section 56) Regulations 2002 (SI 2002/324), item 21. See further below paras **[9.060]** to **[9.061]** regarding the interpretation of 'honestly and responsibly' within the meaning of the Companies Acts. See also Ch **17**.

[194] Consultation Paper C/2002/3 'The Liquidation-Related Functions of the Director of Corporate Enforcement'.

[195] Company Law Enforcement Act 2001 (Section 56) Regulations 2002 (SI 2002/324), item 22.

liquidator must furnish the requisite information separately in respect of each of the directors. The information that is required is largely straightforward, such as the name, address, date of birth, PPS number of the director, the period during which they served as director and their role in the company.[196] The description of the director's role should state whether the director performed an executive function in the company and the extent to which he was involved in the day-to-day conduct of the company's affairs.[197]

[9.059] The liquidator must also furnish full details of any other directorships which the directors held during the 12 months before the commencement of the winding up. The details that must be furnished include the other companies' registration numbers, the dates of appointment of the directors to such companies and the dates of termination of such appointment, if applicable.[198] The liquidator must state expressly if the companies of which these directors also held directorships operated in a similar sector to the company under liquidation. According to the Guidance Notes, this information should be obtained directly from the director in question and it is designed 'to enable the ODCE to consider if a pattern of business failures exists with this individual'.[199]

[9.060] The most important statement that must be included in section three of the report, from the perspective of company law enforcement, is a statement as to whether the director has demonstrated to the liquidator that he acted honestly and responsibly in relation to the conduct of the company's affairs. This statement must be accompanied by details of the factors which support the conclusion reached by the liquidator. The Guidance Notes are instructive with regard to the type of conduct which the DCE may consider to be indicative of a director acting honestly and responsibly. The Guidance Notes state that the liquidator must form this opinion on the basis of his investigation of the company's affairs, as well as on the basis of information received from the directors, but not exclusively on the basis of information received from the directors or others. The DCE will take into account the factors relied upon by the liquidator in deciding whether or not to seek the restriction of the company's directors.[200] However, the Guidance Notes do not state expressly that the DCE will take into account the opinion of the liquidator in this regard. The Decision Notice prepared by the ODCE casts some light on the weight that the liquidator's opinion is likely to carry. The Notice states:

> 'The Director will consider relieving liquidators of the obligation to make application to the High Court for the restriction of a director, where the liquidator makes a clear and unambiguous statement to the effect that the company director

---

[196] Company Law Enforcement Act 2001 (Section 56) Regulations 2002 (SI 2002/324), item 22.

[197] See ODCE, 'Guidance Notes for the Completion of Liquidator's Reports under section 56 of the Company Law Enforcement Act 2001.'

[198] Company Law Enforcement Act 2001 (Section 56) Regulations 2002 (SI 2002/324), item 22.

[199] ODCE, 'Guidance Notes for the Completion of Liquidator's Reports under section 56 of the Company Law Enforcement Act 2001.'

[200] ODCE, 'Guidance Notes for the Completion of Liquidator's Reports under section 56 of the Company Law Enforcement Act 2001.'

has demonstrated that he or she acted honestly and responsibly in the conduct of the company's affairs.'[201]

The liquidator must therefore make a clear and unambiguous statement regarding a director's conduct before the DCE will necessarily take the view of the liquidator into account. Moreover, even in such instances, the DCE does not consider himself to be bound by the opinion of the liquidation in this regard. The Decision Notice states expressly that the Director is under no obligation to accept the liquidator's opinion.[202] The fact that the decision as to whether or not a director has demonstrated that he acted honestly and responsibly is within the exclusive remit of the DCE, rather than that of the liquidator, is reinforced by the following statement in the Decision Notice on this topic:

> 'It should also be understood by liquidators that the Director might be in possession of other information which may be relevant to a decision of the Court on whether or not a restriction declaration should be made. If, for instance, such information suggested that the failure of the company was part of a pattern of failed companies by the directors in question, he would be likely to seek to bring the information in question to the Court for its consideration.'[203]

The DCE clearly reserves the right to require an application for the restriction of directors to be taken where the DCE believes the information available to him warrants it, whatever the source of the information, and irrespective of the view of the liquidator in this regard.

[9.061] The Guidance Notes contain a list of the type of situations in which it is unlikely that the DCE would relieve a liquidator of the obligation to seek the restriction of a company's directors. This list is a non-exhaustive one and includes the following situations:

- the commission of suspected breaches of the CA 1963–2006 by a director, including failures to keep proper books of account;

- a director placing his or her personal interests ahead of the company's, including discharging liabilities to a bank to which he or she has given personal guarantees prior to liquidation;

- a director purchasing company assets below market value, particularly when the company's financial position was fragile;

- misapplication or retention of company money or property by a director;

- a company continuing to trade while insolvent and when the director knew or ought to have known that the company was insolvent;

---

[201] Decision Notice D/2002/3: 'The Liquidation-Related Functions of the Director of Corporate Enforcement' at para 5.8. See also Consultation Paper C/2002/3 'The Liquidation-Related Functions of the Director of Corporate Enforcement'.

[202] Decision Notice D/2002/3: 'The Liquidation-Related Functions of the Director of Corporate Enforcement' at para 5.8. See also Consultation Paper C/2002/3 'The Liquidation-Related Functions of the Director of Corporate Enforcement'.

[203] Decision Notice D/2002/3: 'The Liquidation-Related Functions of the Director of Corporate Enforcement' at para 5.8. See also Consultation Paper C/2002/3 'The Liquidation-Related Functions of the Director of Corporate Enforcement'.

- a company continuing to trade without reasonable prospect of paying creditors' claims, especially where a company accepts consumer prepayments/deposits while insolvent;

- a selective discharge of company debts by the company in the period prior to liquidation and a consequent failure to discharge debts due to State Authorities;

- evidence of past 'phoenix syndrome' practices, such as acquisition of significant assets from another company in a similar business sector, close in time to the failure of that other company;

- evidence of suspected future 'phoenix syndrome' practices, such as unexplained disposals of assets or transfers of staff to another company particularly during 12 months prior to the commencement of the liquidation;

- evidence of an undervaluing or overvaluing of transactions;

- a company director failing to co-operate with, or refusing to give reasonable assistance to, the liquidator.

The law governing the definition of what is considered to be honest and responsible conduct on the part of the directors of a company in insolvent liquidation is expansive and is considered in detail in Ch **17**.[204] Liquidators should be aware of the general legal principles in this regard when forming their views as to whether or not a director demonstrated honest and responsible conduct.

4. STATEMENT OF AFFAIRS, ACCOUNTS AND REPORT TO CREDITORS

[9.062] The fourth section of a report filed under CLEA 2001, s 56, requires the liquidator to produce to the DCE a number of documents regarding the company's affairs. As in every section of the report, with the exception of the final section,[205] the liquidator must complete this section in the first report and in every subsequent report, if there has been a change in details. The liquidator must annex to the report copies of the following documents and, where there is a failure to annex any of these documents, the liquidators must explain this failure:

- the directors' statement of affairs (or similar document);[206]

- last two sets of the audited accounts of the company;[207]

- the most recent draft or management accounts prepared after the last set of audited accounts;[208]

---

[204] See Ch **17**.

[205] See below para **[9.075]**.

[206] Company Law Enforcement Act 2001 (Section 56) Regulations 2002 (SI 2002/324), item 23.

[207] Item 25.

[208] Item 25.

- the last two sets of accounts laid before the AGM of companies which were exempt from the audit requirement;[209]

- the most recent draft or management accounts of companies which were exempt from the audit requirement;[210]

- report to creditors;[211]

- minutes of the creditors' meeting;[212]

- chairperson's statement to the creditors' meeting;[213]

- any other documents relevant to the creditors' meeting.[214]

[9.063] In the case of a failure to annex the directors' statement of affairs, the liquidator must instead attach details of the company's known assets and liabilities.[215] The liquidator must also state in the report whether the statement of affairs (or similar document) is materially different from the expected final position. There are a number of points to note in this regard. First, the 'similar document' that can be used in lieu of a directors' statement is not defined and leaves this requirement ambiguous. For instance, it may leave open the possibility that a 'similar document' could be submitted in substitution for a statement of affairs that is known to contain errors or misrepresentations. This would counteract the objective of assessing the veracity and accuracy of the statement of affairs. A second point to note is that the information that a liquidator is obliged to furnish where there is no statement of affairs or similar document, is limited to the assets and liabilities of the company. It would have been more thorough and consistent with the overall requirements of the report form, to require the liquidator to supplement this with the type of additional information that should have appeared in the statement of affairs.

[9.064] Thirdly, the requirement that the liquidator must state whether there is a 'material difference' between the statement of affairs and the 'expected final position' may be difficult to satisfy in practice. The term 'material difference' is vague. The 'expected final position' may be quite speculative. This is especially true when one considers that the initial report under CLEA 2001, s 56, which must contain this statement, must be filed within six months of the appointment of the liquidator. In a liquidation which is expected to last for several years, it may not be possible for a liquidator to assess the 'expected final position' of the company within the first six months. In addition, in a large company with many assets and liabilities, it may take

---

[209] Item 25.

[210] Item 25.

[211] Item 26.

[212] Item 26.

[213] Item 26.

[214] Item 26.

[215] Company Law Enforcement Act 2001 (Section 56) Regulations 2002 (SI 2002/324), item 23.

more than six months for the liquidator to assess properly the statement of affairs. A final point to note regarding the obligation of the liquidator to compare the statement of affairs and the expected final position of the company is that the liquidator must provide details of the amount of the material difference between the two and the reasons for this difference. If, at the time the report is required to be filed under CLEA 2001, s 56, the liquidation is at an early stage or the complexity of the company's affairs renders it difficult to assess the statement of affairs, it may not be feasible to require a liquidator to reach firm conclusions regarding the accuracy of the statement or the final position of the company. In such circumstances, it would certainly not be feasible to expect a liquidator to provide specific details of the amount of any divergence between the statement of affairs and the company's expected final position and the reasons for such a divergence. To require a liquidator to explain the difference also suggests that it is explicable within the remit of the liquidator's duties. Any difference between the directors' statement of affairs and the expected final position of the company will not necessarily be based on information to which the liquidator is privy. The requirement that he explain such a difference may not be realistic. The fact that the Guidance Notes contain no guidance on this issue may compound any problems faced by liquidators.[216]

[9.065] In addition to the specific documents that must be annexed to the report and, in some instances, elaborated upon, within section four of the report form, there is certain other information that a liquidator must present and which is also included under the heading, 'Statement of Affairs, Accounts and Report to Creditors.' This information is diverse and relates to topics ranging from committees of inspection to the duration of the winding up and disposals of the company's assets. It is difficult to see the relevance of these topics under the heading 'Statement of Affairs, Accounts and Report to Creditors'. However, it is probably more realistic to view section three of the report as a form of umbrella heading that encompasses information not included elsewhere in the report.

[9.066] Under section four, the liquidator must state whether a committee of inspection has been appointed and, if a committee has been appointed, the names of addresses of its members.[217] The liquidator must also state whether the winding up will be completed within 18 months from the date of the report.[218] It may not be feasible for a liquidator to state definitively, within the first six months after appointment, whether the liquidation will be completed within 18 months of the report. The wording of this requirement in the report form does not permit the furnishing of an opinion or estimate as to whether the liquidation will finish within 18 months. This interpretation is reinforced by the Guidance Notes, which merely require the liquidator to indicate whether the winding up

---

[216] The Guidance Notes merely state, 'please confirm if there is any material difference between the Statement of Affairs or similar document and the expected final position. If yes, please provide details on a separate sheet of the amount of and reason for the difference.' ODCE, 'Guidance Notes for the Completion of Liquidator's Reports under section 56 of the Company Law Enforcement Act 2001.'

[217] Company Law Enforcement Act 2001 (Section 56) Regulations 2002 (SI 2002/324), item 27.

[218] Company Law Enforcement Act 2001 (Section 56) Regulations 2002 (SI 2002/324), item 28.

will be completed within 18 months.[219] This can be contrasted with the draft report form, which required the liquidator to forecast the month and the year by which the liquidation would be completed.[220] While the requirement to furnish a month and year for completion of the liquidation is more exact than a requirement to state whether the liquidation would or would not be completed within a defined time frame, the draft report required a 'forecast' rather than a definitive answer. The flexibility allowed in the draft report is highlighted by the draft Guidance Notes which explained that the addressee 'should include your best estimate of the date by which you anticipate that the winding up should be completed, stating the month and year'. It seems more logical to allow a liquidator to provide an estimate of the expected duration of the liquidation, particularly in light of the fact that liquidators can amend any details of section four which changed since the submission of the previous report to the DCE, and could amend this estimate as necessary.[221]

[9.067] The liquidator must state whether there was any material transfer of assets of the company to any person between a date 12 months before the commencement of the winding up and the date of submission of the report as required by CLEA 2001, s 56.[222] If such a transfer did occur, the liquidator must furnish certain details of the transfer, such as the date of the transfer, the nature of the asset and the beneficiary.[223] The Guidance Notes state that 'a material transfer of assets' is to be defined as

> '... any arrangement or series of arrangements by which any assets of the company are transferred to, or held for the benefit of, any party where the value of such assets is greater than 10% of the called up share capital of the company or 10% of the net assets of the company. Net assets are total assets minus total liabilities.'[224]

This disclosure requirement appears to be directed towards the detection of certain breaches of company law. The types of transaction which are prohibited by the Companies Acts and which could come within the scope of the obligation to disclose a

---

[219] ODCE, 'Guidance Notes for the Completion of Liquidator's Reports under section 56 of the Company Law Enforcement Act 2001.'

[220] See draft Report Form, attached to ODCE, Consultation Paper C/2002/3 'The Liquidation-Related Functions of the Director of Corporate Enforcement'.

[221] Note that, the longer the liquidation lasts, the more likely there are to be further reports, which would permit the forecasted completion date of the liquidation to be amended. See also Decision Notice D/2002/3: 'The Liquidation-Related Functions of the Director of Corporate Enforcement' at para 3.9.

[222] Company Law Enforcement Act 2001 (Section 56) Regulations 2002 (SI 2002/324), item 29.

[223] Company Law Enforcement Act 2001 (Section 56) Regulations 2002 (SI 2002/324), item 29.

[224] ODCE, 'Guidance Notes for the Completion of Liquidator's Reports under section 56 of the Company Law Enforcement Act 2001.'

'material transfer of assets' within the meaning of the report form could include the following:

1. Transfer of non-cash assets to directors; CA 1990, s 29 prohibits the sale of non-cash assets of the requisite value from the company to a director, (or a person connected with the director), or by the director (or a person connected with the director) to the company, unless such transaction is first approved by a resolution of the company in general meeting; [225]

2. Dispositions that occurred after the commencement of the liquidation; CA 1963, s 218 renders void any disposition of a company's assets or transfer of its shares, after the commencement of the winding up, subject only to a court order to the contrary; [226]

3. Fraudulent dispositions of corporate property; CA 1990, s 139(1) provides that, where it is established to the satisfaction of the court that the company's property was disposed of with the effect of perpetrating fraud on the company, its creditors or members, the court can order the person in possession of such property or the proceeds of the transaction, to deliver the property to the liquidator or to pay such sum of money as the court deems appropriate; [227]

---

[225] CA 1990, s 29(1) provides that, subject to defined exceptions, a company is not permitted to '… enter into an arrangement (a) whereby a director of the company or its holding company or a person connected with such a director acquires or is to acquire one or more non-cash assets of the requisite value from the company; or (b) whereby the company acquires or is to acquire one or more non-cash assets of the requisite value from such a director or a person so connected; unless the arrangement is first approved by a resolution of the company in general meeting and, if the director or connected person is a director of its holding company or a person connected with such a director, by a resolution in general meeting of the holding company.' See Ch **6**. See also Courtney, *The Law of Private Companies* (2nd edn, Tottel Publishing, 2002), paras 11.023 *et seq.*

[226] CA 1963, s 218 provides that, 'In a winding up by the court, any disposition of the property of the company, including things in action, and any transfer of shares or alteration in the status of the members of the company, made after the commencement of the winding up, shall, unless the court otherwise orders, be void.' See also Courtney, *The Law of Private Companies* (2nd edn, Tottel Publishing, 2002), paras 27.058 *et seq.*

[227] CA 1990, s 139(1) provides that, 'Where, on the application of a liquidator, creditor or contributory of a company which is being wound up, it can be shown to the satisfaction of the court that (a) any property of the company of any kind whatsoever was disposed of either by way of conveyance, transfer, mortgage, security, loan, or in any way whatsoever whether by act or omission, direct or indirect, and (b) the effect of such disposal was to perpetrate a fraud on the company, its creditors or members, the court may, if it deems it just and equitable to do so, order any person who appears to have the use, control or possession of such property or the proceeds of the sale or development thereof to deliver it or pay a sum in respect of it to the liquidator on such terms or conditions as the court sees fit.' See CA 1990, s 251, according to which this provision can be invoked in respect of companies which are not being wound up, if the criteria of that provision are met. See also Courtney, *The Law of Private Companies* (2nd edn, Tottel Publishing, 2002), paras 27.092 *et seq.*

4. Fraudulent preferences; CA 1963, s 286 invalidates any property transaction
    involving a company which is unable to pay its debts as they fall due, in favour
    of a creditor, with a view to preferring that creditor over other creditors, where
    the winding up of that company commences within six months of the
    transaction, at which date the company is also unable to pay its debts as they fall
    due.[228]

[9.068] The interpretation that the requirement to disclose transfers of material assets
could be influenced or motivated by an interest in detecting breaches of the provisions of
the Companies Acts is reinforced by the wording of the draft Guidance Notes. The draft
Guidance Notes gave an example of the type of material transfer of the assets of the
company of which disclosure was required, as a transfer specified in the CA 1990, s 9.[229]

However, the duty to disclose material transfers of assets could also serve the purpose of
indicating, on a more general level, whether the assets of the company were being
handled honestly and prudently prior to, and immediately after, the liquidation, and
whether the directors were making responsible and honest decisions in that regard,
without violating their duties to the company, its members, creditors or their duties
under the Companies Acts.

[9.069] The final requirement of section four of the report form is that the liquidator
must state the date at which the company was unable to trade out of its financial
difficulties.[230] While the wording of the report form requires the liquidator to state
specifically the date on which the company was unable to trade out of its difficulties, the
Guidance Notes are more flexible. They require the liquidator to

> '... state the date on which it appears to you that, based on the company's financial
> situation, it was unable to trade out of its financial difficulties (which may be
> some time in advance of the winding up).'[231]

This allows a liquidator to state his view as to the company's affairs, rather than being
obliged to furnish a definitive date at which the financial position became untenable. In

---

[228] CA 1963, s 286(1), as amended by CA 1990, s 135, provides that 'any conveyance,
mortgage, delivery of goods, payment, execution or other act relating to property made or
done by or against a company which is unable to pay its debts as they become due in favour
of any creditor, or of any person on trust for any creditor, with a view to giving such
creditor, or any surety or guarantor for the debt due to such creditor, a preference over the
other creditors, shall, if a winding-up of the company commences within six months of the
making or doing the same and the company is at the time of the commencement of the
winding-up unable to pay its debts (taking into account the contingent and prospective
liabilities), be deemed a fraudulent preference of its creditors and be invalid accordingly.'
See also Courtney, *The Law of Private Companies* (2nd edn, Tottel Publishing, 2002),
paras 27.072 *et seq.*

[229] See draft Guidance Notes, attached to ODCE, Consultation Paper C/2002/3 'The
Liquidation-Related Functions of the Director of Corporate Enforcement'.

[230] Company Law Enforcement Act 2001 (Section 56) Regulations 2002 (SI 2002/324), item
30.

[231] ODCE, 'Guidance Notes for the Completion of Liquidator's Reports under section 56 of the
Company Law Enforcement Act 2001.'

light of the fact that the directors of the company may not have had a clear view of when the company was unable to trade out of its difficulties, it may not be realistic or fair to require the liquidator to select a specific point in time. The flexibility allowed by the Guidance Notes in its interpretation of this disclosure requirement may therefore be welcomed.

5. PROCEEDINGS

[9.070] In this section of the report, the liquidators are called upon to notify the DCE of any legal proceedings, actual or prospective, pending against the company or its directors. The liquidator is also obliged to set out his views as to whether proceedings should be taken to restrict or disqualify the directors of the company. One of the most important functions of this section of the report form is that the liquidator can ask the DCE to relieve him of the obligation to apply for the restriction of directors.

The first answer that a liquidator must furnish under section five is to the question whether the liquidator is asking the DCE to relieve him of the obligation to apply for the restriction of one or more of the company's directors, under CA 1990, s 15, and, if so, in respect of which directors relief is sought.[232] Where the liquidator is seeking relief in respect of certain directors, he must name those directors and state the grounds on which he believes those individuals should not be restricted.[233] Where no relief is being sought in respect of other directors, the liquidator must name these directors and state the grounds that would be relied upon in making the application to restrict those directors.[234]

The answers that the liquidator will already have furnished, in section three, to the question of whether each director has demonstrated to the liquidator that he acted honestly and responsibly in relation to the conduct of the company's affairs, will largely pre-judge the answers that will be given to this question under section five.[235] If the liquidator is satisfied that a particular director acted honestly and responsibly, it must follow logically that the liquidator will seek relief from the obligation to apply for the restriction of that director. There will be considerable duplication in this regard. Under section three, the liquidator has to explain the reasons for believing whether a director acted honestly and responsibly. Under section five, he is then called upon to explain the grounds for his views as to whether he should be relieved of the obligation to apply for the restriction of each of the same directors.[236] The grounds for believing directors acted honestly and responsibly will, inevitably, be the same as the grounds for believing those directors should not be restricted within the meaning of CA 1990, s 150. In the event that a liquidator forms the view that a director did not act honestly and responsibly, he will have to explain the reasons for this view in section three. In section five of the report form, these grounds will be repeated as the grounds for making an application to

---

[232] Company Law Enforcement Act 2001 (Section 56) Regulations 2002 (SI 2002/324), item 31.

[233] Item 31.

[234] Item 31.

[235] Company Law Enforcement Act 2001 (Section 56) Regulations 2002 (SI 2002/324), item 22. See above paras **[9.058]** to **[9.061]**.

[236] Company Law Enforcement Act 2001 (Section 56) Regulations 2002 (SI 2002/324), item 31.

have those directors restricted. The Guidance Notes provide no insight into the answers and information that should be furnished by a liquidator as to his view of the institution of restriction proceedings.[237] However, the detailed Guidance Notes that accompany section three deal with proceedings for the restriction of directors and apply squarely to the questions facing liquidators under section five.

[9.071] While the application for restriction of directors will require the attention of all liquidators, as every liquidator is obliged to seek restriction, unless relieved of the obligation to do so, there are other proceedings that can be taken against a company's directors and/or officers at the discretion of the liquidator. Where such further proceedings are being taken, the liquidator must furnish information in that regard to the DCE. In the first instance, the liquidator must state whether he will be applying for the disqualification of any directors within CA 1990, s 60, and, if so, the names of such persons and the grounds for making an application to disqualify them.[238] If the liquidator is taking, or contemplating taking, any additional proceedings against the company's officers, he must also state this fact and must specify the nature of these proceedings, the names of the persons being proceeded against, the date of institution of the proceedings and, if already commenced, the court in which the proceedings have been filed and their record number.[239]

[9.072] In addition to proceedings being taken or contemplated by the liquidator, if there are proceedings being taken, or contemplated, by anyone else against the company or its officers, the liquidator must notify the DCE of this fact.[240] The liquidator must also inform the DCE of the nature of such proceedings, the persons being proceeded against, the date (or projected date) of commencement of the proceedings, the name, address and telephone number of the person taking the proceedings and, if the proceedings have already commenced, the court in which they have been instituted and the record number.[241]

Where proceedings have commenced, the liquidator will be aware of this fact, and will be in possession of all of the categories of information sought in the report form. However, it is difficult to see how a liquidator can state definitively whether anyone is contemplating taking proceedings against the company or its officers. It would be more logical to require the liquidator to furnish such information as is available to him regarding any contemplated proceedings, rather than requiring him to furnish a direct answer as to whether anyone is contemplating issuing proceedings. In contrast to other questions on the report form, the wording of this question does not allow the liquidator's answer to be qualified by reference to the information available to him.

---

[237] Draft Guidance Notes, attached to ODCE, Consultation Paper C/2002/3 'The Liquidation-Related Functions of the Director of Corporate Enforcement'.

[238] Company Law Enforcement Act 2001 (Section 56) Regulations 2002 (SI 2002/324), item 32.

[239] Company Law Enforcement Act 2001 (Section 56) Regulations 2002 (SI 2002/324), item 33.

[240] Company Law Enforcement Act 2001 (Section 56) Regulations 2002 (SI 2002/324), item 34.

[241] Company Law Enforcement Act 2001 (Section 56) Regulations 2002 (SI 2002/324), item 34.

A further point to note about this aspect of the report form is that neither the question nor the accompanying Guidance Notes is limited by reference to proceedings that relate to the company's affairs. It is quite conceivable that an officer of the company could be the subject of distinct personal or professional proceedings, unrelated to the company, and, although these would not be relevant to the liquidation, a literal reading of the report form would require information about all and any such proceedings to be supplied to the DCE. It would be more appropriate to employ language that qualifies the nature of the proceedings about which information must be furnished, by reference to the company or the liquidation.

[9.073] The final question in section five of the report form requires the liquidator to state whether he has made, or is contemplating making, a report to the DPP and to the DCE under CA 1963, s 299.[242] If such a report is being made, the liquidator must further specify the nature of the offence, the person being reported, the relationship between that person and the company and the date, or expected date, of submission of the report.[243]

CA 1963, s 299 is addressed in more detail below.[244] For present purposes, it should be noted that there is no time limit within which a liquidator must invoke s 299. To require a liquidator to disclose whether he has, or intends to, make a report under s 299, within six months of the commencement of the liquidation, may therefore be unrealistic. In addition, s 299 can arise in a liquidation by virtue of court intervention.[245] It is a strange omission that the report form does not include an obligation to disclose whether a court has ordered the liquidator to refer a matter to the DPP and to the DCE. It is also curious that the report form, as it is prescribed by regulation, refers to the amendment of CA 1963, s 299 by CLEA 2001, s 51, but not the amendment of that provision by CA 1990, s 143. Section 143 substituted a new s 299(1), which addresses the power of the court to direct a liquidator to refer a matter to the DPP. This may be further evidence that the report form does not include situations where the liquidator is directed by court to refer a matter to the appropriate authorities. It is more likely, however, that it is due to an oversight that the report form fails to include a reference to CA 1990, s 143, and to situations where the court directs the liquidator to refer matters to the DPP and to the DCE.

[9.074] One of the significant amendments that CLEA 2001, s 51, introduced to CA 1963, s 299, is the creation of an obligation on liquidators to refer certain matters to the DCE. According to CA 1963, s 299(2), as will be seen, a liquidator is obliged to report certain matters to the DPP.[246] Since the introduction of CLEA 2001, a liquidator who makes such a report, must also refer the matter to the DCE and must furnish the DCE with such information and facilities and assistance as the Director may

---

[242] As amended by CA 1990, s 143 and CLEA 2001, s 51. See paras [9.086] *et seq*. Company Law Enforcement Act 2001 (Section 56) Regulations 2002 (SI 2002/324), item 35.

[243] Company Law Enforcement Act 2001 (Section 56) Regulations 2002 (SI 2002/324), item 35.

[244] As amended by CA 1990, s 143 and CLEA 2001, s 51. See below paras [9.086] *et seq*.

[245] CA 1963, s 299(1), as amended by CA 1990, s 143 and CLEA 2001, s 51. See further below paras [9.086] *et seq*.

[246] See below paras [9.086] *et seq*.

require.[247] In light of the fact that the obligation to furnish information to the DCE in this context is expressly required by statute, it may be superfluous to require a liquidator to furnish this information in the context of the report form.

6. FINAL REPORT

[9.075] The final substantive section of the report form differs from each of the preceding sections in that it is the only section which does not have to be completed in the initial report and in each successive report, where changes have occurred. On the contrary, section six appears only to apply to reports filed at, or close to, the conclusion of a liquidation. This is confirmed by the Guidance Notes, which state:

> 'Section 56 of the CLEA envisages that more than one report may be filed by liquidators during the liquidation process and this Section of the Report Form is intended for use in the context of follow-up and final reports.'[248]

The information that must be presented in section six of the report represents largely the culmination of the proceedings referred to in section five. The liquidator must notify the DCE of the outcome of any proceedings taken for the restriction of directors, with details of the outcome in the case of each individual director.[249] The liquidator must also specify the outcome of any other civil or criminal proceedings taken against the company, its directors or officers, by the liquidator or any other person.[250] This category is defined by reference to the proceedings of which disclosure is required under section five. This could be seen as limiting the category of proceedings within the scope of the report form, as, in liquidations in which there is only an initial report and a final report, and in which proceedings are contemplated against the company, its directors or officers, whether by the liquidator or other persons, only after the first report is made, these proceedings will not have been included in section five of the initial report. Section six requires disclosure of the outcome of 'court proceedings taken under the circumstances set out in ...' section five.[251] It may be that proceedings that did not come within the scope of the reporting obligation of section five, may not then fall within the reporting obligation contained in section six.

The final disclosure that a liquidator must make in the CLEA 2001, s 56 report form, relates to the form that must be submitted to the Companies Registration Office at the completion of a liquidation. Where the liquidation is completed, the liquidator must send to the DCE a copy of this form.[252]

---

[247] CA 1963, s 299(2A), as inserted by CLEA 2001, s 51.

[248] ODCE, 'Guidance Notes for the Completion of Liquidator's Reports under section 56 of the Company Law Enforcement Act 2001.'

[249] Company Law Enforcement Act 2001 (Section 56) Regulations 2002 (SI 2002/324), item 36.

[250] Company Law Enforcement Act 2001 (Section 56) Regulations 2002 (SI 2002/324), item 37.

[251] Company Law Enforcement Act 2001 (Section 56) Regulations 2002 (SI 2002/324), item 37.

[252] The so-called 'Form 14'. Company Law Enforcement Act 2001 (Section 56) Regulations 2002 (SI 2002/324), item 38.

7. LIQUIDATOR'S STATEMENT

[9.076] The final section of a report form that must be filed under CLEA 2001, s 56, is the so-called 'liquidator's statement'. This statement must be made at the end of each and every report filed under s 56. The statement, which must be signed and dated by the liquidator, is worded as follows:

> I, _____, being the liquidator of the above company, state that the details and particulars contained in this Report and all associated documentation prepared by me are true, correct and complete, to the best of my knowledge and belief.

In the draft report form that was prepared by the DCE, a similar statement was required to be made, but it was worded somewhat differently.[253] The most significant difference was that the statement, as it was originally drafted, did not include the caveat that it must be 'true, correct and complete, to the best of my knowledge and belief': there was no carve-out to accommodate the extent of the 'knowledge and belief' of the liquidator. This would have operated harshly, particularly in light of the fact that certain aspects of the report form require the liquidator to furnish unequivocal statements in respect of matters of which he may not necessarily have direct knowledge.[254] It is therefore eminently sensible to confine the liquidator's statement by reference to the limits of the liquidator's knowledge and belief.

(iii) Additional reports

[9.077] Liquidators are also obliged to file further reports subsequent to the initial s 56 report. This obligation is formulated vaguely, as s 56 merely refers to an obligation to file reports '...at intervals as required by the Director...' after the initial report.[255] The DCE considered this provision in the Consultation Paper and Decision Notice on the Liquidation-Related Functions of the DCE.[256] These documents note that the decision whether to require further reports after the submission of the initial report will be determined by the information contained in the initial report and the time frame for completion of the liquidation and any related court proceedings.[257] The Consultation Paper and Decision Notice further note that additional reports will probably not be

---

[253] Draft Report Form, attached to ODCE, Consultation Paper C/2002/3 'The Liquidation-Related Functions of the Director of Corporate Enforcement'.

[254] See, eg, item 29 which requires an answer to the following question: 'Was there any material transfer of assets of the Company ... to any person during the period commencing 12 months prior to the date of commencement of its winding up and ending on the date of this report?' See also item 34, which requires an answer to the following question: 'Are any other civil or criminal proceedings being undertaken, or contemplated, by any other person against the Company or any of its officers?'

[255] CLEA 2001, s 56(1).

[256] Decision Notice D/2002/3: 'The Liquidation-Related Functions of the Director of Corporate Enforcement'; Consultation Paper C/2002/3 'The Liquidation-Related Functions of the Director of Corporate Enforcement'.

[257] Decision Notice D/2002/3: 'The Liquidation-Related Functions of the Director of Corporate Enforcement' at para 3.9.

required sooner than six months after the submission of the initial report, although the period may be shorter in certain circumstances.[258] With regard to the type of circumstances that may require the submission of additional reports, it appears that applications to court for the restriction of directors may be among the circumstances that would warrant the filing of a further report. The Decision Notice states, '[f]ollowing the making of a restriction application, the Director envisages that he will almost always require a final report to be furnished by the liquidator immediately prior to the conclusion of the liquidation'.[259]

[9.078] As has already been seen, there are different provisions and arrangements in place for the oversight and supervision of liquidations, depending on how and by whom the liquidator is appointed.[260] There is considerably more court involvement in the course of an official liquidation than in a voluntary liquidation, for instance. This has a bearing on the reporting obligations of liquidators. The DCE has acknowledged this distinction:

> 'The Director does not consider that identical reporting arrangements will apply to official and voluntary liquidations. In the case of official liquidations, the Director recognises that the High Court will be regularly supervising the conduct of these liquidations, and he expects that only two reports (an initial and final section 56 report) will be required from official liquidators in most cases.'[261]

The requirement to file additional reports is therefore more likely to be imposed on voluntary liquidators, as a means of supervision of voluntary liquidations.

(iv) Sanctions

[9.079] It is an offence for a liquidator to fail to make a report as required by CLEA 2001, s 56. [262] The DCE has considered the sanctions that would attach to a failure by a liquidator to make the requisite report.[263] The DCE specifically listed the following three steps that could be taken in the event of a failure to comply with s 56:[264]

1. Prosecution;
2. Administrative fine;
3. Court order.

---

[258] Decision Notice D/2002/3: 'The Liquidation-Related Functions of the Director of Corporate Enforcement' at para 3.9.

[259] Decision Notice D/2002/3: 'The Liquidation-Related Functions of the Director of Corporate Enforcement' at para 3.9.

[260] See above paras **[9.023]** to **[9.033]**.

[261] Decision Notice D/2002/3: 'The Liquidation-Related Functions of the Director of Corporate Enforcement' at para 3.9.

[262] CLEA 2001, s 56(3).

[263] ODCE, Decision Notice D/2002/3: 'The Liquidation-Related Functions of the Director of Corporate Enforcement' at para 3.12. See also ODCE, Consultation Paper C/2002/3 'The Liquidation-Related Functions of the Director of Corporate Enforcement'.

[264] ODCE, Decision Notice D/2002/3: 'The Liquidation-Related Functions of the Director of Corporate Enforcement' at para 3.12. See also ODCE, Consultation Paper C/2002/3 'The Liquidation-Related Functions of the Director of Corporate Enforcement'.

1. PROSECUTION

[9.080] The DCE can prosecute a liquidator for the offence of failing to comply with CLEA 2001, s 56. The penalties that would apply for a conviction under this section are set out in CA 1990, s 240(1).[265] A liquidator convicted summarily of failing to comply with s 56 could be liable to a fine of up to €1904.61 or a term of imprisonment of a maximum of 12 months, or both. If convicted on indictment, a liquidator could face a fine of up to €12,697.38 or a term of imprisonment of a maximum of five years, or both.

2. ADMINISTRATIVE FINE

[9.081] The DCE has suggested that another remedy that could be pursued is the payment of an administrative fine by the liquidator.[266] The default would also need to be remedied under CLEA 2001, s 109, which permits the Director to deliver a notice to the person in default, requiring them to remedy the default as far as practicable to the satisfaction of the Director and to make a payment of the prescribed amount. This could be used as an alternative to prosecution, according to the DCE.[267]

3. COURT ORDER

[9.082] The DCE can apply to the High Court for an order to remedy the default of the liquidator in failing to comply with CLEA 2001, s 56. The basis for this application would be CA 1963, s 371,[268] which provides that, where an officer of a company fails to make good a failure to comply with a provision of the Companies Acts after receipt of a notice requiring the officer to do so, the court can make an order directing the company and the officer to make good the default.[269] The DCE is among the persons who can apply to court for such an order. The DCE has noted that, where such an application is made, the Director would require the costs of the application to be borne by the liquidator.[270]

---

[265] As amended by CLEA 2001, s 104(c).

[266] ODCE, Decision Notice D/2002/3: 'The Liquidation-Related Functions of the Director of Corporate Enforcement' at para 3.12. See also ODCE, Consultation Paper C/2002/3 'The Liquidation-Related Functions of the Director of Corporate Enforcement'.

[267] See CLEA 2001, s 109(2)(c): 'a prosecution in respect of the alleged offence shall not be instituted in the period specified in the notice and, if the default is remedied to the satisfaction of the Director and the payment specified in the notice is made during that period, no prosecution in respect of the alleged offence shall be instituted at all.' See also ODCE, Decision Notice D/2002/3: 'The Liquidation-Related Functions of the Director of Corporate Enforcement' at para 3.12. See also ODCE, Consultation Paper C/2002/3 'The Liquidation-Related Functions of the Director of Corporate Enforcement'.

[268] As amended by CLEA 2001, s 96.

[269] CA 1963, s 371(1), as amended by CLEA 2001, s 96.

[270] ODCE, Decision Notice D/2002/3: 'The Liquidation-Related Functions of the Director of Corporate Enforcement' at para 3.12. See also ODCE, Consultation Paper C/2002/3 'The Liquidation-Related Functions of the Director of Corporate Enforcement'.

[9.083] When considering which of these three remedies to pursue, the DCE stated that 'The remedy selected by the DCE will depend on its likely effectiveness in achieving a timely remedy of the default.'[271] The DCE further noted that, 'In the event of repeated non-compliance, the Director will also consider applying to disqualify the liquidator under s 160 of the Companies Act 1990.'[272] A liquidator who is in default under CLEA 2001, s 56, could therefore face the prospect of imprisonment, a fine and disqualification. As noted above, strict compliance with the obligation to complete the prescribed report form, may not always be straightforward, or even, in limited instances, feasible. It remains to be seen how the DCE will sanction a liquidator who is guilty of failing to satisfy the requirements of s 56 in such circumstances. It is to be hoped, however, that, where the failure to satisfy the strict requirements of s 56 is not due to any fault, bad faith or breach of duty on the part of the liquidator, that the DCE will neither invoke any of the three categories of sanction outlined above, nor pursue disqualification proceedings.

(v) Approach of the ODCE

[9.084] The ODCE has released information regarding its assessment of s 56 reports. For example, in 2006, the ODCE published a list of all insolvent companies in liquidation, in respect of which s 56 reports were required, with the objective of enabling 'interested parties to bring any matters of concern in relation to the insolvent company to the attention of the liquidator and the ODCE'.[273] In a subsequent information notice, the ODCE published a list of insolvent companies in liquidation, in respect of which relief was granted.[274] With regard to other insolvent companies in liquidation, the ODCE clarified that, 'details of cases where no relief or "partial" relief decisions were made will be published in the ODCE Annual Report following the determination of such cases by the High Court'.[275]

[9.085] The terms employed by the ODCE in describing its assessment of s 56 reports, are 'full relief', 'relief at this time', 'partial relief' and 'no relief'. 'Full relief' refers to cases in which the Director has decided that the liquidator is relieved of the obligation to apply to the High Court for the restriction of the company's directors.[276] 'Relief at this

---

[271] ODCE, Decision Notice D/2002/3: 'The Liquidation-Related Functions of the Director of Corporate Enforcement' at para 3.12. See also ODCE, Consultation Paper C/2002/3 'The Liquidation-Related Functions of the Director of Corporate Enforcement'.

[272] ODCE, Decision Notice D/2002/3: 'The Liquidation-Related Functions of the Director of Corporate Enforcement' at para 3.12. See also ODCE, Consultation Paper C/2002/3 'The Liquidation-Related Functions of the Director of Corporate Enforcement'.

[273] ODCE, List of Insolvent Companies in Liquidation, Information Notice I/2006/1. Available at www.odce.ie.

[274] ODCE, List of 'Relief' Decisions Issued in 2006 for Insolvent Companies in Liquidation, Information Notice I/2007/1. Available at www.odce.ie.

[275] ODCE, List of 'Relief' Decisions Issued in 2006 for Insolvent Companies in Liquidation, Information Notice I/2007/1. Available at www.odce.ie.

[276] ODCE, List of 'Relief' Decisions Issued in 2006 for Insolvent Companies in Liquidation, Information Notice I/2007/1. Available at www.odce.ie.

time' refers to cases in which the Director has decided to relieve the liquidator of the obligation to apply to the High Court for the restriction of the company's directors, 'for the present'. This is further defined by reference to the Decision Notice and, in particular, para 5.5 thereof, which states:

> 'On receipt of an initial s 56 report, it may be evident that substantial further work requires to be undertaken by the liquidator, before he/she will be in a position to make a restriction application to the High Court. The Director will consider on a case-by-case basis any genuine request from a liquidator for relief under s 56, so that he/she may be afforded additional time to conclude his or her examination of the conduct of the company directors and, in appropriate cases, to prepare properly for a restriction application. Any such relief will only be given in exceptional circumstances, and the Director will specify when he requires the subsequent s 56 report to be submitted. The submission of this subsequent report will, of course, impose an obligation on the liquidator to apply to the court for a restriction order unless relieved of that obligation in accordance with the terms of s 56 ...'[277]

The term 'no relief' refers to cases in which the DCE has not relieved the liquidator of the obligation to apply to the High Court for the restriction of the insolvent company's directors, either because the liquidator has not sought such relief, or because the DCE disagrees with the liquidator's assessment that no such application is warranted. 'Partial relief' is granted if the DCE considers that relief from the obligation to bring restriction proceedings, should be granted in respect of some, but not all, of the company's directors.[278]

(d) Duty to report to the Director of Public Prosecutions

[9.086] There is an important tool in the enforcement of company law contained in CA 1963, s 299.[279] This provision is designed to ensure that any criminal offences that appear to have been committed by a company's directors, officers or members, are brought to the attention of the Director of Public Prosecutions ('DPP') and the DCE and that the appropriate information and assistance is furnished to facilitate the investigation and prosecution of such offences. There are three distinct means by which this provision operates. First, in official liquidations the court can direct matters to be referred to the DPP and to the DCE under s 299(1) and (1A).[280] Secondly, the liquidator in a voluntary liquidation can refer the commission of suspected offences to the DPP and to the DCE.[281] Thirdly, the court can direct a liquidator in a voluntary liquidation to refer

---

[277] ODCE, Decision Notice D/2002/3: 'The Liquidation-Related Functions of the Director of Corporate Enforcement' at para 5.5. Available at www.odce.ie.

[278] ODCE, List of 'Relief' Decisions Issued in 2006 for Insolvent Companies in Liquidation, Information Notice I/2007/1. Available at www.odce.ie.

[279] As amended by CA 1990, s 143 and CLEA 2001, s 51. This provision is reproduced in CLRG, General Scheme of the Draft Companies Consolidation and Reform Bill 2007, Pt A11, Head 153.

[280] CA 1963, s 299(1) and (1A), as amended by CA 1990, s 143 and CLEA 2001, s 51. The scope of s 299(1) as being limited to official liquidations is clear from the reference to 'a winding up by the court'. See CA 1963, s 299(1), as amended by CA 1990, s 143 and CLEA 2001, s 51.

[281] CA 1963, s 299(2) and (2A), as amended by CA 1990, s 143 and CLEA 2001, s 51.

suspected offences to the DPP and to the DCE where the liquidator in a voluntary liquidation has failed to do so.[282]

The requirement to refer the suspected commission of criminal offences to the DPP and to the DCE will now be considered in the context of official liquidations and voluntary liquidations.

(i) Official liquidations

[9.087] Section 299(1) provides that a court may direct a liquidator to refer a matter to the DPP if it appears to the court in the course of the winding up that any director, officer or member of the company has been guilty of an offence in relation to the company to which criminal liability attaches. It provides:

> If it appears to the court in the course of a winding up by the court that any past or present officer, or any member, of the company has been guilty of an offence in relation to the company for which he is criminally liable, the court may either on the application of any person interested in the winding up or of its own motion direct the liquidator to refer the matter to the Director of Public Prosecutions and in such a case the liquidator shall furnish to the Director of Public Prosecutions such information and give to him such access to and facilities for inspecting and taking any copies of any documents, being information or documents in the possession or under the control of the liquidator and relating to the matter in question, as the Director of Public Prosecutions may require.

According to s 299(1A),[283] where a court directs a liquidator to refer such a matter to the DPP, the court shall also make a similar direction to report the matter to the DCE.

1. APPLICANTS

[9.088] The persons who can apply for a direction to be made under CA 1963, s 299(1) are persons who are interested in the company's winding up. This would include creditors, contributories and members of the company.[284] In the alternative, the court can issue directions under CA 1963, s 299, of its own motion.

2. SCOPE

[9.089] The category of persons to whom CA 1963, s 299(1), applies, is broadly formulated. It applies to past and present officers and any members of the company. The category of offences to which it applies is also a broad one. The offences covered are any offences in relation to the company which attract criminal liability: there is no stipulation that the offence must be an offence under the CA 1963–2006, or that it must be an indictable offence. The only requirement is that it must be an offence 'in relation to the company' provided that they relate to the company. The type of situations that would most obviously be captured by this provision include the commission of fraud in

---

[282] CA 1963, s 299(3), as amended by CA 1990, s 143 and CLEA 2001, s 51.

[283] As inserted by CLEA 2001, s 51.

[284] By analogy with the category of persons who are entitled to petition the court for the winding up of a company. CA 1963, s 215.

the management of the company. It will be interesting to see whether the broadening scope of corporate criminal liability will cause CA 1963, s 299 to be invoked for broader categories of offences than the traditional company law offences and whether offences under the Competition Act 2002, for example, may trigger the reporting obligation of s 299.

3. GROUNDS

[9.090] The grounds on which a court will direct a liquidator to refer a matter to the DPP and to the DCE are that it appears to the court that past or present officers or any member of the company has been guilty of an offence in relation to the company for which he is criminally liable. As has been seen, the category of offences that are potentially captured by s 299(1) is a broad one.[285] The grounds which must exist for believing such offences to have been committed are not set out in s 299(1). That provision merely states that, 'if it appears to the court in the course of a winding up by the court that any past or present officer, or any member, of the company has been guilty of an offence in relation to the company for which he is criminally liable', the court may direct the matter to be referred to the DPP and to the DCE. There is no evidential threshold in this regard. The stipulation that the court must believe the person 'has been guilty' indicates a level of certainty regarding the commission of the offence is required, however: it will not be within the scope of s 299(1) if it appears that an offence may have been committed.

4. LIQUIDATOR'S DUTIES

[9.091] If a court invokes its powers under s 299(1) to direct a liquidator to refer the commission of a suspected criminal offence to the DPP and to the DCE, the liquidator is under a number of distinct obligations:

- the liquidator must comply with the direction and refer the matters in question to the DPP and to the DCE;

- the liquidator must furnish to the DPP and to the DCE information in the possession or under the control of the liquidator and relating to the matter in question, as they each may require;

- the liquidator must give the DPP and the DCE access to any documents in the possession or under the control of the liquidator and relating to the matters in question, as they may require;

- the liquidator must give the DPP and the DCE facilities for inspecting and taking copies of any documents in the possession or under the control of the liquidator and relating to the matters in question, as they may require.[286]

---

[285] See above para **[9.089]**.

[286] CA 1963, s 299(1), 299(1A), (2) and (2A), as amended by CA 1990, s 143 and CLEA 2001, s 51. The same duties are imposed on liquidators in voluntary and in official liquidations.

(ii) Voluntary liquidations

[9.092] Section 299(2), (2A) and (3)[287] address the obligation of voluntary liquidators to report the apparent commission of criminal offences by a company's past or present officers, or members, to the DPP and to the DCE. There are two alternative means by which a voluntary liquidator can refer such matters to the appropriate authorities. First, the liquidator can make such a referral of his own volition. Secondly, where the liquidator fails to make such a report, the liquidator may be directed by court to do so. Section 299 addresses each of these situations.

1. VOLUNTARY LIQUIDATOR'S REPORT

[9.093] Section 299(2) and (2A) provide that, if it appears to a liquidator that any past or present officer or member of the company has committed an offence in relation to the company for which criminal liability attaches to that person, he shall report this forthwith to the DPP (s 299(2)) and further refer the matter to the DCE (s 299(2A)). Section 299(2) provides:

> If it appears to the liquidator in the course of a voluntary winding up that any past or present officer, or any member, of the company has been guilty of any offence in relation to the company for which he is criminally liable, he shall forthwith report the matter to the Director of Public Prosecutions and shall furnish to the Director of Public Prosecutions such information and give to him such access to and facilities for inspecting and taking copies of any documents, being information or documents in the possession or under the control of the liquidator and relating to the matter in question, as the Director of Public Prosecutions may require.[288]

The language used in this provision is similar in many respects to the provision governing the power of the court to require an official liquidator to refer matters to the DPP and to the DCE.[289] The scope of the provisions are the same, as are the grounds on which the apparent offences should be referred to the DPP and to the DCE. The duties of the liquidators consequent on making on such a report are the same, whether in a voluntary or an official liquidation. There are a number of points of distinction, however. First, where it appears that an offence has been committed, a voluntary liquidator is under a mandatory obligation to report this to the DPP and the DCE. In the case of an official liquidator, the court has a discretion whether to require the matter to be referred to the DPP and to the DCE. Secondly, in the case of an official liquidation, the court can direct the liquidator to 'refer' the matter to the DPP and to the DCE. In a voluntary liquidation, the obligation is expressed as an obligation to 'report' the matter to the DPP and to 'refer' it the DCE. While nothing may hinge on this distinction, the duty to 'report' a matter may be seen as a more concrete and formal obligation and as a stronger indication of the existence of an offence capable of prosecution, than the term 'refer'. The third difference between official and voluntary liquidations in this regard, is

---

[287] As amended by CA 1990, s 143 and CLEA 2001, s 51.

[288] CA 1963, s 299(2), as amended by CA 1990, s 143 and CLEA 2001, s 51.

[289] See above paras **[9.087]**–**[9.091]**.

that a voluntary liquidator must report the commission of a suspected offence to the DPP 'forthwith', whereas there is no such requirement in situations where the court directs the liquidator to refer a matter to the DPP.

2. COURT DIRECTIONS

[9.094] Where a voluntary liquidator fails to report a matter to the DPP or to the DCE even though it appears that an officer or member of the company has committed an offence in relation to the company, the court can direct the liquidator to make such a report. CA 1963, s 299(3)[290] provides:

> If it appears to the court in the course of a voluntary winding up that any past or present officer, or any member, of the company has been guilty as aforesaid, and that no report relating to the matter has been made by the liquidator to the Director of Public Prosecutions under sub-s (2), or to the Director under sub-s (2A), the court may, on the application of any person interested in the winding up or of its own motion, direct the liquidator to make such a report, and on a report being made accordingly, this section shall have effect as though the report had been made in pursuance of sub-s (2) or sub-s (2A), as the case may be.

This provision has the effect that, where a person interested in the voluntary liquidation of a company, such as a creditor, is aware of the apparent commission of a criminal offence by an officer in relation to the company, and the liquidator fails or refuses to report this matter to the DPP, the creditor can make an application to court to require the liquidator to make such a report. The persons who can make the application are persons interested in the winding up, which would include creditors, members and contributories. The court can also, of its own motion, direct a voluntary liquidator, who has not already done so, to report the apparent commission of an offence to the DPP and to the DCE. If the court issues a direction in this regard, and the voluntary liquidator accordingly reports the suspected offence to the DPP and to the DCE, the provisions that would apply if the liquidator had made the report of his own volition,[291] will apply.[292]

[9.095] There is nothing in s 299(3) which confers a right on persons interested in a winding up to request the voluntary liquidator to make a report under s 299(2), without the necessity of making a court application. There is no provision that deals specifically with the costs of such a court application.[293] Finally, there is nothing in s 299 that suggests that a liquidator who fails to make a report, despite the apparent commission of an offence, is guilty of an offence.

---

[290] As amended by CA 1990, s 143 and CLEA 2001, s 51.

[291] CA 1963, s 299(2) and (2A), as amended by CA 1990, s 143 and CLEA 2001, s 51.

[292] See above paras **[9.091]**–**[9.093]**.

[293] This can be contrasted with CA 1963, s 299(5), as amended by CA 1990, s 143 and CLEA 2001, s 51, which provides for liquidators to be personally liable for the costs of an application to court requiring them to assist in the prosecution of offences reported to the DPP and to the DCE under that section. See below para **[9.098]**.

(iv) Prosecution

[9.096] A liquidator, whether in an official or a voluntary winding up, who has referred the apparent commission of an offence by a member or officer of the company to the DPP and the DCE under s 299, must provide certain assistance to those entities. Section 299 requires the liquidator to furnish such information and to provide such access to documents in his possession or under his control, relating to the matter in question, as the DPP and the DCE may require.[294]

If the DPP or the DCE then consider that a prosecution is necessary and proceedings are instituted, there are further duties on the liquidator, among others, to assist in the prosecution. Section 299(4)[295] provides:

> If, where any matter is reported or referred to the Director of Public Prosecutions and the Director under this section, either the Director of Public Prosecutions or the Director considers that the case is one in which a prosecution ought to be instituted and institutes proceedings accordingly, it shall be the duty of the liquidator and of every officer and agent of the company past and present (other than the defendant in the proceedings) to give all assistance in connection with the prosecution which he is reasonably able to give.

1. OBLIGATION TO ASSIST

[9.097] As the prosecution of indictable offences remains within the exclusive remit of the DPP, only the DPP can institute proceedings for such offences.[296] The DCE could, however, decide to institute proceedings for summary offences under the Companies Acts. In either case, the persons who can be obliged to provide assistance in the prosecution of an offence committed in relation to a company in liquidation by an officer or member of that company, are the liquidator, the past and present officers of the company and the past and present agents of the company. The term 'agents' is defined as including 'any banker or solicitor of the company and any person employed by the company as auditor, whether that person is or is not an officer of the company'.[297] There is no exemption in respect of legal professional privilege or banker-client confidentiality. The assistance which those persons must furnish to the DPP and/or the DCE is 'all assistance ... which he is reasonably able to give', which may permit valid claims of privilege to be invoked.

2. FAILURE TO ASSIST

[9.098] If a person who is obliged to assist in the prosecution of an offence under s 299(4), fails or neglects to do so, the DPP or the DCE can make an application to court.[298] On such an application, the court can direct the person in question to comply

---

[294] CA 1963, s 299(1), (1A), (2), (2A), as amended by CA 1990, s 143 and CLEA 2001, s 51.

[295] As amended by CA 1990, s 143 and CLEA 2001, s 51.

[296] See *Report of the Working Group on Company Law Compliance and Enforcement* (November 1998) at para 4.28: 'Legal responsibility for prosecuting all indictable offences under the Companies Acts rests with the DPP'. See Ch **15**.

[297] CA 1963, s 299(4), as amended by CA 1990, s 143 and CLEA 2001, s 51.

[298] CA 1963, s 299(5), as amended by CA 1990, s 143 and CLEA 2001, s 51.

with the duty to provide assistance. If the person in default is the company's liquidator, the court can direct that the liquidator must bear the costs of the application personally. However, if it appears that the liquidator's failure or neglect to comply with s 299(4) was due to 'the liquidator not having in his hands sufficient assets of the company to enable him so to do', the court will not direct the liquidator to bear the costs of the application.[299]

It is curious that there is an exception from the costs penalty for liquidators who do not have sufficient assets to be able to assist in the prosecution of an offence. The obligation to assist in the prosecution of an offence is described explicitly as an obligation to provide all assistance which the individual in question is 'reasonably able to give'.[300] If a liquidator lacked the resources to be able to provide the assistance sought by the DPP or the DCE, this should be regarded as good grounds for asserting that he was not 'reasonably able' to give that assistance. There should therefore be no question of the liquidator failing or neglecting to comply with s 299(4), and such a situation should not be subject of a court application under s 299(5).[301]

The fact that the power to render liquidators liable for the costs of a court application under CA 1963, s 299(5) is expressly provided for, suggests that no such power exists in respect of the other persons who may be found to have failed or neglected to assist in the prosecution of an offence in relation to the company in liquidation.

3. ROLE OF THE DIRECTOR OF PUBLIC PROSECUTIONS

[9.099] The role of the DPP under CA 1963, s 299 was analysed by the Working Group on Company Law Compliance and Enforcement in the following terms:[302]

> '... the Group is satisfied that the Director of Public Prosecutions has no investigative function and, accordingly, simply refers any such cases to the Gardaí for investigation. It should be emphasised that the delivery to the DPP of a very damning liquidation report does not, of itself, provide any admissible evidence for a criminal prosecution. Thus, although the Companies Acts provide for an obligation to assist the Director of Public Prosecutions, and for access for the DPP to documents and information relating to the suspected offences, the Office of the Director of Public Prosecutions can take no independent investigatory steps, and must rely exclusively on An Garda Síochána, to whom he refers such matters, to further investigate such cases.'[303]

This view of the role of the DPP in the investigation of suspected offences, such as offences that are referred or reported to the DPP under CA 1963, s 299, is a limited one. However, the investigation of such offences is likely to have been bolstered by the establishment of the ODCE.

---

[299] CA 1963, s 299(5), as amended by CA 1990, s 143 and CLEA 2001, s 51.

[300] CA 1963, s 299(4), as amended by CA 1990, s 143 and CLEA 2001, s 51.

[301] As amended by CA 1990, s 143 and CLEA 2001, s 51.

[302] *Report of the Working Group on Company Law Compliance and Enforcement* (November 1998) at para 2.14.

[303] *Report of the Working Group on Company Law Compliance and Enforcement* (November 1998) at para 2.14.

4. ROLE OF THE DCE

[9.100] Since the introduction of CLEA 2001, the DCE must also be referred any suspected offences that are referred to the DPP under s 299.[304] While the prosecution of indictable offences remains within the exclusive remit of the DPP, the investigative role of the ODCE must now be an important aspect of the investigation of offences reported or referred by a liquidator under s 299.[305] This is confirmed by the following recommendation of the Working Group on Company Law Compliance and Enforcement:

> '... the Director of Corporate Enforcement should play an active role in assisting the preparation of cases for possible criminal proceedings for breaches of the Companies Acts. We envisage that the Director and his staff will work closely with An Garda Síochána in identifying the indictable offences in any particular case and in supporting Garda enquiries ... Such support would, we believe, be useful prior to the Gardaí submitting a case for possible criminal proceedings to the DPP.'[306]

In addition to this role in support of the prosecution of indictable offences reported under CA 1963, s 299,[307] the DCE also has jurisdiction to prosecute offences summarily.[308]

(e) Duty to report to court

[9.101] There are a number of provisions of the Companies Acts which impose obligations on liquidators to report certain matters to the court or to make certain applications to the court. In some instances, the duty to make such reports is contingent on the occurrence of specified events. For example, a liquidator who was appointed by the members in a creditors' voluntary winding up, must apply to the court for directions where the company or its directors default in their obligation to summon a meeting of the company's creditors.[309] It is an offence for a liquidator to fail to comply with this obligation.[310]

[9.102] There is a particular reporting obligation that is imposed on directors of insolvent companies. According to CA 1990, s 151, if it appears to a liquidator that a person who is the subject of a declaration of restriction[311] is acting directly or indirectly as a director of another company, or is otherwise involved in the promotion or formation

---

[304] See s 299(1A) and (2A), as inserted by CLEA 2001, s 51.

[305] See further Ch **11** regarding the interaction between the DPP and the DCE.

[306] Report of the Working Group on Company Law Compliance and Enforcement (November 1998) at para 4.29.

[307] As amended by CA 1990, s 143 and CLEA 2001, s 51.

[308] CLEA 2001, s 12(1)(a). See further Ch **11**.

[309] See CA 1990, s 131; See also CA 1963, s 266, as amended by CA 1990, s 130.

[310] CA 1990, s 131(7).

[311] Within the meaning of CA 1990, s 150, as amended by CLEA 2001, s 41. See further Pt **D**, Declarations of Restriction.

of another company, the liquidator must inform the court of this fact forthwith. This reporting obligation arises in the following circumstances:

> Where it appears to the liquidator of a company to which under this Chapter applies that the interests of any other company or its creditors may be placed in jeopardy by the relevant matters referred to in sub-s (2) the liquidator shall inform the court of his opinion forthwith and the court may, on receipt of such report, make whatever order it sees fit.[312]

There are a number of pre-conditions to the imposition of this obligation. First, the company to which the liquidator was appointed must be a company which has been proven to be unable to pay its debts either at the date of the commencement of the liquidation or during the course of the liquidation.[313] It is therefore only liquidators of insolvent companies who are bound by this duty. Secondly, the circumstance that must exist before the obligation to notify the court is triggered, is set out in CA 1990, s 151(2) as follows: '... a person to whom s 150 applies is appointed or is acting in any way, whether directly or indirectly, as a director or is concerned or is taking part in the promotion or formation of such other company ...'.

The persons to whom CA 1990, s 150 applies are persons who the court has declared should not be appointed, or act in any way, directly or indirectly, as a director or secretary of a company or take part in the promotion or formation of any company.[314] Where the liquidator is of the opinion that a person in respect of whom such a declaration has been made, is appointed or acting, directly or indirectly, as a director, or is taking part in the promotion or formation of another company, he must then make a further enquiry before he is obliged to inform the court of the situation.

The liquidator must consider whether the fact that a restricted person is involved in a company in contravention of the declaration of restriction is placing the interests of that company or its creditors in jeopardy.[315] The fact that a person is in breach of a declaration of restriction is not sufficient to trigger the duty of the liquidator to inform the court of the matter. It is only if such involvement presents a risk to the other company or its creditors that the liquidator must inform the court of the situation.

Where the criteria set out above are met, it is an offence for the liquidator not to report the matter to court, an offence which may be tried summarily or on indictment.[316] Where the criteria are met and the liquidator duly informs the court of the actions of the restricted person, the court can then make whatever order the court deems fit. [317]

[9.103] There are a number of points to note about this reporting obligation. First, the pre-conditions to the imposition of the obligation are not entirely coherent. For instance, there is no correlation between the company in liquidation, the company in respect of which the restricted person was acting when the declaration of restriction was made, and

---

[312] CA 1990, s 151(1).

[313] CA 1990, s 149(1) (Pt VII, Ch I).

[314] See further Pt **D**.

[315] CA 1990, s 151(1).

[316] CA 1990, s 151(3).

[317] CA 1990, s 151(1).

the company in which the restricted person now appears to be acting. This has the illogical consequence that a liquidator of an insolvent company (Company A) may be bound by statute to report the fact that a person who was the subject of a declaration of restriction arising from the liquidation of another company (Company B), is now acting as a director or secretary, or otherwise, in relation to a third company (Company C). It should perhaps be stipulated in this provision that a liquidator is only under this duty if the declaration of restriction was made in the course of the liquidation of Company A. Otherwise, every liquidator of any insolvent company could bear a duty, unrelated to their duties as a liquidator and the insolvency of the company to which they have been appointed, to inform the court of the actions of restricted persons, however the liquidator may become aware of such actions. The fact that it is an offence for 'any liquidator' to fail to comply with CA 1990, s 151(1) renders the potential breadth of this obligation worrying.[318]

[9.104] A further point to note about the obligation to inform the court that an individual appears to be acting in violation of a declaration of restriction, is that proving the commission of an offence under CA 1990, s 151, may be difficult. The obligation that is imposed on liquidators arises where 'it appears to the liquidator...' that the requisite circumstances exist.[319] This obligation is premised on the subjective view formed by the liquidator as to whether or not the interests of another company or its creditors may be placed in jeopardy. The offence is premised on a liquidator contravening the requirements of the section.[320] To establish that an offence was committed would therefore require proof that it appeared to the liquidator that a restricted person was acting in another company and that such involvement may place the interests of that company or its creditors in jeopardy. In the event that the liquidator did not inform the court of a situation where a restricted person was acting in another company, as a director, secretary or otherwise, it may be open to the liquidator to raise the defence that it did not appear to him that the interests of that other company or its creditors were in danger.

The utility of this provision may be questioned, as the duty could be imposed very widely and without any logical connection between the liquidator on whom the duty is imposed and the person or the company to which the report would relate. The history of the provision was described in the following terms by the Working Group on Company Law Compliance and Enforcement:

> At present, there is provision under ss 151 and 154 of the 1990 Act allowing both official and voluntary liquidators and receivers to report certain matters to the High Court. Notwithstanding this provision, few, if any, of these reports are made, presumably because the costs of court representation could dilute the funds available for members and creditors ... The Group is of the view that a large number of company law offences never come to light due to the absence of a compulsory reporting requirement by voluntary liquidators in particular ...[321]

---

[318] CA 1990, s 151(3).

[319] CA 1990, s 151(1).

[320] 'Any liquidator who contravenes sub-s (1) shall be guilty of an offence', CA 1990, s 151(3).

[321] *Report of the Working Group on Company Law Compliance and Enforcement* (1998) at para 4.15.

[9.105] There is another provision of the Companies Acts the objective of which is similar to that underlying CA 1990, s 151. CA 1990, s 161 renders it an offence for an individual to contravene a declaration of restriction or a disqualification order to which he is subject.[322] That section also creates reporting obligations for liquidators.[323] Two conditions must be satisfied before these obligations arise. First, a restricted person must act as a director of a company (Company B), the liquidation of which commences within five years of the commencement of the liquidation of the company (Company A) in connection with which the person was restricted.[324] Secondly, it must appear to the liquidator of Company B that that company is unable to pay its debts, at the commencement, or in the course, of its winding up.[325] Where these conditions are met, the liquidator must report this to the court.[326] Upon receipt of this report, the court may disqualify that person for such period as it thinks fit, if the court considers it proper to do so. If the liquidator fails to report the required report, he is guilty of an offence.[327]

The reporting obligations imposed on a liquidator by CA 1990, s 161, can be distinguished from those that arise by virtue of CA 1990, s 151. In the first instance, it is not necessary under s 161 that the involvement of the restricted person in another company had an impact on that company's welfare or that of its creditors. In particular, and by contrast with CA 1990, s 151, it is not necessary that the involvement of the restricted person placed the interests of the company in jeopardy or contributed towards its insolvency. Another point of distinction is that it is only liquidators of the company in liquidation in relation to which the restricted person is acting that are bound by the reporting obligation of s 161, whereas the reporting obligation that was created by s 151, is not confined to liquidators of a company with which a restricted person is or ever has been involved.

D. Investigations during winding up

(a) Introduction

[9.106] Since the enactment of the Companies Act 1963, the court has extensive powers over companies in respect of which it has made winding up orders. For instance, the court has the power to summon persons before it for examination; it can order the inspection of a company's books and papers; and a court can order the arrest of an individual and seizure of his property in certain circumstances.[328] The powers available

---

[322] CA 1990, s 161(1).

[323] CA 1990, s 161(5).

[324] CA 1990, s 161(5)(a).

[325] CA 1990, s 161(5)(b).

[326] CA 1990, s 161(5).

[327] CA 1990, s 161(6), as amended by CA 1990 s 240(7), as inserted by CLEA 2001, s 104. See Pt E.

[328] Eg, CA 1963, ss 243, 245 and 247 provided, respectively, for the inspection of a company's books and papers, the summoning of persons for examination and the arrest of persons who are likely to abscond. These provisions are substantially reproduced in the CLRG, General Scheme of the Draft Companies Consolidation and Reform Bill 2007, Pt A11, Heads 101 *et seq*. Available at www.clrg.org.

to a court in a compulsory winding up have been considerably bolstered by the CA 1990 1990 and the CLEA 2001, and, as will be seen in this section, now include such extensive powers as the power to order the search of a person's dwelling by the DCE.

A further significant amendment that has been introduced to the powers of the court in relation to liquidations, is the scope of these powers. Under the CA 1963 and 1990, the investigative powers of the court to order inspections of documents, summon witnesses, and order arrests, for example, only applied in the context of compulsory liquidations. This situation has been changed and the CLEA 2001 has now extended most of these powers to voluntary liquidations.

A final point to note about the powers of the court regarding companies being wound up, is that the role of the DCE has now been incorporated into these powers. The DCE can now make applications to court for orders and can acquire the right to inspect documents, search premises, among others.[329]

(b) Inspection of books

(i) Compulsory liquidations

[9.107] In the context of compulsory liquidations, CA 1963, s 243 permits the court to make orders for inspection of the company's books and papers by creditors or members and such books and papers may be inspected in accordance with such an order.[330] Section 243(1) provides:

> The court may, at any time after making a winding up order, make such order for inspection of the books and papers of the company by creditors and contributories as the court thinks just, and any books and papers in the possession of the company may be inspected by creditors or contributories accordingly, but not further or otherwise.

Since the introduction of the CLEA 2001, the court can also make orders for inspection of books and papers to be carried out by the DCE.[331] The new s 243(1A) provides:

> The court may, on the application of the Director, make an order for the inspection by the Director of any books and papers in the possession of a company the subject of a winding-up order and the company, every officer of the company and the liquidator shall give to the Director such access to and facilities as are necessary for inspecting and taking copies of those books and papers as the Director may require.

There are certain points of distinction between the order that a court may make for inspection by creditors or members of the company, and the order that may be made for inspection by the DCE.

    (1)   The DCE must apply for an order of inspection, whereas there is no requirement that an application be made on behalf of the company's creditors or members for the court to make the order in their favour.

---

[329] See further Ch **12**.

[330] CA 1963, s 243(1), as amended by CLEA 2001, s 43.

[331] CA 1963, s 243(1A), as inserted by CLEA 2001, s 43.

(2)   The order allowing for inspection by the creditors or members, is for inspection of the 'books and papers of the company', whereas an order for inspection by the DCE is for inspection of 'any books and papers in the possession of the company'. The latter could clearly encompass a broader category of books and papers than the former and could include, for example, books and papers that do not relate directly to the company in liquidation, but which are in its possession.

(3)   The order a court may make for inspection by creditors and members is such order 'as the court thinks just'. In the context of inspection by the DCE, there is no requirement that the court must consider the order to be just.

(4)   Finally, creditors or members in favour of whom an order has been made under s 243, may inspect the books and papers in accordance with the terms of the order. Where an order is made in favour of the DCE, s 243(1A) expresses the right of inspection in stronger terms, stipulating that, 'the company, every officer of the company and the liquidator shall give to the Director such access to and facilities as are necessary for inspecting and taking copies of those books and papers as the Director may require.'[332]

(ii) Voluntary liquidations

[9.108] In the context of voluntary liquidations, there is no equivalent of s 243. It therefore appears that the court does not have the power to order inspection of the company's documents by a creditor or member of the company. This is underscored by the fact that s 243 refers to the court having made a winding up order, which language would not be appropriate in the case of a voluntary liquidation. Moreover, CLEA 2001, s 49 introduced a provision identical to s 243(1A),[333] to apply in the case of voluntary liquidations, but significantly, did not introduce an equivalent of s 243(1). As will be seen below, most of the powers of the court in relation to detection and investigation of the affairs of a company in compulsory liquidation, were extended to voluntary liquidations by the CLEA 2001. This makes it an almost inescapable conclusion that the failure to extend the power to order inspection under s 243(1) to voluntary liquidations was a deliberate omission.

With regard to inspection by the DCE, s 282A(1) provides:

> The court may, on the application of the Director, make an order for the inspection by the Director of any books and papers in the possession of a company which is in voluntary liquidation and the company, every officer of the company and the liquidator shall give to the Director such access and facilities as are necessary for inspecting and taking copies of those books and papers as the Director may require.

As will be seen below, CLEA 2001, s 57 gives the DCE the power to require the liquidator to produce all books in a liquidation, without the necessity of a court

---

[332] CA 1963, s 243(1A), as inserted by CLEA 2001, s 43.

[333] CA1963, s 282A.

application.[334] As this facility exists, it is likely that ss 243(1A) and 282A will only be invoked by the DCE where s 57 is inadequate.

(c) Examination of persons

[9.109] The court may, at any time after the appointment of a provisional liquidator or the making of a winding up order, either of its own motion, or on the application of the DCE, summon persons to appear before it.[335] In the context of a voluntary liquidation, the court has an identical jurisdiction, pursuant to s 282B.[336]

The persons who may be summoned before the court are the following:[337]

– any officer of the company;

– any person known or suspected of having company property;

– any person supposed to be indebted to the company; and

– any person who the court deems capable of giving information in relation to the promotion, formation, trade, dealings, affairs or property of the company.

[9.110] There is no requirement that particular grounds be established for summoning a person before the court. All that is necessary is that the person be an officer of the company, or it may be sufficient for the person to be 'supposed' to be indebted to the company or 'suspected' of having company property. In light of the some of more draconian consequences of being summoned before the court under s 245,[338] the fact that there is no requirement that the persons be shown to have a definite connection with the company being wound up in a manner which will be of assistance to the liquidation process, could be questioned.

A person who is summoned to answer questions before the court cannot refuse to answer questions on the grounds of self-incrimination.[339] Sections 245(6) and 282B(6) moreover provide that, 'any answer by him to such a question may be used in evidence against him in any proceedings whatsoever (save proceedings for an offence (other than perjury in respect of such answer))'. Section 245(6) was amended by the CLEA 2001,[340] as formerly, the answers given were not admissible in either civil or criminal

---

[334] See below para **[9.128]**.

[335] CA 1963, s 245(1), as substituted by CA 1990, s 126 and as amended by CLEA 2001, s 44.

[336] CA 1963, s 282B, as inserted by CLEA 2001, s 49.

[337] CA 1963, s 245(1), as substituted by CA 1990, s 126 and as amended by CLEA 2001, s 44; CA 1963, s 282B(1), as inserted by CLEA 2001, s 49.

[338] Note that a person who fails to attend for examination can be arrested and his property seized and detained, CA 1963, s 245(8), as substituted by CA 1990, s 126 and as amended by CLEA 2001, s 44; CA 1963, s 282B(8), as inserted by CLEA 2001, s 49.

[339] CA 1963, s 245(6), as substituted by CA 1990, s 126 and as amended by CLEA 2001, s 44; CA 1963, s 282B(6), as inserted by CLEA 2001, s 49.

[340] CLEA 2001, s 44.

proceedings, with the exception of proceedings for perjury in respect of the answer given.[341]

In the event that a person fails without reasonable cause to attend the examination to which he is summoned, this will constitute a punishable contempt of court.[342] Furthermore, in the event of such a failure to attend, or if there are reasonable grounds for believing the person has, or is likely to, abscond, for the purpose of delaying or avoiding the examination, the court may cause that person to be arrested and detained and his books, documents and moveable property to be seized and detained.[343]

The court is empowered to examine any person so summoned on oath, to reduce the answers to writing, and to require that person to sign them.[344] The court can also require a person summoned to produce any document or paper in his custody or power that relate to the company[345] and to place before it a statement of any transactions between him and the company, of such a nature and in such form as the court may direct.[346] A requirement to produce such a statement of transactions must be made before the court examines the person in question.

A further order that can be made by the court in respect of a person who is summoned to appear before it, is that the person so examined should pay the costs of the examination.[347]

It should be noted that the DCE and the court are the only entities which can instigate the issue of a summons for a person to appear for an examination before the court. The liquidator of a company does not have the right, according to the wording of the legislation, to apply to court for the examination of persons involved in the company.

(d) Power of arrest

[9.111] In addition to the power to summon persons for examination and to require such persons to produce books and documents, the court has a broader power to prevent a

---

[341] CA 1963, s 245(6), as substituted by CA 1990, s 126 provided, that 'none of the answers of such person shall be admissible in evidence against him in any other proceedings, civil or criminal'.

[342] CA 1963, s 245(7), as substituted by CA 1990, s 126 and as amended by CLEA 2001, s 44; CA 1963, s 282B(7), as inserted by CLEA 2001, s 49.

[343] CA 1963, s 245(8), as substituted by CA 1990, s 126 and as amended by CLEA 2001, s 44; CA 1963, s 282B(8), as inserted by CLEA 2001, s 49.

[344] CA 1963, s 245(2), as substituted by CA 1990, s 126 and as amended by CLEA 2001, s 44; CA 1963, s 282B(2), as inserted by CLEA 2001, s 49.

[345] CA 1963, s 245(3), as substituted by CA 1990, s 126 and as amended by CLEA 2001, s 44; CA 1963, s 282B(3), as inserted by CLEA 2001, s 49.

[346] CA 1963, s 245(4), as substituted by CA 1990, s 126 and as amended by CLEA 2001, s 44; CA 1963, s 282B(4), as inserted by CLEA 2001, s 49.

[347] CA 1963, s 245(5), as substituted by CA 1990, s 126 and as amended by CLEA 2001, s 44; CA 1963, s 282B(5), as inserted by CLEA 2001, s 49. This order can be made if the court considers it 'just and equitable' to do so.

person from absconding in the course of a compulsory winding up. This power was extended to companies being wound up voluntarily by virtue of the CLEA 2001, s 49.[348]

Sections 247 and 282D provide that the court may:

> … on proof of probable cause for believing that a contributory, director, shadow director, secretary or other officer is about to quit the State or otherwise to abscond or to remove or conceal any of his property for the purpose of evading payment of calls or of avoiding examination about the affairs of the company, may, of its own motion or on the application of the Director, a creditor of the company or any other interested person, cause the contributory, director, shadow director, secretary or other officer to be arrested, and his books and papers and movable personal property to be seized and him and them to be detained until such time as the court may order.[349]

The only difference between this provision as it applies in relation to compulsory and voluntary liquidations, is that the court may make an order for arrest and seizure in relation to the former, 'at any time either before or after making a winding-up order',[350] whereas such an order may be made 'at any time in respect of a voluntary winding up'.[351] This difference in language suggests that a company must already be in voluntary liquidation before the court will order the arrest of a director, for example, but such an order may be made before the making of an order for compulsory liquidation.

[9.112] There is a degree of overlap between these provisions and CA 1963, s 245(8) and 282B(8).[352] The latter provides for the arrest and detention of an individual and the seizure of his property, if he fails to attend an examination to which he was summoned by the court under s 245 or if there are reasonable grounds for believing he has, or is about to, abscond, with a view to delaying or avoiding the examination.

Among the points of distinction between the provisions are the following:

- as noted above, an order can be made under s 247 before a winding up order is made, while ss 245 and 282B can only be invoked after a winding up order is made;

- ss 247 and 282D are not dependent on the issue of a summons for examination by the court;

- the category of persons to whom ss 247 and 282D apply is more limited than the scope of ss 245 and 282B, as it affects only members, directors, shadow directors or other officers of the company;

- there must be 'probable cause' to believe the person is going to abscond or remove or conceal property under ss 247 and 282D, whereas ss 245(8) and 282B(8) require only 'reasonable grounds';

---

[348] CLEA 2001, s 49, inserted a new s 282D.

[349] CA 1963, s 247, as substituted by CLEA 2001, s 46 and CA 1963, s 282D, as inserted by CLEA 2001, s 49.

[350] CA 1963, s 247, as substituted by CLEA 2001, s 46.

[351] CA 1963, s 282D, as inserted by CLEA 2001, s 49.

[352] CA 1963, s 245(8), as substituted by CA 1990, s 126 and as amended by CLEA 2001, s 44; CA 1963, s 282B(8), as inserted by CLEA 2001, s 49.

- the DCE, a creditor or other interested party, can make an application for an order under ss 247 and 282D, whereas it appears that an order under ss 245(8) and 282B(8) can only be made of the court's own motion;

- the fact that a person may be about to remove or conceal property is not a ground for invoking ss 245(8) or 282B(8), but may justify an order under ss 247 or 282D.

There are some areas of duplication between the two sets of provisions. For example, where a person plans to abscond for the purpose of evading examination about the affairs of the company, this is one of the grounds on which ss 247 and 282D can be invoked. However, there is no requirement that the person must have been summoned to attend such an examination. It may be expected that, in the event that the person had been so summoned, ss 245(8) or 282B(8) would be invoked, involving as it does, a lower burden of proof. There is therefore some incongruity in providing for the arrest of an individual for attempting to evade an examination to which he had not been summoned.

(e) Orders for payment, delivery up, search and seizure

[9.113] CA 1963, s 245A[353] is a further provision conferring specific powers on the court in relation to compulsory liquidations. According to this provision, if it appears during an examination of a person under s 245, that the person is indebted to the company or is in possession of money, property, books or papers of the company, there are certain orders the court may make.[354] Since the enactment of the CLEA 2001, these orders can also be made in the context of a voluntary winding up.[355]

First, the court may, on the application of the DCE or of its own motion, order the person to pay or deliver to the liquidator all or part of the amount of the debt or money, property, books or papers as the court may order.[356]

Secondly, where the court has made such an order for payment or delivery, it may also, on the application of the DCE or the liquidator, make an order permitting the DCE or the liquidator, as the case may be, to do the following:[357]

- enter any premises[358] owned or occupied by the person in question at any time or times within one month from the date of issue of the order;

- be accompanied by such persons as the DCE or liquidator, as the case may be, considers appropriate;

- search the premises;

---

[353] As inserted by CA 1990, s 127, and as amended by CLEA 2001, s 45.

[354] CA 1963, s 245A(1), as inserted by CA 1990, s 127, and as amended by CLEA 2001, s 45.

[355] CA 1963, s 282C, as inserted by CLEA 2001, s 49.

[356] CA 1963, s 245A(1), as inserted by CA 1990, s 127, and as amended by CLEA 2001, s 45; CA 1963, s 282C(1), as inserted by CLEA 2001, s 49.

[357] CA 1963, s 245A(2), as inserted by CA 1990, s 127, and as amended by CLEA 2001, s 45; CA 1963, s 282C(2), as inserted by CLEA 2001, s 49.

[358] The premises that can be searched expressly include the dwelling of the person in question.

    – use such force as is reasonably necessary; and

    – seize any property, money, books or papers of the company found.

These powers of entry, search and seizure are bolstered by the fact that it is an offence for an individual to obstruct their exercise or to obstruct the exercise of the right to take possession of property, money, books or papers, found at the premises.[359]

This provision confers extensive powers on the DCE or liquidator and it should be noted that it is not predicated on a failure by the person the subject of an order under ss 245A(1) or 282C(1), to comply with such an order. In these circumstances, it is conceivable that a person may be ordered to pay a debt under ss 245A(1) or 282C(1) and, having complied with that order, may nonetheless be the subject of a search order. This is particularly egregious in light of the fact that there is no evidential burden that must be discharged in an application for a search order under ss 245A(2) or 282C(2).

[9.114] It is curious to note that a liquidator of a company that is being wound up by the court or voluntarily, has neither the right to apply to the court for a summons to be issued for the examination of a particular person under ss 245 or 282B,[360] nor the right to apply for an order for the payment or delivery of company money, property, books or papers, under ss 245A(1) or 282C(1), but is entitled to apply for an order for search of that person's premises and seizure of their property. The reason for this discrepancy in the liquidator's right to apply to the court for some orders, but not others, is unclear.

[9.115] When the court has made an order for search and seizure under ss 245A(2) or 282C(1), the DCE or the liquidator, as the case may be, must report back to the court on the outcome of any search conducted on foot of the court order.[361] The court will then issue directions as to the disposition of anything seized, but no such direction will be issued to the DCE except directions as to the DCE's costs and expenses.[362]

(f) Prevention of removal or dissipation of assets

[9.116] A new power that was conferred on the court by the CLEA 2001, is the power to prevent the removal or dissipation of assets from the State. CLEA 2001, s 55, provides that:

> The court may, on the application of a company, director, member, liquidator, receiver, creditor or the Director, order a director or other officer of a company not to remove his or her assets from the State or to reduce his or her assets within or

---

[359] CA 1963, s 245A(5), as inserted by CA 1990, s 127, and as amended by CLEA 2001, s 45; CA 1963, s 282C(5), as inserted by CLEA 2001, s 49. Proceedings for such an offence are without prejudice to the power of the court to issue contempt proceedings for failure to comply with the court order. See CA 1963, s 245A(6), as inserted by CA 1990, s 127, and as amended by CLEA 2001, s 45; CA 1963, s 282C(6), as inserted by CLEA 2001, s 49.

[360] See above para **[9.110]**.

[361] CA 1963, s 245A(3), as inserted by CA 1990, s 127, and as amended by CLEA 2001, s 45; CA 1963, s 282C(3), as inserted by CLEA 2001, s 49.

[362] CA 1963, s 245A(4), as inserted by CA 1990, s 127, and as amended by CLEA 2001, s 45; CA 1963, s 282C(4), as inserted by CLEA 2001, s 49.

outside the State below an amount to be specified by the court, where the court is satisfied that—

(a) the applicant has a substantive civil cause of action or right to seek a declaration of personal liability or claim for damages against the director, other officer or the company, and

(b) there are grounds for believing that the respondent may remove or dispose of his, her or the company's assets with a view to evading his, her or the company's obligations and frustrating an order of the court.

[9.117] Before the enactment of s 55, the courts had exercised their inherent jurisdiction to prevent the dissipation of assets by means of the issue of mareva injunctions. In *Re John Horgan Livestock Ltd*,[363] for example, the official liquidator, appointed pursuant to the petition of the Revenue Commissioners, applied for interlocutory injunctions to prevent a director of the company from dissipating the company's assets. In particular, the liquidator sought an interlocutory injunction restraining a director from collecting the sum of £71,000, which represented monies payable under a policy of insurance. In the alternative, the liquidator sought an interlocutory injunction restraining the director from disposing of, dissipating or charging that sum of money.

The High Court granted the application. On appeal, the Supreme Court analysed the law applicable to mareva injunctions. Hamilton CJ, delivering the judgment of the Supreme Court, cited the decision in *Z Ltd v A-Z and AA-LL*[364] to the effect that a Mareva injunction should be granted:

'... but granted only, when it appears to the court that there is a combination of two circumstances. First, when it appears likely that the plaintiff will recover judgment against the defendant for a certain or approximate sum. Secondly, when there are also reasons to believe that the defendant has assets within the jurisdiction to meet the judgment, in whole or in part, but may well take steps designed to ensure that these are no longer available or traceable when judgment is given against him.'[365]

Hamilton CJ concluded that:

'... the cases establish that there must be an intention on the part of the defendant to dispose of his assets with a view to evading his obligation to the plaintiff and to frustrate the anticipated order of the court. It is not sufficient to establish that the assets are likely to be dissipated in the ordinary course of business or in the payment of lawful debts.'[366]

The Supreme Court emphasised the requirement that the liquidator must establish the likelihood that the assets would be dissipated with the intention that they would not be

---

[363] *Re John Horgan Livestock Ltd, O'Mahony v Horgan* [1995] IESC 6; [1995] 2 IR 411; [1996] 1 ILRM 161 (Supreme Court, 7 November 1995).

[364] *Z Ltd v A-Z and AA-LL* [1982] 1 QB 558, [1982], 2 WLR 288, [1982] 1 All ER 556, [1982] 1 Lloyd's Rep 240 (*per* Kerr LJ).

[365] *Re John Horgan Livestock Ltd, O'Mahony v Horgan* [1995] 2 IR 411, 418, quoting *Z Ltd v A-Z and AA-LL* [1982] 1 QB 558 at 585.

[366] *Re John Horgan Livestock Ltd, O'Mahony v Horgan* [1995] 2 IR 411, 422.

available to meet a decree made against them.[367] It was on this basis that the Court allowed the appeal and refused the liquidator's application for a mareva injunction.

[9.118] CLEA 2001, s 55 preserves the requirement that the person against whom an order is sought must be attempting to remove the assets in question 'with a view to evading his, her or the company's obligations and frustrating an order of the court'. This mirrors the legal requirements for a successful application for a mareva injunction and decisions such as *Re John Horgan Livestock Ltd*,[368] will therefore be of relevance to liquidators seeking to invoke s 55.

(g) Order for return of company property

[9.119] A court has the power to direct the return of property to a liquidator, if the court is satisfied that the property was disposed of with the effect of perpetrating a fraud on the company, its creditors or members. CA 1990, s 139(1) provides:

> Where, on the application of a liquidator, creditor or contributory of a company which is being wound up, it can be shown to the satisfaction of the court that—
>
> (a) any property of the company of any kind whatsoever was disposed of either by way of conveyance, transfer, mortgage, security, loan, or in any way whatsoever whether by act or omission, direct or indirect, and
>
> (b) the effect of such disposal was to perpetrate a fraud on the company, its creditors or members, the court may, if it deems it just and equitable to do so, order any person who appears to have the use, control or possession of such property or the proceeds of the sale or development thereof to deliver it or pay a sum in respect of it to the liquidator on such terms or conditions as the court sees fit.

An application for such an order may be made by the liquidator, a creditor or member of the company. The application must be made by way of notice of motion in an official liquidation, or by means of originating notice of motion in a voluntary liquidation.[369]

The criteria for the making of an order under s 139 are the following:

– The company must be in course of being wound up;

– The court must be satisfied that property of the company of any kind was disposed of by a direct or indirect act or omission, such as a conveyance, transfer, mortgage, security, or loan;

– The court must be satisfied that the effect of the disposal was to perpetrate a fraud on the company, its creditors or members; and

– The court must consider it just and equitable to make the order sought.[370]

---

[367] *Re John Horgan Livestock Ltd, O'Mahony v Horgan* [1995] 2 IR 411, 421.

[368] *Re John Horgan Livestock Ltd, O'Mahony v Horgan* [1995] IESC 6; [1995] 2 IR 411; [1996] 1 ILRM 161 (Supreme Court, 7 November 1995).

[369] Rules of the Superior Courts (No 4) of 1991 (SI 278/1991), substituting ord 74, r 136.

[370] CA 1990, s 139(1). Note that this provision does not apply to fraudulent preferences within the meaning of CA 1963, s 286. See CA 1990, s 139(2).

If all of these criteria are met, the court may order 'any person who appears to have the use, control of such property' to return that property to the liquidator. Alternatively, the court may order that 'any person who appears to have the use, control or possession of … the proceeds of sale or development' of the property must pay a sum in respect of that sale or development to the liquidator. The court may make these orders on such terms or conditions as the court sees fit.

While there is no express requirement that the person who is in possession or control of the property or the proceeds of its sale or development, must have notice of the fraudulent nature of the conveyance or transaction, it may be expected that a court would only consider it 'just and equitable' to return the order of such property or proceeds, if the person in possession or control thereof did not acquire the property in good faith and without notice of the fraud. This is confirmed by s 139(3): 'In deciding whether it is just and equitable to make an order under this section, the court shall have regard to the rights of persons who have *bona fide* and for value acquired an interest in the property the subject of the application.'

A court may also make an order under s 139 in respect of a company that is in receivership[371] and a company to which an examiner has been appointed.[372]

(h) Contribution toward debts of related companies

[9.120] A court may order that a company that is related to a company that is being wound up, whether voluntarily or compulsorily, must contribute to the debts of that company.[373] Section 140 is the governing provision in this regard and requires that the

---

[371] CA 1990, s 178 provides: 'The provisions of section 139 shall, with the necessary modifications, apply to a company in receivership as if the references therein to the liquidator and to winding up were construed as references to the receiver and to receivership.'

[372] CA 1990, s 180(2) provides: 'section 244A of the Principal Act (inserted by section 125 of the Companies Act 1990) and section 139 of the Companies Act 1990, shall apply to a company under the protection of the court as they apply to a company being wound up, and any references in those sections to a liquidator or provisional liquidator shall be construed for the purposes of this subsection as a reference to an examiner.'

[373] A 'related company' is defined in s 140(5) as follows: 'For the purposes of this Act, a company is related to another company if— (a) that other company is its holding company or subsidiary; or (b) more than half in nominal value of its equity share capital (as defined in section 155 (5) of the Principal Act) is held by the other company and companies related to that other company (whether directly or indirectly, but other than in a fiduciary capacity); or (c) more than half in nominal value of the equity share capital (as defined in section 155(5) of the Principal Act) of each of them is held by members of the other (whether directly or indirectly, but other than in a fiduciary capacity); or (d) that other company or a company or companies related to that other company or that other company together with a company or companies related to it are entitled to exercise or control the exercise of more than one half of the voting power at any general meeting of the company; or (e) the businesses of the companies have been so carried on that the separate business of each company, or a substantial part thereof, is not readily identifiable; or (f) there is another company to which both companies are related.'

court must be satisfied that it is just and equitable to order the related company to pay the whole or part of all or any of the debts of the company that is being wound up.[374] Among the matters to which the court must have regard in reaching this determination are the following:

- The extent to which the related company took part in the management of the company that is being wound up;

- The conduct of the related company towards the creditors of the company being wound up; and

- The effect the order would be likely to have on the creditors of the related company.[375]

Furthermore, the court cannot make an order that a related company contribute to the debts of a company that is being wound up, unless it is satisfied that 'the circumstances that gave rise to the winding up of the company are attributable to the acts or omissions of the related company.'[376]

An application for such an order may be made by the liquidator, or a creditor or contributory of the company that is being wound up.[377] A 'creditor' for the purposes of s 140, means one or more creditors who are owed more than €12,697.38 in the aggregate.[378]

[9.121] A similar provision is CA 1990, s 141, which provides for two or more related companies that are being wound up by the court, to be wound up together as if they are one company. This only applies in relation to compulsory liquidations and a liquidator of one of the companies is the only person who may apply for such an order. The court must be satisfied that it is just and equitable to order that the companies be wound up together and may make the order on such terms and conditions, and to such an extent, as the court orders.[379] In determining the terms and conditions of such an order, the court is required to 'have particular regard' to the interests of those who are members of some, but not all, of the companies being wound up.[380]

---

[374] CA 1990, s 140(1). Note that it is not 'just and equitable' to make an order under s 140 on the sole ground that the companies are related to each other or that the creditors of the company that is being wound up relied upon the fact that it was related to the other company. CA 1990, s 140(4). See generally MacCann and Courtney (eds) *Companies Acts 1963–2006* (Tottel Publishing, 2007) at pp 1258 to 1259, where the origin of this provision, which is modelled on the New Zealand Companies Act 1955, s 245(1)(a) and the New Zealand Companies Act 1993, s 271(1), is considered.

[375] CA 1990, s 140(2).

[376] CA 1990, s 140(3).

[377] CA 1990, s 140(1).

[378] CA 1990, s 140(6).

[379] CA 1990, s 141(1).

[380] CA 1990, s 141(2). See also CA 1990, s 141(4) and (5) regarding the matters that must be taken into account in determining whether it is 'just and equitable' to make an order under s 141.

(i) Extension of powers to companies not in liquidation

[9.122] Some of the orders that may be made in respect of companies that are being wound up, may also be made in relation to companies that are not being wound up. CA 1990, s 251 is the governing provision in this regard. It applies if the following criteria are met:

– 'Execution or other process issued on a judgment, decree or order of any court in favour of a creditor of the company is returned unsatisfied in whole or in part';[381] or

– 'it is proved to the satisfaction of the court that the company is unable to pay its debts, taking into account the contingent and prospective liabilities of the company';[382] and

– 'it appears to the court that the reason or the principal reason for its not being wound up is the insufficiency of its assets.'[383]

Section 251 is essentially directed towards companies which a court is satisfied are insolvent, but which are not being wound up due to the insufficiency of their assets.

If a court determines that a company meets the criteria of s 251(1), the following provisions may be applied to that company:

– CA 1990, s 139, which provides for an order to return property to a liquidator, on the basis that it was disposed of with the effect of perpetrating a fraud on the company;[384]

– CA 1990, s 140, which provides for an order that a company related to a company being wound up must contribute to the debts of that company;[385]

– CA 1990, s 148, which extends the power to assess damages against directors of a company that is being wound up, to directors of the holding company of the company that is being wound up;[386]

---

[381] CA 1990, s 251(1)(a).

[382] CA 1990, s 251(1)(b).

[383] CA 1990, s 251(1).

[384] CA 1990, s 251(2)(a), as amended by CLEA 2001, s 54 and as substituted by reg 9 and Schedule of the European Communities (International Financial Reporting Standards and Miscellaneous Amendments) Regulations 2005 (SI 116/2005). See above para **[9.119]**.

[385] CA 1990, s 251(2)(a), as amended by CLEA 2001, s 54 and as substituted by reg 9 and Schedule of the European Communities (International Financial Reporting Standards and Miscellaneous Amendments) Regulations 2005 (SI 116/2005). See above para **[9.120]**.

[386] CA 1990, s 251(2)(a), as amended by CLEA 2001, s 54 and as substituted by reg 9 and Schedule of the European Communities (International Financial Reporting Standards and Miscellaneous Amendments) Regulations 2005 (SI 116/2005). See further Ch **6**.

- CA 1990, s 149, which defines the scope of CA 1990, Pt VII, Ch I, a chapter which deals with declarations of restriction;[387]

- CA 1990, s 149A, a provision which does not exist in the CA 1990;[388]

- CA 1990, s 203, which permits the prosecution of officers of companies that are being wound up, are insolvent, and have failed to keep proper books of account, on the conditions set out in that provision;[389]

- CA 1990, s 204, which provides for the imposition of personal liability for the debts of a company on officers of the company, where the conditions of that provision are met;[390]

- CA 1963, s 243, which provides for the inspection of the books of a company in compulsory liquidation by its creditors or contributories;[391]

- CA 1963, s 245,[392] which provides for the summoning of persons before the court for examination on oath, and for the production of records and documents, where the criteria of s 245(1) are met;[393]

- CA 1963, 245A,[394] which provides for the delivery up of money, property, books or papers of the company in liquidation by persons who have been examined under s 245;[395]

---

[387] CA 1990, s 251(2)(a), as amended by CLEA 2001, s 54 and as substituted by reg 9 and Schedule of the European Communities (International Financial Reporting Standards and Miscellaneous Amendments) Regulations 2005 (SI No 116/2005). See further Ch **16** and Pt D, Declarations of Restriction, generally.

[388] This provision was added to the list included under CA 1990, s 251(2)(a) by reg 9 and Schedule of the European Communities (International Financial Reporting Standards and Miscellaneous Amendments) Regulations 2005 (SI No 116/2005), and must have been erroneously included.

[389] CA 1990, s 251(2)(a), as amended by CLEA 2001, s 54 and as substituted by reg 9 and Schedule of the European Communities (International Financial Reporting Standards and Miscellaneous Amendments) Regulations 2005 (SI 116/2005). See further Ch **4**.

[390] CA 1990, s 251(2)(a), as amended by CLEA 2001, s 54 and as substituted by reg 9 and Schedule of the European Communities (International Financial Reporting Standards and Miscellaneous Amendments) Regulations 2005 (SI No 116/2005). See further Ch **4**.

[391] CA 1990, s 251(2)(b) and Table. See above paras **[9.107]** to **[9.108]**.

[392] CA 1963, s 245, as substituted by CA 1990, s 126.

[393] CA 1990, s 251(2)(b) and Table. See above paras **[9.109]** to **[9.110]**. See also *Alba Radio v Haltone* [1995] 2 IR 170, for an example of a case in which a successful application was made under CA 1963, s 245 by means of CA 1990, s 251. In that case, s 251 was applied retrospectively, on the basis that, 'there is no right vested in Michael Murphy not to be examined under section 245 of the Companies Act, 1963 unless the company is being wound up. Because the law has been altered as to the circumstances in which an application may be made under section 245 and its provisions have been altered to some extent does not mean that the Act is being operated retrospectively' (per Barron J at 173).

[394] CA 1963, s 245A, as inserted by CA 1990, s 127.

[395] CA 1990, s 251(2)(b) and Table. See above paras **[9.113]** to **[9.115]**.

- CA 1963, s 247[396] which provides for a person to be arrested and his books, papers and property seized and detained, in the circumstances stipulated in that provision;[397]

- CA 1963, s 295, which provides that an officer of a company which is being wound up, may be prosecuted with the offence of having defrauded creditors of the company or fraudulently induced others to give credit to the company;[398]

- CA 1963, ss 297[399] and 297A[400], which address, respectively, criminal liability for fraudulent trading and civil liability for fraudulent trading and reckless trading;[401] and

- CA 1963, s 298,[402] which provides for the assessment of damages against promoters, officers, liquidators, receivers, or examiners, of companies in liquidation, in the circumstances set out in that provision.[403]

[9.123] These provisions must clearly be adapted for the purposes of s 251. Section 251(3) provides in this regard, that where these provisions refer to the date of the winding up order or other such dates, this should be read as referring to the date on which the criteria of s 251 were met, specifically the date of the judgment or order that

---

[396] CA 1963, s 247, as substituted by CLEA 2001, s 46.

[397] CA 1990, s 251(2)(b) and Table. See above paras [9.111] to [9.112].

[398] CA 1990, s 251(2)(b) and Table. See further Ch 6.

[399] CA 1963, s 297, as substituted by CA 1990, s 137. Note that, on the terms of s 297, a company does not have to be wound up for that provision to be applicable. Section 297, as it existed before the enactment of CA 1990, was, however, predicated on a company being wound up. See further Ch 6.

[400] CA 1963, s 297A, as inserted by CA 1990, s 138. Note that an attempt to invoke s 251 retrospectively in an application under ss 297A and 298 in relation to a company that was not being wound up, was rejected by the High Court in *Jones v Gunn* [1997] IEHC 27, [1997] 3 IR 1: 'Section 297A(1)(b) in itself is not retrospective in its application, since by and large it restates existing law and does not impose new penalties or disabilities. However, that is in the context of a company in the course of being wound up. Under the previous law the penalty of personal liability could not have been applied to the directors of the third-named Defendant as it has never been wound up. I do not find it a particularly attractive proposition that a director of a company, who may have treated its creditors in a fraudulent manner, should be able to avoid personal liability simply by ceasing to trade and by not winding up the company. That may, indeed, have been one of the mischiefs which it was sought to cure by the enactment of section 251 of the Companies Act, 1990. Nevertheless, I must conclude that to operate the Sections 297A(1)(b) and section 251 together would be to impose a liability on the first-named Defendant which could not have been imposed on him under the original 1963 Act. The impugned transactions were completed prior to August 1991 and therefore the Plaintiff's claim under Section 297A must fail because it would involve retrospection. The same infirmity would attach to a claim under Section 298 because it, too, would involve the use of Section 251.' (per McGuinness J at p 17).

[401] CA 1990, s 251(2)(b) and Table.

[402] CA 1963, s 298, as substituted by CA 1990, s 142. See further Ch 6.

[403] CA 1990, s 251(2)(b) and Table.

was returned unsatisfied, within the meaning of s 251(1)(a) or the date of the court's determination that the company is unable to pay its debts, within the meaning of s 251(2)(b).[404]

[9.124] If the criteria of s 251(1) are met, the DCE may apply to court for the orders or judgments provided for by any of these provisions.[405] This is without prejudice to the right of persons who may invoke the provisions referred to in s 251, when the company is being wound up, to do so when s 251 is applicable. There is nothing in s 251 which limits its scope to applications by the DCE: s 251 indeed pre-dates the creation of the office of the DCE, and if the standing of other persons was intended to be ousted, this would have to have been expressly provided for. An application under s 251 may be made by way of originating notice of motion.[406]

A person who has a claim against the company, and who does not invoke one of the provisions listed in s 251 directly, may apply for a share of any monies or assets recovered by the DCE, but only if they seek such an enforcement order within one month of the date on which the DCE obtained judgment.[407] Any creditors of companies that are not being wound up, but which appear to be insolvent, would be well advised to monitor any proceedings initiated by the DCE in respect of that company under s 251 and to move quickly to recover monies if a court order is made for the payment of monies or the delivery of property under that provision.

[9.125] A final point that may be noted about s 251 is that, when proceedings are instituted under certain provisions listed in that section[408] by persons other than the DCE, the court may make additional directions regarding the sums recovered, including the following:

- The persons or classes of persons who may be paid from the sums recovered;
- The purposes for which such payments may be made;
- The amounts or proportions of such payments;
- The time or times at which the payments may be made;
- The priorities that will apply to the payment of those sums among the different persons.[409]

---

[404] Note that, whereas CA 1963, s 295 refers to offences by officers of a company 'which is subsequently ordered to be wound up by the court or subsequently passes a resolution for voluntary winding up', s 251(5) provides that those words can be deleted, when s 295 is applied in the context of s 251.

[405] CA 1990, s 251(2A), as inserted by CLEA 2001, s 54(b).

[406] See Rules of the Superior Courts, Order 75B, Rule 3(dd), as inserted by Rules of the Superior Courts (No 4) of 1991 (SI No 278/1991).

[407] CA 1990, s 251(4)(b), as inserted by CLEA 2001, s 54(c).

[408] This applies to applications under CA 1990, ss 139, 140 and 204, and CA 1963, ss 254A, 297A and 298. See CA 1990, s 251(4)(a), as inserted by CLEA 2001, s 54(c).

[409] See CA 1963, s 297A(7)(b), as inserted by CA 1990, s 138 ('Where the court makes any such declaration [of personal liability], it may … provide that sums recoverable under this section shall be paid to such person or classes of person, for such purposes, in such amounts or proportions at such time or times and in such respective priorities among themselves as such declaration may specify.')

This is subject to the qualification that, where the court makes an order under one of these provisions, by means of s 251, on an application by the DCE, no order can be made in favour of the DCE, other than an order for the payment of costs and expenses.[410]

[9.126] An interesting illustration of the application of s 251 arose in *Airscape Ltd v Powertech Logistics Ltd*.[411] The applicant sought an order applying CA 1990, s 251, to a company against which the applicant had obtained judgment in the amount of €289,550. The applicant further sought an order under CA 1963, s 245, that two directors of that company be summoned before the court for examination on oath to provide information in relation to the company.

In relation to the first order sought, the Court had no difficulty in determining that the company was insolvent and that the only reason that it was not being wound up was the insufficiency of its assets. Section 251 therefore applied to the company. Laffoy J then held, 'the consequence of that finding is provided for in sub-s (2) of s 251, which provides that certain sections of the Companies code, with necessary qualification, shall apply to a company to which the section applies, notwithstanding that it is not being wound up. All of the sections invoked by the applicant on the second motion come within the ambit of s 251(2). Accordingly, having found that the first respondent is unable to pay its debts and is not being wound up because of insufficiency of assets, the provisions invoked automatically apply to the first respondent as of now.'[412]

The Court then turned to the application for an order under CA 1963, s 245, noting that the court's powers under that provision are discretionary and that there was no authority opened to the court in which an order under s 245, pursuant to an order under s 251, was sought.

In this regard, it is interesting to note that CA 1963, s 245, permits the court 'of its own motion or on the application of the Director' to summon before it officers of a company or persons known or suspected to have possession of company property, or to be indebted to the company, or any person who the court considers to be capable of providing information in relation to the company.[413] It does not provide expressly for an application to be made by a creditor or contributory of the company or by any person. It is, however, established practice, that a liquidator may make an application under s 245.[414] Moreover, on the authority of *Re Comet Food Machinery Company Ltd*,[415] a

---

[410] CA 1990, s 251(4)(a), as inserted by CA 1990, s 54(c).

[411] *Airscape Ltd v Powertech Logistics Ltd* [2007] IEHC 43.

[412] *Airscape Ltd v Powertech Logistics Ltd* [2007] IEHC 43.

[413] CA 1963, s 245(1), as substituted by CA 1990, s 126.

[414] See MacCann and Courtney (gen eds) *Companies Acts 1963–2006* (Tottel Publishing, 2007) at p 471.

[415] *Re Comet Food Machinery Company Ltd* [1999] 1 IR 485 ('It cannot be said that, in these circumstances, the application is one which is manifestly brought by the applicant without any hope of recovering any benefit but simply in order to initiate an unnecessarily intrusive inquiry because of pique arising from the fact that its proceedings against Comet have so far proved fruitless', *per* Keane J at p 490).

creditor or contributory may make an application under s 245, provided he can show a probability that some benefit will accrue to him from such an examination.

[9.127] In *Airscape Ltd v Powertech Logistics Ltd*,[416] Laffoy J considered the grounds relied upon in the application for an order under s 245, noting that the affidavit grounding the application did not contain a 'specific reason for, or demonstrate that some benefit will accrue to the applicant from, the examinations sought.' The Court further stated that the basis for seeking an order under s 245 was that the manner in which the directors operated the company called for 'further inquiry and examination' and that there was irregularity in the manner in which the directors conducted the affairs of the company. While the Court considered that there was 'some truth' in these contentions, the Court also held that,

> 'there is an onus on a creditor of a company which is not being wound up, who is seeking an order under s 245 in reliance on s 251, to demonstrate that the examination would probably result in a benefit accruing to him. That onus is more rigorous than the onus borne by a contributory or a creditor in a compulsory or a voluntary winding up.'[417]

The applicant did not discharge this onus. On the contrary, according to Laffoy J, the examination sought would amount to a 'fishing expedition'. While it might reveal information that would reflect unfavourably on the directors, there was no evidence that an examination would benefit the applicant. The Court referred in passing to s 297A,[418] in a reference which suggests that, if an examination would probably reveal information which would advance proceedings for personal liability under a provision such as s 297A, that may be a benefit to a creditor that may be taken into account in an application under s 245.

The Court also clarified that a 'public interest' rationale for seeking an order under s 245, 'however commendable' is not sufficient and that the DCE is the appropriate person to pursue such applications in the public interest. The Court therefore refused to make an order under s 245.

It may be expected that this decision will not apply to all cases within the scope of s 251. In relation to CA 1990, ss 139, 140, 148, 204, and ss 247, 297A, 298, a creditor and contributory are among the potential applicants expressly referred to and will not therefore face as heavy an onus of proof as arises under s 245.[419] CA 1990, s 203 and CA 1963, ss 295 and 297 relate to prosecutions for criminal offences. Finally, applications under CA 1990, ss 139, 140, 204, and CA 1963, ss 245A, 297A and 298, envisage the return or payment of monies or property to the company or other persons, in accordance with s 251(4)(a). It would not be difficult for a creditor to demonstrate the benefit to be gained from a successful application under any of those provisions.

---

[416] *Airscape Ltd v Powertech Logistics Ltd* [2007] IEHC 43.

[417] *Airscape Ltd v Powertech Logistics Ltd* [2007] IEHC 43.

[418] *Airscape Ltd v Powertech Logistics Ltd* [2007] IEHC 43 ('there is no evidence from which one could infer that anything would emerge which would be of benefit to the applicant in, say, pursuing proceedings under s 297(A)' per Laffoy J).

[419] See in this regard, *Re Comet Food Machinery Company Ltd* [1999] 1 IR 485.

E. Investigation of liquidator

(a) Production of liquidator's books

[9.128] While a liquidation is underway, the DCE possesses extensive powers to investigate the company in general, and, more particularly, to examine the execution of the liquidator's duties. CLEA 2001, s 57 is significant in this regard. It provides as follows:

> The Director may on his or her own motion or where a complaint is made to the Director by a member, contributory or creditor of the company, request, specifying the reason why the request is being made, the liquidator of a company in liquidation to produce to the Director the liquidator's books for examination, either in relation to a particular liquidation process or to all liquidations undertaken by the liquidator,[420] and the liquidator shall comply with the request.[421]

The DCE can also put questions to the liquidator about the content of any books produced under s 57 and about the conduct of the liquidation in question, or any other liquidations. The liquidator is obliged to answer any questions put by the DCE and to furnish such assistance as the liquidator is reasonable capable of furnishing.[422] It is an offence for a liquidator to fail to comply with a request under s 57.[423]

According to the DCE, this provision will be used in the following manner:

> 'The Director envisages that he may require to use these powers from time to time in implementing his supervisory functions with respect to insolvent companies and the conduct of their directors. He may also require to use these powers to evaluate the conduct of a liquidator in one or more liquidations.'[424]

While this provision may facilitate the investigation of a liquidator's conduct, it is important to bear in mind that it is broad in scope and may be used to investigate the affairs of a company more generally.

(b) Investigation by professional body

[9.129] A final provision that is relevant to the investigation of companies in liquidation concerns the conduct of the liquidator. According to CLEA 2001, s 58, a prescribed

---

[420] According to CLEA 2001, s 57(3), such a request shall not be made in respect of a liquidation which concluded more than six years previously.

[421] CLEA 2001, s 57(1). The CLRG General Scheme of Draft Companies Consolidation and Reform Bill 2007, Pt A11, Head 84, represents an extended version of s 57, applying that power to require the production of documents to officers, auditors and receivers, as well as liquidators. Available at www.clrg.org.

[422] CLEA 2001, s 57(2).

[423] CLEA 2001, s 57(4).

[424] Consultation Paper C/2002/3, 'The Liquidation-Related Functions of the Director of Corporate Enforcement' at p 22.

professional body of which a liquidator is a member is obliged to report certain matters regarding the conduct of liquidators to the DCE. Section 58 provides:

> Where a disciplinary committee or tribunal (however called) of a prescribed professional body finds that a member conducting a liquidation or receivership has not maintained appropriate records, or it has reasonable grounds for believing that a member has committed an indictable offence under the Companies Acts during the course of a liquidation or receivership, the body shall report the matter, giving details of the finding or, as the case may be, of the alleged offence, to the Director forthwith and if the body fails to comply with this section it, and every officer of the body to whom the failure is attributable, is guilty of an offence.

The DCE recommended that the following bodies be included for the purposes of s 58:[425]

- the Institute of Chartered Accountants in Ireland;

- the Institute of Certified Public Accountants in Ireland;

- the Association of Chartered Certified Accountants;

- the Institute of Incorporated Public Accountants Ltd;

- the Law Society of Ireland;

- the Bar Council;

- the Institute of Taxation in Ireland;

- the Chartered Institute of Management Accountants.

The CLEA 2001 (Section 58) Regulations 2002 prescribe the above mentioned bodies for the purpose of s 58, with the exception of the Bar Council, which is not therefore a prescribed body for the purposes of s 58.[426]

The First Report of the Company Law Review Group noted in relation to CLEA 2001, s 58 that:[427]

> 'This provision is to allow the Director to discharge his general supervisory role in respect of liquidators and receivers and also his role of investigating offences under the Companies Acts.'

This provision therefore facilitates the supervision of liquidators, but only if they are members of a professional body.

---

[425] Consultation Paper C/2002/3, 'The Liquidation-Related Functions of the Director of Corporate Enforcement' at p 23.

[426] CLEA 2001(S 58) R 2002, SI 544/2002.

[427] *First Report of the Company Law Review Group* (February 2002) at para 13.8.5. The Group further recommended that, in addition to the bodies recognised by the Minister under s 187 of the Companies Act 1990, the Law Society of Ireland should be included as a prescribed professional body.

Chapter 10

EXAMINERS' OBLIGATIONS

A. Introduction

[10.001] This chapter considers the obligations and powers of examiners under the CA 1963–2006 and, in particular, C(A)A 1990, as amended by the C(A)(No 2)A 1999. While the C(A)A 1990 Act contains detailed provisions regarding the grounds and procedures for the appointment of examiners, the focus of this chapter is on the rules applicable to a duly appointed examiner and the duties he must discharge to ensure compliance with the Companies Acts.[1]

[10.002] Before considering these duties of examiners, it is important to note the effects of an examinership. C(A)A 1990, s 5(2) provides that, while the court is under the protection of the court, the following rules apply:

- no winding up proceedings may be commenced, nor resolutions passed;[2]

- no receiver may be appointed;[3]

- no attachment, sequestration, distress or execution may be put in force against the company, other than with the examiner's consent;[4]

- if a claim against the company is secured by a mortgage, charge, lien or other charge, on the company's property, this may not be realised except with the examiner's consent;[5]

- no steps may be taken to repossess goods in the company's possession under a hire purchase agreement, except with the examiner's consent;[6]

- if someone other than the company is liable to pay the company's debts, no proceedings shall be commenced, nor attachments, sequestration, distress, or execution, put in force against that person;[7]

---

[1]   For an analysis of the grounds and procedures for the appointment of examiners, see Courtney, *The Law of Private Companies* (2nd edn, Tottel Publishing, 2002), Ch 23.

[2]   C(A)A 1990, s 5(2)(a).

[3]   C(A)A 1990, s 5(2)(b). Note that, according to C(A)A 1990, s 6, as amended by C(A)(No 2)A 1999, s 16, if a receiver is already appointed at the date of commencement of the protection period, the court may order that he cease acting; that he act only in respect of particular assets; that the receiver all books and documents in his possession to the examiner; and that the receiver give the examiner full particulars of all dealings with the company.

[4]   C(A)A 1990, s 5(2)(c).

[5]   C(A)A 1990, s 5(2)(d), as amended by C(A)(No 2)A 1999, s 14.

[6]   C(A)A 1990, s 5(2)(e).

[7]   C(A)A 1990, s 5(2)(f).

– no order for relief may be made under s 205 (for oppression of the interests of a minority shareholder) in respect of matters that occurred before the period of protection;[8]

– no other proceedings in relation to the company may be commenced other than with the leave of, and subject to the conditions imposed by, the court;[9] and

– the court may, on the examiner's application, make such orders as it considers proper in relation to proceedings in being against the company, including an order staying such proceedings.[10]

This period of protection commences when the petition for the appointment of an examiner is filed in the Central Office of the High Court. Section 5(1) provides that, from that date, referred to as the date of presentation of the petition, the company shall be under the protection of the court for a period of 70 days, unless the petition is withdrawn or rejected within that period ('the protection period').[11]

B. General provisions regarding examiners

(a) Qualifications

[10.003] There is nothing in the Companies Acts specifying the qualifications that must be possessed by an examiner. While it is usual for the persons appointed to that office to be qualified and trained as accountants, there is no such requirement.[12] There have been judicial determinations that an examiner appointed to a company should not have

---

8   C(A)A 1990, s 5(2)(g), as inserted by CA 1990, s 180. Note that there is nothing in C(A)A 1990, which prevents an order under s 205 being made during the period of protection that arises out of events that occurred after the commencement of the period of protection. However, C(A)A 1990, s 5(4) provides that, 'complaints concerning the conduct of the affairs of the company while it is under the protection of the court shall not constitute a basis for the making of an order for relief under s 205 of the Principal Act.'

9   C(A)A 1990, s 5(3). Note that, according to O 75A, r 8, Rules of the Superior Courts, any application by an examiner under s 5(3), must be brought by motion on notice to all parties to such existing proceedings, including the company in examinership, and any applications by any persons seeking leave to commence proceedings in relation to the company must be brought by way of motion on notice to the examiner and to the company.

10   C(A)A 1990, s 5(3).

11   C(A)A 1990, s 5(1), as amended by C(A)(No 2)A 1999, s 14. Note that, according to C(A)A 1990, s 18(3), as amended by C(A)(No 2)A 1999, ss 22 and 18(4), this period may be extended for a further 30 days by the court. See paras **[10.059]** to **[10.063]**. In the *Irish Current Law Statutes Annotated*, Declan Murphy notes that, 'Section 14(a) amends s 5(1) by reducing the notional maximum period of Court protection from three months to 70 days, although this may be extended in appropriate circumstances. This contraction in the period of protection is a consequence of the investigative phase of the procedure occurring (with the exception of cases of interim protection under new s 3A) prior to the presentation of the petition.'

12   See ODCE, Decision Notice D/2002/1, 'The Principal Powers and Duties of Liquidators, Receivers and Examiners under the Companies Acts 1963–2001' at para 4.3.

previously acted for the company, but there is no rule prohibiting the independent accountant who submits the report in favour of the petition from being appointed to the office of examiner.[13]

[10.004] There are certain persons who may not act as a company's examiner. The primary rule is that any person who may not act as a liquidator of a company is also prohibited from acting as an examiner of that company.[14] A body corporate is therefore not qualified to act as a company's examiner.[15] In addition, CA 1963, s 300A as inserted by CA 1990, s 146 disqualifies the following persons from acting as a liquidator, and, therefore, also as an examiner, of a company:

- anyone who is, or who was in the twelve months preceding the commencement of the winding up, an officer or servant of the company;

- a parent, spouse, brother, sister or child of an officer of the company;

- a partner or employee of an officer or servant of the company; or

- a person who is disqualified (on one of the aforementioned grounds) from acting as the liquidator of another company which is a subsidiary or holding company of the company in liquidation, or which is a subsidiary of the company in liquidation's holding company.[16]

If a prospective liquidator has a parent, spouse, brother, sister or child who is a servant of the company, this does not give rise to any disqualification. Moreover, with the leave of the court, a person whose parent, spouse, brother, sister or child is an officer of the company, may act as liquidator of that company.[17]

If a prospective examiner has any of the aforementioned connections with a company, he is also prohibited from acting as an examiner of that company. There are two areas of ambiguity that arise from the extension of the provisions governing liquidators' qualifications to examiners. First, a person who was an officer or servant of a company within twelve months prior to the commencement of its winding up, may not be appointed as its liquidator. The basis for calculating the twelve month period is clear.

---

[13] See *Re Tuskar Resources plc* [2001] IEHC 27; [2001] 1 IR 668 ('It should be noted that in *Re Wogans (Drogheda) Limited (No 3)* (9 February 1993, unreported), HC Costello J held that the Court would be very slow to appoint an accountant previously associated with the company as examiner, as his impartiality could be questioned. However, on the other side it can be argued that there would considerable additional expense involved if two accountants had separately to investigate the prospects of the company, and there is also merit in that argument. In view of the fact that the Legislature did not take on itself to prohibit the independent accountant from acting as examiner, I do not think that there is any statutory restriction on the Court in so appointing him, although I can see there may be cases where it would be undesirable to do so.' *per* McCracken J).

[14] C(A)A 1990, s 28(1). ('A person shall not be qualified to be appointed or act as an examiner of a company if he would not be qualified to act as its liquidator.')

[15] CA 1963, s 300(a) and (b). See further Ch **9**.

[16] See also Ch **9**.

[17] CA 1963, s 300A(1)(b), as inserted by CA 1990, s 146.

By contrast, the Companies Acts do not specify the basis for calculating the twelve month prohibition on an examiner acting as a company officer or servant. This may be problematic, as the legislation applicable to examiners alternates between referring to the date of presentation of the petition[18] and the date of appointment of the examiner.[19] Some of the important periods, such as the period of protection of a company in examinership, run from the date of presentation of the petition.[20] In the case of examiners, there is no obvious equivalent to the commencement of a winding up. It is therefore not clear how the twelve month period of prohibition on an examiner acting as an officer or servant of a company should be computed.

[10.005] A second ambiguity in the application of the rules governing the disqualification of liquidators to examiners is that C(A)A 1990 does not specifically extend all of the provisions governing the qualifications of liquidators to examiners. In particular, a liquidator must resign if any of these grounds of disqualification arise after his appointment,[21] but there is no specific statutory requirement that an examiner must resign in such circumstances. While the duration of an examinership is limited and renders it unlikely that an examiner would become disqualified while in office, it is not impossible that an examiner may become disqualified.

If a ground of disqualification, within the meaning of CA 1963, s 300A, does arise, it would be advisable for the examiner to resign. This interpretation is supported by the language in s 28(1) that an examiner 'shall not be qualified to be appointed *or act* as an examiner of a company if he would not be qualified to act as its liquidator' (emphasis added). From this provision, it is apparent that it is not only connections that exist at the date of appointment, but also any that arise in the course of the examinership, that will give rise to a disqualification. The most likely effect of s 28(1), is that any examiner who becomes subject to one of the disqualifications listed in CA 1963, s 300A, is subject to the same rules as a liquidator and must therefore resign.

[10.006] An examiner who acts as such despite the existence of one of the relationships listed in s 300A, is guilty of an offence and liable to a fine. On summary conviction, an examiner in default may be liable to a maximum fine of €1,904.61 and, on conviction on indictment, he may be liable to a maximum fine of €12,697.38.[22]

[10.007] In addition to the grounds of disqualification that apply to liquidators, there are certain other grounds on which a person may not be permitted to act as an examiner of a company. First, a person who is an undischarged bankrupt may not act as an examiner of a company.[23] If an examiner acts in contravention of that prohibition, he shall be guilty of an offence and shall be deemed to be subject to a disqualification order

---

[18] See, eg, C(A)A 1990, s 5(1), as amended by C(A)(No 2)A 1999, s 14; C(A)A 1990, s 6(1), as substituted by C(A)(No 2)A 1999, s 16.

[19] See C(A)A 1990, s 12(3).

[20] See C(A)A 1990, s 5(1), as amended by C(A)(No 2)A 1999, s 14.

[21] CA 1963, s 300A(3), as inserted by CA 1990, s 146.

[22] C(A)A 1990, s 28(2), as amended by CA 1990 s 240(7) as inserted by CLEA 2001, s 104(c).

[23] CA 1963, s 183(1), as substituted by CA 1990, s 169.

from the date of conviction.[24] Secondly, a person who is subject to an order of disqualification may not act as an examiner of a company.[25]

The rules governing the appointment of an examiner and examiners' qualifications notwithstanding, it should be noted that, according to s 13(5), 'The acts of an examiner shall be valid notwithstanding any defects that may afterwards be discovered in his appointment or qualification.'[26]

(b) Publication

[10.008] Upon his appointment, an examiner is under certain specific duties to publicise this appointment. First, within three days after his appointment, the examiner must deliver a copy of the order appointing him to the Registrar of Companies.[27] Secondly, within three days after his appointment, he must 'cause' notice of his appointment and the date of the appointment to be published in two daily newspapers circulating in the district in which the registered office or principal place of business of the company are located.[28] Thirdly, within 21 days of the appointment, the examiner must publish a notice of the appointment and the date of such appointment in the *Companies Registration Office Gazette.*[29]

It is an offence for an examiner to fail to comply with the publication and notification requirements of s 12 and any examiner guilty of such offence is liable, on summary conviction, to a maximum fine of €1,904.61, or €12, 697.38, on conviction on indictment.[30]

Throughout the period of protection, any invoices, orders, or business letters that are issued by or on behalf of the company and on which the company's name appears, must include the words 'in examination (under the Companies (Amendment) Act 1990)' after the company name.[31] This obligation is not imposed specifically on examiners, but any person responsible for a failure to comply with this requirement is guilty of an offence.[32]

---

[24] CA 1963, s 183(1) and (2), as substituted by CA 1990, s 169.

[25] CA 1990, s 159(a). See further Pt **E**, Disqualification Orders.

[26] C(A)A 1990, s 13(5).

[27] C(A)A 1990, s 12(3). Note that, pursuant to s 12(1), the petitioner should already have notified the Registrar of the presentation of the petition ('Where a petition is presented under s 2, notice of the petition in the prescribed form shall, within three days after its presentation, he delivered by the petitioner to the registrar of companies.')

[28] C(A)A 1990, s 12(2), as substituted by C(A)(No 2)A 1999, s 20.

[29] C(A)A 1990, s 12(2), as substituted by C(A)(No 2)A 1999, s 20 and IFCMPA 2005, s 72, which substituted references to *Iris Oifigiúil* for '*The Companies Registration Office Gazette*'.

[30] C(A)A 1990, s 12(5), as amended by CA 1990, s 240(7) as inserted by CLEA 2001, s 104(c).

[31] C(A)A 1990, s 12(4), as substituted by C(A)(No 2)A 1999, s 20.

[32] The penalties are those set out in C(A)A 1990, s 12(5), namely a maximum fine of €1,904.61 on summary conviction, or €12,697.38, on conviction on indictment.

(c) Termination of office

[10.009] The period of protection of a company in examinership ceases when the compromise or scheme of arrangement that is proposed by the examiner takes effect, or on such earlier date as the court may direct.[33] The appointment of the examiner terminates on the same date that the court protection ends.[34]

[10.010] Another means by which the appointment of an examiner may terminate is that the examiner may at any time resign. C(A)A 1990, s 13(1) expressly permits an examiner to resign. However, this provision neither stipulates grounds of resignation, nor requires that the court be notified of such resignation. By contrast, if a liquidator resigns due to an intervening disqualification, he must notify the entity responsible for his appointment, whether the court (in an official liquidation), the company (in a members' voluntary liquidation) or the company and the creditors (in a creditors' voluntary liquidation), of his disqualification and resignation within 14 days and is guilty of an offence if he fails to do so.[35] While there is no statutory equivalent for examiners, O 75A, r 13(1) of *The Rules of the Superior Courts*, stipulates that, if an examiner wishes to resign, he must do so by making an *ex parte* application to court, which must be grounded on an affidavit sworn by the examiner. The grounding affidavit must specify the reasons for, and date of, the proposed resignation. On hearing such an application, the court may direct that notice of the application be served on the petitioner, the company, the directors, or any members or creditors of the company, as the court considers appropriate. In relation to the application, the court may make such order as appears just and proper in the circumstances.[36]

[10.011] A company may remove an examiner if cause is shown.[37] An application for the removal of an examiner must be made by motion on notice to the examiner, the petitioner, the company and its directors, and any other party that the court may direct and must be grounded on an affidavit of the moving party specifying the cause alleged to justify the removal of the examiner.[38] Order 75A, r 13(2) further provides as follows:

> On the hearing of the application, the Court may make such order as appears just in the circumstances and, if satisfied that cause has been shown for the removal of the Examiner by the Court shall order that he be removed forthwith or upon such date as the Court shall specify. The Court may either before or after ruling upon the application for the removal of the Examiner make such order for the production of any document or documents, or the preparation of such report or reports as it thinks fit.

---

[33] C(A)A 1990, s 26(1). Note that, when a compromise or scheme of arrangement is confirmed by the court, it will take effect from such date as is fixed by the court and this date must be within 21 days of the date of the court confirmation (C(A)A 1990, s 24(9)).

[34] C(A)A 1990, s 26(2).

[35] CA 1963, s 300A(3) and (4), as inserted by CA 1990, s 146.

[36] Rules of the Superior Courts, (SI 15/1986), O 75A, r 13(1).

[37] C(A)A 1990, s 13(1).

[38] Rules of the Superior Courts, (SI 15/1986), O 75A, r 13(2).

If a vacancy arises in the office of examiner, the company, a member or creditor of the company or a committee of creditors, if such a committee was established, may apply for a court order filling such a vacancy.[39] This application should generally be made *ex parte*, but the court may adjourn the application and give such directions as are proper, including directions for service of notice of the application on the appropriate parties.[40]

(d) Title

[10.012] From the time of his appointment, the person appointed as examiner shall be described by that title. More specifically, he shall be described as the examiner of the company to which he has been appointed and not by his individual name.[41]

(e) Contractual liability

[10.013] As a general rule, an examiner will be personally liable in respect of a contract which he enters into in the course of the performance of his functions. This applies whether the examiner enters the contract in his own name as the examiner or in the name of the company or otherwise.[42] However, such liability will not be imposed if the contract provides that the examiner is not to be personally liable.

If the examiner does incur personal liability in the performance of his functions, he is entitled to an indemnity from the assets of the company. This does not qualify any right to an indemnity that the examiner may otherwise have.[43]

The provisions of s 13(6) notwithstanding, an examiner will be liable on any contracts that he enters without authority and will not be entitled to any indemnity in respect of such liability.[44]

(f) Directions

[10.014] If any questions arise in the course of the examinership regarding the performance of the examiner's functions, the company or a member or creditor of the company may apply to court for a determination of such questions.[45] This ensures that any potential disputes regarding the examiner's discharge of his functions may be brought before the court at an early stage and that the company, and other interested parties, can seek a judicial determination, rather than being obliged to wait until the examiner makes an application to court, or the court considers the examiner's report on his proposals.[46] An application under s 13(7) should be made by motion on notice to the

---

[39] C(A)A 1990, s 13(2) and (3).

[40] Rules of the Superior Courts, (SI 15/1986), O 75A, r 13(3).

[41] C(A)A 1990, s 13(4).

[42] C(A)A 1990, s 13(6).

[43] C(A)A 1990, s 13(6).

[44] C(A)A 1990, s 13(6).

[45] C(A)A 1990, s 13(7).

[46] C(A)A 1990, s 24.

examiner and the company or any interested party, as appropriate. Order 75A, r 9(3) provides in this regard:

> An application by the company or by an interested party pursuant to s 13(7) of the Act shall be made by motion on notice to the Examiner and to any other interested party or the company, as the case may be, and the Court may deal with any such application as if it were an application under s 7(6) of the Act and make such order as appears just and proper in the circumstances.

(g) Committee of creditors

[10.015] It is possible to have a committee of creditors appointed to assist the examiner in the discharge of his functions.[47] The examiner may do this of his own volition or may be directed by the court to do so.[48] Such a committee must generally include a maximum of five members, including the three largest unsecured creditors who are willing to serve on the committee, unless otherwise directed by the court.[49] The appointment of a committee of creditors gives rise to two related obligations on the part of the examiner.

First, as soon as practicable after the appointment of the committee, the examiner must meet the committee 'to transact such business as may be necessary'.[50] Secondly, when the examiner has formulated proposals for a compromise or scheme of arrangement, he must provide a copy of these to the creditors' committee and the committee may express an opinion on these proposals, on behalf of the committee or on behalf of the creditors or classes of creditors represented on the committee.[51] It may be inferred that the examiner must supply a copy of the proposals to the committee at an early stage in the discharge of his functions and, at a minimum, before he convenes a meeting of the creditors. Otherwise, the obligation to deliver a copy of the proposals to the creditors' committee would entirely duplicate the obligation on every examiner to convene meetings of the creditors to consider the proposed compromise or arrangement.[52]

C. Powers of examiners

(a) Auditors' rights and powers

[10.016] An examiner has the same rights and powers as an auditor and enjoys the same rights to information of co-operation. Section 7(1) provides as follows:

> Any provision of the Companies Acts relating to the rights and powers of an auditor of a company and the supplying of information to and co-operation with such auditor shall, with the necessary modifications, apply to an examiner.[53]

---

[47] C(A)A 1990, s 21.

[48] C(A)A 1990, s 21(1).

[49] C(A)A 1990, s 21(2).

[50] C(A)A 1990, s 21(4).

[51] C(A)A 1990, s 21(3).

[52] C(A)A 1990, s 18. See further paras **[10.055]** to **[10.058]**.

[53] C(A)A 1990, s 7(1). See further Ch **7**.

(b) Meetings

[10.017] An examiner has extensive powers regarding meetings of the members and the board of directors of the company to which he is appointed. These powers override the general rules in the Companies Acts regarding notice of such meetings.[54] First, an examiner is entitled to convene meetings of the members and the board. Secondly, he can set the agenda for such meetings. Thirdly, he can preside at such meetings. Fourthly, an examiner may propose motions and resolutions at meetings of the members or the directors. Fifth, an examiner may give reports to meetings of the members or the board of directors.[55] Finally, an examiner is entitled to reasonable notice[56] of, and to attend and be heard at, all meetings of the board of directors and all general meetings of a company to which he is appointed.[57]

(c) Prevent detriment

[10.018] An examiner may have the power to modify or prevent certain actions by or on behalf of the company in examinership. Before an examiner may exercise this power, there are certain criteria that must exist:

- there must be an 'actual or proposed act, omission, course of conduct, decision or contract' ('the action');

- this action must be done by or on behalf of the company, its officers, employees, members or creditors or by any other person;

- the action in question must relate to the income, assets or liabilities of the company; and

- the examiner must form the opinion that this action 'is or is likely to be to the detriment of that company, or any interested party'.[58]

If these criteria are met, the examiner has full power to take 'whatever steps are necessary to halt, prevent or rectify the effects of such act, omission, course of conduct, decision or contract'. This power is subject to the 'rights of parties acquiring an interest in good faith and for value in such income, assets or liabilities'.[59]

[10.019] There are two points that may be noted about this provision. First, according to the terms of s 7(5), an examiner's view that an action is likely to be to the detriment of 'any interested party' may be a basis for the exercise of the power created by that subsection. 'Interested party' is defined in s 1 as a creditor or member of a company in examinership. In light of the fact that there is no prohibition on an examiner having connections or relationships with creditors or members of a company, this provision may

---

[54] C(A)A 1990, s 7(2).

[55] C(A)A 1990, s 7(2).

[56] According to C(A)A 1990, s 7(4), '"reasonable notice" shall be deemed to include a description of the business to be transacted at any such meeting.'

[57] C(A)A 1990, s 7(3).

[58] C(A)A 1990, s 7(5).

[59] C(A)A 1990, s 7(5).

leave an excessively wide scope for an examiner to intervene in the management of the company without the leave of the court.

A second point to note is that it is a matter within the discretion of the examiner whether he chooses to halt, prevent or rectify, any of the conduct which is listed in s 7(5). If, for example, the company enters a contract that relates to the company's assets, which the examiner considers is likely to be to the detriment of the company, there is no obligation on the examiner to take any steps.

(d) Pre-petition contracts

[10.020] An examiner is not permitted to repudiate contracts that were entered into by the company prior to the presentation of the examinership petition.[60] However, the examiner may determine that certain specified contractual provisions should not be enforceable against the company in examinership.[61] The conditions for the exercise of this power to render contractual provisions unenforceable are as follows:

- the provision must be contained in a contact that was entered by the company at any time, before or after the presentation of the examinership petition;[62]

- the provision must state that the company shall not, or shall only in specified circumstances, either (a) borrow monies or obtain credit from anyone other than the party to the contract, or (b) create or permit the existence of any mortgage, charge, lien or other encumbrance or pledge over all or any part of the company's undertaking or property ('a negative pledge clause');[63]

- the examiner must form the opinion that the negative pledge clause, if it was enforced, would be likely to prejudice the survival of the company or the whole or any part of its undertaking as a going concern;[64] and

- the examiner must serve a notice on the other party or parties to the contract containing the negative pledge clause, informing him or them of that opinion.[65]

When this occurs, the negative pledge clause that is the subject of the notice shall not be binding on the company from the date of service of that notice until the expiry of the period of court protection.[66] The remainder of the contract remains enforceable and valid throughout the period of protection.

---

[60] C(A)A 1990, s 7(5A), as inserted by C(A)(No 2)A 1999, s 18 ('Without prejudice to sub-s (5B), nothing in this section shall enable an examiner to repudiate a contract that has been entered into by the company prior to the period during which the company is under the protection of the court.').

[61] C(A)A 1990, s 7(5B), as inserted by C(A)(No 2)A 1999, s 18. As noted in the Irish Current Law Statutes Annotated by Declan Murphy, 'Section 7(5B) and (5C), in essence, codify the position reached by Irish courts in cases such as *Re Holidair Ltd* [1994] 1 IR 434.'

[62] C(A)A 1990, s 7(5C), as inserted by C(A)(No 2)A 1999, s 18.

[63] C(A)A 1990, s 7(5C), as inserted by C(A)(No 2)A 1999, s 18.

[64] C(A)A 1990, s 7(5B), as inserted by C(A)(No 2)A 1999, s 18.

[65] C(A)A 1990, s 7(5B), as inserted by C(A)(No 2)A 1999, s 18.

[66] C(A)A 1990, s 7(5B), as inserted by C(A)(No 2)A 1999, s 18.

[10.021] In certain circumstances, a company in examinership may affirm or repudiate a contract in respect of which the performance of both the company and the other contracting party has not yet been completed.[67] The obligations that remain to be discharged may not, however, be payment obligations. Section 20(1) provides as follows:

> Where proposals for a compromise or scheme of arrangement are to be formulated in relation to a company, the company may, subject to the approval of the court, affirm or repudiate any contract under which some element of performance other than payment remains to be rendered both by the company and the other contracting party or parties.

Order 75A, r 19 provides that the following procedure applies to an application under s 20:

> An application by the company pursuant to s 20 of the Act to repudiate any contract or any application arising out of such repudiation shall be made by motion on notice to the Examiner and on notice to the other contracting party or parties and on notice to any person referred to in s 20(2) of the Act.[68]

The conditions for the exercise of this right by a company are threefold. First, it must be a company in respect of which proposals for a compromise or scheme of arrangement are to be formulated. This condition clearly requires that the company be in examinership and its language suggests that the compromise or arrangement must not yet have been formulated.[69] Secondly, there must be outstanding performance obligations on the part of both the company and the other contracting party. It appears that, while there must be some obligations remaining to be performed, each of the parties must already have performed some elements of the contract. Thirdly, the court must approve the affirmation or repudiation of any such contract. If the court grants such approval, it make such orders as it considers appropriate to give effect to that approval, including declaring the rights of any person affected by such approval and directing notice to be served on those persons.[70]

[10.022] There are a number of matters which are ambiguous in the formulation of this provision. First, it is not clear from the formulation of s 20 who can apply to court for leave to repudiate or affirm a partly performed contract. As the company must be in examinership for that provision to arise, it may be expected that the examiner would be an appropriate person to make the application. However, under C(A)A 1990, an

---

[67] C(A)A 1990, s 20(1). Note that, according to C(A)A 1990, s 20(2), 'Any person who suffers loss or damage as a result of such repudiation shall stand as an unsecured creditor for the amount of such loss or damage.'

[68] Rules of the Superior Courts, O 75A, r 19.

[69] This interpretation is supported by the terms of C(A)A 1990, s 20(3), which provides that, 'In order to facilitate the formulation, consideration or confirmation of a compromise or scheme of arrangement, the court may hold a hearing and make an order determining the amount of any such loss or damage and the amount so determined shall be due by the company to the creditor as a judgement debt.'

[70] C(A)A 1990, s 20(5).

examiner cannot generally repudiate pre-petition contracts.[71] Section 20(4) casts some light on this question, providing as follows:

> Where the examiner is not a party to an application to the court for the purposes of sub-s (1), the company shall serve notice of such application on the examiner and the examiner may appear and be heard on the hearing of any such application.

This provision suggests that an examiner may be a party to an application for leave to affirm or repudiate a contract, but does not have to be a party in all instances. From the terms of O 75A, r 19, it is clear that the company itself has standing to apply for an order approving the affirmation or repudiation of a contract under s 20(1). If the company makes such an application, the examiner must be notified and may be heard at the hearing.

Secondly, it is unclear how s 20 interacts with the general prohibition on examiners repudiating contracts that were entered into before the commencement of the protected period.[72] One possible means of reconciling the terms of ss 7(5A) and 20, is to interpret s 20 as relating only to contracts entered after the commencement of the period of protection. However, s 20 is not so limited on its own terms. In addition, it would be difficult to conceive of a notable number of contracts being entered into after the commencement of the protected period, and partly performed before the formulation of the proposed compromise or arrangement, particularly in light of the short time frames applicable in examinerships. An alternative interpretation is that s 20 overrides the general prohibition on the repudiation of contracts entered into before the commencement of the examinership, and that the requirement of court approval justifies this deviation. Under this interpretation, s 20 presents a means for an examiner or a company to repudiate an onerous contract that was formed by the company before the commencement of the examinership, and partly performed by both the company and the other party. A third and most plausible interpretation, is that only a company may apply for the right to repudiate a pre-petition contract under s 20. This is consistent with the terms of O 75A, r 19 and the language of s 20. It leaves open the possibility, however, that if an examiner is vested with the powers of the directors under s 9, he may effectively be the person who makes an application to court under s 20, thereby by-passing the general prohibition on the repudiation of pre-petition contracts by an examiner.

(e) Application for directions

[10.023] An examiner has the right to apply to the court for the determination of any question that arises in the course of the examinership, or for the court to exercise the powers conferred upon it under the CA 1963–2006, in relation to the company in examinership.[73] Section 7(6) provides as follows:

> The examiner may apply to the court to determine any question arising in the course of his office, or for the exercise in relation to the company of all or any of the powers which the court may exercise under this Act, upon the application to it of any member, contributory, creditor or director of a company.

---

[71]   C(A)A 1990, s 7(5A), as inserted by C(A)(No 2)A 1999, s 18. See para **[10.020]**.

[72]   C(A)A 1990, s 7(5A), as inserted by C(A)(No 2)A 1999, s 18. See para **[10.020]**.

[73]   C(A)A 1990, s 7(6).

There are two alternative interpretations of this provision. First, the provision may be interpreted as permitting an examiner to exercise this right to apply to court only if a member, creditor or director of the company makes an application to the examiner.[74] This interpretation is anomalous as the examiner should have the right to apply to court for the determination of questions related to the examinership, without the necessity of an application to the examiner by another party.

The alternative interpretation is that the examiner can make an application to court for directions, or an application for the exercise by the court of powers that the court is otherwise permitted under the Companies Acts to exercise on the application of a member, creditor, or director of the company. This interpretation is more compelling, both in light of the objective of the provision to confer a power on the examiner, and in light of the words 'application to it' in the final clause of the provision, words which are more likely to refer to an application to the court, than an application to the examiner.

The latter interpretation is further supported by the terms of O 75A, r 9(1), *Rules of the Superior Courts*, which provides that an application by an examiner under s 7(6) may be made *ex parte*. However, the terms of O 75A, r 9(2) provide for an application by a company, creditor or member to the court under s 7(6), which is difficult to reconcile with the terms of s 7(6).[75]

(f) Claims against a company

[10.024] If there are claims against a company in examinership, the examiner may have power to ascertain and agree these claims.[76] Section 7(7) provides that, 'The examiner shall, if so directed by the court, have power to ascertain and agree claims against the company to which he has been appointed.'

An examiner only has this power if the court makes a direction to this effect. It is interesting to note that the nature of a court order, which may be made under s 7(7) is an order that an examiner 'shall... have power to ascertain and agree claims'. A court order within the scope of s 7(7) will not compel the examiner to ascertain and agree claims against the company.

(g) Co-operation of officers and agents

(i) Scope of obligation to co-operate

[10.025] As a general rule, the officers and agents of a company in examinership must co-operate with the examiner. However, the category of persons who are obliged to co-operate with that examiner is broad in a number of respects.[77] First, it is not just the officers and agents of the company in examinership who are bound to co-operate with

---

74 C(A)A 1990, s 7(6).

75 O 75A, r 9(2) provides as follows: 'Any application, by any member, contributory, creditor or director of a company pursuant to s 7(6) of the Act shall be by way of motion on notice to the Examiner and to the company and the Court may make such order upon such application as if it had been brought by the Examiner.'

76 C(A)A 1990, s 7(7).

77 C(A)A 1990, s 8.

the examiner. Officers and agents of related companies are also bound by the same obligations of co-operation. For the purposes of C(A)A 1990, companies are related to each other if:

- one is a holding company or subsidiary of the other;[78]

- most of the nominal value of the equity share capital[79] of one company is held, directly or indirectly,[80] by the other company and companies related to it;[81]

- most of the nominal value of the equity share capital of each of the companies is held by members of the other;[82]

- one of the companies[83] can control the exercise of more than half of the voting power at a general meeting of the other company;[84]

- the businesses of the two companies have been carried on in such a manner that the separate business of each company, or a substantial portion of their business, is not readily identifiable;[85] or

- there is a third company to which both companies are related.[86]

Secondly, both past and present officers and agents are obliged to co-operate with the examiner.[87] There is no time limitation upon the category of past officers and agents captured by this obligation. According to the terms of the C(A)A 1990, anyone who was at any time in the past an officer or agent of the company in examinership or a related company, may be bound to co-operate with the examiner.

Thirdly, the term 'agents' is broadly defined to include the company's bankers, solicitors and auditors, whether those persons are officers of the company or not.[88] However, it

---

78   C(A)A 1990, s 4(5)(a).

79   'Equity share capital' is defined in CA 1963, s 155(5) as 'in relation to a company, its issued share capital excluding any part thereof which, neither as respects dividends nor as respects capital, carries any right to participate beyond a specified amount in a distribution'.

80   While the capital may be held directly or indirectly, it may not be held in a fiduciary capacity. C(A)A 1990, s 4(5)(b).

81   C(A)A 1990, s 4(5)(b).

82   C(A)A 1990, s 4(5)(c). As with s 4(5)(c), the shares may held directly or indirectly, but not in a fiduciary capacity.

83   This provision also applies if any company, or any related companies of the company have this voting power, or if one of companies, in conjunction with companies related to it, would have such voting power. C(A)A 1990, s 4(5)(d).

84   C(A)A 1990, s 4(5)(d).

85   C(A)A 1990, s 4(5)(e).

86   C(A)A 1990, s 4(5)(f), as amended by CA 1990, s 181.

87   C(A)A 1990, s 8(6).

88   C(A)A 1990, s 8(6).

should be noted in this regard that CA 1990, s 23(1) applies to this provision of the C(A)A 1990, and provides that:

> Nothing in this [section] shall compel the disclosure by any person of any information which he would, in the opinion of the court, be entitled to refuse to produce on the grounds of legal professional privilege or authorise the taking of possession of any document containing such information which is in his possession.[89]

This exemption is predicated on an 'opinion of the court' and there is nothing in s 8 which would permit a solicitor simply to refuse to answer a question or produce a document on the ground of legal professional privilege.

Finally, the obligation to co-operate with an examiner may extend beyond the broadly defined category of officers and agents of the company in examinership. Section 8(2) provides that 'if the examiner considers that a person other than an officer or agent of any such company is or may be in possession of any information concerning its affairs,' that person may be subject to the same obligations of co-operation as an officer or agent of the company.[90] Any person who the examiner considers may be in possession of any information in relation to the company, may therefore be under a duty to co-operate with the examiner.

(ii) Forms of co-operation

[10.026] When an examiner is appointed, there are four forms of co-operation which the company's officers and agents, as broadly defined in the C(A)A 1990, are obliged to provide to the examiner. First, they must produce to the examiner all books and documents in their custody or power that belong, or relate, to the company.[91] Second, officers and agents must attend before the examiner when required to do so.[92] Thirdly, they must give the examiner all assistance in connection with his functions which they are reasonably able to give.[93] Fourthly, any such persons may be obliged to appear in front of the examiner and be examined on oath.[94] On consideration by the examiner that a person who is not an agent or officer of the company possesses information

---

[89] CA 1990, s 23(1), as applied by C(A)A 1990, s (5B), as inserted by CA 1990, s 180 ('s 23(1) of the Companies Act 1990 shall apply for the purposes of this section').

[90] C(A)A 1990, s 8(2) provides that, 'If the examiner considers that a person other than an officer or agent of any such company is or may be in possession of any information concerning its affairs, he may require that person to produce to him any books or documents in his custody or power relating to the company, to attend before him and otherwise to give him all assistance in connection with his functions which he is reasonably able to give; and it shall be the duty of that person to comply with the requirement.'

[91] C(A)A 1990, s 8(1).

[92] C(A)A 1990, s 8(1).

[93] C(A)A 1990, s 8(1).

[94] C(A)A 1990, s 8(4). The examination on oath may be conducted orally or by written interrogatories and the examiner may administer the oath, reduce the answers to writing and require the person under examination to sign them.

concerning the company's affairs, the examiner may require that person to adhere to these same four forms of co-operation[95].

(iii) Refusal to co-operate

[10.027] If a person refuses to comply with the duty to produce any book or document to the examiner; refuses to attend before the examiner when requested to do so; or refuses to answer a question from the examiner regarding the company's affairs, the examiner may certify this refusal and refer it to court.[96]

The procedure to be followed is that the examiner may certify the refusal to court and the court may then make an enquiry. As part of this enquiry, the court may hear any witnesses who may be produced against or on behalf of the person allegedly in default and may hear any statement in defence of that person. The court may make then any order or direction it considers appropriate.[97] In particular, the court may direct the person to comply with the obligation to attend before the examiner, produce specific books or documents or answer specific questions by the examiner.[98] Alternatively, the court may direct that the person allegedly in default is not obliged to produce a particular book or document or answer a particular question.[99] In this regard, it should be recalled that nothing in s 8 can compel a person to disclose information which the court considers is covered by legal professional privilege.[100] This exemption is premised on the 'opinion of the court' and it therefore appears most likely that the question of legal professional privilege will arise pursuant to an enquiry by a court under s 8(5).

[10.028] Applications under s 8(5) are governed by O 75A, r 10. This requires that, once the examiner has certified a refusal to comply with the duty to produce any book or document to the examiner; to attend before the examiner; or to answer a question from the examiner regarding the company's affairs, he must apply *ex parte* to the court for leave to produce this certificate. The examiner must verify the facts stated in the certificate by affidavit. The court may then make such enquiries and give such directions, as it sees fit, on notice to the party concerned. The court shall further hear such evidence as may be produced and make such order as appears just and proper.[101]

---

95.   C(A)A 1990, s 8(2) and (4).

96.   C(A)A 1990, s 8(5), as substituted by C(A)(No 2)A 1999, s 19. As noted by Declan Murphy in the *Irish Current Law Statutes Annotated*, 'This amendment to s 8(5) of the Act of 1990 is a rather belated amendment required on constitutional grounds. The original s 8(5) was in similar form to s 10(5) of the Companies Act, 1990 which was subject to constitutional challenge in the case of *Desmond v Glackin* [1993] 2 IR 106'.

97.   C(A)A 1990, s 8(5), as substituted by C(A))(No 2)A 1999, s 19.

98.   C(A)A 1990, s 8(5A)(a), as inserted by CA 1990, s 180 and substituted by C(A)(No 2)A 1999, s 19.

99.   C(A)A 1990, s 8(5A)(b), as inserted by CA 1990, s 180 and substituted by C(A)(No 2)A 1999, s 19.

100.   CA 1990, s 23(1), as applied by C(A)A 1990, s 5(5B), as inserted by CA 1990, s 180.

101.   Rules of the Superior Courts, O 75A, r 10.

(h) Access to bank details

[10.029] In certain circumstances, an examiner has the right to require a director of the company in examinership to produce all documents in their possession or control, relating to a bank account in their name.[102] The grounds on which this power may be exercised are limited. The examiner must have 'reasonable grounds' to believe that particular criteria are met.[103] It is not sufficient for the examiner to form the opinion, or have a reasonable suspicion, that this is the case. The criteria that the examiner must have reasonable grounds to believe exist before he can exercise the power to require information in relation to a bank account are as follows:

- a bank account[104] must be, or have been, held in the name of the director,[105] either alone, or jointly with other persons, and either in the State or elsewhere; and

- monies must have been paid into or out of the account which resulted from, or were used in, the financing of any transaction, arrangement or agreement, the particulars of which were not disclosure in the company's accounts, as required by law;[106] or

- monies must have paid into or out of the account which were connected with any act or omission, or series of acts or omissions, which constituted misconduct on the part of the director (whether fraudulent or not) towards the company or its members.[107]

(i) Powers of directors

[10.030] An examiner may apply to court for an order vesting all or any of the functions and powers of the company's directors solely in the examiner. C(A)A 1990, s 9(1) provides in this regard:

> Where it appears to the court, on the application of the examiner, that, having regard to the matters referred to in sub-s (2), it is just and equitable to do so, it may make an order that all or any of the functions or powers which are vested in or exercisable by the directors (whether by virtue of the memorandum or articles of association of the company or by law or otherwise) shall be performable or exercisable only by the examiner.

---

[102] C(A)A 1990, s 8(3), as amended by CA 1990, s 180.

[103] C(A)A 1990, s 8(3), as amended by CA 1990, s 180.

[104] Note that, according to C(A)A 1990, s 8(3), as amended by CA 1990, s 180, '"bank account" includes an account with any person exempt by virtue of s 7(4) of the Central Bank Act 1971, from the requirement of holding a licence under s 9 of that Act'.

[105] 'Director' is broadly defined for the purpose of s 8(3) to include, 'any present or past director or any person connected, within the meaning of s 26 of the Companies Act 1990, with such director, and any present or past shadow director.'

[106] C(A)A 1990, s 8(3)(a), as amended by CA 1990, s 180.

[107] C(A)A 1990, s 8(3)(b), as amended by CA 1990, s 180.

The court must therefore have regard to the matters set out in s 9(2) and further determine that it is just and equitable to make the order sought, before such an order should be made. The matters to which the court must have regard are the following:

- that the company's affairs are being, or are likely to be, conducted in a manner which is calculated or likely to prejudice the interests of the company, its employees or its creditors as a whole;[108]

- that it is expedient, for the preservation of the company's assets or to safeguard the interests of the company, its employees or its creditors as a whole, that the carrying on of the company's business by, or the exercise of the powers of, the directors and management should be curtailed or regulated in any particular respect;[109]

- that the company's members or directors have passed a resolution that such an order should be sought;[110] or

- any other matter in relation to the company that the court considers to be relevant.[111]

The broad scope of the court's discretion under s 9 is apparent from the power of the court to make an order under that section on the basis of 'any ... matter in relation to the company the court thinks relevant' provided the court considers it just and equitable to do so.

In *Re Clare Textiles Ltd*[112] Costello J considered a situation in which the powers of the directors were conferred on the examiner, and noted that 'special circumstances' should exist before this occurs. The Court commented:

> '... as the directors have duties to the company and its members and as these continue when the company is under the protection of the court the examiner should not be required to undertake these duties in the absence of special circumstances.'[113]

[10.031] An order under s 9 may include such conditions and such ancillary or other orders as the court considers appropriate for the purpose of giving full effect to the order.[114] In addition, an order under s 9 may confer on an examiner all or any of the

---

[108] C(A)A 1990, s 9(2)(a). It should be noted that it must be interests of the creditors as a whole that are affected. It is not sufficient that an individual creditor, or a category of creditors, would suffer such prejudice.

[109] C(A)A 1990, s 9(2)(b).

[110] C(A)A 1990, s 9(2)(c).

[111] C(A)A 1990, s 9(2)(d).

[112] *Re Clare Textiles Ltd* [1993] 2 IR 213.

[113] *Re Clare Textiles Ltd* [1993] 2 IR 213 at 223.

[114] C(A)A 1990, s 9(3).

powers of an official liquidator. If this occurs, the court has all of the powers that it would have in the case of an official liquidation.[115]

The procedure applicable to an application under s 9 is set out in O 75A, r 11 which requires the examiner to make the application by notice of motion served on the directors, and grounded on an affidavit of the examiner, specifying which, if not all, of the powers he seeks to have conferred on him. The court may give such directions in relation to the hearing of such an application as it deems fit.

(j) Power to dispose of charged property

[10.032] In certain circumstances, an examiner may dispose of property despite the fact that it is subject to a charge or other security. C(A)A 1990, s 11, permits an examiner to make an application to court for the right to dispose of such property. Such an application must be made by notice of motion grounded on an affidavit sworn by the examiner, which must be served on the holder of the security or the hire purchase company, or any other person who appears to have an interest in the property. On such an application, the court may make such order under s 11 as it considers just and proper and may give directions concerning the proceeds of any such disposals as are authorised by the court.[116]

[10.033] The pre-condition to the exercise of the court's discretion in this regard is that the court must be satisfied the disposal of the property, alone or with other assets, 'would be likely to facilitate the survival of the whole or any part of the company as a going concern'.[117] If the court is satisfied that this is the case, the court may do any of the following:

– authorise the examiner to dispose of property which is subject to a security which was created as a floating charge, as if it was not subject to such security;[118]

– authorise the examiner to exercise his powers in relation to property which is subject to a security which was created as a floating charge, as if it was not subject to such security;[119]

– authorise the examiner to dispose of property subject to a security other than a floating charge as if it was not subject to such security;[120] or

---

[115] C(A)A 1990, s 9(4) ('Without prejudice to the generality of sub-ss (1) and (3), an order under this section may provide that the examiner shall have all or any of the powers that he would have if he were a liquidator appointed by the court in respect of the company and, where such order so provides, the court shall have all the powers that it would have if it had made a winding-up order and appointed a liquidator in respect of the company concerned.')

[116] See Rules of the Superior Courts, O 75A, r 12.

[117] C(A)A 1990, s 11(1).

[118] C(A)A 1990, s 11(1).

[119] C(A)A 1990, s 11(1).

[120] C(A)A 1990, s 11(2)(a).

> – authorise the examiner to dispose of goods in the possession of the company under a hire purchase agreement,[121] as if the rights of the owner under that agreement were vested in the company.[122]

The examiner must deliver to the Registrar of Companies an office copy of a court order which is made under s 11(1) or (2) within seven days after the making of that order.[123] If the examiner fails to comply with this duty without reasonable excuse, he is guilty of an offence and liable to a maximum fine of €1,904.61.[124]

[10.034] If the property disposed of is subject to a floating charge, the holder of that security retains his priority over any property of the company which represents the property disposed of. Section 11(3) provides as follows:

> Where property is disposed of under sub-s (1), the holder of the security shall have the same priority in respect of any property of the company directly or indirectly representing the property disposed of as he would have had in respect of the property subject to the security.

This ensures that the interest of the holder of the floating charge is protected and that, while the property itself may be disposed of, the interest of the charge holder transfers onto the proceeds, or products, of that sale. This protection does not depend on the formulation of the court order but arises automatically, on the disposal of the property.

[10.035] If the property which is disposed of is subject to a security other than a floating charge, the court order permitting such disposal shall include a condition that the proceeds of the disposal shall be applied towards discharging the sums subject to the security or outstanding under the hire purchase agreement.[125] If the net proceeds of the sale are less than what the court considers to be the net amount that would be realised in the open market by a willing vendor, such sums as are required to make good this deficiency ('top-up'), should be added to the proceeds of sale and applied to satisfy the security.[126] If such a court condition relates to two or more securities, the order must require the application of the proceeds and top-up (if any) to be applied to discharge those debts in the order of their priorities.[127]

[10.036] In the context of the an examiner's right to deal with charged property, there are three points of distinction between the treatment of holders of floating charges over a company's property and holders of other forms of security. First, the court may confer on an examiner the right to dispose of, or to exercise his powers in relation to, property

---

[121] According to C(A)A 1990, s 11(8) 'References in this section to a hire-purchase agreement include a conditional sale agreement, a retention of title agreement and an agreement for the bailment of goods which is capable of subsisting for more than three months.'

[122] C(A)A 1990, s 11(2)(b).

[123] C(A)A 1990, s 11(6).

[124] C(A)A 1990, s 11(7), as amended by C(AA)A 2003, s 57 and Sch 2 and CA 1990 s140(7) as inserted by CLEA 2001 s 104(c).

[125] C(A)A 1990, s 11(4).

[126] C(A)A 1990, s 11(4)(b).

[127] C(A)A 1990, s 11(5), as amended by CA 1990, s 181.

which is subject to a floating charge (or a security which was created as a floating charge), whereas an examiner may only dispose of property which is subject to other forms of security. There is no provision for an examiner to exercise his powers in relation to property subject to a security other than a floating charge.

Secondly, the holder of a floating charge automatically retains priority in respect of any property that directly or indirectly represents the property disposed of. The court order must include a condition conferring the right on holders of other forms of security to look to the proceeds of sale for satisfaction of their debts. Finally, the holder of a floating charge can look to any property which represents the property sold for satisfaction of the debt. By contrast, holders of other forms of security can only look to the proceeds of sale for satisfaction of their debt, and can only recoup an amount in excess of that to the extent that the court considers that less than the market price was obtained.[128]

(k) Related companies

[10.037] The Companies Acts also provide for the appointment of an examiner, or the extension of the powers of the examiner, to companies related to the company in examinership.[129] This avoids the possibility of numerous examiners being appointed to different companies within a group.[130] While s 4 does not state so specifically, the criteria of s 2 for the appointment of an examiner must be taken to apply to the appointment of an examiner to a related company. Otherwise, a company which was not insolvent or which was in liquidation could face an application to be placed in examinership, which would appear to be beyond the scope and policy of the legislation. Moreover, as will be seen, one of the conditions for the exercise of the court's discretion to appoint an examiner to a related company is that the court must be satisfied 'that there is a reasonable prospect of the survival of the related company, and the whole or any part of its undertaking, as a going concern'.[131] This criterion is not logical unless the other criteria for the appointment of an examiner under s 2, particularly the requirement that the company be insolvent, are satisfied by the company in question.

[10.038] A court order extending the appointment or powers of an examiner to a related company may be made at the same time as the appointment of the examiner or at any

---

[128] C(A)A 1990, s 11(4).

[129] The definition of related companies is set out in C(A)A 1990, s 4(5), and was considered above in the context of C(A)A 1990, s 8. Note that, according to C(A)A 1990, s 4(4), 'Where an examiner stands appointed to two or more related companies, he shall have the same powers and duties in relation to each company, taken separately, unless the court otherwise directs'.

[130] See McCormack, *Irish Current Law Statutes Annotated* on the C(A)A 1990, 'The aim is to short-circuit a practice which might otherwise have developed of multiple petitions to the court and simultaneous appointment of an examiner to all the companies within a group. The section means that in a group situation an examiner may be appointed to related companies. This obviates the need for individual examiners to be appointed to individual companies within the group (121 Seanad Debates Col. 59).'

[131] C(A)A 1990, s 4(2), as amended by C(A)(No 2)A 1999, s 12.

time thereafter.[132] In determining whether to make such an order, there are two matters which the court must consider. First, the court must have regard to 'whether the making of the order would be likely to facilitate the survival of the company, or of the related company, or both, and the whole or any part of its or their undertaking, as a going concern'.[133] Secondly, the court must not, in any case, make an order appointing, or extending the powers of, the examiner to a related company, 'unless it is satisfied that there is a reasonable prospect of the survival of the related company, and the whole or any part of its undertaking, as a going concern'.[134]

The court must therefore be satisfied that there is a reasonable prospect of the survival of the related company as a going concern and, if satisfied that this criterion is met, the court may proceed to consider whether appointing the examiner of the company in examinership to the related company, or extending his powers to that related company, would be likely to facilitate the survival of the company, the related company, or both.

If the court makes an order under s 4, the related company shall be deemed to be under the protection of the court from the date on which the order is made.[135] The protection of the related company will then continue for so long as the other company is under such protection.[136]

(l) Pre-petition debts

[10.039] There is a limitation on the powers of an examiner in C(A)A 1990, s 5A.[137] According to s 5A, during the period of protection, any debts that were contracted by the company before the commencement of the period of protection, may not be discharged or satisfied in whole or in part, subject to two exceptions.

The first exception is that liabilities may be discharged, if the report of the independent accountant that accompanied the petition recommends that the whole or, as the case may be, part of those liabilities should be discharged or satisfied.[138] Secondly, on an application by the examiner or an interested party, the court may authorise the discharge

---

[132] C(A)A 1990, s 4(1) as amended by C(A)(No 2)A 1999, s 12.

[133] C(A)A 1990, s 4(2), as amended by C(A)(No 2)A 1999, s 12.

[134] C(A)A 1990, s 4(2), as amended by C(A)(No 2)A 1999, s 12.

[135] C(A)A 1990, s 4(3). Note that, according to McCormack, *Irish Current Law Statutes Annotated,* 'This subsection was amended at the Dáil Report stage to make it clear that a protection order under this section cannot be backdated to the date of the protection order on the first company.'

[136] C(A)A 1990, s 4(3).

[137] Inserted by the C(A)(No 2)A 1999.

[138] C(A)A 1990, s 5A(1), as inserted by C(A)(No 2)A 1999, s 15. Note that C(A)A 1990, s 3(3B)(k), as inserted by C(A)(No 2)A 1999, s 7 requires the independent accountant's report to include 'his recommendations as to which liabilities incurred before the presentation of the petition should be paid.'

or satisfaction, in whole or in part, of pre-petition liabilities. To grant such authorisation, the court must be satisfied that a failure to so discharge or satisfy that liability would considerably reduce the prospects of the company's survival as a going concern.[139]

(m) Costs of examinership

(i) Costs, expenses and remuneration payable

[10.040] During the course of the examinership, the court may from time to time make such orders as it considers proper of the payment of the examiner's costs, remuneration and properly incurred expenses.[140]

Expenses will be deemed to have been incurred properly if the examiner certifies such expenses, at the date they are incurred, as being expenses which were necessary to prevent serious prejudice to the survival of the company as a going concern during the protection period.[141] It is clear, however, that the expenses referred to in s 10 are ones for which the company, not the examiner, is liable.[142]

It should be noted that, if a court appoints an *interim* examiner under s 3A, any liabilities incurred by the company during that interim period may not be certified by the examiner under s 10(2).[143]

The costs, remuneration and expenses that a court orders to be paid to an examiner will generally be paid out of the revenue of the business of the company or the proceeds of sale of the company's assets or investments.[144]

---

[139] C(A)A 1990, s 5A(2), as inserted by C(A)(No 2)A 1999, s 15. It may also be noted that a court may order a person to return property to an examiner, if the court is satisfied that the disposal of that property perpetrated a fraud on the company, its creditors or members. CA 1990, s 139, as applied by CA 1990, s 180(2). See further Ch **9**.

[140] C(A)A 1990, s 29(1).

[141] C(A)A 1990, s 10(1) (as amended by CA 1990, s 180) and (2). See *Re Don Bluth Entertainment Ltd* [1994] 3 IR 141.

[142] C(A)A 1990, s 10(1), as amended by CA 1990, s 180 provides that, 'Any liabilities incurred by the company during the protection period which are referred to in sub-s (2) shall be treated as expenses properly incurred, for the purpose of s 29, by the examiner.'

[143] C(A)A 1990, s 3A(8) as inserted by C(A)(No 2)A 1999, s 9. The period of interim protection is a maximum of ten days from the presentation of the interim petition. C(A)A 1990, s 3A(2), as inserted by C(A)(No 2)A 1999, s 9 provides as follows: 'That period shall be a period that expires not later than the 10th day after the date of making of the order concerned or, if the 10th day after that date would fall on a Saturday, Sunday or public holiday, the first following day that is not a Saturday, Sunday or public holiday.'

[144] C(A)A 1990, s 29(2). This is subject to the qualification that the court may order otherwise and, in particular, may order that the examiner's costs, remuneration and expenses be paid from monies other than the company's business revenue or proceeds of the sale of company assets.

(ii) Application to court

[10.041] Order 75A, r 22, requires that an application under s 29 must be made *ex parte*, grounded on an affidavit of the examiner. The examiner must set out the following:

- a full account of the work carried out by the examiner up to the date of the application;

- a full account of the costs and expenses incurred by the examiner;

- vouch these accounts and the basis for the remuneration claimed; and

- specify what use, if any, the examiner has made of the staff and facilities of the company and the extent of such use.[145]

The court may order that notice of the application be given to all such persons as the court may direct and may give directions regarding such service and fixing a date for the hearing of the application.

(iii) Court discretion

[10.042] The court has a broad discretion to determine the appropriate level of costs, remuneration and expenses to be paid in an examinership. While it appears from the decision of Costello J in *Re Clare Textiles Ltd*[146] that the courts will scrutinise the costs and remuneration claimed by an examiner, that decision suggests that the amount of expenses that is certified by the examiner will not be disturbed unless the certification itself is challenged.

[10.043] In *Re Don Bluth Entertainment Ltd*[147] the company's creditors challenged the expenses that were certified by the examiner under s 10 on a number of grounds. These included the argument that the certification was bad in form; that the expenses were incurred by the directors rather than the company; that the expenses were incurred before, or to be incurred after, the period of protection; and that some liabilities did not relate to the survival of the company during the period of protection. The examiner argued that a certificate under s 10 could not be reviewed, or could only be reviewed on limited grounds, as in the case of a challenge by way of judicial review.

Murphy J held that the Court does have a discretion to review the liabilities certified under s 10 and considered the nature of the examiner's role under that provision as follows:

> 'As the combined operation of ss 10 and 29 of the Act of 1990 will frequently result in some creditors of a company being paid in full at the expense of the

---

[145] Rules of the Superior Courts, O 75A, r 22. The requirement to specify the use made of the company's staff and facilities, relates to the terms of s 29(4) and (5), which require 'an examiner shall, insofar as is reasonably possible, make use of the services of the staff and facilities of the company to which he has been appointed to assist him in the performance of his functions.'

[146] *Re Clare Textiles Ltd* [1993] 2 IR 213.

[147] *Re Don Bluth Entertainment Ltd* [1994] 3 IR 141.

creditors who hold securities over the assets of the company or creditors who would have enjoyed a statutory preference under s 285 of the Act of 1963 if the insolvency of the company in question had resulted in a liquidation rather than an examinership, it is important that an examiner should exercise great care and professional expertise in issuing certificates under s 10 aforesaid. I would anticipate that an examiner from whom a certificate is sought would require the directors managing the business of the company to submit to him their proposals in relation to any particular liabilities which they proposed to incur and to satisfy him as to how the services or goods to be obtained would benefit the company, and in particular how they would contribute to the survival of the company 'during the "protection period".'[148]

Examiners should note the requirement that 'great care and professional expertise' be exercised in issuing a certificate under s 10, and that examiners should require directors to submit proposals and satisfy the examiners as to how the expenses sought to be incurred would contribute to the survival of the company during the period of protection.

[10.044] It is also important to note that in *Re Don Bluth Entertainment Ltd*[149], Murphy J held that the costs of the presentation of the petition for the appointment of an examiner may not be certified as expenses under s 10:

'The Act of 1990 does not confer any priority on the costs of persons petitioning for the appointment of an examiner ... Furthermore, the general scheme of the Act could not have envisaged the petitioner procuring a priority for his costs by means of certification under s 10, as ordinarily the examiner would not be appointed until after the expense of the petition had been incurred ... In so far as the examiner purported to certify liabilities already incurred, it is clear that the certificate has no statutory effect. In so far as the liabilities related or may have been intended to relate to contemporaneous liabilities in respect of proceedings for the appointment of an examiner, it seems to me that the certificate is likewise invalid for the reason offered by counsel on behalf of the official liquidator, namely, that the protection period during which the survival of the company falls to be considered is a period which commences with and postulates the existence of an examiner so that the appointment of an examiner or proceedings for that purpose can have no bearing on the survival of the company during the relevant period.'[150]

[10.045] There is one matter to which the court is obliged to have regard in determining the appropriate level of costs, expenses and remuneration. Section 29(4) permits an examiner to appoint or employ persons to assist him in his functions. This is qualified by the proviso that, 'an examiner shall, insofar as is reasonably possible, make use of the services of the staff and facilities of the company to which he has been appointed to assist him in the performance of his functions.'[151] The court must have regard to this proviso in considering any matter relating to the costs, expenses and remuneration of an examiner.[152] Examiners should be aware that the cost of employing persons to provide

---

[148] *Re Don Bluth Entertainment Ltd* [1994] 3 IR 141 at 149.

[149] *Re Don Bluth Entertainment Ltd* [1994] 3 IR 141.

[150] *Re Don Bluth Entertainment Ltd* [1994] 3 IR 141 at 151 to 152.

[151] C(A)A 1990, s 29(4).

[152] C(A)A 1990, s 29(5).

assistance, which could have been furnished by employees of the company, may not be recoverable and the court is obliged to consider this question in determining which costs, expenses and remuneration should be paid.

(iv) Priority of examiner's costs, expenses and remuneration

[10.046] Any sums that are sanctioned by the court as costs, remuneration or properly incurred expenses, must be paid in full.[153] Moreover, costs and remuneration that are due to the examiner on foot of a court order have priority over any other secured or unsecured claims, whether arising under any compromise or scheme of arrangement or in a receivership or winding up of the company.[154] The examiner's costs and remuneration will also be paid in priority to any costs, charges and expenses of the winding up of the company, including the liquidator's remuneration.[155] Therefore, whether the examinership is successful or not, payment of the examiner's costs and remuneration takes priority.

[10.047] In *Re Atlantic Magnetics Ltd (in receivership)*[156], the Supreme Court considered an argument to the effect that the claims over which the examiner's costs and remuneration enjoyed priority were limited to charges other than fixed charges. The Court rejected this argument, determining that:

> 'To insert a clause such as has been suggested, in sub-s (3) of s 29, would in my view clearly be to legislate and could not come under any doctrine or principle of interpretation. The phrase "before any other claim secured or unsecured" is unambiguous and must be given its literal meaning.'[157]

[10.048] In considering the appropriate level of costs and remuneration to allow, the court will be mindful of the priority those sums will enjoy in the event of liquidation of the company. In *Re Clare Textiles Ltd,*[158] the costs and remuneration sought by the examiner were in the region of £103,587 and the liquidator of the company filed affidavits to the effect that the company was hopelessly insolvent and that payment of this sum under s 29 would seriously prejudice the position of the company's unsecured creditors. The Court considered the fact that the examiner had engaged in functions

---

[153] C(A)A 1990, s 29(3), as substituted by C(A)(No 2)A 1999, s 28.

[154] C(A)A 1990, s 29(3), as substituted by C(A)(No 2)A 1999, s 28.

[155] C(A)A 1990, s 29(3B), as inserted by C(A)(No 2)A 1999, s 28 provides that, 'In sub-ss (3) and (3A) references to a claim shall be deemed to include references to any payment in a winding-up of the company in respect of the costs, charges and expenses of that winding-up (including the remuneration of any liquidator).' This amendment gives statutory effect to the decision of the Supreme Court in *Re Springline Ltd (in liq)* [1999] 1 IR 467.

[156] *Re Atlantic Magnetics Ltd (in receivership)* [1993] 2 IR 561.

[157] *Re Atlantic Magnetics Ltd (in receivership)* [1993] 2 IR 561 at 574 (*per* Finlay CJ). Although this case was decided under the C(A)A 1990, as it existed before the enactment of the C(A)(No 2)A 1999, the same reference to 'claim, secured or unsecured' appears in s 3 as substituted by the latter.

[158] *Re Clare Textiles Ltd* [1993] 2 IR 213.

which were unauthorised and the fact that the proposals advanced by the examiner, for the liquidation of the company, were beyond the scope of his role. The Court concluded:

> 'Section 29 allows the court to make such order in relation to remuneration as it "thinks proper" and the question for consideration is whether it is proper that the creditors of the company should be asked to bear the cost of remuneration for performing unauthorised functions which resulted from the error of construction to which I have referred. I do not think that it would be fair to them to make such an order and so it would not be proper to do so.'[159]

The Court therefore only allowed the examiner's costs and remuneration to the extent that they were incurred in the course of the proper discharge of the examiner's functions and disallowed any other costs and remuneration. In effect, the Court permitted payment of costs, such as legal costs, and remuneration incurred in the first 12 days of the examiner's appointment to office and did not allow any costs or remuneration, incurred in connection with the carrying on of the company's business or the formulation of the examiner's proposals.

[10.049] Expenses properly incurred by the examiner must also be paid in full before any other claim, such as claims secured by floating charges and including any sums due to a liquidator.[160] However, expenses properly incurred and certified by the examiner rank behind the following:

- claims secured by mortgages, fixed charges, liens or other fixed securities;

- claims under any compromise or scheme of arrangement; and

- claims in any receivership or winding up of the company.[161]

While the examiner will receive his costs and remuneration in priority to other creditors in a receivership, winding up or under a compromise or arrangement, and in priority to fixed charge holders, the expenses properly incurred by the examiner will not rank in priority to such claims.

D. Obligations of examiners

[10.050] The principal function of an examiner is to examine the affairs of the company and formulate proposals to ensure the survival of the company as a going concern.[162] As a general rule, an examiner is also obliged to carry out any duties that the court may direct him to carry out.[163]

---

[159] *Re Clare Textiles Ltd* [1993] 2 IR 213 at 222.

[160] C(A)A 1990, s 29(3A), as inserted by C(A)(No 2)A 1999, s 28.

[161] C(A)A 1990, s 29(3A), as inserted by C(A)(No 2)A 1999, s 28.

[162] Before the enactment of the C(A)(No 2)A 1999, the examiner was also obliged to examine the company to determine whether it was capable of survival as a going concern. The requirement that a report of an independent accountant must accompany the petition and state whether the company is capable of survival as a going concern, has now largely replaced the examiner's obligation in that regard.

[163] C(A)A 1990, s 18(1)(b) as substituted by C(A)(No 2)A 1999, s 22.

There are a number of steps that must be taken in relation to the formulation, dissemination and confirmation of an examiner's proposals for the rescue of the company in examinership.

(a) Formulation of proposals

[10.051] As soon as practicable after his appointment, the examiner must formulate proposals for a compromise or scheme of arrangement in relation to the company.[164] While there is no specific deadline for this formulation to occur, 'as soon as practicable' appears to mean that it should be done within 30 days of the appointment of the examiner. This is apparent from the terms of s 18(2), which require the proposals to be reported to court, within 35 days of the appointment of the examiner, having been considered at meetings of the company and its creditors, convened with three days' notice.[165]

The proposals for a compromise or scheme of arrangement must comply with the following requirements:[166]

- they must specify each class of members and creditors of the company;[167]

- they must specify each class of members and creditors whose interests or claims will not be impaired[168] by the proposals;[169]

- they must specify each class of members and creditors whose interests or claims will be impaired by the proposals;[170]

- they must provide for equal treatment of each claim or interest of a particular class, unless the holder agrees to less favourable treatment than others;[171]

- they must provide for the implementation of the proposals;[172]

- they must specify what changes should be made to the management or direction of the company, if the examiner considers this necessary or desirable for the

---

[164] C(A)A 1990, s 18(1)(a), as substituted by C(A)(No 2)A 1999, s 22.

[165] C(A)A 1990, s 18(2), as amended by C(A)(No 2)A 1999, s 22.

[166] C(A)A 1990, s 22(1).

[167] C(A)A 1990, s 22(1)(a).

[168] According to C(A)A 1990, s 22(5), 'a creditor's claim against a company is impaired if he receives less in payment of his claim than the full amount due in respect of the claim at the date of presentation of the petition for the appointment of the examiner.' C(A)A 1990, s 22(6) provides that a member's interests are impaired if the nominal value of his shareholding is reduced; the amount of the fixed dividend to which he is entitled is reduced; he is deprived of any of his rights as a shareholder; the percentage of his interest in the company's total issued share capital is reduced; or he is deprived of his shareholding in the company.

[169] C(A)A 1990, s 22(1)(b).

[170] C(A)A 1990, s 22(1)(c).

[171] C(A)A 1990, s 22(1)(d).

[172] C(A)A 1990, s 22(1)(e).

survival of the company;[173] specify what changes should be made to the company's memorandum and articles of association, if the examiner considers this necessary or desirable for the survival of the company;[174]

- they must include such other matters as the examiner considers appropriate;[175]

- they must a statement of the company's assets and liabilities at the date of the proposals should be attached to each copy of the proposals to be submitted to the members' and creditors' meetings;[176]

- they must a description of the estimated financial outcome of a winding up of the company for each class of members and creditors should be attached to each copy of the proposals;[177] and

- they must the court may direct that the proposals contain such other provisions as it deems appropriate.[178]

[10.052] The examiner's proposals must provide for the survival of the company and cannot be directed towards the liquidation of the company. In *Re Clare Textiles Ltd*[179], Costello J considered proposals which envisaged the sale of the company's assets and undertaking and concluded as follows:

> 'In my opinion, it is quite clear that the only proposals he is permitted to formulate are those which make it likely that (a) the company and (b) the whole or part of its undertaking will survive as a going concern. The examiner has no authority to prepare proposals involving the sale of the company's assets and its business or its liquidation and in my opinion the court has no power to confirm proposals under s 24 which do not provide for the survival of the company and at least part of its undertaking as a going concern.'[180]

[10.053] There is a further limitation on the matters which the examiner may include in the proposed compromise or arrangement. According to C(A)A 1990, s 25B[181], such proposals may not abrogate the rights of a lessor. In particular, the proposals may not provide for a reduction or extinguishment of the amount of rent due under a lease[182] and may not limit or prevent the exercise of the lessor's rights in respect of a failure to pay

---

[173] C(A)A 1990, s 22(1)(f).

[174] C(A)A 1990, s 22(1)(g).

[175] C(A)A 1990, s 22(1)(h).

[176] C(A)A 1990, s 22(2). This statement must include contingent and prospective liabilities of the company. Note that it is only the proposals which are submitted to the members' and creditors' meetings under s 23 that must include this statement.

[177] C(A)A 1990, s 22(3).

[178] C(A)A 1990, s 22(4).

[179] *Re Clare Textiles Ltd* [1993] 2 IR 213.

[180] *Re Clare Textiles Ltd* [1993] 2 IR 213 at 220.

[181] Inserted by C(A)(No 2) A 1999, s 26.

[182] C(A)A 1990, s 25B(1)(a), as inserted by C(A)(No 2)A 1999, s 26 prohibits provisions of a proposed compromise or arrangement which provide for, 'a reduction in the amount of any rent or other periodical payment reserved under a lease of land that falls to be paid after the compromise or scheme of arrangement would take effect under s 24(9) or the complete extinguishment of the right of the lessor to any such payments …'

rent or comply with the covenants in a lease[183], where the obligations in question would arise after the compromise or arrangement takes effect.[184] This is subject to the qualification that, if the lessor consents in writing to such provisions appearing in a proposed compromise or scheme of arrangement, these provisions will be permissible.[185]

[10.054] With regard to the interaction between the examiner's proposals and the petition, it is interesting to note the following comment by Costello J in *Re Clare Textiles Ltd*[186]:

> '... when the court appoints an examiner, it seems to me desirable that the order should require him to report to the court either by means of affidavit or in the s 15 report as to (a) any material errors in the petition and/or grounding affidavit leading to his appointment, and (b) when proposals for the company's survival had been contained in these documents and are not adopted, the reasons for their non-adoption.'[187]

While that case was decided under the C(A)A 1990, as it existed before the enactment of the C(A)(No 2)A 1999, and before the creation of the requirement that the petition be accompanied by the report of an independent accountant, it may be interpreted as imposing an obligation on an examiner to abide by the content of the petition seeking his appointment. As the legislation is presently formulated, there is no correlation between the petition and the report of the independent accountant, and the proposals and report that the examiner is obliged to formulate. It would be illogical and counter-productive to allow an examiner to formulate proposals that are inconsistent with the terms of the petition. While the legislation does not furnish any clarity in this regard, the above-quoted dicta of Costello J may be a basis for interpreting the terms of the petition as being generally binding on an examiner in the formulation and presentation of his proposals.

(b) Consideration of proposals

[10.055] When the examiner has formulated the proposals for the compromise or scheme of arrangement, he must convene such meetings of the members and creditors as he considers appropriate to consider such proposals, and shall preside at such

---

[183] C(A)A 1990, s 25B(1)(b), as inserted by C(A)(No 2)A 1999, s 26, prohibits provisions in a compromise or scheme of arrangement which require that, in respect of a failure to pay rent or comply with covenants, 'the lessor under such a lease shall not exercise, or shall only exercise in specified circumstances, any right, whether under the lease or otherwise, to recover possession of the land concerned, effect a forfeiture of the lease or otherwise enter on the land or to recover the amount of such rent or other payment or to claim damages or other relief in respect of the failure to comply with such a covenant or obligation.'

[184] C(A)A 1990, s 25B(1), as inserted by C(A)(No 2)A 1999, s 26.

[185] C(A)A 1990, s 25B(3), as inserted by C(A)(No 2)A 1999, s 26.

[186] *Re Clare Textiles Ltd* [1993] 2 IR 213.

[187] *Re Clare Textiles Ltd* [1993] 2 IR 213 at 223.

meetings.[188] There is nothing in the Companies Acts which specifies the criteria that must be considered by the examiner in determining whether and which meetings to convene. However, it may be expected that an examiner should, at a minimum, convene meetings of any members or creditors whose interests would be impaired by the proposed compromise or arrangement.

While the examiner is not bound by the requirements of the Companies Acts regarding the notice requirements for convening meetings, he must furnish at least three days' notice, by post,[189] of any meetings convened to consider the proposed compromise or arrangement.[190] This notice must be sent to every person who appears from the company's books to be a member or creditor of the company, as the case may be.[191] The notice must be accompanied by proxy forms which the creditors or members may use to vote at the meetings.[192] An affidavit by the examiner, a solicitor, or employee or the company, that the notice has been duly posted will be sufficient evidence that such notice was duly sent.[193] If some creditors or members do not receive the notice that was sent to them, the proceedings and resolutions at the meetings, shall be valid, unless the court orders otherwise.[194]

[10.056] Every notice that is sent in advance of such a meeting must be accompanied by a statement explaining the effect of the compromise or scheme of arrangement.[195] Such a statement must also specify any material interests of the company's directors, whether in their capacity as directors, members, creditors of the company or otherwise, and the effect of the compromise or arrangement on these interests, insofar as that effect

---

[188] C(A)A 1990, s 18(2), as amended by C(A)(No 2)A 1999, s 22. Rules of the Superior Courts, O 75A, r 18(4) provides in this regard that, 'The Examiner shall preside at and be chairman of any meeting which he has convened and shall conduct the business of the meeting in an orderly manner so as to ensure the proper discussion of all proposals placed by him before the said meeting.'

[189] Rules of the Superior Courts, O 75A, r 18(1), specifies that notice should be served by post.

[190] C(A)A 1990, s 18(2), as amended by C(A)(No 2)A 1999, s 22.

[191] Rules of the Superior Courts, O 75A, r 18(1). Order 75A, Rule 18(2) states that the address should be the address specified in the examiner's report. However, since the enactment of C(A)(No 2)A 1999, there will have been no examiners report before the formulation of the proposals. It may be inferred that the address that should be used is the address stipulated in the report of the independent accountant which accompanied the petition, although the Rules have not been updated and do not contain guidance in this regard.

[192] Rules of the Superior Courts, O 75A, r 18(11).

[193] Rules of the Superior Courts, O 75A, r 18(3).

[194] Rules of the Superior Courts, O 75A, r 18(5).

[195] C(A)A 1990, s 23(8). Note that, according to CA 1963, s 202(3), 'Where a notice given by advertisement includes a notification that copies of a statement explaining the effect of a compromise or arrangement proposed can be obtained by creditors or members entitled to attend the meeting, every such creditor or member shall, on making application in the manner indicated by the notice, be furnished by the company free of charge with a copy of the statement.' This provision is applied to s 23 by C(A)A 1990, s 23(7).

is different to the effect on the interests of other persons.[196] Any director (or trustee for debenture holders) is under a duty to give notice to the company of such matters related to himself as are necessary to ensure compliance with this provision and he shall be guilty of an offence and liable to a fine if he fails to do so.[197]

[10.057] The meetings of members or creditors may be held at such places as the examiner considers is most convenient for the majority of those attending and the meeting may be held at different places and times.[198] If the meeting consents, the examiner may adjourn any such meeting, but the adjourned meeting must be held at the same place, unless the resolution authorising the adjournment also authorises a change of venue.[199] A meeting must be adjourned if there are less than three creditors who are entitled to vote, or at least two members in the case of a members' meeting.[200] Members and creditors may attend in person or by proxy[201] and an examiner may be appointed to act as a proxy.[202]

The examiner must keep and sign minutes of any meetings of the members or creditors in a book kept for that purpose and must keep a list, signed by him, of the members and creditors present at every meeting.[203]

With regard to the right to vote at meetings, the examiner has the right to allow or disallow the vote of any person claiming to be a creditor or member, if he considers it appropriate to do so, but this decision may be subject to appeal to the court. If the examiner is not certain whether to allow a vote, he must allow the vote, recording it as

---

[196] C(A)A 1990, s 23(8). Note that, according to CA 1963, s 202(2), 'Where the compromise or arrangement affects the rights of debenture holders of a company, the said statement shall give the like explanation in relation to the trustees of any deed for securing the issue of the debentures as it is required to give in relation to the company's directors.' C(A)A 1990, s 23(7) applies this provision to meetings under s 23.

[197] CA 1963, s 202(6), as amended by C(A)A 1982, s 15; CA 1990, s 240(7) as inserted by CLEA 2001, s 104, and C(AA)A 2003, Sch 2, Item 1, and as applied by C(A)A 1990, s 23(7).

[198] Rules of the Superior Courts, O 75A, r 18(3).

[199] Rules of the Superior Courts, O 75A, r 18(6).

[200] Rules of the Superior Courts, O 75A, r 18(7)(a). Rule 18(7)(b) further specifies that, 'If within 15 minutes from the time appointed for the meeting, a quorum of creditors or members as the case may be is not present or represented, the meeting shall be adjourned for the same day in the following week at the same time and place or to such other day or time or place as the Examiner may appoint but so that the day appointed shall be not less than three, nor more than 21 days from the date from which the meeting was adjourned.'

[201] Note that infants may not be appointed as proxies and that, 'Where a company is a creditor, any person who is duly authorised under the seal of such company to act, generally on behalf of the company at meetings of creditors and members, may fill in and sign the instrument of proxy on such company's behalf and appoint himself to be such company's proxy and the instrument of proxy so filled in and signed by such person shall be received and dealt with as a proxy of such company', Rules of the Superior Courts, O 75A, r 18(14).

[202] Rules of the Superior Courts, O 75A, rs 18(9) and 18(13).

[203] Rules of the Superior Courts, O 75A, r 18(8).

being subject to being declared invalid in the event of an objection being taken and sustained by the court.[204]

At a meeting of the members, creditors, or classes of the company's members or creditors, a modification of the proposed compromise or arrangement may be put to the meeting, but it may only be accepted with the consent of the examiner.[205]

[10.058] While there are provisions of the Companies Acts governing voting at meetings of creditors to consider examiners' proposals, there are no specific provisions in relation to meetings of the company's members and it may be assumed that the general provisions of the Companies Acts regarding members' meetings will apply.[206] With regard to creditors' meetings, the proposals advanced by the examiner shall be deemed to have been accepted by a meeting of the company's creditors or a meeting of a class of such creditors, if two conditions are met. First, a majority in number of such creditors, must vote in person or by proxy, in favour of the resolution for the proposals.[207] Secondly, a majority in value of the claims represented at the creditors' meeting must vote in person or by proxy in favour of the proposals.[208] If a State authority is a creditor of the company, it may accept an examiner's proposals despite the fact that the claim would be impaired and despite the provisions of any legislation to the contrary.[209] An abstention from voting, or a failure to vote, by a creditor, in relation to the proposals cannot be construed as a vote against the proposals.[210]

If a meeting of the members or creditors to consider an examiner's proposals is adjourned, a resolution passed at an adjourned meeting shall be treated as if it was passed on the date it was in fact passed and not on any earlier date.[211]

There is no provision of s 23 which renders it an offence for the examiner to fail to comply with any of its obligations in relation to the meetings of members or creditors of the company in examinership. However, s 23(7) provides that CA 1963, s 202[212] applies to meetings held under s 23. Section 202(4) stipulates that, if a company fails to comply with the requirements of s 202, the company and every defaulting officer is guilty of an offence and liable to a fine.[213] Applying this to s 23, it appears that any default by an examiner under s 23 is an offence, which, according to s 202(4), is publishable by a fine

---

[204] Rules of the Superior Courts, O 75A, r 18(15).

[205] C(A)A 1990, s 23(2).

[206] See further Ch **5**.

[207] C(A)A 1990, s 23(4).

[208] C(A)A 1990, s 23(4).

[209] C(A)A 1990, s 23(5) as amended by CA 1990, s 180. Note that, according s 23(5)(b), '"State authority" means the State, a Minister of the Government [, or local authority,] or the Revenue Commissioners.'

[210] C(A)A 1990, s 23(4A) as inserted by C(A)(No 2)A 1999, s 23.

[211] C(A)A 1990, s 23(6), as amended by C(A)(No 2)A 1999, s 23, applying to CA 1963, s 144.

[212] Section 202 concerns the confirmation of proposals for compromises and schemes of arrangements between a company and its members or creditors. See CA 1963, s 201.

[213] CA 1963, s 202(4), as amended by C(A)A 1982, s 15 and C(AA)A 2003, Sch 2 Item 1.

of €1904.61[214]. However, s 202(5) provides that it is a defence to prove that the default was due to the refusal of a director or debenture holder to supply the necessary information regarding this interests, a defence which would also appear to be available to a company's examiner.[215]

(c) Report

[10.059] After holding the creditors' and members' meetings to consider the proposed compromise or arrangement, the examiner must report on those proposals by delivering a copy of his report to the office of the court.[216] This report must be made to the office of the court within 35 days of the examiner's appointment, or such longer period as the court may allow.[217] In this regard, an examiner may apply to court for an extension of time beyond the expiry of the 70 day period of protection stipulated in s 5(1). If the court is satisfied that the examiner would be unable to report to court within that 70 day period, and that the examiner would be able to make a report if that period were extended, the court may extend that period by a maximum of a further 30 days.[218]

[10.060] Order 75A, r 17 governs the procedure for reports to be made under s 18. However, O 75A has not been amended to reflect the terms of C(A)(No 2)A 1999 and continues to refer to provisions of the C(A)A 1990 which have since been repealed. As the terms of s 18 have been amended quite significantly, it is difficult to discern the relevance or workability of O 75A and its provisions are treated here subject to the caveat that these provisions require amendment to reflect the amendments introduced by C(A)(No 2)A 1999. Insofar as it may continue to be relevant, O 75A, r 17 requires that an examiner's report under s 18 must be delivered to the court by making an *ex parte* application to court to deliver it.[219] The examiner may further apply *ex parte* for an extension of time under s 18(4). On such an application, the court may direct the examiner to serve notice on such parties as the court thinks fit. In this regard, the court may adjourn the hearing to allow such service to occur and may extend the period of

---

[214] CA 1963, s 202(4), as amended by C(A)A 1982, s 15 and CA 1990, s 240(7) as inserted by CLEA 2001 s 104(c).

[215] This provision applies to meetings under s 23, by virtue of C(A)A 1990, s 23(7).

[216] C(A)A 1990, s 18(2), as amended by C(A)(No 2)A 1999, s 22 and C(A)A 1990, s 18(5)(a), as substituted by C(A)(No 2)A 1999, s 22.

[217] C(A)A 1990, s 18(2), as amended by C(A)(No 2)A 1999, s 22. See the *Irish Current Law Statutes Annotated*, in which Declan Murphy describes the background to this time limit, and its reduction since the enactment of the C(A)(No 2)A 1999, as follows: 'As an examiner is now only appointed where the Court is of the opinion that that the confirmation of proposals for a compromise or scheme of arrangement would facilitate the survival of the company and the whole or any part of its undertaking, s 18(1) was required to be amended to reflect this. Accordingly, s 18(1) (substituted by s 22(a)) requires the examiner as soon as practicable to formulate such proposals. Previously, an examiner would have 21 days to prepare his report under s 15 and a further 21 days to report back to Court under s 18 with the results of the meetings. With the repeal of s 15, it was felt appropriate to reduce the time necessary for making the s 18 report. Section 22(b) reduces this time to 35 days.'

[218] C(A)A 1990, s 18(3), as amended by C(A)(No 2)A 1999, s 22.

[219] Rules of the Superior Courts, O 75A, r 17(1).

protection until the adjourned hearing date or such other date as the court considers fit.[220]

[10.061] The examiner's report to court must include the following:[221]

– the proposals placed before the meetings;[222]

– any modifications of those proposals adopted at any of those meetings;[223]

– the outcome of each of the meetings;[224]

– the recommendation of the committee of creditors, if any;[225]

– a statement of the assets and liabilities of the company as at the date of the report;[226]

– a list of the creditors of the company, the amount owing to each, the nature and value of any security held, and the priority status of any such creditor;[227]

– a list of the officers of the company;[228]

– the examiner's recommendations;[229] and

– such other matters as the examiner deems appropriate or as the court directs.[230]

Order 75A, r 18(17)(2)(a) requires that:

> The report shall contain a full account of each meeting convened by the Examiner and of the proposals put before each such meeting and shall contain as an appendix to the said report a copy of the said proposals which shall deal with each of the matters specified in s 22 of the Act in the order set out in that section.

(d) Dissemination of report

[10.062] On the same day that an examiner provides its report to the court, it must supply a copy of the report to the company.[231] The examiner must also furnish a copy of the report to any interested party, on receipt of a written application in that regard.[232] The report which is furnished to interested parties may omit certain information. Section

---

[220] Rules of the Superior Courts, O 75A, r 17(3).

[221] C(A)A 1990, s 19.

[222] C(A)A 1990, s 19(a).

[223] C(A)A 1990, s 19(b).

[224] C(A)A 1990, s 19(c).

[225] C(A)A 1990, s 19(d).

[226] C(A)A 1990, s 19(e). Note that this must include any contingent or prospective liabilities.

[227] C(A)A 1990, s 19(f).

[228] C(A)A 1990, s 19(g).

[229] C(A)A 1990, s 19(h).

[230] C(A)A 1990, s 19(i).

[231] C(A)A 1990, s 18(5)(a), as substituted by C(A)(No 2)A 1999, s 22.

[232] C(A)A 1990, s 18(5)(b), as substituted by C(A)(No 2)A 1999, s 22.

18(7) provides that an application may be made to court for an order permitting the omission of certain specified parts of the report from the copy supplied to an interested person.[233] In particular, the court may direct the omission of information which, if it was included in the report, would be likely to prejudice the survival of the company as a going concern.[234]

(e) Confirmation of report

(i) Time limits

[10.063] There is no deadline stipulated in the legislation for the confirmation of the examiner's proposals by the court. However, there are three general rules that are relevant to this question. First, the examiner is obliged to submit the report to court within 35 days of his appointment, but this period may be extended by the court[235] and may even be extended beyond the expiry of the 70 day period of protection, for an additional 30 days, if the court is of the view that this is necessary to allow the report to be made.[236] Secondly, the examiner's report must be set down for consideration by the court as soon as possible after receipt of the report by the court.[237]

Thirdly, even if the examiner's report is submitted to court within the period of protection, whether 70 days or 100 days, if an extension was granted under C(A)A 1990, s 18(3), this period may be extended further at the discretion of the court. Section 18(4) provides that, if the period of protection would expire after the delivery of the report, the court may extend the period of protection for as long as the court considers necessary to enable it to decide whether to confirm the examiner's proposals. This is the only means by which the period of protection may be extended beyond the period of 100 days that is envisaged by s 18(3). It ensures that a company, which is placed in the protection of the court, remains so protected until the court determines whether to confirm the examiner's proposals. C(A)A 1990, s 18(4) provides in this regard that:

> Where the examiner has submitted a report under this section to the court and, but for this subsection, the period mentioned in s 5(1) (and any extended period allowed under sub-s (3) of this section) would expire, the court may, of its own motion or on the application of the examiner, extend the period concerned by such period as the court considers necessary to enable it to take a decision under s 24.

---

[233] C(A)A 1990, s 18(7), as inserted by C(A)(No 2)A 1999, s 22. Note that O 75A, r 18(17)(2)(b) provides that, 'The Examiner shall in his application specify whether and if so, what portions of the report should be omitted from delivery under s 18(5) of the Act and he shall draw to the attention of the Court any particular aspects of the report which are or may be relevant to the exercise by the Court of any other of its functions under the Act.' While this refers to s 18 as it existed before the enactment of C(A)(No 2)A 1999, the requirement that the examiner draw the court's attention to any aspects of the report which are relevant to the exercise of the court's functions should be noted.

[234] C(A)A 1990, s 18(8), as inserted by C(A)(No 2)A 1999, s 22.

[235] C(A)A 1990, s 18(2), as amended by C(A)(No 2)A 1999, s 22.

[236] C(A)A 1990, s 18(3), as amended by C(A)(No 2)A 1999, s 22.

[237] C(A)A 1990, s 24(1).

(ii) Hearing

[10.064] At the court hearing, the company, its examiner, and any creditor or member whose claim or interest would be impaired by the proposals, may appear and be heard.[238] In particular, a member or creditor whose interest or claim would be impaired by the proposals, may object to confirmation of the proposals on grounds including, but not limited to, the following:

- a material irregularity at or concerning the meeting of creditors or members summoned by the examiner to consider the proposals;[239]

- the acceptance of the proposal at the meeting was obtained by improper means;[240]

- the proposals were put forward for an improper purpose;[241] or

- the proposals unfairly prejudice the interests of the objector.[242]

If the creditor or member who appears at the hearing for the confirmation of the examiner's proposals, voted in favour of the proposals at the meeting, the grounds on which he may object to the court confirmation are limited.[243] He may object on the basis that the acceptance was obtained by improper means or on the basis that, since voting in favour of the proposals, he became aware that they were put forward for an improper purpose.[244]

If the court upholds the objections made by a creditor or member to the confirmation of the examiner's proposals, it may make such orders as it considers fit.[245] In particular, the court may set aside the decision of the meeting of creditors or members at which the proposal was approved and order that the meeting in question be reconvened.[246]

(iii) Court determination

[10.065] Upon consideration of the report, the court may make such order in relation to the examiner's proposals as it considers proper, whether an order confirming the proposals, refusing to confirm the proposals, or confirming the proposals subject to

---

[238] C(A)A 1990, s 24(2). See further fn 168 above regarding the meaning of 'impairment' of the interests of members and creditors. Note also that in the case of certain banking companies or those listed in the second schedule of C(A)(No 2)A 1999, the Central Bank is also entitled to appear and be heard: C(A)A 1990, s 2(b) and (c), inserted by C(A)(No 2)A 1999, s 7.

[239] C(A)A 1990, s 25(1)(a).

[240] C(A)A 1990, s 25(1)(b).

[241] C(A)A 1990, s 25(1)(c).

[242] C(A)A 1990, s 25(1)(d).

[243] C(A)A 1990, s 25(2).

[244] C(A)A 1990, s 25(2).

[245] C(A)A 1990, s 25(3).

[246] C(A)A 1990, s 25(3).

modifications.[247] Section 24(8) provides that, if the court confirms the proposals, it may also make such orders for the implementation of its decision as it deems fit.[248] While s 24(8) does not state so specifically, it may be assumed that this power to make implementation orders applies to orders of the court which confirm the examiner's proposals subject to modifications.

[10.066] The court's discretion to confirm the examiner's proposals is subject to the limitation that the court cannot confirm such proposals unless:

–   at least one class of creditors whose interests or claims would be impaired by the proposals has accepted the proposals;[249]

–   the court is satisfied that the proposals are fair and equitable in relation to any class of members or creditors whose claims or interests would be impaired by the proposals and who have not accepted the proposals;[250] or

–   the court is satisfied that the proposals are not unfairly prejudicial to the interests of any interested party;[251] and

–   the sole or primary purpose of the proposals is not the avoidance of tax.[252]

This is subject to the qualification that an examiner is always entitled to submit proposals which will not impair the interests of any members or creditors of the company and nothing in the Companies Acts prevents the court from confirming such proposals.[253]

[10.067] There are certain further limitations on the confirmation of proposed compromises and schemes of arrangement by the court. First, the court must not confirm any proposals which would impair the interests of the creditors of the company in examinership in a manner which favours the creditors or members of a related company to which the examiner has also been appointed.[254] In this regard, it should be recalled that C(A)A 1990, s 22(5) provides that, 'a creditor's claim against a company is impaired if he receives less in payment of his claim than the full amount due in respect of the claim at the date of presentation of the petition for the appointment of the examiner'. The proposals may not therefore involve the payment of less than the full amount of a creditor's claim so as to benefit creditors or members of a related company in examinership. As one example, this provision ensures that an examiner cannot discharge in full the debts owing to creditors of one company at the expense of creditors of a related company.

---

[247] C(A)A 1990, s 24(3).

[248] C(A)A 1990, s 24(8).

[249] C(A)A 1990, s 24(4)(a), as substituted by C(A)(No 2)A 1999, s 24(b).

[250] C(A)A 1990, s 24(4)(c)(i).

[251] C(A)A 1990, s 24(4)(c)(ii).

[252] C(A)A 1990, s 24(4)(b).

[253] C(A)A 1990, s 24(12), as substituted by C(A)(No 2)A 1999, s 24.

[254] C(A)A 1990, s 24(4A), as inserted by C(A)(No 2)A 1999, s 24.

[10.068] Secondly, the court must not modify an examiner's proposals in a manner which would abrogate the rights of a lessor under a lease for land. Section 25B provides that the proposed compromise or scheme of arrangement may not be modified by the court in a manner which reduces or extinguishes the amount of rent due under a lease[255] or limits or prevents the exercise of the lessor's rights in respect of a failure to pay rent or comply with the covenants in a lease,[256] where the obligations in question would arise after the compromise or arrangement takes effect.[257] The same limitation applies by a different means to provisions in relation to leases or hire purchase agreements of property other than land which is of a substantial value.[258] If the following conditions are met, a provision of a proposed compromise or scheme of arrangement will be deemed to be unfairly prejudicial to the interests of an interested party:

– the court must be of the opinion that the provision would reduce or extinguish a right to rent or other periodic payment, which would fall due after the commencement of the compromise or scheme of arrangement, or limit the right to enforce these obligations or other covenants;

– it must relate to a lease or hire purchase agreement in respect of property other than land; and

– the court must be of the opinion that the property is of a substantial value.[259]

The only exception to this rule is that the owner or lessor of the property may furnish his written consent to the inclusion of such provisions in the proposed compromise or scheme of arrangement and the court could then confirm such proposals.[260]

(iv) Consequences of confirmation

[10.069] There are a number of consequences and steps that flow from a court order confirming an examiner's proposals. First, the compromise or scheme of arrangement that is confirmed by the court will take effect from such date as is fixed by the court.[261] This date must be within 21 days of the date of the court confirmation.

Secondly, if the court confirms the examiner's proposals, whether modified or not, the proposals are binding on all members or classes of members of the company who are

---

[255] C(A)A 1990, s 25B(1)(a), as inserted by C(A)(No 2)A 1999, s 26. See further para **[10.053]**.

[256] C(A)A 1990, s 25B(1)(b), as inserted by C(A)(No 2)A 1999, s 26. See further para **[10.053]**.

[257] C(A)A 1990, s 25B(1), as inserted by C(A)(No 2)A 1999, s 26.

[258] C(A)A 1990, s 25B(2), as inserted by C(A)(No 2)A 1999, s 26.

[259] C(A)A 1990, s 25B(2), as inserted by C(A)(No 2)A 1999, s 26. Note that, according to C(A)A 1990, s 25B(4), as inserted by C(A)(No 2)A 1999, 'In deciding, for the purposes of sub-s (2), whether the value of the property concerned is substantial the matters to which the court shall have regard shall include the length of the unexpired term of the lease or hiring agreement concerned.'

[260] C(A)A 1990, s 25B(3), as inserted by C(A)(No 2)A 1999, s 26.

[261] C(A)A 1990, s 24(9).

affected by the proposal; all creditors or classes of creditors who are affected by the proposal; any person who is liable for all or any part of the debts of the company (under any statute, enactment, rule of law or otherwise); and on the company itself.[262]

Thirdly, upon the confirmation of the proposals, the examiner (or such other person as the court may direct) is under a duty to deliver a copy of the court order to the Registrar of Companies for registration.[263] It may be assumed that this applies whether the order confirms the proposals or confirms the proposals with modifications. Fourthly, notice of the delivery of a copy of the order to the Registrar must be published in the *Companies Registration Office Gazette* within 14 days.[264] The obligation to cause this notice to be published rests on the examiner or such other person as the court may direct and it is an offence to fail to comply with this obligation, punishable by a maximum fine of €1,904.61.[265] It may be expected that the obligation to deliver a copy of the order to the Registrar and the obligation to cause notice of this to be published in the *Companies Registration Office Gazette*, will be imposed on the same person, whether the examiner, or such other person as may be directed by the court.

A fifth effect of the confirmation of the examiner's proposals is that any recommendations that the memorandum and articles of association be amended, shall take effect from a date fixed by the court.[266] This provision takes effect irrespective of any provisions of the Companies Acts, and, to that extent, overrides the general requirements of the Companies Acts regarding notice, voting and other procedures applicable to the amendment of a company's articles or memorandum of association.

(v) Revocation of confirmation

[10.070] A company, or a creditor or member of a company may apply for the revocation of a court order confirming an examiner's proposals.[267] This must be done within 180 days of the order. The only ground on which revocation may be sought is on the ground that it was procured by fraud.[268] If satisfied that there was such fraud, the court may revoke the confirmation, although it is not compelled do so. If the court does exercise its discretion to revoke the confirmation, it may do so subject to such terms and conditions as it sees fit, particularly regarding 'the protection of the rights of parties acquiring interests or property in good faith and for value in reliance on that confirmation.'[269] A copy of any order revoking the confirmation of an examiner's

---

[262] C(A)A 1990, s 24(5) and (6).

[263] C(A)A 1990, s 24(10).

[264] C(A)A 1990, s 30(1), as amended by C(A)(No 2)A 1999, s 29 and IFCMPA 2005, s 72.

[265] C(A)A 1990, s 30(1), as amended by C(A)(No 2)A 1999, s 29, and s 30(2) and CA 1990, s 240(7) as inserted by CLEA 2001, s 104.

[266] C(A)A 1990, s 24(7).

[267] C(A)A 1990, s 27(1).

[268] C(A)A 1990, s 27(1).

[269] C(A)A 1990, s 27(1).

proposals must be delivered to the Registrar of Companies as soon as practicable after that order is made, by such person as the court may direct.[270]

(f) Failure of examinership

[10.071] There are two possible means by which it may be determined that the examiner failed to arrive at an acceptable proposed compromise or scheme of arrangement for the survival of the company. First, the examiner may apply to court if he has been unable to enter into an agreement with the necessary persons or to formulate proposals for a compromise or scheme of arrangement in relation to the company.[271] On such an application, the court may give such directions or make such orders as it considers appropriate. In particular, the court, if it considers it just and equitable to do so, may order the winding up of the company.[272]

The second means by which the examinership may fail is for the court to reject the proposals advanced by the examiner. Section 24(3) provides that, on consideration of the examiner's report, the court may refuse to confirm the proposals contained therein.

In either of these circumstances, the court may, if it considers it just and equitable to do so, make an order for the winding up of the company, or such other order as it deems fit.[273]

(g) Report regarding irregularities

[10.072] Where a court considers that there is evidence of a substantial disappearance of the company's property, or other serious irregularities in relation to the company, the court must hold a hearing to consider these matters. Section 13A(1) accordingly provides:

> Where, arising out of the presentation to it of the report of the independent accountant or otherwise, it appears to the court that there is evidence of a substantial disappearance of property of the company concerned that is not adequately accounted for, or of other serious irregularities in relation to the company's affairs having occurred, the court shall, as soon as it is practicable, hold a hearing to consider that evidence.[274]

If the court so directs, the examiner must prepare a report setting out the matters which the examiners considers would be of assistance to the court at the hearing into these irregularities.[275] The examiner must deliver a copy of this report to the office of the

---

[270] C(A)A 1990, s 27(2), as inserted by C(A)(No 2)A 1999, s 27.

[271] C(A)A 1990, s 18(9), as inserted by C(A)(No 2)A 1999, s 22.

[272] C(A)A 1990, s 18(9), as inserted by C(A)(No 2)A 1999, s 22.

[273] C(A)A 1990, s 24(11), as amended by C(A)(No 2)A 1999, s 24. In relation to the conclusion of an examiner that no compromise or arrangement could be arrived at, this is duplicative of the terms of s 18(9) which state that, in such circumstances, 'the court may, on such application, give such directions or make such order as it deems fit, including, if it considers it just and equitable to do so, an order for the winding-up of the company'.

[274] C(A)A 1990, s 13A(1), as inserted by C(A)(No 2)A 1999, s 21.

[275] C(A)A 1990, s 13A(2), as inserted by C(A)(No 2)A 1999, s 21.

court, and to the company, on the same day.[276] Upon receipt of written applications, the examiner must also furnish copies of the report to any person who is mentioned in the report and any interested party.[277] However, copies of the report that are furnished to such person may omit certain information, if the court issues a direction to that effect.[278] In particular, the court may direct that the copies of the report that are supplied to persons named in the report or interested parties, may omit any information the inclusion of which would be likely to prejudice the survival of the company as a going concern.[279]

There are various persons who may appear at the hearing into suspected irregularities. First, the examiner may appear.[280] Secondly, if the evidence of suspected irregularities was contained in report of the independent accountant, the independent accounts may appear.[281] Thirdly, the company in examinership may appear at the hearing.[282] Fourth, any interested party may appear.[283] Finally, any person who is referred to in the independent account's report or the examiner's report regarding suspected irregularities may appear at the hearing into such suspected irregularities.[284]

On a hearing into suspected irregularities, the court may make such orders as it deems fit.[285] In particular, the court may, if it considers it appropriate, direct the examiner or any other person, to deliver an office copy of such orders to the Registrar of

---

[276] C(A)A 1990, s 13A(3), as inserted by C(A)(No 2)A 1999, s 21.

[277] C(A)A 1990, s 13A(4), as inserted by C(A)(No 2)A 1999, s 21. There is no distinction in this regard between the different forms in which a person may be mentioned in the report and any such mention will entitle that person to apply in writing for a copy of the report.

[278] C(A)A 1990, s 13A(5), as inserted by C(A)(No 2)A 1999, s 21.

[279] C(A)A 1990, s 13A(6), as inserted by C(A)(No 2)A 1999, s 21.

[280] C(A)A 1990, s 13A(8)(a), as inserted by C(A)(No 2)A 1999, s 21.

[281] C(A)A 1990, s 13A(8)(c), as inserted by C(A)(No 2)A 1999, s 21.

[282] C(A)A 1990, s 13A(8)(d), as inserted by C(A)(No 2)A 1999, s 21.

[283] C(A)A 1990, s 13A(8)(d), as inserted by C(A)(No 2)A 1999, s 21. Note that 'interested party' means a member or creditor of the company (C(A)A 1990, s 1). C(A)A 1990 s 13A(8)(g) also provides that the Central Bank may appear and be heard in the case of the examinership of companies referred to in C(A)A 1990, s 2(b) and (c) (as inserted by C(A)(No 2)A 1999, s 7), being certain banking companies or those listed in the second schedule of C(A)(No 2)A 1999.

[284] C(A)A 1990, s 13A(8)(e), as inserted by C(A)(No 2)A 1999, s 21.

[285] C(A)A 1990, s 13A(9), as inserted by C(A)(No 2)A 1999, s 21. Note that such orders may include, '... where appropriate, an order for the trial of any issue relating to the matter concerned' (C(A)A 1990, s 13A(9)). In the *Irish Current Law Statutes Annotated*, Declan Murphy notes re C(A)(No 2)A 1999, that, 'If the allegations of serious irregularities or the wrongful disposal of assets were not contested it would seem appropriate for the court to make a substantive order remedying the situation.' It should be noted that a court has a general power to direct a person to return property, or proceeds, to an examiner, if satisfied that the property was disposed of in a manner which perpetrated a fraud on the company, its creditors or members. See CA 1990, s 139, as applied to examinerships by CA 1990, s 180(2). See Ch **9**.

Companies.[286] If a copy of the order is delivered to the Registrar, notice of such delivery must be published in the *Companies Registration Office Gazette* within 14 days.[287] The obligation to cause this notice to be published rests on the examiner or such other person as the court may direct and it is an offence to fail to comply with this obligation, punishable by a maximum fine of €1,904.61.[288]

---

[286] C(A)A 1990, s 13A(10), as inserted by C(A)(No 2)A 1999, s 21.

[287] C(A)A 1990, s 30(1), as amended by C(A)(No 2)A 1999, s 29 and IFCMPA 2005, s 72.

[288] C(A)A 1990, s 30(1), as amended by C(A)(No 2)A 1999, s 29, and s 30(2) and CA 1990, s 240(7) as inserted by CLEA 2001, s 104(c).

PART C
ENFORCEMENT AND INVESTIGATION

Chapter 11: Agencies of Enforcement

A. Office of the Director of Corporate Enforcement 517

B. Companies Registration Office 545

C. Director of Public Prosecutions 553

D. Minister for Enterprise, Trade and Employment 557

E. Irish Auditing and Accounting Supervisory Authority 562

Chapter 12: Powers of Investigation of the Director of Corporate Enforcement

A. Production of books or documents 565

B. Entry and search of premises 619

C. Disclosure of information 635

Chapter 13: Inspectors and Company Investigations

A. Appointment of inspector to investigate company's affairs 641

B. Investigation of membership of company 662

C. Conduct of investigations 666

D. Powers of investigation 675

E. Report 693

F. Expenses 708

Chapter 14: Striking Companies' Names off the Register

A. Grounds for striking off 713

B. Effect of strike-off 729

C. Restoration by court 736

D. Restoration by Registrar 758

E. Effect of restoration 766

Chapter 15: Criminal Prosecutions

A. Nature of offences 775

B. Detection of offences 779

C. Potential Defendants 779

D. Pre-trial 786

E. Trial 793

F. Sanctions 800

G. Illustration of criminal prosecution under the Companies Acts 802

H. Proposed reforms 803

Chapter 11

AGENCIES OF ENFORCEMENT

A. Office of the Director of Corporate Enforcement

[11.001] The Office of the Director of Corporate Enforcement ('ODCE') is vested with responsibility for enforcing the Companies Acts.[1] Since its establishment, the ODCE has been responsible for many of the developments that have occurred in the enforcement of company law in Ireland. Formerly, there was a lacuna to a certain extent in the attribution and discharge of company law.

(a) Background

(i) Establishment

[11.002] The Office of the Director of Corporate Enforcement ('ODCE') was established by the CLEA 2001. This body had its origins in the *Report of the Working Group on Company Law Compliance and Enforcement*.[2] The Working Group made the following recommendation:

> 'An independent statutory officer – to be known as the Director of Corporate Enforcement – who would have general – but not exclusive – responsibility for the enforcement of company law should be appointed. The Director would have a similar role to that of the Director of Consumer Affairs, who has specific responsibility in law for the prosecution of offences under consumer legislation, and should be independent in the discharge of his functions.'[3]

The ODCE was established by the commencement of provisions of the CLEA 2001 on 28 November 2001. It comprises the Director of Corporate Enforcement ('DCE') and a staff that includes accountants, administrators, lawyers, and members of An Garda Síochána, who are seconded to the ODCE.[4] At the time of its establishment, the 'primary mandate' of the ODCE was described as follows:

> ... to improve the compliance environment for corporate activity in the Irish economy by:
>
> – encouraging adherence to the requirements of the Companies Acts, and
>
> – bringing to account those who disregard the law.[5]

---

[1] CLEA 2001, s 12(1)(a).

[2] *Report of the Working Group on Company Law Compliance and Enforcement* (30 November 1998).

[3] *Report of the Working Group on Company Law Compliance and Enforcement* (30 November 1998) at para 11 (Summary).

[4] Introduction to the ODCE (www.odce.ie).

[5] See Introduction to the ODCE (www.odce.ie)

(ii) Appointment

[11.003] The DCE is appointed in writing by the Minister for Enterprise, Trade and Employment, following selection by means of a civil service competition.[6] The DCE, who is a civil servant,[7] holds office for five years and may continue in office for further periods, not exceeding five years, as the Minister for Enterprise, Trade and Employment considers appropriate.[8]

(iii) Functions

[11.004] The general objective in creating the ODCE was to improve compliance with company law by encouraging adherence to its requirements and punishing instances of non-compliance.[9] The specific functions of the DCE are listed in CLEA 2001, s 12(1), as follows:

    (a) to enforce the Companies Acts, including by the prosecution of offences by way of summary proceedings,

    (b) to encourage compliance with the Companies Acts,

    (c) to investigate instances of suspected offences under the Companies Acts,

    (d) at his or her discretion, to refer cases to the Director of Public Prosecutions where the Director of Corporate Enforcement has reasonable grounds for believing that an indictable offence under the Companies Acts has been committed,

    (e) to exercise, insofar as the Director feels it necessary or appropriate, a supervisory role over the activity of liquidators and receivers in the discharge of their functions under the Companies Acts,

    (f) for the purpose of ensuring the effective application and enforcement of obligations, standards and procedures to which companies and their officers are subject, to perform such other functions in respect of any matters to which the Companies Acts relate as the Minister considers appropriate and may by order confer on the Director,

    (g) to perform such other functions for a purpose referred to in para (f) as may be assigned to him or her by or under the Companies Acts or any other Act, and

    (h) to act, under the Companies (Auditing and Accounting) Act 2003 as a member of the Irish Auditing and Accounting Supervisory Authority and, if appointed under s 11 of that Act, as a director of the Authority.[10]

These statutory functions of the ODCE can be summarised as involving compliance, enforcement, investigation and supervision. This list may be expanded, in accordance with s 12(1)(f) and (g), to include such other functions as the Minister may consider appropriate.

---

6   CLEA 2001, s 7(2) and (3).

7   CLEA 2001, s 8(2).

8   CLEA 2001, s 8(1).

9   See Department of Enterprise, Trade and Employment, Press Release, 'Director of Corporate Enforcement formally established, "New era in corporate governance", Tánaiste', 27 November 2001.

10   CLEA 2001, s 12(1), as amended by C(AA)A 2003, s 51.

In the Strategy Statement for 2003–2005,[11] the ODCE described its mission as follows:

'– to encourage compliance by companies and individuals with relevant requirements of the Companies Acts 1963–2001 and

– to bring to account those who disregard the law.'

For the purpose of analysing the role and activities of the ODCE, the compliance and enforcement aspects of its functions will be considered separately.

(b) Compliance role

[11.005] According to the ODCE the goal of 'encouraging compliance' involves three sub-goals, namely:

(1) 'Publishing accessible company law information';

(2) 'Promoting compliance';

(3) 'Improving company law and associated corporate practices.'[12]

The ODCE has engaged in an extensive campaign of informing companies, their directors, officers, employees, and the public, of the need to comply with the CA 1963–2006 and the consequences of non-compliance.

The ODCE has adopted the following strategies for encouraging compliance with company law in Ireland:

– public presentations;

– preparation of publications;

– consultation processes;

– discussions with Government and other parties.

To this list, can be added the strategy of encouraging compliance by publicising enforcement actions which have been taken, and penalties which have been imposed, as a result of breaches of company law. Publications and oral presentations regarding the need to comply with the Companies Acts are not guaranteed to inspire adherence to the requirements of those Acts. Evidence that non-compliance will be detected and prosecuted is, however, likely to provoke a higher level of compliance. In this regard, the fact that the ODCE has been very active and visible in the enforcement of company law,[13] is an important means of encouraging compliance with those laws.

A further means of encouraging compliance is the interaction by the ODCE with other agencies and bodies which deal with, regulate or represent, companies governed by Irish law. This interaction plays an important role in the detection and prosecution of breaches of the Companies Acts. It may also enhance the awareness of the need to comply with the Companies Acts and encourage compliance with the Acts, from a broader perspective.

---

[11] ODCE, *Strategy Statement* 2003–2005 (31 December 2002). All ODCE publications referred to are available on the website of the ODCE, www.odce.ie.

[12] See ODCE, *Annual Report 2006* at p 5. Available at www.odce.ie.

[13] See below paras [11.020] to [11.040].

(i) Public presentations

[11.006] Frequent presentations are given on behalf of the ODCE to a wide variety of audiences. The *Annual Reports* for 2004, 2005 and 2006 record numbers of presentations in the region of 60, 58, and 38 respectively. The topics of the presentations range from the role of the ODCE, to corporate governance and include such topics as directors' compliance statements. The topics appear to vary depending upon the audience addressed, which in turn varies from students, to businesses, to representative bodies, to lawyers, and beyond. The ODCE summarised the audience of their presentations in 2004 as including 'business, professional, regulatory and voluntary groups'.[14]

The ODCE also releases press statements and conducts press briefings, reporting eight press statements in 2006 and responses to 100 press queries.[15]

The ODCE reports in 2006 that, following market research, it is focusing these efforts on small and medium sized companies and sought to promote compliance in this sector 'in partnership with business entities and professional representative bodies'.[16]

(ii) Publications

[11.007] In addition to the obligatory annual reports, the ODCE has published a number of information notices, consultation papers, decision notices and articles, regarding its functions; the general requirements of company law and certain specific questions of company law. The ODCE has distributed these publications widely, including the distribution to every company on the Register of Companies, in early 2003, of Information Books concerning companies, company directors and company secretaries, together with details about where the remaining four books could be obtained. Each of the publications is also freely available on the website of the ODCE.[17]

In addition, the ODCE distributes its publications in response to public enquiries and reports that in 2006 over 15,000 copies of its publications were distributed to improve awareness of corporate governance matters.[18] The ODCE also publishes annual reports and interim reviews of activity, among other publications.

(iii) Consultations

[11.008] One of the means by which the ODCE has encouraged compliance with Irish company law is by embarking on consultation processes. The ODCE has produced a number of consultation papers on topics such as transactions with directors[19] and the

---

14 ODCE, *Annual Report 2004* at p 7.

15 ODCE, *Annual Report 2006* at p 9.

16 ODCE, *Annual Report 2006* at pp 5 and 8.

17 See www.odce.ie.

18 ODCE, *Annual Report 2006* at p 8. Available at www.odce.ie.

19 ODCE, Transactions with Directors, Consultation Paper (C/2003/2).

duty of auditors to report suspected indictable offences.[20] Upon the publication of these papers, the ODCE invites submissions and comments from interested parties and engages in a process of consultation with such parties. At the culmination of the consultation process, the ODCE then presents definitive guidance or a decision notice, which represents the final position of the ODCE regarding the area of law in question. For example, the ODCE decided that there was a problem with the level of unlawful loans which were being made to company directors and accordingly prepared a consultation paper on this topic.[21] Interested parties were invited to furnish any comments in relation to the Paper within one month. The ODCE considered all of the submissions received and issued definitive guidance on the subject of transactions between a company and its directors.[22]

(iv) Discussions

[11.009] The ODCE lists 'discussions with Government and other parties as required to facilitate and support the compliance role of the Director' as one of the means by which that Office encourages compliance with company law in Ireland. The following activities of the ODCE may be regarded as falling within this category.

1. SUBMISSIONS ON LEGISLATION

[11.010] The ODCE has been involved in, and made submissions concerning, the drafting of various pieces of legislation which are relevant to the area of company law. For example, the ODCE made submissions on the Companies (Auditing and Accounting) Bill 2003 and argued successfully for a number of changes to that Bill.[23]

---

[20] ODCE, The Duty of Auditors to Report Suspected Indictable Offences under the Companies Acts to the Director of Corporate Enforcement via Section 74(c) of the Company Law Enforcement Act 2001, Consultation Paper (C/2002/1).

[21] ODCE, 'Transactions with Directors' (C/2003/2). See ODCE, *Annual Report 2004.*

[22] ODCE, 'A Guide to Transactions Involving Directors' (November 2003).

[23] According to ODCE, *Annual Report 2003* at p 7, the ODCE successfully argued for the following provisions to be included:

'– the introduction of an exemption from the duty of auditors to report suspected indictable offences in respect of annual return defaults (ie, instances of late returns and the non-filing of returns), on the basis that such noncompliance was already evident from the CRO database and the reporting of such suspected offences involved an unnecessary burden of work on both auditors and the ODCE;

– an augmentation of the information which auditors are required to provide to the ODCE as a consequence of their reporting a suspected indictable offence, in order to assist the Office in evaluating the circumstances of the indicated non-compliance;

– the introduction of provisions allowing for certain certifications by officers of the Director to be admissible as evidence in legal proceedings in a manner similar to that available for other comparable enforcement authorities; the confirmation that certain defaults in complying with the Companies Acts are criminal as well as civil in character.'

The ODCE also made submissions regarding the implementation of the 'Market Abuse' Directive in Ireland.[24]

[11.011] The ODCE also made policy submissions to the Department of Enterprise, Trade and Employment regarding the IFCMPB 2006, including proposals for inclusion in that Bill. One of the five proposals advanced by the ODCE was included in the IFCMPA 2006.[25]

2. INVOLVEMENT WITH IAASA

[11.012] The DCE is a member of the Irish Auditing and Accounting Supervisory Authority ('IAASA') since its establishment in January 2006. In that capacity, the DCE contributes to the deliberations of the IAASA. The ODCE also executed a memorandum of understanding with the IAASA on the exchange of confidential information.[26]

Prior to January 2006, while the IAASA continued on an interim basis throughout 2003 and 2004, the ODCE was a member of the interim board and contributed to the work of the Authority in that capacity, including making submissions to government regarding the content of the Act.[27]

3. COMPANY LAW REVIEW GROUP

[11.013] The DCE is a member of the Company Law Review Group (the 'CLRG'), a statutory advisory expert group which was established on 1 December 2001[28] to advise the Minister for Enterprise, Trade and Employment on the development and review of company law in Ireland. The ODCE describes its role in this Group as follows:

> 'In its work, the Office has sought to ensure that the proposed chapter contains a
> more user–friendly presentation of the statutory requirements and a simplification
> of the current legislation, in order that the State's corporate insolvency provisions
> are better structured and more accessible to creditors and other stakeholders.'[29]

Any input into the reform of Irish company law, which improves the accessibility of its provisions, would be an important means of enhancing compliance with company law.

---

[24] Directive 2003/6/EC (28 January 2003). Regulation (EC) No 2273/2003 (22 December 2003), Directives 2003/124/EC and 2003/125/EC (22 December 2003). See ODCE, *Annual Report 2004* at p 8.

[25] ODCE, *Annual Report 2006* at p 9. The proposal that was adopted involved the recovery of costs in restriction and disqualification proceedings and is addressed in Pt **D**, Declarations of Restriction, and Pt **E**, Disqualification Orders.

[26] ODCE, *Annual Report 2006* at p 10.

[27] See ODCE, *Annual Report 2003*, and ODCE, *Annual Report 2004*.

[28] The CLRG was established on an administrative basis on 8 December 1999 and was formally established on the commencement of Pt VII of the CLEA 2001 on 1 December 2001.

[29] ODCE, *Annual Report 2004* at p 9.

4. MISCELLANEOUS

[11.014] The ODCE made submissions regarding the work of certain other regulatory bodies.[30] For example, the ODCE made contributions and submissions to the Revenue Powers Group, which was established by the Minister for Finance to advise him on the powers of the Revenue Commissioners. In particular, the ODCE commented upon the powers of the Revenue Commissioners to detect, investigate and enforce non-compliance with tax law and the merits of information sharing between regulatory bodies as a means of improving legal compliance by companies.[31] The ODCE also made submissions to the Department of Enterprise, Trade and Employment on proposals related to the audit exemption and to the European Commissions on questions of EU corporate governance.[32]

(v) Interaction with other bodies

[11.015] The ODCE has interacted with other agencies of enforcement and various representative bodies to enhance the level of compliance with company law in Ireland. This has been done by means of joint presentations, publications, co-operation agreements and other forms of interaction.

1. JOINT PRESENTATIONS

[11.016] The ODCE conducted a number of presentations in conjunction with business and professional representative bodies, such as the Association of Chartered Certified Accountants, the Irish Small and Medium Enterprises Association, the Institute of Directors, the Chambers of Commerce of Ireland, FAS and a number of Country Enterprise Boards. The ODCE also developed and maintained links with third level educational institutions.[33]

2. AGREEMENTS

[11.017] The ODCE has a direct relationship with offices such as the Companies Registration Office and the Director of Public Prosecutions ('DPP'), by virtue of statutory mechanisms for referring cases and issues between each other. For example, s 12 provides that the ODCE is required to refer indictable offences to the DPP.[34] The ODCE has also agreed a memorandum of understanding with the IAASA for the exchange of confidential information.[35]

---

[30] Eg, the ODCE made a submission to the Expert Group on Crime Statistics regarding the means of recording the incidence of crime and the ODCE's approach towards recording breaches of the CA 1963–2003. See ODCE, *Annual Report 2003* at p 8.

[31] See ODCE, *Annual Report 2003* at p 8.

[32] ODCE, *Annual Report 2006* at p 10.

[33] ODCE, *Annual Report 2004*; ODCE, *Annual Report 2006* at p 8.

[34] CLEA 2001, s 12(d). See further paras **[11.033]** and Ch **15**.

[35] ODCE, *Annual Report 2006* at p 10.

3. JOINT PUBLICATIONS

[11.018] The ODCE has published a number of articles in periodicals, magazines and other literature, which are issued by representative bodies of business, and auditing and accounting professions, such as the Irish Construction Industry Magazine and the ACCA's 'In Practice Ireland'. The ODCE has also prepared, in conjunction with the CRO, a newsletter about corporate compliance which has been distributed to every person who is registered as a company director in Ireland.[36]

(vi) Enforcement

[11.019] The ODCE issues press releases regarding aspects of its enforcement policy.[37] This ensures that public attention is drawn to the risks of non-compliance with company law and highlights the developments in the enforcement of company law. This in turn is a means of encouraging compliance with the CA 1963–2006.

(c) Enforcement role

[11.020] The enforcement role of the ODCE encompasses a number of distinct elements. As reported by the ODCE in 2006, the enforcement role includes the uncovering of suspected breaches of company law; the prosecution of such breaches; and the sanctioning of improper conduct relating to insolvent companies.[38] These objectives can, according to the ODCE, be further divided into 'sub-goals' as follows:

- 'Uncovering suspected breaches of company law' involves:

  (i)   'developing detection and reporting arrangements for suspected breaches of the Companies Acts';

  (ii)   'identifying suspected breaches of the Companies Acts'; and

  (iii)   commissioning/supporting formal company investigations'.

- 'Prosecuting detected breaches of the Companies Acts' involves:

  (i)   'developing a balanced enforcement policy';

  (ii)   'upholding the disclosure requirements of the Companies Acts';

  (iii)   'sanctioning parties disregarding company or other interests'; and

  (iv)   'acting against parties denying accountability under the law'.

- 'Sanctioning improper conduct relating to insolvent companies' involves:

  (i)   'supervising liquidators in the discharge of their functions';

---

[36] 'Corporate Compliance Matters'. See www.cro.ie.

[37] According to the ODCE, *Annual Report 2004*, p 7, the ODCE issued 11 press releases in 2004, for example.

[38] ODCE, *Annual Report 2006* at p 5. See www.odce.ie.

> (ii) 'assessing directors' conduct in insolvent liquidation situations'; and
>
> (iii) 'sanctioning fraudulent or abusive behaviour'[39]

There are certain other functions listed in CLEA 2001, s 12(1), which will also be included in this analysis of the ODCE's enforcement role. The following specific functions of the ODCE will be considered:

- detection of breaches of company law;

- investigation of breaches of company law;

- prosecution of breaches of company law;

- imposition of civil sanctions;

- supervision of liquidators and receivers; [40] and

- referral of suspected breaches to other agencies.

(i) Detection

[11.021] There are a number of means by which the commission of suspected offences under the Companies Acts may come to the attention of the DCE. There are several provisions of CA 1963–2006, which require certain agencies and bodies to report specific matters to the ODCE. In addition, there are provisions of the Companies Acts which encourage the supply of information to the ODCE regarding suspected violations of those Acts. The ODCE also receives complaints from members of the public which may lead to the detection of infringements of company law. The ODCE may instigate investigations and inspections, with a view to detecting breaches of the Companies Acts. In this regard, it reports that it conducts 'targeted enquires' and keeps information in the public domain, such as media reports and CRO filings, under review.[41]

The ODCE reports that it is 'anxious to develop other potential sources of information for possible company law breaches in conjunction with other State and regulatory bodies and through its own investigations'.[42]

1. REPORTS BY OTHER AGENCIES

Companies Registration Office

[11.022] There is a mechanism in the Companies Acts whereby any instances of a company not keeping proper books of account should be reported by the CRO to the ODCE.[43] CA 1990, s 194 requires an auditor to notify the Registrar of Companies if he

---

[39] ODCE, *Annual Report 2006* at p 5. See www.odce.ie.

[40] This aspect of the role of the ODCE is considered in Chs **8** and **9** and is therefore not addressed here.

[41] ODCE, *Annual Report 2006* at p 13.

[42] ODCE, *Annual Report 2006* at p 13.

[43] CA 1990, s 194, as amended by CLEA 2001, s 74. See Ch **4**.

forms the view that a company has failed to keep proper books of account.[44] When this occurs, the registrar is obliged to 'forthwith send a copy of the notice to the Director.'[45]

Stock Exchange

[11.023] There are a number of provisions of the CA 1963–2006, which require the Stock Exchange to report particular suspected violations of the Acts to the ODCE.[46] Since the commencement of IFCMPA 2005, s 31, however, these provisions contained in CA 1990, Pt V, only apply to companies which are traded on an Irish stock exchange market other than the main market for listed securities (the so-called 'Official List'), in particular the Irish Enterprise Exchange ('IEX') market. Pt V also applies to trading on the Official List which took place before the commencement of the Market Abuse (Directive 2003/EC) Regulations 2005 on 6 July 2005.

[11.024] First, the Stock Exchange[47] is required by CA 1990, s 92,[48] to report violations of CA 1990, s 91, to the ODCE.[49] If it appears to the Exchange[50] that such a violation has occurred on the IEX (or occurred in respect of the Official List before 6 July 2005), this must be reported forthwith to the ODCE and the Exchange must furnish such information and access to, and facilities for inspecting and taking copies of, such documents relating to the apparent violation, as the ODCE may require.[51] If the ODCE institutes proceedings as a result of the report, or refers the matter to the DPP, the Stock

---

44   CA 1990, s 194, as amended by CLEA 2001, s 74. See Ch 7.

45   CA 1990, s 194(1)(b), as inserted by CLEA 2001, s 74(b).

46   Note that investigations may be undertaken by persons authorised under CA 1990, s 117, to detect such contraventions of Pt V. See DETE, *Companies Report 2006* at p 27. As with all provisions of Pt V, s 117 now only applies in respect of the IEX or trading on the Official List which occurred before 6 July 2005. See IFCMPA 2005, s 31. Authorised persons conducted five investigations under s 117 in 2006, with no report being made to the ODCE in four of these cases. One investigation was ongoing at the end of 2006. DETE, *Companies Report 2006* at p 28.

47   According to CA 1990, s 92(1), the reporting obligation lies on the 'relevant authority', which is defined in CA 1990, s 90 as the committee of management of the Stock Exchange and the manager of the Stock Exchange.

48   CA 1990, s 92, as amended by CLEA 2001, s 36.

49   CA 1990, s 91 requires a shareholder of a public company listed on the Irish Stock Exchange to notify the Stock Exchange if his shareholding exceeds or falls below any of the following percentages of the company's shares: 10%, 25%, 50%, 75%. An investigation may be undertaken under s 92, with the same powers as an authorised person may exercise pursuant to s 117, for the purpose of determining whether a report should be made under s 92. No such investigations were undertaken in 2006. See *Companies Report 2006* at p 30.

50   According to CA 1990, s 92(2), 'where it appears to a member of the Exchange that any person has contravened section 91, he shall report the matter forthwith to a relevant authority of the Exchange, which shall thereupon come under the duty referred to in sub-s (1).' The reporting obligation therefore applies, indirectly, to every member of the Stock Exchange. One such report was made in 2006. See DETE, *Companies Report 2006* at p 30.

51   CA 1990, s 92(1), as amended by CLEA 2001, s 36.

Exchange, the officers of the company in question and every person with relevant information, must give all assistance that they are reasonably able to give.[52]

[11.025] CA 1990, s 115 requires the Irish Stock Exchange[53] to report to the ODCE any suspected incidents of insider dealing on the IEX (or in respect of the Official List before the 6 July 2005).[54] The exchange must also furnish such information and access to, and facilities for inspecting and taking copies of, such documents relating to the apparent violation, as the ODCE may require.[55] If the report leads to a prosecution, whether initiated by the ODCE or by DPP, having been referred by the ODCE, the Stock Exchange, the officers of the company in question and every person with relevant information, must give all assistance that they are reasonably able to give.[56]

[11.026] A final example of a provision which requires the stock exchange to make a report to the ODCE, is CA 1990, s 230.[57] This continues to apply in respect of all companies listed on the Irish Stock Exchange. This obligation is formulated in the same terms as ss 92 and 115, and requires the recognised stock exchange to report offences concerning the acquisition by companies of their own shares or their holding company's shares, contrary to Pt XI of CA 1990, to the ODCE.

Courts

[11.027] There are provisions of the CA 1963–2006, according to which the courts can require apparent breaches of those Acts to be referred to the ODCE. For example, CA 1963, s 299(1) provides that, if, in the course of a winding up by the court, it appears that any officer or member of the company has been guilty of an offence, 'the court may either on the application of any person interested in the winding up or of its own motion direct the liquidator to refer the matter to the DPP.'[58] If this occurs, the liquidator is also obliged to furnish such information, access to documents and facilities for copying documents, as the DCE may require.[59]

This was amended by CLEA 2001, which inserted a new s 299(1A), requiring that, where the court directs the liquidator to make a report to the DPP, the liquidator must

---

[52] CA 1990, s 92(4), as inserted by CLEA 2001, s 36(b).

[53] The reporting obligation actually lies on 'a relevant authority' of a recognised stock exchange' (CA 1990, s 115(1), as amended by CLEA 2001, s 37). This expression is defined in CA 1990, s 107, as 'its board of directors, committee of management or other management body or its manager, however described.'

[54] Similarly to CA 1990, s 92(2), CA 1990, s 115(2), provides that 'where it appears to a member of s recognised stock exchange that any person has committed an offence under this Part, he shall report the matter forthwith to a relevant authority of the recognised stock exchange concerned, who shall thereupon come under the duty referred to in sub-s (1).' The reporting obligation therefore applies, indirectly, to every member of the stock exchange.

[55] CA 1990, s 115(1), as amended by CLEA 2001, s 37.

[56] CA 1990, s 115(4), as substituted by CLEA 2001, s 37(b).

[57] CA 1990, s 230, as amended by CLEA 2001, s 39.

[58] CA 1963, s 299(1), as substituted by CA 1990, s 143. See further Ch **9**.

[59] CA 1963, s 299(1), as substituted by CA 1990, s 143.

also be directed to make the report to the ODCE and the liquidator must furnish such information, access to documents and facilities for copying documents, as the ODCE may require.[60]

The same reporting obligation can arise in a voluntary winding up, either because the liquidator has formed the view that an offence was committed, or because the court has directed the liquidator to make the report to the DPP and the ODCE.[61]

2. Reports by Auditors, Directors, Liquidators

[11.028] The duties imposed on a company's auditor, liquidator and directors to make statements and file reports with the ODCE are very significant aspects of the enforcement of company law and a crucial means of detection of breaches of company law by the ODCE. The topic of the liquidator's report is addressed in detail in Ch **9**, the reporting obligation of auditors is addressed in detail in Ch **7** and director's compliance statements are analysed in Ch **6**.

3. Reports by Professional Bodies

[11.029] CLEA 2001, s 58, requires a disciplinary committee or tribunal of a prescribed professional body,[62] to report to the ODCE a finding that a member conducting a liquidation or receivership has not maintained appropriate records or the existence of reasonable grounds for believing that a member has committed an indictable offence during a liquidation or receivership.[63]

Similarly, a disciplinary committee or tribunal of a recognised accountancy body must report to the ODCE the existence of reasonable grounds for believing that a member may have[64] committed an indictable offence under the Companies Acts while a member of the body.[65]

---

[60]   CA 1963, s 299(1A), as inserted by CLEA 2001, s 51(a).

[61]   CA 1963, s 299(2) and (3), as amended by CLEA 2001, s 51.

[62]   The bodies prescribed for the purpose of s 58 are the Institute of Chartered Accountants in Ireland, the Institute of Certified Public Accountants in Ireland, the Association of Chartered Certified Accountants, the Institute of Incorporated Public Accountants in Ireland, the Law Society of Ireland, the Institute of Taxation in Ireland, and the Chartered Institute of Management Accountants. CLEA 2001 (Section 58) Regulations 2002 (SI 544/ 2002).

[63]   CLEA 2001, s 58. See further Chs **8** and **9**.

[64]   The belief that a member 'may have' committed an offence, to trigger the reporting obligation of CA 1990, s 192(6), as inserted by CLEA 2001, s 73, can be distinguished from the obligation imposed on prescribed professional bodies by CLEA 2001, s 58, which requires the belief that the member 'has' committed an indictable offence. The latter requires a higher level of certainty.

[65]   See CA 1990, s 192(6), as inserted by CLEA 2001, s 73.

Whenever these reporting obligations arise, the committee or tribunal in question must furnish to the ODCE a report with details of the finding or the offence.[66] It is an offence to fail to comply with this reporting obligation.[67]

4. DISCLOSURE OF INFORMATION

[11.030] The CLEA 2001 encourages the disclosure of information regarding offences under the Companies Acts to the DCE. This applies even if the disclosure of the information would otherwise be prohibited. The Act accordingly contains a provision whereby information which may relate to the commission of an offence under the Companies Acts may be brought to the attention of the DCE, despite the existence of other laws which may prevent such disclosure.[68] In particular, if the Competition Authority, a member of An Garda Síochána or an officer of the Revenue Commissioners, is in possession of information which may relate to the commission of an offence under the Companies Acts, they are permitted to disclose that information to the DCE.[69]

[11.031] The ODCE reports that, in 2006, the co-operative relationship between the ODCE and the Revenue Commissioners was further developed, and that Revenue officials provided information regarding the commission of an offence to the ODCE. The ODCE also furnishes information to the Revenue, which included, in 2006, the disclosure of details of 86 large cases of excessive directors' transactions, to enable the Revenue to determine if there were tax liabilities arising from such transactions.[70]

Similarly, while it is generally prohibited for persons[71] to disclose information obtained in the course of the discharge of the functions of a recognised stock exchange,[72] information concerning suspected breaches of the Companies Acts can be disclosed to the ODCE.[73] Moreover, where information exists which concerns suspected breaches of

---

[66] The accountancy bodies are also obliged to furnish to the ODCE 'such other information in relation to the matter' as he may require (CA 1990, s 192(6), as inserted by CLEA 2001, s 73). It is curious that the same obligation was not imposed on the other professional bodies by the terms of CLEA 2001, s 58.

[67] CLEA 2001, s 58 and CA s 192(7), as inserted by CLEA 2001, s 73.

[68] CLEA 2001, s 18.

[69] CLEA 2001, s 18.

[70] ODCE, *Annual Report 2006* at p 13.

[71] The persons to whom this prohibition applies are the board of directors, committee of management, management body or manager of the stock exchange; a person nominated by such board, committee, body or manager; or any present or former employee of the stock exchange. See CA 1990, s 118(1), applying definitions contained in CA 1990, ss 117 and 107.

[72] CA 1990, s 118(1). According to CA 1990, s 118(2), the disclosure of information to the Minister pursuant to CA 1990, s 115 or otherwise, or to a similar authority in another Member State, is not prohibited.

[73] CA 1990, s 118(2A), as inserted by CLEA 2001, s 38.

company law, it is the duty of the persons to report this to the DCE.[74] Section 118(2A) provides:

> Sub-s (1) shall not prevent a member, authorised person, relevant authority or employee or former employee of a recognised stock exchange from disclosing information concerning suspected breaches of the Companies Acts to the Director and it is the duty of each such person to so report any such suspected breach to the Director.

In addition to these statutory bases for the disclosure of information to the ODCE, the ODCE has also signed memoranda of understanding with the Irish Financial Services Regulatory Authority in 2003; with the Stock Exchange and the Revenue Commissioners in 2004; and with the IAASA in 2006, regarding the sharing of confidential regulatory information.[75] These memoranda were described as formalising the 'assistance which currently exists with these authorities.' The DCE expressed the hope that 'it will also deepen mutual co-operation over time and widen the incidence of detected non-compliance in the public interest'.[76]

The ODCE reports that there was also a useful two-way flow of information in 2006 between the Garda members of the ODCE and the Garda Bureau of Fraud Investigation and other areas of the Gardaí and that the CRO provides substantial assistance in retrieving and certifying documentation for use by the ODCE.[77]

5. PUBLIC COMPLAINTS

[11.032] The ODCE encourages the public to report to it any suspected infringements of the CA 1963–2006. The ODCE reports that 284 such complaints were received in 2005 and 344 in 2006.[78] The ODCE has furnished a complaint form, in English and in Irish, for the submission of complaints by the public.[79] The ODCE reports that:

> 'many public complaints are of a general character, and it can require contact with the complainant and other investigations to clarify if a company law default ... is involved. It will often be the case as well that the complaint can best be addressed by the complainant's own legal remedies.'[80]

This fact notwithstanding, the ODCE expects the number of public complaints to continue to increase.[81]

---

[74] CA 1990, s 118(2A), as inserted by CLEA 2001, s 38.

[75] ODCE, *Annual Report 2004*, at p 10; ODCE, *Annual Report 2006* at p 10.

[76] ODCE, *The Interim Review of Activity for 2004* (January 2005). See www.odce.ie.

[77] ODCE, *Annual Report 2006* at p 13.

[78] ODCE, *Annual Report 2006*, App 2.1.1.

[79] See www.odce.ie.

[80] ODCE, *Annual Report 2006* at p 14.

[81] ODCE, *Annual Report 2006* at p 17.

(ii) Investigation

[11.033] The ODCE's powers of investigation are extensive and represent an important aspect of how company law is enforced in Ireland. These powers are complemented by the role of the ODCE in the appointment of inspectors to investigate the affairs and the ownership of companies. These powers and the mechanisms used by the ODCE are addressed in detail in Chs **12** and **13**.

The ODCE reports that 913 cases were concluded in 2006 and that it was 'a particularly successful year in completing investigative work.'[82] A total of 267 cases remained to be addressed at the end of 2006 and 130 further cases were the subject of detailed investigation at that time. Of the 913 that were concluded, most cases involved directors' transactions and were closed after the ODCE secured a remedy of the default and issued a caution in respect thereof. In 19 per cent of the cases concluded, no action was taken, as there was insufficient evidence of company law defaults. In a further 7 per cent of cases, there were private law remedies available to the complainants.[83]

It may be noted that, in response to a question in the Dáil, the Minister for Enterprise, Trade and Employment stated:

> 'The Director does not publish figures for the average time taken to conclude a case, and it is my Department's understanding that he does not regard it as a meaningful or reliable measurement of progress because of the diversity and occasional complexity of the cases under ODCE investigation.'[84]

It is not therefore possible to generalise as to how long the investigation of cases lasts.

(iii) Prosecution

[11.034] One of the specific functions of the ODCE under s 12, is the prosecution of offences by means of summary proceedings.[85] CA 1990, s 240 was amended accordingly and now provides,

> Summary proceedings in relation to an offence under the Companies Acts may be brought and prosecuted by the Director of Public Prosecutions or the Director [of Corporate Enforcement].[86]

Where the DCE has reasonable grounds to believe that an indictable offence under CA 1963–2006 has been committed, it is a function of the DCE, in the exercise of his discretion, to refer the case to the DPP.[87]

---

[82] ODCE, *Annual Report 2006* at p 14.

[83] ODCE, *Annual Report 2006* at pp 14 to 15.

[84] Written Answers, Dáil Debates, 17 May 2006, question 110.

[85] CLEA 2001, s 12(1)(a).

[86] CA 1990, s 240(4), as amended by, CLEA 2001, Sch, Pt 2. See further Ch **15**.

[87] CLEA 2001, s 12(d). Art 30.3, Constitution of Ireland ('All crimes and offences prosecuted in any court constituted under Art 34 of this Constitution other than a court of summary jurisdiction shall be prosecuted in the name of the People and at the suit of the Attorney General [now the DPP] or some other person authorised in accordance with law to act for that purpose'). See further Ch **15**.

[11.035] To date, the ODCE has taken successful proceedings in the District Court in respect of the following summary offences (among others):[88]

–   acting as director while undischarged bankrupt;[89]

–   acting as director while restricted;[90]

–   acting as auditor while disqualified;[91]

–   acting as auditor without being qualified;[92]

–   failure to keep proper books of account;[93]

–   failure to submit annual returns;[94]

–   fraudulent trading;[95]

–   furnishing false information;[96]

–   failure to comply with direction to change company name;[97]

–   failure to produce register of members;[98]

–   failure to produce the register of directors' and secretaries' interests.[99]

The procedures that apply to, and sanctions that arise from, proceedings for such offences are considered in Ch **15**.

(iv) Civil sanctions

[11.036] In addition to criminal sanctions, the ODCE has the power to impose, and apply for the imposition of, civil sanctions in respect of breaches of company law. The most important such sanctions are declarations of restriction and disqualification

---

[88]   See ODCE, *Annual Report 2002*, App 3.1.3; ODCE, *Annual Report 2003*, App 3.2; and ODCE, *Annual Report 2004*, App 3.2.

[89]   CA 1963, s 183, as substituted by CA 1990, s 169. See Ch **7**.

[90]   CA 1990, s 161. See Pts **D** and **E**.

[91]   CA 1990, s 187, as amended by CLEA 2001, s 72, C(AA)A 2003, s 35. See Ch **7**.

[92]   CA 1990, s 187.

[93]   CA 1990, s 202, as amended by EC(IFRSMA) 2005. See Ch **4**.

[94]   CA 1963, s 125, as substituted by CLEA 2001, s 59. See Ch **2**.

[95]   CA 1963, s 297, as substituted by CA 1990, s 137. See Ch **6**.

[96]   CA 1990, s 242, as amended by CLEA 2001, s 106 and IFCMPA 2005, s 71. See Ch **6**.

[97]   CA 1963, s 23, as amended by CLEA 2001, s 87. See Ch **2**.

[98]   CA 1963, s 119. See Ch **3**.

[99]   CA 1990, s 60, as amended by IFCMPA 2005, s 73(2)(a). See Ch **3**.

orders.[100] These sanctions and the role of the ODCE in relation to them, are addressed in detail in Pts **D** and **E**.

[11.037] Another means, short of criminal prosecution, of addressing breaches of the Companies Acts, which is at the disposal of the ODCE, is the injunction procedure contained in CA 1963, s 371, as amended by CLEA 2001, s 96.

Section 371(1) provides:

> If a company or any officer of a company having made default in complying with any provision of this Act fails to make good the default within 14 days after the service of a notice on the company or officer requiring it or him to do so, or such greater period as may be specified in the notice, the court may, on an application made to the court by any member or creditor of the company, by the Director or by the registrar of companies, make an order directing the company and any officer thereof to make good the default within such time as may be specified in the order.[101]

If the DCE wishes to avail of this procedure, the first step is that he must confirm that there is a default in complying with the requirements of the CA 1963–2006. Secondly, the DCE must serve a notice on the company or officer[102] responsible for the default, requiring that the default be made good within 14 days after the service of that notice, or such longer period as the notice may specify. The third step is that the DCE may apply to court for an order directing the officer or company to make good the default within such time as the court may direct. The order of the court may provide that 'all costs of and incidental to' the application must be borne by the company and the officers responsible for the default.[103]

This procedure can also be adopted by a member or creditor of the company, or the Registrar of Companies and it is without prejudice to the operation of any provisions imposing penalties, such as declarations of restriction or disqualification orders, on a company or its officers for the defaults in question.[104] It should be noted that one of the consequences of a default order may be an order of disqualification under s 160.[105]

---

[100] There has been some debate regarding the character of declarations of restriction and disqualification orders, and specifically, regarding whether they are penal sanctions and whether they are designed to punish the individual to whom they apply. This debate is addressed in Pts **D** and **E**. For the purposes of this chapter, they are addressed under the heading of 'civil sanctions', and distinguished from the prosecution of criminal offences.

[101] CA 1963, s 371(1), as amended by CLEA 2001, s 96 and IFCMPA 2005, s 74.

[102] In this context, 'officer' includes 'a director, a shadow director, an officer, a promoter, a receiver, a liquidator or an auditor of the company.' See CA 1963, s 371(4), as inserted by CLEA 2001, s 96.

[103] CA 1963, s 371(2).

[104] CA 1963, s 371(3), as amended by CLEA 2001, s 96.

[105] See definition of 'default order' under CA 1990, s 159. See also *Re Wood Products (Longford) Ltd, ODCE v McGowan* [2005] IEHC 41.

[11.038] In *Brosnan v Sommerville*[106] the directors of a company sought to compel a former secretary of a company to sign certain banking documents and to deliver up certain books and records to the plaintiffs' accountant pursuant to CA 1963, s 371 and CA 1990, s 202. Although there was no reference to the directors holding shares in the company, it must be presumed that that was the case, as otherwise they would not have standing to bring an application before the court under s 371. The interesting issue of interpretation that arose in *Brosnan v Sommerville* was whether an order under s 371 could be made against a former officer of a company. It was common case that the defendant ceased to be a director or secretary of the company and was '*prima facie* not a person against whom an order under s 371 of the Act can be made.'[107] The Court stated that, 'the Plaintiffs are, on a legalistic view of the facts, not entitled to an order under s 371(1) of the Act of 1963'.

The Court considered, however, that 'the range of inquiries being made for and on behalf of the Plaintiffs was of a continuing nature over a period of time'; that the request which preceded the application to Court 'was a mere continuum of same'; and that, at the date of that request, the defendant was an officer of the company and was in breach of her statutory duty with regard to the company's books and records under s 202(10). The Court concluded that, on the particular facts of the case at hand:

> 'the inquiries were and are of a continuing nature and it behoved the Defendant in my judgment to have executed all such documents as were necessary to clearly give the information being sought by the accountant for and on behalf of the other directors which had begun as far back as 2003'.

This was subject to the qualification that, if a person resigned as officer for 'some appreciable time', they could be subject to an application under s 371 'without more'. An order under s 371 may therefore be made in respect of a person who had resigned as officer of a company, provided there are special circumstances which warrant such an order. It appears that a court will be reluctant to allow an officer to evade their duties as such, by means of tendering their resignation.

[11.039] Another mechanism the DCE can employ to address breaches of the Companies Acts, short of initiating criminal prosecutions in respect of such breaches, is contained in the CLEA 2001, s 109.[108] Section 109(1) provides:

> Where the Director has reasonable grounds for believing that a person has committed an offence under the Companies Acts which is subject to summary prosecution, the Director may deliver to the person or, where the person believed to have committed the offence is a company, to an officer of the company, a notice in the prescribed form stating—
>
> (a) that the person or company is alleged to have committed that offence,
>
> (b) that the person to whom the notice is delivered may during a period of 21 days beginning on the date of the notice—
>
>   (i) remedy as far as practicable to the satisfaction of the Director any default that constitutes the offence, and

---

[106] *Brosnan v Sommerville* [2006] IEHC 329.

[107] *Brosnan v Sommerville* [2006] IEHC 329.

[108] This is similar to the power given to the CRO by CLEA 2001, s 66. See further para 11.063.

    (ii) make to the Director a payment of a prescribed amount which shall be accompanied by the notice,

and

(c) that a prosecution of the person to whom the notice is delivered in respect of the alleged offence will not be instituted during the period specified in the notice or, if the default is remedied to the satisfaction of the Director and the payment specified in the notice is made during that period, at all.

This essentially provides for the issue of a 'compliance notice' in respect of the suspected commission of summary offences. Such a notice may only be served if the Director believes, on reasonable grounds, that the person in question has committed an offence which 'is subject to summary prosecution.'[109] A person who receives such a 'compliance notice' must remedy the default in question, to the satisfaction of the DCE, and pay the amount specified in the notice within 21 days, to avoid the possibility of prosecution.

Section 109(2) stipulates that a person who is addressed in a notice under s 109 may make the payment specified in the notice, which shall in no circumstances be recoverable by the person in question. The consequence of a 'warning notice' is that the offence referred to in the notice may not be prosecuted until the expiry of the 21 day period referred to in the notice, or, if the conditions of the notice are satisfied, at all.

The DCE may accept a payment proffered under s 109(2)(a) and, according to s 109(2)(b), 'may ... issue a receipt for it'. The apparent discretion of the DCE as to whether to issue a receipt for a payment which has been received under s 109, may operate unfairly, particularly in light of s 109(3), which provides that, 'In a prosecution for an offence to which this section applies, the onus of showing that a payment pursuant to a notice under this section has been made shall lie on the defendant.' If the DCE exercises his apparent discretion not to issue a receipt in respect of a payment received under s 109, it may be difficult for a defendant to summary proceedings to discharge the onus of proving the payment of that sum.

During the passage of the CLEA 2001 through the Dáil, the then Minister for Enterprise, Trade and Employment, described the objective of this provision as follows:

> Section 98 [enacted as s 109] provides a mechanism whereby the director of corporate enforcement may impose on-the-spot fines in lieu of the institution of proceedings in respect of offences under the Companies Acts. The director will use this power in appropriate cases to impose penalties in respect of such offences, short of criminal prosecution, thereby obviating the need to take up court time. Persons accused of offences will, of course, have the option of going to court but in so doing they will risk incurring a conviction.[110]

While the objective of avoiding the necessity of court proceedings is a laudable one, s 109 has not yet been commenced, and the Director has no power at present to serve compliance notices requiring the rectification of defaults and the payment of administrative fines. The Director does, however, already employ certain comparable

---

[109] CLEA 2001, s 109.

[110] Company Law Enforcement Bill, 2000: Second Stage (Dáil Debates, Vol 523, 5 October 2000).

tools.[111] First, the Director accepts remedial measures or voluntary rectification of minor or inadvertent defaults. Second, the Director issues 'caution warnings' informing the person in default that repeated defaults will be treated seriously. Third, the Director may send a 'warning letter' urging rectification of defaults, failing which High Court proceedings will be instituted to compel compliance with the relevant requirements. These are all measures which may be employed in respect of a company director who is in default of his obligations under the Companies Acts.

[11.040] The general approach of the ODCE in enforcing company law may be summarised as follows:

- legal action is only warranted if misconduct is deliberate, persistent, reckless and/or serious;

- the ODCE focuses on helping people to comply and discouraging non-compliance;

- remedial measures or voluntary rectification are often accepted if the default is minor or inadvertent;

- a caution may be issued that any repeat default will be treated seriously;

- a warning letter may be sent in respect of continuing defaults, failing which High Court proceedings will be initiated to compel compliance;

- disqualification or restriction proceedings may be commenced to sanction non-compliance and protect against future risks of non-compliance;

- summary criminal proceedings for offences of non-major character may be commenced; or

- indictable offences may be referred to the DPP.[112]

(d) Powers

[11.041] The DCE has very broad powers under the CLEA 2001. Section 12(2) provides that, '[t]he Director may do all such acts or things as are necessary or expedient for the purpose of the performance of his or her functions under this or any other Act.'[113] More specifically, the DCE has extensive powers of investigation. These powers are addressed in detail in Chs **12** and **13**.

(e) Duties

[11.042] The functions and objectives of the ODCE have been set out above.[114] In the discharge of these functions and realisation of these objectives, the CLEA 2001 imposes certain specific duties on the ODCE.

---

[111] See ODCE, *Annual Report 2006* at p 20.

[112] ODCE, *Annual Report 2006* at p 20.

[113] CLEA 2001, s 12(2).

[114] See above paras **[11.004]** *et seq*.

(i) Independence

[11.043] The DCE is obliged to be independent in the performance of his functions.[115] This is so, despite the fact that he is a civil servant, and may be obliged to report, furnish information and account to, the Minister for Enterprise, Trade and Employment and committees of the Houses of the Oireachtas regarding the performance of his functions.[116] The interaction between the requirement of independence and the obligation of accountability are considered in more detail below.[117]

(ii) Accountability

[11.044] There are essentially three means by which the DCE is required, and may be called upon, to explain the performance of his functions.

1. ANNUAL REPORT

[11.045] The DCE is obliged to present a report to the Minister not more than three months after the end of each year, regarding the performance of his functions and other relevant activities during the year.[118] Within two months of receiving it, the Minister then causes this report to be laid before both Houses of the Oireachtas.[119] This obligation is common to many other statutory bodies. For example, the Law Reform Commission,[120] the Human Rights Commission,[121] the Director of Consumer Affairs[122] and the DPP, are

---

[115] CLEA 2001, s 12(5): 'The Director shall be independent in the performance of his or her functions.' This is similar to the formulation of the independence of the Director of Public Prosecutions. The Prosecution of Offences Act 1974, s 2(5) provides, 'The Director shall be independent in the performance of his functions.'

[116] CLEA 2001, s 16(2)–(4). See further below paras [11.044] et seq.

[117] See further below paras [11.044] et seq.

[118] CLEA 2001, s 16(1).

[119] CLEA 2001, s 16(1).

[120] See the Law Reform Commission Act 1975, s 6: 'As soon as may be after the end of each year, the Commission shall make a report to the Attorney General of its activities during that year under s 4 of this Act, of any preliminary working papers published by it during that year, of any examination during that year of the legal system of a country other than the State and of the activities during that year of any working party or advisory committee established by it The Attorney General shall, as soon as may be, send a copy of the report to the Taoiseach, who shall submit it to the Government and copies of the report shall, as soon as may be, be laid before both Houses of the Oireachtas.'

[121] See Human Rights Commission Act 2000, s 23: 'The Commission shall not later than the 31st day of March in each year prepare and submit to the Minister a report on its activities in the immediately preceding year and the Minister shall, as soon as may be, cause copies of the report to be laid before each House of the Oireachtas.'

[122] See Consumer Credit Act 1995, s 4(3): 'The Director shall, not more than three months after the end of each year, present a report to the Minister of the Director's activities in that year in relation to the performance of the Director's functions under this Act and the Minister shall cause a copy of the report to be laid before each House of the Oireachtas within two months of receipt of it.'

all obliged to present annual reports to the relevant Government authority, to then be laid before the two Houses of the Oireachtas.

In the case of the DCE, the report shall include 'information in such form and about such matters as the Minister may direct.'[123] However, the DCE cannot be required to include in the report 'information the inclusion of which therein would, in the opinion of the Director, be likely to prejudice the performance by him or her of any of his or her functions.'[124]

The Minister has significant control over the content of the Report. However, the fact that the DCE cannot be required to include information in the Report, where its inclusion would be likely to prejudice the performance of his functions, is an important carve-out. There are a number of aspects of this provision which should be noted.

First, the fact that the DCE cannot be required to disclose information which would be likely to prejudice the discharge of his functions, ensures his independence in relation to his functions and information concerning his functions. It is only information which the DCE considers it safe to disclose, that must be included in the Annual Report.

[11.046] Secondly, there is no obligation on the DCE to explain or justify his opinion that the disclosure of information would be prejudicial. There is further no procedure or means of analysing or challenging the DCE's opinion in this regard. This suggests that the DCE has the a blanket power to refuse to disclose information in the Annual Report, without explanation, and without facing the risk of having his opinion challenged. The same situation pertains in relation to the furnishing of information to the Minister and the obligation to account to committees of the Oireachtas, as will be seen below.[125]

[11.047] Thirdly, s 17 contains a general prohibition on the disclosure of information obtained by the DCE in the performance of his functions which has not come to the notice of the public, subject to certain exceptions.[126] It may be expected that, in determining which information should be disclosed, or protected against disclosure, in an Annual Report, the DCE will bear in mind this duty imposed upon him by s 17 to protect the confidentiality of information.[127] It would appear to be consistent and logical for the ODCE to apply the terms of s 17, when determining whether the disclosure of information in the Annual Report would 'be likely to prejudice the performance by him or her of any of his or her functions.'[128] Furthermore, the disclosure of information in an Annual Report, of which disclosure is prohibited by s 17, would be an offence.[129] Requiring the DCE to commit an offence by wrongly disclosing information, would certainly prejudice him in the discharge of his functions within the meaning of s 16(2).

---

[123] CLEA 2001, s 16(2).

[124] CLEA 2001, s 16(2).

[125] See further below paras **[11.051]** to **[11.054]**. See also comparison with Human Rights Commission Act 2000, s 15, at paras **[11.053]** to **[11.054]**.

[126] CLEA 2001, s 17(1). See further below paras **[11.035]** to **[11.059]**.

[127] CLEA 2001, s 17(1). See further below paras **[11.055]** to **[11.059]**.

[128] CLEA 2001, s 16(2).

[129] CLEA 2001, s 17(4). See further below paras **[11.055]** to **[11.059]**.

[11.048] Fourthly, even if one of the exceptions to the prohibition on disclosure of information under s 17 applied, the DCE could only disclose the information to the extent necessary.[130] It is unlikely that disclosure in an Annual Report, which is submitted to the Minister for Enterprise, Trade and Employment, laid before each of the Houses of the Oireachtas, and made publicly available, could be described as disclosure to the extent necessary. It therefore appears that information obtained by the DCE in the course of performing his functions, which has not otherwise come to the notice of the public, should never be included in an Annual Report prepared in accordance with s 16.

[11.049] Fifthly, one of the exceptions to s 17 is that the DCE may disclose information which is required for the performance of his functions by the Minister for Enterprise, Trade and Employment, to the extent that the DCE considers such disclosure to be necessary.[131] This may be interpreted as permitting the DCE to disclose information in his annual report to the Minister which is required for the discharge of the latter's functions, the breach of the information's confidentiality notwithstanding. However, as noted above, disclosure by means of the Annual Report, is unlikely to qualify as disclosure 'to the extent that, in the opinion of the Director, is necessary for that purpose'.[132]

[11.050] Finally, if it is accepted that the DCE can never be required to disclose in the Annual Report information the disclosure of which is prohibited by s 17, then the category of information which he can refuse to disclose under s 16 must be broader, if that provision is to have any effect. Therefore, s 16(2) must permit the DCE to refuse to disclose in an Annual Report a broader category of information than information which 'has not otherwise come to the notice of the public' within the meaning of s 17. According to this analysis, the DCE cannot be required to present information in an Annual Report, even though this information has already come to the notice of the public, if he considers that its inclusion in the Report would be likely to prejudice the performance of his functions.

To date, the Director has presented Annual Reports in each year from 2001 to 2006, as well as Interim Reviews of Activity in each year since 2003.[133]

2. INFORMATION TO MINISTER

[11.051] The DCE is also obliged to furnish to the Minister for Enterprise, Trade and Employment 'such information about the performance of the Director's functions as the Minister may from time to time require'.[134] This obligation is qualified by the proviso that the DCE is not obliged to furnish 'information the provision of which under this subsection would, in the opinion of the Director, be likely to prejudice the performance by him or her of any of his or her functions.'[135] This is the same proviso that applies in

---

[130] CLEA 2001, s 17(2). See further below paras **[11.055]** to **[11.059]**.

[131] CLEA 2001, s 17(2), applying CA 1990, s 21(3). See further below paras **[11.055]** to **[11.059]**.

[132] CLEA 2001, s 17(2). See paras **[11.055]** to **[11.059]**.

[133] All reports and reviews are available on the ODCE website (www.odce.ie).

[134] CLEA 2001, s 16(3).

[135] CLEA 2001, s 16(3).

respect of information to be included in the Annual Report and the analysis set out above, applies equally in this context.[136]

One point that may arise in connection with this obligation of the DCE to furnish such information about his functions as the Minister may require, is that it does suggest that the DCE is somehow accountable to the Minister. As noted above, the DCE is required to be independent in the discharge of his functions.[137] There may be some inconsistency between the requirement of independence and requirement to account to the Minister regarding the discharge of the DCE's functions.

There are some precedents for this reporting obligation. As seen above[138], the Director of Consumer Affairs was the body on which the Working Group on Company Law Compliance and Enforcement[139] modelled the proposed DCE. According to s 4(4) of the Consumer Credit Act 1995, the Director of Consumer Affairs is obliged to 'furnish to the Minister such information regarding the performance of the Director's functions under this Act as the Minister may from time to time require.' This is similar to the obligation of the DCE under CLEA 2001 and it should be noted that the Director of Consumer Affairs is also, like the DCE, obliged to present an annual report of his activities to the Minister for Enterprise, Trade and Employment.

3. ACCOUNTING TO OIREACHTAS COMMITTEES

[11.052] The DCE may be required to account to a committee of either House of the Oireachtas 'for the performance of his or her functions'.[140] He shall not however be required to furnish any information or answer any questions, the furnishing or answering of which would, in his opinion, be likely to prejudice him in the performance of any of his functions.[141] The wording of this carve-out is the same as that contained in s 16(1) and the analysis conducted in that context applies equally here.[142]

The DCE is required to be independent in the discharge of his functions.[143] As noted above in relation to the duty to furnish such information as the Minister may require,[144] the obligation to account to committees of the Oireachtas may indicate a level of accountability of the DCE. This would not be consistent with the independence of that office.

---

[136] See above paras **[11.045]** to **[11.050]**.

[137] See above para **[11.043]**.

[138] See above paras **[11.002]**.

[139] See *Report of the Working Group on Company Law Compliance and Enforcement* (30 November 1998).

[140] CLEA 2001, s 16(4).

[141] CLEA 2001, s 16(4).

[142] See above paras **[11.045]** to **[11.050]**.

[143] CLEA 2001, s 12(5). See above para **[11.043]**.

[144] See above para **[11.051]**.

[11.053] A similar duty to report to a committee of the Oireachtas was imposed on another independent body[145] by the legislature.[146] According to s 15 of the Human Rights Commission Act 2000, the chief executive of the Human Rights Commission is required to, 'at the request in writing of a Committee, attend before it to give account for the general administration of the Commission.'[147]

This obligation is subject to the qualification that:

> 'The chief executive shall not be required to give account before a Committee for any matter which is or has been or may at a future time be the subject of proceedings before a court or tribunal in the State'.[148]

There is a procedure in the 2000 Act for situations in which the chief executive forms the opinion that this exception applies. The procedure involves the committee being informed of the chief executive's opinion and the reason for the opinion.[149] If the committee does not withdraw the request, the chief executive or the chairman of the committee may apply to the High Court for determination of the question[150] and the request will be dealt with according to that determination.[151]

---

[145] Note, however, that the independence of the Human Rights Commission is somewhat qualified by the wording of the Human Rights Commission Act 2000, s 4(2): 'The Commission shall, *subject to the provisions of this Act*, be independent in the performance of its functions' (emphasis added). There is no such qualification to the requirement of the DCE to be independent in the performance of his functions. It may be queried whether absolute independence is consistent with an obligation to account to committees of the Oireachtas.

[146] Human Rights Commission Act 2000, s 15(1) defines 'committee' as 'a Committee appointed by either House of the Oireachtas or jointly by both Houses of the Oireachtas (other than the Committee referred to in section 14 or the Committee on Members' Interests of Dáil Éireann or the Committee on Members' Interests of Seanad Éireann) or a subcommittee of such a Committee.' This can be contrasted with the broad reference to 'an appropriately established Committee of either House of the Oireachtas' in CLEA 2001, s 16(4).

[147] Human Rights Commission Act 2000, s 15(2).

[148] Human Rights Commission Act 2000, s 15(3).

[149] Human Rights Commission Act 2000, s 15(4).

[150] See Human Rights Commission Act 2000, s 15(5): 'Where the chief executive has informed a Committee of his or her opinion in accordance with sub-s (4) and the Committee does not withdraw the request referred to in sub-s (2) in so far as it relates to a matter the subject of that opinion- (a) the chief executive may, not later than 21 days after being informed by the Committee of its decision not to do so, apply to the High Court in a summary manner for determination of the question whether the matter is one to which sub-s (3) applies or (b) the Chairperson of the Committee may on behalf of the Committee, make such an application, and the High Court may determine the matter.'

[151] Human Rights Commission Act 2000, s 15(7): 'If the High Court determines that the matter concerned is one to which sub-s (3) applies, the Committee shall withdraw the request referred to in sub-s (2), but if the High Court determines that sub-s (3) does not apply, the chief executive shall attend before the Committee to give account for the matter.'

This procedure can be contrasted with the general proposition in CLEA 2001, s 16, that the DCE is not required to furnish information or answer any questions where it 'would, in the opinion of the Director, be likely to prejudice the performance by him or her of any of his or her functions.'[152] There is no procedure or means of analysing or challenging the DCE's opinion in this regard.

[11.054] A further point of contrast between the means by which the Human Rights Commission and the DCE may be called upon to account to committees of the Oireachtas, is that the former may only be required to account for 'the general administration of the Commission,'[153] whereas the DCE may be required to account 'for the performance of his or her functions'.[154] The latter is clearly a more broad and invasive requirement. It is interesting to note that the scope of the duty of the DPP to account to committees of the Oireachtas is similar in scope to the duty of the Human Rights Commission and is limited to 'the general administration of the Office and statistics relevant to a matter referred to in a report of and published by the Director in relation to the activities generally of the Office.'[155] The duty of the Attorney General to account to committees of the Oireachtas is similarly limited to matters concerning the administration of the office of the Attorney General.[156]

(iii) Protection of information

[11.055] Where information which has not otherwise come to the notice of the public, is obtained by virtue of the performance of his functions by the DCE, it is prohibited for any person, including the DCE, an officer or an advisor of the DCE, to disclose this

---

[152] See CLEA 2001, s 16(2)–(4). See further above paras **[11.045]** to **[11.052]**.

[153] Human Rights Commission Act 1975, s 15(2).

[154] CLEA 2001, s 16(4).

[155] DPP, *Annual Report 1999*, at p 18. The relevant statutory provision is Committees of the Houses of the Oireachtas (Compellability, Privileges and Immunities of Witnesses) Act 1997, s 3(6), which provides, 'Sub-s (1) [the power of committees to direct person to appear, produce documents and answer questions] does not apply to the Director of Public Prosecutions or an officer of the Director of Public Prosecutions except—(a) where the committee concerned is the Committee of Public Accounts, and (b) in so far as the subsection relates to evidence, or a document in his or her possession or power, concerning— (i) the general administration of the office of the Director of Public Prosecutions, or (ii) statistics relevant to a matter referred to in a report of and published by the Director of Public Prosecutions in relation to the activities generally of the office aforesaid.'

[156] See Committees of the Houses of the Oireachtas (Compellability, Privileges and Immunities of Witnesses) Act 1997, s 3(5): 'Sub-s (1) does not apply to the Attorney General or an officer of the Attorney General except— (a) where the committee concerned is the Committee of Public Accounts, and (b) in so far as that subsection relates to evidence, or a document in his or her possession or power, concerning the general administration of the office of the Attorney General.'

information.[157] If a person discloses information in breach of this prohibition, that is an offence under CLEA 2001, s 17.[158]

1. INFORMATION PROTECTED

[11.056] There are two criteria which must be fulfilled before information benefits from the protection against disclosure of s 17. First, the information which is protected is information which has not otherwise 'come to the notice of the public'.[159] This requirement is curiously formulated. If the criterion was whether the information was in the public domain, this would be an objective test which could be applied with some certainty. Information having 'come to the notice of the public' is a less objective criterion. This wording suggests that it is not sufficient for the information to be available to, or accessible by, the public. The information must actually have come to the notice of the public. It is difficult to assess how one would prove that information had come to the public's notice. It is also difficult to assess what level of dissemination of the information is required before it can be said to have to come to the notice of 'the public'. These ambiguities favour the protection of the confidentiality of a far broader category of information. Unless the DCE can demonstrate that information has 'come to the notice of the public' or that its disclosure is otherwise justified, disclosure of that information will constitute an offence under s 17(4),

[11.057] The second criterion which information must fulfil to come within the protection of s 17, is that it must have been obtained by the DCE 'by virtue of the performance by the Director of any of his or her functions'. This wording suggests that the information must have been obtained as a direct consequence of the discharge of DCE's functions, rather than having been obtained incidentally to, or 'in the course of', the discharge of the DCE's functions, which would arguably encompass a wider category of information. It may also be open to interpretation whether or not information 'obtained by virtue of the performance' of the DCE's functions, includes information which is obtained by other agencies or persons and subsequently referred to the DCE.

2. EXCEPTIONS

[11.058] There are three *caveats* to this prohibition. First, the information may be disclosed in accordance with law.[160] Secondly, where the information is required in

---

[157] CLEA 2001, s 17(1) ('Information obtained by virtue of the performance by the Director of any of his or her functions which has not otherwise come to the notice of the public, shall not be disclosed, except in accordance with law, by any person ...').

[158] CLEA 2001, s 17(4).

[159] CLEA 2001, s 17(1).

[160] CLEA 2001, s 17(1).

connection with any of the following, it may be disclosed to the extent which is in the opinion of the DCE necessary:[161]

–   for the purpose of criminal proceedings under the Companies Acts, or criminal proceedings involving misconduct in connection with the management of the company's affairs or property;[162]

–   with a view to criminal proceedings under the Exchange Control Acts 1954– 1986, the Insurance Acts 1909–1990, or insurance regulations under the European Communities Act;[163]

–   for the purpose of complying with requirements, or exercising powers, in connection with the report of an inspector appointed by the Court or DCE;[164]

–   with a view to the initiation of proceedings for compulsory liquidation by the Director;[165]

–   for the performance of their functions by the Minister for Enterprise, Trade and Employment, the Minister for Finance, persons authorised by them, an inspector, any court, a supervisory insurance authority, the Central Bank;[166]

–   for the performance of his functions by the DCE.[167]

Thirdly, if the DCE or an officer of the DCE is of the opinion that the information may relate to the commission of an offence, other than an offence under the Companies Acts, this information may be disclosed to any member of An Garda Síochána.[168]

3. Approach of ODCE

[11.059] While the disclosure of information obtained by the ODCE is permitted in the circumstances set out above, the ODCE has indicated that 'In making decisions in this area, the Director will be particularly anxious not to compromise the ODCE's ability to gather sufficient evidence to support and prosecute criminal or other Court proceedings.'[169]

The ODCE explained that the protection of the confidentiality of information is required:

'... to encourage the general public, companies, company officers, professional organisations, State agencies and other authorities to provide to the Office information suggesting corporate malpractice. It is vital that the Office receives a good flow of such information if it is to be successful in remedying such

---

[161] CLEA 2001, s 17(1).

[162] CLEA 2001, s 17(1), applying CA 1990, s 21(1)(a).

[163] CLEA 2001, s 17(1), applying CA 1990, s 21(1)(b).

[164] CLEA 2001, s 17(1), applying CA 1990, s 21(1)(c), as amended by CLEA 2001, s 31(a).

[165] CLEA 2001, s 17(1), applying CA 1990, s 21(1)(d), as amended by CLEA 2001, s 31(a).

[166] CLEA 2001, s 17(2)(b), applying CA 1990, s 212(3).

[167] CLEA 2001, s 17(2)(c).

[168] CLEA 2001, s 17(3).

[169] ODCE, *Introduction to the ODCE*. See www.odce.ie.

behaviour and in bringing before the Courts those who are suspected of breaching company law'.[170]

B. Companies Registration Office

[11.060] The Companies Registration Office ('CRO') originated as the Registrar of Joint Stock Companies.[171] It is the repository of public statutory information regarding Irish companies. Among the functions of the CRO are the registration of companies, the registration and maintenance of a range of documents which companies are statutorily obliged to file, and the enforcement of companies' filing obligations under the Companies Acts.[172] The filing obligations of companies and the role of the CRO in this regard are addressed in more details in Ch **2**.

The CRO occupies a unique role in the enforcement of company law, one which has become more pronounced in recent years. Indeed, there are a number of areas of company law enforcement which depend heavily on the activity of the CRO. There are various different means by which the CRO enforces the filing requirements of the Companies Acts.

(a) Powers of prosecution

[11.061] The CRO has the power to bring prosecutions in respect of a number of specific breaches of the Companies Acts. The CRO may only prosecute summary offences.[173] The following table sets out the offences which the CRO can prosecute.

Summary offences capable of prosecution by CRO	Statutory provision
Failure to comply with direction of CRO to change name of company within six weeks, or such longer period as may be allowed	CA 1963, s 23, as amended by CLEA 2001, s 87
Offences in connection with application for exemption from requirement of word 'limited' or 'teoranta' as part of company name: • delivery of incorrect, false, or misleading information in statutory declaration; • alteration of articles or memorandum of company with effect of ceasing to comply with criteria for exemption; • failure to comply with direction of CRO to amend name of company to include the words 'limited' or 'teoranta'	CA 1963, s 24, as substituted by CLEA 2001, s 88

---

[170] ODCE, *Introduction to the ODCE*. See www.odce.ie.

[171] Established by the Joint Stock Companies Act 1844.

[172] See Companies Registration Office, *Companies Report* (2003).

[173] See, however, ambiguities in this regard in CA 1963, s 320, and C(A)A 1990, 12(5), which both appear to confer on the CRO the power to prosecute offences which may be prosecuted on indictment, as noted below.

Summary offences capable of prosecution by CRO	Statutory provision
Failure to send to the CRO for registration, particulars of charges and debentures as required by CA 1963, s 99	CA 1963, s 100
Offences in connection with registered office: • failure to have a registered office in the State; • failure to notify CRO of situation of registered office prior to incorporation of company; • failure to notify CRO of change in registered office.	CA 1963, s 113, as substituted by C(A)1982, s 4
Failure to file annual return with CRO	CA 1963, s 125, as substituted by CLEA 2001, s 59
• Failure to file annual return within 28 days of the 'annual return date'; • Failure by company and every defaulting officer to deliver to the CRO a copy of a court order extending time for delivery of the annual return to the CRO, as soon as practicable after the making of the order	CA 1963, s 127, as substituted by CLEA 2001, s 60 and as amended by C(AA)A 2003, s 46
Failure to annex to annual report: • certified true copy of every balance sheet laid before AGM; • certified true copy of auditors' and directors' report; • translation, where necessary.	CA 1963, s 128, as amended by C(AA)A 2003, s 57 and Sch 2 and IFCMPA 2005, s 61
Failure of official liquidator to publish in the *Companies Registration Office Gazette* a notice of appointment within 21 days thereof or deliver to CRO copy of court order of appointment	CA 1963, s 227, as applied by C(A)A 1982, s 16 and as amended by IFCMPA 2005, s 72
Failure to deliver to the CRO for registration, a copy of a court order annulling a winding up order	CA 1963, s 234, as applied by C(A)A 1982, s 16
Failure of official liquidator to deliver to the CRO for registration, a copy of a court order dissolving a company	CA 1963, s 249, as applied by C(A)A 1982, s 16
Failure to advertise in the *Companies Registration Office Gazette* the passing of a resolution to wind a company up voluntarily, within 14 days of resolution	CA 1963, s 252, as amended by IFCMPA 2005, s 72 and as applied by C(A)A 1982, s 16
• Failure of liquidator in members' voluntary winding up to summon general meetings of company at end of first year from commencement of winding up and each successive year, or • Failure to lay an account of his acts and dealings and the conduct of the winding up before the meeting; or • Failure to send copy of account to CRO within seven days of meeting.	CA 1963, s 262, as applied by C(A)A 1982, s 16
• Failure of liquidator in members' voluntary winding up to call a general meeting of the company as soon as company's affairs are wound up, in the manner required by s 263;	CA 1963, s 263, as applied by C(A)A 1982, s 16

Summary offences capable of prosecution by CRO	Statutory provision
• Failure by person who obtained court order deferring the date of the company's dissolution, to deliver to the CRO a copy of the order for registration, within 14 days of the order	
• Failure of liquidator in creditors' voluntary winding up, to summon general meeting of company and creditors at end of first year since commencement of winding up and each successive year; or	CA 1963, s 272, as applied by C(A)A 1982, s 16
• Failure to lay an account of his acts and dealings and the conduct of the winding up before the meetings; or	
• Failure to send copy of account to CRO within seven days of meeting.	
• Failure of liquidator in creditors' voluntary winding up to call a general meeting of the company or a meeting of creditors as soon as company's affairs are wound up, in the manner required by s 273; • Failure by person who obtained court order deferring the date of the company's dissolution, to deliver to the CRO a copy of the order for registration, within 14 days of the order.	CA 1963, s 273, as applied by C(A)A 1982, s 16
Failure of voluntary liquidator to deliver, within 14 days, notice of appointment to CRO for registration	CA 1963, s 278, as applied by C(A)A 1982, s 16
Failure by company and every defaulting officer to deliver forthwith to CRO for registration, copy of court order annulling resolution to wind up or staying proceedings in winding up	CA 1963, s 280, as applied by C(A)A 1982, s 16
Failure by liquidator to send to CRO statement about proceedings in and position of liquidation, at prescribed intervals, if the winding up is not concluded within two years after commencement	CA 1963, s 306
• Failure by receiver to send notice of appointment to company;	CA 1963, s 319, as applied by C(A)A 1982, s 16
• Failure by receiver to send to court, company, CRO, debenture holders, copy of statement of affairs of company, and any comments thereon, within two months of receipt of statement;	
• Failure by receiver to send to the CRO every six months after appointment, and one month after ceasing to act, an account of assets of which he took possession (value, proceeds of sale, any receipts and payments during preceding six month period, aggregate amounts of all receipts and payments since appointment).	

Summary offences capable of prosecution by CRO	Statutory provision
Failure by company's directors and secretary or by its officers, promoters, employees, former officers or employees, to submit to the receiver a statement of the company's affairs, showing particulars of company's assets, debts and liabilities, names and addresses of creditors, the securities held by them, dates of creation of securities, and any prescribed further information[174]	CA 1963, s 320, as amended by CA 1990, s 173, as applied by C(A)A 1982, s 16
Failure by receiver to send to the CRO for registration, every six months after appointment, and one month after ceasing to act, an account of assets of which he took possession (value, proceeds of sale, any receipts and payments during preceding six month period, aggregate amounts of all receipts and payments since appointment)	CA 1963, s 321, as applied by C(A)A 1982, s 16
Failure by company, being an investment company, and every defaulting officer to include the expression 'investment company' on its letters and orders forms	C(A)A 1983, s 47
Failure by public limited company to publish in the *Companies Registration Office Gazette* notice of the delivery to the CRO of the required statutory documents, within six weeks of such delivery	C(A)A 1983, s 55, as amended by IFCMPA 2005, s 72
Failure by examiner, without reasonable cause, to deliver to the CRO a copy of a court order, authorising examiner to dispose of property, which is subject to security or a hire purchase agreement, as if it were not so subject, within seven days of such order	C(A)A 1990, s 11(6), and C(A)A 1990, s 36A, as inserted by CA 1990, s 181(1)(e)
• Failure by petitioner for appointment of examiner, to deliver notice of petition, within three days after presentation, to the CRO; • Failure by examiner to publish and advertise notice of his appointment and date of hearing; • Failure by examiner to deliver to CRO, within three days of appointment, copy of order appointing him; • Failure to include on every invoice, order, business letter, on which company name appears, statement 'under the protection of the court'.	C(A)A 1990, s 12, and C(A)A 1990, s 36A, as inserted by CA 1990, s 181(1)(e) and as amended by IFCMPA 2005, s 72[175]
Failure by the examiner, or such other person as the court may direct, to publish in the *Companies Registration Office Gazette* notice of the delivery to the CRO of court orders arising from hearings concerning the examiner's report, within 14 days of such delivery[176]	C(A)A 1990, s 30, and C(A)A 1990, s 36A as inserted by CA 1990, s 181(1)(e) and as amended by IFCMPA 2005, s 72
Failure by company and every defaulting officer to deliver to CRO for registration a return regarding purchase by company of own shares within 28 days of delivery to company of shares, stating number, nominal value and date of delivery of shares	CA 1990, s 226
Failure by company and every defaulting officer, to have at least one director of company who is resident in Ireland	C(A)(No 2)A 1999, s 43

Summary offences capable of prosecution by CRO	Statutory provision
Person becoming or remaining director or shadow director at any one time of more than 25 companies	C(A)(No 2)A 1999, s 45

(b) Striking company off the register

[11.062] In addition to the prosecution of offences, the CRO has the following powers to strike companies off the register of companies.

Power of CRO to strike company which is not carrying on business or which does not have at least one director who is resident in Ireland, off the register of companies	CA 1963, s 311, as amended C(A)A 1982, s 11 and C(A)(No 2)A 1999, ss 43, 49, 50 and IFCMPA 2005, s 72
Power of CRO to strike company off register of companies for failing to make an annual return for one or more years or for failing to make statements to the Revenue Commissioners	C(A)A 1982, s 12, as amended CA 1990, s 245 and as substituted by C(A)(No 2)A 1999, s 46 and IFCMPA 2005, s 72
Power of CRO to strike public limited companies off register of companies for failing to obtain, within one year of its registration, a certificate from the CRO entitling the company to do business	C(A)A 1983, s 8 and IFCMPA 2005, s 72

[11.063] The grounds and procedures for, and the consequences and effects of, striking a company off the register of companies are all addressed in detail in Ch **14**.

---

[174] It should be noted that s 320(5), as substituted by CA 1990, s 173, creates an indictable and a summary offence of failing to furnish the statement of affairs to the receiver. C(A)A 1982, s 16 does not limit the jurisdiction of the CRO to the prosecution of summary offences. It merely provides that the 'proceedings in relation to offences under [s 320 among others] … may be brought and prosecuted by the registrar of companies'. The creation of an indictable offence did post-date the C(A)A 1982. However, there is nothing which limits the scope of that provision. From a literal reading of CA 1963, s 320 (as amended by CA 1990, s 173), combined with C(A)A 1982, s 16, the CRO can prosecute the indictable offence of failing to furnish a statement of affairs to the receiver, which cannot be the intended effect of those provisions.

[175] C(A)A 1990, s 12(5) provides that offences under that section may be tried summarily or on indictment. C(A)A1990, s 36A, as inserted by CA 1990, s 181 merely provides that, 'Proceedings in relation to an offence under s 11(6), 12 or 30 may be brought and prosecuted by the registrar of companies.' This suggests that the CRO has the jurisdiction to prosecute, on indictment, offences under C(A)A 1990, s 12. The DPP has, however, exclusive jurisdiction to prosecute on indictment. See Ch **15**.

[176] It is curious to note that C(A)A 1990, s 30(3), as originally drafted, stated that, 'Proceedings in relation to an offence under this section may be brought and prosecuted by the registrar of companies.' CA 1990, s 181(2) repealed that subsection. However, CA 1990, s 181(1) inserted a new s 36A into C(A)A 1990, which provides that 'proceedings in relation to offences [under section 30] … may be brought and prosecuted by the registrar of companies'. The logic behind repealing and instantly replacing this provision is not clear.

(c) Power to seek order of disqualification

[11.064] The final power of the CRO in relation to the enforcement of company law is the power to seek an order of disqualification. Section 160(6) provides that, where there has been a persistent default in relation to the 'relevant requirements'[177] the CRO may apply for an order of disqualification. The expression 'relevant requirements' is defined in CA 1990, s 159, as follows:

> ... any provision of the Companies Acts (including a provision repealed by this Act) which requires or required any return, account or other document to be filed with, delivered or sent to, or notice of any matter to be given to, the registrar of companies.

This aspect of the enforcement powers of the CRO is addressed in detail in Pt **E**.

(d) Power to require compliance

[11.065] In addition to the sanctions set out above, the CRO may also take certain steps to require compliance with the obligations of the Companies Acts. According to CLEA 2001, s 66, if the CRO has reasonable grounds for believing that:

> a person is in default in the delivery, filing or making to the registrar of a return or similar document required under the Companies Acts, the registrar may deliver to the person or, where the person believed to be in default is a company, to an officer of the company, a notice in the prescribed form ...

This notice will specify the default and state that the person may within 21 days of the date of the notice, remedy the default and make a payment to the CRO in the prescribed amount.[178] The notice will also state that no prosecution for the default will be instituted during that 21 day period.[179]

[11.066] The Registrar may also make an application to court to compel compliance by a company and its officers, with requirements of the Companies Acts. Section 371 provides in this regard:

> If a company or any officer of a company having made default in complying with any provision of this Act fails to make good the default within 14 days after the service of a notice on the company or officer requiring it or him to do so, or such greater period as may be specified in the notice, the court may, on an application made to the court by any member or creditor of the company, by the Director or by the registrar of companies, make an order directing the company and any officer thereof to make good the default within such time as may be specified in the order.[180]

The CRO took its first action under s 371 in 2006, requiring a set of companies which were clients of a particular presenter, who had the highest proportion of out-of-date filings of any presenter. The CRO sought an order compelling four companies to bring

---

[177] See CA 1990, s 160(2)(f). See further Ch **22**.

[178] CLEA 2001, s 66(1).

[179] CLEA 2001, s 66(1).

[180] CA 1963, s 371(1), as amended by CLEA 2001, s 96 and IFCMPA 2005, s 74. See further above paras **[11.036]** to **[11.037]**.

their filings up to date and to meet the costs of the action and orders were made against three of the companies and their directors.[181] There have been indications that these procedures will be deployed more extensively in 2007.[182]

[11.067] A further example of the power of the CRO to take steps to require compliance with the Companies Acts is CA 1963, s 381[183]. This provides that, if a person uses the word 'limited' or 'teoranta' as the last part of the business or trading name, without being incorporated as a limited liability company, which is an offence, the CRO may apply to court for an order directing that person to cease to so trade or carry on business. Before making such an application to court, a notice must have been served requiring the person to cease trading or carrying on business and they must have failed to comply with that notice within 14 days.[184]

(e) Fines/penalties

[11.068] A company which does not submit its annual return by its annual return date is subject to late fining penalties and may also be subject to on-the-spot fines for the default.[185] CLEA 2001, s 66, as noted above[186], provides that the CRO may require the payment of a prescribed sum, where there are reasonable grounds for believing there has been a default in the filing obligations of the Companies Acts. According to the *Companies Report* for 2004, the imposition of late filing penalties yielded the sum of €12.5 million in 2002, €27.8 million in 2003 and €18.2 million in 2004.[187] The reduction in the penalties paid in 2004 was considered by the *Companies Report* to be very encouraging and to be indicative of a reduction in the number of companies in default of their filing obligations.[188] However, the Registrar of Companies has noted that, while the compliance rate for filing returns on time increased from 57 per cent in 1999 to 75 per cent in 2002 and up to 84 per cent in 2003, there was a 'troubling trend underlying these figures'.[189] In particular, the CRO noted that 'a sizeable number' of

---

[181] DETE, *Companies Report 2006* at p 15.

[182] DETE, *Companies Report 2006* at p 15.

[183] CA 1963, s 381(2), as substituted by CLEA 2001, s 98.

[184] CA 1963, s 381(2), as substituted by CLEA 2001, s 98.

[185] The late filing penalty is €100 which becomes due on the day after the expiry of the deadline for filing the annual return, and a daily penalty of €3 thereafter, up to a maximum penalty of €1,200 *per* return. This penalty is in addition to the filing fee of €30 *per* return. In addition, on-the-spot fines may be imposed and fines of €1,904.61 can be imposed on a conviction for breach of the annual return filing requirements. See www.cro.ie. With regard to the interaction between late filing penalties and prosecutions for failing to comply with filing requirements, see *Registrar of Companies v Anderson* [2004] IESC 103. See further Ch **15**.

[186] See above para [11.065].

[187] DETE, *Companies Report 2004*.

[188] DETE, *Companies Report 2004*.

[189] Companies Registration Office, 'Corporate Compliance Matters' (Information Bulletin, Summer 2004).

companies paid late filing penalties on more than one occasion.[190] The CRO therefore indicated its intention to deal with companies which repeatedly paid late filing penalties.[191]

(f) 'Integrated Enforcement Environment'

[11.069] As part of the CRO's drive towards enhancing compliance with the filing requirements of the Companies Acts, it devised the so-called 'Integrated Enforcement Environment'. This system was initiated in May 2004 and was described by the CRO as follows:

> 'The system enables the Office to accurately distinguish one company from another on the basis of its compliance history, and to initiate appropriate enforcement action on the basis of that history. The selection of companies for enforcement action and the selection of the appropriate action are thus now made on a much more rational basis than the comparatively random basis which existed heretofore. Secondly, enforcement actions (especially strike-off) are implemented now on a phased, regular, stepped basis compared to the system of very large, static lists which used to apply.'[192]

The CRO reports that this project is having a 'major impact', particularly on the strike-off process and further notes that it:

> '... represents a radical revision to the way in which the CRO conducts its enforcement activities. The system enables the Office to accurately distinguish one company from another on the basis of its compliance history, and to initiate appropriate enforcement action on the basis of that history.'[193]

(g) Encouraging compliance

[11.070] The CRO has engaged in a campaign of public information to encourage compliance with the filing obligations of the Companies Acts. In 2003, the CRO noted that:

> 'With 30% of companies failing to file their annual returns on time in 2002, it was apparent there was limited awareness among some company directors and their professional advisers of their duties and responsibilities to file documents with the CRO, and a need to promote the importance of corporate compliance.
>
> During 2003 we adopted a proactive approach to communicating with company directors and their professional advisers. Our overall aim was to ensure that no one could say they were not told or could not find out.'[194]

---

[190] Companies Registration Office, 'Corporate Compliance Matters' (Information Bulletin, Summer 2004).

[191] Companies Registration Office, 'Corporate Compliance Matters' (Information Bulletin, Summer 2004).

[192] DETE, *Companies Report 2004*.

[193] CRO, *Annual Report 2005* at pp 1 and 2.

[194] DETE, *Companies Report 2003*, 'Annual Report of the Registrar of Companies'.

As part of this communication effort, the CRO discovered that 81 per cent of companies used external providers to file their annual returns, of whom 99 per cent were accountants. The CRO therefore established a forum, comprising representatives of the various accountancy bodies and the CRO, which the CRO described as 'an opportunity for accountants to represent and articulate the views of members in practice'.[195]

The CRO also conducted an advertising campaign regarding the requirement that companies file annual returns by their 'annual return date'.[196]

C. Director of Public Prosecutions

(a) Overview of role of DPP

[11.071] The office of the Director of Public Prosecutions ('DPP') was established by the Prosecution of Offences Act 1974. That Act had the effect of transferring all of the criminal functions of the Attorney General to the DPP.

The core function of the DPP is to decide whether to prosecute. If the case is being prosecuted on indictment, the decision to prosecute must be taken or confirmed by the DPP.[197] The DPP also bears responsibility for the conduct of criminal prosecutions. If the offence is being tried on indictment, only the DPP can prosecute the case. With regard to summary offences, the DPP can prosecute such cases 'except those which are prosecuted by a Minister, Department of State or other person.'[198] In practice the vast majority of criminal offences are tried summarily at District Court level without the direct involvement of the DPP.[199]

The DPP has a number of other distinct functions. For example, if an offence may be tried summarily or on indictment, the DPP's consent is generally required before the case can be dealt with summarily.[200] It should also be noted that the office of the DPP works closely with:

> 'the Garda Síochána and with other investigative agencies including Government departments, the Revenue Commissioners, Revenue Solicitor, An Post, The Competition Authority, the DCE, the Health & Safety Authority, as well as with other State agencies and local authorities'.[201]

---

[195] DETE, *Companies Report 2003*, 'Annual Report of the Registrar of Companies'.

[196] See Ch 2.

[197] See Director of Public Prosecutions, *Annual Report, 1999*, at para 2.6.

[198] See Director of Public Prosecutions, *Annual Report, 1999*, at para 2.3.

[199] See Director of Public Prosecutions, *Annual Report, 1999*, at para 2.6.

[200] See Director of Public Prosecutions, *Annual Report, 1999*, at para 2.4. The DPP also has a range of specific statutory powers and functions, such as the prosecution of offences under the Offences Against the State Act 1939, functions in relation to election and referendum petitions and in relation to extradition requests and requests for international mutual assistance in criminal matters. See Office of the Director of Public Prosecutions Annual Report 2003, at paras 1.3, 2.3, 2.4 and 2.6.

[201] See Director of Public Prosecutions, *Annual Report, 2003*, at para 2.2.

(b) Role of DPP under Companies Acts

(i) Before the CLEA 2001

[11.072] In the context of company law, the DPP has historically had a range of functions and powers. The DPP bears responsibility for the prosecution of all indictable offences under the Companies Acts and may also prosecute summary offences under the Acts. Before the enactment of the CLEA 2001, the DPP also had the power under CA 1990, s 160, to apply to the High Court for orders of disqualification.[202]

1. Criminal functions

[11.073] The DPP has the power to prosecute summary and indictable offences committed under the Companies Acts. However, as with other areas of criminal law, the DPP does not have the exclusive power to prosecute summary offences. Even before the establishment of the ODCE, the Companies Registration Office and the Minister for Enterprise, Trade and Employment also had the power to initiate summary proceedings for different categories of offences. By contrast, the DPP was the only person who could initiate and pursue prosecutions on indictment under the Companies Acts.

[11.074] The Working Group on Company Law Compliance and Enforcement ('the Working Group') considered the scope of the DPP's role under the Companies Acts, noting his role in relation to summary prosecutions and prosecutions on indictment.[203] The Working Group further observed that:

> 'the great majority of the hundreds of summary offences provided for in the Acts have never been the subject of any criminal proceedings, and there has only been a handful of occasions on which the indictable offences have been prosecuted.'[204]

[11.075] The Group considered the dearth of prosecutions of indictable offences under the Companies Acts, noting that,

> 'We have been assured that any decision of the DPP not to commence criminal proceedings for breaches of the Companies Acts is due entirely to the quality of the evidential material available at the time of the decision.'[205]

In light of this assurance, the Group recommended that, 'the Director of Corporate Enforcement should play an active role in assisting the preparation of cases for possible criminal proceedings for breaches of the Companies Acts'[206] and that, 'the Director of

---

[202] See further Pt **E** regarding disqualification orders.

[203] *Report of the Working Group on Company Law Enforcement and Compliance* (November 30, 1998) at para 2.7.

[204] *Report of the Working Group on Company Law Enforcement and Compliance* (November 30, 1998) at para 2.10.

[205] *Report of the Working Group on Company Law Enforcement and Compliance* (November 30, 1998) at para 4.28.

[206] *Report of the Working Group on Company Law Enforcement and Compliance* (November 30, 1998) at para 4.29.

Public Prosecutions' Office should prosecute indictable offences under the Companies Acts on foot of completed investigations'.[207]

2. CIVIL FUNCTIONS

[11.076] Under the Companies Acts, the DPP has the power to exercise the civil function of applying for an order of disqualification.[208] According to CA 1990, s 160,[209] as it existed before the enactment of the CLEA 2001, the DPP could apply for an order of disqualification on any of the six grounds for making such orders. In relation to most of these grounds of disqualification, the DPP was not the sole person who could seek an order of disqualification. For example, in relation to the first four grounds for disqualification orders, as listed in s 160(2)(a) to (d),[210] a 'member, contributory, officer, employee, receiver, liquidator, examiner or creditor' of a company, had the same entitlement as the DPP to apply for a disqualification order.

There was, however, one ground of disqualification on which only the DPP could make an application for an order of disqualification. Section 160(2)(e) provides that a court may make an order of disqualification if it is satisfied that, 'in consequence of a report of inspectors... the conduct of any person makes him unfit to be concerned in the management of a company.'[211] According to s 160(5), as it existed before the CLEA 2001, the DPP could make an application for an order of disqualification under s 160(2)(e). No other person or entity was empowered by the CA 1990, to invoke that provision. The DPP was therefore the only potential applicant for an order of disqualification, on the basis of disclosures of unfit conduct in an inspector's report.

[11.077] The Working Group on Company Law Enforcement and Compliance considered the DPP's role in relation to disqualification orders. In this regard, the Group noted that:

'although s 160 of the Companies Act 1990, gives the Director of Public Prosecutions power to apply to court to disqualify persons ..., the Office of the Director of Public Prosecutions is not equipped or organised to investigate and institute civil proceedings for disqualification in the manner envisaged by the Act.'[212]

In this regard, the Group concluded that:

'there was an anomaly in providing a civil role in the monitoring of company directors for the Director of Public Prosecutions in matters which may not amount to or disclose the commission of a criminal offence.'[213]

---

[207] *Report of the Working Group on Company Law Enforcement and Compliance* (November 30, 1998) at para 2.17.

[208] See further Pt **E**.

[209] See, in particular, CA 1990, s 160(4)–(6). See further Chs **21** and **22**.

[210] CA 1990, s 160(2)(a)–(d). See further Ch **22**.

[211] CA 1990, s 160(2)(e). See further Ch **22**.

[212] *Report of the Working Group on Company Law Enforcement and Compliance* (30 November 1998) at para 2.15.

[213] *Report of the Working Group on Company Law Enforcement and Compliance* (30 November 1998) at para 2.15.

The Group went on to make the following recommendation:

'... responsibility for making applications to disqualify persons was generally inconsistent with the primary functions of the Director of Public Prosecutions in prosecuting criminal offences on foot of investigations carried out by others. It would be more appropriate for these functions to be carried out by another agency.'[214]

(ii) Effect of CLEA 2001

[11.078] The extent of the DPP's functions and powers under the Companies Acts was reduced by the CLEA 2001, particularly as a result of the establishment of the ODCE.

1. CRIMINAL ROLE

[11.079] The exclusive role of the DPP in the prosecution of indictable offences under the Companies Acts has not been affected by the CLEA 2001. As noted above, this is consistent with the recommendations of the Working Group on Company Law Enforcement and Compliance.[215] While the DPP retains the sole power to initiate and pursue prosecutions on indictment, the DCE has been invested with an important and valuable role in assisting in the investigation of suspected indictable offences. In this regard, CLEA 2001, s 12, lists among the functions of the DCE, the duty 'to investigate instances of suspected offences under the Companies Acts'[216] and 'at his or her discretion, to refer cases to the Director of Public Prosecutions where the Director of Corporate Enforcement has reasonable grounds for believing that an indictable offence under the Companies Acts has been committed.'[217] The DCE has been vested with a wide range of powers and resources to assist in the discharge of these functions.[218]

Although the prosecution of indictable offences remains the domain of the DPP, the work of the DCE should enhance the scale and quality of evidence available for the prosecution of such offences. As noted above, the DPP attributed the poor rate of prosecution of offences under the Companies Acts to the quality of the available evidential material. It may therefore be hoped that the dedication of the DCE to this investigative task will improve the level of prosecution of indictable offences under the Companies Acts. The Working Group expressed the belief that the involvement of the DCE 'will assist in increasing the number of investigations leading to prosecution for indictable offences under the Companies Acts by the DPP in the future.'[219]

---

[214] *Report of the Working Group on Company Law Enforcement and Compliance* (30 November 1998) at para 2.16.

[215] *Report of the Working Group on Company Law Enforcement and Compliance* (November 30, 1998). See above para **[11.075]**.

[216] CLEA 2001, s 12(1)(c).

[217] CLEA 2001, s 12(1)(d).

[218] See further paras **[11.020]** *et seq*. See also Chs **12** and **13**.

[219] *Report of the Working Group on Company Law Enforcement and Compliance* (30 November 1998) at para 4.31.

The indictable offences under the Companies Acts are listed in an appendix to the ODCE Decision Notice on 'Revised Guidance on the Duty of Auditors to Report Suspected Indictable Offences to the Director of Corporate Enforcement'.[220]

With regard to summary offences, it is one of the functions of the DCE to prosecute offences under the Companies Acts summarily.[221] As noted above, the DPP did not have the exclusive power to prosecute summary offences under the Companies Acts before the CLEA 2001 and this remains the case. However, the fact that the DCE, with the enforcement of company law as its brief, now has the power to prosecute summary offences, may, in practice, supplant any role of the DPP in this regard.

2. Civil Functions

[11.080] CLEA 2001, s 42, amended CA 1990, s 160, quite considerably. Three new grounds of disqualification were inserted into s 160. In addition, CLEA 2001, s 42(e), inserted a new provision that the ODCE may apply for an order of disqualification on each of the grounds on which such an order may be made.[222] The effect of these amendments on the role of the DPP in relation to disqualification orders can be summarised as follows:

- the DPP retains the right to apply for an order of disqualification on the same grounds as existed before the enactment of the CLEA 2001;

- the DCE now has a concurrent power to bring applications on precisely the same grounds;

- there are no grounds of disqualification on which the DPP is the sole potential applicant;

- there are three new grounds of disqualification, on which the DPP does not have the right to apply for an order of disqualification.[223]

D. Minister for Enterprise, Trade and Employment

(a) Background

[11.081] The Department of Enterprise, Trade and Employment, Company Law Administration Section, is responsible for the enactment and administration of legislation governing companies in Ireland. That Section also prepares secondary legislation under the Companies Acts and bears responsibility for the CRO and the ODCE, among other statutory offices.

---

[220] ODCE, 'Revised Guidance on the Duty of Auditors to Report Suspected Indictable Offences to the Director of Corporate Enforcement', Decision Notice D/2006/2, List of Offences pursuant to the Companies Acts 1963 to 2005.

[221] CLEA 2001, s 12(1)(a).

[222] CA 1990, s 160(6A), as inserted by CLEA 2001, s 42(e).

[223] See Chs **21** and **22**.

The Minister for Enterprise, Trade and Employment ('the Minister') occupied a central role in the enforcement of company law under the CA 1963–1999. For example, the Minister had authority to prosecute summary offences under the Companies Acts[224] and had the jurisdiction to appoint inspectors under CA 1990, s 8.

The Working Group on Company Law Compliance and Enforcement noted in its Report that:

> 'day to day investigation and prosecution of breaches of company law (other than the Companies Registration Office offences) is close to non-existent and that within the existing resources allocated to these functions there is no realistic prospect that the Department's function of enforcement, as envisaged by the Acts, will be discharged.'[225]

The Group concluded:

> 'If the more complex provisions of the Companies Acts are to be enforced, and if serious breaches of company law are to be remedied as a matter of probability, the enforcement role envisaged by the Acts for the Minister will have to be transferred to a specialist unit with the resources and skills to enforce the law on a consistent and independent basis.'[226]

In line with the recommendations of the Working Group, responsibility for enforcement under the Companies Acts is now vested primarily in specialist agencies. As the Department of Enterprise, Trade and Employment reports, 'the work of administering and enforcing the Companies Acts is now largely carried out by specialised agencies or offices.'[227]

(b) Transferred functions

(i) Functions transferred to DCE

[11.082] The CLEA 2001 changed fundamentally the role of the Minister in the enforcement of company law. The ODCE is now the entity with primary responsibility for the enforcement of company law in Ireland and many of the functions of the Minister in this regard have been transferred to the ODCE.[228] Most significantly, the power to prosecute summary offences and to petition for the appointment of an inspector to

---

[224] See CA 1990, s 240(4), which was amended by the Schedule to CLEA 2001.

[225] *Report of the Working Group on Company Law Compliance and Enforcement* (30 November 1998) at para 2.22.

[226] *Report of the Working Group on Company Law Compliance and Enforcement* (30 November 1998) at para 2.25.

[227] DETE, *Companies Report 2006*, Foreword.

[228] While responsibility for the investigation of company law offences has been vested in the ODCE, the Minister retained responsibility for five ongoing company law investigations, which were undertaken by authorised officers of the Minister prior to the commencement of CLEA 2001. Three of these investigations remained to be concluded at the end of 2006. See DETE, *Companies Report 2006* at p 11.

investigate the affairs of a company, have been transferred to the DCE.[229] The following is an overview of those competences which have been transferred from the Minister.

Function transferred	Statutory provision	Amendment
Annual general meeting	CA 1963, s 131(3), (4), (6)	CLEA 2001, Sch
Production and inspection of books when offence suspected	CA 1963, s 384(1)	CLEA 2001, Sch
Application for appointment of inspector	CA 1990, s 8(1)	CLEA 2001, s 21
Inspectors' report	CA 1990, s 11(3)	CLEA 2001, Sch
Proceedings on inspectors' report	CA 1990, s 12(2)	CLEA 2001, Sch
Appointment and power of inspectors to investigate ownership of company	CA 1990, s 14(1), (2), (5)	CLEA 2001, Sch
Power to require information as to persons interested in shares and debentures	CA 1990, s 15(1)	CLEA 2001, Sch
Power to impose restrictions on shares and debentures	CA 1990, s 16(1), (5)– (8), (13), (16), (18)	CLEA 2001, Sch
Power to require production of books and documents	CA 1990, s 19	CLEA 2001, s 29
Power to obtain and execute warrant for entry and search of premises	CA 1990, s 20	CLEA 2001, s 30
Protection of privileged information	CA 1990, s 32	CLEA 2001, s 32
Security of information obtained under CA 1990, ss 19 and 20	CA 1990, s 21	CLEA 2001, s 31
Investigation of share dealing	CA 1990, s 66(1), (4), (5)	CLEA 2001, Sch
Penalty for failure to provide information	CA 1990, s 85(6)	CLEA 2001, Sch
Obligation of professional secrecy	CA 1990, s 94(2)	CLEA 2001, Sch
Direction to stock exchange to use its powers and report an offence under Pt V, CA 1990[230]	CA 1990, s 115(5)	CLEA 2001, s 37

---

[229] It is of interest to note that the *Report of the Working Group on Company Law Compliance and Enforcement* (30 November 1998) recommended that the Minister should not retain a prosecution role in respect of company law offences, but recommended that 'the Minister should retain the sole power under Pt II of the Companies Act 1990 to petition the Court to appoint an inspector to examine the affairs of a company' (para 14, Summary). This recommendation was not adopted by the CLEA 2001, as the power to apply for the appointment of an inspector has now been vested in the DCE. See Ch **13**.

[230] There is an anomaly in relation to this transfer of functions. The suspected offence must now be reported to the ODCE, rather than the DPP (CLEA 2001, s 37(1), amending CA 1990, s 115). Therefore, the effect of transferring the function of directing the Stock Exchange to exercise its reporting power from the Minister to the DCE, is that the DCE will essentially be directing the Exchange to make a report to himself. The same anomaly arises under s 230, as the DCE now has the power to require to stock exchange to report a suspected offence to himself.

Function transferred	Statutory provision	Amendment
Co-operation with other authorities outside the State	CA 1990, s 116(3)	CLEA 2001, Sch
Authorised persons	CA 1990, s 117(1)	CLEA 2001, Sch
Obligation of professional secrecy	CA 1990, 118(2)	CLEA 2001, Sch
Disqualification of certain persons from acting as directors, or auditors, or managing companies	CA 1990, s 160(2)	CLEA 2001, Sch
Direction to stock exchange to make a report to the DCE or use its powers of investigation regarded alleged offence	CA 1990, s 230(5)	CLEA 2001, s 39
Initiation and prosecution of summary proceedings	CA 1990, s 240(4)	CLEA 2001, Sch

(ii) Functions transferred to the CRO

[11.083] In addition to the transfer of functions to the DCE, there are some former functions of the Minister which were assigned by the CLEA 2001 to the CRO.

Function	Statutory provision	Amendment
Notification of resolution altering objects clause, if company exempt from requirement to use 'limited' or 'teoranta'	CA 1963, s 10(8)	CLEA 2001, s 85
Prohibition of registration of companies under undesirable names	CA 1963, s 21	CLEA 2001, s 86
Approval of change of company's name	CA 1963, s 23	CLEA 2001, s 87
Exemption from requirement to use 'limited' or 'teoranta' as part of company name	CA 1963, s 24	CLEA 2001, s 88
Approval of change of name of company authorised to register under CA 1963	CA 1963, s 334	CLEA 2001, s 95

(iii) Functions transferred to the IAASA

[11.084] The enactment of the Companies (Auditing and Accounting) Act 2003 has caused a further abridgement of the scope of the Minister's role in relation to company law in Ireland. The following table sets out the functions which have been transferred to the Irish Auditing and Accounting Supervisory Authority ('IAASA').

Functions transferred	Statutory provision	Amendment
Qualification for appointment as auditor – authorisation and recognition	CA 1990, s 187(1)(a)	C(A&A)A 2003, Sch 1, Pt 1
Approval of qualifications obtained outside the State	CA 1990, s 189(1), (2), (4)	C(A&A)A 2003, Sch 1, Pt 1
Consultation regarding standards and qualifications of auditors	CA 1990, s 190(1), (2)	C(A&A)A 2003, Sch 1, Pt 1
Recognition of bodies of accountants	CA 1990, s 191	C(A&A)A 2003, Sch 1, Pt 1

Functions transferred	Statutory provision	Amendment
Provisions regarding recognition and authorisation of bodies of accountants or individuals to act as auditors	CA 1990, s 192(1)–(4)	C(A&A)A 2003, Sch 1, Pt 1

(c) Retained functions

[11.085] The Minister retains overall responsibility for company legislation, primary and secondary, and for the policy and administration of the CRO and the ODCE. The Minister continues to discharge certain specific functions under the Companies Acts.

(i) Obligations to show particulars on headed paper

[11.086] CA 1963, s 196(1) requires a company to disclose the name and nationality (if not Irish) of every director of the company on all business letters on which the company's name appears. According to CA 1963, s 196(2), the Minister has the power to grant an exemption from this requirement if 'special circumstances exist which render it in the opinion of the Minister exedient that such an exemption should be granted.'[231] The number of companies which are granted such authorisations is small, with only two of the nine companies which made an application under s 196 being successful in 2006.[232]

(ii) Investigations

[11.087] As noted above, the Minister formerly bore responsibility for the appointment of inspectors to investigate the affairs of a company.[233] While this responsibility has been transferred to the ODCE, the Minister did retain responsibility for the investigations which were initiated at his instigation. The *Companies Report 2004*[234] records that examinations of three company's books and records were ongoing at the end of 2001 and that CLEA 2001, s 34, provided for the continuation of these investigations. The *Companies Report* further records that:

> '[t]he progress of these investigations is being monitored by the Department in order to bring the investigations to a timely conclusion. To this end the Tánaiste made a formal direction to the authorised officer on 29 July 2004 to cease investigative work and to commence writing up the reports with a view to facilitating appropriate follow-up action as soon as possible by relevant authorities.'[235]

This direction notwithstanding, three of the investigations remained to be concluded at the end of 2006.[236]

---

[231] CA 1963, s 196(2).

[232] See DETE, *Companies Report 2006* at p 11.

[233] See above para [11.081]. See further Ch 13.

[234] DETE, *Companies Report 2004*.

[235] DETE, *Companies Report 2004*.

[236] Companies Report 2006 at p 11.

These will be the final investigations at the instigation of the Minister. In addition, reports which are compiled by inspectors appointed on the application of the Minister, will now be delivered to the ODCE and the latter will deal with the findings and repercussions of such reports.[237]

(iii) Postponement of AGM or annual return date

[11.088] In general, a holding company is obliged to ensure that the financial year of each of the subsidiaries will coincide with that of the holding company.[238] The Minister has the power to allow the postponement of the submission of accounts to the annual general meeting or to permit the extension of the date for filing the annual return, for the purpose of ensuring that the financial year of the holding company and the subsidiary coincide.[239]

There are certain other discrete functions of the Minister for Enterprise, Trade and Employment under the Companies Acts and related legislation.[240] As these are not relevant to the enforcement of the Acts, these functions are not considered here.

E. Irish Auditing and Accounting Supervisory Authority

[11.089] The IAASA was established pursuant to C(AA)A 2003, Pt 2. Section 5 provides that the IAASA discharges its functions and exercises its powers through a company limited by guarantee; this company was incorporated on 20 December 2005. Most of its statutory functions were conferred on the IAASA by the C(AA)A 2003 (Commencement) Order 2006, with effect from 3 February 2006.

The objectives of the Authority are the following:

    (a) to supervise how the prescribed accountancy bodies regulate and monitor their members,

    (b) to promote adherence to high professional standards in the auditing and accountancy profession,

    (c) to monitor whether the accounts of certain classes of companies and other undertakings comply with the Companies Acts, and, where applicable Art 4 of the IAS Regulations; and

    (d) to act as a specialist source of advice to the Minister on auditing and accounting matters.[241]

---

[237] Eg the report of the inspector appointed to investigate National Irish Bank Ltd, was delivered to the ODCE. See DETE, *Companies Report 2004*.

[238] CA 1963, s 153(1).

[239] CA 1963, s 153(2), as substituted by CLEA 2001, s 61. See Department of Enterprise, Trade and Employment, *Companies Reports* 2002, 2003, 2004.

[240] See, eg, Designated Investment Funds Act 1985, s 5 (approval of prospectus' and publicity material for BES funds); Investment Limited Partnerships Act 1994, s 44 (annual report of Central Bank and Financial Services Authority to be delivered to the Minister); Companies Act 1990, s 236 (recognition of relevant bodies to ensure that secretaries of public limited companies have adequate knowledge and experience to discharge their functions).

[241] C(AA)A 2003, s 8(1), as amended by EC(IFRSMA)R 2005, Sch 1, Pt 5.

The powers of the IAASA include several powers regarding bodies of accountants and, in particular, the power to grant recognition to such bodies for the purposes of CA 1990, s 187; to attach terms and conditions to such recognition; to require changes to, and approval of, the regulatory plans, constitutions and bye-laws of such bodies; and the power to conduct enquiries under C(AA)A 2003, s 23 into whether a prescribed accountancy body has complied with its investigation and disciplinary procedures.[242] The IAASA also has the power to monitor the effectiveness of provisions of the Companies Acts relating to the independence of auditors, among other powers. The IAASA is more generally vested with the responsibility for doing 'all things necessary and reasonable to further its objects.'[243]

---

[242] C(AA)A 2003, s 9(2).

[243] C(AA)A 2003, s 9(1). See further Ch 7.

Chapter 12

POWERS OF INVESTIGATION OF THE DIRECTOR OF CORPORATE ENFORCEMENT

[12.001] This chapter considers the investigative powers that have been conferred on the ODCE: particular emphasis is placed on the power to require the production of a company's books and documents[1] and the power to apply to the District Court for a search warrant[2] and related powers. Part A is concerned with the parameters and implications of the power to require production of books and documents. Part B considers the issue of search warrants, including the application to court for such warrants, the grounds for such applications, and the execution of search warrants by the ODCE.[3]

A. Production of books or documents

(a) Introduction

[12.002] CA 1990, s 19[4] gives the Director of Corporate Enforcement ('DCE') the power to direct certain entities to produce such books and documents as the DCE may require. According to s 19(1) the DCE may give directions to any body to which that provision applies,[5] 'requiring the body, at such time and place as may be specified in the directions, to produce such books or documents as may be so specified'.[6] Section 19 further defines the entities to which it applies and the circumstances that must exist before this power of enquiry can be exercised. It also provides for the production of documents by third parties and stipulates the circumstances in which the power to direct such third parties to produce documents may be exercised. Section 19[7] confers additional powers on the DCE regarding the collection of documents. It is an offence to fail to comply with directions issued by the DCE under s 19.

CA 1990, s 19 serves the same purpose as (UK) Companies Act 1985, s 447, which provides in material part:[8]

> (2) The Secretary of State may at any time, if he thinks there is good reason to do so, give directions to a company requiring it, at such time and place as may be specified in the directions, to produce such documents as may be so specified.

---

[1] CA 1990, s 19, as substituted by CLEA 2001, s 29.

[2] CA 1990, s 20, as substituted by CLEA 2001, s 30 and amended by IRCMPA 2005, s 68.

[3] Sections 19 and 20 are largely replicated in the CLRG, General Scheme of the Draft Companies Consolidation and Reform Bill 2007, Pt A13, Heads 14 and 15. Available at www.clrg.org.

[4] CA 1990, s 19, as substituted by CLEA 2001, s 29 and amended by IRCMPA 2005, s 67.

[5] See below paras **[12.003]** to **[12.010]**.

[6] CA 1990, s 19(1), as substituted by CLEA 2001, s 29.

[7] CA 1990, s 19, as substituted by CLEA 2001, s 29 and amended by IRCMPA 2005, s 67.

[8] See W Green, *Palmer's Company Law* (Sweet & Maxwell), pp 10028–10042.

(3) The Secretary of State may at any time, if he thinks there is good reason to do so, authorise an officer of his or any other competent person, on producing (if so required) evidence of his authority, to require a company to produce to him (the officer or other person) forthwith any documents which he (the officer or other person) may specify.

The popularity of using the investigative powers of s 19, which facilitate access to documents without requiring a court order, rather than the appointment of an inspector, was explained in the case of *Dunnes Stores Ireland Company Limited v Ryan*.[9] In that case, the decision to require the production of documents via the appointment of an authorised officer under s 19,[10] rather than an inspector, was seen as being less susceptible to a successful judicial review application and therefore as a safer and less cumbersome option. In the United Kingdom the utility of this investigative tool has been recognised by the courts in explicit terms in the context of an investigation prior to an application for an order of disqualification:

> 'An application to the court which was not based on the books and records of the company would be based on incomplete information. It is most unlikely that the Secretary of State would contemplate making an application for a disqualification order without first obtaining information from inside the company itself, either by the use of his powers under s 447, or by requiring an office-holder to provide it.'[11]

In light of this general attitude, the provisions governing the procedures to be followed in respect of a direction to produce books or documents need to be carefully scrutinised.

---

[9]   *Dunnes Stores Ireland Co Ltd v Ryan* [2002] 2 IR 60 at 74 (the Minister 'had deliberately chosen to go down the route of an application under s 19 because, on the advice of her officers, she thought it would be more immune to a judicial review challenge', *per* Keane CJ).

[10] References to the Minister authorising an officer to fulfil the functions set out in CA 1990, s 19 were removed by its substitution by CLEA 2001, s 29, which transferred the power to require the production of documents from the Minister for Trade, Enterprise and Employment to the DCE. The DCE may, by virtue of CLEA 2001 s 13, 'in writing delegate to an officer of the Director any of the Director's powers under this or any other Act'. The interaction of these provisions was considered in *Dunnes Stores (ILAC) v Houlihan* [2003] IEHC 65, (9 May 2003, unreported), HC. At p 15 O'Neill J stated: 'Under s 13 of the Act of 2001 the [Director] can delegate his function to an officer of the [Director] who would appear to me to be then in an analogous position to an 'authorised officer' appointed under the old s 19'. Upon the delegation of the DCE's powers to an officer, that officer becomes known as the 'authorised officer': see *Rogers v Maloney* [2005] IEHC 433, O'Leary J, in which it is noted that the term 'authorised officer' is 'the name by which the delegated person is known following the delegation'. In this chapter, references to an 'authorised officer' therefore include reference to officers authorised by the Minister to investigate under CA 1990, s 19 prior to its substitution by CLEA 2001, s 29; and to officers to whom the DCE has delegated his powers under s 19.

[11] *Secretary of State for Trade and Industry v Ashcroft* [1998] Ch 71, [1997] 3 WLR 319, [1997] 3 All ER 86, *per* Millett LJ.

(b) Entities affected

[12.003] CA 1990, s 19(1) lists the entities that may be directed by the DCE to produce books or documents within the meaning of that section.[12] This list replicates in all respects the list of entities that were subject to the power of the Minister for Enterprise, Trade and Employment to direct the production of documents under the now-repealed CA 1990, s 19. In the context of s 19, these entities will be referred to generically as 'companies'.

(i) Companies formed and registered under the Companies Acts[13]

[12.004] CA 1963, s 2 defines a 'company' as '… a company formed and registered under this Act'.[14] Any company that was formed after 1 April 1964, in accordance with the Companies Acts, and which is registered under those Acts, is therefore subject to the power of the DCE to direct the production of books or documents.

(ii) Companies that already exist within the meaning of the Companies Acts[15]

[12.005] CA 1963, s 2(1) includes '… an existing company' within the definition of a 'company' and defines an 'existing company' as any company that was formed and registered in accordance with the legislation in force prior to the enactment of CA 1963.[16] Companies that were formed and registered prior to 1 April 1964, in accordance with the companies legislation then in place, fall within the scope of CA 1990, s 19, as amended.

(iii) Companies that are covered by CA 1963, s 325[17]

[12.006] Whereas CA 1963, s 2(1), refers to companies that are formed and registered under the Companies Acts and existing companies, s 325 encompasses companies that are registered but not formed under legislation that preceded the enactment of CA 1963. More precisely, s 325 brings within the scope of the Companies Acts, any company that was registered under the Joint Stock Companies Acts,[18] the Companies Act 1862 or the

---

[12] Note that, for ease of reference, this chapter will use the term 'company' on the understanding that CA 1990, s 19 does encompass other bodies, as set out in CA 1990, s 19(1) and as described in this section.

[13] CA 1990, s 19(1)(a), as substituted by CLEA 2001, s 29.

[14] See Courtney, *The Law of Private Companies* (2nd edn, Tottel Publishing, 2002), paras 2.054–2.055.

[15] CA 1990, s 19(1)(b), as substituted by CLEA 2001, s 29.

[16] CA 1963, s 2(1) defines an 'existing company' as 'a company formed and registered in a register kept in the State under the Joint Stock Companies Acts, the Companies Act, 1862, or the Companies (Consolidation) Act, 1908'.

[17] CA 1990, s 19(1)(c), as substituted by CLEA 2001, s 29.

[18] 'Joint Stock Companies Acts' are defined in CA 1963, s 2 as 'the Joint Stock Companies Act, 1956, the Joint Stock Companies Acts, 1856, 1857, the Joint Stock Banking Companies Act, 1857, and the Act to enable Joint Stock Banking Companies to be formed on the principle of limited liability, or any one or more of those Acts as the case may require, but does not include the Act 7&8 Victoria, Ch 110'.

Companies (Consolidation) Act 1908. Each of these companies is within the scope of CA 1990, s 19.

(iv) Companies registered in accordance with Pt IX of CA 1963[19]

[12.007] CA 1963, Pt IX permits the registration of certain entities that existed under legislation that pre-dated the CA 1963. The entities referred to in Pt IX are:

- a company with seven or more members that existed on 2 November 1862, including a joint stock company;[20]

- a company with seven or more members formed after November 2, 1862, pursuant to any statute other than the CA 1963;[21]

- a company with seven or more members formed after 2 November 1862 by letters patent;[22]

- a company with seven or more members formed after 2 November 1862 in accordance with law.[23]

Part IX does not apply to the following entities:

- a company registered under the CA 1862;[24]

- a company registered under the Companies (Consolidation) Act 1908;[25]

- a company which does not have its registered office or principal place of business in the State;[26]

- a company, other than a joint stock company, in which the members' liability is limited by statute or letters patent.[27]

There are particular prerequisites and procedures that govern registration under CA 1963, Pt IX. These must have been validly complied with before CA 1990, s 19(1)(c) will render a company subject to the powers of enquiry contained in s 19.

---

[19]　CA 1990, s 19(1)(c), as substituted by CLEA 2001, s 29.

[20]　CA 1963, s 328(1)(a).

[21]　CA 1963, s 328(1)(b).

[22]　CA 1963, s 328(1)(b).

[23]　CA 1963, s 328(1)(b).

[24]　CA 1963, s 328(2).

[25]　CA 1963, s 328(2).

[26]　CA 1963, s 328(2).

[27]　CA 1963, s 328(3). Pursuant to CA 1963, s 328(4), such entities cannot register under Pt IX as unlimited companies or as companies limited by guarantee.

(v) Bodies corporate to which provisions of CA 1963 apply pursuant to CA 1963, s 377[28]

[12.008] CA 1963, s 377[29] brings unregistered companies within the scope of specific provisions of the Companies Acts.[30] While the list of provisions that applies to such entities is limited, this can be amended by Ministerial order. CA 1990, s 19(1) represents one such addition to the list. The entities affected are all bodies corporate incorporated in the State and having a principal place of business in the State.[31] The following bodies are not, however, covered by s 377 and, by extension, are not within the scope of CA 1990, s 19(1):

- a body corporate incorporated by or registered under any public general statute;

- a body corporate formed for an object other than the acquisition of gains for the body or its members;

- a body corporate which is prohibited, by statute or otherwise, from making a distribution of its income or property to its members;

- any body corporate that is exempted by direction of the Minister for Enterprise, Trade and Employment.

(vi) Bodies corporate incorporated outside Ireland[32]

[12.009] Before a company that is incorporated in a jurisdiction other than Ireland will be subject to the powers of the DCE to direct the production of books or documents, that company must be, or have at any time been, carrying on business in Ireland.

(vii) Insurance undertakings[33]

[12.010] The final category of undertakings that are affected by CA 1990, s 19(1), are insurance undertakings, whether incorporated or not. This encompasses any body which is, or appears to the DCE to be, an insurance undertaking within the meaning of the Insurance Acts, 1909 to 2000 or regulations made under the European Communities Act 1972.

(c) Grounds for directing production of books or documents

[12.011] The DCE must be of the opinion that certain circumstances exist in relation to a company before he can direct that company to produce such books or documents as he may specify.[34] CA 1990, s 19(2)[35] lists these circumstances, and mirrors almost exactly

---

[28] CA 1990, s 19(1)(d), as substituted by CLEA 2001, s 29.

[29] As amended by CA 1990 s 250(1)(a).

[30] The provisions that apply to the entities defined in CA 1963, s 377, are listed in CA 1963, Sch 9.

[31] CA 1963, s 377(1), as substituted by CA 1990, s 250(1)(a).

[32] CA 1990, s 19(1)(e), as substituted by CLEA 2001, s 29.

[33] CA 1990, s 19(1)(f), as substituted by CLEA 2001, s 29.

[34] CA 1990, s 19(1) and (2), as substituted by CLEA 2001, s 29.

[35] As substituted by CLEA 2001, s 29 and amended by IFCPMA 2005, s 67.

the list of grounds on which the Minister for Enterprise, Trade and Employment had power to order the production of books or documents, before the commencement of CLEA 2001, s 29.[36] The DCE must form the opinion that one of the following situations exists.

(i) The necessity of appointing an inspector needs to be investigated[37]

[12.012] If the DCE is of the opinion that a company's books and documents need to be examined in order to determine whether an investigation of the company's affairs is necessary, he can make a direction that those books and documents be produced. Section 19(2)(a) refers to circumstances suggesting that:

> it is necessary to examine the books and documents of the body with a view to determining whether an inspector should be appointed to conduct an investigation of the body under the Companies Acts.

Pursuant to CA 1990, s 14, as amended by CLEA 2001, ss 14 and 26, the DCE can appoint one or more inspectors directly if he forms the opinion that there are circumstances suggesting that such an appointment is necessary for the effective administration of company law, for the effective discharge of the DCE's functions or in the public interest.[38]

[12.013] CA 1990, s 8,[39] sets out the grounds on which the DCE can apply to court to have one or more inspectors appointed to investigate the affairs of a company. The threshold is that the court must be satisfied the circumstances of the company suggest that:

> ... its affairs are being or have been conducted with intent to defraud its creditors or the creditors of any other person or otherwise for a fraudulent or unlawful purpose or in an unlawful manner or in a manner which is unfairly prejudicial to some part of its members, or that any actual or proposed act or omission of the company (including an act or omission on its behalf) is or would be so prejudicial, or that it was formed for any fraudulent or unlawful purpose.[40]

The additional grounds on which the DCE can apply to court for the appointment of an inspector are that persons involved in the company's formation or management have been guilty of fraud, misfeasance or other misconduct[41] or that the members of the company have not received all of the information relating to the company's affairs which they could reasonably expect.[42]

---

[36]   The only ground introduced by CLEA 2001, s 29 is the new CA 1990, s 19(2)(i) and a further ground, s 19(2)(da) was introduced by IFCMPA 2005, s 67. See paras **[12.038]** and **[12.029]** to **[12.031]** below, respectively.

[37]   CA 1990, s 19(2)(a), as substituted by CLEA 2001, s 29.

[38]   CA 1990, s 14(2), as amended by CLEA 2001, ss 14 and 26. See Ch **13** below.

[39]   As amended by CLEA 2001, s 21. See Ch **13**.

[40]   CA 1990, s 8(1)(a), as amended by CLEA 2001, s 21.

[41]   CA 1990, s 8(1)(b), as amended by CLEA 2001, s 21.

[42]   CA 1990, s 8(1)(c), as amended by CLEA 2001, s 21.

As will be apparent from the ensuing description of the other grounds on which the DCE can direct the production of books or documents, there is a notable similarity between the grounds on which the DCE can apply to court for the appointment of an inspector and the grounds on which the DCE can direct the production of books or documents pursuant to CA 1990, s 19.

[12.014] This duplication suggests that, whereas the DCE must form an opinion as to the existence of one of grounds listed in CA 1990, s 19 before invoking his powers under that provision directly, if the DCE directs the production of books or documents on the basis of an opinion that it may be necessary to appoint an inspector, this lowers the threshold and the level of certainty that is required. As an illustration, the DCE may have some suspicion that a company's affairs are being conducted with a fraudulent purpose, but not a sufficiently well-founded suspicion to amount to the 'opinion that there are circumstances suggesting...' such a state of affairs, as required by CA 1990, s 19(c).[43] In such a situation, it may be open to the DCE to form an opinion that there are circumstances suggesting, not that the company's affairs are being conducted for a fraudulent purpose within the meaning of CA 1990, s 8(1)(a), but that it is necessary to examine the company's books and documents in order to determine whether a court could be satisfied that the circumstances suggest that the company's affairs are being conducted for a fraudulent purpose. The latter could satisfy the requirements of CA 1990, s 19(2)(a) and would clearly impose a lesser burden and lower evidential standard than the other grounds contained in s 19(2).

This would render the list of grounds contained in s 19(2)(b)–(i) superfluous. If s 19(2)(a) referred to the appointment of an inspector under s 14 by the DCE, this duplication would be avoided. As s 19(2)(a) is formulated, however, there is a possibility that the evidential thresholds required to invoke s 19(2)(b) to (i) could be circumvented, as the requirements of s 19(2)(a) are more easily met.

[12.015] A further issue that arises in relation to CA 1990, s 19(2)(a), is one of scope. This provision is notably more broadly formulated than the other grounds in s 19(2), a point that was considered by the Supreme Court in *Dunnes Stores Ireland Company Limited v Ryan*.[44] In that case, an authorised officer was appointed by the Minister for Enterprise, Trade and Employment to examine the books or documents of Dunnes Stores in the exercise of the powers conferred by CA 1990, s 19, as it existed before the commencement of s 29 of the CLEA 2001. This appointment was challenged in a first set of judicial review proceedings, entitled *Dunnes Stores Ireland Co Ltd v Maloney*, in which an alleged conflict of interest on the part of the authorised officer, and a failure to give reasons for the appointment under s 19, were challenged. The authorised officer resigned and by judgment dated 18 November 1998, Laffoy J determined that the Minister was obliged to give reasons for her decision.[45] Reasons were subsequently given for the decision to appoint an authorised officer. A second set of judicial review proceedings were then initiated challenging the constitutionality of s 19(5) and (6); claiming that the demand under s 19 was unreasonable in extent and time for

---

[43] See further para **[12.028]**.

[44] *Dunnes Stores Ireland Co Ltd v Ryan* [2002] 2 IR 60.

[45] Reported as *Dunnes Stores Ireland Co Ltd v Maloney* [1999] 3 IR 542.

compliance; the reasons furnished were inadequate, among other matters. Kinlen J determined that the respondent acted unreasonably in requiring the books and documents in question, and struck down the demand under s 19.[46] This decision was reversed by the Supreme Court and the matter was remitted to the High Court.[47] By judgment dated 29 July 2000, Butler J held the appointment of the authorised officer to have been irrational, unreasonable and *ultra vires* the Minister.[48] On appeal to the Supreme Court, this decision was overturned[49] and the constitutional question was remitted to the High Court.[50]

[12.016] Many aspects of s 19 were scrutinised in the second judgment delivered by the Supreme Court. One of the issues that arose was that the authorised officer invoked the necessity of examining the books or documents with a view to determining whether an inspector should be appointed, within the meaning of CA 1990, s 19(2)(a),[51] as one of the grounds for requiring the production of books and documents. Murray J noted at the outset that 'the condition identified in s 19(2)(a) differs from the conditions referred to in any other paragraphs of that subsection. Paragraph (a) does not refer to any suspected wrongdoing, whether civil or criminal, but to the necessity to examine the books and documents of the body with a view to determining whether an inspector should be appointed to conduct an investigation of the body under the Companies Acts 1963 to 1990'.[52] When compelled to give reasons for the formation of the opinion that a direction was necessary under that subsection, the officer in that case stated:

> 'The circumstances outlined under the following heading give substantial cause for concern as to the standards of corporate governance operating in Dunnes Stores Ireland Company and suggest that it is necessary to examine the books and documents of the company to determine whether an inspector should be appointed to conduct an investigation of the body under the Companies Acts.'

Dunnes Stores contended, on various grounds, that this was not a valid reason to appoint an authorised officer under CA 1990, s 19. The grounds relied upon concerned the term 'corporate governance' and the scope of the responsibilities of the Minister for Enterprise, Trade and Employment under s 19. In particular, Dunnes Stores argued that a concern about corporate governance was vague and general and was not a ground for appointing an authorised officer or an inspector; that the term 'corporate governance' embraces a broad range of aspects of the management and control of a company and extends beyond the scope of the Companies Acts; and that the responsibilities of the Minister for Enterprise, Trade and Employment under s 19 are confined to ensuring compliance with the Companies Acts and do not extend to corporate 'best practices' criteria. Dunnes Stores also submitted that the information relied on as support for the

---

[46] *Dunnes Stores Ireland Co Ltd v Ryan* [1999] IEHC 184.

[47] *Dunnes Stores Ireland Co Ltd v Ryan* [2000] IESC 46.

[48] *Dunnes Stores Ireland Co Ltd v Ryan* [2000] IEHC 141.

[49] *Dunnes Stores Ireland Co Ltd v Ryan* [2002] 2 IR 60.

[50] This High Court judgment was delivered on 5 June 2002 and is also reported at *Dunnes Stores Co Ltd v Ryan* [2002] 2 IR 60.

[51] As it existed before the enactment of the CLEA 2001.

[52] *Ibid* at 93, *per* Murray J.

opinion formed had been available to the Minister for some time and the abuses suggested by that information had since been rectified. Dunnes Stores therefore contended that it was no longer 'necessary' to appoint an inspector within the meaning of s 19(2)(a).

[12.017] In *Dunnes Stores Ireland Company Limited v Ryan*[53] Keane CJ considered the submissions of the parties regarding the adequacy of the reference to 'corporate governance' as a ground on which to invoke the powers of CA 1990, s 19, and concluded that, 'This reason, of itself, couched as it is in such general terms, could not justify the appointment of an authorised officer…'.[54]

Murray J, in a judgment with which Denham and Murphy JJ concurred,[55] reached a different conclusion on this point. His judgment analysed the concept of 'corporate governance' in some detail. He stated that the term comprises external and internal elements: the internal concerning the relationship between the members and directors, as governed by the articles and memorandum of association of the company; and the external comprising rules and standards imposed upon the company from external sources such as legislation. Murray J held that Dunnes Stores was mistaken to attribute a solely internal interpretation to the term 'corporate governance'. The following definition of that term was favoured:

> 'It seems to me that the phrase "standards of corporate governance", in its ordinary and natural meaning, refers to the standards according to which the affairs and business of the company are conducted, by reference to the obligations and standards imposed upon them by law as well as the memorandum and articles of association.'[56]

The standards referred to as 'standards of corporate governance' therefore encompass both the internal and external rules which govern the conduct and management of a company and clearly encompass compliance with legislation that governs companies in Ireland, such as the Companies Acts. Murray J moreover noted that such legislation sets the standards for corporate governance.

[12.018] Under the Companies Acts before the enactment of the CLEA 2001, the Minister for Enterprise, Trade and Employment bore responsibility for ensuring compliance with the Acts. Dunnes Stores made the submission that this responsibility did not extend to policing 'corporate governance'. Murray J considered the scope of the Minister's role under the Companies Acts, noting that the responsibilities imposed were accompanied by extensive powers to ensure that companies do not abuse the privilege of corporate status. The object of such a regulatory system is not only to avoid breaches of the Companies Acts, but also to prevent abuses that may have public interest implications. On that basis, Murray J concluded that the concerns which should guide the Minister in discharging his supervisory role under the Companies Acts were not confined to ensuring that breaches of provisions of the Acts be avoided. On the contrary, the Minister should also be concerned with the damage such breaches could do to public

---

[53] *Dunnes Stores Ireland Co Ltd v Ryan* [2002] 2 IR 60.

[54] *Dunnes Stores Ireland Co Ltd v Ryan* [2002] 2 IR 60, 78.

[55] Murphy and Denham JJ concurring.

[56] *Dunnes Stores Ireland Co Ltd v Ryan* [2002] 2 IR 60, 92.

confidence in the conduct of companies' affairs. Murray J concluded that the responsibility of the Minister under the Companies Acts is 'to be concerned with and oversee the standards of corporate governance in companies as laid down or reinforced by those Acts'.[57]

[12.019] On the basis of these conclusions, Murray J held that breaches of standards of corporate governance could be taken into account by the Minister in the exercise of the power conferred by CA 1990, s 19(2)(a). A general statement regarding such breaches would not be an adequate disclosure of the reasons for appointing an authorised officer under that subsection. However, Murray J held that in *Dunnes Stores Ireland Limited v Ryan*,[58] the reasons given were related to specific instances of alleged abuse, which rendered the reasons sufficient 'to disclose a reasonable and rational basis'[59] for the decision to appoint an authorised officer. Murray J further observed that these abuses were relevant to the grounds on which an inspector could be appointed under CA 1990, s 8(1). For these reasons, the concerns of the Minister regarding standards of corporate governance were held to come within the scope of CA 1990, s 19(2)(a) and the Minister was entitled to rely on those concerns as a ground for appointing an authorised officer under that subsection.

[12.020] A further aspect of s 19(2)(a) that needs to be considered is the extent to which an examination of a company's books or documents must be 'necessary' to determine whether an inspector should be appointed. The use of the word 'necessary' suggests that it should be considerably more difficult, if not impossible, to decide whether to appoint an inspector to investigate the affairs of a company, without first conducting an examination of that company's books or documents. The DCE does not have the power to determine whether an application to appoint an inspector will be successful. According to CA 1990, s 8,[60] that application must be made to the court and it is for the court to determine whether the requisite threshold has been met, whereas the necessity of the examination of books or documents that may be conducted under s 19(2)(a), is determined by the DCE alone, and not by a court assessing the merits of an application for the appointment of an inspector. The requirement that it be 'necessary' to examine books or documents 'with a view to determining whether an inspector should be appointed' is clearly not a requirement that relates to a court's determination. On the basis of these factors, it seems that the wording of s 19(2)(a) does not relate to the determination whether to actually appoint an inspector, as that determination is not within the control of the DCE. Rather, the power to examine books or documents under s 19(2)(a) can only relate to the information that is required for the DCE to form a view as to whether an application for an inspector itself is warranted. On the basis of this wording, the provision should only be invoked where the DCE has not reached a decision as to whether to apply for the appointment of an inspector. If the DCE has

---

[57]   *Dunnes Stores Ireland Co Ltd v Ryan* [2002] 2 IR 60, 96.

[58]   *Dunnes Stores Ireland Co Ltd v Ryan* [2002] 2 IR 60.

[59]   *Dunnes Stores Ireland Co Ltd v Ryan* [2002] 2 IR 60, 96.

[60]   As amended by CLEA 2001, s 21. Note that the DCE may, however, appoint an inspector directly, without the necessity of a court order, under CA 1990, s 14, to investigate the ownership of a company. CA 1990, s 14, as amended by CLEA 2001, ss 14 and 26.

decided that an inspector should be appointed and has accordingly decided to make the necessary application, s 19(2)(a) should not be used as a means of bolstering the evidence that the DCE can present to the court in support of that application. Conversely, if the DCE has no information or suspicion that could conceivably warrant an application under s 8, it is arguable that s 19(2)(a) should not be used as a ground on which to examine a company's books or documents.

[12.021] The use of the word 'necessary' in s 19(1)(a) was considered in *Dunnes Stores Ireland Company Limited v Ryan*.[61] Dunnes Stores contended that, in order to invoke s 19(2)(a), it must be established that an examination of the company's books or documents was necessary to determine whether to appoint an inspector and that such necessity did not arise in that case. Murray J considered this submission and arrived at the following interpretation of the term 'necessary' as used in s 19(2)(a):

> '... the word "necessary" clearly relates to the requirement that the second respondent should satisfy herself that appropriate circumstances exist in which to make such an application and that the court be provided first, with appropriate information to prove compliance with the statutory conditions and, secondly, with adequate information on which to base the exercise of the discretion conferred upon it in relation to such an appointment. The word 'necessary' could not be read as an absolute condition precedent to the making of an application to the court for the appointment of an inspector, but as the practical necessity of obtaining sufficient information to justify the decisions which would be involved in making an application to the court, which could have damaging effects for the company in respect of which the application was made.'[62]

Herbert J in a judgment with which Keane CJ agreed, in relation to the circumstances in which the Minister may give a direction in exclusive reliance on s 19(2)(a),[63] also considered the meaning of the term 'necessary'.[64] Herbert J concluded that it was not used 'in any extreme or compelling sense':

> 'In my judgment, it has the meaning of "reasonably required" in contrast to merely optional. Again, it is important to emphasise that the question of whether it is or is not reasonably required is not a matter of objective proof, or an issue to be decided by the court. The determination is that of the second respondent alone and that decision may not be usurped by the court and may only be set aside on clear proof that it flies in the face of fundamental reason and common sense.'[65]

[12.022] The finding that an examination of a company's books or documents is not a condition precedent to an application to appoint an inspector to that company is not contentious. The existence of such a pre-condition is not suggested by the terms of CA 1990, ss 7, 8 or 14, which govern the appointment of inspectors.[66] Moreover, the right to

---

[61] *Dunnes Stores Ireland Co Ltd v Ryan* [2002] 2 IR 60.

[62] *Dunnes Stores Ireland Co Ltd v Ryan* [2002] 2 IR 60 at 97.

[63] *Dunnes Stores Ireland Co Ltd v Ryan* [2002] 2 IR 60 at 82.

[64] *Dunnes Stores Ireland Co Ltd v Ryan* [2002] 2 IR 60.

[65] *Dunnes Stores Ireland Co Ltd v Ryan* [2002] 2 IR 60 at 99–100

[66] See Ch **13**.

apply to court for the appointment of an inspector[67] can be exercised by a much broader category of person than the powers conferred by s 19, the latter being exercisable only by the DCE (or an authorised officer). It would be entirely anomalous to require an examination of books or documents to have been carried out under s 19 as a pre-condition to the appointment of an inspector, in circumstances where persons having the right to apply for the appointment of an inspector have no rights or powers under s 19.

[12.023] An application for the appointment of an inspector by the DCE will only be granted if the court is satisfied that there are circumstances suggesting that specified situations exist in respect of the company.[68] The reasoning adopted by Murray J, as set out above, equates the exercise of the power under s 19(2)(a) with the threshold that must be met for the appointment of an inspector under s 8. This overlooks the fact that s 19(2)(a) addresses the view of the DCE alone as to whether an inspector should be appointed, and not the court's determination in that regard. Clearly, the DCE will not apply for an inspector to be appointed if there is no evidence that suggests the requisite circumstances exist. If that be the case, it will also not be open to the DCE to invoke the power contained in s 19(2)(a), as there will be no question of needing to form a view regarding the appointment of an inspector. If, on the other hand, the DCE is of the view that an inspector should be appointed, it appears from the wording of s 19(2)(a), that it is not open to the DCE to rely on that provision as a means of strengthening a view already formed and of bolstering the case for the appointment of an inspector.

[12.024] In the excerpt from the judgment in *Dunnes Stores Ireland Co Ltd v Ryan* quoted above,[69] Murray J states that the word 'necessary' in s 19(2)(a) should be read as 'the practical necessity of obtaining sufficient information to justify the decisions which would be involved in making an application to the court'.[70] There is a danger that this could be viewed as permitting the DCE to direct the production of books or documents in order to strengthen an application for the appointment of an inspector. Section 19(2)(a) does not, on its face, permit the examination of books or documents to justify decisions already made. However, the effect of the Murray J's judgment in this regard may be to equate the 'necessary' proviso in s 19(2)(a) with the necessity to examine books or documents to justify an application, rather than the necessity of the examination to forming a view as to whether to bring such an application. The importance of the word 'necessary' as a threshold requirement that must be satisfied before there can be a valid exercise of the powers conferred by s 19(2)(a) may therefore be diminished.

[12.025] The interpretation that has been adopted of the scope of s 19(2)(a) is a generous one. The breadth of the interpretation was acknowledged by Murray J in the following terms:

'In my view, the nature of the power conferred upon the second respondent by s 19(2)(a) is deliberately expressed in wide and general terms, relating as it does to a form of preliminary inquiry which would enable the second respondent best to

---

[67] See CA 1990, s 7(1), as amended by CLEA 2001, s 20. See further Ch **13**.

[68] See above paras **[12.012]** and **[12.013]**. See also Ch **13**.

[69] See para **[12.021]**.

[70] *Dunnes Stores Ireland Co Ltd v Ryan* [2002] 2 IR 60 at 97.

determine whether there are sufficient grounds for the appointment of an inspector to conduct an investigation of the company in question. This contrasts to the very specific occasions for such intervention by the second respondent instanced in sub-s (2)(b) to (h).'[71]

As noted above,[72] the general terms of s 19(2)(a) may present a risk that the more specific requirements that exist in relation to the other grounds in s 19 could be evaded. The fact that it has now been given a wide interpretation, permitting that provision to be invoked on the basis of concerns that are expressed in somewhat general terms, may heighten that risk. Permitting broadly formulated grounds to be invoked as a justification for directing the production of books or documents under s 19(2)(a) could encourage the use of that provision, to the exclusion of the more specific and more exacting provisions of s 19(2)(b) to (2)(i). It may be questioned whether this accords with the intention underlying s 19 and whether it affords sufficient respect and protection to the rights of a company not to have the privacy of its books or documents invaded without adequate justification.

(ii) The company's affairs are or were conducted with intent to defraud[73]

[12.026] Section 19(2)(b) provides that a company can be directed to produce books or documents where there are circumstances suggesting that:

> ... the affairs of the body are being or have been conducted with intent to defraud—
>
> (i) its creditors,
>
> (ii) the creditors of any other person, or
>
> (iii) its members.

This category addresses companies which are run in a manner which indicates an intention to defraud the company's creditors, the company's members, or the creditors of any other body or person.

[12.027] In *Dunnes Stores Ireland Company Limited v Ryan*,[74] one of the grounds on which the Minister purported to appoint an authorised officer to direct the production of the company's books or documents, was that there was an intention to defraud the Revenue Commissioners, as the company had been found to have assisted another person in the evasion of tax. Dunnes Stores contended that this was not a valid ground on which to exercise the powers conferred by s 19. Keane CJ accepted this contention, observing that the company had already been found to have made payments for the purpose of tax evasion and an examination of the company's books and records was superfluous if it was for the purpose of assessing whether payments had been made for that purpose. These payments could not therefore be used as a reason to appoint an authorised officer to examine the books or documents of the company under the powers

---

[71] *Dunnes Stores Ireland Co Ltd v Ryan* [2002] 2 IR 60 at 93–94.

[72] See above paras **[12.013]** and **[12.014]**.

[73] CA 1990, s 19(2)(b), as substituted by CLEA 2001, s 29.

[74] *Dunnes Stores Ireland Co Ltd v Ryan* [2002] 2 IR 60.

conferred by s 19(2)(b)(ii).[75] This decision confirms that s 19(2)(b) should not be invoked if it not necessary to the formation of the conclusion at issue.

(iii) The company's affairs are or were conducted with a fraudulent purpose[76]

[12.028] Section 19(2)(c) addresses circumstances in which, '… the affairs of the body are being or have been conducted for a fraudulent purpose other than described in para (b)'. This category is expressly designed to capture any fraud in the conduct of the affairs of a company that is not caught by the previous category.

(iv) The company's affairs are or were conducted in an unfairly prejudicial manner[77]

[12.029] Section 19(2)(d) addresses circumstances in which '…the affairs of the body are being or have been conducted in a manner which is unfairly prejudicial to some part of its members.' Section 19(2)(da) inserts a new ground, that 'the affairs of the body are being or have been conducted in a manner which is unfairly prejudicial to some of all of its creditors'.[78]

Where there are circumstances demonstrating that a company's affairs were conducted in a manner that was unfairly prejudicial to some or all of the members or creditors of the company, the DCE may order the production of the books or documents of that company.

[12.030] With regard to the purposes for which these sections can be invoked, Keane CJ noted in *Dunnes Stores Ireland Company Limited v Ryan*,[79] that this section is not limited to circumstances in which it is necessary to determine whether the affairs of the

---

[75] *Dunnes Stores Ireland Co Ltd v Ryan* [2002] 2 IR 60, 78. This finding was subject to the caveat that, 'it may be possible to envisage circumstances in which even the ample powers of the Revenue Commissioners are not sufficient to enable them to ascertain whether the affairs of a company are being carried out in order to evade the payment of tax, and the examination by the second respondent [the Minister] of the books and documents of the company may in the result be justified under s 19(2)(b)(ii).' (*per* Keane CJ at p 78). However, Keane CJ noted further that, 'this was certainly not such a case.' Note that, in relation to s 19(2)(b), (d) and (f), Denham, Murphy and Murray JJ agreed with the judgment of Keane CJ. See *Dunnes Stores Ireland Co Ltd v Ryan* [2002] 2 IR 60, 97 *per* Murray J.

[76] CA 1990, s 19(2)(c), as substituted by CLEA 2001, s 29.

[77] CA 1990, s 19(2)(d), as substituted by CLEA 2001, s 29.

[78] CA 1990, s 19(2)(da), as inserted by IFCMPA 2005, s 67(a).

[79] *Dunnes Stores Ireland Co Ltd v Ryan* [2002] 2 IR 60 (Denham, Murphy, Murray, Herbert JJ concurring with the judgment of Keane CJ in this regard). While Keane CJ was addressing s 19(2)(d) relating to members rather than s 19(2)(da), inserted by IFCMPA 2005, s 67 which relates to creditors, the subsections are in near identical terms and these comments may therefore, by analogy, be read to apply equally to s 19(2)(da).

company are being conducted in a manner that is or would be unfairly prejudicial to some part of its members. Keane CJ held that:

> 'The power may arise in a case where ... it is beyond argument that they had been so conducted in the past. It may be invoked in such circumstances because the second respondent, in the exercise of her supervisory jurisdiction over companies, may be concerned to establish how such a misuse of the privilege of incorporation took place with a view to ensuring, so far as possible, that similar abuses do not take place in this, or indeed any other companies regulated by the Acts, in the future.'[80]

Keane CJ rejected the submission that, because the conduct detrimental to the shareholders' interests had ceased, the Minister's interest in that aspect of the company's affairs had also ceased. He noted that the Minister:

> '... remains under a statutory duty to take whatever steps are open to her to satisfy herself as to the reasons which led to the use by the person then in control of those assets for purposes which, in terms of the relevant Acts and the constitutions of the companies concerned, were clearly unlawful.'[81]

The conclusion reached in that regard was that, while the investigation may not be relevant to other lines of inquiry regarding the company, it may indicate any frailties or inadequacies in the protection that the Companies Acts provide against abuse. The fact that the prejudicial conduct in a particular company had ceased was not therefore necessarily relevant to a decision by the Minister to undertake an inquiry. On the authority of this decision, s 19(2)(d) and (da) may be invoked in a precautionary manner, to avoid the recurrence of prior misconduct.

[12.031] The scope of CA 1990, s 19(2)(d) and (da) is therefore quite broad, as, on the authority of *Dunnes Stores Ireland Limited v Ryan*,[82] these sections may be invoked where the prejudice that was caused to members or creditors of a company was in the past and has ceased. In those circumstances, while the prejudicial conduct has been terminated, it may nonetheless be considered necessary to examine the company's books or documents to ascertain how such a situation arose and to guard against its recurrence. This suggests that s 19(2)(d) and (da) can be employed in cases where the interests of the company or its members or creditors are no longer at stake, but a broader policy interest may be at issue.

(v) Unfairly prejudicial act or omission[83]

[12.032] Section 19(2)(e) provides for situations in which there are circumstances suggesting that 'any actual or proposed act or omission or series of acts or omissions of

---

[80] *Dunnes Stores Ireland Co Ltd v Ryan* [2002] 2 IR 60 at 80.

[81] *Dunnes Stores Ireland Co Ltd v Ryan* [2002] 2 IR 60 at 80.

[82] *Dunnes Stores Ireland Co Ltd v Ryan* [2002] 2 IR 60.

[83] CA 1990, s 19(2)(e), as substituted by CLEA 2001, s 29 and amended by IFCMPA 2005 s 67.

the body or on behalf of the body have been, are or would be unfairly prejudicial to some part of its members'.[84]

This ground relates to any actual or proposed act or omission or series of acts or omissions by the company or on its behalf that have been, are or would be unfairly prejudicial to some part of its members. This ground for invoking CA 1990, s 19 did not originally encompass past acts or omissions which caused unfair prejudice to its members, but was amended by the IFCMPA 2005 to include past acts or omissions.

It appears that the act or omission or series of acts or omissions must be committed by the company or on its behalf and that any such acts or omissions by an officer of the company or other responsible person acting without the company's authority, cannot justify a direction to produce the company's books or documents.[85]

(vi) Acts or omissions that have been, are or are likely to be unlawful[86]

[12.033] CA 1990, s 19(2)(f) addresses situations where 'any actual or proposed act or omission or series of acts or omissions of the body or on behalf of the body or by an officer of the body acting in his capacity as such officer have been, or are or are likely to be unlawful'.[87]

This provision has the effect that, where any actual or proposed act or omission or series of acts or omissions committed by the company or on its behalf are, or are likely to be, unlawful, this can give rise to a direction by the DCE to produce that company's books or records. This provision did not originally apply to acts or omissions committed in the past; the IFCMPA 2005 amended s 19(2)(f) to include such past acts or omissions.[88]

[12.034] Section 19(2)(f) was considered by the Supreme Court in *Dunnes Stores Ireland Company Limited v Ryan*.[89] In that case, the Minister for Enterprise, Trade and Employment appointed an authorised officer to examine the books and documents of Dunnes Stores. One of the grounds on which this appointment was made was that there were circumstances suggesting that there was a series of acts or omissions by the company that were likely to be unlawful within the meaning of s 19(2)(f). The acts in question were payments made to certain beneficiaries, some of which were alleged to have been in breach of exchange control legislation. There was also a claim that the company had failed to obtain auditor's certificates for a number of years. Keane CJ

---

[84] CA 1990, s 19(2)(e), as substituted by CLEA 2001, s 29 and amended by IFCMPA 2005, s 67. The latter amendment extended the scope of s 19(2)(e) to cover acts or omissions which have been prejudicial to members in the past.

[85] This should be contrasted with the ground contained in CA 1990, s 19(2)(f), discussed below.

[86] CA 1990, s 19(2)(f), as substituted by CLEA 2001, s 29 and amended by IFCMPA 2005, s 67.

[87] CA 1990, s 19(2)(f), as substituted by CLEA 2001, s 29 and amended by IFCMPA 2005 s 67. The latter amendment extended the scope of s 19(2)(f) to cover acts or omissions which have been unlawful in the past.

[88] See IFCMPA 2005, s 67.

[89] *Dunnes Stores Ireland Co Ltd v Ryan* [2002] 2 IR 60.

considered the scope of s 19(2)(f) and made a number of useful observations.[90] First, the competent prosecuting authority in respect of summary offences committed under the Companies Acts[91] is the appropriate person to issue proceedings for offences regarding proper books of account or the laying of audited accounts before the AGM of a company.[92] That person has no function in respect of such legislation as exchange control legislation. Secondly, where there appear to be breaches of legislation other than the Companies Acts, that person can furnish the information in their possession regarding those breaches to the appropriate authorities, where those authorities appear not to be aware of the breaches. Thirdly, Keane CJ held that where there is no suggestion that breaches of the Companies Acts or other legislation are being committed at the time of the appointment of the authorised officer, the fact that such breaches may have been committed in the past did not provide a valid basis for the appointment of an authorised officer under s 19(2)(f). Keane CJ interpreted the subsection as follows:

> 'The language used in s 19(2)(f), using as it does the present tense in contrast to the past tense employed in other subparagraphs, makes it clear that the examination of books or documents authorised under that subparagraph is related to continuing or future illegal acts or omissions of the company and not to acts or omissions which have occurred in the past.'[93]

Since the amendment introduced by IFCMPA 2005, past acts and omissions are now captured by s 19(2)(f).[94]

[12.035] Section 19(2)(f) includes expressly acts or omissions committed by an officer of the company, where he was acting in his capacity as such. As acts or omissions committed on behalf of the company are captured by the more general provisions of the subsection,[95] the inclusion of acts or omissions of an officer of the company must be capable of being more broadly construed, specifically to include acts of officers committed otherwise than on behalf of the company. The result is that, where an officer of a company committed an act that was, or was likely to be, unlawful, in his capacity as officer, but not on behalf of the company, that can be a circumstance that warrants a direction to the company to produce its books or documents.

The fairness of this aspect of the provision may be questioned as it appears to impose an obligation on a company, even though the ground for imposing that obligation does not relate to acts done by the company or on behalf of the company. It is worth noting that the unlawful acts of officers were not included in the equivalent provision of the CA

---

90 Note that the majority of the Supreme Court (Denham, Murphy and Murray JJ) agreed with the judgment of Keane CJ in respect of s 19(2)(b), (d) and (f). See *Dunnes Stores Co Ltd Ireland v Ryan* [2002] 2 IR 60, 97 (*per* Murray J).

91 Formerly the Minister for Enterprise, Trade and Employment; replaced by the DCE since the CLEA 2001.

92 *Dunnes Stores Ireland Co Ltd v Ryan* [2002] 2 IR 60, 79 (*per* Keane CJ).

93 *Dunnes Stores Ireland Co Ltd v Ryan* [2002] 2 IR 60, 80 (*per* Keane CJ).

94 CA 1990, s 19(2)(f), as substituted by CLEA 2001, s 29 and amended by IFCMPA 2005, s 67.

95 The language used in s 19(2)(f), as seen above, is '... act or omission or series of acts or omissions of the body *or on behalf of the body*' (emphasis added).

1990, namely s 19(2)(f). The scope of that section was limited to acts or omissions of, or on behalf of, the company. It seems peculiar that the scope of this provision was altered to include acts or omissions of the company's officers, whereas the preceding provision, CA 1990, s 19(2)(e),[96] which contained the same formula of words, was not altered by the CLEA 2001, s 29.

(vii) Fraudulent purpose[97]

[12.036] Section 19(2)(g) addresses situations in which there are circumstances suggesting that, '...the body was formed for any fraudulent purpose'. Accordingly, where there are circumstances suggesting that a company was formed for any fraudulent purpose, the DCE is justified in making a direction for the production of that company's books or documents.

(viii) Unlawful purpose[98]

[12.037] Where there are circumstances suggesting that the company was formed for any unlawful purpose, the DCE can direct that company to produce its books or documents. This is expressed succinctly in s 19(2)(h) as follows: 'the body was formed for any unlawful purpose'.

(ix) Other company[99]

[12.038] Pursuant to CA 1990, s 19(2)(i), as substituted by CLEA 2001, s 29, the DCE can direct the production of a company's books or documents where there are circumstances to suggest that: '... the body may be in possession of books or documents containing information relating to the books or documents of a body which comes within the terms of one or more of paras (a) to (h).'

This ground for directing the production of books or documents was introduced by the CLEA 2001, s 29. It confers a power on the DCE to direct any entity that may have possession of books or documents that contain information relating to a company that falls within the other grounds listed in CA 1990, s 19(2), to produce such books or documents.

It is of note that the definitions of the other grounds on which production can be ordered under CA 1990, s 19 relate to existing or impending circumstances, indicated by language such as 'are being or have been conducted...',[100] 'actual or proposed act or omission...'[101] and 'was formed...'.[102] CA 1990, s 19(2)(i), however, is based on the

---

[96]   See above, para **[12.032]**.

[97]   CA 1990, s 19(2)(g), as substituted by CLEA 2001, s 29.

[98]   CA 1990, s 19(2)(h), as substituted by CLEA 2001, s 29.

[99]   CA 1990, s 19(2)(i), as substituted by CLEA 2001, s 29.

[100] CA 1990, s 19(2)(b), (c), (d), as substituted by CLEA 2001, s 29. See above at paras **[12.026]** to **[12.031]**.

[101] CA 1990, s 19(2)(e), (f), as substituted by CLEA 2001, s 29. See above at paras **[12.032]** to **[12.035]**.

[102] CA 1990, s 19(2)(g), (h), as substituted by CLEA 2001, s 29. See above at paras **[12.036]** to **[12.037]**.

vague and uncertain circumstance that a company 'may' be in possession of books or documents that 'contain information' relating to another company's books or documents.[103]

This subsection has been described as being 'in the nature of a residual provision'.[104] It does not, according to the High Court in *Dunnes Stores v Houlihan*, 'alter the nature or extent of the functions and powers transferred from the Minister to the second named Respondent in the new s 19'.[105]

(d) Evidential requirement

[12.039] The evidential threshold for the DCE to direct a company to produce books or documents is not defined in the Companies Acts. CA 1990, s 19, merely requires the DCE to be 'of the opinion that there are circumstances suggesting' that one of a list of generally formulated situations may pertain to a particular company.[106] There is no express requirement in the legislation that reasonable grounds must exist for the formation of such an opinion.

[12.040] The inference that CA 1990, s 19(2) does not create any threshold of reasonableness or standard of evidence for the formation of an opinion by the DCE under that subsection, is strengthened by a comparison with a later subsection, namely CA 1990, s 19(4). As will be seen below, s 19(4)(a) requires the DCE to have 'reasonable grounds' for his belief that the books and documents which he may wish to require a third party to produce, are 'related to' other books or documents of the company, within the meaning of CA 1990, s 19(3)(b).[107] The fact that this requirement is imposed explicitly in relation to the production of documents in this one situation, and not in relation to others, reinforces the interpretation that s 19 gives the DCE a wide margin of discretion regarding the level of evidence and the strength of the grounds that must exist before the DCE can decide to exercise his power to direct companies and third parties to produce books or documents.

The breadth of the discretion conferred on the DCE in the formation of the requisite opinion under CA 1990, s 19(2), has been tempered by certain judicial determinations. As is discussed in more detail below,[108] Laffoy J ruled in *Dunnes Stores Ireland Company Limited v Maloney*[109] that the decision to require the production of books or documents under CA 1990, s 19 is subject to judicial review and that an opinion formed

---

[103] The topic of production of books or documents by third parties is addressed in more detail below. See below **[12.064]** to **[12.073]**.

[104] *Dunnes Stores Ireland Co Ltd v Houlihan* [2003] IEHC 689JR, *per* O'Neill J.

[105] *Dunnes Stores Ireland Co Ltd v Houlihan* [2003] IEHC 689JR, *per* O'Neill J.

[106] CA 1990, s 19(2), as substituted by CLEA 2001, s 29 and amended by IFCMPA 2005, s 67.

[107] See below paras **[12.047]** and **[12.067]**.

[108] See below paras **[12.043]** to **[12.044]**.

[109] *Dunnes Stores Ireland Co Ltd v Maloney* [1999] 3 IR 542.

for the purposes of that section must be formed in good faith and must be 'factually sustainable and not unreasonable.'[110]

[12.041] In *Dunnes Stores Ireland Company Limited v Ryan,*[111] Murray J went a step further and commented that:

> '... the requirement in s 19(2) that the second respondent be "of the opinion that there are circumstances suggesting that" one of the reasons enumerated at (a) to (h) of the subsection exists, means no more than that she must have reasonable grounds for her opinion. It is exclusively a matter for the second respondent to form the opinion. It is necessarily a subjective one.'[112]

Herbert J in the same case, considered the opinion that must be formed by the Minister and, noting that it must be the subjective opinion of the Minister alone, stated:

> 'The basis for this opinion is no more than that there are "circumstances" which act upon the mind of the second respondent. What these 'circumstances' are, is not defined in the companies legislation and, in my judgment, it is not for the court to say what they might be, but I venture to suggest that they at least should be identifiable matters of substance.'[113]

On the basis of these statement of the law, it appears that, while the opinion that must be formed for the purpose of CA 1990, s 19 is a subjective one, reasonable grounds must exist for the formation of such an opinion.

[12.042] The English Companies Acts contain a provision for the appointment of inspectors that uses similar terminology to that used in CA 1990, s 19. The Companies Act 1985, s 432(2) (UK) provides that the Secretary of State can appoint inspectors to investigate a company's affairs 'if it appears to him that there are circumstances suggesting...' that one of a number of specified situations existed in respect of such company.[114] This provision was preceded by Companies Act 1948, s 165, which used the same wording and which fell to be considered by the English Court of Appeal in *Norwest Holst Ltd v Secretary of State for Trade.*[115] The particular provision that was considered by the Court in that case was the (UK) Companies Act 1948, s 165(b)(ii), which provided in relevant part:

> '... the Board of Trade – (a) shall appoint one or more competent inspectors to investigate the affairs of a company and to report thereon ... (b) may do so if it appears to the Board that there are circumstances suggesting ... (ii) that persons concerned with its formation or the management of its affairs have in connection therewith been guilty of fraud misfeasance or other misconduct towards it or towards its members.'

---

[110] *Dunnes Stores Ireland Co Ltd v Maloney* [1999] 3 IR 542, 556 quoting *Lynch v Cooney* [1982] IR 337, 361 (*per* O'Higgins CJ).

[111] *Dunnes Stores Ireland Co Ltd v Ryan* [2002] 2 IR 60.

[112] *Dunnes Stores Ireland Co Ltd v Ryan* [2002] 2 IR 60, 88–89.

[113] *Dunnes Stores Ireland Co Ltd v Ryan* [2002] 2 IR 60, 99.

[114] This provision is considered in more detail in Ch **13**.

[115] *Norwest Holst v Secretary of State for Trade* [1978] 1 Ch 201; [1978] 3 WLR 73.

Having considered whether the rules of natural justice applied to a decision to appoint an inspector or to otherwise investigate a company,[116] Lord Denning MR observed:

> 'I see no reason why the minister should disclose the information he has before he makes the order ..., such questions do not arise at that stage. It is sufficient that there are 'circumstances suggesting ... misconduct' within s 165(b)(ii).'[117]

This expression '... if it appears to the Board that there are circumstances suggesting' was also given the following interpretation by Lane LJ in that case:

> 'It is difficult to imagine words which would give a wider discretion to the minister than those. Secondly, the burden is firmly and heavily upon the company in question to make out that the minister is not acting *bona fide* in accordance with his powers under that section ...'.[118]

In response to the argument that only admissible evidence could be relied upon for the formation of the requisite opinion, Lane LJ drew a sharp distinction between the word 'evidence' and the word 'circumstances'. He observed:

> '"Circumstances" is the word used, not "evidence", nor "admissible evidence". It seems to me that the argument founders on that very point. It is indeed the purpose of the inquiry – the investigation which the minister has ordered – to discovery whether the view of the minister about those circumstances in the upshot is an accurate one or not.'[119]

This indicates that the expression 'circumstances suggesting ...' does not necessarily carry with it the connotation that reasons must be shown to exist for the formation of an opinion regarding such circumstances. According to the interpretation of that term as it is used in the United Kingdom, there is no duty to explain the grounds for forming an opinion that such circumstances exist. In that jurisdiction, the requirement to form an opinion regarding specified circumstances, the same requirement as exists under CA 1990, s 19, confers a much wider discretion on the person forming such an opinion than the interpretation of that requirement that was contended for, and endorsed, in *Dunnes Stores Ireland Company Limited v Ryan*.[120]

(e) Review of decision

[12.043] The issue of whether and to what extent a decision to direct the production of books or documents under CA 1990, s 19, is amenable to judicial review, arose squarely for consideration in the case of *Dunnes Stores Ireland Company v Maloney*.[121] That case was decided under the CA 1990, as it existed before the introduction of the CLEA 2001, and concerned a situation in which the Minister for Enterprise, Trade and Employment

---

[116] See below para **[12.051]**.

[117] *Norwest Holst v Secretary of State for Trade* [1978] 1 Ch 201, 225; [1978] 3 WLR 73, 90.

[118] *Norwest Holst v Secretary of State for Trade* [1978] 1 Ch 201, 230 (*per* Lane LJ); [1978] 3 WLR 73, 95.

[119] *Norwest Holst v Secretary of State for Trade* [1978] 1 Ch 201, 230; [1978] 3 WLR 73 at 95 (*per* Lane LJ).

[120] *Dunnes Stores Ireland Co Ltd v Ryan* [2002] 2 IR 60.

[121] *Dunnes Stores Ireland Co Ltd v Maloney* [1999] 3 IR 542.

appointed an authorised officer to direct Dunnes Stores to produce books or documents pursuant to CA 1990, s 19. Dunnes Stores challenged this appointment and various aspects of the direction to produce books and documents that was issued by the authorised officer.

[12.044] The High Court (Laffoy J) confirmed that, '… having regard to the nature of the power conferred on the Minister by s 19, the Court is entitled to review the formation of the opinion which must precede the Minister's decision under s 19 …'.[122] Drawing an analogy between a decision taken under CA 1990, s 19 and a decision taken under the Broadcasting Authority Act 1960, s 31(1), which was considered in the *State (Lynch) v Cooney*,[123] Laffoy J quoted with approval the following dicta of O'Higgins CJ in that case:

> 'The Court is satisfied that the subsection does not exclude review by the Courts and that any opinion formed by the Minister thereunder must be one which is *bona fide* held and factually sustainable and not unreasonable.'[124]

Laffoy J also endorsed the decision of Henchy J in *Lynch v Cooney*[125] to the effect that a power, such as the power conferred by CA 1990, s 19, was intended to be exercised in conformity with the Constitution and within the limits of such a statutory power. This required that the power must be exercised in good faith. Furthermore, as stated by Henchy J:

> '… the opinion or other subjective conclusion set as a precondition for the valid exercise of the power must be reached by a route that does not make the exercise unlawful – such as by misinterpreting the law, or by misapplying it through taking into consideration irrelevant matters of fact or through ignoring relevant matters. Otherwise, the exercise of the power will be held to be invalid for being *ultra vires*.'[126]

Having determined that an opinion that is formed for the purpose of CA 1990, s 19, must be formed in good faith, on the basis of sound and relevant considerations and not on the basis of anything that could render the formation of such opinion unlawful, such as misinterpretation of the law, Laffoy J proceeded to consider other restraints on the exercise of power conferred by that section. The Court noted that, as the power conferred by CA 1990, s 19 is a discretionary one, it is subject to such constraints as were described by the Supreme Court in *East Donegal Co-Operative v Attorney General*.[127] These constraints include the obligation to exercise discretionary powers within the boundaries of the legislation conferring such power, and the duty to act fairly and judicially 'in accordance with the principles of constitutional justice'.[128] Laffoy J

---

[122] *Dunnes Stores Ireland Co Ltd v Maloney* [1999] 3 IR 542 at 555.

[123] *Lynch v Cooney* [1982] IR 337.

[124] *Dunnes Stores Ireland Co Ltd v Maloney* [1999] 3 IR 542 at 556 citing *Lynch v Cooney* [1982] IR 337 at 361.

[125] *Lynch v Cooney* [1982] IR 337 at 361.

[126] *Dunnes Stores Ireland Co Ltd v Maloney* [1999] 3 IR 542 at 556 citing *Lynch v Cooney* [1982] IR 337 at 360.

[127] *East Donegal Co-Operative v Attorney General* [1970] IR 317.

[128] *East Donegal Co-Operative v Attorney General* [1970] IR 317 at 343 (*per* Walsh J).

concluded in this regard that '… the exercise of the power conferred on the Minister by s 19 is reviewable for compliance with the requirement of fair procedures'.[129]

[12.045] When the interpretation of CA 1990, s 19 arose for consideration by the Supreme Court in the related case of *Dunnes Stores Ireland Company Limited v Ryan*,[130] Murray J agreed fully with the decision of Laffoy J referred to above. Having analysed the principles applicable to the exercise of a discretion under CA 1990, s 19, Murray J went on to set out some of the elements that must be taken into account in the exercise of that discretion in the following terms:

'… it seems to me that in exercising her powers under s 19, the second respondent, without intending to be exhaustive as to all the elements which may be taken into account, must do so, so that:

(a) it is exercised for a purpose contemplated by the Act and within the terms of the section;

(b) reasons are given for her decision;

(c) the decision to do so is rational and neither arbitrary nor disproportionate.'[131]

[12.046] In the United Kingdom, the Companies Act 1967, s 109, which created similar powers to those contained in CA 1990, s 19, was the subject of an application for judicial review in *R v Secretary of State, ex p Perestrello*.[132] Woolf J was called upon to consider whether allegations of bias were a sufficient reason to give rise to a right to relief. Reliance was placed on *Norwest Holst Ltd v Secretary of State for Trade*[133] in support of the contention that only bad faith on the part of the officers carrying out the investigation could justify granting the relief sought. Woolf J held that this contention stated the powers of the courts in too narrow a manner and went on to conclude that, '[i]n the case of s 109, to talk of the rules of natural justice is not really helpful'[134] and further that the function of officers appointed under s 109, 'is to see whether their suspicions are justified by what they find'[135] which was a role more akin to a 'potential prosecutor'. The rules that apply to a person exercising a judicial or quasi-judicial role, who is called upon to make a determination, should not apply to an officer appointed under s 109. However, Woolf J accepted that there are certain limits to the exercise of the powers conferred by that section, describing these as follows:

'First of all, the persons exercising the power must not exceed or abuse the discretion which is granted to them by the section … Secondly, the person concerned must not use the discretion for some ulterior purpose … It appears to

---

[129] *Dunnes Stores Ireland Co Ltd v Maloney* [1999] 3 IR 542 at 556.

[130] *Dunnes Stores Ireland Co Ltd v Ryan* [2002] 2 IR 60.

[131] *Dunnes Stores Ireland Co Ltd v Ryan* [2002] 2 IR 60 at 89.

[132] *R v Secretary of State, ex p Perestrello* [1981] QB 19 at 34; [1980] 3 WLR 1.

[133] *Norwest Holst Ltd v Secretary of State for Trade* [1978] Ch 201. See below para **[12.051]**.

[134] *R v Secretary of State, ex p. Perestrello* [1981] QB 19, 34; [1980] 3 WLR 1 at 12 (*per* Woolf J).

[135] *R v Secretary of State, ex p. Perestrello* [1981] QB 19, 34; [1980] 3 WLR 1 at 12 (*per* Woolf J).

me that it is a requirement of this power that it should be exercised fairly in the sense that the statutory discretion which it gives should not be abused.'[136]

It is clear from the standards set out in *Dunnes Stores Ireland Company Limited v Maloney*,[137] as endorsed by the Supreme Court in *Dunnes Stores Ireland Company Limited v Ryan*,[138] that the bar is set somewhat higher in Ireland and the powers that are conferred by s 19 will be more tightly policed in this jurisdiction.

(f) Duty to give reasons

[12.047] According to the terms of CA 1990, s 19, where the DCE forms the opinion that there are circumstances suggesting it is necessary to direct a company to produce specified books or documents, the DCE is not under any express obligation to furnish reasons for the formation of that opinion. The impression that this obligation does not exist in the context of an opinion formed under CA 1990, s 19(2), is reinforced by the terms of CA 1990, s 19(4)(a). The latter was introduced by CLEA 2001 and addresses the production of books or documents by a third party, where that party is in possession of books or documents 'which may relate to any books or documents of the body'.[139] Section 19(4)(a) requires the DCE to have 'reasonable grounds' for his belief that the books and documents which he may wish to require a third party to produce, are 'related to' other books or documents of the company, within the meaning of CA 1990, s 19(3)(b).[140] The DCE is moreover required to furnish a statement of those grounds to the third party in question.[141] As a matter of statutory interpretation, the fact that the DCE is required expressly to state the grounds for the formation of an opinion in that context, and that no such requirement is imposed in the context of a general direction to produce books or documents under CA 1990, s 19(2), suggests that the obligation to state reasons does not apply in the latter context.

[12.048] The question of the duty to give reasons for the formation of an opinion under CA 1990, s 19, as it existed before the enactment of the CLEA 2001, was considered in *Dunnes Stores Ireland Company Limited v Maloney*.[142] Laffoy J considered the various authorities relied on by both parties regarding the scope of the duty to give reasons for an administrative decision, with particular emphasis on the decision of Costello P in *McCormack v The Garda Síochána Complaints Board*[143] and that of Blayney J in *International Fishing Vessels Ltd v Minister for Marine*.[144]

---

[136] *R v Secretary of State, ex p. Perestrello* [1981] QB 19, 34; [1980] 3 WLR 1 at 12–13 (*per* Woolf J).

[137] *Dunnes Stores Ireland Co Ltd* [1999] 3 IR 542 (*per* Laffoy J). See above para **[12.044]**.

[138] *Dunnes Stores Ireland Co Ltd v Ryan* [2002] 2 IR 60. See above para **[12.045]**.

[139] CA 1990, s 19(3)(b), as substituted by CLEA 2001, s 29.

[140] See below paras **[12.064]** *et seq*.

[141] CA 1990, s 19(4)(b), as substituted by CLEA 2001, s 29. See below para **[12.067]**.

[142] *Dunnes Stores Ireland Co Ltd v Maloney* [1999] 3 IR 542.

[143] *McCormack v The Garda Síochána Complaints Board* [1997] 2 IR 489.

[144] *International Fishing Vessels Ltd v Minister for Marine* [1989] IR 149.

The respondents sought to rely on *McCormack v The Garda Síochána Complaints Board* which describes the law regarding the duty to give reasons as follows:

'It is not the law of this country that procedural fairness requires that in every case an administrative decision-making authority must give reasons for its decisions. Where a claim is made that a breach of a constitutional duty to apply fair procedures has occurred by a failure to state reasons for an administrative decision the court will be required to consider (a) the nature of the statutory function which the decision-maker is carrying out, (b) the statutory framework in which it is to be found and (c) the possible detriment the complainant may suffer arising from the failure to state reasons.'[145]

Having considered the possible implications of a failure to give reasons,[146] Costello P concluded that, 'a person aggrieved by a decision has no right to obtain reasons for it merely for the purpose of seeing whether or not the decision-maker had erred'.[147]

[12.049] Dunnes Stores relied on the decision of Blayney J in *International Fishing Vessels Ltd v Minister for Marine*[148] in which the failure of the Minister for Marine to give reasons for refusing to grant a sea fishing licence under the Fisheries (Consolidation) Act 1959 was held not to be in compliance with the requirements of fair procedures. This decision was based on the finding that, while the decision of the Minister was subject to review, the lack of reasons placed a serious obstacle in the way of any exercise of the right of review, as the applicant could not form a view as to whether grounds existed to quash the decision in question. Blayney J noted that:

'As a result, the applicant is at a great disadvantage, firstly, in reaching a decision as to whether to challenge the Minister's decision or not, and secondly, if he does decide to challenge it, in actually doing so, since the absence of reasons would make it very much more difficult to succeed.'[149]

Blayney J concluded that a procedure that placed the applicant at such a disadvantage could not be described as a fair procedure, particularly in light of the importance of the

---

[145] *McCormack v The Garda Síochána Complaints Board* [1997] 2 IR 489 at 500 (*per* Costello P).

[146] *McCormack v The Garda Síochána Complaints Board* [1997] 2 IR 489 at 500 (*per* Costello P): 'There may also be circumstances in which (a) no unfairness arose by a failure to give reasons when the decision was made but (b) the concept of fair procedures might require that reasons should subsequently be given in response to a *bona fide* request for them. Therefore in such cases the court would not grant an order of certiorari (because the decision itself was not an *ultra vires* one) but it would have jurisdiction to grant an order of *mandamus* directing the decision-making authority to carry out its constitutional duty (which the court had found existed) to provide reasons when asked. Finally, there may be circumstances in which the duty to apply fair procedures may not oblige a decision-making authority to state reasons for its decision at the time or after it has made it but which might oblige the authority to explain to an affected person the material on which the decision was based.'

[147] *McCormack v The Garda Síochána Complaints Board* [1997] 2 IR 489 at 502 (*per* Costello P).

[148] *International Fishing Vessels Ltd v Minister for Marine* [1989] IR 149.

[149] *International Fishing Vessels Ltd v Minister for Marine* [1989] IR 149 at 155.

decision to the applicant's business.[150] An order was accordingly made declaring that the applicant was entitled to be furnished with a statement in writing of the reasons for the Minister's decision.

[12.050] In *Dunnes Stores Ireland Company Limited v Maloney*,[151] an affidavit was sworn setting out the source of the material on which the decision of the Minister to appoint an authorised officer was based. It did not, however, set out the reasons for the decision. Laffoy J held that this description of the source of the material contained no real disclosure of information regarding the reasons for the decision to require the production of books or documents. Having determined that the opinion formed under, and the exercise of powers pursuant to, s 19 were reviewable, Laffoy J decided that the stance adopted by the Minister for Enterprise, Trade and Employment 'in effect, rendered her decision unreviewable'.[152] The Court further held that, whereas the applicant had the right to seek to judicially review the decision of the Minister, 'they are utterly stymied in the exercise of that right by reason of the refusal to give reasons for the decision'.[153] This represented a significant detriment to the applicant. A declaration was therefore made that the Minister was obliged to furnish a statement in writing setting out the reasons for the decision to appoint an authorised officer to carry out the functions provided for in CA 1990, s 19.[154] In related proceedings, the Supreme Court endorsed this conclusion in full.[155]

[12.051] There have been decisions in England regarding provisions of the English Companies Acts that govern company law investigations and that use language similar to that of CA 1990, s 19. The Court of Appeal has refused to impose a duty to give reasons in relation to such provisions. In *Norwest Holst Ltd v Secretary of State for Trade*[156] Lord Denning MR considered the (UK) Companies Act 1948, s 165, which addressed the power of the Board of Trade to appoint an inspector.[157] Having decided that there was no obligation on the Board to provide notice of an investigation, Lord Denning MR proceeded to make the following comment in respect of s 165: '... so long as the minister acts in good faith, it is not incumbent upon him to disclose the material he has before him, or the reasons for the inquiry'. He later stated that 'I see no reason why the minister should disclose the information he has before he makes the order ...

---

[150] *International Fishing Vessels Ltd v Minister for Marine* [1989] IR 149 at 155.

[151] *Dunnes Stores Ireland Co Ltd v Maloney* [1999] 3 IR 542.

[152] *Dunnes Stores Ireland Co Ltd v Maloney* [1999] 3 IR 542 at 563.

[153] *Dunnes Stores Ireland Co Ltd v Maloney* [1999] 3 IR 542 at 563.

[154] References to the authorisation by the Minister of an officer appointed to fulfil the functions set out in CA 1990, s 19 were removed by its substitution by CLEA 2001, s 29, which transferred the functions in this regard from the Minister for Industry and Commerce to the DCE.

[155] *Dunnes Stores Ireland Co Ltd v Ryan* [2002] 2 IR 60, 88 (*per* Murray J).

[156] *Norwest Holst Ltd v Secretary of State for Trade* [1978] 1 Ch 201; [1978] 3 WLR 73.

[157] See below para **[12.062]**.

such questions do not arise at that stage. It is sufficient that there are 'circumstances suggesting ... misconduct' within s 165(b)(ii).'[158]

This position clearly contrasts with that which has been adopted by the Irish courts in respect of the duty to give reasons for requiring the production of books or documents.

(g) Books or documents to be produced

[12.052] CA 1990, s 19,[159] defines the entities and the situations to which the power of the DCE to direct the production of books or documents applies. It does not, however, define the categories of books or documents which a company can be required to produce. While it would not be feasible to require an exhaustive definition of what books or documents the DCE is entitled to direct a company to produce in a manner that would address all of the diverse situations in which the DCE may wish to direct such production, some threshold could have been set forward in the legislation.

In this regard, CA 1990, s 19 merely states that the DCE can require a company to produce 'such books or documents as may be so specified'.[160] There is no limit to the breadth of the documents that can be required by the DCE, nor any requirement that the books or documents so required must relate to the circumstances giving rise to the direction to produce. The lack of any requirement that the books or documents that a company is required to produce be connected to the reasons for requiring such production may be criticised on the basis that the DCE's power is unrestricted in this regard and may be open to abuse, imposing unnecessary expense[161] and inconvenience on the company and exposing the company, its officers and employees, to potential liability for any instance of non-compliance.[162]

[12.053] This issue was considered by Laffoy J in *Dunnes Stores Ireland Company Limited v Maloney*.[163] In that case, Dunnes Stores sought to challenge the demand for documents that was made by the authorised officer pursuant to CA 1990, s 19. While this demand was withdrawn before the hearing of the case, the judgment of the High Court considered the legal issues raised in relation to it and the findings made remain relevant to the scope of documents of which an authorised officer can require production and the timeframes within such production can be required under CA 1990, s 19.

The principal ground that Dunnes Stores relied on for challenging the demand for the production of books and documents was that the demand was excessive and unreasonable. Three questions arose in this regard: first, whether the documents sought came within the scope of CA 1990, s 19; secondly, whether the demand for documents

---

[158] *Norwest Holst Ltd v Secretary of State for Trade* [1978] 1 Ch 201 at 225; [1978] 3 WLR 73 at 80–89.

[159] As substituted by the CLEA 2001, s 29.

[160] CA 1990, s 19(1), as substituted by the CLEA 2001, s 29.

[161] See CA 1990, s 19(10), as substituted by CLEA 2001, s 29, allows for the DCE to apply to the court to render the company liable for expenses incidental to the examination.

[162] See CA 1990, ss 19(6), (8)–(10) and 19A, as substituted by CLEA 2001, s 29.

[163] *Dunnes Stores Ireland Co Ltd v Maloney* [1999] 3 IR 542.

was reasonable in terms of content; and thirdly, whether the time allowed for production of the books and documents was reasonable.

In relation to the first question, Laffoy J accepted the submission of Dunnes Stores to the effect that, not having been informed of the reasons for the appointment of an authorised officer or for requiring books or documents to be produced under CA 1990, s 19,[164] they could not form a view as to whether the documents sought came within the scope of the exercise of the powers conferred by that provision.[165] Secondly, Laffoy J considered the submission that the demand for documents was excessive in the sense that too many documents were required. In this regard, Dunnes Stores argued that the demand was nearly total in its nature and could probably never have been complied with. Laffoy J examined the demand for documents and determined that:

> 'The inclusion of the categories which are of a general nature gives the demand as a whole the hallmark of a trawl. That being the case, the only reasonable inference is that the demand was excessive in content.'[166]

The final question regarding the demand for documents was whether the time given for compliance with the demand was too limited and rendered the demand unreasonable. The demand in question was issued on Friday, 24 July 1998 and required that the books and documents referred to therein be produced by Monday, 27 July 1998. Acknowledging that the challenge to the demand was academic, as the demand was no longer extant, Laffoy J nonetheless noted that 'common sense indicates that the demand could not be complied with between Friday and Monday afternoon'.[167]

[12.054] In *Dunnes Stores Ireland Co Ltd v Ryan*,[168] the Supreme Court was called upon to consider whether the request for documents was excessive and in the nature of a 'trawl'. In this regard, Keane CJ concluded that, 'I am satisfied that the range of documents sought is not unduly extensive, having regard to the scale of the misuse of the companies' assets which has already been identified.'[169] This observation is of interest in that it suggests a correlation be drawn between the severity of the apparent breaches of company law and the breadth of documents of which production can be required under CA 1990, s 19.

In *Rogers v Maloney*[170] the court found that a requirement to produce what could amount to 120,000 documents between 28 May 2004 and 31 May 2004 was unreasonable.

---

[164] With regard to the duty to give reasons, see further above paras **[12.047]** to **[12.051]**.

[165] *Dunnes Stores Ireland Co Ltd v Maloney* [1999] 3 IR 542 ('In my view, the applicants' criticisms of the demand are well founded. Without knowing the reasons why the Minister thought it appropriate to appoint an authorised officer, it is impossible to form any view as to whether even the categories of documents sought which are specific fall within the ambit of the entitlement to seek documents under s 19,' *per* Laffoy J at 564.).

[166] *Dunnes Stores Ireland Co Ltd v Maloney* [1999] 3 IR 542 at 564.

[167] *Dunnes Stores Ireland Co Ltd v Maloney* [1999] 3 IR 542 at 565.

[168] *Dunnes Stores Ireland Co Ltd v Ryan* [2002] 2 IR 60.

[169] *Dunnes Stores Ireland Co Ltd v Ryan* [2002] 2 IR 60 at 82.

[170] *Rogers v Maloney* [2005] IEHC 433, O'Leary J.

Further, O'Leary J, who noted that the demand was otherwise well-founded, stated that 'if the remainder of the process depended on this demand then the Court would consider whether the whole proceedings should be vitiated'. He considered that compelling the production of such a vast amount of documents in a short space of time in circumstances in which a criminal penalty for concealment of those documents would arise would require a 'compelling reason'. Such compelling reasons could include the fear of imminent destruction of the documents, but no such concern existed in that case.

[12.055] In the United Kingdom, a statutory provision that was drafted for the same purpose as, and in similar terms to, s 19,[171] was considered in *R v Secretary of State, ex p Perestrello*.[172] In that case, Lord Woolf examined whether the request for the production of documents in that case was too broad and concluded that the notices in that case were unreasonable and excessive for two reasons. First, the notice did not explicitly state that it was limited to documents in the possession of the person to whom it was directed and who was challenging the request. Secondly, while it was contended that the notice only applied to documents located in the United Kingdom, it did not expressly so state and, for that reason, the notice was unreasonably wide. Lord Woolf cautioned that, while the notice may have been intended to apply only to documents located in the United Kingdom:

> 'It should be borne in mind by the Department that this is a case which under this very provision of the Act, the notice can lead to criminal proceedings. It is true that if the notice is not complied with, the person concerned has a defence under the Act, but that, in my view, is no justification for a notice being in unreasonably wide terms as I regard this notice as being.'[173]

This caution could apply equally to a notice to produce books or documents under s 19 that is drafted in excessively broad terms, particularly in light of the fact that it is an offence not to comply with a direction to produce books or documents under that section.

[12.056] A final point that could be noted with regard to s 19 is that the requirement that the DCE specify the books and documents of which production is required may be onerous in practice, particularly in light of the fact that the DCE may not be aware of what books or documents exist within a company. This argument was made in *R v Secretary of State, ex p Perestrello*,[174] the Secretary of State stating that:

> 'It is difficult for inspectors to know what documents they want until they know what documents are available. Section 109 was designed to allow inspectors to range far and wide in order to see what information is available.'[175]

---

[171] Companies Act 1967, s 109.

[172] *R v Secretary of State, ex p Perestrello* [1981] QB 19; [1980] 3 WLR 1.

[173] *R v Secretary of State, ex p Perestrello* [1981] QB 19 at 31; [1980] 3 WLR 1 at 9.

[174] *R v Secretary of State, ex p Perestrello* [1981] QB 19; [1980] 3 WLR 1.

[175] *R v Secretary of State, ex p Perestrello* [1981] QB 19 at 23; [1980] 3 WLR 1. This treatment of s 109 accords somewhat with the view that the Irish courts have taken of the purpose of s 19, as evident from the statements of the Supreme Court in *Dunnes Stores Ireland Co Ltd v Ryan* [2002] 2 IR 60 to the effect that s 19 is a form of 'preliminary inquiry' and 'preliminary screening process'.

The specification of what documents are required could relate, not to the books or documents themselves, but to their relevance to the categories of situations which can justify a direction to produce such books or documents. So, for example, books or documents that relate to a particular suspected fraudulent transaction, or dealings with particular members which are feared to have been unfairly prejudicial, could be required.

(h) Notice of decision and time periods

(i) Advance notice

[12.057] Under CA 1990, s 19, there is no obligation on the DCE to notify a company of his intention to direct the production of that company's books or documents. The company therefore has no statutory right to be notified in advance of the making of a direction to produce books or documents or of the reasons underlying such a direction. The company, furthermore, has no opportunity to make submissions regarding any direction that the DCE may intend to make. The legislation, as drafted, merely provides that the company be required 'at such time and place as may be specified in the directions, to produce such books or documents as may be so specified'.[176]

The lack of procedural requirements before issuing directions to a company to produce books or documents is highlighted by the terms of CA 1990, s 19(4)(b).[177] Section 19(4) addresses the procedures that must be followed in the making of a direction to a third party to produce books or documents which may relate to other books or documents of a company. Section 19(4)(b) describes the obligation on the DCE to notify such third party that the DCE proposes to require the production of books or documents and the grounds for requiring such production. The third party is entitled to make submissions to the DCE within 21 days of the notification and the DCE is obliged to have regard to any such submissions in deciding whether to make the proposed direction.

The existence of such procedures in that particular context strengthens the view already expressed, that no such procedures exist in s 19 for the protection of companies, other than third parties, that are the subject of directions to produce books or documents.

[12.058] It is relevant to note that the notification requirement in CA 1990, s 19(4)(b) is subject to the proviso that the DCE is not bound to furnish such notification, if he is of the opinion that this '... could result in the concealment, falsification, destruction or the disposal otherwise of the books or documents concerned ...'.[178] This *proviso* demonstrates that it is considered to be possible to avoid the potential disadvantages and risks associated with advance notification of a proposal to require the production of books or documents. If this is accepted in the context of production of documents by a third party, it is difficult to see why it should not also be accepted in the context of production of books or documents by the company itself and why there is no general obligation on the DCE to afford a company certain procedural rights, such as a right to be notified of the direction, the grounds for making it and a right to make submissions in

---

[176] CA 1990, s 19(1), as substituted by CLEA 2001, s 29.

[177] See below paras **[12.067]**.

[178] CA 1990, s 19(4)(b), as substituted by CLEA 2001, s 29. See below para **[12.067]**.

respect of the proposal to direct the production of books or documents. In light of the fact that a failure to comply with a direction under CA 1990, s 19 is an offence and can give rise to potentially severe sanctions, this lack of procedural protection could be regarded as particularly unfair.

[12.059] In *Dunnes Stores Ireland Company Limited v Maloney*,[179] Laffoy J determined that the exercise of the powers conferred by CA 1990, s 19, was amenable to judicial review and that such powers must be exercised in accordance with the requirements of fair procedures. Dunnes Stores argued that the obligation to abide by fair procedures encompassed the duty to furnish advance notice before the appointment of an authorised officer and to allow representations to be made to the Minister for Enterprise, Trade and Employment opposing such an appointment. In making this submission, Dunnes Stores relied on the decision of the Supreme Court in *Haughey v Moriarty*[180] and in particular on the decision of Hamilton CJ in that case.[181]

Laffoy J considered the facts of *Haughey v Moriarty*,[182] noting that the order for discovery of documents in that case was directed to the secretary of the Anglo Irish Bank Corporation plc and required discovery of documents in the power, procurement or possession of the bank that related to accounts in the name of, or otherwise connected with, the applicant in that case, Mr Haughey. Laffoy J distinguished the facts of *Haughey v Moriarty*[183] and those of *Dunnes Stores Ireland Company Limited v Maloney*[184] in the following terms:

> 'The fundamental distinction between the factual situation in *Haughey v Moriarty* [1999] 3 IR 1 and the factual situation in this case is that the orders for discovery in Haughey v Moriarty might have been complied with by the bank and discovery made which might have included discovery of matters to which the Tribunal had no entitlement before the persons affected became aware of the discovery orders, whereas the applicants' property and their rights of privacy and confidentiality in relation to their books and documents could not be interfered with without their knowledge on the invoking of the s 19 procedure.'

With regard to the submission that there were certain representations that Dunnes Stores could have made concerning the appointment of the authorised officer and the demand for documents, if advance notice had been given, Laffoy J considered that these representations could have been as effectively made after the demand was issued as before. Laffoy J further concluded that, while any representations made after the issue of

---

[179] *Dunnes Stores Ireland Co Ltd v Maloney* [1999] 3 IR 542.

[180] *Haughey v Moriarty* [1999] 3 IR 1.

[181] *Haughey v Moriarty* [1999] 3 IR 1 at 75. ('Fair procedures require that before making such orders, particularly orders of the nature of the orders made in this case, the person or persons likely to be affected thereby should be given notice by the Tribunal of its intention to make such order, and should have been afforded the opportunity prior to the making of such order, of making representations with regard thereto.')

[182] *Haughey v Moriarty* [1999] 3 IR 1.

[183] *Haughey v Moriarty* [1999] 3 IR 1.

[184] *Dunnes Stores Ireland Co Ltd v Maloney* [1999] 3 IR 542 at 599.

a demand for production of books or documents could be disregarded by the Minister, any grievance in that regard may be aired by way of judicial review. [185] Laffoy J concluded 'the power conferred on the Minister by s 19 is not a power the exercise of which requires advance notice or the giving of an opportunity to make representations.'[186]

[12.060] There is some scope for distinguishing between cases such as *Haughey v Moriarty,* in which the person affected most heavily by a direction to produce documents may not be aware of such a direction until after it has been complied with, and cases such as *Dunnes Stores Ireland Co Ltd v Maloney*[187] in which the demand is issued directly to the entity under investigation. However, this distinction is not a sound basis on which to analyse the effects of CA 1990, s 19 or on which to determine the scope of the rights affected by that provision for two reasons. First, as will be seen below, CA 1990, s 19(3)(a), as substituted by CLEA 2001, s 29, permits the DCE to require a third party to produce books or documents which may be copies of other books or documents, without conferring any right of advance notice of such a direction on the third party or on the company whose books or documents are requisitioned.[188] This situation appears to be entirely analogous with the facts of *Haughey v Moriarty* and the refusal in *Dunnes Stores Ireland Co Ltd v Maloney* to confer a right to receive advance notice or a right to make representations in the context of CA 1990, s 19, may be questioned since the commencement of CLEA 2001, s 29.

[12.061] Secondly, it is an offence not to comply with a direction to produce books or documents if directed to do so under CA 1990, s 19.[189] The same provision existed under the CA 1990 before the enactment of the CLEA 2001 and was therefore applicable at the date of the decision in *Dunnes Stores Ireland Co Ltd v Maloney.*[190] The suggestion made in that case that it is open to a company to make representations regarding a direction to produce books or documents after such a direction has been issued would entail the company failing to comply with a direction under CA 1990, s 19, giving rise to an offence under that section. In addition, a failure to comply with a direction to produce books or documents can justify a warrant for the search and entry of a premises.[191] It is therefore questionable whether a company that receives a direction to produce books or documents has a real right to make representations regarding that direction, if such a course of action may lead to prosecution for the offence of non-compliance.

---

[185] *Dunnes Stores Ireland Co Ltd v Maloney* [1999] 3 IR 542 at 563.

[186] *Dunnes Stores Ireland Co Ltd v Maloney* [1999] 3 IR 542 at 560.

[187] *Dunnes Stores Ireland Co Ltd v Maloney* [1999] 3 IR 542.

[188] See below paras **[12.066]**.

[189] CA 1990, s 19(6), as substituted by CLEA 2001, s 29. Note that the only defence regarding a person's failure to produce books or documents that is stipulated in that subsection is that '… it shall be a defence to prove that they were not in his possession or under his control and that it was not reasonably practicable for him to comply with the requirement'.

[190] *Dunnes Stores Ireland Co Ltd v Maloney* [1999] 3 IR 542.

[191] See below para **[12.113]**.

[12.062] The question of advance notice of an intention to inspect the books or documents of a company was considered by Lord Denning MR in *Norwest Holst Ltd v Secretary of State for Trade*.[192] As has been seen, that case concerned the interpretation of the provisions of the English Companies Acts dealing with the appointment of inspectors. In the course of his judgment, Lord Denning MR considered a submission that the rules of natural justice applied to any decision to appoint an inspector or to require the production of books or documents and that both sides should therefore be heard before any decision to appoint an inspector be made.[193]

Lord Denning MR held that, while there may have been a practice of notifying companies in advance of the intention to appoint an inspector, that practice was never required by the common law.[194] He went on to state:

> '... when the officers of the Department of Trade are appointed to examine the books, there is no need for the rules of natural justice to be applied. If the company was forewarned and told that the officers were coming, what is to happen to the books? In a wicked world, it is not unknown for books or papers to be destroyed or lost. So also with the appointment of inspectors under s 165 (b)(ii). The inspectors are not to decide rights or wrongs. They are to investigate and report. This inquiry is a good administrative arrangement for the good conduct of companies and their affairs. It is not a case to which the rules of natural justice apply. There is no need for them to be given notice of a charge, or a fair opportunity of meeting it.'[195]

(ii) Time limit for compliance

[12.063] Section 19 does not prescribe the time period which the DCE must allow for a company to produce its books or documents: s 19(1) merely states that he may require the body in question to produce such books and documents 'at such time and place as may be specified in the directions'.[196] If the books and documents sought are wide-ranging and numerous, and the persons bearing responsibility for the company's affairs few, a short time limit for compliance with s 19 could be onerous and unfair, particularly

---

[192] *Norwest Holst Ltd v Secretary of State for Trade* [1978] 1 Ch 201; [1978] 3WLR 73. See above para **[12.051]**.

[193] Reliance was placed on the practice of the Board of Trade in this regard, as expressed before Lord Jenkin's Company Law Committee (1962) (Cmnd 1749) at p 79: it is 'very necessary to hear both sides before deciding whether or not an inspector should be appointed. By so doing it is often possible in cases where no fraud is alleged to bring the parties together or for them to reach a mutually satisfactory arrangement so that an investigation is not necessary'. *Norwest Holst v Secretary of State for Trade* [1978] 1 Ch 201 at 224; [1978] 3WLR 73 at 89.

[194] Lord Denning MR adopted the following reasoning: 'There are many cases where an inquiry is held – not a as a judicial or quasi-judicial inquiry – but simply as a matter of good administration. In these circumstances there is no need to give preliminary notice of any charge, or anything of that sort'. *Norwest Holst v Secretary of State for Trade* [1978] 1 Ch 201 at 224; [1978] 3WLR 73 at 89.

[195] *Norwest Holst v Secretary of State for Trade* [1978] 1 Ch 201, 224; [1978] 3WLR 73 at 89.

[196] CA 1990, s 19(1), as substituted by CLEA 2001, s 29.

as failure to comply with such a direction is an offence by the company and any officers who consented, connived or were neglectful in relation to such non-compliance.[197]

In *Rogers v Maloney*[198] O'Leary J considered a direction to produce documents under s 19, which was received on 28 May 2004 and required that the documents be produced by 31 May 2004. The applicant challenged the search warrant that was subsequently issued under s 20 on a number of grounds, including that the time period for compliance with the s 19 direction was unreasonable. The Court considered that the requirement to produce the documents by 31 May 2004 was unreasonable:

> 'The production of 120,000 documents in such a short space of time when there is a criminal penalty for concealment (which may in the view of the Court be inferred in certain circumstances) would require a compelling reason. An example of such an emergency would be a fear of the possible destruction of the documents in the event of delay.'

While the decision of the Court in *Rogers v Maloney* did not hinge on this determination,[199] that decision indicates clearly that severe time limits for the production of documents under s 19 will only be justified if there is a 'compelling reason', such as a risk of destruction of the documents sought.

(i) Production of books or documents by third parties

(i) Grounds for directing third parties to produce books or documents

[12.064] Where the DCE has the power to direct a company to produce its books or documents on one of the grounds listed in CA 1990, s 19(2), this power can also be exercised to direct other persons to produce those books or documents. The persons who may be directed to produce books and documents are not defined and s 19(2) is broad enough to encompass natural persons, not just a company or its officers.

Third parties may be the subject of a direction under s 19(2), if they appear to be in possession of one of the following categories of books or documents:[200]

– books or documents to which CA 1990, s 19(1) applies;

– books or documents which may be copies of any books or documents of the company;

– other books or documents which may relate to any books or documents of the company.

---

[197] CA 1990, s 19(6), as substituted by CLEA 2001, s 29; and CA 1990, s 241(1).

[198] *Rogers v Maloney* [2005] IEHC 433.

[199] The case concerned judicial review proceedings and the Court formed the view that the manner in which the requirement was issued under s 19 was within the reasonable discretion of the respondents; the orders were not defective or unreasonable to such a degree as to permit them to be set aside by way of judicial review. *Rogers v Maloney* [2005] IEHC 433, *per* O'Leary J.

[200] CA 1990, s 19(3), as substituted by CLEA 2001, s 29.

It is clear that before exercising the power to direct a third party to produce books or documents, the DCE must form the opinion that circumstances exist which suggest that there are grounds to direct the company itself to produce specified books or documents, within the context of CA 1990, s 19(1). There is no requirement that the DCE must in fact have exercised his power under s 19(1) to require production of such books or documents.

The DCE must assess whether one of the following circumstances exists.

1. POSSESSION OF S 19(1) BOOKS OR DOCUMENTS

[12.065] If the requirements of CA 1990, s 19(1) and (2) are satisfied, and it appears to the DCE that another person is in possession of such books or documents, that person can also be directed to produce such books or documents. This power was also contained in the now-repealed CA 1990, s 19(3), which permitted the Minister for Enterprise, Trade and Employment to require production of books or documents by any person who appears to be in possession of them, where the Minister had the power to require the production of those books or documents under CA 1990, s 19(1).

Further circumstances in which a third party can be required to produce books or documents were introduced by the CLEA 2001, s 29. These require further consideration.

2. POSSESSION OF COPIES OF BOOKS OR DOCUMENTS

[12.066] According to CA 1990, s 19(3)(a), the DCE can require a third party to produce books or documents where that person appears to be in possession of 'other books or documents which may constitute copies of any books of documents of the body'. This language is vague and potentially anomalous. First, s 19(3)(a) permits the DCE to require a third party to produce books or documents, where that third party is in possession of 'other books or documents' not being the books or documents within the scope of s 19(1), but which may be copies of any other books or documents. This is almost obscure in its formulation.

Secondly, the requirement that the third party must possess books or documents which 'may' be copies of other books or documents is a very weak one. Thirdly, it would be difficult for a person to refute a suggestion that a document in their possession 'may' be a copy of another document. Fourthly, this subsection refers to 'any books or documents' of the company, whereas CA 1990, s 19(1) permits the DCE to require production of 'such books or documents as may be so specified'. The means by which a third party can be directed to produce books or documents appears to be less restrictive than those applicable to the company itself, which is clearly anomalous.

3. POSSESSION OF RELATED BOOKS OR DOCUMENTS

[12.067] According to CA 1990, s 19(3)(b), the DCE can direct a third party to produce books or documents of which the DCE could require production under s 19(1) if it appears to the DCE that such party is in possession of 'other books or documents which may relate to any books or documents of the body'.[201] There are three categories of books and documents referred to in s 19(3)(b). First, there are books and documents of another body of which the DCE has the power to require the production under s 19(1) (the 'other body's books and documents'). Second, there are other books and documents which are in the possession of a third party (the 'third party's books and documents'). Third, s 19(3)(b) refers to 'any books or documents of the other body to which the third party's books and documents may relate ('the related books and documents'). The interaction between these categories is curious. According to s 19(3)(b), the DCE may require production of the 'other body's books and documents' by the third party not on the basis that the third party is in possession of those books and documents, but rather on the basis that the 'third party's books and documents' may relate to the 'related books and documents'. There is no requirement that the 'third party's books and documents' or the 'related books and documents' must be documents of which the DCE could require production under s 19(1). The weaknesses of CA 1990, s 19(3)(a), that were highlighted above,[202] also apply to this provision, particularly regarding the vague and broad language used. However, s 19(3)(b) is qualified by CA 1990, s 19(4), which was introduced by CLEA 2001, s 29.

CA 1990, s 19(4) provides that the power to require a third party who is in possession of books or documents which may relate to any books or documents of another body, to produce books or documents, can only be exercised if two pre-conditions are met.

First, the DCE must be of the opinion that there are 'reasonable grounds' for believing that the books and documents in the possession of the third party and the 'related books and documents', as referred to in CA 1990, s 19(3)(b), are related to one another. Examples of some of the grounds that may satisfy this threshold are mentioned specifically and include grounds related to the relationship between the company and the third party, the common origin of the information contained in the books or documents 'or similar considerations'.[203]

Secondly, the DCE must send a notification to the third party regarding the proposal to require that third party to produce books or documents. [204] This notification must contain the following information:

- a statement that the DCE proposes to require the production of books or documents pursuant to CA 1990, s 19(3)(b);

- a statement of the grounds for the opinion that the books or documents in question are related to each other;

- a statement that the third party is entitled to make submissions to the DCE, if they so wish, within 21 days from the date of making the notification, as to why they believe the DCE's opinion to be erroneous.

---

[201] CA 1990, s 19(3)(b) as substituted by CLEA 2001, s 29.

[202] See above para **[12.066]**.

[203] CA 1990, s 19(4)(a), as substituted by CLEA 2001, s 29.

[204] CA 1990, s 19(4)(b), as substituted by CLEA 2001, s 29.

The DCE is obliged to have regard to any submissions made by the third party before deciding whether to require the production of books or documents under CA 1990, s 19(3)(b).[205]

The notification requirement is subject to a particular *proviso*. The DCE is not obliged to notify a third party of the proposal to require books or documents to be produced, if 'the Director is of the opinion that compliance with this [requirement] could result in the concealment, falsification, destruction or the disposal otherwise of the books or documents concerned...'.[206]

The logic of this *proviso* is inescapable. It avoids the possibility that a direction to produce books or documents could be thwarted by virtue of advance notification of the intention to make such a direction.

Section 19(4) also creates a carve-out in respect of books or documents in respect of which the third party makes a claim of privilege. This is addressed below in the context of the grounds on which a third party can refuse to produce books or documents.[207]

It is important to note that a person who fails to comply with s 19(3)(b) may be subject to a court order directing compliance with the obligation to produce books or documents.[208]

(ii) Documents to be produced by a third party

[12.068] As noted above, the DCE has the power to direct a company to produce such books or documents 'as may be so specified' where one of the grounds set forward in CA 1990, s 19(2) exists.[209] Furthermore, the DCE can direct a third party who appears to be in possession of such books or documents, to produce those books or documents.[210] It would appear that any other categories of books or documents which third parties can be directed to produce should logically be books or documents which do not fall within the scope of CA 1990, s 19(1). However, the wording of CA 1990, s 19(3) suggests that the DCE can only direct a third party to produce those books or documents which the DCE has power to require the production of by virtue of CA 1990, s 19(1). This gives rise to certain anomalies and inconsistencies.

[12.069] First, if the DCE can only require third parties to produce such books or documents as are covered by CA 1990, s 19(1), the third parties would need to be in possession of those books or documents. Accordingly, only the first category of production by a third party, in which the third party appears to be in possession of the books or documents that are covered by CA 1990, s 19(1), as outlined above, could validly be possible.[211]

---

[205] CA 1990, s 19(4)(b): '... the Director shall have regard to any such submissions so made before finally deciding whether to make the said requirement or not ...'.

[206] CA 1990, s 19(4)(b), as substituted by CLEA 2001, s 29.

[207] See below para **[12.071]**.

[208] See CA 1963, s 371A, as inserted by CLEA 2001, s 97. See further below para **[12.088]**.

[209] See above paras **[12.052]** to **[12.056]**.

[210] CA 1990, s 19(3). See above para **[12.065]**.

[211] See above para **[12.065]**.

A second and related anomaly is that, if a third party can only be required to produce the books or documents that are covered by CA 1990, s 19(1), the fact that such third party may appear to be in possession of books or documents that may be copies of any books of documents of a company or that may be related to such books or documents, must be immaterial, as production of those books or documents is not provided for by the general language of CA 1990, s 19(3).

Thirdly, if a third party is categorised by virtue of its apparent possession of copies of books or documents or related books or documents, within the meaning of CA 1990, s 19(3)(a) and (b), the inference that the third party does not have possession of such books or documents as are covered by CA 1990, s 19(1) appears to be inescapable. Otherwise, that entity would fall within the first and least controversial category of third party document production, that which existed in the original CA 1990, s 19(1), namely the category of third party who appears to be in possession of such books or documents as fall within CA 1990, s 19(1). On this interpretation, CA 1990, s 19(3) appears to require a third party who is not in possession of books or documents within the scope of CA 1990, s 19(1), to produce books or documents within the scope of CA 1990, s 19(1). This is entirely anomalous.

[12.070] An alternative interpretation of CA 1990, s 19(3), is that the DCE is permitted to require a third party to produce books or documents other than those that the company itself can be directed to produce under CA 1990, s 19(1). While this interpretation is not supported by the language used, it is the only means by which the anomalous interpretation of the statutory provision introduced by CLEA 2001, s 29, outlined above, can be avoided. It is also the only interpretation that is consistent with the terms of CA 1990, s 19(4), which appears to envisage the production of books or documents other than those covered by CA 1990, s 19(1), by a third party.[212]

If a third party can be required to produce books or documents other than those covered by CA 1990, s 19(1), there are some issues that need to be considered. First, there are certain restrictions and requirements that exist in relation to the exercise by the DCE of his power to direct a company to produce books or documents. As has already been noted, many of these existed since the introduction of the CA 1990.[213] If a third party can be required to produce books or documents, which are not within the scope of the exercise of that power, those restrictions and requirements can be negated.

Secondly, the two new grounds on which third parties can be required to produce books or documents are formulated in vague terms. As noted above,[214] CA 1990, s 19(3)(a) refers to 'books or documents which may constitute copies of any books or documents' and CA 1990, s 19(3)(b) refers to 'other books or documents which may relate to any books or documents of the company'. By contrast, CA 1990, s 19(1) requires the production of 'such books or documents as may be so specified'. If the DCE can require the production of documents which may constitute copies of, or may relate to, any books or documents of a company, this is considerably broader than the power to require the

---

[212] See above para **[12.067]**.

[213] See above para **[12.011]** *et seq.*

[214] See above paras **[12.066]** *et seq.*

company itself to produce specified books or documents and makes no reference to the need to specify the books or documents that need to be produced.

(iii) Grounds for resisting third party production

1. PRIVILEGE

[12.071] CA 1990, s 19(4), as addressed above,[215] sets out the procedures that must be adhered to before the DCE can require a third party to produce books or documents on the basis that the third party is in possession of books and documents that may relate to other books or documents of the company. While these procedures are expressed as prerequisites to any direction to such third party to produce documents, this is overridden by the final caveat which provides:

> … in no case shall the third party be obliged to comply with such a requirement in relation to a particular book or document concerned if he would be entitled, by virtue of any rule of law or enactment, to refuse to produce, in any proceedings, the book or document on the ground of any privilege (whether the privilege to which s 23 applies or not).[216]

This exemption is not expressed to apply in respect of third parties who are in possession of books or documents which may be copies of other books or documents, as described in CA 1990, s 19(3)(a), or third parties that possess books and documents that may be subject to directions under s 19(1).

2. BANKING DOCUMENTS

[12.072] CA 1990, s 23(2)[217] creates a carve-out in respect of the power of the DCE to compel the production of documents pursuant to CA 1990, s 19. This provision relates to banking documents and is addressed in more detail below.[218] It should be noted, however, that is clearly applies in respect of the production of books or documents by third parties.

3. LIEN

[12.073] Where the DCE seeks to require a third party to produce books or documents under any of the three categories set out in CA 1990, s 19(3),[219] this shall be without prejudice to any lien that such third party may claim in respect of those books or documents.

Section 19(3)[220] provides that, '…where any such person claims a lien on books or documents produced by him, the production shall be without prejudice to the lien'.

---

215 See above paras **[12.067]** *et seq.*

216 See below para **[12.084]**.

217 As substituted by CLEA 2001, s 32(a).

218 See below para **[12.085]** to **[12.087]**.

219 See above paras **[12.065]** *et seq.*

220 As substituted by CLEA 2001, s 29.

This exemption applies clearly to all situations in which third parties can be required by the DCE to produce books or documents in accordance with the terms of CA 1990, s 19(3).

(j) Supplemental powers

[12.074] In addition to the power to require a company or third party to produce specified books or documents, the Companies Acts also confer on the DCE certain supplemental powers to aid in the gathering of documentary evidence.

(i) Copies of books or documents

[12.075] CA 1990, s 19(5)(a)(i),[221] provides that the DCE has the power to take copies of, or extracts from, any books or documents that are produced by a company or other person pursuant to s 19. This power already existed under the CA 1990. There no express reference in CA 1990, s 19(5) to the protection of any privilege in, liens over, or other interests in, books or documents. However, where there is a ground for resisting the production of books or documents, those books or documents clearly will not be produced. As CA 1990, s 19(5)(a)(i) only applies to books or documents that have been produced, the power to take copies of or extracts from, books or documents that are protected by legal professional privilege, for example, will not arise. Where a third party asserts a lien in respect of books or documents, production of those books or documents is expressly without prejudice to such liens.[222] The power of the DCE to take extracts from books or documents is not curtailed by reference to any liens that may exist. However, where taking an extract from a book or document may prejudice a third party's lien, this may be a reason to prevent such an extract being taken. Otherwise, the protection against prejudice to any third party's lien, that is guaranteed by CA 1990, s 19(3), could be undermined.

(ii) Explanations of books or documents

[12.076] CA 1990, s 19(5)(a)(ii),[223] confers on the DCE the power to require explanations of any books or documents that were produced. The persons who can be required to give such explanations are the following:

- **Third parties.** The powers contained in CA 1990, s 19(5) are complementary to the power of the DCE 'to require a body or other person to produce books or documents'.[224] The only entities that the DCE has the power to direct to produce books or documents are the company itself and such third parties as are covered by CA 1990, s 19(3).[225] According to CA 1990, s 19(5)(a)(ii), the power to require explanations of books or documents arises if the DCE has the power to

---

[221] As substituted by CLEA 2001, s 29.

[222] CA 1990, s 19(3), as substituted by CLEA 2001, s 29. See above paras **[12.082]** to **[12.083]** and para **[12.073]**.

[223] As substituted by CLEA 2001, s 29.

[224] CA 1990, s 19(5), as substituted by CLEA 2001, s 29.

[225] See above paras **[12.064]** et seq.

require 'a body or other person' to produce books or documents and is described as applying to 'that person', which suggests that it is a reference to the 'other person', a third party which produced books or documents.

- **Officers.** The DCE can require a past or present officer of a company to provide an explanation of books or documents that were produced by the company.[226]

- **Employees.** The power to require an explanation of books or documents extends to past and present employees of the company. This category is broadly formulated. It includes anyone who was 'at any time' employed by the company. Furthermore, this category specifically includes persons who are or were at any time employed 'in a professional, consultancy or similar capacity'.[227] Persons who carry out consultancy or other professional work on behalf of companies typically do not do so as employees, but rather pursuant to contracts for services, as contractors, without an employment relationship. Whether they qualify as being 'employed' by the company may be an issue that will require determination before the scope of the power to require explanations can be assessed accurately. The extension of the power to persons employed 'in a professional, consultancy or similar capacity' was introduced by the CLEA 2001[228] and there is accordingly little guidance available regarding its interpretation. If a broad interpretation is adopted, however, questions may arise as to the fairness and propriety of compelling persons who formerly acted as professional advisers to a company to provide explanations to the DCE. The issue of legal professional privilege may require particular examination.[229]

[12.077] The obligation to give an explanation relates to the books and documents that have been produced. Since the introduction of the CLEA 2001, the obligation to provide an explanation of such books or documents includes an obligation to provide an explanation of '… any apparent omissions from them or any omission of any book or document'.[230] There is a certain inconsistency in the language of the section in this regard. The requirement to provide an explanation of books or documents only arises '… if the books or documents are produced'.[231] To require an explanation of an omitted book or document, where the power to require such explanation is premised on the production of the requested books or documents, may be anomalous. The anomaly becomes more apparent in light of the fact that the DCE is given a particular power to deal with the situation in which books or documents are not produced.[232] That power,

---

[226] CA 1990, s 19(5)(a)(ii), as substituted by CLEA 2001, s 29.

[227] CA 1990, s 19(5)(a)(ii), as substituted by CLEA 2001, s 29.

[228] CLEA 2001, s 29.

[229] See below para **[12.084]**.

[230] CA 1990, s 19(5)(a)(ii), as substituted by CLEA 2001, s 29.

[231] CA 1990, s 19(5)(a), as substituted by CLEA 2001, s 29.

[232] CA 1990, s 19 (5)(b), as substituted by CLEA 2001, s 29. See below para **[12.080]**.

which is addressed below,[233] may be a more appropriate way of addressing a failure to produce books and documents than requiring explanations under s 19(5)(a)(ii).

A further factor that suggests it is anomalous for the DCE to require an explanation of the omission of books or documents within the context of CA 1990, s 19(5)(a)(ii) relates to the addressees of that power. Books or documents are produced by the company or a third party. Section 19(5)(a)(ii) refers to 'that person, or any other person who is a present or past officer of, or is or was at any time employed (including in a professional, consultancy or similar capacity) by the body in question'. The power of the DCE to require a person who may have been employed by the company years previously to explain the omission of a book or document from among the books or documents that were produced is illogical. This is reinforced by the fact that CA 1990, s 19(5)(b), which deals with situations where books or documents are not produced, is directed towards the person who was required to produce the books or documents.[234] This approach, it is suggested, is eminently more sensible.

[12.078] There is a defence available to persons who are called upon to provide an explanation under s 19(5)(a)(ii). The persons to whom CA 1990, s 19(5)(a)(ii) applies are only required to provide explanations of books or documents that were produced 'insofar as the person may be reasonably able to do so'. This is the only ground that can be relied upon by a person for any failure to provide an explanation. While there is no reference to confidentiality or other interests or obligations that may conflict with an obligation to provide explanations to the DCE, these may be regarded as matters which would impede a person from being 'reasonably able' to provide explanations. By that means, a person may be able to invoke conflicting obligations as a defence to the obligation to provide explanations of books or documents.

[12.079] A final point to note regarding this aspect of s 19 is its constitutionality. This was considered at length by Kearns J in *Dunnes Stores Ireland Company Limited v Ryan*.[235] Having considered the governing authorities, it was determined that the privilege against self-incrimination was not infringed by the terms of s 19:

> 'The compulsion to produce books and documents is completely unobjectionable and the requirement to answer questions of a fairly limited nature under s 19 does not, in my view, constitute an infringement of Art 40 of the Constitution of sufficient substance to warrant condemning the section when weighed in the balance with the countervailing public interest in good corporate governance.'[236]

(iii) Location of books or documents

[12.080] Section 19(5)(b)[237] addresses situations in which, despite a direction of the DCE to produce specified books or documents, a body or other person fails to produce

---

[233] See below para **[12.080]**.

[234] See below para **[12.080]**.

[235] *Dunnes Stores Ireland Co Ltd v Ryan* [2002] 2 IR 60.

[236] *Dunnes Stores Ireland Co Ltd v Ryan* [2002] 2 IR 60 at 119. The topics of the right to silence and the privilege against self-incrimination are considered in more detail in Ch **13**.

[237] As substituted by CLEA 2001, s 29.

such books or documents. In those situations, the DCE has the power to require the person who was required to produce the books or documents to state 'to the best of his knowledge and belief' where such books and documents are.

(iv) General assistance

[12.081] When the DCE issues a direction to a company or a third party to produce books or documents, CA 1990, s 19(5) imposes an overriding duty to assist the DCE in connection with examinations of the books or documents, irrespective of whether such books or documents were in fact produced. This obligation is framed in the following language:

> Any power conferred by or by virtue of this section to require a body or other person to produce books or documents shall include power.
>
> .... to give all assistance to the Director as the body or person is reasonably able to give in connection with an examination or proposed examination of books or documents under this section.

As has already been seen,[238] CA 1990, s 19(5)(a) and (b) address different categories of persons. It is therefore not clear from the wording of the duty to assist what persons are bound by this duty. However, the phrase '...as the body or person is reasonably able to give' suggests that it is the company or third party to which the direction to produce books or documents was issued, that bears the obligation of assisting the DCE. Applying this interpretation, the obligation to assist the DCE does not apply to persons such as past or present officers or persons who are or were in the employment of the company and who fall within the scope of CA 1990, s 19(5)(a)(ii).[239]

The obligation to assist the DCE in the examination or proposed examination of books or documents applies whether or not the books or documents were produced.[240] This seems incongruous for the obvious reason that it is only books or documents that have been produced that can be examined, and that can give rise to the duty to assist in connection with such examination.

A final possible frailty in the drafting of the duty to assist the DCE is that it refers to assistance in connection with 'an examination or proposed examination under this section'.[241] CA 1990, s 19,[242] deals with the production of books or documents to the DCE and describes the powers of the DCE in relation to requiring the production of books or documents and certain explanations to be furnished in connection with such books or documents. The section does not address or describe the examination of such books or documents by the DCE. The nature and scope of the obligation to assist in an examination or proposed examination is therefore uncertain.

---

[238] See above paras **[12.074]** to **[12.080]**.

[239] See above para **[12.076]**.

[240] CA 1990, s 19(5), as substituted by CLEA 2001, s 29. Section 19(5) refers to 'in either event' in this regard, indicating that the obligation to provide assistance applies whether the books and documents are produced or not.

[241] CA 1990, s 19(5), as substituted by CLEA 2001, s 29.

[242] As substituted by CLEA 2001, s 29.

(k) Exceptions

(i) Lien

[12.082] There is no general carve-out in CA 1990, s 19 in respect of books or documents that are the subject of a lien. The only express provision in this regard is s 19(3).[243] That subsection relates only to books or documents produced by third parties and provides that, '…where any such person claims a lien on books or documents produced by him, the production shall be without prejudice to the lien'.

One point to note in this regard, is that the newly introduced CA 1990, s 19(2)(i) permits the DCE to require the production of books or documents where there are circumstances to suggest that:

> '… the body may be in possession of books or documents containing information relating to the books or documents of a body which comes within the terms of one or more of paras (a) to (h).'

This appears to refer to a third party. However, the protection of any lien a third party may claim, that is contained in s 19(3) is not extended to any third party which may be required to produce books or documents pursuant to s 19(2)(i). This could undermine any protection in that regard, as it is open to the DCE to require production of the books or documents by exercising his powers under s 19(2)(i) rather than invoking s 19(3) and being constrained by the duty to protect any lien the third party may claim.

[12.083] It is interesting to note that the equivalent of s 19 in the United Kingdom, the Companies Act 1985, s 447,[244] contains the same protection in respect of documents over which a third party claims a lien but, like s 19, does not extend that protection to the company which is directly required to produce documents. Section 447(4) accordingly provides that, where the Secretary of State (or a designated officer or other such person) has the power to require the production of documents under that section, they can also require the production of those documents from a person who appears to be in possession of them, but this is subject to the proviso that, '…where any such person claims a lien on documents produced by him, the production is without prejudice to the lien'.[245]

(ii) Privilege

[12.084] CA 1990, s 23[246] excludes from the scope of Pt II of the Act[247] any obligation of a person to disclose, produce or hand over possession of, information, where that person would 'in the opinion of the court' be entitled to refuse to produce that information on the grounds of legal professional privilege.[248] It further provides that

---

[243] As substituted by CLEA 2001, s 29.

[244] As amended by (UK) CA 1989, s 63.

[245] (UK) CA 1985, s 447(4), as amended by (UK) CA 1989, s 63.

[246] As amended by CLEA 2001, s 32.

[247] CA 1990, Pt II, is entitled 'Investigations' and includes such provisions as CA 1990, s 19.

[248] CA 1990, s 23(1).

nothing in CA 1990, Pt II will authorise the taking of possession of any document in the possession of any person which contains information that that person would be entitled to refuse to produce on the basis of legal professional privilege.

Section 23(1) provides:

> Nothing in this Part shall compel the disclosure by any person of any information which he would, in the opinion of the court, be entitled to refuse to produce on the grounds of legal professional privilege or authorise the taking of possession of any document containing such information which is in his possession.

The wording of this subsection suggests 'the opinion of the court' may be a prerequisite to invoking this legal professional privilege, which could be anomalous in practice, as it could require the person to disclose the document and then assert the privilege over it before a court. Secondly, it appears that, whether or not the person with possession of a document asserts privilege in respect of it, the taking of possession of privileged information is not authorised. This would have the effect that the officer(s) taking production of books or documents would need to ensure that those books or documents do not include information that is covered by legal professional privilege, as their authority to take production does not extend to books or documents which are covered by such privilege.

(iii) Banking documents

[12.085] According to s 23(2),[249] the DCE cannot exercise his powers under s 19 to require a person engaged in the business of banking, to produce documents regarding the affairs of a customer[250] or of any other person. This exclusion does not apply in two circumstances. First, if it appears to the DCE that it is necessary to require production of the documents in question, in order to investigate the affairs of the person carrying on the business of banking, such production can be required, the terms of CA 1990, s 23(2) notwithstanding. Secondly, if it appears to the DCE that the customer or other person, 'is a person on whom a requirement has been imposed by virtue of that section' the DCE can require production of documents relating to the affairs of such persons.[251]

[12.086] There are some ambiguities in this section that merit attention. First, s 23(2) refers to 'the affairs of any other person'. This expression is very vague and does not relate to the terminology used elsewhere in s 23, or in s 19. Secondly, a bank can be required to produce books or documents of its customers or other person if the DCE is of the opinion that it is necessary to do so for the purposes of investigating the affairs of the bank itself. This is anomalous in light of the fact that banks are not among the entities to which s 19 applies. The DCE cannot therefore direct a bank to produce its own books or documents under s 19(1). The effect of s 23(2) is that a bank can be directed to produce its customers, or a third party's, documents, to further an investigation into the bank's own affairs, even though such an investigation is not

---

[249] As substituted by CLEA 2001, s 32.

[250] For the purposes of this section 'customer' includes, 'a person who has in the past availed of one or more services of the person, as defined in s 149(12) of the Consumer Credit Act, 1995', CA 1990, s 23(4), as inserted by CLEA 2001, s 32.

[251] CA 1990, s 23(2), as substituted by CLEA 2001, s 32(a).

envisaged by s 19, the provision to which s 23 is supposedly an exception. This appears to circumvent the limitation in s 19(1) of the entities to which it applies. Whereas the DCE does not have the power to direct a bank to produce its books or documents, by means of the exception created in s 23, the books or customers or other persons can be required as a means of investigating the bank's affairs.

A further point to note regarding s 23(2), is that it permits the DCE to require the production of documents relating to a bank's customer or 'other person' if that customer or 'other person' are persons who have been required to produce documents under s 19. The terminology used in this regard is vague. It refers to whether or not 'a requirement' has been imposed under s 19. This could encompass any of the situations in which requirements can be imposed under s 19, ranging from the requirement that a company produce documents itself, to the requirement of a third party to produce documents, to the requirement of a former employee of a company to provide an explanation regarding books or documents. Under this interpretation of s 23(2), the fact that a former employee of a company was required to provide an explanation under s 19(5)(a)(ii) of that company's documents, may justify the DCE requiring a bank of which that person was not even a customer, to produce documents relating to that person's affairs.

[12.087] On a broader note, s 23(2) has the effect of placing a bank in the same position as any other third party which may be required to produce documents under s 19(3). This is consistent with the decision in *Glackin v Trustee Savings Bank*[252] in which Costello J held that banks could not refuse to give information sought by inspectors appointed under the Companies Acts on the basis that disclosure of that information would breach the relationship of confidentiality between a bank and its customer. The object of s 23(2), however, seems to have been to provide some protection of bank-client confidentiality. The cumulative effect of the provision is to undermine any such protection.

(l) Compel compliance

[12.088] When there is a default by a company in complying with a requirement of the Companies Acts, and, following the service of a notice requiring the rectification of this default, the company continues to be in default, an application may be made to court to compel compliance.[253] The persons who may make such an application under CA 1963, s 371, are the DCE, the Registrar of Companies, a member or creditor of the company. This provision may be employed in the case of a failure by a company to produce books and documents as required by s 19.

Section 371A provides further for such an application to be made to compel compliance with a direction made under s 19(3)(b):

> If a person having made default in complying with a requirement made of him under s 19(3)(b) of the Companies Act 1990 fails to make good the default within

---

[252] *Glackin v Trustee Savings Bank* [1993] 3 IR 55. This approach can be contrasted with that adopted in cases such as *Tournier v National Provincial and Union Bank of England* [1924] 1 KB 461, which protect the confidentiality of the bank-client relationship.

[253] CA 1963, s 371, as amended by CLEA 2001, s 96 and IFCMPA 2005, s 64. See further Ch **11**.

14 days after the service of a notice on him requiring him to do so, the court may, on an application made to the court by the Director, make an order directing the person to make good the default within such time as may be specified in the order.[254]

This is confined to a direction to require production of documents by 'any person who appears to the DCE to be in possession' of books or documents 'which may relate' to the books and documents of a body of which the DCE has power to direct the production pursuant to s 19(1).[255]

There are some aspects of s 371A which may be noted. First, s 19(3)(b) is not confined to a company or its officers, and would not come within the scope of s 371. This explains why s 371A was considered necessary. The reference to 'person' in place of the reference to 'a company or any officer of a company' in s 371, demonstrates the intended breadth of s 371A.

Second, it is not clear why s 371A is confined to s 19(3)(b): s 19(3)(b) refers to only one of three grounds on which the DCE may require a third party to produce books and documents.[256] It appears that, if the DCE requires a third party, not being a company or its officer, to produce books and documents on one of the other grounds listed in s 19(3), there is no means of compelling compliance with that requirement.

Third, s 371 was amended by IFCMPA 2005, to enlarge the time for compliance that may be specified in the default notice. Section 371A continues to provide that the notice may only permit 14 days for the default to be rectified. As a direction to produce books and documents may be extensive in its scope and the logistics of gathering documents, taking legal advice, assessing such issues as privilege, may be time-consuming, the prescribed 14 day time limit could prove insufficient. The rationale, if there is one, for extending this time period in s 371, but not in s 371A is not clear.

(m) Use of statements in legal proceedings

[12.089] CA 1990, s 19(7), as substituted by CLEA 2001, s 29, provides as follows:

> A statement made or an explanation provided by an individual in compliance with a requirement imposed by virtue of this section may be used in evidence against him in any proceedings whatsoever (save proceedings for an offence (other than an offence under sub-s (6) or (8)).

The constitutionality of the predecessor to this provision was considered and adjudicated upon by Kearns J in *Dunnes Stores Ireland Company Limited v Ryan*.[257] Section 19(6), (as the pre-CLEA 2001 equivalent was numbered) did not limit the use of statements made to civil proceedings. It merely provided that, 'A statement made by a person in compliance with a requirement imposed by virtue of this section may be used

---

[254] CA 1963, s 371A, as inserted by CLEA 2001, s 97.

[255] CA 1990, s 19(3)(b), as substituted by CLEA 2001, s 29. See further para **[12.067]**.

[256] CA 1990, s 19(3), as substituted by CLEA 2001, s 29. See further above paras **[12.064]** to **[12.067]**.

[257] *Dunnes Stores Ireland Co Ltd v Ryan* [2002] 2 IR 60. The question of the constitutionality of CA 1990, s 19 was remitted by the Supreme Court to the High Court for consideration.

in evidence against him'. The constitutionality of this provision was struck down on that basis. In the course of his judgment, Kearns J considered the issue of self-incrimination in some detail. In particular, the fact that a refusal to provide an explanation or make a statement constitutes an offence, combined with the fact that any statements made could be used as evidence in subsequent criminal proceedings, was held to render s 19(6) unconstitutional:

> 'The interviewee under s 19 has no ... scope for dissent. Either he answers or he does not. If he does not answer, all the elements of the offence exist ... Can it be said that there is any scope for 'voluntariness' with regard to the answering of questions in this framework? In my view there is not. A refusal seems to me to be akin to a refusal to provide a blood or urine sample when required so to do by a properly designated medical officer in the context of a drink driving offence. Furthermore, the fact that any answer given may be used in later proceedings can only constitute a further pressure on the interviewee to keep silent, so that his only "choice" is between a conviction on refusal, and self-incrimination in the context of a later prosecution on making answer.'[258]

The amendment that was introduced to s 19(6) by the CLEA 2001, s 29 undeniably counters many of the flaws that formerly existed in s 19(6). However, the use of evidence obtained through compulsion in prosecutions taken for offences under s 19 may remain open to challenge.

[12.090] The use of information obtained by virtue of the exercise of the powers conferred by s 447, the equivalent provision of the Companies Act 1985 in the United Kingdom, was considered in *Re Rex Williams Leisure*.[259] An affidavit was sworn by an officer of the Department of Trade and Industry for the purpose of use in disqualification proceedings.[260] The affidavit relied on interviews conducted pursuant to s 447. The directors claimed that this was not admissible, as it was hearsay evidence, and that information gathered pursuant to (UK) CA 1985, s 447 should be distinguished from a report of an inspector duly appointed under the Companies Acts. These submissions were rejected by Sir Donald Nicholls V-C. He concluded that 'similar

---

[258] *Dunnes Stores Ireland Co Ltd v Ryan* [2002] 2 IR 60 at 122.

[259] *Re Rex Williams Leisure* [1994] Ch 1, [1993] 2 All ER 741, [1993] 3 WLR 685, [1993] BCLC 568.

[260] A distinction that should be noted in this regard is that the (UK) Company Directors Disqualification Act 1986, s 8(1) reads: 'If it appears to the Secretary of State from a report made by inspectors under s 437 of the Companies Act or s 94 or 177 of the Financial Services Act 1986, or from information or documents obtained under s 447 or 448 of the Companies Act or s 105 of the Financial Services Act 1986 or s 2 of the Criminal Justice Act 1987 or s 52 of the Criminal Justice (Scotland) Act 1987 or s 83 of the Companies Act 1989, that it is expedient in the public interest that a disqualification order should be made against any person who is or has been a director or shadow director of any company, he may apply to the court for such an order to be made against that person'. This clearly envisages expressly that information obtained pursuant to s 447 may be used in support of an application for a disqualification order, a point that may enable it to be distinguished from similar situations arising under the Irish Companies Acts.

consequences' should flow from information obtained by an inspector and information obtained pursuant to s 447:[261]

> 'I appreciate that a s 447 direction leads to a less formal and less elaborate investigation than the appointment of inspectors under s 431. But under both sections the information is being sought and provided pursuant to statutory powers and obligations. The differences in the two procedures do not dictate that, in the one case the court can take into account the information obtained and in the other case it cannot. Rather, in both cases the evidence is admissible but the court should take the differences into account when deciding, having regard to all the evidence and all the circumstances of the particular proceedings, how much importance or weight should be attached to the information in question. The court is well able to do this. The court will have due regard to the source and nature of the information and also the circumstances in which it was provided. The court will be astute to see that a company or a defendant is not prejudiced by the hearsay nature of the information. If the defendant's evidence raises an issue which needs to be tried, the court will take appropriate steps to ensure that the issue is justly and fairly resolved.'[262]

An interesting aspect of the submissions made concerned the construction of s 447(8) which provides, 'A statement made by a person in compliance with such a requirement [under s 447] may be used in evidence against him'. The directors contended that, while this permitted a statement made by a particular person in compliance with a requirement to provide an explanation of a document to be used in evidence against him, it does not permit statements made by other persons in compliance with such requirements to be used in evidence in that manner. This contention was similarly rejected.

[12.091] It may now be open to parties who are the subject of directions to provide explanations or statements under s 19 to invoke the European Convention of Human Rights, in light of its incorporation into Irish law by virtue of the European Convention of Human Rights Act 2003. Article 6 protects the right to a fair trial and has been held in cases such as *Funke v France*[263] to embody protection of the right to silence. In that case, the applicant was convicted and fined for failing to produce bank statements relevant to the investigation into customs offences that were suspected to have been committed by him. The European Court of Human Rights determined that the attempt to compel the applicant to provide evidence of offences he had allegedly committed violated art 6 and amounted to an unjustified infringement of the right of persons charged with a criminal offence to remain silent and not to incriminate themselves.

[12.092] However, in a case which appears to be of more direct relevance to s 19, *Fayed v United Kingdom*,[264] the Court of Human Rights considered an investigation carried out under the Companies Act 1985 in which the applicants challenged the exercise of the power to compel them to answer questions. The Court held that the powers of

---

[261] This decision was affirmed by the judgment of the Court of Appeal in *Secretary of State for Trade and Industry v Ashcroft* [1998] Ch 71, [1997] 3 WLR 319, [1997] 3 All ER 86.

[262] *Re Rex Williams Leisure* [1994] Ch 1, 13, [1993] 2 All ER 741, [1993] 3 WLR 685, 695, [1993] BCLC 568.

[263] *Funke v France* Series A, No 256-A: 16 EHRR 297.

[264] *Fayed v United Kingdom* Series A, No 294-B; 18 EHRR 393.

compulsion were not of themselves an issue under art 6, on the basis that the functions of the inspectors being essentially investigative in nature and did not involve an adjudication in full or substance. The function of the inspectors was to ascertain and record facts that might subsequently be used as the basis for action by the competent authorities. The Court concluded that imposing judicial procedures on such a preparatory investigation would unduly hamper the effective regulation in the public interest of complex financial and commercial activities.

While the compulsion itself was held not to be contrary to art 6, it is accepted that the use of answers obtained through such compulsion as part of a prosecution case would be a violation of art 6. In *Saunders v United Kingdom*,[265] the Court of Human Rights found that the use of answers given by an applicant in the course of an interview with inspectors in a manner which incriminated him, would violate the right to fair procedures and contravene art 6 of the Convention.

(n) Offences

(i) Failure to comply

[12.093] CA 1990, s 19(6) makes it an offence for any body or person to fail to comply with a requirement issued under s 19, to produce books or documents or to provide an explanation or statement regarding such books or documents:

> If a requirement to produce books or documents or provide an explanation or make a statement which is imposed by virtue of this section is not complied with, the body or other person on whom the requirement was so imposed shall be guilty of an offence ...[266]

The obligation to produce books or documents under s 19(1) only applies to the bodies listed in that subsection, and does not extend to any 'persons'. Similarly, the grounds specified in s 19(2) for directing the production of books or documents all refer to a 'body', as that term is used in s 19(1). The only requirements imposed by s 19 that refer to 'a person' relate to production of books or documents by third parties[267] and the furnishing of explanations or statements regarding books or documents.[268]

[12.094] While there is no explicit provision in s 19 for the imposition of criminal liability on the officers of a company in default under s 19(1), CA 1990, s 241 fills this gap. Section 241 provides:

> (1) Where an offence under s 19, 21, 79 or 242 which is committed by a body to which any such section applies is proved to have been committed with the consent or connivance of or to be attributable to any neglect on the part of any person being a director, manager, secretary or other officer of the body, or any person who was purporting to act in any such capacity, that person shall also be guilty of an offence under that section.

---

[265] Reports 1996 – 62044; (1996) 23 EHRR 313

[266] CA 1990, s 19(6), as substituted by CLEA 2001, s 29.

[267] CA 1990, s 19(3), as substituted by CLEA 2001, s 29. See above paras **[12.064]** to **[12.067]**.

[268] CA 1990, s 19(5)(a)(ii), (b), as substituted by CLEA 2001, s 29. See above paras **[12.076]** and **[12.080]** to **[12.081]**.

(2) Where the affairs of a body are managed by its members, sub-s (1) shall apply in relation to the acts and defaults of a member in connection with his functions of management as if he were a director or manager of the body.[269]

If an offence by a company under s 19 is proven to have been done with the consent or connivance, or due to the neglect, of a director, manager, secretary or other officer of the company (or member or other person purporting to act in that capacity), that person is also guilty of an offence under s 19.

There is a defence available to persons who are charged with an offence of failure to comply. According to s 19(6):

'... where a person is charged with an offence under this subsection in respect of a requirement to produce any books or documents, it shall be a defence to prove that they were not in his possession or under his control and that it was not reasonably practicable for him to comply with the requirement.'

[12.095] There are a number of points that can be made in respect of this defence. First, the defence only applies to 'a person' charged with an offence under s 19(6). Section 19(6) makes it an offence for 'a body' as well as 'a person' to fail to comply with a requirement to produce books or documents. However, it appears from the wording of s 19(6) that there is no defence available to such a body, where, for instance, the books or documents of which production are required are not in the possession of or under the control of that body.

Secondly, this defence only applies to the offence of failing to produce books or documents and does not apply to the offence of failing to provide an explanation or make a statement, which can also give rise to charges under s 19(6). This arises from the fact that the obligations to provide an explanation or make a statement are qualified. Section 19(5)(a)(ii) provides that a person is only obliged to provide explanations of books or documents 'insofar as the person may be reasonably able to do so'. Similarly, pursuant to s 19(5)(b), a person can only be required to state the whereabouts of books or documents that have not been produced 'to the best of his knowledge and belief'.

Thirdly, the defence in s 19(6) arises where there is proof that the books or documents which a person is required to produce 'were not in his possession or under his control and that it was not reasonably practicable for him to comply with the requirement'. The use of the word 'and' indicates that this is a cumulative requirement and that a person seeking to rely on that defence must establish both limbs of the defence to avoid liability. This raises a question regarding the scope of what it is 'reasonably practicable' to expect of a person who is the subject of a direction to produce books or documents. If the person has neither possession of nor control over the books and documents in question, it is difficult to see what more is required to establish that it is not 'reasonably practicable' to require that person to produce those books or documents.

[12.096] A further query that may be raised in respect of s 19(6) is the logic of providing a defence of non-possession of books or documents, where such possession appears to be a pre-requisite to the power to require that person to produce such books or documents. This can be illustrated as follows: the only persons, other than the company, that can be required to produce books or documents under s 19, are third parties who

---

[269] CA 1990, s 241.

appear to be in possession of books or documents.[270] The obligation and the defence become somewhat circular, as third parties should only be required to produce books or documents of which they appear to have possession,[271] yet if they are directed to produce books and documents and fail to do so, they can then raise the defence of not having possession. If that person does not have possession or control of the books or documents sought, it seems arbitrary that they can only raise this fact as a defence to a charge under s 19(6). It would be more logical to limit the direction to produce books or documents to apply only to such books or documents as are in the possession or under the control of such third parties. This is the approach that has been adopted in respect of a requirement to provide an explanation or statement in respect of books or documents. As has been seen, a person is only required to provide explanations of books or documents 'insofar as the person may be reasonably able so to do'.[272] A person is only required to state where books or documents are 'to the best of his knowledge and belief'.[273]

(ii) False or misleading

[12.097] Section 19(8) provides that it shall be an offence to knowingly provide an false or misleading explanation or statement, if required to furnish such an explanation or statement under s 19. The offence arises where, 'a person ... provides an explanation or makes a statement required under this section which is false or misleading in a material respect, knowing it to be so false or misleading ...'.[274]

There are certain defences that are open to a person charged with this offence. First, they can challenge the materiality of the false or misleading aspect of the explanation or statement provided. Secondly, a person could deny knowledge of the false or misleading nature of the explanation or statement.

(iii) Interference

[12.098] Section 19(9) creates an offence where a person or body with notice of a direction to produce books or documents under s 19(1), interferes with the integrity of such books or documents. Under s 19(9), it is an offence to 'destroy, mutilate, falsify or conceal any book or document the subject of a direction'. This offence clearly only relates to directions which have already been issued.

This provision has been strengthened considerably by the addition of s 19A.[275] That provision renders it an offence for a person who knows or suspects that an investigation under the Companies Acts is pending or likely, to interfere with, or permit the

---

[270] CA 1990, s 19(3), as substituted by CLEA 2001, s 29. See above paras **[12.064]** to **[12.067]**.

[271] For further discussion on this point, see further above paras **[12.068]** to **[12.070]**.

[272] CA 1990, s 19(5)(a)(ii), as substituted by CLEA 2001, s 29. See above para **[12.078]**.

[273] CA 1990, s 19(5)(b), as substituted by CLEA 2001, s 29. See above para **[12.080]**.

[274] CA 1990, s 19(8), as substituted by CLEA 2001, s 29.

[275] Inserted by CLEA 2001, s 29. This provision is substantially reproduced in the CLRG, General Scheme of the Draft Companies Consolidation and Reform Bill 2007, Pt A13, Head 17. Available at www.clrg.org.

interference with, any books or documents which would be relevant to such investigation.

Section 19A(1) is broadly formulated:

> A person who—
>
> (a) knows or suspects that an investigation by the Director into an offence under the Companies Acts is being or is likely to be carried out, and
>
> (b) falsifies, conceals, destroys or otherwise disposes of a document or record which he knows or suspects is or would be relevant to the investigation or causes or permits its falsification, concealment, destruction or disposal,
>
> shall be guilty of an offence.[276]

A further aspect of s 19A that is drafted expansively, relates to the burden of proof. In respect of the other offences created by s 19, the burden of proof is on the prosecuting authority. However, where there has been falsification, concealment, destruction or disposal of books or documents of a company, certain presumptions may arise that place the onus on the person charged with such an offence to show that they did not know or suspect that an investigation was underway or pending and that they did not know that the books or documents in question would be relevant to such investigation. Section 19(A)(2) accordingly provides:

> Where a person—
>
> (a) falsifies, conceals, destroys or otherwise disposes of a document or record, or
>
> (b) causes or permits its falsification, concealment, destruction or disposal,
>
> in such circumstances that it is reasonable to conclude that the person knew or suspected—
>
> (i) that an investigation by the Director into an offence under the Companies Acts was being or was likely to be carried out, and
>
> (ii) that the document or record was or would be relevant to the investigation,
>
> the person shall be taken for the purposes of this section to have so known or suspected, unless the court or the jury, as the case may be, is satisfied having regard to all the evidence that there is reasonable doubt as to whether the person so knew or suspected.[277]

(o) Expenses

[12.099] Where the DCE, or a designated officer of the DCE, issues a direction to a company to produce specified books or documents, the DCE can make an application to court to make this company liable to repay the DCE the expenses 'of and incidental to'

---

[276] CA 1990, s 19A(1), as inserted by CLEA 2001, s 29.

[277] CA 1990, s 19A(2), as inserted by CLEA 2001, s 29.

the examination.[278] The court can direct to the extent to which the company will be liable to repay the DCE.

This obligation to make repayment of all or part of the DCE's expenses also extends to persons who, as a result of directions issued under s 19(1), fall into one of the following categories:

     (a)   was convicted on indictment of an offence;

     (b)   was ordered to pay damages or to restore any property in proceedings brought; or

     (c)   was awarded damages or had property restored in proceedings brought.[279]

A person who was awarded damages or to whom property was restored, within the meaning of s 19(11)(c), can not be ordered to repay more than one-tenth of the amount of the damages awarded or of the value of the property restored.[280] Furthermore, any order requiring that person to repay expenses to the DCE shall not be executed until they have received the damages or the property in question has been restored.[281]

It is interesting to note that this provision relates only to directions issued under s 19(1)[282] and not to directions issued to third parties under s 19(3) or directions issued to persons under s 19(5), both of which can also give rise to the commission of an offence. While the powers conferred by s 19(3) and (5) are part of the powers conferred on the DCE under s 19, they are distinct from the directions that can be issued under s 19(1).

With regard to the potential for an award of costs in the other direction, such as the reimbursement of expenses incurred by the company in complying with directions issued under s 19, Kearns J held in *Dunnes Stores Ireland Company Limited v Ryan* that:

> 'There is no question of *mala fides* of any sort, which strikes me as the only possible motivation which might give rise to any question of the applicants seeking relief in respect of costs or expenses incurred in complying with the second respondent's requirements.'[283]

According to this authority it is only if the DCE or the designated officer exercise the powers conferred by s 19 in bad faith, that the company will have any grounds to apply for the reimbursement of expenses incurred.

---

[278] CA 1990, s 19(10), as substituted by CLEA 2001, s 29.

[279] CA 1990, s 19(11), as substituted by CLEA 2001, s 29.

[280] CA 1990, s 19(12), as substituted by CLEA 2001, s 29.

[281] CA 1990, s 19(12), as substituted by CLEA 2001, s 29.

[282] CA 1990, s 19(1) is expressed as being subject to s 19(2) and does not purport to apply to s 19(3) or (5), a point which is reinforced by the fact that the persons who can be required to give explanations or make statement under s 19(5) are unlikely to fall within any of the categories mentioned in s 19(1).

[283] *Dunnes Stores Ireland Co Ltd v Ryan* [2002] 2 IR 60 at 124.

B. Entry and search of premises

(a) Issue of search warrant

[12.100] CA 1990, s 20[284] provides for the issue of a search warrant for the entry and search of a premises in specified circumstances and pursuant to specified procedures. The search warrant can only be issued by a judge of a District Court. CA 1990, s 20(1), provides:

> If a judge of the District Court is satisfied by information on oath laid by a designated officer that there are reasonable grounds for suspecting that any material information is to be found on any premises (including a dwelling), the judge may issue a search warrant under this section.

The search warrant must authorise a named designated officer 'at any time or times within one month from the date of issue of the warrant',[285] to enter and search the premises, and to exercise such other powers as are conferred by CA 1990, s 20, in conjunction with the issue of a search warrant.

The requirement that the search warrant be issued by a judge of the District Court on the demonstration of certain reasonable grounds, is common to other pieces of legislation that provide for the issue of such warrants.[286] There are certain aspects of the search warrant procedure contained in the CA 1990, however, that can be distinguished from search warrants governed by other legislation, and that require further consideration.

Throughout the following analysis of the procedure for entry and search of premises pursuant to s 20, the provisions of the Constitution must be borne in mind. The protection of the inviolability of the dwelling[287] that is afforded by Article 40.5 is a strong one.[288] Legislation which permits the entry onto and search of, premises must be construed in light of the words of Hamilton P (as he then was) in *Byrne v Grey*:

> 'These powers encroach on the liberty of the citizen and the inviolability of his dwelling as guaranteed by the Constitution and the courts should construe a statute which authorises such encroachment so that it encroaches on such rights no more than the statute allows, expressly or by necessary implication.'[289]

---

[284] As substituted by CLEA 2001, s 30.

[285] CA 1990, s 20(2), as substituted by CLEA 2001, s 30.

[286] See, eg, Criminal Justice Act 1994, s 64; Criminal Assets Bureau Act 1996, s 14; Criminal Justice (Theft and Fraud Offences) Act 2001, s 48; Broadcasting Act 1990, s 14; Copyright Act 1963, s 27; Video Recordings Act 1989, s 25; Gaming and Lotteries Act 1956, s 39.

[287] 'Dwelling' has been interpreted broadly, to include places of business.

[288] Article 40.5 provides, 'The dwelling of every citizen is inviolable and shall not be forcibly entered save in accordance with law'. See also art 8, European Convention of Human Rights, which was incorporated into Irish law by the European Convention of Human Rights Act 2003. According to decisions such as *Niemietz v Germany* (1993) 16 EHRR 97, the protection afforded by art 8 can extend to places of business.

[289] *Byrne v Grey* [1988] IR 31 at 38.

(b) Application for search warrant

[12.101] An application for a search warrant under s 20(1) is governed by O 34, r 7 of the District Court Rules, as amended by the District Court (Company Law Enforcement) Rules 2002. The following procedural rules are applicable to such an application:

- the application for a warrant may be made at any sitting of the District Court for the district in which the premises which it is sought to search are situated;[290]

- the application must be made by information on oath and in writing;[291]

- the application must be in form 34.25, Schedule B;[292]

- the application must be laid by an officer of the ODCE designated for the purposes of s 20;[293]

- the application must be laid under the authority of the DCE;[294]

- a warrant issued to a designated officer on foot of such information shall be in the Form 34.16, Schedule B;[295] and

- a warrant issued under s 20 shall continue in force until the end of a one month period from the date on which it is issued.[296]

[12.102] On Form 34.15 the designated officer must state, on oath, that he is an officer designated by the DCE for the purposes of s 20 and is duly authorised by the DCE to make the application. He must also state on oath that he believes there are reasonable grounds for suspecting that there is 'material information' within the meaning of s 20 at the specified premises, being a premises located in the relevant court area and district. The application must specify whether the material information referred to is books or documents of which production has been required under CA 1990, ss 14, 15 or 19, and which have been produced, or books or documents or information which the designated officer has 'reasonable grounds for believing may provide evidence of or relating to the commission of an offence under the Companies Acts'.[297] The designated officer must

---

[290] Rules of the District Court, O 34, r 7(1).

[291] Rules of the District Court, O 34, r 7(2) as substituted by District Court (Company Law Enforcement) Rules 2002, reg 3.

[292] Rules of the District Court, O 34, r 7(2) as substituted by District Court (Company Law Enforcement) Rules 2002, reg 3.

[293] Rules of the District Court, O 34, r 7(2) as substituted by District Court (Company Law Enforcement) Rules 2002, reg 3.

[294] Rules of the District Court, O 34, r 7(2) as substituted by District Court (Company Law Enforcement) Rules 2002, reg 3.

[295] Rules of the District Court, O 34, r 7(3) as amended by District Court (Company Law Enforcement) Rules 2002, reg 3.

[296] Rules of the District Court, O 34, r 7(3) as amended by District Court (Company Law Enforcement) Rules 2002, reg 3.

[297] Rules of the District Court, Order 34, Form 34.15, Sch B, as substituted by District Court (Company Law Enforcement) Rules 2002.

also specify the basis for believing that there is material information at the location in question.

[12.103] If a search warrant is issued, it will be in Form 34.16. The warrant must confirm that the court is satisfied that there are reasonable grounds for suspecting that there is material information located at the premises specified in the warrant. The warrant will authorise the named designated officer, to do the following:

> '... accompanied by such other persons as (s)he thinks necessary, at any time or times, within one month from the date hereof, on production if so requested of this warrant, TO ENTER, if necessary by reasonable force and SEARCH the above-mentioned premises in the said court (area and) district (including, without limitation, to operate or cause to be operated any computer), TO REQUIRE any person found on the premises to give his name, home address and occupation and to produce to him/her any material information (including, without limitation information necessary to facilitate access to information held on any computer) in his/her possession, TO SEIZE and retain any material information found on the premises or in the custody or possession of any person found on the premises and TO TAKE ANY OTHER STEPS which appear to him/her to be necessary for preserving or preventing interference with material information.'[298]

(c) Designated officer

[12.104] When an application is being made to a judge of the District Court for a search warrant under CA 1990, s 20, the person who must satisfy the judge of the existence of reasonable grounds for suspecting that material information is to be found at a premises, is referred to as a 'designated officer'. If the search warrant is then issued, it must 'be expressed and operate to authorise a named designated officer ('the officer'), accompanied by such other persons as the officer thinks necessary ...'[299] to enter and search a premises and exercise such other additional powers as are conferred by CA 1990, s 20.

There is no necessary correlation between the designated officer who must satisfy the judge by information on oath of the requisite grounds for issuing a search warrant, and the designated officer who is named in the search warrant as the person authorised to execute the search warrant. However, CA 1990, s 20(7) defines the 'designated officer' as follows: '... the Director [of Corporate Enforcement] or an officer of the Director authorised in that behalf by the Director ...'.

This definition draws no distinction between the 'designated officer' who satisfies the judge of the District Court of the grounds for issuing the search warrant and the 'designated officer' who is named in the search warrant as the person authorised to execute that warrant. The only reasonable conclusion is that the definition of 'designated officer' contained in the provision applies to both categories of 'designated officer'. The DCE, or an officer authorised by him, is therefore the appropriate person to satisfy a judge of the District Court of the existence of grounds for issuing a search warrant under CA 1990, s 20(1). In relation to the execution of the search warrant, CA

---

[298] Rules of the District Court, Order 34, Form 34.16, Sch B, as substituted by District Court (Company Law Enforcement) Rules 2002.

[299] CA 1990, s 20(2), as substituted by CLEA 2001, s 30.

1990, s 20(2) requires that the warrant must be expressed as authorising a 'named designated officer' to exercise such powers as are conferred by the warrant.

This may lead to a certain incongruity, as CA 1990, s 20(2) requires that the search warrant name a designated officer and the term 'designated officer' is subsequently defined in s 20(7) as the DCE or an officer authorised by him. As the search warrant must contain the name of the relevant officer, it appears that the DCE must authorise the officer in question to act on his behalf in executing the warrant before it is issued.

[12.105] A final point to note regarding the 'designated officer' for the purposes of CA 1990, s 20, is that other legislation governing the issue of search warrants typically provides for the evidence on oath grounding the issue of the warrant, to be given by a member of the Garda Síochána and further provides for the warrant to name a member of the Garda Síochána.[300] The fact that the powers associated with a search warrant issued pursuant to CA 1990, s 20 include the power to enter the premises by force[301] may seem to be a good ground to specify a member of the Garda Síochána as the person having authority to execute the warrant. The logic of the DCE being the primary designated officer with authority to execute such a warrant may be questioned, as may the fact that there is no reference in the CA 1990 to any requirement that a member of the Garda Síochána be involved in the execution of a warrant.[302] In practice, however, it appears likely that the officers designated by the DCE for the purpose of s 20 will typically be members or An Garda Síochána.[303]

(d) Grounds

[12.106] CA 1990, s 20(1),[304] requires that a judge of the District Court, before issuing a search warrant, must be 'satisfied by information on oath laid by a designated officer that there are reasonable grounds for suspecting that any material information is to be found on any premises'.

One issue that arises from the wording of CA 1990, s 20(1) is that the only evidential requirement appears to be one of location. The judge must be satisfied that there are grounds for suspecting that certain information is to be found at a certain location, but there is no requirement that the judge be satisfied as to any other circumstances, such as why the location of the information is of any relevance. It is particularly noteworthy that there nothing in s 20 that requires the judge to be satisfied that there are reasonable grounds to believe an offence was committed or that the information in question is related to, or evidence of, the commission of any such offence. The interpretation that

---

[300] See, eg, Criminal Justice Act 1994, s 64; Criminal Assets Bureau Act 1996, s 14; Criminal Justice (Theft and Fraud Offences) Act 2001, s 48; Electronic Commerce Act 2000, s 27.

[301] CA 1990, s 20(2)(a), as substituted by CLEA 2001, s 30.

[302] It should however be noted that in practice, it seems that warrants under CA 1990, s 20, are applied for and, if granted, executed by a member of the Garda Síochána: see *Rogers v Maloney* [2005] IEHC 433, O'Leary J.

[303] See, eg, *Rogers v Maloney* [2005] IEHC 433 (21 December 2005, unreported), HC, O'Leary J. See further para **[12.111]**.

[304] As substituted by CLEA 2001, s 30.

the procedures for issuing a search warrant under CA 1990, s 20 omit any such requirement, is reinforced by the definition of 'material information' in s 20(7), particularly the first limb of that definition, as is addressed below.[305]

[12.107] In *Byrne v Grey*[306] a warrant was issued under the Misuse of Drugs Act 1977 on the basis of a sworn information by a member of an Garda Síochána to the effect that he had reasonable grounds for believing cannabis plants were being cultivated at a particular location. This warrant was challenged on the basis that the reasonable grounds alleged to exist were not presented to the District Court judge who issued the warrant. Hamilton P held '... the District Justice or Peace Commissioner should himself be satisfied by information on oath that facts exist which constitute reasonable grounds for suspecting that an offence has been or is being committed.'[307]

[12.108] The egregiousness of not requiring any grounds to be established regarding the nature of the information sought to be seized is highlighted by the fact that other legislation governing the issue of search warrants typically contains such a requirement.

In relation to the issue of a search warrant to the Criminal Assets Bureau, the Criminal Assets Bureau Act 1996, s 14(1) provides:

> A judge of the District Court, on hearing evidence on oath given by a bureau officer who is a member of the Garda Síochána, may, if he or she is satisfied that there are reasonable grounds for suspecting that evidence of or relating to assets or proceeds deriving from criminal activities, or to their identity or whereabouts, is to be found in any place, issue a warrant for the search of that place and any person found at that place.

The Criminal Justice (Theft and Fraud Offences) Act 2001, s 48(2) similarly provides:

> A judge of the District Court, on hearing evidence on oath given by a member of the Garda Síochána, may, if he or she is satisfied that there are reasonable grounds for suspecting that evidence of, or relating to the commission of, an offence to which this section applies is to be found in any place, issue a warrant for the search of that place and any persons found there.

Each of these provisions requires the judge to be satisfied that there are reasonable grounds for suspecting that evidence of, or relating to, criminal offences, is to be found in the place in respect of which the warrant is sought, before issuing a search warrant. In those instances, it is clear that the judge must be satisfied as to the reasonableness of the grounds for suspecting that the information or material at the premises, is evidence of, or relating, to the relevant offence, as well as being satisfied of the reasonableness of the belief of the location of such evidence. This contrasts sharply with the evidential requirements imposed by CA 1990, s 20 and may bring the constitutionality of the latter provision into question.

---

[305] See below paras **[12.112]** to **[12.117]**.

[306] *Byrne v Grey* [1988] IR 31.

[307] *Byrne v Grey* [1988] IR 31 at 39.

[12.109] The validity of provisions governing the issue of warrants for the search of a premises needs to be scrutinised carefully in the light of the Constitution. As stated by Kinlen J in *Hanahoe v Hussey*:

> 'This Court accepts without question that any such intrusion on the personal rights of a citizen, building, privacy, property and the inviolability of a dwelling-house must therefore be closely scrutinised and expressly justified.'[308]

It is also firmly established that a decision of a District Court judge to issue a search warrant must be shown:

> '(a)　to be *bona fide*.
>
> (b)　factually sustainable.
>
> (c)　to be decided by a decision maker who directed himself or herself correctly in law. '[309]

[12.110] In the United Kingdom, Diplock LJ issued the following caution regarding the issue and execution of search warrants:

> 'The construing court ought, ... to remind itself, if reminder should be necessary, that entering a man's house or office, searching it and seizing his goods against his will are tortious acts against which he is entitled to the protection of the court unless the acts can be justified either at common law or under some statutory authority.'[310]

In the context of s 20 it is particularly important to bear in mind that any suggestion that the District Court judge can rely on the reasonable grounds and belief held by the designated officer, would be contrary to a long line of authority. As noted by Kinlen J in *Hanahoe v Hussey*:

> 'The *People (Director of Public Prosecutions) v Kenny* [1990] 2 IR 110, the *DPP v Gaffney* [1987] IR 173 and *The State (Lynch) v Cooney* [1982] IR 337 are authority for the fact that the District Judge issuing a warrant must himself or herself be satisfied that there are reasonable grounds for the relevant suspicions which entitle the warrant to be issued. The District Judge is not entitled to rely upon a mere averment of a member of An Garda Síochána that the garda has reasonable grounds or suspicion.'[311]

[12.111] In *Rogers v Maloney*[312] the legality of a District Judge's decision to grant a warrant under CA 1990 s 20 was judicially reviewed on several grounds. O'Leary J analysed, among other elements, whether there was sufficient evidence before the court of an alleged offence under s 19(6), which section renders it an offence not to produce documents as required under s 19. The Court found that the combination of written evidence before the Court and the oral testimony of the garda who made the application comprised sufficient evidence for the District Judge, acting within his jurisdiction, to grant the search warrant. While there is little discussion of the necessity of evidence of

---

[308] *Hanahoe v Hussey* [1998] 3 IR 69 at 92.

[309] *State (Lynch) v Cooney* [1982] IR 337, quoted in *Hanahoe v Hussey* [1998] 3 IR 69 at 93.

[310] *R v IRC Ex p Rossminster* [1980] AC 952 at 1008.

[311] *Hanahoe v Hussey* [1998] 3 IR 69 at 94–95.

[312] *Rogers v Maloney* [2005] IEHC 433, O'Leary J.

an offence in this judgment, it seems that it was considered to be an integral element underlying the legality of a District Judge awarding a search warrant under s 20.

In the subsequent, related case of *Re Barnroe Ltd*[313] the evidence collected under the search warrant which was being used in support of an application for the disqualification of the directors under s 160 was challenged as having been collated by an abuse of process. The main submission was that the statutory power given to the DCE under s 20 was to gather evidence for possible criminal prosecutions, and this material could not be then used in the context of a civil application. The Court accepted that an application under s 160 for an order of disqualification constitutes a civil, rather than criminal, procedure. The Court then examined the background to the warrant, which followed the DCE's direction to the company to furnish books and records under s 19. The company failed to comply with the s 19 direction and a search warrant was accordingly issued. The Court held the DCE had made a valid requirement to the company for the books and records which it now relied on for the s 160 application. The judge noted that these documents constituted 'company records' rather than personal property, which had been seized in order to remedy a company default in providing them and that 'no material other than company records are used for the s 160 application'. The records in question were not the property of the respondents. The s 160 application did not expose the company itself to any adverse findings. The Court allowed this evidence to be used in support of the s 160 application.

(e) Material information

[12.112] 'Material information' is defined in CA 1990, s 20(7) as follows:

(a) any books or documents of which production has been required under or by virtue of s 14, 15 or 19 and which has not been produced in compliance with that requirement, or

(b) any books or documents or other things (including a computer) which the officer has reasonable grounds for believing may provide evidence of or relating to the commission of an offence under the Companies Acts.

(i) Books or documents not produced

[12.113] A direction by the DCE for the production of books or documents under s 19 is grounded merely on the opinion of the DCE regarding circumstances that may suggest the existence of one of the grounds listed in CA 1990, s 19(2).[314]

Under CA 1990, s 20, the DCE can obtain a search warrant on the basis that he has reasonable grounds for believing that books or documents he required to be produced under CA 1990, s 19, but which were not so produced, may be found at the premises in question. The DCE (or such officer as he may have authorised) must satisfy the judge of the District Court as to the reasonableness of the grounds for the belief as to the whereabouts of the books or documents. There is no requirement, however, that the DCE (or authorised officer) satisfy the judge of the District Court that the books or documents of which production were sought were evidence of, or related to, the

---

[313] *Re Barnroe Ltd, Director of Corporate Enforcement v Rogers* [2005] IEHC 443, O'Leary J.

[314] See paras [12.039] to [12.042].

commission of any offence.[315] This omission is particularly glaring when one considers that the grounds on which the production of books or documents can be required, range from such circumstances as the possible necessity of appointing an inspector[316] to an opinion that a proposed act of a company would be unfairly prejudicial to some of its members.[317] These grounds fall far short of the type of beliefs that should typically be established to justify the issue of a search warrant.[318] In particular, it is of note that legislation permitting the issue of a search warrant usually requires proof that the warrant is sought in connection with the commission of an offence or some such connection with criminality.[319] The grounds on which the production of books or documents can be required under CA 1990, s 19(2) do not meet that threshold, as those grounds do not necessarily indicate the commission of any offences, whether under the Companies Acts or otherwise.

It may be noted that a failure to produce documents under s 19 is an offence under s 19(6),[320] but it stretches the notion of collecting evidence of the commission of an offence, to say that the books and documents that were not produced under s 19 are evidence of the commission of an offence under s 19(6): the fact that the documents were not produced is sufficient under s 19(6).

[12.114] Furthermore, the scope of the books or documents of which the DCE may require production under CA 1990, s 19(1), is not defined. There is no requirement that the DCE demonstrate a connection between the circumstances giving rise to the direction to produce books or documents and the categories of books or documents sought.[321] When the failure to produce such books or documents gives rise to an application for a search warrant under CA 1990, s 20, the omission of the need to connect the books or documents with the suspected circumstances is not cured and there is no requirement that such a connection be established. This is another contrast with the typical requirements for the issue of a search warrant, whereby the judge of the District Court must be satisfied that there exist reasonable grounds for the belief that there is evidence of, or related to, the commission of an offence, or elements of an offence, at the premises in question.[322]

[12.115] There is a final point regarding the first limb of the definition of 'material information' in CA 1990, s 20(7). This aspect of the definition encompasses any books or documents of which production was required by the DCE pursuant to CA 1990, s 19 and which were not so produced and appears to significantly heighten the importance of

---

[315] See above paras **[12.106]** et seq.

[316] CA 1990, s 19(2)(a), as substituted by CLEA 2001, s 29. See above paras **[12.012]** to **[12.025]**.

[317] CA 1990, s 19(2)(e), as substituted by CLEA 2001, s 29. See above para **[12.032]**.

[318] See above para **[12.108]**.

[319] See above para **[12.108]**.

[320] See paras **[12.093]** to **[12.096]**.

[321] See above paras **[12.052]** to **[12.054]**.

[322] See, eg, Criminal Justice Act 1994, s 64; Criminal Assets Bureau Act 1996, s 14; Criminal Justice (Theft and Fraud Offences) Act 2001, s 48.

such books or documents. Whereas under CA 1990, s 19, there is no express requirement that the books or documents sought be of any particular significance or note, non-production of these books documents elevates them to the status of 'material information' in the context of CA 1990, s 20(7).

(ii) Evidence of offences under the Companies Acts

[12.116] CA 1990, s 20(7),[323] sets out the second category of books or documents that can be categorised as 'material information' for the purposes of issuing a search warrant:

> … books or documents or other things (including a computer) which the officer
> has reasonable grounds for believing may provide evidence of or relating to the
> commission of an offence under the Companies Acts.[324]

The wording of this category is relatively non-controversial, resembling, as it does, the description of the grounds that must be established for the issue of a search warrant that has been adopted in other legislation. What could be controversial, however, as noted above,[325] is the fact that there is nothing in the CA 1990 that requires the designated officer to satisfy the judge of the District Court of the reasonableness of the grounds for believing that the information in question relates to, or provides evidence of, the commission of an offence.

[12.117] It may be argued that the grounds of which the judge of the District Court must be satisfied under CA 1990, s 20(1) before issuing a search warrant, include a requirement that the judge be satisfied that there are reasonable grounds for believing that the books or documents referred to in CA 1990, s 20(7) 'may provide evidence of or relating to the commission of an offence under the Companies Acts', within the meaning of the definition contained in that subsection. This would be a means of filling an obvious evidential gap and overcoming the potential injustice and unconstitutionality of the section. However, such an interpretation is not warranted by the wording of the section. Moreover, the fact that the first category of 'material information', as defined in CA 1990, s 20(7), contains no reference to a requirement that reasonable, or any, grounds, exist for the belief that an offence has been committed, or that a connection exists between such offence and the information in question, undermines any argument that such an evidential requirement is implicit in respect of the second category of 'material information'.[326]

---

[323] As substituted by CLEA 2001, s 30.

[324] This category of information was not a ground for issuing a search warrant under CA 1990, s 20, as it existed before the CLEA 2001.

[325] See above paras **[12.106]** to **[12.108]**.

[326] See, however, *Rogers v Maloney* [2005] IEHC 433 (21 December 2005, unreported), HC, O'Leary J, in which it appears that the District Court is, in practice, required to satisfy itself that there is 'sufficient evidence' of an offence under s 19(6).

(f) Execution of search warrant

[12.118] There are a number of procedural issues that arise in connection with the execution of a search warrant under CA 1990, s 20.

(i) Duration of validity of search warrant

[12.119] The first issue is the length of time for which the search warrant remains valid. Under legislation such as the Criminal Assets Bureau Act 1996 and the Criminal Justice (Theft and Fraud Offences) Act 2001, there is a short period of time from the issue of a search warrant, within which the entry and search of the premises must occur. In the case of the Criminal Assets Bureau Act 1996, this period is one week.[327] Under the Criminal Justice (Theft and Fraud Offences) Act 2001, the period of time allowed is described as seven days.[328] In other legislation, the most common time period for which a warrant remains valid is one week or one month.[329] CA 1990, s 20(2) provides that the designated officer may enter and search the premises named in the warrant 'at any time or times within one month from the date of issue of the warrant'.[330]

[12.120] The usual rule with search warrants is that they are spent as soon as they have been used, even if the time period referred to above has not lapsed.[331] However, CA 1990, s 20 permits the entry and search of the premises pursuant to a search warrant issued under that provision, to occur on more than one occasion, as evidenced by the language '... time or times ...'. There are some other statutes that provide for a search to be carried out more than once pursuant to the same warrant. These include the Misuse of Drugs Act 1977, s 27(2) which permits a warrant to be executed at 'any time or times' within one month from the date of issue. Similarly, the Consumer Credit Act 1995, s 106, the Investment Intermediaries Act 1995, s 75, the Regulation of Information (Services Outside the State for Termination of Pregnancies) Act 1995, s 9, Stock Exchange Act 1995, s 66, Criminal Damage Act 1991, s 13, among others, provide for a warrant to be executed on more than one occasion. It has been observed that this facility seems to be increasingly availed of in legislation governing the issue of search warrants.[332]

[12.121] In the case of s 20, the fact that the power to execute a search warrant endures for an unusually long period, combined with the fact that it can be exercised repeatedly, may expose that section to a challenge under the Constitution. An argument that may be

---

[327] Criminal Assets Bureau Act 1996, s 14(4).

[328] Criminal Justice (Theft and Fraud Offences) Act 2001, s 48(3)(a).

[329] Walsh, *Criminal Procedure* (Round Hall, 2002), p 414.

[330] CA 1990, s 20(2) (as it existed before the CLEA 2001) similarly provided, 'Every warrant issued under this section shall continue in force until the end of the period of one month after the date on which it is issued'.

[331] Walsh, *Criminal Procedure* (Round Hall, 2002), p 414.

[332] Walsh, *Criminal Procedure* (Round Hall, 2002), p 415.

particularly relevant in this context is that the provision is not proportionate to the objective it seeks to attain. The decision in *Heaney v Ireland* is instructive in this regard:

'In considering whether a restriction on the exercise of rights is permitted by the Constitution, the courts in this country and elsewhere have found it helpful to apply the test of proportionality, a test which contains the notions of minimal restraint on the exercise of protected rights, and of the exigencies of the common good in a democratic society. This is a test frequently adopted by the European Court of Human Rights (see, for example, *Times Newspapers Ltd v United Kingdom* (1979) 2 EHRR 245) and has recently been formulated by the Supreme Court in Canada in the following terms. The objective of the impugned provision must be of sufficient importance to warrant overriding a constitutionally protected right. It must relate to concerns pressing and substantial in a free and democratic society. The means chosen must pass a proportionality test. They must:

(a) be rationally connected to the objective and not be arbitrary, unfair or based on irrational considerations;

(b) impair the right as little as possible; and

(c) be such that their effects on rights are proportional to the objective; see *Chaulk v R* [1990] 3 SCR 1303, at pp 1335 and 1336.'[333]

(ii) Premises

[12.122] A second issue regarding the search warrant procedure of CA 1990, s 20 is that there is nothing in that section that requires expressly that the premises named in the search warrant must be the premises at which it has been established that the material information is to be found. Section 20(1) requires that it be shown to the satisfaction of the judge of the District Court that there are reasonable grounds for suspecting that material information is to be found at 'any premises (including a dwelling)'. When this threshold has been met, the judge may issue a search warrant 'under this section'.[334] Among the powers conferred by such a warrant is the power to 'enter the premises named in the warrant'.[335] There is no cross-reference in the section between the premises at which it has been shown information may be found and the premises named in the warrant. In other enactments, by contrast, the search warrant that may be issued by a judge of the District Court is described as a warrant for the search of the place at which it has been shown, to the satisfaction of the judge, that there are reasonable grounds for suspecting evidence may be found.[336] Under the CA 1990, s 20, as it existed before the enactment of the CLEA 2001, the premises to which the search warrant related, was described as 'the premises specified in the information'.[337] As a matter of logic, it must be assumed that the premises named in the warrant must be the same as the premises at which the information is believed to be located. The manner in which CA 1990, s 20 has

---

[333] *Heaney v Ireland* [1994] 3 IR 593 at 607 (*per* Costello J).

[334] CA 1990, s 20(1), as substituted by CLEA 2001, s 30.

[335] CA 1990, s 20(2)(a), as substituted by CLEA 2001, s 30.

[336] See, eg, the Criminal Assets Bureau Act 1996, s 14(1), Criminal Justice (Theft and Fraud Offences) Act 2001, s 48(2).

[337] CA 1990, s 20(1) (before the enactment of CLEA 2001).

been drafted leaves open the possibility of other interpretations and resultant ambiguity, however.

[12.123] In *Rogers v Maloney*[338] the validity of a warrant was challenged as it did not specify which buildings on a site known as 4, 4A and 4C Kiltalawn Cottages, which included a private dwelling, was the premises at which documents relating to the company were located and the warrant referred to the entire premises known as 4 Kiltalawn Cottages. This was because there was no apparent division between the three premises in question and no notice indicating which was the registered office of the company. O'Leary J held that naming the three related premises was acceptable in these circumstances, commenting that 'insofar as this contained a dwelling this dwelling could also have been the registered office and there was no reason to exclude that portion of the site. In fact the discovery of documents, relating to the company, in all parts of the site search is in itself a vindication of the view that the site was properly considered as an entity.' The latter aspect of this decision suggests that the 'ends justify the means', which is not an approach to be welcomed in the issue of search warrants. The difficulty faced by the designated officer in identifying the relevant portion of the property would appear to be a more sound and reasonable basis for upholding the validity of the search warrant, particularly as this difficulty had been expressly brought to the District Court's attention at the time of the application for the warrant. The decision of the High Court in *Rogers v Maloney*[339] does, nonetheless, demonstrate a broad interpretation of the term 'any premises', an interpretation which may dilute the need for the designated officer to specify particular premises in the application for a search warrant under s 20, if he can attest to his belief that the information required is at one of several premises.

(iii) Use of force

[12.124] Where a warrant has been issued under CA 1990, s 20(1), this authorises the named designated officer to enter the premises named in the warrant 'if necessary by force',[340] among other powers. The right to use force in the execution of a search warrant is not novel. What is unusual about this provision is that the right to use force to enter a premises is not confined to the use of reasonable force. Other enactments governing search warrants typically permit the use of force, if necessary, to enter a premises but limit this power expressly to the use of reasonable force. Section 20(1), as it existed before the enactment of CLEA 2001, for example, stipulated that the member of the Garda Síochána executing a search warrant under that section was authorised to enter the premises 'using such force as is reasonably necessary for the purpose'.[341] There is no readily apparent reason or explanation for the omission of such a reasonableness requirement from CA 1990, s 20, as substituted by CLEA 2001, s 30 and the constitutional considerations already mentioned will apply in this regard.

---

[338] *Rogers v Maloney* [2005] IEHC 433, O'Leary J.

[339] *Rogers v Maloney* [2005] IEHC 433, O'Leary J.

[340] CA 1990, s 20(2)(a), as substituted by CLEA 2001, s 30.

[341] CA 1990, s 20(1) (before the enactment of CLEA 2001).

(iv) Material information

[12.125] The weaknesses of the definition of 'material information' that was adopted in CA 1990, s 20(7) have already been examined from the perspective of the issue of a search warrant.[342] The term 'material information' is also used to define the scope of the material that the designated officer is authorised to seize and retain in the execution of a search warrant. According to CA 1990, s 20(e), a designated officer is moreover entitled to 'take any steps which appear to the officer to be necessary for preserving or preventing interference with material information'.

Many of the frailties of the definition of 'material information' in s 20(7) that were described in connection with the issue of a search warrant apply with equal force in the context of the execution of the search warrant. This is reinforced by the fact that other enactments that describe the powers to seize, retain and preserve material during a search, typically limit such powers to such material as '... the member reasonably believes to be evidence of or relating to the commission of an offence'.[343]

One particular ambiguity in relation to the execution of a search warrant under s 20, is whether computers and other such equipment may be seized. In *Rogers v Maloney*,[344] the applicants argued that the warrant issued under s 20 did not permit the seizure of a computer or other equipment. Among other reliefs, the applicant sought a declaration that:

> '... the servants or agents of the third named respondent were not authorised by the search warrant dated the 10th day of June, 2004, or by the Company Law Enforcement Act 2001, to remove any computer hardware, lap tops, computer software, CCTV, tapes, or electronic equipment from the premises named on the said warrant.'

O'Leary J held that the face of the warrant permitted such equipment to be seized, as it referred to 'other things' in addition to books and documents. With regard to the argument that s 19 does not permit the seizing of equipment, the Court noted that the applicants were 'on firmer ground'. The Court did not determine this question, as it was considered to be moot, but made the following observation:

> 'The Act of 1990 permits the seizing of material information and the taking of other steps which appear to be necessary for preserving or preventing the interference with material information. The exact status of the machines seized and whether they fell within the definition of the Act of 1990 is a matter for plenary hearing in the event of it being relevant.'

Whether a warrant issued under s 20 can authorise the seizing of computers and other such equipment is a question yet to be definitively determined. In light of the terms of s 20(4), however, it is thought most likely that a designated officer may operate

---

[342] See above paras **[12.106]** and **[12.112]** to **[12.117]**.

[343] Criminal Justice (Theft and Fraud Offences) Act 2001, s 48(3)(c).

[344] *Rogers v Maloney* [2005] IEHC 433, O'Leary J.

computers at the location of the search and discharge the other powers in relation to computers that are listed in s 20(4), but not seize such equipment.[345]

(v) Persons at premises

[12.126] A search warrant issued pursuant to CA 1990, s 20(1) confers the power to enter and search a premises, among other powers, which are addressed in more detail below.[346] Unlike other legislation governing the issue of search warrants, s 20 does not permit the search of persons at the premises in question. It does, however, confer certain powers to question such persons and to require them to produce documents. It also permits the seizure of material information found in the custody or possession of any person who is on the premises under search.[347] How such information may be found, without having been produced by the person in question under s 20(2)(c)(ii) and without any power of search under s 20, is not at all clear.

Section 20(2) authorises the designated officer named in the search warrant to:

> (c) require any person found on the premises—
>
> > (i)   to give to the officer his name, home address and occupation, and
> >
> > (ii)   to produce to the officer any material information which is in the custody or possession of that person,
>
> (d) seize and retain any material information found ... in the custody or possession of any person found on the premises.

(vi) Retention of information

[12.127] There is no time limit in the Companies Acts for the retention of material information seized during a search by a designated officer. As originally enacted, CA 1990, s 20(3), permitted books or documents of which possession was taken under that section, to be retained for a period of three months, with no possibility of an extension of that period by the District Court. CLEA 2001, s 30 substituted a new s 20(3) into CA 1990, which provided:

> Any material information which is seized under sub-s (2) may be retained for a period of six months, or such longer period as may be permitted by a judge of the District Court, or if within that period there are commenced any proceedings to which the material information is relevant, until the conclusion of those proceedings.

---

[345] CA 1990, s 20(4), as substituted by CLEA 2001, s 30, permits a designated officer to operate, or cause to be operated, including by means of obtaining passwords, a computer at the location of a search. See further para **[12.128]**.

[346] See below para **[12.128]**.

[347] CA 1990, s 20(2)(d), as substituted by CLEA 2001, s 30.

The ODCE apparently experienced practical difficulties with the operation of this provision, including the need for regular court applications and the risk of missing renewal dates through administrative oversights.[348] Section 20(3) was therefore repealed by IFCMPA 2005:[349] there is now no limit to the period of time for which information seized under s 20 may be retained.

(vii) Computers

[12.128] Section 20 confers quite specific powers on a designated officer who is authorised to execute a search warrant under that section, regarding access to information that is stored on computers. The term 'computer' is used in broad sense for the purposes of CA 199, s 20. A 'computer' is defined as including 'a personal organiser or any other electronic means of information storage or retrieval'.[350] The expression 'a computer at the place which is being searched' includes any other computer, whether at that place or at any other place, which is lawfully accessible by means of that computer'.[351]

A designated officer is authorised by a search warrant issued under s 20(1) to do the following in respect of a computer at the place which is being searched (which will include any computer which is lawfully accessible by means of that computer, in accordance with the definition quoted above):

- operate the computer;[352]

---

[348] See Seanad Éireann (Vol 180, 26 April 2005): Investment Funds, Companies and Miscellaneous Provisions Bill 2005: Committee and Remaining Stages (Mr M Ahern stated 'The Office of the Director of Corporate Enforcement has had considerable difficulties with the operation of s 20(3) of the Companies Act 1990, as inserted by s 30 of the Companies Act 2001. The position under all criminal justice legislation, other than for the ODCE and the Competition Authority, is that material seized on foot of a search warrant is retained until the conclusion of the relevant proceedings. There is no valid reason for the exception that currently pertains to the ODCE and the Competition Authority. The ODCE is currently applying to the District Court on a weekly basis to renew warrants, with all of the associated arrangements, such as preparing court documents, alerting the other parties, briefing counsel, attending court and so on. It is a disruption to genuine investigative work, halts the progress of the investigation and is completely unwarranted. It also gives rise to an increased threat of successful legal action by companies and others under investigation. Not only does the ODCE have to defend the validity of the original warrant, it has to secure each retention application, as well as defending the validity of the resultant retention decisions in the subsequent criminal proceedings. The ODCE is also exposed to the risk of missing a renewal application date through an administrative oversight. The burden of criminal proof is already very high and s 20(3), as it stands, is adding to the difficulties of the ODCE. This amendment provides for the repeal of s 20(3).')

[349] Repealed by IFCMPA 2005, s 68.

[350] CA 1990, s 20(7), as substituted by CLEA 2001, s 30.

[351] CA 1990, s 20(7), as substituted by CLEA 2001, s 30. This definition mirrors the Criminal Justice (Theft and Fraud Offences) Act 2001, s 48(8).

[352] CA 1990, s 20(4)(a), as substituted by CLEA 2001, s 30.

- cause the computer to be operated by a person accompanying the officer;[353]

- require any person at the premises who appears to the officer to be in a position to facilitate access to the information in the computer, or another computer which can be accessed by use of that computer, to give the officer any password necessary to operate it;[354]

- require such a person to otherwise enable the officer to examine the information accessible by the computer in a form in which the information is visible and legible; [355] or

- require such a person to produce the information in a form in which it can be removed and in which it is, or can be made, visible and legible.[356]

(g) Obstruction and failure to comply

[12.129] If a person impedes the execution of any of the powers conferred by a search warrant that was issued under CA 1990, s 20, he is liable to conviction of an offence under that section. Section 20(6) renders it an offence for a person to:

- obstruct the exercise of a right of entry or search conferred by a search warrant issued under s 20;[357]

- obstruct the exercise of a right conferred by a search warrant issued under s 20 to seize and retain material information;[358]

- fail to comply with a requirement of a designated officer to give his name, address or occupation;[359]

- fail to comply with a requirement to produce material information in his custody or possession;[360]

- give a name, address or occupation which is false or misleading; [361] or

- fail to comply with a requirement of a designated officer under s 20(4)(b) to facilitate access to information stored in a computer.[362]

---

[353] CA 1990, s 20(4)(a), as substituted by CLEA 2001, s 30.

[354] CA 1990, s 20(4)(b)(i), as substituted by CLEA 2001, s 30.

[355] CA 1990, s 20(4)(b)(ii), as substituted by CLEA 2001, s 30.

[356] CA 1990, s 20(4)(b)(iii), as substituted by CLEA 2001, s 30.

[357] CA 1990, s 20(6)(a), as substituted by CLEA 2001, s 30.

[358] CA 1990, s 20(6)(b), as substituted by CLEA 2001, s 30.

[359] CA 1990, s 20(6)(c), as substituted by CLEA 2001, s 30.

[360] CA 1990, s 20(6)(c), as substituted by CLEA 2001, s 30.

[361] CA 1990, s 20(6)(c), as substituted by CLEA 2001, s 30.

[362] CA 1990, s 20(6)(d), as substituted by CLEA 2001, s 30.

C. Disclosure of information

[12.130] CA 1990, s 21(1),[363] enshrines the rule that 'no information, book or document relating to a body which has been obtained under s 19 or 20 shall, without the previous consent in writing of that body, be published or disclosed, except to a competent authority, unless the publication or disclosure is, in the opinion of the Director, required …' for the reasons specified reasons in s 21(1)(a) to (j).

There are therefore three general situations in which books, documents, and information obtained under s 19 or 20, may be disclosed. First, books, documents and information may be disclosed or published in any circumstances with the prior consent in writing of the body to which they relate. As noted by Laffoy J in this regard, 'the clear intention of s 21 is to safeguard the body which is the subject of directions under section 19'.[364] Second, books, documents or information may be disclosed to a 'competent authority' without such prior consent. Third, without the consent of the body in question, there may be publication or disclosure to persons other than competent authorities, if the DCE is of the opinion that there exists one of the grounds listed in s 21(1).

Whenever books, documents or information obtained pursuant to s 19 or 20 are published or disclosed, s 23(3) provides, 'the publication, in pursuance of any provision of this Part, of any report, information, book or document shall be privileged'.

[12.131] Information, books and documents relating to a body may be disclosed to a competent authority. The authorities that are categorised as 'competent authorities' for the purposes of s 21(1) are listed in s 21(3)[365] as follows:

(a) the Minister,

(b) a person authorised by the Minister,

(c) an inspector appointed under this Act,

(d) the Minister for Finance,

(e) an officer authorised by the Minister for Finance,

(ea) the Irish Auditing and Accounting Supervisory Authority,

(f) any court of competent jurisdiction,

(g) a supervisory authority within the meaning of regulations relating to insurance made under the European Communities Act 1972,

(h) the Central Bank, and

(i) any authority established outside the State in which there are vested—

    (i) functions of investigating or prosecuting an offence similar to an offence referred to in para (a) of sub-s (1),

    (ii) functions of assessing the liability of a person in respect of a tax or duty or other payment owed or payable to the state in which it is established or any other authority established in that state or of collecting an amount due in

---

[363] As substituted by C(A)(No 2)A 1999, s 53(2). Section 21 is substantially reproduced in the CLRG, General Scheme of the Draft Companies Consolidation and Reform Bill 2007, Pt A13, Head 16. Available at www.clrg.org.

[364] *Dunnes Stores Ireland Co Ltd v Maloney* [1999] 3 IR 542 at 554.

[365] As amended by IFCMPA 2005, s 69 and C(A)(No 2)A 1999, s 53(3).

respect of such a tax or duty or other payment, or

(iii) functions which are similar to the functions referred to in para (c), (d), (e) or (f) of sub-s (1).[366]

[12.132] The relevance of classification as a 'competent authority' was considered in *Dunnes Stores Ireland Co Ltd v Ryan*.[367] One of the grounds on which the Minister appointed an authorised officer to examine the books or documents of Dunnes Stores, related to the fraud that was allegedly perpetrated against the Revenue Commissioners.[368] Among the arguments advanced by Dunnes Stores was that the interests of the Revenue Commissioners should not be taken into account under s 19(2)(b), as the Revenue was not a creditor of the company and was not among the list of competent authorities in s 21. As has been seen, the reliance on s 19(2)(b) in this regard was held not to be valid, as, while there may be circumstances in which the Revenue Commissioners are unable to detect the evasion of tax and an examination of a company's documents under s 19 may be necessary, this was not such a case, as the company had already been found to have assisted in the evasion of tax.[369]

[12.133] The circumstances which may, in the opinion of the DCE, require publication or disclosure, other than to one of the competent authorities listed above, without the consent of the body in question, are set out in CA 1990 s 21(1).[370] These circumstances are all premised on the formation of an opinion by the DCE: there are no circumstances under which books, documents, or information obtained under s 19 or 20, may be published or disclosed to bodies other than 'competent authorities' without the consent of the body in question, unless the DCE determines that one of the grounds for such publication or disclosure exists.

[12.134] The grounds for publishing or disclosing books, documents, or information are wide ranging and may be divided into three approximate sub categories. First, there are grounds of disclosure that relate to the investigation or prosecution of offences. Second, there are grounds of disclosure that relate to the discharge of the functions of other entities, such as the Competition Authority, a tribunal, or a Minister of the Government. Third, there are books or documents that may be published or disclosed in connection with other proceedings under the CA 1963–2006.

[12.135] The first category of grounds of disclosure relates to the investigation or prosecution of offences.[371] The basis of such publication or disclosure is that the DCE is of the opinion that it is required to investigate or prosecute an offence entailing misconduct in connection with the management of the body's affairs; an offence

---

[366] CA 1990, s 21(3)(i) as inserted by C(A)(No 2)A 1999, s 53(3)(b).

[367] *Dunnes Stores Ireland Co Ltd v Ryan* [2002] 2 IR 60.

[368] See above para **[12.027]**.

[369] *Dunnes Stores Ireland Co Ltd v Ryan* [2002] 2 IR 60, 78 (*per* Keane CJ). See above para **[12.027]**.

[370] As substituted by C(A)(No 2)A 1999, s 53 and amended by CLEA 2001, s 31.

[371] CA 1990, s 21(1)(a) as substituted by C(A)(No 2)A 1999, s 53(2).

entailing the misapplication or wrongful retainer of its property; or an offence under one of the following enactments:

- the Companies Acts;

- the Central Bank Acts, 1942 to 1998;

- the Exchange Control Acts 1954 to 1986;

- the Insurance Acts 1909 to 1990;

- the Taxes Consolidation Act 1997;[372] or

- regulations relating to insurance made under the European Communities Act 1972.[373]

[12.136] The second category of grounds for publishing or disclosing books or documents, is that the DCE is of opinion that it is necessary for one of the following purposes:

- to assess a person's liability, or collect payment, in respect of a tax or duty or other payment owed or payable to the State, a local authority or a health board;[374]

- the performance by a tribunal of any of its functions;[375]

- to assist or facilitate the performance of the functions of a Minister of the Government;[376]

- to assist or facilitate the discharge of the disciplinary functions of an accountancy or other professional organisation;[377]

- the performance by the Irish Takeover Panel or any stock exchange established in the State of any of its functions in relation to the body or any other person who, in its opinion, is connected with the body;[378]

- the performance by the Competition Authority of any of its functions;[379] or

---

[372] This also encompasses an offence under an enactment referred to in TCA 1997, s 1078(1), as amended by CLEA 2001, s 31(b).

[373] CA 1990, s 21(1)(a), as substituted by C(A)(No2)A 1999, s 53(2) and as amended by CLEA 2001, s 31.

[374] CA 1990, s 21(1)(b), as substituted by C(A)(No2)A 1999, s 53(2) and as amended by CLEA 2001, s 31.

[375] CA 1990, s 21(1)(c), as substituted by C(A)(No2)A 1999, s 53(2) and as amended by CLEA 2001, s 31.

[376] CA 1990, s 21(1)(d), as substituted by C(A)(No2)A 1999, s 53(2) and as amended by CLEA 2001, s 31.

[377] CA 1990, s 21(1)(e), as substituted by C(A)(No2)A 1999, s 53(2) and as amended by CLEA 2001, s 31.

[378] CA 1990, s 21(1)(f), as substituted by C(A)(No2)A 1999, s 53(2) and as amended by CLEA 2001, s 31.

[379] CA 1990, s 21(1)(fa), as inserted by CLEA 2001, s 31(c).

- the performance by a committee under the Committees of the Houses of the Oireachtas (Compellability, Privileges and Immunities of Witnesses) Act 1997, of any of its functions.[380]

[12.137] The third category of grounds on which the DCE may permit the publication or disclosure, to persons other than 'competent authorities', of books, documents, or information obtained under s 19 or s 20, without the consent of the body in question, relates to proceedings under the Companies Acts. If the DCE is of the opinion that publication or disclosure is required on one of the following grounds, he may permit such publication or disclosure to occur:

- to comply with the requirements of procedural fairness, it is necessary to make disclosure to a company to which an inspector was appointed to investigate the ownership of the company;[381]

- to comply with the requirements of procedural fairness, it is necessary to make disclosure to a person who was required to give information to the DCE under CA 1990, s 15;[382]

- to comply with the requirements of procedural fairness, it is necessary to make disclosure to a body to which the DCE has given a direction under s 19, or to a person named in a report relating to an examination conducted under s 19;[383]

- it is required to comply with a requirement, or exercise a power, under Pt II of the CA 1990, with regard to the report of an inspector appointed by the court or the DCE;[384]

- it is required with a view to the institution of, or for the purposes of, proceedings for the winding up of a body instituted by the DCE under CA 1963;[385]

- it is required for the purpose of proceedings under s 20, to seek an arrest warrant;[386] or

- disclosure or publication of such books, documents or information, is required for proceedings seeking an order of disqualification under s 60.[387]

---

[380] CA 1990, s 21(1)(fb), as inserted by CLEA 2001, s 31(c).

[381] CA 1990, s 21(1)(g), as substituted by C(A)(No2)A 1999, s 53(2) and as amended by CLEA 2001, s 31, referring to CA 1990, s 14.

[382] CA 1990, s 21(1)(g), as substituted by C(A)(No2)A 1999, s 53(2) and as amended by CLEA 2001, s 31.

[383] CA 1990, s 21(1)(g)((ii), as substituted by CLEA 2001, s 31(d).

[384] CA 1990, s 21(1)(h), as substituted by C(A)(No2)A 1999, s 53(2) and as amended by CLEA 2001, s 31(a).

[385] CA 1990, s 21(1)(h), as substituted by C(A)(No2)A 1999, s 53(2) and as amended by CLEA 2001, s 31(a).

[386] CA 1990, s 21(1)(i), as substituted by C(A)(No2)A 1999, s 53(2) and as amended by CLEA 2001, s 31(a).

[387] CA 1990, s 21(1)(j), as substituted by C(A)(No2)A 1999, s 53(2) and as amended by CLEA 2001, s 31(a).

[12.138] One of the grounds for a direction to produce books and documents is that:

> 'the Director ... is of the opinion that there are circumstances suggesting that ... it is necessary to examine the books and documents of the body with a view to determining whether an inspector should be appointed to conduct an investigation of the body under the Companies Acts'.[388]

It is surprising that there is no specific provision in s 21(1) that the DCE may publish or disclose such books or documents if it considers it necessary for the purpose of making of an application to court for the appointment of an inspector. This can be contrasted with the explicit right of the DCE to disclose such books or documents in proceedings initiating the winding up of a company. It would be anomalous if the DCE could require a company to produce its books and documents, on the basis that it may be necessary to appoint an inspector, but not then be able to disclose those books or documents in support of its application for the appointment of an inspector. This anomaly may be overcome in part, however, by the fact that a court is a 'competent authority' for the purposes of s 21, so books or documents obtained under s 19 may be disclosed to the court, without the consent of the company itself.

It is an offence for a person to publish books, documents, or information, contrary to CA 1990, s 21.[389] If such an offence is committed by a company with the consent, connivance, or due to the neglect, of an officer of the company that person shall also be guilty of an offence.[390]

---

[388] CA 1990, s 19(2)(a), as substituted by CLEA 2001, s 29. See above paras **[12.012]** to **[12.025]**.

[389] CA 1990, s 21(2).

[390] CA 1990, s 241. Note that this applies to a company's director, secretary, manager, or person purporting to act in that capacity, as well as members who are managing the company's affairs. See para **[12.094]**.

Chapter 13

INSPECTORS AND COMPANY INVESTIGATIONS

[13.001] Part II of CA 1990 governs the appointment of inspectors to investigate the affairs and the membership of companies.[1] As the Supreme Court noted in *Dunnes Stores Ireland Co Ltd v Ryan*,[2] investigations by inspectors are designed to ensure that companies 'do not abuse the privileges which incorporation confers on them to the detriment of their members, their creditors or indeed the public in general'.[3] The function of an inspector is inquisitorial. In *National Irish Bank (Under Investigation) v Companies Acts*, Kelly J described this function as follows:

'They are obliged to investigate the affairs of that company in order to enquire into matters specified by the court. They are then obliged to report to the court on their investigation. They are conferred with wide powers ... Inspectors are not appointed as evidence gatherers but rather as investigators whose job is to make a report. Their function is inquisitorial.'[4]

A. Appointment of inspector to investigate company's affairs

(a) Applicants

[13.002] There are different procedures by which an inspector can be appointed to investigate the affairs of a company and there are different categories of persons who can initiate these procedures. In each case, the application must be made by means of an originating notice of action and must be served on the company and the directors, if they are not the applicants.[5] The right of these persons to have an inspector appointed to a company is an important tool in the enforcement of company law and will now be examined from that perspective.

(i) Internal applicants

[13.003] Pursuant to CA 1990, s 7(1), the court can appoint an inspector to investigate the affairs of a company and to report to the court as directed. The category of persons who can apply to the court under s 7(1) is limited to persons within, or close to, the

---

[1] CA 1990, Pt II replaces CA 1963, ss 165 to 173.

[2] *Dunnes Stores Ireland Co Ltd v Ryan* [2002] 2 IR 60.

[3] *Dunnes Stores Ireland Co Ltd v Ryan* [2002] 2 IR 60 at 77, *per* Keane CJ.

[4] *National Irish Bank (Under Investigation)* [2006] IEHC 35.

[5] Rules of the Superior Courts 1986, ord 75B, rr 3(a) and 3(b), inserted by Rules of the Superior Courts (No 4) 1991 (SI 278/1991). Note that, unless the Court otherwise orders, such applications will be heard and determined on affidavit: ord 75B, r 7.

company. In circumstances in which the company has a share capital, the following applicants can petition the court for the appointment of an inspector:

-    100 members or more; or
-    member(s) holding at least one tenth of the company's paid up share capital.

Where the company does not have share capital, one-fifth or more of the persons on the company's register of members may apply to the court for such an appointment.

[13.004] The following applicants can seek the appointment of an inspector to investigate a company's affairs in any case:

-    the company itself;
-    a director of the company; or
-    a creditor of the company.

Where an application is made to appoint an inspector under s 7(1), the court may require the applicant or applicants to give security of between €6,348.69 and €317,434.52 towards payment for the costs of the investigation.[6] Section 7(3) provides in this regard:

> Where an application is made under this section, the court may require the applicant or applicants to give security, to an amount not less than £500 and not exceeding £100,000, for payment of the costs of the investigation.

One effect of these provisions is that they may act as a deterrent for persons who have legitimate grievances regarding the conduct of a company's affairs.[7]

As will be seen below, there are certain other obstacles and burdens that face persons seeking to have an inspector appointed to a company. These factors may account for the unpopularity of s 7(1) in practice.[8] The less encumbered power of the DCE (formerly the Minister for Enterprise, Trade and Employment) to have an inspector appointed under s 8(1) may also explain the fact that s 7(1) is rarely invoked.[9]

[13.005] The equivalent of CA 1990, s 7(1) in England, is CA 1985 (Eng), s 431. That provision contains similar definitions of the categories of person that can seek to have an inspector appointed to a company. There are, however, certain significant differences between the English legislation and CA 1990.

The first and most notable difference is that s 431 gives the Secretary of State the power to appoint an inspector directly, where the requisite criteria are met.[10] There is no court

---

6   CA 1990, s 7(3), as amended by CLEA 2001, s 20.

7   The equivalent English provision, CA 1985, s 431(4), provides for significantly lesser security to a maximum of £5,000, subject to the discretion of the Secretary of State. ('The Secretary of State may, before appointing inspectors, require the applicant or applicants to give security, to an amount not exceeding £5,000, or such other sum as he may by order specify, for payment of the costs of the investigation.')

8   See below paras **[13.025]** to **[13.026]**.

9   See below paras **[13.006]** to **[13.008]**.

10   CA 1985, s 431(1), as amended, provides, 'The Secretary of State may appoint one or more competent inspectors to investigate the affairs of a company and to report on them in such manner as he may direct.'

involvement in the appointment of an inspector in such circumstances. This has certain consequences for the conduct of the inspection, which are considered in more detail below.[11]

A second distinction is that the class of persons who can seek the appointment of an inspector in England is restricted to members or the company itself and does not extend to creditors or directors of the company. Other than this distinction, the criteria employed in CA 1985 (Eng), s 431(2) are strikingly similar to those employed in CA 1990, s 7(1). Section 431(2) provides:

> The appointment may be made—
>
> (a) in the case of a company having a share capital, on the application either of not less than 200 members or of members holding not less than one tenth of the shares issued [(excluding any shares held as treasury shares)],
>
> (b) in the case of a company not having a share capital, on the application of not less than one fifth in number of the persons on the company's register of members, and
>
> (c) in any case, on application of the company.

There are other drafting differences between the procedures that have been adopted in England and those that were enacted by the CA 1990. However, one important similarity that should be noted is that neither procedure is invoked frequently. In Ireland, this procedure appears never to have been invoked. In England, there appear to have been no investigations under CA 1985, s 431 since 1990.[12]

(ii) External

[13.006] CA 1990, s 8(1) confers a power on the DCE to apply to court for the appointment of inspectors to investigate the affairs of a company and to report to the court on those affairs. It provides that:

> '… the court may on the application of the Director appoint one or more competent inspectors (who may be or include an officer or officers of the Director) to investigate the affairs of a company and to report thereon in such manner as the court shall direct.'

Before the enactment of the CLEA 2001,[13] this power was vested in the Minister for Enterprise, Trade and Employment and was invoked in certain high profile cases, as will be seen below. By virtue of such cases, the power to appoint inspectors and the powers of inspectors once appointed have been the subject of considerable judicial scrutiny.

[13.007] In England, CA 1985, s 432 provides for the appointment of inspectors in similar circumstances. Pursuant to CA 1985 (Eng), s 432(2), where the requisite circumstances exist, the Secretary of State may appoint an inspector or inspectors

---

[11] See below para **[13.007]**.

[12] P Davies, *Gower and Davies' Principles of Modern Company Law* (7th edn, Sweet and Maxwell, 2003), p 471. See also DTI, 'Company Investigations: Powers for the Twenty-First Century' (2001).

[13] CLEA 2001, s 21, amending CA 1990, s 8.

directly, without the necessity of a court application. This provision will be examined in more detail below.[14]

There is another provision of the CA 1985 (Eng) which governs the appointment of inspectors to investigate a company's affairs. Pursuant to s 432(1), the procedure is almost the inverse of the procedure for the appointment of an inspector under CA 1990, s 8(1), however. Section 432(1) provides:

> The Secretary of State shall appoint one or more competent inspectors to investigate the affairs of a company and report on them in such manner as he directs, if the court by order declares that its affairs ought to be so investigated.

This requires a court order that the affairs of a company should be investigated, followed by the appointment of an inspector by the Secretary of State. CA 1985 (Eng), s 432(1) and (2), can be contrasted with CA 1990, s 8(1), which requires the DCE to make an application to court which, if successful, will result in the appointment of an inspector by the court. Under s 432(1) and (2), the appointment of the inspector is done by the Secretary of State rather than by the court. One effect of this distinction is that an inspector appointed in Ireland under CA 1990, ss 7 and 8 is subject to court supervision and approval throughout the conduct of the inspection, whereas inspectors in England are answerable primarily to the Secretary of State. Inspectors appointed under ss 7 or 8 are specifically subject to court approval in relation to certain aspects of the procedure governing investigations, such as ss 7(4) and 9.[15] In England on the other hand, such court approval is not necessary.[16] The difference between the jurisdictions in the supervision and control of inspections is also evidenced by the fact that inspectors appointed in Ireland under ss 7 or 8 are obliged to report to the court, whereas inspectors appointed under CA 1985 (Eng), s 431 or 432, for example, report to the Secretary of State.[17]

[13.008] There is a final point to note regarding applications for the appointment of an inspector to investigate the affairs of a company in Ireland. The appointment of an inspector under either s 7 or s 8, can only result from an application to court by members of the company, the company itself, a creditor, a director, or the DCE. An Irish court does not appear to have the right to appoint an inspector in the absence of such an application.[18] This can be contrasted with the CA 1985 in England, which provides for the court to make an order to the effect that a company's affairs should be investigated, without the necessity of an application to the court by a qualified applicant.[19]

---

[14]   See below paras **[13.012]**, **[13.031]** and **[13.035]**.

[15]   See below paras **[13.059]** to **[13.061]**.

[16]   See, eg, CA 1985, ss 433 and 437.

[17]   See further below paras **[13.101]** to **[13.124]**.

[18]   See Courtney, *The Law of Private Companies* (2nd edn, Tottel Publishing, 2002) at para [14.012].

[19]   CA 1985 (Eng), s 432(1).

(b) Grounds

[13.009] When an application to appoint an inspector is made by one of the categories of person listed in CA 1990, s 7(1), the grounds for appointment are defined very vaguely. CA 1990, s 7(2), merely provides that: 'The application shall be supported by such evidence as the court may require, including such evidence as may be prescribed.'

This requirement does not provide any clarity regarding the type of situation which may warrant the appointment of an inspector. Members of a company who feel aggrieved at the conduct of a company's affairs, for instance, will have to apply to court to ascertain whether s 7(1) can be invoked in respect of that conduct. By contrast, the circumstances in which the DCE can make an application for the appointment of an inspector are clearly and exhaustively defined in s 8(1).[20] It is difficult to see why the same defined circumstances do not apply to an application under s 7(1). The failure to do so can only be presumed to be deliberate, however, and while the conduct and situations described in s 8(1), may be of guidance to an applicant under s 7(1), they can by no means be invoked or relied directly upon. The ambiguity regarding the circumstances which may warrant the appointment of an inspector under s 7(1), is heightened by the vague evidential threshold that s 7(2) requires an applicant to meet. This aspect of the procedure is addressed in more detail below.[21]

[13.010] The English CA 1985, s 431(3) is somewhat more clear in terms of the grounds that must be established for an application for the appointment of an inspector to succeed. It provides that, in order to succeed:

> The application shall be supported by such evidence as the Secretary of State may require for the purpose of showing that the applicant or applicants have good reason for requiring the investigation.

[13.011] As already mentioned, the power of the DCE to apply to court for the appointment of an inspector is based on defined situations existing in a company. These are set out in CA 1990, s 8(1), which provides that a court may appoint an inspector:

> ... if the court is satisfied that there are circumstances suggesting:
>
> (a) that its affairs are being or have been conducted with intent to defraud its creditors or the creditors of any other person or otherwise for a fraudulent or unlawful purpose or in an unlawful manner or in a manner which is unfairly prejudicial to some part of its members, or that any actual or proposed act or omission of the company (including an act or omission on its behalf) is or would be so prejudicial, or that it was formed for any fraudulent or unlawful purpose; or
>
> (b) that persons connected with its formation or the management of its affairs have in connection therewith been guilty of fraud, misfeasance or other misconduct towards it or towards its members; or
>
> (c) that its members have not been given all the information relating to its affairs which they might reasonably expect.

---

[20] See below paras **[13.011]** to **[13.024]**.

[21] See below paras **[13.025]** to **[13.026]**.

[13.012] The grounds for the appointment of an inspector under s 8 can broken down as follows:

- the company's affairs are being or have been conducted with intent to defraud its creditors;[22]

- the company's affairs are being or have been conducted with intent to defraud the creditors of any other person;[23]

- the company's affairs are being or have been conducted for a fraudulent or unlawful purpose, other than with intent to defraud its creditors or the creditors of any other person;[24]

- the company's affairs are being or have been conducted in an unlawful manner, other than with intent to defraud its creditors or the creditors of any other person;[25]

- the company's affairs are being or have been conducted in a manner which is unfairly prejudicial to some part of its members;[26]

- any actual or proposed act or omission of the company (including an act or omission on its behalf) is or would be prejudicial to some part of its members;[27]

- the company was formed for any fraudulent or unlawful purpose;[28]

- persons connected with the formation of the company or the management of its affairs have been guilty of fraud, misfeasance or other misconduct towards the company or its members in connection with such formation or management;[29]

- the members of the company have not been given all the information relating to the company's affairs which they might reasonably expect.[30]

These grounds are nearly identical to the grounds for the appointment of an inspector by the Secretary of State under the English CA 1985, s 432(2). The only difference between the provisions is that s 8(1) includes situations where the company's affairs are being or have been conducted in an unlawful manner, a situation which is not covered by CA 1985, s 432(2).

The most striking similarity between CA 1990, s 8(1) and the English CA 1985, s 432(2), is the reference to 'unfairly prejudicial'. This language reflects CA 1985, ss 459 and 460, which permit members or the Secretary of State to petition the court

---

[22] CA 1990, s 8(1)(a), as amended by CLEA 2001, s 21.

[23] CA 1990, s 8(1)(a).

[24] CA 1990, s 8(1)(a).

[25] CA 1990, s 8(1)(a).

[26] CA 1990, s 8(1)(a). See below para **[13.013]**.

[27] CA 1990, s 8(1)(a).

[28] CA 1990, s 8(1)(a).

[29] CA 1990, s 8(1)(b).

[30] CA 1990, s 8(1)(c).

where there is evidence of such unfair prejudice towards the company's members. The first point regarding this ground for appointing an inspector, as it is formulated in both jurisdictions, is that it refers to the conduct of a company's affairs '… in a manner which is unfairly prejudicial to *some part of its members'* (emphasis added). CA 1985 (Eng), s 459, on the other hand, refers to 'its members generally or some part of its members'. The omission of 'members generally' from CA 1990, s 8(1), as from CA 1985, s 432(2), may, as one commentator has noted, have the absurd result that inspectors should, strictly speaking, not be appointed, if the court or the DCE, as the case may be, considers that there is unfair prejudice to all the company's members, rather than 'some part' of them.[31]

[13.013] The concept of 'unfair prejudice' in the context of company law petitions has received some consideration in England, with views differing as to whether it extends beyond actual illegality[32] and whether the prejudice must be caused to members in their capacity as members.[33] It now appears to be established that the requirement of independent illegality has been removed and that the restriction of the remedy to members acting in their capacity as such, is not an inflexible one.[34] However, there have been some attempts to clarify the scope of the 'unfair prejudice' remedy. The House of Lords in *O'Neill v Phillips*[35] favoured some legal certainty rather than the vague concept of fairness and focused on whether a bargain or some form of arrangement, whether formal or not, could be relied upon by the shareholders. This category of unfair prejudice appears to have become the dominant, and most clearly defined, category in England.[36] A final point to note regarding the interpretation of 'unfair prejudice,' as that term is used in CA 1985 (Eng), s 459, is that the courts in England have focused on the requirement of 'unfairness,' which has been established to be an objective concept.[37] There have been decisions exploring the requirement of 'unfairness' to the effect that a

---

[31] P Davies, *Gower and Davies' Principles of Modern Company Law* (7th edn, Sweet and Maxwell, 2003), p 471.

[32] This is referred to as 'independent illegality,' a requirement which appears to have originated with the decision of the House of Lords in *Scottish Co-Operative Society Ltd v Meyer* [1959] AC 324 in the context of oppression of minorities.

[33] In cases such as *Anderson v Hogg* 2002 SLT 634, it seems to be accepted that proof of illegality against the company may equate to unfair prejudice to the members, whereas such a proposition was rejected in cases such as *Re Charnley Davies Ltd (No 2)* [1990] BCLC 760, which adhered to the view that, where the wrong is done to the company, the members could only proceed by means of a derivative action, and subject to the restrictions of *Foss v Harbottle* (1843) 2 Hare 461.

[34] In relation to the interpretation of CA 1985, s 459, *Re A Company* [1983] Ch 178, suggested that the requirement of acting *qua* member was imported into this provision, whereas cases such as *Re A Company* [1986] BCLC 376 have since established that this requirement is not so rigid in the context of s 459. See Davies, *Gower and Davies' Principles of Modern Company Law* (7th edn, Sweet and Maxwell, 2003), p 515.

[35] *O'Neill v Phillips* [1999] 1 WLR 1092; [1999] 2 All ER 961; [1999] 2 BCLC 1.

[36] See Davies, *Gower and Davies' Principles of Modern Company Law* (7th edn, Sweet and Maxwell, 2003), p 521. *O'Neill v Phillips* [1999] 2 BCLC 1.

[37] *Re Saul D Harrison & Sons plc* [1995] 1 BLCL 14.

member who benefited from the conduct complained of, cannot subsequently invoke the unfairness of that conduct,[38] and that a member's own conduct may disentitle him to the relief sought.[39]

The interpretation of 'unfair prejudice' as that term is used in the CA 1985 (Eng), may be of assistance in interpreting the grounds for appointment of an inspector in Ireland under CA 1990, s 8. However, as will be seen,[40] it is by no means established that the grounds for appointing an inspector need to be explained by the court and the practice of the courts in Ireland appears to be to set forth the matters which are to form the scope of the investigation and the provision under which the appointment of inspectors is made. It would require a case in which there is a dispute as to the basis for appointing an inspector, or in which the court refuses to accede to an application for the appointment of an inspector, before the exact parameters of what constitutes 'unfair prejudice' within the meaning of CA 1990, s 8, may be explored by an Irish court.

[13.014] The grounds for the appointment of an inspector under s 8 resemble closely the circumstances which warrant an order for the production of a company's books or documents under CA 1990, s 19.[41] However, whereas the situations referred to in s 8 have not received judicial consideration to date, the grounds for invoking s 19 have been considered in a number of cases. This discrepancy may be explained by the fact that the appointment of an inspector under s 8 is done by court order, by contrast with the power of the DCE under s 19 to appoint an inspector to examine the books and records of a company. The latter has therefore attracted more resistance and scrutiny and the interpretations that have been placed on s 19 may be of assistance in interpreting the same grounds as they appear in s 8.[42]

[13.015] There are certain other divergences between CA 1990, ss 8 and 19. One notable difference is how the provisions are drafted: s 19 encompasses situations in which the affairs of the company are being or have been conducted with intent to defraud its members, creditors or the creditors of any other person.[43] Section 8 refers to intent to defraud creditors and creditors of other persons, but omits any reference to intent to defraud members. It could be inferred from this omission that members are intended to make their own application under CA 1990, s 7, in the event of such fraud. An alternative explanation is that conduct which is 'unfairly prejudicial' to the members of a company, within the meaning of s 8(1)(a) could encompass conduct designed to defraud those members.

[13.016] A further distinction between ss 8 and 19, is that s 19(2)(f) covers actual or proposed acts or omissions by or on behalf of a company or by an officer of the

---

[38] *Jesner v Jerad Properties Ltd* [1993] BCLC 1032.

[39] *Re London School of Electronics* [1986] Ch 211, [1985] 3 WLR 474, [1985] BCLC 273.

[40] See below paras **[13.027]** to **[13.030]**.

[41] See Ch **12**.

[42] See Ch **12** for an analysis of the grounds for issuing a direction under CA 1990, s 19, as amended.

[43] CA 1990, s 19(2)(b)(iii), as substituted by CLEA 2001, s 29.

company, 'have been, or are likely to be unlawful'.[44] There is no equivalent provision in s 8. This may be explained, however, by the fact that s 8 includes a reference to the conduct of a company's affairs in an unlawful manner, which may include the unlawful acts or omissions referred to in s 19.

Section 8 and s 19 each cover situations in which there is an actual or proposed act or omission that were, are or would be unfairly prejudicial to part of the company's members. One distinction between ss 8 and 19 in this regard is that s 19(2)(e) includes a series of acts or omissions. While not included expressly in s 8, it is unlikely, however, that a series of prejudicial acts or omissions would be excluded from the scope of that provision.

[13.017] Finally, there are two categories of conduct that can warrant the appointment of an inspector under CA 1990, s 8, which do not appear in s 19. Section 8(1)(b) addresses situations in which persons connected with the formation or management of the company have been guilty of fraud, misfeasance or other misconduct towards the company or its members. The use of the term 'guilty' suggests that there must first be concrete legal findings of such fraud, misfeasance or misconduct. However, in light of the fact that the court must merely be 'satisfied that there are circumstances suggesting …' such guilt, it may not be subject to that limitation.

Section 8(1)(c) addresses a situation in which the court is satisfied that there are circumstances suggesting 'that its members have not been given all the information relating to its affairs which they might reasonably expect'. This category is very broadly formulated. The information that a company's members 'might reasonably expect' could be open-ended. This category certainly addresses the predicament of members who cannot obtain sufficient evidence to apply for the appointment of an inspector under s 7(1). However, the fact that the provision is not limited by reference to some objective criteria, such as the information that is required to be furnished under the Companies Acts, presents the danger that it may be relied upon as a catch-all category, where the other, more specific, situations listed in s 8, cannot be shown to exist.

[13.018] On a general note, both s 8 and s 19 are premised on the formation of a view that there are circumstances suggesting the existence of one of the situations listed in those provisions. The interpretation that has placed on certain subsections of s 19 suggest that it must be necessary to invoke those subsections, before they can be relied upon.[45] There is no mention of necessity in the wording of s 8. Moreover, there is no express correlation between the situations that the court must be satisfied exist, and the affairs which the inspector has the power to investigate. It is not apparent from the wording of s 8 that the appointment of the inspector must be directed towards investigating the situations listed in that provision. This type of language is also missing from s 19. It is conceivable, therefore, that s 8 would be interpreted in the same manner as s 19, with the effect that certain situations which fit the criteria of s 8, but which it is not necessary to investigate, will not warrant the appointment of an inspector.

---

[44] CA 1990, s 19(2)(f), as substituted by CLEA 2001, s 29, as amended by IFCMPA 2005, s 67(c).

[45] See Ch **12**.

[13.019] The most important decision that considered the grounds on which an authorised officer can be appointed to direct the production of a company's books or documents under CA 1990, s 19, is *Dunnes Stores Ireland Company Ltd v Ryan*.[46] In that case there was a challenge to the appointment of an officer by the Minister for Enterprise, Trade and Employment under CA 1990, s 19. The appointment was made on a number of grounds and, as many of these mirror the grounds contained in CA 1990, s 8(1), certain aspects of the judgments of the High Court and the Supreme Court in that case will now be considered.

[13.020] One of the grounds on which the Minister purported to appoint an authorised officer to direct the production of the company's books or documents was that there was an intention to defraud a creditor, namely the Revenue Commissioners. This ground is contained in CA 1990, s 19(2)(b)(ii), which addresses situations in which 'the affairs of the body are being or have been conducted with intent to defraud ... (ii) the creditors of any other person'. This mirrors s 8(1)(a), as outlined above. One aspect of this provision that was relied upon was the fact that it addresses situations in which the conduct complained of is past or current.

Keane CJ accepted Dunnes Stores' contention that this was not a valid ground on which to exercise the powers conferred by s 19, observing that an examination of the company's books and records was superfluous if it was for the purpose of assessing whether payments had been made for the purpose of tax evasion, when it was already established that such payments had been made. These payments could not therefore be used as a reason to appoint an authorised officer to examine the books or documents of the company under the powers conferred by s 19(2)(b)(ii).[47]

[13.021] Another ground that is contained in both CA 1990, ss 8 and 19, is that the affairs of the company are being or have been conducted in a manner which is unfairly prejudicial to some part of its members. With regard to the interpretation of s 19(2)(d), Keane CJ stated in *Dunnes Stores Ireland Co Ltd v Ryan*,[48] that the right to invoke s 19(2)(d) is not limited to situations where it is necessary to determine whether the affairs of the company are being conducted in a manner that is or would be unfairly prejudicial to some part of its members. On the contrary, Keane CJ held that, '...the power may arise in a case where... it is beyond argument that they had been so conducted in the past.[49]'

Keane CJ rejected the submission that, because the conduct detrimental to the shareholders' interests had ceased, the Minister's interest in that aspect of the company's

---

[46] *Dunnes Stores Ireland Co Ltd v Ryan* [2002] 2 IR 60. See Ch **12**.

[47] *Dunnes Stores Ireland Co Ltd v Ryan* [2002] 2 IR 60 at 78. This finding was subject to the caveat that, 'it may be possible to envisage circumstances in which even the ample powers of the Revenue Commissioners are not sufficient to enable them to ascertain whether the affairs of a company are being carried out in order to evade the payment of tax, and the examination by the second respondent [the Minister] of the books and documents of the company may in the result be justified under s 19(2)(b)(ii).' (*per* Keane CJ at p 78). However, Keane CJ noted further that, 'this was certainly not such a case.'

[48] *Dunnes Stores Ireland Co Ltd v Ryan* [2002] 2 IR 60.

[49] *Dunnes Stores Ireland Co Ltd v Ryan* [2002] 2 IR 60 at 80.

affairs had also ceased. The fact that the prejudicial conduct in a particular company had ceased was not therefore necessarily relevant to a decision by the Minister to undertake an inquiry.[50]

The scope of CA 1990, s 19(2)(d) is therefore quite broad and it can be employed in cases where the interests of the company or its members are no longer at stake, but a broader policy interest may be at issue. It remains to be seen whether s 8(1)(a) would be given the same broad interpretation.

[13.022] While CA 1990, s 8 does not contain an equivalent to CA 1990, s 19(2)(f), as was seen above,[51] some aspects of the interpretation of s 19(2)(f) may be of relevance in the interpretation of s 8. Section 19(2)(f) addresses '... any actual or proposed act or omission or series of acts or omissions of the body or on behalf of the body ...'. This resembles one clause of s 8(2)(a), which addresses '... any actual or proposed act or omission of the company (including an act or omission on its behalf)'. Both clauses address actual or proposed acts or omissions by or on behalf of the company.

Section 19(2)(f) was considered by the Supreme Court in *Dunnes Stores Ireland Company Limited v Ryan*,[52] as one of the grounds relied on in that case was that there were circumstances suggesting that there was a series of acts or omissions by the company that were likely to be unlawful within the meaning of s 19(2)(f).[53] Keane CJ considered the scope of s 19(2)(f) and stated that where there is no suggestion that breaches of the Companies Acts or other legislation are being committed at the time of the appointment of the authorised officer, the fact that such breaches may have been committed in the past does not provide a valid basis for the appointment of an authorised officer under s 19(2)(f). Keane CJ interpreted the subsection as follows:

> 'The language used in s 19(2)(f), using as it does the present tense in contrast to the past tense employed in other subparagraphs, makes it clear that the examination of books or documents authorised under that subparagraph is related to continuing or future illegal acts or omissions of the company and not to acts or omissions which have occurred in the past.'[54]

[13.023] It seems appropriate and logical that the same interpretation would be applied to CA 1990, s 8(1)(a), insofar as that provision differentiates between acts or events in the past, present and/or future. In the context of CA 1990, s 8, this means that all situations covered by that provision, other than prejudicial acts or omissions, can relate to past as well as present circumstances.[55] In the context of acts or omissions which are or would be unfairly prejudicial, only existing or future acts or omissions can suffice. A

---

[50] *Dunnes Stores Ireland Co Ltd v Ryan* [2002] 2 IR 60 at 81.

[51] See above para **[13.016]**.

[52] *Dunnes Stores Ireland Co Ltd v Ryan* [2002] 2 IR 60.

[53] The acts in question were payments made to certain beneficiaries, some of which were alleged to have been in breach of exchange control legislation. See Ch **12**.

[54] *Dunnes Stores Ireland Co Ltd v Ryan* [2002] 2 IR 60 at 80.

[55] This remains subject to the *caveat* that the Supreme Court interpreted similar language in s 19(2)(b)(ii), to exclude acts which were already found to have been committed in the past. *Dunnes Stores Ireland Co Ltd v Ryan* [2002] 2 IR 60. See above para **[13.020]**.

company's past acts or omissions which caused unfair prejudice to its members, but which may have been undetected at the time, could not therefore warrant the appointment of an inspector.

[13.024] A final point to note with regard to the interpretation of the grounds that can be invoked under CA 1990, s 8(1), is the definition of 'members' for the purposes of that section. Section 8(2)(b) provides:

> The reference in sub-s (1)(a) to the members of a company shall have effect as if it included a reference to any person who is not a member but to whom shares in the company have been transferred or transmitted by operation of law.[56]

This definition applies to circumstances in which the company's affairs are being or have been conducted in a manner which is unfairly prejudicial to some part of its members, and actual or proposed acts or omissions by or on behalf of the company which are or would be prejudicial to some part of its members.[57] This definition is essentially limited to situations where prejudice is caused to the company's members.

The situations covered by s 8(1)(b) and (c) do not encompass persons to whom shares in the company have been transferred or transmitted by operation of law. The rationale underlying this distinction is not readily apparent. The type of conduct captured by s 8(1)(a) is not vastly different to the conduct covered by s 8(1)(b). Section 8(1)(b), for example, covers situations where persons involved in the management of a company are responsible for misconduct towards the company or its members.

This could overlap considerably with s 8(1)(a) which refers to circumstances where the affairs of a company are conducted 'in an unlawful manner or in a manner which is unfairly prejudicial to some part of its members'. The existence of this overlap between s 8(1)(a) and (b) may counter the criticism that there appears to be no reason for differentiating between the definition of 'member' as it is used in the two subsections. However, in the context of s 8(1)(c), this overlap does not appear to exist and it could seen as invidious that 'members' have their right to information protected, whereas persons who acquire shares by operation of law do not. It is accepted that members may have the right to expect more extensive information regarding the company's affairs, within the context of s 8(1)(c). However, this provision alludes to information which a member can 'reasonably expect', which suggests that it extends beyond the information to which members are entitled. Furthermore, the fact that persons who hold shares, not as members, are not entitled to the same information as members, does not counter the possible right of such persons to expect certain information regarding the company's affairs. As such persons are included among the grounds for appointing an inspector under CA 1990, s 8(1)(a), it seems anomalous that they are not included in s 8(1)(b) and (c).

---

[56] This mirrors CA 1985 (Eng), s 432(4), which provides, '(4) The reference in sub-s (2)(a) to a company's members includes any person who is not a member but to whom shares in the company have been transferred or transmitted by operation of law.'

[57] See above paras **[3.012]** to **[3.013]**.

(c) Evidence

(i) Applications under CA 1990, s 7(2)

[13.025] The level of evidence regarding a company's affairs that a court will require to appoint an inspector depends upon the applicant. Under CA 1990, s 7(2), an application under s 7(1) '… shall be supported by such evidence as the court may require, including such evidence as may be prescribed'. This resembles closely the equivalent English provision, which requires an application for the appointment of an inspector to be 'supported by such evidence as the Secretary of State may require'.[58]

The first issue with CA 1990, s 7(1) is that it is only when the application comes before the court that the applicant can ascertain what evidence is necessary for it to succeed. This fact, combined with the lack of any guidance as to the circumstances which warrant the appointment of an inspector, renders it difficult for an applicant to assess the chances of a successful application. Secondly, the language used in s 7(2) suggests that the evidence in question may be mandatory. In particular, the use of the words 'shall,' 'require' and 'prescribed' indicate that a failure to adduce the evidence may be fatal to an application. More specifically, the language used suggests that, in the absence of such evidence as may be 'prescribed', the application may not be permitted to proceed. 'Prescribe' is defined in CA 1990, s 3(1) as 'prescribe by regulations'. No such regulations have been adopted to date. The evidence that is required to ground an application for the appointment of an inspector under s 7 is therefore solely a matter of judicial discretion.

[13.026] A final point regarding s 7(2) is that it requires that, '…the application shall be supported…' by such evidence as the court may require and/or prescribe. This clearly indicates that the burden on adducing the evidence in question lies on the applicant(s) and must exist before an inspector will be appointed. It may not be easy or even possible for the members of a company, in which there is alleged wrong-doing, to meet such a threshold.

In light of the potential costs implications of making an application to court under s 7(1), as was examined above,[59] an applicant would need to be assured of a high level of impropriety, which could be substantiated by evidence that would satisfy any court, before invoking that provision. These issues, arising from the vague definition of the threshold and grounds for the appointment of an inspector under s 7(1), may account for the unpopularity of that procedure.

(ii) Applications under CA 1990, s 8(1)

[13.027] CA 1990, s 8(1) provides that the court may appoint an inspector if satisfied that there are circumstances suggesting the existence of one of the situations which may warrant the appointment of an inspector, as outlined above.[60] The first point to note is that there is no evidential requirement imposed on the DCE in respect of an application

---

[58] CA 1985 (Eng), s 431(3), as amended.

[59] See above para **[13.004]**.

[60] See above paras **[13.011]** to **[13.024]**.

under s 8(1). There is nothing to indicate that an application by the DCE under that provision must be based on any particular evidence, or any evidence at all. Secondly, the threshold that does exist in s 8(2) is a low one. The court must be satisfied 'that there are circumstances suggesting' that one of a list of circumstances pertains in the company. There is no reference to evidence of the existence of such a situation being required, or even to the existence of reasonable grounds; it is merely necessary that circumstances suggest such a situation exists.

[13.028] There have been no authoritative judicial pronouncements on this aspect of s 8. However, CA 1990, s 19(2) which permits the appointment of an authorised officer to direct the production of a company's books or documents, employs the same language.[61] It provides that the DCE can direct the production of books or documents 'if he is of the opinion that there are circumstances suggesting that…' one of number of stipulated situations exist. There have been judicial determinations regarding the scope and meaning of this aspect of s 19(2) and, these interpretations may be of assistance in the interpretation of s 8.

[13.029] In *Dunnes Stores Ireland Co Ltd v Moloney*[62] Laffoy J ruled that the decision to require the production of books or documents under CA 1990, s 19 is subject to judicial review and that an opinion formed for the purposes of that section must be formed in good faith and must be 'factually sustainable and not unreasonable.'[63]

In *Dunnes Stores Ireland Co Ltd v Ryan*,[64] Murray J went a step further and commented that:

> '… the requirement in s 19(2) that the second respondent be "of the opinion that there are circumstances suggesting that" one of the reasons enumerated at (a) to (h) of the subsection exists, means no more than that she must have reasonable grounds for her opinion. It is exclusively a matter for the second respondent to form the opinion. It is necessarily a subjective one.'

On the basis of these statements of the law, it appears that, while the opinion that must be formed for the purpose of CA 1990, s 19 is a subjective one, reasonable grounds must exist for the formation of such an opinion.

[13.030] In the context of s 8, the issue of judicial review does not arise, as the decision to appoint an inspector is made by the court and the appropriate recourse for a person aggrieved by such a decision, would be an appeal within the judicial system. However, the Supreme Court's indication that reasonable grounds should exist, before an opinion can be formed that there are 'circumstances suggesting' the existence of a particular situation may colour the interpretation of the same wording in s 8(1). The result is that the court would need to have reasonable grounds for being satisfied that the circumstances set out in s 8(1) exist, before an inspector could be appointed under that provision.

---

[61] See Ch **12**.

[62] *Dunnes Stores Ireland Co Ltd v Moloney* [1999] 3 IR 542. See also *Dunnes Stores Co Ltd v Ryan* [2002] 2 IR 60. See further Ch **12**.

[63] *Dunnes Stores Ireland Co Ltd v Moloney* [1999] 3 IR 542 at 556 quoting *Lynch v Cooney* [1982] IR 337, 361 (*per* O'Higgins CJ).

[64] *Dunnes Stores Ireland Co Ltd v Ryan* [2002] 2 IR 60 at 88–89.

[13.031] An analogy can also be drawn with the powers of the Secretary of State in the United Kingdom. Companies Act (Eng) 1985, s 432(2) provides that the Secretary of State can appoint inspectors to investigate a company's affairs 'if it appears to him that there are circumstances suggesting ...' that one of a number of specified situations existed in respect of such company. The predecessor to this provision, Companies Act 1948 (Eng), s 165, which used the same wording, was considered by the English Court of Appeal in *Norwest Holst Ltd v Secretary of State for Trade*.[65]

The expression '... if it appears to the Board that there are circumstances suggesting' was given the following interpretation by Lane LJ in that case:

> 'It is difficult to imagine words which would give a wider discretion to the minister than those. Secondly, the burden is firmly and heavily upon the company in question to make out that the minister is not acting *bona fide* in accordance with his powers under that section ...'[66]

Lane LJ further drew a sharp distinction between the word 'evidence' and the word 'circumstances.' He observed:

> '"Circumstances" is the word used, not "evidence", nor "admissible evidence". It seems to me that the argument founders on that very point. It is indeed the purpose of the inquiry – the investigation which the minister has ordered – to discovery whether the view of the minister about those circumstances in the upshot is an accurate one or not.'[67]

This interpretation is broader than the interpretation of CA 1990, s 19(2), that was adopted in *Dunnes Stores Ireland Co Ltd v Ryan*[68] and may, therefore, be broader than the interpretation that the Irish courts would adopt in respect of CA 1990, s 8(1).

(d) Companies affected

(i) General definition

[13.032] There is nothing in CA 1990, s 7 or s 8, which defines the category of companies to which those provisions apply. In the absence of any specific definition, the term 'company' as it is used in relation to the appointment of inspectors by the court, must be accorded the general interpretation contained in CA 1963[69] of 'a company formed and registered under this Act, or an existing company.'[70]

---

[65] *Norwest Holst Ltd v Secretary of State for Trade* [1978] 1 Ch 201. See further Ch **12**.

[66] *Norwest Holst Ltd v Secretary of State for Trade* [1978] 1 Ch 201, 230 (*per* Lane LJ).

[67] *Norwest Holst Ltd v Secretary of State for Trade* [1978] 1 Ch 201, 230 (*per* Lane LJ).

[68] *Dunnes Stores Ireland Co Ltd v Ryan* [2002] 2 IR 60.

[69] According the CLEA 2001, s 3(1) 'Companies Acts' 'means the Companies Act, 1963, and every enactment (including this Act) which is to be construed as one with that Act.' CA 1990, s 3(1), provides, 'the Companies Acts' 'means the Companies Act, 1963, and every enactment (including this Act) which is to be construed as one with that Act.'

[70] CA 1963, s 2(1). 'Existing company' means 'a company formed and registered in a register kept in the State under the Joint Stock Companies Acts, the Companies Act, 1862, or the Companies (Consolidation) Act. 1908. CA 1963, s 2(1).

This can be contrasted with other categories of investigation, which can be initiated in respect of a category of entities that is broader than a 'company' as defined within the Companies Acts.[71]

(ii) Companies incorporated outside the State

[13.033] The range of entities to which the court can order the appointment of an inspector is broadly formulated, in one instance CA 1990, s 17, provides that:

> Sections 8 to 11, 13, 18 and 22 shall apply to all bodies corporate incorporated outside the State which are carrying on business in the State or have at any time carried on business therein as if they were companies registered under the Principal Act, subject to any necessary modifications.

This brings within the scope of CA 1990, s 8, bodies corporate that are not incorporated in Ireland, but which are carrying on business, or which have at any time carried on business, in the State. The DCE could therefore apply to court for the appointment of an inspector to a company which is incorporated in another jurisdiction but which carried on business in Ireland at some time in the past. One or two isolated transactions in Ireland do not suffice to bring a company that does not otherwise carry on business in the State within the remit of the act: a continuum of activity is required.[72]

[13.034] This provision does not extend to applications by a company, its members, directors, or creditors, for the appointment of an inspector, under CA 1990, s 7. In light of the fact that much of the focus of s 8 is on avoiding prejudice being caused to, or fraud committed against, the members or creditors of a company, the reason for not permitting the members or creditors of a company which is incorporated in a different jurisdiction, to petition the court under s 7, may be questioned. It is particularly curious when one considers that while the members cannot make the application to court, the same petition could be brought by the DCE on the basis of prejudice caused to those same members. It may be undesirable to permit the members of a company which is registered, incorporated and based in a different jurisdiction, to rely on some past business dealings of that company, to invoke the jurisdiction of the Irish courts under CA 1990, s 7 in all instances. There could be a risk of so-called 'forum shopping' in this regard. However, the important threshold in s 7, is that it is only the court that can order the appointment of an inspector. Moreover, there is no obligation on a court to make such an order, even if evidence of serious wrong-doing within a company is presented. The language of both s 7 and s 8 is permissive, providing that the court 'may' appoint an inspector if the requisite circumstances exist. Any risk of forum-shopping could be avoided by the exercise of the court's discretion. It should also be noted in this regard that the application of CA 1990, s 17 to companies which are not incorporated in Ireland, '... may be subject to any necessary modifications'. This clause could be relied upon to narrow the scope of an inspection of a company incorporated in another jurisdiction and to avoid the possibility of abuse in that regard.

In light of these factors, it may be seen as invidious that the members of a company which, for example, carries on a fraudulent business in Ireland without being

---

[71]   See, eg, CA 1990, s 19, as substituted by CLEA 2001, s 29. See Ch **12**.

[72]   *Minister for Justice v Siucre Éireann* [1992] 2 IR 215.

incorporated in the State, could not avail of the procedure contained in CA 1990, s 7, while the DCE could rely on similar grounds to apply to have an inspector appointed to that company under CA 1990, s 8.

(iii) Winding up

[13.035] There is one aspect of the power to apply to court for the appointment of an inspector under CA 1990, s 7 and s 8 that is more broadly formulated than other aspects of those provisions. Unlike other powers of investigation, this power can be exercised in respect of a company that is in the course of being wound-up.

Section 8(2)(a) provides, 'The power conferred by s 7 or this section shall be exercisable with respect to a body corporate not withstanding that it is in course of being wound up.'

This can be contrasted with the equivalent English provision, CA 1985, s 432(3), which provides that the power of the Secretary of State to appoint an inspector under s 432(2) 'is exercisable with respect to a body corporate notwithstanding that it is in course of being voluntarily wound up.' There are two particular points of contrast with s 432(3) that highlight the breadth of s 8(2)(a). First, the power to investigate a company that is being wound-up only arises in England in one of the three situations in which an inspector can be appointed to investigate the affairs of a company. In Ireland, this power arises when an inspector is appointed on the application of the members, the company, the DCE, among others. Secondly, s 432(2) only addresses companies that are being wound-up voluntarily, whereas s 8(2)(a) is broad enough to cover a company being wound-up either compulsorily or voluntarily.

(iv) Related company

[13.036] The appointment of an inspector to investigate the affairs of a company can have implications for other companies. In particular, when an inspector is appointed to a company, companies which are related to that company should be aware of the terms of CA 1990, s 9. This provision permits an inspector to extend his investigation of a company into the affairs of a related company, where the inspector considers this to be necessary for the primary investigation. The approval of the court must be obtained before such an extension will be permitted. Where this occurs, the inspector's report will include a report of the affairs of that related company insofar as they are relevant to the primary investigation. An application under s 9 must be made by means of an originating notice of motion and must be served on the company, its directors, and the applicant for the appointment of the inspector.[73]

CA 1990, s 9(1) provides:

> If an inspector appointed under s 7 or 8 to investigate the affairs of a company thinks it necessary for the purposes of his investigation to investigate also the affairs of any other body corporate which is related to such company, he shall, with the approval of the court, have power so to do, and shall report on the affairs of the other body corporate so far as he thinks the results of his investigation

---

[73] Rules of the Superior Courts 1986, ord 75B, r (3)(c), as inserted by the Rules of the Superior Courts (No 4) 1991 (SI 278/1991).

thereof are relevant to the investigation of the affairs of the first-mentioned company.

The fairness of this provision and its compatibility with the other provisions of CA 1990, Pt II, may be questioned, as it does permit an investigation to be conducted into a company's affairs without the criteria for the appointment of an inspector necessarily being met.[74] However, there are two factors which may quell such concerns. First, court approval is necessary and this should permit any objections to the opening of the secondary investigation to be heard and adjudicated upon.

Secondly, the definition of a 'related company,' as it is contained in CA 1990, s 140,[75] is quite rigorous and, in essence, requires that there be a high level of cross-ownership or control or other close connection between the two companies.

Section 140(5) provides:

> For the purposes of this Act, a company is related to another company if—
>
> (a) that other company is its holding company or subsidiary; or
>
> (b) more than half in nominal value of its equity share capital (as defined in s 155(5) of the Principal Act) is held by the other company and companies related to that other company (whether directly or indirectly, but other than in a fiduciary capacity); or
>
> (c) more than half in nominal value of the equity share capital (as defined in s 155(5) of the Principal Act) of each of them is held by members of the other (whether directly or indirectly, but other than in a fiduciary capacity); or
>
> (d) that other company or a company or companies related to that other company or that other company together with a company or companies related to it are entitled to exercise or control the exercise of more than one half of the voting power at any general meeting of the company; or
>
> (e) the businesses of the companies have been so carried on that the separate business of each company, or a substantial part thereof, is not readily identifiable; or
>
> (f) there is another company to which both companies are related;
>
> and 'related company' has a corresponding meaning.

[13.037] In light of this definition, it is unsurprising that an inspector may consider it necessary to investigate the affairs of a related company to assist in the primary investigation. This could conceivably arise, for instance, where a holding company was under investigation and the inspector considered it necessary to examine the affairs of a subsidiary in order to complete the primary investigation. The only caveat to the application of CA 1990, s 140(5) to s 9(1) arises from the reference in s 9(1) to the related entity as a 'body corporate.' In light of the references in CA 1990, ss 3(1) and 140(5) to companies and related companies, it is curious that s 9(1) adopts the term 'body corporate' and, by extension, 'related body corporate'. This could undermine the use of the s 140(5) definition of 'related company' in the context of s 9(1). There is no alternative definition of bodies corporate which are related to each other, however. For

---

[74]   See CA 1990, ss 7 and 8, as amended by CLEA 2001, ss 20 and 21.

[75]   CA 1990, s 3(1) provides that 'related company' 'has the meaning assigned to it by s 140.'

that reason, it can only be assumed that the definition in s 140 is intended to apply to s 9(1).

[13.038] A significant amendment was introduced to CA 1990, s 9. CLEA 2001, s 22 inserted a new s 9(2) in the following terms:

> For the purposes of this section, a body corporate which is related to a company includes a body corporate with which the company has a commercial relationship, and a commercial relationship exists where goods or services are sold or given by one party to another.

The effect of this amendment is not entirely clear. It does not refer to the definition in CA 1990, s 140, of a company being related to another company or to the fact that that definition applies to CA 1990, s 9. Given the undeniable logic of being able to extend an investigation into companies with the degree of proximity provided for in s 140, it is unlikely that CLEA 2001 intended to displace the definition contained in that provision. The more likely interpretation is that CA 1990, s 9(2) extends the definition of a 'related company.' This widening of the definition expressly only applies to CA 1990, s 9(1).

The right of an inspector to investigate the affairs of a company which has no more than a commercial relationship with the company under investigation, does not sit easily with the scheme of CA 1990, Pt II.

[13.039] Section 9(1) of CA 1990, fell to be considered by the High Court in *Chestvale Properties Ltd v Glackin*.[76] In that case, the inspector sent a written demand to the bankers of a company under investigation seeking, among other things, production of books or documents related to a different company, which was identified by name and described as a 'related company'. No advance approval had been obtained for an extension of the investigation, as required by CA 1990, s 9. The company under investigation challenged the request for documents on that ground, among others. Murphy J noted that even if the company in question was a related company within the meaning of s 9, which it in fact was not, no approval had been obtained under s 9, and the demand for books and documents related to the second company was not authorised by the Companies Acts. That finding is entirely consistent with the purpose and function of CA 1990, s 9.

However, Murphy J made a further observation that could re-open this question. He noted:

> 'On the other hand the fact that particular books and documents may be properly identified as being the property of or relating to one company does not necessarily preclude them from relating also to another company.'[77]

This highlights the breadth of the category of documents which can be captured by the enforcement mechanism at the disposal of inspectors provided for in s 10[78] and the possibility that the requirements of s 9 could be evaded where there is any connection between the documents relating to the company under investigation and those relating to

---

[76] *Chestvale Properties Ltd v Glackin* [1993] 3 IR 35.

[77] At p 49. This was affirmed in *Re Countyglen Plc (under investigation)* [1995] 1 IR 220.

[78] See below, paras **[13.067]**–**[13.082]**.

other entities. If the inspector appointed to investigate Chestvale Properties Ltd had not used the expression 'related company' in the demand for books and documents, but instead referred to the books and documents of and relating to the company under investigation, even where such books and documents would also relate to other companies, many relevant documents of and relating to the other company may have been caught, without the necessity of obtaining approval under s 9.

[13.040] In a subsequent judgment in the same matter,[79] Murphy J considered a submission to the effect that, where the power under s 9 to extend an investigation to a second company could have been, but was not exercised, the documents which are demanded in the course of the investigation should not cover or concern such second companies. Murphy J held:

> 'I see no reason why the range of documents would necessarily be restricted by the
> power of the Minister to extend the inquiry. It seems to me that the test as to what
> documents must be produced by the persons to whom a demand is addressed falls
> to be determined under s 10 of the Act of 1990 as adapted by s 14 and not by
> reference to s 9 of that Act.'

While this interpretation is entirely supported by the wording of the Act, it could heighten the possibility referred to above, that the requirements of s 9 could be evaded by a broad demand for documents of the company under investigation, which would encompass books and documents that are primarily of or relating to other companies, and merely bear some relation to the company under investigation.[80]

[13.041] The extension of an investigation to the affairs of a related company under CA 1990, s 9, can be contrasted with the equivalent English provision. CA 1985, s 433, provides:

> If inspectors appointed under s 431 or 432 to investigate the affairs of a company
> think it necessary for the purposes of their investigation to investigate also the
> affairs of another body corporate which is or at any relevant time has been the
> company's subsidiary or holding company, or a subsidiary of its holding company
> or a holding company of its subsidiary, they have power to do so; and they shall
> report on the affairs of the other body corporate so far as they think that the results
> of their investigation of its affairs are relevant to the investigation of the affairs of
> the company first mentioned above.

The most important point of distinction is that the English provision permits inspectors to extend their investigations to the affairs of a related company, without the necessity of obtaining the approval of the Secretary of State or of the court. A second distinction is the close level of proximity that must exist between companies before the investigation can be extended in England, particularly when contrasted with the breadth of the newly-introduced s 9(2).

---

[79]   *Chestvale Properties Ltd v Glackin (No 2)* (10 March 1992, unreported), HC, Murphy J.

[80]   This interpretation is cited with apparent approval by McCarthy J in *Glackin v Desmond (No 2)* [1993] 3 IR 67 at 126.

(e) Request of other authority

[13.042] The powers of the DCE regarding the investigation of companies is extended by the insertion of CA 1990, s 23A, by CLEA 2001, s 33. This new provision permits the DCE to exercise the powers conferred upon him by CA 1990, Pt II, where he receives a request from a company law authority in another jurisdiction for such assistance.

Section 23A provides:

> (1) The powers conferred on the Director by this Part are also exercisable by the Director on foot of a request from a company law authority for assistance in connection with inquiries being carried out by it or on its behalf where the Director is satisfied that such assistance is for the purpose of the discharge by the authority of its supervisory or regulatory functions.
>
> (2) The Director may decline to accede to a request referred to in sub-s (1) if, in the opinion of the Director, it is not appropriate to so accede or where the company law authority making the request does not undertake to make such contribution to the costs attendant on the request as the Director considers appropriate.
>
> (3) In this section, 'company law authority' means an authority outside the State which performs functions of a supervisory or regulatory nature in relation to bodies corporate or undertakings or their officers, or a person acting on behalf of such an authority.

This extension of the DCE's powers is subject to a number of qualifications. The DCE must be 'satisfied' that the company law authority in question is seeking the assistance in question for the purpose of the discharge of that authority's supervisory or regulatory functions. This requirement is reinforced by the fact that the assistance that is captured by s 23A can only be sought in connection with inquiries being carried out by the other authority or on its behalf. The combination of these provisos should avoid the risk of the powers conferred upon the DCE by Pt II being extended in an unwarranted manner. Even if these two criteria are met, the DCE has the right to refuse the assistance sought. This right arises in two situations. First, if the DCE considers that it is not appropriate to accede to the request for assistance, he has the right to refuse to do so. This is a very general provision and protects the right of the DCE to guard his own powers under Pt II and the extent of his discretion thereunder. In light of the potentially invasive nature of many of the powers contained in Pt II, it would not be desirable from a policy perspective for an overseas authority to be in position to compel the DCE to provide assistance under s 23A.

The second ground on which the DCE can refuse to furnish assistance is of a more practical nature. The DCE can refuse assistance where the other authority does not furnish such undertaking to contribute to the costs of the assistance sought, as the DCE considers appropriate. In respect of both grounds on which the DCE can decline to exercise his powers under Pt II, there is no obligation on the DCE to explain or justify his decision. Moreover, there is no requirement that the appropriateness of the request or the undertaking as to costs be gauged objectively. It is only necessary that the DCE be of the opinion that it is not appropriate to accede to the request or that the appropriate contribution to costs is not forthcoming.

B. Investigation of membership of company

[13.043] The DCE has certain powers to appoint inspectors and to investigate particular aspects of the ownership and management of companies. These provisions are aimed towards ascertaining the true ownership and control of companies and have been invoked in several high profile instances.[81]

(a) Inspector

(i) Appointment

[13.044] Section 14(1)[82] is the provision which governs the appointment of an inspector by the DCE to investigate the membership of a company. It provides:

> The Director may, subject to sub-s (2), appoint one or more competent inspectors to investigate and report on the membership of any company and otherwise with respect to the company for the purpose of determining the true persons who are or have been financially interested in the success or failure (real or apparent) of the company or able to control or materially to influence the policy of the company.

There is no court involvement in the appointment of inspectors under s 14.

(ii) Grounds

[13.045] The grounds on which the DCE can appoint an inspector to investigate the membership of a company are very broad. According to CA 1990, s 14(2):[83]

> An appointment may be made by the Director if he is of the opinion that there are circumstances suggesting that it is necessary—
>
> (a) for the effective administration of the law relating to companies;
>
> (b) for the effective discharge by the Minister of his functions under any enactment; or
>
> (c) in the public interest.

In determining that it is necessary to appoint an inspector, the DCE must comply with the requirements of constitutional justice and, in particular, must ensure that the decision is neither arbitrary nor disproportionate; that it is reasonable; that it is exercised for the purposes contemplated by s 14; and reasons must be given for the decision.[84]

---

[81]   See, eg, *Chestvale Properties Ltd v Glackin* [1993] 3 IR 35.

[82]   As amended by CLEA 2001, Sch.

[83]   As amended by CLEA 2001, s14, which substituted references to 'Minister' for 'Director'.

[84]   See *Dunnes Stores Ireland Co Ltd v Ryan* [2002] 2 IR 60, 89 *per* Murray J. This decision was reached in the context of CA 1990, s 19, as substituted by CLEA 2001, s 29, but would apply to the review of decisions under CA 1990, s 14. See, in particular, the *dicta* of Keane CJ at p 77, which refers specifically to investigations under s 14. See further Ch **12**.

In *Probets v Glackin*,[85] O'Hanlon J considered a submission that the warrant of appointment was invalid as it failed to recite the nature of the public interest underlying the appointment and concluded:

> '... a recital of the nature of the public interest involved is not essential to the validity of the warrant of appointment; that while it might be desirable in many cases to recite it in the warrant of appointment, it was unnecessary in the present case because of the wide publicity already given to the matters of public interest which led up to the appointment of the first respondent.'[86]

Where the matters giving rise to the investigation are notorious, the requirement to specify the public interest underlying the appointment may therefore be waived. A similar circumstance arose in *Desmond v Glackin (No 2)*[87] in which O'Hanlon J reiterated that the Minister did not have to spell out the underlying public interest, but held that the appointment did have to be *bona fide*, factually sustainable and not unreasonable, applying the test laid down in *The State (Lynch) v Cooney*.[88]

(iii) Scope of inspection

[13.046] The scope of an investigation that is commenced under CA 1990, s 14, can be defined by the DCE, by reference to the subject matter, the period of time covered and the scope may even be defined so narrowly as to refer to particular shares or debentures. Section 14(3) provides:

> The appointment of an inspector under this section may define the scope of his investigation, whether as respects the matters or the period to which it is to extend or otherwise, and in particular may limit the investigation to matters connected with particular shares or debentures.

The potential scope of an inspection under s 14 is widened by the discretion which s 14(4) confers on an inspector appointed under that section:

> Subject to the terms of an inspector's appointment his powers shall extend to the investigation of any circumstances suggesting the existence of an arrangement or understanding which, though not legally binding, is or was observed or likely to be observed in practice and which is relevant to the purposes of his investigation.

(iv) Powers

[13.047] An inspector appointed under CA 1990, s 14 possesses all of the same powers as an inspector appointed by the court under s 7 or s 8.[89] The only qualifications are that the provision governing production of directors' banking documentation,[90] does not

---

85 *Probets v Glackin* [1993] 3 IR 134.

86 *Probets v Glackin* [1993] 3 IR 134 at 139.

87 *Desmond v Glackin (No 2)* [1993] 3 IR 67 at 83.

88 *The State (Lynch) v Cooney* [1982] IR 337 at 661. See further *Dunnes Stores Ireland Co Ltd v Ryan* [2002] 2 IR 60. See also Ch **12**.

89 CA 1990, s 14(5) provides, 'For the purposes of any investigation under this section, ss 9 to 11, except s 10(3), shall apply with the necessary modifications of references to the affairs of the company or to those of any other body corporate ...'.

90 CA 1990, s 10(3). See further paras **[13.091]** to **[13.096]**.

apply to inspectors appointed by the DCE, and that references to 'the court' in ss 9 to 11 are largely replaced by references to 'the Director' in the context of s 14.[91] An illustration of this is that an inspector appointed by the DCE, must get the approval of the DCE before extending investigations into the affairs of a related company, within the meaning of s 9, whereas a court-appointed inspector, must apply for court approval of such an extension. The final adaptation of ss 9 to 11 for the purposes of an inspection under s 14, concerns the category of persons to whom those provisions apply. Section 14(5)(a) provides:

> … the said sections shall apply in relation to all persons who are or have been, or whom the inspector has reasonable cause to believe to be or have been, financially interested in the success or failure or the apparent success or failure of the company or any other body corporate whose membership is investigated with that of the company, or able to control or materially to influence the policy thereof, including persons concerned only on behalf of others and to any other person whom the inspector has reasonable cause to believe possesses information relevant to the investigation, as they apply in relation to officers and agents of the company or of the other body corporate, as the case may be.

(v) Publication

[13.048] The general rule, that the provisions governing the conduct of an investigation under s 7 or 8 apply equally to investigations under s 14, is qualified by s 14(5)(b). This provision derogates to a limited extent from the approach of s 11, which governs the publication and dissemination of inspectors' reports. Section 14(5)(b) provides:

> … if the Minister is of opinion that there is good reason for not divulging any part of a report made by virtue of this section he may disclose the report with the omission of that part; and may cause to be kept by the registrar of companies a copy of the report with that part omitted or, in the case of any other such report, a copy of the whole report.

(vi) Expenses

[13.049] CLEA 2001, s 26 introduced a number of changes to inspections under s 14. These changes deal solely with the expenses of such inspections:

> (6) The court may, on the application of the Director, direct that a company the subject of an investigation under this section shall be liable, to such extent as the court may direct, to repay the Director the expenses of and incidental to the investigation.
>
> (7) Without prejudice to sub-s (6) but subject to sub-s (8), a person—
>
> (a) convicted on indictment of an offence on a prosecution instituted,
>
> (b) ordered to pay damages or restore any property in proceedings brought, or

---

91 The only instances in which the references to the court remain, are s 10(5) and (6), which concern the certification to court of refusals to comply with inspections. See above paras **[13.097]** to **[13.100]**.

(c) awarded damages or to whom property is restored in proceedings brought,

as a result of an investigation under this section may, in the same proceedings, be ordered to repay the Director all or part of the expenses referred to in sub-s (6).

(8) The court shall not order a person to whom sub-s (7)(c) relates to make payment in excess of one-tenth of the amount of the damages awarded or of the value of the property restored, as the case may be, and any such order shall not be executed until the person concerned has received his damages or the property has been restored.

(b) Investigations

[13.050] Where the circumstances that could warrant the appointment of an inspector under s 14 exist, but the DCE considers that such an appointment is not necessary, there is an additional power contained in CA 1990, s 15. Pursuant to this provision, the DCE can require certain information, where it appears to him to be necessary to investigate the ownership of any shares or debentures of a company, on one of the three grounds that are listed in s 14, namely, for the effective administration of company law; for the effective discharge of the Director's functions; or in the public interest.

Where these criteria are met, the DCE has the following powers:

… he may require any person whom he has reasonable cause to believe to have or to be able to obtain any information as to the present and past interests in those shares or debentures and the names and addresses of the persons interested and of any persons who act or have acted on their behalf in relation to the shares or debentures to give any such information to the Director.[92]

The persons who are considered to have an interest in a share or debenture are defined very broadly by CA 1990, s 15(2):

For the purposes of this section a person shall be deemed to have an interest in a share or debenture if he has any right to acquire or dispose of the share or debenture or any interest therein or to vote in respect thereof or if his consent is necessary for the exercise of any of the rights of other persons interested therein or if the other persons interested therein can be required or are accustomed to exercise their rights in accordance with his instructions.

Section 15 does not contain much detail regarding the powers of the DCE in the conduct of an investigation under that section. However, where the DCE requests information of an individual, the threat of sanction for non-compliance, should encourage the individual to accede to the DCE's request.

Section 15(3) provides in this regard:

Any person who fails to give any information required of him under this section or who in giving any such information makes any statement which he knows to be false in a material particular, or recklessly makes any statement which is false in a material particular, shall be guilty of an offence …

---

[92] CA 1990, s 15(1), as amended by CLEA 2001, s 14.

(c) Share restrictions

[13.051] There is a power conferred on the DCE by CA 1990, s 16, which complements the powers of the DCE under CA 1990, ss 14 and 15. It permits the DCE to restrict any activity in relation to shares, about which the DCE has found it difficult to ascertain the relevant facts.[93]

(d) Investigations of share dealing

[13.052] The DCE can appoint inspectors to investigate whether there have been contraventions of particular provisions of CA 1990, when it appears to the Director that there are circumstances suggesting such contraventions. CA 1990, s 66 accordingly provides that the DCE may appoint inspectors to investigate suspected contraventions of ss 30,[94] 53[95] and 64(3) to (5).[96] Inspectors appointed under s 66 generally enjoy the same powers as inspectors appointed under ss 7, 8 and 14.[97] Inspectors appointed under s 14 are also required to deliver a final report to the DCE and may also be required to deliver interim reports.[98]

C. Conduct of investigations

(a) Role of inspectors

[13.053] The role of an inspector has attracted considerable scrutiny in this jurisdiction and others. In relation to the classification of the functions of an inspector, there is a relatively high degree of consensus. Before examining Irish case law, it is useful to note that the European Court of Human Rights, adjudicating upon the investigations regime in the UK,[99] made the following observations:

> '... the court recalls its judgment in *Fayed v UK*[100] ... where it held that the functions performed by the inspectors under s 432(2) of the Companies Act 1985

---

[93]   See CA 1990, s 16, as amended by CLEA 2001, ss 14 and 27. See Courtney, *The Law of Private Companies* (2nd edn, Tottel Publishing, 2002) at paras 14.085 to 14.088. Note that applications under s 16(5), (7), (8) and (9) must be made by means of originating notice of motion. Rules of the Superior Courts 1986, ord 75B, r 3(e), as inserted by Rules of the Superior Courts (No 4) 1991 (SI 278/1991).

[94]   CA 1990, s 30, as amended by CLEA 2001, s 102, relates to dealings by directors in options to buy or sell shares or debentures of a company.

[95]   CA 1990, s 53, which relates to the obligation of directors and secretaries to notify the company of any interests in shares and debentures of the company.

[96]   CA 1990, s 63, which extends s 53 to spouses and children of directors and secretaries.

[97]   CA 1990, s 66(3) applies s 10 to investigations under s 66, with certain modifications. Note that CA 1990, ss 9, 16 to 18, 22 and 23(1) and (3) also apply with the necessary modifications to investigations under s 66. See CA 1990, s 66(6).

[98]   CA 1990, s 66(4), as amended by CLEA 2001, s 14.

[99]   *Saunders v United Kingdom* (Case 43/1994/490/572) (1996) 23 EHRR 313, [1998] 1 BCLC 362.

[100] *Fayed v UK* (Case 28/1993/423/502) (A/294-B) (1994) 18 EHRR 393.

were essentially investigative in nature and that they did not adjudicate either in form or in substance. Their purpose was to ascertain and record facts which might subsequently be used as the basis for action by other competent authorities – prosecuting, regulatory, disciplinary or even legislative.[101] As stated in that case, a requirement that such a preparatory investigation should be subject to the guarantees of a judicial procedure as set forth in art 6(1) would in practice unduly hamper the effective regulation in the public interest of complex financial and commercial activities ...'[102]

This clearly treats an inspection as investigative, rather than adjudicative, in nature, and establishes that the imposition of the protections of a judicial procedure would hamper the conduct of an inspection, contrary to the public interest.

[13.054] Irish courts have considered the character of an investigation in a number of cases. *Chestvale Properties Ltd v Glackin*[103] arose from the appointment of an inspector by the Minister for Tourism, Transport and Communications under CA 1990, s 14, to investigate the membership of two companies (Chestvale Properties Ltd and Hoddle Investments Ltd). These companies were involved in a series of transactions, leading to the sale of a site in Dublin to Telecom Éireann, at a substantially higher price than the price for which it was acquired. One of the arguments in that case was that the inspector, a solicitor, was disqualified from acting as inspector on the grounds of bias, as the firm in which he worked had previously represented an individual (Mr Doherty) who was interested in the transactions in question. The High Court (Murphy J) considered this allegation, and analysed the nature of an inspection to determine whether the powers of an inspector could be described as 'quasi-judicial'.

The test of bias that was formulated by the Supreme Court in *O'Neill v Beaumont Hospital Board*[104] was relied upon:

'The test is an objective test as to whether a person in the position of the plaintiff who is a reasonable man might reasonably fear that the pre-judgment expressed by the chairman would prevent a completely fair and independent hearing of the issues which arise.'[105]

Applying this definition to the circumstances of the inspector appointed to investigate Chestvale Properties Ltd and Hoddle Investments Ltd, Murphy J considered that the inspector would be disqualified from acting in a quasi-judicial role in any matter in which Mr Doherty was involved, as the reasonable suspicion of bias would invalidate the exercise of a judicial function. This begged the question of whether the role of the inspector appointed under CA 1990, s 14 is a quasi-judicial one.

---

[101] See *Fayed v UK* (Case 28/1993/423/502) (A/294-B) (1994) 18 EHRR 393 at 427–428 (para 61).

[102] *Saunders v United Kingdom* (Case 43/1994/490/572) (1996) 23 EHRR 313 at para 67.

[103] *Chestvale Properties Ltd v Glackin* [1993] 3 IR 35.

[104] *O'Neill v Beaumont Hospital Board* [1990] ILRM 419.

[105] *O'Neill v Beaumont Hospital Board* [1990] ILRM 419 at 438.

Murphy J regarded the decision in *Re Pergamon Press Ltd*,[106] which related to statutory provisions similar to CA 1990, Pt II, to be 'helpful.'[107] Sach LJ described the functions of an inspector in that case and concluded that:

> 'One way or another it may be a considerable time before the inspectors have before them sufficient information to see any pattern in the affairs of a company. Even when this pattern commences to take shape, they may need further material before the possibility emerges of any criticism attaching to individuals ... more complex the affairs of the company and the greater the number of subsidiary companies, the longer it may take before those respective stages are reached.'[108]

In *Re Haughey*,[109] the Supreme Court examined the nature of proceedings before the Committee of Public Accounts of Dáil Éireann and the duties owed to persons whose conduct was impugned by evidence received by the committee. The court in *Re Haughey*[110] stated that the examination and investigation conducted by the Committee reached the stage at which,

> '... Mr Haughey is more than a mere witness. The true analogy, in terms of High Court procedure, is not that of a witness but of a party. Mr Haughey's conduct is the very subject matter of the Committee's examination and is to be the subject matter of the Committee's report.'[111]

Murphy J summarised these decisions, among others, as demonstrating that an investigating authority is bound to conduct itself in accordance with an appropriate measure of natural justice. However, this was qualified by the observation that:

> 'On the other hand it is, I believe, equally clear that the findings in that regard were directed and relevant only to certain issues within the various investigations and were not intended to be applied and could not in fact be applied to each and every inquiry or communication emanating from the investigating authority.'[112]

This was supported by the analysis of an inspector's duties that was adopted by Buckley LJ in *Re Pergamon Press Ltd*:[113]

> 'Until an inspector has reached a stage at which he thinks that he will, or, at least, may have to report adversely on a director or officer, it will be premature for him to decide what, if anything, he should do to give the director or officer a fair chance of explaining the matter.'[114]

[13.055] Applying this reasoning to the facts of *Chestvale Properties Ltd v Glackin*,[115] Murphy J concluded that the proceedings before him were commenced when the investigation was at a preliminary, exploratory stage. Murphy J further concluded that, if

---

[106] *Re Pergamon Press Ltd* [1971] 1 Ch 388.

[107] *Chestvale Properties Ltd v Glackin* [1993] 3 IR 35 at 49.

[108] *Re Pergamon Press Ltd* [1971] 1 Ch 388 at 404.

[109] *Re Haughey* [1971] IR 217.

[110] *Re Haughey* [1971] IR 217.

[111] *Re Haughey* [1971] IR 217 at 263.

[112] *Chestvale Properties Ltd v Glackin* [1993] 3 IR 35 at 49, *per* Murphy J.

[113] *Re Pergamon Press Ltd* [1971] 1 Ch 388.

[114] *Re Pergamon Press Ltd* [1971] 1 Ch 388 at 407.

[115] *Chestvale Properties Ltd v Glackin* [1993] 3 IR 35.

Mr Doherty's claim to be interested in the companies under investigation proceeded to be substantiated by evidence obtained by the inspector in the course of his investigations, with no conflict of evidence:

> '… there will be no conflict to be resolved by proceedings analogous to a judicial hearing. In these circumstances it must be presumed that the respondent … will not have to "enter a verdict" on any issue between claimants to the shares in question.'[116]

Even if there was a potential conflict of evidence concerning the involvement of Mr Doherty, necessitating a decision by the inspector to resolve such conflict, Murphy J emphasised that this had not yet occurred and the application for disqualification on the grounds of bias was therefore premature.

The most important impact of this decision, from the perspective of the role of an inspector, is the determination that the preliminary investigative phase of an inspection does not involve the discharge of quasi-judicial functions, but that such functions may become part of the role of an inspector when positive determinations fall to be made regarding such matters as conflicts of evidence.

[13.056] This analysis has been followed in subsequent decisions of the High Court. In *Re National Irish Bank Ltd*,[117] the facts of which are set out elsewhere,[118] the inspectors described the procedure they proposed to adopt as involving two stages, the first being information gathering. The second would only arise if, on the basis of information collected in the first stage, there was the possibility of drawing adverse conclusions regarding certain individuals. In the event of a second stage being necessary, the inspectors proposed that the individuals in question would be entitled to attend before them; to hear the evidence against them; to conduct cross-examinations; and to give evidence.

This procedure was challenged in the High Court and there were disputes as to whether the first stage was purely investigative or accusatory. Shanley J determined that, in the first stage of the investigation the documents the inspectors had obtained did not constitute evidence in a strict legal sense and the inspectors were not obliged to afford the protections that would be appropriate to an adversarial process.[119]

[13.057] In a judgment delivered by Kelly J in relation to the same investigation,[120] the High Court considered the rights of individuals affected by an investigation to have access to certain documents and transcripts arising from the investigation. This aspect of the decision is considered elsewhere.[121] What is relevant for present purposes is the analysis of the function of an inspector contained in the judgment. Kelly J stated unequivocally, 'An inspection of this type is primarily investigative. It only becomes adversarial in limited circumstances.'[122] In relation to the investigation into the affairs of

---

[116] *Chestvale Properties Ltd v Glackin* [1993] 3 IR 35 at 51.

[117] *Re National Irish Bank Ltd (No 1)* [1999] 3 IR 145.

[118] See below para **[13.085]**. See also Pt **E**, Disqualification Orders.

[119] *Re National Irish Bank Ltd (No 1)* [1999] 3 IR 145.

[120] *Re National Irish Bank Ltd (No 2)* [1999] 3 IR 190.

[121] See below paras **[3.109]** to **[13.110]**.

[122] *Re National Irish Bank Ltd (No 2)* [1999] 3 IR 190 at 214.

the National Irish Bank, as has been seen, the inspectors proposed a particular two-stage procedure. Applying this approach, Kelly J concluded, 'the inspectors are only at a preliminary stage of their investigation and have not been called upon to exercise any quasi-judicial functions since that will not arise until stage two is reached.' In respect of the implications of an investigation reaching stage two, Kelly J held:

> 'Once one moves into the second stage then, whilst the investigation is not transformed into an adversarial hearing, nonetheless fair procedures have to be observed insofar as any adverse conclusions may be drawn in relation to individuals.'[123]

[13.058] One of the decisions on which the High Court relied was the decision of Lord Denning MR in *Maxwell v Dept of Trade and Industry*,[124] which contained a clear statement of the nature of an inspection:

> 'First and foremost, when a matter is referred to an inspector for investigation and report, it is a very special kind of inquiry. It must not be confused with other inquiries which we have had to consider. Remember what it is not. It is not a trial of anyone, nor anything like it. There is no accused person. There is no prosecutor. There is no charge. It is not like a disciplinary proceeding before a professional body. Nor is it like an application to expel a man from a trade union or a club, or anything of that kind. It is not even like a committee which considers whether there is a *prima facie* case against a person. It is simply an investigation, without anyone being accused.'[125]

In *Re National Irish Bank Ltd*,[126] Kelly J accepted this statement of the law as:

> '... a correct summary of the position which obtains at least insofar as the investigatory stage of the inspectors' task is concerned. Once one moves into the second stage then, whilst the investigation is not transformed into an adversarial hearing, nonetheless fair procedures have to be observed insofar as any adverse conclusions may be drawn in relation to individuals.'[127]

This clarifies that, while the first phase of an inspector's work is simply an investigation not involving accusations, inspections can take on a different character. In Ireland, the legal position appears to be that once an inspection involves the making of decisions regarding conflicts of evidence and the formation of adverse conclusions, for instance, it

---

[123] *Re National Irish Bank Ltd (No 2)* [1999] 3 IR 190 at 215.

[124] *Maxwell v Dep of Trade and Industry* [1974] 1 QB 523.

[125] *Maxwell v Dep of Trade and Industry* [1974] 1 QB 523 at 533.

[126] *Re National Irish Bank Ltd (No 2)* [1999] 3 IR 190.

[127] *Re National Irish Bank Ltd (No 2)* [1999] 3 IR 190, 215. Kelly J also drew an analogy with criminal proceedings, noting, that criminal investigations do not necessarily result in charges and that the rights argued for would hamper an investigation unduly. Applying this analogy, he concluded (at 217): 'In my view, the same result would be had here. When the inspectors come to stage two of their investigation there may be nothing for the applicants to answer. Secondly, the correspondence from the solicitors for the applicants makes it clear that they wish to have these documents so that they may at this stage respond to the allegations made. Such an exercise would merely prove a hindrance to the inspectors in the carrying out of their functions, is unnecessary and would be wasteful of both time and resources.'

is no longer true to say that the procedure is purely investigative. Unless such a stage is reached, it would be costly, wasteful and inefficient to afford the rights sought. However, if the stage is reached in an inspection where adverse conclusions are being drawn, persons affected thereby have certain rights to fair procedures. These will now be examined.

(b) Fair procedure

[13.059] It has been seen that persons affected by an inspection do not have rights, such as the right of access to documents or the right to cross-examine witnesses, during the purely investigative phase of the inspection. However, if an inspection progresses to the stage where conclusions are being formed and decisions made on the evidence before an inspector, certain rights of the individual do intrude. The rights in question were set out in the decision of the Supreme Court in *Re Haughey*[128] and include the right of access to material which reflect on a persons' good name and reputation; the right to give evidence; and the right to cross-examine other witnesses. In that case, accusations were made by evidence under oath before the Public Accounts Committee which reflected on the character and good name of the person in question. The accusations were based upon the hearsay evidence of a witness before the Public Accounts Committee of Dáil Éireann.

As Shanley J pointed out in *Re National Irish Bank Ltd*,[129] this could not be equated with the investigative stage of an inspection. In *Re Haughey*,[130] it was direct evidence that was challenged, whereas in the initial phase of an investigation, under the Companies Acts, the material cannot be categorised as evidence, within the meaning of *Re Haughey*.[131] In the case of *Re National Irish Bank Ltd*,[132] the content of these rights was not explored, as the inspection was at a preliminary stage and did not attract the so-called 'panoply of rights' guaranteed by *Re Haughey*.[133] Moreover, the inspectors made it clear that they intended to respect such rights in the event that the inspection reached a second stage.[134] This indicates that the same rights that were recognised in *Re Haughey*[135] would be extended in the context of an investigation, but only when the investigation reaches a sufficiently advanced stage at which adverse conclusions may be drawn. Other decisions regarding the rights to fair procedure of persons who are affected by company inspections, will be examined in the context of the powers of inspectors.[136]

---

[128] *Re Haughey* [1971] IR 217.

[129] *Re National Irish Bank Ltd (No 1)* [1999] 3 IR 145.

[130] *Re Haughey* [1971] IR 217.

[131] *Re Haughey* [1971] IR 217.

[132] *Re National Irish Bank Ltd (No 1)* [1999] 3 IR 145.

[133] *Re Haughey* [1971] IR 217.

[134] *Re National Irish Bank Ltd (No 2)* [1999] 3 IR 190. 'At stage two of their investigation they have, in my view, made it clear that all of the rights to which a party might be entitled under the decision in *Re Haughey* [1971] IR 217 will be respected.' (*per* Kelly J at 215).

[135] *Re Haughey* [1971] IR 217.

[136] See below paras [13.085] to [3.086] for example.

(c) Court directions

[13.060] While an inspector is expressly subject to court approval or control only in very limited circumstances, such as the extension of the investigation into the affairs of a related company under CA 1990, s 9,[137] there is a useful provision of Pt II that permits court intervention in the conduct of an inspection.

Section 7(4) provides:

> Where the court appoints an inspector under this section or s 8, it may, from time to time, give such directions as it thinks fit, whether to the inspector or otherwise, with a view to ensuring that the investigation is carried out as quickly and as inexpensively as possible.

An application for directions may be made by motion *ex parte* grounded on the affidavit of the applicant and will be heard and determined on affidavit, unless the court otherwise directs.[138]

This provision has arisen for consideration in cases such as *Re National Irish Bank Ltd (No 2)*.[139] This case is examined in more detail elsewhere.[140] It concerned a refusal to answer the questions of an inspector, on the basis of the right to silence. There is a mechanism in CA 1990, s 10(5), as will be seen, for the certification of such refusals to the court. However, where the inspectors were aware in advance that the witnesses would refuse to answer questions, it was impractical and cumbersome to require them to go through the procedure of summoning these witnesses and receiving the expected refusals, before being in a position to certify the matter to the court.[141] This was particularly cumbersome in light of the fact that there were many witnesses in this position. Kelly J was of the view that it is more appropriate for the matter to come to court by means of a motion for directions under s 7(4). This illustrates the potential usefulness of the provision, where intractable issues do arise during an investigation, necessitating judicial intervention.

[13.061] In *Re National Irish Bank Ltd (No 2)*,[142] Kelly J considered a submission that s 7(4) should be invoked, as the investigation was not being conducted as inexpensively and efficiently as possible. In particular, the applicants sought orders under s 7(4) restricting the inspectors from investigating matters that were also being investigated by the Comptroller and Auditor General, as that represented a duplication of process. Having determined that the object of the investigation by the Controller and Auditor General was 'fundamentally different' to the object of the inspection, Kelly J concluded

---

[137] See above paras **[13.036]** to **[13.041]**.

[138] Rules of the Superior Courts 1986, ord 75B, rr 5(a) and 7, as inserted by Rules of the Superior Courts (No 4) 1991 (SI 278/1991).

[139] *Re National Irish Bank Ltd (No 2)* [1999] 3 IR 190 at 206–207.

[140] See below paras **[13.085]** *et seq.*

[141] *Re National Irish Bank Ltd (No 2)* [1999] 3 IR 190. 'I am also satisfied that it would not be in the interest of an expeditious and efficient conduct of the investigation or indeed in the public interest that these matter be left to be dealt with under the procedures prescribed in s 10(5) of the Act.' (*per* Kelly J).

[142] *Re National Irish Bank Ltd (No 2)* [1999] 3 IR 190.

that, while there was some degree of overlap, there was no duplication of process.[143] He went on to consider the relevance of s 7(4). The applicants contended that the effect of the alleged duplication was that the inspection was not being carried out as quickly and inexpensively as possible. This was countered by allegations of inconsistency, on the basis of the applicant's previous approach to the investigation. The inspectors further opined that it was necessary to continue with each aspect of the inspection and that, to do otherwise, would hamper the effectiveness of the investigation.

[13.062] Kelly J considered these submissions and concluded that the inspectors were in the best position to know how the order sought would impact on their investigation, and therefore rejected the application. Kelly J noted that, even if the application succeeded on its merits, he would not be willing to make the order sought, as:

> To do so would, it appears to me, give rise to the possibility of endless applications
> to the court asking it to in effect second guess decisions made by the inspectors as
> to what steps they consider necessary in order to report upon the issues. The
> inspectors appointed under these provisions are carrying out an important public
> duty in the public interest. They should not have to carry out their duties whilst
> constantly looking over their shoulders at the court in anticipation of decisions
> made by them in the course of the investigation being the subject matter of a form
> of judicial review … It puts no strain on the imagination to conceive of situations
> where argument would be made to the court that decisions of the inspectors as to
> what they considered necessary were wrong in law or irrational. Such a process
> would only tend to impede an investigation which is designed to be carried out
> thoroughly but efficiently.[144]

This establishes clearly that the right of the court to give directions to inspectors under s 7(4), should not be relied on as a means of second guessing the decisions of inspectors and that courts will be vigilant to ensure that inspectors will not be impeded in the execution of their tasks by the threat of constant court intervention.

(d) Information regarding offences

[13.063] Inspectors are obliged to deliver final reports on the completion of the inspection and may deliver interim reports, as will be seen.[145] There is an additional provision of CA 1990, which permits inspectors to inform the court of certain matters arising in the course of an investigation. Section 11(2) provides:

> Notwithstanding anything contained in sub-s (1), an inspector appointed under s 7
> or 8 may at any time in the course of his investigation, without the necessity of
> making an interim report, inform the court of matters coming to his knowledge as
> a result of the investigation tending to show that an offence has been committed.

This ensures that criminal matters coming to light will be dealt with expeditiously, without the necessity of waiting for the submission of an interim or final report.

---

[143] *Re National Irish Bank Ltd (No 2)* [1999] 3 IR 190 at 202–203.

[144] *Re National Irish Bank Ltd (No 2)* [1999] 3 IR 190 at 207–208.

[145] See below paras **[13.101]** to **[13.124]**.

[13.064] Section 7(4) can be contrasted with the English CA 1985, s 437 which provides:

> (1A) Any persons who have been appointed under s 431 or 432 may at any time and, if the Secretary of State directs them to do so, shall inform him of any matters coming to their knowledge as a result of their investigations.
>
> (1B) If it appears to the Secretary of State that matters have come to light in the course of the inspectors' investigation which suggest that a criminal offence has been committed, and those matters have been referred to the appropriate prosecuting authority, he may direct the inspectors to take no further steps in the investigation or to take only such further steps as are specified in the direction.
>
> (1C) Where an investigation is the subject of a direction under sub-s (1B), the inspectors shall make a final report to the Secretary of State only where—
>
> (a) they were appointed under s 432(1) (appointment in pursuance of an order of the court), or
>
> (b) the Secretary of State directs them to do so.

This provision has the considerable merit of addressing the implications for an ongoing investigation of concurrent criminal proceedings.

(e) Privacy of investigations

[13.065] The general rule is that investigations under the Companies Acts are conducted in private. However, in the course of an investigation, this can become a pertinent issue. In *Re Countyglen Plc*,[146] a case arising from the appointment of an inspector under s 8 to investigate the affairs of Countyglen Plc, the inspector applied to the High Court for directions under s 7(4). In particular, the inspector sought to engage a firm of lawyers in Guernsey to make an application under the Criminal Justice (Fraud Investigation) (Bailiwick of Guernsey) Law, 1991, to initiate an investigation into the affairs of a company related to Countyglen plc. At the hearing of the application the inspector applied successfully to have the proceedings heard *in camera*.

Murphy J considered arguments to the effect that the application regarding the company in Guernsey was an application under CA 1990, s 9, an argument which he rejected on the basis that his order related to the application being heard *in camera* and it did not permit the inspector to extend his investigations into the affairs of the other company. The *in camera* application was an application for directions under s 7(4). Murphy J also addressed arguments that an order giving directions under s 7(4) constitutes the administration of justice. Relying on the *dicta* of Walsh J in *The State (O) v O'Brien*,[147] that '[t]he quality of the act is to be determined by the act itself, not by the person who is doing the act,' Murphy J concluded, 'The fact that orders under that subsection must be made by a judge of the High Court does not of itself determine whether such orders constitute the administration of justice.'[148]

---

[146] *Re Countyglen Plc* [1995] 1 IR 220.

[147] *The State (O) v O'Brien* [1973] IR 50 at 67.

[148] *Re Countyglen Plc* [1995] 1 IR 220 at 224.

In relation to the terms of s 7(4), Murphy J further noted:

> 'It seems to me that most of the matters in respect of which the court would make an order under s 7, sub-s 4 are matters which the inspector might do within his own discretion but which he might prefer for his own protection or some reason to have sanctioned by an order of the court confirming the propriety of his action. When it is recognised that the investigation by the inspector is not itself the administration of justice – though from time to time it may involve the requirement to act judicially – it is difficult to see how or why guidance or directions as to how those functions should be carried out could themselves constitute the administration of justice.'[149]

On the basis of this decision, there is no duty to hear an application under s 7(4) in public, as it does not involve the administration of justice.

D. Powers of investigation

[13.066] An inspector who is appointed to investigate the affairs of a company is given far-reaching powers under the Companies Acts. These powers include the right to compel a broad range of persons to produce an extremely broad category of books or documents and to answer questions and otherwise assist in the investigation.[150] An inspector also has the power to examine persons on oath.[151] The breadth of the powers of an inspector is particularly evident when one considers the range of companies, other than the company under investigation, whose affairs can fall within the scope of the investigation.[152] The strength of an inspector's powers is moreover reinforced by the fact that any failure to co-operate, such as a failure to produce documents or to answer questions, can be referred to the court to make such order or give such directions as the court deems fit.[153]

(a) Production of documents

[13.067] When an inspector is appointed to investigate a company, all of the officers and agents of that company, as well as any related company which is being investigated, are under a duty to produce all books and documents of the company or relating to the company, which are in their custody or power. They are also under a duty to attend

---

[149] *Re Countyglen Plc* [1995] 1 IR 220 at 225.

[150] CA 1990, s 10(1), (2), as amended by CLEA 2001, s 23. Note that these powers apply to inspectors appointed to investigate the affairs of a company. They also apply to inspectors appointed under s 14, by means of s 14(5), as adapted by that provision. See para **[13.047]**. See below paras **[13.067]–[3.090]**.

[151] CA 1990, s 10(4). See below paras **[13.084]–[3.087]**.

[152] See, eg, CA 1990, s 9, as amended by CLEA 2001, s 22. See above paras **[13.032]** to **[13.041]**.

[153] CA 1990, s 10(5), (6), as substituted by CLEA 2001, s 23. See below paras **[13.097]** to **[13.100]**.

before the inspector and to give all assistance which they are reasonably able to give. CA 1990, s 10(1),[154] defines the obligations of a company's officers and agents as follows:

> It shall be the duty of all officers and agents of the company and of all officers and agents of any other body corporate whose affairs are investigated by virtue of s 9 to produce to the inspectors all books and documents of or relating to the company, or, as the case may be, the other body corporate which are in their custody or power, to attend before the inspectors when required so to do and otherwise to give to the inspectors all assistance in connection with the investigation which they are reasonably able to give but where any such person claims a lien on books or documents produced by the person, the production shall be without prejudice to the lien.

This provision is very wide and imposes a heavy burden on a company's officers or agents. CA 1990, s 10(2),[155] extends the inspector's right of access to a company's books and document even further. It provides:

> If the inspectors consider that a person other than an officer or agent of the company or other body corporate is or may be in possession of any information concerning its affairs, they may require that person to produce to them any books or documents in his custody or power relating to the company or other body corporate, to attend before them and otherwise to give them all assistance in connection with the investigation which he is reasonably able to give; and it shall be the duty of that person to comply with the requirement but where any such person claims a lien on books or documents produced by the person, the production shall be without prejudice to the lien.

There are various aspects of these provisions which need to be considered, and these will now be addressed individually.

(i) General

[13.068] The formulation of CA 1990, s 10(1) is unusually broad. It requires all officers and agents to produce all books and documents of 'or relating to' the company. There is no limit regarding the type or number of books or documents that should be produced. Moreover, the imposition of the obligation to produce books and documents on officers and agents directly, without the necessity of a request or direction from the inspector, denies them the guidance that such a request or direction may have provided. In the absence of such a request or direction, all officers or agents of a company under investigation have no choice but to produce every book and document in their custody or control, of or concerning the company, to the inspector. There is no reference in the provision to timing, means of production or such practical questions as to whether copies or originals should be produced. This lack of detail may render it difficult for officers and agents to be certain of compliance with their duties under s 10, which is particular egregious in light of the fact that failure to comply with that provision can lead to court sanctions.

---

[154] As amended by CLEA 2001, s 23.

[155] As amended by CLEA 2001, s 23.

(ii) Officers or agents

[13.069] Section 10(1) imposes the obligation to produce books and documents on 'all officers and agents' of the company under investigation, including the officers or agents of a related body corporate within the meaning of s 9.[156] Section 10(2) extends the scope of document production further to include books or documents in the possession of persons other than officers or agents of the companies under investigation or related companies.

The definition of officers and agents for the purposes of s 10 is contained in CA 1990, s 10(7):[157]

> In this section, any reference to officers or to agents shall include past, as well as present, officers or agents, as the case may be, and 'agents', in relation to a company or other body corporate, shall include the bankers and solicitors of the company or other body corporate and any persons employed by the company or other body corporate as auditors, accountants, book-keepers or taxation advisors, whether those persons are or are not officers of the company or other body corporate.

This definition is very inclusive, drawing in a broad category of person who may be or have formerly been, associated with the company in question. The term 'officer' in relation to a body corporate is defined in CA 1963, s 2(1) as including a director or secretary. It is appropriate that officers, within the meaning of this definition, would be subject to the duty to produce a company's books or documents. The definition of 'agents', on the other hand, is very wide. According to CA 1990, s 10(7), the term 'agents' includes bankers, solicitors and any person employed by the company as auditors, accountants, book-keepers and taxation advisers.[158] The fact that s 10(1) imposes the obligation to produce on these agents directly, without the precondition of receiving any notice of the appointment of an inspector, or other intervention or communication by the inspector, could cause particular difficulty for agents who may have worked for the company some years in the past. As an illustration, a person may have been employed as a taxation adviser to a company ten years before that company became the subject of an investigation under s 8. From the wording of s 10(1), that person is obliged to produce all books or documents of or relating to that company. The fact that they may be unaware of the appointment of an inspector is no defence under the section and would not prevent that person falling foul of s 10, and possibly facing an order under s 10(5) or (6).[159]

[13.070] The power of an inspector appointed under CA 1990, s 14, to invoke the powers contained in s 10[160] was challenged in *Chestvale Properties Ltd v Glackin*.[161]

---

[156] See paras **[13.036]** to **[13.041]**.

[157] As amended by CLEA 2001, s 23.

[158] The latter three, 'accountants, book-keepers or taxation advisers' were added by the CLEA 2001, s 23(d).

[159] See paras **[13.097]** to **[13.100]**.

[160] See CA 1990, s 14(5), as amended by CLEA 2001, s 14. See para **[13.047]**.

[161] *Chestvale Properties Ltd v Glackin* [1993] 3 IR 35.

Murphy J considered whether there was an unconstitutional intrusion on the property rights of the company under investigation and examined the implications for the relationship between a client and its banker or solicitor. Murphy J noted that, 'It is common case that the customary and contractual right of a client to confidentiality from his banker or solicitor is and always has been subject to a very wide range of exceptions' and reached the following conclusion:

> 'I am satisfied that this limited intrusion on the contractual rights of the applicants could not be seen as an unjust attack on the applicants' property rights or a failure to vindicate them as far as practicable. The minimal interference is fully justifiable as a means of reconciling the exercise of property rights with the exigencies of the common good as provided by Art 43, s 2, sub-s 1 of Bunreacht na hEireann.'[162]

[13.071] With regard to the sanction for a breach of the duty to produce books or documents, s 10(5), provides that, where a person refuses 'to produce to the inspectors any book or document which it is his duty under this section so to produce', this could be referred to the court. The requirement that there be a refusal to produce a book or document suggests that this provision is intended to address specific requests and specific documents. CLEA 2001, s 23(c) amends this wording inserting a new s 10(5) into CA 1990. The breach of duty that can be referred to the court under s 10(5) now includes a 'failure' to produce books or documents. This could include a more inadvertent breach of duty than a deliberate refusal, and raises the possibility that former agents of a company who are oblivious to the appointment of an inspector could inadvertently commit a breach of their duty to produce books or documents, which could lead to a court order under s 10(5).

(iii) Other persons

[13.072] CA 1990, s 10(2) extends the category of persons who can be required to produce books or documents to an inspector. Despite the breadth of the definition of 'agents', as examined above, it was considered necessary to provide for the production of books and documents by persons other than officers or agents of the company under investigation. The basis for requiring such persons to produce books or documents is that 'the inspectors consider that a person other than an officer or agent of the company or other body corporate is or may be in possession of any information concerning its affairs ...'.[163] There is no definition of the persons who may be affected by this provision and it appears to be unlimited. The threshold is also low, as the inspector only needs to consider that the person in question 'is or may be' in possession of information about the company's affairs. There is no requirement that there be grounds for the formation of such an opinion or that the information which the person may possess be relevant to the investigation. Furthermore, in the context of the production of books or documents, it is potentially anomalous that an obligation on a person to produce books or documents can be based on the opinion that they may possess information about a company. It would be more logical if the threshold for imposing a requirement on persons to produce books or documents was that they have possession of such books or documents. The fact that a

---

[162] *Chestvale Properties Ltd v Glackin* [1993] 3 IR 35 at 45–46.

[163] CA 1990, s 10(2), as amended by CLEA 2001, s 23(b).

person may possess information is not a suitable basis on which to require them to produce books or documents.

[13.073] *Glackin v Trustee Savings Bank*[164] was one of a number of cases which arose out of the investigation into the sale of a site of land and its re-sale at a substantially higher price.[165] In the course of the investigation, the inspector required the bank at which an account that held the monies under investigation was kept, to furnish certain information in accordance with CA 1990, s 10(2). This direction was refused. In proceedings arising from this refusal,[166] Costello J held that the inspector was entitled, in the discharge of his functions, to seek information about the company in whose name the account was held, as that company had some level of interest in the proceeds of sale and was closely connected with other persons relevant to the investigation.

Costello J went on to state:

'It seems to me that the bank has misunderstood its statutory duty. Its statutory duty has been made perfectly clear in the judgment of Murphy J in *Chestvale Properties Ltd v Glackin (No 2)* (Unreported, High Court, Murphy J, 10 March, 1992). It is a duty to give assistance if requested to do so under s 10, sub-s 2 of the Act of 1990. It is not permitted to refuse assistance, because of a contractual arrangement with a customer which may have involved a term of confidentiality.'[167]

Having determined that the bank was obliged to give assistance to the inspector within the terms of s 10(2), Costello J elaborated further on the nature of the assistance which the bank was obliged to give:

'The Oireachtas has made perfectly clear, to my mind, what people, statutory organisations such as the Trustee Savings Bank, are required to do. They are required to assist the inspector, who has been appointed by the Minister. They are not entitled to obstruct him and they must observe his requests. They have a statutory obligation to do so. They are not entitled to ask their customer whether or not the customer objects. Whatever contractual arrangement there has been between the bank and the customer has been clearly over-ridden by the provisions put into this section by the Oireachtas and the manner in which it should comply with the request has been made clear by Mr. Justice Murphy. They are to give assistance to the inspector when requested to do so. The inspector is, by the nature of things, enquiring into a situation in which it is very possible that efforts have been made to conceal the true position which is believed to exist .... What the bank has to do, and other persons who are subject to a request by an inspector under the section, is to comply with the request and to assist the inspector in the work which he has to perform and which is clearly set out in the section.'[168]

Following this decision, a third party who is required by an inspector to provide assistance in accordance with CA 1990, s 10(2), has considerably less scope for

---

[164] *Glackin v Trustee Savings Bank* [1993] 3 IR 55.

[165] See above para [13.054].

[166] See further below at para [13.075] regarding this aspect of the case.

[167] *Glackin v Trustee Savings Bank* [1993] 3 IR 55 at 62.

[168] *Glackin v Trustee Savings Bank* [1993] 3 IR 55 at 62–63.

resisting compliance with such a requirement. *Glackin v Trustee Savings Bank*[169] establishes clearly that, when s 10(2) is invoked, there is a statutory obligation to comply with it, and any conflicting contractual arrangements that may exist are overridden.

(iv) Books or documents to be produced

[13.074] There is no limit in s 10(1) or (2) to the scope of books or documents that officers, agents or other persons can be obliged to produce. Section 10(1) simply refers to '... all books or documents of or relating to the company ...'.[170] There is no requirement that the books or documents being produced must be relevant to the investigation or that they must in any way relate to the object of the investigation. In addition, the language used is broad enough to encapsulate books or documents that may only be remotely connected with the company and expressly includes books or documents that do not belong to, or emanate from, the company. This raises the possibility that any documents generated by officers, agents, or such other persons as are covered by s 10(2), that bear any relation to the company under investigation or a related company, would need to be produced. Finally, certain practical issues, such as the lack of any requirement that the inspector specify the nature of the documents sought and the absence of a carve-out in respect of copies of documents, where the originals have already been obtained, for instance, heighten the already heavy burden on officers, agents and the company, and could lead to unnecessary and excessive expense and disruption.

[13.075] The range of books and documents that may be captured by s 10 was hinted at in *Chestvale Properties Ltd v Glackin*,[171] where Murphy J considered an inspector's demand for documents of a company other than the company under investigation. Having determined that such a demand was not authorised by the Companies Acts, as the requirements for extending an investigation into the affairs of a related company were not met, Murphy J noted:

> 'On the other hand the fact that particular books and documents may be properly identified as being the property of or relating to one company does not necessarily preclude them from relating also to another company.'

This acceptance of the wide scale of documents of which production could be required under s 10, was also apparent in the following statement by Costello J in *Glackin v Trustee Savings Bank*:[172]

> 'In carrying out an enquiry as required by the Minister pursuant to the provisions enacted by the Oireachtas, it may well be that the inspector may obtain information from the documents which are completely irrelevant to what he is inquiring into. He does not know until he has seen the documents, and the

---

[169] *Glackin v Trustee Savings Bank* [1993] 3 IR 55.

[170] The phrase 'books or documents' is defined in CA 1990, s 3(1) as including 'accounts, deed, writing and records made in any other manner.'

[171] *Chestvale Properties Ltd v Glackin* [1993] 3 IR 35 at 53.

[172] *Glackin v Trustee Savings Bank* [1993] 3 IR 55 at 62–63.

documents which may appear to be irrelevant may subsequently, as a result of investigations in other areas, prove to be relevant.'[173]

[13.076] Section 10 can be contrasted with CA 1990, s 19, which states that the DCE can require a body to produce 'such books or documents as may be so specified'.[174] The requirement that a specification must be furnished may assist in the task of producing books or documents. It may also help to ensure that only books or documents that are relevant will be produced.

The scope of s 19 was considered above.[175] In the present context, it is worth noting the decision of Laffoy J in *Dunnes Stores Ireland Co Ltd v Moloney*.[176] One of the submissions in that case was that the demand for the production of books and documents was excessive and unreasonable as too many documents were required. Dunnes Stores argued that the demand was nearly total in its nature and could probably never have been complied with. Laffoy J examined the demand for documents and determined that:

> 'The inclusion of the categories which are of a general nature gives the demand as a whole the hallmark of a trawl. That being the case, the only reasonable inference is that the demand was excessive in content.'[177]

[13.077] In a subsequent appeal to the Supreme Court in related proceedings, this issue again arose for consideration. In *Dunnes Stores Ireland Co Ltd v Ryan*,[178] Keane CJ examined whether the request for documents in that case was excessive and in the nature of a 'trawl' and reached the following conclusion:

> 'I am satisfied that the range of documents sought is not unduly extensive, having regard to the scale of the misuse of the companies' assets which has already been identified.'[179]

This observation is of interest in the context of s 10. Keane CJ clearly considered that a demand for the production of almost all of a company's documents may not be excessive. As s 10 provides for the production of books or documents on precisely such a scale, this dicta may be called in support of the breadth of the obligation contained in s 10.

[13.078] A final point to note regarding the scope of the books and documents of which production can be required under s 10, is that documents which came into existence

---

[173] *Glackin v Trustee Savings Bank* [1993] 3 IR 55.

[174] CA 1990, s 19(1), as substituted by the CLEA 2001, s 29.

[175] See above Ch **12**.

[176] *Dunnes Stores Ireland Co Ltd v Moloney* [1999] 3 IR 542.

[177] *Dunnes Stores Ireland Co Ltd v Moloney* [1999] 3 IR 542 at 564.

[178] *Dunnes Stores Ireland Co Ltd v Ryan* [2002] 2 IR 60. See further Ch **12**.

[179] *Dunnes Stores Ireland Co Ltd v Ryan* [2002] 2 IR 60 at 82.

before CA 1990 was enacted are covered by that provision. In *Chestvale v Glackin*,[180] this question was considered by Murphy J:

> 'The issue between the parties to the present proceedings is whether an inspector thus appointed could exercise the powers apparently vested in him under the Act of 1990 so as to procure documents or obtain information relating to events which pre-dated the coming into operation of the Act. Whilst the Act does not state in express terms whether it should operate in that manner, I have no doubt at all that this was indeed the intention of the legislature.'[181]

The principal reason for this decision was that the equivalent provisions in CA 1963 were repealed and, if the powers created by CA 1990, Pt II, were not retrospective, an inspector would be impeded in the execution of his duties.

(v) Time frame

[13.079] The obligation to produce books or documents under s 10(1) and (2), is very broadly formulated, both in terms of the persons to whom the obligation applies and the category of books or documents which need to be produced, as has already been seen. A final aspect of s 10 that may be noted is that there is no stipulation of the time which is allowed for production of books or documents. In light of the breadth of the documents which may need to be produced, the fact that there is no particular period of time allowed to ensure compliance with the obligation to produce, may be of concern to officers, agents, or other persons who are directed to produce books or documents.

There is some relief, however, in s 10(5), which provides that it is only when a person 'refuses or fails within a reasonable time' to comply with their duty to produce books or documents, that the inspector can certify this matter to the court. An inspector is therefore obliged to allow a reasonable time for compliance with s 10(1) or (2), before taking any steps to challenge non-compliance. What is a 'reasonable time' will necessarily depend on the scale of the books or documents which a given individual is under a duty to produce and the ease of their access to those books or documents.

[13.080] This issue arose in the context of CA 1990, s 19, in *Dunnes Stores Ireland Company Limited v Moloney*,[182] where one of the grounds for challenging the demand for the production of books and documents was that the time given for compliance with the demand was too limited and rendered the demand unreasonable. The demand in question was issued on Friday, 24 July 1998 and required that the books and documents referred to therein be produced by Monday, 27 July 1998. Although this issue was academic, as the demand had been withdrawn, Laffoy J nonetheless noted that 'common sense indicates that the demand could not be complied with between Friday and Monday afternoon'.[183] This suggests that the courts will adopt a commonsense view of what is involved in producing books and documents and the time that is required, even where no such accommodation exists in the legislation.

---

[180] *Chestvale Properties Ltd v Glackin* [1993] 3 IR 35.

[181] *Chestvale Properties Ltd v Glackin* [1993] 3 IR 35 at 44.

[182] *Dunnes Stores Ireland Co Ltd v Moloney* [1999] 3 IR 542. See Ch **12**.

[183] *Dunnes Stores Ireland Co Ltd v Moloney* [1999] 3 IR 542 at 565. See Ch **12**.

(vi) Lien

[13.081] The only amendment that CLEA 2001 introduced to s 10(1) and (2), was the insertion of the right to claim a lien in respect of books and documents. Section 23(a) and (b) accordingly added the following phrase:

> ... but where any such person claims a lien on books or documents produced by the person, the production shall be without prejudice to the lien.

This is the only exception in s 10(1) and (2) to the obligation to produce books and documents of a company under investigation.

(vii) Privilege

[13.082] In addition to the protection of a person's right to claim a lien, CA 1990, s 23(1), provides that:

> Nothing in this Part shall compel the disclosure by any person of any information which he would, in the opinion of the court, be entitled to refuse to produce on the grounds of legal professional privilege or authorise the taking of possession of any document containing such information which is in his possession.

This protection will be particularly relevant to such officers and agents as may have been involved with the company under investigation in a legal professional capacity. The fact that the court must first form an opinion as to the validity of the claim of privilege should prevent any abuse of this exception.[184]

(b) Attendance, examinations and other assistance

(i) Obligation to attend and assist

[13.083] A person[185] who may be obliged to produce books and documents of a company under investigation[186] to an inspector, also bears certain other obligations. Section 10(1) requires a company's officers or agents 'to attend before the inspectors when required so to do and otherwise to give to the inspectors all assistance in connection with the investigation which they are reasonably able to give.' The same language is applied in s 10(2) to persons other than officers or agents who are in possession of information regarding the company.[187]

The scope of these obligations is less vague and ambiguous than the obligation to produce books and documents and it is likely that compliance with these obligations would be considerably more straight-forward. In particular, the requirement to attend before the inspectors will be communicated to the persons in question by the inspector.

---

[184] See *Desmond v Glackin (No 2)* [1993] 3 IR 67 for an example of the application of CA 1990, s 10. See paras **[13.097]** to **[13.098]**.

[185] This includes officers, agents and persons covered by CA 1990, s 10(2).

[186] This applies to inspectors appointed under CA 1990, ss 7 and 8, and by virtue of CA 1990, s 14(5), as amended. See para **[13.047]**.

[187] See *Desmond v Glackin (No 2)* [1993] IR 67 for an example of the application of CA 1990, s 10. See paras **[13.098]** to **[13.099]**.

Furthermore, the obligation to give assistance is limited to such assistance as the person is 'reasonable able to give' and is expressly confined to assistance 'in connection with the investigation'. This approach makes the task of persons who do wish to comply with their obligations under s 10 considerably easier and more justifiable than the approach adopted in relation to the production of books and documents.

[13.084] These obligations can be read in conjunction with s 10(4) which clarifies that an inspector of a company has the power to administer oaths and examine witnesses. It provides:

> An inspector may examine on oath, either by word of mouth or on written interrogatories, the officers and agents of the company or other body corporate and such person as is mentioned in sub-s (2) in relation to its affairs and may—
>
> (a) administer an oath accordingly,
>
> (b) reduce the answers of such person to writing and require him to sign them.

The right of an inspector to certify instances of non-compliance with s 10 to the court extends to any refusal or failure to:

> …
>
> (b) attend before the inspectors when required so to do, or
>
> (c) answer a question put to him by the inspectors with respect to the affairs of the company or other body corporate as the case may be …[188]

(ii) Self-incrimination

[13.085] One issue that has attracted attention with regard to the obligation to answer questions, is the extent to which persons can assert a right to silence, an issue which was determined by the Supreme Court in the case of *Re National Irish Bank Ltd (No 1)*.[189] The background to that case was that two inspectors were appointed by the High Court on the application of the Minister for Enterprise and Employment, pursuant to s 8(1) of CA 1990, to investigate and report on the improper charging of interest and fees to accounts of customers, the improper removal of funds from accounts of customers, the manner in which the company's books and records reflected these matters, the identity of any persons responsible and any other unlawful or improper practices regarding the evasion of any revenue or other obligations on the part of the bank or third parties or otherwise.

In the course of the inspection, the inspectors intended to interview employees of the company, but solicitors representing such employees queried whether interviewees, in the context of an investigation under Pt II of CA 1990, have a right to refuse to answer questions put by the inspectors on grounds of possible self-incrimination, and, if no such right exists, whether answers or other evidence obtained from the employees can be used against them in any subsequent criminal trial. The inspectors applied to the High Court

---

[188] CA 1990, s 10(5), as substituted by CLEA 2001, s 23(c). See further paras **[13.097]** to **[13.100]**.

[189] *Re National Irish Bank Ltd (No 1)* [1999] 3 IR 145.

(Kelly J) for directions and these issues were determined by the High Court (Shanley J), and subsequently, the Supreme Court.

[13.086] The Supreme Court considered the constitutional protections of the right to free expression, the personal rights of citizens and the right to a trial in due course of law contained in Art 40.6.1, Art 40.3 and Art 38.1 of the Constitution. The Court further considered a number of judgments, including the judgment of the Supreme Court in *Heaney v Ireland*.[190] That judgment established that the right to silence derived from the right to freedom of expression, as guaranteed to citizens by Art 40.6, and that this right was not absolute but might in certain circumstances have to give way to the exigencies of the common good provided the means used to curtail the right of silence are proportionate to the public object to be achieved.

The Supreme Court also considered the decision of *Saunders v United Kingdom*,[191] a decision of the European Court of Human Rights regarding the powers of inspectors appointed under the English CA 1985, which established that the nature of an inspection is essentially investigative and should not be subject to the same rigours as a judicial procedure, as that would 'unduly hamper the effective regulation in the public interest of complex financial and commercial activities'.[192]

In light of these decisions, the Supreme Court considered that it was essential in the public interest that there should be effective powers to investigate the operation of the banking system and that the powers of inspectors under s 10 were no greater than necessary and met the requirements of proportionality. On this basis, the Supreme Court held that persons who were required to attend and answers questions in the course of an inspection, were not entitled to refuse to answer such questions.

(iii) Use of answers

[13.087] As has been seen,[193] among the extensive powers given to inspectors, whether they are appointed under CA 1990, s 7, s 8 or s 14, are the powers to require persons to attend before them, to give all the assistance which they are reasonably able to give,[194] and the power to examine certain persons on oath.[195] A significant issue that arises from the exercise of these powers is the use that can be made of answers that the inspector receives. This question is particularly significant in light of the decision in *Re National*

---

[190] *Heaney v Ireland* [1996] 1 IR 580.

[191] *Saunders v United Kingdom* (1997) 23 EHRR 313. See above paras **[13.053]**–**[13.054]**.

[192] *Saunders v United Kingdom* (1997) 23 EHRR 313 at para 67.

[193] See above paras **[13.083]** to **[13.090]**.

[194] CA 1990, s 10(1), (2). See above paras **[13.083]** to **[13.084]**.

[195] CA 1990, s 10(4). 'An inspector may examine on oath, either by word of mouth or on written interrogatories, the officers and agents of the company or other body corporate and such person as is mentioned in sub-s (2) in relation to its affairs and may—(a) administer an oath accordingly, (b) reduce the answers of such person to writing and require him to sign them.' See above para **[13.084]**.

Irish Bank Ltd (No 1)[196] to the effect that such persons are not entitled to invoke the right to silence.

Section 18 provided the straightforward solution that an answer given by a person who is questioned under s 10 'may be used in evidence against him.' This was qualified by CLEA 2001, s 28, and s 18 now provides that answers furnished by an individual under s 10, 'may be used in evidence against him in any proceedings whatsoever (save proceedings for an offence (other than perjury in respect of such an answer))'.

To appreciate fully the reason for this amendment, it is necessary to examine further the decision of the Supreme Court in the case of *Re National Irish Bank Ltd (No 1)*.[197] Having determined that the right to silence cannot be relied upon by a person who is required to attend before an inspector, the Supreme Court considered the use to which answers furnished by such a person could be put.

The constitutional protection at issue was the right to a trial in due course of law, as guaranteed by Art 38 and reinforced by Art 40.3 of the Constitution. The Court doubted whether the principle of proportionality could apply to an analysis of that right, on the basis that, 'a criminal trial is conducted "in due course of law" or "with due process of law" or it is not.'[198] The issue which had to be determined, therefore, was whether the admission in evidence of a confession obtained from a person under threat of a penal sanction, would render a trial unfair or a trial not in due course of law.

[13.088] The Court cited the decision of the European Court of Human Rights in *Saunders v United Kingdom*[199] that reliance in a criminal trial on a self-incriminating statement that was made in the course of an inspection, was contrary to the right to a fair trial and infringed Art 6(1) of the European Convention on Human Rights. The Court of Human Rights stated in that case:

> 'The public interest cannot be invoked to justify the use of answers compulsorily obtained in a non-judicial investigation to incriminate the accused during the trial proceedings ... Moreover the fact that statements were made by the applicant prior to his being charged does not prevent their later use in criminal proceedings from constituting an infringement of the right.'

The Supreme Court also cited the decision of the South African Constitutional Court in *Ferreira v Levin*,[200] that s 417 of the South Africa Companies Act, 1973, regarding the examination of directors and officers of insolvent companies, was unconstitutional, as it required such a person to answer questions notwithstanding that the answer might tend to incriminate him and that 'any answer given to any such question may thereafter be used in evidence against him'.

---

[196] *Re National Irish Bank Ltd (No 1)* [1999] 3 IR 145.

[197] *Re National Irish Bank Ltd (No 1)* [1999] 3 IR 145.

[198] *Re National Irish Bank Ltd (No 1)* [1999] 3 IR 145 at 180 *per* Barrington J.

[199] *Saunders v United Kingdom* (1997) 23 EHRR 313 at para 74. See also para **[13.053]**.

[200] *Ferreira & Others v Levin & Others* [1996] ISA 484, cited by Barrington J in *Re National Irish Bank Ltd (No 1)* [1999] 3 IR 145 at 181–182.

[13.089] Having analysed a number of Irish decisions on the question of the admission of statements made involuntarily,[201] the Supreme Court in *Re National Irish Bank Ltd (No 1)*[202] stated that:

> '... the better opinion is that a trial in due course of law requires that any confession admitted against an accused person in a criminal trial should be a voluntary confession and that any trial at which an alleged confession other than a voluntary confession were admitted in evidence against the accused person would not be a trial in due course of law within the meaning of Art 38 of the Constitution and that it is immaterial whether the compulsion or inducement used to extract the confession came from the executive or from the legislature.'[203]

[13.090] The Court then considered whether CA 1990, s 18 was sufficiently broad to cover evidence in both civil and criminal cases and whether it was intended to remove the privilege against self-incrimination. In this regard, the most persuasive fact, which rendered the debate regarding the retention or otherwise of the privilege against self-incrimination, irrelevant in the Court's opinion, was that the CA 1990 benefits from a presumption of constitutionality.[204] In the light of the Court's finding that Art 38 does protect the right of an accused person not to have statements made involuntarily admitted in evidence in a criminal trial, the following interpretation of s 18 was therefore arrived at:

> '... the better interpretation of s 18 in the light of the Constitution is that it does not authorise the admission of forced or involuntary confessions against an accused person in a criminal trial, and it can be stated, as a general principle, that a confession, to be admissible at a criminal trial must be voluntary. Whether however a confession is voluntary or not must in every case in which the matter is disputed be a question to be decided, in the first instance, by the trial judge.'[205]

On the basis of this interpretation of s 18, the Supreme Court concluded that:

> ... a confession of a bank official obtained by the inspectors as a result of the exercise by them of their powers under s 10 of the Companies Act, 1990, would not, in general, be admissible at a subsequent criminal trial of such official unless, in any particular case, the trial judge was satisfied that the confession was voluntary.

This interpretation has now been adopted into the statutory formulation of CA 1990, s 18, but without the *caveat* that a court can determine that an answer given to an

---

[201] Including the following *dicta* in *The People (AG) v Cummins* [1972] IR 312 at p 322. 'It should be said at once that a trial judge has no discretion to admit an inculpatory or an exculpatory confession, or statement, made by an accused person which is inadmissible in law because it was not voluntary. It is a matter for the trial judge to decide, when he has heard the evidence on the point, whether or not he will admit a statement, but if he is satisfied that it was not voluntary then his decision can be only to exclude it.' (*per* Walsh J, delivering the judgment of the Supreme Court).

[202] *Re National Irish Bank Ltd (No 1)* [1999] 3 IR 145 at 186.

[203] *Re National Irish Bank Ltd (No 1)* [1999] 3 IR 145 (*per* Barrington J, delivering the unanimous judgment of the Supreme Court).

[204] Quoting *East Donegal Co-Operative v Attorney General* [1970] IR 317 at 341.

[205] *Re National Irish Bank Ltd (No 1)* [1999] 3 IR 145 at 188.

inspector was in fact voluntary. Section 18 now ensures that answers received by the inspector under s 10 will not be used in any proceedings for an offence, with the exception of criminal proceedings for perjury, arising directly from the answers given.

(c) Banking documents

[13.091] There is a particular provision of CA 1990 which empowers an inspector to require a director to produce documents relating to certain private bank accounts. Section 10(3) is directed towards bank accounts held by a director and into or out of which monies have been paid that relate to a transaction, arrangement or agreement that should have been, but was not disclosed, in the notes to the company's accounts, or to some other misconduct on the part of the director. It provides:

> If an inspector has reasonable grounds for believing that a director of the company or other body corporate whose affairs the inspector is investigating maintains or has maintained a bank account of any description, whether alone or jointly with another person and whether in the State or elsewhere, into or out of which there has been paid—
>
> (a) any money which has resulted from or been used in the financing of any transaction, arrangement or agreement—
>
>   (i) particulars of which have not been disclosed in a note to the accounts of any company for any financial year as required by s 41; or
>
>   (ii) in respect of which any amount outstanding was not included in the aggregate amounts outstanding in respect of certain transactions, arrangements or agreements as required by s 43 to be disclosed in a note to the accounts of any company for any financial year; or
>
>   (iii) particulars of which were not included in any register of certain transactions, arrangements and agreements as required by s 44; or
>
> (b) any money which has been in any way connected with any act or omission, or series of acts or omissions, which on the part of that director constituted misconduct (whether fraudulent or not) towards that company or body corporate or its members;
>
> the inspector may require the director to produce to him all documents in the director's possession, or under his control, relating to that bank account; and in this subsection 'bank account' includes an account with any person exempt by virtue of s 7(4) of the Central Bank Act 1971, from the requirement of holding a licence under s 9 of that Act, and 'director' includes any present or past director or any person connected, within the meaning of s 26, with such director, and any present or past shadow director.

[13.092] The relevant obligations of disclosure are set out in CA 1990, ss 41 to 45 and these essentially relate to the category of transactions that are prohibited by CA 1990, s 31.[206] The transactions in question are loans and quasi-loans by a company to a director;[207] credit transactions where the company acts as creditor for a director;[208] and

---

[206] See Ch **6**.

[207] CA 1990, s 31(1)(a) refers to 'a loan or a quasi-loan to a director of the company or of its holding company or to a person connected with such a director'.

[208] CA 1990, s 31(1)(b) prohibits a company entering '… into a credit transaction as creditor for such a director or a person so connected.'

the provision of guarantees or security in connection with a loan, quasi-loan or credit transaction made on behalf of a director.[209] Mechanisms by which the same result could be achieved without actually entering one of these prohibited transactions are similarly prohibited by CA 1990, s 31(2)[210] and (3).[211]

[13.093] With regard to the obligations of disclosure that are relevant to CA 1990, s 10(3), s 41 requires disclosure by way of notes[212] to company accounts, including group accounts prepared by a holding company, of particulars[213] of the transactions outlined above, as well as any agreement to enter such transactions.[214] Section 41(1)(c) also requires disclosure of:

> 'any other transaction or arrangement with the company or with a subsidiary of the company in which a person who at any time during the relevant period was a director of the company or its holding company had, directly or indirectly, a material interest.'[215]

[13.094] Certain transactions are exempted specifically from the disclosure obligations of s 41. These relate to such matters as directors' contracts of service, transactions entered into before s 41 commenced and not subsisting thereafter, and transactions between two companies in which a director of one company is interested only by virtue of holding the position of director in the second company.[216]

Furthermore, s 41(6) exempts licensed banks from the obligation to disclose transactions covered by s 31, where the bank is a party to the transactions. However,

---

[209] CA 1990, s 31(1)(c) provides that a company shall not, 'enter into a guarantee or provide any security in connection with a loan, quasi-loan or credit transaction made by any other person for such a director or a person so connected.'

[210] CA 1990, s 31(2) provides, 'A company shall not arrange for the assignment to it or the assumption by it of any rights, obligations or liabilities under a transaction which, if it had been entered into by the company, would have contravened sub-s (1); but for the purposes of this Part the transaction shall be treated as having been entered into on the date of the arrangement.'

[211] CA 1990, s 31(3) provides, 'A company shall not take part in any arrangement whereby— (a) another person enters into a transaction which, if it had been entered into by the company, would have contravened sub-s (1) or (2); and (b) that other person, in pursuance of the arrangement, has obtained or is to obtain any benefit from the company or its holding company or a subsidiary of the company or its holding company.'

[212] CA 1990, s 41(3).

[213] The particulars that must be disclosed are described in CA 1990, s 42.

[214] CA 1990, s 41(1)(a) covers the transactions described in s 31, where these are 'entered into by the company or by a subsidiary of the company for a person who at any time during the relevant period was a director of the company or its holding company or was connected with such a director.'

[215] According to CA 1990, s 41(5)(b), '... an interest in such a transaction or arrangement is not material if in the opinion of the majority of the directors (other than that director) of the company which is preparing the accounts in question it is not material (but without prejudice to the question whether or not such an interest is material in any case where those directors have not considered the matter).'

[216] CA 1990, s 41(7).

such banks are obliged by s 44 to keep a register containing copies of every transaction, arrangement or agreement which would otherwise have been subject of the disclosure obligation of s 41[217] and a statement of the particulars of these transactions must be made available to the members of the company at least 15 prior to an annual general meeting and at such a meeting.[218]

Section 43 addresses a similar class of transactions as those that are covered by s 41 and requires group accounts and company accounts to include a statement of the aggregate value of any such outstanding transactions as were entered into by officers of the company, as well as the number of officers involved.[219]

[13.095] The effect of CA 1990, s 10(3), is that where an inspector has reasonable grounds for believing that there was a breach of these disclosure obligations of ss 41 to 44, and the monies related to such breach have been paid into or out of a director's bank account, the inspector can require that director to produce all documents related to the bank account.[220] This power to require production of banking documents also arises where the inspector has reasonable grounds for believing that monies which were connected with misconduct by the director towards the company or its members have been paid into or out of the director's bank account.[221]

[13.096] Before the power to require the production of documents can be exercised, the inspector must have reasonable grounds for the belief that the director has a bank account into or out of which the impugned monies have been paid. This can be contrasted with the other powers conferred on the inspector by s 10, which are unfettered by the obligation to show reasonable grounds.[222] As against this, the scope of s 10(3) is quite broad in a number of respects. First, a director can be required to produce banking documents, even if the bank account is held jointly with another person. There no requirement that a joint account holder be involved in, or even aware of, the breaches of company law that can activate s 10(3). Secondly, the power to require the production of documents can arise, whether the account is held in this or another jurisdiction. Thirdly, the bank account investigated does not have to be an existing one, as s 10(3) covers accounts which a director 'maintains or has maintained'.[223] Fourthly, the documents of which production can be required are unlimited. There is no reference, for instance, to the documents being related or relevant to the breach of company law at issue. This is particularly invasive from the perspective of a joint account holder who is a stranger to the acts or omissions complained of.

A fifth point to note is that there no correlation between the investigation into the company's affairs and the source of the monies referred to in s 10(3). Banking

---

[217] CA 1990, s 44(1).

[218] CA 1990, s 44(3). CA 1990, s 44(1) and (3) are subject to the exceptions set out in CA 1990, s 44(2) and (4).

[219] CA 1990, s 43(2).

[220] CA 1990, s 10(3)(a).

[221] CA 1990, s 10(3)(b).

[222] See, eg, CA 1990, s 10(1) and (2).

[223] CA 1990, s 10(3).

documents can therefore be obtained, even though they relate to issues entirely different to those that form the subject of the investigation. A sixth point regarding the scope of s 10(3), is the definition of 'director', which expressly includes '... any present or past director or any person connected, within the meaning of s 26,[224] with such director, and any present or past shadow director.' Furthermore, the bank accounts that fall within the scope of s 10(3) include accounts held at institutions such as certified trustee savings banks, building societies, friendly societies, credit unions, industrial and provident societies, among others that are exempt from the obligation to hold a licence by virtue of s 7(4) of the Central Bank Act, 1971.

A final point to note is the conduct described in s 10(3)(b) that can give rise to an obligation to produce documents. It refers to money 'which has been in any way connected with any act or omission, or series of acts or omissions, which on the part of that director constituted misconduct (whether fraudulent or not).' The use of the term 'misconduct' suggests that breaches of the duties of directors at common law, as well as under the Companies Acts, will be captured.[225] The breadth of this provision is further indicated by the proviso that the misconduct at issue does not necessarily need to be fraudulent.

(d) Failure to comply

[13.097] The provisions of CA 1990 of which the inspector can avail when there is a failure or refusal to comply with his directions, were replaced by CLEA 2001. These provisions are designed to allow the inspectors to certify any such failure or refusal to the court. Section 10(5) provides:

> If an officer or agent of the company or other body corporate, or any such person as is mentioned in sub-s (2), refuses or fails within a reasonable time to—
>
> (a) produce to the inspectors any book or document which it is his duty under this section so to produce,
>
> (b) attend before the inspectors when required so to do, or
>
> (c) answer a question put to him by the inspectors with respect to the affairs of the company or other body corporate as the case may be,
>
> the inspectors may certify the refusal or failure under their hand to the court, and the court may thereupon enquire into the case and, after hearing any witnesses who may be produced against or on behalf of the person alleged to have so refused or failed and any statement which may be offered in defence, make any order or direction it thinks fit.[226]

One change introduced by CLEA 2001 was to include a failure, as opposed to a refusal, to comply with the inspection as a ground for certification to the court. The more significant amendment was to the last sentence of the provision, which formerly

---

[224] CA 1990, s 26(1) provides, '... a person is connected with a director of a company if, but only if, he is—(a) that director's spouse, parent, brother, sister or child; (b) a person acting in his capacity as the trustee of any trust, the principal beneficiaries of which are the director, his spouse or any of his children or any body corporate which he controls; or (c) a partner of that director; unless that person is also a director of the company.'

[225] See further Ch **6**.

[226] As substituted by CLEA 2001, s 23(c).

provided that the court was empowered to 'punish the offender in like manner as if he had been guilty of contempt of court'. This has been substituted by the power to 'make any order or direction it thinks fit.'[227] Consistently with this amendment, the previous reference to an 'alleged offender' has been replaced by a reference to the more neutral 'the person alleged to have so refused or failed'.

[13.098] The reason for removing the reference to contempt of court stems from a decision of the Supreme Court in *Desmond v Glackin (No 2)*.[228] The background to that case was that the Minister for Enterprise, Trade and Employment appointed an inspector under CA 1990, s 14(1) to investigate the membership of two companies on the grounds of public interest. The investigation arose out of the purchase in 1989 of a site in Dublin for a price of £4 million, and its sale in 1990 to a semi-state body for £9 million, transactions in which the companies under investigation were involved. In the course of the inspection, the inspector sought certain information under s 10(2) from a person who had played a significant role in those transactions, including information about his own business affairs and certain other companies in which he had an interest. This person refused to furnish such information and issued judicial review proceedings seeking to quash the appointment of the inspector and prohibiting the inspector from proceeding with the investigation while seeking the information referred to above. Among the determinations of the High Court (O'Hanlon J), was the determination that s 10(5) was unconstitutional insofar as it provided for a person who refused to comply with an inspector's direction to be punished as if for contempt of court.[229] This was appealed to the Supreme Court. The Supreme Court considered the decision in *Re Haughey*[230] which declared a provision similar to s 10(5)[231] to be unconstitutional, on the basis that the punishment which could be imposed for contempt of court was imprisonment or fine without limit, which could not be constitutionally construed as providing for summary trial, and the impugned section could not be construed as providing for trial of the offence in the High Court, with a jury.[232] The provision was therefore invalid having regard to the provisions of Art 38.

---

[227] The power of the court to 'make any order it thinks fit' was contained in CA 1990, s 10(6) before the enactment of CLEA 2001.

[228] *Desmond v Glackin (No 2)* [1993] 3 IR 67.

[229] *Desmond v Glackin (No 1)* [1993] 3 IR 1.

[230] *Re Haughey* [1971] IR 217.

[231] The provision at issue was Committee of Public Accounts of Dáil Éireann (Privilege and Procedure) Act 1970, s 3(4) which provided: 'The committee may certify the offence of that person under the hand of the chairman of the committee to the High Court and the High Court may, after such inquiry as it thinks proper to make, punish or take steps for the punishment of that person in like manner as if he had been guilty of contempt of the High Court.'

[232] *Re Haughey* [1971] IR 217, 254: 'It is, in the opinion of this Court, beyond the reach of the presumption of constitutionality to read into the simple inquiry formula of the subsection an intention to authorise trial by jury. The statute in this case created an offence which was not prohibited by the common law. It indicated a particular manner of proceeding against the alleged offender by express reference to contempt of court in terms which clearly indicated a summary manner of disposal of the trial and of the offender, if convicted; and the procedure thus indicated clearly excludes that of indictment.' (*per* O'Dalaigh CJ).

[13.099] The Supreme Court in *Desmond v Glackin (No 2)* reached the following conclusion regarding the applicability of *Re Haughey*:[233]

> 'The Court is satisfied that it should, and sees no reason to depart from that decision. It provides a freedom and protection concerning the possible or conceivable imposition of severe penalties, appropriate only to the commission of major offences, by a trial held otherwise than with a jury.'[234]

The Court moreover noted, in respect of the practical repercussions of a finding that s 10(5) was unconstitutional insofar as it provided for punishment in the same manner as contempt of court, that:

> 'There does not appear to the Court to be any insuperable obstacle to providing effective sanctions in respect of the refusal to co-operate with statutory investigations or tribunals which avoid this particular constitutional invalidity by the provision of statutory offences triable, in the alternative, summarily or with a jury, and appropriate limits on the penalties applicable to them.'[235]

On the question of the constitutionality of s 10(5), the Court's final conclusion was that the unconstitutional aspect of the provision was severable and other than the deletion of 'punish in like manner as if he had been guilty of contempt of court' from s 10(5), the provision remained intact.[236]

[13.100] The directions which can be made by the court following a hearing under s 10(5), include the following, as set out in s 10(6):

> Without prejudice to the generality of sub-s (5), the court may, after a hearing under that subsection, direct—
>
> (a) the person concerned to attend or re-attend before the inspectors or produce particular books or documents or answer particular questions put to him by the inspectors, or
>
> (b) that the person concerned need not produce a particular book or document or answer a particular question put to him by the inspectors.[237]

This replaces a provision that permitted the court to 'make any order or direction it thinks fit,' which expressly included the powers that are now represent s 10(6)(a) and (b). The power to make any order or direction the court thinks fit, is now contained in s 10(5) and the powers set out in s 10(6) are illustrative of the orders that may be considered appropriate and useful in the context of an inspection.

E. Report

(a) Form of report

[13.101] There are two types of report that can result from the appointment of an inspector to investigate the affairs of a company. There is always a final report at the

---

[233] *Re Haughey* [1971] IR 217.
[234] *Desmond v Glackin (No 2)* [1993] 3 IR 67 at 117 *per* Finlay CJ.
[235] *Desmond v Glackin (No 2)* [1993] 3 IR 67 at 117.
[236] To ensure consistency, s 10(6) was also amended by the deletion of a reference to s 10(5).
[237] As substituted by CLEA 2001, s 23(c).

completion of the investigation. The obligation to produce such a report is built into the provisions governing the appointment of inspectors. For instance, s 7(1) provides for the appointment of an inspector to investigate the affairs of a company 'and to report thereon in such manner as the court directs'. This is mirrored in CA 1990, s 8(1) and a similar obligation to report is contained in s 14(1).

There can also be an interim report, depending upon the circumstances of the investigation. CA 1990, s 11(1) is the governing provision and states, 'Inspectors appointed under s 7 or 8 may, and if so directed by the court shall, make *interim* reports to the court and on the conclusion of the investigation, shall make a final report to the court.'[238] If an inspector wishes to deliver an interim or a final report, he may make an application by motion *ex parte* which will generally be heard and determined on affidavit.[239]

One case which illustrates the making of an interim and a final report is *Countyglen plc v Carway*.[240] In that case an inspector was appointed pursuant to CA 1990, s 8, to investigate the affairs of Countyglen plc, with reference to particular transactions. Approximately seven months later, the court granted the inspector leave to deliver an interim report to the Court under s 11(1) of CA 1990. There were subsequent civil proceedings which demonstrate some of the possible consequences of the making of interim reports and final reports and the uses to which they can be put. These aspects of the case will be examined below.[241]

[13.102] Where an inspector has sought and obtained court approval to extend the investigation into the affairs of a related company, within the meaning of CA 1990, s 9, that provision states that he:

> '... shall report on the affairs of the other body corporate so far as he thinks the results of his investigation thereof are relevant to the investigation of the affairs of the first-mentioned company.'

It is only if, and to the extent that, the inspector considers the related company's affairs to be relevant to the primary inspection that he is under an obligation to report on the affairs of that related company.

[13.103] The scope of a report by an inspector appointed under CA 1990, s 14, to investigate the membership of any company, for the purpose of determining the true persons with a financial interest in the company, was considered in *Lyons v Curran*.[242] That inspection arose from the so-called Greencore affair. The final report issued by the inspector contained a reference to the ownership of a company (Talmino) other than the company under investigation. The case of *Lyons v Curran*[243] arose from a challenge to the inclusion of this company in the report. Blayney J considered the submission that the

---

[238] This is identical to the English CA 1985, s 437(1), subject to the significant *proviso* that the reports are made to the Secretary of State in England, rather than to the court.

[239] Rules of the Superior Courts 1986, ord 75B, rr 7(c), 7(d) and 7, as inserted by Rules of the Superior Courts (No 4) of 1991 (SI 278/1991).

[240] *Countyglen plc v Carway* [1998] 2 IR 540.

[241] See below paras **[13.122]** and **[13.123]**.

[242] *Lyons v Curran* [1993] ILRM 375.

[243] *Lyons v Curran* [1993] ILRM 375.

inspector had no power to investigate Talmino because it was not one of the companies he was appointed to investigate, and also because it was a foreign company. Blayney J concluded that an inspector seeking to ascertain the true persons with a financial interest in a company, must go further than the names of the companies that are members of the company under investigation. The inspector must determine the persons who are beneficially interested in the corporate member also. With regard to the duty to report where an inspector has carried out such investigations, Blayney J stated:

> 'If he does determine who such persons are, then clearly he has the duty and the power to include that determination in his report. And if he is unable to make a positive determination, but is able to form an opinion as to who the persons probably are, I consider that he still has a duty to include his findings in his report as it is something which it would be relevant to include and, furthermore, Section 22 clearly envisages an Inspector expressing opinions as his report is admissible in civil proceedings as evidence of the opinion of the Inspector in relation to any matter contained in the report.'[244]

The result of this interpretation of CA 1990, s 14(1) is that the inspector:

> 'had both the duty and the power to investigate Talmino for the purpose of determining the true persons who had been financially interested in the success or failure of Gladebrook ... He was in addition entitled to report his findings.'[245]

An inspector appointed under s 14(1) therefore has the right, but not necessarily the duty, to report on companies other than the company under investigation, which fall within the scope of the investigation. It will depend on the circumstances of the inspection and the conclusions of the inspector, whether there will be a duty to report on the membership of other companies.

(b) Challenge to report

[13.104] It has been seen that the rules of natural justice do not generally bind inspectors in the execution of their investigative tasks.[246] However, inspectors must act fairly and, in the context of the preparation of an inspector's report, the scope of this duty to act fairly has been explored, both in this jurisdiction and in England.

[13.105] In 1998, inspectors were appointed under CA 1990, s 8(1) to investigate the affairs of National Irish Bank Ltd ('NIB') and National Irish Bank Financial Services Ltd ('NIBFS'). The inspectors so appointed set out in writing the procedures they intended to follow, including a statement to that 'In the light of these procedures we consider it would be inappropriate and inconsistent with the statutory procedure to provide copies of the draft report to witnesses and invite comments on it.'[247] The procedures, among other issues, were challenged, and the ensuing decisions of the High Court and the Supreme Court in this regard are considered elsewhere.[248] In a subsequent

---

[244] *Lyons v Curran* [1993] ILRM 375.

[245] *Lyons v Curran* [1993] ILRM 375.

[246] See above paras [13.053] to [13.059].

[247] See *Re National Irish Bank Ltd (No 2)* [1999] 3 IR 190 at 194–195.

[248] See *Re National Irish Bank Ltd (No 2)* [1999] 3 IR 145. See also above paras [13.056] to [13.062] and [13.085] to [13.086].

decision of the High Court (Kelly J) entitled *Re National Irish Bank Ltd (No 2)*,[249] the companies under investigation sought to challenge the inspectors' conduct on the basis of duplication with an investigation by the Controller and Auditor General and on the basis that they were not afforded the right of access to all transcripts and documents related to interviews conducted before the interim report was submitted. It is the latter application that is relevant to the present topic as it was the content of the report that brought about that challenge.

The inspectors appointed to investigate NIB and NIBFS submitted two interim reports to the court and the final paragraph of the second such report read as follows:

> 'In setting out the more salient details of evidence given to us, we wish to emphasise that we have not yet formed any concluded view on these matters and cannot do so until officials of the [first applicant] have been given an opportunity of giving evidence to us … Until we have had the opportunity of interviewing the relevant employees of the [first applicant], it is not possible even to commence the process of considering whether the evidence should be accepted or not. We considered it proper nonetheless that we should report to the court now what we have done to date in the conduct of our investigations.'

[13.106] This statement notwithstanding, the applicants criticised the report for reaching conclusions and making findings without affording them the rights to which they claimed to be entitled. Kelly J considered the report and the criticisms made of it and decided as follows:

> 'For my part I can find no conclusions drawn in the inspectors' report. In fact the contrary is the case. They are careful to indicate that they have not even yet made a decision on whether the evidence outlined in para 10 [of the report] should be accepted or not.'[250]

The court found that, as the inspection was still in its investigative, information-gathering phase, the rights contended for by the applicants did not arise.[251] From the perspective of challenging a report, this decision is of interest, as it indicates that the submission of an interim report, or even two interim reports, does not necessitate any conclusions or imply that the investigative phase of the inspection is at an end.

[13.107] There is an English decision that addresses the circumstances surrounding the submission of an inspector's report and the problems that could be encountered, in some detail. In *R (Clegg) v Secretary of State*,[252] the applicant sought to challenge the decision of inspectors to complete their report and deliver it to the Secretary of State. This was based on the allegation that the report was delivered without giving the applicant any adequate opportunity to answer the criticisms against him. The background was that the inspectors notified the applicant of the provisional criticisms of him. His response was to request any underlying material on which the inspectors were placing reliance. The inspectors, relying on in *Re Pergamon Press Ltd*,[253] refused this request. The applicant

---

[249] *Re National Irish Bank Ltd (No 2)* [1999] 3 IR 190.

[250] *Re National Irish Bank Ltd (No 2)* [1999] 3 IR 190 at 213.

[251] See above paras **[13.056]** to **[13.058]**.

[252] *R (Clegg) v Secretary of State* [2002] EWCA Civ 519.

[253] *Re Pergamon Press Ltd* [1971] Ch 388, [1970] 3 All ER 535.

persisted in requesting the material in question and attended two interviews with the inspectors, but did not respond to the provisional criticisms originally notified to him by the inspectors.

Having received no such written response to the criticisms, the inspectors proceeded to complete and deliver the report some five years later. The question addressed by the Court was whether the inspectors had acted unfairly in completing and submitting the report without receiving such a response. The Court was called upon to consider the implications of a letter from the applicant requesting the inspectors to revise their provisional criticisms, to which the inspectors did not reply. The Court of Appeal analysed the failure to respond to this letter in the following manner:

> '... it does not lead to the conclusion that they treated the appellant unfairly. It cannot be said, in the circumstances of the present case, that the inspectors' failure to respond to that letter led the appellant to believe that they would not complete and submit their report without first telling him that they intended to proceed notwithstanding that they had received no written response from him. Nor can it be said, in my view, that fairness – as distinct from prudence and good administration – required that (even though they had done nothing to encourage that belief) they would not proceed without telling him that that was their intention.'[254]

This case confirms that, even when inspectors have been in communication with persons regarding criticisms of them that have arisen in the course of the investigation, there is no obligation on the inspectors to keep such persons informed of their intentions with regard to the completion and submission of reports.

[13.108] An important English decision regarding the duty of inspectors is the decision of the Court of Appeal in *Maxwell v Department of Trade and Industry*.[255] The plaintiff was the chairman and chief executive of the company under investigation and sought to challenge the conduct of the inspectors on a number of grounds, including that the interim report was completed and submitted without allowing the plaintiff the opportunity to respond to the criticisms made of him and that the inspectors had failed to put to the plaintiff all relevant statements made by other witnesses, or in documents, which were prejudicial to him so as to give him an opportunity of answering them.

Lord Denning MR analysed what is involved in making a report in the following terms:

> '... the inspectors have to make their report. They should state their findings on the evidence and their opinions on the matters referred to them. If their report is to be of value, they should make it with courage and frankness, keeping nothing back. The public interest demands it. It may on occasion be necessary for them to condemn or criticise a man. Before doing so, they must act fairly by him. But what does fairness demand? That is the question.'[256]

---

[254] *R (Clegg) v Secretary of State* [2002] EWCA Civ 519 (*per* Chadwick LJ) at para 35.

[255] *Maxwell v Department of Trade and Industry* [1974] QB 523, [1974] 2 All ER 122, [1974] 2 WLR 338.

[256] *Maxwell v Department of Trade and Industry* [1974] QB 523, [1974] 2 All ER 122, [1974] 2 WLR 338 at 344.

In answering this question, Denning MR rejected the argument (which was based on the decision of the High Court (Forbes J) in the same case) that, after hearing the evidence and studying the documents, the inspectors ought to come to a tentative conclusion and put the substance of that conclusion to the witness. Denning MR considered the practical consequences of such an approach:

> 'Just think what it means. After hearing all the evidence the inspectors have to sit down and come to tentative conclusions. If these are such as to be critical of any of the witnesses, they have to re-open the inquiry, recall those witnesses, and put to them the criticisms which they are disposed to make. What will be the response of those witnesses? They will at once want to refute the tentative conclusions by calling other witnesses, or by asking for further investigations. In short, the inquiry will develop into a series of minor trials in which a witness will be accused of misconduct and seek to answer it. That would hold up the inquiry indefinitely. I do not think it is necessary. It is sufficient for the inspectors to put the points to the witnesses as and when they come in the first place. After hearing the evidence, the inspectors have to come to their conclusions. These need not be tentative in the least. They can be final and definite, ready for their report.'[257]

This clarifies that a witness does not have the right to know of all of the conclusions that will be contained in an inspector's report, which allows inspectors considerably more flexibility in the execution of their tasks and the formulation of their conclusions. This is a point that was emphasised by Lord Denning MR:

> 'It must be remembered that the inspectors are doing a public duty in the public interest. They must do what is fair to the best of their ability. They will, of course, put to a witness the points of substance which occur to them – so as to give him the chance to explain or correct any relevant statement which is prejudicial to him. They may even recall him to do so. But they are not to be criticised because they may on occasion overlook something or other. Even the most skilled advocate, expert in cross-examination, forgets now and again to put this or that point to a witness. And we all excuse him, knowing how difficult it is to remember everything. The inspector is entitled to at least as much consideration as the advocate. To borrow from Shakespeare, he is not to have "All his faults observ'd, Set in a note-book, learn'd, and conn'd by rote", to make a lawyers' holiday. His task is burdensome and thankless enough as it is. It would be intolerable if he were liable to be pilloried afterwards for doing it. No one of standing would ever be found to undertake it. The public interest demands that, so long as he acts honestly and does what is fair to the best of his ability, his report is not to be impugned in the courts of law.'[258]

On the basis of these conclusions, Lord Denning MR refused the relief sought, observing that, as a court could not set aside the report or declare it to be null or void, in whole or in part, the only available relief was a declaration that natural justice was not

---

[257] *Maxwell v Department of Trade and Industry* [1974] QB 523, [1974] 2 All ER 122, [1974] 2 WLR 338.

[258] *Maxwell v Department of Trade and Industry* [1974] QB 523, [1974] 2 All ER 122, [1974] 2 WLR 338 at 345–346.

observed in the making of the report and that it was only in rare cases that it would be appropriate for the court 'to make such a bare declaration in the air.'

[13.109] Lord Denning's approach in both *Maxwell* and *Pergamon Press* was endorsed by the High Court in *Re National Irish Bank Ltd*, an unreported judgment of Kelly J.[259] In that case, the DCE sought discovery of documents collated by the inspectors during their investigation in circumstances in which the DCE was pursuing s 160 proceedings against certain company directors. Those company directors resisted the DCE's disqualification proceedings, which the DCE characterised as a collateral attack on the inspectors' report. In order to meet that challenge, the DCE submitted that he required access to the documentation upon which the inspectors had based their findings. Kelly J noted that the inspectors had fulfilled their obligations under s 11 to make a final report to the Court. Endorsing *Maxwell v Department of Trade*,[260] Kelly J stated:

'In my view the inspectors are correct when they argue that just as there is a need for finality in litigation so there is also a need for finality in investigations. That is what the legislature has ordained by speaking of the presentation of a final report. I do not believe that the legislation and s 12 in particular envisage some form of rolling process where, notwithstanding the delivery of a final report by them, inspectors might be asked to revisit all of the documents in their possession in order to identify which documents support particular findings made by them. Such an exercise would be inconsistent both with the notion of a final report and indeed the task which the statute requires inspectors to undertake. Inspectors are not appointed as evidence gatherers but rather as investigators whose job is to make a report. Their function is inquisitorial. When they produce a final report they ought not to be asked to conduct further work for others who may wish to challenge or to stand over the report prepared by them.'

[13.110] Kelly J gave the following as further reasons for his refusal to accede to the application: firstly, the statutory scheme provided for a report of a final nature. Secondly, whereas costs for the investigation leading to the final report were recoverable by inspectors under s 13 of the Act, no further costs were recoverable after the delivery of the final report. Thirdly, as a practical consideration, Kelly J felt that if he granted such an order, potential respondents would also seek documents pertaining to inspectors' reports, rendering the inspectors' task an 'endless obligation' which was 'never envisaged nor contemplated by the legislation'. Finally, Kelly J noted that the evidential status given to the inspectors' report by s 22 of the Act related to the conclusions and opinions set out in the report, rather than the information gathered.

It seems from this judgment that, once the final inspectors' report is delivered, any documents gathered in the preparation of the report are not accessible to third parties. Only the inspectors' conclusions and opinions and the information they select to form part of their final report enjoy the evidential status bestowed by CA 1990, s 22.

---

[259] *National Irish Bank (Under Investigation) v Companies Act* [2006] IEHC 35, (10 February 2006, unreported), HC, Kelly J.

[260] *Maxwell v Department of Trade* [1974] 1 QB 523.

(c) Publication

[13.111] Where an inspector's interim or final report is filed with the court, the court is obliged to furnish a copy of every such report to the DCE and has a discretion, if the court thinks fit, to furnish copies to other entities listed in CA 1990, s 11(3):

> Where inspectors were appointed under s 7 or 8, the court shall furnish a copy of every report of theirs to the Director and the court may, if it thinks fit—
>
> (a) forward a copy of any report made by the inspectors to the company's registered office,
>
> (b) furnish a copy on request and payment of the prescribed fee to—
>
> > (i)   any member of the company or other body corporate which is the subject of the report;
> >
> > (ii) any person whose conduct is referred to in the report;
> >
> > (iii) the auditors of that company or body corporate;
> >
> > (iv) the applicants for the investigation;
> >
> > (v)   any other person (including an employee) whose financial interests appear to the court to be affected by the matters dealt with in the report whether as a creditor of the company or body corporate or otherwise;
> >
> > (vi) the Central Bank, in any case in which the report of the inspectors relates, wholly or partly, to the affairs of the holder of a licence under s 9 of the Central Bank Act, 1971;
>
> (ba) furnish a copy to—
>
> > (i)   an appropriate authority in relation to any of the matters referred to in s 21(1)(a) to (fb);[261] or
> >
> > (ii) a competent authority as defined in s 21(3)(a) to (i)[262]...

[13.112] A further discretion which is conferred on the courts in connection with the dissemination of an inspector's report, is contained in s 11(3)(c), which provides that the court may, if it thinks fit, 'cause any such report to be printed and published.' The discretion of the court to print and publish a report under this provision, or to forward a copy of the report to the company's registered office or to such other persons as request a copy pursuant to s 11(3)(b), is complemented by the terms of s 11(4). Section 11(4) provides that, when a court determines that it is appropriate to forward or publish a report under s 11, that court can further determine that a part of the report be omitted from the copy that is to be forwarded or published:

> Where the court so thinks proper it may direct that a particular part of a report made by virtue of this section be omitted from a copy forwarded or furnished under sub-s (3)(a), (b) or (ba), or from the report as printed and published under sub-s (3)(c).[263]

---

[261] See above Ch **12** in relation to CA 1990, s 21, as amended by C(A)(No 2)A 1999, s 53 and CLEA 2001, s 31.

[262] CA 1990, s 11(3), as amended by CLEA 2001, s 24(1).

[263] CA 1990, s 11(4), as amended by CLEA 2001, s 24(2).

[13.113] A decision in which the publication of an inspector's report arose for consideration was *Re Ansbacher (Cayman) Ltd.*[264] That case arose from the appointment of inspectors by the High Court on 22 September, 1999, under CA 1990, s 8(1), to investigate the affairs of Ansbacher (Cayman) Limited (formerly Guinness Mahon Cayman Trust Limited Ansbacher Limited and Cayman International Bank and Trust Company Limited). At the conclusion of the inspection and before the report was submitted to the court, the inspectors made it known to certain individuals that their names would appear in the report as customers of the company under investigation. These individuals, through their solicitors, sought to challenge the disclosure of their names in the report and, specifically, sought to have any applications relating to the inspectors' report heard *in camera*. This was determined as a preliminary point by the High Court (McCracken J), on the basis that there existed what he referred to as a 'chicken and egg' situation, because if the application for a private hearing was heard in open court, the names would be disclosed in any event.

McCracken J considered Art 34.1 of the Constitution, which requires that justice be administered in public, except in 'such special and limited circumstances as may be prescribed by law', and Art 40.3.2, which protects the right to a good name. He also considered submissions to the effect that the jurisprudence of the Irish courts confirms that the courts have jurisdiction to hear legal proceedings *in camera* and/or to permit a party to use a pseudonym in circumstances where such a jurisdiction has not been conferred by law and that such a jurisdiction should be exercised in favour of the applicants. The Court concluded that the submissions made would involve a distortion of the wording of Art 34.1 and that the phrase 'as may be prescribed by law' can extend beyond statute law to such special and limited cases as 'may expressly or by inference be prescribed in the Constitution itself.'[265] In this regard, McCracken J formed the view that 'there is no possible harmonious construction of the Constitution whereby the applicants' personal rights could be considered to give rise to any special or limited case prescribed by law as an exception to Art 34.1.'

[13.114] Having determined that any applications arising in connection with the inspectors' report should be heard in public, McCracken J noted that:

> 'The fact that Art 34.1 requires courts to administer justice in public by its very nature requires the attendant publicity, including the identification of parties seeking justice. It is a small price to be paid to ensure the integrity and openness of one of the three organs of the State, namely, the judicial process, in which openness is a vital element. It is often said that justice must not only be done, but must also be seen to be done, and if this involves innocent parties being brought before the courts in either civil or criminal proceedings, and wrongly accused, that is unfortunate, but is essential for the protection of the entire judicial system. I do not believe I am called upon to consider any hierarchy of rights in the present case, but if I had to do so, I have no hesitation whatever in saying that the right to have justice administered in public far exceeds any right to privacy, confidentiality or a good name.'[266]

---

[264] *Re Ansbacher (Cayman) Ltd* [2002] 2 IR 517.

[265] *Re Ansbacher (Cayman) Ltd* [2002] 2 IR 517 at 526.

[266] *Re Ansbacher (Cayman) Ltd* [2002] 2 IR 517 at 531–532.

This decision confirms that the protection of the privacy of persons who are named in inspectors' reports is by no means certain. In the case of the inspection of the affairs of Ansbacher (Cayman) Limited, exactly two months after McCracken J's judgment was delivered, Finnegan P ordered that the entire inspectors' report be printed and published.[267]

[13.115] The discretion of the court to omit parts of a report from the copy that is to be distributed or published,[268] was considered in *Countyglen plc v Carway.*[269] The main issue in that case was the use of an inspector's report in subsequent civil proceedings, an issue which is governed by CA 1990, s 22, and in the context of which the decision is considered in more detail elsewhere.[270] In that case, parts of the inspector's report had been omitted from publication or distribution, in accordance with s 11(4). The Court ruled, however, that the reference to the 'report of an inspector' in s 22, was to the entire report, including any parts of the report which may have been excluded from publication or distribution. The entire report could therefore be admissible in subsequent civil proceedings, even where a court may have previously made an order under s 11, that the entire report should be not disclosed. This could present a risk of unfairness to a litigant who may not have received access to certain portions of an inspector's report. Laffoy J acknowledged this risk, noting that:

> 'In applying s 22, the court must have regard to the constitutional right of every party to fair procedures and it may be that in the instant actions the embargo on the disclosure of the contents of appendix 23 will give rise to difficulties. However, these difficulties will have to be addressed as they arise. It was not contended by any party that non-circulation and the non-publication of appendix 23 has vitiated the use of the final report as permitted by s 22.'[271]

[13.116] In *Re National Irish Bank (No 3)*,[272] Kelly J refused an application by the bank and the company to be furnished with an advance copy of the report. He rejected submissions which related to their ability to prepare for the report's publication, whilst stating that the bank and the company were entitled to a copy of the report. On the other hand, Kelly J did grant the Central Bank and the Irish Financial Services Regulatory Authority immediate access to the report (ie prior to its general publication) on the grounds that they did not have access to any preparatory drafts of the report and required such access in order to prepare for its regulatory implications.

Kelly J further refused an application by company directors against whom negative findings were made to adjourn the proceedings pending their sight of a draft of the report, in order to determine whether they would apply for redaction of the report under

---

[267] *Re Ansbacher (Cayman) Ltd,* Order of High Court, 24 June 2004 (Finnegan P).

[268] CA 1990, s 11(4).

[269] *Countyglen v Carway* [1998] 2 IR 540.

[270] See below paras **[13.122]** to **[13.123]**.

[271] *Countyglen v Carway* [1998] 2 IR 540 at 551.

[272] *Re National Irish Bank (No 3)* [2004] 4 IR 186.

s 11(4). The serious nature of the enquiry warranted its full publication and Kelly J stated:

> 'Prospective customers, staff and employees, as well as the general public are entitled to know the outcome of the investigation particularly where as counsel for the bank pointed out it forms part of the banking structure in the State'.[273]

The judge did, however, express some misgivings regarding publication, arising from the fact that DPP would receive a copy of the report. The Court was ultimately satisfied that any prosecution would take a considerable time to initiate and a trial judge would be in a position to make the appropriate directions to a jury to negative any prejudicial impact of publishing the report.[274]

[**13.117**] The provisions governing the publication and dissemination of inspector's reports in Ireland can be contrasted to some extent with the equivalent provisions in England. The first observation that should be made is that reports of inspectors appointed under CA 1985 are made to the Secretary of State, as opposed to the court.[275] CA 1985, s 437 provides that the Secretary of State must send a copy of the report to the court but only if the inspector was appointed under CA 1985, s 432(1) pursuant to an order of the court. If the inspector was appointed by any means other than s 432(1), it does not appear that the Secretary of State has the discretion to send the report to the court. In respect of all inspectors, however appointed, the Secretary of State may forward a copy of the report to the same or similar entities as are provided for in CA 1990, s 11(3).[276] Unlike CA 1990, s 11(4), the Secretary of State does not have any discretion to omit particular parts of a report that is to be disseminated or published. There have been decisions in England arising from refusals by the Secretary of State to publish or distribute inspectors' reports. There was a series of decisions in connection with the inspection of the acquisition of the House of Fraser by the Al Fayed brothers. The inspectors were appointed by the Secretary of State under s 432(2) and, at the conclusion of the inspection, the Secretary of State deferred publication of the report

---

[273] *Re National Irish Bank (No 3)* [2004] 4 IR 186 at 193.

[274] Kelly J ordered that the report be furnished to the bank and the company (pursuant to s 11(3)(a); persons whose conduct was referred to in the report and the auditors whose conduct was also referred to in the report (pursuant to s 11(3)(b)(ii)); the DCE and the Minister for Enterprise, Trade and Employment if he so requested (pursuant to s 11(3)(b)(iv)); a creditor (pursuant to s 11(3)(b)(v)); the Central Bank and the Irish Financial Regulatory Authority due to their regulatory functions (pursuant to s 11(3)(b)(vi)); the Revenue Commissioners, the Director of Public Prosecutions, the Minister for Finance and the Institute for Chartered Accountants in Ireland (pursuant to s 11(3)(ba)); and at the request of the Director and the Bank, the report was also sent to regulatory authorities in the UK, Australia, New Zealand, the United States of America and the Isle of Man.

[275] CA 1985, ss 431, 432, 437, 442.

[276] The only differences between the entities to which copies can be forwarded in Ireland and England are that CA 1990, s 11(3)(b)(v) expressly includes employees among the persons whose financial interests appear to be affected by the report, and CA 1990, s 11 contains three categories that do not have an equivalent in CA 1985, s 437, namely the Central Bank, an appropriate authority in relation to any of the matters referred to in s 21(1)(a) to (fb) and a competent authority as defined in s 21(3)(a) to (i).

pending investigations and any eventual prosecutions, by the Serious Fraud Office, a decision which was challenged and affirmed.[277]

[13.118] There are other provisions of the English legislation which address the publication of inspectors' reports and which have no equivalent in the CA 1990. There is an interesting aspect of CA 1985, s 432, which provides for the appointment of an inspector to investigate a company's affairs where the Secretary of State considers that one or more of the requisite circumstances pertain to that company. CA 1985, s 432(2A), was inserted by CA 1989, s 55, and provides:

> Inspectors may be appointed under sub-s (2) on terms that any report they may make is not for publication; and in such a case, the provisions of s 437(3) (availability and publication of inspectors' reports) do not apply.

This provision essentially permits the findings of an inspection to remain private and may facilitate the co-operation of persons who are involved in the company under investigation, particularly where the public interest considerations are minimal. One commentator has noted that, while the Secretary of State already had a discretion as to whether to publish or distribute inspectors' report, there are two advantages flowing from s 432(2A):

> 'It protects the Secretary of State from pressure to publish even though he is advised that that might prejudice possible criminal prosecutions, and it makes it clear to the proposed appointees that they will not be able to bask in publicity resulting from their efforts.'[278]

(d) Consequences

[13.119] There are certain consequences that the Companies Acts envisage as flowing directly from an inspector's report. This should be distinguished from the use to which such a report can be put in separate subsequent proceedings, a topic which will is addressed below.[279]

CA 1990, s 12, sets out the range of orders that a court can make, having considered a report that was delivered by inspectors pursuant to s 11:

> (1) Having considered a report made under s 11, the court may make such order as it deems fit in relation to matters arising from that report including—
>
> (a) an order of its own motion for the winding up of a body corporate, or
>
> (b) an order for the purpose of remedying any disability suffered by any person whose interests were adversely affected by the conduct of the affairs of the company, provided that, in making any such order, the court shall have regard

---

[277] See, eg, *R v Secretary of State, ex p Lonrho* [1989] 1 WLR 525. See also *Re Lonrho plc and others* [1990] 2 AC 154, [1989] 3 WLR 535, [1989] 2 All ER 1100, which concerned contempt of court proceedings that arose from the distribution of the report by a newspaper, while the challenge to the Secretary of State's decision not to publish the report was pending.

[278] P Davies, *Gower and Davies' Principles of Modern Company Law* (7th edn, Sweet and Maxwell, 2003), p 472.

[279] See below paras **[13.122]** to **[13.124]**.

to the interests of any other person who may be adversely affected by the order.

(2) If, in the case of any body corporate liable to be wound up under the Companies Acts, it appears to the Director from—

(a) any report made under s 11 as a result of an application by the Director under s 8, or

(b) any report made by inspectors appointed by the Director under this Act, or

(c) any information or document obtained by the Director under this Part,

that a petition should be presented for the winding up of the body, the Director may, unless the body is already being wound up by the court, present a petition for it to be so wound up if the court thinks it just and equitable for it to be so wound up.[280]

[13.120] In *Re National Irish Bank (No 3)*[281] Kelly J commented on the 'extraordinarily wide jurisdiction' s 12(1)(a) grants the court, even in circumstances in which neither the DCE advocates the winding up of the company:

'The court is given an express power, unique to the company law of this jurisdiction, to order of its own motion the winding up of a body corporate, having considered a report under s 11. That power is given to the court, notwithstanding the express entitlement conferred upon the Director, to himself petition the court for a winding up order as a result of matters disclosed in a report under s 11. It was clearly the intention of the legislature that, even in circumstances where the Director does not wish to present a petition for the winding up of a company that has been investigated, nonetheless the court may order it to be liquidated.'[282]

While Kelly J noted that the DCE, the inspectors and the regulator did not advocate the winding up of the company, he nevertheless deemed the decision as to whether to make such an order to be exclusively the preserve of the court. Kelly J noted that the court must only effect such an order if to do so would serve the public interest. Kelly J adopted the approach of the House of Lords in *Re Walter L Jacob & Co Ltd*[283] in which the leading judgment in relation to the independent role the court had to play as against a petitioner who applied for the winding up of a company in the public interest was handed down by Lord Nicholls:

'In the case of "public interest" petitions, the court will, of course, carry out that evaluation with the assistance of evidence and submissions from the Secretary of State and from other parties. When doing so the court will take note that the source of the submissions that the company should be wound up is a government department charged by Parliament with wide-ranging responsibilities in relation to the affairs of companies. The department has considerable expertise in these matters and can be expected to act with the proper sense of responsibility when

---

[280] CA 1990, s 12 as amended by CLEA 2001, s 14. For an example of the adoption of this procedure, see *Honiball v McGrath* (23 March 2000, unreported), HC, where a company was wound up following an inspection which found that there were breaches of the Companies Acts, including fraudulent activity.

[281] *Re National Irish Bank (No 3)* [2004] 4 IR 186.

[282] *Re National Irish Bank (No 3)* [2004] 4 IR 186 at 195.

[283] *Re Walter L Jacob & Co Ltd* [1989] BCLC 345 at 353.

seeking a winding-up order. But the cogency of the submissions made on behalf of the Secretary of State will fall to be considered and tested in the same way as any other submissions. His submissions are not *ipso facto* endowed with such weight that those resisting a winding-up petition presented by him will find the scales loaded against them. At the end of the day the court must be able to identify for itself the aspect or aspects of the public interest which, in the view of the court, would be promoted by making a winding-up order in the particular case. In many, perhaps most, cases that would be a simple exercise in which the answer would be self-evident. In other cases the answer may not be so obvious.'

Kelly J therefore undertook a review of the inspectors' report, which revealed a situation of the 'utmost gravity'.[284] He weighed this against contrition on behalf of the bank (backed up by concrete actions of repayment programmes); the impact on the bank's employees and the banking sector in the event of the winding up; and gave weight to the attitudes of the DCE and the inspectors. He concluded that it would not be in the public interest to wind up the bank.

[13.121] This case illustrates the court's willingness to exercise the broad discretion granted to it under s 12(1)(a) and highlights, in this instance, five factors which swayed the court's resolve from winding up the company in the public interest. These factors were: (a) the company's evident seriousness in addressing the problems highlighted by the inspectors; (b) the negative impact winding up the company would have on its employees and (c) the negative impact winding up the company would have on the banking sector; (d) the DCE's opinion that winding up the company was not appropriate and (e) the inspectors' opinion that winding up the company was not appropriate.

If a court does not consider that an order should be made for the winding up of a company, it may direct the person who applied for the appointment of the inspector under s 7 or s 8, or 'such other person as the court shall think fit', to present a petition for the winding up of the company. The court may also give such further directions in relation to the proceedings as it thinks fit.[285]

(e) Use of report

[13.122] There is a particular provision of the CA 1990, which provides for the report of an inspector to be admissible in evidence in subsequent civil proceedings. Section 22 provides:

> A document purporting to be a copy of a report of an inspector appointed under the provisions of this Part shall be admissible in any civil proceedings as evidence—
>
> (a) of the facts set out therein without further proof unless the contrary is shown, and
>
> (b) of the opinion of the inspector in relation to any matter contained in the report.

---

[284] *Re National Irish Bank (No 3)* [2004] 4 IR 186 at 199.

[285] Rules of the Superior Courts, 1986, ord 75B, r 4, as inserted by Rules of the Superior Courts (No 4) 1991 (SI 278/1991).

In *Countyglen plc v Carway,*[286] Laffoy J considered the interpretation of s 22 and noted that the provision it replaced, CA 1963, s 172, merely provided that a copy of the report of an inspector appointed under that Act should be admissible in any legal proceedings as evidence of the opinion of the inspector in relation to any matter contained in the report. The Court further noted that there is no equivalent provision in the UK, the closest comparator being CA 1985, s 441, which was amended by the Company Directors Disqualification Act, 1986, to permit true copies of an inspector's report to be admissible in proceedings on an application under the Act of 1986 'as evidence of any fact stated therein'. Laffoy J therefore considered English authorities not to be of assistance in the interpretation of s 22.[287] In *Countyglen plc v Carway,* [288] one of the issues was whether parts of the report, which were omitted from publication and distribution in accordance with CA 1990, s 11(4), could be relied upon in court under s 22.

The plaintiff in that case contended that the meaning of s 22 was clear and unambiguous and permitted the use of an inspector's report in civil proceedings, in the sense that the production of the report gives the facts set out therein the status of evidence, whether or not those facts relate to the party to the civil action against whom it is sought to prove them. The defendant argued that this construction would be unconstitutional, on the basis that it would introduce an inquisitorial system into a civil adversarial process and on the basis that it would infringe Art 34.1 of the Constitution; the rights of fair procedure;[289] and the principle of equality of arms.

Laffoy J considered these submissions and, on the basis of the following interpretation of s 22, concluded that primary facts in an inspector's report, as distinct from findings, would be admissible as proven facts:

> 'In my view, on a literal interpretation of s 22 the word "facts" means primary or basic facts and not secondary or inferred facts. The words "without further proof", in my view, indicate that what the legislature intended was that facts which would be provable by witnesses in the ordinary way, and not deductions from facts found or admitted, should acquire the status of proven facts under s 22. Therefore, I accept the contention of the bank and the solicitors that the expression 'facts' in s 22 means only findings of primary fact clearly expressed as such and I reject the alternative construction contended for by the plaintiff.'[290]

It should also be noted that, where such primary facts are admissible under s 22, Laffoy J did not consider that they were accorded any special probative value:

> 'Section 22 does not prescribe that facts thereby given the status of proven facts have any special probative value or that any particular weight should be attached thereto.'

---

[286] *Countyglen plc v Carway* [1998] 2 IR 540.

[287] *Countyglen plc v Carway* [1998] 2 IR 540 at 546.

[288] *Countyglen plc v Carway* [1998] 2 IR 540.

[289] The right of a person to confront and cross-examine persons giving evidence against him was particularly relied upon.

[290] *Countyglen plc v Carway* [1998] 2 IR 540 at 550–551.

[13.123] With regard to the material which was omitted from the published report, Laffoy J considered that the reference to an inspector's report in s 22 was to the entire report, including any part which had been omitted from circulation under s 11(4). Acknowledging the difficulties that could arise from the admission into evidence of such material, Laffoy J noted:

> 'In applying s 22, the court must have regard to the constitutional right of every party to fair procedures and it may be that in the instant actions the embargo on the disclosure of the contents of appendix 23 will give rise to difficulties. However, these difficulties will have to be addressed as they arise.'[291]

Having made that observation, Laffoy J further observed that no party had challenged the implications the non-circulation or non-publication of a report would have on the use of such a report under s 22. This may be an area in which special attention will need to be paid to ensure the rights of parties to civil litigation are not unfairly disadvantaged by the admission into evidence of material which the courts did not consider it appropriate to publish and of which the party against whom it is being invoked, may be unaware.

[13.124] Inspectors' reports have been admitted as evidence in disqualification actions taken by the DCE under CA 1990, s 160, in a number of cases.[292]

F. Expenses

[13.125] The general rule governing the expenses incurred in the course of an investigation, is that they are borne by the relevant Minister. However, the court can make directions to the effect that particular persons may be liable to contribute to these expenses. When one considers the potential cost of a large scale investigation, such as the £8.5 million bill for the investigation into Mirror Group Newspapers plc[293] in the UK, this issue assumes real importance.

[13.126] CA 1990, s 13(1)[294] provides that the persons who may be directed by the court to be liable for expenses include a body corporate which is dealt with in the report or the applicant(s) for the investigation. An application for an order under s 13(1) must be made by means of originating notice of motion and must be served on the person on whom liability for expenses is sought to be imposed.[295] The court may order these

---

[291] *Countyglen plc v Carway* [1998] 2 IR 540 at 551.

[292] See, eg *Re NIB Ltd: Director of Corporate Enforcement v D'Arcy* [2006] 2 IR 163; *Re Ansbacher (Cayman) Limited: Director of Corporate Enforcement v Collery* [2006] IEHC 67, (9 March 2006, unreported), HC, Finlay Geoghegan J. See Pt E, Disqualification Orders.

[293] The then Secretary of State, the Rt Hon Stephen Byers MP announced, on the publication of the report into the Mirror Group Newspapers plc, that it had taken nearly nine years and cost £8.5 million, and that, 'I do not regard this as an acceptable state of affairs.' DTI, *Company Investigations: Powers for the 21st century.*

[294] As amended by CLEA 2001, s 25.

[295] Rules of the Superior Courts 1986, ord 75B, r 3(d), as inserted by Rules of the Superior Courts (No 4) 1991 (SI 278/1991).

persons to be liable to repay expenses to the relevant Minister to the extent that the court directs. In the case of the applicants, the maximum liability for expenses is £250,000. There is no such threshold stipulated in respect of companies dealt with in the report. Pursuant to s 13(2), another category of persons who may be held liable for the costs of a company inspection are persons who are convicted on indictment of offences arising from the investigation; persons who are ordered to pay damages or restore property in proceedings brought as a result of the investigation; and persons who are awarded damages or to whom property is restored in proceedings resulting from the investigation. These persons may, in the same proceedings, be ordered to repay 'all or part' of the expenses of the investigation to the Minister or to any person on whom liability has been imposed. In respect of persons who receive damages or property, there is some protection against full liability. Section 13(2) provides that such persons shall not be required to pay more than one-tenth of the damages or value of property they receive and an order for expenses against such persons will not be executed until they receive the damages or property.

The inspector has the right, pursuant to CA 1990, s 13(3), to include recommendations in the report, regarding the liability for expenses of companies dealt with in the report or applicants for the appointment of the inspector. If the court so directs, the inspector is obliged to include such directions in the report.

[13.127] In the *Minister for Justice v Siucre Éireann cpt*,[296] the application of s 13 arose for consideration. The inspectors were appointed to investigate the affairs of the respondent under CA 1990, s 8. The investigation was subsequently extended, pursuant to s 9, to the affairs of a number of related companies. After the submission of two interim reports and a final report, which found the existence of various irregularities and possible and probable irregularities in the conduct of the enterprise, the Minister for Justice applied, pursuant to s 13, to be re-imbursed in respect of certain expenses. The expression 'dealt with in the report' as it appears in s 13(1)(a), was considered. One company in particular, which was not under investigation, either pursuant to s 8 or s 9, resisted the submission that it was 'dealt with' in the report. Another issue arose due to the fact that Siucre Éireann had been recently privatised and it was argued that the matters giving rise to the investigation all occurred during the time when the enterprise was owned and controlled by the State and the State should therefore bear the costs of the investigation. The Minister argued that it would be wrong for the State to have the bear the cost of such investigations.

[13.128] The High Court (Lynch J) agreed generally with the latter submission, on the basis that companies are creatures of the law and are controlled by the law and it is the task of the executive power of the State to supervise them. He went on to consider the issue of security for costs under ss 7 and 8, and the appropriate allocation of liability for expenses of an investigation:

> 'If, under s 7, the court may require security for the costs ... from the applicant for the investigation, but if, under s 8, it is a matter of such public concern, even though the State has no direct interest in the company, that no security for the costs is required, in such circumstances it is *prima facie* only right and proper that the company or companies dealt with in the report, even though not adversely dealt

---

[296] *Minister for Justice v Siucre Éireann cpt* [1992] 2 IR 215.

with therein, should reimburse the State the costs and expenses pursuant to s 13, sub-s (1) and then in appropriate circumstances such companies can seek reimbursement themselves under sub-s (2).'[297]

This was subject to the significant *caveat*, however, that the allocation of liability fell to be determined on the facts of each individual case. Lynch J was persuaded by the fact that the alleged wrongdoing in the enterprise giving rise to the investigation all took place when the enterprise was wholly owned by the State and under the control of the State. While, at the time of privatisation, neither the State nor the public were aware of these irregularities, the State did benefit financially, and Lynch J considered it would be unjust to permit the State to effectively make a double recovery, by subsequently recouping the expenses of the investigation against shareholders, most of whom were not members of the company at the relevant times. The Court concluded:

> 'it is more equitable that those in ultimate control at the time of the wrongdoing (even though unaware of it at that time) should bear the costs of the investigation rather than their successors especially to the extent that such successors were wholly unaware of any such wrongdoing.'

The Court was also influenced by the fact that the company itself had already incurred substantial costs in complying with the inspection. On these grounds, the Court held:

> 'In all the very special circumstances of this case I do not think that it would be just or equitable to direct that any of the first nine respondents being part of the enterprise should be liable to repay to the applicant, the Minister for Justice, any of the expenses of and incidental to the investigation by the inspectors and I accordingly refuse the Minister's application as against those respondents.'[298]

This decision demonstrates that it is not an automatic right of the Minister to have expenses of investigations reimbursed, pursuant to s 13. However, it should also be noted that the facts of *Minister for Justice v Siucre Éireann cpt*,[299] are very particular and unusual and the decision is very much a product of those facts.

[13.129] In that case, the Court also considered the situation of a different company, from which the Minister sought to recover expenses, on the basis that the company in question was 'dealt with' in the report. This company was not formally under investigation, in the meaning of the Companies Acts, although it was relevant to the investigation. Lynch J reached the following conclusion:

> 'If the court has power to order a company dealt with in the report, but not actually under investigation, to pay these expenses it could lead to strange results in that the company might never have had a proper opportunity of itself putting its case to the inspectors who might nevertheless have power under s 13, sub-s (3) to recommend that such company should bear such expenses.
>
> I have come to the conclusion that the intention of the legislature and the meaning of the words "a body corporate dealt with in the report" is to limit the power of the court to order repayment of the expenses by such bodies corporate only as were under investigation and are dealt with in the report and not to extend the power to

---

[297] *Minister for Justice v Siucre Éireann cpt* [1992] 2 IR 215.

[298] *Minister for Justice v Siucre Éireann cpt* [1992] 2 IR 215.

[299] *Minister for Justice v Siucre Éireann cpt* [1992] 2 IR 215.

bodies corporate which are dealt with in the report but were not under investigation.'[300]

This limits the scope of s 13(1) considerably and it may now be read as referring to companies under investigation, rather than companies 'dealt with in the report'. This interpretation protects the position of other companies that fall within the scope of an inspector's report, without formally being under investigation. This is more consistent with the terms of CA 1990, s 14(6),[301] which permits the court, on the application of the DCE, to direct a company 'subject of an investigation under this section' to be liable for the expenses of the investigation, to the extent directed by the court. The fact that this provision refers explicitly to companies under investigation, however, highlights the lower threshold contained in s 13(1) of companies 'dealt with in the report' and may cast some doubt on the interpretation reached in *Minister for Justice v Siucre Éireann cpt*.[302]

---

[300] *Minister for Justice v Siucre Éireann cpt* [1992] 2 IR 215.

[301] As inserted by CLEA 2001, s 26. See above para **[13.049]**.

[302] *Minister for Justice v Siucre Éireann cpt* [1992] 2 IR 215.

Chapter 14

STRIKING COMPANIES' NAMES OFF THE REGISTER

[14.001] The sanction of a company's name being struck off the register of companies has risen to considerable prominence since it was first enacted in 1982. This is largely due to the number of companies on which this sanction has been imposed. By way of illustration, the names of 28,731 companies were struck off the register in 1999. This number has decreased in more recent years, but has not completely abated, with 9,456 company names being struck off in 2006. While a company's name may be struck off the register of companies for a relatively inoffensive omission, typically a failure to file an annual return, the repercussions of this administrative act and the expense of reversing it, can be considerable.[1]

A. Grounds for striking off

[14.002] The number of companies which face the sanction of being struck off the register of companies, and the attendant difficulties and ignominy, has increased dramatically in recent years. There are a number of different grounds on which such a fate may befall a company.

(a) Failure to file annual returns

[14.003] The most common ground on which companies are struck off the register of companies is for failure to file an annual return.[2] As the CRO reports, 'From September 1998, the Office began a vigorous campaign of company strike-offs to address the non-filing of returns. From September 1998 to end-January 2003, 67,000 companies were struck off.'[3] Since the beginning of 2003, a further sizable number of companies have been struck off the register of companies by the CRO, with 14,836 companies struck off in 2003; 1,401 in 2004; 9,514 in 2005; and 5,255 in 2006.[4] While figures are not furnished by the CRO or the ODCE as to the precise proportion of these proceedings which relate to failures to file annual returns, as opposed to other grounds on which the

---

[1] Note that the provisions regarding striking companies' names off the register, and restoring such names to the register, are substantially reproduced in the General Scheme of the Draft Companies Consolidation and Reform Bill 2007, Pt A12. See www.clrg.org.

[2] See further Ch **2** regarding to the obligation to file an annual return.

[3] CRO, *Notice on Involuntary Strike Off*. www.cro.ie.

[4] ODCE, *Annual Report 2006*, p 26. Available at www.odce.ie.

CRO may strike companies off the register involuntarily, it appears likely that the vast majority of these companies were struck off for failing to file annual returns.[5]

[14.004] C(A)A 1982, s 12,[6] is the provision which governs the power of the CRO to strike companies' names off the register for failure to file annual returns. This provides:

> (1) Without prejudice to the generality of s 311 of the Principal Act,[7] where a company does not, for one or more years, make an annual return required by s 125 or 126[8] of the Principal Act, the registrar of companies may send to the company by post a registered letter stating that, unless all annual returns which are outstanding are delivered to him within one month of the date of the letter, a notice will be published in the Companies Registration Office Gazette with a view to striking the name of the company off the register.

> (2) If the registrar of companies either receives an answer to the effect that the company is not carrying on business, or does not within one month after sending the letter receive all annual returns which are outstanding, he may publish in the Companies Registration Office Gazette a notice stating that, at the expiration of one month from the date of that notice, the name of the company mentioned therein will, unless all outstanding returns are delivered to the registrar, be struck off the register, and the company will be dissolved.

> (3) Subject to sub-s (1) and (2) of s 12B of this Act,[9] at the expiration of the time mentioned in the notice, the registrar of companies may, unless cause to the contrary is previously shown by the company, strike its name off the register, and shall publish notice thereof in the Companies Registration Office Gazette and on the publication in the Companies Registration Office Gazette of this notice, the company shall be dissolved.

---

[5]   Note that the CRO in its *Report 2005*, states that of the companies that were struck off in 2005, 9,514 were struck off for failure to file annual returns (the same figure employed in the *ODCE Annual Report 2006* to describe the total number of companies struck off involuntarily by the CRO); 3,316 were struck off voluntarily; and 794 were struck off at the request of the Revenue Commissioners. While the CRO does have the power to strike companies off the register on other grounds (as will be addressed below), no such strike offs appear to be reflected in the statistics published by the CRO and the ODCE. Most, if not all, companies which are cited as being struck off involuntarily by the CRO, other than at the request of the Revenue Commissioners, therefore appear to have been struck off for failure to file annual returns.

[6]   C(A)A 1982, s 12, as substituted by C(A)(No 2)A 1999, s 46, as amended by IFCMPA 2005, s 72.

[7]   CA 1963, s 311 concerns the striking off the register of companies which have ceased to carry on business. See further para **[14.013]**.

[8]   See further: Ch **2** regarding the obligation to file annual returns.

[9]   C(A)A 1982, s 12B(1) and (2), as inserted by C(A)(No 2)A 1999, s 46, concern the continuing liability of the company's directors, officers and members, and the power of the court to wind up the company, the dissolution notwithstanding. See further paras **[14.028]** to **[14.029]**.

This provision envisages a five-step procedure for striking the name of a company which has failed to file its annual return off the register of companies:

1. The company must fail to file an annual return for one or more years;

2. The Registrar of Companies must send a registered letter to the company stating that, unless all outstanding annual returns are delivered within one month, a notice will be published in the *CRO Gazette*;

3. If the Registrar does not receive the outstanding annual returns within one month, or receives a response that the company is no longer carrying on business, a notice may be published in the *CRO Gazette* stating that the company will be struck off within one month of that date and dissolved, unless all outstanding returns are delivered ('the first *CRO Gazette* notice');

4. After one month expires, the Registrar may strike the company's name off the register, unless cause has been shown to the contrary; and

5. The Registrar must publish a notice in the *CRO Gazette* of the company's name being struck off; and

6. Upon publication of that notice, the company is dissolved.

[14.005] A company therefore has a number of opportunities to prevent its name being struck off the register. It has one month from receipt of the letter from the Registrar, to deliver the outstanding annual returns. It may then deliver the annual returns during the one month period following publication of the first *CRO Gazette* notice. This is apparent from the language of s 12(2) that requires such a notice to state that, 'at the expiration of 1 month from the date of that notice, the name of the company mentioned therein will, *unless all outstanding returns are delivered to the registrar*, be struck off the register ...' (emphasis added).[10]

Furthermore, it appears from the wording of s 12(3) that a company is entitled to make representations seeking to prevent its name being struck off the register, after the publication of the first *CRO Gazette* notice. Section 12(3) provides that the Registrar may strike the company's name off the register one month after publication of the first *CRO Gazette* notice, 'unless cause to the contrary is previously shown by the company.'[11] There are three points to note about this provision. First, it envisages representations by the company, other than the delivery of its annual returns. If the annual returns are delivered within the one month period specified in the notice, this comes within the scope of s 12(2). Second, it appears from the words 'previously shown' that such representations must be made within the one month period following the publication of the first *CRO Gazette* notice. Thereafter, the Registrar is entitled, in the exercise of his discretion, to strike the company's name off the register. Third, it is only the company that may show 'cause' as to why it should not be struck off the register. A

---

[10] C(A)A 1982, s 12(2), as substituted by C(A)(No 2)A 1999, s 46, as amended by IFCMPA 2005, s 72.

[11] C(A)A 1982, s 12(3), as substituted by C(A)(No 2)A 1999, s 46, as amended by IFCMPA 2005, s 72.

creditor, member or potential litigant who wishes to prevent the company being struck off the register for failing to file its annual returns, has no status to make representations to the Registrar in this regard.

[14.006] Section 12 confers on the Registrar a wide margin of discretion in a number of respects. The Registrar 'may' send a notice to a company which is in default in filing its annual returns for one or more years, under s 12(1). This letter must state that, unless the outstanding annual returns are delivered within one month, a notice 'will' be published in the *CRO Gazette*.[12] However, if the outstanding returns are not delivered, the Registrar 'may' publish a notice in the *CRO Gazette*. This notice must state that, unless the outstanding annual returns are delivered within one month, the company 'will' be struck off the register and dissolved.[13] At the expiration of that month, the Registrar 'may' strike the company off the register and in such circumstances 'shall' publish a further notice in the *CRO Gazette*.[14] Therefore, while it must be represented to the company that, once the Registrar sends a letter under s 12(1), this will lead to a notice in the *CRO Gazette* and to the company being struck off, unless the outstanding returns are delivered within the specified deadlines, the Registrar in fact has a discretion whether to pursue either of those steps. The Registrar may, therefore, issue a letter under s 12(1), but never publish a notice under s 12(2), or publish a notice under s 12(2), but never exercise its discretion to strike a company's name off the register under s 12(3). It could also be problematic that the Registrar is not bound to act promptly or within any stipulated timeframe, after the expiry of the one month deadlines specified in ss 12(1) and 12(2). The Registrar could, as the provision is formulated, wait considerable periods of time before publishing a notice under s 12(2) or striking a company off under s 12(3). This could prejudice a company which proceeded to carry on its business on the assumption that no further action was being taken, as well as those dealing with the company in the intervening periods.

[14.007] In addition, the stipulation that companies must deliver all outstanding annual returns within one month of either receipt of the s 12(1) letter, or publication of the s 12(2) notice, could be interpreted as precluding later delivery of those returns. So, for example, a company which received a letter from the Registrar under s 12(1), and failed to deliver its returns within one month, but, the Registrar having taken no further action, delivered the outstanding returns at a later stage, could nonetheless be the subject of a subsequent notice under s 12(2). While such an exercise of the Registrar's discretion must be highly unlikely, a company has little protection and would have little recourse under s 12 for any prejudice caused by such a sequence of events. A further issue that

---

[12] C(A)A 1982, s 12(1), as substituted by C(A)(No 2)A 1999, s 46, as amended by IFCMPA 2005, s 72.

[13] C(A)A 1982, s 12(2), as substituted by C(A)(No 2)A 1999, s 46, as amended by IFCMPA 2005, s 72.

[14] C(A)A 1982, s 12(3), as substituted by C(A)(No 2)A 1999, s 46, as amended by IFCMPA 2005, s 72.

arises from the stipulation that outstanding annual returns must be delivered within one month of a letter under s 12(1) or a notice under s 12(2), is that this could be interpreted as precluding a company from delivering its outstanding annual returns outside of those deadlines, whether or not the Registrar has taken action in the intervening period.

[14.008] The CRO refers to 'initial warning periods' in respect of striking companies' names off the register and states that, in 2005, they reduced 'the initial warning period we allow to such companies from 16 to eight weeks'.[15] It is not clear whether the CRO is referring to the letter which may be sent under s 12(1). However, it appears that this 'initial warning period' must refer to a warning which the CRO furnishes to companies before sending a letter under s 12(1), as, while the Registrar has discretion as to whether to send a letter, publish a notice, or strike a company's name off the register, s 12 does not formulate the one month deadlines stipulated in s 12(1) and (2) in similarly permissive language. If a letter is sent under s 12(1), it must refer to a deadline of one month from the date of such letter for the delivery of outstanding annual returns.

[14.009] If a company has not filed an annual return for more than 20 years and the Registrar has not been notified of its registered office, the Registrar will clearly find it difficult to deliver the letters to the company that are required for the company's name to be struck off the register under C(A)A 1982, s 12. In those circumstances, instead of sending the letter required by s 12(1), the Registrar may:

> publish a notice in the Companies Registration Office Gazette stating that he proposes to take that course of action in relation to the company, and where the registrar publishes such a notice the reference in sub-s (2) of s 12 of this Act to the sending of a letter of the foregoing kind shall be construed as a reference to the publishing of that notice.[16]

(b) Failure to deliver statement to Revenue Commissioners

[14.010] The second ground on which a company's name may be struck off the register of companies is that it failed to deliver to the Revenue Commissioners the statement which it is required to deliver pursuant to the Taxes Consolidation Act 1997 ('TCA 1997'), s 882.[17] Section 882(2) sets out the scope and content of the obligation to deliver this statement. The obligation essentially applies to every company which is incorporated in the State and every company which commences a trade, profession or business in the State. The deadline for delivery of the statement is 30 days from either the date on which the company commences to carry on the trade, profession, or business; the date of a material change in information previously delivered under s 882;

---

15 CRO *Report 2005* at p 3. Available at www.cro.ie.

16 C(A)A 1982, s 12B(8A), as inserted by IFCMPA 2005, s 65.

17 Taxes Consolidation Act 1997, s 882, as substituted by Finance Act ('FA') 1999, s 83, as amended FA 2000, s 78.

or the date of the giving of notice by an inspector requiring delivery of such a statement.[18]

The information that must be contained in the statement varies depending on whether the company is incorporated in the State or not. Certain information must be provided by all companies, whether resident or incorporated in the State or not. This includes the company's name; registered office; address of principal place of business; secretary's name and address; date of commencement, and nature of trade, profession or business; the date to which the accounts will be made up; and such other information as the Revenue Commissioners consider necessary under the Tax Acts.[19]

If the company is incorporated, but not resident in the State, the statement must specify where the company is resident for tax purposes.[20] If the company is incorporated in Ireland, but is regarded as not being resident in Ireland as it is a 'relevant company'[21] and either carries on a trade in the State, or is related[22] to a company which carries on a trade in the State, the name and address of the latter company must also be included in the statement.[23]

If a company which is incorporated in Ireland is treated as non-resident, as it is regarded for the purposes of any arrangements as resident in a territory other than the State and not resident in the State,[24] one of two matters must be included in the statement.[25] First, if the company is controlled by another company whose principal shares are traded on a recognised stock exchange in a relevant territory,[26] the name of this company and its

---

[18]   TCA 1997, s 882(2), as substituted by FA 1999, s 83.

[19]   TCA 1997, s 882(2)(i), as substituted by FA 1999, s 83.

[20]   TCA 1997, s 882(2)(ii), as substituted by FA 1999, s 83.

[21]   A 'relevant company' is defined in TCA 1997, s 23A(1)(a), as inserted by FA 1999, s 82, as 'a company—(i) which is under the control, whether directly or indirectly, of a person or persons who is or are—(I) by virtue of the law of any relevant territory, resident for the purposes of tax in a relevant territory or relevant territories, and (II) not under the control, whether directly or indirectly, of a person who is, or persons who are, not so resident, or (ii) which is, or is related to, a company the principal class of the shares of which is substantially and regularly traded on one or more than one recognised stock exchange in a relevant territory or territories.' 'Relevant territories' are described in TCA 1997, s 23A(1)(a), as inserted by FA 1999, s 82, as '(i) a Member State of the European Communities, or (ii) not being such a Member State, a territory with the government of which arrangements have been made.'

[22]   A company is 'related' for the purposes of this provision if, 'one company is a 50 per cent subsidiary of the other company or both companies are 50 per cent subsidiaries of a third company'. TCA 1997, s 23A(1)(b), as inserted by FA 1999, s 82.

[23]   TCA 1997, s 882(2)(ii), as substituted by FA 1999, s 83.

[24]   See TCA 1997, s 882(2)(ii), as substituted by FA 1999, s 83, referring to TCA 1997, s 23A(4), as inserted by FA 1999, s 82.

[25]   TCA 1997, s 882(2)(ii), as substituted by FA 1999, s 83.

[26]   'Relevant territories' are described in TCA 1997, s 23A(1)(a), as inserted by FA 1999, s 82, as '(i) a Member State of the European Communities, or (ii) not being such a Member State, a territory with the government of which arrangements have been made.'

registered office must be included in the statement.[27] In any other case, the names and addresses of the individuals who are the ultimate beneficial owners[28] of the shares of the company must be included in the statement.[29]

If a company is neither incorporated nor resident in the State, but carries on a trade, profession or business in the State, the statement must contain the address of the company's principal place of business in the State; the name and address of the company's agent, manager, or other representative; and the date on which the company commenced its trade, profession or business in the State.[30]

[14.011] If a company fails to deliver a statement required by TCA 1997, S 882, then the Revenue Commissioners or such officer of the Revenue Commissioners as is nominated by the Commissioners for the purpose of s 882, may give a notice of this fact to the Registrar of Companies.[31] This notice may be in writing, or in such other form as the Revenue Commissioners may decide. The Commissioners, or the nominated officer, have the power of give such a notice, any obligations as to secrecy or 'other restriction upon disclosure of information imposed by or under any statute or otherwise' notwithstanding.[32] The notice should state that the company in question has failed to deliver the statement required by s 882.[33]

[14.012] Upon receipt of a notice from the Revenue Commissioners under s 882, the Registrar may send a letter to the company named in the notice by registered post, stating that, unless the statement is delivered within one month of the date of the letter, a notice will be published in the *CRO Gazette* with a view to striking the company's name off the register of companies.[34] The Registrar has a discretion whether to send such a letter and is not obliged to react to the notice from the Revenue Commissioners, or officer nominated by the Commissioners.

---

[27] TCA 1997, s 882(2)(ii), as substituted by FA 1999, s 83.

[28] According to TCA 1997, s 882(1)(a), as substituted by FA 1999, s 83, '"ultimate beneficial owners", in relation to a company, means- (i) the individual or individuals who have control of the company, or (ii) where a person, whether alone or together with other persons, who controls the company controls it in the capacity as the trustee of a settlement, any person who in relation to the settlement- (I) is a settlor, or (II) is, or can under any scheme or arrangement reasonably expect to become, a beneficiary under the settlement, or (III) where such settlor or beneficiary, as the case may be, is a company, the ultimate beneficial owners of that company.'

[29] TCA 1997, s 882(2)(ii), as substituted by FA 1999, s 83.

[30] TCA 1997, s 882(2)(iii), as substituted by FA 1999, s 83.

[31] TCA 1997, s 882(3), as substituted by FA 1999, s 83 and as further substituted by FA 2000, s 78.

[32] TCA 1997, s 882(3), as substituted by FA 1999, s 83 and as further substituted by FA 2000, s 78.

[33] TCA 1997, s 882(3), as substituted by FA 1999, s 83 and as further substituted by FA 2000, s 78.

[34] C(A)A 1982, s 12A(1), as inserted by C(A)(No 2)A 1999, s 46, as amended by IFCMPA 2005, s 72.

Following this letter, the procedure is the same as that applicable in the case of companies which fail to deliver annual returns.[35] If the company does not deliver the s 882 statement within one month, the Registrar may publish a notice in the *CRO Gazette* stating that the name of the company will be struck off and the company dissolved, unless the statement is delivered to the Revenue Commissioners within one month from the date of the notice.[36]

At the expiry of this one month period, the Registrar may 'unless cause to the contrary is previously shown by the company' strike the company's name off the register and publish a notice in the *CRO Gazette*, upon which publication the company will be dissolved.[37]

(c) Ceasing to carry on business

[14.013] If the Registrar has 'reasonable cause' to believe that a company which is registered is not carrying on business, the Registrar can take steps with a view to ascertaining whether the company is carrying on business and, if not, to strike its name off the register.

If it has come to the attention of the CRO that there are no persons recorded as directors of the company, due to the notification of the resignation of all registered directors, this constitutes good grounds for the Registrar to believe that the company is not carrying on business and will justify the exercise of the Registrar's powers under s 311.[38]

CA 1963, s 311, provides that, if the Registrar has reasonable cause to believe a company is not carrying on business, the Registrar can send a letter by registered post to the company[39] enquiring whether the company is carrying on business and specifying that, if no response is received within one month from the date of that letter, the Registrar will publish a notice in the *CRO Gazette*.[40]

If, within one month of the letter, the Registrar receives a response to the effect that the company is not carrying on business, or receives no response, he may publish a notice in the *CRO Gazette* to the effect that the name of the company would be struck off the register and dissolved within one month of that notice, unless cause be shown to the

---

35   See paras **[14.003]** to **[14.009]**.

36   C(A)A 1982, s 12A(2), as inserted by C(A)(No 2)A 1999, s 46, as amended by IFCMPA 2005, s 72.

37   C(A)A 1982, s 12A(3), as inserted by C(A)(No 2)A 1999, s 46, as amended by IFCMPA 2005, s 72.

38   C(A)(No 2)A 1999, s 48.

39   Note that, pursuant to CA 1963, s 311(9), '… a letter or notice to be sent under this section to a company may be addressed to the company at its registered office, or, if no office has been registered, to the care of some officer of the company, or, if there is no officer of the company whose name and address are known to the registrar of companies, may be sent to each of the persons who subscribed the memorandum, addressed to him at the address mentioned in the memorandum.'

40   CA 1963, s 311(1), as substituted by C(A)A 1982, s 11, and as amended by IFCMPA 2005, s 72.

contrary. It is a distinctive feature of this means of striking a company off the register, that, if the Registrar publishes such a notice in the *CRO Gazette*, he must also send such a notice to the company by registered post.[41]

At the expiration of that one month period, the Registrar may strike the company's name off the register, unless 'cause to the contrary is previously shown by the company.'[42] If the Registrar does strike the company's name off the register, he must publish a notice in the *CRO Gazette*, and upon that publication, the company will be dissolved.

(d) Failure to have an Irish resident director

(i) Irish resident director

[14.014] There is a general requirement that every company must have at least one director who is resident in the State. C(A)(No 2)A 1999, s 43(1), provides that, 'one, at least, of the directors for the time being of a company...shall, on and from the commencement of this section, be a person who is resident in the State.'

A person is 'resident' in the State at a particular time, if he is present in the State during the preceding 12 months, for an aggregate period of at least 183 days; or if he is present during the preceding 24 months, for an aggregate period of at least 280 days, so long as he was present for at least 30 of those days during the preceding 12 months; or if he has made an election to be treated as resident in respect of that year of assessment within the meaning of the TCA 1997, s 819(3).[43]

(ii) Exceptions

[14.015] There are two circumstances in which the Irish-resident director requirement does not apply to a company. First, if the company holds a bond, in the prescribed form, in the value of €25,394.74.[44] The form to use for this purpose is set out in the C(A)(No 2)A 1999 Bonding Order 2000. This bond must provide that monies become payable under the bond in any of the following four circumstances:

1. if the company fails to pay the whole or part of a fine imposed on the company as a result of an offence committed by the company under the Companies Acts, being an offence prosecutable by the Registrar;[45]

---

[41] CA 1963, s 311(2), as substituted by C(A)A 1982, s 11, and as amended by IFCMPA 2005, s 72.

[42] CA 1963, s 311(5), as amended by IFCMPA 2005, s 72.

[43] C(A)(No 2)A 1999, s 44(8)(a). Note that, pursuant to C(A)(No 2)A 1999, s 44(10), '(a) references in this section to a person's being present in the State are references to the person's being personally present in the State, and (b) a person shall be deemed to be present in the State for a day if the person is present in the State at the end of the day.'

[44] C(A)(No 2)A 1999, s 43(3).

[45] C(A)(No 2)A 1999, s 43(3)(a).

2.   if the company fails to pay the whole or part of a fine under of the TCA 1997, s 1078 in respect of an offence by the company, in failing to deliver a statement required under of the TCA 1997, s 882; [46]

3.   if the company fails to pay the whole or part of a fine under of the TCA 1997, s 1078, in respect of an offence by the company, in failing to comply with a notice served under s 884 of that Act; [47] or

4.   if the company fails to pay the whole or part of a penalty imposed under of the TCA 1997, ss 1071 or 1073.[48]

In such circumstances, a sum of money shall be payable under the bond, to be applied in discharging, in whole or in part, the company's liability in respect of that fine or penalty.[49] The monies must be paid to a person nominated for the purpose, by the Registrar or the Revenue Commissioners, or both jointly, as appropriate, and the nominated person must apply the monies received under the bond towards that end.[50]

[14.016] The bond must also provide that, in addition to the monies payable towards the fine or penalty, a sum of money shall be payable in respect of the expenses reasonably incurred by the person nominated to receive the monies.[51] This sum becomes payable to that person, when he makes a demand for such payment, with the consent of the Revenue Commissioners.[52] This sum must not exceed the amount sanctioned by the Revenue Commissioners and the Minister.[53]

[14.017] The bond required under C(A)(No 2)A 1999, s 43, must be attached to the following:

–   the statement required under of C(A)A 1982, s 3, if there is no Irish resident director at the date of the incorporation of the company;

–   the notification which a director who resigns, being, to his knowledge, the last resident director, must send to the Registrar under s 43(9); or

---

[46]   See further paras **[14.010]** to **[14.012]**.

[47]   C(A)(No 2)A 1999, s 43(3)(b)(i).

[48]   C(A)(No 2)A 1999, s 43(3)(b)(ii).

[49]   C(A)(No 2)A 1999, s 43(3). Note that, pursuant to s 43(4), 'The bond referred to in sub-s (3) may be entered into and shall have effect according to its terms notwithstanding any rule of law whereby any agreement to insure or indemnify a person in respect of any punishment or liability imposed on him or her in relation to any offence or unlawful act committed by him or her is void or unenforceable.'

[50]   C(A)(No 2)A 1999, s 43(3).

[51]   Note that, pursuant to C(A)(No 2)A 1999, s 43(6), 'The nominated person shall keep all proper and usual accounts, including an income and expenditure account and a balance sheet, of all moneys received by him or her on foot of the bond referred to in sub-s (3) and of all disbursements made by him or her from any such moneys.'

[52]   C(A)(No 2)A 1999, s 43(5). Strangely, there is no reference to the consent of the Registrar in respect of payment of monies to persons nominated by him under s 43(3).

[53]   C(A)(No 2)A 1999, s 43(5).

– if there are no Irish resident directors during the period to which an annual return relates, to that annual return.[54]

Section 43(9) requires that when a company's only Irish resident director ceases to so act, knowing that there is no other Irish resident director, he must notify the Registrar in writing of this fact within 14 days.[55] If he fails to deliver such a notification, he will be jointly and severally liable with the company of which he has ceased to act, for any fine or penalty imposed on the company after that cessation, which should be covered by a bond provided for that purpose.[56] Any such fine or penalty may be recovered by the Registrar or the Revenue Commissioners, as appropriate, from that former director as a simple contract debt.[57]

[14.018] The second means by which a company can overcome the requirement to have an Irish resident director is by obtaining a certificate from the Registrar of Companies to the effect that it has a real and continuous link with one or more economic activities being carried on in the State.[58] A company can obtain this certificate by presenting proof of such a link, the application to be used for this purpose being CRO Form B67.[59] A written statement from the Revenue Commissioners is deemed to be proof for this purpose.[60] This written statement must be given to the company by the Revenue within two months before the company makes an application to the Registrar for a certificate and it must state that the Revenue Commissioners have reasonable grounds for believing that the company has a real and continuous link with one or more economic activities being carried on in the State.[61] The Registrar may revoke a certificate if he comes into possession of information which leads him to form the opinion that the company in question has ceased to have a real and continuous link with an economic activity being carried on in the State.[62] If the Revenue Commissioners come into possession of such information, they may give the Registrar a notice in writing stating their opinion that the company has ceased to have a real and continuous link with an economic activity being carried on in the State, any obligations of secrecy or restrictions on disclosure imposed by statute or otherwise notwithstanding.[63]

(iii) Consequences

[14.019] If a company does not have an Irish resident director, and neither has a bond nor certificate disapplying this requirement, the company and every officer of the

---

[54] C(A)(No 2)A 1999, s 43(8). See Ch **2**.

[55] C(A)(No 2)A 1999, s 43(9).

[56] C(A)(No 2)A 1999, s 43(11).

[57] C(A)(No 2)A 1999, s 43(11).

[58] C(A)(No 2)A 1999, s 44(1) and (2).

[59] C(A)(No 2)A 1999, s 44(2) and (3). See also Companies (Forms) Order 2000. Form B67 is available at www.cro.ie.

[60] C(A)(No 2)A 1999, s 44(3) and (4).

[61] C(A)(No 2)A 1999, s 44(5).

[62] C(A)(No 2)A 1999, s 44(6).

[63] C(A)(No 2)A 1999, s 44(7).

company who is in default, is guilty of an offence.[64] The Registrar of Companies may bring and prosecute summary proceedings in relation to such an offence.[65]

If the Registrar has reasonable grounds for believing that a company does not have an Irish resident director, he may further initiate the procedure to strike the company's name off the register, by sending a letter by registered post requesting the company to furnish evidence of compliance with that requirement within one month, failing which the Registrar will publish a notice in the *CRO Gazette*.[66] At the expiry of that month, if the Registrar does not receive evidence of compliance with C(A)(No 2)A 1999, s 43, he may publish a notice in the *CRO Gazette* and send a notice to the company that, after a month, the name of the company will be struck off the register, and the company dissolved, unless cause is shown to the contrary.[67] At the expiry of that further month, the Registrar may 'unless cause is previously shown', strike the company's name off the register and publish a notice in the *CRO Gazette*, causing the company to be dissolved.[68]

[14.020] The propriety of this regime, particularly from the perspective of European Union law, has been queried. It has been noted that: 'The regime sets hurdles, if not impediments, before EU entrepreneurs who might wish to exercise a right of secondary establishment in Ireland' and that:

> 'non-Irish-resident EU nationals are clearly put at a disadvantage *vis-à-vis* their Irish counterparts, and, to that extent, it might be argued that the regime in ss 43 and 44 constitute a discriminatory measure in respect of the right of establishment which is not justified by as a proportionate response to pressing reasons of public policy.'[69]

The rationale for requiring a bond in respect of the payment of fines and penalties, or certificates of links with Ireland, only in respect of companies without Irish resident directors, has also been questioned:

> 'If there were an overriding objective of public policy that Irish companies be in a financial position to pay the fines mentioned in s 43(3)(a) and (b) and the costs referred to in s 43(5), then one would think that such a requirement should be imposed on *all* Irish companies (whether such companies have Irish resident directors or not). Similarly, if it were an overriding objective of public policy that companies satisfy the registrar on an ongoing basis (and not merely at incorporation) that they have a continuous link with Ireland such a requirement should be placed on *all* Irish companies (whether such companies have Irish

---

[64]   C(A)(No 2)A 1999, s 43(13).

[65]   C(A)(No 2)A 1999, s 43(14).

[66]   C(A)(No 2)A 1999, s 43(15) contains the curious provision that, 'The provisions of s 311 of the Principal Act shall apply for the purposes of this section as they apply for the purposes of that s 311, subject to the following modifications ...' and then sets out alternative formulations of CA 1963, s 311(1), (2) and (8). As this provision does not purport to amend s 311 for all purposes, it essentially requires two versions of s 311 to co-exist.

[67]   CA 1963, s 311(2), as adapted for the purposes of C(A)(No 2)A 1999, s 43, as amended by IFCMPA 2005, s 72.

[68]   CA 1963, 311(5), as amended by IFCMPA 2005, s 72.

[69]   Murphy, Companies (Amendment) (No 2) Act 1999, ICLSA.

resident directors or not). The fact of the Irish residency of a director hardly demonstrates the ability of a company to pay £20,000 in fines or penalties. It does not necessarily prove a greater willingness to comply with relevant law, nor does it prove the real and continuous link with the jurisdiction.[70]

(e) Failure of public limited company to have certificate

[14.021] A company which is registered as a public limited company on its original incorporation must not do business or exercise any borrowing powers without first obtaining a certificate from the Registrar for that purpose, unless it re-registers as a different form of company.[71] The company must make an application to the Registrar on Form 70, which is entitled 'application by a public limited company to commence business and declaration of particulars'.[72] The 'particulars' that must be declared are those required by s 6(3), which states:

> The statutory declaration shall be in the prescribed form and signed by a director or secretary of the company and shall state—
>
> (a) that the nominal value of the company's allotted share capital is not less than the authorised minimum;
>
> (b) the amount paid up, at the time of the application, on the allotted share capital of the company;
>
> (c) the amount, or estimated amount, of the preliminary expenses of the company and the persons by whom any of those expenses have been paid or are payable; and
>
> (d) any amount or benefit paid or given or intended to be paid or given to any promoter of the company, and the consideration for the payment or benefit.[73]

[14.022] If the Registrar is satisfied that the nominal value of the company's allotted share capital[74] is not less than the authorised minimum and that the duly completed Form 70 complies with all of the requirements of section 6(3), the Registrar shall issue a section 6 certificate to the company.[75] The issuing of such a certificate is not a matter within the discretion of the Registrar. If the statutory declaration is in order and he is satisfied regarding the nominal value of the company's allotted share capital, s 6(2) requires that the Registrar 'shall' issue the certificate. It is noteworthy that the Registrar is entitled to accept such a statutory declaration as 'sufficient evidence of the matters stated therein'.[76] The only matter on which the Registrar is obliged to make an enquiry is

---

[70] Murphy, Companies (Amendment) (No 2) Act 1999, ICLSA.

[71] C(A)A 1983, s 6(1).

[72] Form 70 available at www.cro.ie.

[73] C(A)A 1983, s 6(3). Note that notice of delivery of a statutory declaration under s 6 must be published in the *CRO Gazette*. C(A)A 1983, s 55(1)(a), as amended by IFCMA 2005, s 72.

[74] Note that, pursuant to C(A)A 1983, s 6(4), '... a share allotted in pursuance of an employees' share scheme may not be taken into account in determining the nominal value of the company's allotted share capital unless it is paid up at least as to one-quarter of the nominal value of the share and the whole of any premium on the share.'

[75] C(A)A 1983, s 6(2).

[76] C(A)A 1983, s 6(5).

whether the nominal value of the company's allotted share capital is not less than the authorised minimum.

[14.023] The effect of a certificate under s 6 is that it is 'conclusive evidence' that the company is entitled to do business and exercise borrowing powers.[77] However, if a company contravenes s 6 and does business or exercises borrowing powers without a certificate, the company and any officer of the company who is in default shall be guilty of an offence and shall be liable on summary conviction to a maximum fine of €1,904.61.[78] Furthermore, if a public limited company enters into a transaction without a certificate and fails to comply with this requirement within 21 days of being called upon to do so, the directors will be jointly and severally liable to indemnify the other party to the contract against any loss or damage suffered due to the company's failure to obtain a section 6 certificate. The general rule is that the requirements of s 6 are without prejudice to the validity of transactions entered into by the company, and a transaction will not therefore be invalidated solely on the ground that the company did have obtain a section 6 certificate.[79]

[14.024] A further consequence of failing to obtain a section 6 certificate, is that the Registrar may initiate procedures to strike the company's name off the register of companies. C(A)A 1983, s 8, provides that, if a company registered on its original incorporation as a public limited company has not been issued with a section 6 certificate within one year from the date of its registration, the Registrar may send a letter to the company by registered post notifying it that, unless a certificate is issued to the company within one month of the date of the letter, a notice will be published in the *CRO Gazette* with a view to striking the company's name off the register.[80] It may be noted that this time limit could operate oppressively, as the issue of the certificate is not within the control of the company, being a document which only the Registrar can issue. Even if the company files a duly completed Form 70, it would be difficult for the company to ensure that the certificate is issued within one month. This concern notwithstanding, if the certificate is not issued within one month, the Registrar may publish a notice in the *CRO Gazette* and 'proceed to strike the name of the public limited company off the register in accordance with s 311(5) of the Principal Act.'[81]

The procedure for striking the name of a company off the register for failing to obtain a section 6 certificate, differs in a material respect from the other grounds on which companies' names may be struck off the register. The usual procedure is that the Registrar sends a letter notifying the company of its intention, if there is not compliance

---

[77] C(A)A 1983, s 6(6).

[78] CA)A 1983, s 6(7), as amended by CA 1990, s 240(7), as inserted by CLEA 2001, s 104(c).

[79] C(A)A 1983, s 6(8) ('The provisions of this section are without prejudice to the validity of any transaction entered into by a public limited company').

[80] C(A)A 1983, s 8(1), as amended by IFCMPA 2005, s 72.

[81] C(A)A 1983, s 8(2). Note that CA 1963, s 311(5), as amended by IFCMPA 2005, s 72, addresses the final step in the striking-off procedure and provides, '… at the expiration of the time mentioned in the notice [in the *CRO Gazette*], the registrar may, unless cause to the contrary is previously shown by the company, strike its name off the register, and shall publish notice thereof in the *CRO Gazette* and on the publication in the *CRO Gazette* of this notice, the company shall be dissolved.'

within one month, to publish a notice in the *CRO Gazette*; one month later, the Registrar may publish such a notice in the *CRO Gazette* of its intention to strike the company's name off the register, if the relevant requirement is not complied with within a month; at the expiry of that further month, the Registrar may, unless cause is shown to the contrary, strike the company's name off the register and publish a final notice in the *CRO Gazette*, with the effect of dissolving the company.[82] There are therefore three steps and two separate month-long periods within which the company may essentially rectify its non-compliance with the relevant requirement or make representations as to why the company's name should not be struck off the register.

However, if the company's default relates to a certificate under C(A)A 1983, s 6, the Registrar may send the first letter notifying the company of its intention to publish a notice in the *CRO Gazette* and, at the expiry of that one month period, immediately proceed to strike the company's name off the register and publish a notice in the *CRO Gazette* dissolving the company. The first public notification of this procedure would therefore be the notice in the *CRO Gazette* that the company's name has been struck off the register and the company dissolved. The rationale for introducing a more severe procedure for dealing with a public limited company's failure to obtain a section 6 certificate is not apparent.

(f) Incomplete winding up

[14.025] If a company is being wound up and the Registrar has reasonable cause to believe that no liquidator is acting, or that the company is fully wound up, but the liquidator has not made the necessary returns for six consecutive months, the Registrar shall initiate proceedings to strike the company's name off the register.[83] It should be noted that the Registrar does not have discretion whether to act, but 'shall' begin the proceedings, if he has reasonable cause to believe the existence of these matters.

The procedure applicable to striking a company's name off the register in the context of an incomplete winding up differs from the procedures applicable to striking company's name off the register on other grounds.[84] The first step the Registrar must take is to publish in the *CRO Gazette* and send to the company[85] or the liquidator,[86] a notice that, at the expiration of one month from the date of that notice, the name of the company will

---

[82] See, eg, C(A)A 1982, s 12, as inserted by C(A)(No2)A 1999, s 46, as amended by IFCMPA 2005, s 72. See paras **[14.003]** to **[14.009]**.

[83] CA 1963, s 311(3), as substituted by C(A)A 1982, s 11, and amended by IFCMPA 2005, s 72.

[84] See paras **[14.003]** to **[14.009]** regarding the procedure applicable under C(A)A 1982, s 12 as substituted by C(A)(No 2)A 1999, s 46, as amended by IFCMPA 2005, s 72.

[85] Note that, pursuant to CA 1963, s 311(9), '… a letter or notice to be sent under this section to a company may be addressed to the company at its registered office, or, if no office has been registered, to the care of some officer of the company, or, if there is no officer of the company whose name and address are known to the registrar of companies, may be sent to each of the persons who subscribed the memorandum, addressed to him at the address mentioned in the memorandum.'

[86] Note that, pursuant to CA 1963, s 311(9), 'A notice to be sent under this section to a liquidator may be addressed to the liquidator at his last known place of business.'

be struck off the register, and the company dissolved, unless cause is shown to the contrary.[87] There is no requirement that the Registrar first send a letter to the company indicating its intention to publish a notice in the *CRO Gazette* one month thereafter, unless cause is shown to the contrary. The second and final step which the Registrar may take, is that, one month after the publication of the notice in the *CRO Gazette*, he may 'unless cause to the contrary is previously shown by the company' strike its name from the register of companies and publish a notice in the *CRO Gazette*, with the effect of dissolving the company.[88] The second step in this procedure, by contrast with the first, is framed in permissive language and, having published the first notice in the *CRO Gazette*, the Registrar 'may' strike the company off the register and publish a further notice to this effect in the *CRO Gazette*.

(g) Voluntary striking off

[14.026] A company can volunteer to have its name struck off the register. The procedure applicable is the same as that applicable to companies being struck off for ceasing to carry on business, as set out in CA 1963, s 311. The ODCE reports that, in 2002, 3,125 companies were struck off voluntarily, 5,483 in 2003; 3,595 in 2004; 3,316 in 2005; and 3,757 companies were struck off voluntarily in 2006.[89]

Section 311 is cited as the legal basis for the voluntary striking of companies' names off the register. That provision does not refer to companies' names being voluntarily struck off the register. However, the CRO has adopted the practice of allowing companies to make a request to the Registrar to have their names struck off the register. According to the CRO, the power of the Registrar under s 311 'is a discretionary power which he will use only if a director of a company makes a formal request to him to strike the name of his/her company off the register and such request is accompanied by the following steps.' The steps which the CRO requires to be followed are the following:

(1)   A director must issue a formal request containing the full company name and registration number, which states that the company has ceased trading or has never traded and will not commence or re-commence trading during the period before its name is struck off the register; that the company has no assets or outstanding liabilities; and requesting that the Registrar strike the company's name off the register under s 311.

(2)   The company must file all outstanding annual returns and pay all relevant fees and penalties.

(3)   The company must deliver a letter of 'no objection' from the Revenue Commissioners.

(4)   After the preceding two steps are completed, and within the four weeks before delivering to the CRO the application to be struck off the register, the company must publish an advertisement in one daily newspaper circulating in the

---

[87]   CA 1963, s 311(3), as substituted by C(A)A 1982, s 11, and amended by IFCMPA 2005, s 72.

[88]   CA 1963, s 311(5), and amended by IFCMPA 2005, s 72.

[89]   ODCE, *Annual Report 2006*, at p 26. Available at www.odce.ie.

Republic of Ireland, and must submit the full newspaper page on which the advertisement appears, to the CRO.[90]

When the CRO is satisfied that the appropriate steps have been completed, and the application duly submitted, the Registrar may then initiate the procedure to strike the company's name off the register. The Registrar will advertise the intention to strike the company's name off the register and, one month later, the company will be dissolved and its name struck off the register of companies. It is proposed to put modified rules applicable to striking companies' names off the register voluntarily on a statutory footing in the Draft Companies Consolidation and Reform Bill 2007.[91]

B. Effect of strike-off

(a) Dissolution

[14.027] When a company's name is struck off the register, a notice of this fact must be published in the *CRO Gazette* and, upon such publication, the company is dissolved. The fact that a company's name is struck off the register does not of itself have the effect of dissolving the company. It is the publication of the notice in the *CRO Gazette* that is synonymous with the dissolution of the company. This is apparent from the formulation of the relevant provisions of the CA 1963–2006. CA 1963, s 311(5) provides that:

> Subject to sub-ss (6) and (7), at the expiration of the time mentioned in the notice, the registrar may, unless cause to the contrary is previously shown by the company, strike its name off the register, and shall publish notice thereof in the Companies Registration Office Gazette *and on the publication in the Companies Registration Office Gazette of this notice*, the company shall be dissolved (emphasis added).[92]

C(A)A 1982, s 12(3), similarly provides:

> Subject to sub-ss (1) and (2) of s 12B of this Act,[93] at the expiration of the time mentioned in the notice, the registrar of companies may, unless cause to the contrary is previously shown by the company, strike its name off the register, and shall publish notice thereof in the Companies Registration Office Gazette and *on*

---

[90] See CRO, 'Voluntary Strike Off' at www.cro.ie, where the format of the appropriate advertisement is illustrated.

[91] See General Scheme of the Draft Companies Consolidation and Reform Bill, Pt A12, Head 7.

[92] CA 1963, s 311(5), as amended by IFCMPA 2005, s 72. This provision applies when a company's name is struck off the register for ceasing to carry on business (CA 1963, s 311); failing to obtain a certificate to carry on business in the case of public limited companies (C(A)A 1983, s 8); failing to have an Irish resident director (C(A)(No2)A 1999, s 43(15)); or when the company's name is struck off the register voluntarily (see www.cro.ie).

[93] C(A)A 1982, s 12B(1) and (2), as inserted by C(A)(No 2)A 1999, s 46, concern the continuing liability of the company's directors, officers and members, and the power of the court to wind up the company, the dissolution notwithstanding.

> *the publication in the Companies Registration Office Gazette of this notice*, the
> company shall be dissolved[94] (emphasis added).

The dissolution of a company therefore requires a distinct separate step, beyond the striking of the company's name off the register. The effect of dissolution is also a distinct one. Upon dissolution, the company loses its legal existence. By contrast, the striking of a company's name off the register will have certain consequences, but does not of itself annul the company's existence.

These distinctions notwithstanding, the relevant legislative provisions seem to refer to the two events interchangeably. It may be inferred that the CA 1963–2006 regard the dissolution of a company and the striking of its name off the register, as almost contemporaneous.

(b) Director and officer liability

[14.028]   The fact that a company's name has been struck off the register does not affect the liability of its directors, officers and members. C(A)A 1982, s 12B(1), provides that:

> The liability, if any, of every director, officer and member of a company the name
> of which has been struck off the register under s 12(3) [for failure to file annual
> returns] or 12A(3) [for failure to deliver the requisite statement to the Revenue
> Commissioners] of this Act shall continue and may be enforced as if the company
> had not been dissolved.[95]

In the case of companies whose names were struck off the register for ceasing to carry on business; failing to have an Irish resident director; failing to obtain a certificate for a public limited company to commence business; or companies whose names are voluntarily struck off the register, s 311(6) provides, 'The liability, if any, of every director, officer and member of the company shall continue and may be enforced as if the company had not been dissolved.'[96]

These provisions neither create an additional cause of action against directors, officers or members of companies which were dissolved, nor impose personal liability on such persons arising from that dissolution. However, if a director, officer or member would otherwise face liability for acts or omissions committed in the course of the discharge of their functions, the fact that a company's name was struck off the register will not prevent the imposition and enforcement of that liability.

---

[94]   C(A)A 1982, s 12(3), as substituted by C(A)(No2)A 1999, s 46, as amended by IFCMPA 2005, s 72. This provision applies to the striking off the register of the names of companies which fail to file annual returns. C(A)A 1982, s 12A(3), as substituted by C(A)(No2)A 1999, s 46, as amended by IFCMPA 2005, s 72, which concerns striking companies' names of the register for failing to deliver the requisite statement to the Revenue Commissioners, is in identical terms.

[95]   C(A)A 1983, s 12B(1), as inserted by C(A)(No2)A 1999, s 46.

[96]   CA 1963, s 311(6).

(c) Winding up

[14.029] While a company which has been dissolved has no legal existence, it can nonetheless be wound up by the court. C(A)A 1982, s 12B(2), provides that, 'Nothing in sub-s (1) of this section or s 12(3) or 12A(3) of this Act shall affect the power of the court to wind up a company the name of which has been struck off the register.'[97]

CA 1963, s 311(7), similarly provides, 'Nothing in sub-s (5) or (6) shall affect the power of the court to wind up a company the name of which has been struck off the register.'

There are some matters that may be noted about these provisions. First, they do not permit companies to be wound up voluntarily. Only compulsory liquidations may be commenced in respect of a company whose name has been struck off the register. Second, they do not require that the company's name be restored to the register before it may be wound up. Third, the provisions do not refer to companies which have been dissolved, but only to the name of the company being struck off the register of companies. It must be assumed that the power of the court to wind up companies the names of which have been struck off the register, extends to companies which have been dissolved.

(d) Company's property

[14.030] When a company is dissolved, its property vests in the State. The State Property Act 1954, s 28(2) provides:

> Where a body corporate is dissolved, ... the following provisions shall apply and have effect ... :—
>
> (a) all land which was vested in or held in trust for such body corporate immediately before its dissolution (other than land held by such body corporate upon trust for another person) shall, immediately upon such dissolution, become and be the property of the State, subject however to any incumbrances or charges affecting the land immediately before such dissolution,
>
> (b) all personal property (excluding chattels real but including choses-in-action) which is vested in or held in trust for such body corporate immediately before its dissolution (other than personal property held by such body corporate upon trust for another person) shall, immediately upon such dissolution become and be State property.

On the date on which the Registrar publishes a notice in the *CRO Gazette* that a company's name has been struck off the register of companies, the company is dissolved and all real and personal property which the company owns vests immediately in the Minister for Finance.[98] This does not apply to property which the company holds on

---

[97] C(A)A 1982, s 12B(2), as inserted by C(A)(No 2)A 1999, s 46.

[98] State Property Act 1954, s 29(3) provides in this regard, '(3) Where any personal property becomes on or after the operative date the property of the State as *bona vacantia* or by virtue of s 28, such personal property shall, upon so becoming the property of the State, vest in the Minister.' Section 27 provides more generally that, 'Every right and every prerogative which, by virtue of Art 49 of the Constitution, belong to the People and relate to any property (including choses-in-action) shall be exercised by the Government through and by the Minister.'

trust for other beneficiaries. While the company's land is held by the State subject to any charges or encumbrances which affect that land, there is no such saver in respect of charges over the company's personal property.

[14.031] The Minister for Finance may, if he thinks fit, apply to the High Court for a declaration that the property of a dissolved company has become the property of the State.[99] Such an application should be made *ex parte* initially, with the High Court then giving such directions as it thinks proper regarding service or publication of notice of the application. The High Court must not finally determine such an application unless all directions have been complied with, and such time as the Court considers reasonable has elapsed since such service or publication of notice of the application.[100]

An order of the High Court that a dissolved company's property has become the property of the State, is subject to appeal to the Supreme Court, but is otherwise conclusive evidence of that fact and shall be binding upon all persons, whether or not they had notice of the application.[101] Such an application or order is not necessary for the property of a dissolved company to vest in the Minister. However, if there is a likelihood of controversy in relation to the dissolved company's property or if there is a need to confirm the title to property (for example, if there is property which is derelict and in respect of which steps need to be taken to secure its condition), the Minister may consider it appropriate to obtain a court order confirming that the property is the property of the State.

[14.032] An alternative approach which may be taken by the Minister, is that he may waive the right of the State to the property of a dissolved company. The State Property Act 1954, s 31 provides:

> Whenever ... any property of whatsoever nature or kind ... becomes the property of the State ... by virtue of s 28, the Minister may, if he thinks proper so to do, waive, in whole or in part and in favour of such person and upon such terms (whether including or not including the payment of money) as he thinks proper having regard to all the circumstances of the case, the right of the State to such property.

When an application is made to restore a company's name to the register, that name having been struck off by the Registrar, this may be a situation in which the Minister would consider it appropriate to waive the State's claim to that company's property.[102]

It is worth noting that there is an unofficial mechanism whereby the Department of Finance is likely to become aware of the names of companies, which have substantial assets, being struck off the register of companies. The ODCE reports in this regard:

> 'Where companies are struck off the Companies Register, the assets of every company are vested in the Minister for Finance in accordance with the provisions of the State Property Acts. It is the policy of the Office to bring to the attention of

---

[99] State Property Act 1954, s 30(1).

[100] State Property Act 1954, s 30(2).

[101] State Property Act 1954, s 30(3).

[102] See further below paras **[14.040]** *et seq.*

the Department of Finance cases where a company held significant assets at the time of strike-off.'[103]

[14.033] The application of s 28 of the State Property Act 1954 can be seen in *Re Clarkes of Ranelagh Ltd.*[104] In respect of two separate liquidations, the liquidators envisaged that there were dividends payable to creditors. In each case, however, one of the creditors was a company which was formerly incorporated outside Ireland, and which was now dissolved. The primary issue was whether s 28 applied to the monies due to a foreign company, which was dissolved. Finlay Geoghegan J described the 'purpose and intent' of s 28 as follows: 'to provide for the vesting in the State of property which might otherwise be or become ownerless following the dissolution of a body corporate'.[105] While the Court expressly reserved its position in relation to the application of s 28 to property of Irish companies that is situated outside Ireland, the Court did conclude that:

> 'The ownership by a dissolved body corporate is the precondition to the application of s 28 of the [State Property Act 1954] to the relevant property. There is nothing in the Act which indicates that such body corporate must be one incorporated or formed in the State. It does not appear to me that in construing s 28 as applying, at minimum, to all property whether land or personal property of the type set out located in the State, the Act of 1954 is offending against the presumption of or rules in relation to territoriality in the application of statutes.'[106]

Section 28 of the State Property Act 1954 therefore applies to the property of all dissolved companies, wherever incorporated, that is located in Ireland. Any unfairness arising from the operation of this provision in this manner, may be mitigated by the exercise of the Minister's power of waiver under s 31. As Finlay Geoghegan J noted:

> 'it appears to me that the Oireachtas, in enacting s 31 of the State Property Act 1954 ... envisaged that there could be circumstances in which, notwithstanding his entitlement pursuant to the provisions of ss 28 and 29 of the Act of 1954, the Minister for Finance could form the view that there existed another person with a valid claim to the ownership of the property upon the dissolution of the body corporate and that it was proper having regard to the circumstances of the case to waive the right of the State to the property.'[107]

(e) Litigation

[14.034] When a company is dissolved, it has no legal status and cannot sue or be sued. If a third party wishes to pursue proceedings against a company the name of which was struck off the register, the third party must first take the appropriate steps to have the company's name restored to the register.[108] If proceedings are instituted by or against a company, and its name is subsequently struck off the register, the company will be

---

[103] ODCE, *Annual Report 2006* at p 33.

[104] *Re Clarkes of Ranelagh Ltd* [2004] IEHC 320, [2004] 3 IR 264.

[105] *Ibid* at para 7.

[106] *Ibid* at para 11.

[107] *Ibid* at para 16.

[108] See, eg, *Re New Ad Advertising Ltd* [2006] IEHC 19. See further paras **[14.064]** to **[14.068]**.

struck out as a party to those proceedings, unless its name is first restored to the register.[109]

If the company had accrued a cause of action (which is a chose in action) before its dissolution, this will have vested in the State, pursuant to the State Property Act 1954, s 28.[110] For this cause of action to be pursued on behalf of the company, the company's name must be restored to the register and the Minister must waive the right of the State to that *chose in action* under the State Property Act 1954, s 31.

(f) Disqualification of directors

[14.035] A final consequence of a company's name being struck off the register is that its directors may face disqualification proceedings. This only applies if the company's name is struck off on the ground that it failed to file its annual returns.[111] Section 160(2)(h) provides:

> Where the court is satisfied in any proceedings or as a result of an application under this section that ... a person was a director of a company at the time of the sending, after the commencement of s 42 of the Company Law Enforcement Act 2001, of a letter under sub-s (1) of s 12 of the Companies (Amendment) Act 1982, to the company and the name of which, following the taking of the other steps under that section consequent on the sending of that letter, was struck off the register under sub-s (3) of that section ... the court may, of its own motion, or as a result of the application, make a disqualification order against such a person for such period as it sees fit.[112]

This ground of disqualification must be read in light of s 160(3A)[113] which provides:

> The court shall not make a disqualification order under para (h) of sub-s (2) against a person who shows to the court that the company referred to in that paragraph had no liabilities (whether actual, contingent or prospective) at the time its name was struck off the register or that any such liabilities that existed at that time were discharged before the date of the making of the application for the disqualification order.[114]

---

[109] See, eg, *Re Amantiss Enterprises Ltd, Framus Ltd v CRH plc* [2000] 2 ILRM 177, where proceedings are commenced in the name of the company, after it had, unbeknownst to its directors, been struck off the register. See further paras **[14.099]–[14.101]**.

[110] State Property Act 1954, s 28(2)(b) provides, 'all personal property (excluding chattels real but *including choses-in-action*) which is vested in or held in trust for such body corporate immediately before its dissolution (other than personal property held by such body corporate upon trust for another person) shall, immediately upon such dissolution become and be State property' (emphasis added).

[111] Note, however, that a company being struck off the register on other grounds may provide evidence which would support an application to disqualify or restrict a director. See further Pt **E**, Disqualification Orders.

[112] CA 1990, s 160(2)(h), as inserted by CLEA 2001, s 42(b)(ii). See further Ch **22**.

[113] CA 1990, s 160(3A) as inserted by CLEA 2001, s 42(c).

[114] CA 1990, s 160(3A), as inserted by CLEA 2001, s 42(c).

[14.036] If the company which was struck off the register of companies did not, at the date of being struck off, or does not, at the date of the application for disqualification, have any outstanding liabilities, the court cannot make an order of disqualification under s 160(2)(h). In either of these circumstances, the court no longer has a discretion to make an order of disqualification.

[14.037] The deadline for discharging a dissolved company's liabilities is described in s 160(3A) as 'the date of the making of the application for the disqualification order,' which appears to refer to the actual date of the application to court for the order of disqualification, rather than the date on which the proceedings were issued. If this interpretation is correct, a person who faces disqualification proceedings under s 160(2)(h) has until the day of the hearing of the disqualification application to discharge the dissolved company's outstanding liabilities, thereby avoiding an order of disqualification.

In the decision of Finlay Geoghegan J in *Re Clawhammer Ltd*[115] it was established that the DCE does not have to demonstrate that a company has liabilities, but the onus lies on the respondent to demonstrate as a matter of probability the non-existence or discharge of, a company's liabilities.

[14.038] The ODCE reports that, in the context of applications for orders of disqualification under CA 1990, s 160(2)(h), 'In considering the penalty to be imposed, the Court may, as an alternative to disqualification, make a restriction declaration against the directors.' The ODCE further reports that nine directors of struck-off companies were disqualified for five years each during 2006, and two such directors were restricted for five years each. The ODCE further reports that eight further such cases were pending before the High Court at the end of 2006, including the first proceedings against directors of multiple struck-off companies, and that, 'many additional cases remain open at year-end, and it is anticipated that several more cases will be initiated before the Court in 2007.'[116] The risk of disqualification or restriction for directors of companies which are struck off the register is therefore a real one, and may be increasingly so.

In this regard, the ODCE specifically stated:

> 'In many cases, it was apparent that former directors used the involuntary strike-off process as a mechanism for terminating the corporate structure without recourse to other formal mechanisms of liquidation or voluntary strike off. In some of these cases, the former directors alleged that they did so on the basis of professional advice received. The Director wishes to point out clearly that involuntary strike off should not be seen as a replacement for more formal terminations of companies and that those resorting to such a route are now likely to be selected by the ODCE for disqualification proceedings and thus likely to incur disqualification or the expense of preparing accounts and declarations and defending their position before the High Court. Involuntary strike-off should not be seen as a mechanism for directors of insolvent companies to avoid the scrutiny

---

[115] *Re Clawhammer Ltd, Director of Corporate Enforcement v McDonnell* [2005] 1 IR 503. See further Ch **22**.

[116] ODCE, *Annual Report 2006* at pp 32–33. Available at www.odce.ie.

of their conduct that is applied to directors of insolvent companies in liquidation under the s 56 process described earlier.'[117]

[14.039] The determination of the ODCE to pursue directors who permit companies to be struck off involuntarily, leaving creditors with no recourse, was reiterated in a statement by the ODCE that, 'we are devoting a significant amount of resources to this area and it is one of our main priorities.'[118] Commenting on the pursuit of disqualification applications against directors of companies struck off in such circumstances, the ODCE warned, 'we anticipate that we will be making a number of similar applications in the near future.'[119] Any company directors who regard the company being struck off the register as a mechanism for terminating the company's business without discharging outstanding liabilities or incurring the cost of liquidation proceedings, would be well-advised to heed this warning. Persons who are directors of a number of companies which are struck off involuntarily leaving undischarged debts should expect to be subject to the ODCE's particular scrutiny.

C. Restoration by court

[14.040] There are three separate statutory provisions applicable to the restoration of companies' names to the register of companies by the courts, namely C(A)A 1982, s 12B(3);[120] C(A)A 1982, s 12B(7);[121] and CA 1963, s 311(8).[122] These will be considered in turn under the following headings:

    (i)   scope;

   (ii)   applicants;

  (iii)   requirements;

  (iv)   procedure;

   (v)   orders.

(a) Section 12B(3) of CA(A) 1982

[14.041] C(A)A 1982, s 12B(3), provides:

> If any member, officer or creditor of a company is aggrieved by the fact of the company's having been struck off the register under s 12(3) or 12A(3) of this Act, the court, on an application made (on notice to the registrar of companies, the Revenue Commissioners and the Minister for Finance) by the member, officer or

---

[117] ODCE, *Annual Report 2006* at p 33.

[118] See Sunday Business Post, 'ODCE Clamps down on Involuntary Closures' (5 August 2007), an article apparently triggered by orders of disqualification obtained against two directors of companies, the names of which were struck off the register in the preceding week.

[119] Sunday Business Post, 'ODCE Clamps down on Involuntary Closures' (5 August 2007).

[120] C(A)A 1982, s 12B(3), as inserted by C(A)(No2)A 1999, s 46, as amended by IFCMPA 2005, s 72.

[121] C(A)A 1982, s 12B(7), as inserted by C(A)(No2)A 1999, s 46, as amended by IFCMPA 2005, s 72.

[122] CA 1963, s 311(8), as amended by C(A)(No2)A 1999, s 49(a) and IFCMPA 2005, s 72.

creditor, before the expiration of 20 years from the publication in the Companies Registration Office Gazette of the notice referred to in s 12(3) or, as the case may be, 12A(3) of this Act, may, if satisfied that it is just that the company be restored to the register, order that the name of the company be restored to the register, and, subject to sub-s (4) of this section, upon an office copy of the order being delivered to the registrar for registration, the company shall be deemed to have continued in existence as if its name had not been struck off; and the court may by the order give such directions and make such provisions as seem just for placing the company and all other persons in the same position as nearly as may be as if the name of the company had not been struck off or make such other order as seems just (and such other order is referred to in sub-s (4) of this section as an 'alternative order').[123]

(i) Scope

[14.042] This provision applies when a company is struck off the register for failing to file its annual returns or for failing to deliver to the Revenue Commissioners a statement required by TCA 1997, S 882.[124]

(ii) Applicants

[14.043] The persons who may apply for the restoration of a company's name under s 12B(3) are a member, officer or creditor of the company who are 'aggrieved by the fact of the company's having been struck off the register'.[125] These persons must have that status as members, officers or creditors, at the date on which the company's name was struck off the register of companies.[126] The company itself cannot make an application under s 12B(3).

[14.044] The category of creditors who can bring an application to restore to the register the name of a company which was struck off under s 12 or s 12A, was considered in *Re Deauville Communications Worldwide Ltd.*[127] In that case, an application was made to the High Court for an order to restore the name of a dissolved company to the register by a company which had initiated proceedings against the dissolved company since the date on which its name was struck off. The applicant company also issued a motion seeking to fix the directors of the dissolved company with personal liability for the company's debts and directing that the directors deliver all outstanding annual returns to the Registrar. The application was resisted on behalf of the dissolved company on three grounds. First, it was argued that, as the applicant company was attempting to bring the application as a creditor of the company, it could only bring the proceedings in the Circuit Court. Second, it was argued that the applicant company was only a prospective or contingent creditor and did not have standing to apply for the restoration of the company's name. Third, it was contended that the applicant company

---

[123] C(A)A 1982, s 12B(3), as inserted by C(A)(No2)A 1999, s 46, as amended by IFCMPA 2005, s 72.

[124] See paras **[14.003]** to **[14.009]** and **[14.010]** to **[14.012]**.

[125] C(A)A 1982, s 12B(3), as inserted by C(A)(No2)A 1999, s 46, as amended by IFCMPA 2005, s 72.

[126] See *Re New Timbiqui Gold Mines Ltd* [1961] 1 Ch 319. See further para **[14.092]**.

[127] *Re Deauville Communications Worldwide Ltd, Orlaford Ltd v Wetherhill* [2002] 2 IR 32.

had adduced insufficient evidence to satisfy the court that the claim was *bona fide*. The High Court found in favour of the applicant company on all three points and made an order restoring the company's name to the register.

[14.045] On appeal, Keane CJ, delivering the judgment of the Supreme Court, considered these arguments in turn. The first argument, regarding the appropriate forum for the institution of proceedings by a creditor, is considered below.[128] In relation to the second argument, that a prospective creditor was not within the scope of the legislation, Keane CJ stated:

> 'Unless there were authority to the contrary, I would be inclined to the view that the word "creditor" in s 12B(3) should be read as extending to contingent or prospective creditors. It would seem unjust that the question whether a person is entitled to have the company restored to the register for the purpose of recovering a judgment against him, should be determined by whether his claim against the company is for a liquidated sum – in which case he would unarguably be a "creditor" – or takes the form of a claim for unliquidated damages.'[129]

Keane CJ concluded that, while the proceedings against the dissolved company were not initiated until after the date on which the company was struck off, the cause of action accrued before that date and the applicant did have the status of a creditor for the purposes of s 12B(3).[130]

[14.046] With regard to the argument that there was insufficient evidence of a *bona fide* claim, the Court applied the test expounded in *Re Nelson Car Hire Ltd*,[131] a case which concerned a petition by the Revenue Commissioners to have the dissolution of a company declared void under CA 1963, s 310.[132] In that case, the order was sought for

---

[128] See paras **[14.057]** to **[14.059]**.

[129] *Re Deauville Communications Worldwide Ltd, Orlaford Ltd v Wetherhill* [2002] 2 IR 32 at 41.

[130] *Re Deauville Communications Worldwide Ltd, Orlaford Ltd v Wetherhill* [2002] 2 IR 32 at 413: 'Since the events which are claimed to give rise to the cause of action are alleged to have happened before the 18th April, 1999, the day on which Deauville was struck off, it is clear that, adopting the reasoning of the English courts in the two cases to which I have referred, the applicant should be regarded as being a creditor for the purposes of the application to restore Deauville to the register.'

[131] *Re Nelson Car Hire Ltd* (1971) 107 ILTR 97.

[132] CA 1963, s 310(1) provides, 'Where a company has been dissolved, the Court may at any time within two years of the date of the dissolution, on an application being made for the purpose by the Liquidator of the company or by any other person who appears to the Court to be interested, make an order, upon such terms as the Court thinks fit declaring that this dissolution to have been void, and thereupon such proceedings may be taken as might have been taken if the company had not been dissolved. ...' This provision has been interpreted as applying to companies which have been wound up. See *Re Amantiss Enterprises Ltd, Framus Ltd v CRH plc* [2000] 2 ILRM 177 at 188: 'This section makes provision for declaring void a dissolution of a company where the company has been dissolved either as a result of a voluntary liquidation or a Court liquidation, in contradistinction to s 12 sub-s (6) which provides for the situation where a dissolution of a company results from the company being struck off the register under the provisions of s 12 of the 1982 Act.'

the purpose of assessing the company for income tax and corporation profits tax. Kenny J held that the Revenue Commissioners were not creditors within the meaning s 310, as no assessments were raised before the company's name was struck off the register. The Court also held in that case, in a passage quoted with approval by Keane CJ in *Re Deauville Communications Worldwide Ltd*,[133] that '[t]he court has a discretion in granting the application and the decisive matter must be whether the claim, which it is sought to make against the company, is one which might succeed.'[134]

Keane CJ applied this test of whether claim is one which 'might succeed', reaching the following conclusion:

> 'Assuming that the test adopted by Kenny J. in that case is also appropriate where a court is deciding whether 'it is just' that the company should be restored to the register, I have no doubt that it was satisfied by the applicant in this case ... It is clear that the High Court Judge was entitled to conclude that, at the least, the claim by the applicant might succeed and that there was nothing to indicate that the proceedings were frivolous or vexatious or were not being *bona fide* maintained by the applicant.'[135]

[14.047] On the authority of *Re Deauville Communications Worldwide Ltd*, an application may be made under s 12B(3) by a prospective or contingent creditor, so long as the cause of action accrued before the date on which the company's name was struck off the register, the creditor 'might succeed' in his claim against the company and the proceedings are being *bona fide* maintained.

(iii) Requirements

[14.048] An application to restore a company's name to the register under s 12B(3) can be made at any time up to 20 years from the date on which notice was published in the *CRO Gazette* of the fact that the company's name was struck off the register. In practice, as the name of a company which was struck off the register for failing to file annual returns or deliver the statement required by TCA 1997, S 882, may be restored by the Registrar for up to 12 months from the date on which it was dissolved, s 12B will only be availed of after the expiry of that 12 month period.[136]

(iv) Procedure

[14.049] An application for the restoration to the register of a company's name under s 12B(3) must be made 'on notice to the registrar of companies, the Revenue Commissioners and the Minister for Finance' by the member, officer or creditor.[137] The

---

[133] *Re Deauville Communications Worldwide Ltd, Orlaford Ltd v Wetherhill* [2002] 2 IR 32.

[134] *Re Nelson Car Hire Ltd* (1971) 107 ILTR 97 at 101, quoted in *Re Deauville Communications Worldwide Ltd, Orlaford Ltd v Wetherhill* [2002] 2 IR 32 at 45 to 46.

[135] *Re Deauville Communications Worldwide Ltd, Orlaford Ltd v Wetherhill* [2002] 2 IR 32 at 46.

[136] See further paras **[14.083]** to **[14.097]**.

[137] C(A)A 1982, s 12B(3), as inserted by C(A)(No2)A 1999, s 46, as amended by IFCMPA 2005, s 72.

Chief State Solicitor's Office represents the Registrar and the Minister for Finance, and the Revenue Solicitor represents the Revenue Commissioners. Each have their own procedural requirements for issuing a letter of consent to the restoration of a company's name to the register of companies.

[14.050] The CRO has issued an Information Leaflet regarding the restoration of companies' names to the register of companies. This Leaflet must be regarded with some circumspection as it contains certain interpretations of ss 12B(3) and 311(8) which seem to go beyond the scope of those provisions, and other interpretations which are at variance with the language of the provisions. For example, the CRO states that 'if the company was struck off involuntarily, the application for restoration is made under s 12B(3) Companies (Amendment) Act 1982. The following steps are required to be followed by the director, member, or solicitor acting on behalf of the company...'.[138] Section 12B(3) is not the only provision to be availed of in respect of a company which was struck off the register involuntarily.

Both C(A)A 1982, s 12B(7), and CA 1963, s 311(8),[139] provide for the restoration to the register of the names of companies which were struck off involuntarily. Moreover, in spite of the administrative practice of the CRO of permitting companies to apply for their names to be struck off the register voluntarily, there is nothing in the Companies Acts which refers to such a practice.[140] In the absence of any statutory basis for restoring companies' names to the register voluntarily, the Companies Acts are not open to the interpretation that only one of the three provisions governing restoration to the register can apply to companies which are struck off involuntarily. The suggestion implicit in the Information Leaflet that CA 1963, s 311(8), can only be availed of in respect of a company which was struck off voluntarily, is certainly not sustainable.

A further difficulty with the statement by the CRO quoted above, is that is advises that a 'director, member, or solicitor acting on behalf of the company'[141] may make an application under s 12B(3), whereas s 12B(3) in fact refers to a 'member, officer or creditor of a company' as a potential applicant. A company cannot make an application under s 12B(3).[142] Similar errors appear in the Leaflet regarding the potential applicants under CA 1963, s 311(8). Section 311(8) refers to the right of 'a company or any member or creditor' to apply for the restoration of a company's name under that provision, whereas the CRO suggests that, 'If the company was struck off voluntarily and it intends to apply to the court pursuant to s 311(8) Companies Act 1963 to have itself restored, the following steps are required to be followed by the director, member

---

138 CRO, 'Restoration of a Company to the Register', Information Leaflet No 11 (October 2005) at p 5.

139 See further paras **[14.071]** to **[14.076]** and **[14.077]** to **[14.082]**.

140 See para **[14.026]**.

141 CRO, 'Restoration of a Company to the Register', Information Leaflet No 11 (October 2005) at p 5. Available at www.cro.ie.

142 This interpretation by the CRO that a company can make an application under s 12B(3) is also apparent from the fact that, under the heading 'Company/member/officer & Restoration' there is a heading 'Involuntary strike off' which deals with s 12B(3).

applying for restoration or the solicitor acting on behalf of the company ...'.[143] This is misleading, as it is clear from s 311(8) that a director is not one of the persons who has standing to bring that application.

These qualifications to the accuracy of the Information Leaflet notwithstanding, there is some useful information in the Leaflet regarding the practice and procedures that should be followed in making an application for the restoration to the register of a company's name.

[14.051] In the case of an application under s 12B(3), the requirements vary depending upon whether the application is made by a member or officer of the company, or its creditor.

If a member or officer of a company wishes to make an application under s 12B(3), he must follow these steps. First, he must write to the CRO, Enforcement Section, requesting confirmation that the Registrar has no objection to the restoration of the company. According to the CRO:

> 'The Registrar will furnish a letter of no objection to an application pursuant to s 12B(3) to restore a company to the register, subject to compliance with the following:
>
> (i) If all outstanding annual returns (including the accounts which are required to be annexed pursuant to the provisions of the Companies Acts 1963–2005) are delivered to the CRO, and are in order ... or
>
> (ii) If all outstanding annual returns (including the accounts which are required to be annexed pursuant to the provisions of the Companies Acts 1963–2005) are delivered in final draft format to the CRO, and are in order, together with the applicant's personal undertaking to file signed returns and audited accounts in identical form following the making of the restoration order.'[144]

If one of these conditions is met, the Registrar will issue a letter of 'no objection', subject to the requirement that the restoration order must include a provision that it will lapse unless it is delivered by the applicant to the Registrar within three months of the date on which the order is pronounced.

[14.052] Second, he must obtain a letter from the Chief State Solicitor's Office, on behalf of Minister for Finance, stating that there is no objection to the restoration of the company. Third, he must obtain a letter of 'no objection' from the Revenue Solicitor, on behalf of the Revenue Commissioners. Fourth, he may then issue a petition in the High Court for an order to restore the company. The CRO advises that the petition not be issued until all letters of 'no objection' have been received. Fifth, within three months of the date on which the High Court makes an order restoring the company's name to the register, the applicant must deliver to the CRO for registration an attested copy of the order, together with the filing fee. Finally, if the outstanding annual returns were not previously delivered to the CRO, they must be lodged without delay.

---

[143] CRO, 'Restoration of a Company to the Register', Information Leaflet No 11 (October 2005) at p 4.

[144] CRO, 'Restoration of a Company to the Register', Information Leaflet No 11 (October 2005) at p 5. Available at www.cro.ie.

[14.053] If a creditor wishes to make an application under s 12B(3), he must comply with the following requirements. First, he must write to the CRO, Enforcement Section, requesting confirmation that the Registrar has no objection to the restoration of the company. According to the CRO, if the company's name was struck off the register for failing to file annual returns, the letter of 'no objection' which the CRO must issue before a company can be restored to the register, on the application of a creditor, is:

> 'strictly subject to notice being given by or on behalf of the creditor to the last recorded (as *per* CRO records) directors of the dissolved company:
>
> (i) of the hearing date of the restoration application, and
>
> (ii) that, pursuant to s 12B(6) Companies (Amendment) Act 1982, a direction will be included in the court order that one or more specified members or officers of the company file all outstanding annual returns with the CRO within such period as the court may specify.'[145]

[14.054] If, on the other hand, the company's name was struck off the register for a failure to deliver a statement required by TCA 1997, S 882, to the Revenue Commissioners:

> 'the Registrar will furnish a letter of no objection to a creditor or solicitor strictly subject to notice being given by or on behalf of the creditor to the last recorded (as *per* CRO records) directors of the dissolved company of the hearing date of the restoration applications.'[146]

According to the CRO, such an application by a creditor must also be preceded by a request for an alternative order to be made by the court under C(A)A 1982, s 12B(3), directing the last recorded officers of the company to deliver all outstanding returns to the CRO within such period as the court may specify.

The Registrar will issue a letter of 'no objection', subject to the requirement that the restoration order must include a provision that it will lapse unless it is delivered by the applicant to the Registrar within three months of the date on which the order is pronounced.

[14.055] Second, the creditor must obtain a letter from the Chief State Solicitor's Office, on behalf of Minister for Finance, stating that there is no objection to the restoration of the company. Third, he must obtain a letter of 'no objection' from the Revenue Solicitor, on behalf of the Revenue Commissioners.[147] Fourth, he may then issue a petition in the High Court or in the Circuit Court for an order to restore the company. The CRO advises that the petition not be issued until all letters of 'no objection' have been received. Finally, within three months of the date on which the High Court or Circuit Court makes an order restoring the company's name to the

---

[145] CRO, 'Restoration of a Company to the Register', Information Leaflet No 11 (October 2005).

[146] CRO, 'Restoration of a Company to the Register', (Information Leaflet No 11 (October 2005) at p 8.

[147] Note that this requirement applies whether the company was struck off the register for failing to deliver annual returns, or for failing to deliver a statement to the Revenue Commissioners under TCA 1997, S 882.

register, the applicant must deliver to the CRO for registration an attested copy of the order, together with the filing fee.

[14.056] The requirement that a petitioner who obtains a court order restoring the name of a company to the register must deliver a copy of this order to the Registrar within a specified period of time, was considered in *Re Barrowland Ltd.*[148] In that case, the order for the restoration of a company's name was not delivered to the Registrar until more than five and a half years after the date on which the order was made. The decision of Smyth J includes significant pronouncements regarding the requirement that a court order for the restoration of a company's name be delivered to the Registrar and the effect of failing to comply with that requirement. It indicates clearly that, unless a court order is delivered promptly to the Registrar, it will lapse and a fresh application to court will be necessary. Applicants for a court order restoring a company's name to the register must therefore be vigilant to ensure that such an order is delivered promptly to the Registrar.[149]

[14.057] The significant difference between an application brought by a member or an officer of a company under s 12B(3) and an application by a creditor under the same provision, is that a creditor may bring the petition in the Circuit Court, whereas members or officers must bring the petition in the High Court. Section 12B(9) provides:

> Without prejudice to s 2(1) of the Principal Act[150] where such an application is made by any other person, in the case of an application under this section that is made by a creditor of the company or the registrar of companies, 'the court', for the purposes of this section, means the Circuit Court.[151]

This suggests that the generality of s 2(1) applies when the application is brought by persons other than a creditor, namely a member or officer, but that, if the application is brought by a creditor, the Circuit Court is the appropriate forum. However, the Supreme Court has determined that it is not obligatory for a creditor to bring the application in the Circuit Court, but may alternatively issue such a petition in the High Court. In *Re Deauville Communications Worldwide Ltd*[152] the petition to have the company restored to the register was issued in the High Court by a company claiming to be a creditor of the dissolved company. It was argued that, due to s 12B(9), this petition could only be

---

[148] *Re Barrowland Ltd* [2003] IEHC 54.

[149] *Re Barrowland Ltd* [2003] IEHC 54 *per* Smyth J: 'Orders not lodged forthwith and at the very outside within three months should and do automatically lapse. In such circumstances a renewed fresh application to the Court is necessary: such must not only comply with this subsection but also aver to the exact state of the business and affairs of the company as from the date of the pronouncement of the lapsed Order and give a full and satisfactory explanation to the Court as to why its original Order was not complied with in the interim.' See further paras **[14.102]** to **[14.105]**.

[150] CA 1963, s 2(1), as substituted by CA 1990, s 235, defines 'the court' as follows: 'unless the context requires otherwise, 'the court' used in any provision of the Companies Acts in relation to a company means: (a) the High Court or (b) where another court is prescribed for the purposes of that provision, that court.'

[151] C(A)A 1982, s 12B(9), as inserted by C(A)(No2)A 1999, s 46.

[152] *Re Deauville Communications Worldwide Ltd, Orlaford Ltd v Wetherhill* [2002] 2 IR 32.

brought by a creditor in the Circuit Court and that it was not open to a creditor to initiate such proceedings in the High Court. This argument was rejected in the High Court. On appeal, Keane CJ, delivering the judgment of the Supreme Court, noted that this was a 'somewhat difficult issue of statutory construction.'[153] The Court considered the legislative history of s 12B(3) and the related provisions of s 12B. Keane CJ noted that s 12B(9) was clearly intended to confer the right to bring restoration proceedings in the Circuit Court only upon certain applicants:

> 'It is beyond argument that the subsection was, at the least, intended to enable a creditor or the first notice party to apply under the section to the Circuit Court. It is also beyond argument that the facility thus afforded to those parties was not intended to apply to any other person and that may have been the reason for the use of the opening words.'[154]

[14.058] The Court considered the rationale behind allowing the Registrar of Companies and creditors to initiate restoration proceedings in the Circuit Court and noted that there was no equivalent reason for denying those applicants the right to bring such proceedings in the High Court:

> 'It is obvious that the Oireachtas thought it desirable that the first notice party should be in a position, if it seemed a convenient course, to make an application in the Circuit Court, where it was considered appropriate, to have a company, which had been in default in making returns, restored to the register. One can see good reasons why a similar facility should be afforded to persons in the position of creditors who had not been in any way in default. One can also understand why it was not thought necessary to afford such a facility to members or officers of the company which had been in default. But there seems no reason – and none has been suggested – why the legislature, while enabling creditors and the first notice party to avail of what might be a more convenient forum, should at the same time have chosen to deny them access to a forum, ie the High Court, which, depending on the circumstances, could have been as convenient, if not more convenient, than the Circuit Court.'[155]

The Court concluded:

> 'I am satisfied that, when the subsection is placed in its appropriate statutory context, it becomes clear that the intention of the Oireachtas was more likely to have been to enable the application to be brought either in the High Court or the Circuit Court.'[156]

It is now therefore established that a creditor can bring proceedings for the restoration of a company's name to the register under s 12B(3) in either the Circuit Court or the High Court.

---

[153] *Re Deauville Communications Worldwide Ltd, Orlaford Ltd v Wetherhill* [2002] 2 IR 32 at 35.

[154] *Re Deauville Communications Worldwide Ltd, Orlaford Ltd v Wetherhill* [2002] 2 IR 32 at 38.

[155] *Re Deauville Communications Worldwide Ltd, Orlaford Ltd v Wetherhill* [2002] 2 IR 32 at 38 to 39 (*per* Keane CJ).

[156] *Re Deauville Communications Worldwide Ltd, Orlaford Ltd v Wetherhill* [2002] 2 IR 32 at 40.

[14.059] If a creditor does being an application under s 12B(3) in the Circuit Court, it should be brought before the judge in one of the following three circuits:

– the circuit in which the company's registered office was situated, immediately before the company's name was struck off the register;

– if no office was registered at the time at which the company's name was struck off the register, the circuit in which the creditor resides; or

– if the creditor resides outside the State, Dublin Circuit Court.[157]

[14.060] When the preliminary matters have been attended to and the petitioner is ready to issue a petition for the restoration of a company's name to the register, he must file the following documents:[158]

1.   A petition in the form of Appendix N to the Rules of the Superior Courts setting out the following information in numbered paragraphs:

(i)   Name and description of petitioner;

(ii)   Name and registered office of company;

(iii)   Company's objects;

(iv)   Company's nominal and issued share capital;

(v)   Business carried on by company;

(vi)   Reasons for company being struck off;

(vii)   Statement that all outstanding annual returns or statements under s 882 of the Taxes Consolidation Act 1997 have been filed or delivered, as applicable (or appropriate undertakings);

(viii)   Statement that all tax liabilities have been paid;

(ix)   Prayer for order restoring company's name to the register;

(x)   Statement of intention to serve petition on Registrar, Minister for Finance and Revenue Commissioners;

(xi)   This petition should be dated and signed on behalf of the company.

2.   A notice of motion, stating that the petitioner will apply for an order for the restoration of the company's name to the register, on notice to the Registrar of Companies; the Minister for Finance; the Chief State Solicitor; the Revenue Commissioners; and the Revenue Solicitor.

---

[157] C(A)A 1982, s 12B(10), as inserted by C(A)(No2)A 1999, s 46.

[158] Rules of the Superior Courts, O 75, r 4 addresses the appropriate procedure to be followed and, in provisions which are now out-dated as they do not reflect the changes introduced by the C(A)(No2)A 1999, states that '(o) applications to restore a company's name to the register under s 12(6) of the 1982 Act' shall be by way of petition.

3.   A grounding affidavit, sworn by the petitioner, should ideally include the following information:[159]

     (i)   Petitioner's name and means of knowledge;

     (ii)   Description of company's formation and memorandum and articles of association and these documents should be exhibited to the affidavit;

     (iii)   Reasons and explanations for the company's name being struck off the register;

     (iv)   Grounds on which the name should be restored to the register;

     (v)   An averment that the Minister for Finance has not intermeddled in the company's property since the date on which its name was struck off the register;

     (vi)   Confirmation that all outstanding tax liabilities have been paid to the Revenue Commissioners, and statements under s 882 delivered, if applicable, (or appropriate undertakings or commitments furnished);

     (vii)   Confirmation that all returns have been filed with the Registrar, if applicable (or appropriate undertakings or commitments furnished);

     (viii)   Confirmation that letters of 'no objection' were received from the Registrar; the Revenue Commissioners (typically issued by the Revenue Solicitor) and the Minister for Finance (typically issued by the Chief State Solicitor);

     (ix)   These letters of 'no objection' must be exhibited to the affidavit; and

     (x)   An averment that it is just that the company's name be restored to the register.

(v) Orders

[14.061] On an application under s 12B(3), the court 'may, if satisfied that it is just that the company be restored to the register, order that the name of the company be restored to the register.'[160] The only requirement is that the court must be satisfied that it is 'just' to restore the company's name to the register.

The court must moreover ensure that the defaults which lead to the company's name being struck off the register will be rectified. The form of this order depends upon the applicant and on the ground on which the company's name was struck off the register:

    –   In the case of an application made by a member or officer of the company for the restoration of a company which was struck off under s 12(3), for failing to file annual returns, the order restoring the company's name must, 'unless cause

---

[159] Note that, if the applicant is a creditor of the company, the petition and affidavit must include additional information, such as the basis of the creditor's claim and the names of the persons (such as directors) to whom the necessary directions to file outstanding returns should be made.

[160] C(A)A 1982, s 12B(3), as inserted by C(A)(No2)A 1999, s 46, as amended by IFCMPA 2005, s 72.

is shown to the contrary' include a provision that the order will not have effect unless within one month of that order, all outstanding annual returns are delivered to the Registrar;[161]

- In the case of an application made by a member or officer of a company which was struck off for failing to deliver a statement required by s 883 of the Taxes Consolidation Act 1997, the order restoring the company's name must, 'unless cause is shown to the contrary' include a provision that the order will not have effect unless within one month of that order, all such outstanding statements must be delivered to the Revenue Commissioners;[162]

- In the case of an application by a creditor of a company which was struck off for failing to file annual returns, the court shall direct that one or more specified members or officers of the company shall, within a specified period, deliver all outstanding annual returns to the Registrar; [163] and

- In the case of an application by a creditor of a company which was struck off for failing to deliver statements to the Revenue Commissioners under s 882 of the Taxes Consolidation Act, 1997, the court shall direct that one or more specified members or officers of the company shall, within a specified period, deliver all such outstanding statements to the Revenue Commissioners.[164]

[14.062] Before the enactment of C(A)(No2)A 1999, there was a practice that the restoration of companies' names, which were struck off the register for failing to file annual returns, was conditional on the prior filing of all annual returns. However, *Re Haltone (Cork) Ltd*[165] demonstrates that this was not an unwavering requirement. In that case, a company (the 'Creditor') had obtained judgment in England against Haltone (Cork) Ltd (the 'Company'), before the latter's name was struck off the register. In order to enforce this judgment against the Company and against its directors, the Creditor brought a petition for the Company's name to be restored to the register. The Registrar did not object to the application.

O'Hanlon J noted that, '[s]uch application is usually made on behalf of the company itself and when relief is granted it is normally conditional upon the prior filing of all annual returns then outstanding' and that:

> 'Obviously, the petitioner is not in a position to file annual returns on behalf of the company to make good the default which has taken place in the past and is

---

[161] C(A)A 1982, s 12B(5)(a), as inserted by C(A)(No2)A 1999, s 46. The CRO describes the effect of this provision as follows: 'A restoration order made by the Court will not have effect unless all outstanding returns, including accounts, are delivered to the CRO within one month from the date of the making of the order. In the event that it is not complied with within the period specified, the company will remain dissolved.' (CRO, 'Restoration of a Company to the Register' Information Leaflet No 11 (October 2005) at p 5.

[162] C(A)A 1982, s 12B(5)(b), as inserted by C(A)(No2)A 1999, s 46.

[163] C(A)A 1982, s 12B(6)(a), as inserted by C(A)(No2)A 1999, s 46.

[164] C(A)A 1982, s 12B(6)(b), as inserted by C(A)(No2)A 1999, s 46.

[165] *Re Haltone (Cork) Ltd* [1996] 1 IR 32.

unlikely to secure the co-operation of the company or its officers in carrying out this procedure.'[166]

The Court determined that:

'Notwithstanding this circumstance, I am of opinion that I should accede to the present application so that the petitioner may be allowed a reasonable opportunity to pursue whatever remedy may be available to it under the provisions of the Companies Acts for the recovery of the sums due by the company in respect of which it has already recovered judgment against the company, without being inhibited in any way by the dissolution of the company which took place when the company was struck off the register.'[167]

[14.063] On the authority of this case, a company's name could be restored to the register without outstanding annual returns being filed or any prospect of such returns being filed in the future. As mentioned, *Re Haltone (Cork) Ltd*[168] was determined under C(A)A 1982, s 12(6), as it existed before the changes introduced by C(A)(No2)A 1999. Under s 12B as it is now formulated, it would no longer be possible to obtain an order restoring a company's name to the register without a direction that the outstanding annual returns or Revenue statements be delivered to the Registrar within such period as may be specified by the court.[169] A creditor who wishes to make such an application, must therefore name the directors of the company to whom that direction to file outstanding returns may be made and those persons are typically named as notice parties to such applications.

[14.064] This issue, among others, arose in *Re New Ad Advertising Company Ltd*.[170] The petitioner in that case was a former director and member of a company who initiated proceedings in June 2005 under CA 1963, s 205, arising from his membership of that company. Orders for costs were made in favour of the petitioner in these proceedings in November 1995, and March 1996. The company's name was struck off the register for failing to deliver annual returns in January 1999. The s 205 proceedings were listed for hearing in 2004, and shortly before the date fixed for hearing, a director of the company notified the court that the company had been struck off the register. The court adjourned the hearing to allow an application to be made to restore the company's name to the register. The petitioner brought this application under s 12B(3) in his role as a member and creditor of the company, in order to prosecute the s 205 proceedings. A director of the company was joined as a notice party to the restoration application (the 'Notice Party'), as the petitioner was not a director of the company. As the Court stated:

'Mr McNulty was joined as a notice party because, as the application has been treated by the Registrar as an application by a creditor, and as the Registrar and the Revenue Commissioners are pressing for orders directed to the directors to comply with their obligations to make statutory returns under the Company Law

---

[166] *Re Haltone (Cork) Ltd* [1996] 1 IR 32 at 35.

[167] *Re Haltone (Cork) Ltd* [1996] 1 IR 32 at 35.

[168] *Re Haltone (Cork) Ltd* [1996] 1 IR 32.

[169] C(A)A 1982, s 12B(6)(a), as inserted by C(A)(No2)A 1999, s 46.

[170] *Re New Ad Advertising Company Ltd* [2006] IEHC 19.

code and their obligations to make returns under the Revenue code, the directors were necessary parties.'[171]

This statement demonstrates that, contrary to the position adopted in *Re Haltone (Cork) Ltd*,[172] if a creditor now wishes to bring an application for the restoration of a company's name, its directors are necessary parties to such an application.

[14.065] In *Re New Ad Advertising Company Ltd*[173] the Registrar's letter of 'no objection' was strictly subject to a direction under s 12B(6) being included in the court order; the Revenue Commissioners' agreement not to object was strictly subject to a court order directing the directors of the company to deliver all outstanding tax returns to the Revenue Commissioners within one month of the restoration order; and the Minister for Finance supported the Revenue position.

The Notice Party resisted the restoration of the company's name to the register on a number of grounds. In particular, the Notice Party argued that it was not 'just' that the company be restored and that the only purpose of the restoration was to enable the petitioner to prosecute the s 205 proceedings, there being no other creditors. While the Court considered that, as he was the person who would have to comply with any orders of the Court, it was appropriate to hear the Notice Party on the application, the Court rejected the arguments advanced by the Notice Party. On the contrary, the Court determined that it would be unjust to prevent the petitioner from pursuing the s 205 proceedings.

[14.066] A further argument raised by the Notice Party involved the interpretation of s 12B(5) and (6). As already noted, s 12B(5) provides that, in the case of an application made by a member or officer of the company for the restoration of a company, the order restoring the company's name must, 'unless cause is shown to the contrary' include a provision that the order will not have effect unless within one month of that order, all outstanding annual returns are delivered to the Registrar or all outstanding statements are delivered to the Revenue Commissioners, as appropriate.[174] Section 12B(6), by contrast, provides that, in the case of an application by a creditor of a company, the court shall direct that one or more specified members or officers of the company shall, within a specified period, deliver all outstanding annual returns to the Registrar or all outstanding statements to the Revenue Commissioners, as appropriate.[175]

[14.067] In *Re New Ad Advertising Company Ltd*[176] the Notice Party claimed that, if the petition were to succeed, it should be treated as a petition by a member, rather than a creditor, and that, according to the terms of s 12B(5), the Court therefore had a discretion whether to require outstanding returns to be filed. In favour of his contention that the Court should not direct outstanding annual returns to be filed, the Notice Party

---

[171] *Re New Ad Advertising Company Ltd* [2006] IEHC 19.

[172] *Re Haltone (Cork) Ltd* [1996] 1 IR 32. See para **[14.062]**.

[173] *Re New Ad Advertising Company Ltd* [2006] IEHC 19.

[174] C(A)A 1982, s 12B(5), as inserted by C(A)(No2)A 1999, s 46. See further para **[14.061]**.

[175] C(A)A 1982, s 12B(6), as inserted by C(A)(No2)A 1999, s 46. See further paras **[14.061]** to **[14.063]**.

[176] *Re New Ad Advertising Company Ltd* [2006] IEHC 19.

cited practical difficulties, including uncertainty regarding the company's directors; the expense of having the accounts prepared and audited; the fact that company records were put in storage in 1998 and subsequently destroyed in a fire, among others.

Laffoy J considered the extent of the court's discretion under s 12B(5) and (6) and concluded:

> 'In my view, a very limited discretion is given to the court in sub-s (5). The court is mandated to make the effect of the restoration order conditional on the outstanding returns being delivered "unless cause is shown to the contrary". The obvious situation in which cause is shown to the contrary is where, before the matter is heard in court, the outstanding returns have been delivered and there is confirmation from the relevant State authority that such is the case. In my view, it would be erroneous to assume that sub-s (6) is more rigorous than sub-s (5). The contrary, is, in fact, the case because under sub-s (5) the effect of the order is postponed until delivery of the outstanding returns within the period of one month, whereas in the case of sub-s (6) the order takes effect immediately, although there is an ancillary direction to the members or officers of the company to deliver the outstanding returns within a time period stipulated by the court. The reason for the different approach in the two subsections is because almost invariably a creditor petitioner will not be in a position to deliver returns on behalf of the company. In relation to both subsections, the legislative intent is clear. It is to ensure that the striking-off mechanism as a deterrent against breach of company law and tax law is not devalued. It would be devalued if a company could be restored to the Register without the breach which gave rise to its striking-off being remedied.'[177]

In the circumstances of the case, the Court concluded that the petitioner, whether as a member or creditor, was not in a position to deliver the outstanding returns, and decided to treat the petitioner as a creditor for the purposes of s 12B(6), as requested by the Registrar. The Court proceeded to direct the Notice Party to deliver all outstanding annual returns within a period of three months from the date of the order.

[14.068] On the authority of *Re New Ad Advertising Company Ltd*[178] a court, in restoring a company's name to the register under s 12B(3), must ensure that either all outstanding annual returns are filed with the Registrar, or outstanding statements delivered to the Revenue Commissioners, depending on the ground on which the company's name was struck off. This requirement must be imposed whether the petitioner is a creditor, member, or officer of the company. The only difference that appears to exist between the different categories of applicant is that there is more flexibility regarding the time to be allowed to members or officers who are directed to file returns or deliver statements, on the application of a creditor for the company's name to be restored.

[14.069] A further order that may be made by a court in restoring a company's name to the register under s 12B(3), is that the court may:

> ... give such directions and make such provisions as seem just for placing the company and all other persons in the same position as nearly as may be as if the

---

[177] *Re New Ad Advertising Company Ltd* [2006] IEHC 19.

[178] *Re New Ad Advertising Company Ltd* [2006] IEHC 19.

name of the company had not been struck off or make such other order as seems just (and such other order is referred to in sub-s (4) of this section as an 'alternative order').[179]

Section 12B(4) further provides:

An alternative order may, if the court considers it appropriate that it should do so, include a provision that, as respects a debt or liability incurred by, or on behalf of, the company during the period when it stood struck off the register, the officers of the company or such one or more of them as is or are specified in the order shall be liable for the whole or a part (as the court thinks just) of the debt or liability.[180]

The role of the court on an application under s 12B(3) is a somewhat circumscribed one, and the court cannot, for example, penalise the company in relation to its conduct in other proceedings, since the date of striking off, by means of an order of costs in connection with the restoration proceedings. *Re Bloomberg Developments Ltd*[181] was a case in which a company initiated proceedings against another company ('the notice party'), but was struck off the register of companies before the trial of the proceedings. The notice party sought to have the proceedings struck out on the basis that the company no longer existed. The court granted this application, subject to a stay of five weeks to permit the applicant, a director and member of the dissolved company, to obtain an order restoring its name to the register. Approximately four weeks later, the Court granted a further extension of time for the restoration of the company's name to the register. In determining each of these motions, the Court made orders that the costs of the notice party be discharged by the company.

[14.070] When the application to restore the company's name to the register under C(A)A 1982, s 12B(3), came before the High Court, the notice party made an appearance objecting to the restoration. While the Court did order that the company's name be restored to the register, the Court also directed that the notice party's costs should be discharged by the company. The company appealed to the Supreme Court, against the order for the discharge of the notice party's costs, and contended that the High Court erred in giving the notice party *locus standi* on the application.

Murphy J, delivering the judgment of the Supreme Court, described the nature of restoration proceedings as follows:

'On principle it is difficult to see what legal right Philips had to intervene in the proceedings for the restoration of Bloomberg to the Register of Companies. Restoration is primarily a matter between the petitioner on the one part and the regulatory authority – who has the duty to ensure compliance with the relevant provisions of the Companies Acts – and the Minister for Finance – in whom would vest the assets of the company as *bona vacantia* – of the other part.'[182]

---

[179] C(A)A 1982, s 12B(3), as inserted by C(A)(No2)A 1999, s 46, as amended by IFCMPA 2005, s 72.

[180] C(A)A 1982, s 12B(4), as inserted by C(A)(No2)A 1999, s 46.

[181] *Re Bloomberg Developments Ltd, Bloomberg Developments Ltd v Philips Electrical (Ireland) Ltd* [2002] 2 IR 613.

[182] *Re Bloomberg Developments Ltd, Bloomberg Developments Ltd v Philips Electrical (Ireland) Ltd* [2002] 2 IR 613 at 616.

The Court did however conclude that, in the circumstances of the case, the right of the notice party to be heard on the application under s 12B(3) was a matter within the discretion of the trial judge:

> 'Whilst no directions were given in relation to persons to be served or advertisements to be published in relation to the application, it would seem that the Court was satisfied to hear counsel on behalf of Philips and that this course was not opposed by Bloomberg. In the circumstances I believe that it was within the discretion of the Court to treat Philips as a notice party to the proceedings.'[183]

With regard to the order for costs that was made in that case, Murphy J considered that it was imposed by way of a sanction or penalty and that, insofar as there may have been some conduct by the company in the proceedings against the notice party which warranted such a penalty, it should have been imposed in the context of those proceedings. Murphy J concluded:

> 'I am satisfied that the law in practice in this jurisdiction does confer power on the High Court to ensure that the power to restore a company to the Register is used for the purpose for which it was intended but does not extend to the imposition of a penalty, such as was imposed in the present case, by an award of costs – whether taxed or otherwise – in proceedings which fall to be dealt with on their own merits independently of the application for restoration.'[184]

The decision of the Supreme Court in *Re Bloomberg Developments Ltd* indicates that proceedings for the restoration of a company's name to the register should typically only involve the petitioner, the regulatory authority (CRO) and the Minister for Finance, although there may be additional notice parties. The Court has the power to examine the application so as to assess that the power to restore a company's name to the register is being used for the proper purpose, but it does not have the power to impose penalties, such as awards of costs. It should be noted, however, that the entities that are required to furnish letters of 'no obligation' such as the Revenue Commissioners may, and often do, require a contribution towards their expenses.

(b) Section 12B(7) of C(A)A 1982

[14.071] C(A)A 1982, s 12B(7), provides:

> The court, on an application made by the registrar of companies (on notice to each person who, to his knowledge, is an officer of the company) before the expiration of 20 years from the publication in the Companies Registration Office Gazette of the notice referred to in s 12(3) or, as the case may be, 12A(3) of this Act, may, if satisfied that it is just that the company be restored to the register, order that the name of a company which has been struck off the register under the said s 12(3) or 12A(3) be restored to the register and, upon the making of the order by the court, the company shall be deemed to have continued in existence as if its name had not been struck off; and the court may by the order give such directions and make such provisions as seem just for placing the company and all other persons in the same

---

[183] *Re Bloomberg Developments Ltd, Bloomberg Developments Ltd v Philips Electrical (Ireland) Ltd* [2002] 2 IR 613 at 617.

[184] *Re Bloomberg Developments Ltd, Bloomberg Developments Ltd v Philips Electrical (Ireland) Ltd* [2002] 2 IR 613 at 618.

position as nearly as may be as if the name of the company had not been struck off or make such other order as seems just (and such other order may, if the court considers it appropriate that it should do so, include a provision of the kind referred to in sub-s (4) of this section).[185]

(i) Scope

[14.072] Section 12B(7) applies to an application by the Registrar of Companies to restore to the register the name of a company which was struck off the register for failing to file its annual returns or for failing to deliver a statement to the Revenue Commissioners as required by TCA 1997, s 882.[186]

(ii) Applicants

[14.073] The only potential applicant under s 12B(7) is the Registrar of Companies, although an application may be made in the same circumstances by an officer, member or creditor of the company under s 12B(3).[187]

(iii) Requirements

[14.074] An application under s 12B(7) can be made any time up until 20 years from the date on which the notice that the company's name was struck off the register was published in the *CRO Gazette*. The only requirement for a successful application under s 12B(7) that is specified in that provision, is that court must consider it 'just' that the company's name be restored to the register. The court therefore has a wide discretion regarding the matters which may justify an order under s 12B(7). There are no particular matters of which the Registrar must satisfy the court on such an application.

(iv) Procedure

[14.075] A petition by the Registrar must be made 'on notice to each person who, to his knowledge, is an officer of the company'.[188] There is no requirement that the application be on notice to the Minister for Finance or the Revenue Commissioners.

Like a creditor, the Registrar has the right to bring proceedings for the restoration of a company's name to the register, in the Circuit Court. Section 12B(9) provides:

> Without prejudice to s 2(1) of the Principal Act[189] where such an application is made by any other person, in the case of an application under this section that is

---

[185] C(A)A 1982, s 12B(7), as inserted by C(A)(No2)A 1999, s 46.

[186] See further paras **[14.003]** *et seq*.

[187] C(A)A 1982, s 12B(3), as inserted by C(A)(No2)A 1999, s 46. See paras **[14.041]** to **[14.070]**.

[188] C(A)A 1982, s 12B(7), as inserted by C(A)(No2)A 1999, s 46.

[189] CA 1963, s 2(1), as substituted by CA 1990, s 235, defines 'the court' as follows: 'unless the context requires otherwise, 'the court' used in any provision of the Companies Acts in relation to a company means: (a) the High Court or (b) where another court is prescribed for the purposes of that provision, that court.'

made by a creditor of the company or the registrar of companies, 'the court', for the purposes of this section, means the Circuit Court.[190]

The Supreme Court has interpreted this provision as giving a creditor a choice as to whether to proceed in the High Court or the Circuit Court and the same interpretation must apply to the appropriate forum for an application by the Registrar to restore a company to the register.[191]

By contrast with the rules applicable to the circuit in which a creditor must issue a petition for the restoration of a company's name, s 12B(11) provides, 'An application under this section to the Circuit Court by the Registrar of Companies shall be made to the judge of the Circuit Court for the Dublin Circuit.'[192] This rule applies irrespective of the location of the registered office of the company on the date at which its name was struck off the register.[193]

(v) Orders

[14.076] On an application under C(A)A 1982, s 12B(7), the court may, if it is satisfied that it is just to do so, order that the company's name be restored to the register. The court may further:

> ... give such directions and make such provisions as seem just for placing the company and all other persons in the same position as nearly as may be as if the name of the company had not been struck off or make such other order as seems just (and such other order may, if the court considers it appropriate that it should do so, include a provision of the kind referred to in sub-s (4) of this section).[194]

(c) Section 311(8) of CA 1963

[14.077] CA 1963, s 311(8) provides as follows:

> If a company or any member or creditor thereof feels aggrieved by the company having been struck off the register, the court, on an application made (on notice to the registrar) by the company or member or creditor before the expiration of 20 years from the publication in the Companies Registration Office Gazette of the notice aforesaid, may, if satisfied that the company was at the time of the striking off carrying on business or otherwise that it is just that the company be restored to the register, order that the name of the company be restored to the register and

---

[190] C(A)A 1982, s 12B(9), as inserted by C(A)(No2)A 1999, s 46.

[191] See *Re Deauville Communications Worldwide Ltd, Orlaford Ltd v Wetherhill* [2002] 2 IR 32. See further paras **[14.057]** to **[14.058]**.

[192] C(A)A 1982, s 12B(11), as inserted by C(A)(No2)A 1999, s 46.

[193] Note that the CRO *Report 2005* indicates that there may be difficulties with such an approach in relation to prosecution of companies: ' A number of further difficulties arose towards the end of the year ... involving the issue of whether the court in Dublin has jurisdiction in cases where the defendant company has its registered office located outside of the Dublin area. The Office is in discussion with the Attorney-General's Office in the matter.' (CRO *Report 2005* at p 4). It is likely that these concerns will not affect restoration proceedings to the same extent, if at all.

[194] C(A)A 1982, s 12B(7), as inserted by C(A)(No2)A 1999, s 46.

upon an office copy of the order being delivered to the registrar for registration, the company shall be deemed to have continued in existence as if its name had not been struck off; and the court may by the order give such directions and make such provisions as seem just for placing the company and all other persons in the same position as nearly as may be [as if the name of the company had not been struck off or make such other order as seems just (and such other order is referred to in sub-s (8A) as an 'alternative order').[195]

(i) Scope

[14.078] There is nothing in s 311(8) which defines or limits its scope. It could therefore be relied upon as a basis for attempting to restore to the register of companies the names of companies which were struck off the register, on any of the grounds to which s 311 applies, namely for ceasing to carry on business; for failing to have an Irish resident director;[196] for the failure by a public limited company to obtain a certificate to commence business; and could also apply to companies the names of which were voluntarily struck off the register.[197]

(ii) Applicants

[14.079] The persons who may make an application under s 311(8), are the company itself or its members or creditors, on the condition that they are 'aggrieved by the company having been struck off the register'. It is notably not open to a company's officers or directors to make such an application.

---

[195] CA 1963, s 311(8), as amended by C(A)(No2)A 1999, s 49(a) and IFCMPA 2005, s 72.

[196] It should be noted that, when s 311(8) is applied to a company which was struck off the register for failing to have an Irish resident director under C(A)(No2)A 1999, s 43, it is adapted as follows: 'If a company or any member or creditor thereof feels aggrieved by the company having been struck off the register, the court, on an application made (on notice to the registrar) by the company or member or creditor before the expiration of 20 years from the publication in the Companies Registration Office Gazette of the notice aforesaid, may, if satisfied that sub-s (1) or, as the case may be, sub-s (2) of s 43 of the Companies (Amendment) (No 2) Act, 1999, was at the time of the striking off being complied with in relation to the company, or otherwise that it is just that the company be restored to the register, order that the name of the company be restored to the register and upon an office copy of the order being delivered to the registrar for registration, the company shall be deemed to have continued in existence as if its name had not been struck off; and the court may by the order give such directions and make such provisions as seem just for placing the company and all other persons in the same position as nearly as may be [as if the name of the company had not been struck off or make such other order as seems just (and such other order is referred to in sub-s (8A) as an 'alternative order').' CA 1963, s 311(8), as amended by C(A)(No2)A 1999, s 49(a) and IFCMPA 2005, s 72, as adapted and modified by C(A)(No2)A 1999, s 43(15)(b).

[197] See CRO, 'Restoration of a Company to the Register' Information Leaflet No 11 (October 2005), which confirms that s 311(8) is regarded as a basis for restoring to the register the name of a company which was struck off voluntarily.

(iii) Requirements

[14.080] An application under s 311(8) can be made up to 20 years from the date on which the notice that the company has been struck off the register is published in the *CRO Gazette*. The court may make an order for the restoration of a company's name to the register, 'if satisfied that the company was at the time of the striking off carrying on business or otherwise that it is just that the company be restored to the register'.[198] The first aspect of this provision is that an applicant may succeed in having the company's name restored to the register, if it can be shown that the company was carrying on business at the time it was struck off the register. Secondly, the court must be satisfied that it is just that the company's name be restored.

In the case of an application for the restoration of the name of a company which was struck off the register for failing to have an Irish resident director, the first of these requirements is substituted with the requirement that the court must be satisfied that, 'sub-s (1) or, as the case may be, sub-s (2) of s 43 of the Companies (Amendment) (No 2) Act, 1999, was at the time of the striking off being complied with in relation to the company.'[199]

(iv) Procedure

[14.081] An application under s 311(8) must be made on notice to the Registrar and must be made by way of petition.[200] There is nothing in the Companies Acts which requires that an application under s 311(8) must be made on notice to the Registrar, the Revenue Commissioners or the Minister for Finance.

The CRO, which treats s 311(8) as a basis for restoring to the register the names of companies which were struck off the register voluntarily, sets forth the following procedural steps to be followed in an application under that section by a company or a member of a company:[201]

> '(a) Submit a letter to Enforcement Section, CRO, requesting confirmation that the Registrar of Companies has no objection to the restoration of the company.

---

[198] CA 1963, s 311(8), as amended by C(A)(No2)A 1999, s 49(a) and IFCMPA 2005, s 72.

[199] CA 1963, s 311(8), as amended by C(A)(No2)A 1999, s 49(a) and IFCMPA 2005, s 72, as adapted and modified by C(A)(No2)A 1999, s 43(15)(b).

[200] Rules of the Superior Courts, O 75, r 4(n) provides that 'applications to restore a company's name to the register under s 311(8)' shall be by way of petition. The form of the petition is set out in App N to the Rules. See further paras **[14.049]** to **[14.060]**, in the context of applications under s 12B(3).

(o) applications to restore a company's name to the register under s 12(6) of the 1982 Act;

[201] The CRO states that these steps are 'required to be followed by the director, member applying for restoration or the solicitor acting on behalf of the company'. As s 311(8) only applies to creditors, members and the company itself, and a separate section of the Information Leaflet deals with applications by creditors, it is presumed that the steps enumerated are intended for use by members and the company itself. See CRO, 'Restoration of a Company to the Register' Information Leaflet No 11 (October 2005) at p 4.

(b) File all outstanding annual returns (including the accounts which are required to be annexed pursuant to Companies Act 1963–2005) and ensure they are in order ... When the annual returns have been filed and checked, a letter of no objection to the restoration application will issue from CRO, subject to the restoration order including a provision that it will lapse unless delivered by the applicant to the Registrar of Companies within three months of the date of perfection of the restoration order.

(c) Obtain a letter from the Chief State Solicitor's Office ... on behalf of Minister for Finance, stating that there is no objection to the restoration of the company.

(d) Petition the High Court for an order to restore the company. Do not issue the petition until the letters of no objection are to hand.

(e) Following the making of a High Court order restoring the company, deliver to the CRO for registration an attested copy of the order, together with the filing fee, within three months of the date of pronouncement of the order.'[202]

In the case of an application by a creditor under s 311(8) for the restoration to the register of the name of a company which was voluntarily struck off, the CRO requires the same steps, subject to the qualification that steps (a) and (b) above, are substituted with the sole requirement that the creditor must submit a letter to the CRO requesting confirmation that the Registrar has no objection to the restoration of the company, which confirmation will be forthcoming, 'provided the restoration order includes a provision that it will lapse unless it is delivered by the applicant creditor to the Registrar within three months of the date on which the order is pronounced.'[203]

(v) Orders

[14.082] In addition to ordering that the company's name be restored to the register, the court may 'give such directions and make such provisions as seem just for placing the company and all other persons in the same position as nearly as may be as if the name of the company had not been struck off or make such other order as seems just (and such other order is referred to in sub-s (8A) as an 'alternative order').'[204]

The alternative order which may be made under s 311(8A) is as follows:

An alternative order may, if the court considers it appropriate that it should do so, include a provision that, as respects a debt or liability incurred by, or on behalf of, the company during the period when it stood struck off the register, the officers of

---

202 CRO, 'Restoration of a Company to the Register', Information Leaflet No 11 (October 2005) at pp 4 to 5. Available at www.cro.ie.

203 CRO, 'Restoration of a Company to the Register', Information Leaflet No 11 (October 2005) at p 6. See further paras **[14.102]** to **[14.105]** regarding the obligation to deliver the order to the Registrar. See also *Re Barrowland Ltd* [2003] IEHC 54.

204 CA 1963, s 311(8), as amended by C(A)(No2)A 1999, s 49(a) and IFCMPA 2005, s 72.

the company or such one or more of them as is or are specified in the order shall be liable for the whole or part (as the court thinks just) of the debt or liability.[205]

D. Restoration by Registrar

(a) Scope of the statutory provisions

[14.083] There are two statutory provisions which provide for the restoration to the register by the Registrar of Companies of the names of companies which were struck off the register. C(A)A 1982, s 12C[206] provides for the restoration to the register of the names of companies which were struck off for failing to deliver the requisite statement to the Revenue Commissioners.[207] The scope of this provision is clear. Section 12C(1) accordingly provides:

> Without prejudice to the provisions of section 311(8) or 311A(1) of the Principal Act or subsection (3) or (7) or section 12B of this Act, if a member or officer of a company is aggrieved by the fact of the company's having been struck off the register under section 12A(3) of this Act, the registrar of companies, on an application made in the prescribed form by the member or officer before the expiration of 12 months from the publication in the Companies Registration Office Gazette of the notice striking the company name from the register, and provided he has received confirmation from the Revenue Commissioners that all outstanding, if any, statements required by section 882 of the Taxes Consolidation Act 1997 have been delivered to the Revenue Commissioners, may restore the name of the company to the register.[208]

Section 311A[209] provides for the restoration of company names to the register by the Registrar of Companies. This provision does not specify the means and grounds of striking a company's name off the register to which it applies. It merely states, in material part:

> ... if a company feels aggrieved by having been struck off the register, the registrar of companies ..., on an application made in the prescribed form by the company before the expiration of twelve months after the publication in the Companies Registration Office Gazette of the notice striking the company name from the register, and provided he has received all annual returns outstanding, if any, from the company, may restore the name of the company to the register.[210]

---

[205] CA 1963, s 311(8A), as inserted by C(A)(No2)A 1999, s 49(a).

[206] C(A)A 1982, s 12C, as inserted by C(A)(No2)A 1999, s 46.

[207] See further paras **[14.010]** to **[14.012]**.

[208] C(A)A 1982, s 12C(1), as inserted by C(A)(No 2)A 1999, s 46, as amended by IFCMPA 2005, s 72.

[209] CA 1963, s 311A, as inserted by CA 1990, s 246, and as amended by C(A)(No2)A 1999, s 50 and IFCMPA 2005, s 72.

[210] CA 1963, s 311A, as inserted by CA 1990, s 246, and as amended by C(A)(No2)A 1999, s 50 and IFCMPA 2005, s 72.

[14.084] The interpretation of the scope of s 311A advanced by Courtney is that it applies to companies the names of which were struck off on any of the following grounds:[211] failing to deliver annual returns;[212] ceasing to carry on business;[213] or failing to have an Irish resident director.[214] MacCann appears to adopt the interpretation that s 311A applies only in the case of companies of which the names were struck off the register for failing to file annual returns.[215]

The formulation of s 311A is ambiguous as to its scope. In particular, it refers to a company feeling aggrieved by being struck off the register, without specifying the ground on which that company may have been struck off. This can be contrasted with s 12C which specifies that it applies when companies are aggrieved at being struck off under s 12A(3). This may suggest that s 311A should be broader in scope. However, s 311A proceeds to state that the Registrar can only restore a company's name to the register if he has 'received all annual returns outstanding, if any, from the company.' This can be equated with the terminology of s 12C, which provides that the Registrar can only restore a company's name to the register under that provision if he has 'received confirmation from the Revenue Commissioners that all outstanding, if any, statements required by TCA 1997, S 882, have been delivered to the Revenue Commissioners.'

[14.085] If s 311A is read together with s 12C, it seems that s 311A can only permit the restoration of the names of companies which were struck off for failing to deliver annual

---

[211] Courtney, *The Law of Private Companies* (2nd edn, Tottel Publishing, 2002) at para 12.158 ('The second method of restoration by administrative action is provided for by CA 1963, s 311A(1). This applies to applications for restoration to the Registrar where strike-off resulted from any of the other four grounds.' Note that Courtney includes as a distinct ground of striking off, situations where companies have no directors. This is addressed in this chapter, as a ground for the Registrar to believe that the company has ceased to carry on business. See C(A)(No2)A 1999, s 48 ('The fact that, for the time being ... there are no persons recorded in the office of the registrar of companies as being directors of a particular company shall, for the purposes of s 311 of the Principal Act, afford the registrar good grounds for believing that the company is not carrying on business, and for so believing with the cause requisite for the exercise by him or her of the powers conferred by sub-s (1) of that s 311 in relation to the company.') Courtney does not consider whether s 311A applies to striking off the name of a public limited company for failing to obtain a certificate to commence business (C(A)A 1983, s 8(1), as amended by IFCMPA 2005, s 72); or companies the names of which were struck off voluntarily (CA 1963, s 311(5), as amended by IFCMPA 2005, s 72).

[212] C(A)A 1982, s 12(3), as inserted by C(A)(No2)A 1999, s 46, as amended by IFCMPA 2005, s 72. See further paras **[14.003]** to **[14.009]**.

[213] CA 1963, s 311(5), as amended by IFCMPA 2005, s 72. See further para **[14.013]**.

[214] C(A)(No2)A 1999, s 43(15), applying CA 1963, s 311, provides, 'The provisions of s 311 of the Principal Act shall apply for the purposes of this section as they apply for the purposes of that s 311, subject to the following modifications ...' and then sets out alternative formulations of CA 1963, s 311(1), (2) and (8). See paras **[14.014]** to **[14.020]**.

[215] MacCann & Courtney (eds), *Companies Acts 1963–2006* (2nd edn, Tottel Publishing, 2007) at p 573 (annotation to CA 1963, s 311A): 'In the case of striking-off for failure to file annual returns, restoration may be effected by the Registrar upon application by the company itself ...').

returns. This interpretation is reinforced by the following illustration of the alternative interpretation: if s 311A applies to all grounds for striking companies' names off the register, a company which was struck off for failing to have an Irish resident director could have its name restored to the register, subject to the requirement of filing any outstanding annual returns, but it would not be a condition of such restoration that the company have an Irish resident director. It is difficult to imagine this is the intended interpretation of s 311A.

[14.086] As against this, if s 311A was intended to apply only to companies the names of which were struck off the register for failing to file annual returns, it may have been expected that this provision would appear in the same Act as the provision governing that ground for striking companies' names off the register. C(A)A 1982, s 12, applies to failure to file annual returns, whereas s 311 addresses companies which have ceased to carry on business and has also been extended to apply to companies which are struck off for failing to have Irish resident directors and public limited companies which fail to obtain certificates to commence business.[216]

Of course, the legislative history accounts for much of the difficulty in interpretation in this regard. Section 311A was inserted by the CA 1990, whereas the provision for striking companies' names off the register for failing to have Irish resident directors, for example, was only enacted in 1999.[217]

[14.087] The Registrar has adopted the interpretation that his powers under s 311A can be exercised to restore to the register the names of companies which were struck off for failing to file annual returns or which were struck off voluntarily. The CRO website states: 'Where a company has been struck off voluntarily under s 311 Companies Act 1963 or was struck off under s 12(3) Companies (Amendment) Act 1982 for failure to file annual returns, it may apply for restoration by filing within 12 months of the date of dissolution.'[218]

[14.088] Whatever the precise scope of s 311A, there can be no dispute that it applies to companies, the names of which were struck off for failing to file annual returns. However, the basis for permitting companies which were struck off voluntarily under s 311, to make an application under s 311A, without permitting companies which were struck off under s 311 for ceasing to carry on business, is not clear. If s 311A does apply to companies which were struck off under s 311, there is no indication in the legislation that there can be differentiation between the grounds on which the Registrar can strike companies' names off the register under s 311. This interpretation, which has been adopted by the CRO, seems particularly curious, when one considers that the power of the Registrar to strike a company off the register for ceasing to carry on business under s 311 has existed in largely the same form since 1963, and was in existence when s 311A was inserted by the CA 1990. By contrast, the practice of striking companies' names off the register voluntarily, does not have any express legislative basis. How, as a

---

[216] See further paras **[14.013]** to **[14.024]**.

[217] C(A)(No2)A 1999, s 43(15). See paras **[14.014]** to **[14.020]**.

[218] Business Termination: Company: Restoration: Administrative at www.cro.ie. See CRO, 'Restoration of a Company to the Register' Information Leaflet No 11 (October 2005) at www.cro.ie.

matter of legislative interpretation, s 311A could be applied in the latter instance, but not in the other cases to which s 311 expressly applies, is not at all clear. However, the interpretation adopted by the Registrar is the administrative reality of which companies should be aware. The analysis in this chapter is therefore premised on this interpretation and s 311A is treated as applying to companies the names of which were either struck off the register voluntarily, or for failing to file annual returns.

[14.089] As the CA 1963–2006 are applied by the Registrar at present, if a company's name has been struck off the register involuntarily, on any ground other than failing to deliver an annual return, or failing to deliver the requisite statement to the Revenue Commissioners, restoration by the Registrar will not be possible.

It should be noted that the power of the Registrar to restore companies to the register under s 311A is expressed to be 'Without prejudice to the provisions of s 311(8) of this Act or sub-s (3) or (7) of s 12B, or sub-s (1) of s 12C, of the Companies (Amendment) Act 1982.'[219] Similarly, the power to restore under C(A)A 1982, s 12C, is 'Without prejudice to the provisions of s 311(8) or 311A(1) of the Principal Act or sub-s (3) or (7) of s 12B of this Act'.[220] CA 1963, s 311(8),[221] and C(A)A 1982, s 12B(3) and (7),[222] provide for the restoration of a company's name to the register of companies by the court. While restoration by the Registrar may not be possible, this will not prejudice any right to make an application to court to have a company's name restored to the register.[223]

(b) Applicants

[14.090] The persons who may apply to the Registrar for the restoration of a company's name to the register vary depending upon the basis of the application. If the company's name was struck off for failing to deliver the requisite statement to the Revenue Commissioners,[224] an officer or member of the company who is 'aggrieved' by the company's name being struck off the register, may apply to the Registrar for its name to be restored.[225]

[14.091] The decision of the Scottish Court of Sessions in *Inner House Conti v UeberseeBank AG*[226] suggests that the grievance does not have to exist at the date on which the company is struck off, but can arise subsequently. The member who sought to

---

[219] CA 1963, s 311A(1), as inserted by CA 1990, s 246 and as amended by C(A)(No2)A 1999, s 50.

[220] C(A)A 1982, s 12C(1), as inserted by C(A)(No2)A 1999, s 46.

[221] CA 1963, s 311(8), as amended by C(A)(No2)A 1999, s 49 and IFCMPA 2005, s 72.

[222] C(A)A 1982, s 12B(3) and (7), as inserted by C(A)(No2)A 1999, s 46 and amended by IFCMPA 2005, s 72.

[223] For the rules and procedures applicable to restorations by the court, see further paras **[14.040]** to **[14.082]**.

[224] See further paras **[14.010]** to **[14.012]**.

[225] See C(A)A 1982, s 12C, as inserted by C(A)(No 2)A 1999, s 46.

[226] *Inner House Conti v UeberseeBank AG*, (2000) TLR, 15 March 2000.

have a company's name restored to the register in that case had in fact chaired the meeting at which it was resolved to have the company's name struck off the register voluntarily, but a grievance which subsequently arose as a result of the company's dissolution was sufficient to give that member standing to seek to have the company's name restored to the register. Lord Prosser stated:

> 'If at a subsequent date it emerged in some way that there was a benefit which would otherwise have accrued to him, it did not appear to be contrary to the ordinary use of language to say that at that later date he was aggrieved, not by his original act of striking off the company, but by the fact that at the date of the new event, the company had been struck off.'

The language of s 12C is also open to this interpretation. It refers to a member or officer who 'is aggrieved by the fact of the company's having been struck off the register'. This could encompass a grievance which arises as a consequence of the company's name being struck off, rather than just grievances related directly to the fact that the company's name was struck off.

[14.092] A further point which should be noted is that the person must have been an officer or member of the company at the date on which it was struck off the register. A person who purports to acquire shares in a company after the date on which its name was struck off the register will be unlikely to have standing to apply to have the company's name restored.

In *Re New Timbiqui Gold Mines Ltd*,[227] this issue arose for consideration. The person seeking to have the company's name restored to the register in that case acquired a number of bearer shares in a company some four years after its name was struck off the register for ceasing to carry on business under s 353 of the Companies Act 1948 (England). Section 353(6) permitted the following persons to apply to court for the restoration of the company's name: 'a company or any member or creditor' of the company who 'feels aggrieved by the company having been struck off the register.' The petitioner sought to argue that the provision pre-supposed the existence of a company, members and creditors, the fact that the company had been struck off notwithstanding, and that there was:

> '... no reason to restrict that language to persons who were members or creditors of the company at the date when it was struck off; but that it is legitimate and it would be sensible to construe the language so as to extend to persons who have become members or creditors of the company since the company has been struck off, in this sense, that if the company had not been struck off, having regard to the course of events which in fact occurred, the particular person would have been a member or would have been a creditor of the company.'[228]

As against this, it was argued that a person could not become a member or creditor of a company which did not exist. Adopting the view that, 'I think that the right way to approach this sort of problem of construction is to adopt that interpretation which would give a working effect to the subsection without extending the operation of inference or

---

227 See *Re New Timbiqui Gold Mines Ltd* [1961] 1 Ch 319.
228 *Re New Timbiqui Gold Mines Ltd* [1961] 1 Ch 319 at 325.

imagination further than is necessary for that purpose',[229] Buckley J reached the following conclusion:

> 'Although I think the point is a difficult one, I reach the conclusion that, in order to qualify to be a petitioner under this subsection, the petitioner must show that, at the date when the company was dissolved, he was a member or a creditor; and that anyone who, whether in ignorance of the dissolution of the company or otherwise, purports to become a member or creditor of the company afterwards is not a member or a creditor within the subsection.'[230]

The Court further noted that, even if this conclusion were flawed, there was a suggestion that the petitioners in *Re New Timbiqui Gold Mines Ltd*[231] were aware at the date on which they acquired the shares, that the company's name had been struck off the register and they could not claim to be aggrieved by that fact. While this suggestion was disputed, Buckley J noted:

> 'It seems to me it would be impossible for such a person to say that he was aggrieved. He would, in fact, be an officious interloper who, with knowledge of the fact that the company has been struck off, chooses to buy his shares or acquire the debt in the hope that he can get something out of it. Such a person, in my judgment, could not genuinely be said to be aggrieved by the company having been struck off the register.'[232]

This decision indicates that a person must be a member or creditor of a company on the date on which that company's name was struck off the register, to have standing to apply for the restoration of that company's name. Even if this interpretation is not adopted in Ireland in the context of s 12C, it is highly unlikely that a person who acquires shares in a company, knowing its name has been struck off the register, could bring an application to have that company's name restored to the register.

In the case of an application to restore a company's name to the register under s 311A, it is only the company itself who can bring the application. Section 311A can be invoked 'if a company feels aggrieved by having been struck off the register'. The artificiality of this language was highlighted clearly by Buckley J in *Re New Timbiqui Gold Mines Ltd*[233] in the context of s 353(6) of the Companies Act 1948 (England):

> 'The opening words of the subsection refer to a company or a member or creditor feeling aggrieved by the company having been struck off the register, which creates a somewhat artificial state of affairs in which it has to be assumed that the company or some member or creditor thereof can still be properly so described although the company has been struck off the register and consequently has become dissolved. It is one of the anomalies of company law that a company which has been dissolved can petition the court under this section to have its name restored to the register. The opening words of the subsection clearly relate to a

---

[229] *Re New Timbiqui Gold Mines Ltd* [1961] 1 Ch 319 at 326.

[230] *Re New Timbiqui Gold Mines Ltd* [1961] 1 Ch 319 at 326 to 327.

[231] *Re New Timbiqui Gold Mines Ltd* [1961] 1 Ch 319.

[232] *Re New Timbiqui Gold Mines Ltd* [1961] 1 Ch 319 at 327.

[233] *Re New Timbiqui Gold Mines Ltd* [1961] 1 Ch 319 at 324.

date after the company has been struck off and, therefore, they necessarily involve some latitude in the construction of the reference to 'a company or any member or creditor thereof.'

Although a company ceases to have legal existence at the date of its dissolution, it remains the only potential applicant for its restoration by the Registrar under CA 1963, s 311A.

(c) Requirements

[14.093] There is one very important pre-condition to an application to the Registrar to have a company's name restored to the register under both C(A)A 1982, s 12C, and CA 1963, s 311A. Such an application can only be made within 12 months of the date on which the notice that the company's name was struck off the register was published in the *CRO Gazette*. The Registrar has no jurisdiction to entertain an application for the restoration of a company's name beyond that period of time. Once 12 months expires from the dissolution of the company by means of the publication of the notice in the *CRO Gazette*, an application must be made to court before a company's name can be restored to the register.

[14.094] There are four further conditions that must be met before the Registrar will restore the name of a company to the register under s 12C. First, an aggrieved officer or member who wishes to have a company's name restored under s 12C, must make an application on Form H1R to have the company's name restored.[234] Form H1R merely requires the full name of the company and the following statements:

- 'I hereby apply for the restoration of the above named company to the register of companies under s 12C of the Companies (Amendment) Act, 1982 (substituted by s 46 of the Companies (Amendment)(No 2)Act, 1999)'; and

- 'The company was dissolved pursuant to s 12A(3) of the Companies (Amendment) Act, 1982 (substituted by s 46 of the Companies (Amendment) (No 2) Act, 1999) on [date on which the company was dissolved].'

This Form must state the date, the name, address and telephone number, of the presenter. It must also be signed by a director or secretary of the former company and state their name and address in full.[235]

Second, any and all outstanding statements that are required to be delivered to the Revenue Commissioners under TCA 1997, s 882 must be delivered, and the Revenue Commissioners must confirm this fact.[236] It should be noted that s 12D specifically allows the Revenue Commissioners to furnish information to the Registrar which may

---

[234] Form H1R available at www.cro.ie.

[235] Note that, even though it is only officers or members of the company, rather than the company itself, who can make an application under s 12C, it does not appear necessary that the presenter sign Form H1R, as the only signature line appears next to the title of director or secretary.

[236] C(A)A 1982, s 12C(1), as inserted by C(A)(No2)A 1999, s 46.

help in the discharge of his functions under s 12C, any obligations as to secrecy or confidentiality notwithstanding:

> If the question of whether a statement which a company has failed to deliver to the Revenue Commissioners in accordance with s 882(3) of the Taxes Consolidation Act 1997, has or has not been subsequently delivered to them falls to be determined for the purpose of the exercise by the registrar of companies of any of the powers under ss 12A to 12C of this Act, the Revenue Commissioners may, notwithstanding any obligations as to secrecy or other restriction upon disclosure of information imposed by or under statute or otherwise, disclose to the registrar any information in their possession required by him for the purpose of that determination.[237]

Third, any fees prescribed for such an application must be paid.[238] A fourth requirement is stipulated by the Registrar on Form H1R, although it is not specified as a requirement in s 12C. According to the Registrar, all outstanding annual returns must be filed before an application under s 12C will succeed.[239]

[14.095] For the purposes of an application to restore a company's name to the register under s 311A, there are also three conditions to be met. First, the company must make an application on Form H1 to the Registrar.[240] Second, the Registrar must receive all outstanding annual returns from the company.[241] Third, the company must pay the fee prescribed for the application.[242]

Form H1 requires the name of the company to be stated in full, and requires the applicant to state that they are applying to have the company restored under CA 1963, s 311A. The date on which the company was dissolved must be inserted. The Form must state the date and, the name, address and telephone number, of the presenter. It must also be signed by a director or secretary of the former company and state their name and address in full.

[14.096] In respect of both applications under C(A)A 1982, s 12C, and CA 1963, s 311A, it is possible to avail of a 'fast track' process at the CRO. This procedure requires an officer of the company to attend at the CRO cashier between 10am and 11am or between 14.15 and 15.15 (presumably on a business day) with all outstanding documentation and fees, informing the cashier that he wishes to avail of the 'fast track process'. He will then be required to complete a form to apply for this process and, after waiting up to two hours, during which time any necessary additional forms (such as

---

[237] C(A)A 1982, s 12D, as inserted by C(A)(No2)A 1999, s 46.

[238] C(A)A 1982, s 12C(2), as inserted by C(A)(No2)A 1999, s 46. The fees for such an application are €300. See reg 4 of the Companies (Fees) Order 2000, as amended by reg 7 of the Companies (Fees) Order 2001.

[239] See Form H1R at www.cro.ie.

[240] See www.cro.ie.

[241] CA 1963, s 311A(1), as inserted by CA 1990, s 246, as amended by C(A)(No2)A 1999, s 50.

[242] CA 963, s 311A(2), as inserted by CA 1990, s 246. Note that, pursuant to the Companies (Fees) Order 1997, reg 4 as amended by the Companies (Fees) Order 2001, reg 6 the fee for such an application is €300.

Forms B2/B10) will be completed and fees paid, if all documentation is in order, the company's name will be restored to the register.[243] It may be noted that, with the decentralisation of the CRO to Carlow, a process which commenced in July 2007, the utility of this 'fast track' process may be diminished.[244]

(d) Restoration

[14.097] When an applicant for the restoration of a company's name to the register under C(A)A 1982, s 12C, or CA 1963, s 311A, has satisfied all of the requirements listed in those provisions, the Registrar 'may restore the name of the company to the register.'[245] It is clear that even if all of the documentation is correct, all necessary returns have been filed, and fees paid, the Registrar retains a discretion not to restore the company's name to the register. There is no indication of the factors which should be taken into account by the Registrar in exercising this discretion. The discretion of the Registrar on an application under s 12C or s 311A is not wholly consistent with the second clause of both provisions, which provide:

> Upon the registration of an application under sub-s (1) of this section and on payment of such fees as may be prescribed, the company shall be deemed to have continued in existence as if its name had not been struck off.[246]

These provisions suggest that, upon the registration of an application which complies with the requirements of the sections, and payment of the relevant fees, the company's name is automatically restored to the register. This could not be the intended interpretation of these provisions. The CRO documents and forms make it clear that it is only when the relevant fees have been paid, documents filed and application duly completed, that a company's name will be restored to the register. It is suggested that, what ss 12C(2) and 311(A)(2) intend to convey is that, upon the restoration of the company's name to the register, it shall be deemed to have continued in existence as if its name had not been struck off. The registration of an application should not be synonymous with the company's name being restored to the register.

E. Effect of restoration

[14.098] In relation to every ground on which a company's name may be restored to the register by the court, when the court makes an order restoring a company's name, 'the

---

[243] See http://www.cro.ie/en/business-termination-fast-track-restoration.aspx. See also CRO, 'Restoration of a Company to the Register' Information Leaflet No 11 (October 2005).

[244] See announcement by Tanaiste on 30 July 2007 welcoming the commencement of the relocation of the CRO to Carlow (www.entemp.ie.)

[245] C(A)A 1982, s 12C(1), as inserted by C(A)(No2)A 1999, s 46, and CA 1963, s 311A(1), as inserted by CA 1990, s 246, as amended by C(A)(No2)A 1999, s 50.

[246] C(A)A 1982, s 12C(2), as inserted by C(A)(No2)A 1999, s 46, and CA 1963, s 311A(2), as inserted by CA 1990, s 246 (the only difference in the formulation of the two provisions is that the latter omits the words 'of this section' after 'sub-s (1)'.)

company shall be deemed to have continued in existence as if its name had not been struck off.'[247] The same effect ensues when a company's name is restored to the register by the Registrar of Companies.[248]

In addition, it should be recalled that a court, in making an order for the restoration of a company's name, under s 12B(3), (7) or 311(8) may:

> ... give such directions and make such provisions as seem just for placing the company and all other persons in the same position as nearly as may be as if the name of the company had not been struck off or make such other order as seems just.[249]

Sections 12B(4) and 311(8A) further specify that, in relation to the orders that a court may make to place the company and other persons in the same position as if the company had not been struck off:

> An alternative order may, if the court considers it appropriate that it should do so, include a provision that, as respects a debt or liability incurred by, or on behalf of, the company during the period when it stood struck off the register, the officers of the company or such one or more of them as is or are specified in the order shall be liable for the whole or a part (as the court thinks just) of the debt or liability.[250]

The legislative provisions regarding the effect of the restoration of a company's name to the register by the court are therefore identical, whatever the means by which the court came to restore the company's name.[251]

[14.099] The consequences of the restoration of a company's name to the register have been addressed in a number of decisions of the Irish High Court and Supreme Court. In *Re Amantiss Enterprises Ltd*[252] the name of Amantiss Enterprises Ltd ('the Company') was struck off the register on 19 May 1993 for failing to file returns with the CRO. Unaware of this fact, the members and creditors of the Company placed it in voluntary liquidation by resolution dated 1 April 1994. On 4 December 1996, the Company (in voluntary liquidation) was one of three plaintiffs which issued plenary proceedings against a number of defendants ('the Notice Parties'), alleging anti-competitive practices and conspiracy which, it was claimed, drove the plaintiffs out of business.

---

[247] CA 1963, s 311(8), as amended by C(A)(No2)A 1999, s 49(a) and IFCMPA 2005, s 72; C(A)A 1982, s 12B(3), as inserted by C(A)(No2)A 1999, s 46, as amended by IFCMPA 2005, s 72; C(A)A 1982, s 12B(7), as inserted by C(A)(No2)A 1999, s 46.

[248] C(A)A 1982, s 12C(2), as inserted by C(A)(No2)A 1999, s 46, and CA 1963, s 311A(2), as inserted by CA 1990, s 246. See further para **[14.097]**.

[249] C(A)A 1982, s 12B(7), as inserted by C(A)(No2)A 1999, s 46; C(A)A 1982, s 12B(3), as inserted by C(A)(No2)A 1999, s 46, as amended by IFCMPA 2005, s 72; and CA 1963, s 311(8), as amended by C(A)(No2)A 1999, s 49(a) and IFCMPA 2005, s 72.

[250] C(A)A 1982, s 12B(4), as inserted by C(A)(No2)A 1999, s 46; and CA 1963, s 311(8A), as inserted by C(A)(No2)A 1999, s 49(a).

[251] It should be noted that the 'alternative orders' provided for by ss 12B(4) and 311(8A) cannot be made in the case of companies which are restored to the register by the Registrar of Companies under ss 12C or 311A.

[252] *Re Amantiss Enterprises Ltd, Framus Ltd v CRH plc* [2000] 2 ILRM 177.

On 27 April 1999, one of the Notice Parties issued a motion to strike out the Company's name from the plenary proceedings, and to strike out those portions of the pleadings which related to the Company's claim, as the Company had been dissolved. The Petitioner (an officer and member of the Company) issued a petition to restore the company's name to the register under C(A)A 1982, s 12(6), as it then was.[253] In this petition, the Petitioner claimed not to have been aware that the company's name was struck off the register until service of the motion to strike its name from the plenary proceedings.

The defendants to the plenary proceedings appeared as notice parties ('the Notice Parties') to the petition to restore the company's name, claiming, not that they resisted the restoration *per se*, but stating their objections to any order of the court which would have the effect of validating retrospectively things done by or on behalf of the company during the period in which its name was struck off the register. The Petitioner's case was that the effect of restoration would be to validate all things done in the company's name since the date on which it was struck off the register, including the voluntary liquidation and the initiation of plenary proceedings against the Notice Parties.

The determination of the Court hinged on the interpretation of the phrase, 'the company shall be deemed to have continued in existence as if its name had not been struck off'.

[14.100] The Court considered the submission of the Notice Parties that the Court may make a specific order conferring validity retrospectively on acts done by the company during the period of dissolution, in exercise of the power of the court to '… give such directions and make such provisions as seem just for placing the company and all other persons in the same position as nearly as may be as if the name of the company had not been struck off or make such other order as seems just,' but that the fact that a company is deemed to have continued in existence, does not have that effect. The Notice Parties contended that the words, 'the company shall be deemed to have continued in existence as if its name had not been struck off' have the effect '… merely of restoring the status of incorporation of the company and its identity but do not have the effect of validating retrospectively any acts done between dissolution and restoration to the register.'[254]

O'Neill J considered the submissions of the Petitioner and the Notice Parties and concluded:

> '… the words "the company shall be deemed to have continued in existence as if its name had not been struck off" have the effect of validating retrospectively all acts done in the name or on behalf of the company during the period between its dissolution and the restoration of its name to the register, and that the words "and the Court may by order give such directions and make such provisions as seem just

---

[253] Note that C(A)A 1982, s 12(6), as it existed before the enactment of C(A)(No2)A 1999, s 46, was largely identical to the current provisions of s 12B(3), s 12B(7) and 311(8), insofar as is relevant in the present context, contained exactly the same provision that: '… upon an office copy of the order being delivered to the registrar for registration, the company shall be deemed to have continued in existence as if its name had not been struck off; and the court may by the order give such directions and make such provisions as seem just for placing the company and all other persons in the same position as nearly as may be as if the name of the company had not been struck off.'

[254] *Re Amantiss Enterprises Ltd, Framus Ltd v CRH plc* [2000] 2 ILRM 177 at 187.

for placing the company and all other persons in the same position as nearly as may be as if the name of the company had not been struck off'" are not expository qualifying the scope of the proceeding general word but are complementary only to those general words so as to enable the Court to achieve to the fullest extent consistent with justice the "as you were" position of the company.'[255]

The Court further concluded:

'In my view the plain and very reasonable and sensible intendment of sub-s (6) of s 12 is to preserve the validity of transactions entered into during a period of dissolution where frequently that dissolution is unknown to either the company and its officers or third parties dealing with it, and who conduct their business with each other and enter into engagements with each other on the basis that the company enjoys lawful existence. To remove legal validity from all of these transactions in circumstances where the parties to them at the time of their making intended them to have legal validity would in a great many instances work injustices and would provide the unscrupulous with much opportunity for mischief. I have no doubt that the legislature, in selecting the very clear language used in sub-s (6) of s 12, intended that such unfortunate consequences would not occur by reason of an unintended dissolution where no orderly process of winding up had taken place.'[256]

[14.101] The effect of the decision in *Re Amantiss Enterprises Ltd* is that anything that is done in the name of a company while that company's name is struck off the register, is retrospectively validated as soon as that company's name is restored to the register, provided the company has not been wound up during that period of time. It is not necessary for a court to make a specific order validating things done in the company's name during its period of dissolution. That validation occurs automatically upon the restoration of the company's name. As O'Neill J determined, '... an order restoring a company to the register under s 12(6) of the Companies (Amendment) Act 1982 has the automatic effect of rendering valid in law all acts done by or on behalf of the company or in its name during the period from its dissolution until restoration to the register.'[257]

[14.102] Another aspect of the effect of a court order for the restoration of a company's name to the register was addressed in *Re Barrowland Ltd*.[258] In that case, the order for the restoration of a company's name was not delivered to the Registrar until more than five and a half years after the date on which the order was made. The Registrar was concerned as to the correct approach to take in such cases, as a practice had apparently developed of waiting considerable periods of time before delivering court orders for the restoration of company's names to the Registrar. The Registrar therefore sought the directions of the Court. In particular, the Registrar sought the directions of the Court as to whether he was obliged to accept and register such orders without any further order of the Court, or whether a further Court order extending time or confirming the original order was necessary, in light of the significant period of time that lapsed since the making of the original order of restoration.

---

[255] *Re Amantiss Enterprises Ltd, Framus Ltd v CRH plc* [2000] 2 ILRM 177 at 187 at 190.

[256] [2000] 2 ILRM 177 at 187 at 191.

[257] [2000] 2 ILRM 177 at 194.

[258] *Re Barrowland Ltd* [2003] IEHC 54.

Smyth J noted that:

> 'The Registrar was of the view that as registration is an integral part of the restoration process that by necessary implication, the order ought to be delivered to the Companies Registration Office for registration within a reasonable time from the date of its perfection.'[259]

The Court considered that the words: 'Upon an office copy of the order being delivered to the Registrar for registration' are:

> 'a clear indication by the Oireachtas that it was not sufficient merely for the Court to make the pronouncement and make its order but that an office copy of the order should be delivered to the Registrar and it is upon the completion of both the making of the Court order and its delivery to the Registrar that the company is deemed to have continued in existence.'

The Court further noted, 'The Order of the Court must not merely be pronounced in Court, but perfected in written form and delivered to the Registrar to bring into operation the deemed provision or consequence.'[260]

[14.103] It is significant to note that it is only upon the delivery of the court order to the Registrar that the company shall be restored to the register and deemed to have continued in existence. With regard to the time that may be allowed to lapse between the date of the court order and its delivery to the Registrar, Smyth J. stated:

> 'As the effect of an Order which is complied with as to its terms is to validate retrospectively all acts done in the name and on behalf of the company during the period between its dissolution and the restoration of its name to the registrar: it follows that it is imperative that the copy of the Order of the Court be lodged as soon as ever possible with the Registrar of Companies. The Court Order does not act prospectively, the retrospective date of effect is the date not of the making of the Court Order but of compliance with it. However as the Order can only be made if the Court is satisfied with a given state of facts on a given day it is mandatory that the shortest interval possible should exist between the date of the perfected Court Order and a copy of its being lodged with the Registrar of Companies.'

[14.104] This decision highlights clearly that it is 'imperative' and 'mandatory' that a court order for the restoration of a company's name must be delivered to the Registrar 'as soon as ever possible', with the 'shortest interval possible' between the date of the court order and its delivery to the Registrar. With regard to failures to comply with this requirement, Smyth J stated unequivocally: 'In my judgment the Registrar ought not to be bound to register restoration orders which are not lodged with him forthwith' and, more specifically, that:

> 'Orders not lodged forthwith and at the very outside within three months should and do automatically lapse. In such circumstances a renewed fresh application to the Court is necessary: such must not only comply with this subsection but also aver to the exact state of the business and affairs of the company as from the date of the pronouncement of the lapsed Order and give a full and satisfactory

---

[259] *Re Barrowland Ltd* [2003] IEHC 54.

[260] [2003] IEHC 54.

explanation to the Court as to why its original Order was not complied with in the interim.'[261]

[14.105] A company is therefore only restored to the register, and to corporate existence, when the court order so directing is delivered to the Registrar. If the order is not so delivered as soon as possible and, at the latest, within three months of that order, the order will lapse. The applicant will then have to make a fresh application to court for the restoration of the company's name, which application must overcome the additional hurdle of explaining why the original order was not complied with. Every applicant for a court order to restore the name of a company to the register, must be vigilant in ensuring that this order is delivered to the Registrar promptly, if they wish to avoid the unnecessary expense, inconvenience and risk of having to make a second application to the court.

[14.106] The meaning of a company being 'deemed to have continued in existence as if its name had not been struck off' was again considered in *Richmond Building Products Ltd v Soundgables Ltd.*[262] The second and fourth defendants were directors of a company the name of which was struck off the register of companies on 25 August 2000 (the first defendant). On dates between 26 August 2000 and 31 December, 2000, the plaintiff sold and delivered goods to the first defendant. The first defendant's name was restored to the register on 20 April 2001. By summary summons dated 28 August 2001, the plaintiffs sought to recover payment from the directors, among others.

[14.107] While the application to restore the company's name could have been made to the Registrar under s 12C(1), the Court stated that the matter proceeded on the basis that the application was made under C(A)A 1982, s 12B(3), as inserted by C(A)(No2)A 1999, s 46, although the Court also acknowledged that documents produced in evidence in the case suggested that the application may have been made under s 12C(1). The Court did not resolve this issue, but stated that, 'this it seems to me makes no difference to the issue before me as if the application to restore was made under the latter provision the court is nonetheless deemed to have continued in existence as if its name had not been struck off.' [263] The Court also considered that the application for restoration of the company's name could have been made pursuant to s 311A to the Registrar and stated in this regard, 'Again the effect will be the same as a company so restored is deemed to have continued in existence as if its name had not been struck off.' [264] This demonstrates that the effect of the restoration of a company's name to the register is the same, however that restoration is brought about.

Finnegan P considered the meaning of this effect of restoration of a company's name to the register, concluding that, 'I am satisfied that the order restoring the company had the

---

[261] *Re Barrowland Ltd* [2003] IEHC 54.

[262] *Richmond Building Products Ltd v Soundgables Ltd* [2005] 1 ILRM 497.

[263] [2005] 1 ILRM 497.

[264] [2005] 1 ILRM 497.

effect of releasing directors from the personal liability which they incurred while the company was struck off.'[265] The Court further concluded:

> On the authorities I am satisfied that the effect of the restoration of the first named defendant and whether effected under the Companies (Amendment) Act 1982, ss 12(3), 12B, or 12C, is that the personal liability which might otherwise have attached to the directors is extinguished.

The plaintiff therefore failed in the action against the directors of the company. On the authority of *Richmond Building Products Ltd v Soundgables Ltd*, while a director of a dissolved company may incur personal liability as a result of things done in the company's name during the period of dissolution, one of the effects of the restoration of the company's name to the register, is that this liability is extinguished and the company is deemed never to have ceased to exist.

[14.108] An important point of distinction that should be noted about restoration by the Registrar and restoration by a court is that the former does not alter the rights or liabilities of the company that may have arisen during the period between the company's dissolution and the date of the restoration of its name to the register. In both s 12C and s 133(A) there are provisions to the effect that:

> Subject to any order made by the court in the matter, the restoration of the name of a company to the register under this section shall not affect the rights or liabilities of the company in respect of any debt or obligation incurred, or any contract entered into by, to, with or on behalf of, the company between the date of its dissolution and the date of such restoration.[266]

[14.109] The plaintiff in *Richmond Building Products Ltd v Soundgables Ltd*, sought to rely on s 12C(3) in support of its claim against the directors of a company which had been struck off the register. The defendants in that case had purchased goods from the plaintiff, on behalf of the dissolved company, before its restoration to the register. While it was not resolved in that case whether s 12C was applicable at all, Finnegan P considered the terms of s 12C(3) and concluded: 'This provision does not avail the plaintiff. It enables the company to sue and be sued on any contract entered into by it or on its behalf: it has nothing to say as to the position of those purporting to act on the company's behalf.'[267]

The Court further noted that the interpretation advanced by the plaintiffs, that the restoration did not affect the personal liability of the company's directors, 'ignores the provisions of s 12C(2) which provides as follows: "Upon the registration of an application under sub-s (1) of this section and upon payment of such fees as may be prescribed, the company should be deemed to have continued in existence as if its name had not been struck off".'[268]

---

[265] *Richmond Building Products Ltd v Soundgables Ltd* [2005] 1 ILRM 497.

[266] C(A)A 1982, s 12C(3), as inserted by C(A)(No2)A 1999, s 46, and CA 1963, s 311A(3), as inserted by CA 1990, s 246.

[267] *Richmond Building Products Ltd v Soundgables Ltd* [2005] 1 ILRM 497. See further para **[14.106]**.

[268] *Richmond Building Products Ltd v Soundgables Ltd* [2005] 1 ILRM 497.

The reference in s 12C(3) to the rights and liabilities of the company does not therefore have any bearing on the rights or liabilities of the company's directors or members.

Chapter 15

CRIMINAL PROSECUTIONS

[15.001] The CA 1963–2006 contain a wide range of offences, some of which may be prosecuted only summarily; and many of which may be prosecuted on indictment or summarily.

The rules and procedures that are applicable to the prosecution of these offences will vary depending on whether the offence is prosecuted summarily or on indictment; it is beyond the scope of this book to examine all such rules and procedures.[1]

The aim of this chapter, is to consider certain legal and procedural questions that are unique to the prosecution of offences under the CA 1963–2006. Insofar as the rules of criminal procedure more generally are considered, emphasis is placed on the procedures applicable in the District Court, being the jurisdiction in which most offences under the Companies Acts are tried.[2]

A. Nature of offences

[15.002] An offence may be a summary offence or an indictable offence. The distinction is an important one, as it determines the manner in which offences can be tried. Summary offences may be tried by courts of summary jurisdiction, ie the District Court, before a judge alone. Indictable offences may be tried on indictment before a judge and a jury, in the Circuit Court or the Central Criminal Court.[3] This is subject to the qualification that indictable offences may generally be tried before the District Court in certain circumstances, such as where the offence is of a minor nature, and the accused and the DPP consent to such trial. There is a third category of offences, which are offences that may be tried summarily or on indictment.

[15.003] The CA 1963–2006 contain approximately 138 offences that may be prosecuted on indictment.[4] However, these offences may generally be tried either

---

1. For a more general analysis of the procedure applicable to criminal prosecutions, see Walsh, *Criminal Procedure* (Thomson Round Hall, 2002). See also District Court Rules 1997 (as amended).

2. See ODCE, *Annual Report 2003*: 'ODCE has deemed it appropriate in a number of cases to initiate criminal proceedings on a summary basis, and this is likely to continue to be a primary enforcement option for the foreseeable future.'

3. See generally Walsh, *Criminal Procedure* (Thomson Round Hall, 2002) at p 10.

4. See ODCE, List of Indictable Offences pursuant to the Companies Acts 1963–2005, available at www.odce.ie.

summarily or on indictment. By way of example, CA 1963, s 187(9) provides that a person who acts as auditor while disqualified pursuant to that section from so acting:

> shall be guilty of an offence and liable (a) on summary conviction, to a fine not exceeding €1,904.61, and, for continued contravention, to a daily default fine not exceeding €63.49, or (b) on conviction on indictment, to a fine not exceeding €6,348.69 and, for continued contravention, to a daily default fine not exceeding €126.97.[5]

The distinction between summary offences and indictable offences is not therefore a neat one, and has been described as follows:

> 'The choice between summary trial and trial on indictment in such cases would appear to lie with the prosecutor. If he opts for the former then the offence is summary, and if he opts for the latter the offence is indictable. It is almost as if they are two distinct criminal offences sharing the same substantive definition and differing only in the degree of punishment that may be imposed on conviction.'[6]

These offences may be referred to as 'hybrid' offences.

One area of company law in which the distinction between summary and indictable offences has some relevance relates to the duty of an auditor to report to the DCE if he forms the opinion that there are reasonable grounds for believing an indictable offence has been committed.[7] In this regard, the ODCE advises that, even if it is the policy of the DCE and DPP to prosecute certain offences summarily, 'this is not a matter which should affect the formation of the auditor's opinion in respect of the reporting of any suspected indictable offence.'[8] Therefore, unless and until a decision is taken to prosecute an offence summarily, it is to be regarded as an indictable offence for the purposes of the auditors' report.[9]

[15.004] Summary proceedings under the Companies Acts may be prosecuted by the DCE or the DPP. CA 1990, s 240(4), accordingly provides: 'Summary proceedings in relation to an offence under the Companies Acts may be brought and prosecuted by the Director of Public Prosecutions or the Director.'[10] The formulation of this provision is clearly wide enough to encompass the summary prosecution of offences which may be

---

5   CA 1990, s 187(9), as amended by CA 1990, s 240(7), as inserted by CLEA 2001, s 104(c). See Ch **7**.

6   Walsh, *Criminal Procedure* (Thomson Round Hall, 2002) at p 11.

7   CA 1990, s 194(5). See Ch **7**.

8   ODCE, *Revised Guidance on the Duty of Auditors to Report Suspected Indictable Offences to the Director of Corporate Enforcement* (Decision Notice D/2006/2) at paras 9.1 to 9.4. Available at www.odce.ie.

9   Note that a similar approach applies with regard to the power of arrest without warrant conferred by the Criminal Law Act 1997, s 4. To exercise that power, it is sufficient if the offence is one which could be punished by a maximum of five years imprisonment: the person carrying out the arrest does not appear to be bound to consider whether it is possible that the offence may be tried summarily. See further paras **[15.028]** to **[15.032]**.

10   See also CLEA 2001, s 12(1)(a), which provides that one of the functions of the DCE is, '… to enforce the Companies Acts, including by the prosecution of offences by way of summary proceedings.'

tried either on indictment or summarily.[11] Certain offences under the Companies Acts may also be prosecuted summarily by the CRO.[12]

A 'summary trial' was described in *Clune v DPP*[13] as follows:

> 'A summary trial is a trial which could be undertaken with some degree of expedition and informality without departing from the principles of justice. The purpose of summary procedures for minor offences is to ensure that such offences are charged and tried as soon as reasonably possible after their alleged commission so that the recollection of witnesses may still be reasonably clear, that the attendance of witnesses and presentation of evidence may be procured and presented without great difficulty or complexity, and that there should be minimal delay in the disposal of the work load of minor offences.'

Only the DPP can prosecute offences on indictment.[14] The ODCE describes the division of functions as follows:

> 'It is a matter for the Director of Corporate Enforcement to determine in any particular case if the suspected indictable offence reported to him by an auditor should be prosecuted summarily or referred to the DPP. Where a case is referred to

---

[11] See *TDI Metro Ltd v Delap (No 2)* [2000] 4 IR 520, where the Local Government (Planning and Development) Act 1963, s 80(1), as amended by the Local Government (Planning & Development) Act 1982, s 13 ('An offence under this Act may be prosecuted summarily by the planning authority in whose area the offence is committed') was interpreted as permitting the statutory authority to initiate summary proceedings in respect of an offence which was triable either summarily or on indictment. Geoghegan J, delivering a judgment with which the majority of the Supreme Court concurred, held at p 535, 'I am of opinion that there is no reason whatsoever to give the expression "prosecuted summarily" a narrow interpretation so as to confine it to prosecutions for summary offences. Even applying the strict canons of construction it does not require such an interpretation and I cannot believe that such an interpretation would have been the intention of the Oireachtas. A failure to comply with a planning permission or a failure to obtain a planning permission contrary to s 24 of the Act of 1963 may in numerous instances be a very minor matter and it would be strange if the Oireachtas intended that although the planning authority would be the normal prosecuting authority for the summary offences it could not deal with minor incidents of indictable offences clearly thought fit to be tried summarily. An objection to this line of reasoning which was aired at the hearing of the appeal was that if the District Court Judge ultimately held that the offence was of a nature that it should not be tried summarily, then the commencement of the prosecution by the planning authority was *ultra vires*. I do not agree with that objection. What the Act allows the planning authority to do is a certain activity namely to 'prosecute summarily'. Up to the stage when the District Court declines jurisdiction the planning authority, is doing nothing unlawful.'

[12] For a list of these offences, see Ch **11**.

[13] *Clune v DPP* [1981] ILRM 17, *per* Gannon J.

[14] Constitution of Ireland, Art 30.3 ('All crimes and offences prosecuted in any court constituted under Art 34 of this Constitution other than a court of summary jurisdiction shall be prosecuted in the name of the People and at the suit of the Attorney General [now the DPP] or some other person authorised in accordance with law to act for that purpose'); and Criminal Justice (Administration) Act 1924, s 9(1) ('All criminal charges prosecuted upon indictment in any court shall be prosecuted at the suit of the Attorney-General of Saorstát Éireann [now the DPP]').

the DPP by the Director of Corporate Enforcement, the DPP will subsequently make an independent decision as to whether or not it should actually be prosecuted on indictment.'[15]

[15.005] Those offences under the Companies Acts which are prosecutable either on indictment, or summarily, may accordingly be regarded as 'hybrid offences.' 'Hybrid offences' can be distinguished from indictable offences that may be prosecuted summarily, in two important respects. First, if the offences were indictable offences, which may be tried summarily, the DPP would have to consent to the offences being tried summarily.[16] In respect of offences under the Companies Acts, the ODCE clearly exercises the right to determine whether the offences should be tried summarily or referred to the DPP.

Secondly, if an offence is an indictable offence, which may be tried summarily, rather than a 'hybrid offence', the accused would have a right to veto a decision to try the case summarily rather than on indictment. By contrast, as the DPP reports, 'Hybrid offences do not give the accused a right to choose a trial on indictment.'[17]

There are certain provisions of the Companies Acts which contain indictable offences, rather than 'hybrid' offences. By way of example, s 57, C(A)A 1983, permits certain offences to be prosecuted summarily, subject to the requirements that the judge must determine that the matter is suitable for summary trial, and the consent of the of the DPP and the defendant to the summary trial must be obtained, before such summary trial can

---

[15] ODCE, *The Duty of Auditors to Report to the Director of Corporate Enforcement*, Decision Notice D/2002/2 at para 10.2. See also Revised Guidance on the Duty of Auditors to Report Suspected Indictable Offences to the Director of Corporate Enforcement, Decision Notice D/2006/2. Available at www.odce.ie. Note that the ODCE reported in 2003, that no offences had yet been referred to the DPP for trial on indictment: '... ODCE has deemed it appropriate in a number of cases to initiate criminal proceedings on a summary basis, and this is likely to continue to be a primary enforcement option for the foreseeable future. No case has as yet been formally referred to the Director of Public Prosecutions, although a handful of cases was the subject of correspondence and discussions. It is expected that a small number of the cases currently under investigation will in due course be referred to the DPP for consideration.' ODCE, *Annual Report 2003* at p 16. In 2004, the ODCE referred the first case to the DPP relating to breaches of company law obligations. ODCE *Annual Report 2004* at p 17.

[16] DPP, *Annual Report 1999*: 'the Director also has an important role in relation to a wide range of offences which may be tried either summarily (before a judge sitting alone) or on indictment (before a judge and jury). In some cases the Director has a choice which option should be followed. Generally the Director's consent is required if such a case is to be dealt with summarily.'

[17] DPP, *Annual Report 2002*. See O'Donnell J. 'Summary v Indictable: Choices in the Disposal of Criminal Cases' (2006) JSIJ 15 at 23, citing the *Report of the Working Group on the Jurisdiction of the Court*: 'The working group in it own report pointed out that in respect of hybrid offences, it was curious that the accused, whose liberty might be at stake, has no say on the issue of trial venue.'

proceed.[18] That offence may be categorised as an 'indictable offence' that may be tried summarily, rather than a 'hybrid' offence.

A final point to note about the distinction between summary and indictable offences under the CA 1963–2006, is that every offence which is punishable by a fine of not more than €1,904.61 or a term of imprisonment not exceeding 12 months, or both, may be prosecuted summarily.[19]

B. Detection of offences

[15.006] In most cases, the ODCE will be the authority which investigates suspected offences under the CA 1963–2006 and it has wide ranging powers for this purpose.[20] There are a number of different means by which suspected offences under the Companies Acts may come to the attention of the ODCE. These include information contained in auditors' reports, liquidators' reports and reports from the public.[21] According to the ODCE, 'Auditor reports and public complaints continued to be the primary sources of potential detected misconduct in 2006.'[22] The ODCE also undertakes its own efforts to detect breaches of company law, including by means of reviewing information in the public domain, such as media reports, CRO filings and tax settlements.[23]

C. Potential Defendants

[15.007] The appropriate defendant to a prosecution under the CA 1963–2006, depends on the offence being prosecuted. There are certain offences with which only particular persons, such as the company's liquidator,[24] auditor,[25] or receiver,[26] may be charged. In

---

[18] C(A)A 1983, s 57(4) provides, 'A Justice of the District Court shall have jurisdiction to try summarily an offence under s 20, 24, 31, 36, 40 or 41 if— (a) the Justice is of the opinion that the facts proved or alleged against the defendant charged with any such offence constitute a minor offence fit to be tried summarily; (b) the Director of Public Prosecutions consents; and (c) the defendant (on being informed by the Justice of his right to be tried by a jury) does not object to being tried summarily.' Note that this mirrors the terms of other legislation, such as the Local Government (Planning and Development) Act 1982, s 9.

[19] CA 1990, s 240(3), as amended by CLEA 2001, s 104.

[20] See Ch **12**. In 2006, the ODCE concluded its deliberations regarding 913 cases, with 594 such cases being resolved by securing a remedy for the default and a caution to the relevant persons. In 19% of the cases, the ODCE considered no action to be warranted as there was no, or insufficient, evidence of a default. In 7% of the cases, the complainant had a civil remedy available to him, and the ODCE refuses to get involved in commercial disputes. In a further 9% of the cases, matters were not pursued for reasons such as that the matter was not relevant to the ODCE. See ODCE, *Annual Report 2006* at pp 16 to 17 and app 2.2.4.

[21] See Ch **11**.

[22] ODCE, *Annual Report 2006* at p12.

[23] ODCE, *Annual Report 2006* at p 13.

[24] Eg, CA 1963, ss 300A(4), 306(2); CA 1990, ss 144(2), 151(3).

[25] Eg, CA 1990, s 187(9), (12)(a), 194(4).

[26] Eg, CA 1963, ss 315(5), 319(8), 321(2).

respect of other offences under the Companies Acts, it may be necessary to charge the company itself or an officer 'who is in default', each of which is more problematic.[27]

(a) Company

[15.008] A company can face liability for summary and indictable offences under various provisions of the CA 1963–2006. Such liability is not confined to provisions which state specifically that a company may be liable for the offence created, but also extends to provisions which create offences capable of commission by a 'person'. In this regard, the Interpretation Act 2005 makes it clear that, 'a reference to a person in relation to an offence (whether punishable on indictment or on summary conviction) shall be read as including a reference to a body corporate.'[28] There are many provisions of the Companies Acts which do refer to offences by a 'person' and in theory a company may be charged under any of these provisions. However, many such offences are not capable of commission by a corporation and the provisions would have to be examined individually to assess whether a company could come within their scope. An example of an offence with which it is unlikely a company could be charged is CA 1963, s 90, which provides:

> If any person falsely and deceitfully personates any owner of any share or interest in any company, or of any share warrant or coupon, issued in pursuance of this Act, and thereby obtains or endeavours to obtain any such share or interest or share warrant or coupon, or receives or endeavours to receive any money due to any such owner, or votes at any meeting, as if the offender were the true and lawful owner, he shall be liable, on conviction on indictment, to imprisonment for a term not exceeding five years or to a fine not exceeding €3,174.35 or to both, or, on summary conviction to imprisonment for a term not exceeding six months or to a fine not exceeding €1,904.61 or to both.[29]

[15.009] Most of the offences with which a company may specifically be charged are of a regulatory nature and do not require proof of intention or *mens rea* on the part of the company. This overcomes many of the issues that have been debated in relation to corporate criminal liability.[30] However, there are certain practical questions that need to be considered. In particular, there is authority to the effect that a company must be legally represented in court and cannot be represented by its members or directors. In

---

[27] See eg, CA 1963, ss 125(2), 127(12), regarding the obligation to file a company's annual return that is made up to the company's annual return date, by the date specified in s 127.

[28] Interpretation Act 2005, s 18(j). Note that s 18(c) also provides, '"Person" shall be read as importing a body corporate (whether a corporation aggregate or a corporation sole) and an unincorporated body of persons, as well as an individual, and the subsequent use of any pronoun in place of a further use of "person" shall be read accordingly.'

[29] CA 1963, s 90, as amended by CA 1990, s 240(7), as inserted by CLEA 2001, s 104(c).

[30] See Law Reform Commission, *Consultation Paper on Corporate Killing* (LRC CP 26–2003) at paras 1.29 to 1.80 for an examination of the different bases on which companies may be made criminally liable. See also Courtney, *The Law of Private Companies* (2nd edn, Tottel Publishing, 2002) at paras 4.051 to 4.058 for an analysis of the topic of corporate criminal responsibility.

Battle v Irish Art Promotion Centre Ltd, O'Dalaigh CJ described the law on this topic as follows:

> '... the law is ... that, in the absence of statutory exception, a limited company cannot be represented in court proceedings by its managing director or other officer or servant. This is an infirmity of the company which derives from its own very nature. The creation of the company is the act of its subscribers; the subscribers, in discarding their own *personae* for the persona of the company, doubtless did so for the advantages which incorporation offers to traders. In seeking incorporation they thereby lose the right of audience which they would have as individuals; but the choice has been their own. One sympathises with the purpose which the appellant has in mind, to wit, to safeguard his business reputation; but, as the law stands, he cannot as major shareholder and managing director now substitute his *persona* for that of the company.'[31]

[15.010] One of the difficulties this causes is that a company which lacks resources and cannot afford legal representation will not be represented in court. This general rule is abrogated by CA 1963, s 382, which provides that, when a company[32] is charged with an indictable offence, either jointly with another person, or alone,

> The company may appear at all stages of the proceedings by a representative and the answer to any question to be put to a person charged with an indictable offence may be made on behalf of the company by that representative but if the company does not so appear it shall not be necessary to put the questions and the District Court may, notwithstanding its absence, take depositions and send forward the company for trial.[33]

The effect of this provision is that a company may appoint a representative to appear in court on its behalf in respect of indictable offences, for the purpose of doing any act or thing which the representative is permitted to do by s 382.[34] Such a representative 'shall not, by virtue only of being so appointed, be qualified to act on behalf of the company before any court for any other purpose.'[35] It is important to emphasise that this provision only applies if the company is charged with an indictable offence. The ODCE clearly identifies every offence under the CA 1963–2006 that is capable of being tried on indictment as an indictable offence.[36] As many 'indictable offences' under the

---

[31] *Battle v Irish Art Promotion Centre Ltd* [1968] 1 IR at p 254. This decision was confirmed in subsequent cases including *Re Friends of the Curragh Environment Ltd* [2006] IEHC 243.

[32] Note that CA 1963, s 184(7) provides, a '"company" includes a company incorporated outside the State which has an established place of business in the State.'

[33] CA 1963, s 382(2).

[34] Note that a representative does not have to be appointed under the seal of the company, and 'a statement in writing purporting to be signed by a managing director of the company or by some other person (by whatever name called) having, or being one of the persons having, the management of the affairs of the company, to the effect that the person named in the statement has been appointed as the representative of the company for the purposes of this section shall be admissible without further proof as evidence that that person has been so appointed.' CA 1963, s 382(6).

[35] CA 1963, s 382(5).

[36] See, eg, Table of Indictable Offences at www.odce.ie. See para **[15.003]**.

Companies Acts are hybrid offences, which may be tried summarily or on indictment, it is only if the company is charged on indictment that the offence will be regarded as an indictable one. This gives rise to the anomalous situation that, if a company is charged with a summary offence, it must retain legal representation. However, if the company is charged with a more serious indictable offence, it may appoint a representative other than a legal representative. There is no visible justification for this dichotomy. The potential injustice of this provision is heightened by the fact that a person prosecuted in respect of a hybrid offence has no right to elect to be tried on indictment. This can be contrasted with the right of persons who are charged with indictable offences, which may be tried summarily, to choose not to be tried summarily.[37]

There are certain things that a company's representative, appointed in accordance with s 382, may do on behalf of the company in the course of proceedings for which he was appointed. He may answer any question put to the company;[38] he may exercise any right of objection or election that the accused person may have;[39] or enter a plea in writing on behalf of the company.[40]

The ODCE has prosecuted several companies in the District Court in relation to such offences as failing to keep proper books of account.[41] Applying s 382, these companies could have been represented by someone other than a legal representative, if they were prosecuted on indictment but not when charged with a summary offence.

(b) Officer in default

[15.011] There are many provisions of the CA 1963–2006 which provide for the prosecution of offences by a company and its officers who are 'in default'.[42] Section 383 of the CA 1963 originally defined an 'officer in default' as follows:

> For the purpose of any provision in this Act which provides that an officer of a company who is in default shall be liable to a fine or penalty, 'officer who is in default' means any officer of the company who knowingly and wilfully authorises or permits the default, refusal or contravention mentioned in the provision.[43]

---

[37] See para [15.005].

[38] CA 1963, s 382(2).

[39] CA 1963, s 382(3).

[40] CA 1963, s 382(4) ('Any plea which may be entered or signed by an accused person, whether before the District Court or before the trial judge, may be entered in writing on behalf of the company by its representative, and, if the company does not appear by its representative or, though it does so appear, fails to enter any such plea, the trial shall proceed as though the company had duly entered a plea of not guilty.')

[41] *Director of Corporate Enforcement v Cloudbury Developments Limited* (22 June 2007), Newport District Court; *Director of Corporate Enforcement v Mediasatellite Ireland Ltd* (20 June 2007), Cork District Court; *Director of Corporate Enforcement v This N' That Athenry Ltd* (14 November 2006), Athenry District Court. See www.odce.ie for information regarding additional prosecutions of companies under the Companies Acts.

[42] See Chs **2**, **3** and **4** for examples of such offences.

[43] CA 1963, s 383.

This definition required a prosecutor to adduce proof that an officer of a company knowingly and wilfully authorised or permitted the offence in question to be committed.[44] The threshold of 'knowingly and wilfully' was a high one and prosecutions of officers in default were rare.

[15.012] The Working Group on Company Law Compliance and Enforcement recommended that s 383 be amended to provide that:

> '... officer in default shall mean any officer who authorises or, in breach of his or her duty as such officer, permits the default, refusal or contravention mentioned in the provision, and an officer shall be presumed to have permitted any default, refusal or contravention by the company unless the officer shows that he or she took all reasonable steps to prevent the default, refusal or contravention concerned, or by reason of circumstances beyond his or her control was unable to do so. For the avoidance of doubt it shall be the duty of each individual director and of the company secretary to ensure that the requirements of the Companies Acts 1963 to 1990 are complied with by the company.'[45]

The Working Group also recommended that the definition of the term 'officer in default' in s 383 should be amended to place the onus of disproving fault on an officer who faces prosecution for permitting a default, refusal or contravention under the Companies Acts, where he had a duty to prevent such a breach.[46]

[15.013] This recommendation was reflected in CLEA 2001, s 100, which inserts a new s 383 in CA 1963, an amendment which eases significantly the burden on prosecutors. CA 1963, s 383, now provides:

> (1) For the purpose of any provision of the Companies Acts which provides that an officer of a company who is in default shall be liable to a fine or penalty, an officer who is in default is any officer who authorises or who, in breach of his duty as such officer, permits, the default mentioned in the provision.

> (2) For the purposes of this section, an officer shall be presumed to have permitted a default by the company unless the officer can establish that he took all reasonable steps to prevent it or that, by reason of circumstances beyond his control, was unable to do so.

> (3) It is the duty of each director and secretary of a company to ensure that the requirements of the Companies Acts are complied with by the company.

> (4) In this section 'default' includes a refusal or contravention.

[15.014] As can be seen from a perusal of the Companies Acts, in respect of many defaults for which a company can be liable, every officer in default can also be prosecuted. According to the amended formulation of s 383, it is no longer necessary to demonstrate that the default was wilfully and knowingly permitted or authorised by the

---

44 Note that 'an officer' is defined in CA 1963, s 2(1) as follows: '"officer" in relation to a body corporate includes a director or secretary'.

45 *Report of the Working Group on Company Law Compliance and Enforcement* (November 1998) at para 7.30.

46 *Report of the Working Group on Company Law Compliance and Enforcement* (November 1998) at para 3.28.

company's officer. There is no requirement of knowledge or intention on the part of the officer. Recklessness or even negligence may now be sufficient for an officer to be prosecuted as an 'officer in default' under the CA 1963–2006.

[15.015] Another consequence of the amendment of s 383 is that, whenever there is a default in relation to the Companies Acts, every officer shall be presumed to have permitted the default to occur and shall therefore be liable for that default.[47] The only way to rebut this presumption is to prove either that the officer took all reasonable steps to prevent the default or that, because of circumstances beyond his control, he was unable to prevent the default occurring. Whenever a company is in breach of a requirement of the Companies Acts, the burden of proof is therefore on each and every officer of that company to prove that he took all reasonable steps to prevent the default or that it was beyond his control to prevent the default occurring. If an officer fails to discharge this burden, he will be liable for the company's default.[48]

[15.016] A further effect of s 383 is that it is a breach of duty for a director to fail to ensure that the company complies with the requirements of the Companies Acts.[49] The requirement that a director must 'ensure' such compliance is an onerous one. This scope of this requirement is not defined by reference to s 383(2), which permits an officer to disprove that they permitted a default to occur. There is also nothing in s 383(3) which envisages a director or secretary overcoming or avoiding the finding that there was a breach of duty. According to s 383(3), therefore, whenever a company fails to comply with a requirement of the Companies Acts, every director has automatically committed a breach of duty. This heightens considerably the likelihood of enforcement of the provisions of the Companies Acts against individual directors.

[15.017] A final provision of the Companies Acts that is relevant to the prosecution of individual persons involved in the company, is CA 1990, s 241. This provision relates to particular offences with which companies may be charged, and extends the net to specified individuals. Section 241(1) accordingly provides:

> Where an offence under s 19, 21, 79 or 242 which is committed by a body to
> which any such section applies is proved to have been committed with the consent
> or connivance of or to be attributable to any neglect on the part of any person

---

47   CA 1963, s 383(1) and (2), as substituted by CLEA 2001, s 100.

48   CA 1963, s 383(1) and (2), as substituted by CLEA 2001, s 100.

49   CA 1963, s 383(3), as substituted by CLEA 2001, s 100. In *Re USIT World plc* [2005] IEHC 285, the liquidator, in the course of an application for declarations of restriction, submitted that it was incompatible with CA 1963, s 383(3) (as substituted by CLEA 2001, s 100) to draw any distinction between directors on the basis of their relative levels of involvement in the management of the company. In relation to the interpretation of s 383(3), Peart J held, 'I would be of the view that this should be interpreted as meaning exactly what it says, namely that each director is responsible in that regard. But in the context of an application under s 150 it does not appear to run contrary to the section to draw a distinction in an appropriate case to the level or degree of that responsibility as between one director and another. No director can close his eyes completely to this responsibility, and it may in the end boil down to the question identified by McCracken J in Gasco, namely *"whether his reliance on the actions of another director was itself responsible".'*

being a director, manager, secretary or other officer of the body, or any person who was purporting to act in any such capacity, that person shall also be guilty of an offence under that section.[50]

The offences in question broadly concern a failure to produce books and documents in response to a direction from the DCE; the unauthorised publication or disclosure of books or documents obtained pursuant to CA 1990, ss 19 or 20; a failure to make the requisite notifications or disclosures in connection with share transfers; and the furnishing of false information.

In respect of each of these offences, if a body is found guilty of an offence and it is proved that the offence was committed with the consent, connivance, or due to the neglect, of a director, manager, secretary of other officer, or person purporting to act in that capacity, that person is also guilty of an offence. The same may apply to a member, if the affairs of the body are being managed by its members, and the acts and defaults in question were carried out by a member in connection with his management functions.[51] This provision facilitates responsibility for corporate offences being attributed to those bearing responsibility for the company's management.

[15.018] There is no common thread among the offences to which this provision applies. Other than the connection between ss 19 and 21,[52] the areas of law are disparate and unconnected. It is also curious that, while s 241 is premised on the commission of an offence by a 'body', only s 19 contains any reference to an offence by a 'body'.[53] Sections 21, 79 and 242 solely provide for the imposition of fines and penalties on a 'person'. It may be recalled, however, that the Interpretation Act 2005 mandates that, a '"person" in relation to an offence (whether punishable on indictment or on summary conviction) shall be read as including a reference to a body corporate.'[54] Insofar as the offences created by ss 19, 21, 79 and 242 may only be committed by a company/body, s 241 may facilitate the prosecution of members of management who were responsible for that offence. It is by no means clear from the formulation of those provisions, however, that such persons could not be prosecuted directly. By way of illustration, it is an offence under s 242(1) for a person to answer a question, in purported compliance with a provision of the Companies Acts, knowing it to be false. This seems to be an offence with which any director or officer of a company could be charged, an

---

[50] CA 1990, s 241(1).

[51] CA 1990, s 241(2) provides: 'Where the affairs of a body are managed by its members, sub-s (1) shall apply in relation to the acts and defaults of a member in connection with his functions of management as if he were a director or manager of the body.'

[52] See further Ch **12**.

[53] CA 1990, s 19(6), as substituted by CLEA 2001, s 29. Note that in s 19(8)-(9) there are also references to the commission of offences by a 'person.' See Ch **12**.

[54] Interpretation Act 2005, s 18(j). Note that s 18(c) also provides, '"Person" shall be read as importing a body corporate (whether a corporation aggregate or a corporation sole) and an unincorporated body of persons, as well as an individual, and the subsequent use of any pronoun in place of a further use of "person" shall be read accordingly.'

interpretation which is reinforced by the fact that, if convicted on indictment, the person may be liable to a sentence of imprisonment.[55] The utility of s 242 in such contexts is not clear.

D. Pre-trial

(a) Commencement of prosecution

[15.019] Criminal proceedings may be commenced in one of three ways: by laying a complaint or information before a District Court judge for the issue of a summons or arrest warrant; by issuing a summons through an administrative process; or by presenting a suspect who has been arrested without warrant before the District Court to be charged.

(i) Laying a complaint or information

[15.020] A complaint or information, which is a statement of the facts constituting the offence,[56] must generally be made to a District Court judge. This made be made on oath or otherwise, as the judge may direct.[57] If the complaint is made on oath, it must be by sworn information.[58] The complaint or information is laid by the person prosecuting the offence which, under the Companies Acts, would typically be the DCE, the DPP, or the Registrar of Companies.[59] The information should state the name and address of the alleged offender, the name and address of the complainant, the date of the information and a brief description of the offence. In the case of an offence under the Companies Acts it is recommended that the information include the words, 'contrary to section [the applicable section] of the Companies Act ...'.[60]

If the judge has jurisdiction in the district to which he is assigned, he may then issue a summons, which will specify the particulars of the alleged offence and the name and address of the person against whom the offence is alleged.[61] The summons will require the person to whom it is addressed to appear at a sitting of the court which has

---

[55]   CA 1990, 242(2), as amended by CLEA 2001, s 106.

[56]   See Walsh, *Criminal Procedure* (Thomson Round Hall, 2002) at para 13-09, citing *AG (McDonnell) v Higgins* [1964] IR 374 at 385.

[57]   District Court Rules, O 15, r 1 as substituted by District Court (Summonses) Rules 2005, reg 3 ('(1)Where in the first instance a summons is sought pursuant to s 10 of the Petty Sessions (Ireland) Act 1851 to require the attendance before the Court of a person against whom a complaint is made, the complaint shall be made to a Judge and may be made with or without oath as the Judge shall direct.')

[58]   District Court Rules, O 15, r 2 as substituted by District Court (Summonses) Rules 2005, reg 3.

[59]   See Ch 11.

[60]   See Walsh, *Criminal Procedure* (Thomson Round Hall, 2002) at para 13-09, citing *AG (McDonnell) v Higgins* [1964] IR 374 at 385.

[61]   District Court Rules, O 15, r 3 as substituted by District Court (Summonses) Rules 2005, reg 3.

jurisdiction to deal with the matter, which must be a court in the same jurisdictional area as the judge issuing the summons.[62]

The summons may contain allegations of several complaints or offences.[63]

There is a particular provision of the District Court Rules which would be of relevance to prosecutions under the CA 1963–2006. Order 15, r 9 provides:

> In alleging an offence contrary to any statute or statutes it shall be sufficient to state the substance of the offence in ordinary language with such particulars of the offence as may be necessary for giving reasonable information as to the nature of the complaint, and it shall not be necessary to negative any exception or exemption from or qualification to the operation of a statute creating such offence.[64]

This permits the substance of an offence to be stated, using 'ordinary language': the summons does not have to address every qualification, exception, and technical aspect of the alleged offence, as formulated in the relevant statute.

If the offence is an indictable offence and a summons is considered unsuitable, an arrest warrant might be issued. Order 16 of the District Court Rules 1997 governs the procedure and provides that the complaint seeking a warrant must be made by information in writing and on oath.[65] The judge may issue a summons instead of a warrant,[66] but if a warrant is issued it must be signed by the judge.[67]

---

[62] District Court Rules, O 15, r 3(3)(a), as substituted by District Court (Summonses) Rules 2005, reg 3.

[63] District Court Rules, O 15, r 4 as substituted by District Court (Summonses) Rules 2005, reg 3. Note that, pursuant to O 15, r 6, 'In the case of every summons issued otherwise than by transmitting it by electronic means to the person who applied for it or a person acting on his or her behalf, there shall be issued with such summons a copy thereof for service upon each person to whom the summons is directed. Where a summons is issued by transmitting it by electronic means to the person who applied for it or a person acting on his or her behalf, a true copy of such summons shall be served upon each person to whom the summons is directed by electronic means.'

[64] District Court Rules, O 15, r 9 as substituted by District Court (Summonses) Rules 2005, reg 3.

[65] District Court Rules 1997, O 16, r 1.

[66] District Court Rules 1997, O 16, r 4.

[67] District Court Rules 1997, O 16, r 2. Note that, O 15, rr 8 and 9 are equally applicable to summons and provide: 'Where an enactment constituting an offence states the offence to be the doing or the omission to do any one of a number of different acts in the alternative, or states any part of the offence in the alternative, the acts, omissions or other matters stated in the alternative in the enactment may be stated either in the alternative or in the conjunctive in the summons alleging such offence,' and 'In alleging an offence contrary to any statute or statutes it shall be sufficient to state the substance of the offence in ordinary language with such particulars of the offence as may be necessary for giving reasonable information as to the nature of the complaint, and it shall not be necessary to negative any exception or exemption from or qualification to the operation of a statute creating such offence.' (O 16, r 3).

(ii) Administrative procedure

[15.021] A criminal prosecution may be commenced in the District Court through an administrative procedure, whereby an officer of the court issues the summons.[68] An application for a summons by way of this administrative procedure may be made to an officer of the District Court by the DPP, the AG, a member of An Garda Síochána, 'or any person authorised by or under statute to prosecute the offence.'[69] The DCE or the Registrar of Companies may therefore avail of this procedure in respect of offences which they are empowered to prosecute under the CA 1963–2006. By contrast with the procedure outlined above, the complaint is not made until the alleged offender appears in court to answer the summons.[70]

A summons issued under this procedure must state 'in ordinary language' the particulars of the alleged offence; the name and address of the alleged offender; and it must notify him that he will be accused of that offence at a sitting of the District Court, which is specified by reference to its date and location and, insofar as is practicable, its time.[71] It is substantially identical to a summons issued by the court under O 15.[72] In practice, most summonses are issued by means of the administrative procedure governed by the Courts (No 3) Act 1986.

(iii) Arrest without warrant

[15.022] The final means of commencing a criminal prosecution is by presenting a person who has already been arrested without a warrant, before the court to be formally charged.[73] If a person is charged while in the custody of An Garda Síochána, particulars of the alleged offence must be set out on a charge sheet.[74] The alleged offender must be furnished with a copy of that charge sheet 'as soon as may be',[75] and it must also be lodged, 'as soon as possible' with the District Court clerk for the area in which the offence will be prosecuted.[76] If the offence is tried summarily, the charge sheet is usually treated as the information.[77]

---

[68]   Courts (No 3) Act 1986, s 1.

[69]   Courts (No 3) Act 1986, s 1(4).

[70]   Walsh, *Criminal Procedure* (Thomson Round Hall 2002) at para 13–24.

[71]   Courts (No 3) Act 1986, s 1(3).

[72]   Note that there has been some debate as to the status of a summons issued under the Courts (No 3) Act 1986. See Walsh, *Criminal Procedure* (Thomson Round Hall, 2002) at para 13–24.

[73]   See further paras **[15.028]** to **[15.029]** regarding the power to arrest a suspect without a warrant in the context of the Companies Acts 1963–2006.

[74]   District Court Rules 1997, O 17, r 1(1).

[75]   District Court Rules 1997, O 17, r 1(2).

[76]   District Court Rules 1997, O 17, r 1(3).

[77]   Walsh, *Criminal Procedure* (Thomson Round Hall, 2002) at para 13–27.

(b) Limitation periods

[15.023] The general rule is that a complaint alleging a criminal offence must be laid within six months of the commission of the offence. This is dictated by s 10(4) of the Petty Sessions (Ireland) Act 1851. This requirement has been abrogated, however. Section 7 of the Criminal Justice Act 1951 provides that s 10(4) 'shall not apply in respect of an indictable offence.' This provision has been replaced by s 177 of the Criminal Justice Act 2006 and now provides that the time limit of s 10(4) of the 1851 Act shall not apply to either of the following:

– 'an offence that is triable ... at the election of the prosecution, either on indictment or summarily', or

– 'an offence that is triable ... either on indictment or, subject to certain conditions including the consent of the prosecution, summarily.'[78]

The Explanatory Memorandum to the Criminal Justice Act 2006 explains this amendment as follows:

> This section amends the Criminal Justice Act 1951 by the substitution of a new s 7. Section 7 of the Criminal Justice Act 1951 provides that the time limits prescribed by s 10(4) of the Petty Sessions (Ireland) Act 1851 for the making of complaints in cases of summary jurisdiction (currently six months) do not apply to an indictable offence. The amendment further clarifies that the restriction does not apply to a scheduled offence under the 1951 Act and provides that it does not apply to an offence that is triable either on indictment and, subject to certain conditions including the consent of the prosecution, summarily. The effect of this amendment is that the six month time limit for prosecuting offences applies to offences that can only be tried as summary offences. The section also provides that the amendment shall not have effect in relation to an offence committed before the commencement of this section.

The effect of this amendment is therefore that a six-month time limit only applies to the commencement of proceedings in respect of offences which can only be prosecuted summarily. This will be significant for offences which may be categorised as 'hybrid offences'. While these offences may be prosecuted summarily or on indictment, at the option of the prosecutor, the six-month time limit does not apply, even if they are prosecuted summarily.

[15.024] The general rule that the six-month time limit continues to apply to offences which may only be prosecuted summarily, has been further abrogated in the context of the CA 1963–2006. CA 1990, s 240(5) provides:

> Notwithstanding s 10(4) of the Petty Sessions (Ireland) Act, 1851, summary proceedings in relation to an offence under the Companies Acts may be commenced—
>
> (a) at any time within three years from the date on which the offence was committed, or

---

[78] Criminal Justice Act 1951, s 7(b), as substituted by Criminal Justice Act 2006, s 177(1). Note that, according to s 177(2), 'This section shall not have effect in relation to an offence committed before the commencement of this section.'

    (b) if, at the expiry of that period, the person against whom the proceedings are to be brought is outside the State, within six months from the date on which he next enters the State, or

    (c) at any time within three years from the date on which evidence that, in the opinion of the person by whom the proceedings are brought, is sufficient to justify the bringing of the proceedings comes to that person's knowledge, whichever is the later.[79]

Section 240(5) does not differentiate between summary proceedings which may be prosecuted on indictment and those which may not. It therefore removes the six-month time limit in respect of all offences that are prosecuted summarily under the Companies Acts. The new time limit is three years from the commission of the offence; three years from the date on which sufficient evidence to justify proceedings comes to the knowledge of the prosecutor; or six months from the date on which the alleged offender enters the State.

[15.025] These time limits are not very restrictive. If a person is outside the State at the expiry of the three-year period (wherever he was located during that three-year period), proceedings may be brought at any time, without limitation, within six months of his next return to the State. Section 240(5)(c) is even more open-ended: if a prosecutor forms the subjective opinion that he has sufficient evidence to bring proceedings, he then has three years within which to do so. This provision is widened further by s 240(5A), which provides:

> For the purpose of sub-s (5)(c), a certificate signed by or on behalf of the person bringing the proceedings as to the date on which the evidence referred to in that provision relating to the offence concerned came to his knowledge shall be *prima facie* evidence thereof and in any legal proceedings a document purporting to be a certificate issued for the purpose of this subsection and to be so signed shall be deemed to be so signed and shall be admitted as evidence without proof of the signature of the person purporting to sign the certificate.[80]

It would be very difficult to challenge the delay in prosecuting an offence under this provision, as the certificate by the prosecutor as to the date on which the evidence came to his knowledge is *prima facie* evidence of that fact.

[15.026] The net effect of s 7 of the Criminal Justice Act 1851, as amended, combined with s 240(5), CA 1990, as amended, is as follows:

    — there is no time limit for the commencement of proceedings in respect of an indictable offence under the Companies Acts;

    — there is no time limit for the commencement of proceedings in respect of offences which may be tried summarily or on indictment;

    — proceedings in respect of offences under the Companies Acts which may only be tried summarily, can be commenced within three years after the commission of the offence; within three years from the date on which the prosecutor became aware of evidence which he considered sufficient to justify bringing such

---

[79] CA 1990, s 240(5), as substituted by C(A)(No2)A 1999, s 41.

[80] CA 1990, s 240(5A), as inserted by C(A)(No2)A 1999, s 41.

proceedings; or within six months of the return to Ireland of the alleged offender, beyond the expiry of three years from the commission of the offence.

(c) Collecting evidence

[15.027] In addition to the powers of investigation of the ODCE, there are particular provisions of the Companies Acts which permit books, documents, and information to be obtained. By way of example, when a company is in liquidation, there are various provisions of the CA 1963–2006 which provide for orders directing documents to be produced and persons to be summoned for examination.[81]

More generally, CA 1963, s 384, provides that the AG, the DCE or a Superintendent of An Garda Síochána may apply to a judge of the High Court for an order authorising the inspection of a company's books or papers or requiring the company's secretary or any officer to produce such books or papers.[82]

Two criteria must be met before such an order may be made. First, there must be 'reasonable cause to believe that any person has, while an officer of the company, committed an offence in connection with the management of the company's affairs'. Second, there must be 'reasonable cause to believe that ... evidence of the commission of the offence is to be found in any books or papers of or under the control of the company.'[83]

Such an order may also be made in relation to 'any books or papers of a person carrying on the business of banking so far as they relate to the company's affairs', but no order for the production of such documents may be made.[84] A decision of the High Court on an application under s 384 is final subject only to an appeal to the Supreme Court on a question of law.[85]

(d) Arrest

[15.028] The rules and procedures that apply to the arrest of suspects generally are also applicable to offences under the Companies Acts.[86] An important amendment that was introduced by the CLEA 2001 in this regard was the increase in the maximum sentence of imprisonment to five years for indictable offences.[87] This brings indictable offences

---

[81] See, eg, CA 1963, s 243(1), as amended by CLEA 2001, s 43; CA 1963, s 243(1A), as inserted by CLEA 2001, s 43; CA 1963, s 282B, as inserted by CLEA 2001, s 49. See further Ch **9**.

[82] CA 1963. s 384, as amended by CLEA 2001, s 14. Note that 'company' includes 'a company incorporated outside the State which has an established place of business in the State'. CA 1963, s 384(4).

[83] CA 1963, s 384(1), as amended by CLEA 2001, s 14.

[84] CA 1963, s 384(2).

[85] CA 1963, s 384(3).

[86] It is beyond the scope of this text to examine every aspect of the law and practice governing the arrest of suspects. See Walsh, *Criminal Procedure* (Thomson Round Hall, 2002), Ch 4.

[87] CA 1990, s 240(1) and (8), as amended by CLEA 2001, s 104.

under the Companies Acts within the threshold of 'arrestable offences', a term defined in the Criminal Law Act 1997 as:

> an offence for which a person of full capacity and not previously convicted may, under or by virtue of any enactment, be punished by imprisonment for a term of five years or by a more severe penalty and includes an attempt to commit any such offence.[88]

[15.029] One consequence of an offence being 'arrestable' is that persons suspected of committing such an offence may be arrested without a warrant. According to s 4(2) of the Criminal Law Act 1997, a person suspected of an 'arrestable offence' may be arrested by any person: 'where an arrestable offence has been committed, any person may arrest without warrant anyone who is or whom he or she, with reasonable cause, suspects to be guilty of the offence.'

For this power to be exercised by a person other than a member of An Garda Síochána, three conditions must be met. First, the person must believe that the suspected offender is avoiding, or would otherwise attempt to avoid, arrest by a member of An Garda Síochána.[89] Second, there must be certainty that an offence was committed, and third, there must be 'reasonable cause' to believe the arrestee was the offender. Most serious offences under the CA 1963–2006 will come to light following detailed and extensive investigation. By contrast, the power of arrest without warrant by a civilian appears to be directed towards offences which are witnessed and the commission of which is readily apparent. This power of arrest does not appear to be particularly appropriate to offences under the Companies Acts, due to the nature of those offences.

[15.030] Section 4(3) of the Criminal Law Act 1997 confers a wider power of arrest on a member of An Garda Síochána:

> 'Where a member of the Garda Síochána, with reasonable cause, suspects that an arrestable offence has been committed, he or she may arrest without warrant anyone whom the member, with reasonable cause, suspects to be guilty of the offence.'

There does not have to be certainty regarding the fact that the offence was committed for a member of An Garda Síochána to exercise this power of arrest: it is sufficient if there is 'reasonable cause' to suspect that an arrestable offence has been committed.

[15.031] Another consequence of an offence being an 'arrestable offence' is that the detention periods specified in s 4 of the Criminal Justice Act 1984 are applicable. Section 4 states that when a person is arrested by a member of An Garda Síochána on suspicion of having committed an 'arrestable offence', and the member in charge of the station to which the person is taken has reasonable grounds for believing that his detention is 'necessary for the proper investigation of the offence,'[90] that person may be

---

[88] Criminal Law Act 1997, s 2(1).

[89] Criminal Law Act 1997, s 4(4) provides, 'An arrest other than by a member of the Garda Síochána may only be effected by a person under sub-s (1) or (2) where he or she, with reasonable cause, suspects that the person to be arrested by him or her would otherwise attempt to avoid, or is avoiding, arrest by a member of the Garda Síochána.'

[90] Criminal Justice Act 1984, s 4(2).

detained for six hours from the time of arrest. He may be detained for a further six hours if a member of An Garda Síochána not below the rank of superintendent 'has reasonable grounds for believing that such further detention is necessary for the proper investigation of the offence.'[91]

[15.032] The extension of this power of arrest and detention without warrant to indictable offences under the Companies Acts is not accidental. The Working Group on Company Law Compliance and Enforcement recommended that, 'all indictable offences under the Companies Acts should carry a maximum term of imprisonment of at least five years. This would make suspected offenders liable to arrest without warrant under the Criminal Law Act 1997 and detention under the Criminal Justice Act 1984.'[92] This recommendation was fully implemented. Section 240(1) provides that, in respect of convictions on indictment for which no penalty is specifically provided, the maximum term of imprisonment shall be five years.[93] Section 240(8) covers all other convictions on indictment under the Companies Acts and provides that, where a sentence of less than five years is provided for a conviction on indictment, the maximum sentence 'shall be taken to be five years.'[94] The maximum sentence of imprisonment for all convictions on indictment under the CA 1963–2006 is now five years.

The ODCE has demonstrated its willingness to use the power of arrest in respect of persons suspected of committing offences under the Companies Acts. In 2003, the ODCE reported that Garda officers seconded to the ODCE arrested ten individuals in 2003, five of whom were detained for questioning.[95]

E. Trial

(a) Venue

[15.033] For the trial of criminal offences in the District Court, there are two jurisdictional divisions to be considered. The State is divided into districts, and the districts are in turn divided into areas. A judge has jurisdiction to hear any case in respect of an offence which was committed in his district or an accused who resides or was arrested in his district.[96] However, the District Court Rules, insofar as relevant, provide that criminal proceedings should be brought, heard and determined in one of the following:

  – the court area in which the offence charged is stated to have been committed;

---

[91] Criminal Justice Act 1984, s 4(3).

[92] *Report of the Working Group on Company Law Compliance and Enforcement* (November 1998) at para 4.30.

[93] CA 1990, s 240(1), as amended by CLEA 2001, s 104.

[94] CA 1990, s 240(8), as inserted by CLEA 2001, s 104(c).

[95] ODCE, *Annual Report* 2003 at p 16. Available at www.odce.ie.

[96] See generally Walsh, *Criminal Procedure* (Thomson Round Hall 2002) at para 13-02.

- if more than one offence is stated to have been committed within a judge's district, the area in which any one of such offences is stated to have been committed;
- the court area in which the accused was arrested;
- the court area in which the accused resides; or
- in the court area determined by order made pursuant to s 15 of the Courts Act 1971.[97]

The combined effect of these rules is that a judge from the district with jurisdiction may hear a case, but only in the court area in which the offence was committed; the court area in which the accused was resident or arrested; or an area determined pursuant to s 15 of the Courts Act 1971. In respect of an indictable prosecution, proceedings may be dealt with in any court area within the judge's district.[98]

[15.034] There is a particular rule applicable to the summary trial of offences under the CA 1963–2006. CA 1990, s 240A, provides:

> For the purposes of any provision of the Companies Acts which provides that the company and every officer of the company is guilty of an offence, summary proceedings against the company or an officer of the company may be brought, heard and determined either—
>
> (a) in the court area in which the offence charged or, if more than one offence is stated to have been committed, any one of the offences charged, is stated to have been committed,
>
> (b) in the court area in which the accused has been arrested,
>
> (c) in the court area in which the accused resides,
>
> (d) in the court area specified by order made pursuant to s 15 of the Courts Act 1971, or
>
> (e) in the court area in which the registered office of the company is situated.'[99]

[15.035] For the summary trial of certain offences under CA 1963–2006, there is therefore an additional basis for conferring jurisdiction on a court: the proceedings may be brought, heard and determined in the court area in which the registered office of the company is situated.

[15.036] It is important to be aware that this extension of jurisdiction does not apply in respect of every offence under the Companies Acts. It is expressed to apply only to a provision of the Acts 'which provides that the company and every officer of the company is guilty of an offence.' It must be assumed that this is intended to encompass provisions that create offences on the part of a company and 'every officer of the company who is in default': there are no provisions of the Companies Acts that refer to offences by a 'company and every officer of the company'. The only offences to which

---

[97] District Court Rules 1997, O 13, r 1, as substituted by District Court (Criminal Justice Act 2006) Rules 2007. Courts Act 1971, s 15, applies where the Minister for Justice, Equality and Law Reform certifies that it is desirable that there be early trial or disposal in the District Court of specified summary offence and makes different provision for the *locus* of such trial.

[98] District Court Rules 1997, O 13, r 2.

[99] CA 1990, s 240A, as inserted by CLEA 2001, s 105.

s 240A applies therefore are offences with which a company and its officers who are in default, may be prosecuted. It does not provide a uniform basis for the prosecution of a company's officers in the court area in which the company is registered.

[15.037] The objective of s 240A was to overcome certain difficulties that were experienced in prosecuting offences by a company and its officers. Prior to the commencement of the CLEA 2001, such an offence could only be prosecuted in the area in which the accused was resident, arrested, or in which the offence was committed.[100] According to the Explanatory and Financial Memorandum to the Company Law Enforcement Bill, this was problematic as 'For certain offences under the Companies Acts, it is not possible to identify the place where an act or omission occurred.' As a result, the practice was to issue proceedings against officers in the court area in which they resided, and against companies in the area of their registered office, which lead to 'unnecessary duplication of work' and was 'wasteful of court time.'[101] The effect of s 240A, as inserted by CLEA 2001, s 105, is that where an offence is committed for which every officer of the company in default may be liable, both the company and its officers may be prosecuted in the court area in which the company has its registered office.

[15.038] It does not seem that this amendment has overcome all difficulties in determining the correct venue for the prosecution of company law offences. On the contrary, the CRO has experienced difficulties regarding the question of whether the Dublin District Court has jurisdiction in respect of prosecutions of companies which have a registered office outside Dublin.[102] In 2006, the CRO similarly reported that:

> 'Difficulties arose at the end of 2005 which kept the number of company and director prosecutions in 2006 lower than would otherwise be the case as pre-booked court days had to be cancelled. In two instances Justices of the District Court raised issues on CRO procedures viz. the summonses used by the Office and the jurisdiction of the Dublin District Court in prosecutions of companies with a registered office elsewhere than in Dublin. In both instances the procedures questioned had been in place for some time. Those issues have now been resolved.'[103]

The Department of Enterprise Trade and Employment refers to the same issues regarding the prosecution of companies with registered offices outside Dublin in the Dublin District Court and reports, 'Those issues have now been resolved, the wording of summonses was revised and the Dublin jurisdiction was accepted in subsequent cases'.[104] The procedure of the CRO which leads to prosecutions in the Dublin District Court is not explained in these reports. If and to the extent that the jurisdiction of the

---

[100] District Court Rules 1997, O 13, r 1.

[101] *Explanatory and Financial Memorandum* to the Company Law Enforcement Bill.

[102] CRO Annual Report 2005 at p 4: 'A number of further difficulties arose towards the end of the year ... involving the issue of whether the court in Dublin has jurisdiction in cases where the defendant company has its registered office located outside of the Dublin area. The Office is in discussion with the Attorney-General's Office in the matter.' Available at www.cro.ie.

[103] CRO *Annual Report 2006* at p 2. Available at www.cro.ie.

[104] DETE *Companies Report 2006* at pp 14–15.

Dublin District Court is invoked on the basis that the CRO is located in Dublin, and offences such as omissions to file annual returns, are therefore committed in Dublin, the decentralisation of the CRO to Carlow will surely have an impact on the selection of Dublin District Court as the appropriate forum for the prosecution of such offences.

[15.039] On a general note, it is understandable that the CRO would prefer to prosecute proceedings in a District Court which may attain some level of familiarity and expertise in relation to offences under the CA 1963–2006. In this regard, it is perhaps regrettable that the following recommendation of the Working Group on Company Law Compliance and Enforcement has not been adopted: 'We consider that it would be helpful, in the interests of consistency and in order to build up a body of expertise, if a District Judge with experience of company law were to be designated to hear company law prosecutions.'[105]

[15.040] Among the disadvantages of prosecutions under the CA 1963–2006 being conducted in various District Courts is the potential disparity of outcomes and sentences and the cost and time involved in duplicating prosecutions. One illustration of this issue was the successful appeal by a partner in an audit firm against his conviction for acting as an auditor of a company while not qualified to so act contrary to CA 1990, s 187. The appeal was successful and conviction quashed, a factor in this decision appearing to be that the Probation Act was applied to other partners of the audit firm who faced similar charges before a different Judge sitting in a different District Court area.[106]

The ODCE made a submission to the DETE that, where the same facts apply, the ODCE should be able to prosecute multiple persons within the same summary proceedings. The ODCE comments that, 'in certain instances at present, proceedings have to be duplicated in different District Court areas with associated time and cost expenditures.'[107] According to the ODCE, this proposal would have the following effect: 'as well as removing the scope for what might be perceived as inconsistent outcomes at District Court level, this change would save Court time and legal costs.'[108] This submission has not been acted upon; it was not reflected in the IFCMPA 2006.

(b) Jury

[15.041] A jury trial will only arise in respect of a prosecution on indictment. When a jury is called upon to consider an offence under the Companies Acts, however, the elements of the offence may be technical and complex. CLEA 2001, s 110 is designed to counter some of the difficulties that may arise in this regard. It provides that, when an offence under the Companies Acts is tried on indictment, the trial judge may order that copies of various documents be given to the jury in such form as the judge considers appropriate. An application for such documents to be supplied to the jury may be made

---

[105] *Report of the Working Group on Company Law Compliance and Enforcement* (November 1998) at para 3.24.

[106] See ODCE *Annual Report 2006* at pp 18 and 23. Available at www.odce.ie. See Ch **7**.

[107] ODCE *Annual Report 2006* at p 9. Available at www.odce.ie.

[108] ODCE *Annual Report 2006* at p 23. Available at www.odce.ie.

on behalf of the DPP.[109] It is curious that there is no indication in s 110 that an application may be made on behalf of an accused person to have certain documents furnished to the jury.[110] The documents which may be furnished are:

(a) any document admitted in evidence at the trial,

(b) the transcript of the opening speeches of counsel,

(c) any charts, diagrams, graphics, schedules or summaries of evidence produced at the trial,

(d) the transcript of the whole or any part of the evidence given at the trial,

(e) the transcript of the trial judge's charge to the jury,

(f) any other document that in the opinion of the trial judge would be of assistance to the jury in its deliberations including, where appropriate, an affidavit by an accountant summarising, in a form which is likely to be comprehended by the jury, any transactions by the accused or other persons relevant to the offence.[111]

Two points may be noted in relation to s 110(1)(f). First, if the prosecutor proposes to seek an order that the jury be furnished with a document to assist them within the meaning of s 110(1)(f), such as an affidavit by an accountant, he must give a copy of this document to the accused before the trial. In determining that application, the judge must take account of any representations made on behalf of the accused in relation to the document.[112] Second, if a trial judge has directed that an affidavit prepared by an accountant should be furnished to the jury, he may also require that accountant to explain any relevant accounting procedures or principles to the jury.[113]

(c) Documentary evidence

[15.042] There is a particular provision of the Companies Acts which facilitates the presentation of certificate evidence, copies of documents, and extracts from documents, in legal proceedings. CLEA 2001, s 110A was introduced by C(AA)A 2003, s 52,[114] to ease some of the practical difficulties of presenting evidence in proceedings under the

---

[109] This is apparent from the terms of s 110(2), which refers to a situation in which, '... the prosecutor proposes to apply to the trial judge for an order that a document mentioned in sub-s (1)(f) shall be given to the jury.' Note however that it is only if the document which the DPP wishes to have furnished to the jury is within s 110(1)(f), that an advance copy must be given to the accused.

[110] See CLEA 2001, Annotation, ICLSA ('One criticism which may be made is the slight bias inherent in the fact that the section envisages an order under s 110(1) made on the application of the prosecution or on the trial judge's own motion, with any representations, by or on behalf of the accused to be taken into account, whilst the accused is not given standing to actually apply for an order. This would seem to ignore the fact that an accused may equally have an interest in the presentation of the issues in proceedings to the jury being made in as clear and comprehensible a way as is reasonably possible.')

[111] CLEA 2001, s 110(1).

[112] CLEA 2001, s 110(2).

[113] CLEA 2001, s 110(3).

[114] Note that this provision was also amended by IFCMPA 2005, s 74, to incorporate references to the Irish Financial Services Regulatory Authority, amendments which are not relevant in the present context.

Companies Acts. This provision applies to specified officers, who, for the purpose of s 110A, may be any of the following:

- the Minister or an officer of the Minister, in respect of functions to be discharged by the Minister under the Companies Acts;

- the DCE or an officer of the DCE, in respect of functions to be discharged by the DCE under the Acts;

- an inspector or, if more than one is appointed, any inspector, in respect of functions to be performed by inspectors under the Acts; and

- the Registrar of Companies, an assistant registrar, or any person so authorised by the Minister, in respect of functions to be performed by the Registrar under the Acts.[115]

[15.043] Any of the following certificates signed by such an official in the course of discharging his functions shall, 'in the absence of evidence to the contrary' be proof of its content in any legal proceedings, including criminal proceedings. It is also unnecessary to prove the signature of the officer or the authority of the officer to sign the certificate.[116] Section 110A does not universally excuse the need to prove the content of certificates in proceedings under the Companies Acts, but contains a list of particular matters which, once certified, do not have to be otherwise proven. If the certificate states that an officer examined relevant records, and that it appears from those documents that an event did or did not occur, the certificate shall be proof of the occurrence or non occurrence of that event. The following are the events that may be proven by way of certificate:

- that an item which was not received from a stated person during a particular period, was not furnished by that person during that period and was not received;

- that a stated notice[117] which was not issued to a stated person, was not received by that person;

- that a notice which was given to a person on a stated date, was received by that person on that date;

- that a stated notice, which was posted to a stated person at a stated address on a stated date, was received by that person at that address three days after the date of posting;

---

[115] CLEA 2001, s 110A(1), as inserted by C(AA)A 2003, s 52. Note that the Chief Executive of IFSRA or a person appointed by a person to whom he has delegated responsibility for making such appointments, is a recognised officer for the purpose of s 110A in respect of functions to be discharged under the Companies Acts by the Financial Authority or the Central Bank. See IFCMPA 2005, s 74.

[116] CLEA 2001, s 110A(3), as inserted by C(AA)A 2003, s 52.

[117] For the purposes of this provision, 'notice' includes '(a) any request, notice, letter, demand, pleading or other document, and (b) any form of obligation that an individual may have under the Companies Acts by reason of a demand or request made by an appropriate officer, whether communicated in writing, orally or by other means. CLEA 2001, s 110A(1), as inserted by C(AA)A 2003, s 52.

    — that a document was filed or registered with, or delivered at, a stated place, on a stated date or at a stated time.[118]

[15.044] There are particular provisions of CLEA 2001, s 110A, which also abrogate the requirement for formal proof of copies or extracts of documents. Any document that purports to be a copy of, or extract from, any document kept by or on behalf of the DCE, the Minister or an inspector, and certified to have been a true copy or extract, shall be admissible as evidence in all legal proceedings. It is not necessary to prove the official position of the person certifying the copy or extract to be true, who may be any of the following:

    — the DCE, Minister, or inspector, as appropriate;

    — an officer of the DCE or Minister, as appropriate; or

    — any person authorised by the DCE, Minister or inspector, as appropriate.[119]

Section 110A also contains provisions which overcome the need for persons to attend in court to prove signatures, consent, or the creation of particular documents. These may be useful evidential aids. First, s 110A(4) provides:

> 'A document prepared pursuant to any provision of the Companies Acts and purporting to be signed by any person is deemed, in the absence of evidence to the contrary, to have been signed by that person.'

The effect of this provision is that it is not necessary for every person who signs a document that was prepared pursuant to the Companies Acts, such as an auditors report, for example, to attend in court to prove their signature.

Second, s 110A(5) provides:

> 'A document submitted under the Companies Acts on behalf of a person is deemed to have been submitted by the person unless that person proves that it was submitted without that person's consent or knowledge.'

This provision removes the necessity of proving that a document that was submitted on behalf of a person was in fact furnished with their consent or knowledge. It is presumed, unless proved by that person to the contrary, that the document was submitted with his consent and knowledge.

The third general evidential aid contained in s 110A, is s 110A(9), which provides:

> 'A document that purports to have been created by a person is presumed, in the absence of evidence to the contrary, to have been created by that person, and any statement contained in the document is presumed to have been made by the person unless the document expressly attributes its making to some other person.'

The presumptions are rebuttable, but have the effect of overcoming the need for oral evidence to verify the matters set out in s 110A(4), (5) and (9) in proceedings under the Companies Acts.

(d) Double jeopardy

[15.045] The principle of double jeopardy ensures that a person will not face trial on the same charges twice. This topic has arisen in the context of the prosecution of a company

---

[118] CLEA 2001 s 110A(2), as inserted by C(AA)A 2003, s 52.

[119] CLEA 2001, s 110A(6)-(8), as inserted by C(AA)A 2003, s 52.

for failing to file its annual returns, in circumstances where the company had also paid a late filing penalty in respect of that failure. In the *Registrar of Companies v Anderson*,[120] the District Judge decided that the prosecution of a company under CA 1963, s 125, would offend against the principle of double jeopardy, as the company had already paid a late filing penalty in respect of those failures, and struck out the summons on this ground. In judicial review proceedings, the High Court refused to grant an order of *certiorari*, a refusal which was appealed to the Supreme Court.

Murray CJ, delivering the judgment with which the other members of the Court concurred, considered the administrative benefit of encouraging timely filing of annual returns, noting that it was 'a foreseeable, objective and automatic consequence for lateness in filing an annual return by any company' and that it was 'clearly designed to encourage timely filing and discourage the dilatory.' The imposition of this late filing charge was therefore 'in the interest of good and efficient administration.' The Court concluded, 'It is manifest that the statutory requirement to pay late filing fees is not in any sense something which involves a criminal process let alone a criminal prosecution.' The obligation to pay extra fees for filing the annual return late was therefore an administrative sanction. As the rule against double jeopardy applies only in relation to the prosecution of offences, and there was only ever one criminal process against the company, the question of double jeopardy did not arise and the order of the District Judge was set aside.[121]

F. Sanctions

[15.046] There are various sanctions specified in the CA 1963–2006, for offences and defaults under the Acts, ranging from fines, terms of imprisonment, daily default fines,[122] to orders of personal liability for the debts of a company, among others.[123] The

---

[120] *Registrar of Companies v Anderson* [2004] IESC 103.

[121] *Registrar of Companies v Anderson* [2004] IESC 103 ('Since there was no other criminal process, no charge, no trial of guilt or innocence, the question of double jeopardy in relation to the District Court prosecution could not arise,' *per* Murray CJ).

[122] Note that, in respect of default fines, CA 1990, s 240(6), provides: 'Where, in relation to a contravention of any provision of the Companies Acts, it is provided that for continued contravention a person shall be liable to a daily default fine, he shall be guilty of contravening the provision on every day on which the contravention continues after conviction of the original contravention and for each such offence he shall be liable to a fine not exceeding the amount specified in the provision, instead of the penalty specified for the original contravention.' The effect of this is that liability to pay the daily default fine only arises after the person has been convicted of the default in question, and when the default is ongoing, the daily default fine shall be substituted for the penalty which he would otherwise face.

[123] For a table of all indictable offences under CA 1963–2005, see appendix to ODCE, Revised Guidance on the Duty of Auditors to Report Suspected Indictable Offences to the Director of Corporate Enforcement, Decision Notice, D/2006/2. Available at www.odce.ie. Civil sanctions such as declarations of restriction; disqualification orders and orders striking the names of companies off the register are addressed separately. See Pt **D**, Pt **E** and Ch **14**, respectively.

sanction applicable to an offence is typically specified in the legislative provision that creates the offence. There are, however, certain provisions of the Acts which set out penalties applicable where none are otherwise specified. CA 1990, s 240, is the governing provision in this regard. In respect of summary convictions for which no penalty is specified in the Acts, the rule is that the maximum fine shall be €1,904.61 or, at the discretion of the court, a maximum sentence of imprisonment of 12 months, or both. When a person is convicted on indictment of an offence for which no penalty is specified in the Acts, the maximum fine is €12,697.38 or, at the discretion of the court, a maximum sentence of imprisonment of five years, or both.[124]

[15.047] Section 240 also substitutes certain penalties for those specified elsewhere in the Companies Acts. In particular, if a fine of less than €1,904.61 is provided for summary conviction of any offence, the maximum fine for that offence shall be taken to be €1,904.61. When a person is convicted summarily of an offence under the CA 1963–2006, the maximum fine will therefore never be less €1,904.61, although it may be more.[125] In respect of convictions on indictment, the maximum fine may vary, but if the maximum sentence of imprisonment is less than five years, the maximum sentence shall be taken to be five years.[126]

The penalties which are in fact imposed by the courts depend on all of the circumstances of the case. This is illustrated by the fact that the same offence, acting as an auditor while not qualified to do so, has attracted penalties ranging from a €20 fine,[127] to a €4,900 fine[128] and including the imposition of a three-month suspended sentence.[129]

There was a particular penalty applicable to persons who face second and subsequent convictions under the Companies Acts. Before the enactment of CLEA 2001, CA 1963, s 386, provided that:

> Where a person is convicted of an offence under this Act and is subsequently convicted of another offence under this Act, the fine to be imposed by the court in respect of such second or subsequent offence shall not be less than €317.43 unless the court, having regard to all the circumstances of the case, otherwise decides.[130]

As a result of the substitution of the maximum penalty for summary convictions with the sum of €1,904.61, the maximum penalty for second and subsequent offences is now also €1,904.61. This renders the intended sanction of s 386 meaningless. If it is intended to punish serial offenders, the maximum sanction provided for by s 386 will need to be increased.

[15.048] As an alternative to the sanctions applicable under the Companies Acts, it is open to a court to apply the Probation of Offenders Act 1907 and to direct the payment

---

124 CA 1990, s 240(1), as amended by CLEA 2001, s 104.

125 CA 1990, s 240(7), as amended by CLEA 2001, s 104.

126 CA 1990, s 240(8), as inserted by CLEA 2001, s 104(c).

127 Conviction of two offences.

128 Conviction of 14 separate offences.

129 See ODCE, *Annual Report 2004*, App 3.3. See further Ch **7**.

130 CA 1963, s 386, as amended by C(A)A 1982, s 15.

of monies to charity.[131] This possibility is inconsistent with the recommendation of the Working Group on Company Law Compliance and Enforcement that, 'to assist in prosecutions, the Group recommends that summary offences under the Companies Acts be removed from the ambit of the Probation of Offenders Act 1907'.[132] In spite of the Working Group recommendation, the Probation of Offenders Act is in fact frequently applied by courts in relation to offences under the CA 1963–2006.[133]

The ODCE has cautioned that, 'primarily from a concern for the effectiveness of our law enforcement functions, we are anxious insofar as penalties are concerned that breaches of the law should be capable of being sanctioned by effective, proportionate and dissuasive penalties.' The ODCE referred to the statistic that in 2006 the aggregate amount of fines levied in criminal cases was €23,000, having amounted to €35,000 in 2005, but noted that charitable donations in excess of €7,000 were directed in other cases.[134]

G. Illustration of criminal prosecution under the Companies Acts

[15.049] An illustration of the detection, investigation, prosecution, and sentencing of a person in relation to an offence under the CA 1963–2006 can be seen in the case of the *ODCE v Gannon*.[135] In this case, the liquidator of Corran Building Services Ltd (in voluntary liquidation) made a report to the ODCE under CLEA 2001, s 56, which suggested that an offence had been committed. The liquidator made a further report under CA 1963, s 299, regarding his belief that an offence had been committed. As a result of the information contained in these reports, members of An Garda Síochána who were seconded to the ODCE, applied to court for a search warrant under CA 1990, s 20, which they then executed, seizing documents and other information from the company's registered office.

In a follow-up search (the legal basis for which is not specified by the ODCE), the officers seized two vehicles which were purchased with company funds, but were in the personal use of a director of the company and his wife. These vehicles were subsequently handed over to the liquidator, on foot of a court order granted under s 9 of the Police Property Act 1897. Following further investigation, members of An Garda

---

[131] A probation order is effectively a formal warning to a person that if he does not abide by conditions imposed by the court he will be liable to be brought before the court for punishment. The making of a so-called 'probation order' may or may not involve the conviction of the alleged offender. See Walsh, *Criminal Procedure* (Thomson Round Hall, 2002), paras 21.29 to 21.31.

[132] *Report of the Working Group on Company Law Compliance and Enforcement* (November 1998) at para 3.23.

[133] See App 3.3 to ODCE *Annual Report 2006* at pp 56–60. While convictions were secured by ODCE on 48 charges in 2006, the Probation Act was applied in respect of 36 charges. See ODCE *Annual Report 2006* at p 18. See further examples of cases in which the Probation Act was applied or charitable donations ordered, at ODCE *Annual Report 2006* at p 23.

[134] ODCE *Annual Report 2006* at p 17. Available at www.odce.ie.

[135] See ODCE *Annual Report 2003* at p 19. Available at www.odce.ie.

Síochána who were seconded to the ODCE, arrested and charged a director of the company in liquidation with fraudulent trading contrary to CA 1963, s 297 (as amended); failing to keep proper books of account, contrary to CA 1990, s 202; and failing to file annual returns, contrary to CA 1963, s 125 (as amended).

In the District Court, the director pleaded guilty to all three charges. The Court imposed two concurrent sentences of six months, which were suspended for 12 months, in respect of the fraudulent trading and failure to keep proper books of account charges. The director was also bound to keep the peace for 12 months, on a bond of €250. On the application of the liquidator, the High Court subsequently made a declaration of restriction in respect of the director. This case illustrates the investigative and prosecutorial functions of the DCE and the prosecution of summary offences under CA 1963–2006.

H. Proposed reforms

[15.050] If the recommendations of the CLRG regarding offences under the Companies Acts are enacted into law, the landscape of this area of company law will change considerably and some of the issues discussed in this chapter will no longer be pertinent. In particular, the CLRG General Scheme on the Draft Companies Consolidation and Reform Bill 2007 contains a novel provision proposing to categorise offences under the Companies Acts into category one, category two, category three, and category four offences.

Head 57 of Pt A13 of the General Scheme provides that, where no punishment is specified, a 'Category 1' offence will be punishable, on summary conviction, by a maximum fine of €5,000 or, at the discretion of the court, to imprisonment for a term not exceeding 12 months, or both. On conviction on indictment, a 'Category 1' offence is punishable by a maximum fine of €500,000 or, at the discretion of the court, a maximum term of imprisonment of 10 years, or both.[136] A 'Category 2' offence is punishable, on summary conviction, by a maximum fine of €5,000 or maximum sentence of imprisonment of 12 months, or both. On conviction on indictment, a 'Category 2' offence is punishable by a maximum fine of €50,000, or a maximum sentence of imprisonment of 5 years, or both.[137] A 'Category 3' offence is punishable, on summary conviction, by a maximum fine of €5,000 or a maximum term of imprisonment of 6 months, or both.[138] A 'Category 4' offence is punishable, on summary conviction, to a maximum fine of €5,000.[139] There is no provision for convictions on indictment in respect of Category 3 and Category 4 offences.

---

[136] CLRG, General Scheme of the Draft Companies Consolidation and Reform Bill 2007, Pt A13, Head 57(1)(a). Available at www.clrg.org.

[137] CLRG, General Scheme of the Draft Companies Consolidation and Reform Bill 2007, Pt A13, Head 57(1)(b). Available at www.clrg.org.

[138] CLRG, General Scheme of the Draft Companies Consolidation and Reform Bill 2007, Pt A13, Head 57(1)(c). Available at www.clrg.org.

[139] CLRG, General Scheme of the Draft Companies Consolidation and Reform Bill 2007, Pt A13, Head 57(1)(d). Available at www.clrg.org.

Head 57 also proposes that:

> 'Following a conviction for a category 1 offence, or category 2 offence or category
> 3 offence or category 4 offence, the Court in which that conviction has been
> recorded or affirmed may order that the convicted person should remedy the
> breach of the Companies Acts in respect of which they were convicted.'[140]

The CLRG envisages that this categorisation of offences would apply to all offences
under the Companies Acts, subject to some narrow exceptions involving the most
serious offences, such as fraudulent trading and market abuse.[141] The CLRG describes
the manner in which these categories have been compiled as follows:

> 'This four-fold system will allow for an appropriately graduated system of
> penalties as between different offence provisions. In preparing these Heads, the
> CLRG has undertaken a comprehensive exercise, in conjunction with ODCE
> officials, of classifying the offences on what is thought to be the appropriate basis.
> In addition, it leads to the law being more easily understood because in each of the
> many provisions throughout the Bill creating offences, it is now possible to simply
> add a phrase along the lines of "which will be a Category 2 offence".'[142]

The CLRG describes this approach as a 'new initiative'[143] and as a 'root and branch
review of all criminal offences arising under the Companies Acts':[144] it remains to be
seen, however, whether this proposed re-categorisation of criminal offences will form
part of the new companies legislation and how it would operate in practice.

---

[140] CLRG, General Scheme of the Draft Companies Consolidation and Reform Bill 2007,
Pt A13, Head 57(3). Available at www.clrg.org.

[141] See CLRG, Report on the General Scheme of the Draft Companies Consolidation and
Reform Bill 2007, at p 68. It may be noted that Pt A13, Head 57(2) envisages only four
categories of indictable offences: Category 1 and 2 offences; offences under the Market
Abuse Regulations, and offences under the Prospectus Regulations.

[142] CLRG, Report on the General Scheme of the Draft Companies Consolidation and Reform
Bill 2007, at p 68. Available at www.clrg.org.

[143] CLRG, Report on the General Scheme of the Draft Companies Consolidation and Reform
Bill 2007, at p 68.

[144] CLRG, Report on the General Scheme of the Draft Companies Consolidation and Reform
Bill 2007, at p 3.

PART D
DECLARATIONS OF RESTRICTION

Chapter 16: Nature and scope of restriction proceedings
A. Introduction 807
B. Nature of restriction proceedings 808
C. Persons affected 817

Chapter 17: Defences to restriction proceedings
A. Introduction 841
B. Honesty and responsibility 842
C. 'Just and equitable' 875
D. Delay 877
E. Relief 881

Chapter 18: Procedure of restriction proceedings
A. Applicants under s 150 887
B. Parties to restriction proceedings 888
C. Rules of procedure 891
D. Practice direction 892
E. Service of restriction proceedings 893
F. Discovery in restriction proceedings 897
G. Restriction undertakings 898

Chapter 19: Consequences of declarations of restriction
A. Period of restriction 903
B. Effect of declaration of restriction 904
C. Notification and reporting requirements 905
D. Consequences for restricted companies 906
E. Register of restricted persons 914
F. Breach of declaration of restriction 915
G. Costs 916

Chapter 16

NATURE AND SCOPE OF RESTRICTION PROCEEDINGS

A. Introduction

[16.001] An area in which the enforcement of company law is particularly visible relates to the restriction of directors. The idea of restricting directors of insolvent companies from acting as directors of other companies was introduced into Irish company law by the CA 1990. The number of directors who were restricted in the years between the enactment of the CA 1990 and the introduction of the CLEA 2001, was few. Since the introduction of the CLEA 2001, however, the number of persons who have faced restriction proceedings has risen quite dramatically. By way of illustration, there were 118 restricted persons at the end of 2001[1] and at the end of 2006, 691 names appeared on the register of restricted persons.[2]

The governing provisions are CA 1990, ss 149 and 150. Section 150(1), in particular, provides:

> The court shall, unless it is satisfied as to any of the matters specified in subsection (2), declare that a person to whom this Chapter applies shall not, for a period of five years, be appointed or act in any way, whether directly or indirectly, as a director or secretary or be concerned or take part in the promotion or formation of any company unless it meets the requirements set out in subsection (3); and in subsequent provisions of this Part, the expression 'a person to whom section 150 applies' shall be construed as a reference to a person in respect of whom such a declaration has been made.

[16.002] As restriction orders are an important and prominent aspect of the enforcement of company law, the rules, procedures and interpretations that have been applied in this area warrant close scrutiny. It is first necessary to examine the nature of restriction proceedings under CA 1990, s 150, in order to understand what restriction applications are designed to achieve, how they operate in practice and how their outcome is determined; and the scope of restriction proceedings.

---

[1] See Department of Enterprise, Trade and Employment, Companies Report 2001 at p 42. Available at www.cro.ie.

[2] See CRO, *Annual Report 2006* at p 28. Available at www.cro.ie.

[3] CA 1990, s 150(1) reads as follows: 'The court shall, unless it is satisfied as to any of the matters specified in sub-s (2), declare that a person to whom this chapter applies shall not, for a period of five years, be appointed or act in any way, whether directly or indirectly, as a director or secretary or be concerned or take part in the promotion or formation of any company unless it meets the requirements set out in sub-s (3); (contd .../)

B. Nature of restriction proceedings

(a) Introduction

[16.003] The basis for the making of a restriction order is described pithily in CA 1990, s 150 as follows: 'the court shall, unless it is satisfied as to any of the matters specified in sub-s (2)' restrict a person 'to whom this chapter applies…'.[3]

A person to whom that chapter[4] applies is 'any person who was a director[5] of a company to which this section applies at the date of, or within 12 months prior to, the commencement of its winding-up.'[6] The companies to which the section refers are companies which are unable to pay their debts, whether this is proved at the commencement, or in the course of the winding up.[7]

Section 150 essentially requires the court to make an order of restriction in respect of any person who was a director or shadow director of a company, within 12 months prior to that company going into insolvent liquidation. The only basis on which the court can decide not to make a restriction order, is that the director has established one of the grounds set out in s 150(2).[8]

[16.004] If a court is satisfied that a person was a director or shadow director of a company within 12 months of that company entering insolvent liquidation that is sufficient to make a declaration of restriction. As will be seen, the onus is on the director to satisfy the court that such a declaration should not be made.[9] Little attention has focused upon the grounds for making an order of restriction. As will be seen below, the category of persons to whom the order applies,[10] and the defences which may be raised to an application for restriction,[11] as well as the procedures applicable to such an application,[12] have attracted considerably more attention.

---

[3] (contd) and, in subsequent provisions of this Part, the expression '"a person to whom s 150 applies" shall be construed as a reference to a person in respect of whom such a declaration has been made.'

[4] CA 1990, Pt VII, Ch 1.

[5] According to CA 1990, s 149(5), 'This Chapter applies to shadow directors as it applies to directors'. The definition and scope of the term 'director' for the purpose of restriction proceedings is considered further below at paras **[16.021]** to **[16.067]**.

[6] CA 1990, s 149(2).

[7] CA 1990, s 149(1) reads, 'This Chapter applies to any company if—

    (a) at the date of the commencement of its winding-up it is proved to the court, or

    (b) at any time during the course of its winding-up the liquidator of the company certifies, or it is otherwise proved, to the court,

    that it is unable to pay its debts (within the meaning of s 214 of the Principal Act).'

[8] See further Ch **17**.

[9] See paras **[16.014]** to **[16.018]**.

[10] See below paras **[16.021]** to **[16.067]**.

[11] See Ch **17**.

[12] See Ch **18**.

(b) Public interest

[16.005] The objectives of the Companies Acts include the protection of the public and this encompasses protecting the public against fraudulent, unscrupulous, incompetent or imprudent management of companies. The restriction of a director who has acted as a director of an insolvent company, is one means of providing such protection. Declarations of restriction are often cited as a means of overcoming the 'phoenix syndrome', whereby persons form a company, which becomes insolvent, liquidate the company and then form a new company from its ashes, potentially exposing new creditors to the same detriment and losses suffered by the first company's creditors. This underlying objective of protecting the public against such conduct has an impact on the nature of restriction proceedings, and has affected the procedures and outcomes of such proceedings in a number of significant ways.

In *Re Verit Hotel and Leisure (Ireland) Ltd*,[13] Fennelly J observed that 'the intrinsic nature' of proceedings seeking restriction orders must be taken into account[14] and that s 150 'gives effect to a public interest in seeing that persons should no longer enjoy the unqualified right to become involved in the formation of companies, where they have been directors of companies which have failed due to insolvency'.[15]

The public interest dimension to restriction proceedings was also emphasised by the Court in *Re Colm O'Neill Engineering Services Ltd*.[16] Finlay Geoghegan J described the 'legal framework which has been established by s 150 and the authorities on the section' as demonstrating:

> '... that the purpose of the Section is to protect the public against the future supervision and management of companies by persons whose past record as directors of insolvent companies have shown them to be a danger to creditors and others. It is also established that it is not the purpose of the Section to punish the individuals concerned.'

(c) Non-adversarial

[16.006] The practice and procedure of an application seeking a declaration of restriction is quite different to other adversarial court applications. There are a number of reasons for this distinction. First, most restriction applications come before the courts as a result of the ODCE's refusal to relieve liquidators of the duty to bring restriction

---

13 *Re Verit Hotel and Leisure (Ireland) Ltd (In Receivership and in liquidation), Re Verit Hotel and Leisure (Ireland) Ltd (In Receivership and in liquidation), Duignan v Carway* [2001] IESC 74.

14 *Re Verit Hotel and Leisure (Ireland) Ltd (In Receivership and in liquidation), Re Verit Hotel and Leisure (Ireland) Ltd (In Receivership and in liquidation), Duignan v Carway* [2001] IESC 74 at para 16.

15 *Re Verit Hotel and Leisure (Ireland) Ltd (In Receivership and in liquidation), Re Verit Hotel and Leisure (Ireland) Ltd (In Receivership and in liquidation), Duignan v Carway* [2001] IESC 74 at para 16.This case is addressed further below in the context of delay in the bringing of restriction proceedings. See paras **[17.071]** to **[17.072]**.

16 *Re Colm O'Neill Engineering Services (in liq)* [2004] IEHC 83.

proceedings in accordance with s 56(2).[17] As every liquidator is compelled to bring restriction proceedings in those circumstances, there will inevitably be some applications which the liquidators themselves do not consider to be warranted. Secondly, the onus of proof in an application for a restriction order is a low one, with the applicant bound only to establish that the company was in insolvent liquidation and that the respondent was a director of the company at, or within 12 months prior to, the date of commencement of the winding up. Most restriction applications revolve around a consideration of the honesty and responsibility of the director, which are not matters on which the liquidator has to express a view. In many cases, the liquidator will engage with the director's defence of their conduct, but there is no obligation to do so. Thirdly, the application for restriction is a matter between the directors and the court. It is in the public interest that restriction orders are made and the view of the liquidator with regard to the merits of making such an order are not necessarily relevant to the protection of the public interest.

[16.007] In *Re Verit Hotel and Leisure (Ireland) Ltd*,[18] the High Court was called upon to consider the nature of restriction proceedings in some detail. One of issues with which the Court was confronted was the evidential burdens on the respective parties to an application for a restriction order. In that case, it was argued on behalf of the directors opposing the restriction orders, that any evidence which was not controverted by the liquidator must be accepted by the court. This argument was based on the premise that proceedings seeking a restriction order are adversarial proceedings between the liquidator and the director.

McCracken J rejected these propositions, stating, 'I think this objection is really based on a total misconception of the nature of proceedings under s 150' and that, 'in fact, these are not adversarial proceedings in that sense'.[19] This case was not determined under the CLEA 2001. However, the analysis of the Court is equally relevant to proceedings taken after 2001. In particular, the Court analysed the nature of the obligation on a liquidator to bring a s 150 application, emphasising that, 'there is in fact no obligation on a liquidator who brings the matter before the Court to put forward any facts which would tend to show that the directors had acted dishonestly or irresponsibly, nor indeed is he obliged to so argue'.[20] On the contrary, the Court acknowledged that 'in practice, there are occasions when the liquidator will bring an application under this Section, and will tell the Court that he believes that the directors acted honestly and responsibly'.

---

[17] Ch **9**.

[18] *Re Verit Hotel and Leisure (Ireland) Ltd (In Receivership and in liquidation), Re Verit Hotel and Leisure (Ireland) Ltd (In Receivership and in liquidation), Duignan v Carway* [2002] IEHC 1.

[19] *Re Verit Hotel and Leisure (Ireland) Ltd (In Receivership and in liquidation), Re Verit Hotel and Leisure (Ireland) Ltd (In Receivership and in liquidation), Duignan v Carway* [2002] IEHC 1 at para 8.

[20] *Re Verit Hotel and Leisure (Ireland) Ltd (In Receivership and in liquidation), Re Verit Hotel and Leisure (Ireland) Ltd (In Receivership and in liquidation), Duignan v Carway* [2002] IEHC 1 at para 9.

In that case the High Court commented further that:

> 'Most proceedings brought by a liquidator against the directors are for the benefit of the creditors. There is no such benefit in s 150 Proceedings, and once the formal application has been brought, together with the formal proof that the company is insolvent, it is a matter for the liquidator whether he should take any further part in the proceedings. In many cases the liquidators feel that they do have an obligation to pursue the directors to some degree, but if they do so, they do so in the public interest.'[21]

[16.008] Similarly, in *Re Tralee Beef and Lamb Ltd*[22] the Court noted that, even though the liquidator may be satisfied with the conduct of the director and satisfied that no grounds for restriction existed, if the liquidator is not relieved of his obligation to bring restriction proceedings under s 56, there may be, as occurred in respect of one of the respondents in that case, 'no formal *legitimus contradictor*'.

[16.009] Another aspect of the non-adversarial nature of restriction proceedings is that it is firmly established that, irrespective of an applicant's own views of the merits of the case or the desirability of a restriction order, he cannot settle the proceedings or discourage the making of an order. There have been instances in which the applicant has indicated expressly their satisfaction with the conduct of the respondent director, only for the court to determine that it is not a matter to which the applicant's level of satisfaction is relevant. One example is the case of *Re Dunleckney Ltd*[23] in which the respondent failed to comply with his statutory duty to file a statement of affairs. The liquidator was satisfied with the co-operation provided by the respondent and expressed the view that the statement of affairs would not have revealed any additional information. The Court nonetheless made an order of restriction, noting the respondent's failure to explain the lack of a statement of affairs and commenting that, 'In my opinion it is not for the Official Liquidator to excuse a director from his statutory obligation.'

[16.010] This examination of proceedings taken under s 150 highlights an important point. Proceedings for a restriction order are taken before the court where a certain set of circumstances exists and there is not necessarily any party to the proceedings who believes that the making of the order sought is necessary, desirable or even warranted. This is a highly unusual feature of applications made under s 150, and one which is particularly prevalent since the introduction of CLEA 2001. As will be seen, a liquidator of an insolvent company is now obliged to bring restriction proceedings against any person who acted as a director or shadow director of the company within 12 months of its winding up, unless the ODCE relieves the liquidator of this obligation. The possibility that a liquidator may find himself applying for a restriction order which he does not believe to be necessary, desirable or warranted, is therefore heightened since the CLEA 2001 came into force.

---

[21] *Re Verit Hotel and Leisure (Ireland) Ltd (In Receivership and in liquidation), Re Verit Hotel and Leisure (Ireland) Ltd (In Receivership and in liquidation), Duignan v Carway* [2002] IEHC 1.

[22] *Re Tralee Beef and Lamb Ltd, Kavanagh v Delaney* [2004] IEHC 139.

[23] *Re Dunleckney Ltd* [1999] IEHC 109 (Carroll J).

[16.011] The statements of McCracken J in *Re Verit Hotel and Leisure (Ireland) Ltd,*[24] to the effect that proceedings seeking restriction orders are not adversarial in nature and may in some circumstances not have any actual proponent, are therefore even more apt since the amendments introduced by the CLEA 2001 and should be borne in mind in relation to any proceedings under s 150.

In that case, McCracken J contrasted proceedings under s 150 with proceedings taken pursuant to CA 1990, s 160. The relevant point of comparison in the context of that case, and in the present context, is that, whereas an application under s 160 is not mandatory, applications under s 150 are. McCracken J concluded that, if a party chooses to make an application under s 160, 'then a truly adversarial situation does arise.'[25]

McCracken J pointed to a further contrast between s 150 proceedings and most other proceedings which may be taken by a liquidator against the company's directors, noting that, whereas the objective of most proceedings against directors was the benefit of the company's creditors: 'there is no such benefit in s 150'.[26] According to the Court, one consequence of this is that, in relation to s 150 proceedings:

> 'once the formal application has been brought, together with the formal proof that the company is insolvent, it is a matter for the liquidator whether he should take any further part in the proceedings. In many cases the liquidators feel that they do have an obligation to pursue the directors to some degree, but if they do so, they do so in the public interest.'

[16.012] The following points can be distilled from the dicta of McCracken J in *Re Verit Hotel and Leisure (Ireland) Ltd,*[27] and the other cases addressed above, regarding the nature of proceedings seeking declaration of a restriction under s 150:

- the proceedings are not adversarial in nature;

- there will not necessarily be a party advocating the making of a restriction order;

- the proceedings are mandatory;

- if the liquidator does actively pursue the application, he does so in the public interest; and

- evidence which is presented on behalf of respondent directors, and on which there is no cross-examination, does not have to be accepted by the court.

---

[24] *Re Verit Hotel and Leisure (Ireland) Ltd (In Receivership and in liquidation), Duignan v Carway* [2002] IEHC 1.

[25] *Re Verit Hotel and Leisure (Ireland) Ltd (In Receivership and in liquidation), Duignan v Carway* [2002] IEHC 1 at para 10.

[26] *Re Verit Hotel and Leisure (Ireland) Ltd (In Receivership and in liquidation), Duignan v Carway* [2002] IEHC 1 at para 11.

[27] *Re Verit Hotel and Leisure (Ireland) Ltd (In Receivership and in liquidation), Duignan v Carway* [2002] IEHC 1.

(d) Role of applicant

[16.013] The persons who may apply to court for a declaration of restriction, as set out in s 150(4A), are the Director of Corporate Enforcement, a liquidator or a receiver. In practice, the vast majority of applications under s 150[28] are brought by liquidators, which is largely due to the obligation of liquidators to bring such applications, unless relieved of that obligation by the ODCE.[29]

A person applying for an order of restriction must establish all of the factors set out in CA 1990, s 149. Once the applicant has demonstrated that the respondent was a director of a company which went into insolvent liquidation at the time of the commencement of the winding up or within 12 months before that date, the applicant has fulfilled this task. The rules of procedure and law which have been formulated for the purpose of restriction proceedings, however, clarify that the applicant, at least if he is a voluntary liquidator, is obliged to put before the court any material that touches upon the honesty or responsibility of the respondent; whether it is just and equitable to restrict the person in question; and whether the respondent is the nominee of a financial institution within the meaning of s 150(2)(b).

In *Re SPH Ltd*[30] the Court commented that the obligation of a liquidator who was taking restriction proceedings pursuant to s 56, was 'to put before the court those matters which he considers the court should take into account in determining whether the director has acted honestly and responsibly' as required by the Practice Direction of the President of the High Court.

(e) Burden of proof

[16.014] One unusual aspect of proceedings for a restriction order under s 150, is that the onus on the person making the application is a limited one. It is evident from the terms of CA 1990, ss 149 and 150, and from a number of decisions of the Irish courts, that the only burden on the applicant is the burden to show that the company in liquidation was insolvent and that the person against whom the order of restriction is sought was a director of the company at the date of commencement of the winding up or within 12 months before that date.[31]

The person defending the proceedings, on the other hand, bears a heavier burden of proof. As will be seen, s 150(2) imposes on the respondent the burden of satisfying the court that they acted 'honestly and responsibly in the conduct of the affairs of the company' and there is no other reason why it would be just and equitable to make a declaration of restriction.

---

[28] CA 1990, s 150(4A), as inserted by CLEA 2001, s 41(1)(c).

[29] CLEA 2001, s 56(2). See Ch **9**. See also Ch **18**.

[30] *Re SPH Ltd, Fennell v Shanahan* [2005] IEHC 152.

[31] See decision of Peart J in *Re USIT World plc* [2005] IEHC 285: 'There is no onus on the Liquidator in an application under this section.'

[16.015] In cases such as *Re Mitek Ltd,*[32] *Re Tralee Beef and Lamb Ltd*[33] and *Re 360Atlantic (Ireland) Ltd,*[34] the Irish courts have acknowledged that:

> 'An application such as this brought by a liquidator under s 150(4) pursuant to his obligation under s.56 of the Act of 2001 is not a normal *inter partes* adversarial application. The onus of establishing that he/she acted honestly and responsibly rests on the director.'[35]

The High Court has also noted that the burden of proof which rests on a director is not limited to the matters listed in s 150(2), but also extends to dealing in the course of the application with any matters which arise, including matters raised by their fellow directors.[36]

In *Re Tralee Beef and Lamb Ltd,*[37] the Court, having described the general burden of proof on an applicant for an order of restriction, went on to state:

> 'It is of course, also open to a director to bring to the attention of the court any other matter which he/she considers the court should take into account when considering the overall conduct of that person as this Court is required to do in accordance with the decision of the Supreme Court in *Re Squash (Ireland) Limited* [2001] 3 IR 35.'

In *Re Newcastle Timber (in liq),*[38] the High Court drew a distinction between disqualification and restriction proceedings in relation to the respective burdens of proof borne by the applicant and the respondent. The Court noted that, whereas under s 160, the onus is on liquidators to satisfy the court that the conditions for the making of a disqualification order have been satisfied, under s 150:

> 'the Court must make a Restriction Order unless it is satisfied that the person acted honestly and responsibly, and therefore the onus is on the Director concerned to satisfy the Court as to his honesty and responsibility.'

The restriction procedure is therefore much more heavily weighted against the director and it is a matter for the director to satisfy the court that there are reasons for the court not to exercise its otherwise mandatory jurisdiction under s 150.

[16.016] This does not, however, mean that a director who does not participate in restriction proceedings will automatically be restricted. In *Re USIT World plc*[39] two of the directors against whom restriction orders were sought, neither filed affidavits in, nor

---

[32] *Re Mitek Ltd, Grace v Kachkar* [2005] IEHC 63. The Court also noted in that case, 'Whilst in practical terms a director may primarily seek to address the matters raised by the liquidator, pursuant to the practice direction referred, the director is not relieved of the general onus established by s 150 of the Act of 1990.'

[33] *Re Tralee Beef and Lamb, Kavanagh v Delaney* [2004] IEHC 139.

[34] *Re 360Atlantic (Ireland) Ltd, O'Ferral v Coughlan* [2004] IEHC 410.

[35] *Re 360Atlantic (Ireland) Ltd, O'Ferral v Coughlan* [2004] IEHC 410.

[36] See *Re Tralee Beef and Lamb, Kavanagh v Delaney* [2004] IEHC 139.

[37] *Re Tralee Beef and Lamb Ltd Kavanagh v Delaney* [2004] IEHC 139.

[38] *Re Newcastle Timber (in liq)* [2001] IEHC 146. See further Ch **22**.

[39] *Re USIT World plc* [2005] IEHC 285.

were represented at, the proceedings seeking a declaration of restriction. Peart J posed the question whether a court, which is satisfied that a director who is not present or represented in restriction proceedings, acted honestly and responsibly, is nonetheless obliged to make an order of restriction in respect of that director.

Peart J noted that a court may be satisfied from the information and evidence advanced by a liquidator or from affidavits of other respondents or information otherwise before the court, that an unrepresented director acted honestly and responsibly. There is, according to the Court, no presumption that a director against whom an order of restriction is sought acted irresponsibly or dishonestly.[40]

Reiterating that there is no burden of proof on a liquidator under s 150, the Court determined that:

> '... it seems to be contrary to common-sense, if nothing worse, that a Court could be satisfied that the conduct of all the directors was responsible in all the circumstances from its consideration of such a volume of documentation as in this case, as well as perhaps the submissions of other parties, and yet have to decide, in a way which flies in the face of that finding, that a particular director should be restricted because, for whatever reason – perhaps lack of means – he/she had not engaged lawyers to participate in the application.'

The Court referred to the position of directors of insolvent companies and the impact that insolvency may have had on their finances, noting that there may be financial reasons for a director not to be represented on a s 150 application. Peart J expressed a concern over directors conceding that they acted dishonestly or irresponsibly to avoid the expense of court proceedings:

> '... For a director to be forced to concede the matter rather than resist, on the basis of it being the lesser of two evils, the greater being perhaps to try and borrow funds to meet the application, cannot be necessary or, more importantly, just and equitable.'

The conclusion in *Re USIT World plc*[41] is a noteworthy one:

> 'In my view, justice requires that the court, even where there is no response by the respondent, should first consider whether it can be satisfied from the facts placed before it by the liquidator that the respondent has acted honestly and responsibly. If it is so satisfied, then it follows that no order should be made, even in the absence of participation by the respondent, as to do otherwise is to presume that an absence of participation gives rise to a presumption of dishonesty and irresponsibility, and the Act provides for no such presumption. It is undesirable that a director should be deemed to have conceded a matter about which the court can be satisfied to the contrary on the documentation before it, especially where

---

[40] *Re USIT World plc* [2005] IEHC 285, *per* Peart J: 'The section cannot be fairly interpreted, in the absence of express wording to such effect, as meaning that a presumption of dishonesty and irresponsibility is to be inferred where a director takes no step to participate in the application. Such a presumption could fly in the face of matters glaring from the application itself from which the Court is satisfied as to honesty and responsibility. The task of the court is to be satisfied. The section does not confine the Court as to the source of that satisfaction.'

[41] *Re USIT World plc* [2005] IEHC 285.

the consequences of so doing are penal in nature, if not intent. The effect is to provide protection to the public against someone in respect of whom the public has no need to be protected. That is nonsensical, absurd and unjust.'

[16.017] This decision does abrogate to some extent the principle that a director bears the burden of proving to the satisfaction of the court that he acted honestly and responsibly. This is particularly apparent from statements such as 'it is important to note that the section does not state that the director must satisfy the Court. It says that "unless the Court is satisfied"', and 'The task of the court is to be satisfied. The section does not confine the Court as to the source of that satisfaction.' The burden of proof is only removed to the extent, however, that it may be satisfied by evidence from sources other than the director. The court still has to be satisfied that a director acted honestly and responsibly and if the director wishes to resist a restriction application, the burden will rest on him rather than on any other person making submissions to the court.

[16.018] For directors who do not wish or cannot afford, to resist restriction proceedings, *Re USIT World plc*[42] is significant. This decision clarifies that a director who is not represented will not automatically be restricted. This may provide most comfort in cases where there are several respondents, with similar allegations and facts applicable to each. Information and submissions advanced by other respondents may satisfy the court of the honesty and responsibility of unrepresented directors. It would be open to the respondents in such a case, for example, to put resources into resisting one of the applications, in the hope that a successful defence would also avail the other respondents. This is not without risks, however. It is by advancing his own case, indicting all exculpatory material and all subjective evidence of honesty and responsibility, that a director has the best prospect of satisfying the court that he acted honestly and responsibly.

(f) Lack of discretion

[16.019] It has already been seen that the structure and practice of restriction proceedings is not like other adversarial court proceedings. The same applies to the role of the court in relation to the restriction proceedings. If the criteria of s 149 are met, and the court is not satisfied on the balance of probabilities[43] that the director acted honestly and responsibly or that there is any other reason why it is just and equitable that he not be restricted, the court has no discretion. It is mandatory for the court to make a declaration of restriction in those circumstances. This was noted by the High Court in *Re 360 Atlantic (Ireland) Ltd*,[44] in which the Court, under the heading 'limit of court's jurisdiction' stated that potential prejudice to the respondents 'is not a matter which the Court may take into account under s 150 of the Act of 1990. The restriction for five

---

[42]   *Re USIT World plc* [2005] IEHC 285.

[43]   *Re USIT World plc* [2005] IEHC 285 clearly applies the 'balance of probabilities' standard: 'It is clear from what I have said that I am satisfied on the balance of probabilities in view of certain conflicts of evidence that both Gordon Colleary and Mairín Colleary have acted honestly and responsibly.'

[44]   *Re 360 Atlantic (Ireland) Ltd: O'Ferral v Coughlan* [2004] IEHC 410.

years is mandatory where a respondent fails to satisfy the Court that he acted responsibly in relation to the conduct of the affairs of the Company[45].'

(g) Extra-territorial jurisdiction

[16.020] It has been established, through decisions of the High Court, that an order of restriction can be made against directors of Irish companies who are not resident in this jurisdiction. In *Re Euroking Miracle (Ireland) Ltd*,[46] the Court stated the reasoning behind this aspect of a section 150 declaration as follows:

> 'Having regard to the frequency with which persons resident outside the State are appointed directors of Irish companies, it would clearly be absurd to suggest that the Oireachtas, in enacting these provisions in the public interest, only intended to restrict directors of insolvent companies who happened to be resident within the State and leave dishonest or irresponsible non-resident directors unrestricted freedom to be directors of any Irish companies in the future. The use of the phrase 'any person' in s 149(2) underlines what appears to be the obvious intent of the Oireachtas that the restrictions provided for in s 150 should apply to all persons who agree to act as directors of Irish companies irrespective of where they happen to be resident.'

The application of s 150 to directors of Irish companies who are not resident in Ireland can also be seen in cases such as *Re 360Networks (Ireland) Ltd*,[47] *Re 360Atlantic (Ireland) Ltd*,[48] and *Re Mitek Ltd*.[49]

C. Persons affected

[16.021] The possibility of restriction of a company's directors arises whenever a company enters into liquidation, the company being, or transpiring to be, insolvent.[50]

Where these criteria are met, any person who acted as a director of the company in question faces the risk of restriction. In many companies, the category of persons who are within the scope of s 150 will be clear and unambiguous, being the directors sitting on the board of directors at the date of the winding up of the company. However, the history of section 150 proceedings demonstrates that there may be other categories of persons in respect of whom the application of that provision is not without controversy. This topic has been addressed, and to a large extent, resolved, by a number of decisions of the Irish courts.

---

45 *Re 360 Atlantic (Ireland) Ltd: O'Ferral v Coughlan* [2004] IEHC 410. Finlay Geoghegan J further commented that, 'The only discretion in the Court is where an application is subsequently made under s 152.'

46 *Re Euroking Miracle (Ireland) Limited (In Voluntary Liquidation), Fennell v Frost* [2003] IEHC 15 (5 June 2003, unreported), HC, Finlay Geoghegan J).

47 *Re 360Networks (Ireland) Ltd, O'Ferral v Coughlan* [2004] IEHC 410.

48 *Re 360 Atlantic (Ireland) Ltd: O'Ferral v Coughlan* [2004] IEHC 410.

49 *Re Mitek Ltd, Grace v Kachkar* [2005] IEHC 63.

50 See above para **[16.003]**.

(a) Onus of proving fact of directorship

[16.022] It is well established that the heavier onus of proof in restriction proceedings lies on the directors seeking to resist the making of a restriction order.[51] However, the liquidator pursuing the restriction application must demonstrate that the respondent to the application was a director of a company at the date of its winding up or within 12 months prior to that date.[52]

[16.023] The case of *Re Visual Impact and Displays Ltd*[53] provides a strong illustration of the onus on the applicant for a restriction order, to show that the person against whom the order is sought was a director of the company at, or within 12 months before, the commencement of the winding up. In that case, the liquidator's affidavit stated that the respondent was 'apparently appointed director of the company... However, no form B10 to this effect has been lodged in the Company's Registration Office'. The respondent in question swore an affidavit to the effect that he never became nor acted as a director of the company in liquidation, an averment to which the liquidator made no response. The liquidator further failed to put forward evidence in support of his claim that the respondent was a director. The High Court (Finlay Geoghegan J) ruled that the liquidator failed to prove, as a matter of probability, that the respondent was a director of the company.

[16.024] The liquidator in *Re Visual Impact and Displays Ltd*[54] attempted to rely on the fact that he was not relieved by the ODCE of the obligation to apply for the restriction of the respondent. The Court rejected this argument, noting that the liquidator must have included the respondent among the directors of the company for the purposes of the report to the ODCE and cautioning that:

> 'If a liquidator so includes a person then he must be able to foresee that if not relieved by the Director he will be obliged to bring the application under s 150 in respect of that person and discharge the onus of proof placed on him to establish before the Court on credible evidence that as a matter of probability the named person was a director of the company at the date of commencement of the winding up or within the prior 12 months.'[55]

As a result of the inclusion of the respondent in the section 56 report without evidence to prove that he was a director of the company at the date of commencement of the winding up or within the preceding 12 months, the Court noted that the respondent 'has been put unnecessarily to the expense of defending this application.' On that basis, the Court proceeded to award costs in favour of the respondent, and further ordered that the

---

[51] See above paras **[16.014]** to **[16.018]**.

[52] It must also be shown that the company was insolvent. This requirement was addressed above. See para **[16.013]**.

[53] *Re Visual Impact and Displays Ltd, Murphy v Murphy* [2003] IEHC 91.

[54] *Re Visual Impact and Displays Ltd, Murphy v Murphy* [2003] IEHC 91.

[55] *Re Visual Impact and Displays Ltd, Murphy v Murphy* [2003] IEHC 91.

liquidator, rather than the company, should be liable for the award of costs. The costs' implications of the case are addressed in more detail below.[56]

[16.025] This case has a number of implications for restriction proceedings:

- an applicant for a declaration of restriction bears the onus of proving that the respondent was a director of the company at, or within 12 months before, the commencement of the company's winding up;

- the applicant must adduce credible evidence to support the contention that the respondent was a director;

- the standard of proof is that the applicant must prove as a matter of probability, that the respondent was a director of the company;

- a liquidator must not include a person as a director in the section 56 report, unless he can satisfy the burden of proving that fact, as a matter of probability, on the basis of credible evidence; and

- if a liquidator includes a person as a director in the section 56 report, without being able to prove as a matter of probability on the basis of credible evidence, that the person was a director, he may be personally liable to the respondent for the costs of the application.

It may further be supposed that if an applicant other than a liquidator (such as a receiver or the ODCE)[57] makes an application for a declaration of restriction and fails to discharge the onus of proving that the respondent was a director of the company in liquidation at, or within 12 months before, the commencement of winding up, that applicant may be liable for an award of costs in favour of the respondent.[58]

(b) Directors at date of winding up

[16.026] CA 1990, s 149(2), defines the category of persons to whom s 150 applies as follows: 'This Chapter applies to any person who was a director of a company to which this section applies at the date of, or within 12 months prior to, the commencement of its winding-up.'

The term 'director' is defined in CA 1963, s 2(1), as 'any person occupying the position of director by whatever name called'.[59]

The term 'director' for the purpose of restriction proceedings, as defined in CA 1963, s 2(1) and as applied by CA 1990, s 149, clearly encompass any person who was formally appointed as a director of the company and remained on the board of directors until the date of the company's winding up. This is the category of persons to whom the

---

[56] See below paras **[19.045]** to **[19.047]**.

[57] See CA 1990, s 150(4A), as inserted by CLEA 2001, s 41(1)(c).

[58] See further Ch **19** regarding the costs of restriction proceedings generally.

[59] This definition can encompass persons who acted as directors without being duly appointed as such. See below paras **[16.056]** to **[16.065]**.

provisions of s 150 most clearly and uncontroversially apply. It is also the category of persons who were most visibly responsible for the phoenix syndrome which s 150 sought to conquer.

[16.027] It may be imagined that it would be difficult for a person who was a duly appointed director of a company at the date of the winding up to argue that the terms of s 150 do not apply to them. There have, however, been cases in which persons who were duly appointed directors of companies at the date of commencement of the insolvent liquidation of those companies, have attempted to argue that the terms of s 150 do not apply to them with the same rigour as other directors. The arguments advanced in such cases were that the persons in question were non-executive directors, nominee directors or otherwise not responsible or active on the board of directors, arguments which will be examined in more detail below.[60]

(i) Executive and non-executive directors

[16.028] Many companies appoint executive and non-executive directors to their board of directors and the non-executive directors may delegate the day-to-day management of the company to the executive directors. The High Court has acknowledged that, 'It is a fact of commercial life which the courts should not ignore that persons are appointed as non-executive directors to act alongside executive directors.'[61] The courts have further acknowledged that, 'The non-executive directors normally do not participate in the day-to-day management of a company. The directors collectively delegate the day-to-day management of the company to *inter alia* the executive directors.'[62]

[16.029] In the context of restriction proceedings, the appointment of non-executive directors has raised a number of issues. The first point is that the scope of CA 1990, s 150, is not confined to executive directors. The legislative provisions governing the restriction of directors draws no distinction between those directors who are appointed to act as executive directors and those who adopt a non-executive role.

[16.030] As a consequence of the uniform inclusion in the scope of CA 1990, s 150, of all directors of a company, without distinction, the second point that should be noted is that there is nothing in the formulation of that provision or its application in practice, which exempts non-executive directors from the threat of restriction in the event of a company becoming insolvent and being wound up. This is consistent with the general approach of Irish company law that the occupation by a person of the office of non-executive director does not absolve him of the responsibilities of a director. In *Re Tralee*

---

[60] See below paras **[16.028]** to **[16.038]** and **[16.066]** to **[16.067]**, for example.

[61] *Re Tralee Beef and Lamb Ltd, Kavanagh v Delaney* [2004] IEHC 139 (20 July 2004, unreported), HC. See also the following dicta in *Re RMF (Ireland) Ltd, Kavanagh v Riedler* [2004] IEHC 334 (27 May 2004, unreported), HC: 'The distinction between executive and non executive directors is well established in commercial life, if not expressly recognised in the relevant company's legislation.'

[62] *Re Tralee Beef and Lamb Ltd, Kavanagh v Delaney* [2004] IEHC 139 (20 July 2004, unreported), HC.

Beef and Lamb Ltd,[63] while the Court accepted the reality of delegation of daily management to executive directors, the Court also cautioned that, 'such delegation does not absolve the non-executive directors from the duty to acquire information about the affairs of the company and to supervise the discharge of delegated functions.'[64] The Court summarised the obligations of a non-executive director as involving an obligation to inform themselves about the affairs of the company and to supervise and control the affairs of the company. While *Re Tralee Beef and Lamb Ltd* is a significant judgment and is cited extensively here, it should be noted that the judgment of Finlay Geoghegan J was the subject of an appeal to the Supreme Court, an appeal which was heard on 14 November 2007 and on which judgment is awaited.

[16.031] The third point regarding the treatment of non-executive directors in the context of restriction proceedings is that, while the legislation recognises no distinction between executive and non-executive directors, the lesser role played by non-executive directors in the management of a company is not completely disregarded by the courts.

The need to recognise the differing roles of executive and non-executive directors was acknowledged by the High Court in *Re RMF (Ireland) Ltd,*[65] in the following terms:

> 'In considering whether a person has acted responsibly whilst a director of the company it appears to me that this court must recognise the distinction between executive and non executive directors. A person may, from to time be appointed as a non executive director to bring a particular expertise to a board of directors. Where this is done it appears appropriate to consider such persons conduct as a director *inter alia* in relation to any such particular agreement or purpose.'[66]

[16.032] This recognition of the differing roles of each director can be seen in relation to the burden of proof that a director bears to show that he acted honestly and responsibly within the meaning of CA 1990, s 150(2). In a number of cases, it has been shown that a director's non-executive role may lighten that burden of proof. The effect of

---

[63] *Re Tralee Beef and Lamb Ltd, Kavanagh v Delaney* [2004] IEHC 139 (20 July 2004, unreported), HC.

[64] Similarly, in *Re RMF (Ireland) Ltd Kavanagh v Riedler* [2004] IEHC 334 (27 May 2004, unreported), HC, the High Court held that, 'In relation to the obligation of a director to supervise and control the affairs of the company it is well established that directors may collectively delegate to executives or management certain functions but that such delegation does not absolve the directors from their obligation of ultimate supervision.'

[65] *Re RMF (Ireland) Ltd, Kavanagh v Riedler* [2004] IEHC 334 (27 May 2004, unreported), HC.

[66] *Re RMF (Ireland) Ltd, Kavanagh v Riedler* [2004] IEHC 334 (27 May 2004, unreported), HC. In *Re Tralee Beef and Lamb Ltd, Kavanagh v Delaney* [2004] IEHC 139 (20 July 2004, unreported), HC the High Court also recognised that, 'the Court should take into account the differing roles of each director.' In *Re DCS Ltd, Fitzpatrick v Henley* [2006] IEHC 179, MacMenamin J made the following determination in respect of an application for an order restricting a non-executive director: 'While the courts have been careful to point out that a non-executive director, no matter how small their involvement, cannot wash their hands of responsibility, no specific evidence of wrongdoing has been adduced in relation to the second named respondent and therefore I do not think that the applicant is entitled to the relief sought against her.'

the distinction between the role of an executive and non-executive director on the outcome of s 150 proceedings was stated by the High Court in *Re RMF (Ireland) Ltd*[67] as follows:

> 'In considering whether a non executive director has acted responsibly for the purposes of s 150 of the Act of 1990 it appears to me that the courts should also recognise that, in general, a non executive director is entitled both to rely upon information provided by his fellow executive directors and to rely upon the executive directors carrying out what might be considered to be normal executive or management functions.'[68]

[16.033] An example of a case in which the non-executive status of a director appears to have weighed very heavily in his favour and against the making of a restriction order, is *Re Lynrowan Enterprises Ltd*.[69] This case concerns a family business in which the father, although holding the title 'managing director', was held to have effectively handed over control of the company to his son and to have had virtually no involvement with the company in the 18 months before its winding up. He was not a signatory to the cheques and carried out no transactions on behalf of the company. He was not involved in the company's day-to-day business, took no active part in its affairs and appeared to have been unaware of the detail of the company's business.

On the basis of these findings, the Court determined that there was no dishonesty on the part of this respondent and concluded that it would not be fair to make a finding of irresponsibility leading to an order of restriction against the respondent on the following basis:

> 'In the ordinary course it could be said that this complete neglect of his responsibilities as a managing director could be said to be evidence of irresponsibility justifying the restriction under Section 150. However I am inclined to the view that his failures both in regard to the management of the company up to the time of the winding up and in relation to the preparation of the two statement of affairs thereafter can be attributed to having effectively passed all control of the affairs of the company to his son … and in the context of a small family business, having effectively permitted his son to take over control of the business, he having arrived at the stage of retirement.'[70]

[16.034] Fourth, it should be noted that while it may be easier for a non-executive, rather than an executive, director to resist the making of a restriction order, there have been cases in which non-executive directors have been the subject of restriction orders despite the limited role they may have played in the company's affairs and irrespective of

---

[67]   *Re RMF (Ireland) Ltd, Kavanagh v Riedler* [2004] IEHC 334 (27 May 2004, unreported), HC.

[68]   The Court noted, however, that 'There may be factual circumstances which will put a non executive director on notice that he should not continue to rely either upon information provided or upon executive duties being properly performed and require further action from him or her.' *Re RMF (Ireland) Ltd, Kavanagh v Riedler* [2004] IEHC 334 (27 May 2004, unreported), HC.

[69]   *Re Lynrowan Enterprises Ltd* [2002] IEHC 90 (31 July 2002, unreported), HC.

[70]   *Re Lynrowan Enterprises Ltd* [2002] IEHC 90 (31 July 2002, unreported), HC at para 29.

any understandings or agreements that may be in place regarding the low level of responsibility of that director.

The standard to be expected of non-executive directors for the purposes of defending restriction proceedings was stated as follows in *Re Tralee Beef and Lamb Ltd*:[71]

> 'It is difficult… to envisage that a director could establish that he or she has acted responsibly in relation to the conduct of the affairs of a company within the meaning of s 150(2) of the Act of 1990, if during a significant period he or she either failed to inform himself or herself about its affairs or if he or she did not take steps to join with his or her co-directors in supervising and controlling the affairs of the company at least in the sense of taking reasonable steps to guide and monitor the management of the company.'

That case provides an example of a case in which a non-executive director was the subject of a restriction order. The respondent in question was the wife of the executive director. She was held to have been aware of the company's financial difficulties and to have failed to inform the other two non-executive directors of these difficulties or to have convened a meeting of the board. In these circumstances, despite her limited involvement in the company; her relationship with the executive director; the fact that she was unremunerated and ill-experienced to manage the affairs of a company; it was held that she could not be said to have acted responsibly for the purposes of s 150 and a declaration of restriction was therefore made.[72]

[16.035] The outcome of the application for a restriction order in *Re Lynrowan Enterprises Ltd*[73] may be contrasted with the fate of the respondent in *Re Tralee Beef and Lamb Ltd*.[74] In the former case, the inactivity of the director was excused on the basis that he placed reliance on his son in the context of a family-run business and had effectively retired and the Court refused to make the order of restriction sought.[75] In *Re Tralee Beef and Lamb Ltd*,[76] the wife of the executive director was restricted on the basis of her inactivity, the Court ruling that it could not be regarded as responsible conduct for a director to fail to inform him or herself about the company's affairs or to fail to take reasonable steps to guide and monitor the management of the company.

[16.036] A final point about the treatment of non-executive directors in restriction proceedings is that the size of the company may have an impact on the level of responsibility with which the director is fixed. In *Re Dublin Sports Cafe Ltd*,[77] Peart J

---

[71] *Re Tralee Beef and Lamb Ltd, Kavanagh v Delaney* [2004] IEHC 139 (20 July 2004, unreported), HC.

[72] As noted above, this decision is the subject of an appeal to the Supreme Court, which was heard on 14 November 2007 and on which judgment was reserved.

[73] *Re Lynrowan Enterprises Ltd* [2002] IEHC 90 (31 July 2002, unreported), HC.

[74] *Re Tralee Beef and Lamb Ltd, Kavanagh v Delaney* [2004] IEHC 139 (20 July 2004, unreported), HC.

[75] *Re Lynrowan Enterprises Ltd* [2002] IEHC 90 (31 July 2002, unreported), HC.

[76] *Re Tralee Beef and Lamb Ltd, Kavanagh v Delaney* [2004] IEHC 139 (20 July 2004, unreported), HC.

[77] *Re Dublin Sports Cafe Ltd, Farrell v Long* [2005] IEHC 458.

considered an application under s 150 in respect of a company with two directors, one being an executive director, the other being a non-executive director based in British Colombia:

> 'the fact that he was a non-executive director is neither her nor there. He was a director and as such shares the responsibility to ensure that all is in order, and I venture to suggest that in a company where there are but two directors, the obligation on the non-executive director is even higher than a non-executive director of a much larger company who may have certain identifiable and particular responsibilities within the company, but who may rely on other directors to carry out their particular functions, even though he would be remiss not to be concerned and satisfied as a member of the Board of directors that all the affairs of the company were being properly attended to.'

There was a failure to keep proper books and records in that case, which the Court found to be irresponsible conduct on the part of the non-executive director and to warrant a declaration under s 150.

(c) Former directors

[16.037] Section 150 applies to any person who was a director of a relevant company 'within 12 months prior to, the commencement of its winding-up'.[78] A director of a company who resigned or was removed from office within 12 months before the commencement of the company's winding up, irrespective of the reasons or the circumstances, can therefore be the subject of restriction proceedings.

(i) Justifications for restricting former directors

[16.038] There are strong and clear justifications for extending the threat of restriction to persons who acted as directors of a company before the commencement of the company's winding up.

First, directors are free to resign of their own volition and there is no obligation under the Companies Acts that they provide a reason for so doing. There is therefore nothing in the Companies Acts to prevent directors from tendering their resignation to the company when it becomes clear that the company is facing imminent insolvent liquidation.[79] If s 149 did not capture persons who acted as directors before the commencement of the winding up, all directors could use timely resignations to evade restriction. A director who had played a role in the failure of the company could thereby avoid the consequences of his actions or inactions.

[16.039] A second justification for the extension of s 150 to persons who acted as directors in the year before commencement of a company's winding up, is that there are mechanisms under the Companies Acts whereby a director can be removed from office. There are two means by which this can occur. The directors can resolve to remove a

---

[78]   CA 1990, s 149(2).

[79]   CA 1963, s 195(6) requires a company to notify the CRO, within 14 days, of any change of directors.

director or the members can pass an ordinary resolution under CA 1963, s 182(1).[80] It is conceivable that, upon detecting that a director's conduct was responsible for causing damage to a company's interests and its solvency, the directors or the members may seek to remove that director from office. If this occurred, but failed to redeem the company's fortunes, it would be entirely unjust and contrary to the objectives of the restriction regime, if the errant former director avoided restriction because of his removal from office before the commencement of the winding up.

[16.040] Finally, while it is possible that the extension of s 150 to former directors may operate unfairly in some circumstances, such as where the director ceased to so act before the company was in any detectable difficulties, this should be taken into account by the liquidator, by the ODCE and, if there is no relief granted under CLEA 2001, s 56, by the courts. It is hoped that the potential harshness of extending s 150 to directors who could neither have known of, nor been in any way responsible for, the company's insolvency, due to the timing of their cessation in office, should be overcome by the ODCE relieving the liquidator of the obligation to bring restriction proceedings in respect of such former directors. The possibility of restricting directors who may have resigned as long as 12 months before the commencement of the winding up, may therefore be justified on the basis that the scheme of the legislation can ensure that any former directors for whom that time period operates unfairly and of whom restriction is not warranted, will not be restricted and should not even face restriction proceedings before the courts.

(ii) Resignation

[16.041] As has been seen, there are different means by which a director can cease to so act. Where the director resigned to evade restriction, or was removed from office, it can only be considered appropriate and just that they would face the possibility of being restricted from acting as directors. Where, on the other hand, the director was guilty of no wrongdoing and could not have been aware of the company's future difficulties at the date of resignation, it is to be hoped that the legislative regime will ensure they do not face a real risk of restriction.

In between these two extremes, however, there have been cases, of which there will no doubt be more, in which a director, aware of the company's failing condition, resigned prior to the winding up of a company, because of dissatisfaction, concern and frustration at the company's state of affairs and management. Such cases highlight the predicament of persons appointed to a board of directors who, with the best intentions and efforts, cannot overcome or prevent the deterioration of the company's situation, which may or may not result from mismanagement by others.

The courts, liquidators and the ODCE appear to have adopted varying approaches to directors who resigned before the commencement of winding up, in circumstances where the company's ill fate already was or should have been, apparent.

---

[80] See Courtney, *The Law of Private Companies* (2nd edn, Tottel Publishing, 2002) at paras 8.075 to 8.880.

[16.042] At one end of the spectrum, the High Court has refused to make declarations of restriction against directors who, having become aware of a company's difficulties, attempted to save the company and, when such attempts were futile, due to management conflicts, resigned. In *Re Gasco Ltd*,[81] for example, McCracken J considered the position of a director who had resigned from office in the course of the year before the commencement of the winding up. The director in question realised, more than a year before the winding up, that the company was in difficulties and helped to draw up a business plan to resolve the situation. In the circumstances, he was not satisfied with the plan, and appears to have been excluded from management as a result. Within a few months of these events, he resigned as a director of the company. The Court considered the conduct of this director and concluded that he did act honestly and responsibly and that a restriction order was not warranted.

At the other end of spectrum, it could be imagined that a director who chose to resign, upon realising the difficulties which the company faced, rather than attempting to join in controlling and supervising the affairs of the company, whether this meant accepting the company's insolvency, or attempting to rescue the company, would be liable to be restricted.

(iii) Temporal scope of restriction

[16.043] The inclusion of the 12-month time period as a means of defining the scope of s 150 was examined by McCracken J in *Re Gasco Ltd*.[82] In that case, the Court considered the implications of the 12-month period, noting that:

> 'I think it is quite significant that no restrictions can attach to somebody who ceased to be a director of the Company more than 12 months before the winding up. This seems to me to indicate that the primary aim of s 150 is to deal with directors who have behaved irresponsibly or dishonestly during the last 12 months of the life of the Company.'

In light of this aim, the Court deduced that s 150 requires the actions of a director who faces restriction proceedings 'to be looked at primarily in the light of his actions' during the last 12 months of the company's life. This aspect of the judgment in *Re Gasco Ltd*[83] is addressed in more detail below.[84] However, in the present context it is interesting to note that McCracken J went one step further with this interpretation of the effect of s 149. Having held that the last 12 months of the company's life was the relevant period in which to examine the directors' conduct, McCracken J held that this aspect of s 149:

> '... is presumably intended to focus attention on the behaviour of the directors in the period leading up to the winding up, and to try to ensure that they deal responsibly with creditors when a company is in difficulties. In my view, therefore, there should be particular scrutiny of the actions of directors during the final months before winding up.'

---

[81] *Re Gasco Ltd* [2001] IEHC 20.

[82] *Re Gasco Ltd* [2001] IEHC 20.

[83] *Re Gasco Ltd* [2001] IEHC 20.

[84] See paras **[17.035]** to **[17.036]**.

[16.044] If the person facing restriction proceedings was a director of a company at the date of the commencement of the winding up, scrutinising his conduct in the final months before winding up will usually be the appropriate approach. However, s 150 also applies to persons who were directors of the company at any time during the 12 months before the commencement of the winding up. It is impossible and unworkable to seek to scrutinise the conduct of such a director during the final months before winding up, when that director may have ceased to so act as much as a year prior to that date.

[16.045] This analysis may call into question the choice of 12 months as the means of defining the scope of s 150. If, as McCracken J considered, the pivotal period is the final months before the commencement of the winding up, the extension of s 150 to persons who may not have acted as directors for a year prior to that, could be regarded as unnecessary and harsh. As noted above, there are clear justifications for extending s 150 to persons who ceased to act as directors before the commencement of a company's winding up. Whether it is justifiable to extend this to persons who may have resigned a year before the commencement of winding up, is not so clear.

As against this, a company's demise can extend over a period longer than a few months and can originate in events which occurred many months before the company's eventual winding up.[85] Moreover, if the scope of s 150 was confined to less than 12 months prior to the winding up, it may be feared that certain former directors who did not act honestly and responsibly in relation to the company, may be beyond the scope of the restriction regime.

[16.046] The *dicta* in *Re Gasco Ltd* to the effect that the appropriate timeframe within which to assess a director's conduct is the final months before the commencement of the company's winding up, may be doubted in the light of certain decisions of the High Court and Supreme Court. In *Re Squash (Ireland) Ltd*,[86] the Supreme Court, approving the decision of Shanley J in *La Moselle Clothing Company Ltd v Soualhi*,[87] stated, 'I would agree with Shanley J that the court should look at the entire tenure of the director and not simply at the few months in the run up to the liquidation.'

This approach was subsequently applied by the High Court in cases such as *Re Tralee Beef and Lamb Ltd*[88] and *Re SPH Ltd*.[89]

[16.047] In conclusion, it could be said that it is preferable to include directorships dating back so far as 12 months before the winding up, to ensure that errant former directors are caught in the net of the restriction regime. However, this is only justifiable so long as honest and responsible former directors can escape that net. It is therefore important that the ODCE should relieve liquidators of the obligation to seek the restriction of directors who resigned before any difficulties in the company's state of

---

[85] See, eg, *Re Gasco Ltd* [2001] IEHC 20.

[86] *Re Squash (Ireland) Ltd* [2001] IESC 200, [2001] 3 IR 35.

[87] *La Moselle Clothing Company Ltd v Soualhi* [1998] IEHC 66, [1998] 2 ILRM 345.

[88] *Re Tralee Beef and Lamb Ltd, Kavanagh v Delaney* [2004] IEHC 139 (20 July 2004, unreported), HC.

[89] *Re SPH Ltd, Fennell v Shanahan* [2005] IEHC 152.

affairs could have been detected. The justification for pursuing directorships dating back to a year before winding up weakens if, as McCracken J commented in *Re Gasco Ltd*,[90] the most relevant period is the final months before the winding up, but the ODCE nonetheless refuses to relieve liquidators of the obligation to pursue restriction proceedings against persons who had long before resigned as directors. If that occurs, the unfairness of honest and responsible former directors having to defend restriction proceedings arising from an unprecedented winding up which occurred a number of months after their resignation, could outweigh the benefit to be gained from being able to pursue errant former directors who resigned a considerable time before the winding up. If the injustice of the temporal scope of s 150 is outweighing its benefit, one means of redressing this imbalance would be to reduce the period during which a former director must have acted as such from twelve to six months, or other such period.

(iv) Obligation to restrict former directors

[16.048] The duty of a liquidator to bring restriction proceedings against a company's directors under CLEA 2001, s 56, unless relieved of the obligation to do so, applies equally to former directors. This has been considered in one High Court decision. In *Re USIT Ireland Ltd*[91] a former director of the company, who had ceased to so act before the winding up and before the coming into force of CLEA 2001, s 56, made the preliminary argument that s 56 did not apply to his directorship. The director in question was appointed to the board of directors on 18 January 2001 and ceased to be a director on 2 July 2001. The winding up of the company commenced on 15 May 2002. The director contended that the obligation contained in s 56 only concerned persons who were directors at the date that the obligation arose, or at the date of commencement of the winding up. He further contended that s 56 was a penal provision and should be construed accordingly.

The High Court (Finlay Geoghegan J) rejected these arguments, concluding that:

> 'the obligation imposed in s 56(2) is not limited to those persons who either are a director of the company at the time that the obligation arises or were a director at the date of commencement of the winding-up. I have concluded that in referring to "each of the directors of the company" the legislature intended, at minimum, that the obligation exist in relation to any person whom the official liquidator considers to be a director to whom s 150 applies and in respect of whom he had not been relieved by the Director.'[92]

(d) Shadow Directors

(i) Definition

[16.049] Section 149(5) states expressly that, 'This Chapter applies to shadow directors as it applies to directors'. The classification of 'shadow director' was first formally

---

[90]   *Re Gasco Ltd* [2001] IEHC 20.

[91]   *Re USIT Ireland Ltd* [2003] IEHC 44.

[92]   *Re USIT Ireland Ltd* [2003] IEHC 44.

introduced into Irish company law by CA 1990, s 27,[93] which defines a 'shadow director' as '…a person in accordance with whose directions or instructions the directors of a company are accustomed to act'. That section further provides that a shadow director 'shall be treated for the purposes of this Part as a director of the company unless the directors are accustomed so to act by reason only that they do so on advice given by him in a professional capacity'.[94]

There are a number of components to the definition of a 'shadow director':

- a shadow director will not be formally appointed as a director of the company;
- a shadow director will be someone who gives directions and instructions to the directors of the company;
- the directors will be accustomed to acting in accordance with these directions and instructions;
- the directors do not only act in accordance with his directions and instructions because of advice given by him in a professional capacity.

(ii) Restriction of shadow directors

[16.050] It is in the context of proceedings taken against directors, such as restriction proceedings, that the importance of the designation 'shadow director' comes to the fore. This is demonstrated by the increasing number of cases before the Irish courts which raise the issue of 'shadow directors'.

The original rationale behind including shadow directors among the persons who could be restricted under s 150 was to ensure that persons who would otherwise fall within the scope of s 150 could not escape restriction by appointing nominee directors to act on their instructions.

[16.051] In *Re Lynrowan Enterprises Ltd*,[95] the liquidator brought restriction proceedings against three respondents, one of whom was not formally appointed to the board of directors of the company. It was agreed that the application could only succeed against this respondent if he was shown to be a *de facto* director within the meaning of CA 1963, s 2(1)[96] or a shadow director within the meaning of CA 1990, s 27. The High Court (O'Neill J) observed that:

'The question of the precise kind of activity or role which will result in a person being deemed to be either a *de facto* director or a shadow director does not appear to have been considered in any reported judgments in this jurisdiction.'[97]

---

93 It has been observed elsewhere that the definition of 'director' in s 2(1), CA 1963, as 'any person occupying the position of director by whatever name called' is similar to the definition of 'shadow directors' in s 27, CA 1990. See MacCann, *Companies Acts 1963–1990* (1993) at p 21.

94 For more detailed analysis of the concept of 'shadow director' in company law, see Courtney, *The Law of Private Companies* (2nd edn, 2002) at paras 8.058 to 8.068.

95 *Re Lynrowan Enterprises Ltd* [2002] IEHC 90 (31 July 2002, unreported), HC.

96 See further below paras **[16.056]** to **[16.065]**.

97 *Re Lynrowan Enterprises Ltd* [2002] IEHC 90 (31 July 2002, unreported), HC at para 10.

The Court examined the jurisprudence of other jurisdictions including the following dicta of Millett LJ in *Re Hydrodan (Corby) Limited*:[98]

> 'A de facto director, I repeat, is one who claims to act and purports to act as a director although not validily appointed as such. A shadow director by contrast does not claim or purport to act as a director. On the contrary claims not to be a director. He lurks in the shadows, sheltering behind others who he claims, are the only directors of the company to the exclusion of himself.'

In *Re Lynrowan Enterprises Ltd*,[99] O'Neill J considered the nature of the role of a shadow director and concluded that:

> 'Thus it would appear that an invariable characteristic of a shadow director is that his role is hidden behind that of the validly appointed or indeed de facto directors, through whom, in a concealed way, the shadow director directs the affairs of the company.'

In the circumstances of that case, the respondent, though not appointed to act as a director, openly and overtly controlled the affairs of the company, to the extent of carrying out all of the company's banking transactions. On the basis of these facts, the Court held that he was not a 'shadow director' as he did not direct the affairs of the company by means of instructions or directions to the other director. The Court further noted that his role was 'not hidden or concealed in any way'.[100] The conduct of the respondent and his involvement with the company did, however, expose him to the finding that he was *de facto* a director of the company, a finding which is addressed in more detail below.[101]

[16.052] An example of a case in which a person was held to be a shadow director for the purpose of restriction proceedings was *Re Gasco Ltd*.[102] The respondent to that application owned between 50% and 100% of the shareholding of the company in liquidation. The respondent claimed not to have been involved in the day-to-day management of the company, evidence which was contradicted by the company's two appointed directors. These directors gave evidence to the effect that the respondent in question controlled the company's affairs. It appears that he was also a signatory of the company's cheques, while at least one of the directors was not a signatory. All of these factors were mentioned by the Court, as was the fact that, after both directors had resigned, the alleged shadow director did not appoint replacement directors. McCracken J held that he effectively ran the company on his own from that time and was a shadow director for the purposes of s 150.[103]

This judgment could be welcomed for its recognition and application of the principle that a person, not being duly appointed as a director of a company, may be subject to a

---

[98] *Re Hydrodan (Corby) Limited* (1994) 2 BCLC 180, cited in *Re Lynrowan Enterprises Ltd* [2002] IEHC 90 (31 July 2002, unreported), HC at para 20.

[99] *Re Lynrowan Enterprises Ltd* [2002] IEHC 90 (31 July 2002, unreported), HC.

[100] *Re Lynrowan Enterprises Ltd* [2002] IEHC 90 (31 July 2002, unreported), HC at para 21.

[101] See below paras **[16.057]** to **[16.062]**.

[102] *Re Gasco Ltd* [2001] IEHC 20.

[103] *Re Gasco Ltd* [2001] IEHC 20 at para 11.

restriction order, if he instructs and directs the company's directors in their management of the company. It is also an important illustration of the dangers of controlling shareholders directing the affairs of a company without formally occupying the office of director. However, the designation of the respondent in that case as a 'shadow director' may be questioned.

[16.053] The facts relied upon by the Court in support of the finding that the respondent was a shadow director included that there were no duly appointed directors for a period of time; that he controlled the company's affairs on his own during that time; and that he was a signatory to the company's cheques, for example. If one recalls the essential characteristic of a 'shadow director' as someone who conceals his role in a company, instructing the directors in their actions from behind the scenes, this is not consistent with the facts of *Re Gasco Ltd*,[104] as set out in the judgment of the High Court in that case. For example, the fact that the respondent was a cheque signatory may be more indicative of the status of a *de facto* director than a shadow director. More fundamentally, there was a period during which there were no directors in place and the Court held that, during that period, the respondent ran the company on his own.[105] While this fact was relied upon as a ground for finding that the respondent was a shadow director, it is difficult to see how this level of involvement could be described as a covert role in the company. It certainly could scarcely be described as the instruction or direction of the directors of the company, within the meaning of CA 1990, s 27.

From the facts of the case, as set out in the judgment, it appears that the respondent deserved to be the subject of a restriction order, but as a *de facto*, rather than a shadow, director. In the circumstances of *Re Gasco Ltd*, this distinction is more semantic than substantive, as it would not have affected the outcome of the proceedings. Nonetheless, there may be circumstances in which a person could fall within the definition of *de facto* director, but not shadow director, and *vice versa*. In such circumstances, the distinction between the two designations bears some significance. More generally, it would advance the clarity and certainty of the law in this area if the characteristics of a shadow director and *de facto* director were clearly defined. It is regrettable that *Re Gasco Ltd* may have created some confusion in relation to the distinctive features of the two designations.

(iii) Companies as shadow directors

[16.054] The position of a company as a shadow director which may be made subject to an order of disqualification arose squarely for consideration in *Re Worldport (Ireland) Ltd*.[106] The official liquidator in that case sought an order of restriction against three directors of the company in liquidation, one being a corporate entity incorporated in the US, Worldport Communications Ltd. The issues raised were whether a company may be a shadow director for the purposes of s 150 and whether a company incorporated in another jurisdiction may be a shadow director.

---

[104] *Re Gasco Ltd* [2001] IEHC 20 at paras 10 to 11.

[105] *Re Gasco Ltd* [2001] IEHC 20 at para 11.

[106] *Re Worldport (Ireland) Ltd* [2005] IEHC 467.

O'Leary J referred to the Interpretation Act 1937, s 11(d) of which defines a 'person' as 'importing a body corporate'[107] and the terms of CA 1990, s 27, that:

> 'a person in accordance with whose directions or instructions the directors of a company are accustomed to act (in this Act referred to as a "shadow director") shall be treated for the purposes of this part as a director of the company unless the directors are accustomed to so act by reason only that they do so on advice given by him in a professional capacity.'

The Court placed emphasis on the expression 'shall be treated for the purposes of this part as a director' among other aspects of the provisions applicable to shadow directors:

> 'It is of significance that in establishing the status or office of "shadow director" the legislation was enacted in a manner, which uses the formula that the person who falls within the definition shall be treated as a director, rather than providing, for example, that the person so appointed shall be deemed to be a director.'[108]

The Court concluded that a 'shadow director' is an independent category, distinct from the category of director and that, 'the nature of the status enjoyed by shadow directors is that they are a separate entity than directors.' The Court concluded on this basis that there was no reason why a company could not be a shadow director for the purposes of s 150.

The Court also rejected the submission that s 150 was never intended to apply to companies. O'Leary J noted that the restrictions attendant on a s 150 order went beyond prohibiting a person from acting as director, but also precluded direct or indirect involvement in the promotion or formation of a company. If a restriction order was made in respect of a company, this would have the effect of preventing the company from being involved in the promotion and formation of an Irish company for five years.

This decision is clear authority that a body corporate can be a shadow director, both generally and in the particular context of s 150.

[16.055] With regard to the position of companies that are incorporated in another jurisdiction, the court referred to the definition of 'body corporate' in s 2(3) as including 'a company incorporated outside the State' and to the fact that s 150 makes no distinction between Irish based company promoters and promoters based in other jurisdictions. The Court concluded, 'There appears to be no reason why the conclusion on the eligibility of bodies corporate to be shadow directors should not apply equally to Irish and foreign entities.'[109] A company that is incorporated in another jurisdiction may therefore be a shadow director and may be subject to a restriction order under s 150.

---

[107] Note that Interpretation Act 2005, s 18(c) similarly provides that, '"Person" shall be read as importing a body corporate (whether a corporation aggregate or a corporation sole) and an unincorporated body of persons, as well as an individual, and the subsequent use of any pronoun in place of a further use of "person" shall be read accordingly.'

[108] *Re Worldport (Ireland) Ltd* [2005] IEHC 467.

[109] *Re Worldport (Ireland) Ltd* [2005] IEHC 467.

(e) De facto directors

[16.056] The next category of persons who may become the subject of restriction orders without being formally appointed to act as a director of a company in liquidation are so-called '*de facto*' directors. This term refers to persons who hold themselves out or represent themselves as being directors of a company without being duly appointed as such. The definition of a 'director' in CA 1963, s 2(1), as 'any person occupying the position of director by whatever name called' clearly envisages the extension of the rules of company law to persons who, without being formally appointed to the office, act as if they are a director of a company. *De facto* directors have been defined as follows: 'Essentially a *de facto* director is a person who assumes to occupy the position of a director or assumes to act as a director of the company.'[110] In a number of instances, such persons have been restricted from acting as directors.[111]

[16.057] In *Re Lynrowan Enterprises Ltd*,[112] the Court held that the respondent to that restriction application was not a shadow director but did fit the criteria of a *de facto* director and was restricted from acting as a director on that basis.

The High Court (O'Neill J) analysed certain decisions of the English courts to ascertain the factors necessary to establish that a person was a *de facto* director of a company. The Court referred to *Re Richborough Furniture Ltd*[113] in which the disqualification of an alleged *de facto* director arose for consideration. The English High Court in that case relied on the decision in *Re Lo-Line Electric Motors Limited*[114] to the effect that disqualification proceedings applied to persons 'acting as a director whether validly appointed, invalidly appointed, or just assuming to act as a director without any appointment at all' and that 'the Court must have regard to the conduct of the respondent as director when validly appointed or invalidly appointed or merely *de facto* acting as a director.'[115]

In *Re Richborough Furniture Ltd*[116] the High Court went on to state, as quoted in *Re Lynrowan Enterprises Ltd*,[117] that 'directors' in the context of disqualification

---

[110] *Re First Class Toy Traders Ltd (in liquidation), Gray v McLoughlin* [2004] IEHC 289, Finlay Geoghegan J, *ex tempore*.

[111] See *Re Kelly Technical Services (Ireland) Ltd, Kavanagh v Kelly* [2005] IEHC 421 for an example of a case in which the Court refused to find that the respondent was a de facto director ('I do not consider there is evidence that Mr O'Flaherty directed the affairs of the company on an equal or more influential footing than the first, second and fourth respondents, or in any way conduct and himself so as to constitute a shadow or *de facto* director,' *per* MacMenamin J).

[112] *Re Lynrowan Enterprises Ltd* [2002] IEHC 90 (31 July 2002, unreported), HC. See further para **[16.051]**.

[113] *Re Richborough Furniture Limited* (1996) 1 BCLC 507, as cited in *Re Lynrowan Enterprises Ltd* [2002] IEHC 90 (31 July 2002, unreported), HC.

[114] *Re Lo-Line Electric Motors Limited* (1998) BCLC 696, [1998] Ch 477.

[115] *Re Lo-Line Electric Motors Limited* (1998) BCLC 696, [1998] Ch 477.

[116] *Re Richborough Furniture Limited* (1996) 1 BCLC 507, as cited in *Re Lynrowan Enterprises Ltd* [2002] IEHC 90 (31 July 2002, unreported), HC.

[117] *Re Lynrowan Enterprises Ltd* [2002] IEHC 90 (31 July 2002, unreported), HC.

proceedings 'includes the case where he has acted as a director even though not validly appointed or even if there has been no appointment at all' and that:

> 'Given the purpose of the legislation it seems to me that it would be bizarre if a person was liable to the jurisdiction if he had acted as a validly appointed director or as a shadow director, but not if he had acted as a director under an appointment which was for some technical reason invalid or if he had acted in the absence of any appointment at all.'

With regard to the criteria for demonstrating that a person acted as a *de facto* director, O'Neill J, in the course of his judgment in *Re Lynrowan Enterprises Ltd*,[118] quoted further from the decision of the English High Court in *Re Richborough Furniture Ltd*.[119] The English High Court held in that case that, for a person who was alleged to be a *de facto* director to be made liable to a restriction order:

> 'the Court would have to have clear evidence that he had been either the sole person directing affairs of the company (or acting with others all equally lacking in a valid appointment...) or, if there were others who were true directors, that he was acting on an equal footing with the others in directing the affairs of the company.'

The English High Court also noted, significantly, that:

> '... if it is unclear whether the acts or the person in question are referable to an assumed directorship, or to some other capacity such as shareholder or as here, consultant, the person in question must be entitled to the benefit of the doubt.'

[16.058] In *Re Lynrowan Enterprises Ltd*,[120] O'Neill J regarded these passages as persuasive, emphasising that the objective of restriction proceedings was to protect the public from persons who are unfit to hold the office of director.[121] O'Neill J concluded that:

> 'I am of opinion that a person although not validly appointed a director of a company may nonetheless be said to be a *de facto* director and thus deemed to be "a director" within the meaning of s 2(1) of the Companies Act 1993 and thus amenable to the restriction contained in s 150 of the Companies Act 1990, in the following circumstances:
>
> 1. Where there is clear evidence that that person has been either the sole person directing the affairs of the company or

---

[118] *Re Lynrowan Enterprises Ltd* [2002] IEHC 90 (31 July 2002, unreported), HC at para 16.

[119] *Re Richborough Furniture Limited* (1996) 1 BCLC 507, as cited in *Re Lynrowan Enterprises Ltd* [2002] IEHC 90 (31 July 2002, unreported), HC.

[120] *Re Lynrowan Enterprises Ltd* [2002] IEHC 90 (31 July 2002, unreported), HC at para 17.

[121] Quoting the following passage from the judgment of Shanley J in *La Moselle Clothing Co Ltd v Soualhi* [1998] 2 ILRM 345: 'Quite apart from the injustice that results from the failure to restrict directors whose conduct merits restriction, there is the fact that the primary purpose of the Section 150 restriction is the protection of the public from persons who by their conduct, have shown themselves unfit to hold the office of, and discharge the duties of, a director of a company and, in consequence, represent a danger to potential investors and traders dealing with such companies.'

2. Is directing the affairs of the company with others equally lacking in valid appointment or

3. Where there were other validly appointed directors that he was acting on an equal or more influential footing with the true directors in directing the affairs of the company.

4. In the absence of clear evidence of the foregoing and when there is evidence that the role of the person in question is explicable by the exercise of a role other than director, the person in question should not be made amenable to the s 150 restriction.

5. Where the object of the Section is the protection of the public from dishonest or irresponsible persons the absence of a valid appointment should not permit an escape from the restriction in s 150. It would be nonsensical if a person who had been validly appointed a director was to be treated differently to someone who lacked valid appointment but nevertheless assumed in all other respects the role of director. I would agree that "liability cannot sensibly depend upon the validity of the defendant's appointment".

6. In the light of all of the foregoing then in my view the Companies Act 1963 to 1990 recognise and embrace in the provision of s 2(1) of the Act of 1963 and s 150 of the Act of 1990, the concept of the '*de facto* director.'[122]

[16.059] According to this decision, the applicant for a restriction order must prove that the alleged *de facto* director was the sole person directing the affairs of the company, or that he directed the company with others who were similarly not formally appointed as directors, or that he acted on an equal or more influential footing with the appointed directors, in directing the affairs of the company. This must moreover be established on the basis of clear evidence. If there is no clear evidence of the existence of one of these three situations, and there is evidence that the role of the person is explicable by reason of a role other than director, that person should not be within the scope of s 150.

[16.060] One of the features of this judgment is that it presents a narrow interpretation of the term '*de facto* director'. The restrictiveness of this interpretation is heightened by the fact that the judgment purports to define exhaustively the circumstances in which a person can be deemed to be a *de facto* director. In particular, it is of note that the only circumstance in which a person can be a *de facto* director of a company with directors, duly appointed and acting as such, is if he acted on an equal or more influential footing with those directors. This essentially eliminates from the scope of the designation '*de facto* director' a person who may describe themselves as, present themselves as, and act as, a director of the company, without acting or purporting to act with the same or more authority than the chairman of the board of directors, for example.

[16.061] Another aspect of the test set out by O'Neill J in *Re Lynrowan Enterprises Ltd*,[123] which is of note to a person seeking to prove, or to refute, the status of a *de facto* director, is the consequence of failing to establish one of the three criteria of the test. According to the fourth limb of the test, if there is no evidence of the existence of one of the three situations outlined in the judgment, this is not sufficient to overcome the

---

[122] *Re Lynrowan Enterprises Ltd* [2002] IEHC 90 (31 July 2002, unreported), HC at para 18.

[123] *Re Lynrowan Enterprises Ltd* [2002] IEHC 90 (31 July 2002, unreported), HC at para 17.

allegation of *de facto* directorship. It appears that there must also be evidence that the alleged *de facto* director's role in the company was explicable by his occupation of a role other than director in the company. The formulation of this aspect of the test is unfortunate, particularly as the two components are framed in a cumulative, rather than alternative, fashion. This suggests that if there is no evidence that the person in question was directing the affairs of the company, whether alone, with other unappointed directors, or with duly appointed directors, he may still be a *de facto* director unless there is evidence of another role in the company which explains his involvement. If the evidence of his involvement in the company is lacking, it is illogical to require evidence of the occupation of a role to explain his involvement. If, on the other hand, there is evidence of involvement, but not sufficient to meet the requirements of the test put forward in *Re Lynrowan Enterprises Ltd*, it may be considered to be unfair to allow the designation of *de facto* director to be made, unless the person adduces evidence of an alternative role in the company.

This concern is particularly pressing if one considers that the Court in *Re Lynrowan Enterprises Ltd* purported to approve the following dicta of the English High Court in *Re Richborough Furniture Ltd* to the effect that, 'if it is unclear whether the acts or the person in question are referable to an assumed directorship, or to some other capacity such as shareholder or as here, consultant, the person in question must be entitled to the benefit of the doubt.' This permits a person to refute the allegation of *de facto* directorship by reference to a different role in the company. It does not suggest that where the evidence of involvement is lacking, the alleged *de facto* director must demonstrate the occupation of a different role in the company.

Therefore, while it may be said that the test for establishing the existence of a *de facto* directorship under *Re Lynrowan Enterprises Ltd* was a narrow one, the means of countering an allegation of such directorship was also tightly framed.

[16.062] The facts of *Re Lynrowan Enterprises Ltd*[124] were that the respondent was found to have had almost complete control over the affairs of the company, as illustrated by the fact that he carried out all of the banking transactions on behalf of the company, without ever being formally appointed to act as director of the company. The Court held that the fact that all of the banking transactions were carried out by the respondent, rather than the only director then remaining on the board, was indicative that the respondent had a 'decisive role in the direction of the affairs of the company.'[125] This finding was bolstered by the fact that the director was not a signatory for the purposes of the company bank accounts, whereas the respondent was. The Court concluded that the respondent was in control of, and directed, the affairs of the company, that he was a *de facto* director, and that he was therefore amenable to s 150.[126]

[16.063] The authority of the decision of the Irish High Court in *Re Lynrowan Enterprises Ltd*[127] and the persuasiveness of the decision of the English High Court in

---

[124] *Re Lynrowan Enterprises Ltd* [2002] IEHC 90 (31 July 2002, unreported), HC at para 17.

[125] *Re Lynrowan Enterprises Ltd* [2002] IEHC 90 (31 July 2002, unreported), HC at para 22.

[126] *Re Lynrowan Enterprises Ltd* [2002] IEHC 90 (31 July 2002, unreported), HC at para 23.

[127] *Re Lynrowan Enterprises Ltd* [2002] IEHC 90 (31 July 2002, unreported), HC at para 17.

Re Richborough Furniture Ltd[128] may be doubted since the decision of Finlay Geoghegn J in *Re First Class Toy Traders Ltd.*[129] In that case, the Court revisited the jurisprudence of the English courts in relation to the designation '*de facto* director' and reached different conclusions to those arrived at in *Re Lynrowan Enterprises Ltd.*[130] This decision may be regarded as easing the burden on persons seeking to establish the existence of a *de facto* directorship and as expanding the circumstances in which such a directorship may be found to exist.

[16.064] In *Re First Class Toy Traders Ltd*[131] it was accepted that *de facto* directors were amenable to s 150; that the onus of proving an individual was a *de facto* director lay on the person seeking an order of restriction; and that this onus must be discharged on the balance of probabilities. The central issue which the Court addressed was the appropriate approach to adopt in determining whether a person was a *de facto* director.

On the question of the appropriate approach to adopt, Finlay Geoghegan J cited the three circumstances in which a *de facto* director may be shown to have acted, as set out by O'Neill J in *Re Lynrowan Enterprises Ltd*[132] and the limitation set out by O'Neill J to the effect that, 'That in the absence of clear evidence of the foregoing and when there is evidence that the role of the person in question is explicable by the exercise of a role other than director, the person in question should not be made amenable to the s 150 restriction'.

The Court noted that the formulation of the three-prong test in *Re Lynrowan Enterprises Ltd*, followed a decision of the English High Court, *Re Richborough Furniture Ltd*,[133] which 'has been subsequently the subject matter of some consideration and, I think it is fair to say, some criticism in subsequent decisions of the English courts.'[134] In this regard, Finlay Geoghegan J cited a number of authorities of the English courts to the effect that it was not possible for formulate a single decisive test to determine whether a person was a *de facto* director and that this was essentially a question of degree.[135] The

---

[128] *Re Richborough Furniture Ltd* (1996) 1 BCLC 507, as cited in *Re Lynrowan Enterprises Ltd* [2002] IEHC 90 (31 July 2002, unreported), HC.

[129] *Re First Class Toy Traders Ltd (in liquidation), Gray v McLoughlin* [2004] IEHC 289 (9 July 2004, unreported), HC, Finlay Geoghegan J, *ex tempore*.

[130] *Re Lynrowan Enterprises Ltd* [2002] IEHC 90 (31 July 2002, unreported), HC at para 17.

[131] *Re First Class Toy Traders Ltd (in liquidation), Gray v McLoughlin* [2004] IEHC 289 (9 July 2004, unreported), HC, Finlay Geoghegan J, *ex tempore*.

[132] *Re Lynrowan Enterprises Ltd* [2002] IEHC 90 (31 July 2002, unreported), HC at para 17.

[133] *Re Richborough Furniture Ltd* (1996) 1 BCLC 507, as cited in *Re Lynrowan Enterprises Ltd* [2002] IEHC 90 (31 July 2002, unreported), HC.

[134] *Re First Class Toy Traders Ltd (in liquidation), Gray v McLoughlin* [2004] IEHC 289 (9 July 2004, unreported), HC, Finlay Geoghegan J, *ex tempore*.

[135] Citing *Secretary of State for Trade and Industry v Tjolle* [1998] BCC 282, and *Re Kaytech International plc, Secretary for State for Industry v Kaczer* [1999] BCC 390.

Court further quoted the following passage from the judgment of Jacob J in *Secretary of State for Trade and Industry v Tjolle*:[136]

> 'The court takes into account all the relevant factors. Those factors include at least whether or not there was a holding out by the company of the individual as a director, whether the individual used the title, whether the individual had proper information (eg management accounts) on which to base decisions, and whether the individual had to make major decisions and so on. Taking all these factors into account, one asks "was this individual part of the corporate governing structure?", answering it as a kind of jury question. In deciding this, one bears very much in mind why one is asking the question ... There would be no justification for the law making a person liable to misfeasance or disqualification proceedings unless they were truly in a position to exercise the powers and discharge the functions of a director. Otherwise they would be made liable for events over which they had no real control, either in fact or law.'

The Court also quoted the following guidance from the judgment of Robert Walker LJ in *Re Kaytech Ltd*:[137]

> 'I do not understand Jacob J, in the first part of that passage, to be enumerating tests which must all be satisfied if de facto directorship is to be established. He is simply drawing attention to some (but not all) of the relevant factors, recognising that the crucial issue is whether the individual in question has assumed the status and functions of a company director so as to make himself responsible under the 1986 Act as if were a *de jure* director.'

The effect of these decisions was that the exhaustive definition of the circumstances in which a person may be found to be a *de facto* director, as set out in *Re Richborough Furniture Ltd*,[138] is no longer favoured. On the contrary, the test for determining the existence of a *de facto* directorship was a question of degree and, while certain factors such as whether the person used the title of director, whether he made important decisions, whether he was held out as being a director, were relevant, the crucial issue was whether the individual had assumed the status of functions of a director.

[16.065] Having considered the decisions in *Re Kaytech Ltd*[139] and *Secretary of State for Trade and Industry v Tjolle*,[140] Finlay Geoghegan J concluded that:

> 'the task which this court must perform is to determine... whether the individual in question has assumed the status and functions of a company director so as to make himself amenable to s 150 of the Act of 1990.'[141]

---

[136] *Secretary of State for Trade and Industry v Tjolle* [1998] BCC 282 at 290.

[137] *Re Kaytech International plc, Secretary for State for Industry v Kaczer* [1999] BCC 390.

[138] *Re Richborough Furniture Limited* (1996) 1 BCLC 507, as cited in *Re Lynrowan Enterprises Ltd* [2002] IEHC 90 (31 July 2002, unreported), HC.

[139] *Re Kaytech International plc, Secretary for State for Industry v Kaczer* [1999] BCC 390.

[140] *Secretary of State for Trade and Industry v Tjolle* [1998] BCC 282 at 290.

[141] *Re First Class Toy Traders Ltd (in liquidation), Gray v McLoughlin* [2004] IEHC 289 (9 July 2004, unreported), HC, Finlay Geoghegan J, *ex tempore*.

In order to determine whether a person has assumed that status and function, the Court recalled the essential duties of a director at common law[142] and concluded that:

> 'what I must decide is whether the official liquidator has established on the balance of probabilities that [the respondent] on the facts of this case assumed the status and function of a director bearing in mind the above formulation of the duties or function of a director.'

Applying this test to the circumstances of the case, the Court held that the respondent was a *de facto* director relying primarily on the following factors:

- the two appointed directors considered the respondent to be a director of the company, and to have been so appointed;

- the respondent accepted that he agreed to be described as the finance director;

- the respondent met the other two directors regularly at what he argued were management meetings, but which were as a matter of probability, board meetings;

- the respondent was a cheque signatory, although not an employee;

- the respondent had full information about the affairs of the company and controlled the availability of financial information;

- although not an employee, the respondent had responsibility for the financial function in the company;

- the respondent's control and supervision of the company's affairs went beyond a purely financial function and also involved negotiations in relation to property matters.

(f) Nominee directors

[16.066] It is clear from decisions such as *Re Tralee Beef and Lamb Ltd*[143] that a director who is nominated to a board of directors by another company is subject to the same rules and standards in the context of restriction proceedings, as any other directors. Moreover, his conduct as a director of the nominating company, or of any other entity, will not be taken into account by the court in the context of restriction proceedings.

[16.067] However, s 150(2)(b) and (c) do provide some protection for directors who are appointed to the board of a company in connection with the provision of credit or financing by a financial institution or venture capital company. Accordingly, a court is

---

[142] *Re First Class Toy Traders Ltd (in liquidation), Gray v McLoughlin* [2004] IEHC 289 (9 July 2004, unreported), HC, Finlay Geoghegan J, *ex tempore*, citing the following dicta in *Re Barings PLC (No 5) Secretary of State For Trade and Industry v Baker* [1991] BCLC 433: 'Each individual director owes duties to the company to inform himself about its affairs and to join with his co-directors in supervising and controlling them'.

[143] See *Re Tralee Beef and Lamb Ltd, Kavanagh v Delaney* [2004] IEHC 139 (20 July 2004, unreported), HC.

not obliged to make a restriction order under s 150, if satisfied that the director against whom the order is sought:

> (b) ... was a director of the company solely by reason of his nomination as such by a financial institution in connection with the giving of credit facilities to the company by such institution, provided that the institution in question has not obtained from any director of the company a personal or individual guarantee of repayment to it of the loans or other forms of credit advanced to the company, or
>
> (c) ... was a director of the company solely by reason of his nomination as such by a venture capital company in connection with the purchase of, or subscription for, shares by it in the first-mentioned company.

Chapter 17

DEFENCES TO RESTRICTION PROCEEDINGS

A. Introduction

[17.001] There are few evidentiary requirements for a successful application to restrict a company director. The applicant must show that the winding up of the company has commenced; that the company is insolvent (whether proven at the commencement, or in the course of, the winding up); and that the person against whom the declaration of restriction is sought was a director of the company at, or within 12 months prior to, the commencement of the winding up.[1] If these elements are in place, there are limited grounds on which the person against whom the order is sought can resist the making of a restriction order.

As has been seen, s 150(2) contains exemptions for directors who are appointed to so act as nominees of financial institutions and venture capital companies in certain circumstances.[2] If a director does not fit either of those categories, the only basis on which he can resist a restriction order is if he can satisfy the court:

> ... 'that the person concerned has acted honestly and responsibly in relation to the conduct of the affairs of the company and that there is no other reason why it would be just and equitable that he should be subject to the restrictions imposed by this section.[3]

To avail of this defence, the director must show that he acted honestly, responsibly and that there is no other reason why it would be just and equitable to make an order of restriction. The requirements are clearly stated to be cumulative. As noted by the High Court in the *La Moselle Clothing Company Ltd v Soualhi*:[4]

> '... there are three hurdles that a director has to surmount:
>
> (a) He must establish that he has acted honestly in relation to the affairs of the company.
>
> (b) He must establish that he has acted responsibly in relation to the affairs of the company.
>
> (c) He must satisfy the Court that there is no other reason why it would be just and equitable that he should be subject to the restrictions imposed by the section.'[5]

The CLRG now recommends that a fourth hurdle be added to those which a director seeking to resist the making of a declaration of restriction, must surmount. According to Head 32(3)(b) of Pt A13 of the General Scheme of the Draft Companies Consolidation

---

[1] See para **[16.013]**.

[2] See above para **[16.067]**.

[3] CA 1990, s 150(2)(a).

[4] *La Moselle Clothing Company Ltd v Soualhi* [1998] IEHC 66, [1998] 2 ILRM 345.

[5] *La Moselle Clothing Company Ltd v Soualhi* [1998] IEHC 66, [1998] 2 ILRM 345 at para 6.

and Reform Bill 2007, a director must satisfy the court, in addition to the matters currently set out in s 150(2)(a); that 'he has when requested to do so by the liquidator, cooperated with the liquidator insofar as he may reasonably be expected to do so in connection with the conduct of the winding up'.[6]

The only other means by which a declaration of restriction may be avoided are by an application for relief under CA 1990, s 152, or by arguing successfully that there was inordinate and inexcusable delay in bringing the application.[7]

B. Honesty and responsibility

[17.002] The decisive issue in the vast majority of restriction proceedings is whether the director can satisfy the court that he acted honestly and responsibly within the meaning of s 150(2)(a). In practice, few, if any, cases turn on the honesty of the director. *La Moselle Clothing Company Ltd v Soualhi*[8] is one of the few cases in which the honesty of the director was impugned to any degree and even there, the Court reached the decision to restrict the director on the basis that there was 'improper conduct and if it was not to be described as actually dishonest it was certainly irresponsible', thereby avoiding a direct finding that the director was guilty of dishonesty. The term 'dishonesty' was defined in *Re USIT World plc*:[9]

> 'Dishonesty implies something akin to improper dealing with money or other assets belonging to the company, or some form of fraudulent trading. In an extreme case this would involve a director depleting the assets of the company directly for his own benefit, rather than settling his creditors, thereby leading to the collapse of the company; or obtaining funds from others with a fraudulent intent. Clearly such a director who is prepared to steal or deal with the company's or another's assets in such a fashion, or behave in any other way in which dishonesty is manifest will have demonstrated that the trust invested in him in exchange for the privileges attaching to limited liability through the mechanism of a limited liability company has been abused to the extent that he should be restricted within the terms of the section from being a director. Such dishonesty will of course also amount to irresponsibility.'

[17.003] In practice, the outcome of s 150 applications generally hinges on the central question of whether the director can satisfy the court that he acted 'responsibly' in relation to the company's affairs. From the decisions of the Irish courts on this topic, it is possible to derive certain general principles and specific guidance regarding what conduct may or may not be found to be responsible, and, to a lesser extent, honest in relation to the conduct of a company's affairs.

---

[6]   Available at www.clrg.org.

[7]   See paras **[17.070]** to **[17.080]**.

[8]   *La Moselle Clothing Company Ltd v Soualhi* [1998] IEHC 66, [1998] 2 ILRM 345.

[9]   *Re USIT World plc* [2005] IEHC 285.

(a) Scope of directors' 'honesty and responsibility'

(i) Relevant period of time

[17.004] At the outset, it is important to note the timeframe during which the conduct of a director facing restriction proceedings will be assessed by the court. Decisions such as *Re Gasco Ltd*[10] encourage courts to direct their attention principally to the final months of the company's life. However, more recent decisions establish that the appropriate period of time in which to assess the conduct of a director, is the entire tenure of his directorship of the company.

In *Re Squash (Ireland) Ltd*,[11] the Supreme Court held that, in applying s 150, 'the court should look at the entire tenure of the director and not simply at the few months in the run up to the liquidation.' This approach was subsequently applied by the High Court in cases such as *Re Tralee Beef and Lamb Ltd*[12] and *Re SPH Ltd*.[13] As confirmed in *Re Tralee Beef and Lamb Ltd*:[14]

> '... in considering an application under s 150 the court is confined to considering the respondents conduct in relation to the affairs of the company in liquidation. Section 150 does not appear to give a court any discretion to consider how a respondent acted or acts as a director of any other company. The respondent must satisfy the court he or she acted responsibly as a director in relation to the conduct of the affairs of the company in liquidation in which the application is made.'

[17.005] As will be seen, the courts have also encouraged the examination of a director's conduct after the commencement of winding up, but under the heading of whether it would be 'just and equitable' to make an order of restriction. This distinction was drawn in *La Moselle Clothing Company Ltd v Soualhi*[15] on the basis that the criteria of 'honesty and responsibility' are framed by reference to the 'conduct of the affairs of the company', a phrase which could not be applied to the period of time after the commencement of the company's winding up. The assessment of whether it would be 'just and equitable' to make an order of restriction is not so confined and therefore allows courts to take into account a director's conduct in the period after the commencement of the winding up.

[17.006] The application of this approach can be seen vividly in *Re CMC (Ireland) Ltd*.[16] An unusual feature of this case, acknowledged as such by the Court, was that the conduct of the directors that gave rise to the s 150 application related entirely to the

---

10 *Re Gasco Ltd* [2001] IEHC 20. See further above paras [16.043] to [16.046].

11 *Re Squash (Ireland) Ltd* [2001] IESC 200, [2001] 3 IR 35.

12 *Re Tralee Beef and Lamb Ltd, Kavanagh v Delaney* [2004] IEHC 139 (20 July 2004, unreported), HC.

13 *Re SPH Ltd, Fennell v Shanahan* [2005] IEHC 152.

14 *Re Tralee Beef and Lamb Ltd, Kavanagh v Delaney* [2004] IEHC 139 (20 July 2004, unreported), HC.

15 *La Moselle Clothing Company Ltd v Soualhi* [1998] IEHC 66, [1998] 2 ILRM 345.

16 *Re CMC (Ireland) Ltd, Fennell v Carolan* [2005] IEHC 59.

period after the commencement of the winding up of the company.[17] Applying *La Moselle Clothing Company Ltd v Soualhi*,[18] Clarke J observed that the test to be applied in these circumstances, was whether it was 'just and equitable' to make orders under s 150, rather than whether the directors acted honestly and responsibly.[19]

[17.007] Three factual matters were relied upon by the Court in making a declaration of restriction in respect of the respondents. First, the respondents took and retained certain company property (a forklift truck), refusing to respond to enquiries from the liquidator about the whereabouts of that property. The respondents subsequently returned the forklift truck, claiming that they had kept it as a form of 'self help' for monies owed to them by the company. Clarke J addressed this situation as follows:

> 'It is axiomatic that the duties of persons who have served as directors include an obligation to be of any assistance which they can to the liquidator in the conduct of the liquidation. The rights of the creditors of a company are likely to be compromised not only by the fact that a company is insolvent and unable to pay its debts as of the date of liquidation but also such rights can be further compromised where, due to inappropriate action or inaction on the part of directors or former directors, the liquidator is prevented from being in a position to effectually get in the assets of the company for the purposes of discharging the liabilities due to the creditors to the greatest extent possible and as soon as possible. In the circumstances I am satisfied that the court is entitled to take into account any conduct on the part of directors or former directors which amounts to an inappropriate retention of the companies assets subsequent to the commencement of the winding up.'[20]

[17.008] The second factual matter raised was that the respondents failed generally to co-operate with the liquidator, including declining to meet with him. It was only after the commencement of the restriction proceedings, almost one year after the commencement of the winding up, that the respondents met with the liquidator. The Court considered that this failure to co-operate with the liquidator was a matter to be taken into account in an application under s 150:

> '... anything which places a significant barrier in the way of the efficient conduct of the liquidation is likely to lead to a diminution in the extent to which the creditors of the company will be paid. Even if there is no ultimate failure to

---

[17] Both the DCE and the liquidator accepted that the company kept proper books and records and was up to date with its statutory returns. As the Court noted, '... the liquidator has expressed the view that the company appears to have kept proper books and records and was up to date with its statutory returns. The liquidator has also given evidence to the effect that the directors kept their taxation returns up to date, which fact enabled him to complete returns that were outstanding at the date of his appointment. It seems clear that the only basis upon which the liquidator and the Director considered it appropriate to bring this application before the court stemmed from certain matters that occurred in the course of the winding-up and after the company had gone into liquidation.' *Re CMC (Ireland) Ltd, Fennell v Carolan* [2005] IEHC 59.

[18] *La Moselle Clothing Company Ltd v Soualhi* [1998] IEHC 66, [1998] 2 ILRM 345.

[19] This case is a useful example of the application of the 'just and equitable' criteria in restriction proceedings. See further 'C. Just and Equitable' at paras **[17.066]** to **[17.069]**.

[20] *Re CMC (Ireland) Ltd, Fennell v Carolan* [2005] IEHC 59.

recover the assets of the company, delay in their recovery can effect the legitimate interests of the creditors not least because an elongation of the liquidation is likely to mean greater costs which all have to come out of the same pool which ought, properly, be available for the creditors.'[21]

[17.009] The third factual issue related to proceedings initiated by the liquidator in the Netherlands on behalf of the company to recover monies owing to it. Both respondents filed statements in these proceedings which supported the defendant's case and were against the interests of the company. While the Court emphasised that it would be 'wholly inappropriate' to suggest that directors should not give evidence in court proceedings, even if against the interests of the company, the statements made in this case were found to be at variance with the company's records. The Court further found that the respondents did not seek to check those records before furnishing their statements and that they should, at a minimum, have exercised care when taking actions which were against the company's interest. Clarke J determined that, if a director of a company in liquidation intervenes in proceedings against the company's interest, without regard to the company's books and records, 'he may well be said to do so at his peril.'

On the basis of these findings, Clarke J was satisfied that the respondents 'engaged in activity which, at least taken cumulatively, amounts to a sufficient departure from the reasonable standards that can be expected of a director or former director during a winding up so as to make it just and equitable to make an order under s 150'. The Court did however observe that the respondents' actions were 'on the lower end of the range of seriousness of such actions.'[22]

There was nothing reprehensible about the conduct of the respondents in *Re CMC (Ireland) Ltd*[23] prior to the date of commencement of the winding up. This decision is a clear caution to directors that it is important to continue to act in the interests of a company beyond the commencement of the winding up, and to co-operate fully with the liquidator, to avoid being the subject of restriction proceedings under s 150.

(ii) Conduct in relation to other companies

[17.010] It has consistently been stated by the courts that the conduct to be examined for the purpose of determining whether a director acted 'honestly and responsibly' within the meaning of s 150(2)(a) is his conduct in relation to the company in liquidation. No matter how exemplary, the conduct of the director as a director of other companies, even a company which nominated him to the board of the company in liquidation, is not relevant to the decision whether to make a restriction order.[24]

---

[21] *Re CMC (Ireland) Ltd, Fennell v Carolan* [2005] IEHC 59.

[22] *Re CMC (Ireland) Ltd, Fennell v Carolan* [2005] IEHC 59.

[23] *Re CMC (Ireland) Ltd, Fennell v Carolan* [2005] IEHC 59.

[24] See *Re Tralee Beef and Lamb Ltd, Kavanagh v Delaney* [2004] IEHC 139 (20 July 2004, unreported), HC.

This limitation also applies firmly in the context of subsidiary companies. It has been established in cases such as *Re 360Atlantic (Ireland) Ltd*[25] and *Re Mitek Holdings Ltd*,[26] that the conduct of the director in relation to the group of companies of which the company in liquidation is a member, or other members of a group, is not relevant to the analysis the court must undertake of his conduct in relation to the company in liquidation to assess whether it was honest and responsible.

(b) General interpretation of 'honestly and responsibly'

[17.011] In cases have which revolved around the term 'honestly and responsibly' in the context of restriction proceedings, Irish courts have advanced a number of helpful interpretations of that phrase as it appears in s 150(2)(a).

(i) Failure of company

[17.012] The fact that a company makes significant losses may be a factor in determining whether its directors acted honestly and responsibly, but should not be determinative. In *Re USIT World plc*,[27] Peart J noted, '... the size of the deficit should not of itself be determinative, although obviously the greater sums involved in the business the greater the care required to accompany decisions taken.'

In *Business Communications v Baxter*[28] Murphy J observed that the fact that a company has failed is not of itself evidence of a lack of responsibility. This observation was endorsed by Shanley J in *La Moselle Clothing Company Ltd v Soualhi*, but was qualified, albeit to a limited extent, by the statement that:

> '... there may well be circumstances where a business will fail due to a lack of
> business probity or indeed sheer incompetence (without actual dishonesty or non-
> compliance with the principal features of the Companies Acts) such as to amount
> to such a want of responsibility as to permit a restriction under s 150, sub-s (1), of
> the Companies Act, 1990.'[29]

This suggests that where the company's failure was attributable to incompetence or lack of business sense, this could be a basis for a finding of irresponsibility against a director and the making of a declaration of restriction. The extent to which a director's conduct contributed to the company's insolvency will clearly be a decisive criterion in determining whether to make a declaration of restriction.[30]

---

[25] *Re 360Atlantic (Ireland) Ltd, O'Ferral v Coughlan* [2004] IEHC 410.

[26] *Re Mitek Ltd, Grace v Kachkar* [2005] IEHC 63. See also *Re 360Networks (Ireland) Ltd, O'Ferral v Coughlan* [2004] IEHC 412.

[27] *Re USIT World plc* [2005] IEHC 285.

[28] *Business Communications v Baxter* (21 July 1995, unreported), HC, (Murphy J).

[29] *La Moselle Clothing Co Ltd v Soualhi* [1998] IEHC 66, [1998] 2 ILRM 345 at para 9.

[30] See *La Moselle Clothing Co Ltd v Soualhi* [1988] IEHC 66 and *Re Money Markets International Stock Brokers Ltd* [2006] IEHC 350.

(ii) Compliance with Companies Acts

[17.013] A company's compliance with the requirements of the CA 1963–2006 may be a factor in deciding whether to make a declaration of restriction in respect of its directors.[31] In *Business Communications v Baxter*,[32] Murphy J stated:

> 'Ordinarily "responsibly" will entail compliance with the principal features of the Companies Acts and the maintenance of the records required by those Acts. The records must be basic in form and modest in appearance. But they must exist in such a form as to enable the directors to make a reasonable commercial decision and auditors (or liquidators) to understand and follow the transactions in which the company was engaged.'

This decision suggests that evidence that a company complied with the requirements of the Companies Acts and kept proper books and records will be a factor in an application under s 150.

[17.014] In *Re USIT World plc*,[33] the liquidator raised concerns regarding non-compliance with certain statutory requirements by both companies under consideration in that case, USIT Ltd (a Northern Ireland registered company) and USIT World plc. In particular, those companies were alleged to have failed to have kept and filed audited accounts; failed to have kept proper books and records; and failed to have kept statutory registers. The Court noted that such failures may be relevant to a restriction application:

> 'In some situations, there is no doubt that in the absence of these documents being filed, some creditor may be deprived of relevant information prior to lending money, or providing services to a company which later goes into liquidation, and had it seen the up to date state of affairs of the company from an examination of the company file in the CRO it may say that it would have chosen not to do business. In such a situation clearly there is a causative link between the culpable behaviour of the directors and the loss sustained by the creditor on liquidation.'[34]

In the case of *Re USIT World plc*, however, Peart J found that there was no such causative link and, while the failure to file returns was important it was 'so incidental to the collapse of the group as not to be capable of being a matter of irresponsibility for the purposes of an application of this kind, and in the sense of being connected causally to the collapse of the group.' The Court distinguished the situation in *Re USIT World plc*

---

[31] See *Business Communications v Baxter* (21 July 1995, unreported), HC, (Murphy J); *La Moselle Clothing Company Ltd v Soualhi* [1998] IEHC 66, [1998] 2 ILRM 345; *Re Tralee Beef and Lamb Ltd, Kavanagh v Delaney* [2004] IEHC 139 (20 July 2004, unreported), HC; *Re SPH Ltd, Fennell v Shanahan* [2005] IEHC 152; *Re Dublin Sports Cafe Ltd, Farrell v Long* [2005] IEHC 458; *Re Greenmount Holdings Ltd, Stafford v O'Connor* [2007] IEHC 246.

[32] *Business Communications v Baxter* (21 July 1995, unreported), HC, (Murphy J).

[33] *Re USIT World plc* [2005] IEHC 285.

[34] Peart J also stated, in relation to allegations of failing to keep proper books and records and statutory registers, 'In any event, I do not believe that even if there was a failure to observe the requirements in these respects, they went in any way towards the demise of the company in the circumstances of this case, and while it is right that the Court would have regard to a matter such as this when making its assessment of responsibility, it could not in this case be persuasive.' *Re USIT World plc* [2005] IEHC 285.

from more serious cases, suggesting that if the non-compliance was particularly egregious, it may warrant a finding of irresponsibility without such a causal connection:

> 'It is unlike a worse situation where over perhaps many years of trading, officers of the company have ignored completely the obligations under the Companies Acts regarding the requirement to file returns, and/or other statutory requirements, where such behaviour would be demonstrative of such a degree of irresponsibility of attitude generally, and such egregious and wanton disregard of the obligations upon officers of limited companies as to liabilities as to indicate their complete lack of suitability for the entrustment of the privileges of limited liability. From such persons the public are entitled to be protected in the future.'[35]

[17.015] In *Re USIT World plc*[36] one of the directors filed an affidavit to the effect that, while the liquidator claimed not to have been able to locate the statutory registers and books and records, such registers, books and records were kept[37] and that responsibility lay with the director of corporate governance for the group. The Court held:

> 'I believe that in a group as large and spread and to which directors with particular expertise had been appointed to various specialist positions, it was not irresponsible for Mr Olivares to leave matters such as these to the director of corporate governance. He cannot have been expected to have any direct responsibility in that regard as part of his day-to-day activity with the company, even though as a director he has a shared responsibility for all matters.'

This indicates that it may not be irresponsible for a director to leave responsibility for compliance matters such as the maintenance of statutory registers and even the maintenance of proper books and records, to a designated individual.

(iii) 'La Moselle' test

[17.016] The most frequently cited test to determine whether a director acted responsibly for the purpose of restriction proceedings, is the following test, as put forward by Shanley J in *La Moselle Clothing Company Ltd v Soualhi*:[38]

> '... it seems to me that in determining the "responsibility" of a director for the purposes of s 150(2)(a) the Court should have regard to:
>
> (a) The extent to which the director has or has not complied with any obligation imposed on him by the Companies Acts 1963–1990.
>
> (b) The extent to which his conduct could be regarded as so incompetent as to amount to irresponsibility.
>
> (c) The extent of the director's responsibility for the insolvency of the company.
>
> (d) The extent of the director's responsibility for the net deficiency in the assets of the company disclosed at the date of the winding up or thereafter.

---

[35]	*Re USIT World plc* [2005] IEHC 285.

[36]	*Re USIT World plc* [2005] IEHC 285, *per* Peart J.

[37]	The Court concluded that, while the liquidator could not locate the statutory registers, they were, on the balance of probabilities, maintained: 'in relation to this conflict in the evidence I cannot resolve it conclusively, but I am left on the basis of a probability that these records were kept and maintained even though the liquidator for whatever reason never obtained them, except for the minutes.' *Re USIT World plc* [2005] IEHC 285.

[38]	*La Moselle Clothing Company Ltd v Soualhi* [1998] IEHC 66, [1998] 2 ILRM 345.

(e) The extent to which the director, in his conduct of the affairs of the company, has displayed a lack of commercial probity or want of proper standards.'[39]

[17.017] According to this test, if a director complied with his duties under the Companies Acts; was not guilty of any incompetence, lack of probity, or otherwise lacking in ability; and was not responsible for the insolvency of the company or the deficiency of its assets, he should not be the subject of a declaration of restriction. It should be noted, however, that this list is not exhaustive and the items in it are not necessarily dispositive of s 150 applications:

> 'The list I am sure cannot be regarded as exhaustive, and neither in my view does the presence of one or more of these factors in a particular case mean that in that case the director must be regarded as having acted either dishonestly and/or irresponsibly to such an extent as to warrant restriction. Each case will have to be looked at on its own particular facts. In one case a director may have been culpable in respect of a number of the factors on the list, but in the heel of the hunt none of those factors had any direct or meaningful bearing on the failure of the company. In another case, a director may fall foul of only one of the factors, yet that one lapse may be of such a degree and have such a direct bearing on the insolvency of the company that it outweighs all the other ways in which the director conducted himself/herself honestly and responsibly as a director, and be such that the public should be protected for the period of restriction from any risk that it might happen again.'[40]

[17.018] In *La Moselle Clothing Company Ltd v Soualhi*[41] Shanley J acknowledged that the five limbs of the test for responsibility are not mutually exclusive and that there was some overlap between them, as illustrated by the following: '...a failure to keep proper books of account may directly contribute to the company becoming insolvent and may be caused by the incompetence of a director.'[42] He also stated, however, that there are circumstances in which conduct, not amounting to breaches of the Companies Acts, could amount to a want of responsibility and cited the example of a director extracting excessive sums by way of salary from the company without regard to the company's financial situation.

[17.019] There are some aspects of the 'La Moselle' test for determining whether a director acted 'responsibly' within the meaning of s 150(2)(a) which could be potentially unfair. First, the subjectivity of some of the limbs of the test may introduce arbitrariness and lack of consistency and certainty. If conduct amounts to a breach of the Companies Acts or a clear violation of the duties attendant on the role of a director, a person cannot have any grievance about being the subject of a declaration of restriction. If, on the other hand, a director's conduct is regarded as lacking in probity and as

---

[39] *La Moselle Clothing Company Ltd v Soualhi* [1998] IEHC 66, [1998] 2 ILRM 345 at para 11, as approved by the Supreme Court in *Re Squash (Ireland) Limited* [2001] 3 IR 35 and as followed in a number of High Court cases, such as *Re SPH Ltd, Fennell v Shanahan* [2005] IEHC 152.

[40] *Re USIT World plc* [2005] IEHC 285, *per* Peart J.

[41] *La Moselle Clothing Company Ltd v Soualhi* [1998] IEHC 66, [1998] 2 ILRM 345.

[42] *La Moselle Clothing Company Ltd v Soualhi* [1998] IEHC 66, [1998] 2 ILRM 345 at para 11.

amounting to irresponsibility on that basis, the director may feel aggrieved at the subjectivity of the assessment.

A second potential difficulty with the 'La Moselle' test for responsibility is that some of the prongs of the test may suffer from the 'benefit of hindsight' syndrome. There may be circumstances in which it is far easier for a liquidator to allege that a director's conduct contributed to the company's insolvency, whereas, viewed in the context of the company's state of affairs at the time of the conduct in question, it may have been reasonable for the director to adopt the course of action that he did.

A third difficulty is that at least one limb of the 'La Moselle' test is very ambiguously framed. The fifth aspect of the test focuses upon 'the extent to which the director, in his conduct of the affairs of the company, has displayed a lack of commercial probity or want of proper standards'. There is no definition of 'commercial probity' and the expression a 'want of proper standards' is meaningless in the absence of any assistance or guidance as to what type of standards are in question. It would be very difficult for a director of a company to assess whether his conduct would meet the threshold of 'proper standards' without any direction as to what standards were in question, and what sources he could rely on to ensure compliance with such 'proper standards'. A final issue regarding the test for determining whether a director acted responsibly, as set out in *La Moselle Clothing Co Ltd v Soualhi*,[43] is that the standard of 'a lack of commercial probity or want of proper standards' is derived from the jurisprudence of English courts under s 300 of the Companies Act 1985, which mirrors CA 1990, s 160(2)(d).[44] The test of 'commercial probity' and 'proper standards' was therefore formulated and applied in the context of determining whether a person was 'unfit to be concerned in the management of a company'. It is a test for disqualification, not restriction, proceedings, Duplicating this test in restriction proceedings blurs the distinction between restriction and disqualification proceedings and does not enhance clarity or certainty in relation to the forms of conduct which may merit a declaration of restriction under s 150.[45]

[17.020] While these concerns exist and the potential for the infliction of unfair adjudications of the conduct of directors is a real one, it must be stated that the Irish courts have to date applied the test of responsibility with common sense and with an understanding of the reality that it may be more difficult for a director of a company in difficulty to assess the correct course of action at the time, than it is for the court to say what should have been done, with the benefit of hindsight after the company has become insolvent and is being wound up. Indeed it has been acknowledged specifically by the High Court in a case involving s 150 that:

> 'the Courts must be careful in considering applications under this section not to,
> as was described in one judgment, permit the conducting of witch hunts against
> directors and, perhaps more importantly from the Courts' perspective, not to view

---

[43] *La Moselle Clothing Co Ltd v Soualhi* [1998] IEHC 66, [1998] 2 ILRM 245.

[44] See, in particular, *Re Lo-Line Ltd* [1988] Ch 477. See further paras **[22.032]** to **[22.047]**.

[45] See paras **[22.036]** to **[22.041]**, 'Overlap between ss 150 and 160'.

the matter with the inevitable benefit of hindsight which arises in the course of the liquidation.'[46]

[17.021] Another consideration that must be weighed is the need not to stifle entrepreneurial endeavours. In *Re USIT World plc*[47] Peart J sets out the balance to be struck in this regard as follows:

'It is the very essence of entrepreneurial endeavour that risks are taken. Risks can differ in character. Something can be characterised as a risk simply because the outcome cannot be known with certainty, whereas those with responsibility to see it through and with the knowledge base from which to assess and weigh the magnitude or reasonableness of the risk may see the risk of failure as being far less than the likelihood of success.

A risk taken against such a background of planning and knowledge, and with appropriate advice taken, might be reasonably characterised as a calculated risk without any element of carelessness, rashness or recklessness attached to it which could attract to it the tag of irresponsibility. Clearly the greater the amount of money involved in the risk the greater is the obligation on all concerned to ensure that appropriate care is taken in all aspects of its planning, so that all factors, reasonably foreseeable, which may cause the venture to fail, will be anticipated and guarded against.

If an entrepreneur were to be obliged, on pain of being found to be irresponsible and of being restricted under the section, to avoid taking any decision which at some date in the future might be found to have risk attached to it, the business life and a large component of the economic driver of the economy of the State would stultify. I do not believe that this is what the legislature had in mind when enacting s 150.'

(iv) The extension of 'La Moselle'

[17.022] In *Re Tralee Beef and Lamb Ltd*[48] the High Court considered the test that was expounded in *La Moselle Clothing Company Ltd v Soualhi*[49] and suggested the insertion of a new criteria among the matters to which a court should have regard in determining whether a director acted responsibly within the meaning of s 150(2)(a). Finlay Geoghegan J suggested the following amplification of the test for responsibility:

'Shanley J at paragraph (a) refers only to the obligations imposed on a director by the Companies Acts. At common law, directors owe duties to the company which are normally divided into duties of loyalty based on fiduciary principles, developed initially by the Courts of Equity and duties of skill and care developed initially by the Common Law Courts from the principles in the law of negligence ... Accordingly, it appears to me that when considering the matters referred to by Shanley J in *La Moselle Clothing Limited v Soualhi* [1998] 2 ILRM 345 under paragraph (a) a court should have regard not only to the extent to which a director

---

[46] *Re Colm O'Neill Engineering Services Ltd* [2004] IEHC 83 (13 February 2004, unreported), HC, Finlay Geoghegan J, *ex tempore*.

[47] *Re USIT World plc* [2005] IEHC 285.

[48] *Re Tralee Beef and Lamb Ltd, Kavanagh v Delaney* [2004] IEHC 139 (20 July 2004, unreported), HC.

[49] *La Moselle Clothing Company Ltd v Soualhi* [1998] IEHC 66, [1998] 2 ILRM 345.

has or has not complied with any obligation imposed on him/her by the Companies Acts but also with duties imposed by common law.'[50]

[17.023] From one perspective, this expansion of the test for responsibility is to be welcomed. Insofar as possible, it is preferable that the standards to which directors are expected to adhere and the non-attainment of which could lead to restriction, should be clear and ascertainable by directors. The common law duties imposed on directors under Irish law are well documented and, if a director was concerned to be vigilant and compliant in his observance of his duties as a directors, it would not be difficult for him to ascertain the content of those duties. The same can be said of the obligations of a director under the Companies Acts, as already contained in the first limb of the 'La Moselle' test.

[17.024] The dangers of subjectivity, lack of clarity and unpredictability still exist in relation to the other limbs of the '*La Moselle*' test. It would be preferable if the considerations listed at (b) to (e) of that test were defined more tightly. It is suggested that this could be achieved if the terms, such as 'want of proper standards' and 'lack of commercial probity,' were defined or analysed by reference to the standards and requirements imposed on directors by the Companies Acts and the common law. This may be possible, if the expansion of the first limb of the 'La Moselle' test to include the duties of directors at common law, as effected by *Re Tralee Beef and Lamb Ltd*,[51] was also applied to aid in the interpretation of the other limbs of the test for responsibility.

[17.025] There is another perspective from which the amplification of the test expounded in *La Moselle Clothing Company Ltd v Soualhi*,[52] to include the common law duties of a director, may not be a positive development. As a result of the extension of that test by *Re Tralee Beef and Lamb Ltd*,[53] a court is still obliged to have regard to the factors listed in *La Moselle Clothing Company Ltd v Soualhi*,[54] but is now also obliged to have regard to the common law duties imposed on a director.

[17.026] It is worth listing briefly some of the duties which are imposed on directors by the rules of common law. Directors of a company must:[55]

- exercise their powers in good faith;

- carry out their functions with due skill, care and diligence;

---

[50] This extension of the criteria for determining whether a director acted responsibly within the meaning of s 150(2)(a) has been approved and reiterated in a number of subsequent decisions of the High Court, including *Re SPH Ltd, Fennell v Shanahan* [2005] IEHC 152.

[51] *Re Tralee Beef and Lamb Ltd, Kavanagh v Delaney* [2004] IEHC 139 (20 July 2004, unreported), HC.

[52] *La Moselle Clothing Company Ltd v Soualhi* [1998] IEHC 66, [1998] 2 ILRM 345.

[53] *Re Tralee Beef and Lamb Ltd, Kavanagh v Delaney* [2004] IEHC 139 (20 July 2004, unreported), HC.

[54] *La Moselle Clothing Company Ltd v Soualhi* [1998] IEHC 66, [1998] 2 ILRM 345.

[55] It is beyond the scope of this chapter to analyse the common law duties of directors in details. See further Ch **6**. See also Courtney, *The Law of Private Companies* (2nd edn, Tottel Publishing, 2002) at 10.022.

- exercise their powers in the interests of the company as a whole;
- not make an undisclosed personal profit;
- account for any profit they make from their position;
- not allow their personal interests to conflict with the company's interests.

If these aspects of a director's duties, as well as their duties under the Companies Acts, are taken into account in restriction proceedings, it is difficult to see the justification for continuing to require that regard must also be had to the other limbs of the 'La Moselle' test. It should be recalled that (b) to (e) of that test address the following types of conduct:

- incompetence such as to amount to irresponsibility;
- responsibility for the insolvency of the company;
- responsibility for net deficiency in the company's assets;
- lack of commercial probity; and
- want of proper standards.

[17.027] It seems inevitable that if a director displayed such incompetence as to amount to irresponsibility, he would be in breach of his common law duty to exercise his powers with due skill, care and diligence or his statutory duty to keep proper books of account, for example. If a director was guilty of conduct which caused the company's insolvency or the deficiency in its assets, it is impossible to imagine that such conduct would not be categorised as a violation of one of the aspects of a director's duties at common law or under the Companies Acts. Finally, if a director demonstrated a lack of commercial probity, sufficient to reach a finding of irresponsibility, this should also be sufficient to reach the threshold of being a want of due skill, care and diligence within the common law meaning of that term. As regards the reference to a 'want of proper standards', it is reiterated that this phrase could and should only be defined by reference to the existing standards imposed on directors at common law and under the Companies Acts.

[17.028] This analysis is bolstered by the *dicta* of Shanley J in *La Moselle Clothing Company Ltd v Soualhi*.[56] In the course of his judgment, he accepted that there was certain overlap between the different elements of the test for responsibility, but that, in certain circumstances, the different limbs stood alone, citing the examples that 'a director's inability to see the 'writing on the wall' (eg an inability to see from a perusal of the company's management accounts that the company was trading while insolvent) may result from sheer incompetence and justify a restriction' without amounting to an infringement of the Companies Acts, and that 'a director who takes excessive sums from the company by way of drawings for salary without regard to the financial state of health of the company may be said to have acted without commercial probity although he did not necessarily fail to comply with his obligations under the Companies Acts 1963–1990.'[57]

---

[56] *La Moselle Clothing Company Ltd v Soualhi* [1998] IEHC 66, [1998] 2 ILRM 345.

[57] *La Moselle Clothing Company Ltd v Soualhi* [1998] IEHC 66, [1998] 2 ILRM 345 at para 12.

[17.029] Under the test as it has been revised by *Re Tralee Beef and Lamb Ltd*,[58] these examples of the distinct functions of the different limbs of the test no longer hold up. First, the failure to see 'the writing on the wall' would be very likely to amount to a breach of the duty to exercise the powers of a director with due skill, care and diligence. Secondly, the taking of excessive sums from the company would certainly amount to a breach of the duty of a director to exercise his powers in good faith and in the interests of the company, for example, and may also amount to a breach of the director's fiduciary duties at common law.

[17.030] The consequence of the extension of the 'La Moselle' test therefore appears to have been to include among the indicators of a lack of responsibility a wide variety of types of conduct which were not formerly part of the test for responsibility. This has therefore broadened the test to the extent that it may now be considered to be evidence of irresponsibility if a director violated any of the duties of a director at common law or under the Companies Acts, irrespective of whether the conduct in question had any bearing on, or relevance to, the ultimate liquidation or insolvency of the company. Whereas the scope of the jurisdiction to restrict a director was, under *Business Communications v Baxter*[59] and *La Moselle Clothing Company Ltd v Soualhi*,[60] confined to a breach of the Companies Acts and certain other breaches, the effect of *Re Tralee Beef and Lamb Ltd*[61] is that, unless a director complies with every obligation imposed upon him by the common law and the Companies Acts, he may be found to have acted irresponsibly and have a declaration of restriction made in respect of him. It is by no means clear or automatic that a failure to comply with obligations set out in the common law and the Companies Acts should be equated with a lack of responsibility, nor indeed that such a failure would necessarily have any relevance to the insolvency and dissolution of the company.

Another implication of the extension of the first limb of the 'La Moselle' test to include a director's duties at common law is that it has deprived the remaining four limbs of the test of any relevance, as their content is encompassed in the rules of common law. Finally, while it was cited as a possible advantage of the reference to a director's duties at common law that these duties should be ascertainable by a conscientious director, it could equally be said that confining the first limb of the 'La Moselle' test to the provisions of the Companies Acts was more transparent and certain for directors facing the risk of restriction.

(c) Relevant factors

[17.031] There are certain recurring themes running through the various decisions of the courts under s 150. Directors of failed companies are frequently accused of certain types of conduct, on the basis of which they are confronted with restriction proceedings.

---

58 *Re Tralee Beef and Lamb Ltd, Kavanagh v Delaney* [2004] IEHC 139 (20 July 2004, unreported), HC.

59 *Business Communications v Baxter* (21 July 1995, unreported), HC, (Murphy J).

60 *La Moselle Clothing Co Ltd v Soualhi* [1998] IEHC 66, [1998] 2 ILRM 345.

61 *Re Tralee Beef and Lamb Ltd, Kavanagh v Delaney* [2004] IEHC 139 (20 July 2004, unreported), HC.

There are different specific facts and nuances in each instance, which colour the outcome of the restriction proceedings. Furthermore, there are certain categories of action or inaction and certain defences and allegations which arise on the basis of the very particular facts of individual cases. The following are the categories of conduct which have been considered in relation to the overriding question of whether the directors in question acted 'honestly and responsibly in relation to the conduct of the affairs of the company'.[62] It is hoped that this overview of the jurisprudence of the Irish courts in relation to the restriction of directors will help to clarify the type of conduct for which directors have been restricted and the type of conduct which has been held to represent evidence of responsibility and to justify the refusal to make a declaration of restriction.

(i) Proper books and records

[17.032] One of the criteria for determining whether a director acted responsibly is whether they complied with the terms of the Companies Acts.[63] It has further been held repeatedly that the keeping of proper books and records is an important indicator of a director's responsibility, or lack thereof.[64] Furthermore, a director's attitude towards the books and records of a company after the commencement of the winding up is a factor which does weigh heavily with the court.

In a number of restriction proceedings, the directors' alleged failure to keep proper books and records has been raised and relied upon as an indication of lack of responsibility.

[17.033] The High Court conducted a very detailed analysis of the obligation of directors to keep books of account under CA 1990, s 202, in *Re Mantruck Service Ltd.*[65] That case concerned proceedings seeking to make a director of the company in liquidation personally liable for the company's debts, under s 204, as a result of the failure to comply with s 202. The liquidator also pursued restriction proceedings against the director. In that case, the principal issue was the order of personal liability sought against the director. The declaration of restriction, presumably being of lesser consequence for the respondent, received little attention, the Court delivering the following finding under s 150:

> 'having regard to the mandatory words of s 150 of the 1990 Act (in relation to which See *Re Business Communications Limited* Murphy J 21st July, 1995) I am satisfied that I have no discretion but to impose the five year restriction, contained

---

[62]   CA 1990, s 150(2)(a).

[63]   See *Business Communications v Baxter* (21 July 1995, unreported), HC, (Murphy J); *La Moselle Clothing Company Ltd v Soualhi* [1998] IEHC 66, [1998] 2 ILRM 345; *Re Tralee Beef and Lamb Ltd, Kavanagh v Delaney* [2004] IEHC 139 (20 July 2004, unreported), HC; *Re SPH Ltd, Fennell v Shanahan* [2005] IEHC 152; *Re Dublin Sports Cafe Ltd, Farrell v Long* [2005] IEHC 458.

[64]   See *Business Communications v Baxter* (21 July 1995, unreported), HC, (Murphy J). Under the Companies Acts, a company is obliged to keep proper books of account. CA 1990, ss 202 and 203.

[65]   *Re Mantruck Services Ltd, Mehigan v Duignan* [1996] IEHC 18, [1997] 1 IR 340, [1997] 1 ILRM 171.

in the section, on Mr Duignan: he does not bring himself within any of the three exceptions of sub-s 2 (of s 150).'[66]

The other aspects of this case are addressed in more detail elsewhere.[67]

[17.034] In *La Moselle Clothing Company Ltd v Soualhi*,[68] one of the grounds relied upon by the liquidator in support of the application for a declaration of restriction against Mr Soualhi was the difficulty faced by the liquidator in obtaining books and records related to the two companies in liquidation. The liquidator claimed to have experienced extreme difficulty in obtaining the companies' books and records and cited the respondent's 'cavalier attitude to the books and records' of one of the companies.

The liquidator cited an affidavit sworn by Mr Soualhi as evidence of this 'cavalier attitude'. The explanation used by Mr Soualhi for the difficulty encountered by the liquidator in accessing books and documents is an example to any directors of how not to deal with a company's books and records. In his affidavit, Mr Soualhi averred:

> 'I say that when the company ceased trading I caused the offices to be shut down and all possessions, documents and equipment belonging to the company or otherwise were removed from the offices and/or thrown out.
>
> ... I say and believe that any documents relating to the company which were removed from the said offices (if any) were brought to another premises ... I say that I subsequently moved from these premises in December, 1994 and further caused another clear-out of documentation, equipment and possessions ... Since that date I caused a further clear-out of documentation, equipment and possessions to an office premises ...'

In relation to the books and records of the companies, the Court noted, 'the cavalier approach of Mr Soualhi' and went on to state that the actions of the respondent:

> 'are the actions of a person who does not realise that the protection afforded by limited liability carries with it certain obligations which he clearly failed to discharge in not ensuring the safety of all the books and records of Rosegem, despite the fact that it had ceased trading.'[69]

[17.035] In *Re Gasco Ltd*,[70] the two directors of the company resigned at different points in time, some seven months and four months before the company was wound up. After their resignations, the controlling shareholder of the company, Mr Rooney, effectively ran the company on his own and was held to have been a shadow director of the company.[71] One of the former directors gave evidence that there were certain monthly accounts and records in existence at the date of his resignation, and the other director verified that there were monthly management accounts in place at the date of his resignation, four months before the commencement of the winding up. When the

---

[66] *Re Mantruck Services Ltd, Mehigan v Duignan* [1996] IEHC 18, [1997] 1 IR 340, [1997] 1 ILRM 171.

[67] See Ch **4**.

[68] *La Moselle Clothing Co Ltd v Soualhi* [1998] IEHC 66, [1998] 2 ILRM 345.

[69] *La Moselle Clothing Co Ltd v Soualhi* [1998] IEHC 66, [1998] 2 ILRM 345.

[70] *Re Gasco Ltd* [2001] IEHC 20.

[71] This aspect of the judgment is addressed above. See paras **[16.052]** to **[16.053]**.

liquidator was appointed, he found virtually no books or records and could not locate the monthly accounts and management accounts referred to by the company's former directors.

There were a number of implications for the company in liquidation, and criticisms directed at Mr Rooney, as a result of the dearth of books and records available or in existence at the commencement of the company's winding up. First, the Court concluded from the facts set forth by the liquidator and the two former directors that, 'The clear implication is that either these records never existed, or they were in some way destroyed during the last few months of the life of the company when Mr. Rooney was effectively in charge.'[72]

Secondly, the Court noted that there was a poor recovery of debts by the liquidator as a result of the lack of records. McCracken J emphasised that, by the time of the resignation of the two former directors, 'the company was in serious difficulties, and if only for the purpose of collecting in as many debts as possible, it was very important that the company should have kept proper records.'[73]

Thirdly, the egregiousness of the Mr Rooney's failure to keep the books and records was substantially compounded by the fact that there were sizable debts owed to the company in liquidation by a second company ('Hutchinson and Rooney Ltd') of which he was also the controlling shareholder. Mr Rooney alleged that a substantial amount of these debts were discharged in the period after the resignation of the directors of Gasco Ltd and before the commencement of the winding up of the latter company. The Court dealt with this claim as follows:

> '... because of the lack of records, the liquidator has been unable to find evidence
> of substantial payments to the company in the last few months of its existence.
> One would expect that if such substantial payments were made to reduce the debt
> to these sort of figures, Mr. Rooney would have been very careful to keep records
> to demonstrate that Hutchinson and Rooney Limited had paid off most of their
> debt.'[74]

Having indicated a number of ways in which the failure to keep proper books and records was improper and deleterious to the company's interests, and those of its creditors, the Court held, 'The fact that no such records exist may make me suspect many things, but certainly is clear evidence of serious irresponsibility by Mr. Rooney during the last few months of the trading life of the company.'[75] A restriction order was made against Mr Rooney on that ground, among others.

[17.036] It is noteworthy that, despite the suggestions that the director may have deliberately destroyed the company's records during the final months of the company's existence and that the director may have exploited that circumstance to falsely claim the repayment of debts by his company to the company in liquidation, the Court determined that the director had acted irresponsibly, but did not state that he acted dishonestly. This

---

[72]   *Re Gasco Ltd* [2001] IEHC 20 at para 13.

[73]   *Re Gasco Ltd* [2001] IEHC 20 at para 13.

[74]   *Re Gasco Ltd* [2001] IEHC 20 at para 14.

[75]   *Re Gasco Ltd* [2001] IEHC 20 at para 14.

highlights the reluctance of courts to make findings of dishonesty within the context of restriction proceedings. If there were to be a case in which a finding of dishonesty may be warranted, it surely would be a case such as *Re Gasco Ltd*.[76]

[17.037] A failure to keep proper books and records was also relied upon by the High Court in *Re Capital Auto Group Ltd*, [77] Peart J rejecting the defence that the respondent delegated responsibility for such matters to a co-director:

> 'It is not sufficient for Mr Swords to say that these were the responsibility of his co-director and that he presumed that all was being attended to. Each director as part of acting responsibly has a duty to inform himself without any doubt, as to whether books and records are being kept. Sometimes this is achieved by the employment of suitable staff. Other times it is achieved by each director himself or herself making sure that all matters of that kind are looked after and being attended to as required. I am not left with anything like an assurance that Mr Swords concerned himself adequately with matters of this kind.'[78]

The Court emphasised that directors have a 'shared responsibility' and that the onus is on each of them to ensure that the affairs of the company are conducted in an honest and responsible manner.

[17.038] An example of a case in which a failure to keep books and records was alleged, and rejected, as a ground for seeking an order of restriction, in circumstances where an order of disqualification was also sought, was *Re Newcastle Timber Ltd*.[79]

In that case, the directors claimed that they employed a full-time bookkeeper and that full records were maintained, but that they were destroyed in a fire in the company's premises after it ceased trading but before it was wound up. The directors also relied upon the fact there were a number of inspections of the records of the company by the Revenue Commissioners while it was still trading. McCracken J held, 'There is no doubt that such a fire did take place, and there is no suggestion that this fire was caused by anything other than vandalism. It is now really impossible to say what books and records did exist[80].'

In all of the circumstances of the case, declarations of restriction, but no orders of disqualification, were ultimately made against the directors. The allegation of failure to keep proper books and records was not one of the grounds for making the declaration of restriction. This case turns on its very particular facts. However, it does demonstrate that a court will not assume that a company which appeared to suffer many forms of mismanagement, necessarily also suffered from a failure to keep proper books and records.

[17.039] In addition to the duty to keep proper books of account, a company and its directors must also ensure that they keep books of account in Ireland, as required by CA

---

[76] *Re Gasco Ltd* [2001] IEHC 20.

[77] *Re Capital Auto Group Ltd, Foster v Swords* [2005] IEHC 434.

[78] *Re Capital Auto Group Ltd, Foster v Swords* [2005] IEHC 434.

[79] *Re Newcastle Timber Ltd* [2001] IEHC 146.

[80] *Re Newcastle Timber Ltd* [2001] IEHC 146 at para 5.

1990, s 202(6). In *Re 360Atlantic (Ireland) Ltd*,[81] the directors of an Irish subsidiary of a multinational company were restricted on a number of grounds. One of the grounds invoked by the liquidator was the alleged failure to keep books of account in Ireland as required by s 202(6). In making the declarations of restriction sought, the Court took into account that the accounts presented appeared to have been inaccurate and that books of account were not kept in Ireland, among other factors.

(ii) Financial affairs

[17.040] One of the most crucial and unwavering duties of a director is the duty to keep himself informed about the company's affairs, which includes the duty to acquire and maintain an understanding of the company's business.[82] In the context of restriction proceedings, the awareness that a director possesses of the company's financial state of health can be critical. It has been established by the cases interpreting s 150 that it is not acceptable for a director of a company to plead ignorance of the company's financial predicament and, although a non-executive director is entitled to delegate the day-to-day management of the company to executive directors,[83] such delegation does not absolve directors of their duties to the company.[84] This duty to be informed of the company's financial situation has a number of dimensions, as will now be addressed.

[17.041] If a company enters liquidation with very sizable deficits, this automatically raises questions about the conduct of the directors. One such question is whether they were informed about, and monitored, the company's financial situation. In *Re SPH Ltd*[85] that issue arose for consideration in circumstances where the company owed very substantial debts to the Revenue Commissioners. The liquidator raised the issue of 'whether the respondents acted responsibly in relation to the control and supervision of the financial affairs of the Company having regard in particular to the amount of the liability to the Revenue and the manner and period over which this had been allowed to accumulate.'[86]

The Court noted that the company did employ an accountant, but emphasised that, if day-to-day management of the company finances was delegated to the accountant, 'it cannot relieve the first and second named respondents of their obligations to inform themselves about the financial affairs of the Company and with their fellow directors to supervise and control the delegated functions.'[87] The Court concluded that, if the directors did not knowingly permit the debts to accrue, and were unaware of the

---

[81] *Re 360Atlantic (Ireland) Ltd, O'Ferral v Coughlan* [2004] IEHC 410.

[82] See *Re SPH Ltd, Fennell v Shanahan* [2005] IEHC 152 and *Re Cookes Events Company Ltd, Kavanagh v Cooke* [2005] IEHC 225.

[83] See above paras **[16.028]** to **[16.036]**.

[84] See, eg, *Re Tralee Beef and Lamb Ltd Kavanagh v Delaney* [2004] IEHC 139 (20 July 2004, unreported), HC: 'such delegation does not absolve the non-executive directors from the duty to acquire information about the affairs of the company and to supervise the discharge of delegated functions.'

[85] *Re SPH Ltd, Fennell v Shanahan* [2005] IEHC 152.

[86] *Re SPH Ltd, Fennell v Shanahan* [2005] IEHC 152.

[87] *Re SPH Ltd, Fennell v Shanahan* [2005] IEHC 152.

company's liabilities, that 'they failed to have in place appropriate systems to inform themselves of the financial position of the Company to allow them properly control and manage the affairs of the Company.'[88]

This case demonstrates three potential factors which a court may find to be indicative of irresponsibility on the part of a company's directors. First, there was a failure to control and supervise the company's financial affairs. Secondly, there was a failure to have in place systems to keep informed about the company's financial situation. The Court held that, if directors do not adopt direct responsibility for the day-to-day management of the company's financial affairs, they must have appropriate systems in place to inform themselves of the company's financial position. Finally, this judgment suggests that the existence of very substantial deficits may be indicative of the inadequacy of the director's knowledge, control and management of, the company's financial affairs.

[17.042] In *Re Colm O'Neill Engineering Services Ltd*[89] the liquidator advanced a number of distinct grounds for seeking restriction of the company's four directors. One was the allegation that the directors failed to obtain sufficient financial information from the company's executives and failed to recognise in due time the company's deteriorating financial situation. The Court took into account the fact that the company complied with all of its statutory obligations and that its books and records were accepted to be reasonable. On this basis, the Court concluded that insofar as there may have been any inadequacy in the financial information received by the board and the manner in which the board addressed the company's financial situation, 'such inadequacy of the actions of the Board could not be considered to be either incompetent, as such, or certainly not incompetent so as to amount to irresponsibility.' The factors which were taken into account by the Court in reaching this conclusion were the following:

- there was no executive director acting as financial controller of the company;

- one of the directors of the company did bring the financial information to the board in the latter periods;

- even though there was no financial director, the board took steps to strengthen the financial reporting to the board in the company's final periods;

- on the advice of auditors, the board appointed first one, and then another, individual, to act as financial controller.[90]

In all of the circumstances of the case, the Court refused the declarations of restriction sought against the four directors. This judgment suggests that, while directors are obliged to keep informed about the company's affairs, there may be circumstances in which the appointment of financial controllers and the absence of a director with a financial role in the company, may ease the burden on directors of demonstrating that

---

[88]   *Re SPH Ltd, Fennell v Shanahan* [2005] IEHC 152.

[89]   *Re Colm O'Neill Engineering Services Ltd* [2004] IEHC 83 (13 February 2004, unreported), HC, Finlay Geoghegan J, *ex tempore*.

[90]   *Re Colm O'Neill Engineering Services Ltd* [2004] IEHC 83 (13 February 2004, unreported), HC, Finlay Geoghegan J, *ex tempore*.

the inadequacy of their insight into the company's financial situation may not be irresponsible. The keeping of adequate and statutorily-compliant books and records would clearly assist in the discharge of this burden.

[17.043] In *Re Tralee Beef and Lamb Ltd*,[91] the liquidator raised the inadequacy of the financial information available to the company as a factor to be considered in the restriction proceedings. On the facts of the case, which involved large deficits, the Court concluded that the financial information available to the directors 'must have been inadequate'. The managing director (Mr Delaney) bore responsibility for furnishing the other directors with financial information about the company. He was held to have been aware of the company's financial difficulties but not of their full scale. From the evidence presented, the Court concluded that Mr Delaney failed to inform the other directors about the company's difficulties. The Court concluded that Mr Delaney:

> 'must be considered to have been under an obligation as part of his duty to exercise skill and diligence to inform his fellow directors of the financial difficulties and to arrange for the holding of board meetings in order that the directors could collectively seek to discharge their duties of supervising and controlling the affairs of the Company at least during this crucial period for the Company.'[92]

One of the non-executive directors was also restricted on the basis that she was aware of the company's financial predicament and failed to inform the other directors of same, or to convene a meeting of the board of directors. The other two non-executive directors were held not to have been aware of the company's financial difficulties. However, this did not absolve them of responsibility or protect them from exposure to the penalties of s 150. Both of these directors played a minimal role in the company and the Court was satisfied that, in all of the circumstances, they could not be regarded as having discharged their duties as director to keep themselves informed about the affairs of the company and to join with their co-directors in supervising the controlling the affairs of the company.

[17.044] The overriding principle to be derived from these, among others,[93] cases, is that whether a director, an officer or an employee of the company is responsible for a company's financial information, it is not sufficient or acceptable for the other directors to abdicate responsibility in relation to that information. A director must obtain and monitor the financial situation of the company and it is no excuse to s 150 proceedings to plead ignorance of the company's financial demise.

---

91 *Re Tralee Beef and Lamb Ltd, Kavanagh v Delaney* [2004] IEHC 139 (20 July 2004, unreported), HC.

92 *Re Tralee Beef and Lamb Ltd, Kavanagh v Delaney* [2004] IEHC 139 (20 July 2004, unreported), HC.

93 See, eg, '*Re, Lynrowan Enterprises Ltd* [2002] IEHC 90 (31 July 2002, unreported), HC; *Re 360Networks (Ireland) Ltd, O'Ferral v Coughlan* [2004] IEHC 412; *Re 360 Atlantic (Ireland) Ltd: O'Ferral v Coughlan* [2004] IEHC 410.

[17.045] From a review of the cases regarding the failure of directors to be informed about the company's financial situation, the following types of conduct appear to be taken into account by the courts as indicators of irresponsibility:

- failing to recognise the company's deteriorating financial situation;[94]

- failing to be involved in monitoring or controlling the company's financial affairs;[95]

- not taking an active part in the company's affairs;[96]

- failing to take steps to remedy a deteriorating financial situation;[97]

- failing to inform other directors of the company's financial difficulties;[98]

- failing to have systems in place to obtain financial information;[99]

- it is not sufficient to delegate all responsibility for financial information to an executive director, an officer or an employee, without supervising and monitoring the company's financial affairs.

(iii) Non-financial information

[17.046] A director's obligation to keep informed about the company's situation is not limited to financial information, although that will typically be the most critical type of information in a company which is facing insolvency. In *Re Tralee Beef and Lamb Ltd*,[100] Finlay Geoghegan J noted that: 'Whilst financial information is very important it is not the only relevant information in relation to the affairs of a trading company such as this.' The Court placed reliance on the fact that, in that case, there was no evidence that the director facing restriction made efforts to inform himself about any non-financial aspects of the affairs of the company.[101]

---

[94] See *Re Colm O'Neill Engineering Services Ltd* [2004] IEHC 83 (13 February 2004, unreported), HC, Finlay Geoghegan J, *ex tempore*.

[95] See *Re Tralee Beef and Lamb Ltd, Kavanagh v Delaney* [2004] IEHC 139 (20 July 2004, unreported), HC and *Lynrowan Enterprises Ltd, Re* [2002] IEHC 90 (31 July 2002, unreported), HC.

[96] See *Re Tralee Beef and Lamb Ltd, Kavanagh v Delaney* [2004] IEHC 139 (20 July 2004, unreported), HC.

[97] See *Re Colm O'Neill Engineering Services Ltd* [2004] IEHC 83 (13 February 2004, unreported), HC, Finlay Geoghegan J, *ex tempore*.

[98] See *Re Tralee Beef and Lamb Ltd, Kavanagh v Delaney* [2004] IEHC 139 (20 July 2004, unreported), HC.

[99] See *Re Colm O'Neill Engineering Services Ltd* [2004] IEHC 83 (13 February 2004, unreported), HC, Finlay Geoghegan J, *ex tempore*.

[100] *Re Tralee Beef and Lamb Ltd, Kavanagh v Delaney* [2004] IEHC 139 (20 July 2004, unreported), HC.

[101] *Re Tralee Beef and Lamb Ltd, Kavanagh v Delaney* [2004] IEHC 139 (20 July 2004, unreported), HC.

(iv) Board meetings

[17.047] If a company's board of directors failed to hold board meetings, particularly at a time when the company's affairs were critical, this can be a factor to be taken into account by the court in determining whether the directors acted responsibly for the purposes of s 150.

In *Re Tralee Beef and Lamb Ltd*, for example, declarations of restriction were made in respect of three non-executive directors. One of the factors considered by the court in that case was that there appeared to have been no board meetings for the final two years of the company's existence, during a period in which the company's finances became critical. In the absence of any evidence of board meetings, the court could not conclude that the directors had joined collectively in supervising, guiding and monitoring the company.[102]

[17.048] In *Re 360Atlantic (Ireland) Ltd*,[103] the High Court made declarations of restrictions against each of the directors of an Irish subsidiary of a multinational company. The central issue in that case was the allegation that the company was run as a division of the parent company and that the directors failed to act responsibly in the context of the subsidiary as a separate legal entity. One of the factors taken into account by the Court in deciding to make the orders of restriction sought, was that the minutes of the company's board meetings 'suggest that they related primarily to regulatory matters which required compliance in this jurisdiction. There is no evidence of any meeting which included a consideration of any substantive issue (other than the approval of Annual Accounts) relating to the operation or business of the company.'

This case indicates that, in relation to the question of board meetings, the fact that such meetings were held is not sufficient to demonstrate responsibility in the context of s 150. The meetings must also involve consideration of substantive matters concerning the company.

(v) Relationship with other companies

[17.049] The law recognises the commercial reality that companies often operate as a member of a group of companies.[104] The interaction between related companies has arisen as a factor to be considered in relation to restriction proceedings, where one company in a group becomes insolvent and is wound up. In particular, the courts have been called upon to determine whether there are any specific factors which the court should take into account, when considering whether a director of a wholly-owned subsidiary acted responsibly.

---

[102] As already noted, this decision is under appeal to the Supreme Court, an appeal which was heard on 14 November 2007 and on which judgment has been reserved.

[103] *Re 360Atlantic (Ireland) Ltd, O'Ferral v Coughlan* [2004] IEHC 410.

[104] See Courtney, *The Law of Private Companies* (2nd edn, Tottel Publishing, 2002), Ch 17.

[17.050] The two related cases of *Re 360Atlantic (Ireland) Ltd*[105] and *Re 360Networks (Ireland) Ltd*[106] address the responsibility of directors of a wholly owned subsidiary company in the context of restriction applications.

In *Re 360Atlantic (Ireland) Ltd*,[107] the Court identified the issue raised by cases in which the directors of a wholly owned subsidiary face restriction in the following terms:

> 'whether and to what extent the Court should have regard to the fact that the company is a wholly owned subsidiary within a worldwide group of companies and to what extent if any that fact alters the matters to which the Court should have regard when determining whether the respondents acted responsibly as a director of the subsidiary company.'[108]

At the outset, the Court noted that any analysis of the responsibility of a director in relation to the conduct of the affairs of a company for the purposes of s 150(2)(a), relates only to his conduct in relation to the company in liquidation. Courts should not take account of the director's conduct as a director of other companies. Finlay Geoghegan J decided that the fact that a company is a wholly-owned subsidiary operating within a group of companies does not 'alter the legal principles applicable to the duties of directors'. It was however, a 'particular factual scenario', which should be taken into account in relation to the discharge of the duties of a director.

[17.051] The company in liquidation being a member of a group of companies does not alter the legal principles applicable to the directors' duties and the standard of 'responsibility' required under s 150(2)(a). In particular, the factors which courts take into account in determining whether a director acted responsibly for the purposes of s 150(2)(a), apply equally and without deviation to directors of companies which are wholly owned subsidiaries within groups of companies.

[17.052] Before applying these legal standards to the facts of the case before it, the Court in *Re 360Atlantic (Ireland) Ltd*[109] reached a number of factual conclusions regarding the organisation and the structure of the company in liquidation, including the following:

- the operations of the group of companies were 'financed managed and controlled as part of worldwide operations on essentially a group divisional basis;'

- the management of the Irish company's site appears to have been primarily under the control of the group whose management team were primarily based in Barbados;

- the company was formed by reason of professional advice with the intention that there be a separate corporate structure in each jurisdiction to hold assets and operate the group's network;

---

[105] *Re 360Atlantic (Ireland) Ltd, O'Ferral v Coughlan* [2004] IEHC 410.

[106] *Re 360Networks (Ireland) Ltd, O'Ferral v Coughlan* [2004] IEHC 412.

[107] *Re 360Atlantic (Ireland) Ltd, O'Ferral v Coughlan* [2004] IEHC 410.

[108] *Re 360Atlantic (Ireland) Ltd, O'Ferral v Coughlan* [2004] IEHC 410.

[109] *Re 360Atlantic (Ireland) Ltd, O'Ferral v Coughlan* [2004] IEHC 410.

- the company was part of a 'closely intertwined group of companies whose activities were in reality centrally planned;'

- it was not open to the Company to operate independently of the group;

- the financing of the Irish operations, including those under the control of the Irish company, were determined in Barbados by the group management team;

- the financial information that was furnished to the directors of the Irish company, was consolidated information and did not separately represent the financial position of the Irish company; and

- the board meetings were held to ensure compliance with Irish regulatory requirements and did not consider substantive issues regarding the operation or business of the company.

In summary, the company was so closely intertwined with the group of companies of which it was a member that it had no separate financial control, no independent financial information, no independent management and little or no control over its operations, which were controlled as if it were a division of the parent company. Having acknowledged the intertwined relationship between the company and the group of which it was a member, the Court also drew attention to the fact that the company was a separate corporate and legal entity, with its own employees, creditors and directors.

[17.053] Finlay Geoghegan J then set out the following important guidance for directors of a wholly owned subsidiary:

'In such a factual scenario it would appear totally permissible and indeed a proper exercise of the duties of directors in the interests of the Company for the directors to fully take into account and indeed to even to follow the policies adopted for the entire group when managing the business of the Irish Company. However, notwithstanding such a factual scenario and indeed the almost total dependence of the Company on other companies within the group it does not seem permissible for directors of the Company to effectively abdicate all decision-making in relation to the affairs of the Company. They must be considered to remain under a duty to inform themselves about the affairs of the Company as distinct from any other corporate part of the group and to join with each other in supervising and controlling the affairs of the Company. Otherwise their position as directors is meaningless. In real terms the directors may have a very small margin of discretion in the decisions to be taken but this cannot absolve them of the obligation to take the decisions.

Accordingly, it appears to me that where a group corporate structure exists, such as in the present case, and the issue under s 150 of the Act of 1990 is whether a director of the wholly owned Irish subsidiary company acted responsibly in the sense of discharging the minimum common law duties, he must be able to establish at a minimum that he did inform himself about the affairs of the Irish subsidiary company as distinct from any other company within the group and together with his fellow directors that he did take real steps to consider and take decisions upon at least significant transactions to be entered into or projects undertaken by the Irish subsidiary company. There must be evidence of a real consideration by the directors of whether significant transactions or operations to be undertaken were desirable in the interest of the Irish subsidiary company or could be said to be for the benefit of the Irish subsidiary company. I readily recognise that in many instances the interests of the Irish subsidiary company may be so intertwined with the affairs of the group as a whole that the answer may be obvious. However, the fact that the answer is obvious does not appear to absolve the directors from at least addressing the question.

If the issue of the responsibility relates to the nature of decisions taken (which it does not on the facts of this application) as distinct from the absence of any decisions different and further considerations may apply. It is not necessary to consider those on the facts of this case.'[110]

[17.054] In light of the facts of the case and the principles and standards set out above, Finlay Geoghegan J held that the directors could not be held to have acted responsibly within the meaning of s 150(2)(a).[111] They did not keep informed about the financial affairs of the company and they did not join together in supervising and controlling the affairs of the company, as directors are obliged to do. It was not permissible for directors to abdicate the entire responsibility for making decisions regarding the affairs of the company to another entity and, in this case, there was held to have been a total abrogation of responsibility for the company's financial affairs. In particular, the directors failed to consider whether certain substantial transactions were in the interests of the company as a separate corporate entity. A declaration of restriction was made against each of the directors of the company in liquidation.

[17.055] The same background and legal issues that were set out in *Re 360Atlantic (Ireland) Ltd*[112] also applied to another case in which judgment was delivered on the same date, *Re 360Networks (Ireland) Ltd.*[113] In the latter case, declarations of restriction were also made against the directors of the Irish subsidiary. The Court noted in that case that, when the directors agreed to become directors of the Irish subsidiary, an independent, separate legal entity, incorporated under Irish law:

'they became obliged to discharge the minimum duties required at common law and under statute as directors of the company as distinct from any other entity within the 360networks group ... It is only in respect of the discharge of those duties that this Court has concluded they have failed to satisfy that they acted responsibly. The Court is not considering any other responsibilities of the respondents within the 360networks group in respect of which they may not be subject to any criticism.'[114]

This aspect of the decision in *Re 360Networks (Ireland) Ltd*,[115] highlights that the conduct of directors of a subsidiary company which is being wound up in relation to other companies of which they may also be directors, even if such conduct may have greatly favoured the other companies in the group, will not aid them in establishing that they acted responsibly in their capacity as directors of the subsidiary company.

---

[110] *Re 360Atlantic (Ireland) Ltd, O'Ferral v Coughlan* [2004] IEHC 410.

[111] Two of the respondents presented no evidence in opposition to the application for orders of restriction.

[112] *Re 360Atlantic (Ireland) Ltd, O'Ferral v Coughlan* [2004] IEHC 410.

[113] *Re 360Networks (Ireland) Ltd, O'Ferral v Coughlan* [2004] IEHC 412.

[114] *Re 360Networks (Ireland) Ltd, O'Ferral v Coughlan* [2004] IEHC 412.

[115] *Re 360Networks (Ireland) Ltd, O'Ferral v Coughlan* [2004] IEHC 412.

[17.056] The decision of the High Court in *Re 360Atlantic (Ireland) Ltd*[116] was also applied in *Re Mitek Ltd*.[117] That case concerned the application to restrict two directors of a group of Irish companies, which formed part of a larger multinational group of companies. One of the issues which arose in that case was that the Irish companies entered into certain intra-group transactions, such as the payment of sums of money and transfer of assets, allegedly on foot of inter-company charges, and provided security for other companies in the group, at a time when the financial situation of the Irish companies was precarious. In relation to the facts of the application, Finlay Geoghegan J, concluded that the directors did not appear to have taken steps to supervise and control the financial affairs of the companies during the critical time period, particularly regarding the transfer of monies from the Irish companies to other companies in the group, and that there was no evidence that the directors took any decisions whatsoever about the appropriateness of these transfers. In light of the poor financial situation of the Irish companies, this failure could be regarded as particularly egregious. Applying the principles set out in *Re 360Atlantic (Ireland) Ltd*,[118] Finlay Geoghegan J held that the directors had failed to demonstrate that they acted responsibly in relation to the affairs of the Irish companies and they were accordingly restricted.

[17.057] The following advice can be gleaned from these decisions for directors of wholly-owned subsidiaries who are faced with the possibility of restriction:

- it is permissible and proper for such directors to take into account the policies adopted for the group of companies in the management of the subsidiary;

- it is permissible and proper to follow the policies of the group in the management of the subsidiary;

- in no circumstances is it permissible for the directors to abdicate all responsibility for decision-making regarding the affairs of the company;

- the directors must keep informed about the affairs of the company at all times;

- the directors must consider the affairs of the company as a separate legal entity, distinct from the group of companies;

- the directors must join together in supervising and controlling the affairs of the company

- even if the directors have little control or discretion over the decisions to be taken in relation to the company's affairs, they must still take those decisions;

- at a minimum, a director must consider and take decisions concerning the significant transactions and projects to be undertaken by the subsidiary company;

- with regard to any significant transactions or operations the company is to engage in, the directors must prove that they gave real consideration to whether

---

[116] *Re 360Atlantic (Ireland) Ltd, O'Ferral v Coughlan* [2004] IEHC 410.

[117] *Re Mitek Ltd, Grace v Kachkar* [2005] IEHC 63.

[118] *Re 360Atlantic (Ireland) Ltd, O'Ferral v Coughlan* [2004] IEHC 410.

these transactions or operations were desirable, in the interests of, or for the benefit of, the subsidiary company;

- the fact that the conduct of the director may have been in the interests of the group or other members of the group is not relevant;

- any conduct of the director in relation to other companies is not relevant;

- if there is a question about the responsibility of a director arising from the actual decisions taken (rather than the failure to take such decisions), different considerations apply.[119]

(vi) Dealings with Revenue Commissioners

[17.058] In a number of restriction proceedings which have been heard by the Irish courts, the companies in liquidation have owed substantial sums of money to the Revenue Commissioners. These debts attract particular scrutiny and their accumulation has frequently been considered to be a relevant factor in determining whether the directors of the company acted responsibly or whether a declaration of restriction was warranted.[120]

[17.059] In *Re Euroking Miracle (Ireland) Ltd*,[121] the main issues which arose for consideration concerned the extra-territorial jurisdiction of declarations of restriction and certain questions of procedure, such as the service of proceedings.[122] Having determined these issues, Finlay Geoghegan J considered the factors which the liquidator contended were relevant to the honesty and responsibility of the four directors of the company. One of the facts relied upon was that the directors failed to keep the returns to the Revenue Commissioners up to date. Another was that there was a failure to discharge debts owed to the Revenue Commissioners, the directors choosing instead to discharge debts selectively, including to an associated company of the company, in the period prior to liquidation. Applying the test formulated in *La Moselle Clothing Company Ltd v Soualhi*,[123] the Court was not satisfied that the directors had acted honestly and responsibly and declarations of restriction were made against the four directors. This case illustrates that a failure to comply with a company's obligations to the Revenue Commissioners to file returns and make payments due, can be indicative of a lack of responsibility on the part of the company's directors. Moreover, it is an example of the court taking into account the discharge of debts owed to an associated company of the company in liquidation, in preference to discharging liabilities to the

---

[119] *Re 360Atlantic (Ireland) Ltd, O'Ferral v Coughlan* [2004] IEHC 410; *Re 360Networks (Ireland) Ltd, O'Ferral v Coughlan* [2004] IEHC 412; *Re Mitek Ltd, Grace v Kachkar* [2005] IEHC 63.

[120] See *Re Pineroad Distribution Ltd, Stafford v Fleming* [2007] IEHC 55; *Re Cherby Ltd, Kavanagh v Cooke* [2005] IEHC 219; *Re Kelly Technical Services (Ireland) Ltd, Kavanagh v Kelly* [2005] IEHC 421; *Re Club Tivoli Ltd Foster v Davies* [2005] IEHC 468; *Re Finchley Construction Ltd, Roache v Culloo* [2005] IEHC 448.

[121] *Re Euroking Ltd, Fennell v Frost* [2003] IEHC 15.

[122] See further paras **[18.011]** to **[18.017]**.

[123] *La Moselle Clothing Company Ltd v Soualhi* [1998] IEHC 66, [1998] 2 ILRM 345.

Revenue Commissioners, a course of action which clearly will not assist directors in demonstrating their responsibility under CA 1990, s 150(2)(a).

[17.060] The judgment of McCracken J in *Re Verit Hotel and Leisure (Ireland) Ltd*[124] provides a strong indication that a company's failure to discharge monies owing to the Revenue Commissioners can be an important factor in determining the honesty and responsibility of the company's directors. The company owned a number of hotels and bars and, having fallen into arrears in the payment of tax liabilities, reached an agreement with the Revenue Commissioners in 1993 which involved a payment of £300,000 to be paid within the following year. It was intended to make this payment out of the proceeds of sale of one of the company's hotels. The directors ultimately entered into an agreement with another company they controlled for the sale of the hotel, which culminated in that company discharging the liability of £300,000 to the Revenue Commissioners directly. The Court considered these circumstances and concluded from a review of the statement of affairs, and the fact that Revenue liabilities remained outstanding at the date of the winding up, in the order of £561,526 in respect of VAT and £229,394 in respect of PAYE and PRSI, that £300,000 was not the entire sum owing to the Revenue at the date of the agreement.

The circumstances of the sale of the hotel were examined by the Court and the Court expressed concern at the fact that 'the panic to put through this sale showed that the directors were well aware in January, 1994 that if they did not immediately pay £300,000.00 to the Revenue, the Company was going to go under.'[125] The Court further noted that, having made the payment of £300,000, the directors made no further payments whatsoever to the Revenue prior to the winding up of the company. The Court concluded that:

> 'Indeed it is clear that at least from the beginning of 1993 this Company was being
> kept alive by the fact that it was in effect trading on monies due to the Revenue,
> and allowing huge arrears to build up, together with the attendant interest.'[126]

The directors attempted to justify their treatment of revenue debts on the basis that a company which is temporarily short of funds may be justified in not making revenue payments and, as the court summarised their submissions, 'in effect taking a loan on interest to keep the company going,' an argument which McCracken J observed was 'quite astonishingly' made.

The Court went on to describe the importance of revenue payments in the context of restriction proceedings:

> 'PAYE and PRSI are monies which a company pays to the Revenue on behalf of its
> employees, and constitutes its employees tax and its employees social insurance.
> To try to justify trading by using what is in effect its employees money without
> their knowledge or consent, is to me a quite bizarre and totally irresponsible
> attitude. This appears to have been a policy of the Board of Directors, and is not

---

[124] *Re Verit Hotel and Leisure (Ireland) Ltd, Duignan v Carway* [2002] IEHC 1, McCracken J.
[125] *Re Verit Hotel and Leisure (Ireland) Ltd, Duignan v Carway* [2002] IEHC 1, McCracken J.
[126] *Re Verit Hotel and Leisure (Ireland) Ltd, Duignan v Carway* [2002] IEHC 1.

something which can be attributable to any one particular director. On this ground alone I have no doubt that the directors must be restricted under s 150.'[127]

This case demonstrates that it is not acceptable for directors of a company to continue trading and accruing liabilities to the Revenue Commissioners, in the knowledge that the company is not a viable going concern. A company cannot trade on the basis of non-payment of Revenue liabilities and a board of directors which permits a company, which is unable to discharge its liability to the Revenue Commissioners, to continue trading, will face a high hurdle in attempting to convince a court that they acted responsibly in the conduct of the company's affairs.

[17.061] Another example of the relevance of revenue debts as a potential indicator of a director's level of responsibility in restriction proceedings, is *Re SPH Ltd*.[128] That company had a large deficit in the region of €1.7 at the date of commencement of winding up. The liquidator raised the extent of the liability to the Revenue Commissioners and the manner and period in which this liability had been allowed to accumulate, as a factor in determining whether the directors acted responsibly in the supervision and control of the company's financial affairs.

The Court noted that there was an aggregate liability to the Revenue Commissioners in the order of €345,000 and liability for Relevant Contracts Tax of approximately €212,000. On this basis, Finlay Geoghegan J concluded that the respondents either knowingly permitted these liabilities to the Revenue Commissioners to accrue without providing for their discharge, or, if they did not know of the accrual of such liabilities, 'they failed to have in place appropriate systems to inform themselves of the financial position of the company to allow them properly control and manage the affairs of the company.'[129] The Court concluded that the directors, 'knew or ought to have known (if proper financial management had been in place) of the accrual of significant liabilities… to the Revenue Commissoner.'[130] The Court noted that the directors did not appear to have taken steps to discharge these liabilities and used the sums due to the Revenue Commissioners to continue trading. Declarations of restriction were made in respect of each of the respondents.

[17.062] Similarly, in *Re Newcastle Timber Ltd*[131] the company failed to discharge tax liabilities and the Court was called upon to take this into account in restriction proceedings. In that case, the company failed to file the requisite returns with the Revenue Commissioners in time, and there were discrepancies in respect of some of the returns which were filed, a fact which the Court did not find to be 'unduly serious' and it does appear to have been taken into account in relation to the restriction orders sought.

This approach to the importance of tax returns as a factor in restriction proceedings seems to be emulated in *Re RMF Ltd*.[132] In that case, Finlay Geoghegan J considered the

---

[127] *Re Verit Hotel and Leisure (Ireland) Ltd, Duignan v Carway* [2002] IEHC 1.

[128] *Re SPH Ltd, Fennell v Shanahan* [2005] IEHC 152.

[129] *Re SPH Ltd, Fennell v Shanahan* [2005] IEHC 152.

[130] *Re SPH Ltd, Fennell v Shanahan* [2005] IEHC 152.

[131] *Re Newcastle Timber Ltd* [2001] IEHC 146.

[132] *Re RMF (Ireland) Ltd, Kavanagh v Riedler* [2004] IEHC 334.

responsibility of a non-executive director in the context of the failure of the company to file tax returns and concluded that the non-executive director was entitled to rely on the company's executives. In that case, it was not suggested that the failure to make the requisite tax returns was brought to the attention of the director in question or that he had in any sense condoned the failure to make returns. No declaration of restriction was made against the director.

In *Re Newcastle Timber Ltd*[133] the Court regarded with much more seriousness the failure of the company to discharge its tax liabilities while continuing to trade. The applicant contended that the company traded insolvently without discharging debts owing to the Revenue Commissioners. While the Court had some sympathy with the circumstances of the company's downfall, involving a fire at the company's premises and other related circumstances, the Court concluded, 'the fact remains that the trading losses were of a considerable magnitude and the clear implication is that there was a deliberate policy not to discharge the Revenue debts.' The Court held in this regard,:

> 'To trade while insolvent for one year, or perhaps two years, in the hope that the company may trade out of its problems is understandable, but to have kept Newcastle trading insolvently for some four years, and allowing Revenue debts to build up, appears to me to be totally irresponsible.'[134]

In addition, the directors were found to have discharged certain debts to trade creditors after the company ceased to trade, while ignoring the debts owing to the Revenue Commissioners. The Court considered this preference of trade creditors over the Revenue Commissioners as evidence of the directors' desire to keep trade creditors happy so that they could continue in the same kind of business in the future. However, the Court also determined that the factors raised by the liquidator demonstrated incompetence on the part of the directors and that trading while insolvent and preferring trade creditors to the detriment of the Revenue Commissioners, were factors which indicated irresponsibility on the part of the directors. Declarations of restriction were accordingly made.[135]

[17.063] Another example of a case in which the company continued to trade while insolvent, accruing Revenue debts, and discharged the debts of trade creditors in preference to the Revenue Commissioners was *La Moselle Clothing Company Ltd v Soualhi*.[136] Shanley J concluded on the facts of that case:

> 'I have no doubt whatsoever that Mr Soualhi traded at a time when he knew that Rosegem and La Moselle were insolvent. I am quite satisfied that he used monies due to the Collector-General and CCL to finance his trading activities and his travel. I have little doubt that he was aware that Rosegem and La Moselle could not trade and at the same time discharge their liabilities to the Collector-General

---

[133] *Re Newcastle Timber Ltd* [2001] IEHC 146.

[134] *Re Newcastle Timber Ltd* [2001] IEHC 146.

[135] The Court refused to make the orders of disqualification sought against the directors. See further Ch **22**.

[136] *La Moselle Clothing Company Ltd v Soualhi* [1998] IEHC 66, [1998] 2 ILRM 345.

and CCL. Such conduct was, in my view, improper conduct and if it was not to be described as actually dishonest it was certainly irresponsible.'[137]

(vii) Dealings between director and company

[17.064] In restriction proceedings, a factor which can influence the court in determining whether a director acted responsibly is the extent to which the director profited personally, such as by way of loans,[138] expenses, salary,[139] or share transactions,[140] from his position as director.

This can be seen quite graphically in *La Moselle Clothing Ltd v Soualhi*[141] where the Court referred to a number of aspects of Mr Soualhi's expenses and salary which were drawn from the two companies in liquidation. The Court referred to the liquidator's claim that:

'The credit card statements relating to Mr Soualhi disclosed that payments to credit card companies were made by La Moselle between 1991 and 1994 in the amount of £99,447.99, of which £35,259.96 represents payments by La Moselle to restaurants and night-clubs. These payments are described as "motor and travel expenses" in the management accounts of the company.'[142]

The Court also referred to claims that Mr Soualhi drew £39,034 from one of the companies between 1992 and 1994 at a time when it was alleged that he must have known that the company was clearly insolvent, and drew £29,950 from the other company, both of which sums were drawn without any provision for tax being made.

The Court described the following travel expenses of the director:

'In circumstances where both Rosegem and La Moselle were insolvent in 1993 and 1994, Mr Soualhi was nonetheless maintaining a very busy and indeed expensive lifestyle, all of which according to himself was business related. His

---

[137] *La Moselle Clothing Company Ltd v Soualhi* [1998] IEHC 66, [1998] 2 ILRM 345 at para 24.

[138] See *Re Dunleckney Ltd* [1999] IEHC 109 (Carroll J); *Re Lynrowan Enterprises Ltd* [2002] IEHC 90 (31 July 2002, unreported), HC.

[139] See *Re Lynrowan Enterprises Ltd* [2002] IEHC 90 (31 July 2002, unreported), HC; *La Moselle Clothing Ltd v Soualhi* [1998] IEHC 68.

[140] On a related question, O'Leary J determined in *Re Camoate Construction Ltd, Coyle v Callanan* [2005] IEHC 346, that a restriction order should not be made in respect of directors who had obtained erroneous legal advice to the effect that the sale of shares by one of them to the company, was not contrary to CA 1963, s 60, as they were entitled to rely on that advice. See also *Re Greenmount Holdings Ltd, Stafford v O'Connor* [2007] IEHC 246: 'I am not entirely convinced that the company was solvent or had adequate distributable reserves to make the decision to purchase the first named respondent's share capital in the company for €130,000.00 a responsible decision. However there appears to have been some good reasons why she should be bought out in view of the long standing disagreements between her and the second named respondent. In any event I am satisfied that the respondents obtained proper professional advice in the matter and that this advice did not go against the completion of the transaction. In the circumstances I make no restriction order in relation to the respondents in respect of that issue,' *per* McGovern J.

[141] *La Moselle Clothing Ltd v Soualhi* [1998] IEHC 68.

[142] *La Moselle Clothing Ltd v Soualhi* [1998] IEHC 68 at para 18.

credit card statements (paid for by his companies) disclosed that in 1994 alone (when he surely knew that Rosegem and La Moselle were insolvent) he managed to travel to Bangkok, Ho Chi Minh City, Hanoi, Hong Kong, Seoul, Taiwan, San Francisco, Shanghai, Boston, Jamaica, Paris, New York, London and San Tropez.'[143]

The Court noted that there was no evidence of any sales or purchases resulting from any of the travel and further observed that:

'even if one did allow that the trips were for business purposes, the travel and associated costs show a want of commercial probity on Mr Soualhi's part, having regard to the overall parlous financial position of La Moselle and Rosegem.'[144]

(viii) Miscellaneous factors

[17.065] There are a large number of other factors which may be, and many of which have been, taken into account by courts in determining whether a director acted responsibly in the context of restriction proceedings. The following examples are derived from cases which have applied the criteria of 'honest and responsible' conduct as it appears in CA 1990, s 150(2)(a):

1. The discharge of debts owed to related companies in preference to other creditors;[145]

2. Allowing the company to extend a significant level of credit to a second company, such as a company in which the director facing restriction had a substantial interest, at a time when the first company was in financial difficulties;[146]

3. Continuing to trade when the directors are, or ought to be, aware that the company is insolvent;[147]

4. The creation of securities in favour of related companies, without considering the benefit to the company itself or the fact that it is in financial difficulties;[148]

---

[143] *La Moselle Clothing Ltd v Soualhi* [1998] IEHC 68 at para 23.

[144] *La Moselle Clothing Ltd v Soualhi* [1998] IEHC 68 at para 23.

[145] See *Re Euroking Miracle (Ireland) Ltd, Fennell v Frost* [2003] IEHC 15.

[146] *Re Gasco Ltd* [2001] IEHC 20.

[147] See *Re Pineroad Distribution Ltd, Stafford v Fleming* [2007] IEHC 55; *Re Verit Hotel and Leisure (Ireland) Ltd, Duignan v Carway* [2002] IEHC 1; Re Mitek Ltd, Grace v Kachkar [2005] IEHC 63, HC; *Re La Moselle Clothing Ltd, La Moselle Clothing Ltd v Soualhi* [1998] IEHC 68; *Re Lynrowan Enterprises Ltd* [2002] IEHC 90 (31 July 2002, unreported), HC; *Re Newcastle Timber Ltd* [2001] IEHC 146. It should be noted in this regard that the courts are aware of the importance that, as the Court observed in *Re Mitek Ltd, Grace v Kachkar* [2005] IEHC 63, 'the court must be very careful not to judge such decisions made by directors with the benefit of hindsight.'

[148] *Re Mitek Ltd, Grace v Kachkar* [2005] IEHC 63; *Re 360Atlantic (Ireland) Ltd, O'Ferral v Coughlan* [2004] IEHC 410.

5.   Failing to prepare or file proper audited accounts;[149]

6.   Failing to keep proper books of account;[150]

7.   Writing off debts owed by other companies which are owned and/or controlled by the director;[151]

8.   Allowing the company to accrue very significant liabilities;[152]

9.   Allowing the company to create securities, such as debentures, over its assets in favour of related companies, when insolvent;[153]

10.   Transferring monies and assets to related companies within a group of companies, without considering the interests of, and benefit to, the company;[154]

11.   Placing undue reliance on another director in relation to the conduct of the company's affairs;[155]

12.   The fact that the company was undercapitalised;[156]

13.   Failing to hold annual general meetings;[157]

14.   Failing to stay informed about, and join in, the control and supervision of the company's affairs;[158]

---

[149] *Re Cookes Events Company Ltd, Kavanagh v Cooke* [2005] IEHC 225; *Re Dublin Sports Cafe Ltd, Farrell v Long* [2005] IEHC 458 ('The respondents carried a serious responsibility as directors to ensure that these accounts were audited in a timely manner, and that annual returns were filed. These are responsibilities which matter, and simply because some dispute breaks out with the auditors over fees is not a reason to remove the need to have these accounts available,' *per* Peart J) While no order of restriction was made on this ground, the liquidator did raise the issue of failures to file audited accounts in *Re USIT World plc* [2005] IEHC 285.

[150] See, eg, *Re Greenmount Holdings Ltd, Stafford v O'Connor* [2007] IEHC 246, in which McGovern J found that the respondents failed to keep proper books of account contrary to CA 1990, s 202. The Court did not however make the restrictions order sought in that case, one of the grounds being that the respondents had made attempts to regularise the situation.

[151] *La Moselle Clothing Ltd v Soualhi* [1998] IEHC 68.

[152] *Re SPH Ltd, Fennell v Shanahan* [2005] IEHC 152.

[153] *Re Mitek Ltd, Grace v Kachkar* [2005] IEHC 63.

[154] *Re Mitek Ltd, Grace v Kachkar* [2005] IEHC 63.

[155] *Re Gasco Ltd* [2001] IEHC 20 is an example of a case where the reliance was held to be understandable and the directors in question were not restricted, the Court cautioning that, 'This does not mean, of course, that a director can disclaim responsibility altogether on the basis that financial matters were the responsibility of another director, but nevertheless one of the matters to be considered in assessing whether he acted responsibly was whether his reliance on the actions of another director was itself responsible.'

[156] *Re First Class Toy Traders Limited (in liquidation), Gray v McLoughlin* [2004] IEHC 289 (9 July 2004, unreported), HC, Finlay Geoghegan J, *ex tempore*.

[157] *Re First Class Toy Traders Limited (in liquidation), Gray v McLoughlin* [2004] IEHC 289 (9 July 2004, unreported), HC, Finlay Geoghegan J, *ex tempore*.

[158] *Re Tralee Beef and Lamb Ltd, Kavanagh v Delaney* [2004] IEHC 139; *Re Lynrowan Enterprises Ltd* [2002] IEHC 90 (31 July 2002, unreported), HC.

15. Failure to make annual returns to the Companies Registration Office;[159]

16. Undervaluation of the company's assets;[160]

17. Failing to co-operate with the liquidator;[161]

18. Repaying certain liabilities that have not fallen due at a time when the directors know, or should know, that this repayment would render the company incapable of paying its debts;[162]

19. Preferential payments to certain creditors between the cessation of trading and the decision to wind up a company;[163]

20. Excessive delegation of responsibility for the company's financial affairs without staying informed about the company's affairs and controlling and supervising the exercise of the delegated functions.[164]

C. 'Just and equitable'

[17.066] Section 150(2)(a) of CA 1990 provides that an order of restriction will not be made if the director in question satisfies the court that he 'acted honestly and responsibly in relation to the conduct of the affairs of the company and that there is no other reason why it would be just and equitable that he should be subject to the restrictions imposed by this section'. The second limb of this test is therefore, that, having demonstrated honesty and responsibility, the director must satisfy the court that there is no just and equitable reason why an order of restriction should be made.

[17.067] The courts have identified one manner in which the 'just and equitable' proviso may be particularly important in restriction proceedings. In *La Moselle Clothing*

---

[159] *Re Lynrowan Enterprises Ltd* [2002] IEHC 90 (31 July 2002, unreported), HC; *Re Newcastle Timber Ltd* [2001] IEHC 146.

[160] *Re Verit Hotel and Leisure (Ireland) Ltd, Duignan v Carway* [2002] IEHC 1.

[161] See *Re DCS Ltd, Fitzpatrick v Henley* [2006] IEHC 179 and *Re CMC (Ireland) Ltd, Fennell v Carolan* [2005] IEHC 59. In a number of cases, this ground of restriction has been rejected. See *Re Club Tivoli Ltd Foster v Davies* [2005] IEHC 468 and *Re USIT World plc* [2005] IEHC 285 ('I am satisfied that while the liquidator for whatever reason felt that he was not receiving cooperation, matters required to be dealt with were dealt with, and there remains an offer of a meeting ...', per Peart J).

[162] *Re Swanpool Ltd, McLaughlin v Lannen* [2005] IEHC 341 ('One of the most important obligations of any director is to ensure that when a company is facing an insolvency situation, its assets are dealt with in accordance with law. For the reasons identified by McCracken J in *Gasco* the actions taken at such a time must be subject to particular scrutiny. While understanding the pressures which may have been on the directors it does have to be noted that all directors in insolvent circumstances are likely to be subjected to significant pressure. It is their job to resist such pressure and to ensure that the company's assets are properly dealt with. Any significant failure in that regard has to be taken as demonstrating a level of irresponsibility sufficient to warrant making an order under the section,' per Clarke J).

[163] *Re DCS Ltd, Fitzpatrick v Henley* [2006] IEHC 179.

[164] *Re SPH Ltd, Fennell v Shanahan* [2005] IEHC 152.

Company Ltd v Soualhi,[165] Shanley J considered the wording of s 150(2)(a) and, in particular, the relevant timeframe during which the conduct of a director fell to be considered for the purposes of that provision. The Court observed that the phrase 'honestly and responsibly in relation to the conduct of the affairs of the company' as it appears in s 150(2)(a):

> 'arguably such bears no relation to any period after the commencement of a winding-up or receivership of the particular company where the person may not be involved any further in the conduct of the affairs of the company.'[166]

The Court therefore concluded that the only period during which the conduct of the director fell to be considered was the time before the winding up commenced. However, Shanley J proceeded to note that a director facing restriction proceedings must additionally satisfy the court that there is 'no other reason why it would be just and equitable that he should be subject to' a restriction order. This phrase, according to Shanley J:

> 'allows the Court to take into account ... any relevant conduct of the director after the commencement of the winding-up or the receivership (for example, any failure to co-operate with the liquidator or receiver) in deciding whether or not to make an Order under s 150, sub-s (1), of the Companies Act 1990.'[167]

[17.068] In this regard, the courts have since taken account of various aspects of the conduct of directors in the period after the commencement of the winding up.

For example, if a director of a company in liquidation was somehow deficient in relation to the filing of the company's statement of affairs, this may be a factor to be taken into account by a court in assessing whether to make an order of restriction.

In *Re Dunleckney Ltd*,[168] the High Court was confined to analysing the conduct of the director after the commencement of the winding up. The director in that case failed to file a statement of affairs, and further failed to explain this deficiency. The liquidator in that case stated that the director had co-operated in the liquidation and that a statement of affairs would not have furnished any additional information. Nonetheless, Carroll J determined that it was just and equitable to make a declaration of restriction, stating:

> 'In my opinion it is not for the Official Liquidator to excuse a director from his statutory obligation.
>
> ... I am satisfied that the failure to fulfil his statutory obligation by filing a Statement of Affairs and the failure to explain why, is sufficient reason to make the declaration under s 150 of the Companies Act, 1990 that he should not for a period of five years be appointed or act in any way, whether directly or indirectly, as a Director or Secretary or be concerned with or take part in the promotion or formation of any company unless that company meets the requirements set out in sub-s (3) of s 150 of the Companies Act, 1990.'[169]

---

[165] *La Moselle Clothing Ltd v Soualhi* [1998] IEHC 68.

[166] *La Moselle Clothing Ltd v Soualhi* [1998] IEHC 68.

[167] *La Moselle Clothing Ltd v Soualhi* [1998] IEHC 68.

[168] *Re Dunleckney Ltd* [1999] IEHC 109 (Carroll J).

[169] *Re Dunleckney Ltd* [1999] IEHC 109 at paras 12 and 13.

This 'just and equitable' criterion was applied by the High Court in *Re CMC (Ireland) Ltd*.[170] In that case, there was no issue or allegation regarding the respondents' conduct prior to the commencement of the winding up. Clarke J held that the respondents could not therefore be restricted on the basis of whether they acted honestly and responsibility in relation to the conduct of the company's affairs, but their conduct after the commencement of the winding up could be examined to determine whether it was just and equitable that declarations of restriction be made. In the circumstances of that case, the Court did make declarations of restriction, on the ground that it was just and equitable to do so.[171] This decision illustrates the importance of the 'just and equitable' criteria in cases in which the impugned conduct post-dates the commencement of a company's winding up.

[17.069] As against this, there have been cases in which the preparation of two different, inconsistent, statements of affairs have been held by the High Court not to be a ground for restricting the directors of the company under s 150.[172]

The court may also take into account any allegations that the directors were guilty of failing, or refusing to co-operate fully with the liquidator. However, the courts have at times looked sympathetically at the circumstances of directors of companies being wound up and the difficulties they face in presenting the books, records and other assistance required by the liquidator.[173]

D. Delay

[17.070] The issue of delay has been raised by some respondents to restriction applications. It should be noted at the outset that a liquidator of an insolvent company must apply for a restriction order under s 150 'not earlier than three months nor later than five months (or such later time as the court may allow and advises the Director) after the date on which he or she has provided to the Director a report under sub-s (1)', unless he has been relieved of the obligation to do so.[174] This time limit is a restriction of a regulatory nature. Failure to comply with the time limit is an offence on the part of the liquidator, but does not preclude the power of a liquidator to bring proceedings under s 150.[175] This time limit will be extended if the court considers that justice and fairness

---

[170] *Re CMC (Ireland) Ltd, Fennell v Carolan* [2005] IEHC 59. See paras **[17.006]** to **[17.009]**.

[171] *Re CMC (Ireland) Ltd, Fennell v Carolan* [2005] IEHC 59. See paras **[17.005]** to **[17.009]**.

[172] See *Lynrowan Enterprises Ltd, Re* [2002] IEHC 90 (31 July 2002, unreported), HC.

[173] See, eg, *Re Colm O'Neill Engineering Services Ltd* [2004] IEHC 83 (13 February 2004, unreported), HC.

[174] CLEA 2001, s 56(2).

[175] *Re E-Host Europe Ltd, Coyle v O'Brien* [2003] 2 IR 627 ('I have concluded on balance that the time limitation imposed by s 56(2) of the Act of 2001 is a regulatory limitation imposed on the liquidator which potentially has for him the consequence of committing the offence specified in s 56(3) of the Act of 2001 but does not bar his entitlement to bring an application under s 150 of the Act of 1990 for a declaration of restriction of the directors', *per* Finlay Geoghegan J).

requires the liquidator to be excused of the statutory consequence of such delay.[176] There have been several decisions regarding delay at different stages of restriction proceedings.

[17.071] In *Re Verit Hotel and Leisure Ltd*[177] the respondents attempted to preclude a restriction application from proceeding on the grounds of delay. The alleged delay occurred between the issue of the notice of motion and the date on which the liquidator sought to re-enter that motion. On the facts of the case, the lapse of time was due to a number of different sets of proceedings between the liquidators and the respondents arising from the liquidation. The liquidator accepted there was a delay between the conclusion of the other proceedings and the application to re-enter, a delay he described as 'inexcusable' but not 'inordinate'. The directors argued that they had a right, by virtue of, or by analogy with, the European Convention on Human Rights and Fundamental Freedoms, to a fair trial, which encompassed the notion of a speedy trial and that they would be prejudiced by the making of an order of restriction after such delay, as 'the longer the period of delay the greater the prejudice' and that general prejudice was caused by the delay, due to the lapse of time.

[17.072] The Supreme Court cited the decision in *Primor plc v Stokes Kennedy Crowley*[178] to the effect that 'even where the delay has been both inordinate and inexcusable the court must exercise a judgment on whether, in its discretion, on the facts the balance of justice was in favour of or against the case proceeding'. The Court went on to state that, 'It is common case that, in an appropriate case, the Court has jurisdiction to dismiss an application of the sort at issue here on the ground of excessive delay'.[179]

The Supreme Court cited the following criteria from the judgment of Hamilton CJ in *Primor plc v Stokes Kennedy Crowley*:[180]

> 'The principles of law relevant to the consideration of the issues raised in this appeal may be summarised as follows:
>
> (a) the courts have an inherent jurisdiction to control their own procedure and to dismiss a claim when the interests of justice require them to do so;
>
> (b) it must, in the first instance, be established by the party seeking a dismissal of proceedings for want of prosecution on the ground of delay in the prosecution thereof, that the delay was inordinate and inexcusable;
>
> (c) even where the delay has been both inordinate and inexcusable the court must exercise a judgment on whether, in its discretion, on the facts the balance of justice is in favour of or against the proceeding of the case;
>
> (d) in considering this latter obligation the court is entitled to take into consideration and have regard to:
>
>   (i) the implied constitutional principles of basic fairness of procedures,

---

[176] See *Re E-Host Europe Ltd, Coyle v O'Brien* [2003] 2 IR 627.

[177] *Re Verit Hotel and Leisure Ltd Duignan v Carway* [2001] IESC 74, [2001] 4 IR 550.

[178] *Primor plc v Stokes Kennedy Crowley* [1996] 2 IR 459.

[179] *Re Verit Hotel and Leisure Ltd Duignan v Carway* [2001] IESC 74, [2001] 4 IR 550 at para 15.

[180] *Primor plc v Stokes Kennedy Crowley* [1996] 2 IR 459 at 475.

(ii)   whether the delay and consequent prejudice in the special facts of the case are such as to make it unfair to the defendant to allow the action to proceed and to make it just to strike out the plaintiff's action,

(iii) any delay on the part of the defendant – because litigation is a two party operation, the conduct of both parties should be looked at,

(iv)   whether the delay or conduct of the defendant amounts to acquiescence on the part of the defendant in the plaintiff's delay,

(v)   the fact that conduct by the defendant which induces the plaintiff to incur further expense in pursuing the action does not, in law, constitute an absolute bar preventing the defendant from obtaining a striking out order but is a relevant factor to be taken into account by the judge in exercising his discretion whether or not to strike out the claim, the weight to be attached to such conduct depending upon all the circumstances of the particular case,

(vi)   whether the delay gives rise to a substantial risk that it is not possible to have a fair trial or is likely to cause or have caused serious prejudice to the defendant,

(vii) the fact that the prejudice to the defendant referred to in (vi) may arise in many ways and be other than that merely caused by the delay, including damage to a defendant's reputation and business.'

In *Re Verit Hotel and Leisure Ltd*,[181] the Court referred to the mandatory nature of restriction proceedings and the public interest underlying such orders. The Court determined that the prejudice caused to the respondents was not sufficient to prevent the restriction application from proceeding and ruled accordingly.

[17.073]   In the subsequent case of *Re Supreme Oil Company Ltd*[182] the High Court commented that it was 'undisputed that the Court has jurisdiction to dismiss an application under s 150 of the Act of 1990 on grounds of delay'. The Court cited the decision of the Supreme Court in *Re Verit Hotel and Leisure Ltd*[183] and the matters considered in *Primor v Stokes Kennedy Crowley*[184] as cited therein. The High Court commented in *Re Supreme Oil Company Ltd*[185] that, 'Those matters were indicated in *inter partes* proceedings and may not all be relevant to the procedure under s 150, which is not a normal *inter partes* proceeding.' The Court further interpreted the judgment of the Supreme Court in *Re Verit Hotel and Leisure Ltd*[186] as envisaging:

'two separate circumstances in which the Court might determine the balance of justice was against proceeding with an application under s 150 of the Act of 1990:

(i) Where the delay is such as to put a just hearing at risk;

---

[181] *Re Verit Hotel and Leisure Ltd Duignan v Carway* [2001] IESC 74, [2001] 4 IR 550.

[182] *Re Supreme Oil Company Ltd, Hughes v Duffy* [2005] IEHC 145.

[183] *Re Verit Hotel and Leisure Ltd Duignan v Carway* [2001] IESC 74, [2001] 4 IR 550.

[184] *Primor plc v Stokes Kennedy Crowley* [1996] 2 IR 459 at 475.

[185] *Re Supreme Oil Company Ltd, Hughes v Duffy* [2005] IEHC 145.

[186] *Re Verit Hotel and Leisure Ltd Duignan v Carway* [2001] IESC 74, [2001] 4 IR 550.

and

(ii) Where the delay would render it unjust to permit the application to proceed by reason of being in breach of the respondents' constitutional right to fair procedures including the right to have determined whether their normal rights to become directors and promote and take part in the formation of companies should be limited, restricted or taken away by reason of their prior involvement as a director of an insolvent company.'

In relation to these circumstances, the Court in *Re Supreme Oil Company Ltd*[187] emphasised the fact that s 150 orders are mandatory in nature and that the director bears a heavy burden of proof under such applications.

[17.074] On the basis of the facts of *Re Supreme Oil Company Ltd*,[188] the Court ruled that there was both inordinate and inexcusable delay in the bringing of this application, as communications ceased in 1995 and no application was made under s 150 until December 2003, without any explanation for the delay. The Court determined that the liquidation appeared to have simply remained dormant and that:

'if the Court were now to permit this application to proceed and put the respondents at jeopardy of a declaration of restriction against them that it would be in breach of their constitutional rights to fair procedures as identified by Fennelly J in *Duignan v Carway* [2001] 4 IR 550.'

[17.075] In *Re Knocklofty House Hotel Ltd*[189] Finlay Geoghegan J determined that a delay of eleven years between the commencement of the winding up and the initiation of the restriction proceedings was inordinate and inexcusable and should be stayed. While *Re Verit Hotel and Leisure Ltd*[190] and *Primor v Stokes Kennedy Crowley*[191] concerned delay after the initiation of proceedings, the Court held that similar principles applied to delay in initiating proceedings. In determining whether the balance of justice lies in favour of, or against, the proceedings continuing, however, the Court considered that the principles set out in *Primor v Stokes Kennedy Crowley*[192] were suited to *inter partes* proceedings and not restriction applications. The factors taken into account by the Court in determining where the balance of justice lay were the following:

- the legislative intent of s 150 including the public interest in ensuring that persons who have been directors of insolvent companies should not have an unqualified right to be involved in companies;

- the constitutional rights of respondents to fair procedures, including the right to a fair and speedy trial of applications under s 150;

- the imposition of the onus of proving that they acted honestly and responsibly on the respondents;

---

[187] *Re Supreme Oil Company Ltd, Hughes v Duffy* [2005] IEHC 145.

[188] *Re Supreme Oil Company Ltd, Hughes v Duffy* [2005] IEHC 145.

[189] *Re Knocklofty House Hotel Ltd* [2005] IEHC 105.

[190] *Re Verit Hotel and Leisure Ltd Duignan v Carway* [2001] IESC 74, [2001] 4 IR 550.

[191] *Primor plc v Stokes Kennedy Crowley* [1996] 2 IR 459 at 475.

[192] *Primor plc v Stokes Kennedy Crowley* [1996] 2 IR 459 at 475.

- the lack of any discretion on the part of the court as to the duration of an order under s 150;

- the fact that the respondents in *Re Knocklofty House Hotel Ltd*[193] would bear an onus of proving that they acted honestly and responsibly in relation to the conduct of the company's affairs since 1991;

- among the issues raised by the liquidator which would need to be considered were events that occurred in 1989, 15 years prior to the date of the hearing of the application;

- any actual prejudice to the respondent as a result of the delay; and

- the constitutional right to earn a livelihood and the right of directors to put behind them the consequences of an insolvent liquidation at a certain point in time.

Applying these considerations, Finlay Geoghegan J determined that the directors had faced the consequences of the company's insolvent liquidation and had started a new business of which they were both directors seven or eight years after that liquidation. The Court considered:

> 'It appears to me that that is a reasonable time at which these directors should have been able to put behind them the consequences of this liquidation and start moving forward and should be entitled to do so now without having to face, at this stage, the threat of a declaration of restriction which potentially would interfere with their ability to conduct their present business through a limited company.'

An order was granted staying the restriction proceedings.

E. Relief

[17.076] Once a declaration of restriction has been made, there is only one means by which a former director can attempt to overcome the effects of that order.

CA 1990, s 152 provides that:

> (1) A person to whom s 150 applies may, within not more than one year after a declaration has been made in respect of him under that section, apply to the court for relief, either in whole or in part, from the restrictions referred to in that section or from any order made in relation to him under s 151 and the court may, if it deems it just and equitable to do so, grant such relief on whatever terms and conditions it sees fit.

According to s 152(2), notice of an intention to make such an application must be served on the liquidator of the company in connection with which the director was restricted. This notice must be served at least 14 days in advance of the application. Upon receipt of such notice, s 152(3) requires the liquidator to notify 'such creditors and contributories of the company as have been notified to him or become known to him, that he has received such notice'. At the hearing of the application, the liquidator and

---

[193] *Re Knocklofty House Hotel Ltd* [2005] IEHC 105.

any creditor or member of the company may appear and give evidence.[194] It is an offence for the liquidator to fail to comply with these requirements, according to s 152(5).

[17.077] The case of *Re Ferngara*[195] concerned an application under CA 1990, s 152 and was the first application under the provision. The Court made the procedural point that, on an application under s 152, the liquidator should personally swear an affidavit that he has notified all of the creditors and contributories of the company who have been notified to him or become known to him of receipt by him of the application under s 152 and of the return date of that application.

The Court further noted the nature of restriction proceedings, focusing on the mandatory nature of the orders and the intransigence of the five-year period of restriction. The Court quoted the decision in *Business Communications v Baxter*[196] and the comments of Murphy J regarding the inflexibility of s 150 and concluded that:

> 'In contrast to s 150, the Court is given a very broad discretion under s 150. The discretion is so broad that the Court may accede to an application for relief in whole from the restrictions thereby imposed and, in effect, wholly negative the effect of the Order under s 150. The only criterion stipulated in s 152 for the guidance of the Court is that it should be "just and equitable" to grant the relief.'[197]

On the facts of the case before it, the Court granted the relief sought under s 152.

[17.078] Another case in which an application under s 152 was considered was *In Re CMC (Ireland) Ltd*,[198] in which the DCE sought to be joined as a notice party to an application for relief under s 152.[199] The applicants for relief relied upon s 152(4) as a ground for resisting this application. It provides:

> 'On the hearing of an application under this section the liquidator or any creditor or contributory of the company, the insolvency of which caused the applicant to be subject to this chapter may appear and give evidence.'

The Court considered that, while the persons named in s 152(4) have a statutory right to appear, that provision does not specify exhaustively the persons who might appear and

---

[194] The CLRG replicates these provisions in the General Scheme of the Draft Companies Consolidation and Reform Bill 2007, Pt A13, Head 34, subject to the changes that the DCE also has the right to appear and give evidence, and there is no longer a requirement that the application be made within one year of the declaration of restriction. Available at www.clrg.org.

[195] *Re Ferngara, Robinson v Forrest* [1999] IEHC 103 [1999] 1 IR 429, [1999] 2 ILRM 169 (11 February 1999, unreported), HC.

[196] *Business Communications v Baxter* (21 July 1995, unreported), HC, (Murphy J).

[197] *Re Ferngara, Robinson v Forrest* [1999] IEHC 103 [1999] 1 IR 429, [1999] 2 ILRM 169 (11 February 1999, unreported), HC at para 10.

[198] *Re CMC (Ireland) Ltd, Carolan v Fennell* [2005] IEHC 340.

[199] The Court referred to O 15, r 13, which provides in relevant part: 'The Court may at any stage of the proceedings, either upon or without the application of either party, and on such terms as may appear to the Court to be just, order that ... the names of any parties, whether plaintiffs or defendants, who ought to have been joined, or whose presence before the Court may be necessary in order to enable the Court effectually and completely to adjudicate upon and settle all the questions involved in the cause or matter, be added ...'.

give evidence. It does not, moreover, 'exclude the jurisdiction of the court to add as parties to the application such persons as it might consider necessary or desirable in the interests of justice.'[200]

The Court distinguished the position applicable to applications under s 150, noting that s 150(4A) specified the persons who may commence s 150 proceedings and that the Oireachtas intended only those persons to be able to bring such proceedings.[201] In an application under s 152, by contrast, there was nothing to limit the jurisdiction of a court to permit persons to be added as parties. On this basis, the Court was not precluded from joining the DCE as a notice party, if such joinder was 'necessary or desirable in the interests of justice'.

[17.079] There were a number of factors which the Court took into account in determining that it was necessary and desirable to join the DCE to that application. First, Finlay Geoghegan J noted that the liquidator did not propose to tender evidence in relation to the application, as such participation could only be undertaken at a cost to the liquidation:

> 'To participate in such an application and either oppose it or even seek to be represented and put before the Court matters which he thinks the Court should take into account can only be done at a cost to the liquidation. Even if there are funds in this liquidation (about which I am not aware) it is doubtful that the creditors would appreciate such funds being expended in response to an application under s 152.'[202]

There was therefore no person who intended to appear to oppose, test or controvert the application under s 152. The Court commented that it was desirable that there be an adversary in relation to an application under s 152:

> 'It is desirable in our adversarial system of justice that there is a party before the court who is either opposing the application or at minimum has an interest in examining with the benefit of relevant facts and expertise, the validity of the application and making relevant submissions to the court.'[203]

[17.080] A second consideration taken into account in *Re CMC (Ireland) Ltd*,[204] was the DCE's submission that he could put relevant information and evidence before the Court in relation to companies referred to in the applicants' affidavits. The Court accepted that it was relevant to consider the applicants' positions as directors of the other companies they referred to and that the DCE was an appropriate person to present admissible evidence and make submissions to the Court.

---

[200] *Re CMC (Ireland) Ltd, Carolan v Fennell* [2005] IEHC 340.

[201] See further paras **[18.001]** to **[18.007]**.

[202] *Re CMC (Ireland) Ltd, Carolan v Fennell* [2005] IEHC 340.

[203] *Re CMC (Ireland) Ltd, Carolan v Fennell* [2005] IEHC 340.

[204] *Re CMC (Ireland) Ltd, Carolan v Fennell* [2005] IEHC 340.

In deciding to grant the DCE's motion to be joined as a notice party to the s 152 application, the Court also made some general observations regarding the nature of that application, observations that demonstrate the breadth of such an application:

'The jurisdiction intended to be exercised by the court under s 152(1) is not confined to the facts pertaining to the company in liquidation nor the facts considered in the application for the declaration of restriction under s 150. It is not in any sense an appeal from the decision making the declaration of restriction. Rather it is a consideration of the issue as to whether, notwithstanding the declaration of restriction, there are other facts pertaining to the applicants which make it just and equitable to grant them relief (either in whole or in part) from the restrictions imposed by the declaration of restriction and on whatever terms and conditions as the court sees fit.'

A final aspect of the judgment of Finlay Geoghegan J which is interesting in the context of s 152, is the Court's clear indication that the DCE will not automatically be granted the right to appear in relation to such applications. The Court cautioned:

'In deciding to join the Director in this application I wish to make clear that I am not deciding that he should be joined in all applications under s 152 of the Act of 1990. The Oireachtas has not specified that he is a person to whom notice must be given by the liquidator under s 152(3). Also, the Oireachtas has created a class of persons with an automatic right to appear and give evidence in s 152(4). Whether the Director should be joined in any particular application will depend on the relevant facts and the court determining that it is necessary or in the interests of justice to do so.'[205]

The DCE will clearly have a strong case for being joined as a notice party to a s 152 application, when he has relevant evidence to present and no person, other than the applicant for relief, intends to appear or make submissions in relation to that application. It will fall to be determined on a case by case basis and in each individual case, the DCE (or any other person who wishes to appear as a notice party) will have to file a motion seeking to be joined and satisfy the court that, in all of the circumstances, it is necessary and desirable in the interests of justice that he be so joined. The CLRG recommends that the DCE should be given the same right to appear and give evidence in relation to an application for relief, as is currently conferred on the liquidator, creditors and contributories.[206]

[17.081] The decision of O'Neill J in *Re XNet Information Systems Ltd*[207] is an example of an application under s 152 to which the DCE was a notice party. The Court held that, in considering an application for relief from the consequences of a declaration of restriction, the Court must consider 'the fundamental purpose of the restriction declaration', which is to protect the public. Before granting partial or total relief, the Court must be satisfied that such relief will not harm the public. O'Neill J stated that, while hardship is a factor in applications under s 152, it is an inevitable consequence of restriction and cannot outweigh 'the paramount consideration which is the protection of

---

[205] *Re CMC (Ireland) Ltd, Carolan v Fennell* [2005] IEHC 340.

[206] See General Scheme of the Draft Companies Consolidation and Reform Bill 2007, Pt A13, Head 34(4). Available at www.clrg.org.

[207] *Re XNet Information Systems Ltd, Higgins v Stafford* [2006] IEHC 289.

the public'. Other matters which the Court considered to be relevant were the grounds on which the declaration of restriction was made; the applicant's need or interest in having the declaration removed; whether the capitalisation requirement of s 150(3) is an 'insurmountable obstacle'; the conduct of the applicant since the winding up; and the deterrent effect of the declaration of restriction.

Applying these criteria to the application in *Re XNet Information Systems Ltd*,[208] O'Neill J referred to the following features of the application:

- the applicant was impecunious and unable to raise capital and demonstrated a 'need' for the relief sought;

- there was a risk that the applicant's ideas could be exploited unfairly if no relief was granted;

- the applicant had suffered great financial hardship due to the company's collapse and the declaration of restriction;

- the factors which led to the declaration of restriction were 'serious', but 'not at the worst end of the scale of turpitude';

- the applicant's behaviour for most of the company's life was responsible;

- the applicant demonstrated responsible conduct since the winding up of the company, including by repayment of monies to the liquidator, in spite of his impecunious state;

- there was very little risk to the public if the applicant was permitted to act as a company director again; and

- the applicant had already suffered the stigma of restriction, as he had been restricted between May 2004 and the date of the judgment (10 October 2006), and the deterrent effect of the declaration of restriction would not be undermined by the granting of relief.

On the basis of these considerations, the Court determined that the appropriate order was one of partial relief. The declaration of restriction was therefore removed to the extent that the applicant could act as a director or secretary or otherwise be concerned or take part in the promotion or formation of a company, so long as that company has fully paid-up allotted share capital of the nominal value of €7,500, rather than the threshold of €63,487 stipulated in s 150(3).[209] The Court directed that all other aspects of the declaration of restriction remain in place and imposed the additional requirement on the applicant to notify the DCE of the name of any company to which he is appointed. The Court further granted to the DCE liberty to apply to court to vary or revoke the relief granted, which application must be on notice to the applicant.

---

[208] *Re XNet Information Systems Ltd, Higgins v Stafford* [2006] IEHC 289.

[209] See paras **[19.010]** to **[19.015]**.

Chapter 18

PROCEDURE OF RESTRICTION PROCEEDINGS

A. Applicants under s 150

[18.001] Before the enactment of the CLEA 2001, there was no person or entity with a definitive duty to institute restriction proceedings against directors of companies which went into insolvent liquidation. Moreover, the relevant provisions of the CA 1990 did not mention who the appropriate applicants were or should be for the purpose of bringing an application for a declaration of restriction. Section 150 did not impose a duty or confer a power on any person or entity to make such an application.

In *Re Verit Hotel and Leisure (Ireland) Ltd*,[1] McCracken J noted that, 'Strangely, neither the Section nor any of the rules made under the Act gave any guidance as to how the matter is to come before the Court, or indeed who is to bring it before the Court.'[2] He noted the reality that, 'As a matter of practice in the case of Court Liquidations, the liquidator almost invariably will bring an application by Notice of Motion and indeed on occasion will be directed to do so by the Court.'[3]

The Court contrasted this situation with the situation pertaining under s 160, according to which the courts may make a disqualification order on its own motion, or, alternatively, the application may be made by the DPP, or any member, contributory, officer, employee, receiver, liquidator, examiner or creditor of the company.[4]

[18.002] The absence of a provision in the CA 1990 requiring or even expressly permitting certain individuals or entities to apply for restriction orders must have been largely, if not exclusively, accountable for the relative rarity of applications for restriction orders in the period between the enactment of the CA 1990 and the CLEA 2001.[5] As noted by the Working Group on Company Law Compliance and Enforcement:

> 'The basic problem with s 150 is that it does not specifically require any liquidator
> (or receiver) to make application to the court to have a director "restricted". Where

---

[1]   *Re Verit Hotel and Leisure (Ireland) Ltd, Duignan v Carway* [2002] IEHC 1.

[2]   *Re Verit Hotel and Leisure (Ireland) Ltd, Duignan v Carway* [2002] IEHC 1 at para 9.

[3]   *Re Verit Hotel and Leisure (Ireland) Ltd, Duignan v Carway* [2002] IEHC 1 at para 9.

[4]   CA 1990, s 160(4); See *Re Verit Hotel and Leisure (Ireland) Ltd, Duignan v Carway* [2002] IEHC 1 at para 10. See Ch **22**.

[5]   This may have been tempered to some extent by the fact that, in the period before the introduction of the CLEA 2001, Murphy J did issue a practice direction requiring all official liquidators of insolvent companies to bring applications for the restriction of the directors of those companies under s 150. See *Re Euroking Miracle (Ireland) Ltd (In Voluntary Liquidation), Fennell v Frost* [2003] IEHC 15 (5 June 2003, unreported), HC, Finlay Geoghegan J.

> liquidators chose not to make application under s 150(1), the legislation contains no penalty or sanction whatsoever.'[6]

[18.003] The law governing the applicants and applications for restriction orders was changed quite profoundly by CLEA 2001.[7] Section 41 inserted a new s 150(4A) which now provides that an application for a restriction order may be made by the DCE, a liquidator or a receiver. This is a crucial clarification of the source from which applications for restriction orders can be expected. It is also noteworthy that the range of applicants for restriction orders remains considerably more limited than the range of persons who are empowered by s 160(4) to apply for orders of disqualification.[8]

[18.004] A further change of considerable significance that was introduced by the CLEA 2001 in the area of restriction applications, was CLEA 2001, s 56(2). This provision, as has been seen in more detail elsewhere, [9] now requires liquidators of companies in insolvent liquidation to bring restriction proceedings against the company's directors, unless the ODCE relieves them of the obligation to do so. This provision has heralded an unprecedented increase in the number of restriction applications made to the High Court by liquidators of insolvent companies and accounts for the fact that the vast majority of applications under s 150 are brought by liquidators.

B. Parties to restriction proceedings

[18.005] In most applications for declarations of restriction, the parties will be the applicant (typically the company's liquidator) and the director or directors in respect of whom the declarations are sought. There have, however, been cases in which other persons have sought to be joined as parties to restriction proceedings.

In the case of *Re Document Imaging Systems Ltd*,[10] for example, a creditor of a company in liquidation applied to be joined as a party in support of an application for declarations of restriction. This applicant was also a contributory and former director of the company. The applicant argued that he had direct knowledge of the circumstances of the company and that the evidence he could furnish would be relevant to the s 150 application. He further submitted that the jurisdiction of the court to join parties to proceedings under O 15, r 13 of the Rules of the Superior Courts[11] was a broad one, relying on the following passage from the judgment of Hardiman J in *TDI Metro Limited*

---

[6]   Working Group on Company Law Compliance and Enforcement, *Report* (November 30, 1998) at para 6.11.

[7]   The High Court acknowledged the significance of these changes in the judgment in *Re Euroking Miracle (Ireland) Ltd In Voluntary Liquidation), Fennell v Frost* [2003] IEHC 15 (5 June 2003, unreported), HC, Finlay Geoghegan J, the first case arising from an application for restriction made in the exercise of the obligation of the voluntary liquidator under s 56(2).

[8]   See further Ch **22**.

[9]   CLEA 2001, s 56. See further Ch **9**.

[10] *Re Document Imagining Systems Ltd* [2005] IEHC 250.

[11] SI 15/1986.

v Delap (No 1),[12] which concerned an application by the Attorney General to intervene in an appeal against an order of the High Court:

> 'Although the Attorney General has not in my view any entitlement as of right to intervene and be heard in the present proceedings he has applied to do so. That is something which the court should consider very seriously. The court has a jurisdiction in its discretion to allow a party to be joined in the proceedings even at the appeal stage where this is considered to be necessary in the interest of justice and where there is no specific rule of law excluding the additional parties at that stage of the proceedings.'

The Court agreed in *Re Document Imaging Systems Ltd*[13] that the court does have a wide discretion under O 15, r 13,[14] but noted that:

> 'in an application such as this, where a person is seeking voluntarily to be joined in proceedings, the court must be satisfied that he is a person "whose presence before the court may be necessary in order to enable the court effectually and completely to adjudicate upon and settle all the questions involved in the cause or matter".'

The Court went on to state that the necessity of a party 'will primarily depend upon the nature of the proceedings and the issues to be determined' and that, 'Where, as in this application, a person is seeking to be joined to support the applicant, it appears relevant also to consider whether he has *locus standi* to pursue the application.'

[18.006] The Court considered the fact that s 150, as originally enacted, did not stipulate the parties who could or should bring applications under that provision. The Court quoted the following dicta of Shanley J in *Re Steamline Limited (In Voluntary Liquidation):*[15]

> 'All enactments should be given a purposive construction: that is, a construction which promotes the remedy the Oireachtas has provided to cure a particular mischief. Armed with such a canon of construction, this court approaches Part VII of the Act of 1990 noting that the legislature has expressly provided a particular restriction for particular types of conduct; it is a restriction to be imposed by the court, but which cannot realistically be imposed in the absence of a procedure whereby applications for such a restriction are made to the court by parties with an interest in making such an application. I believe that the court ought to construe s 150(1) in such a way as to promote, rather than restrict, the remedy provided for in that subsection: while the grounds for the disqualification of a director and other officers of a company differ from the grounds warranting restriction of a director, nonetheless, it does appear to me that the persons authorised by s 160(4)(b) to bring an application for a disqualification order are, broadly, the

---

[12] *TDI Metro Limited v Delap (No 1)* [2000] 4 IR 337.

[13] *Re Document Imagining Systems Ltd* [2005] IEHC 250.

[14] RSC, O 15, r 13 of the Rules of the Superior Courts states, insofar as relevant: 'The Court may at any stage of the proceedings, either upon or without the application of either party, and on such terms as may appear to the Court to be just, order that ... the names of any parties, whether plaintiffs or defendants, who ought to have been joined, or whose presence before the Court may be necessary in order to enable the Court effectually and completely to adjudicate upon and settle all the questions involved in the cause or matter, be added ...'.

[15] *Re Steamline Limited (In Voluntary Liquidation)* [2001] 1 IR 103.

same category of persons who would have an interest in seeking an order for the restriction of a director. In promoting, rather than restricting, the remedy provided for in s 150(1), this court ought, in my view, to construe the mandatory power provided therein as exercisable on the application of any one of the class of persons identified in s 160(4)(b) of the Act of 1990 being persons identified by the legislature as having an interest in moving an application for a disqualification order and whom the legislature would have intended to have a like interest in relation to applications to restrict directors. Accordingly, in my view, Musgrave Ltd, as a creditor of Steamline Ltd, is entitled to maintain this application.'

The Court in *Re Document Imaging Systems Ltd*[16] noted that s 150 as it currently exists is 'quite different' to the provision which was considered by Shanley J in *Re Steamline Limited (In Voluntary Liquidation)*.[17] The Court referred to the insertion by CLEA 2001, s 41 of a new s 150(4A) which provides expressly that an application under s 150 can be made by the DCE, a liquidator or a receiver.

Despite this amendment, the applicant argued that the Court should permit creditors and contributories to initiate applications under s 150. The Court rejected this submission in the following terms:

'The Oireachtas has specifically, by the 2001 amendment, provided that the jurisdiction conferred on the High Court under s 150 should be exercised on the application of one of the persons named in subs. (4A). They have done so in circumstances where they have in s 160(4) of the Act of 1990 specified a different class of persons who may bring applications under s 160(2) of the Act of 1990. Applying the well established principle of construction that the intention of the Oireachtas should be construed from the words used when given their ordinary meaning, I must conclude that the Oireachtas intend (since the passing of the Act of 2001) that applications under s 150 be brought by the persons named in s 150(4A) and not by any other person. If it were intended that other persons could bring such an application then the Oireachtas would have specified such additional categories as it has done in s 160(4) of the Act of 1990. Accordingly I have concluded that the court has no jurisdiction to permit a person who is not the Director of Corporate Enforcement, a liquidator or a receiver to be an applicant in proceedings under s 150(1) of the Act of 1990.'

[18.007] This decision clarifies that there are two very different categories of applicants for orders of restriction and disqualification and that only the persons referred to explicitly in the legislation can initiate such proceedings. The result is that nobody other than the DCE, a company's liquidator or receiver, can make an application to court to have a director restricted under s 150.

The Court in *Re Document Imaging Systems Ltd*[18] did note that the decision to limit the category of applicants to those enumerated in s 150(4A) left open the question of whether the court has a discretion under O 15, r 13 to join a person as a notice party to a s 150 application. The Court determined that, as this issue was not addressed by counsel

---

[16] *Re Document Imagining Systems Ltd* [2005] IEHC 250.

[17] *Re Steamline Limited (In Voluntary Liquidation)* [2001] 1 IR 103.

[18] *Re Document Imagining Systems Ltd* [2005] IEHC 250.

in *Re Document Imagining Systems Ltd,*[19] the question should be reserved until it arose properly and was fully argued. However, the Court did note that:

> 'even if such a discretion exists, where, as on the facts of this application, a person wishes to be joined for the purpose of making submissions in support of the application by a liquidator... there would have to be exceptional circumstances in which a court would permit such a person to be joined as a notice party.' The Court further noted that, 'No such exceptional circumstances arise on the facts of this case.'

The Court concluded that the creditor should not be joined as a party to the restriction application in *Re Document Imagining Systems Ltd.*[20] By contrast, it should be noted that the DCE requires that he be joined as a notice party to all s 150 applications initiated pursuant to s 56 reports.[21]

C. Rules of procedure

[18.008] Neither the Rules of the Superior Courts, nor the Companies Acts, provide any specific guidance about the procedures that should be adopted in relation to s 150 restriction proceedings. In 1991, O 75B was inserted into the Rules of Superior Courts by statutory instrument[22] to govern proceedings under the Companies Acts. Order 75B, r 3 states that certain applications under the Companies Acts shall be made by way of originating notice and motion. Order 75B, r 3(z) applies this rule to applications for disqualification orders and provides:

> (z) An application for a disqualification Order in relation to a person under s 160(2) or in relation to a disqualification Order under s 160(8). Such an application shall be served on the person in relation to whom the disqualification Order is sought and on any other party to the proceedings and on the applicant for the original disqualification Order, as the case may be.

There is no provision of O 75B which addresses the procedures to be adopted in applications for orders of restrictions under s 150. However, the same statutory instrument did insert into O 74, which deals with the winding up of companies, a new r 136 which provided that:[23]

> In any winding up an application under s 234 of the Companies Act 1962 or under s 139 of the Companies Act 1990 *or under any other section of the Acts not herein expressly provided for,* shall, in the case of a winding up by the Court, be made by motion on notice and in the case of a voluntary winding up by originating notice of motion[24] (emphasis added).

---

19 *Re Document Imagining Systems Ltd* [2005] IEHC 250.

20 *Re Document Imagining Systems Ltd* [2005] IEHC 250.

21 ODCE, The Liquidator-Related Functions of the Director of Corporate Enforcement, Decision Notice D/2002/3 at para 5.6.

22 The Rules of the Superior Courts (No 4) (SI 278/1991).

23 See consideration of SI 278/1991 in *Re Euroking Miracle (Ireland) Ltd In Voluntary Liquidation), Fennell v Frost* [2003] IEHC 15.

24 The Rules of the Superior Courts (No 4) (SI 278/1991), s 2(3).

[18.009] In *Re Verit Hotel and Leisure (Ireland) Ltd*,[25] the liquidator filed a motion seeking a declaration of restriction against the directors of the company in liquidation. The respondents claimed that, as the Rules of the Superior Courts did not provide that an application under s 150 could be brought by means of notice of motion, that such an application should be brought by plenary summons, in accordance with O 1, r 1 of the Rules of the Superior Courts.

The Court agreed that there was no provision of the Rules governing applications under s 150,[26] noting, however, that O 74, r 136 contained a number of provisions under which applications could be brought by means of notice of motion. McCracken J did comment that, 'It does seem a strange omission from the rules and one which should possibly be rectified.' However, in the circumstances of that particular case, it was held that the respondents had brought a number of challenges to the application, without raising this procedural argument, and were now precluded from doing so.

D. Practice direction

[18.010] The President of the High Court issued a practice direction regarding the procedures to be followed in certain applications under s 150. This direction came into effect on 24 March 2003. The following aspects of the direction should be noted:

1. It applies to any application for an order of restriction, whether made by a liquidator pursuant to his obligation under CLEA 2001, s 56 or by a receiver, the DCE or a liquidator pursuant to CA 1990, s 150(4A);

2. The practice direction does not apply to official liquidations;

3. An application for a restriction order must be commenced by an originating notice of motion, grounded on the affidavit of the applicant;

4. Applications in respect of several directors are to be made on the same notice of motion;

5. The grounding affidavit must set out all of the facts which the applicant considers should be brought to the court's attention for the purpose of determining whether the respondent(s) acted honestly and responsibly, whether there is any reason why it would be just and equitable to make orders of restriction or whether the respondent(s) are nominees with the meaning of s 150(2)(b);[27]

---

[25] *Re Verit Hotel and Leisure (Ireland) Ltd, Duignan v Carway* [2002] IEHC 1.

[26] The Court contrasted this with the situation in relation to s 160, noting that, '... Furthermore, under Order 75 B. Rule 3 of the Superior Court Rules it is provided that a s 160 application shall be brought by way of Notice of Motion.' *Re Verit Hotel and Leisure (Ireland) Ltd, Duignan v Carway* [2002] IEHC 1.

[27] See Kirwan, 'Restriction of Company Directors' Journal of Civil Practice and Procedure, Vol 1, No 1, Spring 2005 8 at 10: 'it is arguable that if the Practice Direction is strictly followed, the grounding affidavit, because of its focus on the directors, may not provide an adequate account of the trading history of the company and the reason for its insolvency, which would be of assistance to the court. The better approach, it is submitted, would be to treat the information required by the Practice Direction as a minimum and adopt a more expansive approach in terms of matters sworn in the affidavit'.

6. Motions must be issued in the Central Office of the High Court and must be returnable for not less than 28 days from issue;

7. The motion, a grounding affidavit and a copy of the Practice Direction, must be served on the respondent(s) at least 21 days before the return date;

8. The respondent(s) must enter an appearance in the Central Office and serve the appearance on the applicant (or his solicitor) within ten days of service of the notice of motion;

9. If the respondent(s) wish to oppose the application, they must file an affidavit setting out the facts on which the opposition is based in the Central Office and serve this on the applicant or his solicitor at least four days before the return date;

10. The court may exceptionally allow further time for the filing and service of the respondent's affidavit;

11. If the respondent(s) enters no appearance, the applicant must file an affidavit of service in the Central Office at least two days before the return date;

12. The court will only grant extensions of time for filing affidavits exceptionally, where the court is satisfied that the extension is required for good reason;

13. An application which is properly served may be determined by the court on the return date.

This Practice Direction ensures that the procedural uncertainties identified in *Re Verit Hotel and Leisure (Ireland) Ltd*[28] should no longer cause concern, as it is now clear how restriction proceedings are to be initiated and what steps both parties should take up to the date that the motion is first listed before the High Court. It should be noted that, in practice, if a respondent is contesting an application for restriction, there will often be further exchanges of affidavits between the applicant and the respondent. This is particularly likely if there are a number of respondents and each raise different and possibly conflicting issues. The timeframes that are applicable to the service of any such supplemental affidavits are fixed by the court. Either side may serve a notice to cross examine a deponent in order to test the assertions contained in his affidavit.[29]

E. Service of restriction proceedings

(a) General rule

[18.011] The Practice Direction did not resolve all procedural aspects of applications under s 150. In *Re Euroking Miracle (Ireland) Ltd,*[30] the High Court considered an

---

[28] *Re Verit Hotel and Leisure (Ireland) Ltd, Duignan v Carway* [2002] IEHC 1.

[29] See comment by Peart J in *Re USIT World plc* [2005] IEHC 285: '... there is the usual procedure available to any party to serve Notice to Cross-examine any deponent in order to test what has been stated.'

[30] *Re Euroking Miracle (Ireland) Ltd In Voluntary Liquidation), Fennell v Frost* [2003] IEHC 15.

application which was initiated by originating notice of motion in accordance with the above Practice Direction. The Court noted that the Practice Direction contained 'no specific provision as to the manner of service of the originating notice of motion.' The Court referred instead to O 9 of the Rules of the Superior Courts and held that, in general, an originating notice of motion in s 150 proceedings should be served by means of personal service 'if it be reasonably practicable'.

In this regard, it should be noted that O 9, r 2[31] provides that, 'Service of any summons on the defendant shall, except in the cases in the following rules of this Order specified, be effected by personal service if it be reasonably practicable.' Otherwise, if 'due and reasonable diligence … in endeavouring to effect such personal service' has failed, the Rules state that:

> 'service of such summons may be effected by delivering a copy thereof at the defendant's house or place of residence, or at his or her office, warehouse, counting house, shop, factory, or place of business, to the wife, husband, child, father, mother, brother, or sister of the defendant, or to any servant or clerk of the defendant (the person to whom such copy shall be delivered being of the age of sixteen years or upwards) and showing to such person the original or duplicate original of such summons.'[32]

Order 9, r 16 as relied upon in *Re Euroking Miracle (Ireland) Ltd*,[33] provides, 'This Order, so far as practicable, shall apply to the originating document in proceedings not commenced by summons and to notice in lieu of service.'[34]

On the authority of *Re Euroking Miracle (Ireland) Ltd*,[35] applying the provisions of O 9, r 2 of the Rules of the Superior Courts, the appropriate means of serving an originating notice of motion of an application for a restriction order under s 150, on a respondent who is resident in Ireland, is by personal service. If it is not reasonably practicably to execute personal service, O 9, r 2 sets out alternative means of service which may be employed by an applicant.

(b) Service out of the jurisdiction

[18.012] In *Re Euroking Miracle (Ireland) Ltd*,[36] the respondents were not resident in this jurisdiction and the issue before the Court was therefore not service on a respondent within the jurisdiction, such as would be provided for by O 9, r 2.[37] The Court was instead obliged to consider the question of service out of the jurisdiction of an originating notice of motion in restriction proceedings.

---

[31]   Rules of the Superior Courts (SI 15/1986), O 9.

[32]   Rules of the Superior Courts (SI 15/1986), O 9, r 2.

[33]   *Re Euroking Miracle (Ireland) Ltd In Voluntary Liquidation), Fennell v Frost* [2003] IEHC 15.

[34]   Rules of the Superior Courts (SI 15/1986), O 9, r 16.

[35]   *Re Euroking Miracle (Ireland) Ltd In Voluntary Liquidation), Fennell v Frost* [2003] IEHC 15.

[36]   *Re Euroking Miracle (Ireland) Ltd In Voluntary Liquidation), Fennell v Frost* [2003] IEHC 15.

[37]   Rules of the Superior Courts (SI 15/1986), O 9.

The rule of court which governs service out of the jurisdiction is O 11 of the Rules of the Superior Courts. This requires the leave of the court to serve an originating summons out of the jurisdiction. According to O 11, r 11 'This Order shall apply, so far as practicable and applicable, to proceedings whether instituted by originating summons or in some other manner, and to any order or notice in any such proceedings.' Finlay Geoghegan J stated that O 11 would 'on its face' apply to the application for an order of restriction commenced by means of originating notice of motion. However, O 11 contains an exhaustive list of the causes of action to which it applies and it was accepted by the liquidator that restriction proceedings did not fall within that category.[38]

[18.013] The liquidator sought to rely on O 11, r 12, which provides:

> Nothing herein contained shall in any way prejudice or affect any practice or power of the Court under which when lands, funds, chooses in action, rights or property within the jurisdiction are sought to be dealt with or affected, the Court may, without affecting to exercise jurisdiction over any person out of the jurisdiction, cause such person to be informed of the nature or existence of the proceedings with a view to such person having an opportunity of claiming, opposing or otherwise intervening.[39]

The liquidator sought to argue that the power of a court to make a declaration of restriction involves dealing with 'rights... within the jurisdiction' within the meaning of O 11, r 12. Finlay Geoghegan J conceded that, 'There is some merit in this argument.' However, the Court considered that, in making an order of restriction, it could not be said that the court was not 'affecting to exercise jurisdiction over any person out of the jurisdiction' within the meaning of O 11, r 12, as an order of restriction does affect directors personally. For that reason, the terms of O 11, r 12 could not be relied upon for the service out of the jurisdiction of an originating notice of motion in restriction proceedings.

[18.014] In the absence of any explicit rules or directions governing the service out of the jurisdiction of an originating notice of motion in restriction proceedings, the Court proceeded to consider some general points regarding restriction proceedings and service of proceedings generally. The following points were noted:

– directors resident outside the jurisdiction are amenable to the jurisdiction of the Irish courts under s 150;

– an order of restriction is mandatory when the requirements of s 149 are met, unless the criteria of s 150(2) are established;

– the CA 1990 does not expressly require directors to be made respondents to applications under s 150(4A);

– the CA 1990 does not expressly require that directors must be heard prior to the court reaching a decision on a restriction application;

---

[38] Rules of the Superior Courts (SI 15/1986), O 11, r 1, lists the causes of action to which that Order applies.

[39] Rules of the Superior Courts (SI 15/1986), O 11, r 12.

- section 150 must be construed in accordance with principles of constitutional justice, including notice of the proceedings and an opportunity to be heard;[40]
- the absence of a rule of court permitting service out of the jurisdiction in relation to restriction proceedings could not preclude the court from exercising its jurisdiction under s 150.[41]

[18.015] In *Re Euroking Miracle (Ireland) Ltd*,[42] copies of the originating notice of motion, the grounding affidavit, the Practice Direction of the President of the High Court and an explanatory covering letter, were sent by registered pre-paid post to the directors at the addresses which they furnished to the Companies Registration Office as their residential addresses. The Court concluded that this mode of service was 'a sufficient discharge of this Court's obligation to ensure that applications under s.150 are heard and determined in accordance with the principles of constitutional justice.'

The reasons given by the Court for reaching this conclusion were as follows:

- The lack of an applicable rule of court;
- The mandatory nature of the court's jurisdiction and the rules of constitutional justice made it necessary that notice should be given to the non-resident director, insofar as was practicable;
- As it was an application under CLEA 2001, s 56, there were facts which the ODCE considered should be brought to the attention of the court;
- As the costs of restriction applications are liable to be discharged from the proceeds available in the winding up, the costs should be minimised insofar as practicable; personal service out of the jurisdiction being a costly option;
- The directors are obliged by CA 1963, s 195, to furnish their regular residential address, and any change thereto, to the Companies Registration Office and there will frequently be contact between the liquidator and directors in the course of a winding up;
- If the director is no longer resident at the address furnished under s 195, the papers would, as a matter of probability, be returned;
- If, through error or change of address, the director does not receive notice of the application and does not appear, it would be open to them to seek to set aside any order made if there are grounds on which the order should not have been

---

[40] Citing *East Donegal Co-Operative Livestock Mart Limited v Attorney* General [1970] IR 317.

[41] Citing the decision of Finnegan J in *McKenna v EH* [2001] IEHC 139 to the effect that, 'If it is the intention of the Oireachtas, and I am satisfied that it is, that person resident outside the jurisdiction with assets inside the jurisdiction which represents the proceeds of crime should be subject to the procedures of the Act, then I am satisfied that *it is the duty of the Court to give effect to that intention and if necessary have resort to the inherent jurisdiction of the Court pending the introduction of appropriate rules of procedure to give effect to the intention*' (emphasis added).

[42] *Re Euroking Miracle (Ireland) Ltd In Voluntary Liquidation), Fennell v Frost* [2003] IEHC 15.

made, by analogy with O 36, r 33. The Court also noted the terms of CA 1990, s 152.

[18.016] Having determined that service by registered post was sufficient to notify directors not resident in the jurisdiction of restriction proceedings, the Court went on to caution:

> '... whilst I have determined that, in this case, the service by registered post to the usual residential address, particulars of which were filed in the Companies Office, is sufficient service, I have done so on the facts of this case. It would be a matter for each individual applicant liquidator to satisfy the court that, insofar as practicable, he has attempted to give actual notice of the application to a non-resident director by sending same, by registered post, to an address where he believes the director for stated reasons to be residing or having a place of business. Further that by reason of information supplied to the person effecting service by the post office, he has allowed sufficient time to elapse during which the registered letter would, as a matter of probability, either have been delivered or returned. The affidavit of service sworn should cover the several elements to satisfy the court that, as a matter of probability, the non-resident director has received actual notice of the application.'[43]

[18.017] A liquidator attempting to bring restriction proceedings against directors not resident in the jurisdiction would be well advised to resist the temptation to simply serve the originating notice of motion, grounding affidavit and copy of the Practice Direction on the director at the address which was furnished to the Companies Registration Office under CA 1963, s 193, on the basis that this is permissible on the authority of *Re Euroking Miracle (Ireland) Ltd*.[44] Instead, pending the introduction of rules of court or other definitive guidance on the topic, liquidators should undertake all of the steps referred to in the above passage from the judgment of Finlay Geoghegan J in *Re Euroking Miracle (Ireland) Ltd* and should be aware that, before obtaining a court order, they will face the relatively high hurdle of having to prove as a matter of probability that the director received actual notice of the application.

F. Discovery in restriction proceedings

[18.018] An application for discovery in restriction proceedings may be brought in accordance with ord 31, r 12 of the Rules of the Superior Courts 1986. In *Re Silken Construction Ltd*,[45] the respondent brought a motion under ord 31, r 12 seeking discovery of the report compiled by the liquidator pursuant to CLEA 2001, s 56. The DCE was joined as a notice party to the application.

The issues which the Court considered were whether the s 56 report was a document 'relating to any matter in question' within the meaning of ord 31, r 12 and whether

---

43   *Re Euroking Miracle (Ireland) Ltd In Voluntary Liquidation), Fennell v Frost* [2003] IEHC 15.

44   *Re Euroking Miracle (Ireland) Ltd In Voluntary Liquidation), Fennell v Frost* [2003] IEHC 15.

45   *Re Silken Construction Ltd, Kavanagh v O'Donoghue* [2003] 4 IR 443.

discovery of this report was necessary to enable the s 150 application to be fairly disposed of or to save costs.

Finlay Geoghegan J referred to the prescribed content of a report under s 56 and that it is possible to identify precisely the nature of those contents. In the Court's determination, much of the report could not be considered to be relevant and there were parts of it which a liquidator may disclose to the DCE without necessarily disclosing them to the directors. The question in the s 56 report which the Court considered to be relevant to the s 150 application, were question 22 (which concerns factual information about the directors, including the liquidator's view as to whether the directors satisfied him that they acted honestly and responsibly) and question 31 (which concerns whether the liquidator was seeking relief from the obligation to bring restriction proceedings).[46] Finlay Geoghegan J directed discovery be made of those aspects of the s 56 report, on the basis that they were necessary to fairly dispose of the s 150 application. The fact that there may be duplication between the affidavit sworn by the liquidator in the restriction proceedings and the material contained in the s 56 report did not alter this conclusion.

[18.019] A further discovery issue which has arisen, but remains largely unresolved, is the extent to which non-party discovery may be obtained against the DCE. The ODCE reports that a respondent to restriction proceedings has attempted to obtain non-party discovery against the Director in respect of a District Court summons which the Director issued against the respondent in 2003.[47] Following correspondence between the respondent and the ODCE, the motion for discovery was struck out. The ODCE's position in relation to this issue is that: 'the Director does not consider that it is appropriate for respondents to restriction proceedings to seek non-party discovery against the ODCE, and he intends to oppose vigorously any and all such applications that may arise in the future.'[48]

G. Restriction undertakings

[18.020] There is no provision or facility under the CA 1963-2006 for a director to whom s 50 applies to consent to the making of or a declaration of restriction. The CLRG has recommended the introduction of 'restriction undertakings', a recommendation which 'is aimed primarily at reducing unnecessary use of resources in the making of court applications'.[49] The effect of such an undertaking would be the same as if the declaration of restriction was made by the court on the application of the liquidator. The person giving the undertaking should also be obliged to pay the costs of investigating the matters that gave rise to that undertaking.

---

46   See further Ch **9**.

47   See ODCE, *Annual Report 2006* at p 28. Available at www.odce.ie.

48   See ODCE, *Annual Report 2006* at p 28. Available at www.odce.ie.

49   CLRG, General Scheme of the Draft Companies Consolidation and Reform Bill 2007, Pt A13, Head 51. Available at www.clrg.org.

APPENDIX

Form of application under Section150, CA 1990

Originating Notice of Motion for section 150 Order

in a voluntary liquidation

THE HIGH COURT

NOTICE OF MOTION

In the matter of (insert full name of company) (In voluntary liquidation)

and in the matter of Section 150 of The Companies Act 1990 and Section 56 of the Company Law Enforcement Act 2001

Between

_____ Applicant

and

_____ and _____ Respondents

TAKE NOTICE that on Monday the __ day of 2008 at the hour of __ o'clock in the forenoon or at the first available opportunity thereafter Counsel on behalf of the applicant will apply to this Honourable Court sitting at the Four Courts, Inns Quay in the City of Dublin for the following reliefs:

1. A declaration that __ and, __ the respondents hereto, being persons to whom Ch 1 of Pt VII of the Companies Act, 1990 applies, shall not for a period of 5 years be appointed or act in any way, whether directly or indirectly, as a director or secretary or be concerned or take part in the promotion or formation of any company unless that company meets the requirements set out in subsection (3) of section 150 of the Companies Act 1990 (as amended).

2. Such further or other Orders as to this Honourable Court may seem just

3. An Order for the costs of this application

[Where necessary]

An order pursuant to section 56(2) of the Company Law Enforcement Act 2001 extending the time for the making of the above application

WHICH SAID APPLICATION will be grounded upon this Notice of Motion together with the Affidavit of service thereof the Affidavit of sworn on the day of 200_ together with the exhibits referred to therein the nature of the case and the reasons to be offered

Dated this day of 2008

Signed:_____

Solicitors for the Applicant

To: The Registrar

       High Court

       Four Courts

       Dublin 7

To: [Names and addresses of the respondents]

Affidavit to ground the application for an order under section 150.

THE HIGH COURT

Title – as above

I, ___ , liquidator, of _____ aged 18 years and upwards make oath and say as follows:

1. On the __ day of _____ 20__ it was resolved pursuant to section ___ of the Companies Act 1963 that the above company be wound up and that the deponent herein be appointed to act as liquidator. I beg to refer to a copy of the said resolution which before swearing this affidavit I have marked with the letter 'A' and have indorsed my name thereon.

2. __ and __ to whom the Notice of Motion herein is addressed were and each of them was a Director of the Company at the date of [or within 12 months prior to] the commencement of its winding up. I beg to refer to a search in the Companies Registration Office in relation to the Company upon which marked with the letter 'B' I have signed my name prior to the swearing hereof

    and/or

    Set out facts which establish any relevant respondent was a director or shadow director within meaning of s 149 of 1990 Act

3. The Company is [or was at the date of commencement of the winding up] unable to pay its debts within the meaning of Section 214 of the Companies Act 1963. I beg to refer to a Certificate given by me to that effect dated the __ day of _____ 200_ upon which marked with the letter 'C' I have signed my name prior to the swearing hereof.

4. I provided my report to Director of Corporate Enforcement pursuant to Section 56 of the Company Law Enforcement Act 2001on the __ day of _____ 200_ and have not been relieved by him of the obligation to bring this application before the Court. I refer to a copy letter from the Director of Corporate Enforcement to that effect dated __ day of _____ 200_ upon which marked with the letter 'D' I have signed my name prior to the swearing hereof.

    [Set out all facts applicant considers should be brought to the attention of the court for the purpose of determining

    i. whether each of the respondents has acted honestly in relation to the conduct of the affairs of the company

    ii. whether each of the respondents has acted responsibly in relation to the conduct of the affairs of the company

    iii. whether there is any other reason for which it would be just and equitable to restrict any of the respondents

    iv. if appropriate whether any of the circumstances set out in s.150(2)(b) apply.]

I make this Affidavit from facts within my own knowledge and belief save as where otherwise appears.

> SWORN by the said at in the City of this __ day of _____ 200_ before me a Commissioner for Oaths/a practising Solicitor and I know the Deponent

Filed this __ day of _____ 200_ by _____ Solicitors for the applicant

Chapter 19

CONSEQUENCES OF DECLARATIONS OF RESTRICTION

A. Period of restriction

[19.001] If a company goes into insolvent liquidation and restriction proceedings are taken against the company's directors, it is mandatory for a court to make the orders sought, unless the directors establish that they acted honestly and responsibly.[1] The consequences of an order of restriction are also mandatory. In particular, an order of restriction can only be made for a period of five years. The effect is that a restricted person is not generally permitted to act as a director or secretary or to take part in a company for a period of five years.[2] Section 150(1) provides:

> The court shall, unless it is satisfied as to any of the matters specified in sub-s (2), declare that a person to whom this Chapter applies shall not, for a period of five years, be appointed or act in any way, whether directly or indirectly, as a director or secretary or be concerned or take part in the promotion or formation of any company unless it meets the requirements set out in sub-s (3).[3]

It is evident from the terms of this provision that a court has no discretion whatsoever to impose a period of restriction of more or less than five years' duration.

[19.002] This point was noted by the High Court in *Business Communications v Baxter*.[4] Murphy J analysed the mandatory nature of s 150 in the following terms:

> '... the introductory words to s 150, that is to say, the phrase "the Court shall" are clearly mandatory and leave the Court with no discretion in those cases to which the Chapter applies unless the persons concerned establish that the case falls within one or other of the three exceptions set out in sub-s (2) of Section 150. Again it is notable that the period of restriction is a fixed period of five years and that, in the first instance at any rate, the Court has no discretion to impose a lesser restriction.'[5]

In a later passage of the judgment, Murphy J reiterated the mandatory period of restriction, stating:

> '[t]he mandatory duty to impose the restraint or declare it applicable for the full period of five years arises unless the Court is satisfied that the person concerned falls within one of the specified three exemptions.'[6]

---

[1] CA 1990, s 150(2). See further Ch **17**.

[2] This is subject to certain qualifications which are set out in CA 1990, s 150(3) and which are addressed below at paras **[19.010]** to **[19.015]**.

[3] CA 1990, s 150(1).

[4] *Business Communications v Baxter* (21 July 1995, unreported), HC, (Murphy J,).

[5] *Business Communications v Baxter* (21 July 1995, unreported), HC at p 5.

[6] *Business Communications v Baxter* (21 July 1995, unreported), HC at p 12.

The final comment made by Murphy J in *Business Communications v Baxter* in relation to the mandatory five year restriction period was that, 'I have some concern about the duration of the period of restraint and in general the lack of flexibility in the particular section'.[7]

[19.003] This feature of restriction orders can be contrasted with disqualification orders made under s 160. As noted by Murphy J in *Business Communications v Baxter*, the court has a discretion with regard to the imposition of disqualification orders.[8] In particular, the period of disqualification may be for such duration as the court sees fit.[9] There is no such discretion in relation to the making of declarations of restriction.

[19.004] It should be noted that the mandatory and intransigent nature of declarations of restriction may be tempered by a number of factors. First, a restriction order does not absolutely prevent a person from being involved in a company and, in particular, does not expressly preclude appointment to roles such as auditor, liquidator, examiner or receiver.[10] Secondly, a person who is subject to a declaration of restriction can act in relation to a company which is sufficiently capitalised, as stipulated in s 150, even during the currency of the restriction order.[11] Thirdly, a person in respect of whom a declaration of restriction is made can make an application under s 152 for relief against that order.[12]

B. Effect of declaration of restriction

[19.005] A person in respect of whom a declaration of restriction is made, cannot 'be appointed or act in any way, whether directly or indirectly, as a director or secretary or be concerned or take part in the promotion or formation of a company ...'.[13]

The effect of a declaration of restriction is therefore that the person against whom the order was made cannot be a company's director (which would include *de facto* and shadow directors), secretary or promoter. Moreover, a restricted person cannot take part in the promotion or formation of a company.

---

[7] *Business Communications v Baxter* (21 July 1995, unreported), HC at p 18.

[8] *Business Communications v Baxter* (21 July 1995, unreported), HC at p 12.

[9] See further Ch **23**.

[10] See further below paras **[19.005]** to **[19.006]**.

[11] CA 1990, s 150(3)(a), as amended by CLEA 2001, s 41(1). See further below paras **[19.010]** to **[19.015]**.

[12] CA 1990, s 152(1) accordingly provides, '(1) A person to whom s 150 applies may, within not more than one year after a declaration has been made in respect of him under that section, apply to the court for relief, either in whole or in part, from the restrictions referred to in that section or from any order made in relation to him under s 151 and the court may, if it deems it just and equitable to do so, grant such relief on whatever terms and conditions it sees fit.' See further paras **[17.076]** to **[17.080]**.

[13] CA 1990, s 150(1).

[19.006] There is a very noticeable distinction between the effect of a declaration of restriction and an order of disqualification. By contrast with the list of roles which a restricted person is precluded from occupying, a person who is disqualified cannot be appointed or act as any of the following: a director, auditor, liquidator, officer, receiver, or examiner.[14] A disqualified person is also precluded from being 'in any way, whether directly or indirectly, concerned or take part in the promotion, formation or management of any company…'.[15] The effect of a disqualification order is considerably more far-reaching than an order of restriction. This is particularly striking in light of the fact that a restricted person can act as a director, secretary, or otherwise take part in the promotion or formation of a company, if that company meets certain criteria.[16] There is no such limit to the effect of disqualification orders.

C. Notification and reporting requirements

(a) Restricted person's notification duty

[19.007] From the date that a declaration of restriction is made, the restricted person cannot accept appointment as a director or secretary of a company or otherwise be concerned or take part in the promotion or formation of a company, unless he has notified that company of the fact that he is a restricted person. CA 1990, s 155(5) provides:

> From the date of a declaration under s 150 a person in respect of whom the declaration was made shall not accept appointment to a position or act in any manner mentioned in sub-s (1) of this section in relation to a company unless he has, within the 14 days immediately preceding such appointment or so acting, sent to the registered office of the company a notification that he is a person to whom s 150 applies.[17]

(b) Liquidator's reporting duty

[19.008] In certain circumstances, a liquidator must immediately report the activities of a restricted person to court.[18] The first circumstance which triggers this obligation is that a restricted person is acting as a director or secretary of a company or otherwise taking part in the promotion or formation of a company, contrary to the declaration of restriction.[19] The second necessary circumstance is that the liquidator must be acting in respect of a company which is insolvent.[20] Thirdly, the liquidator must be of the opinion

---

14 See further Ch **23**.

15 CA 1990, s 160(1). See Ch **23**.

16 See below paras **[19.010]** to **[19.015]**.

17 CA 1990, s 150(5).

18 CA 1990, s 151(1). See further Ch **9**.

19 CA 1990, s 151(2).

20 CA 1990, s 151(1).

that 'the interests of any other company or its creditors may be placed in jeopardy' by the fact that the restricted person is acting in breach of the declaration of restriction.[21]

Where these circumstances arise, and the liquidator immediately makes the requisite report to court, the court may make such order as it sees fit.[22] If the liquidator fails to make the requisite report in these circumstances, he is guilty of an offence which is triable summarily or on indictment.[23]

D. Consequences for restricted companies

[19.009] A person who is subject to a declaration of restriction can be concerned or take part in the promotion or formation of a company or act as a company's director or secretary during the period of restriction, if certain conditions and requirements are met. It is the company which must satisfy these requirements. For the purposes of this section, these companies in relation to which restricted persons act, will be referred to as 'restricted companies'.

(a) Capital requirements

[19.010] The most important requirement which must be fulfilled before a restricted person can act as a director of a company is that the company must be capitalised to a particular extent. Section 150(3)(a) requires that:

 the nominal value of the allotted share capital of the company shall—

  (i) in the case of a public limited company, be at least £250,000,[24]

  (ii) in the case of any other company, be at least £50,000.[25]

CA 1990 moreover stipulates that the allotted shares which form the aggregate capital of the company for the purposes of s 150(3), must be fully paid up, including the entirety of any premium.[26] Each such share and premium must be paid for in cash.[27]

---

[21] CA 1990, s 151(1).

[22] CA 1990, s 151(1).

[23] CA 1990, s 151(3) provides, 'Any liquidator who contravenes sub-s (1) shall be guilty of an offence and shall be liable— (a) on summary conviction, to a fine not exceeding £1,000 and, for continued contravention, to a daily default fine not exceeding £50, or (b) on conviction on indictment, to a fine not exceeding £10,000 and, for continued contravention, to a daily default fine not exceeding £250'. The maximum fine on summary conviction has been increased to €1,904.61. See CA 1990, s 240(7), as amended by CLEA 2001, s 104(c). See Ch **9**.

[24] €317,435.

[25] €63,487. CA 1990, s 150(3)(a), as amended by CLEA 2001, s 41(1).

[26] CA 1990, s 150(3)(b) provides: 'each allotted share to an aggregate amount not less than the amount referred to in subparagraph (i) or (ii) of paragraph (a), as the case may be, shall be fully paid up, including the whole of any premium thereon …'.

[27] CA 1990, s 150(3)(c).

[19.011] If a restricted company allots a share which is not fully paid up, or which is not fully paid up in cash, as required by s 150(3)(b) and (c), the share is treated as if it were fully paid up. However, the person to whom the share was allotted is liable to pay the company in cash the full amount which should have been paid, together with interest.[28] The value of any consideration actually paid for the share is deducted from the amount of that liability.[29] Section 156(1) provides:

> Where a company to which s 155 applies allots a share which is not fully paid up as required by s 150(3)(b) the share shall be treated as if its nominal value together with the whole of any premium had been received, but the allottee shall be liable to pay the company in cash the full amount which should have been received in respect of the share under that subsection less the value of any consideration actually applied in payment up (to any extent) of the share and any premium on it, and interest at the appropriate rate on the amount payable under this subsection.[30]

[19.012] Section 156(2) governs the consequences of a breach of the requirement that the paid up shares must be paid up in cash and provides:

> Where a company to which s 155 applies allots a share which is not fully paid for in cash as required by s 150(3)(c) the allottee of the share shall be liable to pay the company in cash an amount equal to its nominal value, together with the whole of any premium, and shall be liable to pay interest at the appropriate rate on the amount payable under this subsection.[31]

There is no deduction allowed under this provision for non-cash consideration paid for the shares. It therefore appears that, where shares are allotted and paid up, other than in cash, contrary to s 150(3)(c), any non-cash consideration paid will not be deducted from the amount owing to the company. However, as noted by MacCann:

> 'In such circumstances he may apply to the court for relief pursuant to C(A)A 1983 s 34 as extended by CA 1990 s 155(3) … Presumably the court will grant relief on the basis that the non-cash consideration is independently valued and the allottee is only ordered to pay whatever cash balance is found to be due and owing after deduction of the independently valued non-cash consideration from the total price.'[32]

[19.013] Certain persons do not incur liability to pay the company the value of shares which are allotted and not paid up, contrary to s 150(3):

- Persons to whom bonus shares are allotted, who did not know the shares were not paid up as required by s 150(3);[33]

---

28 According to CA 1990, s 156(5), the rate of interest is that defined in C(A)A 1983, s 2, which is 'five per cent. *per* annum or such other rate as may be specified by order made by the Minister.'

29 CA 1990, s 156(1).

30 CA 1990, s 156(1).

31 CA 1990, s 156(2).

32 MacCann, *Companies Acts 1963–1990* (1993) at p 1009.

33 CA 1990, s 156(3).

   – Employees to whom shares are allotted in pursuance of an employees' share scheme;[34]

   – Persons who purchased shares for value from the original allottee without actual notice of the contravention of s 150(3); [35] and

   – Persons who, directly or indirectly, derived title to the non-paid up shares from a person who became the holder of those shares after the contravention of s 150(3) and who was not liable for that contravention.[36]

[19.014] The amount of paid up share capital which a company must have was increased by the CLEA 2001 from £100,000 in the case of public companies to £250,000 (€317,435) and from £20,000 for private limited companies to £50,000 (€63,487).[37] According to CA 1990, s 158, the Minister may also vary these amounts by order.[38] Such orders may include certain other requirements, such as a requirement that a company must increase its nominal share capital,[39] and may specify different amounts in relation to companies of different classes.[40]

[19.015] In *Business Communications v Baxter*,[41] Murphy J considered the effect of declarations of restriction and distinguished such orders from disqualifications orders made under s 160. He noted:

> 'It is hardly unreasonable to require a person who was a director of a failed company in respect of which he committed no misconduct but for which he neglected to exercise an appropriate degree of responsibility from resuming such an office in another company, again with the privilege of limited liability except on condition that a stipulated and not excessive sum was provided for the paid-up share capital thereof.'[42]

---

[34] CA 1990, s 156(4). 'Employees' share scheme' is defined in C(A)A 1983, s 2, as follows: 'any scheme for the time being in force, in accordance with which a company encourages or facilitates the holding of shares or debentures in the company or its holding company by or for the benefit of employees or former employees of the company or of any subsidiary of the company including any person who is or was a director holding a salaried employment or office in the company or any subsidiary of the company.'

[35] C(A)A 1983, s 26(4), as applied by CA 1990, s 156(6).

[36] C(A)A 1983, s 26(4), as applied by CA 1990, s 156(6).

[37] CA 1990, s 150(3), as amended by CLEA 2001, s 41(1).

[38] CA 1990, s 158. The CLRG recommends that the capital requirements should be that a public limited company have €350,000 in par value of allotted share capital, and that any other company should have an allotted share capital of a par value of €70,000. General Scheme of the Draft Companies Consolidation and Reform Bill 2007, Pt A13, Head 32(4). Available at www.clrg.org.

[39] CA 1990, s 158(a).

[40] CA 1990, s 158(c).

[41] *Business Communications v Baxter* (21 July 1995, unreported), HC.

[42] *Business Communications v Baxter* (21 July 1995, unreported), HC at p 14.

The Court considered the amount of the paid-up capital requirement which, at the time, was £20,000 and observed, 'The figure of £20,000 must represent a very modest sum as the capital for any commercial enterprise and a very limited obstacle to anyone wishing to engage in trade through the medium of a limited liability company.' The Court went one step further in this regard, noting, 'it might not be unreasonable to suggest that every limited liability company should be required to have paid up capital of at least that amount.' This comment illustrates that the capitalisation requirement imposed on restricted companies is not as prohibitive or exacting as the legislature may have intended. While the thresholds have been increased by the CLEA 2001, a capital requirement of €63,487 for a private limited company is nonetheless a modest requirement and one which is unlikely to impede many restricted directors from continuing to act, or to provide adequate protection of all creditors of 'restricted companies'.

(b) Limitations on a restricted company

[19.016] A restricted company is subject to particular rules, which do not apply to private companies generally. CA 1990, s 155 provides that restricted companies cannot avail of certain exceptions and exemptions from provisions of the Companies Acts of which other companies can avail.

(i) Funding purchase of company's shares

[19.017] There is a general prohibition in the Companies Acts against companies funding the purchase of their shares.[43] The relevant provision, CA 1963, s 60, can be broadly summarised as prohibiting any company from giving any financial assistance, direct or indirect, in connection with the purchase of, or subscription for, the company's shares.[44]

Despite this overall prohibition, s 60 does prescribe a 'whitewash' procedure which, if followed by a company, would allow the company to fund the purchase of its own shares. This procedures involves the following:

- The directors must issue a statutory declaration stating the form and purpose of the financial assistance, the persons to whom such assistance is to be given;[45]
- The statutory declaration must state that the directors have made a full inquiry into the affairs of the company and have formed the opinion that, after the transaction, the company will be able to pay its debts in full as they become due;[46]

---

[43] See generally Courtney, *The Law of Private Companies* (2nd edn, Tottel Publishing, 2002) at paras 18.041 to 18.075.

[44] CA 1963, s 160(1) provides: 'it shall not be lawful for a company to give, whether directly or indirectly, and whether by means of a loan, guarantee, the provision of security or otherwise, any financial assistance for the purpose of or in connection with a purchase or subscription made or to be made by any person of or for any shares in the company, or, where the company is a subsidiary company, in its holding company.'

[45] CA 1963, s 60(2)–(4), as amended by CLEA 2001, s 89.

[46] CA 1963, s 60(2)–(4), as amended by CLEA 2001, s 89.

- This declaration must be made at a meeting of the directors held within 24 days before a special meeting of the members;[47]

- A copy of this declaration must be sent to the company's members together with a notice of that special meeting;[48]

- At the special meeting of the members, which must be held within 12 months before the financial assistance is provided, the members must pass a special resolution authorising the assistance.[49]

A restricted company does not have the right to avail of this authorisation procedure and, subject to the limited exemptions provided in s 60(13),[50] it is not permissible for a restricted company to fund the purchase of its own shares.

(ii) Loans to directors

[19.018] The Companies Acts prohibit the extension of any credit by a company to its directors or persons connected with its directors, whether by means of loans, quasi-loans, credit transactions, guarantees, the provision of security, or any arrangements to the same effect.[51]

---

[47] CA 1963, s 60(3).

[48] CA 1963, s 60(2), as amended by CLEA 2001, s 89.

[49] CA 1963, s 60(2), as amended by CLEA 2001, s 89.

[50] CA 1963, s 60(13) provides: 'Nothing in this section shall be taken to prohibit – (a) where the lending of money is part of the ordinary business of the company, the lending of money by the company in the ordinary course of its business; (b) the provision by a company, in accordance with any scheme for the time being in force, of money for the purchase of, or subscription for, fully paid shares in the company or its holding company, being a purchase or subscription of or for shares to be held by or for the benefit of employees or former employees of the company or of any subsidiary of the company including any person who is or was a director holding a salaried employment or office in the company or any subsidiary of the company; (c) the making by a company of loans to persons, other than directors, *bona fide* in the employment of the company or any subsidiary of the company with a view to enabling those persons to purchase or subscribe for fully paid shares in the company or its holding company to be held by themselves as beneficial owners thereof.'

[51] CA 1990, s 31 provides, '(1) … a company shall not—(a) make a loan or a quasi-loan to a director of the company or of its holding company or to a person connected with such a director; (b) enter into a credit transaction as creditor for such a director or a person so connected; (c) enter into a guarantee or provide any security in connection with a loan, quasi-loan or credit transaction made by any other person for such a director or a person so connected. (2) A company shall not arrange for the assignment to it or the assumption by it of any rights, obligations or liabilities under a transaction which, if it had been entered into by the company, would have contravened sub-s (1); but for the purposes of this Part the transaction shall be treated as having been entered into on the date of the arrangement. (3) A company shall not take part in any arrangement whereby— (a) another person enters into a transaction which, if it had been entered into by the company, would have contravened sub-s (1) or (2); and (b) that other person, in pursuance of the arrangement, has obtained or is to obtain any benefit from the company or its holding company or a subsidiary of the company or its holding company.' See Ch **6**. See generally Courtney, *The Law of Private Companies* (2nd edn, Tottel Publishing, 2002) at paras 11.051 to 11.114.

There are certain exceptions to this general prohibition. These can be summarised as follows:

- A credit arrangement with a director is not prohibited, if the value of the arrangement, together with the total value of any amounts outstanding under other such arrangements, is less than ten per cent of the company's relevant assets;[52]

- A credit arrangement between companies which are members of the same group will not be prohibited on the sole ground that a director of one member of the group is connected with another;[53]

- A credit arrangement in favour of a company's holding company is not prohibited;[54]

- It is not forbidden for a company to provide funds to a director to meet vouched expenses properly incurred or to be incurred for the purposes of the company, or to avoid such expenses, but any liability of any person arising from that funding must be discharged within six months;[55]

- A company is permitted to enter credit arrangements if the company does so in the ordinary course of its business and the arrangement is not of higher value or on more favourable terms, than is reasonable or usual for the company to offer to a person who is unconnected with the company.[56]

A restricted company is not entitled to avail of all of these exemptions. Section 155(4) provides, '[w]ithout prejudice to s 39, ss 32 and 37 shall not apply to any company to which sub-s (1) applies.'[57]

CA 1990, s 32 is the provision which permits a company to enter into a credit arrangement, if the value of the arrangement, together with the total value of any amounts outstanding under other such arrangements, is less than ten per cent of the company's relevant assets.[58] Section 37 permits a company to enter into credit arrangements with its directors, if it does so in the ordinary course of its business, and

---

[52] CA 1990, s 32(2). 'Relevant assets' are defined in CA 1990, s 29(2) as follows: '(a) except in a case falling within *paragraph (b)*, the value of its net assets determined by reference to the accounts prepared and laid in accordance with the requirements of section 148 of the Principal Act in respect of the last preceding financial year in respect of which such accounts were so laid; (b) where no accounts have been prepared and laid under that section before that time, the amount of its called-up share capital.' See CA 1990, s 32(b).

[53] CA 1990, s 34.

[54] CA 1990, s 35.

[55] CA 1990, s 36(1)–(2). Note that it is an offence to fail to discharge that liability within six months (CA 1990, s 36(3)).

[56] CA 1990, s 37.

[57] CA 1990, s 155(4).

[58] CA 1990, s 32(1).

on its usual terms.[59] A restricted company cannot enter either of these categories of arrangements.

The reference in s 155(4) to s 39 is perplexing. CA 1990, s 39 essentially provides that, where a credit arrangement is entered into under s 32, which materially contributes to the company's insolvency and substantially impedes the orderly winding up of the company, the court may declare that the beneficiary of the credit arrangement should be personally liable for all or part of the company's debts and liabilities.[60] If a restricted company is not entitled to avail of s 32, there will be no means by which the provisions of s 39 could come into effect. There is no logical reason why the fact ss 32 and 37 do not apply to restricted companies, should be 'without prejudice to s 39.'

The effect which s 155(4) has on restricted companies is that a restricted company, unlike all other companies, cannot enter into a credit arrangement with any director, or person connected with a director, even if the value of the arrangement is less than ten per cent of the company's assets, and even if the company enters such arrangements in the ordinary course of its business.

If a company contravenes s 31, the transaction or arrangement may be voidable at the instance of the company[61] and the director may be liable to account to the company for any gain which he made from the transaction or arrangement and to indemnify the company for any loss suffered as a result of the transaction or arrangement.[62] In addition, pursuant to s 40, if an officer of a company authorised or permitted a company to enter into an arrangement or transaction in breach of s 31, knowing, or having reasonable cause to believe that it was such a violation, he shall be guilty of an offence.[63] Similarly, it is an offence for any person to procure a company to enter into such a transaction or arrangement with knowledge or cause to believe it was a contravention of s 31.[64]

---

[59]   CA 1990, s 37(1).

[60]   CA 1990, s 39(1).

[61]   CA 1990, s 38(1). The transaction is not voidable in the following circumstances as set out in s 38(1): '(a) restitution of any money or any other asset which is the subject matter of the arrangement or transaction is no longer possible, or the company has been indemnified in pursuance of sub-s (2)(b) for the loss or damage suffered by it; or (b) any rights acquired *bona fide* for value and without actual notice of the contravention by any person other than the person for whom the transaction or arrangement was made would be affected by its avoidance.'

[62]   CA 1990, s 38(2). This is subject to the following exception, as set out in s 38(3): 'Where an arrangement or transaction is entered into by a company and a person connected with a director of the company or its holding company in contravention of *section 31* that director shall not be liable under sub-s (2) if he shows that he took all reasonable steps to secure the company's compliance with that section and, in any case, a person so connected and any such other director as is mentioned in the said sub-s (2) shall not be so liable if he shows that, at the time the arrangement or transaction was entered into, he did not know the relevant circumstances constituting the contravention.'

[63]   CA 1990, s 40(1).

[64]   CA 1990, s 40(2).

(iii) Consideration for transfer of non-cash assets by members

[19.019] Another effect of a company having on its board of directors a restricted person is that C(A)A 1983, ss 32–36, which generally only apply to public companies, will also apply to such companies.

A company to which ss 32–36 applies is not permitted to enter into an agreement for the transfer of non-cash assets by a member, director or any person involved in the promotion or formation of the company, for consideration which equals one-tenth or more of the nominal value of the company's issued share capital.[65]

This prohibition does not apply if the asset in question and any non-cash consideration are valued by a report of an independent person[66] within the preceding six months and the terms of the agreement have been approved by an ordinary resolution of the company, the notice of which was accompanied by a copy of the report and the resolution.[67] Within 15 days of passing such a resolution, the company must deliver a copy of it to the Registrar of Companies, together with the independent valuation report.[68]

The prohibition is also inapplicable where the transaction is part of the company's ordinary business and where the agreement is entered under the supervision of the court or an authorised officer of the court.[69]

(c) Relief for a restricted company

[19.020] If there was a violation of a provision of the Companies Acts, by means of s 155, the court may grant relief to the company or person adversely affected, if the court deems it just and equitable to do so, and on such terms and conditions as the court considers fit.[70] The court is expressly empowered to grant exemption from any such provision.

---

[65] C(A)A 1983, s 32(1), as applied by CA 1990, s 155(3).

[66] See C(A)A 1983, s 32(5)–(6). Section 32(6) provides, '(6) The report of the independent person under this section shall— (a) state the consideration to be received by the company, describing the asset in question, specifying the amount to be received in cash, and the consideration to be given by the company, specifying the amount to be given in cash; (b) state the method and date of valuation; (c) contain or be accompanied by a note as to the matters mentioned in s 30(8)(a) to (c); and (d) contain or be accompanied by a note that on the basis of the valuation the value of the consideration to be received by the company is not less than the value of the consideration to be given by it.'

[67] C(A)A 1983, s 32(3)(a).

[68] C(A)A 1983, s 33(2). If the company fails to do this, 'the company and every officer of the company who is in default shall be liable on summary conviction to a fine not exceeding £250 together with, in the case of a continuing offence, a fine not exceeding £25 for every day on which the offence continues, but not exceeding £500 in total' (C(A)A 1983, s 33(2)). The maximum fine on a summary conviction was increased from £250 to £1,500 (€1,904.61) by the CLEA 2001, s 104(1), inserting CA 1990, s 240(7).

[69] C(A)A 1983, s 32(4)(a)–(b).

[70] CA 1990, s 157(1).

The exercise of this power to grant relief may be warranted where the company or officer who was in violation of s 60, for example, may not have realised that a director of the company was restricted, or that a company with a restricted director was not permitted to avail of the statutory declaration procedure of s 60(2).

It should be noted that the court is not permitted to grant relief where the restricted person notified the company of the fact of his restriction as required by s 155(5).[71] It should also be noted that there is nothing in s 157 regarding the means by which such an application may come before the court or the grounds on which the court's determination may be made. However, the fact that notification by the restricted person, eliminates the possibility of a company obtaining relief, may be an indication that the lack of such a notification would be a ground for seeking relief under s 157. This would be a fair outcome, as a company should not be held liable for a breach of the Companies Acts, where it was not aware of the essential fact which caused its actions to constitute a breach of the Acts.

There are particular consequences of a company continuing to carry on business, and failing to meet the capitalisation requirements of s 150(3) within a reasonable period after receiving a notification under s 155(5). If such a company is subsequently wound up without being able to pay its debts as they fall due, its officers who knew or ought to have known of the notification under s 155(5), may be made personally responsible for the debts of the company.[72]

E. Register of restricted persons

[19.021] Where a declaration of restriction is made, a prescribed officer of the court is obliged to cause the Registrar of Companies to be notified of certain particulars. The officers prescribed for the purpose of s 150 are the examiner and the registrars of the High Court[73] and the particulars which must be notified are essentially the fact of restriction; the company in relation to which the application for a declaration of restriction was made; the name, address and date of birth of the restricted person; and any relief which has been granted.[74]

Having been notified of the prescribed particulars of restriction, the Registrar of Companies is obliged to maintain a register of these particulars.[75] If partial relief is granted under s 152, the particulars of this relief must be included on the register.[76] In the event of full relief being granted to a restricted person, the Registrar must remove all particulars regarding that person from the register as soon as possible.[77] Finally, the Registrar of Companies is obliged to remove from the register any particulars regarding

---

[71] CA 1990, s 157(2). See further above para **[19.007]**.

[72] CA 1990, s 163(3).

[73] Companies Act 1990 (Pts IV and VII) Regulations, 1991 (SI 209/1991), reg 3(1).

[74] Companies Act 1990 (Pts IV and VII) Regulations, 1991 (SI 209/1991), Sch.

[75] CA 1990, s 153(1).

[76] CA 1990, s 153(2).

[77] CA 1990, s 153(3).

a restricted person at the expiry of five years from the date of the declaration of restriction.[78] At the end of 2006, there were 691 names on the register of restricted persons.[79]

[19.022] In real terms, the effect of a declaration of restriction is relatively easily overcome.[80] One of the effects of restriction which is not so easily overcome, however, is the stigma which attaches to a director being subject to a court order that he should not be involved in companies. This was noted by Murphy J in *Business Communications v Baxter*.[81] Murphy J considered the nature of a declaration of restriction and the consequences of such a declaration. Having described the capitalisation requirement imposed on restricted companies as 'very modest',[82] he went on to observe, 'It would seem that the more serious penalty which the restraining order imposes is the stigma which attaches as a result of the making of the Order and its filing in the Companies Office.'[83]

The fact that a publicly accessible register is kept with particulars of declarations of restriction and the persons against whom they are made, may be a real deterrent, particularly as the DCE is now increasingly publicising the making of such restriction orders.

F. Breach of declaration of restriction

[19.023] There are several potential repercussions for a person who acts in contravention of a declaration of restriction. First, a person who is subject to a declaration of restriction and acts in a manner contrary to that order, is guilty of an offence. CA 1990, s 161(1), provides:

> Any person who, in relation to any company, acts in a manner or capacity which,
> by virtue of being a person to whom s 150 applies or being subject or deemed to
> be subject to a disqualification order, he is prohibited from doing shall be guilty of
> an offence.[84]

A number of individuals have been convicted of acting contrary to declarations of restriction.[85]

---

[78] CA 1990, s 153(4).

[79] CRO, *Annual Report 2006*, at p 28. Available at www.cro.ie.

[80] See further above paras **[19.010]** to **[19.015]**.

[81] *Business Communications v Baxter* (21 July 1995, unreported), HC.

[82] *Business Communications v Baxter* (21 July 1995, unreported), HC at p 14. See further above para **[19.015]**.

[83] *Business Communications v Baxter* (21 July 1995, unreported), HC at p 14.

[84] CA 1990, s 161(1).

[85] Eg, in *ODCE v O'Donohue* (6 December 2005, unreported), Swords District Court, the defendant pleaded guilty to a charge of acting as a director while restricted contrary to s 161(1) and was convicted. The defendant was fined €1,500, ordered to pay prosecution costs of €250, and a six-month term of imprisonment suspended for 24 months was imposed. (conts .../)

Second, if convicted of the offence of acting in a 'manner or capacity' which is prohibited, the restricted person shall be deemed to be subject to a disqualification order from the date of that conviction.[86] Third, the company in relation to which the restricted person acted may recover from him as a simple contract debt in any court, any consideration that was paid to him for acts or services performed when he was restricted.[87] Fourth, if that company goes into liquidation, within 12 months of the restricted person acting in a prohibited manner, the court may declare him personally liable for the debts incurred by the company during the period in which he so acted.[88]

G. Costs

[19.024] The award of costs in restriction proceedings has been a somewhat vexed issue. Before the enactment of the CLEA 2001, there was no specific provision governing the award of costs in such proceedings. The general discretion of the High Court to award costs, as enshrined in O 99, r 1 of the Rules of the Superior Courts, therefore applied:

> Subject to the provisions of the Acts and any other statutes relating to costs and except as otherwise provided by these Rules:
>
> (1) The costs of and incidental to every proceeding in the Superior Courts shall be in the discretion of those Courts respectively.
>
> (2) No party shall be entitled to recover any costs of or incidental to any proceeding from any other party to such proceeding except under an order or as provided by these Rules.
>
> (3) ...
>
> (4) The costs of every issue of fact or law raised upon a claim or counterclaim shall, unless otherwise ordered, follow the event.[89]

Section 150(4B) was then introduced, providing that:

> The court, in hearing an application for a declaration under sub-s (1) from the Director, a liquidator or a receiver, may order that the directors against whom the declaration is made shall bear the costs of the application and any costs incurred by the applicant in investigating the matter.[90]

---

[85] (contd) The defendant was also made subject to a deemed order of disqualification. See also *ODCE v Scanlon* (20 December 2005, unreported), Dunshaughlin District Court in which one defendant was convicted under s 161(1) on 8 counts of acting as a director or secretary contrary to an order of restriction and fined a total of almost €8,000. See www.odce.ie.

[86] CA 1990, s 161(2). See further Ch **20**. It should also be noted that if a restricted person is a director of a company (Company A) which commences to be wound up within five years of the commencement of the winding up of the company in connection with which he was restricted (Company B), and it appears to the liquidator that Company A is unable to pay its debts as they fall due, the liquidator must report this to the court and the court may make a disqualification order in respect of that person. See CA 1990, s 161(5).

[87] CA 1990, s 163(2).

[88] CA 1990, s 163(3).

[89] RSC (SI 15/1986), O 99, r 1.

[90] CA 1990, s 150(4B), as inserted by CLEA 2001, s 41(1).

This jurisdiction to award costs was considered not to be vastly different to the general power of a court to make an award of costs.[91] In line with recommendations submitted by the ODCE, the IFCMPA 2006 replaced s 150(4B) with the more extensive power to award the costs of collecting evidence, investigating, and prosecuting, restriction proceedings.[92] Section 150(4B) now provides:

> The court, on the hearing of an application for a declaration under sub-s (1) by the Director, a liquidator or a receiver (in this subsection referred to as the 'applicant'), may order that the directors against whom the declaration is made shall bear—
>
> (a) the costs of the application, and
>
> (b) the whole (or such portion of them as the court specifies) of the costs and expenses incurred by the applicant—
>
> > (i) in investigating the matters the subject of the application, and
> >
> > (ii) in so far as they do not fall within paragraph (a), in collecting evidence in respect of those matters, including so much of the remuneration and expenses of the applicant as are attributable to such investigation and collection.[93]

[19.025] In *Re Tipperary Fresh Foods Ltd*[94] Finlay Geoghegan J considered the retrospective effect of s 150(4B), as originally enacted. The Court noted that s 150(4B) imposed a new monetary obligation on the respondents and that exposure to the costs of investigating an application was not merely a change of a procedural nature. The Court also noted that s 150(4B) was not in force when the winding up of the company commenced, which was the date on which respondents became potentially liable under

---

[91] See *dicta* of Finlay Geoghegan J in relation to the comparable provision governing disqualification proceedings, s 160(9B) in *Re Clawhammer Ltd, Director of Corporate Enforcement v McDonnell; Re Shinrone Food Market Ltd, Director of Corporate Enforcement v Hoctor; Re Cautious Trading Ltd, Director of Corporate Enforcement v Forristal* (15 March 2005, unreported), HC (Finlay Geoghegan J): 'It is difficult to understand the purpose of s 160(9B) insofar as it gives to the court a power to make an order for the costs of the application against a person in respect of whom a disqualification order or declaration of restriction is made. This appears to be a power which the court already had under Order 99 of the Rules of the Superior Courts 1986. However there is no indication that such power is to be exercised in any different way to the existing power under Order 99. In accordance with Order 99 where, as in these three cases, the applications were successful an order for costs in favour of the Director would ordinarily follow unless the court in its discretion considers that the interests of justice require a different order.'

[92] See ODCE, *Annual Report 2006* at p 9, where the ODCE describes submissions it made to the Department regarding the proposed IFCMPA 2006, including a proposal for 'an amendment of the law in relation to the recovery of legal costs in disqualification or restriction proceedings so that it permitted not just the legal costs of the proceedings to be recovered but also the associated costs of investigation from the disqualified or restricted person'.

[93] CA 1990, s 150(4B), as inserted by CLEA 2001, s 41(1), as substituted by IFCMPA 2006, s 11.

[94] *Re Tipperary Fresh Foods Ltd, O'Riordan v O'Connor* [2005] IEHC 96.

s 150. The presumption against retrospective effect would therefore have prevented the application of s 150(4B) to the restriction proceedings under consideration. That presumption did not resolve the matter, however. The terms of CLEA 2001, s 41, in the judgment of the Court, demonstrated the intention of the legislature that s 150(4B) should have retrospective effect and should apply to companies the winding up of which commenced before s 41 came into effect.

> 'Accordingly, I have concluded, notwithstanding that the presumption against retrospectivity applies to s 41 of the Act of 2001 inserting s 150(4B) to the Act of 1990 insofar as it authorises the court to make an order against respondent directors for the costs incurred by the applicant in investigating the matter that the Oireachtas has clearly and unequivocally in the terms of s 41 of the Act of 2001 declared its intention that such section should take effect retrospectively in the sense of applying to a liquidation which commenced prior to the coming into operation of s 41 of the Act of 2001.'

[19.026] On the authority of *Re Tipperary Fresh Foods Ltd*[95] there must be a presumption that s 150(4B), as substituted by IFCMPA 2006, does not have retrospective effect. Like its predecessor, it imposes a new monetary obligation on a respondent, namely the obligation to pay the costs of collecting evidence, and the remuneration and expenses of an applicant, as well as the costs of investigating the application and the costs of the application itself. By contrast with CLEA 2001, s 41, there is nothing in IFCMPA 2006, s 11, to indicate that it is intended to have retrospective effect. There is certainly no clear and unequivocal declaration of such intention, as relied upon in *Re Tipperary Fresh Foods Ltd*.[96] IFCMPA 2006, s 11, was commenced by the IFCMPA 2006 (Commencement) Order 2007 on 29 January 2007. The changes it introduces to s 150(4B) will only apply to liquidations which commence after that date.

[19.027] There are a number of matters to note about the terms of s 150(4B) as it (and its predecessor) have been interpreted by the High Court, which will be examined under the following headings:

(a)   Costs recoverable under s 150(4B);

(b)   Costs of unsuccessful applications;

(c)   Order of costs in favour of respondent;

(d)   Applicant's liability for costs;

(e)   Recovery of costs in winding up; and

(f)   Notice party costs order.

(a) Costs recoverable under s 150(4B)

[19.028] Section 150(4B)[97] provides that the court 'may' make an order of costs: this is similar to the general discretion of the High Court to make an order of costs under O 99,

---

[95]   *Re Tipperary Fresh Foods Ltd, O'Riordan v O'Connor* [2005] IEHC 96.

[96]   *Re Tipperary Fresh Foods Ltd, O'Riordan v O'Connor* [2005] IEHC 96.

[97]   CA 1990, s 150(4B), as inserted by CLEA 2001, s 41(1).

r 1. There are three categories of costs which an applicant for a restriction order may recover:

(a)   the costs of the application;

(b)   the costs and expenses of investigating the matters the subject of the application, including the applicant's remuneration and expenses;

(c)   the costs and expenses of collecting evidence in respect of those matters, including the applicant's remuneration and expenses.

Insofar as s 150(4B) refers to the 'costs of the application', this is a discretion which the court may have exercised under O 99, r 1. The High Court confirmed in *Re Visual Impact and Displays Ltd*[98] and in *Re GMT Engineering Services Ltd*[99] that, insofar as s 150(4B) refers to the power of the court to award the costs of the application, it adds nothing to O 99, r 1:

> 'This appears to be a power which the court already had under Order 99 of the Rules of the Superior Courts 1986. However there is no indication that such power is to be exercised in any different way to the existing power under Order 99.'[100]

[19.029] Under s 150(4B), however, the court may also order the restricted person to pay the whole or a portion of the applicant's costs and expenses of collecting evidence and investigating the relevant matters, including his remuneration and expenses of such investigation and collection. This is broader than the power conferred by O 99, r 1 to order costs 'incidental to' the application for a declaration of restriction. This enhancement of the court's powers was confirmed by the High Court in *Re Tipperary Fresh Foods Ltd*[101] as follows:

> 'It is common case that the costs of investigation now sought would not come within the ambit of an order for costs made under O 99 of the Superior Court Rules. Hence … the court could not have made an order that they pay to the Official Liquidator the costs of his investigating the matters raised in the s 150

---

[98]   *Re Visual Impact and Displays Ltd, Murphy v Murphy* [2003] IEHC 91.

[99]   *Re GMT Engineering Services Limited (in voluntary liquidation) Luby v McMahon and Anor* [2003] 4 IR 133.

[100] See *dicta* of Finlay Geoghegan J in relation to the comparable provision governing disqualification proceedings, s 160(9B) in *Re Clawhammer Ltd, Director of Corporate Enforcement v McDonnell; Re Shinrone Food Market Ltd, Director of Corporate Enforcement v Hoctor; Re Cautious Trading Ltd, Director of Corporate Enforcement v Forristal* [2005] IEHC 15 (15 March, 2005, unreported), HC.

[101] *Re Tipperary Fresh Foods Ltd, O'Riordan v O'Connor* [2005] IEHC 96. That case concerned the retrospectivity of CA 1990, s 150(4B). The Court concluded that: '… notwithstanding that the presumption against retrospectivity applies to s 41 of the Act of 2001 inserting s 150(4B) to the Act of 1990 insofar as it authorises the court to make an order against respondent directors for the costs incurred by the applicant in investigating the matter that the Oireachtas has clearly and unequivocally in the terms of s 41 of the Act of 2001 declared its intention that such section should take effect retrospectively in the sense of applying to a liquidation which commenced prior to the coming into operation of s 41 of the Act of 2001.'

application. Section 150(4B) has now given the court such power where it makes a declaration of restriction.'[102]

That case concerned s 150(4B) as it existed before the IFCMPA 2006. The breadth of the court's power to award costs is more pronounced since then and further exceeds the jurisdiction which the court may otherwise have exercised under O 99.

[19.030] Certain questions have arisen regarding the scope of the costs which may be recovered under s 150(4B).[103] In *Re Mitek Holdings Ltd*[104] the issue was whether the phrase 'any costs incurred by the applicant in investigating the matter', as it appeared in s 150(4B) before the enactment of IFCMPA 2006, included the liquidator's remuneration for time spent investigating the matters involved in the restriction application and reporting to the ODCE on these matters pursuant to CLEA 2001, s 56. The Court held that s 150(4B) did not include the amounts charged by the liquidator for the investigative work done, as those amounts could not be regarded as 'costs incurred by the applicant'. To be 'incurred by' the liquidator, the costs would have to be sums payable to a third party. The liquidator's remuneration did not come within this category. As s 150(4B) imposes a pecuniary burden on respondents, 'the intent of the Oireachtas as to the burden to be imposed must be clear and unequivocal'. Finlay Geoghegan J found that there was no clear and unequivocal intention to impose a burden for costs which would include the liquidator's remuneration.

This position has been reversed by IFCMPA 2006: s 150(4B) now expressly includes 'so much of the remuneration and expenses of the applicant as are attributable to such investigation and collection'.[105]

[19.031] The recovery of legal costs was considered in *Re Moypool Ltd*.[106] The applicant claimed legal costs that were incurred in investigating the matters under consideration in the restriction proceedings. The respondent contended that the

---

[102] See also *Re GMT Engineering Services Limited (in voluntary liquidation) Luby v McMahon and Anor* [2003] 4 IR 133 at 139: 'Insofar as s 150(4B) authorises the court to make an order that restricted directors bear 'any costs incurred by the applicant in investigating the matter', it is conferring an additional jurisdiction and discretion on the court over and above that contained in O. 99, r. 1.'

[103] Many of the decisions considered in this regard concern s 150(4B) as it existed before the enactment of IFCMPA 2006. The principal change introduced by IFCMPA 2006, s 11, is the inclusion of the power to award costs of collecting evidence, including remuneration and expenses. It may be expected that the analysis that has been applied to the court's discretion to order payment of the costs of investigating an application will also be applied to the costs of collecting evidence.

[104] *Re Mitek Holdings Ltd, Grace v Kachkar* [2005] IEHC 160. See also *Re Tipperary Fresh Foods Ltd, O'Riordan v O'Connor* [2005] IEHC 153.

[105] CA 1990, s 150(4B), as inserted by CLEA 2001, s 41(1), as substituted by IFCMPA 2006, s 11.

[106] *Re Moypool Ltd, Gannon v O'Hora* [2006] IEHC 149.

liquidator could only recover costs incurred in litigation and not costs incurred outside the context of litigation. This submission was rejected:

> 'The intention of the Oireachtas as indicated by the words used in the subsection appears to be that the Court has jurisdiction to make an order that a director against whom a declaration has been made, pay to an applicant liquidator not only the costs of the application but also costs incurred by the liquidator in investigating those matters which were the subject matter of the s 150 application. There is no warrant in the words used in s 150(4B) for confining such costs of investigation to costs incurred in litigation.'[107]

[19.032] Two more general issues regarding the award of costs under s 150(4B) also arose in *Re Moypool Ltd*.[108] First, the respondent claimed that, in order to recover investigative costs, the applicant must prove that these costs claimed were necessary to the proceedings and would not have been otherwise incurred in the liquidation. Finlay Geoghegan J considered the general rule applicable to the taxation of costs, as set out in O 99, r 10(2):

> 'costs to which this rule applies shall be taxed on the party and party basis, and on a taxation on that basis there shall be allowed all such costs as were necessary or proper for the attainment of justice or for enforcing or defending the rights of the party whose costs are being taxed'.

Applying this rule to investigative costs, Finlay Geoghegan J determined that:

> 'By analogy it appears to me that the intention of the Oireachtas must be construed as being that where the Court makes an order for the costs of investigating the matter there be allowable "all such costs as were necessary or proper for the investigation of the application under s 150".'

Legal costs for work done at the request of the liquidator in relation to investigating the restriction proceedings, were, according to the Court, *prima facie* within the scope of this test. Any dispute in this regard could be resolved on taxation.

This case confirms that the test for awarding investigative costs arising from a restriction application, as well as the costs of the application itself, is whether the costs are 'necessary or proper.'

[19.033] The second general point raised in *Re Moypool Ltd*[109] relates to the exercise of the court's discretion in relation to costs. The respondent argued that, as there was no finding of dishonesty, the Court should exercise its discretion and refuse to make an award of costs. Rejecting this contention, Finlay Geoghegan J considered the alternative outcome:

> 'Insofar as the solicitors for the liquidator carried out work which may be considered (upon taxation if necessary) to have been necessary or proper for the investigation of the subject matter of the application under s 150 of the Act of 1990, then it appears to me on the facts herein such costs should be borne by the

---

[107] *Re Moypool Ltd, Gannon v O'Hora* [2006] IEHC 149.

[108] *Re Moypool Ltd, Gannon v O'Hora* [2006] IEHC 149.

[109] *Re Moypool Ltd, Gannon v O'Hora* [2006] IEHC 149.

first named respondent and not by either the liquidator personally or, if there are funds in the liquidation, the creditors of the liquidation.'[110]

The absence of a finding that a respondent was dishonest in an application under s 150, is not therefore a ground for refusing to award costs in favour of the applicant.

(b) Costs of unsuccessful applications

[19.034] Section 150(4B)[111] provides that the court may order 'the directors against whom the declaration is made', to pay the applicant's costs. This reference indicates clearly that it is only when a declaration of restriction is made, that the discretion to award costs under s 150(4B) arises. A related issue is whether the applicant can recover costs under O 99 in a case in which no declaration of restriction is made.

[19.035] Before the commencement of s 150(4B), the practice adopted by the High Court was to order directors to make a contribution towards the costs of restriction proceedings, even in cases in which a declaration of restriction was refused. The High Court described this practice in *Re GMT Engineering Services Ltd*:[112]

'In many applications, where the court was satisfied that a declaration of restriction should not be made, it nevertheless ordered that the respondent directors should make a contribution in a measured sum to the official liquidator's costs of the application. This was in exercise of the court's discretion under O 99, r 1. The reasoning of the court, insofar as I made such orders (and I understand also it was the reasoning of my colleagues who so decided), was that, because of the mandatory wording of s 150(1) and the onus placed on the directors thereunder, it was an inevitable consequence of being a director (within 12 months of the commencement of winding-up) of an insolvent company in liquidation that the issue as to whether a declaration of restriction should be made would come before the High Court. Further, if the respondent director did not make a contribution towards the official liquidator's costs of the application, the reality was that, in an insolvent liquidation where funds were available, such costs were borne by the creditors or, if there were no funds, by the official liquidator and/or his lawyers. On balance, it appeared just and equitable, having regard to the intent of the legislation and, in particular, the absence of any mechanism for avoiding the matter coming before the High Court, to require, in certain applications, the respondent directors either to make a contribution to the costs or to bear all the costs of the official liquidator of the application, rather than effectively imposing them on the creditors or the official liquidator.'[113]

[19.036] In *Re GMT Engineering Services Ltd*,[114] the applicant sought to recover costs against the respondent directors after the court refused to make the declarations of restriction sought. This raised the issue of whether s 150(4B) limited the court's

---

[110] *Re Moypool Ltd, Gannon v O'Hora* [2006] IEHC 149.

[111] CA 1990, s 150(4B), as inserted by CLEA 2001, s 41(1).

[112] *Re GMT Engineering Services Limited (in voluntary liquidation) Luby v McMahon and Anor* [2003] 4 IR 133.

[113] *Re GMT Engineering Services Limited (in voluntary liquidation) Luby v McMahon and Anor* [2003] 4 IR 133 at 136 to 137.

[114] *Re GMT Engineering Services Limited (in voluntary liquidation) Luby v McMahon and Anor* [2003] 4 IR 133.

discretion to make such orders under O 99, r 1. The Court considered the principle that statutory provisions should be construed as being intended to have a purpose and effect, and observed that the discretion of a court to order the director to bear the costs of a s 150 application, was a discretion which the court already had under O 99. Finlay Geoghegan J therefore held:

> 'Accordingly, if these words are to be given any meaning and effect, it appears to me that they must be construed as limiting the discretion conferred on the court under O 99, r 1, so as to exclude the court from having a discretion to make any order for the applicant's costs other than against the persons expressly referred to, namely 'directors against whom the declaration of restriction is made.'

In *Re Visual Impact and Display Ltd*,[115] Finlay Geoghegan J described her decision in *Re GMT Engineering Services Ltd*,[116] interpreting s 150(4B) as follows:

> '… the subsection expressly refers to the costs of an applicant and provides that the Court 'may order that the directors against whom the declaration is made shall bear the costs of the application'. That was an order which the Court already had jurisdiction and discretion to make under Order 99, Rule 1, prior to the passing of s 150(4B). Accordingly to give those words any meaning and effect I concluded they must be construed as limiting the discretion conferred on the Court under Order 99, Rule 1, so as to exclude the Court from having a discretion to make any order for the applicant's costs other than against the persons expressly referred to therein.'[117]

[19.037] The jurisdiction of the court to award costs in favour of an applicant for a restriction order, is now limited to the jurisdiction to award such costs when the application is successful. According to the interpretations of s 150(4B) set out above, the general discretion of the courts under O 99, r 1[118] is therefore curtailed to the extent that an applicant cannot recover costs other than against an unsuccessful respondent. As Finlay Geoghegan J held in *Re GMT Engineering Services Ltd*:[119]

> 'It appears consistent with the filtering system established by the Oireachtas and the respect for the constitutionally guaranteed rights to one's good name and property that the director should become obliged to bear the applicant's costs of an application so brought only in the event that the declaration of restriction is made against him or her.'[120]

---

[115] *Re Visual Impact and Displays Ltd, Murphy v Murphy* [2003] IEHC 91.

[116] *Re GMT Engineering Services Limited (in voluntary liquidation) Luby v McMahon and Anor* [2003] 4 IR 133.

[117] *Re Visual Impact and Displays Ltd, Murphy v Murphy* [2003] IEHC 91.

[118] Rules of the Superior Courts (SI 15/1986), O 99, r 1.

[119] *Re GMT Engineering Services Limited (in voluntary liquidation) Luby v McMahon and Anor* [2003] 4 IR 133.

[120] *Re GMT Engineering Services Limited (in voluntary liquidation) Luby v McMahon and Anor* [2003] 4 IR 133 at 140.

(c) Order of costs in favour of respondent

[19.038] Section 150(4B)[121] does not make any reference to the possibility of costs being awarded in favour of a respondent.[122] By contrast, O 99, r 1[123] confers a general discretion on the High Court regarding the award of costs of both parties. The question of whether s 150(4B)[124] restricts the jurisdiction of the High Court to award costs under O 99, r 1 in this regard has been a vexed one. For instance, in *Re Visual Impact and Displays Ltd,*[125] one issue which the Court was called upon to consider was:

> 'whether or not s 150(4B) has restricted or excluded the discretion of the Court under Order 99 Rule 1 to make an order for costs in favour of a respondent in respect of whom an unsuccessful application for a declaration of restriction under s 150 has been brought.'[126]

That case concerned the very particular finding that a respondent was not a director within the twelve months before the commencement of the winding up and should not therefore be restricted. Following the refusal to make the declaration of restriction, the respondent applied to the Court for an award of costs against the liquidator.

[19.039] In resisting the application for costs, the liquidator cited the fact that the DCE did not relieve him of the obligation to bring restriction proceedings. The Court held, however, that the obligation imposed on the liquidator to bring restriction proceedings under CLEA 2001, s 56, arose from the inclusion by the liquidator of the respondent's name as a director of the company. The Court stated in this regard that:

> 'If a liquidator so includes a person then he must be able to foresee that if not relieved by the Director he will be obliged to bring the application under s 150 in respect of that person and discharge the onus of proof placed on him to establish before the Court on credible evidence that as a matter of probability the named person was a director of the company at the date of commencement of the winding up or within the prior 12 months.'[127]

The Court concluded that the decision of the liquidator to include the respondent in the s 56 report without having sufficient evidence to show that he was a director of the company within 12 months prior to the commencement of the winding up, has the consequence of putting the respondent to the unnecessary expense of defending the restriction proceedings. In these circumstances, the Court determined that the discretion regarding costs should be exercised in favour of the respondent.

---

[121] CA 1990, s 150(4B), as inserted by CLEA 2001, s 41(1).

[122] In *Re Visual Impact and Displays Ltd, Murphy v Murphy* [2003] IEHC 91, the Court noted that s 150(4B) made 'no express reference to the costs of a respondent, whether successful or unsuccessful.'

[123] Rules of the Superior Courts (SI 15/1986), O 99, r 1.

[124] CA 1990, s 150(4B), as inserted by CLEA 2001, s 41(1).

[125] *Re Visual Impact and Displays Ltd, Murphy v Murphy* [2003] IEHC 91.

[126] *Re Visual Impact and Displays Ltd, Murphy v Murphy* [2003] IEHC 91.

[127] *Re Visual Impact and Displays Ltd, Murphy v Murphy* [2003] IEHC 91. See further Ch **9** regarding liquidators' duties under CLEA 2001, s 56.

[19.040] In relation to the court's discretion, the applicant for costs argued that the court's discretion under O 99, r 1[128] was not interfered with by s 150(4B),[129] relying on the presumption against implicit changes in the law.[130] The Court analysed the terms of s 150(4B) noting that there was no provision of the Companies Acts governing the award of costs of restriction proceedings prior to its enactment and that O 99 governed the court's jurisdiction in that regard. The Court also noted that s 150(4B) does not address the costs of the director, whether the application against him is successful or not. Finlay Geoghegan J held in this regard:

> 'There is nothing in the wording of the subsection which could be considered to include a clear implication that the Oireachtas intended that the Court's jurisdiction and discretion in relation to the costs of a respondent be restricted or interfered with.'[131]

In reaching this conclusion, the Court stated that, '[t]he impact of s 150(4B) upon the Court's jurisdiction to deal with the costs of a respondent must be distinguished from its impact upon the Court's jurisdiction to deal with the costs of an applicant ...'. The Court concluded that, 'the Court does retain jurisdiction and a discretion to deal with the costs of the respondents under O 99, r 1'.

[19.041] The case of *Re Visual Impact and Displays Ltd*[132] is authority for the proposition that a court may make an order of costs in favour of a successful respondent to restriction proceedings, the limited terms of s 150(4B)[133] notwithstanding. The outcome in that case, however, is premised on a finding of fact that the restriction proceedings were at the instigation, and due to the actions, of the applicant liquidator. This does not address the situation in which the proceedings are not at the behest of the applicant. This could arise if a liquidator states in the s 56 report that he believed the director to have acted honestly and responsibly, but is not relieved of the obligation to bring restriction proceedings against that director. If the application is subsequently unsuccessful, the right of the respondent to recover costs is not entirely beyond doubt. As noted above, *Re Visual Impact and Displays Ltd*[134] confirms the discretion of the court to make an order of costs in favour of a respondent, but indicates that the exercise of that discretion may be influenced by the extent to which the decision to take restriction proceedings is attributable to the applicant. This left a certain amount of

---

[128] Rules of the Superior Courts (SI 15/1986), O 99, r 1.

[129] CA 1990, s 150(4B), as inserted by CLEA 2001, s 41(1).

[130] The applicant for costs cited the dicta of Henchy J in *Minister for Industry and Commerce v Hales* [1967] 1 IR 50 at 67 to the effect that, 'One of these presumptions is that the legislature does not intend to make any substantial alteration in the law beyond what it explicitly declares, either in express terms or by clear implication, or, in other words, beyond the immediate scope and object of the statute. In all general matters outside those limits the law remains undisturbed.'

[131] *Re Visual Impact and Displays Ltd, Murphy v Murphy* [2003] 4 IR 451.

[132] *Re Visual Impact and Displays Ltd, Murphy v Murphy* [2003] 4 IR 451.

[133] CA 1990, s 150(4B), as inserted by CLEA 2001, s 41(1).

[134] *Re Visual Impact and Displays Ltd, Murphy v Murphy* [2003] IEHC 91.

uncertainty regarding the right of successful respondents to restriction proceedings to recoup costs.

[19.042] In *Re Doherty Advertising Ltd*[135] the respondents to a restriction application were found to have acted honestly and responsibly and sought to recover their costs from the liquidator. O'Leary J described *Re Visual Impact and Displays Ltd*[136] as a case in which it was decided that s 150(4B) did not remove the court's discretion to award costs under O 99, r 1 and stated, 'this Court sees no reason to depart from the aforementioned decisions.' The Court therefore determined that s 150(4B) does not limit the discretion of the court in applications falling outside the scope of that provision: O 99, r 1 remains the basis on which courts must exercise their discretion.

The Court went on to consider the rules applicable to the exercise of the court's discretion under O 99, r 1, including the rule that costs should follow the event, with the 'successful' party typically being awarded his costs as against the 'unsuccessful' party. The Court queried whether this approach applies to restriction proceedings:

> 'Does this general rule have any application in the present case? It is clear that the directors feel that they have succeeded as they have proved to the satisfaction of the court that they had acted in an honest and responsible fashion. Therefore they submit they are justified in claiming that as they have won (ie were successful) they should as a matter of normal practice, get costs. But has anybody "lost" (ie been unsuccessful)? Is there any reason why the applicant cannot also maintain that he was equally successful in the sense that he put before the court an application for the court's determination and the decision of the court (irrespective of the outcome) is the fulfilment by him of his legal duty. When the necessity to make the application, on the instructions of the Director of Corporate Enforcement, is backed by a criminal sanction is the application itself not the "event" in question rather than the adjudication of the court.'[137]

The Court referred to the special position of a liquidator in restriction proceedings, noting that, 'the liquidator is merely the presenter of the application not a claimant or party with any interest in the outcome either for himself or on behalf of the creditors.' The Court also drew an analogy with an accused person in criminal proceedings: 'When an accused in a criminal matter is charged with an offence he is under an obligation to use his/her funds to fight the case. In such cases the awarding of costs is very unusual and limited to cases where the prosecution has misbehaved in some way.'

On the basis of these considerations and analogies, the Court concluded that, in exercising its discretion under O 99, r 1, costs should not normally be awarded to a director who successfully resists an application under s 150.

[19.043] There may be cases in which it is, however, appropriate to make an order of costs in favour of a respondent to restriction proceedings. In *Re Doherty Advertising Ltd*[138] the Court referred to certain factors that may be relevant in this regard, such as the Court's criticism of some of the allegations made by the liquidator and the imprecision

---

[135] *Re Doherty Advertising Ltd, Stafford v Beggs* [2006] IEHC 258.

[136] *Re Visual Impact and Displays Ltd, Murphy v Murphy* [2003] 4 IR 451.

[137] *Re Doherty Advertising Ltd, Stafford v Beggs* [2006] IEHC 258.

[138] *Re Doherty Advertising Ltd, Stafford v Beggs* [2006] IEHC 258.

of some of the allegations advanced. If there are sufficient factors of that nature, it appears that the court could award costs in favour of the respondent. There were counterveiling considerations in that case, however, such as legitimate issues the liquidator raised regarding the company's accounts and failures to hold a board meeting. The court also considered that it was extremely unlikely that the liquidator could have been relieved of his obligation to bring s 150 proceedings. No costs order was therefore made.

[19.044] The decision in *Re Doherty Advertising Ltd*[139] resolves some of the uncertainty that remained in the wake of *Re Visual Impact and Displays Ltd*.[140] While a court has a discretion to award costs in favour of a respondent who successfully resists a restriction application, it is not one that should be exercised lightly. A liquidator who has no choice but to pursue a s 150 application, and who does so in an appropriate and balanced manner, should not be in fear of a negative costs order.

(d) Applicant's liability for costs

[19.045] As has been seen, the persons who may pursue an application for an order of restriction are the DCE, a liquidator or a receiver.[141] Where an application is successful, s 150(4B)[142] clearly provides that the court may order the director to pay the costs of the applicant in investigating and pursuing the application.[143] However, s 150(4B) does not address the question of who should bear liability for the costs of the application, in the event that costs are awarded in favour of the respondent.

In *Re Visual Impact and Displays Ltd*,[144] the High Court was called upon to consider this question. It was submitted to the Court that the company in liquidation, rather than the liquidator, should bear the costs of the application.[145] The applicant attempted to rely on the decision of the Supreme Court in *Comhlucht Páipéar Ríomhaireachta Teo v Údarás na Gaeltachta*.[146] That case concerned an application for security for costs against a company in liquidation. The Supreme Court stated that the costs incurred in successfully defending an action taken by a company in liquidation, rank in priority to all other claims. The High Court in *Re Visual Impact and Displays Ltd*[147] held that this decision was not of assistance in determining whether the order of costs of restriction proceedings should be made against the company or against the liquidator. The Court noted, 'it is clear from the facts of the case as recited that at the time the matter was

---

[139] *Re Doherty Advertising Ltd, Stafford v Beggs* [2006] IEHC 258.

[140] *Re Visual Impact and Displays Ltd, Murphy v Murphy* [2003] 4 IR 451.

[141] CA 1990, s 150(4A), as inserted by CLEA 2001, s 41(1). See further paras **[18.001]** to **[18.007]**.

[142] CA 1990, s 150(4B), as inserted by CLEA 2001, s 41(1).

[143] CA 1990, s 150(4B), as inserted by CLEA 2001, s 41(1). See further above paras **[19.028]** to **[19.033]**.

[144] *Re Visual Impact and Displays Ltd, Murphy v Murphy* [2003] IEHC 91.

[145] *Comhlucht Páipéar Ríomhaireachta Teo v Údarás na Gaeltachta* [1990] 1 IR 320.

[146] *Re Visual Impact and Displays Ltd, Murphy v Murphy* [2003] IEHC 91.

[147] *Re Visual Impact and Displays Ltd, Murphy v Murphy* [2003] IEHC 91.

before the Supreme Court the company in liquidation was the plaintiff in the proceedings.'[148]

In *Re Visual Impact and Displays Ltd*,[149] the Court observed that the only applicant was the liquidator. The Court considered the nature of the liquidator's role in bringing an application for restriction and the role played by the company in such applications and reached the following determination:

> 'Undoubtedly [the liquidator] ... is bringing this application in his capacity as liquidator of the company. However, it is clear from the provisions of s 56 and in particular the potential offence created that the obligation to bring the application is an obligation personal on the liquidator. Further s 150 (4A) refers expressly to the liquidator as a potential applicant. It does not refer to the Company in liquidation. Accordingly it is the liquidator as distinct from the company in liquidation which is the party to the application. The Company is a distinct legal person to the liquidator and is not a party to the application. The liquidator for this purpose cannot be considered to be the agent of the Company. Further a s 150 application is not a proceeding of a type envisaged in s 231(1)(a) (applied to this voluntary winding up by s 276(1)(b)) namely a proceeding 'in the name and on behalf of the company'. Accordingly in exercising the Court's jurisdiction under Order 99 the order must be made against the person who is the applicant, namely [the liquidator] ...'

This decision clarifies that, where a liquidator of a company pursues an application for restriction against a director, the only parties to the application are the liquidator and the director. The company is not a party to an application. Therefore, where the director is entitled to an award of costs, the party who is liable for that award is the liquidator. The same principle must apply to applications for restriction orders taken by a receiver or by the DCE.

[19.046] On the basis of this decision, a liquidator or receiver would be well-advised to investigate carefully whether each person they name in the report filed under CLEA 2001, s 56, as directors of the company in liquidation, were in fact directors within 12 months prior to the commencement of the winding up. *Re Visual Impact and Displays Ltd*[150] is now authority for the proposition that, in the event that the liquidator names an individual as a director, without sufficient evidence to prove that fact, he may be liable for the costs of the application.

On the facts of *Re Visual Impact and Display Ltd*,[151] the Court determined that the origin of the restriction application lay in the decision of the liquidator to include the name of the respondent as a director in the s 56 report, without sufficient evidence to prove that fact. The Court therefore rejected the liquidator's argument that the reason for the application was the decision of the DCE not to grant relief from the obligation to bring restriction proceedings.

---

[148] *Re Visual Impact and Displays Ltd, Murphy v Murphy* [2003] IEHC 91.

[149] *Re Visual Impact and Displays Ltd, Murphy v Murphy* [2003] IEHC 91.

[150] *Re Visual Impact and Displays Ltd, Murphy v Murphy* [2003] IEHC 91.

[151] *Re Visual Impact and Displays Ltd, Murphy v Murphy* [2003] IEHC 91. See further above paras **[19.038]** to **[19.041]**.

Applying this aspect of the decision, it may be expected that in cases where the decision to bring an application for restriction cannot be attributed to the liquidator, the liquidator should not be liable for an award of costs. As noted above,[152] such circumstances may arise if the liquidator, despite being of the opinion that the director acted honestly and responsibly,[153] is obliged to bring restriction proceedings, which are subsequently rejected on the ground that the director did act honestly and responsibly. In those circumstances, the application for restriction should not be deemed to have originated with the liquidator and it would be invidious for the costs of the unsuccessful application, of which the liquidator was not in favour, to be awarded against him.

However, the ultimate reasoning of the High Court in awarding costs against the liquidator in *Re Visual Impact and Display Ltd*,[154] was that the liquidator was the only party to the proceedings. Therefore, even though the liquidator may have been neither responsible for, nor even in favour of, the application for restriction, he would still be the only applicant and as such may face the risk of an adverse costs' order.

[19.047] On the other hand, it is suggested by the judgment in *Re Visual Impact and Display Ltd*,[155] that, if the liquidator was not responsible for the decision to pursue restriction proceedings, the court may exercise its discretion under O 99, r 1, to refuse an order of costs. This outcome is not beyond reproach and it will be of little consolation to a director who incurred costs in successfully defending restriction proceedings, to discover that, as the application itself did not originate with the applicant, an order of costs should not be made against that applicant.

It this regard, it should be recalled that restriction proceedings are unlike other forms of adversarial proceedings, in a number of respects, including the fact that the applicant may not necessarily advocate the making of a declaration of restriction.[156] While this is an accepted feature of such applications, it does not favour the situation of respondents who successfully contest restriction applications, only to discover that there is no other party to the application who is accountable for its initiation or liable for the costs incurred. The general discretion of the High Court under O 99, r 1,[157] would allow this potential injustice to be evaded. However, the more limited terms of s 150(4B) and the unique nature of the restriction proceedings, may leave some room for concern.

(e) Recovery of costs in a winding up

[19.048] The final issue which needs to be considered is the liquidator's ability to recover an award of costs that may be made against him. In *Re Visual Impact and Display Ltd*[158] the Court was requested to make orders regarding the priority of the order

---

[152] See above para **[19.041]**.

[153] With regard to this aspect of a liquidator's report, see further Ch **9**.

[154] *Re Visual Impact and Displays Ltd, Murphy v Murphy* [2003] IEHC 91.

[155] *Re Visual Impact and Displays Ltd, Murphy v Murphy* [2003] IEHC 91.

[156] See above paras **[16.006]** to **[16.012]**.

[157] Rules of the Superior Courts (SI 15/1986), O 99, r 1.

[158] *Re Visual Impact and Displays Ltd, Murphy v Murphy* [2003] IEHC 91.

for costs in the liquidation. The Court refused to make such orders, noting, however, that:

> 'Section 281 of the Act of 1963 which applies to a company in voluntary liquidation provides that all costs, charges and expenses properly incurred in the winding up, including the remuneration of the liquidator shall be payable out of the assets of the company in priority to all other claims. If the order for costs against the applicant as the liquidator of the Company is an expense properly incurred in the winding up then it is payable in accordance with that section.'

The Court declined to determine whether the costs of the application for restriction counted as an expense properly incurred in the winding up. The Court concluded that, 'If such a dispute were to arise then it would be a matter for the liquidator to bring that dispute before the Court, putting on notice an appropriate creditor who would be affected by the decision.'

[19.049] Section 150(4B), as substituted by IFCMPA 2006, s 11 does contain a reference to the expenses and remuneration of the application in restriction proceedings. However, this relates exclusively to the recovery of costs from the respondent. It casts no light on the classification of an award of costs against a liquidator in a winding up.

[19.050] The position of a liquidator who has had an order of costs made against him in the pursuit of a declaration of restriction, is therefore unresolved. It remains to be determined whether such an award of costs can be claimed as an expense in the winding up, an issue which is critical to any liquidator. It may be envisaged that pending, and depending upon, the resolution of this matter, liquidators may be cautious and dissuasive of the bringing of restriction proceedings in s 56 reports, to avoid any finding that the proceedings were at their instigation and that they should be liable for the costs of the application.

(f) Notice party costs order

[19.051] The ODCE reports that it was joined as a notice party to proceedings in respect of an application for costs arising from an application for a declaration of restriction in 2006.[159] The liquidator was not relieved of the obligation to bring those proceedings and, when the court refused the declarations, the DCE was joined as a notice party for the purpose of the costs' application. According to the ODCE, the Director indicated his intention to resist the application and issued a motion to have the order joining him as a notice party struck out. The liquidator ultimately decided not to pursue the application for costs against the Director. The ODCE has indicated that, 'the Director does not consider that it is appropriate to seek to join him to such applications and intends to oppose vigorously any and all such applications that may arise in the future.[160]

---

[159] See ODCE, *Annual Report 2006*, at p 27. Available at www.odce.ie.

[160] ODCE, *Annual Report 2006*, at pp 27–28. Available at www.odce.ie.

PART E
DISQUALIFICATION ORDERS

Chapter 20: Deemed disqualifications
A. Introduction 933
B. Conviction on indictment 935
C. Failure to disclose disqualification in other jurisdiction 944
D. Acting in breach of order of restriction or under instructions
    of disqualified or restricted person 950
E. Undischarged bankruptcy 952

Chapter 21: Applications for Disqualification Orders
A. Introduction 955
B. Purpose of a disqualification order 957
C. Discretion of the Court 960
D. Onus of proof 961
E. Procedure 962
F. Test of fitness 969
G. Considerations 977

Chapter 22: Grounds of discretionary disqualification
A. Fraud in relation to company, creditors or members 987
B. Breach of duty 989
C. Civil liability for fraudulent and reckless trading 997
D. Unfit to be concerned with the management of a company 1000
E. Finding of unfitness in inspector's report 1008
F. Persistent default 1010
G. Failing to keep proper books of account 1013
H. Company struck off the register 1016
I. Disqualification in another state 1025
J. Undischarged bankruptcy 1028
K. Restricted persons 1029

Chapter 23: Consequences of Disqualification Orders
A. General 1031
B. Conditional disqualification 1032
C. Period of disqualification 1036
D. Substitution of restriction order 1044
E. Costs 1046
F. Relief 1047
G. Register of disqualified persons 1049
H. Acting while disqualified 1050

Chapter 20

DEEMED DISQUALIFICATIONS

A. Introduction

[20.001] An order of disqualification is an order that prohibits a person from occupying any role of significance in a company. A disqualified person may not be an auditor, officer, director, receiver, liquidator, or examiner of any company. He is also precluded from being, directly or indirectly, concerned in, or taking part in, the promotion, formation or management of a company.[1]

[20.002] There are two broad categories of disqualification orders. A person may be subject to an automatic or 'deemed' disqualification. Alternatively, a court may make a discretionary order of disqualification, following the hearing of an application for such an order. The law governing 'deemed' disqualifications and 'discretionary' disqualifications is quite different. However, the two forms of disqualification share certain common features, features which distinguish such orders from declarations of restriction under CA 1990, s 150:[2]

- (a) both can arise without a company being insolvent or in liquidation, by contrast with restriction proceedings under s 150;

- (b) both can be imposed in respect of persons who are not directors, by contrast with restriction proceedings;

- (c) both can entail varying periods of disqualification, unlike restriction proceedings;

- (d) both prohibit all forms of involvement with companies, unlike the more limited impact of declarations of restriction; and

- (e) there is no carve out in respect of companies which are capitalised to a particular extent, unlike that applicable to restricted persons.[3]

[20.003] The distinctions between automatic or 'deemed' disqualifications and discretionary disqualifications are prominent. The most fundamental difference is, as the titles suggest, that the former arises automatically without the necessity of a court order, whereas discretionary orders of disqualification may only be made in the exercise of the court's discretion. A further point of distinction is that the period of automatic disqualification is generally fixed,[4] whereas the determination of the appropriate period of discretionary disqualification rests with the court.

---

[1]   See CA 1990, s 159. See also Ch **23**.

[2]   See Pt **D**, Declarations of Restriction.

[3]   See Ch **19**.

[4]   This is subject to certain qualifications, which are addressed at paras **[20.008]** to **[20.010]**.

[20.004] The law applicable to discretionary disqualifications bears a closer resemblance to the law governing declarations of restriction under s 150, than to the law governing automatic disqualifications. There are, however, certain important differences between proceedings under s 150 and proceedings for discretionary disqualification orders under s 160(2).[5]

While the sanction of disqualification has been on the statute books since 1990, it has been imposed on many more persons in recent years than ever before. At the end of 2004, there were ten names on the register of disqualified persons; at the end of 2006, there were 1781 names on the register.[6] Most of these names arise from enhanced systems for reporting and recording the names of persons who are deemed to be disqualified.[7] There are also many more persons subject to discretionary disqualification orders than previously was the case. This is due to increased enforcement action by the ODCE, arising from, among other sources, the reports of inspectors into the National Irish Bank Ltd and Ansbacher (Cayman) Ltd.

[20.005] There are certain situations in which a person will be 'deemed' to be disqualified.[8] The main grounds of 'deemed' disqualification are the following:

–   that a person was convicted on indictment of an offence involving fraud or dishonesty, or an offence in relation to a company;[9]

---

5   See *Re Newcastle Timber Ltd* [2001] 4 IR 586 at 589: 'A very important distinction between these two sections is that under s 160 where, as in the present case, an application is made by a liquidator for a disqualification order, the onus is clearly on the liquidator to satisfy the court that the conditions of the section have been complied with, while on the other hand, under s 150, the court must make a restriction order unless it is satisfied that the person acted honestly and responsibly, and therefore the onus is on the director concerned to satisfy the court as to his honesty and responsibility. It is probably also relevant to note that s 150 applies only to directors and secretaries of companies, while s 160 applies to a much wider range of persons connected with a company. Even more relevant in the present case is that the use of the word 'may' in s 160 gives the court a discretion which does not exist under s 150,' *per* McCracken J See further Ch **16** and Ch **23**.

6   See ODCE, *Annual Report 2005* and ODCE, *Annual Report 2006* (available at www.odce.ie) and CRO, *Annual Report 2006* (available at www.cro.ie). It may be of interest to note that 1,675 of these are deemed to be disqualified; 74 were disqualified by Order of the High Court; 21 were disqualified arising from their failure to notify their disqualification in another jurisdiction; and 10 were disqualified on the basis of having acted as a director while restricted. See ODCE, *Annual Report 2006* at p 31.

7   The ODCE reports that, 'In cooperation with the Courts Service and the Registrar of Companies, the Office secured during 2005 the updating of the CRO's Register of Disqualified Persons to include those individuals subject to deemed disqualifications. This led to the identities of 985 individuals, who were deemed to be disqualified during the past five years, being notified to the CRO in 2005 with the result that more than 1,000 persons are now listed on the Register. This was a substantial increase on the ten individuals who were registered at end-2004.' See ODCE, *Annual Report 2005*, available at www.odce.ie.

8   The law governing deemed disqualifications is largely reproduced in the CLRG, General Scheme of the Draft Companies Consolidation and Reform Bill 2007, Pt A13, Head 42. Available at www.clrg.org.

9   CA 1990, s 160(1).

- that a person failed to disclose their disqualification in another jurisdiction;[10]

- that a person was convicted of the offence of acting in breach of a declaration of restriction, in breach of a disqualification order, or under the directions of a restricted or disqualified person;[11] or

- that a person acted in relation to a company while an undischarged bankrupt.[12]

In *Re Wood Products (Longford) Ltd*,[13] Laffoy J described the first two of these categories as illustrating 'the gravity of the type of wrongdoing which the Oireachtas considered merited automatic disqualification ...'.

B. Conviction on indictment

[20.006] A person who is convicted on indictment of particular types of offences will be deemed to be subject to a disqualification order under the Companies Acts.[14] Section 160(1) of CA 1990 provides:

> Where a person is convicted on indictment of any indictable offence in relation to a company, or involving fraud or dishonesty, then during the period of five years from the date of conviction or such other period as the court, on the application of the prosecutor and having regard to all the circumstances of the case, may order—
>
> (a) he shall not be appointed or act as an auditor, director or other officer, receiver, liquidator or examiner or be in any way, whether directly or indirectly, concerned or take part in the promotion, formation or management of any company or any society registered under the Industrial and Provident Societies Acts, 1893 to 1978;
>
> (b) he shall be deemed, for the purposes of this Act, to be subject to a disqualification order for that period.

The effect of this provision is that a person who is convicted on indictment of either an indictable offence in relation to a company or an indictable offence involving 'fraud or dishonesty' shall be deemed to be subject to a disqualification order, as defined in CA 1990, s 159. It should be noted that s 160(1)(a) is entirely superfluous as the wording of that sub-section is identical to the definition of 'disqualification' in s 159.[15]

---

[10] CA 1990, s 160(1A), as inserted by CLEA 2001, s 42(a).

[11] CA 1990, ss 161 and 164.

[12] CA 1963, s 183(2), as substituted by CA 1990, s 169.

[13] *Re Wood Products (Longford) Ltd, Director of Corporate Enforcement v McGowan* [2005] IEHC 41.

[14] CA 1990, s 160(1).

[15] According to s 159, 'disqualification order' means, 'an order under this Part that the person against whom the order is made shall not be appointed or act as an auditor, director or other officer, receiver, liquidator or examiner or be in any way, whether directly or indirectly, concerned or take part in the promotion, formation or management of any company, or any society registered under the Indus trial and Provident Societies Acts, 1893 to 1978 ...'.

(a) Offences which trigger disqualification

[20.007] 'Indictable offences' are offences which are liable to be tried by a judge and jury and which may only be prosecuted by the DPP.[16] There are many offences under the Companies Acts which may be regarded as 'hybrid offences', prosecutable either summarily or on indictment.[17] From the wording of s 160(1), such offences may give rise to an automatic disqualification only if they are in fact prosecuted on indictment.

There is no definition in the Companies Acts or elsewhere of offences 'in relation to a company' or offences 'involving fraud or dishonesty'. These are extremely broad categories. First, the term 'an offence in relation to a company' could involve any offence which injures a company, such as theft of a company's property or arson at a company's premises. Second, an offence involving dishonesty could range from theft to bigamy. There is no requirement in the Act that the offence involving fraud or dishonesty must be an offence in relation to a company or that it must involve the offender's dealings with a company or his position, ability or honesty as a director of a company.

An alternative formulation of s 160(1) would have been to automatically disqualify a person convicted on indictment of an indictable offence under the CA 1963–2006. It would be difficult to argue that such an offence was not relevant to the person's fitness to be involved in the promotion, formation or management of a company. The net of s 160(1) is far wider, however, and has been used to capture persons who are convicted of offences under the Competition Act 1991, as amended, for example.[18]

(b) Period of disqualification

[20.008] The period of disqualification which is imposed under s 160(1) is generally five years from the date of the conviction of the offence.[19] The court may, however, on

---

[16] See Ch **15**.

[17] See Ch **15**.

[18] See Competition Authority, *Annual Report 2006*, at p 9, reporting on the conviction on indictment of JP Lambe on to two counts of aiding and abetting price-fixing. In addition to a sentence of six months imprisonment, suspended for a period of 12 months (the first such custodial sentence under the Competition Act) and a fine of €15,000, which the Competition Authority describe as 'the largest single fine levied by an Irish court on either an undertaking or individual for a competition law offence', he was automatically disqualified and his name was entered on the register of disqualified persons on 2 October 2006, there to remain until 2 October 2011.

[19] This provision was inserted when the Companies (No 2) Bill 1987 was at Committee Stage before Seanad Éireann. The Minister of State at the Department of Industry and Commerce (Mr S Brennan) explained that there was formerly no provision stipulating the length of a period of automatic disqualification and stated, 'This is a new section which will fill a gap which seems to exist in Ch 3 of Pt VII. There seems to be the difficulty where a person is, following conviction of certain offences under Ch 3, deemed to be subject to a disqualification order, and no provision exists for determining how long the order should run. (Seanad Éireann, Vol 120, 12 July 1988. Companies (No 2) Bill, 1987: Committee Stage (Resumed)).

the application of the prosecutor, make a disqualification order for a period other than five years from the date of conviction. This is apparent from the description in s 160(1) of the period of disqualification:

> '... the period of five years from the date of conviction or such other period as the court, on the application of the prosecutor and having regard to all the circumstances of the case, may order ...'.

It appears from the wording of the section, that the general five year disqualification can only be varied by the court in the following circumstances:

– if the prosecutor makes an application seeking the imposition of a period other than five years from the date of conviction; and

– if, having regard to all of the circumstances of the case, the court considers that a period of disqualification other than five years is warranted.

[20.009] While the general principle that disqualification under s 160(1) endures for five years, is laudable for its certainty, the power of a court to make an order for 'such other period as the court, on the application of the prosecutor and having regard to all the circumstances of the case, may order' is very vague and unclear. As indicated by Finlay Geoghegan J in *Re Clawhammer Ltd*:[20]

> '... whilst there is a reference to a period of five years from the date of conviction there is an alternative of "such other period as the court, on the application of the prosecutor and having regard to all the circumstances of the case, may order." It is not clear from these sections what the Oireachtas intended by referring to five years. It is not specified to be a minimum period or a maximum period nor is there any indication as to the circumstances in which the court might consider it appropriate to fix a different period.'[21]

This appears to be a matter which requires further clarification.

[20.010] Another point to note about the duration of deemed disqualifications under s 160(1), is that there does not appear to be any ground for a person convicted of an offence to which s 160(1) applies, to make an application to court for the imposition of a period of disqualification of less than five years. It may be expected that, in practice, only disqualification periods in excess of five years would be sought by the prosecution. If this expectation is well-founded, the five year period of disqualification specified in s 160 will only be revised upwards and will effectively serve as a minimum period of disqualification.

---

20 *Re Clawhammer Ltd, Director of Corporate Enforcement v McDonnell*; *Re Shinrone Food Market Ltd, Director of Corporate Enforcement v Hoctor*; *Re Cautious Trading Ltd, Director of Corporate Enforcement v Forristal* (15 March 2005, unreported), HC (Finlay Geoghegan J).

21 *Re Clawhammer Ltd, Director of Corporate Enforcement v McDonnell*; *Re Shinrone Food Market Ltd, Director of Corporate Enforcement v Hoctor*; *Re Cautious Trading Ltd, Director of Corporate Enforcement v Forristal* (15 March 2005, unreported), HC (Finlay Geoghegan J).

(c) Role of the court

[20.011] A separate court order is not necessary to disqualify a person who is convicted of an offence within the meaning of s 160(1). The only role that is conferred on a court in relation to a disqualification order under s 160(1) is to vary the period of disqualification, upon the application of the prosecutor. The disqualification does not arise from a specific order of the court but is triggered by the conviction itself and will, unless the prosecutor invokes the discretion of the court to vary the period of disqualification, automatically last for five years from the date of the conviction. This may be contrasted with the position in England, where the Company Directors Disqualification Act 1986 provides in s 2(1) that:

> The court may make a disqualification order against a person where he is convicted of an indictable offence (whether on indictment or summarily) in connection with the promotion, formation, management, liquidation or striking off of a company, with the receivership of a company's property or with his being an administrative receiver of a company.[22]

(d) Implementation of deemed disqualification

[20.012] Section 167 of CA 1990 addresses one of the consequences of a person being convicted of an offence within the meaning of s 160(1) and thereby deemed to be disqualified. Where this occurs, s 167 requires a prescribed officer of the court to furnish particulars of the conviction to the Registrar of Companies. Section 167 accordingly provides:

> Where a court … convicts a person of an offence … which has the effect of his being deemed to be subject to a disqualification order, a prescribed officer of the court shall cause the registrar of companies to be furnished with prescribed particulars of the order, relief or conviction at such time and in such form and manner as may be prescribed.

The Companies Act 1990 (Parts IV and VII) Regulations, 1991,[23] designated the following officers for the purposes of s 167:

   (a) in the case of proceedings in the Supreme Court, the Registrar of the Supreme Court,

   (b) in the case of proceedings in the Court of Criminal Appeal, the Registrar of the Court of Criminal Appeal,

   (c) in the case of proceedings or an application in the High Court, the Examiner and Registrars of the High Court,

---

[22] Company Directors Disqualification Act 1986, s 2(1), as amended by Insolvency Act 2000, Sch 4, Pt I. While the court has a role regarding disqualifications arising from convictions in England, the *Report on Parallel Proceedings* by the Financial Regulation Working Group of the Society for Advanced Legal Studies (chaired by George Staple QC) (December 1999) records at para 7.13 that, 'Although there are exceptions, criminal courts have not always been willing to exercise their powers in the field of company director's disqualification, perhaps because it is a jurisdiction that is slightly esoteric and with which they are not familiar.'

[23] Companies Act 1990 (Parts IV and VII) Regulations, 1991 (SI 209/1991).

(d) in the case of proceedings or an application in the Central Criminal Court, the Registrar of the Central Criminal Court,

(e) in the case of proceedings in the Special Criminal Court, the Registrar of the Special Criminal Court,

(f) in the case of proceedings in the Circuit Court, the County Registrar for the county in which the proceedings are heard,

(g) in the case of proceedings in the District Court, in the Dublin Metropolitan District or in the District Court Area of Cork City, the Chief Clerk for the district or area concerned, as the case may be,

(h) in the case of proceedings elsewhere in the District Court, the principal Clerk assigned to the District Court area in which the proceedings are heard.

The Regulations prescribed a particular form for the purposes of notification under s 167, which is 'Form H8'.[24] This form must be completed by the relevant court official and must state:

- the full name, address, and date of birth, of the disqualified person;

- the statutory provision under which the person is deemed to be disqualified;

- the period of disqualification;

- the date of the court order (which, in the case of s 160(1), must be the date of conviction);

- the date of expiration of the disqualification period, if varied by the court; and

- full particulars of any relief granted under s 160(8).

The form stipulates that it must be delivered to the Registrar of Companies within 21 days of the relevant court order.[25]

[20.013] As noted above, where a conviction within the meaning of s 160(1) is handed down, the court does not need to make any order of disqualification or any reference to such an order. The only visible means by which a conviction under s 160(1) is translated into a disqualification order is by means of the notification to the Registrar of Companies, as required by s 167.

A delay in the notification of automatic disqualifications, beyond 21 days after the conviction on indictment, is contrary to the Companies Act 1990 (Parts IV and VII) Regulations, 1991. Upon receipt of a notification under s 167, even a delayed notification, it appears that the CRO should date the entry on the register of disqualified

---

[24] See Schedule to Companies Act 1990 (Parts IV and VII) Regulations, 1991 (SI 209/1991).

[25] Form H8 is available at www.cro.ie. See Schedule to Companies Act 1990 (Parts IV and VII) Regulations, 1991 (SI 209/1991).

persons back to the date of the conviction.[26] The date of commencement of the period of disqualification will typically, if not always, pre-date its notification to the CRO.

(e) Notification by director

[20.014] A provision of the Companies Acts which appears to relate to the practice of automatic disqualifications under s 160(1) is s 166(1),which provides:

> Where—
>
> (a) a director of a company is charged with an offence or civil proceedings are instituted against such a director, and
>
> (b) the charge or proceedings relate to the company or involve alleged fraud or dishonesty,
>
> the court before which the proceedings consequent on that charge or those civil proceedings are pending may (either of its own motion or at the request of any of the parties to the proceedings), if satisfied that it is appropriate to do so, require the director to lodge with the office of the court a notice in writing-
>
> (i) giving the names of all companies of which he is a director at the date of the notice,
>
> (ii) giving the names of all companies of which he was a director within a period commencing not earlier than 12 months prior to his being charged with the offence or the commencement of the civil proceedings and ending at the date of the notice,
>
> (iii) stating whether he is at the date of the notice or ever was subject or deemed to be subject to a disqualification order, and
>
> (iv) giving the dates and duration of each period in respect of which he is or was disqualified.[27]

---

[26] It appears that convictions that give rise to automatic disqualifications are not always promptly notified to the Registrar of Companies. By way of example, on 27 October 2005, JP Lambe pleaded guilty to two counts on a bill of indictment concerning certain offences under the Competition Act 1991, as amended. He was sentenced on 6 March 2006. According to s 160(1), the automatic disqualification should have commenced on the date of conviction and lasted for five years from that date, unless, which does not appear to be the case, the court made an order varying that time period. Applying s 160(1), the period of disqualification should therefore have commenced on 27 October 2005 and terminated on 26 October 2010. The register of disqualified persons maintained by the Registrar of Companies, however, records the period of disqualification as commencing on 2 October 2006, for a period of five years. This suggests that there may have been a delay in notifying the automatic disqualification to the Registrar of Companies, a delay that was treating as postponing the commencement of the official period of disqualification, as recorded by the Registrar. This is wholly contrary to the terms of s 160(1), which states clearly that the period of disqualification, whether five years or some other period, shall run 'from the date of conviction'.

[27] CA 1990, s 166(1), as substituted by IFCMPA 2005, s 70(a), with effect from 30 June 2005. Note that, prior to 30 June 2005, there was a mandatory obligation on such directors to lodge a notice containing those particulars in all such cases.

According to this provision, the court may require a person who faces civil or criminal proceedings alleging fraud or dishonesty or related to the company of which he is a director, to lodge a notice specifying any companies of which he is, or was within the preceding 12 months, a director and any disqualification orders to which he was subject. Therefore, where a person faces criminal charges within the meaning of s 160(1), and he is or was within the previous 12 months a director of a company, or was disqualified from so acting, he may be required to lodge a notice to this effect with the office of the court. This may provide a mechanism for the court to require directors to notify the court office of directorships and disqualification orders, in the context of proceedings which may lead to the person being deemed to be disqualified under s 160(1).

[20.015] There are a number of points that may be noted about s 166. First, s 166 does not provide for the companies of which the person is a director to be notified of the proceedings. There is no requirement that the CRO or the DCE be notified if the person is acting in breach of a disqualification order. Second, the terminology used to define the scope of ss 160(1) and 166 differs in a number of potentially important respects. Section 166(1) refers to the director of a company facing proceedings in relation to 'the company.' By contrast, s 160(1) refers to offences in relation to 'a company'. This difference in terminology is minor but may have the following consequence: s 160(1) provides for automatic disqualification upon conviction of an offence in connection with any company, whether the person convicted played any role in the company or not. Section 166, by contrast, refers only to charges or proceedings in relation to the company of which the director is a director. The notification obligation in s 166 does not, therefore, apply to every category of convictions which may cause a person to be deemed to be disqualified under s 160(1).

By way of practical illustration, if a person was a director of a company, resigned, and subsequently faced charges of defrauding the creditors of that company, he would not be within the scope of s 166(1). Similarly, if a person who is a director of one company, faces charges of fraud in relation to another company, of which he is not director, he will not be bound by the notification obligation of s 166(1). In both of these cases, the accused would face the possibility of being deemed to be disqualified under s 160(1).

Another distinction between sub-ss 160(1) and 166(1) is that the latter refers to offences generally and is not confined to indictable offences prosecuted on indictment.

Third, the reference to civil proceedings in s 166 is not easily explicable. There is no provision of the Companies Acts which provides for disqualification consequent on general civil proceedings in relation to a company or involving allegations of fraud or dishonesty, as referred to in s 166(1)(b). There are certain provisions of s 160(2), which refer to specific civil proceedings, such as the reference in s 160(2)(c) to proceedings under s 297A. However, there is no general provision for disqualification consequent on civil proceedings involving companies or alleging fraud or dishonesty.

In particular, the reference to 'charges or proceeding' which involve 'alleged fraud or dishonesty' in s 166(1)(b) is very broad. Any number of civil proceedings could contain allegations of dishonesty against an individual. On one view of standard civil litigation, the denial by a defendant of a plaintiff's case, may amount to an allegation of dishonesty on the part of the plaintiff. It appears that an individual who faces any allegation of dishonesty in civil proceedings, irrespective of the context, may be directed to comply with s 166.

A final point that may be noted is that, before the commencement of the IFCMPA 2005, s 70 on 30 June 2005, the notification obligation set out in s 166 applied automatically to every director who was charged with an offence or faced civil proceedings related to the company or involving fraud or dishonesty. Moreover, according to s 166(3), it was an offence to fail to comply with this notification requirement. Since the IFCMPA 2005, this notification requirement may be imposed at the discretion of the court, and is not automatic. Furthermore, it is no longer an offence for a director to fail to comply with s 166.

(f) Persons affected

[20.016] The category of persons who may be 'deemed' to be disqualified under s 160(1) is a very wide one; the only criterion to fit within this category is that the person must have been convicted on indictment of an indictable offence in relation to a company, or an indictable offence involving fraud or dishonesty. An automatic disqualification order under s 160(1) does not necessarily have anything to do with the person's role or responsibility in a company.

This was confirmed by the *Report of the Working Group on Company Law Compliance and Enforcement*,[28] which described the automatic disqualification provisions of s 160(1) in the following terms: 'Rather than simply preventing persons from "re-offending", this provision enables a person who has never been a director or other officer of a company to be disqualified from acting as such for a specified period'.

(g) Discretion to substitute restriction order

[20.017] Section 160(9A)[29] confers a general discretion on a court to make an order of restriction under s 150, rather than a disqualification order, where the court considers disqualification to be unwarranted. That provision provides specifically that:

> In considering the penalty to be imposed under this section, the court may as an alternative, where it adjudges that disqualification is not justified, make a declaration under section 150.

The reference to penalties 'to be imposed under this section ...' could be interpreted as encompassing all disqualification orders under s 160. If this interpretation was adopted, it would be possible for a person who has been convicted of an indictable offence within the meaning of s 160(1) to request a court to exercise its discretion to substitute a declaration of restriction for a disqualification order. On balance, it appears most likely that s 160(9A) does not apply to 'deemed' disqualifications: s 160(9A) only relates to situations in which the court has a discretion to decide that 'disqualification is not justified'. There is no such discretion under s 160(1).

---

[28]   *Report of the Working Group on Company Law Compliance and Enforcement* (30 November 1998) at para 6.2.

[29]   CA 1990, s 160(9A), as inserted by CLEA 2001, s 42(f).

A person who is deemed to be disqualified under s 160(1) clearly does have the right to apply for relief under s 160(8).[30]

(h) Comparative legislation

[20.018] The approach of s 160(1), that there are certain offences, conviction of which should lead automatically to a person's disqualification from acting as a director of a company, can be seen in certain other jurisdictions.

In Australia, s 206B of the Corporation Act 2001 provides that:

(1) A person becomes disqualified from managing corporations if the person:

(a) is convicted on indictment of an offence that:

    (i) concerns the making, or participation in making, of decisions that affect the whole or a substantial part of the business of the corporation; or

    (ii) concerns an act that has the capacity to affect significantly the corporation's financial standing; or

(b) is convicted of an offence that:

    (i) is a contravention of this Act and is punishable by imprisonment for a period greater than 12 months; or

    (ii) involves dishonesty and is punishable by imprisonment for at least three months; or

(c) is convicted of an offence against the law of a foreign country that is punishable by imprisonment for a period greater than 12 months.

The offences covered by paragraph (a) and subparagraph (b)(ii) include offences against the law of a foreign country.

This section encompasses a very similar category of offences to the offences covered by s 160(1). In particular, the reference to conviction on indictment for offences involving dishonesty in s 206B(1)(b)(ii) of the Australian Corporation Act 2001 mirrors CA 1990, s 160(1).

The company laws of New Zealand and Singapore also contain provisions whereby conviction of certain offences can automatically cause a person to be disqualified from acting as the director of a company.

[20.019] By way of contrast with the position adopted by the Irish Companies Acts, the English Company Directors Disqualification Act 1986 ('CDDA 1986') provides in s 2(1) that:

The court may make a disqualification order against a person where he is convicted of an indictable offence (whether on indictment or summarily) in connection with the promotion, formation, management, liquidation or striking off of a company, or with the receivership or management of a company's property.

Section 2 of the CDDA 1986 can be distinguished from the automatic disqualification provision of CA 1990, s 160(1), in a number of important respects.

---

[30] CA 1990, s 160(8). See further Ch **23**.

First, disqualification on the basis of a criminal conviction is at the discretion of the court. In Ireland, by contrast, disqualification occurs automatically upon conviction on indictment.

Secondly, the range of offences which may give rise to disqualification is limited to offences 'in connection with the promotion, formation, management, liquidation or striking off of a company, or with the receivership or management of a company's property'. In Ireland, disqualification is automatic upon conviction on indictable of any offence 'in relation to a company or involving fraud or dishonesty.' There is very considerable disparity between the formulation of the offences which may lead to disqualification in the two jurisdictions.

Thirdly, in England the offence must be an indictable one, but may have been tried either on indictment or summarily. In Ireland, the person who becomes subject to an order of disqualification, must have been convicted on indictment.

Fourthly, according to CDDA 1986, s 2(3), the maximum period of disqualification which can be imposed by a court of summary jurisdiction is five years and, in all other cases, fifteen years is the maximum period. Under the Companies Acts, five years is the period of automatic disqualification under s 160(1), unless the court, on the application of the prosecutor, and having regard to the circumstances of the case, orders otherwise.[31]

There has been some concern expressed in England regarding the operation of CDDA 1986 s 2. The *Report on Parallel Proceedings* which was presented by the Financial Regulation Working Group of the Society for Advanced Legal Studies noted:

> 'Although there are exceptions, criminal courts have not always been willing to exercise their powers in the field of company director's disqualification, perhaps because it is a jurisdiction that is slightly esoteric and with which they are not familiar.'[32]

C. Failure to disclose disqualification in other jurisdiction

(a) Duty to notify of disqualification in other jurisdiction

[20.020] To be registered as a limited liability company in Ireland, every company must furnish to the Registrar of Companies, together with the company's memorandum of association, a statement setting out certain information about the company's directors. This is known as 'Form A1'.[33] Companies are also obliged to keep a register of its directors and secretaries at the companies registered office, which must include certain specific information about the company's directors.[34] A company must also notify the

---

[31]   CA 1990, s 160(1). See paras **[20.008]** to **[20.010]**.

[32]   Financial Regulation Working Group of the Society for Advanced Legal Studies (chaired by George Staple QC), *Report on Parallel Proceedings* (December 1999) at para 7.13.

[33]   C(A)A 1982, s 3, as amended by C(A)A 1983 and CLEA 2001, s 101. See Ch **2**.

[34]   CA 1963, s 195, as substituted by CA 1990, s 51 and as amended by CLEA 2001, s 91.

Registrar of any change in its directors or the particulars of its directors as recorded on the register.[35] The form for this purpose is Form B10.[36]

The information which the Companies Acts require a company to maintain and furnish to the Registrar of Companies regarding a company's directors is as follows:

- present and former names;

- dates of birth;

- usual residential address;

- nationality;

- business occupation; and

- any directorships held within the previous ten years, whether in Ireland or elsewhere.[37]

[20.021] The CLEA 2001 introduced certain amendments to the obligations of companies to notify the Registrar of Companies regarding its directors. First, if any of the persons named as directors of the company on Form A1 are disqualified in another jurisdiction C(A)A 1982, s 3A(1), requires that a separate statement to this effect must be attached to Form A1.[38]

Secondly, if a company appoints a new director, who is disqualified in another jurisdiction, s 195(8) requires that the Form B10 which must be delivered to the Registrar of Companies must be accompanied by a separate statement containing particulars of this disqualification.[39]

The wording of the new C(A)A 1982, s 3A(1), and CA 1963, s 195(8), are largely identical and provide that if the person who is named as a director on Form A1 (as required by C(A)A 1982, s 3) or named as a newly appointed director on Form B10 (as required by CA 1963, s 195(6)):

> … is a person who is disqualified under the law of another state (whether pursuant to an order of a judge or a tribunal or otherwise) from being appointed or acting as a director or secretary of a body corporate or an undertaking, that person shall ensure that [the statement[40] or notification[41]] is accompanied by (but as a separate

---

[35] CA 1963, s 195(6), as substituted by C(A)A 1982, s 8.

[36] Available at www.cro.ie. See Ch **2**.

[37] CA 1963, s 195(2), as substituted by CA 1990, s 51. See Ch **2**.

[38] C(A)A 1982, s 3A(1), as inserted by CLEA 2001, s 101.

[39] CA 1963, s 195(7), as substituted by CA 1990, s 51; CA 1963, s 195(8), as inserted by CLEA 2001, s 91(a), which by the CLEA 2001 (Commencement) (No 5) Order 2002 (SI 53/2002), came into effect on 1 March 2002.

[40] C(A)A 1982, s 3A(1), as inserted by CLEA 2001, s 101.

[41] CA 1963, s 195(8), as inserted by CLEA 2001, s 91.

document from [the statement[42] or notification[43]]) a statement in the prescribed form signed by him specifying—

(a) the jurisdiction in which he is so disqualified,

(b) the date on which he became so disqualified, and

(c) the period for which he is so disqualified.

[20.022]   The form that must be used for this purpose is Form B74. It can be used either for a statement under C(A)A 1982, s 3(A), or under CA 1963, s 195(8). The presenter must indicate which of the following categories it falls into:

– A 'Statement accompanying form for the incorporation of a company (Form A1) by a person where he or she is one of the first directors of the company and is a person who is disqualified under the law of another state (whether pursuant to an order of a judge, or a tribunal or otherwise) from being appointed or acting as a director or secretary of a body corporate or an undertaking;' or

– A 'Statement accompanying notice of appointment of director (Form B10) by the person being appointed as such, where he or she is a person who is disqualified under the law of another state (whether pursuant to an order of a judge, or a tribunal or otherwise) from being appointed or acting as a director or secretary of a body corporate or an undertaking.'

This form must also state the name of the company and of the director and the particulars of the disqualification, including the jurisdiction in which it was imposed, the date and period of disqualification. The director in question must sign this form, certifying that all of the particulars contained therein are correct.

[20.023]   The net effect of these requirements is that if a company has among its directors at the time of its first registration, or appoints as a director, a person who is disqualified from so acting in another jurisdiction, this fact must be notified to the Registrar of Companies in a separate statement, together with the notification or statement which the company is otherwise obliged to send to the Registrar.

It should be noted that, while the obligation to notify the Registrar of Companies of the appointment of the first directors and new directors is imposed on the company,[44] the obligation to ensure that a separate statement is filed regarding disqualification in other jurisdictions, lies on the disqualified person himself, rather than on the company.

[20.024]   There is a potential loophole in the obligation to disclose any disqualifications in other jurisdictions to the Registrar of Companies. The notification obligations of ss 3A(1) and 195(8) deal with the original board of directors of a company at the date of submission of the memorandum of association, and any directors who are newly appointed thereafter. These provisions do not capture any duly appointed, existing directors who subsequently become disqualified from so acting in other jurisdictions and continue to act as directors of companies registered in Ireland.

---

[42] C(A)A 1982, s 3A(1), as inserted by CLEA 2001, s 101.

[43] CA 1963, s 195(8), as inserted by CLEA 2001, s 91.

[44] CA 1963, s 195(6). Form B10 is the form to use for this purpose. See Ch **2**.

[20.025] CA 1963, s 195(6) does require notification to be sent to the Registrar of Companies of any changes in the particulars contained in the register. These particulars were set out above and include such matters as the name, address, date of birth and business occupation of the director.[45] An order of disqualification is not one of the particulars listed in s 195(2). Therefore, so long as a person was not disqualified at the date of submission of the statement required by C(A)A 1982, s 3, and is not appointed to a company's board of directors subsequent to the date of disqualification in another jurisdiction, triggering the notification obligation of s 195(8), there is nothing in the Companies Acts which requires such a person, or the company to which they are appointed, to notify the Registrar of Companies or otherwise publicise their disqualification in another jurisdiction.

[20.026] A final point to note regarding the terms of C(A)A 1982, s 3A(1), and CA 1963, s 195(8), is that while these provisions require a statement to be sent to the Registrar of Companies regarding a director's disqualification in another jurisdiction, no consequences flow directly from the making of such a statement. The Registrar of Companies is neither obliged nor specifically empowered to transmit any information regarding disqualifications in other jurisdictions to other agencies. There is no automatic disqualification in this jurisdiction, on the basis of disqualification orders made in other jurisdictions.[46]

[20.027] It should be mentioned that under s 160(2)(i),[47] as will be seen below, the court may make an order of disqualification on the ground that a person is disqualified in another jurisdiction and the court considers that it would have been proper to make a disqualification order in this state in the same circumstances. However, there is no correlation drawn between the obligation to notify the Registrar of Companies of disqualification in another jurisdiction under C(A)A 1982, s 3A(1),[48] and CA 1963, s 195(8),[49] and the penalty of disqualification in CA 1990, s 160(2)(i).[50] The provisions governing the duty to notify the Registrar of Companies of disqualification orders made in other jurisdictions[51] do not refer to any duty, power or role of the Registrar to refer such notifications to other agencies. The potential utility of C(A)A 1982, s 3A(1),[52] and CA 1963, s 195(8)[53] is not invoked directly.

---

[45] CA 1963, s 195(2). See above para **[20.020]**.

[46] This is subject to the caveat that, where a person fails to comply with the requirements of C(A)A 1982, s 3A(1) or CA 1963, s 195(8), he is deemed to be disqualified under CA 1990, s 160(1A). See below paras **[20.029]** to **[20.033]**.

[47] CA 1990, s 160(2)(i), as inserted by CLEA 2001, s 42(b)(ii). See further Ch **21**.

[48] C(A)A 1982, s 3A(1), as inserted by CLEA 2001, s 101.

[49] CA 1963, s 195(8), as inserted by CLEA 2001, s 91.

[50] CA 1990, s 160(2)(i), as inserted by CLEA 2001, s 42(b)(ii).

[51] C(A)A 1982, s 3A(1), as inserted by CLEA 2001, s 101 and CA 1963, s 195(8), as inserted by CLEA 2001, s 91.

[52] C(A)A 1982, s 3A(1), as inserted by CLEA 2001, s 101.

[53] CA 1963, s 195(8), as inserted by CLEA 2001, s 91.

[20.028] Moreover, the Registrar of Companies, who it may be expected would be in the best position to be aware of a director's disqualification in other jurisdictions, by virtue of C(A)A 1982, s 3A(1),[54] and CA 1963, s195(8),[55] does not have the power to make an application for disqualification on the grounds of disqualification in other jurisdictions. Only the DCE can make an application for the disqualification of a director on the ground that he is disqualified in another jurisdiction.[56] In light of the exclusive role of the DCE in this regard, it may be expected that there would be some connection between the obligations to make notification of disqualifications in other jurisdictions, and the power of the DCE to prosecute applications for disqualification in this state on that basis. However, there is no apparent connection in the Companies Acts between the duty to notify the Registrar of Companies of a director's disqualification in another jurisdiction, and the power of the DCE to seek the disqualification of that person in this jurisdiction, on that ground.

(b) Automatic disqualification for failure to notify

[20.029] The CLEA 2001 introduced a new category of automatic disqualification into s 160(1). This disqualification arises when a person who is a director of a company being first registered in Ireland, or who is appointed as a director of a company registered in Ireland, fails to ensure that a separate statement is sent to the Registrar of Companies specifying that he is subject to a disqualification order in another jurisdiction. According to CA 1990, s 160(1A),[57] if such a person fails to ensure the notification requirements are complied with, or permits the requisite statement or notification to be accompanied by a statement signed by him which is 'false or misleading in a material respect,' he shall be deemed to be disqualified:[58]

> Without prejudice to subsection (1), a person who—
>
> (a) fails to comply with s 3A(1) of the Companies (Amendment) Act 1982, or s 195(8) of the Principal Act, or
>
> (b) in purported compliance with the said s 3A(1) or 195(8), permits the first-mentioned statement in the said s 3A(1) or, as the case may be, the first-mentioned notification in the said s 195(8) to be accompanied by a statement signed by him which is false or misleading in a material respect,
>
> shall, upon the delivery to the registrar of companies of the said first-mentioned statement or notification or, as the case may be, the said statement or notification accompanied by a statement as aforesaid, be deemed, for the purposes of this Act, to be subject to a disqualification order for the period referred to in subsection (1B).[59]

---

54   C(A)A 1982, s 3A(1), as inserted by CLEA 2001, s 101.

55   CA 1963, s 195(8), as inserted by CLEA 2001, s 91.

56   See CA 1960, s 160(6A), as inserted by CLEA 2001, s 42(e). See Ch **22**.

57   CA 1990, s 160(1A), as inserted by CLEA 2001, s 42(a).

58   CA 1990, s 160(1A), as inserted by CLEA 2001, s 42(a).

59   CA 1990, s 160(1A), as inserted by CLEA 2001, s 42(a).

[20.030] This disqualification arises upon the delivery to the Registrar of Companies of the statement or notification, without a signed statement as to the overseas disqualification, or with a false or misleading statement. The period of disqualification is defined in s 160(1B) as follows:

    (a) so much as remains unexpired, at the date of the delivery mentioned in that subsection, of the period for which the person concerned is disqualified under the law of the other state referred to in s 3A(1) of the Companies (Amendment) Act, 1982, or s 195(8) of the Principal Act from being appointed or acting in the manner described therein, or

    (b) if the person concerned is so disqualified under the law of more than one other such state and the portions of the respective periods for which he is so disqualified that remain unexpired at the date of that delivery are not equal, whichever of those unexpired portions is the greatest.[60]

[20.031] In summary, where a person fails to ensure that a notification or statement of his appointment which is sent to the Registrar of Companies, on the first registration of the company or on his appointment as a director, is not accompanied by a separate statement to the effect that he disqualified in another jurisdiction, or is accompanied by a false or misleading statement in that regard, he shall be deemed to be disqualified from the date of delivery of that notification or statement. The period of disqualification will be the duration of the unexpired period of disqualification in that other jurisdiction. If the person is subject to more than one period of disqualification in other jurisdictions, he shall be deemed to be disqualified for the longest of the remaining unexpired periods of disqualification. The following example demonstrates how this may operate in practice: A person who is appointed as a director of an Irish company in September 2007, having been disqualified for five years pursuant to an order of an English court of 10 October 2005 and being deemed to be disqualified for five years due to a conviction for an offence involving dishonesty in Australia on 17 August 2007, must ensure that the CRO is sent a separate statement, together with the Form B10, setting out the particulars of these disqualifications. If the director fails to ensure that this statement is sent, or if the statement is false or misleading in a material respect, he will be deemed to be disqualified in Ireland until 17 August 2012, which is the longest of the unexpired periods of disqualification to which he is subject.

[20.032] The most obvious question in relation to this category of automatic disqualification is the enforceability of a period of disqualification which commences from the date of non-disclosure of its basis. A person who does not reveal the fact that he is disqualified in another state may be deemed to be disqualified, in spite of the fact that nobody may be aware of this 'deemed' disqualification. If no regulatory or enforcement agencies are aware of the individual being deemed to be disqualified under s 160(1B), it is not easily apparent how that disqualification can be policed or enforced. This raises the further issue that the person may act as a director for a considerable period of time without the deemed disqualification coming to anyone's attention (his

---

[60] CA 1990, s 160(1B), as inserted by CLEA 2001, s 42(a).

own included). In such circumstances, he may face prosecution and substantial penalties for acting while disqualified.[61]

[20.033] The ODCE did prosecute an individual on 2 March 2006 for acting as a director without notifying the Registrar that he was disqualified in England and Wales.[62] In the case of *Director of Corporate Enforcement v O'Brien*, the defendant was charged at Midleton District Court with contravening CA 1990, s 161(1), with acting as a director of two Irish companies while deemed to be disqualified under s 161(1A), due to his failure to ensure that the Registrar of Companies was notified of his disqualification in England and Wales. The defendant was disqualified in England and Wales for a period of seven years by an order dated 11 February 2000. The defendant pleaded not guilty. On conviction, he was fined €1,900 on each charge and ordered to pay prosecution costs of €1,000. His disqualification from acting as a director in the State was extended to 1 January 2008.[63]

D. Acting in breach of order of restriction or under instructions of disqualified or restricted person

[20.034] If a person is convicted of the offence of acting in breach of a restriction order or of knowingly acting under the instructions or directions of a disqualified person, he shall be deemed to be disqualified.[64]

---

[61]   CA 1990, ss 161, 163. See further Ch **23**.

[62]   *Director of Corporate Enforcement v O'Brien* (2 March 2006, unreported), Midleton District Court. See www.odce.ie for details of all prosecutions by the ODCE.

[63]   How this period of disqualification was arrived at is not entirely clear. The report of the decision states that his disqualification was extended to 1 January 2008, pursuant to CA 1990, s 161(3). However, if the defendant was deemed to be disqualified under s 160(1A), the period of such deemed disqualification should have been fixed according to s 160(1B), as the period that remained unexpired under the foreign disqualification order. In this case, the defendant should have been deemed to be disqualified until seven years from 11 February 2000, ie 11 February 2007. On conviction of the offence of acting contrary to a deemed disqualification under s 161(1), the rule in s 161(3) is that the existing period of disqualification should be extended by a further ten years from the date of that conviction. In this case, the deemed disqualification should have been extended for ten years from 11 February 2007, to 11 February 2017. As an alternative to the ten year extension of an existing period of disqualification, CA 1990, s 161(3), does refer to 'such other further period as the court, on the application of the prosecutor and having regard to all the circumstances of the case, may order.' The only explanation for the period of disqualification ordered in *Director of Corporate Enforcement v O'Brien* is that the court must have ordered that the statutory disqualification period of ten years should be substituted with a period of eleven months, the justification or basis for which is not apparent. This matter is currently under appeal by way of case stated to the High Court. The conviction and disqualification have been suspended pending the outcome of this appeal.

[64]   See Ch **23** regarding the consequences of acting contrary to an order of disqualification.

A person convicted of the offence of acting in contravention of a declaration of restriction is not entitled to apply for relief under s 160(8),[65] although it appears that a person convicted of acting under the directions or instructions of such a person may apply for relief.

(a) Breach of declaration of restriction

[20.035] It is an offence for a person to act in violation of a declaration of restriction.[66] In addition, s 161(2) provides that:

> Where a person is convicted of an offence under subsection (1) he shall be deemed to be subject to a disqualification order from the date of such conviction if he was not, or was not deemed to be, subject to such an order on that date.

The period of disqualification to which a person will be deemed to be subject is five years from the date of conviction, although this period may be varied by the court on the application of the prosecutor having regard to the circumstances of the case. Section 162 is the governing provision in this regard:

> Where a person is, as a consequence of his conviction of an offence under this Chapter, deemed to be subject to a disqualification order, he shall be deemed to be so subject for a period of five years from the date of such conviction or such other period as the court, on the application of the prosecutor and having regard to all the circumstances of the case, may order.

[20.036] The first conviction under s 161 was prosecuted successfully by the DCE on 26 November 2004.[67] The respondent was charged with the offence of contravening CA 1990, s 161(1), by acting as a director of a company between 10 December 2001 and 22 September 2004 while subject to an order of restriction, and with failing to abide by the conditions prescribed in the Act for continuing to act as a company director. On a plea of guilty, the respondent was convicted of failing to comply with an order of restriction. He was fined €600 and ordered to pay prosecution costs of €218. The court noted that, having been convicted of an offence under the Companies Act 1990, s 161, the respondent was deemed to be disqualified for a period of five years from the date of the conviction in accordance with, CA 1990, ss 161(1) and 162.

Commenting on this decision, the DCE expressed concern that there appeared to be a small number of company directors who were acting in breach of declarations of

---

[65] CA 1990, s 161(4) provides, 'Section 160(8) shall not apply to a person convicted of an offence under subsection (1) of this section.'

[66] CA 1990, s 161(1) defines this offence as follows: 'Any person who, in relation to any company, acts in a manner or capacity which by virtue of being a person to whom section 150 applies or being subject or deemed to be subject to a disqualification order, he is prohibited from doing shall be guilty of an offence.'

[67] Mr William McCormack of 3 Firgrove Park, Bishopstown, Cork, was convicted by Cork District Court under s 161 of the Companies Act 1990 on 26 November 2004. See www.odce.ie.

restriction. The conviction obtained on 26 November 2004, was the first of its kind. However, the Director stated:

> 'My Office is determined to ensure that directors who are restricted by the High Court comply with the conditions of their restriction. We have a number of further cases in this area in the pipeline ... All restricted directors who fail to abide by their obligations under the law are at risk of prosecution and disqualification.[68]

(b) Acting under the directions of a disqualified or restricted person

[20.037] If a person in a position of responsibility in a company acts pursuant to the directions or instructions of a second person, knowing that second person is disqualified or that it is otherwise contrary to Pt VII of CA 1990 for that second person to give those directions or instructions, he is guilty of an offence and deemed to be disqualified. Section 164(1) provides:

> If any person while a director or other officer or a member of a committee of management or trustee of any company acts in accordance with the directions or instructions of another person knowing that such other person is disqualified or that, in giving the directions or instructions, he is acting in contravention of any provision of this Part he shall be guilty of an offence.

Upon conviction of such an offence, the person so convicted shall be deemed to subject to a disqualification order from that date, if he not already subject to such an order.[69] There have been no reported cases to date of convictions for acting under the directions or in accordance with the instructions of a disqualified or restricted person.

E. Undischarged bankruptcy

[20.038] The Companies Acts prohibit a person who is an undischarged bankrupt from acting as an officer, auditor, liquidator or examiner of a company or from otherwise taking part in the promotion, formation or management of a company, other than with the leave of court.[70] It is an offence for a person who is an undischarged bankrupt to act in any of those capacities.[71] An 'undischarged bankrupt' is defined in CA 1963, s 2(1) as 'a person who is declared bankrupt by a court of competent jurisdiction, within the State

---

[68]   ODCE, *Press Release*, 26 November 2004.

[69]   CA 1990, s 164.

[70]   CA 1963, s 183(1), as substituted by CA 1990, s 169. The same law has been adopted in other jurisdictions. Eg, in Singapore 'Every person who, being an undischarged bankrupt (whether he was adjudged bankrupt by a Singapore Court or a foreign court having jurisdiction in bankruptcy), acts as director of, or directly or indirectly takes part in or is concerned in the management of, any corporation, except with the leave of the Court or the written permission of the Official Assignee, shall be guilty of an offence and shall be liable on conviction to a fine not exceeding $10,000 or to imprisonment for a term not exceeding 2 years or to both.' (Companies Act, s 148(1)).

[71]   CA 1963, s 183(1), as substituted by CA 1990, s 169.

or elsewhere, and who has not obtained a certificate of discharge or its equivalent in the relevant jurisdiction'.[72]

If a person is convicted of the offence of acting in relation to a company while an undischarged bankrupt, he is automatically subject to a disqualification order. Section 183(2) accordingly provides:

> Where a person is convicted of an offence under subsection (1) he shall be deemed to be subject to a disqualification order from the date of such conviction if he was not, or was not deemed to be, subject to such an order on that date.[73]

[20.039] There is nothing in s 183, or any other provision, however, which indicates the period of time for which the person will be disqualified. It should be noted that s 162 provides:

> Where a person is, as a consequence of his conviction of an offence under this Chapter, deemed to be subject to a disqualification order, he shall be deemed to be so subject for a period of five years from the date of such conviction or such other period as the court, on the application of the prosecutor and having regard to all the circumstances of the case, may order.

This may be of assistance if CA 1963, s 183, was contained in Ch 2 of Pt VII of CA 1990: that is clearly not the case.[74] This provision may provide guidance to a court. Disqualification under s 182 is automatic, however, and does not require any court order for its activation. There is therefore uncertainty about the duration of the period of disqualification under CA 1963, s 183. This makes it difficult for an individual who has been convicted under s 183(1) to know when he can resume activities in relation to a company, without fearing prosecution for acting contrary to a deemed disqualification.[75]

[20.040] An example of disqualification on this ground arose before the Dublin District Court on 6 May 2003. The Court handed down a conviction of the offence of acting as a director while an undischarged bankrupt.[76] The individual in question was convicted, on a guilty plea, of three offences under s 183, as a result of acting as an officer of those companies while an undischarged bankrupt.[77] He was fined a total of €1,200 and was also made the subject of a disqualification order for a period of five years.

---

[72] CA 1963, s 2(1), as inserted by CLEA 2001, s 84(b).

[73] CA 1963, s 183(2), as substituted by CA 1990, s 169.

[74] CA 1990, s 159, does define a 'disqualification order' as including 'an order under s 184 of the Principal Act. However, this does not apply for two reasons: While the reference is to s 184, may be mistaken, as s 184 was repealed by CA 1990, s 6, it nonetheless cannot be read as encompassing deemed disqualifications under s 183. Second, s 162 refers to 'offences under this Chapter' which clearly does not apply to deemed disqualifications under CA 1963, s 183.

[75] CA 1963, s 183(2), as substituted by CA 1990, s 169.

[76] *Director of Corporate Enforcement v Jeffrey Norman Burton* (6 May 2003, unreported), (Dublin District Court), Watkin J. See www.odce.ie.

[77] CA 1963, s 183, as substituted by CA 1990, s 169.

Another example of automatic disqualification on the ground of undischarged bankruptcy arose before Dundalk District Court on 12 October 2004.[78] In that case, two respondents were charged with violations of CA 1990, s 202 (regarding the obligation to keep proper books of account). One of the respondents was also charged under CA 1963, s 183[79] with acting as a director when an undischarged bankrupt. The charges under s 183 were contested and found by the Court to have been proven. The respondent was convicted, fined €50 and ordered to pay prosecution costs of €217.08 and witness expenses of €250. The Court further noted that, having been convicted of an offence under CA 1963, s 183(1), the respondent was deemed to be subject to an order of disqualification under s 183(2). The respondent was therefore disqualified for a period of five years commencing on 12 October 2004.[80]

[20.041] It should be noted that, as s 183 is not within CA 1990, Pt VII, the provisions of that Part do not apply to persons who face automatic disqualification on the ground of bankruptcy. Therefore, the right to apply for relief against the disqualification which other respondents to disqualification proceedings enjoy, is not afforded to respondents under s 183.[81]

---

[78] *Re Tenants First (Ireland) Ltd, Director of Corporate Enforcement v McGovern* (12 October 2004, unreported), Dundalk District Court.

[79] CA 1963, s 183, as substituted by CA 1990, s 169.

[80] In November 2005, two further persons were convicted of the offence of acting as directors while undischarged bankrupts at Mullingar District Court. On a plea of guilty, the defendants were convicted and fined €750 each; they were ordered to pay prosecution costs of €1,000; the Court noted that they were deemed to be subject to a disqualification order under CA 1963, s 183(2). See www.odce.ie.

[81] CA 1990, s 160(8). See further Ch **23**.

Chapter 21

APPLICATIONS FOR DISQUALIFICATION ORDERS

A. Introduction

[21.001] Section 160(2) of CA 1990 provides the basis for a court to make an order of disqualification, referred to here as a 'discretionary disqualification order'. It provides:

> Where the court is satisfied in any proceedings or as a result of an application under this section that—
>
> (a) a person has been guilty, while a promoter, officer, auditor, receiver, liquidator or examiner of a company, of any fraud in relation to the company, its members or creditors; or
>
> (b) a person has been guilty, while a promoter, officer, auditor, receiver, liquidator or examiner of a company, of any breach of his duty as such promoter, officer, auditor, receiver, liquidator or examiner; or
>
> (c) a declaration has been granted under s 297A of the Principal Act (inserted by s 138 of this Act) in respect of a person; or
>
> (d) the conduct of any person as promoter, officer, auditor, receiver, liquidator or examiner of a company, makes him unfit to be concerned in the management of a company; or
>
> (e) in consequence of a report of inspectors appointed by the court or the Director under the Companies Acts, the conduct of any person makes him unfit to be concerned in the management of a company; or
>
> (f) a person has been persistently in default in relation to the relevant requirements; or
>
> (g) a person has been guilty of 2 or more offences under s 202(10); or
>
> (h) a person was a director of a company at the time of the sending, after the commencement of s 42 of the Company Law Enforcement Act 2001, of a letter under subsection (1) of s 12 of the Companies (Amendment) Act 1982, to the company and the name of which, following the taking of the other steps under that section consequent on the sending of that letter, was struck off the register under subsection (3) of that section; or
>
> (i) a person is disqualified under the law of another state (whether pursuant to an order of a judge or a tribunal or otherwise) from being appointed or acting as a director or secretary of a body corporate or an undertaking and the court is satisfied that, if the conduct of the person or the circumstances otherwise affecting him that gave rise to the said order being made against him had occurred or arisen in the State, it would have been proper to make a disqualification order otherwise under this subsection against him.
>
> the court may, of its own motion, or as a result of the application, make a disqualification order against such a person for such period as it sees fit.[1]

---

[1]   CA 1990, s 160(2) as amended by CLEA 2001, ss 14 and 42.

[21.002] Certain issues vary depending on the category of discretionary disqualification which is under consideration, including the appropriate applicant; the potential respondents; and the necessary proofs.

These, among other issues which are particular to the various sub-headings of s 160(2)(a) to (i), are considered under those respective headings.[2]

[21.003] There are other themes that are common to applications under each of the sub-headings of s 160(2)(a) to (i). These include:

– the purpose of an order of disqualification;

– the discretion of the court;

– the onus of proof;

– the procedure;

– the standard of 'fitness' to be applied; and

– the considerations in determining whether to disqualify.

[21.004] There are a number of decisions of the High Court arising from the investigation into the affairs of National Irish Bank Ltd. The background to these cases was the appointment of inspectors by the High Court on 30 March 1998 to investigate the affairs of National Irish Bank Ltd. The scope of the investigation was broadened on 15 June to include the affairs of National Irish Bank Financial Services Limited. The inspectors reported to the court on 9 July 2004 and the Report was published on 30 July 2004.

The inspectors' report ('the Report') concluded that National Irish Bank Limited and National Irish Bank Financial Services Limited (collectively referred to as 'NIB') were involved in a number of improper practices. The Report summarised these practices into six headings:

1. bogus non-resident accounts, opened and maintained in the bank's branches, enabling customers to evade tax through concealment of funds from the Revenue Commissioners;

2. fictitiously named accounts, opened and maintained in the branches, enabling customers to evade tax through concealment of funds from the Revenue Commissioners;

3. Clerical Medical Insurance (CMI) policies, that were promoted as a secure investment for funds undisclosed to the Revenue Commissioners;

4. special saving accounts had deposit interest retention tax (DIRT) deducted at the reduced rate, notwithstanding that the applicable statutory conditions were not observed;

---

[2]   See Ch **22**.

5. improper charging of interest to customers;

6. improper charging of fees to customers.[3]

The DCE issued motions seeking orders of disqualification in respect of nine individuals, arising from the NIB Report.[4]

As of October 2007, judgments have been delivered in respect of three individuals: Nigel D'Arcy, Kevin Curran and Barry Seymour.[5] These judgments contain important statements of the law governing disqualification proceedings and will be relied upon extensively in this chapter.

B. Purpose of a disqualification order

[21.005] The objective of an order of disqualification is usually considered in the context of discretionary orders, rather than deemed disqualifications. The prevailing authorities indicate that disqualification orders are primarily designed to protect the public from directors who would be a danger to creditors and others. The decision of Brown Wilkinson VC in *Re Lo-Line Ltd*[6] to this effect has been approved by the Supreme Court in *Re CB Readymix Ltd*[7] and in numerous decisions of the High Court.[8] This approach is now firmly part of Irish law:

'What is the proper approach to deciding whether someone is unfit to be a director? The approach adopted in all the cases to which I have been referred is

---

3 See *Re National Irish Bank Ltd, Director of Corporate Enforcement v D'Arcy* [2006] 2 IR 163 at 165 to 166.

4 By press release dated 28 July 2005, the DCE announced that he had initiated proceedings under s 160(2)(b), (d), and (e) against the following persons:

Jim Lacey, former Chief Executive, NIB; Barry Seymour, former Executive Director, NIB; Frank Brennan, former General Manager – Retail Banking, NIB and other titles; Michael Keane, former General Manager – Banking, NIB and other titles; Dermott Boner, former Head of Retail, NIB and other titles; Kevin Curran, former Head of Retail Banking, NIB and other titles; Tom McMenamin, a former Regional Manager, NIB and other titles; Patrick Byrne, former Head of Finance, NIB, and Nigel D'Arcy, former Head of the Financial Advice and Services Division, NIB.

Available at www.odce.ie.

5 It appears from the *Legal Diary* that the application in respect of Jim Lacey was listed for hearing on 2 October 2007 and those in respect of Patrick Byrne and Dermott Boner were listed for hearing on 13 November 2007 and 27 November 2007 respectively. Available at www.courts.ie. The applications in respect of Tom McMenamin and Michael Keane do not appear to have been heard to date.

6 *Re Lo-Line Ltd* [1988] Ch 477.

7 *Re CB Readymix Ltd, Cahill v Grimes* [2002] 1 IR 372.

8 See, eg, *Re National Irish Bank Ltd, Director of Corporate Enforcement v Seymour* [2007] IEHC 102; *Re Ansbacher (Cayman) Ltd, Director of Corporate Enforcement v Stakelum* (31 July 2007, unreported), HC; and *Re National Irish Bank Ltd, Director of Corporate Enforcement v D'Arcy* [2006] 2 IR 163.

broadly the same. The primary purpose of the section is not to punish the individual but to protect the public against the future conduct of companies by persons whose past records as directors of insolvent companies have shown them to be a danger to creditors and others. Therefore, the power is not fundamentally penal. But, if the power to disqualify is exercised, disqualification does involve a substantial interference with the freedom of the individual. It follows that the rights of the individual must be fully protected. Ordinary commercial misjudgment is in itself not sufficient to justify disqualification. In the normal case, the conduct complained of must display a lack of commercial probity, although I have no doubt that in an extreme case of gross negligence or total incompetence disqualification could be appropriate.'[9]

The application of this approach can be seen in *Re Kentford Securities Ltd*.[10] Peart J set out the purpose of orders under s 160 as follows:

'The purpose of an order under s 160 of the Act is not punitive in nature, but rather protective of the community. The fact that the Court is satisfied that the respondent during the years in question failed to conduct himself in a manner that was proper and responsible, is not something for which the Court must inflict a punishment. That is not the Court's function under the section. The only function of the Court is to, where necessary, and for such period as the Court might consider necessary, prevent a respondent from acting as an auditor or other officer of a company, where the evidence is sufficient to demonstrate that as a matter of probability that the person in question would present a current risk to members of the public who may be adversely affected.'

Applying this approach to the respondent's conduct in *Kentford*, the Court found that:

'... whatever irregular and improper conduct he was mixed up in all those years ago at the behest of his employer and Mr Traynor is a thing of the past, and that the experience of being caught up in other peoples' deceptions and illegality has been a chastening one for him and one to which he will never risk returning.'

Peart J concluded that the respondent did not present a danger from which the public needed to be protected and that it was appropriate for the Court to exercise its discretion against making the order of disqualification sought. It is interesting to note the following aspect of that decision, which suggests that the impact of a disqualification order on a respondent who is guilty of misconduct, should be balanced against the imperative of protecting the public against risks:

'His capacity to earn his living from his chosen profession would be seriously compromised, and the Court must balance such consequences against the legislative intention that the public should be protected from auditors who have fallen short of the standards expected of such an important profession in the commercial life of the country.'

[21.006] Another case which endorses the 'protection of the public' focus of disqualification orders, is *Re National Irish Bank Ltd, Director of Corporate*

---

9   *Re Lo-Line Ltd* [1988] Ch 477 at 485–486.

10 *Re Kentford Securities Ltd, Director of Corporate Enforcement v McCann* [2007] IEHC 1. This case, including its facts, are considered in more detail at paras **[21.016]**, **[21.035]** and **[21.042]**–**[21.043]**.

Enforcement v Seymour.[11] Mr Seymour was appointed as executive director of NIB in April 1994, having no prior management role and no previous executive responsibility in NIB. He spent approximately 27 months in office before his resignation in July 1996. The DCE sought orders of disqualification under s 160(2)(a), (d) and (e). The Court noted that, in respect of the six practices at NIB which were found to be inappropriate, findings were made in respect of the respondent regarding five of these, including the finding that he knew, or should have known, about those practices.

Mr Seymour raised the question of his constitutional right to earn a livelihood and to a good name. Murphy J addressed these submissions by reference to the nature of a disqualification order:

> 'It is clear that an order made under s 160 is not penal in nature – it is not a criminal sanction nor a determination of liability in respect of any losses that accrued to members, creditors or the regulatory authorities – but an indication of a lack of commercial probity in relation to the management of a company.'[12]

[21.007] In addition to the objective of protecting the public, disqualification orders may also have a deterrent purpose. The observations of Lord Woolf MR in *Re Westmid Packing Ltd*[13] in this regard have been cited with approval in a number of decisions of the High Court:[14]

> 'There are occasions when disqualification must be ordered even though, by reason of the director's recognition of his previous failing and the way he has conducted himself since the conduct complained of, he is in fact no longer a danger to the public at all. In such cases it is no longer necessary for the director to be held "off the road" for the protection of the public, but other factors come into play in the wider interests of protecting the public, ie a deterrent element in relation to the director himself and a deterrent element as far as other directors are concerned. Despite the fact that the courts have said disqualification is not a "punishment", in truth the exercise that is being engaged in is little different from any sentencing exercise. The period of disqualification must reflect the gravity of the offence. It must contain deterrent elements. That is what sentencing is all about, and that is what fixing the appropriate period of the disqualification is all about. What Vinelott J (in *Re Pamstock Ltd* [1994] 1 BCLC 716 at 737) called "tunnel vision", ie concentration on the facts of the offence, is necessary when considering whether a director is unfit. In relation to the period of disqualification

---

11 *Re National Irish Bank Ltd, Director of Corporate Enforcement v Seymour* [2007] IEHC 102.

12 *Re National Irish Bank Ltd, Director of Corporate Enforcement v Seymour* [2007] IEHC 102. See further para **[21.038]**.

13 *Re Westmid Packing Ltd* [1998] 2 All ER 124.

14 See, eg, *Re Ansbacher (Cayman) Ltd, Director of Corporate Enforcement v Stakelum* (31 July 2007, unreported), HC; *Re National Irish Bank Ltd, Director of Corporate Enforcement v D'Arcy* [2006] 2 IR 163; *Re Ansbacher (Cayman) Ltd, Director of Corporate Enforcement v Collery* [2006] IEHC 67.

the facts of the offence are still obviously important but many other factors ought (and in reality do) come into play.'[15]

[21.008] In *Re Ansbacher (Cayman) Ltd, Director of Corporate Enforcement v Stakelum*[16] McGovern J noted that 'in certain circumstances a deterrent element may be necessary in deciding whether or not to make a disqualification order.'

In *Re Ansbacher (Cayman) Ltd, Director of Corporate Enforcement v Collery*,[17] Finlay Geoghegan J set out a number of principles that should be taken into account in determining the appropriate disqualification period:

'(1) The primary purpose of an order of disqualification is not to punish the individual but to protect the public against future conduct of companies by persons whose past record has shown them to be a danger to creditors and others.

(2) The period of disqualification should reflect (in relation to and order under s 160(2)(e)) the gravity of the conduct as found by the Inspectors which makes the respondent unfit to be concerned in the management of a company.

(3) The period of disqualification should contain deterrent elements.

(4) A period of disqualification in excess of ten years should be reserved for particularly serious cases.

(5) The court should firstly assess the correct period in accordance with the foregoing and then take into account mitigating factors prior to fixing the actual period of disqualification.'

[21.009] On these authorities, while the primary purpose of a disqualification order is to protect the public, rather than to punish the respondent, the period of disqualification that is imposed should 'contain deterrent elements.' Even if it is apparent that a person is unlikely to pose a future risk to the public, the severity of the wrongdoing may nonetheless warrant a substantial period of disqualification, to deter the recurrence of such wrongdoing.

C. Discretion of the Court

[21.010] On an application under s 160(2), the Court enjoys full discretion in determining whether to make an order of disqualification and the appropriate period of disqualification. Indeed, the court can make an order of disqualification on any of the grounds set out in s 160(2) 'of its own motion'.[18] This can be contrasted with the

---

15   *Re Westmid Packing Ltd* [1998] 2 All ER 124 at 131 to 132. Different portions of this quote were contained in the judgments of Kelly J in *Re National Irish Bank Ltd, Director of Corporate Enforcement v D'Arcy* [2006] 2 IR 163, and McGovern J in *Re Ansbacher (Cayman) Ltd, Director of Corporate Enforcement v Stakelum* (31 July 2007, unreported), HC, but each contain the essential statements that a period of disqualification must contain 'deterrent elements.'

16   *Re Ansbacher (Cayman) Ltd, Director of Corporate Enforcement v Stakelum* (31 July 2007, unreported), HC.

17   *Re Ansbacher (Cayman) Ltd, Director of Corporate Enforcement v Collery* [2006] IEHC 67.

18   See CA 1990, s 160(2).

mandatory nature of declarations of restriction and the automatic nature of disqualifications under s 160(1).[19]

Cases such as *Re National Irish Bank Ltd, Director of Corporate Enforcement v D'Arcy*[20] and *Re Ansbacher (Cayman) Ltd, Director of Corporate Enforcement v Collery*[21] in which the respondents did not contest the disqualification applications demonstrate the extent of the court's discretion on an application under s 160(2). As Kelly J noted in *Re National Irish Bank Ltd, Director of Corporate Enforcement v D'Arcy*,[22] in spite of the decision of the applicant not to contest the application, 'Nonetheless, as the power given to the court is a discretionary one, the court has to be satisfied that the statutory conditions have been met and that the onus of proof has been discharged by the applicant.'[23]

The scope of the Court's discretion under s 160(2) was also described by Peart J in *Re Kentford Securities Ltd*:[24]

> 'Under s 160 the Court has a discretion whether or not to grant the order, even where findings of fact are made which are consistent with the respondent being guilty of a breach of his duty as auditor, and/or that his conduct makes him unfit to be concerned in the management of a company.'

On this authority, a court may refuse to make an order of disqualification, even if satisfied that the grounds for making such an order have been fully established. In that case, the Court found in favour of the applicant in relation to each of the allegations advanced in support of the application; no order of disqualification was nonetheless made.

D. Onus of proof

[21.011] The onus of proof in a restriction application under s 150 is on the director to prove that he acted honestly and responsibly within the meaning of that section.[25] In disqualification proceedings, by contrast, the onus of proof lies on the applicant. In *Re Newcastle Timber Ltd*,[26] McCracken J described this distinction as follows:

> 'A very important distinction between these two sections is that under s 160 where, as in the present case, an application is made by a liquidator for a disqualification order, the onus is clearly on the liquidator to satisfy the court that the conditions of the section have been complied with, while on the other hand,

---

[19] See Chs **16** and **20**.

[20] *Re National Irish Bank Ltd, Director of Corporate Enforcement v D'Arcy* [2006] 2 IR 163.

[21] *Re Ansbacher (Cayman) Ltd, Director of Corporate Enforcement v Collery* [2006] IEHC 67.

[22] *Re National Irish Bank Ltd, Director of Corporate Enforcement v D'Arcy* [2006] 2 IR 163.

[23] *Re National Irish Bank Ltd, Director of Corporate Enforcement v D'Arcy* [2006] 2 IR 163 at 171.

[24] *Re Kentford Securities Ltd, Director of Corporate Enforcement v McCann* [2007] IEHC 1.

[25] See Ch **16**.

[26] *Re Newcastle Timber Ltd* [2001] 4 IR 586.

under s 150, the court must make a restriction order unless it is satisfied that the person acted honestly and responsibly, and therefore the onus is on the director concerned to satisfy the court as to his honesty and responsibility.'[27]

This approach was endorsed by the Supreme Court in *Re CB Readymix Ltd*:[28]

'The onus does fall on the applicant to establish the allegations on which he relies and, even where a case is made out, the use of the word "may" in s 160(2) confers a discretion on the court whether or not to make the order as was pointed out in *Re Newcastle Timber Ltd (in liquidation)* [2001] 4 IR 586.'[29]

[21.012] In *Re National Irish Bank Ltd, Director of Corporate Enforcement v D'Arcy*,[30] Kelly J considered these authorities, noting that:

'In the light of these authorities it is hardly surprising that the applicant fully accepts that the onus is upon him to satisfy the court that the necessary conditions prescribed in the relevant provisions of s 160(2) of the Act of 1990 are established.'

In cases such as *Re National Irish Bank Ltd, Director of Corporate Enforcement v D'Arcy*[31] and *Re Ansbacher (Cayman) Ltd, Director of Corporate Enforcement v Collery*[32] the respondents to disqualification proceedings did not contest the applications. In spite of such non-opposition, the Court considered the applications carefully: these cases are a good illustration of the onus on the applicant to prove that one of the grounds for making an order of disqualification under s 160(2) exists.

It is now firmly established that the onus of proving the constituent elements of a disqualification application lies on the applicant.

E. Procedure

[21.013] Four questions of procedure under s 160 will be considered here:

   (a)   the initiation of applications under s 160(2);

   (b)   delay in respect of disqualification proceedings;

   (c)   the hearing of disqualification applications; and

   (d)   undertakings.

These matters relate to applications under s 160(2): it should be borne in mind that a court can make an order of disqualification under s 160(2) 'of its own motion'.[33]

---

[27]   *Re Newcastle Timber Ltd* [2001] 4 IR 586 at 589.

[28]   *Re CB Readymix Concrete Ltd, Cahill v Grimes* [2002] 1 IR 372.

[29]   *Re CB Readymix Concrete Ltd, Cahill v Grimes* [2002] 1 IR 372 at 381, *per* Murphy J.

[30]   *Re National Irish Bank Ltd, Director of Corporate Enforcement v D'Arcy* [2006] 2 IR 163 at 171.

[31]   *Re National Irish Bank Ltd, Director of Corporate Enforcement v D'Arcy* [2006] 2 IR 163.

[32]   *Re Ansbacher (Cayman) Ltd, Director of Corporate Enforcement v Collery* [2006] IEHC 67.

[33]   CA 1990, s 160(2).

(a) Initiation of disqualification applications

[21.014] Section 160(7) requires that an applicant for an order of disqualification under s 160(2) must give ten days' notice of his intention to do so, to the person in respect of whom the order is sought.[34] The Rules of the Superior Courts (No 4) 1991 substituted O 75B of the Rules. Order 75B(3)(z) provides that the following shall be initiated by way of originating notice of motion:

> An application for a disqualification Order in relation to a person under section 160(2) or in relation to a disqualification Order under section 160 (8). Such an application shall be served on the person in relation to whom the disqualification Order is sought and on any other party to the proceedings and on the applicant for the original disqualification Order, as the case may be ...

According to O 75B(7), 'Every application under the Act shall be grounded upon the affidavit of the party making such application and shall be heard and determined on affidavit unless the Court otherwise orders.' Order 40 of the Rules of the Superior Courts sets out the rules applicable to the form and content of such affidavits.

[21.015] The court has a discretion to direct that an application for an order of disqualification should be heard by way of plenary hearing. Order 75B, r 9 accordingly provides:

> The Court may, in any case in which the Court considers that it is either necessary or desirable in the interests of justice so to do, direct a plenary hearing in the matter and may make such Order and give such directions in relation to the exchange of pleadings and the settling of issues between the parties as shall appear proper in the circumstances.

There are no further rules or directions regarding the procedure of disqualification applications. This can be contrasted with the position in England where there is a detailed Practice Direction on Directors Disqualification Proceedings.[35] It can also be contrasted with the position applicable to restriction proceedings in Ireland, in respect of which a Practice Direction has been formulated.[36]

(b) Delay

[21.016] In *Re Kentford Securities Ltd*,[37] the respondent sought the dismissal of disqualification proceedings on the ground that there was excessive delay in the commencement of those proceedings. The respondent claimed that the application was 'grossly prejudicial,' as it was brought over fifteen years after the date of the first allegation in 1990; that the delay was inordinate and inexcusable; that it would be unjust to allow the application to proceed; and that a disqualification order would be very serious for him due to his practice as an auditor. The applicant contended that the

---

[34] CA 1990, s 160(7).

[35] See 'Practice Direction: Directors Disqualification Proceedings,' Ministry of Justice. Available at www.justice.gov.uk.

[36] See Ch **18**.

[37] *Re Kentford Securities Ltd, Director of Corporate Enforcement v McCann* [2006] IEHC 57.

complaints against the respondent arose from the report of the authorised officer which was not received until the end of 2002 and that some of the allegations related to events during the course of the investigation.

The Court concluded that, while the proceedings were not initiated until 2005, the report that grounded the proceedings did not come to the attention of the applicant until the end of 2002 and that, 'it is only from that date that the Court should consider whether there has been any excessive or unreasonable delay which has resulted in an unfair prejudice to the applicant's ability to meet the application.'

Peart J noted that there is no statutory time limit for the commencement of disqualification proceedings, and went on to state:

> 'That of course cannot mean that in no circumstances could a person against whom such an application is brought, seek a stay or similar relief such as the present applicant seeks on the grounds of excessive delay, especially where a sufficient case of prejudice to the ability to defend against the application is made out. There must be implied an obligation on the part of an applicant for such an order to proceed with a degree of expedition which in all the circumstances is reasonable. Many factors may interfere with the capacity of the Director to proceed with the application forthwith upon receipt of the necessary information which would ground the application.'[38]

In that case, the DCE was entitled to consider the report of the authorised officer and decide how to proceed, including taking legal advice and commissioning a report of an auditing expert. The Court also made the observation that:

> 'the fact that matters go back many years would, in my view, give rise to a greater need, in the interests of justice, to proceed with all reasonable and possible haste from whatever moment a decision to proceed could be made, and of course from the date of commencement to actual determination.'

[21.017] There was no inordinate or excessive delay in that case, but if there was found to be a delay between the date of delivery of the report and the initiation of proceedings, this was explained sufficiently by the DCE. The Court also determined that the applicant had not discharged the onus of proving a real prejudice 'to the extent that it would be unjust to require him to defend himself against the application which is brought, as a result of any delay,' and that, 'the applicant is in a position to resist the application made in these proceedings without injustice or unfairness'. The lapse of time between the events at issue and the disqualification proceedings can however be taken into account in the disqualification proceedings.[39]

(c) Hearing of disqualification applications

[21.018] An application for a disqualification order is generally heard on affidavit. If the respondent is represented, there will typically be exchanges of affidavits before the application is set down for hearing. These affidavits will then be opened to the court,

---

[38]   *Re Kentford Securities Ltd, Director of Corporate Enforcement v McCann* [2006] IEHC 57.

[39]   See further paras **[21.048]** to **[21.049]**.

and legal submissions made, to assist the court in determining whether to grant the order sought.

There have been cases where the respondents have been cross examined on their affidavits. Order 40, r 1, of the Rules of the Superior Courts, is the governing provision in this regard. It provides that:

> Upon any petition, motion, or other application, evidence may be given by affidavit, but the Court may, on the application of either party, order the attendance for cross-examination of the person making any such affidavit.[40]

[21.019] In *Re National Bank Ltd, Director of Corporate Enforcement v Seymour*[41] the applicant filed a motion under O 75B, r 7 and/or O 40, r 1 and/or the inherent jurisdiction of the court, seeking an order of the High Court directing the respondent to attend and be cross-examined on his affidavits, failing which the respondent may not rely on those affidavits at the trial of the substantive application.

The respondent in that case filed three affidavits which raised few if any material points of factual disagreement with the applicant's affidavits but which did challenge the findings of the inspectors' report which were critical of his conduct and which gave rise to the disqualification proceedings. The respondent's objections were to the opinions and conclusions formed in the inspectors' report, rather than its factual findings. On that ground, he argued that it was not an appropriate case in which to direct cross-examination on the affidavits.

O'Donovan J noted the function of cross-examination, 'to cast doubt upon the veracity, accuracy or reliability of evidence given by a witness' and described the situations in which an order to cross-examine should be made:

> 'In my view, it is axiomatic that, when, in the course of applications to the court which are required to be heard and determined on affidavit, as is the situation in this case, it becomes apparent from the affidavits sworn in those proceedings that there are material conflicts of fact between the deponents of those affidavits, the court must, if requested to do so, consider whether or not to direct a plenary hearing of the proceedings or that one or more of the deponents should be cross examined on his or her affidavit. This is so because it is impossible for a judge to resolve a material conflict of fact disclosed in affidavits.'

The Court then considered the appropriate approach when the conflicts of fact are less obvious:

> '... while it seems to me that, where it is debatable as to whether or not the cross examination of a deponent on his or her affidavit is either necessary or desirable, the court should tend towards permitting the cross examination, at the end of the day it is within the discretion of the court as to whether or not such a cross examination should be directed and that discretion should only be exercised in

---

[40] See also O 75B, r 7. See para **[21.014]**.

[41] *Re National Bank Ltd, Director of Corporate Enforcement v Seymour* [2006] IEHC 369 (16 November 2006, unreported), HC, O'Donovan J.

favour of such a cross examination if the court considers that it is necessary for the purpose of disposing of the issues which the court has to determine.'[42]

The Court considered that there was 'substance to the suggestion' that the respondent did not dispute the facts relied on by the inspectors in a material way, but it did not follow that the applicant was not entitled to test the respondent's interpretations of these facts. The respondent argued that it was neither desirable nor appropriate to require cross-examination in the absence of a dispute regarding material facts. The Court posed the following question:

> 'While the respondent may not dispute material facts upon which the inspectors base their findings, given that he challenges virtually every conclusion that the inspectors drew from those facts which reflect unfavourably on himself, is it reasonable to ask a judge to resolve that challenge in the absence of its being tested by cross examination of the respondent?'

In considering the answer to this question, O'Donovan J noted that the report of an inspector is evidence of the opinion of the inspector[43] and that, if that opinion is challenged, even if the facts underlying it are not, 'the court is entitled to know the mindset of the challenger and, in my view, the only way that that can be ascertained is by confronting the challenger under cross examination.'

O'Donovan J further referred to the volume of affidavit evidence which was filed on behalf of the applicant, including the total rejection by the respondent of the opinions and conclusions in the inspectors' report. This was, according to the Court, 'in itself, a justification for testing by cross-examination of the respondent the reliability and, indeed, reasonableness of the contrary views expressed by him.' Recalling that the test to be applied was that of 'commercial probity', O'Donovan J concluded:

> 'In my view, in the absence of such a cross examination, it would be difficult, if not impossible, for the trial judge to come to a reasoned conclusion with regard the commercial probity of the respondent and, accordingly, it seems to me that the interests of justice require that such a cross examination be conducted.'

The Court therefore directed that the respondent must attend the trial for the purpose of being cross examined and that, failing such attendance, the affidavits could not be relied upon at the hearing of the application.

[21.020] While there are means by which disqualification proceedings may be made more protracted, there is no means of expediting the hearing of a disqualification application in Ireland. If a person is not resisting the application, this does reduce the documentation and shorten the court time involved, but the application, supported by evidence, nonetheless has to be heard by the court before an order can be made. It may be noted that a procedure was introduced in England to expedite disqualification

---

[42]   *Re National Bank Ltd, Director of Corporate Enforcement v Seymour* [2006] IEHC 369 (16 November 2006, unreported), HC, O'Donovan J.

[43]   CA 1990, s 22(b).

proceedings. The background to the so-called 'Carecraft' process[44] was described as follows by Hart J in *Re INS Realisations Ltd*:[45]

> '18. Prior to the 2000 [Insolvency] Act there was no ability to dispose of disqualification proceedings on the basis of a consent order embodying the agreement of the parties to an appropriate period of disqualification. The court itself had to be satisfied that the jurisdictional conditions for the making of a disqualification order were met, that it was appropriate to make (or the Act required the making of) a disqualification order, and as to the relevant period of order that should be made on the facts of the case.
>
> 19. To temper that difficulty, the summary procedure approved in *In Re Carecraft Construction Co Ltd* [1994] 1 WLR 172 (with slight amendment and the approval of the Court of Appeal in *Secretary of State for Trade and Industry v Rogers* [1996] 1 WLR 1569) was developed. Under that procedure a statement of facts was put before the court on an agreed basis and no oral evidence was called by either party. The parties generally submitted to the court that the agreed facts satisfied the conditions of the relevant section of the 1986 Act and submitted what would be an appropriate period of disqualification. The court was not bound either to determine that the conditions of the relevant section were met nor that an order should be made for the period suggested.'[46]

Due to concerns about the cost and time expended under the Carecraft process, the legislature intervened and there is now a statutory process for disqualification undertakings to be furnished.[47] In the present context, it is interesting to contrast the development of a summary procedure for disqualifications in England with the absence of any such process in Ireland.

(d) Undertakings

[21.021] An issue that has been raised by the High Court is that there is no procedure under s 160 for a respondent to furnish an undertaking not to be involved in companies in the manner prohibited by disqualification orders. In *Re National Irish Bank Ltd, Director of Corporate Enforcement v D'Arcy*[48] the respondent did not contest the disqualification application and, as Kelly J recorded:

> 'He went somewhat further than that because even before these proceedings were commenced his solicitors wrote, on his instructions, tendering his resignation with immediate effect from the two companies of which he is a director. He also

---

[44] This process was named after the case from which it originated: *Re Carecraft Construction Co Ltd* [1994] 1 WLR 172.

[45] *Re INS Realisations Ltd Secretary of State for Trade and Industry v Jonkler* [2006] EWHC 135 (Ch), [2006] 1 WLR 3433.

[46] *Re INS Realisations Ltd Secretary of State for Trade and Industry v Jonkler* [2006] EWHC 135 (Ch), [2006] 1 WLR 3433 at 3440 to 3441.

[47] The Insolvency Act 2000 inserted a new s 1A (and related provisions) into the Directors Disqualification Act 1986, which permits disqualification undertakings, having the same effect and consequences as disqualification orders, to be furnished. See further paras **[21.021]** to **[21.023]**.

[48] *Re National Irish Bank Ltd, Director of Corporate Enforcement v D'Arcy* [2006] 2 IR 163.

indicated a willingness to give an undertaking in writing to the applicant that he would not act as director, promoter, officer or involve himself in any way in the formation or management of both those companies or any company whatsoever.'[49]

[21.022] In *Director of Corporate Enforcement v Curran,* Mr Curran submitted that the DCE did not contact him before initiating the disqualification proceedings to seek information regarding his future plans or inviting an undertaking as to the level of responsibility he would take in any business in which he might be involved.[50] Murphy J made the following observation:

'The question arises whether the legislation should be amended with a view to compelling the Director to require an undertaking from such a director/officer. There would appear to be no provision whereby such undertaking could be a matter of public record. It could be noted by the Director of Corporate Enforcement and/or by the Company Registration Office. It would be an immediate remedy and a saving in court time and of costs.'[51]

A similar proposal was made by the ODCE, but was not enacted in the IFCMPA 2006:

'... the introduction of "consent" procedures for disqualification and restriction in recognition of the fact that many such Court proceedings were not contested. These consent undertakings would have a similar legal status to the present Court orders and would therefore save the associated legal costs of proceeding to Court. In relevant cases, this would benefit the liquidation and make more funds available for distribution to the company's creditors.'[52]

[21.023] There is no statutory provision permitting a person to furnish an undertaking not to do those things that would be prohibited by an order of disqualification. This can be contrasted with the position in England, where a person can give an undertaking in the terms of a disqualification order for such period between two and fifteen years as may be agreed.[53] As reported by the Department of Trade and Industry:

'On 2 April 2001, amendments to s 6 of [Directors Disqualification Act 1986] made by the Insolvency Act 2000 came into force. Amongst other things, this allows directors, whom the Secretary of State considers to have exhibited unfit conduct, to avoid the need for a court hearing by offering a Disqualification Undertaking acceptable to the Secretary of State. A Disqualification Undertaking has exactly the same legal effect as a Disqualification Order made by the court and usually includes a Schedule identifying the unfit conduct upon which it was accepted. The consequences of breaching a Disqualification Undertaking are the

---

[49] *Re National Irish Bank Ltd, Director of Corporate Enforcement v D'Arcy* [2006] 2 IR 163 at 180.

[50] *Re National Irish Bank Ltd, Director of Corporate Enforcement v Curran* [2007] IEHC 181. At para 9.13.

[51] *Re National Irish Bank Ltd, Director of Corporate Enforcement v Curran* [2007] IEHC 181. At para 9.13.

[52] ODCE, *Annual Report 2006* at p 9.

[53] See DTI, 'Fast Track Disqualifications results in Record Bans' (2 January 2002).

same as those for breaching a Disqualification Order. This undertaking is enforceable in the same manner as an order of disqualification.'[54]

In light of the decision of some persons who face disqualification proceedings in Ireland not to resist those applications,[55] an undertaking would be a more cost-effective and efficient means of achieving the objectives of disqualification orders, than lengthy and costly court proceedings. The CLRG indeed recommends the introduction of disqualification undertakings, pursuant to which the person giving the undertaking will be disqualified for the period specified in the undertaking, subject to a minimum period of one year's disqualification.[56]

F. Test of fitness

[21.024] While it is not universal to all applications under s 160(2), one of the most heavily analysed grounds of disqualification is that of 'unfitness to be concerned in the management of a company'. This ground is contained in both sub-ss 160(2)(d) and (e).

The decision of the Supreme Court in *Re CB Readymix Ltd*[57] is an example of the application of s 160(2)(d) and is the first decision of the Supreme Court under s 160. This decision was the culmination of one of a series of legal proceedings which arose from the liquidation of a company incorporated as 'Readymix Limited'. The company was struck off the register of companies for failure to file annual returns. While struck off, the company purported to pass a resolution winding up the company and appointing Mr Grimes to act as liquidator. The company having been restored to the register of companies, the Revenue Commissioners brought an application to have the company wound up. A provisional liquidator and, subsequently, an official liquidator, were appointed to act and the High Court held the earlier resolution of the company to be invalid. The official liquidator then brought an application to have Mr Grimes disqualified under CA 1990, s 160.[58] Among the grounds for seeking the order of disqualification was the allegation that Mr Grimes had destroyed books and records of the company.

---

[54] DTI, 'Fast Track Disqualifications results in Record Bans' (2 January 2002). The Department also reports that, 'Under the new rules directors can give an undertaking not to act as a director for an agreed period between 2 and 15 years. The undertakings are made to The Insolvency Service and registered at Companies House. They are accessible by public search and if contravened will constitute criminal offence. Today's figures show that of the 935 disqualifications recorded in the half year period (Q2&3), 57% were on the basis of undertakings given to and accepted by The Insolvency Service.'

[55] See, eg, *Re National Irish Bank Ltd, Director of Corporate Enforcement v D'Arcy* [2006] 2 IR 163 at 180 and *Re Ansbacher (Cayman) Ltd, Director of Corporate Enforcement v Collery* [2006] IEHC 67.

[56] See General Scheme of the Draft Companies Consolidation and Reform Bill 2007, Pt A13, Head 51. Available at www.clrg.org.

[57] *Re CB Readymix Ltd, Cahill v Grimes* [2002] 1 IR 372.

[58] CA 1990, s 160, as amended by CLEA 2001, s 42.

The High Court (Smyth J) disqualified the respondent from being involved in the management of a company or as liquidator, receiver or examiner of a company for a period of seven years. With regard to the offices of auditor, director and secretary, the Court ordered that the respondent could only occupy those offices if he had the necessary professional qualifications and further ordered that:

> 'at no stage or time is he to have possession, custody or control of the seal of any such company or any of its books or records of any kind whatsoever, so however he is entitled to have access to such books and records only as are necessary to enable him to discharge his legal obligations.'

The Court further ordered that the respondent 'may only act as a director of a company whose constitution and management provide for a board of directors of three or more persons'.[59] The respondent appealed the decision to the Supreme Court.

[21.025] The Supreme Court noted that the onus is on the applicant to establish the allegations on which he relies and that, '[t]he appropriateness of the sanction imposed by the trial judge must be considered in the light of the conduct of the respondent and the purpose for which the section was enacted.'[60] In relation to the approach to be adopted, Murphy J quoted the following dicta of Browne-Wilkinson VC in *Re Lo-Line Ltd*:[61]

> 'What is the proper approach to deciding whether someone is unfit to be a director? The approach adopted in all the cases to which I have been referred is broadly the same. The primary purpose of the section is not to punish the individual but to protect the public against the future conduct of companies by persons whose past records as directors of insolvent companies have shown them to be a danger to creditors and others. Therefore, the power is not fundamentally penal. But, if the power to disqualify is exercised, disqualification does involve a substantial interference with the freedom of the individual. It follows that the rights of the individual must be fully protected. Ordinary commercial misjudgment is in itself not sufficient to justify disqualification. In the normal case, the conduct complained of must display a lack of commercial probity, although I have no doubt that in an extreme case of gross negligence or total incompetence disqualification could be appropriate.'

Murphy J noted that this *dicta* was quoted with approval by the High Court in *Re CB Readymix Ltd* and was adopted by Shanley J in *La Moselle Clothing Ltd v Soualhi*,[62] by McGuinness J in *Re Squash (Ireland) Ltd*[63] and by McCracken J in *Re Newcastle Timber Ltd*.[64] He concluded, 'It is I believe a correct statement of the law and represents a proper approach to the application and interpretation of s 160 of the Companies Act 1990.'[65]

---

[59] *Re CB Readymix Ltd, Cahill v Grimes* [2002] 1 IR 372 at 379.

[60] *Re CB Readymix Ltd, Cahill v Grimes* [2002] 1 IR 372 at 383.

[61] *Re Lo-Line Ltd* [1988] Ch 477 at 485–486. See *Re CB Readymix Ltd, Cahill v Grimes* [2002] 1 IR 372 at 383.

[62] *La Moselle Clothing Ltd v Soualhi* [1998] 2 ILRM 345.

[63] *Re Squash (Ireland) Ltd* [2001] 3 IR 35.

[64] *Re Newcastle Timber Ltd* [2001] 4 IR 586.

[65] *Re CB Readymix Ltd, Cahill v Grimes* [2002] 1 IR 372 at 382.

[21.026] The most important aspect of the decision in *Re CB Readymix Ltd*[66] is its approval and adoption of the test of 'unfitness' advanced in *Re Lo-Line Electric Motors Ltd*[67] as the 'proper approach to the application and interpretation of s 160.'[68] This position was also confirmed in the decision of McCracken J in *Re Newcastle Timber Ltd*,[69] in which he stated, in the context of an application for an order of disqualification under s 160(2)(b) and (d), '[t]he approach to be taken by the Court has been very clearly set out by Browne-Wilkinson VC in *In Re: Lo-line Motors Limited* (1988) BCLC 698.'[70]

[21.027] The essential elements of this approach to determining whether someone is 'unfit to the concerned in the management of a company' are that:

1. Ordinary commercial misjudgment is not enough in itself to justify an order of disqualification.

2. The conduct that is alleged to make the person unfit, must display a lack of commercial probity; and

3. In an extreme case of gross negligence or total incompetence, an order of disqualification may be justified.

The test set out by Brown-Wilkinson VC in *Re Lo-Line Ltd*[71] and adopted by Murphy J in *Re CB Readymix Ltd*,[72] has been adopted and applied in many decisions of the High Court.[73]

[21.028] At the time of the decision in *Re Wood Products (Longford) Ltd*,[74] the Court noted that 'there are very few authorities on the nature of the conduct which renders a person unfit.' The Court found that the respondents acted irresponsibly; blatantly disregarded their statutory duties to file annual returns over a protracted period of time;[75] defaulted in making returns to the Revenue Commissioners; disregarded the

---

[66] *Re CB Readymix Ltd, Cahill v Grimes* [2002] 1 IR 372.

[67] *Re Lo-Line Ltd* [1988] Ch 477.

[68] *Re CB Readymix Ltd, Cahill v Grimes* [2002] 1 IR 372 at 382.

[69] *Re Newcastle Timber Ltd* [2001] IEHC 146.

[70] *Re Newcastle Timber Ltd* [2001] IEHC 146 at para 13.

[71] *Re Lo-Line Ltd* [1988] Ch 477.

[72] *Re CB Readymix Ltd, Cahill v Grimes* [2002] 1 IR 372.

[73] See, eg, *Re National Irish Bank Ltd, Director of Corporate Enforcement v Seymour* [2007] IEHC 102; *Re Ansbacher (Cayman) Ltd, Director of Corporate Enforcement v Stakelum* (31 July 2007, unreported), HC; and *Re National Irish Bank Ltd, Director of Corporate Enforcement v D'Arcy* [2006] 2 IR 163; *Re National Irish Bank Ltd, Director of Corporate Enforcement v Curran* [2007] IEHC 181; *Re Barnroe Ltd, Director of Corporate Enforcement v Rogers* [2005] IEHC 433.

[74] *Re Wood Products (Longford) Ltd, Director of Corporate Enforcement v McGowan* [2005] IEHC 41.

[75] In this regard, Laffoy J stated that, 'I think it is not unreasonable to conclude that to some extent this was facilitated by a failure on the part of the CRO to take action to ensure compliance with s 125 until the late 1990s.' *Re Wood Products (Longford) Ltd, Director of Corporate Enforcement v McGowan* [2005] IEHC 41.

order of the court to file such returns; and, most reprehensibly, failed to discharge the company's revenue liabilities. Laffoy J cited the decision of Browne-Wilkinson VC in *Re Lo-Line Ltd*,[76] as approved by the Supreme Court in *Re CB Readymix Ltd*,[77] and went on to find that:

> 'In the context of the application of s 160, the question which arises is whether they have displayed a lack of commercial probity or, as it is sometimes put, whether they have fallen below the standards of commercial morality. In my view, the conduct of the respondents has come very close to that threshold, but has not quite reached it. The saving grace is that the first respondent eventually, albeit when faced with an application by the Director for a disqualification order, remedied the breaches of the Companies Acts and the taxation code in relation to making returns. Both parties combined in restructuring the corporate governance of the Company, which, hopefully, will prevent a repetition of the defaults which occurred in the past. The first respondent, on behalf of the Company, has evinced an intention to discharge the Company's indebtedness to the Revenue Commissioners. While, given that the "sword of Damocles" in the form of the mortgage suit hangs over the Company, little credit accrues to the respondents on this account, it is in the interests of the employees of, and third parties dealing with, the Company that the eventuality of a forced sale of the Company's premises be avoided. On the evidence, that can be achieved. In the circumstances, I consider it appropriate not to make a disqualification order against either respondent. I am satisfied it is not necessary to do so to protect the public.'

[21.029] The test of 'unfitness' was considered in each of the decisions arising from the NIB Report. The first such case was *Re National Irish Bank Ltd, Director of Corporate Enforcement v D'Arcy*.[78] The respondent (Mr D'Arcy) was recruited to establish and head up the financial advice and services division (FASD), reporting to the Chief Executive and subsequently the Executive Director. All financial services managers in FASD reported to the respondent. The inspectors' report found that Mr D'Arcy was aware of a number of issues concerning CMI, including that funds undisclosed to the Revenue Commissioners were being targeted by bank personnel for investment in CMI; that prospective investors were being assured by the FASD managers that their investment would be confidential from the Revenue Commissioners; that CMI was being used by the bank to regularise bogus non-resident accounts and fictitious and incorrectly named accounts; and that the manner in which the CMI policies were being promoted facilitated the evasion of tax by persons investing in the policies.

Mr D'Arcy was found by the inspectors to have been aware of these practices since 1992. As head of FASD, he could have stopped the manner in which CMI policies were promoted by FASD managers: he was, in the opinion of the inspectors, primarily responsible for the continuation of that practice. According to the inspectors, this practice continued for a period of six years.

---

[76] *Re Lo-Line Ltd* [1988] Ch 477.

[77] *Re CB Readymix Ltd, Cahill v Grimes* [2002] 1 IR 372.

[78] *Re National Irish Bank Ltd, Director of Corporate Enforcement v D'Arcy* [2006] 2 IR 163.

[21.030] In *Re National Irish Bank Ltd, Director of Corporate Enforcement v D'Arcy*[79] the applicant relied upon the findings in the inspectors' report as a ground for making an order of disqualification in respect of the respondent. In relation to test to be applied to determine whether a person is 'unfit to be concerned in the management of a company,' Kelly J cited the decision of the Supreme Court in *Re CB Readymix Ltd*[80] approving the *dictum* of Browne-Wilkinson VC in *Re Lo-Line Ltd*[81] noting that that *dictum* has been approved in several decisions of the Irish courts. Kelly J also adopted this test, noting the distinction between the context in which 'unfitness' was interpreted in *Re Lo-Line Ltd* and its use in s 160(2)(e):

> 'Whilst the observations of Browne-Wilkinson V.C. were related to the unfitness
> of a director and dealt with an insolvent company, a similar line of reasoning is
> applicable to the question of the disqualification of a person whose conduct is
> alleged to have made him unfit to be concerned in the management of a company.
> His conduct must show a lack of commercial probity or gross negligence or total
> incompetence before disqualification can be ordered.'[82]

Kelly J referred to prior decisions of the Irish courts under s 160, *Re Newcastle Timber Ltd*,[83] *Re Wood Products (Longford) Ltd*,[84] and *Re CB Readymix Ltd*.[85] The Court noted, however, that:

> 'It is a truism that every case has to be decided upon its own facts and whilst these
> cases are helpful in demonstrating the general approach of the court, ultimately I
> have to decide whether, on the material put in evidence here, the respondent's
> conduct was such as to make him unfit to be concerned in the management of a
> company.'

[21.031] In relation to the facts of *Re National Irish Bank Ltd, Director of Corporate Enforcement v D'Arcy*,[86] the Court recalled that Mr D'Arcy was fully aware of the manner in which CMI policies were being promoted by financial services managers who reported to him. This was one of the practices condemned in the inspectors' report, which the inspectors found he could have stopped and for which he was primarily responsible. Kelly J cited a number of factors in determining whether the respondent was 'unfit to be concerned in the management of a company.' First, the practice in question continued for a long time and involved large sums of money. Second, Mr

---

[79] *Re National Irish Bank Ltd, Director of Corporate Enforcement v D'Arcy* [2006] 2 IR 163.

[80] *Re CB Readymix Ltd, Cahill v Grimes* [2002] 1 IR 372.

[81] *Re Lo-Line Ltd* [1988] Ch 477 at 381.

[82] *Re National Irish Bank Ltd, Director of Corporate Enforcement v D'Arcy* [2006] 2 IR 163 at 175.

[83] *Re Newcastle Timber Ltd* [2001] 4 IR 586.

[84] *Re Wood Products (Longford) Ltd, Director of Corporate Enforcement v McGowan* [2005] IEHC 41.

[85] *Re CB Readymix Concrete Ltd, Cahill v Grimes* [2002] 1 IR 372.

[86] *Re National Irish Bank Ltd, Director of Corporate Enforcement v D'Arcy* [2006] 2 IR 163.

D'Arcy was 'in the upper echelons of bank management' and, while he was not at 'the very top level of management,' he was 'at just one remove from it.'[87]

Third, the Court referred to the special position of banks in society:

> 'An extremely serious element of the conduct was that all of it was taking place within a bank. Banks are not just ordinary corporate entities of the type that the court had to deal with in the various cases which I have cited. They occupy a special position in society ... The edifice of banking is built on a foundation of trust.'[88]

This was a trust which had been broken according to the findings of the inspectors' report, by dishonesty in the operation of the CMI policies. A fourth consideration cited by Kelly J was that the operation of the CMI policies was carried out 'in a deliberate fashion,' and the respondent could have stopped it, but did not. The inspectors held Mr D'Arcy primarily responsible for the inappropriate manner in which the CMI policies were promoted. The Court concluded that Mr D'Arcy's responsibility for this practice was 'demonstrative of a lack of commercial probity on his part.' The respondent was found to be unfit to be concerned in the management of a company, within the meaning of s 160(2)(e).

[21.032] Murphy J in *Re National Irish Bank Ltd, Director of Corporate Enforcement v Seymour*[89] compared s 160(2)(e) and (d) with the other provisions of s 160, noting that:

> 'Sub-s (2)(d) appears wider in scope. There is no requirement of guilt or of breach. Sub-s (2)(e) is not restricted to officers, nor is there any requirement of guilt or of breach. Where a person's conduct, in consequence of a report of inspectors, makes him unfit to be concerned in the management of a company, the court make a disqualification order.'[90]

Murphy J reiterated the standard for determining whether a person is 'unfit', as set out in *Re Lo-Line Ltd* and considered: 'What is critical is the enforcement of standards of management.' This can be distinguished from cases involving insolvent trading, failure to keep records or make returns; 'it extends to a situation where a director fails to act as he is required to act, fails to take action which should have been taken and fails to realise that which ought to have been realised.'

[21.033] In *Re National Irish Bank Ltd, Director of Corporate Enforcement v Curran*[91] the Court also referred to the test in *Re Lo-Line Ltd,*[92] as confirmed by the Supreme

---

87 *Re National Irish Bank Ltd, Director of Corporate Enforcement v D'Arcy* [2006] 2 IR 163 at 177.

88 *Re National Irish Bank Ltd, Director of Corporate Enforcement v D'Arcy* [2006] 2 IR 163 at 177.

89 *Re National Irish Bank Ltd, Director of Corporate Enforcement v Seymour* [2007] IEHC 102.

90 *Re National Irish Bank Ltd, Director of Corporate Enforcement v Seymour* [2007] IEHC 102 at para 11.3.

91 *Re National Irish Bank Ltd, Director of Corporate Enforcement v Curran* [2007] IEHC 181.

92 *Re Lo-Line Ltd* [1988] Ch 477 at 381.

Court in *Re CB Readymix Limited*[93] that the approach in deciding whether someone is unfit to be a director is not to punish but to protect the public and that ordinary commercial misjudgement is not sufficient to justify disqualification. Murphy J confirmed that, 'There would not seem to be any deviation in principles underlying such approach.'

In *Re National Irish Bank Ltd, Director of Corporate Enforcement v Curran*[94] the respondent was a regional manager and, laterally, the Head of Retail Banking. He was not a director and did not occupy a position of management. Distinguishing the situation in *Re National Irish Bank Ltd, Director of Corporate Enforcement v Seymour*, in which the respondent was found to be in a position to secure compliance, Murphy J found that Mr Curran was not in such a position, even as Head of Retail Banking: 'Mr Curran did not appear to have had any line of communication with the Audit Committee nor, indeed, with the Board of Directors.'

Referring to the words of s 160, that a person must be considered to be 'unfit to be concerned in the management of a company,' Murphy J noted that 'management in that sense is direction or governance.' In the case of Mr Curran, the Court found that 'he was not involved in the direction or governance of the Bank.' On grounds which are considered in more detail below, the Court did not make an order of disqualification in respect of Mr Curran.

[21.034] In *Re Ansbacher (Cayman) Ltd, Director of Corporate Enforcement v Stakelum*[95] the DCE applied for an order of disqualification under s 160(2)(e), based on the findings in an inspectors' report that the Ansbacher (Cayman) Ltd's affairs had been conducted with intent to defraud the Revenue Commissioners, among other findings. The inspectors' report made certain findings in respect of the respondent, including that he assisted the company in its Irish business; made use of a non-interest bearing account to hide the business from the Revenue Commissioners; provided a mechanism for Irish residents to withdraw offshore funds in Ireland; and that he carried on this business with intent to defraud the Revenue Commissioners. The inspectors concluded that there was evidence tending to show that the respondent had committed certain offences, such as conspiracy to defraud and breaches of the Taxes Consolidation Act 1997.

McGovern J repeated the test set out in *Re Lo-Line Ltd* and adopted in *Re CB Readymix Ltd* that, 'ordinarily commercial misjudgement is not in itself sufficient to justify disqualification. In the normal case the conduct complained of must display a lack of commercial probity ...'. The Court also noted the decision in *Re National Irish Bank Ltd, Director of Corporate Enforcement v Seymour*[96] that, 'a failure to comply with legislation by a person who had responsibility and who could have resolved issues of non-compliance, is sufficient to justify disqualification.' The Court concluded that the

---

[93] *Re CB Readymix Limited, Cahill v Grimes* [2002] 1 IR 372.

[94] *Re National Irish Bank Ltd, Director of Corporate Enforcement v Curran* [2007] IEHC 181.

[95] *Re Ansbacher (Cayman) Ltd, Director of Corporate Enforcement v Stakelum* (31 July 2007, unreported), HC.

[96] *Re National Irish Bank Ltd, Director of Corporate Enforcement v Seymour* [2007] IEHC 102.

findings of the inspectors were reasonable in light of the facts established by them and, applying the test of *Re Lo-Line Ltd*, made the following determination:

> 'the respondent was engaged in activity designed to conceal funds from the Revenue Commissioners. On that ground alone it seems that his conduct displayed 'a lack of commercial probity' as referred to in *Re Lo-Line*.'

These matters made the respondent unfit to be concerned in the management of a company and the Court imposed a period of disqualification of five years.

[21.035] In another case related to the Ansbacher affair, *Re Kentford Securities Ltd*,[97] Peart J considered whether the respondent, an auditor and former director of a company, was 'unfit to be concerned in the management of a company.' This decision adds an interesting dimension to the interpretation of that phrase: the Court must be satisfied that the respondent is, at present, unfit to be so concerned. It is not sufficient if the person was 'unfit to be concerned in the management of a company' in the past:

> 'It is important to note the use of the present tense in relation to unfitness to be involved in the management of a company. That is relevant in the present case where the conduct complained of and found to have occurred, did so between twelve and eighteen years ago. The question to be considered is whether at the time of this application the past conduct makes him presently unfit to be so involved. The reason for this being so is, as I have just referred to, that the section's purpose is not to punish the respondent, but rather to ensure as far as possible that members of the public are protected from harm. If the respondent is not now somebody against who the public should be protected, then the Court ought not to make the order sought, even if the matters alleged to give rise to disqualification have been established, as they have in this case.'

[21.036] In *Re Barnroe Ltd*[98] the Court considered an application for an order of disqualification of two directors under s 160(2)(a), (b) and (d), following the investigations of an authorised officer. The Court found that the respondents:

- Failed to keep proper books of accounts;
- Operated a bank account not recorded in the company's books;
- Failed to disclose the aforementioned account to the company's auditor;
- Appropriated funds of the company for personal use;
- Failed to file revenue returns; and
- Caused the company to trade while insolvent for a considerable period of time.

O'Leary J quoted the dicta of Brown-Wilkinson VC in *Re Lo-Line Ltd* setting out the test of unfitness as 'a lack of commercial probity', and determined that the matters set out above, particularly the operation of a bank account in the company's name outside the books and records of the company; the failure to disclose this account to the auditor; and the appropriation of company funds, were evidence of 'a lack of commercial probity.' The Court further concluded that, 'taken together they represent a formidable

---

[97] *Re Kentford Securities Ltd, Director of Corporate Enforcement v McCann* [2007] IEHC 1.

[98] *Re Barnroe Ltd, Director of Corporate Enforcement v Rogers* [2005] IEHC 433.

body of evidence on the lack of commercial probity of the respondents.' An order of disqualification was therefore made in that case.

G. Considerations

[21.037] There are certain matters which are taken into account by the courts in determining whether an order of disqualification is warranted. While these matters are often considered in determining whether the person is 'fit to be concerned in the management of a company,' they may have broader application. These include, to varying degrees:

(a)   the seniority of the respondent and his ability to control the matters complained of;

(b)   the experience or qualifications of the respondent;

(c)   the extent to which the respondent attempted to rectify or stop the matters complained of;

(d)   the potential impact of a disqualification order on the respondent;

(e)   the lapse of time; and

(f)   the attitude taken in the proceedings.

There is some overlap between these factors and the mitigating factors that may be taken into account by a court in determining the appropriate period of disqualification. The distinction is blurred in some instances. The decisions cited in this section invoke these factors in determining whether to make an order of disqualification, not the duration of the period.[99]

(a) Seniority

[21.038] The most vivid illustration of the importance of the seniority of an individual in determining whether to make an order of disqualification can be seen in *Re National Irish Bank Ltd, Director of Corporate Enforcement v Seymour*.[100] The Court pointed to the fact that the inspectors identified serious defaults in the management and legal compliance at NIB and that, 'Mr Seymour, for a period of 27 months, was the single most senior and responsible employee in the company.' The Court referred to the findings in the Report that Mr Seymour was or should have been aware of the condemned practices and stated:

> 'Mr Seymour should have been more decisive and effective in eliminating issues of non-compliance and redressing the consequence of improper practices. His successor adopted a tougher stance by giving bank staff a warning of the consequences of breaking bank procedures and of participating in fraudulent acts.'

---

[99]   See Ch **23** regarding the appropriate periods of disqualification.

[100]   *Re National Irish Bank Ltd, Director of Corporate Enforcement v Seymour* [2007] IEHC 102.

While making this determination, the Court was also mindful of the need not to approach the application 'with the benefit of hindsight'. The Court referred to the duty of a bank's director, which cannot be delegated:

> 'A director must familiarise himself or herself with the business of the company in order to carry out his or her duties. The business of banking requires adherence to and compliance with the statutory provisions relating to deposit taking. While a director may rely on delegating to others, there remains an ultimate responsibility with regard to the discharge of the statutory obligations.'[101]

Kelly J also noted the absence of any requirement that the company must have become insolvent as a result of the director's conduct; or that the director must be guilty of wrongdoing:

> 'Moreover, there is clearly no requirement that the company becomes insolvent as a result of the director's conduct. Nor, indeed, is it necessary that the director's conduct involves the commission of wrongdoing. Non-feasance in relation to systemic non-compliance may be sufficient. The clear evidence was that Seymour did know of the recurrent problems and, at least in respect to the bogus non-resident accounts could have re-designated these, accounted for the DIRT unpaid and disciplined senior and branch management for non-compliance. The failure to do so is, in the opinion of the court, a lack of a proper standard of conduct.'

The Court cited the decisions in *Re National Irish Bank Ltd, Director of Corporate Enforcement v D'Arcy*[102] and *Re Ansbacher (Cayman) Ltd, Director of Corporate Enforcement v Collery*[103] as authority that, 'a failure to comply with legislation by a person who had responsibility and who could have resolved issues of non-compliance, is sufficient to justify disqualification.'

As Mr Seymour was in a position of responsibility at NIB, described as 'the single most senior and responsible employee in the company', it was not necessary to demonstrate any wrong doing on his part. The failure to ensure that the company discharged its obligations was sufficient, where that non-compliance was systematic.

[21.039] In *Re National Irish Bank Ltd, Director of Corporate Enforcement v D'Arcy*,[104] the Court referred to the seniority of the respondent's position in determining that he was 'unfit to be concerned in the management of a company': Mr D'Arcy was 'in the

---

[101] The Court acknowledged, however, that responsibilities may be shared between the directors and management: 'In order to ascertain the duties that a person appointed to a board of an established company undertakes to perform, it is necessary to consider not only the nature of the company's business, but also the manner in which the work of the company is in fact distributed between the directors and the other officials of the company, provided always that this distribution is a reasonable one in the circumstances.' *Re National Irish Bank Ltd, Director of Corporate Enforcement v Seymour* [2007] IEHC 102.

[102] *Re National Irish Bank Ltd, Director of Corporate Enforcement v D'Arcy* [2005] IEHC 333.

[103] *Re Ansbacher (Cayman) Ltd, Director of Corporate Enforcement v Collery* [2006] IEHC 67.

[104] *Re National Irish Bank Ltd, Director of Corporate Enforcement v D'Arcy* [2006] 2 IR 163.

upper echelons of bank management' and, while he was not at 'the very top level of management,' he was 'at just one remove from it.'[105]

The opposite outcome can be seen in *Re National Irish Bank Ltd, Director of Corporate Enforcement v Curran*.[106] Mr Curran was a regional manager of NIB from 1988 until his appointment as Head of Retail Banking in 1996. He retired in 1997. He was never a director of NIB. The inspectors made a number of factual findings in relation to Mr Curran and concluded that he was aware of various improper practices that prevailed in NIB. The report further concluded that Mr Curran, together with others, was responsible for the continuation of these practices; for failing to address NIB's liabilities arising from a number of those improper practices; and for NIB's legal and professional failures in this regard.

The DCE sought orders of disqualification under s 160(2)(b), (d) and (e). The DCE's case was that Mr Curran, while an officer of NIB, for nine years, breached his duty as an officer by failing to ensure that the company's legal requirements were complied with and by failing to carry out his common law duties with due care, skill and diligence, within the meaning of s 160(2)(b). The DCE also contended that Mr Curran engaged in conduct which made him unfit to be concerned in the management of a company within the meaning of s 160(2)(d) and (e).[107]

[21.040] Mr Curran did not accept the findings of the inspectors and argued that he had no authority, implied or otherwise, to change any of NIB's corporate governance policies or procedure. He further contended that he was not responsible for the matters complained of in the report: the main perpetrators were the managers who were directly involved in those matters. In his affidavit, Mr Curran noted that the main allegations against him were ones of omission and that it would be unjust to punish him severely for such alleged omissions.

The DCE's position was that, whether or not he had the authority to change these policies and procedures, Mr Curran was a member of senior management and had a responsibility to ensure that NIB complied with its legal and professional obligations. Mr Curran was an officer of NIB, in respect of whom the inspectors had made relevant findings of fact. He had, according to the Director, demonstrated unfitness, lack of commercial probity, negligence and/or incompetence in the discharge of his duties as an officer of NIB.

Murphy J was satisfied that Mr Curran was aware, from internal audit reports, of the 'deficiencies and irregularities' in relation to the non-resident, DIRT exempt accounts held at branches in his region and that he ought to have been aware, at least since his promotion to Head of Retail Banking, of the widespread existence of bogus non-resident accounts.

---

[105] *Re National Irish Bank Ltd, Director of Corporate Enforcement v D'Arcy* [2006] 2 IR 163 at 177.

[106] *Re National Irish Bank Ltd, Director of Corporate Enforcement v Curran* [2007] IEHC 181.

[107] See further Ch **22**.

The Court determined that, while there was a 'systems error in the management and control of the Bank', which had permitted the improper practices found in the Report to continue, Mr Curran 'did not have the authority to bring about a cessation of the improper practices.' Although the Court did consider that a 'more assiduous approach to compliance' could have been adopted by Mr Curran, it was not appropriate to make a disqualification order.[108]

(b) Experience and qualifications

[21.041] The relevance of the respondent's qualifications and experience is demonstrated in *Re Ansbacher (Cayman) Ltd, Director of Corporate Enforcement v Stakelum*.[109] In that case, McGovern J placed some emphasis on the qualifications and experience of the respondent: 'I simply do not accept that the respondent, as a Chartered Accountant was not aware of the implications of what he was doing.' The respondent had engaged in a calculated and elaborate scheme for the evasion of tax and had destroyed all records on his retirement. These matters made the respondent unfit to be concerned in the management of a company and the Court imposed a period of disqualification of five years.

[21.042] In *Re Kentford Securities Ltd*[110] the respondent was, at the relevant times, a newly qualified accountant in his twenties, occupying a junior position. That application arose from the appointment of an authorised officer to examine the books and documents of Kentford Securities Limited ('Kentford'), a company formed by Mr Des Traynor. There were suspicions that the company was involved in tax evasion schemes and, in particular, that it was involved in the Ansbacher deposits.[111] The respondent was an employee of a company secretarial service and was also an auditor and a former director of Kentford.

The applicant cited a number of matters which he claimed evidenced conduct by an auditor which merited an order of disqualification under s 160(2)(a) or 160(2)(b). First, the respondent acted as auditor of Kentford while still a director, contrary to s 163, CA 1963. Second, his resignation as a director was deliberately back-dated to make it appear that he was not acting as auditor while a director, while he was in fact continuing to act as a director, by signing certain documents, such as bank mandates after his purported resignation.

---

[108] *Re National Irish Bank Ltd, Director of Corporate Enforcement v Curran* [2007] IEHC 181 at para 9.14.

[109] *Re Ansbacher (Cayman) Ltd, Director of Corporate Enforcement v Stakelum* (31 July 2007, unreported), HC.

[110] *Re Kentford Securities Ltd, Director of Corporate Enforcement v McCann* [2007] IEHC 1.

[111] The authorised officer believed that Kentford was the company primarily used by Mr Des Traynor during the period 1989–1994 to facilitate cash withdrawals by his friends and business associates from the Ansbacher deposits held in Ireland. The authorised officer also reported that Kentford's bank accounts were part of the Ansbacher secret ledger maintained by Mr Traynor, and that during the relevant period a sum in excess of IR£2.27 million passed through these accounts. See *Re Kentford Securities Ltd, Director of Corporate Enforcement v McCann* [2007] IEHC 1.

Third, the respondent, as auditor, issued unqualified auditor's reports on Kentford's financial statements for four successive years, when he knew or ought to have known that the impression given by the statements that the company was a dormant company showing assets and share capital of IR£2 each was false and misleading since there were large transactions going through the company's bank accounts, and that there were balances held in those accounts. The applicant contended that the respondent committed offences under C(A)A 1986, s 22(3) and CA 1990, s 242, in issuing unqualified reports in such circumstances, and that he facilitated the defrauding of the Revenue Commissioners. The authorised officer rejected the respondent's contentions that he always believed, from assurances received, that Kentford was a trust company which did not trade and had no assets or liabilities, that his audits were of an acceptable standard at all times and that he had no knowledge that the company was used for tax evasion.

Fourth, the applicant submitted that the respondent submitted a forged document in support of his assertion that he was told Kentford was a trust company with no assets or liabilities. This document was accepted by the respondent to be a forgery, but one which he did not create and on which he did place reliance in good faith.

The respondent's case was that he was not aware of any involvement by Kentford with tax evasion until it emerged publicly; that he was never part of any scheme to defraud the Revenue Commissioners; and that he never had any intention of committing any wrongful act. The Court accepted these assertions. The respondent was not, according to the Court, aware that anything illegal was taking place. The Court did, however, find against the respondent in respect of each of the matters complained of by the applicant.

[21.043] Peart J referred to the junior position and lack of experience of the respondent at the relevant dates. The Court pointed out that he qualified as an accountant in about 1988; was employed in a junior capacity by a company secretarial service in 1987 or 1988; and that 'a person such as the respondent, a junior figure in the organisation, would certainly do as he was asked to do by either of these men [his employer and Mr Traynor] and without asking questions.'

Peart J found that the respondent did act as a director while he was still an auditor; that he did backdate his resignation notice to conceal this fact; and that he did sign blank forms in advance, and backdated other documentation. The Court made a number of observations about these occurrences. First, the practice of signing documents in advance, or even backdating such documents, 'spread beyond documents such as appointment and resignation of directors and share transfer forms.' Second, the practice of signing blank forms and backdating documents was not an acceptable practice, but 'it was a feature of the time'.[112] Third, the breaches of law by the respondent are referred to as 'unwitting', and were 'not a deliberate or conscious breach of the law' and the Court doubted 'very much if he was always aware of what he was signing.' Third, the respondent was in a position of junior employment and was immersed in the culture that 'anything required to be signed by him, or that he was requested to sign by his employer or Mr Traynor was signed without any consideration being given to such documents by

---

[112] Note that a similar point was dismissed in *Re National Irish Bank Ltd, Director of Corporate Enforcement v Seymour* [2007] IEHC 102 with the contrary finding that: 'Neither is it an answer to say that the problem was endemic in Irish banking.'

him.' Fourth, the respondent did not gain financially from the matters complained of. The Court held:

> 'One cannot escape the conclusion that the respondent was at the time a very small and insignificant cog in the larger wheel being turned by Mr Des Traynor. It is he and his friends and acquaintances involved in the tax evasion scheme who were the beneficiaries of the respondent's undoubted naivety, lack of attention to his responsibilities, and carelessness at the time.'[113]

No order of disqualification was made in that case. If the respondent was more experienced, more qualified, and older, it may be expected that the Court would not have lightly concluded that he did not know the consequences of what he was doing and was immersed in a culture which accepted such breaches of the law. This is indicated by the statement that:

> '... central to the Court's decision not to make the order sought is the fact that the matters complained of occurred so long ago between 1988 and 1994 and when the respondent was an employee in CSC, and starting when he was a very recently qualified accountant.'[114]

(c) Attempts to rectify or stop the misconduct

[21.044] If a respondent made real attempts to address the problems that gave rise to the disqualification proceedings, this may be taken into account by a court. In *Re National Irish Bank Ltd, Director of Corporate Enforcement v Seymour*,[115] it was argued on behalf of Mr Seymour that he made 'strenuous efforts' to resolve the problems that he became aware of during his tenure; that he was 'broadly complying with his obligations under the Companies Act;' and that he acted with 'a degree of commercial probity'.

Murphy J addressed these submissions as follows:

> 'It seems to the court that, broadly complying with obligations under the Companies Act is too narrow a test. This is particularly so in relation to persistent non-compliance. More importantly, in relation to an investigation by the Court the conduct of the directors may be looked at in relation to all legal compliance, including compliance with the Finance Acts and legislation generally. The courts are entitled to look into all the circumstances of the conduct within the particular business.'

The Court also stated:

> 'It is, in the view of the court, not an answer that he was making a strenuous effort in the difficult circumstances to resolve the increasing problems that were dawning upon him during his tenure. Neither is it an answer to say that the problem was endemic in Irish banking nor, indeed, that taxation matters were dealt with outside the Bank.'

---

[113] *Re Kentford Securities Ltd, Director of Corporate Enforcement v McCann* [2007] IEHC 1.

[114] *Re Kentford Securities Ltd, Director of Corporate Enforcement v McCann* [2007] IEHC 1.

[115] *Re National Irish Bank Ltd, Director of Corporate Enforcement v Seymour* [2007] IEHC 102.

At a further extreme, the conduct of the respondent in *Re Ansbacher (Cayman) Ltd, Director of Corporate Enforcement v Stakelum*[116] who was found to have destroyed documents on his retirement, was cited as a ground for making an order of disqualification.

By contrast, in *Re National Irish Bank Ltd, Director of Corporate Enforcement v Curran*.[117] the Court was satisfied that Mr Curran 'did take steps perhaps, in retrospect, in a somewhat desultory way, to get assurances from the branch managers.' No order of disqualification was made in that case.

(d) Impact of disqualification order

[21.045] In *Re National Irish Bank Ltd, Director of Corporate Enforcement v Curran*[118] the Court considered submissions on behalf of Mr Curran that a disqualification order would bring his working career to an end, as 'the basic currency in banking was honesty and integrity;' that the media attention had a very traumatic effect on his personality, on his health and on his family; that he had no intention or plans of any description to be a director of any company. No order of disqualification was made in that case.

[21.046] In *Re Kentford Securities Ltd,*[119] Peart J refused to make an order of disqualification. Among the grounds for this decision was that the respondent was an auditor who acted for client companies, with his own practice, having qualified as an accountant in 1988:

> 'A disqualification order in such circumstances would have the gravest consequences for the respondent since it would prevent him earning his livelihood as an auditor to client companies, as well as attaching to him the inevitable and serious stigma which will attach to him professionally as an accountant and auditor against whom such an order has been made.'

The Court noted that the respondent had developed his practice since the events that gave rise to the disqualification proceedings; that he has been audited by a professional body and received 'a clean bill of health'; and repeated that 'the consequences of a disqualification order being made against an accountant in private practice are devastating.'

[21.047] When a court does propose to make an order of disqualification, the impact of a disqualification order on the personal and professional life of a respondent, is considered in relation to the appropriate duration of the period of disqualification.[120] It would be preferable to have more consistency in the treatment of these considerations: it is not clear why the personal and professional impact of a disqualification order should

---

[116] *Re Ansbacher (Cayman) Ltd, Director of Corporate Enforcement v Stakelum* (31 July 2007, unreported), HC.

[117] *Re National Irish Bank Ltd, Director of Corporate Enforcement v Curran* [2007] IEHC 181.

[118] *Re National Irish Bank Ltd, Director of Corporate Enforcement v Curran* [2007] IEHC 181.

[119] *Re Kentford Securities Ltd, Director of Corporate Enforcement v McCann* [2007] IEHC 1.

[120] See, eg, *Re National Irish Bank Ltd, Director of Corporate Enforcement v Seymour* [2007] IEHC 102. See Ch **23**.

be a reason not to make an order in some cases, and a reason to reduce the duration of the disqualification period in others.

Another way these factors could appropriately be taken into account, other than as grounds for refusing to make an order of disqualification, is under s 160(9A).[121] In cases such as *Re Kentford Securities Ltd*,[122] the Court acknowledged that a declaration of restriction would operate less harshly than a disqualification order from the perspective of the respondent: 'The effect is worse even that the restriction of a director under s 150 of the Act. In that case the director restricted can still pursue his livelihood by trading other than with the benefit of limited liability.'[123] While the disqualification proceedings in *Re Kentford Securities Ltd*[124] were taken against the respondent in his capacity as an auditor, it seems that there were grounds in that case on which he may have been subject to a declaration of restriction arising from his conduct as director. In such circumstances, the fairness of making neither a declaration of restriction, nor an order of disqualification, in that case may be queried.

(e) Lapse of time

[21.048] The time that has passed since the events that are relied upon in an application for an order of disqualification may be taken into account by a court.[125] In *Re Kentford Securities Ltd*[126] Peart J held that:

> 'central to the Court's decision not to make the order sought is the fact that the matters complained of occurred so long ago between 1988 and 1994 and when the respondent was an employee in CSC, and starting when he was a very recently qualified accountant.'

Applying this approach to Mr McCann's involvement in Kentford, the Court found that '... whatever irregular and improper conduct he was mixed up in all those years ago at the behest of his employer and Mr Traynor is a thing of the past.' On this, among other grounds, no order of disqualification was made in that case.

[21.049] Another way that a lapse of time may be raised as a defence to disqualification applications was also highlighted by Peart J in *Re Kentford Securities Ltd*.[127] In determining whether a respondent is 'unfit to be concerned in the management of a company,' the Court must be satisfied that the respondent is, at present, unfit to be so concerned. When an application is brought under s 160(2) a number of years after the relevant events, it is not sufficient to show that the person was, at that time, 'unfit to be concerned in the management of a company.' According to Peart J, 'The question to be

---

[121] See Ch **23**.

[122] *Re Kentford Securities Ltd, Director of Corporate Enforcement v McCann* [2007] IEHC 1.

[123] *Re Kentford Securities Ltd, Director of Corporate Enforcement v McCann* [2007] IEHC 1.

[124] *Re Kentford Securities Ltd, Director of Corporate Enforcement v McCann* [2007] IEHC 1.

[125] See further paras **[21.016]–[21.017]**.

[126] *Re Kentford Securities Ltd, Director of Corporate Enforcement v McCann* [2007] IEHC 1.

[127] *Re Kentford Securities Ltd, Director of Corporate Enforcement v McCann* [2007] IEHC 1.

considered is whether at the time of this application the past conduct makes him presently unfit to be so involved.'

(f) Attitude in the proceedings

[21.050] A matter that has been cited in a number of decisions under s 160(2) is the attitude of the respondent in the disqualification proceedings: whether he contested the application; whether he took responsibility for the wrongdoing that occurred; whether he co-operated with any investigations by authorised officers or inspectors that were undertaken; and whether he was honest in his evidence, among other considerations. In many cases, these factors are taken into account in determining the appropriate period of disqualification.[128] In other cases, the attitude of the respondent is referred to in determining not to make an order of disqualification.

[21.051] It may be of interest to note that, In *Re Kentford Securities Ltd,*[129] the Court referred to the answers given by the respondent to the authorised officer as 'vague and even at times evasive.' Peart J noted that some of the answers to the authorised officer 'attempted to answer the unanswerable or justify the unjustifiable' and that it would 'have served the respondent better if at interview he had been more open in that respect, rather than try and justify what had happened.' This finding notwithstanding, no order of disqualification was made in that case.

---

[128] See, eg, *Re National Irish Bank Ltd, Director of Corporate Enforcement v Seymour* [2007] IEHC 102, where the Court commented on the polite and open attitude of the respondent, among the mitigating factors which led the Court to reduce the period of disqualification from twelve to nine years. See Ch **23**.

[129] *Re Kentford Securities Ltd, Director of Corporate Enforcement v McCann* [2007] IEHC 1.

Chapter 22

GROUNDS OF DISCRETIONARY DISQUALIFICATION

[22.001] There are nine grounds on which a court may, either of its own motion or on the application of one of the designated applicants, make an order of disqualification.[1] Each of these grounds is considered separately in this chapter.[2]

A. Fraud in relation to company, creditors or members

[22.002] The first ground on which a court has a discretion to make an order of disqualification is that a person, while occupying a role in a company, committed fraud in relation to that company or its member or creditors. Section 160(2)(a) accordingly provides that a court may make an order of disqualification where 'a person has been guilty, while a promoter, officer, auditor, receiver, liquidator or examiner of a company, of any fraud in relation to the company, its members or creditors'.[3]

(a) Respondents under s 160(2)(a)

[22.003] An order of disqualification may be sought under s 160(2)(a) in respect of a person acting in their capacity as a promoter, officer, auditor, receiver, liquidator or examiner of a company. Two points may be noted about the persons whom may come within the scope of s 160(2)(a). First, any fraudulent conduct of a person in relation to a company in which they did not occupy one of the specified roles, will not justify an order of disqualification under s 160(2)(a). Applying this to a hypothetical factual situation, a person may be a director of one company, and commit fraud in relation to a different company, such as a subsidiary of the company of which he is officer, without falling within the scope of s 160(2)(a).

[22.004] Second, fraud committed by a person in relation to a company before they began to act as a promoter, officer, auditor, receiver, liquidator or examiner of that company, or after resignation from such a position, will not justify a disqualification order under s 160(2)(a). This is true, even if the fraud was committed by use of information or knowledge received during the person's tenure at the company. Section 160(2)(a) requires specifically that the person must have been guilty of fraud 'while' occupying the position of promoter, officer, auditor, receiver, liquidator or examiner of the company. There is nothing in the provision which extends the scope of the disqualification to fraud which related to, or arose from, the person's tenure as promoter,

---

[1] CA 1990, s 160(2).

[2] These grounds, and the rules applicable to them, are substantially reproduced in the General Scheme of the Draft Companies Consolidation and Reform Bill 2007, Pt A13, Head 42. Available at www.clrg.org.

[3] CA 1990, s 160(2)(a).

officer, auditor, receiver, liquidator or examiner. There is no basis for interpreting the provision to include such an extended scope.

(b) Applicants under s 160(2)(a)

[22.005] Section 160(4) provides that an application under s 160(2)(a) may be made by the following persons:

    (a) the Director of Public Prosecutions; or

    (b) any member, contributory, officer, employee, receiver, liquidator, examiner or creditor of any company in relation to which the person who is the subject of the application—

        (i) has been or is acting or is proposing to or being proposed to act as officer, auditor, receiver, liquidator or examiner, or

        (ii) has been or is concerned or taking part, or is proposing to be concerned or take part, in the promotion, formation or management of any company.

In addition to these persons, s 160(6A)[4] also permits the DCE to make an application pursuant to s 160(2)(a).

(c) Meaning of 'guilty'

[22.006] It has been suggested that the reference in s 160(2)(a) to the requirement that the person must be 'guilty' of any fraud suggests that the person must have been convicted by a court of fraud in relation to the company, its members or creditors.[5] It has also been noted elsewhere, that this could encompass summary conviction, as well as conviction on indictment, unlike the automatic disqualification provision of s 160(1).[6] This issue was raised by the respondents in *Re Barnroe Ltd*.[7] The applicants in that case argued that guilt in respect of a 'civil wrong' was sufficient. The case was determined on the basis of s 160(2)(d), however, and the question of whether a criminal conviction is required for s 160(2)(a) to apply remains unresolved.

[22.007] If s 160(2)(a) does require a criminal conviction, it should be noted that, unless s 160(2)(a) includes summary convictions, it is entirely superfluous. Section 160(1), as has already been seen,[8] causes a person to be disqualified automatically if they are convicted on indictment of any offence in relation to any company or involving fraud, whether or not that fraud related to any company. This is very substantially wider than the scope of s 160(2)(a). Any conviction on indictment that may fall within the scope of s 160(2)(a), namely a conviction for fraud in relation to the company in which

---

    4   CA 1990, s 160(6A), as inserted by CLEA 2001, s 42(e).

    5   See Courtney, *The Law of Private Companies* (2nd edn, Tottel Publishing, 2002) at para 12.107.

    6   See Courtney, *The Law of Private Companies* (2nd edn, Tottel Publishing, 2002) at para 12.107.

    7   *Re Barnroe Ltd, Director of Corporate Enforcement v Rogers* [2005] IEHC 433. See para **[22.021]**.

    8   See further Ch **20**.

the person held an office, would unavoidably be captured by the automatic disqualification of s 160(1). If criminal convictions are a necessary prerequisite to the exercise of the court's power to disqualify under s 160(2)(a), only summary convictions could fall within the scope of the court's power to make an order of discretionary disqualification under s 160(2)(a).

(d) Applications under s 160(2)(a)

[22.008] The experience of s 160(2)(a) in practice is limited, as no-one has ever been disqualified in Ireland on the specific basis of a fraud committed while they occupied the office of promoter, officer, auditor, receiver, liquidator or examiner within the meaning of s 160(2)(a). This is not to suggest that no such fraud has ever been committed. However, in cases where such fraud has been found to have been committed, no court has exercised their discretion, whether of its own motion, or on the application of a prosecutor, to make an order of disqualification under s 160(2)(a).

It should be mentioned that, in the case of *Re CB Readymix Ltd*,[9] the Supreme Court did refer to, and quote, s 160(2)(a), (b) and (d), in the course of a judgment which upheld an order of disqualification made by the High Court. However, as the order of the High Court purported to be based on s 160(2)(b) and (d), and not s 160(2)(a), and there was no analysis of the terms of s 160(2)(a), the usefulness of that case as an authority under s 160(2)(a) is limited.[10]

B. Breach of duty

[22.009] The second ground on which a court can make an order of discretionary disqualification is that a person acted in breach of his duty as a promoter, officer, auditor, receiver, liquidator or examiner of a company. CA 1990, s 160(2)(b), provides that a court may order disqualification where:

> a person has been guilty, while a promoter, officer, auditor, receiver, liquidator or examiner of a company, of any breach of his duty as such promoter, officer, auditor, receiver, liquidator or examiner.[11]

(a) Respondents under s 160(2)(b)

[22.010] For s 160(2)(b) to apply, the respondent must be 'a promoter, officer, auditor, receiver, liquidator or examiner of a company' and in breach of his duty as such. The

---

[9] *Re CB Readymix Ltd, Cahill v Grimes* [2002] 1 IR 372.

[10] The same applies in respect of the judgment of O'Leary J in *Re Barnroe Ltd, Director of Corporate Enforcement v Rogers* [2005] IEHC 433, in which s 160(2)(a) was invoked by the applicant, but did not for form the basis for the Court's decision. It may also be noted that disqualification proceedings under s 160(2)(a), b) and (d) are pending against Michael and Thomas Bailey, the directors of Bovale Developments Ltd. See ODCE, *Press Release*, 31 October 2006. Available at www.odce.ie.

[11] CA 1990, s 160(2)(b).

decision of Peart J in *Re Kentford Securities Ltd*[12] is an example of the application of s 160(2)(b) to an auditor.

[22.011] In *Re National Irish Bank Ltd, Director of Corporate Enforcement v D'Arcy*[13] the only category into which the respondent could fall was that of 'officer'. In this regard, Kelly J noted that the term 'officer' in CA 1990, s 159, is non-exhaustive and could cover persons other than directors, secretaries and shadow directors.[14]

The DCE contended, relying on a decision of the English Court of Appeal in *Re A Company*[15] that an 'elevated management position', such as that occupied by the respondent, was within the meaning of the term 'officer'. The reliance on *Re A Company* was questioned by Kelly J as the definition of 'officer' under consideration in that case[16] included a 'manager': 'It is therefore arguable that, having regard to this distinction, the respondent does not fall within the definition of 'officer' as prescribed by the Irish legislation.'[17] Kelly J further concluded in relation to the application of English authorities on the definition of 'officer': 'English authorities are at best persuasive but their persuasive value must be lessened when they are dealing with a different definition to that which obtains in the Irish legislation.'

[22.012] With regard to the definition of 'officers' in s 159, Kelly J noted that:

> 'If s 159 of the Companies Act 1990 defined "officer" in the same terms as did the English Companies Act 1948, as including a "manager", there would be no doubt but that the respondent would fall within that definition. As s 159, although framed non-exhaustively, does not include the term "manager", it is arguable that the respondent does not fall within it.'[18]

This question was not determined by the Court, however, as the respondent did not raise any arguments in this regard:

> 'I think that the applicant is probably correct in his submissions but I do not propose to make a finding on the issue since it is not necessary. Such a finding

---

12 *Re Kentford Securities Ltd, Director of Corporate Enforcement v McCann* [2007] IEHC 1.

13 *Re National Irish Bank Ltd, Director of Corporate Enforcement v D'Arcy* [2006] 2 IR 163.

14 CA 1990, s 159 defines 'officer' as follows: '"Officer" in relation to any company, includes any director, shadow director or secretary of the company.'

15 *Re A Company* [1980] Ch 138 ('It seems to me that whenever anyone in a superior position in a company encourages, directs or acquiesces in defrauding creditors, customers, shareholders or the like, then there is an offence being committed by an officer of the company in connection with the company's affairs,' *per* Lord Denning MR at p 143).

16 Companies Act 1948, s 455 provided that an '"officer" includes a director, manager, or secretary'.

17 *Re National Irish Bank Ltd, Director of Corporate Enforcement v D'Arcy* [2006] 2 IR 163 at 172.

18 *Re National Irish Bank Ltd, Director of Corporate Enforcement v D'Arcy* [2006] 2 IR 163 at 173.

would be of little precedent value as the question was not argued before me. A point not argued is a point not decided.'[19]

As the respondent was clearly covered by other provisions of s 160(2), it was unnecessary to reach a determination under s 160(2)(b). The same issue regarding the scope of the term 'officer' was cited by the Court in relation to the application under s 160(2)(d). As the respondent was clearly within the scope of s 160(2)(e), reliance on s 160(2)(d) was also eschewed.

The scope of the term 'officer' as it is used in sub-ss 160(2)(b) and (d) and, indeed, in Chs **2** and **3** of Pt VII more generally, therefore remains unresolved.

(b) Applicants

[22.013] Section 160(4) provides that an application under s 160(2)(b) may be made by the following persons:

(a) the Director of Public Prosecutions; or

(b) any member, contributory, officer, employee, receiver, liquidator, examiner or creditor of any company in relation to which the person who is the subject of the application—

(i) has been or is acting or is proposing to or being proposed to act as officer, auditor, receiver, liquidator or examiner, or

(ii) has been or is concerned or taking part, or is proposing to be concerned or take part, in the promotion, formation or management of any company.

In addition to these persons, s 160(6A)[20] also permits the DCE to make an application pursuant to s 160(2)(b).

(c) Scope of s 160(2)(b)

[22.014] According to s 160(2)(b), any promoter, officer, auditor, receiver, liquidator or examiner of a company, who commits a breach of his duty in that capacity, is liable to be disqualified. The duties which may trigger the operation of s 160(2)(b) are not defined and could encompass any statutory, common law, or contractual duty of the person in question. In addition, the category of duties, the breach of which could give rise to an order of disqualification under s 160(2)(b), is not limited to duties owed to the company and could include duties owed to the company's members, employees, shareholders, and creditors.

(d) Applications under s 160(2)(b)

[22.015] There have been some applications to the courts for disqualification orders under s 160(2)(b). In many instances, s 160(2)(b) has been one of a number of provisions of s 160(2) which is invoked to justify the making of an order of

---

[19] *Re National Irish Bank Ltd, Director of Corporate Enforcement v D'Arcy* [2006] 2 IR 163 at 173.

[20] CA 1990, s 160(6A), as inserted by CLEA 2001, s 42(e).

disqualification. Applications have been made to court invoking s 160(2)(b), (d)[21] and (e)[22] as the basis for the disqualification orders sought. By way of example, following the publication of the inspector's report into National Irish Bank Ltd, the DCE instituted proceedings seeking orders of disqualification against a number of named individuals under CA 1990, s 160(2)(b), (d) and (e).[23]

[22.016] *Re Newcastle Timber Ltd*[24] is an example of a decided case in which an order of disqualification was sought on the basis of breach of duty[25] and unfitness to be concerned in the management of a company.[26] The liquidator in that case relied on five grounds in support of the application for a disqualification order:

1. The directors failed to keep proper books and records of accounts;

2. The directors failed to lodge the required returns to both Revenue and to the Companies Office on time;

3. The directors traded while being unable to discharge their liabilities, in particular the Revenue liabilities;

4. The directors exercised preference in the payment of debts to certain trade creditors rather than to the Revenue Commissioners when the company ceased to trade;

5. There were irregularities with regard to the sale of a particular property by the company to a director.

The Court appears to have analysed each of these allegations to assess whether the directors acted 'honestly and responsibly'. McCracken J concluded, in this regard, that:

> 'insofar as the proceedings under s 160 are concerned, the liquidator has discharged the onus on him in relation to the failure by the company to make company office returns, the fact that the company traded while insolvent for some four years and the fact that after the company ceased to trade, they discharged trade creditors in priority to the Revenue.'[27]

In light of these factors, the Court went on to state:

> 'the primary questions remains as to whether these actions on the part of the Directors amounted to a breach of duty or were actions which made the Directors

---

21   CA 1990, s 160(2)(d) provides, '... the conduct of any person as promoter, officer, auditor, receiver, liquidator or examiner of a company, makes him unfit to be concerned in the management of a company.' See further paras **[22.032]** to **[22.047]**.

22   CA 1990, s 160(2)(e) provides, '... in consequence of a report of inspectors appointed by the court or the Minister under the Companies Acts, the conduct of any person makes him unfit to be concerned in the management of a company'. See further below paras **[22.048]** to **[22.051]**.

23   See further Ch **21**.

24   *Re Newcastle Timber Ltd* [2001] IEHC 146. Another example of a case in which s 160(2)(b) and (d) were both invoked was *Re CB Readymix Ltd, Cahill v Grimes* [2002] 1 IR 372.

25   CA 1990, s 160(2)(b).

26   CA 1990, s 160(2)(d).

27   *Re Newcastle Timber Ltd* [2001] IEHC 146 at para 11.

unfit to be concerned in the management of a company, and secondly, whether, if so, I should exercise the undoubted discretion given by making an Order under the section.'[28]

[22.017] Up to this point, the Court continued to acknowledge that two separate grounds were being invoked for the disqualification orders sought, one being the directors' breach of duty. McCracken then went on to cite the decision of Browne-Wilkinson VC in *Re Lo-Line Motors Ltd*[29] which analysed the criteria for determining whether someone is unfit to be a director and which essentially recommended the test that 'in the normal case the conduct complained of must display a lack of commercial probity, although … in the extreme case of gross negligence or total incompetence, disqualification could be appropriate.'[30] That judgment did not address the criteria for determining whether a person was in breach of duty, such as to justify the making of an order of disqualification, within the meaning of s 160(2)(b).

McCracken J applied *Re Lo-Line Motors Ltd*[31] as follows:

'While these comments were made in the context of slightly different legislation in the United Kingdom, I, like my colleagues, have no doubt that it is the proper approach to be taken both under s 150 and s 160. As I have already said, many faults can be found in the conduct of the Directors in the present case. I have no doubt that they acted incompetently, and, particularly in relation to insolvent trading and preference of trade creditors, I think they behaved irresponsibly. However, the liquidator has not satisfied me that the Directors were so much in breach of their duties, that they are unfit to be concerned of the management of a company particularly in view of the undoubted discretion which I have in this regard.'[32]

The Court ultimately made declarations of restriction in respect of the directors, but refused to make the disqualification orders sought under s 160(2).

[22.018] A number of issues arise from the rationale adopted by the High Court in *Re Newcastle Timber Ltd*.[33] Some of these issues are addressed elsewhere.[34] For present purposes, the most striking aspect of the decision of McCracken J is that he appears to mould 'breach of duty' and 'fitness to be concerned in the management of a company' into one single test for disqualification. He does not assess whether the directors of the company breached the duties they owed to the company, its members, or creditors. The basis for the Court's decision not to grant an order of disqualification was that 'the liquidator has not satisfied me that the Directors were so much in breach of their duties, that they are unfit to be concerned of the management of a company'. There is nothing

---

[28] *Re Newcastle Timber Ltd* [2001] IEHC 146 at para 12.

[29] *Re Lo-Line Motors Ltd* [1988] BCLC 698.

[30] *Re Lo-Line Motors Ltd* [1988] BCLC 698. See *Re Newcastle Timber Ltd* [2001] IEHC 146 at para 13.

[31] *Re Lo-Line Motors Ltd* [1988] BCLC 698.

[32] *Re Newcastle Timber Ltd* [2001] IEHC 146 at para 14.

[33] *Re Newcastle Timber Ltd* [2001] IEHC 146.

[34] See Ch **17**, para **[22.024]** and paras **[22.039]** to **[22.040]**.

in s 160(2)(b) which requires the breach of duty to be such as to render the directors unfit to be concerned in the management of a company.

The application of s 160(2)(b) in *Re Newcastle Timber Ltd* deprives that provision of any real substance. If the standard required under s 160(2)(b) is that the breach of duty must be such as to render the person guilty of the breach unfit to be concerned in the management of a company, that criteria is already covered by s 160(2)(d).

[22.019] In the NIB cases which have been decided to date, the applications were based on s 160(2)(b), as well as s 160(2)(e) and (d). In *Re National Irish Bank Ltd, Director of Corporate Enforcement v Seymour*[35] Murphy J considered the duties of directors, noting that 'Mr Seymour, as director, owes a duty of care, diligence and skill to the Bank as fully considered by Romer J in *City Equitable Fire Insurance Co Ltd Re (No 1)* (1925) Ch 407, 427,' and that:

> 'The court is of the view that the duty of care and skill owed by a director in relation to these matters is a serious responsibility and cannot be compared to the oversight of an individual tax payer or the reliance of an individual tax payer on his accountant or tax adviser. While, of course, such an oversight does not excuse the tax payer from discharging his liability, including interest and penalties, the duty of a director is more explicit and demanding. Not alone is there an obligation towards the members of the company there is also a duty towards its creditors, especially to the Revenue Commissioners in respect of retention tax preferential debts. Directors of a bank have a particular responsibility to its customers to advise and account for such tax from a relevant deposit where they are aware of circumstances where it was obliged to deduct.'

Murphy J also stated that, 'There is an overlap between the breach of duties to the company and breaches leading to disqualification.' In that case, the Court determined that the making of a substantial payment to the Revenue Commissioners for DIRT liability after Mr Seymour left office, attributable in part to the period of his tenure, highlighted his non-compliance with his statutory duty. The Court concluded that, '... a failure to comply with legislation by a person who had responsibility and who could have resolved issues of non-compliance, is sufficient to justify disqualification.'

These aspects of the decision are helpful in setting out the duties applicable to a director and the relevance of these duties to an order of disqualification. It is somewhat regrettable that the Court also made the following statement:

> 'The application before the court is not, however, an allegation of breach of such duty but that the director's conduct makes him unfit to be concerned in the management of a company. The former duty is owed to the company, the latter to the public.'

This is difficult to reconcile with the passage quoted above, which refers to duties owed to members and creditors. It is even more difficult to reconcile with the fact that the application in *Re National Irish Bank Ltd, Director of Corporate Enforcement v*

---

[35]   *Re National Irish Bank Ltd, Director of Corporate Enforcement v Seymour* [2007] IEHC 102.

Seymour[36] was an application under s 160(2)(b), based on allegations of breach of duty by Mr Seymour, as well as under sub-ss 160(2)(d) and (e).

While the Court did make findings which were indicative of a breach of duty by the respondent, it is not clear whether s 160(2)(b) was relied upon in making the disqualification order in that case. This decision does, therefore, blur the distinction between being 'unfit' within the meaning of sub-ss 160(2)(d) or (e) and being in breach of duty within the meaning of s 160(2)(b) to some extent.

[22.020] In *Re Kentford Securities Ltd*[37] Peart J was satisfied that the respondent failed in his duty as an auditor by signing unqualified reports on the financial statements, noting that it was not sufficient to rely on assurances that the company was only a trust company with no assets or liabilities.

> 'He was required to do more, and to pro-actively satisfy himself from an examination of the bank accounts and books and records of the company that what he was told was in fact the situation. The purpose and obligations of an auditor are not fulfilled by the mere going through the motions of signing off on a company's financial statements in the same manner as he may have signed blank forms of resignation as director already referred to, without actually doing anything to verify the true position.'

While this case contains a clear finding that the respondent was in breach of his duty as an auditor,[38] no order of disqualification was made in that case.

(e) Requirement of 'guilty'

[22.021] The same issue arises in connection with s 160(2)(a) and (b) regarding the interpretation of the word 'guilty' as it is used in those provisions. In particular, there is a question as to whether a criminal conviction is required to fulfil the criteria of s 160(2)(b).[39]

In *Re National Irish Bank Ltd, Director of Corporate Enforcement v Seymour*[40] the Court noted that s 160(2)(d) is wider in its scope than s 160(2)(b), as there is 'no requirement of guilt or of breach'. In *Re Barnroe Ltd*[41] the application was brought

---

[36] *Re National Irish Bank Ltd, Director of Corporate Enforcement v Seymour* [2007] IEHC 102.

[37] *Re Kentford Securities Ltd, Director of Corporate Enforcement v McCann* [2007] IEHC 1.

[38] Peart J held: 'in respect of all the matters about which the applicant makes complaint against the respondent, I find against the respondent.' *Re Kentford Securities Ltd, Director of Corporate Enforcement v McCann* [2007] IEHC 1.

[39] See Courtney, *The Law of Private Companies* (2nd edn, Tottel Publishing, 2002), at para 12.108.

[40] *Re National Irish Bank Ltd, Director of Corporate Enforcement v Seymour* [2007] IEHC 102.

[41] *Re Barnroe Ltd, Director of Corporate Enforcement v Rogers* [2005] IEHC 433.

under s 160(2)(a), (b) and (d). The interpretation of the word 'guilty' was considered by the Court:

> 'Both s 160(2)(a) and s 160(2)(b) refer to the person to be disqualified as being "guilty" of either a fraud or breach of his duty. It is submitted by the respondents that the meaning of "guilty" in this context is "guilty of a criminal charge" of fraud of breach of a company law duty. It is submitted by the applicant that the word should be given a meaning which includes "civil guilt".'

An order of disqualification was made in that case under s 160(2)(d) and the interpretation of the word 'guilty' in s 160(2)(b) was not resolved.[42]

[22.022] While it remains unclear whether a criminal conviction is necessary for a court to rely on s 160(2)(b), it may be noted that s 160(2)(b) has been invoked in several cases in which there was no criminal charges or convictions arising from the alleged breach of duty.[43] In decided cases, there appears to have been no suggestion of any requirement that there should have been a finding of guilt in criminal proceedings in relation to the alleged breach of duty.[44]

(f) Relationship between s 160(2)(b) and other grounds

[22.023] There is a degree of overlap between some of the grounds listed in s 160(2) for the making of a discretionary order of disqualification. As already seen, there may be some overlap between a breach of duty committed under s 160(2)(b) and a finding of unfitness to be concerned in the management of a company under s 160(2)(d). Similarly, there may be some overlap between a breach of duty under s 160(2)(b) and the following grounds for making a disqualification order:

- the commission of fraud within the meaning of s 160(2)(a);

- fraudulent or reckless trading within the meaning of s 160(2)(c);

- unfitness to be concerned in the management of a company as disclosed in an inspector's report under s 160(2)(e);

- persistent default within the meaning of s 160(2)(f); and

- allowing a company to be struck-off within the meaning of s 160(2)(g).

[22.024] Despite the potential overlap between the different grounds of disqualification contained in s 160(2), each of them should continue to be treated as a self-sufficient

---

[42]   Note that this issue was reached in neither *Re National Irish Bank Ltd, Director of Corporate Enforcement v D'Arcy* [2006] 2 IR 163, as the Court resolved that application on the basis of s 160(2)(e); nor in *Re National Irish Bank Ltd, Director of Corporate Enforcement v Curran* [2007] IEHC 181, as no order of disqualification was made in that case.

[43]   See, eg, *Re Newcastle Timber Ltd* [2001] IEHC 146; *Re National Irish Bank Ltd, Director of Corporate Enforcement v D'Arcy* [2006] 2 IR 163; *Re National Irish Bank Ltd, Director of Corporate Enforcement v Curran* [2007] IEHC 181; and *Re National Irish Bank Ltd, Director of Corporate Enforcement v Seymour* [2007] IEHC 102.

[44]   See, eg, *Re Newcastle Timber Ltd* [2001] IEHC 146; and *Re National Irish Bank Ltd, Director of Corporate Enforcement v Seymour* [2007] IEHC 102.

basis for making an order of disqualification. If the various grounds of discretionary disqualification are combined and intermingled, as occurred in *Re Newcastle Timber Ltd*,[45] this does not favour the interests of clarity and certainty. A further reason for treating each of the grounds of disqualification under s 160(2) separately, is that the legislature has chosen to include these various grounds for the making of an order of disqualification. By enumerating the various grounds on which a court may make disqualifications orders, the legislature has rejected a generic 'unfitness' test for disqualification. However, if every aspect of s 160(2) is to be interpreted by reference to the 'fitness' of the director to be concerned in the management of the company, the legislature's intention of permitting disqualification on other specific grounds will be thwarted.

[22.025] A final point to note about the relationship between disqualification on the ground of breach of duty under s 160(2)(b) and the other grounds for disqualification under s 160(2), is that there may be cases in which an order of disqualification is sought on the basis of a breach of duty alone. In such cases, the combined analysis of the various grounds listed in s 160(2), will not be of assistance to the prosecutor, the defendant or the court. It will become difficult to decipher the interpretations placed on the distinct grounds for disqualification under s 160(2) if each ground is not treated separately in the decisions of the courts interpreting that provision.

C. Civil liability for fraudulent and reckless trading

[22.026] If a court has granted a declaration that a person was personally responsible for the debts of a company, due to fraudulent or reckless trading, that person may be disqualified. Section 160(2)(c) provides that a court may grant an order of disqualification, if 'a declaration has been granted under s 297A of the Principal Act (inserted by s 138 of this Act) in respect of a person.'[46]

Section 297A(1) provides that:

> if in the course of the winding up of a company or in the course of proceedings under the Companies (Amendment) Act 1990, it appears that – (a) any person was, while an officer of the company, knowingly a party to the carrying on of any business of the company in a reckless manner; or (b) any person was knowingly a party to the carrying on of any business of the company with intent to defraud creditors of the company, or creditors of any other person or for any fraudulent purpose; the court, on the application of the receiver, examiner, liquidator or any creditor of contributory of the company, may, if it thinks it proper to do so, declare that such person shall be personally responsible, without any limitation of liability, for all or any part of the debts or other liabilities of the company as the court may direct.[47]

It is important to be aware that a court can, of its own motion, or on the application of the persons permitted to make such applications, make an order of disqualification

---

45 *Re Newcastle Timber Ltd* [2001] IEHC 146 at para 14.

46 CA 1990, s 160(2)(c).

47 CA 1990, s 297A(1), as inserted by CA 1990, s 138. See further Ch **6** regarding CA 1990, s 297.

against a person who is found to have been a party to the carrying on of the company's business in a reckless or fraudulent manner within the meaning of CA 1963, s 297A.[48]

(a) Respondents under s 160(2)(c)

[22.027] The persons who may face disqualification under s 160(2)(c) are persons who a court has declared to be personally responsible for the debts of a company, as a result of having been, while an officer, 'knowingly a party' to the carrying on of the company's business in a reckless manner or otherwise 'knowlingly a party' to the carrying on of a company's business with a fraudulent intent or purpose. For the purpose of this provision, an 'officer' includes an auditor, liquidator, receiver and shadow director.[49] Therefore, any officer, which term includes directors, auditors, liquidators, receivers and shadow directors, may face disqualification under s 160(2)(c) on the ground of being 'knowingly a party' to reckless trading.[50]

With regard to fraudulent trading, the criteria are that a person, not necessarily being an officer of the company, must have been 'knowingly a party' to the carrying on of the company's business with a fraudulent intent or purpose. The persons who have been held to come within the scope of this provision are primarily persons involved in the management or control of a company.[51] Such persons may therefore face disqualification under s 160(2)(c), if they have been declared personally responsible for all or part of a company's debts under s 297A.

(b) Applicants under s 160(2)(c)

[22.028] Section 160(4) provides that an application under s 160(2)(c) may be made by the following persons:

    (a) the Director of Public Prosecutions; or

    (b) any member, contributory, officer, employee, receiver, liquidator, examiner or creditor of any company in relation to which the person who is the subject of the application—

        (i) has been or is acting or is proposing to or being proposed to act as officer, auditor, receiver, liquidator or examiner, or

        (ii) has been or is concerned or taking part, or is proposing to be concerned or take part, in the promotion, formation or management of any company.

---

[48] CA 1963, s 297A, as substituted by CA 1990, s 138. It is beyond the scope of this book to examine the topic of s 297A is detail. See Courtney, *The Law of Private Companies* (2nd edn, 2002, Tottel Publishing) at Ch **10**.

[49] See CA 1990, s 297A(10), as inserted by CA 1990, s 138.

[50] See Courtney, *The Law of Private Companies* (2nd edn, Tottel Publishing, 2002) at paras 10.081 to 10.100 in relation to reckless trading and, specifically, paras 10.095 to 10.096 regarding the 'Potential Respondents'.

[51] See *O'Keeffe v Ferris* [1993] 3 IR 165. See also Ch **6**, paras **[6.119]** to **[6.147]**, at which CA 1990, s 297A, is considered in detail.

In addition to these persons, s 160(6A)[52] also permits the DCE to make an application pursuant to s 160(2)(c).

(c) Applications under s 160(2)(c)

[22.029] *Re Kelly's Carpetdrome Ltd*[53] is one example of a case in which a person was found to have traded fraudulently, and was disqualified from acting in relation to a company as a result. This case was decided before the enactment of the CA 1990 and fell to be decided instead under the disqualification provision of CA 1963, s 184. It appears to be the sole example of a disqualification order being imposed consequent upon a finding of civil liability for fraudulent trading.

The standard necessary to establish a case of fraudulent or reckless trading and to justify the making of a declaration of personal liability under CA 1990, s 297A, is difficult to attain.[54]

(d) Comparative

[22.030] Section 10 of the Company Directors Disqualification Act 1986 ('CDDA') contains a similar provision to s 160(2)(c): '(1) where the court makes a declaration under section 213 or 214 of the Insolvency Act that a person is liable to make a contribution to a company's assets, then, whether or not an application for such an order is made by any person, the court may, if it thinks fit, also make a disqualification order against the person to whom the declaration relates'. The equivalent of s 297A in England, which is 'wrongful trading', is also difficult to establish. In the case of *Re Bath Glass Ltd*,[55] the Court of Appeal considered the difficulty of making out a case of wrongful trading and compared this with the standard that is required to establish that a person is unfit to act as a director within the meaning of s 6 of CDDA 1986.

The Court considered a submission to the effect that the test for wrongful trading in the Insolvency Act 1986, s 214(1) should be applied in deciding whether a director should be disqualified under CDDA 1986, s 6. The test for wrongful trading in the Insolvency Act 1986, s 214(1) includes that the person knew or ought to have concluded that there was no reasonable prospect that the company would avoid going into insolvent liquidation.

The Court concluded that, in a case of wrongful trading, the fact that the director allowed the company to continue to trade for a short time before liquidation within the meaning of s 214 might lead to a finding of wrongful trading and a small contribution might be awarded on that basis. However, the Court considered that:

> 'the test in s 6 is quite different: there is no single specified offence that is the condition to be satisfied for the court to make a disqualification order. What the court must have regard to is the director's conduct; that is a term of great generality and I do not doubt that it was deliberately so chosen. The court must be

---

[52] CA 1990, s 160(6A), as inserted by CLEA 2001, s 42(e).

[53] *Re Kelly's Carpetdrome Ltd* (1 July 1983, unreported), HC, Costello J,

[54] See Courtney, *The Law of Private Companies* (2nd edn, 2002) at paras [10.081] to [10.113].

[55] *Re Bath Glass Ltd* [1988] BCLC 329.

> satisfied that the conduct in question is sufficiently serious to lead it to the conclusion that the director is unfit and that is emphasised by the mandatory disqualification for at least two years to be imposed by the court if that conclusion is reached.'

The Court went on to state that:

> '[t]o reach a finding of unfitness the court must be satisfied that the director has been guilty of a serious failure or serious failures, whether deliberately or through incompetence, to perform those duties of directors which are attendant on the privilege of trading through companies with limited liability. Any misconduct of the respondent *qua* director may be relevant, even if it does not fall within a specific section of the Companies Acts or the Insolvency Act.'

The Court concluded that the conduct that may be taken into account in relation to the fitness of the director to act under s 6 would not necessarily justify a finding of wrongful trading under s 214:

> Even if such conduct does not amount to wrongful trading within s 214, in my judgment it would still be conduct amounting to misconduct and so relevant to s 6.

The case of *Re Bath Glass Ltd*[56] is an example of the application of grounds of disqualification, similar to s 160(2)(c) and (d) of the Irish CA 1990. There are two aspects of the decision in *Re Bath Glass* that are of relevance in the present context. First, the court indicated that conduct that may justify an order of disqualification on the ground of unfitness will not necessarily justify a finding of wrongful trading, even where the context and the conduct are similar in nature. Conversely, the court stated that conduct that may justify a finding of wrongful trading may not be so serious as to warrant an order of disqualification on the ground of unfitness.

[22.031] In Ireland, it has proven difficult to obtain a declaration of reckless or fraudulent trading under s 297A. In light of this fact, if the attainment of an order of disqualification is an important objective, it appears that an application grounded on an allegation of unfitness under s 160(2)(d), would have a better chance of success than an application which would require a declaration of reckless or fraudulent trading under CA 1990, s 297A.

As against this, it appears likely that the declaration of personal liability under s 297A would be the primary objective of an applicant. If the aim of the applicant is to recover monies to repay some of the company's debts, the declaration of personal liability will be crucial and the application for a disqualification order could follow upon such a declaration. If the primary aim is not to recover monies for the company's liabilities, an applicant may be advised to pursue an order of disqualification on a ground other than fraudulent or reckless trading under s 160(2)(c).

D. Unfit to be concerned with the management of a company

[22.032] The most important and frequently invoked ground of disqualification is s 160(2)(d). This permits a court to make an order of disqualification if it is satisfied

---

[56]   *Re Bath Glass Ltd* [1988] BCLC 329.

that: 'the conduct of any person as promoter, officer, auditor, receiver, liquidator or examiner of a company, makes him unfit to be concerned in the management of a company'.

The Companies Acts contain no guidance or criteria to assist in the interpretation of this phrase. It is therefore necessary to examine judicial interpretations of this provision to garner an understanding of the circumstances in which a person may be considered to be 'unfit to be concerned in the management of a company'.[57]

(a) Respondent under s 160(2)(d)

[22.033] Any person who acts as a promoter, officer, auditor, receiver, liquidator or examiner of a company may be the subject of an application under s 160(2)(d).

(b) Applicant under s 160(2)(d)

[22.034] Section 160(4) provides that an application under s 160(2)(d) may be made by the following persons:

(a) the Director of Public Prosecutions; or

(b) any member, contributory, officer, employee, receiver, liquidator, examiner or creditor of any company in relation to which the person who is the subject of the application—

(i) has been or is acting or is proposing to or being proposed to act as officer, auditor, receiver, liquidator or examiner, or

(ii) has been or is concerned or taking part, or is proposing to be concerned or take part, in the promotion, formation or management of any company.

In addition to these persons, s 160(6A)[58] also permits the DCE to make an application pursuant to s 160(2)(d).

(c) Conduct in other companies

[22.035] One point which was left open by the decision of the Supreme Court in *Re CB Readymix Ltd*[59] was whether a respondent could make the argument that he should not be disqualified on the basis of his conduct in relation to one company, if there are no allegations of misconduct in relation to other companies in which he is involved. In that case, the respondent argued that a liquidator or a director 'should not be severely penalised for one error in relation to a particular company in a context where no allegations of inappropriate conduct are made against him in respect of many other such offices held by him.'[60] The Court did not address that argument because of the respondent's failure or refusal to accept the gravity of his conduct of the affairs of Readymix Ltd. However, the Court did note that, '[t]hat argument has considerable force.' In an appropriate case, in which the respondent accepts the misconduct

---

[57] See further Ch **21** at paras **[21.024]** to **[21.036]**.

[58] CA 1990, s 160(6A), as inserted by CLEA 2001, s 42(e).

[59] *Re CB Readymix Ltd, Cahill v Grimes* [2002] 1 IR 372.

[60] *Re CB Readymix Ltd, Cahill v Grimes* [2002] 1 IR 372.

complained of in relation to one company, and in which the misconduct is of a lesser order than that complained of in *Re CB Readymix Ltd*, it may be open to a respondent to raise arguments based on his proper conduct in relation to other companies and to seek to avoid an order of disqualification under s 160(2)(d) on that basis.

(d) Overlap between ss 150 and 160

[22.036] In *Re CB Readymix Ltd*,[61] Murphy J stated that the approach of *Re Lo-Line Electric Motors Ltd*[62] was approved in other decisions of the Irish High Court and Supreme Court. However, each of the cases cited (with the exception of the High Court judgment which was under appeal) was decided under CA 1990, s 150, and did not purport to consider the test for 'unfitness' as that term is used in s 160(2)(d).

[22.037] *Re Lo-Line Electric Motors Ltd* was applied in a number of cases decided under s 150. In *La Moselle Clothing Ltd v Soualhi*[63] Shanley J quoted, with approval, the passage from the judgment of Browne-Wilkinson V-C cited above. In *Re Squash Ireland Ltd*,[64] McGuinness J stated, '[i]n a number of judgments in the High Court both Murphy J and the late Shanley J, have drawn attention to matters which are to be considered in deciding whether directors have acted responsibly.' She went on to cite the passage of the judgment of Shanley J in *La Moselle Clothing Ltd v Soualhi*[65] in which he quoted the test from *Re Lo-Line Motors Ltd* and then stated:

> 'The conduct referred to by Brown Wilkinson VC is similar to the conduct identified by Murphy J [in *Business Communications v Baxter*[66]], namely, that a director broadly complying with his obligations under the provisions of the Companies Acts and acting with a degree of commercial probity during his tenure as a director of the company will not be restricted on the grounds that he has acted irresponsibly.'[67]

[22.038] In *Re Cooke's Events Co Ltd*[68] MacMenamin J considered the appropriate test for determining whether directors have acted honestly and responsibly within the meaning of s 150(2)(a) and, referring to *Re Squash Ireland Ltd*,[69] he stated that, 'In deciding whether a director is unfit McGuinness J quoted a passage from the English case of *Re Lo-Line Motors Limited* [1998] BCLC 698, 703, a decision of Browne-Wilkinson QC, which was also quoted by Shanley J in the case of *La Moselle Clothing Limited v Soualhi* [1998] 2 ILRM 345.'

---

61   *Re CB Readymix Ltd, Cahill v Grimes* [2002] 1 IR 372.

62   *Re Lo-Line Ltd* [1988] Ch 477.

63   *La Moselle Clothing Ltd v Soualhi* [1998] 2 ILRM 345 at 352.

64   *Re Squash Ireland Ltd* [2001] IESC 200, [2001] 3 IR 35.

65   *La Moselle Clothing Ltd v Soualhi* [1998] 2 ILRM 345 at 352.

66   *Business Communications Ltd v Baxter* (21 July 1995, unreported), HC, Murphy J.

67   *Re Squash Ireland Ltd* [2001] IESC 200, [2001] 3 IR 35 at para 12.

68   *Re Cooke's Events Co Ltd, Kavanagh v Cooke* [2005] IEHC 225.

69   *Re Squash Ireland Ltd* [2001] IESC 200, [2001] 3 IR 35.

[22.039] In the course of his judgment in *Re Newcastle Timber Ltd*,[70] a case which did concern an application for an order of disqualification, McCracken J adopted the test formulated in *Re Lo-Line Motors Ltd*.[71] In the context of the test for disqualification under s 160(2)(d) that is not controversial. However, he went on to observe: 'While these comments were made in the context of slightly different legislation in the United Kingdom, I, like my colleagues, have no doubt that it is the proper approach to be taken both under s 150 and s 160'.[72]

[22.040] This line of authority raises an important issue.[73] The standard for determining whether to make a declaration of restriction in a contested case is whether the person acted 'honestly and responsibly'. Section 160(2)(d) states that it is a ground of disqualification if the court finds that a person's conduct makes him 'unfit to be concerned in the management of a company.' As will be seen, s 6 of the English Company Directors Disqualification Act 1986, provides for disqualification of persons who are 'unfit to be concerned in the management of a company'.

There have been a number of applications for declarations of restriction in which the Irish courts have employed standards and tests devised in England. While comparative analysis is often useful, in this instance, the reliance on English cases seems misplaced, because the Irish courts have applied English cases concerning the fitness of respondents 'to be concerned in the management of a company' in the context of s 150 applications. These tests of unfitness would be appropriate to determining whether a respondent should be disqualified on the ground of unfitness under s 160(2)(d), rather than being used to determine whether a person acted 'honestly and responsibly' within the meaning of s 150(2)(a).

[22.041] One danger of relying on tests of 'unfitness' in cases under s 150 is that a respondent to a restriction application would be able to avoid restriction by showing that he did not reach the threshold of being 'unfit to be concerned in the management of a company.' Conversely, there is a danger of a court imposing higher standards of proof on respondents under s 150, than is warranted by that provision. The legislative intent, that a person should be restricted unless they can show that they acted 'honestly and responsibly,' is readily apparent from the terms of s 150(2)(a). The applicant for a declaration of restriction bears no burden of proof and, in particular, does not have to demonstrate that the respondent is 'unfit'.[74] On the contrary, if an applicant is in a position to show that a person's conduct rendered them 'unfit to be concerned in the management of a company', the path designated by the legislature is that the person should be subject to an order of disqualification under s 160(2)(d). If a person reaches the threshold of being 'unfit', he should not face restriction proceedings, but should be subject to a disqualification order under s 160(2)(d). It is regrettable that the courts have blurred the distinction between the standards applicable to declarations of restriction and disqualification orders, and have used the more exacting test of 'unfitness' to determine

---

[70] *Re Newcastle Timber Ltd* [2001] IEHC 146.

[71] *Re Lo-Line Ltd* [1988] Ch 477.

[72] *Re Newcastle Timber Ltd* [2001] IEHC 146 at para 14.

[73] This issue is also addressed in Chs **17** and **21**.

[74] See further Ch **17**.

whether a person acted 'honestly and responsibly' in the context of restriction proceedings.

(e) Factors

[22.042] The facts and decision of the Supreme Court in *Re CB Readymix Ltd*[75] are important in the context of s 160(2)(d). In that case, as has been seen, a *de facto* liquidator of a company destroyed the company's documents, with the result that the official liquidator who was ultimately appointed to act had no access to the documents.

Murphy J, delivering the judgment of the Supreme Court, held that:

> 'It is common case that the respondent destroyed – or dumped with a view to their destruction – documents relating to the financial affairs of Readymix. In my view the inescapable conclusion is that those documents included the books and records of that company and that this was done with a view to depriving the official liquidator of access thereto.'[76]

In this regard, the Court noted that, '[a]n experienced liquidator – and the respondent rightly claims to be such – would immediately appreciate the importance of the records to which the respondent admits he had access.'[77] Murphy J proceeded to criticise the respondent's conduct and his destruction of the company's documents in the following terms:

> 'The fact that the respondent deprived the official liquidator of the books and records of Readymix was, to my mind, extremely serious. The grace with which the respondent defended his conduct was attractive but alarming. His apparent belief that the commendable motive of saving employment would justify the destruction of documents and the frustration of the liquidation of a company shows a completely mistaken view as to the duties of a liquidator and would undoubtedly raise concern as to the propriety of his being involved in the management of companies which are subject to detailed regulations for the protection of the interests of the public whether as shareholders, creditors or employees.'

The Court focused on the importance of a company's documents and the need to maintain and preserve documents and to have such documents available for a company's liquidators, noting that:

> 'Carrying on business as a corporate entity necessarily involves meetings of shareholders and meetings of directors. Of its nature this type of enterprise must generate substantial documentation. In addition, since the formation of corporate status by registration, the Companies Acts have required the creation, maintenance and preservation of documents relating to the affairs and finances of companies and public access to much of that information. The obligation to maintain such records is imposed on directors and failure to do so may, in addition to particular penalties, leave directors open to a charge of acting irresponsibly.'[78]

---

[75] *Re CB Readymix Ltd, Cahill v Grimes* [2002] 1 IR 372.

[76] *Re CB Readymix Ltd, Cahill v Grimes* [2002] 1 IR 372 at 378.

[77] *Re CB Readymix Ltd, Cahill v Grimes* [2002] 1 IR 372 at 378.

[78] *Re CB Readymix Ltd, Cahill v Grimes* [2002] 1 IR 372 at 382.

In this regard, the Court referred to the judgment of the High Court in *Business Communications Ltd v Baxter*,[79] a case decided under CA 1990, s 150, to the effect that:

> 'To obtain exemption from the restraint which must otherwise be imposed by virtue of s 150 of the Act of 1990, all that is required is the exercise of a suitable degree of responsibility. Ordinarily responsibility will entail compliance with the principal features of the Companies Acts and the maintenance of the records required by those Acts. The records may be basic in form and modest in appearance. But they must exist in such a form as to enable the directors to make reasonable commercial decisions and auditors (or liquidators) to understand and follow the transactions in which the company was engaged.'

The Court considered that:

> '[t]he fortuitous reference in that passage to the importance of appropriate documentation being available for liquidators underscores the gravity of the misconduct of the respondent in the present case. Adequate records are necessary to enable a liquidator to perform his statutory functions properly and some records are necessary to enable him to perform his functions at all.'

[22.043] Despite the severity of the criticism of the respondent's conduct, the Court did not consider that he acted maliciously. However, in the light of the Court's conclusion that 'his decision to destroy or permit the destruction of the books and records of Readymix was a very serious wrong indeed', which was exacerbated by the respondent's refusal to accept the wrongfulness of his actions, the Court upheld the order of disqualification. The Court concluded as follows:

> 'It was the fact that the respondent could not then – and does not now – appreciate the gravity of his misconduct that justifies the conclusion that he is unfit to hold the office of liquidator and casts serious doubt upon his suitability to participate in the management of any company.'[80]

The facts of that case were particularly egregious, as the respondent admitted to deliberately destroying the company's documents. It might be expected that such conduct would lead to an order of disqualification under any circumstances. The judgment of Murphy J also reveals that a failure or refusal to accept the wrongfulness of the conduct complained of, may increase the likelihood of a disqualification order being made. Finally, the fact that the Court accepted there was no malice in the actions of the respondents did not preclude the making of a disqualification order under s 160(2)(d).

[22.044] In *Re Newcastle Timber Ltd*,[81] McCracken J considered an application to disqualify the directors of a company which went into insolvent liquidation. The most serious allegation against the directors was that they traded while unable to discharge their liabilities, in particular liabilities owed to the Revenue Commissioners. The Court noted that the only attempt the directors made to justify the insolvent trading was their belief that the problems were not insuperable and that the company could be turned around. While the Court considered that this was 'a genuine, although highly unrealistic belief' as evidenced by the fact that the directors invested their own money in the

---

[79] *Business Communications Ltd v Baxter* (21 July 1995, unreported), HC, Murphy J.

[80] *Re CB Readymix Ltd, Cahill v Grimes* [2002] 1 IR 372 at 383.

[81] *Re Newcastle Timber Ltd* [2001] IEHC 146.

company during the period in question, the Court stated, 'The fact remains that the trading losses were of a considerable magnitude and the clear implication is that there was a deliberate policy not to discharge the Revenue debts.'[82] There was also evidence that the company failed to make returns and that, when the company ceased to trade, the directors discharged trade creditors in preference to the debts owed to the Revenue Commissioners.

[22.045] McCracken J summarised the issues to be decided as follows:

> 'The primary questions remains as to whether these actions on the part of the Directors amounted to a breach of duty or were actions which made the Directors unfit to be concerned in the management of a company, and secondly, whether, if so, I should exercise the undoubted discretion given by making an Order under the section.'[83]

In this regard, the Court held:

> '... many faults can be found in the conduct of the Directors in the present case. I have no doubt that they acted incompetently, and, particularly in relation to insolvent trading and preference of trade creditors, I think they behaved irresponsibly. However, the Liquidator has not satisfied me that the Directors were so much in breach of their duties, that they are unfit to be concerned of the management of a company, particularly in view of the undoubted discretion which I have in this regard. The Liquidator did rely to a considerable degree on the fact that the Revenue debts remained unpaid, and cited a number of authorities as to the importance of this aspect of the case, but taking the overall behaviour of the Directors I do not think it could be said that a Disqualification Order is necessary to protect the public against their future conduct.'[84]

The Court was influenced in reaching this decision by the fact that the respondent had been 'intimately concerned' in another company in the six years since the winding up of Newcastle Timber Ltd and this company was trading successfully and in compliance with its tax obligations. Rather than making an order of disqualification, the Court made a declaration of restriction, noting that:

> 'To trade while insolvent for one year, or perhaps two years, in the hope that the company may trade out of its problems is understandable, but to have kept Newcastle trading insolvently for some four years, and allowing Revenue debts to build up, appears to me to be totally irresponsible.'[85]

[22.046] A further case which involved an order of disqualification, in somewhat different circumstances, is *Re C (N) (A Bankrupt)*.[86] In the context of bankruptcy proceedings, Court determined that an order of disqualification was appropriate on the basis that the respondent was 'unfit to be concerned in the management of a company' within the meaning of s 160(2)(d). In the course of the hearing in that case, the

---

[82]   *Re Newcastle Timber Ltd* [2001] IEHC 146 at para 8.

[83]   *Re Newcastle Timber Ltd* [2001] IEHC 146 at para 12.

[84]   *Re Newcastle Timber Ltd* [2001] IEHC 146 at para 14.

[85]   *Re Newcastle Timber Ltd* [2001] IEHC 146 at para 15.

[86]   *Re C (N) (A Bankrupt)* [1999] IEHC 203 (26 November, 1999).

arranging debtor indicated that he would be willing to submit to a declaration of restriction or order of disqualification.

The Court noted that 'If the Arranging Debtor were adjudicated a bankrupt he would be debarred from being an officer of a company while an undischarged bankrupt' and went on to state, 'While most of the matters stipulated in sub-s (2) [s 160] are of a specific nature, para (d) is framed in general terms and stipulates that – "the conduct of any person as promoter, officer ... of a company makes him unfit to be concerned in the management of a company".'[87]

Applying this provision, Laffoy J held:

> 'On the facts of this case, in which the indebtedness of the Arranging Debtor is inextricably linked to the management and business of the Company, I think that the protection of the public and of the commercial community, which must be a factor which the Court should have regard to in determining whether to approve a proposal under section 92 will be adequately met by the making of a disqualification order under s 160. However, this case turns very much on its own facts and the approach adopted by the Court in this case would not necessarily be appropriate in the case of an individual debtor who traded or practised his profession in his own name.

> Accordingly, I make a disqualification order under section 160 of the Act of 1990 for the period of five years from today's date.'[88]

[22.047] From the cases which have considered disqualification on the ground of unfitness, some general principles can be noted:

1. The test to be applied is whether the respondent displayed a lack of commercial probity.[89]

2. Commercial misjudgment will not justify an order of disqualification.[90]

3. The non-payment of revenue debts will not be sufficient to demonstrate unfitness.

4. Any interference with (such as destruction of) a company's documents may be evidence of unfitness.[91]

5. A respondent's attitude towards allegations of misconduct may have a bearing on the court's determination as to whether a person is unfit.[92]

6. The absence of malice in the conduct complained of will not necessarily prevent a disqualification order being made.[93]

---

[87] *Re C (N) (A Bankrupt)* [1999] IEHC 203 (26 November, 1999) at para 9.

[88] *Re C (N) (A Bankrupt)* [1999] IEHC 203 (26 November, 1999) at paras 11–12.

[89] See Ch **21** at paras **[21.024]** to **[21.036]**.

[90] See Ch **21** at paras **[21.024]** to **[21.036]**.

[91] *Re CB Readymix Ltd, Cahill v Grimes* [2002] 1 IR 372.

[92] *Re CB Readymix Ltd, Cahill v Grimes* [2002] 1 IR 372.

[93] *Re CB Readymix Ltd, Cahill v Grimes* [2002] 1 IR 372.

7. Continuing to trade while insolvent will not necessarily result in disqualification.[94]

8. The non-payment of revenue debts, or the payment of trade creditors in preference to the Revenue Commissioners, is not necessarily indicative of unfitness. [95]

9. The fact that a respondent has been involved in the management of a successful company for a period of time since the alleged misconduct may be relevant. [96]

E. Finding of unfitness in inspector's report

[22.048] This ground of disqualification is a very specific one. It is predicated upon the appointment of an inspector to investigate the affairs of a company and the description in the inspector's report of conduct that demonstrates the person to be unfit to be concerned in the management of a company.[97] CA 1990, s 160(2)(e), provides that a court may order a person to be disqualified where: 'in consequence of a report of inspectors appointed by the court or the Minister under the Companies Acts, the conduct of any person makes him unfit to be concerned in the management of a company.'[98]

(a) Respondents under s 160(2)(e)

[22.049] The category of persons who may be the subject of an order of disqualification under s 160(2)(e) is broad: any person whose conduct makes him unfit to be concerned in company's management, may be disqualified. There is no requirement that a person against whom a disqualification order is made under that provision must have been acting as a promoter, officer, auditor, receiver, liquidator or examiner at the time of the conduct that is considered to render him unfit to be concerned in the management of a company.

(b) Applicants under s 160(2)(e)

[22.050] Section 160(5) stipulates that, '[a]n application under para (e) or (g) of subsection (2) may be made by the Director of Public Prosecutions.' In addition, s 160(6A)[99] permits the DCE to make an application pursuant to s 160(2)(e). It should be noted that the wider category of persons who can make applications to court for an order of disqualification under s 160(2)(a)–(d)[100] cannot make such an application on

---

[94] *Re Newcastle Timber Ltd* [2001] IEHC 146.

[95] *Re Newcastle Timber Ltd* [2001] IEHC 146.

[96] *Re Newcastle Timber Ltd* [2001] IEHC 146.

[97] CA 1990, s 160(2)(e).

[98] CA 1990, s 160(2)(e).

[99] CA 1990, s 160(6A), as inserted by CLEA 2001, s 42(e).

[100] Namely 'any member, contributory, officer, employee, receiver, liquidator, examiner or creditor of any company in relation to which' the person in question acted or proposed to act. See CA 1990, s 160(4)(a).

the basis of unfitness to be concerned in the management of a company, where the conduct in question is in consequence of an inspectors' report.

The only persons who can seek a disqualification order under s 160(2)(e) are the DPP and the DCE.

(c) Scope of s 160(2)(e)

[22.051] The framing of this provision is curious. The language suggests that it is the inspector's report itself which causes the conduct to make a person unfit to be concerned in the management of a company. Clearly what the provision is intended to provide is that where a report of inspectors appointed to investigate the affairs of a company discloses conduct which renders a person unfit, or makes a specific finding that the person was responsible for conduct which rendered him unfit to be concerned in the management of the company, that the person may be the subject of a disqualification order.

The question of whether a finding of disqualification under s 160(2)(e) could relate to conduct which pre-dated the commencement of s 160 in August 1991, was raised in *Re Ansbacher (Cayman) Ltd, Director of Corporate Enforcement v Collery*,[101] but not resolved. The parties consented to the application being confined to conduct which post-dated the commencement of that subsection.

(d) Applications under s 160(2)(e)

[22.052] In each of the decisions which have been delivered arising from the inspectors' report into National Irish Bank Ltd,[102] the applications were based on sub-ss 160(2)(b), (d) and (e), but, where orders of disqualification were made, the Court focused on s 160(2)(d) as a ground for such an order. In *Re Ansbacher (Cayman) Ltd, Director of Corporate Enforcement v Collery*[103] and *Re Ansbacher (Cayman) Ltd, Director of Corporate Enforcement v Stakelum*,[104] s 160(2)(e) was the only ground on which orders of disqualification were sought, and those judgments are therefore useful illustrations of s 160(2)(e). In particular, they demonstrate that the same standard of fitness applies under s 160(2)(d) and (e).[105]

---

[101] *Re Ansbacher (Cayman) Ltd, Director of Corporate Enforcement v Collery* [2006] IEHC 67.

[102] *Re National Irish Bank Ltd, Director of Corporate Enforcement v Seymour* [2007] IEHC 102; *Re National Irish Bank Ltd, Director of Corporate Enforcement v D'Arcy* [2006] 2 IR 163 and *Re National Irish Bank Ltd, Director of Corporate Enforcement v Curran* [2007] IEHC 181.

[103] *Re Ansbacher (Cayman) Ltd, Director of Corporate Enforcement v Collery* [2006] IEHC 67.

[104] *Re Ansbacher (Cayman) Ltd, Director of Corporate Enforcement v Stakelum* (31 July 2007, unreported), HC.

[105] See further paras **[21.024]** to **[21.036]**.

F. Persistent default

[22.053] Section 160(2)(f) provides that a court may disqualify a person who 'has been persistently in default in relation to the relevant requirements.'

(a) Respondents under s 160(2)(f))

[22.054] Section 160(2)(f) purports to permit a court to make an order of disqualification against any person if they have been proven to be persistently in default in relation to the filing requirements of the Companies Acts. It is clear from the wording of CA 1963, s 371, that the only person who may be the subject of a default order, as that term is invoked as a means of proof of 'persistent default', is an officer of the company. It therefore appears that only an officer of the company can be disqualified on the basis of proof that three default orders were made against him in five years, for failing to comply with the filing requirements of the Companies Acts.

While the application of s 160(2)(f) is not limited expressly to officers of a company, it appears consistent with the formulation and focus of that provision that it should only apply to officers, or former officers, of a company. It is difficult to envisage how an auditor, receiver, liquidator or examiner, could be responsible for persistent default in relation to the filing requirements of the Companies Acts. Similarly, if a promoter was persistently in default in relation to the filing requirements of the Companies Acts, one would imagine that the company would simply not be registered.

(b) Applicants under s 160(2)(f)

[22.055] Section 160(6) provides that an application under s 160(2)(f) may be made by the DPP or the Registrar of Companies. In addition, s 160(6A)[106] permits the DCE to make an application pursuant to s 160(2)(f). The wider category of persons who can make applications to court for an order of disqualification under s 160(2)(a)–(d)[107] cannot make such an application on the basis of persistent default in relation to the filing requirements of the Companies Acts.

(c) Means of proof under s 160(2)(f)

[22.056] Section 160(2)(f) must be read together with s 160(3) which provides:

    (a) For the purposes of subsection (2)(f) the fact that a person has been persistently in default in relation to the relevant requirements may (without prejudice to its proof in any other manner) be conclusively proved by showing that in the five years ending with the date of the application he has been adjudged guilty (whether or not on the same occasion) of three or more defaults in relation to those requirements.

    (b) A person shall be treated as being adjudged guilty of a default in relation to a relevant requirement for the purposes of this subsection if he is convicted of

---

[106] CA 1990, s 160(6A), as inserted by CLEA 2001, s 42(e).

[107] Namely 'any member, contributory, officer, employee, receiver, liquidator, examiner or creditor of any company in relation to which' the person in question acted or proposed to act. See CA 1990, s 160(4)(a).

any offence consisting of a contravention of a relevant requirement or a
default order is made against him.

Laffoy J described the evidential aid of s 160(3) in *Re Wood Products (Longford) Ltd*[108]
as follows:

'What might be called the "three strikes" philosophy which underlies sub-s. (3)
suggests that, on the proper construction of paragraph (f), persistent default is not
merely default which has continued over a long period of time but is default which
has continued in the teeth of intervention on the part of the courts more than
once.'

This provision was not applicable in that case as there was 'no evidence that the
respondents were prosecuted, let alone convicted, of an offence under s 125 of the Act of
1963, as amended, for failure to make annual returns, nor is there any evidence that
s 371 of the Act of 1963, as amended, was invoked, let alone successfully invoked,
against the Company or the respondents'.

[22.057] The expression 'relevant requirements' is defined in CA 1990, s 159, as
follows:

'relevant requirement' means any provision of the Companies Acts (including a
provision repealed by this Act) which requires or required any return, account or
other document to be filed with, delivered or sent to, or notice of any matter to be
given to, the registrar of companies.

A 'default order' is defined as follows in CA 1990, s 159:

'"default order" means an order made against any person under s 371[109] of the
Principal Act by virtue of any contravention of or failure to comply with any
relevant requirement (whether on his own part or on the part of any company).'

[22.058] The effect of s 160(2)(f) is as follows:

– A person may be disqualified if he has been proven to have persistently in
 default in relation to the requirements under the Companies Acts to file with,
 deliver or send to, the Registrar of Companies, a return, account or other
 document or otherwise notify the Registrar of a matter ('a filing requirement');

– Persistent default may be proven by any means and may be conclusively proven
 if the person was found to have been guilty of three defaults in relation to the
 filing requirements in the preceding five years; and

– A default consists of a conviction for contravention of a filing requirement, or
 an order directing the company and its officers to make good a default in

---

[108] *Re Wood Products (Longford) Ltd, Director of Corporate Enforcement v McGowan* [2005]
IEHC 41.

[109] CA 1963, s 371(1) provides, 'If a company or any officer of a company having made default
in complying with any provision of this Act fails to make good the default within 14 days
after the service of a notice on the company or officer requiring it or him to do so, the court
may, on an application made to the court by any member or creditor of the company or by
the registrar of companies, make an order directing the company and any officer thereof to
make good the default within such time as may be specified in the order.'

complying with the filing requirements, having failed to comply with a notice requiring such default to be made good.

(d) Applications under s 160(2)(f)

[22.059] *Re Wood Products (Longford) Ltd*[110] appears to be the only decision of the High Court in which the application of s 160(2)(f) has been considered. Wood Products (Longford) Ltd ('the Company') was struck off the register and dissolved due to its failure to file annual returns. The court subsequently restored the Company to the register on the application of a creditor, with additional orders that all outstanding annual returns and Revenue returns be filed within three months of that order. None of these returns having been delivered within the intervening two and a half years, the applicant issued a notice of motion seeking orders of disqualification under sub-ss 160(2)(d) and (f) against the two directors of the Company.

The respondents, a husband and wife, admitted the failures in question, and raised pleas in mitigation, such as the contention that the company suffered financial difficulties due to the inability to get payment from main contractors and that the second respondent suffered from depression as a result of this and other matters. In addition, following the commencement of the disqualification proceedings, the Company filed all outstanding annual returns and tax returns. A sum in excess of €400,000 remained due to the Revenue Commissioners.

[22.060] The Court made a number of useful observations regarding the scope of s 160(2)(f). First, there must be persistent default in compliance with provisions of the Companies Acts, in relation to making returns to the CRO. Failure to comply with other statutory requirements to make returns, such as returns to the Revenue Commissioners, is not within the scope of s 160(2)(f).

Second, if there is no conviction or default order within the meaning of s 160(3), 'the question which falls to be considered is whether the Director has proved in any other manner that the respondents have been persistently in default in relation to making annual returns.'

Third, in determining the meaning of 'persistent default' the Court referred to the ordinary meaning of the verb 'persist' as: 'to continue firmly or obstinately in a state, opinion, purpose, or course of action *esp.* against opposition' (Shorter *Oxford English Dictionary*, 3rd edn.).' In light of this definition and what the Court referred to as the 'three strikes' philosophy if s 160(3), the Court made the following determination: 'persistent default is not merely default which has continued over a long period of time but is default which has continued in the teeth of intervention on the part of the courts more than once'.

In that case, although there was default over a protracted period of time, as no annual returns were filed for thirteen consecutive years, the only action taken by the CRO was to strike the company off the registers after nine years of such default. While the default of the respondents in failing to file the annual returns and failing to comply with the

---

[110] *Re Wood Products (Longford) Ltd, Director of Corporate Enforcement v McGowan* [2005] IEHC 41.

order of the Court was 'to be deprecated', Laffoy J was '... not satisfied that it has been established on the evidence that the respondents have been "persistently in default" in relation to their obligations under s 125 in the sense in which that expression is used in para (f).'

[22.061] This decision suggests that an order will only be made under s 160(2)(f) when the evidential aid of s 160(3) is applicable, or the respondents have persisted in the defaults in question in spite of other forms of court intervention. As it was clearly considered insufficient in *Re Wood Products (Longford) Ltd*[111] that the court directed the defaults to be made good on an application to restore a company to the register, it seems that either a number of convictions for defaults under the Companies Acts or default orders under s 371 must exist, before a person will be adjudged guilty of 'persistent default' within the meaning of s 160(2)(f). It is also apparent from the decision in *Re Wood Products (Longford) Ltd* that a 'persistent default' under s 160(2)(f) can only arise from defaults under the Companies Acts and that, irrespective of the number of default convictions or default orders, these must occur over a long period of time.

G. Failing to keep proper books of account

[22.062] If a person has been responsible for the failure by a company to keep proper books of account, he may be the subject of a disqualification order. Section 160(2)(g) provides that an order of disqualification may be made where, 'a person has been guilty of two or more offences under s 202(10)'. This provision was inserted by the CLEA 2001.[112]

(a) Respondents under s 160(2)(g)

[22.063] Only a director of a company can be disqualified on the basis of s 160(2)(g). The offence of failing to secure compliance by a company with its obligation to keep proper books of account or causing a company's default in this regard, can only be committed by a company's directors. CA 1990, s 202(10) stipulates that:

> '... a person who, being a director of a company, fails to take all reasonable steps to secure compliance by the company with the requirements of this section, or has by his own wilful act been the cause of any default by the company thereunder, shall be guilty of an offence.'

There is no possibility of any person, other than a director of a company, being adjudged guilty for a company's failure to keep proper books of account.

[22.064] There is one caveat to this, which, while probably lacking any real significance, is curious. The reference in s 202(10) is to '*a* company' being in contravention under s 202. The reference to the person who may be convicted in relation to such a default is to 'a director of *a* company'. The components of the offence are formulated by reference to '*the* company', namely the failure by a director to 'take all

---

[111] *Re Wood Products (Longford) Ltd, Director of Corporate Enforcement v McGowan* [2005] IEHC 41.

[112] CLEA 2001, s 42(b)(ii).

reasonable steps to secure compliance by the company with the requirements of this section' or causing 'default by the company'. A literal reading of s 202(10) could suggest that, where a company is in breach of s 202, a director of any company could be found guilty of an offence under s 202(10), if he failed to secure compliance by the company in breach with the requirements of s 202 or caused such default. This would mean that any person who happens to be a director of any company could come within the scope of s 202(10) and, accordingly, could be disqualified under s 160(2)(g). It seems likely that the reference to a person 'being a director of *a* company' should more accurately refer to a person 'being a director of *the* company' and that the possible consequence outlined above was unintended.

[22.065] A further potential ambiguity regarding the scope of s 160(2)(g) is whether a former director of a company may come within the scope of s 202(10). That provision refers to a person 'being a director of a company.' It does not include any reference to former directors. This can be contrasted with the terms of s 204, which governs civil liability of a company's officers for the company's failure to keep proper books of account. According to s 204(1), a court may, in the circumstances set out in that provision, make a declaration of personal liability against 'any one or more of the officers and former officers of the company who is or are in default.'[113] The failure to refer to 'former directors' in s 202(10) may be an accidental omission but it does suggest that someone who resigned as a director of a company which was in contravention of the obligation to keep proper books of account, before that contravention was detected, may not be prosecuted for that contravention.

(b) Applicants under s 160(2)(g)

[22.066] According to s 160(5), the DPP may make an application for an order of disqualification under s 160(2)(g). In addition, the DCE may make such an application, pursuant to s 160(2), (6A).[114]

(c) Offence of failing to keep proper books of account

[22.067] The obligation to keep proper books of account is addressed in more detail in Ch 4. However, for present purposes, it should be noted that s 202 requires a company to keep proper books of account which give a true and fair view of the state of affairs of the company and explain its transactions and that s 202(10) provides as follows:

> A company that contravenes this section and a person who, being a director of a company, fails to take all reasonable steps to secure compliance by the company with the requirements of this section, or has by his own wilful act been the cause of any default by the company thereunder, shall be guilty of an offence:
>
> Provided, however, that—
>
> (a) in any proceedings against a person in respect of an offence under this section consisting of a failure to take reasonable steps to secure compliance by a company with the requirements of this section, it shall be a defence to prove that he had reasonable grounds for believing and did believe that a competent

---

[113] CA 1990, s 204(1).

[114] As inserted by CLEA 2001, s 42(e).

and reliable person was charged with the duty of ensuring that those requirements were complied with and was in a position to discharge that duty, and

(b) a person shall not be sentenced to imprisonment for such an offence unless, in the opinion of the court, the offence was committed wilfully.

[22.068] Disqualification for failing to secure compliance by a company with its obligations to keep proper books of account, or causing a company to fail in its obligations in that regard, is premised on a criminal conviction. It is only if a person has been found guilty of two or more offences in relation to the company's failure to keep proper books of account that an order of disqualification may be warranted.

It is interesting to compare s 160(2)(g) with s 160(2)(f). One of the means of proving that a person was persistently in default of the filing requirements of the Companies Acts within the meaning of s 160(2)(f) is to show that, 'in the five years ending with the date of the application he has been adjudged guilty (whether or not on the same occasion) of three or more defaults.'[115] By contrast, s 160(2)(g) simply refers to the requirement that the person 'has been guilty of 2 or more offences' in connection with the company's failure to keep proper books of account. The fact that s 160(2)(f) expressly provides for the possibility that the three convictions may have been obtained on the same occasion, while s 160(2)(g) makes no such provision, may be regarded as limiting the scope of s 160(2)(g) to situations in which two separate convictions of offences under s 202(10) took place. However, it seems more likely that the reference in s 160(2)(g) was intended to include single convictions of a number of offences of failing to keep proper books of account.

[22.069] A final point to note with regard to the requirement of a conviction for a disqualification order under s 160(2)(g), is that a declaration of personal liability may be made against an officer or former officer of a company which is in contravention of the obligation to keep proper books of account.[116] Where such a declaration is made, this will not be a sufficient basis for making an order of disqualification under s 160(2)(g). The criteria for a conviction under s 202(10) and a declaration under s 204(1) are not vastly different. For example, in both cases, a director who demonstrates that he took reasonable steps to secure the company's compliance with s 202, will avoid liability.[117] Despite the similarity between the provisions, however, an order of disqualification can only be made if a director is convicted of an offence under s 202(10).

---

[115] CA 1990, s 160(3)(a).

[116] CA 1990, s 204(1) provides: '… if— (a) a company that is being wound up and that is unable to pay all of its debts has contravened s 202, and (b) the court considers that such contravention has contributed to the company's inability to pay all of its debts or has resulted in substantial uncertainty as to the assets and liabilities of the company or has substantially impeded the orderly winding up thereof, the court, on the application of the liquidator or any creditor or contributory of the company, may, if it thinks it proper to do so, declare that any one or more of the officers and former officers of the company who is or are in default shall be personally liable, without any limitation of liability, for all, or such part as may be specified by the court, of the debts and other liabilities of the company.'

[117] See CA 1990, s 202(1)(a) and CA 1990, s 204(4)(a).

(d) Applications under s 160(2)(g)

[22.070] No disqualification orders have been made under s 160(2)(g) to date and there is no equivalent to this provision in England, from which to draw comparative assistance. There have been cases in which people have been found guilty of contravening s 202, but these cases have not led to applications under s 160(2)(g) for orders of disqualification. For example, in the case of *Re Tenants First (Ireland) Ltd*[118] two respondents were charged with, and found guilty of, nine charges of contravening s 202 in three consecutive years. The Court imposed fines totalling €150 against each respondent and awarded prosecution costs totalling €1,041.93. In addition, witness expenses totalling €300 were awarded against the company. In the circumstances of that case, one of the respondents was also charged with violating s 183 and was disqualified automatically as a result. It would have been open to the DCE to make an application for the disqualification of the other respondent on the basis of s 160(2)(g), but no such application was made.

In light of the dearth of authorities under s 160(2)(g), it is not possible to furnish guidance regarding the interpretation of this provision and its application in practice, until such time as applications are brought before the courts for disqualification orders on the ground of offences under s 202(10).

H. Company struck off the register

[22.071] A director of a company which was struck off the register of companies may be the subject of a disqualification order on that basis.[119] Section 160(2)(h), which was inserted by the CLEA 2001,[120] provides that a person may be disqualified on the ground that he:

> '... was a director of a company at the time of the sending, after the commencement of s 42 of the Company Law Enforcement Act, 2001,[121] of a letter under sub-s (1) of s 12 of the Companies (Amendment) Act 1982, to the company and the name of which, following the taking of the other steps under that section consequent on the sending of that letter, was struck off the register under subsection (3) of that section.'[122]

This ground of disqualification must be read in light of s 160(3A)[123] which provides:

> The court shall not make a disqualification order under paragraph (h) of subsection (2) against a person who shows to the court that the company referred

---

[118] *Re Tenants First (Ireland) Ltd, Director of Corporate Enforcement v McGovern* (12 October 2004, unreported), Dundalk District Court.

[119] The topics of companies being struck off the register of companies and the obligation to make annual returns are addressed in more detail in Ch **2** and Ch **14**.

[120] CA 1990, s 160(2)(h), as inserted by CLEA 2001, s 42(b)(ii).

[121] CLEA 2001, s 42 was commenced by the CLEA 2001 (Commencement) (No 5) Order 2002, SI 53/2002 on 1 March 2002.

[122] CA 1990, s 160(2)(h), as inserted by CLEA 2001, s 42(b)(ii).

[123] CA 1990, s 160(3A) as inserted by CLEA 2001, s 42(c).

to in that paragraph had no liabilities (whether actual, contingent or prospective) at the time its name was struck off the register or that any such liabilities that existed at that time were discharged before the date of the making of the application for the disqualification order.[124]

(a) Respondents under s 160(2)(h)

[22.072] The only persons who may be disqualified on the basis of s 160(2)(h) are people who were directors of the company when a s 12 letter was sent, and pursuant to which the company was subsequently struck off the register of companies for failing to make annual returns.[125]

It should be noted that s 160(2)(h) requires that the person must have been a director at the date that the section 12 letter was sent. There is nothing in the provision which requires that the person facing disqualification must have continued to act as a director of the company in the period after the sending of the section 12 letter. This leaves open the possibility that a person who was a director when the section 12 letter was sent, but who resigned before the company was struck off, may face disqualification. In many cases, little sympathy would be felt for the director of the delinquent company. However, there may be circumstances in which the director was not responsible for, or in support of, the failure to reply to the s 12 letter, for example. In such circumstances, even though the director would be captured by the scope of s 160(2)(h), it may be hoped that the court would exercise its general discretion regarding the making of disqualification orders, in favour of the former director.

(b) Applicants under s 160(2)(h)

[22.073] Section 160(2)(h) was introduced by the CLEA 2001 and, according to that Act, only the DCE has jurisdiction to bring an application to have a director disqualified on the basis that he was a director of a company when that company was struck off the register of companies.[126]

(c) Criteria of s 160(2)(h)

[22.074] The first requirement for a successful application for a disqualification order under s 160(2)(h) is that a letter must have been sent pursuant to C(A)A 1982, s 12[127] (a 's 12 letter'). Section 12(1) provides:

> … where a company does not, for two consecutive years, make the annual returns required by ss 125 and 126 of the Principal Act,[128] the registrar of companies may send to the company by post a registered letter inquiring whether the company is carrying on business and stating that, if an answer is not received within one

---

[124] CA 1990, s 160(3A), as inserted by CLEA 2001, s 42(c).

[125] CA 1990, s 160(2)(h), as inserted by CLEA 2001, s 42(b)(ii).

[126] CA 1990, s 160(6A), inserted by CLEA 2001, s 42(e).

[127] C(A)A 1982, s 12, as amended by CA 1990, s 245.

[128] With regard to the requirement to make annual returns, and enforcement of that obligation, see further Ch **2**.

month from the date of that letter, a notice will be published in Iris Oifigiúil with a view to striking the name of the company off the register.[129]

[22.075] The next requirement is that the section 12 letter must have been sent after the commencement of CLEA 2001, s 42. There is no requirement that the grounds for sending a letter under s 12 must arise after the commencement of s 42. As a result, the fact that a company may have failed to make annual returns for two consecutive years in the 1990s, for example, could form the basis for an application for an order of disqualification under s 160(2)(h), so long as the Registrar of Companies did not send the section 12 letter until after the commencement of s 42.

[22.076] The third requirement for an application for an order of disqualification under s 160(2)(h) is that the name of the company was in fact struck off the register of companies 'following the taking of the other steps under that section consequent on the sending of that letter'.[130] The steps which are taken after a section 12 letter is sent are as follows:

–   Unless the registrar receives, within one month of sending the section 12 letter, (a) a response, (b) all outstanding annual returns, or (c) a response indicating that the company is not carrying on business, the registrar may publish in Iris Oifigiúil and send to the company, a notice;[131]

–   The notice will state that the company will be struck off within one month unless cause is shown to the contrary or the outstanding annual returns are received;[132]

–   If no reason to the contrary is shown by the company within one month, the registrar may strike the company's name off the register of companies;[133] and

–   Upon publication in Iris Oifigiúil of the notice that the company was struck-off, the company shall be dissolved.[134]

[22.077] In the most important decision under s 160(2)(h) to date, *Re Clawhammer Ltd,*[135] the High Court considered the proofs which are required for an application for a disqualification order under that provision. Finlay Geoghegan J accepted the submission of the DCE that the applicant only had to prove that a letter was sent under C(A)A 1982, s 12, pursuant to which the company was struck off the register of companies, and that the respondents were directors of the company at that time. As the respondents in one of

---

[129]   C(A)A 1982, s 12(1), as amended by CA 1990, s 245.

[130]   Expression used in CA 1990, s 160(2)(h), as inserted by CLEA 2001, s 42(b)(ii).

[131]   C(A)A 1982, s 12(2). See further Ch **14**.

[132]   C(A)A 1982, s 12(2). See further Ch **14**.

[133]   C(A)A 1982, s 12(3). See further Ch **14**.

[134]   C(A)A 1982, s 12(3). See further Ch **14**.

[135]   *Re Clawhammer Ltd, Director of Corporate Enforcement v McDonnell; Re Shinrone Food Market Ltd, Director of Corporate Enforcement v Hoctor; Re Cautious Trading Ltd, Director of Corporate Enforcement v Forristal* (15 March 2005, unreported), HC, Finlay Geoghegan J.

the cases were not represented at the hearing of the application, the DCE also had to produce evidence of service of the application, which the DCE did by means of an affidavit of personal service.

(d) Defence to disqualification application under s 160(2)(h)

[22.078] If the company which was struck off the register of companies did not, at the date of being struck off, or does not, at the date of the application for disqualification, have any outstanding liabilities, the court cannot make an order of disqualification under s 160(2)(h). The person facing disqualification proceedings must demonstrate either:

(a) that the company had no liabilities (actual, contingent or prospective) at the date of being struck off; or

(b) that any liabilities which did exist at the date the company was struck off, were discharged before the application for the disqualification order was made.[136]

If either of these is established, the court no longer has a discretion to make an order of disqualification. The language used in s 160(3A) firmly demonstrates that a court 'shall not make a disqualification order' if the director demonstrates the company had no liabilities, or had discharged all such liabilities before the application for a disqualification order.[137]

[22.079] The deadline for discharging a dissolved company's liabilities is described in s 160(3A) as 'the date of the making of the application for the disqualification order.' It seems to refer to the actual date of the application to court for the order of disqualification, rather than the date on which the proceedings were issued. This is confirmed by the terms of s 160(7), which requires an applicant for a disqualification order to give ten days' notice to a person of his intention 'to make an application under subsection (2)' in respect of that person.[138] It would be nonsensical if this required an applicant to give notice of his intention to issue proceedings. The reference to an intention 'to make an application' must therefore refer to the intention to make an application to court. Similarly, it appears that the use of the expression 'the making of the application for the disqualification order' as it is used in s 160(2)(h), could not be interpreted to refer to the initiation of proceedings. On the contrary, it appears that a person who faces disqualification proceedings under s 160(2)(h) has until the day of the hearing of the disqualification application, to discharge the dissolved company's outstanding liabilities, thereby avoiding an order of disqualification.

[22.080] In the decision of Finlay Geoghegan J in Re Clawhammer Ltd[139] it was established that the DCE does not have to demonstrate that a company has liabilities. It

---

[136] CA 1990, s 160(3A), as inserted by CLEA 2001, s 42(c).

[137] CA 1990, s 160(3A), as inserted by CLEA 2001, s 42(c).

[138] CA 1990, s 160(7).

[139] *Re Clawhammer Ltd, Director of Corporate Enforcement v McDonnell; Re Shinrone Food Market Ltd, Director of Corporate Enforcement v Hoctor; Re Cautious Trading Ltd, Director of Corporate Enforcement v Forristal* (15 March 2005, unreported), HC, Finlay Geoghegan J.

is a matter for the respondent to demonstrate that the company has no outstanding liabilities, if the respondent wishes to avoid a disqualification order. The respondent must show to the court 'as a matter of probability' that the company had no such liabilities. The onus is therefore firmly on the respondent to demonstrate as a matter of probability the non-existence or discharge of, a company's liabilities.

(e) Applications under s 160(2)(h)

[22.081] The DCE has taken a number of cases seeking the disqualification of directors of companies which were struck off the register of companies for failing to make annual returns. On 15 November 2004, a director of a company which had been struck off the register of companies for failing to make annual returns, was disqualified for a period of two years, the directors having failed to make any annual returns since the company was incorporated in 2000.[140] The company was indebted to the Revenue Commissioners in the order of €275,000 when it was struck off. The costs of the application were awarded to the Director. This was the first successful application by the DCE under s 160(2)(h). He welcomed the outcome of the case, stating:

> 'Today's outcome sends a clear signal to company directors that abandoning an indebted company, failing to comply with statutory filing obligations and leaving it to be struck off the Register of Companies is no solution. Too often in the past, directors have adopted such a strategy in the belief that it represented some sort of alternative to restructuring or liquidation. Thanks to recent legislative changes, my Office now has power to call the directors to account and in appropriate cases, to ask the Courts to sanction such behaviour.'[141]

[22.082] On 15 March 2005, the High Court delivered a combined judgment in three cases.[142] In the cases of *Re Clawhammer Ltd, Re Shinrone Food Market Ltd* and *Re Cautious Trading Ltd*, Finlay Geoghegan J ordered the disqualification of six directors of three companies that had been struck off the register of companies for failing to make annual returns. Each of the companies was insolvent when it was struck off the register of companies.

Certain aspects of the judgment have already been examined, in the context of the proofs required for an application under s 160(2)(h) and the defence available under s 160(3A).[143] The judgment also addressed the appropriate period of a disqualification

---

[140] *Re Norse Security Ltd* (15 November 2004, unreported), HC, Laffoy J.

[141] ODCE, *Press Release*, 15 November 2004.

[142] *Re Clawhammer Ltd, Director of Corporate Enforcement v McDonnell; Re Shinrone Food Market Ltd, Director of Corporate Enforcement v Hoctor; Re Cautious Trading Ltd, Director of Corporate Enforcement v Forristal* (15 March 2005, unreported), HC, Finlay Geoghegan J. Four of the directors were disqualified for four years and the remaining two were disqualified for two years.

[143] See above paras **[22.077]** to **[22.081]**.

order and the criteria to be applied in this regard. This aspect of the judgment is addressed in more detail elsewhere.[144]

In the course of the judgment in *Re Clawhammer Ltd*, The High Court made some general observations about the scope and objective of s 160(2)(h). The Court agreed with the submission of the DCE that, in the application of s 160(2)(h), a court should have regard to the scheme of the Companies Acts and CA 1990, Pt VII, in particular. Finlay Geoghegan J further accepted that a court should take into account the fact that s 160(2)(h) 'reflects a serious legislative concern abut the practice whereby, to the detriment of creditors, insolvent companies are allowed by their directors to be struck off the register rather than wound up in an proper fashion.'[145]

Finlay Geoghegan J went on to state that allowing a company to be struck off the register of companies, rather than winding the company up in an orderly fashion, caused potential prejudice to creditors and may also 'benefit the directors in the sense of escaping the scrutiny of their conduct of the company's affairs which might follow an investigation by a liquidator.' The Court also stated that the Oireachtas regards 'the fact that directors may have permitted a company to be struck off the register as a result of their failing to make annual returns as more than a technical breach of the obligations of the Companies Acts.'

[22.083] Having established the serious nature of proceedings for a disqualification order under s 160(2)(h), the Court went on to observe that, if the respondent directors appear and offer evidence regarding the likely scale of the company's undischarged liabilities, their role in the company, or other circumstances leading to the company being struck off the register, it is appropriate for the court to take those factors into account in relation to the period of disqualification or in deciding whether to make a declaration of restriction rather than an order of disqualification under s 160(9A).[146]

In that case, none of the respondents contested the DCE's entitlement to the orders of disqualification sought under s 160(2)(h). However, the former directors of Clawhammer Ltd did appear personally and filed a sworn affidavit setting out the company's liabilities and their role in the company. The former directors of Shinrone Food Markets Ltd did not appear before the Court, but they did sent two letters to the DCE, which were drawn to the attention of the Court. In relation to Cautious Trading Ltd, the respondents were represented by counsel, but did not present any evidence to the court.[147]

---

[144] See Ch **23**.

[145] *Re Clawhammer Ltd, Director of Corporate Enforcement v McDonnell; Re Shinrone Food Market Ltd, Director of Corporate Enforcement v Hoctor; Re Cautious Trading Ltd, Director of Corporate Enforcement v Forristal* (15 March 2005, unreported), HC, Finlay Geoghegan J.

[146] CA 1990, s 160(9A), as inserted by CLEA 2001, s 42(f). See further Ch **23**.

[147] See further below Ch **23**.

[22.084] The Court set out the following guidelines regarding the approach to be adopted in making an order of disqualification under s 160(2)(h):

- If the DCE satisfies the court of the necessary proofs for an order under s 160(2)(h) and the respondents do not present any exculpatory evidence, it is generally appropriate to make an order under that section;

- If the respondents appear and offer evidence to the court, it is appropriate to take that evidence into account in determining whether to make an order of disqualification and whether to make an order of restriction;

- If the respondents adduce evidence of the likely quantum of the company's undischarged liabilities, the role the respondents played in the company, and other circumstances in relation to the striking off of the company, it will be appropriate for a court to take that into account in determining the period of disqualification;

- A court should to take into account any impact on the respondent's future employment prospects in the making of a disqualification order;

- The scheme of s 160(2)(h) is such that, on satisfaction of the necessary proofs, it may be appropriate for a court to make an order of disqualification in the absence of any evidence about the liabilities of the company or the respondent's role in the company or regarding the events leading to the company being struck off the register of companies;

- A court should attempt to apply a consistent period of disqualification where there is no evidence of the respondent's conduct or role in the company or the company's liabilities;

- In determining the appropriate period of disqualification the court should have regard to the fact that the Oireachtas intended disqualification to be a more serious sanction than a declaration of restriction under s 150 of the Act of 1990 and that the mandatory period for an order of restriction is five years;

- In the absence of any evidence on behalf of a respondent, it is difficult to conclude that a disqualification order for any period less than five years will be a more onerous sanction for the respondent than a declaration of restriction which must be five years;

- If a respondent by failing to put evidence before the court, overlooked drawing the court's attention to evidence which might have persuaded the court to order a lesser period of disqualification or to make a declaration of restriction, that respondent has the possibility of seeking relief under s 160(8); and

- 'In the absence of any relevant evidence in relation to a respondent other than the minimum proofs to satisfy s 160(2)(h) of the Act of 1990 a period of disqualification for five years appears appropriate.

[22.085] The DCE, welcoming the decision, drew attention to the following aspects of the judgment:

'The High Court accepted my submission that the relevant legal provision permitting such disqualification applications was indicative of a serious concern on the part of the Oireachtas about the practice whereby, to the detriment of creditors, insolvent companies are allowed by their directors to be involuntarily struck off the Companies Register. The Court has confirmed that the onus is on the directors of each such company to demonstrate to the Court that the company had no liabilities at the time it was involuntarily struck off the Register or that such liabilities that existed were discharged prior to the date of any disqualification action. It has also affirmed my belief that the ODCE only requires to present to the Court a minimum level of proof to warrant a disqualification order being made under the provision. Finally, the Court expressed the view that in the absence of any relevant evidence from company directors in mitigation against the minimum proofs, a period of disqualification of five years is appropriate.'[148]

In summary, the DCE clearly regards the judgment in *Re Clawhammer Ltd*[149] as authority for the following propositions regarding s 160(2)(h):

– That provision addresses an issue of serious concern in the Companies Acts;

– The respondent must discharge the onus of establishing that the company either had no, or had discharged all, outstanding liabilities;

– The DCE must only establish a minimal level of proof to justify a disqualification order; and

– In the absence of any relevant mitigating evidence, a period of five years disqualification is appropriate.

[22.086] In light of the decision in *Re Clawhammer Ltd*, the DCE indicated his intention to seek more disqualification orders under s 160(2)(h):

'It is now my intention to roll out a series of similar disqualification applications which we have in the pipeline. Today's outcome makes it clear that company directors can no longer abandon an indebted company, fail to comply with statutory filing obligations and leave it to be involuntarily struck off the Register of Companies. Every effort should be made by them to discharge all of the company's liabilities. I see this decision and the future actions of my Office in this area improving legal compliance, supporting the interests of creditors and contributing to improved conditions for enterprise development in the future.'[150]

---

[148] ODCE, *Press Release* 'ODCE Secures Disqualification of six more Directors of Struck-off Companies', 15 March 2005.

[149] *Re Clawhammer Ltd, Director of Corporate Enforcement v McDonnell; Re Shinrone Food Market Ltd, Director of Corporate Enforcement v Hoctor; Re Cautious Trading Ltd, Director of Corporate Enforcement v Forristal* (15 March 2005, unreported), HC, Finlay Geoghegan J.

[150] ODCE, *Press Release* 'ODCE Secures Disqualification of six more Directors of Struck-off Companies', 15 March 2005.

[22.087] There have been several applications taken by the DCE under s 160(2)(h).[151] For example, a successful application was brought under that provision on 5 July 2005, against the directors of a company which was struck off the register for failing to make annual returns.[152] By the order of the High Court (Finlay Geoghegan J), the respondents were each disqualified from being appointed or acting as auditor, director or other officer, receiver, liquidator, examiner or being in any way whether directly or indirectly concerned or taking part in the promotion, formation or management of any company for a period of three years commencing on 5 July 2005. The Court also made an order that the respondents were jointly and severally liable to contribute to the DCE's costs in the sum of €2,500.

[22.088] The usual period of disqualification under s 160(2)(h) is five years when the respondent is the director of one company which is insolvent and struck off the register. When the respondent is the director of several such companies, the period of disqualification increases. In *Re Champion Telecom Ltd,*[153] for example, the respondent was a director of eight insolvent companies at the time they were struck off the register. On an application by the DCE under s 160(2)(h), Finlay Geoghegan J made an order of disqualification of a period of twelve years. Commenting on this decision, and two other

---

[151] See, eg, *Re Merit Marketing Limited and Royal Associates Limited, Director of Corporate Enforcement v Browne* (30 July 2007, *ex tempore*), HC, Finlay Geoghegan J (disqualified for seven years arising from two companies which were struck off); *Re Kinsella Hire Limited, Director of Corporate Enforcement v Kinsella* (16 April 2007, *ex tempore*), HC, Finlay Geoghegan J (disqualified for five years arising from the striking off of one company's name); *Re Diamond Telecom Ltd, Director of Corporate Enforcement v Banks* (16 February 2007, *ex tempore*), HC, Finlay Geoghegan J (A director of a number of insolvent companies at the time they were struck off the Companies Register, was made the subject of a disqualification order for a period of 8 years, with costs in favour of the respondent); *Re Specified Aluminium Limited, Director of Corporate Enforcement v Donoghue* (16 February 2007, *ex tempore*), HC Finlay Geoghegan J) (a director of a number of insolvent companies at the time they were struck off the register, was made the subject of a disqualification order for a period of 6 years, with an order of costs in favour of the applicant); *Re Champion Telecom Limited, Director of Corporate Enforcement v Allen* (19 February 2007, *ex tempore*), HC, Finlay Geoghegan J (a director of a number of insolvent companies at the time they were struck off register, was made the subject of a disqualification order for a period of 12 years. The Court made an order for costs in favour of the DCE, such costs to be taxed in default of agreement); *Re James Pierce & Sons Limited, Director of Corporate Enforcement v Pierce* (18 December 2006, *ex tempore*), HC, Finlay Geoghegan J (Directors of an insolvent company at the time it was struck off were each made the subject of a disqualification order for a period of five years. The Court ordered a contribution to the costs of the DCE measured in the sum of €2,000.); *Re MC Plant Sales Limited, Director of Corporate Enforcement v Christy* (27 November 2006, *ex tempore*), HC, Finlay Geoghegan J (A director of a company at the time it was struck off the register was made the subject of disqualification order for a period of five years, with costs in favour of the DCE).

[152] *Re Allied Mechanical Holdings Ltd, Director of Corporate Enforcement v Mongey* (5 July 2005, *ex tempore*), HC, Finlay Geoghegan J.

[153] *Re Champion Telecom Ltd, Director of Corporate Enforcement v Allen* (19 February 2007, *ex tempore*), HC, Finlay Geoghegan J.

cases in which periods of disqualification of six and eight years were imposed,[154] the DCE stated:

> 'What was different about today's cases was that evidence of persistent and/or serial abuse of company law obligations was before the Court.
>
> Previously, all similar ODCE disqualification cases have involved single struck-off companies. The High Court has consistently accepted that in the absence of mitigating factors, disqualification for five years was appropriate in the light of the serious concern of the Oireachtas about the practice whereby, to the detriment of creditors, insolvent companies are allowed by their directors to be involuntarily struck off the Companies Register. In today's cases, the Court has accepted that aggravating circumstances may lead to disqualification periods in excess of five years particularly where there is evidence of persistent unscrupulous behaviour by directors who walk away from insolvent companies and allow them to be involuntarily struck off.'[155]

[22.089] Any director of a company which is in receipt of a section 12 letter, or in default of its obligations to make annual returns, may now face a real risk of disqualification proceedings under s 160(2)(h), particularly if the company is not in a position to discharge its liabilities. Directors should be aware that it will be difficult to avoid a disqualification order if they allow a company, with undischarged liabilities, to be struck off the register of companies.

I. Disqualification in another state

[22.090] A person who is disqualified from acting as a director of a company in another jurisdiction may be the subject of a disqualification order in Ireland. Section 160(2)(i), which was inserted by CLEA 2001,[156] provides that a disqualification order may be made in the following circumstances:

> a person is disqualified under the law of another state (whether pursuant to an order of a judge or a tribunal or otherwise) from being appointed or acting as a director or secretary of a body corporate or an undertaking and the court is satisfied that, if the conduct of the person or the circumstances otherwise affecting him that gave rise to the said order being made against him had occurred or arisen in the State, it would have been proper to make a disqualification order otherwise under this subsection against him.

---

[154] *Re Diamond Telecom Ltd, Director of Corporate Enforcement v Banks* (16 February 2007, *ex tempore*), HC, Finlay Geoghegan J; *Re Specified Aluminium Limited, Director of Corporate Enforcement v Donoghue* (16 February 2007, *ex tempore*), HC, Finlay Geoghegan J.

[155] ODCE, *Press Release* 19 February 2007. Available at www.odce.ie. The DCE also commented, 'This result reinforces the message that company directors can no longer abandon an indebted company, fail to comply with statutory filing obligations and leave it to be involuntarily struck off the Companies Register. We will continue as best we can to target significant cases of suspected serious misconduct.'

[156] CLEA 2001, s 42(b)(ii).

This provision must be read in conjunction with s 160(3B), which provides:

> A disqualification order under paragraph (i) of subsection (2) may be made against a person notwithstanding that, at the time of the making of the order, the person is deemed, by virtue of subsection (1A), to be subject to a disqualification order for the purposes of this Act, and where a disqualification order under the said paragraph (i) is made, the period of disqualification specified in it shall be expressed to begin on the expiry of the period of disqualification referred to in subsection (1B) to which the person, by virtue of subsection (1A), is subject or the said period of disqualification as varied, if such be the case, under subsection (8).

(a) Applicants under s 160(2)(i)

[22.091] The only person who can make an application for disqualification on the basis of a disqualification order in another jurisdiction, is the DCE.[157] As noted above,[158] in light of the fact that the Registrar of Companies is the person to whom notification of disqualification in another jurisdiction must be sent,[159] it is curious that the Registrar plays no role in relation to applications for orders of disqualification which may be expected to arise from such notifications.

The ODCE has confirmed that its detection work has 'targeted enquiries in a number of areas', including, 'those disqualified in other jurisdictions acting in the State in the absence of the registration of their disqualification.'[160]

(b) Overview

[22.092] This provision essentially aims to provide protection to creditors of Irish companies by ensuring that persons who have been deemed unsuitable or unfit, or have otherwise been disqualified from acting, as directors in other jurisdictions, do not act as directors of Irish companies. The impact of the foreign disqualification order is not automatic, however. An Irish court must examine the basis for the disqualification order, including the conduct and circumstances that gave rise to the order, and must be satisfied that the same conduct or circumstances would justify the making of an order of disqualification under s 160(2), if they occurred in Ireland.

(c) Interaction with automatic disqualification

[22.093] It has already been seen that a person who is subject to a disqualification order in another jurisdiction and who is appointed to act as a director of an Irish company, must send a statement to the Registrar of Companies setting out details of the disqualification order.[161] If this requirement is not met, that person is automatically disqualified for the portion of the period of disqualification which has not expired (or

---

[157] CA 1990, s 160(6A), inserted by CLEA 2001, s 42(e).

[158] See Ch **20**.

[159] C(A)A 1982, s 3A(1) and CA 1963, s 195(8). See further Ch **20**.

[160] ODCE, *Annual Report 2006* at p 13.

[161] CA 1990, s 160(1A), as inserted by CLEA 2001, s 42(a). See Ch **20**.

the longest remaining period of disqualification, if there is more than one order of disqualification).[162]

The sanction of automatic disqualification under s 160(1A) interacts with the discretionary disqualification under s 160(2)(h) as follows: if a person is subject to automatic disqualification under s 160(1A) and a discretionary order of disqualification is also made under s 160(2)(i), the latter period of disqualification shall begin on the expiry of the automatic period of disqualification deemed to have been imposed under s 160(1A).

[22.094] It may be useful to illustrate the operation of these provisions as follows: If a person who was disqualified in one jurisdiction for a period of fifteen years, relocated to Ireland ten years after that order was made, and became appointed to a company's board of directors, without notifying the Registrar of Companies of the existing disqualification order, he will be deemed under s 160(1A) and (1B) to be subject to an automatic disqualification order for the unexpired portion of the disqualification period, namely five years. In those circumstances, the DCE may also make an application to court for the disqualification of the person under s 160(2)(i). If the court makes such a discretionary order of disqualification, the period of disqualification ordered will run from the date of the expiry of the automatic five year disqualification period.

(d) Period of disqualification

[22.095] Under s 160(2)(i), the court must be satisfied that it would have been proper to make an order of disqualification in Ireland on the basis of the same facts and circumstances which grounded the disqualification order made in another jurisdiction. It should be noted that the Irish court does not have to determine whether it would have been proper to order disqualification for the same period of time. Moreover, s 160(2)(i) does not state whether the period of disqualification to which the person will be subject in Ireland should be same period to which he was subject in the other jurisdiction. This leaves open the question of whether an Irish court can substitute its own judgment regarding the appropriate length of the period of disqualification, for the decision of the court or tribunal of the jurisdiction which originally made the order of disqualification.

[22.096] The fact that there is no guidance regarding the appropriate period of disqualification under s 160(2)(i) also leaves open the possibility that a person may be disqualified for a period of time in another jurisdiction and, close to the expiry of that period, be disqualified for an additional period of time under the Irish Companies Acts. This could occur despite the fact that the person may have been deemed to be disqualified in Ireland for the entire period of the original disqualification order. In the example given above, the director could find himself disqualified in this jurisdiction for considerably longer than the fifteen years for which he was originally disqualified in the other jurisdiction, on the basis of precisely the same facts and circumstances. Whether this possibility is consistent with the primary aim of s 160 to protect creditors, rather than punish directors, is a valid question.

---

[162] CA 1990, s 160(1B), as inserted by CLEA 2001, s 42(a). See Ch **20**.

[22.097] As an antidote to the possibility of a director being subject to an excessively extended period of disqualification, it may be suggested that a court, in deciding whether to make an order of disqualification under s 160(2)(i), should take into account the following factors:

- The amount of time for which the respondent has already been disqualified under the original disqualification order; and

- The period, if any, during which the respondent has been the subject of automatic disqualification under s 160(1A).

J. Undischarged bankruptcy

[22.098] In addition to the grounds stipulated in s 160(2), if a director is an undischarged bankrupt, this can be a ground for making an order of disqualification. CA 1963, s 183A(3),[163] provides:

> The court may, on the application of the Director, make a disqualification order (as defined in s 159 of the Companies Act 1990) against a director of a company on the grounds that he is an undischarged bankrupt.

(a) Information gathering

[22.099] The DCE has wide powers to gather information regarding the financial position of a director of a company. According to s 183A(1):

> Where the Director has reason to believe that a director of a company is an undischarged bankrupt, the Director may require the director of the company to produce by a specified date a sworn statement of all relevant facts pertaining to the company director's financial position, both within the State and elsewhere, and, in particular, to any matter pertaining to bankruptcy as at a particular date.[164]

The only prerequisites to the exercise of this power are that the person must be a director of a company and the DCE must have a mere 'reason to believe' that he is an undischarged bankrupt. On the basis of these bare assertions, the DCE has the far-reaching power to require a person to deliver a sworn statement of all relevant facts regarding his own financial position, which must relate to his finances in Ireland and elsewhere. The strength of the DCE's power in this regard is bolstered by s 182A(4), which renders it an offence for a person to fail to comply with the DCE's requirements.

The DCE's powers are further bolstered by s 183A(2), which provides that the DCE may apply to court to require a person who has made a sworn statement under s 183A(1), to appear before the court and answer on oath any questions regarding the statement.

(b) Interaction with Pt VII of CA 1990

[22.100] As the power to make an order of disqualification under s 183A is not within CA 1990, Pt VII, a respondent to an application under s 183A does not have the

---

[163] CA 1963, s 183A(3), as inserted by CLEA 2001, s 40.

[164] CA 1963, s 183A, as inserted by CLEA 2001, s 40.

protections which are generally afforded to respondents to disqualification applications. First, a person facing an application for disqualification on the ground of bankruptcy does not have the right to ten days' notice of the making of that application. In other disqualification applications, s 160(7) ensures that ten days' notice of the application is afforded to the respondent. Secondly, a court dealing with a disqualification application has the discretion, under s 160(9A),[165] to substitute a declaration of restriction, if an order of disqualification is not considered to be warranted. This discretion does not exist under s 183A. Finally, a respondent to an application for disqualification on the ground of bankruptcy does not have the right to apply for relief from the disqualification, a right which is afforded to other respondents to disqualification orders by s 160(8).[166]

K. Restricted persons

[22.101] A final ground on which a court may order the disqualification of a person is where a restricted person acts in relation to a company which subsequently goes into insolvent liquidation.

Section 161(5) provides:

> Where—
>
> (a) a person who is a person to whom s 150 applies is or becomes a director of a company which commences to be wound up within the period of five years after the date of commencement of the winding-up of the company whose insolvency caused that section to apply to him; and
>
> (b) it appears to the liquidator of the first-mentioned company that that company is, at the date of commencement of its winding-up or at any time during the course of its winding up, unable to pay its debts;
>
> the liquidator shall report those matters to the court and the court, on receiving the report and if it considers it proper to do so, may make a disqualification order against that person for such period as it thinks fit.

The criteria for the operation of this provision are that:

– The person must have been the subject of a declaration of restriction arising from the insolvent liquidation of one company (Company A);[167]

– He must be or become a director of another company (Company B);

– The winding up of Company B must commence within five years of the date of the commencement of the winding up of Company A;

– The liquidator of Company B must be of the view that Company B is not able to pay its debts as they fall due;

– The liquidator of Company B must report this to the court; and

---

[165] CA 1990, s 160(9A), as inserted by CLEA 2001, s 42(f).

[166] CA 1990, s 160(8). See Ch **23**.

[167] According to CA 1990, s 150(1): '... the expression 'a person to whom s 150 applies shall be construed as a reference to a person in respect of whom such a declaration [of restriction] has been made.'

– The court, if its considers it proper to do so, may then make a disqualification order for such period as it thinks fit.

[22.0102] There is only one situation in which this provision can logically apply. Company B must be a company which satisfies the requirements of s 150(3): it must be a company which has a minimum allotted share capital of the nominal value of €317,434.52, in the case of a public company, or €63,489.00, in the case of any other company; and each allotted share and any premium must be fully paid up and must be paid for in cash.[168] Otherwise, the restricted person is guilty of an offence under s 161(1) for the fact of being appointed as a director of Company B and, upon conviction, would be deemed to be disqualified from the date of that conviction.[169]

It should be noted that a person who is restricted is not subject to the risk of disqualification under s 161(5) for the entirety of the period of restriction: the restriction will last for five years from the date of the court order under s 150, whereas the danger of disqualification under s 161(5) only applies to companies the winding up of which is commenced within five years of the commencement of the winding up of Company A, a period which will necessarily expire first.

It should also be noted that it is an offence for a liquidator to fail to make a report to the court when the criteria of s 161(5) are met.[170]

---

[168] CA 1990, s 150(3), as amended by CLEA 2001, s 41(1). See Ch **19**.

[169] CA 1990, s 161(2). See Ch **20**.

[170] CA 1990, s 161(6), as amended by IFCMPA 2005, s 73 and CA 1990, s 240(7), as inserted by CLEA 2001, s 104: 'If the liquidator fails to comply with sub-s (5) he shall be guilty of an offence and liable to a fine not exceeding €1904.61'.

Chapter 23

CONSEQUENCES OF DISQUALIFICATION ORDERS

A. General

[23.001] A 'disqualification order' is defined in s 159 as follows:

> (a) an order under this Part that the person against whom the order is made shall not be appointed or act as an auditor, director or other officer, receiver, liquidator or examiner or be in any way, whether directly or indirectly, concerned or take part in the promotion, formation or management of any company, or any society registered under the Industrial and Provident Societies Acts, 1893 to 1978, or
>
> (b) an order under s 184 of the Principal Act.'[1]

'A company' is defined in s 159 as including:

> 'every company and every body, whether corporate or unincorporated, which may be wound up under Pt X of The Principal Act and, without prejudice to the generality of the foregoing, includes a friendly society within the meaning of the Friendly Societies Acts, 1896 to 1977.'[2]

[23.002] The effect of such an order on a person is that he cannot be appointed or act in any company as:

- auditor;
- director;
- officer;
- receiver;
- liquidator; or
- examiner.

In addition, the person in respect of whom an order of disqualification is made cannot be in any way, directly or indirectly, concerned or take part in any company's:

- promotion;
- formation; or
- management.

A disqualification order is therefore very far-reaching and essentially prohibits a disqualified person from having any involvement whatsoever in a company. The courts have acknowledged the breadth and potential harshness of such orders. In some cases,

---

[1]   CA 1990, s 159.

[2]   CA 1990, s 159.

the courts have even indicated that the terms of a disqualification order may be tempered in an appropriate case. *Re CB Readymix Ltd*³ is one example of such a case.

B. Conditional disqualification

[23.003] In *Re CB Readymix Ltd*,⁴ the facts of which were examined above,⁵ the High Court made an order of disqualification against a liquidator. The order made was not, however, in the same terms as the definition of a 'disqualification order' in s 159. The High Court adapted the order as follows:

- The respondent was disqualified from being involved in the management of a company as liquidator, receiver or examiner of a company for a period of seven years.

- The respondent was disqualified from acting as a director of a company whose constitution and management did not provide for a board of directors of three or more persons;

- The respondent could only act as auditor, director or secretary of a company if:

    (a)   he had the necessary professional qualifications; and

    (b)   'at no stage or time is he to have possession, custody or control of the seal of any such company or any of its books or records of any kind whatsoever, so however he is entitled to have access to such books and records only as are necessary to enable him to discharge his legal obligations.' ⁶

[23.004] The respondent appealed the decision to the Supreme Court. One of the grounds of appeal was that the order of the High Court was 'misconceived because it was in part a disqualification and in part a restriction.'⁷ The respondent argued that s 160 was an 'all or nothing section' and that a court could only make a disqualification order within the terms of s 159. He contended that, 'The court had no power to differentiate between the different offices or to impose conditions as to the terms on which anyone or more of the offices might be exercised.'⁸

The Supreme Court considered this argument, noting the danger to the respondent that, if the argument succeeded, he faced the risk of being fully disqualified. Despite his awareness of this danger and of the care taken by the High Court 'to balance the need for a sanction with the desirability of the respondent continuing certain commercial activities,' the respondent advocated a rigid interpretation of s 160.⁹

---

³   *Re CB Readymix Ltd, Cahill v Grimes* [2002] 1 IR 372.

⁴   *Re CB Readymix Ltd, Cahill v Grimes* [2002] 1 IR 372.

⁵   See above paras **[21.024]** to **[21.026]**.

⁶   *Re CB Readymix Ltd, Cahill v Grimes* [2002] 1 IR 372 at 379.

⁷   *Re CB Readymix Ltd, Cahill v Grimes* [2002] 1 IR 372 at 379.

⁸   *Re CB Readymix Ltd, Cahill v Grimes* [2002] 1 IR 372 at 379.

⁹   *Re CB Readymix Ltd, Cahill v Grimes* [2002] 1 IR 372 at 379.

Murphy J, delivering the judgment of the Supreme Court, rejected the rigid interpretation of s 160 contended for as an 'all or nothing section'. The Court determined:

> 'In my view this argument is refuted by the provisions of s 160(8). The express power of the court to grant relief to a person who is subject or deemed subject to a disqualification order "either in whole or in part" and to "grant such relief on whatever terms and conditions it see fit" would enable the court to review a disqualification order in the days immediately following the making thereof by imposing precisely those terms which Smyth J had required in the first instance. In my view it would be unthinkable that the court could have a power to revise its own order in that way and in that time frame and not have the same powers in the first instance. I am fully satisfied that the trial judge did have the powers which he purported to exercise so humanely in disqualifying the respondent from filling certain offices and yet permitting him to fill others subject to stipulated conditions.'[10]

[23.005] This decision represents a clear and unequivocal endorsement of the approach adopted by Smyth J in relation to the disqualification of the liquidator of Readymix Ltd. The Supreme Court has thereby established, as an unambiguous principle, that a court can attach whatever conditions to, and temper whatever aspects of, an order of disqualification as the court sees fit, at the time of making the order. While the outcome is undoubtedly proper and desirable, one could express some misgiving about the reasoning underlying the outcome. The power conferred upon a court under s 160(2) is the power to 'make a disqualification order against such a person for such period as it sees fit'. The court has a specific margin of discretion, namely discretion as to the appropriate period of disqualification. With regard to the order itself, however, no such discretion is conferred on the court. The means by which the terms of 'a disqualification order' may be tempered is governed by s 160(8).[11]

The point relied upon by Murphy J, that it would be nonsensical that a court would be able to adapt a disqualification order a few days after, but not at the time of, making it, is a compelling one. However, it presupposes that an application under s 160(8) can only be made some days after the making of a disqualification order. No such limitation exists in s 160. It is conceivable that an application for relief against a disqualification order, in whole or in part, could be made directly to a court upon the making of a disqualification order. This would have the same effect as permitting a court to temper and adapt a disqualification order as it sees fit. One issue that this may raise is whether the party seeking the disqualification order should receive notice in advance of the respondent's intention to apply for relief under s 160(8). While no such notice requirement is stated in the legislation, by contrast with the notice requirement of s 160(7),[12] if notice is necessary, a respondent clearly could not make an application for relief on the day of the making of the disqualification order.

---

10   *Re CB Readymix Ltd, Cahill v Grimes* [2002] 1 IR 372 at 380.

11   See further paras **[23.027]** to **[23.030]**.

12   CA 1990, s 160(7). See further para **[21.014]**.

[23.006] Some of these issues were mooted by Finlay Geoghegan J in *Re Clawhammer Ltd*.[13] In that case, orders of disqualification of varying durations were imposed on six directors of companies which were struck off the register for failing to make annual returns. The Court considered the severity of disqualification orders and noted that they could have the effect of precluding a person from holding a position of employment in any company. In this regard, Finlay Geoghegan J stated:

> 'It will be appropriate for the court to take into account any impact on the respondent of the making of a disqualification order in the context of any evidence offered of future proposals to earn a livelihood'.

While the orders of disqualification made in that case were comprehensive orders in the terms of s 159, the Court did note that s 160(8) 'would appear to allow a court to grant relief from one aspect of a disqualification order alone, such as the prohibition on involvement in the management of a company'. The Court then observed that, in light of the fact that s 160(8) is not subject to the same notice requirements as are contained in s 152, it remains to be seen whether a respondent can ask for relief against part of a disqualification order simultaneously with the granting of an order of disqualification order. This question was not resolved, as no such application was made by the respondents in *Re Clawhammer*.[14]

[23.007] This intimation by Finlay Geoghegan J that it may be possible to make an application for relief against a disqualification order immediately upon the making of such an order, would lead squarely to a very similar outcome to that achieved by the decision of the Supreme Court in *Re CB Readymix Ltd*.[15] Under *Re CB Readymix Ltd*, a court can, in the exercise of its discretion, attach such conditions to a disqualification order as it deems fit. Depending on the resolution of the issues raised in *Re Clawhammer*,[16] it may be possible for a respondent to seek relief from a disqualification order immediately upon the making of that order, which would permit the court to grant relief from any aspect of the disqualification order. As Finlay Geoghegan J noted, it remains to be seen whether the latter is possible. However, in the event that a respondent can invoke the jurisdiction of the court to vary the terms of a disqualification order, by applying for relief immediately upon the making of the order, it is submitted that this basis for the exercise of that jurisdiction is preferable to reliance on a general discretion of the court under s 160.

---

[13] *Re Clawhammer Ltd, Director of Corporate Enforcement v McDonnell; Re Shinrone Food Market Ltd, Director of Corporate Enforcement v Hoctor; Re Cautious Trading Ltd, Director of Corporate Enforcement v Forristal* (15 March 2005, unreported), HC, Finlay Geoghegan J.

[14] *Re Clawhammer Ltd, Director of Corporate Enforcement v McDonnell; Re Shinrone Food Market Ltd, Director of Corporate Enforcement v Hoctor; Re Cautious Trading Ltd, Director of Corporate Enforcement v Forristal* (15 March 2005, unreported), HC, Finlay Geoghegan J.

[15] *Re CB Readymix Ltd, Cahill v Grimes* [2002] 1 IR 372.

[16] *Re Clawhammer Ltd, Director of Corporate Enforcement v McDonnell; Re Shinrone Food Market Ltd, Director of Corporate Enforcement v Hoctor; Re Cautious Trading Ltd, Director of Corporate Enforcement v Forristal* (15 March 2005, unreported), HC, Finlay Geoghegan J.

[23.008] A related point to note regarding the decision in *Re CB Readymix Ltd* and the only aspect of its outcome that is not entirely clear, is whether the power of a court to adjust a disqualification order can be exercised by the court of its own motion, or must be contended for in submissions on behalf of the respondent. The power of a court to grant relief in respect of a disqualification order under s 160(8) can only be exercised on the application of the respondent.[17] If the power of the court to adapt an order under s 160, as confirmed by the Supreme Court in *Re CB Readymix Ltd*, is dependent on the application of the respondent, then the effect truly is the same as the immediate application for relief under s 160(8).

[23.009] With regard to the actual conditions imposed by the High Court in *Re CB Readymix Ltd*,[18] the respondent argued that they represented an unfair and unwarranted interference with the regulation and management of companies which might wish to retain his services. In particular, the respondent objected to the condition that he could only act in a company with at least three directors on the basis that this 'was an impermissible intrusion into the affairs of a company which was not a party to the proceedings.'[19] The Court rejected this argument, describing it as a 'mistaken analysis of the particular condition.' The Court explained that the condition as to the number of directors 'does not impose any obligation on the company', but rather:

> 'imposes a limitation on the respondent with the result that any company seeking to avail of his managerial skills can only do so if its corporate structure is such that will permit the respondent to comply with the condition.'[20]

The Court noted that the conditions imposed by the High Court to the effect that the respondent should not have possession, custody or control of a company's seal or its books and records, was 'difficult to police', but concluded that, in light of the facts of the case, involving the destruction of the company's documents, 'the inclusion of such a condition is entirely appropriate'.[21]

The Court considered that the only alternative to the insertion of such a condition in the disqualification order was a comprehensive disqualification order. The Court concluded, 'it is a matter for the respondent to comply with these conditions. If he fails to do so it must be anticipated that a comprehensive order will then be made.'[22]

[23.010] *Re CB Readymix Ltd* confirms that the courts have a wide discretion as regards the conditions they can attach to a disqualification order. In formulating the terms of a disqualification order, it appears that a court can take into account all of the facts of the case; the nature of the conduct complained of; the personal situation of the respondent and the hardship which a disqualification order would cause. The Supreme Court accepted that a court is justified in attempting to reach a balance between the need

---

17 See further below paras **[23.027]** to **[23.030]**.

18 *Re CB Readymix Ltd, Cahill v Grimes* [2002] 1 IR 372.

19 *Re CB Readymix Ltd, Cahill v Grimes* [2002] 1 IR 372 at 383.

20 *Re CB Readymix Ltd, Cahill v Grimes* [2002] 1 IR 372 at 383.

21 *Re CB Readymix Ltd, Cahill v Grimes* [2002] 1 IR 372 at 384.

22 *Re CB Readymix Ltd, Cahill v Grimes* [2002] 1 IR 372 at 384.

to sanction the respondent by means of disqualification and the desirability of relieving him of undue hardship by attaching conditions to the order of disqualification.

C. Period of disqualification

[23.011] There is nothing in the Companies Acts to indicate the appropriate period of disqualification of a person who the subject of a discretionary disqualification order under s 160(2). Where a court makes an order of disqualification under that provision, it can order that person be disqualified 'for such period as it sees fit.'[23] This can be contrasted with the position in England, for example, where the Company Directors Disqualification Act 1986 stipulates maximum periods of disqualification, and, in one respect, a minimum period of disqualification.[24]

[23.012] In the High Court decision in *Re Clawhammer Ltd*[25] Finlay Geoghegan J addressed the issue of the appropriate period of disqualification in some detail. As has been seen, the Court in that case was called upon to apply s 160(2)(h), which governs the disqualification of directors of companies which were struck off the register of companies for failing to make annual returns.[26] In its judgment, the Court considered three separate applications concerning three companies which were insolvent and were struck off the register of companies for failing to make annual returns. The DCE sought disqualification orders against six respondents, each of whom were formerly directors of one of the dissolved companies.

[23.013] In relation to the appropriate period of disqualification, Finlay Geoghegan J drew attention to the fact that, 's 160 offers no direct guidance to the court as to the appropriate length of a disqualification order made under that subsection'. The Court went on to examine other provisions of CA 1990, Pt VII. In particular, the Court considered the provisions governing declarations of restriction and automatic disqualifications.

The Court noted that a declaration of restriction entails a mandatory period of restriction of five years and went on to state, 'Section 160(9A) clearly envisages that a declaration of restriction under s 150 is to be considered as a lesser sanction than an order of disqualification under s 160'.[27]

---

[23]   CA 1990, s 160(2).

[24]   See CDDA 1996, ss 1(2), 2(3), 3(5), 4(3), 5(5), 6(4). The maximum periods of disqualification are either five years or 15 years, depending on the ground of disqualification. If a person is disqualified on the ground of unfitness under s 6, the minimum period of disqualification is 2 years. Section 6(4) accordingly provides, 'Under this section the minimum period of disqualification is 2 years, and the maximum period is 15 years.'

[25]   *Re Clawhammer Ltd, Director of Corporate Enforcement v McDonnell; Re Shinrone Food Market Ltd, Director of Corporate Enforcement v Hoctor; Re Cautious Trading Ltd, Director of Corporate Enforcement v Forristal* (15 March 2005, unreported), HC, Finlay Geoghegan J.

[26]   See further above Ch **22**.

[27]   See further paras **[23.022]** to **[23.023]** in relation to CA 1990, s 160(9A), as inserted by CLEA 2001, s 42(f).

The Court also considered ss 160(1) and 161, which provide for a mandatory five year disqualification period. Having observed that 'limited further assistance' could be derived from these provisions, Finlay Geoghegan J proceeded to query the significance of the designation of five years in the context of the power of the court under ss 160(1) and 161 to substitute 'such other period' of disqualification as the court may order.[28]

[23.014] In the course of the judgment in *Re Clawhammer Ltd*, the Court set out some important guidance regarding the appropriate duration of disqualification periods. Some of these principles apply more to applications under s 160(2)(h), than other grounds on which discretionary disqualification orders may be sought, but are nonetheless important in the general context of determining the proper periods of disqualification under s 160(2):

- If the respondents adduce evidence of the likely quantum of the company's undischarged liabilities under s 160(2)(h), the role the respondents played in the company, and other circumstances in relation to the striking off of the company, it will be appropriate for a court to take that into account in determining the period of disqualification;

- 'It will be appropriate for the court to take into account any impact on the respondent of the making of a disqualification order in the context of any evidence offered of future proposals to earn a livelihood';

- The scheme of s 160(2)(h) is such that, on satisfaction of the necessary proofs, it may be appropriate for a court to make an order of disqualification in the absence of any evidence about the liabilities of the company or the respondent's role in the company or regarding the events leading to the company being struck off the register of companies. In such circumstances, 'it appears appropriate that the court should attempt to apply a consistent period of disqualification';

- 'In determining a period of disqualification the court must have regard to the fact that the Oireachtas intended such order as a more serious sanction than a declaration of restriction under s 150 of the Act of 1990. This follows from the express wording of s 160(9A) of the Act of 1990';

- The mandatory period for an order of restriction is five years;

- 'Whilst a full disqualification is in its terms more restrictive than a declaration of restriction in practice the latter may operate to prevent certain respondents from acting as directors. This depends upon the particular circumstances of a

---

[28] *Re Clawhammer Ltd, Director of Corporate Enforcement v McDonnell; Re Shinrone Food Market Ltd, Director of Corporate Enforcement v Hoctor; Re Cautious Trading Ltd, Director of Corporate Enforcement v Forristal* (15 March 2005, unreported), HC, Finlay Geoghegan J: 'However in both such sections whilst there is a reference to a period of five years from the date of conviction there is an alternative of 'such other period as the court ... may order' It is not clear from these sections what the Oireachtas intended by referring to five years. It is not specified to be a minimum period or a maximum period nor is there any indication as to the circumstances in which the court might consider it appropriate to fix a different period.'

respondent director. In the absence of a respondent putting before the court any relevant evidence, it is difficult to conclude that a disqualification order for any period less than five years will be a more onerous sanction for the respondent than a declaration of restriction which must be five years';

- If a respondent by failing to put evidence before the court, overlooked drawing the court's attention to evidence which might have persuaded the court to order a lesser period of disqualification or to make a declaration of restriction, that respondent has the possibility of seeking relief under s 160(8); and

- 'In the absence of any relevant evidence in relation to a respondent other than the minimum proofs to satisfy s 160(2)(h) of the Act of 1990 a period of disqualification for five years appears appropriate.'

Applying these principles to the three companies involved in *Re Clawhammer Ltd*,[29] the Court concluded that, as there was no appearance before the court by the former directors of *Re Shinrone Food Market Ltd*, periods of disqualification of five years should be imposed on each of the respondents. The same period of disqualification was ordered in respect of the former directors of *Re Cautious Trading Ltd*.

In relation to *Clawhammer Ltd*, by contrast, the respondents presented evidence that the amount of undischarged liability was relatively small, as the directors had discharged nearly all of the company's creditors. However, the Court held that it could not overlook the fact that the company failed to make annual returns since 1999 and failed to put the company into liquidation. In light of all of the circumstances, the Court considered that 'the lesser option' of a declaration of restriction might be warranted, but the respondent appeared personally and indicated that in their personal circumstances a declaration of restriction for five years would be more onerous than an order of disqualification for a shorter period. The Court's attention was drawn to the *ex tempore* decision of Laffoy J in *Re Norse Security Ltd* in which an order of disqualification for a period of two years was made against the sole executive director of a company in circumstances where the company had outstanding revenue liability in the sum of €275,000. In light of this decision and the factors mentioned above, the Court made an order of disqualification for one year against the former directors of Clawhammer Ltd.

[23.015] In England, the case of *Re Sevenoaks Stationers Ltd*[30] provides useful guidance regarding the appropriate duration of disqualification orders. In that case, the respondent appealed against the order of disqualification on the principal ground that the seven year period of disqualification was excessive. Dillon LJ considered the facts of the case and various submissions which were made, noting that, as this was the first appeal against a disqualification order to come before the Court of Appeal, it had 'an

---

[29] *Re Clawhammer Ltd, Director of Corporate Enforcement v McDonnell; Re Shinrone Food Market Ltd, Director of Corporate Enforcement v Hoctor; Re Cautious Trading Ltd, Director of Corporate Enforcement v Forristal* (15 March 2005, unreported), HC, Finlay Geoghegan J.

[30] *Re Sevenoaks Stationers Ltd* [1991] BCLC 325.

importance beyond its own facts'. Dillon LJ set out the following approach, which has been followed and applied in many decision of the English courts:

> 'I would for my part endorse the division of the potential 15-year disqualification period into three brackets ..., viz: (i) The top bracket of disqualification for periods over ten years should be reserved for particularly serious cases. These may include cases where a director who has already had one period of disqualification imposed on him falls to be disqualified yet again. (ii) The minimum bracket of two to five years' disqualification should be applied where, though disqualification is mandatory, the case is, relatively, not very serious. (iii) The middle bracket of disqualification for from six to ten years should apply for serious cases which do not merit the top bracket.'[31]

[23.016] The Court in *Re Sevenoaks Stationers Ltd* also considered the factors which should be taken into account by a court in determining the appropriate period of disqualification. The Court rejected emphatically the submission of the official receiver that matters which were not taken into account in the making of the order, could be taken into account in computing the period of disqualification. The Court held that this approach would be inconsistent with the requirement that exists in England, that a respondent must have notice of the charges he has to meet. On the other hand, the Court noted that:

> 'Matters of mitigation can of course be taken into account in favour of the director in fixing the period of disqualification; but otherwise the period should be fixed by reference only to the matters properly alleged against him which have been found to be established and to make him unfit to be concerned in the management of a company.'[32]

[23.017] The following are examples of the application of the three brackets of the *Re Sevenoaks Stationers Ltd* approach to determining periods of disqualification:

1. In *Secretary of State for Trade and Industry v Swan*[33] Etherton J considered that the conduct of the respondent 'plainly does not fall within the most serious of the three categories specified in *Re Sevenoaks Stationers (Retail) Ltd* (11–15 years).'[34] The Court took into account the following factors in determining whether the respondent's conduct fell within the lowest category of two to five years, or the middle category of six to ten years:

   – The fact there was no want of probity on the part of the respondent;

   – There was no evidence of his direct involvement (such as by signing cheques or being aware of) in the company's policies ('cheque kiting') which were complained of;

   – It was not established that the company's cheque kiting policy was for a dishonest purpose;

---

[31] *Re Sevenoaks Stationers Ltd* [1991] BCLC 325.

[32] *Re Sevenoaks Stationers Ltd* [1991] BCLC 325.

[33] *Secretary of State for Trade and Industry v Swan* [2005] EWHC 603 (Ch).

[34] *Secretary of State for Trade and Industry v Swan* [2005] EWHC 603 (Ch) at para 220.

— The respondent's want of competence related to a lack of vigilance rather than any active role in the formulation or promotion of the company's cheque kiting policy;

— It was not alleged or shown that the cheque kiting policy caused loss to any person or caused any insolvency.

In light of all of these factors, the Court made an order of disqualification in the lowest bracket and disqualified the respondent for four years.

2. In *Re JA Chapman Ltd*[35] Peter Smith J took into account the dishonesty of the respondent, the size of the sums of money obtained from clients and the fact that he fought the disqualification order for days in court, as a justification for determining, 'that a period of disqualification should be towards the upper end of the middle *Sevenoaks* bracket of six to ten years'.[36] The Court ultimately made an order of disqualification for nine years.

3. *Official Receiver v Stern*[37] is an example of the imposition of a disqualification order in the highest bracket of the *Re Sevenoaks Stationers Ltd*[38] test. That case was designated by the court as a serious one, as the two companies continued to trade for a protracted period of time while insolvent and the respondent was drawing substantial funds from the companies at a time when creditors were not being paid. The Court therefore imposed a period of disqualification of 12 years. On appeal, it was held that either one of the charges of trading while insolvent or drawing substantial funds from the companies, would have been sufficient to render the case a serious one, meriting a period of disqualification within the middle bracket of the *Re Sevenoaks Stationers Ltd*.[39] The fact that both charges were made out was held to exacerbate the seriousness of each. The Court agreed that it was a serious case meriting a period of disqualification in the top bracket and agreed that a period of twelve years was appropriate.

[23.018] *Re Ansbacher (Cayman) Ltd, Director of Corporate Enforcement v Collery*,[40] was the first disqualification order arising from the publication of the inspectors' report with respect to Ansbacher (Cayman) Ltd in July 2002.[41] Finlay Geoghegan J considered

---

[35] *Re J A Chapman & Co Ltd, Secretary of State for Trade and Industry v Amiss* [2003] EWHC 532 (Ch), [2003] 2 BCLC 206.

[36] *Re J A Chapman & Co Ltd, Secretary of State for Trade and Industry v Amiss* [2003] EWHC 532 (Ch), [2003] 2 BCLC 206 at 221.

[37] *Official Receiver v Stern* [2001] EWHC Civ 1787.

[38] *Re Sevenoaks Stationers Ltd* [1991] BCLC 325.

[39] *Re Sevenoaks Stationers Ltd* [1991] BCLC 325.

[40] *Re Ansbacher (Cayman) Ltd, Director of Corporate Enforcement v Collery* [2006] IEHC 67.

[41] By decision of Finlay Geoghegan J dated 30 January 2007, a second person (Mr Sam Field-Corbett) was disqualified for three years, as the inspectors' report into Ansbacher (Cayman) Ltd demonstrated that he was unfit to be concerned in the management of a company within the meaning of s 160(2)(e). The appropriate period would have been six years, but with mitigating factors taken into account a disqualification period of three years was imposed. See ODCE, *Press Release* (30 January 2007). The disqualification period was postponed for four weeks to allow the respondent to extricate himself from companies in which he was involved. Available at www.odce.ie.

an application for an order of disqualification under s 160(2)(e), on the basis of the findings in that report. This application was not contested by the respondent. The inspectors' report found evidence that the respondent assisted in operating a bank without a licence; in failing to provide the Registrar of Companies with requisite information; in conducting the bank's business so as to defraud creditors of other persons; and in failing to make proper tax returns and payments. Having determined that the conduct of the respondent, as found in the inspectors' report, made him unfit to be concerned in the management of a company, the Court considered the appropriate period of disqualification. In this regard, Finlay Geoghegan J set out a number of principles that should be taken into account:

'(1) The primary purpose of an order of disqualification is not to punish the individual but to protect the public against future conduct of companies by persons whose past record has shown them to be a danger to creditors and others.

(2) The period of disqualification should reflect (in relation to and order under s 160(2)(e)) the gravity of the conduct as found by the Inspectors which makes the respondent unfit to be concerned in the management of a company.

(3) The period of disqualification should contain deterrent elements.

(4) A period of disqualification in excess of ten years should be reserved for particularly serious cases.

(5) The court should firstly assess the correct period in accordance with the foregoing and then take into account mitigating factors prior to fixing the actual period of disqualification.'

Applying these principles, the Court held that the conduct alleged was of a particularly serious nature and that a period of disqualification of twelve years was warranted. This was reduced by three years to take account of the mitigating factors that the respondent did not contest the application; took responsibility for the matters identified in the inspectors' report; that the matters alleged against the respondent took place a consideration time before the application; that there were no allegations against the respondent in the intervening period; and that he had assisted and cooperated with the inspectors.

In arriving at that period of disqualification, the Court agreed with the approach of Lord Woolf MR in *Re Westmid Packing Services Limited*[42] that, 'The citation of cases as to the period of disqualification will, in the great majority of cases, be unnecessary and inappropriate.'

Finlay Geoghegan J determined that 'the appropriate period of disqualification should be the application of the principles now established to the facts of the particular case and that the citation of the facts of other cases and periods of disqualification is unnecessary and inappropriate.'

---

[42] *Re Westmid Packing Services Limited* [1998] 2 ALL ER 124 at 234.

[23.019] In *Re National Irish Bank Ltd, Director of Corporate Enforcement v D'Arcy*,[43] the Court applied the decision of Finlay Geoghegan J in *Re Clawhammer Ltd*.[44] As the respondent put no evidence before the Court and made no application under s 160(8), the minimum period of disqualification should be five years. Kelly J noted that there is no maximum period of disqualification.

In determining the appropriate period of disqualification, Kelly J derived some guidance from the decision in *Re Sevenoaks Stationers (Retail) Ltd*[45] and the three brackets of over ten years, two to five years, and six to ten years described by Dillon LJ in that case. The Court also derived assistance from the decision of Lord Woolf MR in *Re Westmid Packing Ltd*[46] that:

> 'Despite the fact that the courts have said disqualification is not a "punishment", in truth the exercise that is being engaged in is little different from any sentencing exercise. The period of disqualification must reflect the gravity of the offence. It must contain deterrent elements. That is what sentencing is all about, and that is what fixing the appropriate period of the disqualification is all about ... In relation to the period of disqualification the facts of the offence are still obviously important but many other factors ought (and in reality do) come into play.'[47]

Kelly J further quoted the decision of Lord Woolf MR that:

> 'We do not consider that it would send out a wrong message to fix the period of disqualification by starting with an assessment of the correct period to fit the gravity of the conduct, and then allowing for the mitigating factors, in much the same way as a sentencing court would do.'[48]

Kelly J determined that the appropriate period of disqualification was one of twelve years, which would include a deterrent element. The respondent put no material before the court in relation to his personal circumstances, but the Court did consider that he deserved credit for not contesting the application. On the contrary, the Court noted that the respondent consented to the application. This was a mitigating factor and the period

---

[43] *Re National Irish Bank Ltd, Director of Corporate Enforcement v D'Arcy* [2006] 2 IR 163.

[44] *Re Clawhammer Ltd, Director of Corporate Enforcement v McDonnell* [2005] IEHC 85, [2005] 1 IR 503. See, in particular, the following dicta at p 513: 'Whilst a full disqualification order is in its terms more restrictive than a declaration of restriction, in practice the latter may operate to prevent certain respondents from acting as directors. This depends upon the particular circumstances of a respondent director. In the absence of a respondent putting before the court any relevant evidence, it is difficult to conclude that a disqualification order for any period less than five years will be a more onerous sanction for the respondent than a declaration of restriction which must be for five years,' *per* Finlay Geoghegan J.

[45] *Re Sevenoaks Stationers (Retail) Ltd* [1991] Ch 164 at 176. See further paras **[23.015]** to **[23.017]**.

[46] *Re Westmid Packing Ltd* [1998] 2 All ER 124.

[47] *Re Westmid Packing Ltd* [1998] 2 All ER 124 at 131 to 132.

[48] *Re Westmid Packing Ltd* [1998] 2 All ER 124 at 132.

of disqualification was accordingly reduced by two years. The respondent was therefore disqualified for ten years from the date of the Court order.

[23.020] In *Re National Irish Bank Ltd, Director of Corporate Enforcement v Seymour*[49] the Court determined that, without mitigating factors, the appropriate period of disqualification was twelve years. In light of factors such as the respondent's age, openness, politeness, and his attempts to rectify the non-compliance complained of, the Court reduced this period by three years. Among the factors taken into account were, 'his age, his retirement and his non-involvement in banking or any commercial activities.' It may be remarked that factors such as these make the duration of the disqualification period somewhat less relevant to the respondent.

[23.021] In relation to the appropriate duration of a period of disqualification, the Court in *Re Barnroe Ltd*[50] quoted the principles set out in *Re Clawhammer* and stated:

> 'This Court is conscious of the logic of this decision which may well be a correct interpretation of the law. If required the Court would also have to give some weight to its own view that a disqualification, no matter for how short a period, will be seen in the business community as a far greater sanction than a restriction.'

This comment is *obiter*, as O'Leary J stated that he arrived at a period of disqualification of five years without reference to any minimum. The Court further made clear that 'the length chosen in this case was independently arrived at and did not depend on the *"Director of Corporate Enforcement and Martin Forristal and Linda Forristal"* formulae.'

There are four points to note about the final conclusion in *Re Barnroe Ltd*.[51] First, the Court held that a 'lengthy period of disqualification' was warranted in the case to protect the public from future misuse of company law structures by the respondents and then made an order that the respondents be disqualified for five years. Five years is not typically regarded as a 'lengthy period of disqualification': Applying the *Sevenoaks* brackets, it is within the lowest bracket. Second, there is no reference by O'Leary J to any mitigating factors which led to that decision. Indeed, the Court indicates early in the judgment that the respondents presented no evidence on the applications. The justification for that period of disqualification in light of the 'formidable body of evidence' of unfitness, which the Court found to exist, is not apparent. Third, the Court leaves open a doubt as to the proper approach to take in relation to periods of disqualification and, in particular, whether any guidance should be drawn between the mandatory five-year period of declarations of restriction. Fourth, the Court directed that the period of disqualification should commence from the date of the judgment, but that the respondents should have one month to divest themselves of corporate involvement.

---

[49] *Re National Irish Bank Ltd, Director of Corporate Enforcement v Seymour* [2007] IEHC 102.

[50] *Re Barnroe Ltd, Director of Corporate Enforcement v Rogers* [2005] IEHC 433.

[51] *Re Barnroe Ltd, Director of Corporate Enforcement v Rogers* [2005] IEHC 433.

D. Substitution of restriction order

[23.022] On an application for a disqualification order under s 160, a court has the right to make a declaration of restriction, rather than an order of disqualification. Section 160(9A),[52] which was inserted by the CLEA 2001, provides:

> In considering the penalty to be imposed under this section, the court may as an alternative, where it adjudges that disqualification is not justified, make a declaration under section 150.[53]

There are three points that may be made about this provision. First, the court appears to have the right to substitute a declaration of restriction for a disqualification order, even in the absence of an application from the respondent for such an order. It is a matter within the discretion of the Court. Second, it should be noted that cases such as *Re Newcastle Timber Ltd*[54] illustrate that the practice of making declarations of restriction where the court does not consider an order of disqualification to be warranted, existed before the introduction of s 160(9A). In that case, the liquidator applied for an order of disqualification or, failing that, a declaration of restriction. Section 160(9A) essentially has the effect of removing the requirement that an applicant for an order of disqualification must specifically seek, as an alternative, a declaration of restriction. Third, a declaration of restriction made under s 160(9A) will not necessarily have the features common to a declaration made under s 150: the respondent may not necessarily be a director and there is no requirement that there be a company in insolvent liquidation.

Finally, on its terms, s 160(9A) is not confined to discretionary disqualifications under s 160(2). There are two possible approaches to this question. On the one hand, the phrase 'in considering the penalty to be imposed under this section' in s 160(9A) could extend to situations where the prosecutor makes an application under s 160(1) for the variance of the otherwise mandatory five-year period of automatic disqualification. On this interpretation, once the prosecutor invokes the court's jurisdiction to consider the appropriateness of a five year 'deemed' disqualification, the court is 'considering the penalty to be imposed', within the meaning of s 160(9A) and that provision may be invoked.

On the other hand, s 160(1) refers only to the right of the prosecutor to apply to court for a period of disqualification of 'such other period as the court ... may order'. The application which may be made by the prosecutor, and the discretion of the court on such an application, appear to be confined to varying the otherwise mandatory five year duration of the period of 'deemed' disqualification. There is no scope for a court to determine that, the other criteria of s 160(1) being met, an order of disqualification 'is

---

[52]   CA 1990, s 160(9A), as inserted by CLEA 2001, s 42(f).

[53]   CA 1990, s 160(9A), as inserted by CLEA 2001, s 42(f). For an example of a case in which s 160(9A) was invoked by the applicant, as an alternative to an order of disqualification, see *Re Barnroe Ltd, Director of Corporate Enforcement v Rogers* [2005] IEHC 433 ('The Court has considered the alternative s 150 restriction and is of the view that it would be an inadequate protection in this case,' *per* O'Leary J).

[54]   CA 1990, s 160(9A), as inserted by CLEA 2001, s 42(f).

not justified': s 160(1) states that the person to whom it applies 'shall be deemed ... to be subject to a disqualification order.'

The latter interpretation is more compelling. It may be noted, however, that a person who is subject to a 'deemed' disqualification order may undoubtedly make an application for relief under s 160(8). As s 160(9A) expressly provides for the power to substitute a declaration of restriction for an order of disqualification, and is more limited in its scope than s 160(8), it may be inferred that this discretion does not exist in the broader circumstances to which s 160(8) applies.[55] An application for relief under s 160(8) cannot, therefore, have the effect of an application for the substitution of a declaration of restriction.

[23.023] The application of s 160(9A) can be seen in the decision of Laffoy J in *Re Wood Products (Longford) Ltd.*[56] The respondents were the only directors of a company which failed to file its annual returns for thirteen years; failed to file returns with the Revenue Commissions; was struck off the register; and was restored to the register, subject to directions to file all outstanding returns, with which it did not comply. The company further failed to pay Revenue debts, which resulted in the registration of a judgment mortgage against the company. Since the initiation of the disqualification proceedings, the Revenue and annual returns were filed; there were plans in place to repay the Revenue indebtedness; and the second respondent was replaced as a director of the company.

The Court considered its discretion under s 160(9A), in light of its finding that the respondents had acted irresponsibly:

> 'The court has a discretion under sub-s (9A) to make a declaration under s 150. Having regard to the finding that the respondents have acted irresponsibly, if the court was dealing with a separate application under s 150 in the context of the Company being wound up as an insolvent company, on the basis of that finding, the making of a restriction order under s 150 in the case of each respondent would be mandatory. However, I am satisfied on the evidence that the Company is solvent, that it is capable of discharging its indebtedness to the Revenue Commissioners, and that it is operating satisfactorily as a going concern. To make a restriction order against the first respondent would undoubtedly impact on the ability of the Company to give effect to its intention to discharge its liabilities to the Revenue Commissioners and to carry on as a going concern. Because of the pending mortgage suit, if it is to continue as a going concern, it must discharge its tax liabilities. In the circumstances I think it appropriate not to make a restriction order against the first respondent.

> The second respondent has already resigned as a director of the Company. In view of the evidence as to the health of the second respondent, which is supported by a medical certificate from her general practitioner, I think it appropriate not to make a restriction order against the second respondent.'

When a disqualification order is sought against a person in a position of responsibility in a solvent, viable company, this case demonstrates that the courts may be slow to exercise

---

[55] See further paras **[23.027]** to **[23.030]** regarding s 160(8).

[56] *Re Wood Products (Longford) Ltd, Director of Corporate Enforcement v McGowan* [2005] IEHC 41.

its discretion under s 160(9A) to make a declaration of restriction in respect of that person.

E. Costs

[23.024] According to s 160(9B),[57] a court may make an order of costs against a person who is made the subject of a declaration of restriction or an order of disqualification. That section provides:

> The court, on the hearing of an application for a declaration under subsection (2), may order that the persons disqualified or against whom the declaration under section 150 is made as a result of the application shall bear—
>
> (a) the costs of the application, and
>
> (b) in the case of an application by the Director, the Director of Public Prosecutions, a liquidator, a receiver, or an examiner (in this paragraph referred to as 'the applicant'), in addition to the costs referred to in paragraph (a), the whole (or such portion of them as the court specifies) of the costs and expenses incurred by the applicant—
>
> > (i) in investigating the matters the subject of the application, and
> >
> > (ii) in so far as they do not fall within paragraph (a), in collecting evidence in respect of those matters,
>
> including so much of the remuneration and expenses of the applicant as are attributable to such investigation and collection.[58]

[23.025] In *Re Clawhammer Ltd*,[59] Finlay Geoghegan J considered the jurisdiction of a court to make an order for costs of disqualification proceedings and the terms of s 160(9B) as follows:

> 'It is difficult to understand the purpose of s 160(9B) insofar as it gives to the court a power to make an order for the costs of the application against a person in respect of whom a disqualification order or declaration of restriction is made. This appears to be a power which the court already had under Order 99 of the Rules of the Superior Courts 1986. However there is no indication that such power is to be exercised in any different way to the existing power under Order 99. In accordance with Order 99 where, as in these three cases, the applications were successful an

---

[57] CA 1990, s 160(9B), as inserted by CLEA 2001, s 42(f) and as substituted by IFCMPA 2005, s 11(2), with effect from 29 January 2007.

[58] CA 1990, s 160(9B), as inserted by CLEA 2001, s 42(f). See further Ch **19**, regarding applications of this provision in relation to declarations of restriction.

[59] *Re Clawhammer Ltd, Director of Corporate Enforcement v McDonnell; Re Shinrone Food Market Ltd, Director of Corporate Enforcement v Hoctor; Re Cautious Trading Ltd, Director of Corporate Enforcement v Forristal* (15 March 2005, unreported), HC, Finlay Geoghegan J. Four of the directors were disqualified for four years and the remaining two were disqualified for two years.

order for costs in favour of the Director would ordinarily follow unless the court in its discretion considers that the interests of justice require a different order.'[60]

In *Re Clawhammer Ltd*, the respondents raised the point that of the 14,800 companies which were struck off the register in 2003 they were singled out for disqualification proceedings, despite the fact that the company's outstanding liabilities were small and the respondents had used personal loans to repay some of the company's debts. The Court concluded that in the circumstances of that case, it was appropriate to exercise its discretion to make a limited order for costs and accordingly ordered that the respondents, jointly and severally, contribute €2,000 towards the costs of the DCE.

In relation to *Shinrone Ltd*, the Court took into account the fact that the respondents were nearing retirement age and had significant personal liabilities and, in the exercise of its discretion, made a limited order for costs against the respondents in the sum of €2,000. The former directors of Cautious Trading Ltd did not present any evidence to the Court and an order for costs was made against those respondents, to be taxed in default of agreement.

[23.026] The allocation of costs in *Re Clawhammer Ltd*[61] demonstrates that, while the courts can make an order of costs against the respondent to an application for a disqualification order, there is a wide discretion in this regard. On the authority of that case, a respondent would be well advised to appear and present evidence to court on an application for disqualification. It is also worthwhile for a respondent to present evidence of their own personal situation and means. While such evidence may not prevent the making of an order of disqualification, or even mitigate the length of the period of disqualification, it may influence the court in relation to the award of costs.

The formulation of s 160(9B) is substantially the same as s 150(4B) and the analysis of that provision is also highly relevant in this context.[62]

F. Relief

[23.027] A person who is made the subject of an order of disqualification can apply to court for relief against the order, in whole or in part. Section 160(8) accordingly provides:

> Any person who is subject or deemed subject to a disqualification order by virtue of this Part may apply to the court for relief, either in whole or in part, from that disqualification and the court may, if it deems it just and equitable to do so, grant such relief on whatever terms and conditions it sees fit.

---

60 *Re Clawhammer Ltd, Director of Corporate Enforcement v McDonnell; Re Shinrone Food Market Ltd, Director of Corporate Enforcement v Hoctor; Re Cautious Trading Ltd, Director of Corporate Enforcement v Forristal* (15 March 2005, unreported), HC, Finlay Geoghegan J.

61 *Re Clawhammer Ltd, Director of Corporate Enforcement v McDonnell; Re Shinrone Food Market Ltd, Director of Corporate Enforcement v Hoctor; Re Cautious Trading Ltd, Director of Corporate Enforcement v Forristal* (15 March 2005, unreported), HC, Finlay Geoghegan J.

62 See Ch **19**.

While there appear to be no reported decisions in which this provision has been considered in any detail[63] it was addressed in the cases of *Re CB Readymix Ltd*[64] and *Re Clawhammer Ltd*.[65] As noted above,[66] the decision of the Supreme Court in *Re CB Readymix Ltd* established that a court can attach conditions to a disqualification order and is not confined to making a full disqualification order as defined in s 160. The reasoning by which the Court arrived at this conclusion was that a court can grant relief under s 160(8) 'in the days immediately following the making' of the order and that 'it would be unthinkable that the court could have a power to revise its own order in that way and in that time frame and not have the same powers in the first instance.' [67]

[23.028] In *Re Clawhammer Ltd*, Finlay Geoghegan J referred to the potential implications of a disqualification order and the impact such an order could have on someone whose profession and occupation involved the management of companies. The Court observed in this regard that s 160(8) 'would appear to allow a court to grant relief from one aspect of a disqualification order alone, such as the prohibition on involvement in the management of a company'. The Court then observed that, in light of the fact that s 160(8) is not subject to the same notice requirements as are contained in s 152, it remains to be seen whether a respondent can ask for relief against part of a disqualification order immediately upon the making of that order. This question was not resolved, as no such application was made by the respondents in *Re Clawhammer Ltd*.

[23.029] The power of the court under s 160(8) is a very wide one and would permit the court to accommodate any aspect of the respondent's situation, if the court considers it just and equitable to do so. With regard to the timing and other procedural aspects of an application for relief, *Re CB Readymix Ltd* suggests that the application can be made in the days after the order is granted, whereas *Re Clawhammer Ltd* raises the possibility that it may be made immediately upon the making of the order. The question of whether notice of the application is necessary will be important to resolving this issue. There is nothing in s 160 which indicates that such a notice requirement does exist. As Finlay Geoghegan J noted in *Re Clawhammer Ltd*, this is an issue which remains to be resolved.

---

[63] It may be noted that there are certain cases such as *Re Kentford Securities Ltd, Director of Corporate Enforcement v McCann* [2007] IEHC 1, in which no disqualification order was made, although all grounds alleged by the applicant were, according to the Court, well-founded, in which relief under s 160(8) may be more appropriate than no order of disqualification being made.

[64] *Re CB Readymix Ltd, Cahill v Grimes* [2002] 1 IR 372.

[65] *Re Clawhammer Ltd, Director of Corporate Enforcement v McDonnell; Re Shinrone Food Market Ltd, Director of Corporate Enforcement v Hoctor; Re Cautious Trading Ltd, Director of Corporate Enforcement v Forristal* (15 March 2005, unreported), HC, Finlay Geoghegan J. Four of the directors were disqualified for four years and the remaining two were disqualified for two years.

[66] See above paras **[23.003]** to **[23.005]**.

[67] *Re CB Readymix Ltd, Cahill v Grimes* [2002] 1 IR 372 at 380, *per* Murphy J.

[23.030] It should be noted that declarations of certain persons who were subject to restriction and disqualification orders have made applications to the High Court for relief from those orders. The DCE described one such application:

> 'In one case, a director disqualified in the UK involved himself in a company in the State without making his disqualification known to the Registrar of Companies as required by law. Following investigation and with our consent, he sought and secured relief on a conditional basis to continue to act as a director of a single company here.'[68]

The CLRG recommends in the General Scheme of the Draft Companies Consolidation and Reform Bill 2007 that any application for relief from disqualification must be made on notice to the applicant for the order of disqualification and, if the DCE was not the applicant, to the DCE.[69]

G. Register of disqualified persons

[23.031] The Registrar of Companies keeps a register of disqualified persons. Section 167[70] provides that:

> Where a court—
>
> (a) makes a disqualification order;
>
> (b) grants or varies relief under section 160(8); or
>
> (c) convicts a person of an offence:
>
>> (i)   which has the effect of his being deemed to be subject to a disqualification order, or
>>
>> (ii) under section 161(1) or 164,
>
> a prescribed officer of the court shall cause the registrar of companies to be furnished with prescribed particulars of the order, relief or conviction at such time and in such form and manner as may be prescribed.'[71]

CA 1990, s 168(1) further provides that the Registrar shall 'keep a register of the particulars which have been notified to him under section 167'. If the court has granted full relief from disqualification under s 160(8), the particulars in respect of that person should be removed from the register.[72] It is curious to note that s 168 specifically

---

68 ODCE, Press Release, 9 March 2005, stating, 'Certain individuals subject to disqualification or restriction orders have applied for relief to the High Court in the last 12 months or so.'

69 General Scheme of the Draft Companies Consolidation and Reform Bill 2007, Pt A13, Head 42(13). Available at www.clrg.org.

70 This provision was contended for by many deputies during the passage of the Companies Bill. See Dáil Éireann, Vol 384, 23 November, 1988. Companies (No 2) Bill, 1987 [Seanad]; Second Stage (Resumed). 'On Part VII of the Bill a number of Deputies suggested that a black list of restricted or disqualified directors should be available to ensure that people establishing companies did not invite disqualified people on to the board.' (Mr A Reynolds, Minister for Industry and Commerce.)

71 CA 1990, s 167.

72 CA 1990, s 168(2).

requires the Registrar to remove from the register the names of persons who were subject to 'deemed' disqualifications, at the date of expiry of that disqualification, unless a further notification was received in respect of that person, but no such requirement exists to remove the names of persons who are subject to discretionary disqualifications, upon the expiry of that period of disqualification.[73] It must be assumed that a similar obligation exists in relation to persons disqualifed under s 160(2).

[23.032] At the end of 2006, 1781 names of disqualified persons were recorded on the register that is kept pursuant to s 167. This register is accessible on the website of the CRO and readily searchable by means of the surname of the disqualified person. The register includes the name, address, date of disqualification, and reason for disqualification, of the person subject to the disqualification order, and date of expiry of the period of disqualification.[74]

H. Acting while disqualified

[23.033] A number of consequences may flow from a person acting in breach of an order of disqualification or an automatic disqualification. First, the disqualified person is guilty of an offence. Second, upon conviction, he will be disqualified for a further period of ten years, or such other period as the court may, on the application of the prosecutor, direct. Third, he may not apply for relief from the consequences of being disqualified. Fourth, any consideration paid to him in relation to this activity may be recovered. Fifth, he may be made liable for the debts of the company in which he is acting. Finally, there are consequences for any directors, officers, or other such persons who knowingly act under the directions or in accordance with the instructions, of a disqualified person.

(a) Offence of acting while disqualified

[23.034] Section 161(1) provides that:

> Any person who, in relation to any company, acts in a manner or capacity which by virtue of being a person to whom s 150 applies or being subject or deemed to be subject to a disqualification order, he is prohibited from doing shall be guilty of an offence.[75]

---

[73] See CA 1990, s 168(3) ('The registrar shall also remove from the register any particulars in relation to a person on the expiry of five years from the date of the original notification under s 167, or such other period in respect of which the person concerned is deemed to be subject to a disqualification order, unless the registrar has received a further notification in respect of that person under this section.' (emphasis added)).

[74] See www.cro.ie.

[75] As no sanction is specified under s 161, CA 1990, s 240 will be applicable to this offence. See Ch **15**.

It is therefore an offence for a person who is disqualified to do any of the following:

- to be appointed or to act as any company's auditor, director, officer, receiver, liquidator, or examiner;

- to be in any way, directly or indirectly, concerned or take part in any company's promotion, formation or management.[76]

(b) Extension of period of disqualification

[23.035] A person who was disqualified immediately prior to his conviction under s 161(1), shall have his period of disqualification extended for a further period of ten years from the date of the conviction. The court may vary this period of ten years, on the application of the prosecutor, and in light of all of the circumstances of the case. CA 1990, s 161(3) provides:

> Where a person convicted of an offence under subsection (1) was subject, or deemed to be subject, to a disqualification order immediately prior to the date of such conviction, the period for which he was disqualified shall be extended for a further period of ten years from such date, or such other further period as the court, on the application of the prosecutor and having regard to all the circumstances of the case, may order.

The net effect is that, if a person acts in violation of an order of disqualification, the period of disqualification to which he was subject shall be extended by a further period of ten years from the date of conviction, unless this period is varied by the court on the application of the prosecutor and having regard to the circumstances of the case. The respondent has no standing to apply for a period of disqualification of less than ten years. Section 161(3) is open to two possible interpretations. The additional period of ten years for which the person is disqualified, may be added on to the existing period of disqualification to which he is subject: this is suggested by the expression that the disqualification period 'shall be extended for a further period of ten years'. The alternative interpretation is that the period of ten years runs from the date of the conviction of the offence of acting while disqualified: this is suggested by the statement that the ten year period is from the date of the conviction. On balance, the preferred interpretation is that the further period of ten years must be added to the existing disqualification period, with effect from the date of conviction. If a period of disqualification was due to expire four months after the date of conviction, for example, that period will be substituted with a period of ten years and four months from the date of conviction.

(c) No relief

[23.036] When a disqualified person is convicted of the offence of acting in a prohibited manner, he may not apply for relief from the consequences of being disqualified. Section 160(8) generally permits a disqualified person to apply for relief

---

[76] CA 1990, s 159.

from a deemed or discretionary disqualification.[77] Section 161(4) provides, however, that: 'Section 160(8) shall not apply to a person convicted of an offence under subsection (1) of this section'.

A person who is convicted of acting while disqualified, and whose period of disqualification is extended under s 161(3), may not apply for relief for the entire duration of that extended period of disqualification.

(d) Repayment of consideration

[23.037] When a disqualified person acts in relation to a company in a manner which is prohibited, that company may recover any consideration which it paid to that person for so acting. Section 163 is addressed towards any person 'who acts, in relation to a company, in a manner or capacity which by virtue of being a person to whom s 150 applies or being subject or deemed to be subject to a disqualification order, he is prohibited from doing.'[78] Section 163(2) provides:

> Where any consideration is given by or on behalf of a company for an act done or service performed by a person referred to in subsection (1) while he was acting in a manner or capacity described in that subsection, the company shall be entitled to recover from him, as a simple contract debt in any court of competent jurisdiction, the consideration or an amount representing its value.

[23.038] A disqualified person is not entitled to keep any remuneration he receives while acting in a manner or capacity prohibited by that disqualification. There is no direct correlation in s 163(2) between the acts or services for which the remuneration is paid and the means by which the disqualified person is contravening the disqualification. It is possible that remuneration which a disqualified person receives for services which he provides to a company of which he is also acts as a director, but which are separate to his role as a director, may come within the scope of s 161(3). A disqualified person who is appointed as a director of a company, and who also provides legal services, for example, to that company, may be compelled to repay that remuneration. While this interpretation may extend the scope of s 163(3) more widely than is intended, it is an interpretation to which the subsection is open: the reference to acts or services done 'while' the disqualified person was acting contrary to his disqualification does not require that the acts or services must themselves be in contravention of the disqualification.

---

[77] CA 1990, s 160(8) provides, 'Any person who is subject or deemed subject to a disqualification order by virtue of this Part may apply to the court for relief, either in whole or in part, from that disqualification and the court may, if it deems it just and equitable to do so, grant such relief on whatever terms and conditions it sees fit.' See further paras **[23.027]** to **[23.030]**.

[78] CA 1990, s 163(1).

If proceedings are brought against a disqualified person to recover remuneration paid to him, the court may grant relief from that liability if it considers it just and equitable to do so, subject to such conditions as the court sees fit.[79]

(e) Liability for company's debts

[23.039] A disqualified person who acts in relation to a company in a manner or capacity which is prohibited by that disqualification, may be personally liable for the debts of that company. Section 163(3) provides:

> Where
>
> (a) a person referred to in subsection (1) acts, in relation to a company, in a manner or capacity described in that subsection, and
>
> (b) the company concerned commences to be wound up—
>
>> (i) while he is acting in such a manner or capacity, or
>>
>> (ii) within 12 months of his so acting, and
>
> (c) the company is unable to pay its debts, within the meaning of section 214 of the Principal Act,
>
> the court may, on the application of the liquidator or any creditor of the company, declare that such person shall be personally liable, without any limitation of liability, for all or any part of the debts or other liabilities of the company incurred in the period during which he was acting in such a manner or capacity.[80]

The conditions that must exist before such personal liability may arise are the following:

- The person must be deemed to be disqualified or subject to an order of disqualification;

- He must act in relation to a company ('the Company') in a manner or capacity which is prohibited;

- The winding up of the Company must commence while he is acting in relation to it in a prohibited manner or capacity, or within 12 months after he ceases to so act;

- The Company must be unable to pay its debts as they fall due;

- The liquidator or a creditor of the Company must make an application to court; and

- The court may declare that the person shall be personally liable for debts incurred by the Company during the time he acted contrary to a disqualification order.

This applies solely to debts incurred during the period in which the person was disqualified and acting in breach of that disqualification. Moreover, a person whose period of disqualification ended more than 12 months before the winding up commenced, will not be within the scope of s 163(3).

---

[79] CA 1990, s 163(5).

[80] CA 1990, s 163(3).

In proceedings to make a person liable for a company's debts under s 163(3), the court may, 'if, having regard to the circumstances of the case, it considers it just and equitable to do so' grant relief in whole or in part from that liability, and may further attach such conditions as it sees fit to that order of liability.[81]

(f) Acting under directions of a disqualified person

[23.040] If a director, officer, or other such person, acts in accordance with the instructions or directions of a person who he knows is disqualified, he is guilty of an offence and, upon conviction, he will also be deemed to be disqualified.[82] He will moreover be liable for the debts of the company. Section 164 provides:

> If any person while a director or other officer or a member of a committee of management or trustee of any company acts in accordance with the directions or instructions of another person knowing that such other person is disqualified or that, in giving the directions or instructions, he is acting in contravention of any provision of this Part he shall be guilty of an offence.[83]

[23.041] When a person is convicted of this offence, he shall be personally liable for the debts that the company incurred during the period in which he was acting in accordance with those directions or instructions.[84] Section 165(1) provides:

> A person who is convicted of an offence under s 164 for acting in accordance with the directions or instructions of a disqualified person shall, subject to subsection (2) be personally liable for the debts of the company concerned incurred in the period during which he was so acting.[85]

This liability arises automatically upon conviction of the offence of knowingly acting in accordance with the directions or instructions of a disqualified person. The only means of avoiding such liability is provided by s 165(2):

> In any proceedings brought against a person for the recovery of any such debt the court may if, having regard to the circumstances of the case, it considers it just and equitable to do so, grant relief in whole or in part from the liability to which he would otherwise be subject under subsection (1) and the court may attach to its order such conditions as it sees fit.

[23.042] There a number of distinctions between the imposition of personal liability on a person who himself is acting in relation to a company ('the Company') in contravention of a disqualification order or a deemed disqualification ('the disqualified person'), and the imposition of such liability on persons who act in accordance with the instructions or directions of such a disqualified person ('the other director or officer'). First, the Company must be in liquidation before a disqualified person may be made personally liable for the company's debts: there is no such requirement to make the other director or officer liable for its debts. Second, the Company must be unable to pay its

---

[81] CA 1990, s 163(5).

[82] CA 1990, ss 164 and 165. See further Ch **20**.

[83] CA 1990, s 164(1).

[84] CA 1990, s 165(1).

[85] CA 1990, s 165(1).

debts for the disqualified person to be made personally liable: there is no such requirement in relation to the other director or officer. Third, an application must be made to court to make the disqualified person personally liable for the Company's debts: the other director or officer is automatically personally liable upon conviction under s 164(1).

[23.043] In all of these respects, the conditions for making a disqualified person personally liable for a company's debts are more restrictive than those applicable to persons who knowingly act in accordance with the instructions or directions of such a person. This is not consistent with the respective levels of culpability of these persons: it may be expected that a person who acts contrary to an order of disqualification that was imposed on him, would be held to a higher level of responsibility than persons who knowingly follow his directions or instructions. A court may, however, grant to both disqualified persons and the directors or officers who knowingly act in accordance with their instructions or directions, relief in whole or in part from such personal liability for a company's debts.[86]

---

[86] CA 1990, ss 163(5) and 165(2).

Index

[all references are to paragraph number]

Access to documents
auditor's rights, and, 7.067

Account and indemnity
loans, and, 6.056
substantial property transactions,
and, 6.087

Accounts
books of account
content, 4.009
criminal liability, 4.019–4.023
currency, 4.011
deemed proper books, 4.010
disqualification, 4.036
form, 4.005
generally, 4.002
inspection, 4.013–4.017
introduction, 4.001
language, 4.006
location, 4.012
personal liability, 4.024–4.035
preservation, 4.018
proper books of account, 4.003–
4.004
statutory basis, 4.002
updating, 4.007–4.008
date, 2.027–2.028
generally, 2.024
groups of companies
parent company exception, 2.055
subsidiary company
exception, 2.056
parent companies, 2.055
small companies, 2.031
subsidiary companies, 2.056

Acquisition of own shares
filing obligations, and, 2.086

Acting in breach of restriction order
deemed disqualification orders,
and, 20.034–20.036

**Acting under directions of disqualified
or restricted person**
deemed disqualification orders,
and, 20.037

discretionary disqualification orders,
and, 23.040–23.043

Acting whilst disqualified
and see **Discretionary
disqualification orders**
extension of disqualification
period, 23.035
introduction, 23.033
liability for company's debts, 23.039
no relief, 23.036
offence of, 23.034
repayment of consideration,
23.037–23.038

Acting whilst not qualified
auditors, and, 7.041–7.053

Activity in State
filing obligations, and, 2.013–2.014

Adjournments
members' meetings, and, 5.041–
5.044

Adverse opinions
auditor's reports, and, 7.021–7.022

Agreements
filing obligations, and, 2.109–2.111

Allotment of shares
filing obligations, and, 2.071

Alteration of company books
criminal offences, and, 6.118

Alterations to share capital
filing obligations, and, 2.072–2.073

Annual general meetings (AGMs)
addressees of notice, 5.011
adjournments, 5.041–5.044
Chairman, 5.040
conduct of business
adjournments, 5.041–5.044
Chairman, 5.040
quorum, 5.036–5.039
venue of meeting, 5.048
voting, 5.046–5.047
content of notice, 5.010
direction of court, 5.049–5.051

Annual general meetings (AGMs) (contd)

  directions to convene, 5.004–5.006

  exemption for single member private companies, 5.016

  failure to convene, 5.007–5.009

  failure to notify, 5.014

  general business 5.003

  intervals between, 5.002

  introduction, 5.001

  location, 5.015

  minutes, 5.052–5.055

  notices

    addressees, 5.011

    content, 5.010

    failure to notify, 5.014

    service, 5.013

    timing, 5.012

  quorum, 5.036–5.039

  resolutions

    extended notice, 5.034–5.035

    special resolutions, 5.030–5.032

    written resolutions, 5.033

  service of notice, 5.013

  special resolutions, 5.030–5.032

  timing of notice, 5.012

  venue, 5.048

  voting, 5.046–5.047

  written resolutions, 5.033

Annual return

  accounts

    date, 2.027–2.028

    generally, 2.024

    groups of companies, 2.055–2.056

    small companies, 2.031

  annexed documents

    accounts, 2.024

    date of accounts, 2.027–2.028

    introduction, 2.022

    medium companies, 2.032

    relevant documents, 2.024–2.028

    reports, 2.025

    scope of obligation, 2.023

    small companies, 2.029–2.031

    translation, 2.026

  consequences of failure to file, 2.058

  content, 2.018–2.021

  date

    change of, 2.045–2.052

    companies formed after 28 February 2002, 2.040

    companies formed before 1 March 2002, 2.039

    definition, 2.034

    delivery, of, 2.041–2.044

    earlier, 2.045–2.047

    groups of companies, 2.053

    introduction, 2.033–2.038

    later, 2.047–2.052

  date for delivery, 2.041–2.044

  failure to file, 2.058

  filing obligations, and

    annexed documents, 2.022–2.032

    consequences of failure, 2.058

    content, 2.018–2.021

    date, 2.033–2.052

    grounds of rejection, 2.057

    groups of companies, 2.053–2.056

    introduction, 2.017

  grounds of rejection, 2.057

  groups of companies

    accounts, 2.055–2.056

    extension of date, 2.053–2.054

  reports, 2.025

  striking company off the register, and, 14.003–14.009

  translation, 2.026

Annual return date

  change of

    earlier, 2.045–2.047

    later, 2.047–2.052

  companies formed after 28 February 2002, 2.040

  companies formed before 1 March 2002, 2.039

  definition, 2.034

  delivery, of, 2.041–2.044

  groups of companies, 2.053

  introduction, 2.033–2.038

Appointment
auditors, and, 7.002
examiners, and
disqualification, 10.003–10.007
introduction, 10.001
publication, 10.008
qualifications, 10.003
termination, 10.009–10.011
liquidators, and
company, by, 9.003
consent, 9.013
court, by, 9.002
creditors, by, 9.004
creditors' disclosure
obligation, 9.010–9.011
disqualification, 9.007–9.009
methods, 9.002–9.006
notification, 9.017–9.021
prohibition on inducement, 9.012
qualifications, 9.007
receivers, and
disqualification, 8.009–8.013
publication, 8.002–8.008
qualifications, 8.009

Appointment of inspectors
company affairs, in respect of
and see **Investigation of
company affairs**
applicants, 13.002–13.008
companies affected,
13.032–13.041
evidence, 13.025–13.031
external applicants,
13.006–13.008
foreign-incorporated companies,
and, 13.033–13.034
grounds, 13.009–13.024
internal applicants,
13.003–13.005
related companies, and,
13.036–13.041
request of other authority, 13.042
introduction, 13.001
membership of company, in respect
of
DCE's powers, 13.050

generally, 13.044
grounds, 13.045
introduction, 13.043
powers, 13.047
scope, 13.046

Arrest
criminal prosecutions, and,
15.028–15.032

Articles of association
filing obligations, and, 2.006–2.009

Attempts to rectify or stop misconduct
discretionary disqualification orders,
and, 21.044

Attitude
discretionary disqualification orders,
and, 21.050–21.051

Audit exemption
generally, 7.129–7.132

Auditors
access to documents, 7.067
acting whilst not qualified,
7.041–7.053
appointment, 7.002
attendance at meetings, 7.070
audit exemption, and, 7.129–7.132
auditor's report
adverse opinions, 7.021–7.022
content, 7.019–7.020
further considerations,
7.023–7.025
generally, 7.018
qualifications, 7.021–7.022
special report, 7.026–7.027
authorisation
generally, 7.028–7.031
grandfather rights, 7.029
Register of Auditors,
7.032–7.038
background, 7.001
directors, as, 6.004
directors' compliance statements,
and, 7.124–7.125
directors' remuneration, and, 7.023
directors' report, and, 7.023

Auditors (contd)

disqualification, 7.039–7.040

fraud detection, and, 7.071–7.077

grandfather rights, 7.029

group accounts, and, 7.024–7.025

independence, 7.054–7.066

indictable offence reporting, and

 certainty, 7.104

 Companies Act, under,
  7.109–7.111

 'company, officer or
  agent', 7.105–7.108

 discretion, and, 7.112

 exceptions to duty to
  report, 7.113

 'in the course and by virtue of'
  audit work, 7.085–7.093

 'information', 7.094–7.097

 introduction, 7.083–7.084

 legal professional
  privilege, 7.119–7.122

 level of certainty, 7.104

 'opinion to be formed',
  7.098–7.100

 other Acts, under, 7.126–7.128

 protection from liability, 7.123

 provision of information, books
  and documents, 7.116–7.118

 'reasonable grounds',
  7.101–7.103

 relevant offences, 7.109–7.111

 timing of notification,
  7.114–7.115

information and
 explanations, 7.068–7.069

integrity

 access to documents, 7.067

 attendance at meetings, 7.070

 independence, 7.054–7.066

 information and
  explanations, 7.068–7.069

 qualifications, 7.028–7.053

legal professional privilege,
 7.119–7.122

liability

 company subject of audit,
  to, 7.135–7.137

creditors, to, 7.143

developments in law, 7.149

general position, 7.133

indictable offence reporting,
 and, 7.123

investors, to, 7.142

other companies, to, 7.138–7.141

potential liability, 7.134–7.148

standard of care, 7.144–7.148

members' meetings, and, 7.070

overview, 7.001

proper books of account, and,
 7.077–7.082

protection from liability, 7.123

qualifications

 acting whilst not
  qualified, 7.041–7.053

 authorisation, 7.028–7.031

 disqualification, 7.039–7.040

 generally, 7.028

 grandfather rights, 7.029

recognition, 7.028–7.031

Register of Auditors, 7.032–7.038

removal

 auditor's rights, 7.006–7.010

 generally, 7.003–7.005

remuneration, 7.017

reporting obligations

 background, 7.071–7.076

 directors' compliance statements,
  on, 7.124–7.125

 indictable offences, 7.083–7.118

 legal professional
  privilege, 7.119–7.122

 other, 7.126–7.128

 proper books of account,
  7.077–7.082

 protection from liability, 7.123

resignation, 7.011–7.016

rights

 access to documents, 7.067

 attendance at meetings, 7.070

 compelling information and
  explanations, 7.068–7.069

 removal, and, 7.006–7.010

special auditor's report, 7.026–7.027

Auditor's report
adverse opinions, 7.021–7.022
content, 7.019–7.020
further considerations, 7.023–7.025
generally, 7.018
qualifications, 7.021–7.022
special report, 7.026–7.027

Authorisation of auditors
generally, 7.028–7.031
grandfather rights, 7.029
Register of Auditors, 7.032–7.038

Automatic disqualification orders
acting in breach of restriction order
generally, 20.035–20.036
introduction, 20.034
acting under directions of
disqualified or restricted
person, 20.037
conviction on indictment
comparative legislation,
20.018–20.019
court's role, 20.011
discretion to substitute restriction
order, 20.017
implementation of
disqualification,
20.012–20.013
indictable offences, 20.007
introduction, 20.006
notification by director,
20.014–20.015
period of disqualification,
20.008–20.010
persons affected, 20.016
trigger offences, 20.007
failure to disclose disqualification in
other jurisdiction
effect, 20.029–20.033
general duty, 20.020–20.028
generally, 20.005
grounds
acting in breach of restriction
order, etc., 20.034–20.037
conviction on
indictment, 20.006–20.019
failure to disclose
disqualification in other
jurisdiction, 20.020–20.033
generally, 20.005
undischarged
bankruptcy, 20.038–20.041
introduction, 20.001–20.004
undischarged bankruptcy, 20.038–
20.041

Avoidance of transaction
loans, and, 6.053–6.056
substantial property transactions,
and, 6.085–6.086

Bankrupts
directors, as, 6.004

Bodies corporate
books of account, and, 4.019–4.020
directors, as, 6.004

Books of account
auditors, and, 7.077–7.082
content, 4.009
criminal liability
company, 4.019–4.020
directors, 4.019–4.020
officers, 4.021–4.023
currency, 4.011
deemed proper books, 4.010
discretionary disqualification orders,
and
applicants, 22.066
applications, 22.070
generally, 4.036
introduction, 22.062
offence of, 22.067–22.069
respondents, 22.063–22.065
form, 4.005
generally, 4.002
inspection, 4.013–4.017
introduction, 4.001
language, 4.006
location, 4.012
personal liability, 4.024–4.035
preservation, 4.018

Books of account (contd)
proper books of account,
4.003–4.004
statutory basis, 4.002
updating, 4.007–4.008

Breach of duty
and see **Discretionary
disqualification orders**
applicants, 22.013
applications, 22.015–22.020
"guilty", 22.021–22.022
introduction, 22.009
relationship with other
grounds, 22.023–22.025
respondents, 22.010–22.012
scope, 22.014

Burden of proof
discretionary disqualification orders,
and 21.011–21.012
restriction proceedings, and,
16.014–16.018

Business name
filing obligations, and, 2.146

Capacity
directors, and, 6.002
substantial property transactions,
and, 6.084

Cessation of business
striking company off the register,
and, 14.013

Chairman
members' meetings, and, 5.040

Change of name
filing obligations, and, 2.144

Charges
commission, 2.099
effect of non-registration, 2.106
effect of registration, 2.101–2.105
filing obligations, and
commission, 2.099
effect of non-registration, 2.106

effect of registration,
2.101–2.105
introduction, 2.087
obligation to register, 2.088
particulars to be
registered., 2.098
register of debenture
holders, 2.107
registrable charges, 2.089–2.097
release from charge, 2.108
time limits for registration, 2.100
foreign-incorporated
companies, 2.095
judgment mortgages, 2.097
obligation to register, 2.088
particulars to be registered., 2.098
property outside the State,
2.090–2.094
registers, and, 3.044
register of debenture holders, 2.107
registrable charges
foreign-incorporated
companies, 2.095
introduction, 2.089
judgment mortgages, 2.097
property outside the State,
2.090–2.094
series of debentures, 2.096
release from charge, 2.108
series of debentures, 2.096
time limits for registration, 2.100

Commission
charges, and, 2.099

Companies' obligations
books of account
content, 4.009
criminal liability, 4.019–4.023
currency, 4.011
deemed proper books, 4.010
disqualification, 4.036
form, 4.005
generally, 4.002
inspection, 4.013–4.017
introduction, 4.001
language, 4.006
location, 4.012

Companies' obligations (contd)
books of account (contd)
personal liability, 4.024–4.035
preservation, 4.018
proper books of account,
4.003–4.004
statutory basis, 4.002
updating, 4.007–4.008
filing
and see **Filing obligations**
annual return, 2.017–2.058
charges, 2.087–2.108
companies established outside
the State, 2.147–2.155
company name, 2.123–2.146
directors and secretaries,
2.112–2.122
form of documents, 2.163–2.170
formation of company,
2.002–2.016
introduction, 2.001
members, 2.066–2.070
prospectus, 2.059–2.065
public limited companies, 2.156
re-registration, 2.157–2.162
resolutions and
agreements, 2.109–2.111
share capital, 2.071–2.086
members' meetings
and see **Members' meetings**
annual general meetings,
5.002–5.016
conduct of business, 5.036–5.048
direction of court, 5.049–5.051
extraordinary general
meetings, 5.017–5.029
introduction, 5.001
minutes, 5.052–5.055
resolutions, 5.030–5.035
registers
and see **Registers**
charges, of, 3.044
debenture holders, of,
3.045–3.047
directors and secretaries,
of, 3.035–3.036
directors' contracts, of,
3.042–3.043
directors' interests, of,
3.037–3.041
form, 3.002–3.003
introduction, 3.001
members, of, 3.004–3.034

Companies Registration Office (CRO)
compliance, 11.065–11.070
disqualification powers, 11.064
fines and penalties, 11.068
functions transferred from
METD, 11.083
Integrated Enforcement
Environment, 11.069
introduction, 11.060
ODCE, and, 11.022
prosecution powers, 11.061
striking companies off the
register, 11.062

Company directors
see **Directors**

Company in liquidation
substantial property transactions,
and, 6.083

Company investigations
affairs of a company, into
and see **Investigation of
company affairs**
appointment of
inspectors, 13.002–13.031
companies affected,
13.032–13.041
evidence, 13.025–13.031
foreign-incorporated companies,
and, 13.033–13.034
grounds, 13.009–13.024
related companies, and,
13.036–13.041
request of other authority,
at, 13.042
attendance and assistance
general obligation,
13.083–13.084

Company investigations (contd)
attendance and assistance (contd)
self-incrimination,
13.085–13.086
use of answers, 13.087–13.090
banking documents, and,
13.091–13.096
conduct
directions by court,
13.060–13.062
fair procedure, 13.059
information regarding
offences, 13.063–13.064
privacy, 13.065
role of inspectors, 13.055–13.058
directions by court, 13.060–13.062
examinations, 13.084
expenses, 13.125–13.129
failure to comply, 13.097–13.100
fair procedure, 13.059
information regarding
offences, 13.063–13.064
introduction, 13.001
liens, and, 13.081
membership of company, into
appointment of
inspectors, 13.044–13.046
DCE's powers, 13.050
expenses, 13.049
grounds, 13.045
introduction, 13.043
powers of inspector, 13.047
publication of reports, 13.048
scope, 13.046
share dealing, 13.052
share restrictions, 13.051
powers
attendance, examinations and
assistance, 13.083–13.090
banking documents, 13.091–
13.096
failure to comply, 13.097–13.100
introduction, 13.066
production of
documents, 13.067–13.082
privacy, 13.065
privilege, and, 13.082

production of documents
agents, by, 13.072
'books and documents', 13.068
books and documents to be
produced, 13.074–13.078
general, 13.068
introduction, 13.067
liens, and, 13.081
'officers and agents', by, 13.069–
13.071
other persons, by, 13.072–13.073
privilege, and, 13.082
time limits, 13.079–13.080
report
challenges to, 13.104–13.110
consequences, 13.119–13.121
form, 13.101–13.103
publication, 13.111–13.118
use, 13.122–13.124
role of inspectors, 13.055–13.058
self-incrimination, 13.085–13.086
share dealings, 13.052
use of answers, 13.087–13.090

Company name
business name, 2.146
change of, 2.144
disclosure, 2.142–2.143
introduction, 2.123
'limited', 'teoranta' or 'plc',
2.124–2.134
prohibited names, 2.135–2.141
publication, 2.142–2.143
reservation of, 2.145

Company property
striking company off the register,
and, 14.030–14.033

Company secretary
changes in, 2.114–2.115
consent to act, 2.112
disclosure of personal information,
and, 6.092–6.093
filing obligations, and
changes in, 2.114–2.115
consent to act, 2.112
formation of company, on, 2.010

Company secretary (contd)
  filing obligations, and (contd)
    Irish resident director,
      2.119–2.122
    particulars, 2.112
    resignation or removal,
      2.116–2.118
    share qualifications, 2.113
  formation of company, and, 2.010
  Irish resident director, 2.119–2.122
  particulars, 2.112
  resignation or removal, 2.116–2.118
  share qualifications, 2.113

Compulsory winding-up
  and see **Liquidators**
  appointment of liquidator, 9.002
  convening meetings, 9.023–9.024
  disclosure duty, 9.021
  inspection of books, 9.107
  notification of appointment, 9.018
  reporting to DPP
    applicants, 9.088
    grounds, 9.090
    introduction, 9.087
    liquidator's duties, 9.091
    scope obligation, 9.089

Conditional disqualification
  disqualification orders, and,
    23.003–23.010

Conduct of business
  adjournments, 5.041–5.044
  Chairman, 5.040
  quorum, 5.036–5.039
  venue of meeting, 5.048
  voting, 5.046–5.047

Conflict of interests
  consequences, 6.022–6.023
  generally, 6.013–6.021

Consent to act
  filing obligations, and, 2.112

Conviction on indictment
  and see **Deemed disqualification**
    orders

comparative legislation,
  20.018–20.019
court's role, 20.011
discretion to substitute restriction
  order, 20.017
implementation of
  disqualification, 20.012–20.013
indictable offences, 20.007
introduction, 20.006
notification by director,
  20.014–20.015
period of disqualification,
  20.008–20.010
persons affected, 20.016
trigger offences, 20.007

Costs
  disqualification orders, and,
    23.024–23.026
  restriction proceedings, and
    applicant's liability,
      19.045–19.047
    generally, 19.024–19.027
    notice party costs orders, 19.051
    recovery in winding up,
      19.048–19.050
    respondent, in favour of,
      19.038–19.044
    s 150(4B) CA 1990,
      under, 19.028–19.033
    unsuccessful applications,
      of, 19.034–19.037

Creditors' winding-up
  convening meetings, 9.031–9.033
  disclosure obligation, 9.010–9.011
  generally, 9.004

Criminal liability
  books of account, and
    company, 4.019–4.020
    directors, 4.019–4.020
    officers, 4.021–4.023
  loans, and, 6.063–6.064
  reporting to DCE, and, 9.080

Criminal prosecutions
  arrest, 15.028–15.032
  commencement, 15.019–15.022

Criminal prosecutions (contd)
company, against, 15.008–15.010
defendants
company, 15.008–15.010
introduction, 15.007
officer in default, 15.011–15.018
detection of offences, 15.006
documentary evidence,
15.042–15.044
double jeopardy, 15.045
evidence collation, 15.027
example, 15.049
introduction, 15.001
jury, 15.041
limitation periods, 15.023–15.026
nature of offences, 15.002–15.005
officer in default, against,
15.011–15.018
penalties, 15.046–15.048
pre-trial procedure
arrest, 15.028–15.032
commencement of
prosecution, 15.019–15.022
evidence collation, 15.027
limitation periods,
15.023–15.026
reform proposals, 15.050
sanctions, 15.046–15.048
'summary trial', 15.004
venue for trial, 15.033–15.040

De facto directors
restriction proceedings, and,
16.056–16.065

Dealings in shares
acquisition of own shares, 2.086
filing obligations, and
acquisition of own shares, 2.086
financing acquisition of own
shares, 2.084–2.085
introduction, 2.081
variation of rights of
shareholders, 2.082–2.083
financing acquisition of own
shares, 2.084–2.085

variation of rights of
shareholders, 2.082–2.083

Debenture holders
registers, and, 3.045–3.047

Debts of related companies
investigation during winding-up,
and, 9.120–9.121

Deemed disqualification orders
acting in breach of restriction order
generally, 20.035–20.036
introduction, 20.034
acting under directions of
disqualified or restricted
person, 20.037
conviction on indictment
comparative legislation,
20.018–20.019
court's role, 20.011
discretion to substitute restriction
order, 20.017
implementation of
disqualification,
20.012–20.013
indictable offences, 20.007
introduction, 20.006
notification by director,
20.014–20.015
period of disqualification,
20.008–20.010
persons affected, 20.016
trigger offences, 20.007
failure to disclose disqualification in
other jurisdiction
effect, 20.029–20.033
general duty, 20.020–20.028
generally, 20.005
grounds
acting in breach of restriction
order, etc., 20.034–20.037
conviction on
indictment, 20.006–20.019
failure to disclose
disqualification in other
jurisdiction, 20.020–20.033
generally, 20.005

Deemed disqualification orders (contd)
grounds (contd)
undischarged
bankruptcy, 20.038–20.041
introduction, 20.001–20.004
undischarged bankruptcy,
20.038–20.041

Defective documents
delivery, 2.167–2.170

Defences
restriction proceedings, and
delay, 17.070–17.075
honesty and
responsibility, 17.001–17.065
just and equitable,
17.066–17.069

Delay
discretionary disqualification orders,
and, 21.016–21.017
restriction proceedings, and,
17.070–17.075

Delivery up
investigation during winding-up,
and, 9.113–9.115

Direction of court
members' meetings, and,
5.049–5.051

Directions to comply
receivers, and, 8.063–8.066

**Director of Corporate Enforcement
(DCE)**
accountability
annual reports, 11.045–11.050
information to METD, 11.051
introduction, 11.044
Oireachtas Committees,
to, 11.052–11.054
agreements with other
bodies, 11.017
annual reports, 11.045–11.050
appointment, 11.003
civil sanctions, 11.036–11.040

Companies Registration Office,
and, 11.022
compliance role
consultations, 11.008
discussions, 11.009–11.014
enforcement, 11.019
interaction with other
bodies, 11.015–11.018
introduction, 11.005
public presentations, 11.006
publications, 11.007
consultations, 11.008
courts, and, 11.027
detection function
disclosure of
information, 11.030–11.031
introduction, 11.021
public complaints, 11.032
reports by auditors, 11.028
reports by directors, 11.028
reports by liquidators, 11.028
reports by professional
bodies, 11.029
reports from other
agencies, 11.022–11.027
disclosure of information
detection, and, 11.030–11.031
investigations, and,
12.130–12.138
discussions
Company Law Review
Group, 11.013
introduction, 11.009
involvement on IAASA, 11.012
miscellaneous, 11.014
submissions on
legislation, 11.010–11.011
duties
accountability, 11.044–11.054
independence, 11.043
introduction, 11.042
protection of
information, 11.055–11.059
enforcement, 11.019
enforcement role
civil sanctions, 11.036–11.040
detection, 11.021–11.032

Director of Corporate Enforcement (DCE) (contd)

enforcement role (contd)
  introduction, 11.020
  investigation, 11.033
  objectives, 11.020
  prosecution, 11.034–11.035
establishment, 11.002
functions, 11.004
functions transferred from
  METD, 11.082
independence, 11.043
information to METD, 11.051
interaction with other bodies
  agreements, 11.017
  introduction, 11.015
  joint presentations, 11.016
  joint publications, 11.018
introduction, 11.001
investigation powers
  disclosure of
    information, 12.130–12.138
  entry and search of
    premises, 12.100–12.129
  introduction, 12.001
  overview, 11.033
  production of books or
    documents, 12.002–12.099
  search of premises,
    12.100–12.129
powers, 11.041
prosecution function, 11.034–11.035
presentations with other
  bodies, 11.016
production of books or documents,
  power to require
  banking documents, and,
    12.085–12.087
  books or documents to be
    produced, 12.052–12.056
  compelling compliance, 12.088
  copies of books or
    documents, 12.075
  duty to give reasons,
    12.047–12.051
  enforcement, 12.088
  entities affected, 12.003–12.010

evidential requirement,
  12.039–12.042
exceptions, 12.082–12.087
expenses of examination, 12.099
explanations of books or
  documents, 12.076–12.079
failure to comply with
  direction, 12.093–12.096
false or misleading
  statements, 12.097
general assistance duty, 12.081
grounds for direction,
  12.011–12.038
interference with integrity of
  books or documents, 12.098
introduction, 12.002
liens, and, 12.082–12.083
location of books or
  documents, 12.080
notice of decision to
  direct, 12.057–12.062
offences, 12.093–12.098
privilege, and, 12.084
reasons, 12.047–12.051
review of decision,
  12.043–12.046
supplemental powers,
  12.074–12.081
third parties, by, 12.064–12.073
time limit for compliance with
  direction, 12.063
use of statements in legal
  proceedings, 12.089–12.092
production of books or documents by
  third parties, power to require
  banking documents, and, 12.072
  documents to be
    produced, 12.068–12.070
  grounds for direction,
    12.064–12.067
  grounds for resisting,
    12.071–12.073
  liens, and, 12.073
  possession of copies of books or
    documents, 12.066
  possession of related books or
    documents, 12.067

Director of Corporate Enforcement (DCE) (contd)

production of books or documents by third parties, power to require (contd)

possession of s 19(1) books or documents, 12.065

privilege, and, 12.071

protection of information

approach of ODCE, 11.059

exceptions to prohibition, 11.058

general prohibition, 11.055

information protected, 11.056–11.057

public complaints, 11.032

public presentations, 11.006

publications

generally, 11.007

jointly with other bodies, 11.018

reports by auditors, 11.028

reports by directors, 11.028

reports by liquidators, 11.028

reports by professional bodies, 11.029

reports from other agencies, 11.022–11.027

search warrants

applications, 12.101–12.103

books or documents not produced, 12.113–12.115

computers, 12.128

designated officers, 12.104–12.105

duration, 12.119–12.121

evidence of offences under Companies Acts, 12.116–12.117

execution, 12.118–12.128

failure to comply with, 12.130

grounds of application, 12.106–12.111

issue, 12.100

'material information', 12.112–12.117

obstruction of, 12.129

persons at premises, and, 12.126

premises, 12.122–12.123

retention of information, 12.127

scope of material authorised to be seized, 12.125

use of force to enter premises, 12.124

validity period, 12.119–12.121

Stock Exchange, and, 11.023–11.026

submissions on legislation, 11.010–11.011

Director of Public Prosecutions (DPP)

civil function, 11.080

criminal functions, 11.079

overview, 11.071

role under Companies Acts

CLEA 2001, 11.078–11.080

pre-CLEA 2001, 11.072–11.077

Directors

auditors, and, 6.004

bankrupts, and, 6.004

bodies corporate, and, 6.004

books of account, and

criminal liability, 4.019–4.020

disqualification, 4.036

personal liability, 4.024–4.035

capacity to act, 6.002

changes in, 2.114–2.115

consent to act, 2.112

directors' interests

and see **Directors' interests**

common law regulation, 6.013–6.023

introduction, 6.011–6.012

loans, 6.026–6.064

registers, 3.037–3.041

remuneration, 6.025

statutory regulation, 6.024–6.090

substantial property transactions, 6.065–6.090

directors reports

accompanying balance sheet, 6.148–6.155

compliance statement, 6.156–6.159

Directors (contd)

disclosure obligations

directors' contracts, 6.097–6.098

directors' interests in company accounts, 6.113–6.114

disqualifications in other jurisdictions, 6.094–6.096

interest in contract with company, 6.099–6.107

interest in shares or debentures, 6.108–6.111

introduction, 6.091–6.093

payments to directors, 6.112

disqualification

and see **Disqualification**

books of account, and, 4.036

consequences of orders, 23.001–23.043

deemed orders, 20.001–20.041

discretionary orders, 21.001–21.051

grounds, 22.001–22.102

striking company off the register, and, 14.035–14.039

excluded persons, 6.004

filing obligations, and

changes in, 2.114–2.115

consent to act, 2.112

formation of company, on, 2.010

Irish resident director, 2.119–2.122

particulars, 2.112

resignation or removal, 2.116–2.118

share qualifications, 2.113

formation of company, and, 2.010

general, 6.001

insolvent companies, of, 6.164–6.169

introduction, 6.001

Irish resident director

filing obligations, 2.119–2.122

generally, 6.006–6.010

offences

alteration of company books, 6.118

falsification of company books, 6.118

fraud by officers of companies in liquidation, of, 6.163

fraudulent trading, 6.119–6.147

furnishing false information, 6.116–6.117

introduction, 6.115

officers of companies in liquidation, by, 6.160–6.162

particulars, 2.112

protection against liability, 6.182–6.187

qualifications, 6.002–6.005

qualifying shareholdings, 6.005

registers, and

contracts, of, 3.042–3.043

general, 3.035–3.036

interests, of, 3.037–3.041

remuneration, 6.025

resignation or removal, 2.116–2.118

restriction proceedings, and

and see **Restriction proceedings**

breach of order, 19.023

costs, 19.024–19.051

defences, 17.001–17.081

effect of declarations, 19.005–19.006

introduction, 16.001–16.002

nature, 16.003–16.020

notification and reporting, 19.007–19.008

period of restriction, 19.001–19.004

persons affected, 16.021–16.067

procedure, 18.001–18.018

register of restricted persons, 19.021–19.022

sanctions

generally, 6.170–6.179

relief, 6.180–6.181

share qualifications, 2.113

striking company off the register, and, 14.035–14.039

Directors' compliance statements

auditors, and, 7.124–7.125

Directors' contracts

disclosure, and, 6.097–6.098

registers, and, 3.042–3.043

Directors' interests

common law regulation, 6.013–6.023

conflict of interests, and

consequences, 6.022–6.023

generally, 6.013–6.021

disclosure, and, 6.113–6.114

independence, and, 6.012

introduction, 6.011–6.012

loans

account and indemnity, 6.056

avoidance of transaction, and, 6.053–6.055

basic rule, 6.027

'credit transaction', 6.029

criminal sanctions, 6.063–6.064

exceptions to prohibition, 6.036–6.051

expenses, and, 6.050

group loans, and, 6.049

'guarantees', 6.030–6.031

introduction, 6.026

liability to account and indemnify, 6.056

ordinary course of business, and, 6.051

personal liability, 6.057–6.062

'quasi-loan', 6.028

sanctions for breach of prohibition, 6.052–6.064

scope of prohibition, 6.027–6.035

special resolutions, and, 6.044–6.048

value of transaction, and, 6.037–6.043

registers, 3.037–3.041

remuneration, 6.025

secret profits, and

consequences, 6.022–6.023

generally, 6.013–6.021

statutory regulation

loans, 6.026–6.064

introduction, 6.024

remuneration, 6.025

substantial property transactions, 6.065–6.090

substantial property transactions

account and indemnity, 6.087

'acquisition', 6.072–6.073

acquisition by companies, 6.070

'arrangement', 6.071

avoidance of transaction, 6.085–6.086

bodies corporate, and, 6.081

capacity as member, 6.084

company approval, and, 6.078–6.080

company in liquidation, and, 6.083

defence, 6.088–6.090

exceptions to prohibition, 6.077–6.084

group arrangements, and, 6.082

introduction, 6.065

liability to account and indemnify, 6.087

'non-cash assets', 6.075

'person connected with such a director', 6.068

prohibited transactions, 6.066–6.076

'requisite value;, 6.076

sanctions for breach of prohibition, 6.085–6.087

'shadow directors', 6.069

special resolutions, and, 6.078–6.080

statutory basis, 6.066

Directors' loans

account and indemnity, 6.056

avoidance of transaction, and, 6.053–6.055

basic rule, 6.027

'credit transaction', 6.029

criminal sanctions, 6.063–6.064

exceptions to prohibition, 6.036–6.051

expenses, and, 6.050

Directors' loans (contd)
group loans, and, 6.049
'guarantees', 6.030–6.031
introduction, 6.026
liability to account and
indemnify, 6.056
ordinary course of business,
and, 6.051
personal liability, 6.057–6.062
'quasi-loan', 6.028
restricted companies, and, 19.018
sanctions for breach of
prohibition, 6.052–6.064
scope of prohibition, 6.027–6.035
special resolutions, and, 6.044–6.048
value of transaction, and, 6.037–
6.043

Directors' remuneration
auditors, and, 7.023
generally, 6.025

Directors reports
accompanying balance sheet, 6.148–
6.155
auditors, and, 7.023
compliance statement, 6.156–6.159

Disclosure
company names, and, 2.142–2.143
directors' contracts, 6.097–6.098
directors' interests in company
accounts, 6.113–6.114
directors' personal
information, 6.092–6.093
disqualifications in other
jurisdictions, 6.094–6.096
interest in contract with company
date for disclosure, 6.102
general notice, 6.103–6.104
interaction with other laws, 6.107
introduction, 6.099
penalty, 6.106
record of disclosure, 6.105
scope, 6.100–6.101
interest in shares or
debentures, 6.108–6.111
introduction, 6.091–6.093

payments to directors, 6.112
restriction proceedings, and, 18.018
secretaries' personal
information, 6.092–6.093

Disclosure of information
detection function, and, 11.030–
11.031
investigation powers, and, 12.130–
12.138

Discovery
restriction proceedings, and, 18.018

Discretion
disqualification orders, and, 21.010
restriction proceedings, and, 16.019

Discretionary disqualification orders
acting under directions of
disqualified person, 23.040–
23.043
acting whilst disqualified
extension of disqualification
period, 23.035
introduction, 23.033
liability for company's
debts, 23.039
no relief, 23.036
offence of, 23.034
repayment of
consideration, 23.037–23.038
applications
delay, 21.016–21.017
hearing, 21.018–21.020
initiation, 21.014–21.015
introduction, 21.013
attempts to rectify or stop
misconduct, 21.044
attitude in the proceedings, 21.050–
21.051
breach of duty (s 160(2)(b))
applicants, 22.013
applications, 22.015–22.020
"guilty", 22.021–22.022
introduction, 22.009
relationship with other
grounds, 22.023–22.025

Discretionary disqualification orders (contd)

breach of duty (s 160(2)(b)) (conts)
  respondents, 22.010–22.012
  scope, 22.014
conditional disqualification,
  23.003–23.010
consequences, 23.001–23.002
considerations to be taken into
  account
    attempts to rectify or stop
      misconduct, 21.044
    attitude in the
      proceedings, 21.050–21.051
    experience and
      qualifications, 21.041–21.043
    impact of disqualification
      order, 21.045–21.047
    introduction, 21.037
    lapse of time, 21.048–21.049
    qualifications, 21.041–21.043
    seniority, 21.038–21.040
costs, 23.024–23.026
delay, and, 21.016–21.017
discretion of court, 21.010
disqualification in another State
  (s 160(2)(i))
  applicants, 22.091
  disqualification period,
    22.095–22.097
  interaction with automatic
    disqualification,
    22.093–22.094
  introduction, 22.090
  overview, 22.092
"disqualification orders", 23.001
duration, 23.011–23.021
experience of respondent,
  21.041–21.043
failing to keep proper books of
  account (s 160(2)(g))
  applicants, 22.066
  applications, 22.070
  generally, 4.036
  introduction, 22.062
  offence of, 22.067–22.069
  respondents, 22.063–22.065

finding of unfitness by inspector
  (s 160(2)(e))
  applicants, 22.050
  applications, 22.052
  introduction, 22.048
  respondents, 22.049
  scope, 22.051
fitness test, 21.024–21.036
fraud in relation to company, etc. (s
  160(2)(a))
  applicants, 22.005
  applications, 22.008
  "guilty", 22.006–22.007
  introduction, 22.002
  respondents, 22.003–22.004
fraudulent and reckless trading
  (s 160(2)(c))
  applicants, 22.028
  applications, 22.029
  comparative law, 22.030–22.031
  introduction, 22.026
  respondents, 22.027
generally, 21.001–21.004
grounds
  breach of duty, 22.009–22.025
  disqualification in another
    State, 22.090–22.097
  failing to keep proper books of
    account, 22.062–22.070
  finding of unfitness by
    inspector, 22.048–22.052
  fraud in relation to company,
    etc., 22.002–22.008
  fraudulent and reckless
    trading, 22.026–22.031
  introduction, 22.001
  persistent default, 22.053–22.061
  restricted persons,
    22.101–22.102
  striking of company off the
    register, 22.071–22.089
  undischarged
    bankruptcy, 22.098–22.100
  unfit to be concerned with
    management of
    company, 22.032–22.047

Discretionary disqualification orders (contd)

hearing of applications,
21.018–21.020

impact of disqualification
order, 21.045–21.047

initiation of applications,
21.014–21.015

introduction, 20.001–20.004

lapse of time, 21.048–21.049

onus of proof, 21.011–21.012

period of disqualification, 23.011–
23.021

persistent default (s 160(2)(f))

applicants, 22.055

applications, 22.059–22.061

introduction, 22.053

means of proof, 22.056–22.058

respondents, 22.054

procedure

delay, 21.016–21.017

hearing of applications,
21.018–21.020

initiation of
applications, 21.014–21.015

introduction, 21.013

undertakings, 21.021–21.023

purpose, 21.005–21.009

qualifications of
respondent, 21.041–21.043

register of disqualified
persons, 23.031–23.032

relief, 23.027–23.030

restricted persons, 22.101–22.102

seniority of respondent,
21.038–21.040

striking of company off the register
(s 160(2)(h))

applicants, 22.073

applications, 22.081–22.089

criteria, 22.074–22.077

defence, 22.078–22.080

introduction, 22.071

respondents, 22.072

substitution of restriction
order, 23.022–23.023

undertakings, 21.021–21.023

undischarged bankruptcy,
22.098–22.100

unfit to be concerned with
management of company
(s 160(2)(d))

applicants, 22.034

conduct in other
companies, 22.035

factors, 22.042–22.047

introduction, 22.032

overlap between ss 150 and
160, 22.036–22.041

respondents, 22.033

unfitness finding by inspector
(s 160(2)(e))

applicants, 22.050

applications, 22.052

introduction, 22.048

respondents, 22.049

scope, 22.051

Disqualification

auditors, and, 7.039–7.040

automatic disqualification orders

acting in breach of restriction
order, etc., 20.034–20.037

conviction on
indictment, 20.006–20.019

failure to disclose
disqualification in other
jurisdiction, 20.020–20.033

generally, 20.005

grounds, 20.005–20.41

introduction, 20.001–20.004

undischarged
bankruptcy, 20.038–20.041

categories of order, 20.002

deemed disqualification orders

acting in breach of restriction
order, etc., 20.034–20.037

conviction on
indictment, 20.006–20.019

failure to disclose
disqualification in other
jurisdiction, 20.020–20.033

generally, 20.005

grounds, 20.005–20.41

Disqualification (contd)
deemed disqualification orders
    (contd)
    introduction, 20.001–20.004
    undischarged
        bankruptcy, 20.038–20.041
directors, and
    books of account, 4.036
    striking company off the
        register, 14.035–14.039
discretionary disqualification orders
    acting whilst
        disqualified, 23.033–23.043
    breach of duty, 22.009–22.025
    conditional disqualification,
        23.003–23.010
    consequences, 23.001–23.002
    considerations to be taken into
        account, 21.037–21.051
    costs, 23.024–23.026
    discretion of court, 21.010
    disqualification in another
        State, 22.090–22.097
    duration, 23.011–23.021
    failing to keep proper books of
        account, 22.062–22.070
    finding of unfitness by
        inspector, 22.048–22.052
    fitness test, 21.024–21.036
    fraud in relation to company,
        etc., 22.002–22.008
    fraudulent and reckless
        trading, 22.026–22.031
    generally, 21.001–21.004
    grounds, 22.001–22.102
    introduction, 20.001–20.004
    onus of proof, 21.011–21.012
    persistent default, 22.053–22.061
    procedure, 21.013–21.023
    purpose, 21.005–21.009
    register of disqualified
        persons, 23.031–23.032
    relief, 23.027–23.030
    restricted persons, 22.101–
        22.102
    striking of company off the
        register, 22.071–22.089

substitution of restriction
    order, 23.022–23.023
undischarged
    bankruptcy, 22.098–22.100
unfit to be concerned with
    management of
    company, 22.032–22.047
introduction, 20.001–20.004
liquidators, and, 9.007–9.009
receivers, and, 8.009–8.013
register of disqualified
    persons, 23.031–23.032
striking company off the register,
    and, 14.035–14.039
types of order, 20.002

Dissipation of assets
investigation during winding-up,
    and, 9.116–9.118

Dissolution
striking company off the register,
    and, 14.027

Distribution of proceeds
receivers, and, 8.052–8.059

Double jeopardy
criminal prosecutions, and, 15.045

Electronic filing agent
generally, 2.165–2.166

Enforcement agencies
Companies Registration Office
    compliance, 11.065–11.070
    disqualification powers, 11.064
    fines and penalties, 11.068
    Integrated Enforcement
        Environment, 11.069
    introduction, 11.060
    prosecution powers, 11.061
    striking companies off the
        register, 11.062
Director of Public Prosecutions
    overview, 11.071
    role under Companies
        Acts, 11.072–11.080

Enforcement agencies (contd)
Irish Auditing and Accounting
Supervisory Authority, 11.089
Minister for Enterprise, Trade and
Employment
background, 11.081
retained functions,
11.085–11.088
transferred functions,
11.082–11.084
Office of the Director of Corporate
Enforcement
appointment, 11.003
compliance role, 11.005–11.019
duties, 11.042–11.059
enforcement role, 11.020–11.040
establishment, 11.002
functions, 11.004
introduction, 11.001
powers, 11.041

Examiners
access to bank details, 10.029
applications for directions, 10.023
appointment
disqualification, 10.003–10.007
introduction, 10.001
publication, 10.008
qualifications, 10.003
termination, 10.009–10.011
claims against a company, 10.024
committee creditors, and, 10.015
contractual liability, 10.013
convening meetings, 10.055–10.058
co-operation of officers and agents
forms, 10.026
refusal to co-operate,
10.027–10.029
scope of obligation, 10.025
costs and expenses
application to court, 10.041
discretion of court,
10.042–10.045
generally, 10.040
priority, 10.046–10.049
directions, 10.014

disposal of charged
property, 10.032–10.036
disqualification, 10.003–10.007
effect of examinership, 10.002
failure of examinership, 10.071
introduction, 10.001–10.002
meetings, 10.017
powers
access to bank details, 10.029
applications for
directions, 10.023
claims against a company, 10.024
co-operation of officers and
agents, 10.025–10.028
costs, expenses and
remuneration, 10.040–10.049
disposal of charged
property, 10.032–10.036
generally, 10.016
meetings, 10.017
pre-petition contracts,
10.020–10.022
pre-petition debts, 10.039
prevention of detriment,
10.018–10.019
related companies, and,
10.037–10.038
vesting directors' powers and
functions, 10.030–10.031
pre-petition contracts,
10.020–10.022
pre-petition debts, 10.039
prevention of detriment,
10.018–10.019
proposals
confirmation, 10.063–10.070
consequences of
confirmation, 10.069
consideration, 10.055–10.058
determination by court,
10.065–10.068
dissemination, 10.062
formulation, 10.051–10.054
hearing, 10.064
introduction, 10.050
reporting, 10.059–10.061

Examiners (contd)
proposals (conts)
revocation of
confirmation, 10.070
qualifications, 10.003
related companies, and,
10.037–10.038
removal, 10.011
remuneration
application to court, 10.041
discretion of court,
10.042–10.045
generally, 10.040
priority, 10.046–10.049
report regarding
irregularities, 10.072
repudiation of contracts, and, 10.020
resignation, 10.010
termination of office, 10.009–10.011
title, 10.012
vesting directors' powers and
functions, 10.030–10.031

Examination of books
receivers, and, 8.060–8.062

Executive directors
restriction proceedings, and,
16.028–16.036

Expenses
loans, and, 6.050

Experience
discretionary disqualification orders,
and, 21.041–21.043

**Extraordinary general meetings
(EGMs)**
adjournments, 5.041–5.044
Chairman, 5.040
conduct of business
adjournments, 5.041–5.044
Chairman, 5.040
quorum, 5.036–5.039
venue of meeting, 5.048
voting, 5.046–5.047
convening
introduction, 5.018

requisition of members,
5.019–5.025
serious loss of capital, 5.026
direction of court, 5.049–5.051
introduction, 5.001
location, 5.027
minutes, 5.052–5.055
nature, 5.017
notices, 5.028–5.029
quorum, 5.036–5.039
requisition of members, 5.019–5.025
resolutions
extended notice, 5.034–5.035
special resolutions, 5.030–5.032
written resolutions, 5.033
serious loss of capital, 5.026
special resolutions, 5.030–5.032
venue, 5.048
voting, 5.046–5.047
written resolutions, 5.033

Failing to keep proper books of account
and see **Discretionary
disqualification orders**
applicants, 22.066
applications, 22.070
introduction, 22.062
offence of, 22.067–22.069
respondents, 22.063–22.065

**Failure to disclose disqualification in
other jurisdiction**
and see **Deemed disqualification
orders**
effect, 20.029–20.033
general duty, 20.020–20.028

Falsification of company books
criminal offences, and, 6.118

Filing obligations
annual return
annexed documents, 2.022–2.032
content, 2.018–2.021
date, 2.033–2.052
failure to file, 2.058
grounds of rejection, 2.057

Filing obligations (contd)
  annual return (contd)
    groups of companies,
      2.053–2.056
    introduction, 2.017
  charges
    commission, 2.099
    effect of non-registration, 2.106
    effect of registration,
      2.101–2.105
    foreign-incorporated
      companies, 2.095
    introduction, 2.087
    judgment mortgages, 2.097
    obligation to register, 2.088
    particulars to be
      registered., 2.098
    property outside the State, 2.090–
      2.094
    register of debenture
      holders, 2.107
    registrable charges, 2.089–2.097
    release from charge, 2.108
    series of debentures, 2.096
    time limits for registration, 2.100
  companies incorporated outside the
    State
    establishing branch in
      State, 2.150–2.155
    establishing place of business in
      State, 2.147–2.149
  company name
    business name, 2.146
    change of, 2.144
    disclosure, 2.142–2.143
    introduction, 2.123
    'limited', 'teoranta' or
      'plc', 2.124–2.134
    prohibited names, 2.135–2.141
    publication, 2.142–2.143
    reservation of, 2.145
  directors and secretaries
    changes in, 2.114–2.115
    consent to act, 2.112
    Irish resident director,
      2.119–2.122
    particulars, 2.112

    resignation or removal,
      2.116–2.118
    share qualifications, 2.113
  form of documents
    delivery of defective
      documents, 2.167–2.170
    electronic filing agent,
      2.165–2.166
    general requirements, 2.164
    introduction, 2.163
  formation of company
    activity in State, 2.013–2.014
    articles of association, 2.006–
      2.009
    directors' particulars, 2.010
    effect of registration, 2.015
    Form A1, 2.010–2.011
    members, 2.016
    memorandum of
      association, 2.002–2.005
    registered office, 2.011–2.012
    secretary's particulars, 2.010
    section 3 statement, 2.010–2.011
  introduction, 2.001
  members
    increase in number, 2.067
    introduction, 2.066
    location of register, 2.068–2.070
  prospectus
    introduction, 2.059
    Investment Funds, Companies etc
      Act 2005, under, 2.061–2.065
    Prospectus Regulations 2005,
      under, 2.060
  public limited companies, 2.156
  re-registration
    introduction, 2.157
    plc as private company, of, 2.162
    private company as plc,
      of, 2.158–2.161
  resolutions and agreements,
    2.109–2.111
  share capital
    allotment of shares, 2.071
    alterations, 2.072–2.073
    increases, 2.074–2.075
    reduction, 2.076–2.080

Filing obligations (contd)
  share dealings
    acquisition of own shares, 2.086
    financing acquisition of own
      shares, 2.084–2.085
    introduction, 2.081
    variation of rights of
      shareholders, 2.082–2.083

Financing acquisition of own shares
  filing obligations, and, 2.084–2.085

Finding of unfitness by inspector
  and see **Discretionary
    disqualification orders**
  applicants, 22.050
  applications, 22.052
  introduction, 22.048
  respondents, 22.049
  scope, 22.051

Fitness test
  discretionary disqualification orders,
    and, 21.024–21.036

Foreign-incorporated companies
  charges, and, 2.095
  filing obligations, and
    establishing branch in
      State, 2.150–2.155
    establishing place of business in
      State, 2.147–2.149

Foreign property
  charges, and, 2.090–2.094

Form A1
  activity in State, 2.013–2.014
  generally, 2.010–2.011
  registered office, 2.012

Formation of company
  activity in State, 2.013–2.014
  articles of association, 2.006–2.009
  directors' particulars, 2.010
  filing obligations
    activity in State, 2.013–2.014
    articles of association,
      2.006–2.009
    directors' particulars, 2.010

  effect of registration, 2.015
  Form A1, 2.010–2.011
  members, 2.016
  memorandum of
    association, 2.002–2.005
  registered office, 2.011–2.012
  secretary's particulars, 2.010
  section 3 statement, 2.010–2.012
  Form A1
    activity in State, 2.013–2.014
    generally, 2.010–2.011
    registered office, 2.012
  members, 2.016
  memorandum of association
    effect of registration, 2.015
    generally, 2.002–2.005
  registered office, 2.011–2.012
  secretary's particulars, 2.010
  section 3 statement, 2.010–2.012

**Fraud by officers of companies in
liquidation**
  criminal offences, and, 6.163

Fraud detection
  auditors, and, 7.071–7.077

Fraud in relation to company, etc.
  and see **Discretionary
    disqualification orders**
  applicants, 22.005
  applications, 22.008
  "guilty", 22.006–22.007
  introduction, 22.002
  respondents, 22.003–22.004

Fraudulent trading
  'carrying on of the business of a
    company', 6.123–6.126
  criteria, 6.119
  discretionary disqualification orders,
    and
    applicants, 22.028
    applications, 22.029
    comparative law, 22.030–22.031
    introduction, 22.026
    respondents, 22.027
  fraudulent purpose, 6.142–6.143
  'intent to defraud', 6.138–6.141

introduction, 6.119–6.121
knowledge requirement, 6.131–6.133
meaning, 6.119
participation requirement,
6.127–6.130
requisite intention, 6.134–6.143
respondents, 6.122
sentencing, 6.144–6.147
standard of proof, 6.121

Funding purchase of company's shares
restricted companies, and, 19.017

Furnishing false information
criminal offences, and, 6.116–6.117

Grandfather rights
auditors, and, 7.029

Group accounts
auditors, and, 7.024–7.025

Group arrangements
substantial property transactions,
and, 6.082

Group loans
generally, 6.049

Groups of companies
auditors, and, 7.024–7.025
filing accounts, and
parent company exception, 2.055
subsidiary company
exception, 2.056

Guarantees
loans, and, 6.030–6.031

Honest and responsible conduct
and see **Restriction proceedings**
attendance at Board
meetings, 17.047–17.048
compliance with Companies
Acts, 17.013–17.015
conduct in relation to other
companies, 17.010
dealings between director and
company, 17.064

dealings with Revenue
Commissioners, 17.058–17.063
failure of company, 17.012
financial affairs, 17.040–17.045
general interpretation,
17.011–17.030
introduction, 17.001–17.003
just and equitable, and, 17.066–
17.069
'La Moselle' test, 17.016–17.030
miscellaneous factors, 17.065
non-financial information, 17.046
proper books and records,
17.032–17.039
relationship with other
companies, 17.049–17.057
relevant factors, 17.031–17.065
relevant period of time,
17.004–17.009
scope, 17.004–17.010

Increases in share capital
filing obligations, and, 2.074–2.075

Independence
auditors, and, 7.054–7.066

Indictable offences, reporting of
certainty, 7.104
Companies Act, under, 7.109–7.111
'company, officer or agent',
7.105–7.108
discretion, and, 7.112
exceptions to duty to report, 7.113
'in the course and by virtue of' audit
work, 7.085–7.093
'information', 7.094–7.097
introduction, 7.083–7.084
legal professional privilege,
7.119–7.122
level of certainty, 7.104
'opinion to be formed', 7.098–7.100
other Acts, under, 7.126–7.128
protection from liability, 7.123
provision of information, books and
documents, 7.116–7.118
'reasonable grounds', 7.101–7.103

Indictable offences, reporting of (contd)
relevant offences, 7.109–7.111
timing of notification, 7.114–7.115

Insolvent companies
directors, and, 6.164–6.169

Inspection
books of account, and, 4.013–4.017
liquidators, and
compulsory winding-up, 9.107
voluntary winding-up, 9.108
register of members, and,
3.013–3.017

Integrated Enforcement Environment
generally, 11.069

Interest in contracts with company
date for disclosure, 6.102
general notice, 6.103–6.104
interaction with other laws, 6.107
introduction, 6.099
penalty, 6.106
record of disclosure, 6.105
scope, 6.100–6.101

Interest in shares or debentures
generally, 6.108–6.111

Investigation during winding-up
companies not in liquidation,
and, 9.122–9.127
debts of related companies,
9.120–9.121
delivery up, 9.113–9.115
examination of persons, 9.109–9.110
inspection of books, 9.107–9.108
introduction, 9.106
orders for payment, 9.113–9.115
power of arrest, 9.111–9.112
prevention of removal or dissipation
of assets, 9.116–9.118
return of company property, 9.119
search and seizure, 9.113–9.115

**Investigation into membership of
company**
appointment of inspectors,
13.044–13.046

attendance and assistance
general obligation,
13.083–13.084
self-incrimination, 13.085–
13.086
use of answers, 13.087–13.090
banking documents, and,
13.091–13.096
conduct
directions by court,
13.060–13.062
fair procedure, 13.059
information regarding
offences, 13.063–13.064
privacy, 13.065
role of inspectors, 13.055–13.058
DCE's powers, 13.050
directions by court, 13.060–13.062
examinations, 13.084
expenses
generally, 13.125–13.129
introduction, 13.049
failure to comply, 13.097–13.100
fair procedure, 13.059
grounds, 13.045
information regarding
offences, 13.063–13.064
introduction, 13.001
liens, and, 13.081
powers
attendance, examinations and
assistance, 13.083–13.090
banking documents,
13.091–13.096
failure to comply, 13.097–13.100
generally, 13.047
introduction, 13.066
production of
documents, 13.067–13.082
privacy, 13.065
privilege, and, 13.082
production of documents
agents, by, 13.072
'books and documents', 13.068
books and documents to be
produced, 13.074–13.078
general, 13.068

Investigation into membership of company (contd)
    production of documents (contd)
        introduction, 13.067
        liens, and, 13.081
        'officers and agents', by,
            13.069–13.071
        other persons, by, 13.072–13.073
        privilege, and, 13.082
        time limits, 13.079–13.080
    publication of reports, 13.048
    report
        challenges to, 13.104–13.110
        consequences, 13.119–13.121
        form, 13.101–13.103
        publication, 13.111–13.118
        use, 13.122–13.124
    role of inspectors, 13.055–13.058
    scope, 13.046
    self-incrimination, 13.085–13.086
    share dealing, 13.052
    share restrictions, 13.051
    use of answers, 13.087–13.090

Investigation of company affairs
    appointment of inspectors
        applicants, 13.002–13.008
        evidence, 13.025–13.031
        external applicants,
            13.006–13.008
        grounds, 13.009–13.024
        internal applicants,
            13.003–13.005
    attendance and assistance
        general obligation,
            13.083–13.084
        self-incrimination,
            13.085–13.086
        use of answers, 13.087–13.090
    banking documents, and,
        13.091–13.096
    companies affected
        companies in process of winding
            up, 13.035
        foreign companies,
            13.033–13.034
        general, 13.032

        related companies,
            13.036–13.041
    conduct
        directions by court,
            13.060–13.062
        fair procedure, 13.059
        information regarding
            offences, 13.063–13.064
        privacy, 13.065
        role of inspectors, 13.055–13.058
    directions by court, 13.060–13.062
    evidence
        s 7(2) CA 1990
            applications, 13.025–13.026
        s 8(1) CA 1990
            applications, 13.027–13.031
    examinations, 13.084
    expenses, 13.125–13.129
    failure to comply, 13.097–13.100
    fair procedure, 13.059
    foreign-incorporated companies,
        and, 13.033–13.034
    grounds, 13.009–13.024
    information regarding
        offences, 13.063–13.064
    introduction, 13.001
    liens, and, 13.081
    powers
        attendance, examinations and
            assistance, 13.083–13.090
        banking documents,
            13.091–13.096
        failure to comply, 13.097–13.100
        introduction, 13.066
        production of
            documents, 13.067–13.082
    privacy, 13.065
    privilege, and, 13.082
    production of documents
        agents, by, 13.072
        'books and documents', 13.068
        books and documents to be
            produced, 13.074–13.078
        general, 13.068
        introduction, 13.067
        liens, and, 13.081

Investigation of company affairs (contd)
    production of documents (contd)
        'officers and agents', by,
            13.069–13.071
        other persons, by, 13.072–13.073
        privilege, and, 13.082
        time limits, 13.079–13.080
    related companies, and,
        13.036–13.041
    report
        challenges to, 13.104–13.110
        consequences, 13.119–13.121
        form, 13.101–13.103
        publication, 13.111–13.118
        use, 13.122–13.124
    request of other authority, at, 13.042
    role of inspectors, 13.055–13.058
    self-incrimination, 13.085–13.086
    use of answers, 13.087–13.090

**Irish Auditing and Accounting
Supervisory Authority**
    functions transferred from
        METD, 11.084
    generally, 11.089

Irish resident director
    filing obligations, 2.119–2.122
    generally, 6.006–6.010
    striking company off the register,
        and, 14.014–14.019

Judgment mortgages
    charges, and, 2.097

Just and equitable defence
    restriction proceedings, and, 17.066–
        17.069

Lapse of time
    and see **Delay**
    discretionary disqualification orders,
        and, 21.048–21.049

Legal professional privilege
    auditors, and, 7.119–7.122

Liens
    production of books or documents,
        and
        generally, 12.082–12.083
        third party disclosure, 12.073

'Limited', 'teoranta' or 'plc'
    exemption from use, 2.127–2.134
    improper use, 2.125–2.126
    obligation to use, 2.124

Liquidators
    appointment
        company, by, 9.003
        consent, 9.013
        court, by, 9.002
        creditors, by, 9.004
        creditors' disclosure
            obligation, 9.010–9.011
        disqualification, 9.007–9.009
        methods, 9.002–9.006
        notification, 9.017–9.021
        prohibition on inducement, 9.012
        qualifications, 9.007
    compliance obligations
        convening meetings, 9.023–9.033
        introduction, 9.022
        reporting to court, 9.101–9.105
        reporting to DCE, 9.037–9.085
        reporting to DPP, 9.086–9.100
        returns, 9.034–9.035
    compulsory winding-up, and
        appointment of liquidator, 9.002
        convening meetings, 9.023–9.024
        disclosure duty, 9.021
        inspection of books, 9.107
        notification of
            appointment, 9.018
        reporting to DPP, 9.087–9.091
    convening meetings
        compulsory winding-up,
            9.023–9.024
        creditors' voluntary winding-
            up, 9.031–9.033
        members' voluntary winding-
            up, 9.025–9.030
    creditors' winding-up, and
        convening meetings, 9.031–9.033

Liquidators (contd)

creditors' winding-up, and (contd)

disclosure obligation,
9.010–9.011

generally, 9.004

disqualification, 9.007–9.009

inspection of books

compulsory winding-up, 9.107

voluntary winding-up, 9.108

introduction, 9.001

investigation during winding-up

delivery up, 9.113–9.115

examination of persons,
9.109–9.110

inspection of books, 9.107–9.108

introduction, 9.106

orders for payment, 9.113–9.115

power of arrest, 9.111–9.112

prevention of removal or
dissipation of assets,
9.116–9.118

search and seizure, 9.113–9.115

investigation of

production of books, 9.128

professional body, by, 9.129

notification of appointment

Chairman's duty, 9.013

company's duty, 9.019

general duty, 9.021

introduction, 9.017

liquidator's duty, 9.018

voluntary liquidator's duty, 9.020

production of books, 9.128

qualifications, 9.007

removal, 9.014–9.016

reporting to court, 9.101–9.105

reporting to DCE (s 56 CLEA 2001)

additional reports, 9.077–9.078

administrative fines for
default, 9.081

approach of ODCE, 9.084–9.085

auditing accounts, 9.062–9.069

company details, 9.052–9.057

company directors, 9.058–9.061

court orders requiring remedy of
default, 9.082–9.083

criminal liability for non-
compliance, 9.080

final report, 9.075

insolvent companies, 9.039

introduction, 9.037–9.038

legal proceedings, 9.070–9.074

liquidator details, 9.051

liquidator's statement, 9.076

minutes of creditors'
meeting, 9.062

pending proceedings, 9.070

prosecution for non-
compliance, 9.080

provisional liquidations,
in, 9.042–9.046

report to creditors, 9.062–9.069

required information,
9.048–9.076

sanctions, 9.079–9.083

scope of obligation, 9.039–9.047

section headings, 9.050

statement of affairs, 9.062–9.069

statement to creditors'
meeting, 9.062

temporal scope of
obligation, 9.047

voluntary liquidations, in, 9.040–
9.041

reporting to DPP (s 299 CA 1963)

compulsory winding-up,
9.087–9.091

failure to assist DCE, 9.098

further duties in event of
prosecution, 9.096–9.100

introduction, 9.086

obligation to assist DCE, 9.097

role of DCE, 9.100

role of DPP, 9.099

voluntary winding-up,
9.092–9.095

reporting to DPP (compulsory
winding-up)

applicants, 9.088

grounds, 9.090

introduction, 9.087

liquidator's duties, 9.091

scope obligation, 9.089

Liquidators (contd)

reporting to DPP (voluntary
winding-up)
court directions, 9.094–9.095
introduction, 9.092
liquidator's report, 9.093
returns, 9.034–9.035
voluntary winding-up, and
appointment of liquidator, 9.003
convening meetings, 9.025–9.030
disclosure duty, 9.021
inspection of books, 9.108
notification of
appointment, 9.019–9.020
reporting to DPP, 9.092–9.095

Litigation

striking company off the register,
and, 14.034

Loans to directors

account and indemnity, 6.056
avoidance of transaction, and,
6.053–6.055
basic rule, 6.027
'credit transaction', 6.029
criminal sanctions, 6.063–6.064
exceptions to prohibition,
6.036–6.051
expenses, and, 6.050
group loans, and, 6.049
'guarantees', 6.030–6.031
introduction, 6.026
liability to account and
indemnify, 6.056
ordinary course of business,
and, 6.051
personal liability, 6.057–6.062
'quasi-loan', 6.028
restricted companies, and, 19.018
sanctions for breach of
prohibition, 6.052–6.064
scope of prohibition, 6.027–6.035
special resolutions, and, 6.044–6.048
value of transaction, and,
6.037–6.043

Maintenance of registers

charges, of, 3.044
debenture holders, of, 3.045–3.047
directors and secretaries, of,
3.035–3.036
directors' contracts, of, 3.042–3.043
directors' interests, of, 3.037–3.041
form, 3.002–3.003
introduction, 3.001
members, of
closing, 3.029–3.033
contents, 3.004–3.008
date of registration, 3.009
index, 3.010
inspection, 3.013–3.017
location, 3.011–3.012
rectification, 3.023–3.028
refusal to register, 3.018–3.022
sanctions for default, 3.034

Members

filing obligations, and
formation of company, 2.016
increase in number, 2.067
introduction, 2.066
location of register, 2.068–2.070
formation of company, and, 2.016
increase in number, 2.067
location of register, 2.068–2.070
meetings, and
and see **Members' meetings**
annual general meetings,
5.002–5.016
conduct of business, 5.036–5.048
direction of court, 5.049–5.051
extraordinary general
meetings, 5.017–5.029
introduction, 5.001
minutes, 5.052–5.055
resolutions, 5.030–5.035
registers, and
closing, 3.029–3.033
contents, 3.004–3.008
date of registration, 3.009
index, 3.010
inspection, 3.013–3.017
location, 3.011–3.012

Members (contd)
registers, and (contd)
rectification, 3.023–3.028
refusal to register, 3.018–3.022
sanctions for default, 3.034

Members' meetings
adjournments, 5.041–5.044
annual general meetings
addressees of notice, 5.011
content of notice, 5.010
directions to convene, 5.004–
5.006
exemption for single member
private companies, 5.016
failure to convene, 5.007–5.009
failure to notify, 5.014
general business 5.003
intervals between, 5.002
location, 5.015
notices, 5.010–5.014
service of notice, 5.013
timing of notice, 5.012
auditors, and, 7.070
Chairman, 5.040
conduct of business
adjournments, 5.041–5.044
Chairman, 5.040
quorum, 5.036–5.039
venue of meeting, 5.048
voting, 5.046–5.047
direction of court, 5.049–5.051
examiners, and
generally, 10.055–10.058
introduction, 10.017
extraordinary general meetings
convening, 5.018–5.026
location, 5.027
nature, 5.017
notices, 5.028–5.029
requisition of members,
5.019–5.025
serious loss of capital, 5.026
introduction, 5.001
liquidators' obligations, and
compulsory winding-up,
9.023–9.024

creditors' voluntary winding-
up, 9.031–9.033
members' voluntary winding-
up, 9.025–9.030
minutes, 5.052–5.055
quorum, 5.036–5.039
resolutions
extended notice, 5.034–5.035
special resolutions, 5.030–5.032
written resolutions, 5.033
special resolutions, 5.030–5.032
venue, 5.048
voting, 5.046–5.047
written resolutions, 5.033

Memorandum of association
effect of registration, 2.015
generally, 2.002–2.005

**Minister for Enterprise, Trade and
Employment (METF)**
background, 11.081
retained functions
introduction, 11.085
investigations, 11.087
postponement of AGM or annual
return date, 11.088
showing particulars on headed
paper, 11.086
transferred functions
to CRO, 11.083
to DCE, 11.082
to IAASA, 11.084

Minutes
members' meetings, and,
5.052–5.055

Name of company
business name, 2.146
change of, 2.144
disclosure, 2.142–2.143
introduction, 2.123
'limited', 'teoranta' or 'plc'
exemption from use, 2.127–2.134
improper use, 2.125–2.126
obligation to use, 2.124

Name of company (contd)
prohibited names
banks, 2.139
insurance, 2.140
introduction, 2.135
legislative restrictions,
2.139–2.140
miscellaneous restrictions, 2.141
similarity to other company
names, 2.137–2.138
undesirable names, 2.136
publication, 2.142–2.143
reservation of, 2.145

Nominee directors
restriction proceedings, and,
16.066–16.067

Non-executive directors
restriction proceedings, and,
16.028–16.036

Notice party costs orders
restriction proceedings, and, 19.051

Offences
alteration of company books, 6.118
falsification of company
books, 6.118
fraud by officers of companies in
liquidation, of, 6.163
fraudulent trading
'carrying on of the business of a
company', 6.123–6.126
criteria, 6.119
fraudulent purpose, 6.142–6.143
'intent to defraud', 6.138–6.141
introduction, 6.119–6.121
knowledge requirement,
6.131–6.133
meaning, 6.119
participation requirement,
6.127–6.130
requisite intention, 6.134–6.143
respondents, 6.122
sentencing, 6.144–6.147
standard of proof, 6.121
furnishing false information,
6.116–6.117
introduction, 6.115
officers of companies in liquidation,
by, 6.160–6.162

**Office of the Director of Corporate
Enforcement (ODCE)**
accountability
annual reports, 11.045–11.050
information to METD, 11.051
introduction, 11.044
Oireachtas Committees,
to, 11.052–11.054
agreements with other
bodies, 11.017
annual reports, 11.045–11.050
appointment, 11.003
civil sanctions, 11.036–11.040
Companies Registration Office,
and, 11.022
compliance role
consultations, 11.008
discussions, 11.009–11.014
enforcement, 11.019
interaction with other
bodies, 11.015–11.018
introduction, 11.005
public presentations, 11.006
publications, 11.007
consultations, 11.008
courts, and, 11.027
detection function
disclosure of
information, 11.030–11.031
introduction, 11.021
public complaints, 11.032
reports by auditors, 11.028
reports by directors, 11.028
reports by liquidators, 11.028
reports by professional
bodies, 11.029
reports from other
agencies, 11.022–11.027
disclosure of information,
11.030–11.031

Office of the Director of Corporate Enforcement (ODCE) (contd)

discussions
  Company Law Review
    Group, 11.013
  introduction, 11.009
  involvement on IAASA, 11.012
  miscellaneous, 11.014
  submissions on
    legislation, 11.010–11.011
duties
  accountability, 11.044–11.054
  independence, 11.043
  introduction, 11.042
  protection of
    information, 11.055–11.059
enforcement, 11.019
enforcement role
  civil sanctions, 11.036–11.040
  detection, 11.021–11.032
  introduction, 11.020
  investigation, 11.033
  objectives, 11.020
  prosecution, 11.034–11.035
establishment, 11.002
functions, 11.004
independence, 11.043
information to METD, 11.051
interaction with other bodies
  agreements, 11.017
  introduction, 11.015
  joint presentations, 11.016
  joint publications, 11.018
introduction, 11.001
investigation powers
  disclosure of
    information, 12.130–12.138
  entry and search of
    premises, 12.100–12.129
  introduction, 12.001
  overview, 11.033
  production of books or
    documents, 12.002–12.099
  search of premises,
    12.100–12.129
powers, 11.041
prosecution function, 11.034–11.035

presentations with other
  bodies, 11.016
production of books or documents,
  power to require
  banking documents, and,
    12.085–12.087
  books or documents to be
    produced, 12.052–12.056
  compelling compliance, 12.088
  copies of books or
    documents, 12.075
  duty to give reasons,
    12.047–12.051
  enforcement, 12.088
  entities affected, 12.003–12.010
  evidential requirement,
    12.039–12.042
  exceptions, 12.082–12.087
  expenses of examination, 12.099
  explanations of books or
    documents, 12.076–12.079
  failure to comply with
    direction, 12.093–12.096
  false or misleading
    statements, 12.097
  general assistance duty, 12.081
  grounds for direction,
    12.011–12.038
  interference with integrity of
    books or documents, 12.098
  introduction, 12.002
  liens, and, 12.082–12.083
  location of books or
    documents, 12.080
  notice of decision to
    direct, 12.057–12.062
  offences, 12.093–12.098
  privilege, and, 12.084
  reasons, 12.047–12.051
  review of decision,
    12.043–12.046
  supplemental powers,
    12.074–12.081
  third parties, by, 12.064–12.073
  time limit for compliance with
    direction, 12.063

Office of the Director of Corporate Enforcement (ODCE) (contd)
production of books or documents, power to require (contd)
use of statements in legal proceedings, 12.089–12.092
production of books or documents by third parties, power to require
banking documents, and, 12.072
documents to be produced, 12.068–12.070
grounds for direction, 12.064–12.067
grounds for resisting, 12.071–12.073
liens, and, 12.073
possession of copies of books or documents, 12.066
possession of related books or documents, 12.067
possession of s 19(1) books or documents, 12.065
privilege, and, 12.071
protection of information
approach of ODCE, 11.059
exceptions to prohibition, 11.058
general prohibition, 11.055
information protected, 11.056–11.057
public complaints, 11.032
public presentations, 11.006
publications
generally, 11.007
jointly with other bodies, 11.018
reports by auditors, 11.028
reports by directors, 11.028
reports by liquidators, 11.028
reports by professional bodies, 11.029
reports from other agencies, 11.022–11.027
search warrants
applications, 12.101–12.103
books or documents not produced, 12.113–12.115

computers, 12.128
designated officers, 12.104–12.105
duration, 12.119–12.121
evidence of offences under Companies Acts, 12.116–12.117
execution, 12.118–12.128
failure to comply with, 12.130
grounds of application, 12.106–12.111
issue, 12.100
'material information', 12.112–12.117
obstruction of, 12.129
persons at premises, and, 12.126
premises, 12.122–12.123
retention of information, 12.127
scope of material authorised to be seized, 12.125
use of force to enter premises, 12.124
validity period, 12.119–12.121
Stock Exchange, and, 11.023–11.026
submissions on legislation, 11.010–11.011

Officers of companies in liquidation
criminal offences, and, 6.160–6.162

Onus of proof
and see **Burden of proof**
discretionary disqualification orders, and, 21.011–21.012

Parent companies
filing accounts, and, 2.055

Persistent default
and see **Discretionary disqualification orders**
applicants, 22.055
applications, 22.059–22.061
introduction, 22.053
means of proof, 22.056–22.058
respondents, 22.054

Personal liability
    books of account, and, 4.024–4.035
    loans, and, 6.057–6.062

'Plc'
    and see **Public limited companies**
    exemption from use, 2.127–2.134
    improper use, 2.125–2.126
    obligation to use, 2.124

Power of arrest
    investigation during winding-up,
      and, 9.111–9.112

Prevention of removal or dissipation of assets
    investigation during winding-up,
      and, 9.116–9.118

Privilege
    production of books or documents,
      and
        generally, 12.084
        third party disclosure, 12.071

Production of books
    liquidators, and, 9.128

Production of books or documents, power to require
    acts of omissions are or are likely to
      be unlawful, 12.033–12.035
    advance decision, 12.057–12.062
    banking documents, and,
      12.085–12.087
    body formed for fraudulent
      purpose, 12.036
    books or documents to be
      produced, 12.052–12.056
    company's affairs conducted in
      unfairly prejudicial
      manner, 12.029–12.031
    company's affairs conducted with
      fraudulent purpose, 12.028
    company's affairs conducted with
      intent to defraud, 12.026–12.027
    compelling compliance, 12.088
    copies of books or
      documents, 12.075

DCE's power, 12.002
duty to give reasons, 12.047–12.051
enforcement, 12.088
entities affected
    companies formed and registered
      under Companies
      Acts, 12.004
    companies registered under Part
      IX of CA 1963, 12.007
    existing companies, 12.005
    foreign-incorporated
      companies, 12.009
    insurance undertakings, 12.010
    introduction, 12.003
    joint stock companies, 12.006
    s 325 CA 1963
      companies, 12.006
    unregistered companies, 12.008
evidential requirement,
    12.039–12.042
exceptions
    banking documents,
      12.085–12.087
    liens, 12.082–12.083
    privilege, 12.084
existing companies, and, 12.005
expenses of examination, 12.099
explanations of books or
    documents, 12.076–12.079
failure to comply with
    direction, 12.093–12.096
false or misleading
    statements, 12.097
foreign-incorporated companies,
    and, 12.009
general assistance duty, 12.081
grounds for direction
    acts of omissions are or are likely
      to be unlawful, 12.033–12.035
    body formed for fraudulent
      purpose, 12.036
    company's affairs conducted in
      unfairly prejudicial
      manner, 12.029–12.031
    company's affairs conducted with
      fraudulent purpose, 12.028

Production of books or documents,
power to require (contd)
  grounds for direction (contd)
    company's affairs conducted with
      intent to defraud,
      12.026–12.027
    introduction, 12.011
    necessity to appoint inspector
      needs investigation,
      12.012–12.025
    other company, 12.038
    unfairly prejudicial act or
      omission, 12.032
    'unlawful purpose', 12.037
  insurance undertakings, and, 12.010
  interference with integrity of books
    or documents, 12.098
  introduction, 12.002
  joint stock companies, and, 12.006
  liens, and
    generally, 12.082–12.083
    third party disclosure, 12.073
  location of books or
    documents, 12.080
  necessity to appoint inspector needs
    investigation, 12.012–12.025
  notice of decision to direct,
    12.057–12.062
  offences, 12.093–12.098
  privilege, and
    generally, 12.084
    third party disclosure, 12.071
  reasons, 12.047–12.051
  review of decision, 12.043–12.046
  s 325 CA 1963 companies,
    and, 12.006
  supplemental powers
    copies of books or
      documents, 12.075
    explanations of books or
      documents, 12.076–12.079
    general assistance duty, 12.081
    introduction, 12.074
    location of books or
      documents, 12.080
  third parties, by
    banking documents, and, 12.072

    documents to be
      produced, 12.068–12.070
    grounds for direction,
      12.064–12.067
    grounds for resisting,
      12.071–12.073
    liens, and, 12.073
    possession of copies of books or
      documents, 12.066
    possession of related books or
      documents, 12.067
    possession of s 19(1) books or
      documents, 12.065
    privilege, and, 12.071
    time limit for compliance with
      direction, 12.063
    unfairly prejudicial act or
      omission, 12.032
    'unlawful purpose', 12.037
    unregistered companies, and, 12.008
    use of statements in legal
      proceedings, 12.089–12.092

Prohibited company names
  banks, 2.139
  insurance, 2.140
  introduction, 2.135
  legislative restrictions, 2.139–2.140
  miscellaneous restrictions, 2.141
  similarity to other company
    names, 2.137–2.138
  undesirable names, 2.136

Proper books of account
  auditors, and, 7.077–7.082
  content, 4.009
  criminal liability
    company, 4.019–4.020
    directors, 4.019–4.020
    officers, 4.021–4.023
  currency, 4.011
  deemed proper books, 4.010
  discretionary disqualification orders,
    and
    applicants, 22.066
    applications, 22.070
    generally, 4.036
    introduction, 22.062

Proper books of account (contd)
 discretionary disqualification orders,
   and (contd)
     offence of, 22.067–22.069
     respondents, 22.063–22.065
 form, 4.005
 generally, 4.002
 inspection, 4.013–4.017
 introduction, 4.001
 language, 4.006
 location, 4.012
 meaning, 4.003–4.004
 personal liability, 4.024–4.035
 preservation, 4.018
 statutory basis, 4.002
 updating, 4.007–4.008

Property outside the State
 charges, and, 2.090–2.094

Prosecutions
 arrest, 15.028–15.032
 commencement, 15.019–15.022
 company, against, 15.008–15.010
 defendants
   company, 15.008–15.010
   introduction, 15.007
   officer in default, 15.011–15.018
 detection of offences, 15.006
 documentary evidence,
   15.042–15.044
 double jeopardy, 15.045
 evidence collation, 15.027
 example, 15.049
 introduction, 15.001
 jury, 15.041
 limitation periods, 15.023–15.026
 nature of offences, 15.002–15.005
 officer in default, against,
   15.011–15.018
 penalties, 15.046–15.048
 pre-trial procedure
   arrest, 15.028–15.032
   commencement of
     prosecution, 15.019–15.022
   evidence collation, 15.027

 limitation periods, 15.023–
   15.026
 reform proposals, 15.050
 sanctions, 15.046–15.048
 'summary trial', 15.004
 venue for trial, 15.033–15.040

Prospectus
 introduction, 2.059
 Investment Funds, Companies etc
   Act 2005, under, 2.061–2.065
 Prospectus Regulations 2005,
   under, 2.060

Protection from liability
 auditors, and, 7.123
 directors, and, 6.182–6.187

Public interest
 restriction proceedings, and, 16.005

Public limited companies
 company name, and
   exemption from use, 2.127–2.134
   improper use, 2.125–2.126
   obligation to use, 2.124
 filing obligations, and, 2.156
 reduction of share capital,
   and, 2.079–2.080
 re-registration, and
   introduction, 2.157
   plc as private company, of, 2.162
   private company as plc,
     of, 2.158–2.161
 striking company off the register,
   and, 14.021–14.024

Publication
 company names, and, 2.142–2.143
 receivers' appointment, and
   general requirements, 8.005
   person appointing, by,
     8.002–8.004
   receiver's duty,. 8.006–8.008

Purchase of company's own shares
 restricted companies, and, 19.017

Qualifications
auditors, and
acting whilst not
qualified, 7.041–7.053
authorisation, 7.028–7.031
disqualification, 7.039–7.040
generally, 7.028
grandfather rights, 7.029
discretionary disqualification orders,
and, 21.041–21.043
examiners, and, 10.003
liquidators, and, 9.007
receivers, and, 8.009

Qualifying shareholdings
filing obligations, and, 2.113
directors, and, 6.005

Quasi-loans
generally, 6.028

Quorum
members' meetings, and, 5.036–
5.039

Receivers
appointment
disqualification, 8.009–8.013
publication, 8.002–8.008
qualifications, 8.009
compliance duties
distribution of proceeds, 8.052–
8.059
information to company, 8.032–
8.039
qualifications, 8.009–8.013
returns, 8.025–8.031
sale of assets, 8.040–8.051
statement of affairs, 8.014–8.024
directions to comply, 8.063–8.066
disqualification, 8.009–8.013
distribution of proceeds, 8.052–
8.059
enforcement under Companies Acts
directions to comply, 8.063–
8.066
examination of receiver's
books, 8.060–8.062

report by professional
body, 8.067
examination of books, 8.060–8.062
information to company, 8.032–
8.039
introduction, 8.001
liability, 8.074–8.076
publication of appointment
general requirements, 8.005
person appointing, by, 8.002–
8.004
receiver's duty,. 8.006–8.008
qualifications, 8.009
removal, 8.077–8.084
remuneration, 8.070–8.073
report by professional body, 8.067
reporting obligations, 8.068
resignation, 8.077–8.084
returns, 8.025–8.031
sale of assets
distribution of proceeds, 8.052–
8.059
generally, 8.040–8.051
statement of affairs, 8.014–8.024

Recognition
auditors, and, 7.028–7.031

Reduction of share capital
introduction, 2.076
notification of Registrar, 2.077
public limited companies,
and, 2.079–2.080
registration, 2.078

Register of Auditors
generally, 7.032–7.038

Register of charges
form, 3.002–3.003
generally, 3.044
introduction, 3.001

Register of companies
restoration by court
effect, 14.098–14.109
introduction, 14.040
s 12B(3) CA(A) 1982,
under, 14.041–14.070

Register of companies (contd)
　restoration by court (contd)
　　s 12B(7) CA(A) 1982,
　　　under, 14.071–14.076
　　s 311(8) CA 1963,
　　　under, 14.077–14.082
　restoration by registrar
　　applicants, 14.090–14.092
　　effect, 14.098–14.109
　　procedure, 14.097
　　requirements, 14.093–14.096
　　scope of provisions,
　　　14.083–14.089
　striking off
　　and see **Striking companies off
　　　the register**
　　effect, 14.027–14.039
　　grounds, 14.002–14.026
　　introduction, 14.001

Register of debenture holders
　charges, and, 2.107
　form, 3.002–3.003
　introduction, 3.001

Register of directors and secretaries
　form, 3.002–3.003
　generally, 3.035–3.036
　introduction, 3.001

Register of directors' contracts
　form, 3.002–3.003
　generally, 3.042–3.043
　introduction, 3.001

Register of directors' interests
　form, 3.002–3.003
　generally, 3.037–3.041
　introduction, 3.001

Register of disqualified persons
　disqualification orders, and,
　　23.031–23.032

Register of members
　closing, 3.029–3.033
　contents, 3.004–3.008
　date of registration, 3.009
　form, 3.002–3.003

　index, 3.010
　inspection, 3.013–3.017
　introduction, 3.001
　location, 3.011–3.012
　rectification, 3.023–3.028
　refusal to register, 3.018–3.022
　sanctions for default, 3.034

Register of restricted persons
　restriction proceedings, and,
　　19.021–19.022

Registered office
　filing obligations, and, 2.011–2.012

Registers
　and see under individual headings
　　above
　charges, of, 3.044
　debenture holders, of, 3.045–3.047
　directors and secretaries, of,
　　3.035–3.036
　directors' contracts, of, 3.042–3.043
　directors' interests, of, 3.037–3.041
　form, 3.002–3.003
　introduction, 3.001
　members, of, 3.004–3.034

Release from charge
　charges, and, 2.108

Relief
　directors, and, 6.180–6.181
　discretionary disqualification orders,
　　and, 23.027–23.030
　restricted companies, and, 19.020
　restriction proceedings, and,
　　17.076–17.081

Removal
　auditors
　　generally, 7.003–7.005
　　rights, 7.006–7.010
　examiners, and, 10.011
　liquidators, and, 9.014–9.016
　receivers, and, 8.077–8.084

Removal of company officers
　filing obligations, and, 2.116–2.118

Remuneration
auditors, and, 7.017
directors, and, 6.025
examiners, and
  application to court, 10.041
  discretion of court, 10.042–
    10.045
  generally, 10.040
  priority, 10.046–10.049
receivers, and, 8.070–8.073

Reporting obligations
auditors, and
  background, 7.071–7.076
  directors' compliance statements,
    on, 7.124–7.125
  indictable offences, 7.083–7.118
  legal professional
    privilege, 7.119–7.122
  other, 7.126–7.128
  proper books of account,
    7.077–7.082
  protection from liability, 7.123
liquidators to DCE, and
  additional reports, 9.077–9.078
  administrative fines for
    default, 9.081
  approach of ODCE, 9.084–9.085
  auditing accounts, 9.062–9.069
  company details, 9.052–9.057
  company directors, 9.058–9.061
  court orders requiring remedy of
    default, 9.082–9.083
  criminal liability for non-
    compliance, 9.080
  final report, 9.075
  insolvent companies, 9.039
  introduction, 9.037–9.038
  legal proceedings, 9.070–9.074
  liquidator details, 9.051
  liquidator's statement, 9.076
  minutes of creditors'
    meeting, 9.062
  pending proceedings, 9.070
  prosecution for non-
    compliance, 9.080

  provisional liquidations,
    in, 9.042–9.046
  report to creditors, 9.062–9.069
  required information,
    9.048–9.076
  sanctions, 9.079–9.083
  scope of obligation, 9.039–9.047
  section headings, 9.050
  statement of affairs, 9.062–9.069
  statement to creditors'
    meeting, 9.062
  temporal scope of
    obligation, 9.047
  voluntary liquidations, in,
    9.040–9.041
liquidators to DPP, and
  compulsory winding-up,
    9.087–9.091
  failure to assist DCE, 9.098
  further duties in event of
    prosecution, 9.096–9.100
  introduction, 9.086
  obligation to assist DCE, 9.097
  role of DCE, 9.100
  role of DPP, 9.099
  voluntary winding-up,
    9.092–9.095
receivers, and, 8.068

Reports
accompanying balance sheet,
  6.148–6.155
annual returns, and, 2.025
compliance statement, 6.156–6.159

Re-registration
introduction, 2.157
plc as private company, of, 2.162
private company as plc, of,
  2.158–2.161

Reservation
company names, and, 2.145

Resignation
auditors, and, 7.011–7.016
examiners, and, 10.010
receivers, and, 8.077–8.084

Resignation of company officers
filing obligations, and, 2.116–2.118

Resignation of directors
restriction proceedings, and,
16.041–16.042

Resolutions
extended notice, 5.034–5.035
filing obligations, and, 2.109–2.111
special resolutions, 5.030–5.032
written resolutions, 5.033

Restoration of companies to register
court, by
effect, 14.098–14.109
introduction, 14.040
s 12B(3) CA(A) 1982,
under, 14.041–14.070
s 12B(7) CA(A) 1982,
under, 14.071–14.076
s 311(8) CA 1963,
under, 14.077–14.082
registrar, by
applicants, 14.090–14.092
effect, 14.098–14.109
procedure, 14.097
requirements, 14.093–14.096
scope of provisions, 14.083–
14.089
s 12B(3) CA(A) 1982, under
applicants, 14.043–14.047
introduction, 14.041
orders, 14.061–14.070
procedure, 14.049–14.060
requirements, 14.048
scope, 14.042
s 12B(7) CA(A) 1982, under
applicants, 14.073
introduction, 14.071
orders, 14.076
procedure, 14.075
requirements, 14.074
scope, 14.072
s 311(8) CA 1963, under
applicants, 14.079
introduction, 14.077
orders, 14.082

procedure, 14.081
requirements, 14.080
scope, 14.078

Restricted companies
see also **Restriction proceedings**
capital requirements, 19.010–19.015
directors' loans, 19.018
funding purchase of company's
shares, 19.017
introduction, 19.009
limitations
directors' loans, 19.018
funding purchase of company's
shares, 19.017
introduction, 19.016
transfer of non-cash
assets, 19.019
loans to directors, 19.018
purchase of company's own
shares, 19.017
relief, 19.020
transfer of non-cash assets by
members, 19.019

Restriction proceedings
see also **Restricted companies**
applicants' role, 16.013
applications, 18.001–18.007
basis, 16.003
breach of restriction order, 19.023
burden of proof, 16.014–16.018
consequences of
declarations, 19.001–19.006
costs
applicant's liability,
19.045–19.047
generally, 19.024–19.027
notice party costs orders, 19.051
recovery in winding up,
19.048–19.050
respondent, in favour of,
19.038–19.044
s 150(4B) CA 1990,
under, 19.028–19.033
unsuccessful applications,
of, 19.034–19.037
de facto directors, 16.056–16.065

Restriction proceedings (contd)
defences
    delay, 17.070–17.075
    honesty and
        responsibility, 17.001–17.065
    just and equitable, 17.066–
        17.069
delay, 17.070–17.075
discovery, 18.018
discretion, and, 16.019
duration of declaration,
    19.001–19.004
effect of declaration, 19.005–19.006
executive directors, 16.028–16.036
extra-territorial jurisdiction, 16.020
former directors
    introduction, 16.037
    justification for
        restriction, 16.038–16.040
    obligation to restrict, 16.048
    resignation, 16.041–16.042
    temporal scope, 16.043–16.047
honest and responsible conduct
    attendance at Board
        meetings, 17.047–17.048
    compliance with Companies
        Acts, 17.013–17.015
    conduct in relation to other
        companies, 17.010
    dealings between director and
        company, 17.064
    dealings with Revenue
        Commissioners, 17.058–
        17.063
    failure of company, 17.012
    financial affairs, 17.040–17.045
    general interpretation, 17.011–
        17.030
    introduction, 17.001–17.003
    just and equitable, and,
        17.066–17.069
    'La Moselle' test, 17.016–17.030
    miscellaneous factors, 17.065
    non-financial
        information, 17.046
    proper books and
        records, 17.032–17.039

relationship with other
    companies, 17.049–17.057
relevant factors, 17.031–17.065
relevant period of time,
    17.004–17.009
scope, 17.004–17.010
introduction, 16.001–16.002
just and equitable defence,
    17.066–17.069
liquidator's reporting duty, 19.008
nature, 16.003–16.004
nominee directors, 16.066–16.067
non-adversarial procedure,
    16.006–16.012
non-executive directors,
    16.028–16.036
notification duty, 19.007
period of restriction, 19.001–19.004
persons affected
    de facto directors, 16.056–16.065
    directors at date of winding
        up, 16.026–16.036
    executive directors,
        16.028–16.036
    former directors, 16.037–16.048
    introduction, 16.021
    nominee directors,
        16.066–16.067
    non-executive directors,
        16.028–16.036
    onus of proof of
        directorship, 16.022–16.025
    shadow directors, 16.049–16.055
procedure
    applicants, 18.001–18.007
    applications, 18.001–18.007
    discovery, 18.018
    practice direction, 18.010
    rules of court, 18.008–18.009
    service, 18.011–18.017
public interest, 16.005
register of restricted
    persons, 19.021–19.022
relief, 17.076–17.081
reporting duty, 19.008
resignation of directors, and,
    16.041–16.042

Restriction proceedings (contd)
restricted person's notification
   duty, 19.007
rules of court, 18.008–18.009
service
      general rule, 18.011
      out of the jurisdiction,
         18.012–18.017
   shadow directors
      companies as, 16.054–16.055
      definition, 16.049
      restriction, 16.050–16.053
      temporal scope, 16.043–16.047

Return of company property
investigation during winding-up,
   and, 9.119

Returns
and see **Annual returns**
liquidators, and, 9.034–9.035
receivers, and, 8.025–8.031

Sale of assets
receivers, and
      distribution of proceeds,
         8.052–8.059
      generally, 8.040–8.051

Search and seizure
investigation during winding-up,
   and, 9.113–9.115

Search warrants
applications, 12.101–12.103
books or documents not
   produced, 12.113–12.115
computers, 12.128
designated officers, 12.104–12.105
duration, 12.119–12.121
evidence of offences under
   Companies Acts, 12.116–12.117
execution
      computers, 12.128
      introduction, 12.118
      material information, 12.125
      persons at premises, and, 12.126
      premises, 12.122–12.123

retention of information, 12.127
use of force to enter
   premises, 12.124
validity period, 12.119–12.121
failure to comply with, 12.130
grounds of application,
   12.106–12.111
issue, 12.100
'material information'
      books or documents not
         produced, 12.113–12.115
      evidence of offences under
         Companies Acts,
         12.116–12.117
      execution, and, 12.125
      introduction, 12.112
obstruction of, 12.129
persons at premises, and, 12.126
premises, 12.122–12.123
retention of information, 12.127
scope of material authorised to be
   seized, 12.125
use of force to enter
   premises, 12.124
validity period, 12.119–12.121

Secret profits
consequences, 6.022–6.023
generally, 6.013–6.021

Secretary
changes in, 2.114–2.115
consent to act, 2.112
disclosure of personal information,
   and, 6.092–6.093
filing obligations, and
      changes in, 2.114–2.115
      consent to act, 2.112
      formation of company, on, 2.010
      Irish resident director,
         2.119–2.122
      particulars, 2.112
      resignation or removal,
         2.116–2.118
      share qualifications, 2.113
formation of company, and, 2.010
Irish resident director, 2.119–2.122
particulars, 2.112

Secretary (contd)
resignation or removal, 2.116–2.118
share qualifications, 2.113

Section 3 statement
activity in State, 2.013–2.014
generally, 2.010–2.011
registered office, 2.012

Seniority of respondent
discretionary disqualification orders,
and, 21.038–21.040

Series of debentures
charges, and, 2.096

Service
restriction proceedings, and
general rule, 18.011
out of the jurisdiction, 18.012–
18.017

Shadow directors
restriction proceedings, and
companies as, 16.054–16.055
definition, 16.049
restriction, 16.050–16.053
substantial property transactions,
and, 6.069

Share allotment
filing obligations, and, 2.071

Share capital
allotment of shares, 2.071
alterations, 2.072–2.073
dealings in shares
acquisition of own shares, 2.086
financing acquisition of own
shares, 2.084–2.085
introduction, 2.081
variation of rights of
shareholders, 2.082–2.083
filing obligations, and
allotment of shares, 2.071
alterations, 2.072–2.073
increases, 2.074–2.075
reduction, 2.076–2.080
increases, 2.074–2.075

reduction
introduction, 2.076
notification of Registrar, 2.077
public limited companies,
and, 2.079–2.080
registration, 2.078
share allotment, 2.071

Share dealings
acquisition of own shares, 2.086
filing obligations, and
acquisition of own shares, 2.086
financing acquisition of own
shares, 2.084–2.085
introduction, 2.081
variation of rights of
shareholders, 2.082–2.083
financing acquisition of own
shares, 2.084–2.085
investigation into membership of
company, and, 13.052
variation of rights of
shareholders, 2.082–2.083

Share qualifications
filing obligations, and, 2.113
directors, and, 6.005

Small companies
annual returns, and
accounts, 2.031
annexed documents, 2.029–2.030
filing obligations, and
accounts, 2.031
annexed documents, 2.029–2.030

Special auditor's report
generally, 7.026–7.027

Special resolutions
loans, and, 6.044–6.048
members' meetings, and, 5.030–
5.032
substantial property transactions,
and, 6.078–6.080

Statement of affairs
receivers, and, 8.014–8.024

Striking companies off the register

discretionary disqualification orders, and

  applicants, 22.073

  applications, 22.081–22.089

  criteria, 22.074–22.077

  defence, 22.078–22.080

  introduction, 22.071

  respondents, 22.072

effect

  company property, 14.030–14.033

  director and officer liability, 14.028

  disqualification of directors, 14.035–14.039

  dissolution, 14.027

  litigation, 14.034

  winding up, 14.029

grounds

  cessation of business, 14.013

  failure of plc to have certificate, 14.021–14.024

  failure to complete winding up, 14.025

  failure to deliver statement to Revenue. 14.010–14.012

  failure to file annual returns, 14.003–14.009

  failure to have Irish resident director, 14.014–14.019

  incomplete winding up, 14.025

  introduction, 14.002

introduction, 14.001

voluntary striking off, 14.026

Subsidiary companies

filing accounts, and, 2.056

Substantial property transactions

account and indemnity, 6.087

'acquisition', 6.072–6.073

acquisition by companies, 6.070

'arrangement', 6.071

avoidance of transaction, 6.085–6.086

bodies corporate, and, 6.081

capacity as member, 6.084

company approval, and, 6.078–6.080

company in liquidation, and, 6.083

defence, 6.088–6.090

exceptions to prohibition, 6.077–6.084

group arrangements, and, 6.082

introduction, 6.065

liability to account and indemnify, 6.087

'non-cash assets', 6.075

'person connected with such a director', 6.068

prohibited transactions, 6.066–6.076

'requisite value;, 6.076

sanctions for breach of prohibition, 6.085–6.087

'shadow directors', 6.069

special resolutions, and, 6.078–6.080

statutory basis, 6.066

Substitution of restriction order

discretionary disqualification orders, and, 23.022–23.023

'Teoranta'

exemption from use, 2.127–2.134

improper use, 2.125–2.126

obligation to use, 2.124

Transfer of non-cash assets

restricted companies, and, 19.019

Translation

annual returns, and, 2.026

Undertakings

discretionary disqualification orders, and, 21.021–21.023

Undischarged bankruptcy

deemed disqualification orders, and, 20.038–20.041

discretionary disqualification orders, and, 22.098–22.100

Unfit to be concerned with management of company
and see **Discretionary disqualification orders**
applicants, 22.034
conduct in other companies, 22.035
factors, 22.042–22.047
introduction, 22.032
overlap between ss 150 and 160, 22.036–22.041
respondents, 22.033

Unfitness finding by inspector
and see **Discretionary disqualification orders**
applicants, 22.050
applications, 22.052
introduction, 22.048
respondents, 22.049
scope, 22.051

Variation of rights of shareholders
filing obligations, and, 2.082–2.083

Venue
members' meetings, and, 5.048

Voluntary striking off
generally, 14.026

Voluntary winding-up
appointment of liquidator, 9.003
convening meetings, 9.025–9.030
disclosure duty, 9.021
inspection of books, 9.108
notification of appointment, 9.019–9.020
reporting to DPP
court directions, 9.094–9.095
introduction, 9.092
liquidator's report, 9.093

Voting
members' meetings, and, 5.046–5.047

Winding up
striking company off the register, and, 14.029

Written resolutions
members' meetings, and, 5.033

Company Law Compliance and Enforcement